Introduction to Business

Introduction to Business

Compiled from:

Business in Action
Eighth Edition
Courtland L. Bovée and John V. Thill

Fundamentals of Management
Tenth Edition
Stephen P. Robbins, Mary Coulter, and David A. DeCenzo

The Business Environment
Seventh Edition
Ian Worthington and Chris Britton

Business Essentials
Eleventh Edition
Ronald J. Ebert and Ricky W. Griffin

E-Commerce: Business. Technology. Society.
Twelfth Edition
Kenneth C. Laudon and Carol Guercio Traver

The Legal Environment of Business and Online Commerce
Seventh Edition
Henry R. Cheeseman

Harlow, England • London • New York • Boston • San Francisco • Toronto • Sydney • Auckland • Singapore • Hong Kong
Tokyo • Seoul • Taipei • New Delhi • Cape Town • Sao Paulo • Mexico City • Madrid • Amsterdam • Munich • Paris • Milan

Pearson Education Limited
Edinburgh Gate
Harlow
Essex CM20 2JE

And associated companies throughout the world

Visit us on the World Wide Web at:
www.pearson.com/uk

Compiled from:

Business in Action
Eighth Edition
Courtland L. Bovée and John V. Thill
ISBN 978-1-292-16063-4
© Pearson Education Limited 2017

Fundamentals of Management
Tenth Edition
Stephen P. Robbins, Mary Coulter, and David A. DeCenzo
ISBN 978-1-292-14694-2
© Pearson Education Limited 2017

The Business Environment
Seventh Edition
Ian Worthington and Chris Britton
ISBN 978-0-273-75672-9
© Ian Worthington and Chris Britton 1994, 1997, 2000, 2003 (print)
© Ian Worthington and Chris Britton 2006, 2009 (print and electronic)
© Pearson Education Limited 2015 (print and electronic)

Business Essentials
Eleventh Edition
Ronald J. Ebert and Ricky W. Griffin
ISBN 978-1-292-15224-0
© Pearson Education Limited 2017

E-Commerce: Business. Technology. Society.
Twelfth Edition
Kenneth C. Laudon and Carol Guercio Traver
ISBN 978-1-292-10996-1
© Kenneth C. Laudon and Carol Guercio Traver, 2017, 2016, 2015, 2014, 2013, 2012

The Legal Environment of Business and Online Commerce
Seventh Edition
Henry R. Cheeseman
ISBN 978-1-292-03968-8
© Pearson Education Limited 2014

ISBN 978-1-78449-365-3

Printed and bound in Great Britain by Clays Ltd, Bungay, Suffolk.

Contents

Section One

Chapter 1
Introduction

1 Developing a Business Mindset

LEARNING OBJECTIVES   After studying this chapter, you will be able to

1 Explain the concept of adding value in a business, and identify the major types of businesses.

2 List three steps you can take to help make the leap from consumer to business professional.

3 Discuss the five major environments in which every business operates.

4 Explain the purpose of the six major functional areas in a business enterprise.

5 Summarize seven of the most important business professions.

6 Identify seven components of professionalism.

BEHIND THE SCENES   YOLANDA DIAZ: BUILDING HER DREAM WITH HARD WORK AND STRONG BUSINESS SENSE

Jim West/Alamy

Yolanda Diaz's hard work, keen business sense, and smart use of available resources turned her dream of business ownership into a multimillion-dollar reality.

www.miradorenterprises.com

Yolanda Diaz's business instincts have been on display since her childhood in El Paso, Texas. To help her mother with household expenses, Diaz approached families in the neighborhood, offering her services at cleaning, cooking, and other chores. In high school, she got formal exposure to business as part of the Vocational Office Education program. Later, while an accounting major at the University of Texas at El Paso, she and her sister launched a part-time clothing company to help cover the cost of tuition.

By the time she graduated with a degree in accounting, Diaz clearly knew the value of hard work—and knew how to create value for customers. She put her degree to good use as an accounting supervisor for several established companies, including the multinational firm United Technologies. After a decade of working for others, though, she was ready to return to her entrepreneurial roots and strike out on her own again.

If you were Diaz, how would you make the transition from employee to business owner? What resources would you use? Which customers would you pursue, and how would you cultivate new opportunities? If you dreamed of starting your own business, how would you make that dream come true?[1]

INTRODUCTION

Like millions of employees before her, Yolanda Diaz (profiled in the chapter opener) made the bold decision to go into business for herself—a decision you might have already made or are contemplating yourself. At the end of the chapter, you can read about how she turned her dream into a successful company. This chapter gets you ready for the whirl-wind tour of the business world you'll get in this course, starting with a quick overview of what businesses do and then some advice on making the leap from consumer to business professional.

Understanding What Businesses Do

The term *business* is used in a number of ways:

- As a label for the overall field of business concepts, as in "I plan to major in business."
- As a collective label for the activities of many companies, as in "This legislation is viewed as harmful to American business."
- As a way to indicate specific activities or efforts, as in "Our furniture business earned record profits last year, but our housewares business has lost money for the third year in a row."
- As a synonym for *company*, as in "Apple is a successful business." Other common synonyms here are *firm* and *enterprise*.

In this last sense, a **business** is any profit-seeking organization that provides goods and services designed to satisfy customers' needs.

ADDING VALUE: THE BUSINESS OF BUSINESS

A good way to understand what any business does is to view it as a system for satisfying customers by transforming lower-value inputs into higher-value outputs (see Exhibit 1.1). If you want a loaf of bread, for instance, a silo full of wheat isn't of much value to you.

business
Any profit-seeking organization that provides goods and services designed to satisfy customers' needs.

EXHIBIT 1.1	Adding Value to Satisfy Customers

Every company in this chain adds value for the next customer and for the ultimate consumer.

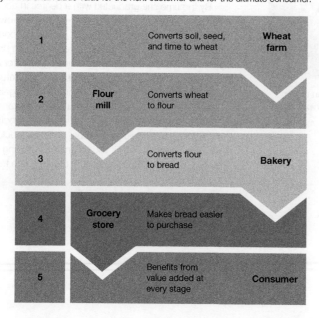

1. Converts soil, seed, and time to wheat — **Wheat farm**
2. **Flour mill** — Converts wheat to flour
3. Converts flour to bread — **Bakery**
4. **Grocery store** — Makes bread easier to purchase
5. Benefits from value added at every stage — **Consumer**

After that wheat is milled into flour, it gets one step closer but is valuable only if you want to bake your own bread. A bakery can take care of the baking, but that helps only if you're willing to travel to the bakery instead of going to the supermarket where you normally shop. At every stage, a company adds value to create the product in a way that makes it appealing to the next customer in the chain.

Each company in this chain has made certain choices about what it will do to generate **revenue**: money the company brings in through the sale of goods and services.

revenue
Money a company brings in through the sale of goods and services.

The result of these decisions is a company's **business model**, which is a clearly stated outline of how the business intends to generate revenue. Of course, generating revenue isn't enough; the business model must also indicate how the company is going to realize **profit**, the amount of money left over after *expenses*—all the costs involved in doing business—have been deducted from revenue.

business model
A concise description of how a business intends to generate revenue.

Competing to Attract and Satisfy Customers

As businesses create value-added products and offer them for sale to customers, they obviously don't do so in a vacuum. Other companies are also trying to sell their products to those same customers, and the result is *competition*. Competition gives customers a wider range of options, and it tends to increase quality, improve customer service, and lower prices.

profit
Money left over after all the costs involved in doing business have been deducted from revenue.

One of the beauties of a free-market economy is that companies usually have a lot of flexibility in deciding which customers they want to focus on and how they want to compete. For instance, one bakery might decide to compete on price and thus structure its business model in such a way as to mass-produce bread at the lowest possible cost. Another might decide to compete on quality or uniqueness and thus structure its business model around handcrafted "artisan" bread that costs two or three times as much as the mass-produced bread. Each company seeks a **competitive advantage** that makes its products more appealing to its chosen customers. Consumers benefit from better products and more choices, and companies get to focus on what they do best.

competitive advantage
Some aspect of a product or company that makes it more appealing to target customers.

Accepting Risks in the Pursuit of Rewards

Take another look at Exhibit 1.1. Notice how every company from the farmer to the grocery store must accept some level of risk in order to conduct its business. Bad weather or disease could destroy the wheat crop. A shift in consumer behavior, such as cash-strapped families in a recession switching to bakery outlet stores instead of regular grocery stores, could leave some bakers, distributors, and retailers with bread nobody wants to buy. Businesses take these risks in anticipation of future rewards.

This linking of risk and reward is critical for two reasons. The first and more obvious is that without the promise of rewards, businesses would have no incentive to take on the risks. And without entrepreneurs and companies willing to accept risk, little would get done in the economy. The second reason that the risk associated with business decisions needs to "stay attached" to those decisions is to encourage smart and responsible decision making. If individuals and companies believe they can pursue rewards without facing the risks that should be attached to those pursuits, they are more likely to engage in irresponsible and even unethical behavior—a situation known as *moral hazard* (see Exhibit 1.2).

IDENTIFYING MAJOR TYPES OF BUSINESSES

The driving forces behind most businesses are the prospects of earning profits and building *assets*, which are anything of meaningful value, from patents and brand names to real estate and company stock. In contrast, **not-for-profit organizations** (also known as *nonprofit organizations*) such as museums, most universities, and charities do not have a profit motive. However, they must operate efficiently and effectively to achieve their goals, and successful nonprofits apply many of the business-management principles you'll learn in this course.

not-for-profit organizations
Organizations that provide goods and services without having a profit motive; also called *nonprofit organizations*.

EXHIBIT 1.2	Risk and Reward

The relationship between risk and reward is fundamental to every modern economy. A company needs to see some promise of reward before it will decide to accept the risks involved in creating and selling products. However, to ensure responsible behavior, these risks need to stay attached to those decisions, meaning that if the decisions turn out bad, that company should suffer the consequences. If the risk gets disconnected from a decision—meaning someone else will suffer from a bad decision—a situation known as *moral hazard* is created. A significant recent example of this problem involved home-mortgage companies lending money to homeowners who were practically guaranteed to default on their loans, but then selling those loans as investments and thereby transferring the risk of nonpayment to someone else.

Healthy connection between risk and reward

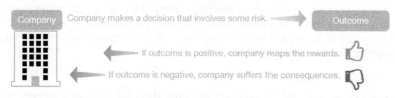

Moral hazard: Link between risk and reward is broken

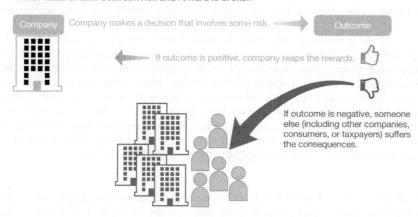

Businesses can be classified into two broad categories. **Goods-producing businesses** create value by making "things," from Pop-Tarts to school furniture to spacecraft. Most goods are *tangible*, meaning they have a physical presence; other goods, such as software, music downloads, and similar digital products, are *intangible*. **Service businesses** create value by performing activities that deliver some benefit to the customer, such as finance, insurance, transportation, construction, utilities, wholesale and retail trade, banking, entertainment, health care, maintenance and repair, and information. Twitter, Jiffy Lube, HBO, and Verizon Wireless are examples of service businesses. Many companies are both goods-producing and service businesses.

Over the past few decades, the U.S. economy has undergone a profound transformation from being dominated by manufacturing to being dominated by services. Although the country remains a manufacturing powerhouse, the service sector now accounts for 70 percent of the economic activity and 80 percent of jobs in the United States.[2]

Because they require large amounts of money, equipment, land, and other resources to get started and to operate, goods-producing businesses are often *capital-intensive businesses*. The capital needed to compete in these industries is a **barrier to entry**, which is a resource or capability a company must have before it can start competing in a given market. Other barriers to entry include government testing and approval, tightly

goods-producing businesses
Companies that create value by making "things," most of which are tangible (digital products such as software are a notable exception).

service businesses
Companies that create value by performing activities that deliver some benefit to customers.

barrier to entry
Any resource or capability a company must have before it can start competing in a given market.

controlled markets, strict licensing procedures, limited supplies of raw materials, and the need for highly skilled employees. Service businesses tend to be *labor intensive*, in that they rely more on human resources than on buildings, machinery, and equipment to prosper. There are exceptions, of course. Airlines require a massive investment in equipment, for example, and the Internet and other technologies have reduced the labor required to operate many types of service businesses.

 Checkpoint

LEARNING OBJECTIVE 1: Explain the concept of adding value in a business, and identify the major types of businesses.

SUMMARY: Businesses add value by transforming lower-value inputs to higher-value outputs. In other words, they make goods and services more attractive from the buyer's perspective, whether it's creating products that are more useful or simply making them more convenient to purchase. Companies fall into two general categories: goods-producing businesses, which create tangible things (except in the case of digital goods), and service businesses, which perform various activities of value to customers. Many companies are both goods-producing and service businesses. Businesses can also be categorized as capital intensive or labor intensive.

CRITICAL THINKING: (1) What inputs does a musical group use to create its outputs? (2) Can not-for-profit organizations benefit from practices used by for-profit companies? Why or why not?

IT'S YOUR BUSINESS: (1) Think back to the last product you purchased; how did the companies involved in its manufacture and sale add value in a way that benefited you personally? (2) Can you see yourself working for a not-for-profit organization after you graduate? Why or why not?

KEY TERMS TO KNOW: business, revenue, business model, profit, competitive advantage, not-for-profit organizations, goods-producing businesses, service businesses, barrier to entry

2 **LEARNING OBJECTIVE**

List three steps you can take to help make the leap from consumer to business professional.

Making the Leap from Buyer to Seller

Even if this course is your first formal exposure to the business world, you already know a lot about business, thanks to your experiences as a consumer. You understand the impact of poor customer service, for example. You have a sense of product value and why some products meet your needs and others don't. In fact, you're an expert in the entire experience of searching for, purchasing, and owning products.

SEEING BUSINESS FROM THE INSIDE OUT

As you progress through this course, you'll begin to look at things through the eyes of a business professional rather than those of a consumer. Instead of thinking about the cost of buying a particular product, you'll start to think about the cost of making it, promoting it, and distributing it. You'll think about what it takes to make a product stand out from the crowd and recognize the importance of finding opportunities in the marketplace. You'll begin to see business as an integrated system of inputs, processes, and outputs. As Yolanda Diaz did when she launched Mirador Enterprises (see page 68), you'll start to develop a business **mindset** as you gain an appreciation for the many decisions that must be made and the many challenges that must be overcome before companies can deliver products that satisfy customer needs (see Exhibit 1.3).

Your experiences as a consumer have taught you a great deal about business already. Now the challenge is to turn those experiences around and view the world from a manager's perspective. Here are a few examples of how a business professional approaches some of the questions you've asked as a consumer.

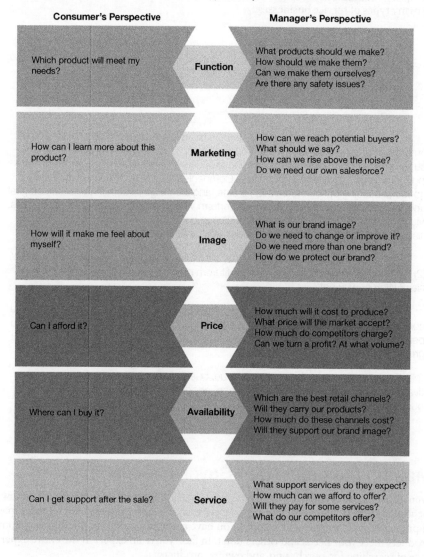

Consumer's Perspective — **Manager's Perspective**

Function
- Which product will meet my needs?
- What products should we make? How should we make them? Can we make them ourselves? Are there any safety issues?

Marketing
- How can I learn more about this product?
- How can we reach potential buyers? What should we say? How can we rise above the noise? Do we need our own salesforce?

Image
- How will it make me feel about myself?
- What is our brand image? Do we need to change or improve it? Do we need more than one brand? How do we protect our brand?

Price
- Can I afford it?
- How much will it cost to produce? What price will the market accept? How much do competitors charge? Can we turn a profit? At what volume?

Availability
- Where can I buy it?
- Which are the best retail channels? Will they carry our products? How much do these channels cost? Will they support our brand image?

Service
- Can I get support after the sale?
- What support services do they expect? How much can we afford to offer? Will they pay for some services? What do our competitors offer?

APPRECIATING THE ROLE OF BUSINESS IN SOCIETY

Your experiences as a consumer, an employee, and a taxpayer have also given you some insights into the complex relationship between business and society. Chapter 4's discussion of *corporate social responsibility* digs deeper into this important topic, but for now, just consider some of the major elements of this relationship. Business has

REAL-TIME UPDATES
Learn More by Exploring This Interactive Website

Use this powerful search tool for easier online searches

Bovée and Thill Web Search is a custom metasearch engine that automatically formats more than 300 types of searches for optimum results. Go to http://real-timeupdates.com/bia8 and click on Web Search in the navigation bar.

EXHIBIT 1.4   Positive and Negative Effects of Business

The relationship between business and society is complex and far reaching. Individuals, communities, and entire nations benefit in multiple ways from the efforts of businesses, but even responsibly managed companies can at times have negative impacts on society in return.

the potential to contribute to society in many useful ways, including the following (see Exhibit 1.4):

- **Offering valuable goods and services.** Most of the goods and services you consider essential to your quality of life were made possible by someone with a profit motive.
- **Providing employment.** In addition to providing salaries, many companies help their employees meet the costs of health care, child care, education, retirement, and other living expenses.
- **Paying taxes.** U.S. businesses pay hundreds of billions in taxes every year,[3] money that helps build highways, fund education, further scientific research, enhance public safety and national defense, and support other vital functions of government.
- **Contributing to national growth, stability, and security.** Beyond the mere dollars from taxes paid, a strong economy helps ensure a strong country. As one example, by providing job opportunities to the vast majority of people who want to work, businesses help the country avoid the social unrest and family disruptions that often result from high unemployment.

Unfortunately, businesses don't always operate in ways that benefit society. As you progress into positions of increasing responsibility in your career, be aware of the potentially negative effects that business can have on society:

- **Generating pollution and creating waste.** Just like individuals, companies consume resources and produce waste and therefore have an impact on the natural environment and the soil, air, and water on which all living creatures depend.
- **Creating health and safety risks.** Many business operations involve an element of risk to the health and safety of employees and surrounding communities. For instance, some of the products you use every day, from your digital music player to your laptop computer, contain toxic materials. If these materials are not created, handled, and disposed of properly, they can cause serious illness or death.
- **Disrupting communities.** From occupying land to displacing existing businesses to overloading schools and roads with employees and their children,

growing businesses can disrupt communities even as they provide employment and other benefits. And when businesses fall into decline, they can leave behind everything from abandoned buildings to laid-off workers.
- **Causing financial instability.** Irresponsible or poorly managed companies can become a liability to society if they are unable to meet their financial obligations and need assistance from the government, for example.

The potential negative effects of business are serious matters, but the good news is that you have a say in how business operates. Even as an employee early in your career, you can conduct yourself in ways that balance the profit motive with society's shared interests. And as you climb the corporate ladder or perhaps launch your own business, you'll be in a position to make decisions that help your company prosper in an ethical and sustainable manner.

REAL-TIME UPDATES
Learn More by Reading This Article

Managing your career in today's workplace: One expert's view

Read these quick tips on succeeding in the new world of work. Go to http://real-timeupdates.com/bia8 and click on Learn More in the Students section.

USING THIS COURSE TO JUMP-START YOUR CAREER

No matter where your career plans take you, the dynamics of business will affect your work and life in innumerable ways. If you aspire to be a manager or an entrepreneur, knowing how to run a business is vital, of course. If you plan a career in a professional specialty such as law, engineering, or finance, knowing how businesses operate will help you interact with clients and colleagues more effectively. Even if you plan to work in government, education, or some other noncommercial setting, business awareness can help you; many of these organizations look to business for new ideas and leadership techniques. *Social entrepreneurs,* people who apply entrepreneurial strategies to enable large-scale social change, use business concepts as well.

As you progress through this course, you'll develop a fundamental business vocabulary that will help you keep up with the latest news and make better-informed decisions. By participating in classroom discussions and completing the chapter exercises, you'll gain some valuable critical-thinking, problem-solving, team-building, and communication skills that you can use on the job and throughout your life.

This course will also introduce you to a variety of jobs in business fields such as accounting, economics, human resources, management, finance, and marketing. You'll see how people who work in these fields contribute to the success of a company as a whole. You'll gain insight into the types of skills and knowledge these jobs require, and you'll discover that a career in business today is fascinating, challenging, and often quite rewarding.

In addition, a study of business management will help you appreciate the larger context in which businesses operate and the many legal and ethical questions managers must consider as they make business decisions. Government regulators and society as a whole have numerous expectations regarding the ways businesses treat employees, shareholders, the environment, other businesses, and the communities in which they operate.

 Checkpoint

LEARNING OBJECTIVE 2: List three steps you can take to help make the leap from consumer to business professional.

SUMMARY: To accelerate your transition from consumer to professional, develop a business mindset that views business from the inside out rather than the outside in, recognize the positive and negative effects that business can have on society, and use this course to develop a business vocabulary and explore the wide variety of jobs in the field of business.

CRITICAL THINKING: (1) How can consumer experiences help a business professional excel on the job? (2) If organized businesses didn't exist and the economy were composed of individual craftspeople, would the result be more or less pollution? Explain your answer.

IT'S YOUR BUSINESS: (1) How might you contribute to society as a business professional? (2) What is your view of business at this point in your life? Negative? Positive? A mixture of both?

KEY TERM TO KNOW: business mindset

---

3 LEARNING OBJECTIVE

Discuss the five major environments in which every business operates.

social environment
Trends and forces in society at large.

Recognizing the Multiple Environments of Business

The potential effects of business, both positive and negative, highlight the fact that no business operates in a vacuum. Every company operates within a number of interrelated environments that affect and are affected by business (see Exhibit 1.5).

THE SOCIAL ENVIRONMENT

Every business operates within the broad **social environment**—the trends and forces in society at large. For instance, all companies are affected by population trends that

EXHIBIT 1.5   The Multiple Environments of Business

Every business operates in an overlapping mix of dynamic environments that continuously create both opportunities and constraints.

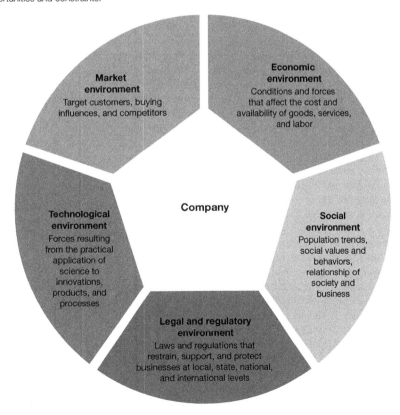

change the composition of consumer markets and the workforce. One great example is the so-called Baby Boom generation, a population "bulge" made up of people born between 1946 and 1964. This large group of people have affected business in numerous ways as they have moved through childhood, then into adulthood as consumers and workers, and finally back out of the workforce now that the first wave of boomers have reached retirement age. The Baby Boomers have occupied a large number of middle- and upper-management positions, frustrating younger professionals who would like to climb the company ladder and causing many to leave and start their own companies.[4]

Various segments of society also have expectations about the appropriate relationship of business and society. The responsibility of a company to its **stakeholders**—all those groups affected by its activities, from employees to local communities to advocacy groups—is a subject of ongoing controversy. You can read more about stakeholders in Chapter 4's discussion of corporate social responsibility.

stakeholders
Internal and external groups affected by a company's decisions and activities.

THE TECHNOLOGICAL ENVIRONMENT

The **technological environment** stems from the practical application of science to innovations, products, and processes. Technological advances have the potential to change every facet of business, from altering internal processes to creating or destroying market opportunities. *Disruptive technologies*, those that fundamentally change the nature of an industry, can be powerful enough to create or destroy entire companies. Many of the technologies that you use in your academic, personal, and social activities, from digital audio and video to the Internet to social media, are disruptive technologies that have shaken up multiple industries.

technological environment
Forces resulting from the practical application of science to innovations, products, and processes.

One of the newest disruptive technologies to hit the business world is mobile connectivity, including smartphones, tablets, app software, and the networking infrastructure that connects all these devices. Venture capitalist Joe Schoendorf call mobile "the most disruptive technology that I have seen in 48 years in Silicon Valley."[5] Researcher Maribel Lopez calls mobile "the biggest technology shift since the Internet."[6]

Companies recognize the value of integrating mobile technology, from employee collaboration systems to banking to retail. Mobile apps and communication systems can boost employee productivity, help companies form closer relationships with customers and business partners, and spur innovation in products and services (see Exhibit 1.6 on the next page). Given the advantages and the rising expectations of employees and customers, firms on the leading edge of the mobile revolution are working to integrate mobile technology throughout their organizations.[7]

For millions of people around the world, a mobile device is their primary way, if not their only way, to access the Internet. Globally, roughly 80 percent of Internet users access the web at least some of the time with a mobile device.[8] Mobile has become the primary communication tool for many business professionals, including a majority of executives under age 40.[9] Email and web browsing rank first and second in terms of the most common nonvoice uses of smartphones, and more email messages are now opened on mobile devices than on PCs.[10] Roughly half of U.S. consumers use a mobile device exclusively for their online search needs, and many online activities that eventually migrate to a PC screen start out on a mobile screen.[11] For many people, the fact that a smartphone can make phone calls is practically a secondary consideration; data traffic from mobile devices far outstrips voice traffic.[12]

Social media pioneer Nicco Mele coined the term *radical connectivity* to describe "the breathtaking ability to send vast amounts of data instantly, constantly, and globally."[13] Mobile plays a major and ever-expanding role in this

REAL-TIME UPDATES
Learn More by Watching This Video

The mobile business advantage

Hear how leading-edge companies are adapting to take advantage of mobile connectivity and communication. Go to http://real-timeupdates.com/bia8 and click on Learn More in the Students section.

REAL-TIME UPDATES
Learn More by Reading This Infographic

Can you run an entire company from a smartphone?

Mobile apps are powerful enough to enable the mobile small business. Go to http://real-timeupdates.com/bia8 and click on Learn More in the Students section.

EXHIBIT 1.6 Disruptive Technologies: The Mobile Revolution

Mobile connectivity is a classic example of a disruptive technology. Here are some of the many ways it is affecting virtually every aspect of business. Mobile simplifies life in some ways but complicates it in others because it creates opportunities for new business models and threatens some existing models.

Inside the Enterprise

Mobile presentation tools, such the ability to stream slides to audience members' phones and tablets, give new life to business meetings and conferences.

Mobile-friendly enterprise communication systems, including collaboration platforms and private Twitter-style microblogging, help colleagues stay in constant contact.

Throughout the organization, employees and managers can get vital information wherever they are, whenever they need it.

For many workers today, the office is wherever they need it to be, from their kitchen tables to local coffee shops to customer facilities.

For better or worse, mobile lets employees stay connected to their work around the clock.

With training apps and real-time information delivery, employees can get important advice and data when and where they need it.

Mobile simplifies transportation and logistics by keeping companies connected to their goods and equipment anywhere in the world.

From location scouting to consumer research, mobile devices help researchers collect vital information live and on the spot.

Through a variety of text-based, audio, and video systems, companies can reach consumers in more ways than ever before.

Outside the Enterprise

For many consumers around the world without PCs, mobile devices are their primary way to access the Internet.

Through services such as Uber, mobile is redefining local transportation options.

Location-based services let companies deliver relevant updates, coupons, and digital products to mobile customers, and consumers influence businesses through on-the-spot reviews and social networking

Business travel no longer forces employees and managers to lose touch with colleagues and customers.

Mobile commerce simplifies life for consumers but disrupts established retail patterns through in-store price comparisons and product research.

Financial apps, from transaction processing to full accounting capabilities, let entrepreneurs take their businesses right to the customer.

Sales and service professionals can use apps for presentations, product configuration, order tracking, troubleshooting, and other in-the-field activities.

phenomenon by keeping people connected 24/7, wherever they may be. Those who've grown up with mobile technology expect to have immediate access to information and the ability to stay connected to their various social and business networks.[14] If *wearable technologies* become mainstream devices, they will contribute even more to this shift in behaviors. You'll read more about mobile in the chapters ahead.

economic environment
The conditions and forces that affect the cost and availability of goods, services, and labor and thereby shape the behavior of buyers and sellers.

THE ECONOMIC ENVIRONMENT

Directly or indirectly, virtually every decision a company makes is influenced by the **economic environment**, the conditions and forces that (1) affect the cost and availability of goods, services, and labor and (2) thereby shape the behavior of buyers and sellers. For example, a growing economy can help companies by increasing demand and supporting higher prices for their products, but it can also raise the costs of labor and the materials the companies need in order to do business. A strong economy can also prompt managers to make decisions that turn out to be unwise in the long term, such as adding costly facilities or employee benefits that the company won't be able to afford when the economy slows down again. A shrinking economy, on the other hand, can damage even well-run, financially healthy companies by limiting demand for their products or the availability of loans or investments needed to expand operations. Chapter 2 explores economic forces in more detail.

THE LEGAL AND REGULATORY ENVIRONMENT

Every business is affected by the **legal and regulatory environment**, the sum of laws and regulations at local, state, national, and even international levels. Some businesses, such as electricity and other basic utilities, are heavily regulated, even to the point of government agencies determining how much such companies can charge for their services. The degree to which various industries should be regulated remains a point of contention, year in and year out.

> **legal and regulatory environment**
> Laws and regulations at local, state, national, and even international levels.

The policies and practices of government bodies also establish an overall level of support for businesses operating within their jurisdictions. Taxation, fees, efforts to coordinate multiple regulatory agencies, the speed of granting permits and licenses, labor rules, environmental restrictions, protection for assets such as patents and brand names, roads and other infrastructure, and the transparency and consistency of decision making all affect this level of support. Not surprisingly, companies prefer to locate and do business in jurisdictions that offer lower costs, lower complexity, and greater stability and predictability.

THE MARKET ENVIRONMENT

Within the various other environments just discussed, every company operates within a specific **market environment** composed of three important groups: (1) its *target customers*, (2) the *buying influences* that shape the behavior of those customers, and (3) *competitors*—other companies that market similar products to those customers. The nature and behavior of these groups and their effect on business strategy vary widely from industry to industry.

> **market environment**
> A company's target customers, the buying influences that shape the behavior of those customers, and competitors that market similar products to those customers.

In commercial aviation, for example, the barriers to entry are extremely high, and the customer decision-making process is lengthy and driven almost entirely by financial considerations. As a consequence, the manufacturers in this industry have to make major investment decisions years in advance of launching new products, but they can do so with the reasonable assumption that a new competitor isn't going to pop up overnight and that their target customers will behave in fairly predictable ways.

In sharp contrast, clothing fashions and fads can change in a matter of weeks or days, and the behavior of celebrities and other buying influences can have a major impact on consumer choices. Moreover, because it is much easier to launch a new line of clothing than a new airplane, competitors can appear almost overnight.

✓ Checkpoint

LEARNING OBJECTIVE 3: Discuss the five major environments in which every business operates.

SUMMARY: Business influences and is influenced by (1) the social environment—the trends and forces in society at large; (2) the technological environment and its ability to create and destroy markets and alter business processes; (3) the economic environment, the conditions and forces that affect the cost and availability of goods, services, and labor and thereby shape the behavior of buyers and sellers; (4) the legal and regulatory environment, comprising all the rules and regulations relating to business activities; and (5) the market environment, composed of target customers, buying influences, and competitors.

CRITICAL THINKING: (1) Is it wise for cities and states to compete with each other to be more business friendly, specifically with regard to lower tax rates on businesses? Why or why not? (2) Even though it never sells directly to consumers, does a company such as Boeing need to pay attention to population trends? Why or why not?

IT'S YOUR BUSINESS: (1) How has technology made your educational experience in college different from your experience in high school? (2) Have current economic conditions affected your career-planning decisions in any way?

KEY TERMS TO KNOW: social environment, stakeholders, technological environment, economic environment, legal and regulatory environment, market environment

4 **LEARNING OBJECTIVE**

Explain the purpose of the six major functional areas in a business enterprise.

Identifying the Major Functional Areas in a Business Enterprise

Throughout this course, you'll have the opportunity to learn more about the major functional areas within a business enterprise. In the meantime, the following sections offer a brief overview to help you see how all the pieces work together (see Exhibit 1.7).

EXHIBIT 1.7   Major Functional Areas in a Business Enterprise

The functional areas in a business coordinate their efforts to understand and satisfy customer needs. Note that this is a vastly simplified model, and various companies organize their activities in different ways.

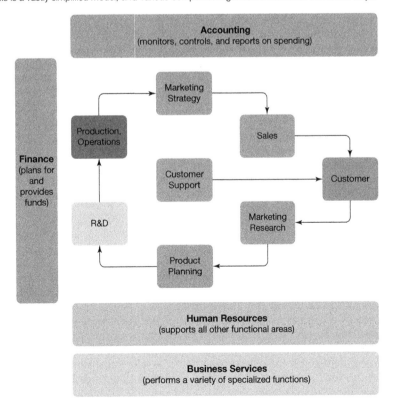

RESEARCH AND DEVELOPMENT

Products are conceived and designed through **research and development (R&D)**, sometimes known as *product design* or *engineering*. Of course, not all companies have an R&D function; many companies simply resell products that other firms make, for example. However, for companies that do develop products, R&D is essential to their survival because it provides the ideas and designs that allow these firms to meet customer needs in competitive markets.

Companies can also engage in *process* R&D to design new and better ways to run their operations. Much of this effort goes into **information technology (IT)** systems that promote communication and information usage through the company or that allow companies to offer new services to their customers.

MANUFACTURING, PRODUCTION, AND OPERATIONS

Variously called *manufacturing, production,* or *operations*, this function concerns whatever the company makes (for goods-producing businesses) or does (for service businesses). In addition to supervising the actual production activity, operations managers are responsible for a wide range of other strategies and decisions, including *purchasing* (arranging to buy the necessary materials for manufacturing), *logistics* (coordinating the incoming flow of materials and the outgoing flow of finished products), and *facilities management* (everything from planning new buildings to maintaining them). Chapter 9 explores operations management in more detail.

MARKETING, SALES, DISTRIBUTION, AND CUSTOMER SUPPORT

Your experience as a consumer probably gives you more insight into marketing, sales, distribution, and customer support than any other functional area in business. Although the lines separating these three activities are often blurry, generally speaking, *marketing* is charged with identifying opportunities in the marketplace, working with R&D to develop the products to address those opportunities, creating branding and advertising strategies to communicate with potential customers, and setting prices. The *sales* function develops relationships with potential customers and persuades customers, transaction by transaction, to buy the company's goods and services. Depending on the type of product, a *distribution* function can be involved both before the sale (helping to promote products to retailers, for example) and after the sale (to physically deliver products). After products are in buyers' hands, *customer support* goes to work, making sure customers have the support and information they need.

Perhaps no aspect of business has been changed as dramatically by recent technological advances as these marketing, sales, distribution, and customer support activities. The advent of *social media* has enabled customers to participate in an unstructured conversation with companies and with each other rather than being passive recipients of broadcast advertising messages. The result has been a profound power shift that puts buyers on much more equal footing with sellers, as you'll read about in Chapters 13 through 16.

FINANCE AND ACCOUNTING

The finance and accounting functions ensure that the company has the funds it needs to operate, monitor, and control how those funds are spent and draft reports for company management and outside audiences such as investors and government regulators. Roughly speaking, *financial managers* are responsible for planning, whereas *accounting managers* are responsible for monitoring and reporting.

Accounting specialists work closely with other functional areas to ensure profitable decision making. For instance, accountants coordinate with the R&D and production departments to estimate the manufacturing costs of a new product and then work with the marketing department to set the product's price at a level that allows the company to be competitive while meeting its financial goals. Chapters 17 through 20 address accounting, finance, and related concepts.

research and development (R&D)
Functional area responsible for conceiving and designing new products.

information technology (IT)
Systems that promote communication and information usage through the company or that allow companies to offer new services to their customers.

HUMAN RESOURCES

As you'll read in Chapter 11, the human resources (HR) function is responsible for recruiting, hiring, developing, and supporting employees. Like finance and accounting, HR supports all the other functional areas in the enterprise. Although managers in other areas are usually closely involved with hiring and training the employees in their respective departments, HR generally oversees these processes and supports the other departments as needed. The HR department is also charged with making sure the company is in compliance with the many laws concerning employee rights and workplace safety.

BUSINESS SERVICES

In addition to these core functions, a wide variety of *business services* exist to help companies with specific needs in law, banking, real estate, and other areas. These services can be performed by in-house staff, external firms, or a combination of the two. For example, a company might have a small permanent legal staff to handle routine business matters such as writing contracts but then engage a specialist law firm to help with a patent application or a major lawsuit. Similarly, all but the smallest companies have accounting professionals on staff to handle routine matters, but companies that sell shares of stock to the public are required to have their financial records *audited* (reviewed) by an outside accounting firm.

 Checkpoint

LEARNING OBJECTIVE 4: Explain the purpose of the six major functional areas in a business enterprise.

SUMMARY: (1) Research and development (R&D) creates the goods and services that a company can manufacture or perform for its customers. (2) Manufacturing, production, or operations is the part of the company where the firm makes whatever it makes or performs whatever services it performs. (3) The related group of functions in marketing, sales, distribution, and customer support are responsible for identifying market opportunities, crafting promotional strategies, and making sure customers are supplied and satisfied with their purchases. (4) Finance and accounting plan for the company's financial needs, control spending, and report on financial matters. (5) Human resources recruits, hires, develops, and supports employees. (6) Various business services provide expertise in law, real estate, and other areas.

CRITICAL THINKING: (1) Do companies that deliver services rather than creating tangible goods ever need to engage in research and development? Why or why not? (2) Why is good customer support essential to the success of marketing and sales activities?

IT'S YOUR BUSINESS: (1) Think of a strongly positive or strongly negative experience you've had with a product or company. What feedback would you like to give the company, and to which functional area would you direct your feedback? (2) Have you already chosen the functional area where you want to work after graduation? If so, what led you to that choice?

KEY TERMS TO KNOW: research and development (R&D), information technology (IT)

5   LEARNING OBJECTIVE

Summarize seven of the most important business professions.

Exploring Careers in Business

Whether you're getting ready to start your career or you've been in the workforce for a while, use this course as an opportunity to explore the many career track options in the world of business. To help stimulate your thinking, this section offers a quick overview of six major business fields.[15] However, don't limit yourself to these six by any means. For just about any professional interest you might have, you can probably find a business-related career to pursue, from entertainment and sports to health care and sciences and everything in between. Also, pay attention to employment trends; as the business environment evolves, employment opportunities in various fields grow and shrink at different rates.

OPERATIONS MANAGER

Operations management encompasses all the people and processes used to create the goods and perform the services that a company sells. The work can involve a wide range of tasks and disciplines, including production engineering, assembly, testing, scheduling, quality assurance, information technology, forecasting, finance, logistics, and customer support. Some degree of technical acumen is always required, and many managers begin their careers in technical positions such as industrial engineering.

The work can be stressful as the organization deals with fluctuating demand levels and with process and supply problems. On the other hand, if you want to balance your business interests with being involved in creating a company's products, one of these management positions might be perfect for you.

HUMAN RESOURCES SPECIALIST

HR specialists and managers plan and direct personnel-related activities, including recruiting, training and development, compensation and benefits, employee and labor relations, and health and safety. In addition, HR managers develop and implement HR systems and practices to accommodate a firm's strategy and to motivate and manage diverse workforces. In the past, top executives and professionals in other functional areas sometimes viewed HR as a tactical function concerned mostly with processing employee records and other nonstrategic duties. However, in many companies, the HR function is becoming more strategic and focused on the global competition to find, attract, and keep the best talent on the market.[16]

INFORMATION TECHNOLOGY MANAGER

Like HR, IT is evolving from a tactical support function into a critical strategic component. Reflecting IT's strategic importance, many midsize and large companies now have a *chief information officer* (CIO) position at the executive level to plot IT strategy. IT specialists design, implement, and maintain systems that help deliver the right information at the right time to the right people in the organization. Jobs in IT typically require a degree in a technical field, but an understanding of business processes, finance, and management is also important, particularly as you move up through the ranks of IT management. Many IT managers and executives also have a business degree, although not all companies require one.[17]

MARKETING SPECIALIST

A wide range of career opportunities exist in the interrelated tasks of identifying and understanding market opportunities and shaping the product, pricing, and communication strategies needed to pursue those opportunities. Whether your interests lie in branding strategy, electronic commerce, advertising, public relations, creative communication, interpersonal relations, or social media, chances are you can find a good fit somewhere in the world of marketing.

Many small companies and virtually all midsize and large companies have a variety of marketing positions, but many of these jobs are also found in advertising agencies, public relations

REAL-TIME UPDATES

Learn More by Exploring This Interactive Website

Explore the wide range of career possibilities

The *Occupational Outlook Handbook* gives insider insights and employment projections for hundreds of careers. Go to http://real-timeupdates.com/bia8 and click on Learn More in the Students section.

operations management
Management of the people and processes involved in creating goods and services.

HR specialists help companies recruit and develop the employees who provide essential skills and capabilities.

Racorn/Shutterstock

Sales can be a highly rewarding career path for motivated professionals with solid communication skills.

(PR) firms, and other companies that offer specialized services to clients. Some marketing jobs are highly specialized (advertising copywriter and e-commerce architect, for instance), whereas others encompass many aspects of marketing (brand managers, for example, deal with a variety of marketing and sales functions).

SALES PROFESSIONAL

If you thrive on competition, enjoy solving problems, and get energized by working with a wide range of people, you should definitely consider a career in sales, becoming one of the professionals responsible for building relationships with customers and helping them make purchase decisions. As a consumer, your exposure to sales might be limited to the retail sector of professional selling, but the field is much more diverse. Salespeople sell everything from design services to pharmaceuticals to airliners.

Many salespeople enjoy a degree of day-to-day freedom and flexibility not usually found in office-bound jobs. On the other hand, the pressure is usually intense; few jobs have the immediate indicators of success or failure that sales has, and most salespeople have specific targets, or *quotas*, they are expected to meet.

ACCOUNTANT

If working at the intersection of mathematics and business sounds appealing, a career in accounting or finance could be just right for you. Accounting tasks vary by job and industry, but in general, *management accountants* are responsible for collecting, analyzing, and reporting on financial matters, such as analyzing budgets, assessing the manufacturing costs of new products, and preparing state and federal tax returns. *Internal auditors* verify the work of the company's accounting effort and look for opportunities to improve efficiency and cost-effectiveness. *Public accountants* offer accounting, tax preparation, and investment advice to individuals, companies, and other organizations. *External auditors* verify the financial reports of public companies as required by law, and *forensic accountants* investigate financial crimes.

Accounting professionals need to have an affinity for numbers, analytical minds, and attention to detail. Their work can have wide-ranging effects on investors, employees, and executives, so accuracy and timeliness are critical. Communication skills are important in virtually every accounting function. Computer skills are also increasingly important, particularly for accountants closely involved with the design or operation of accounting systems.

FINANCIAL MANAGER

Financial managers perform a variety of leadership and strategic functions. *Controllers* oversee the preparation of income statements, balance sheets, and other financial reports; they frequently manage accounting departments as well. *Treasurers* and *finance officers* have a more strategic role, establishing long-term financial goals and budgets, investing the firm's funds, and raising capital as needed. Other financial management positions include *credit managers*, who supervise credit accounts established for customers, and *cash managers*, who monitor and control cash flow.

Unlike accounting tasks, for which there is a long tradition of outsourcing, the work of financial managers is generally kept in-house, particularly in midsize and large companies. The work of a financial manager touches every part of the company, so a broad understanding of the various functional areas in business is a key attribute for this position. The ability to communicate with people who aren't financial experts is also vital. Moreover, awareness of information technology developments is important for chief financial officers (CFOs) and other top financial managers, so that they can direct their companies' investments in new or improved accounting systems as needed.

Checkpoint

Achieving Professionalism

As you map out your career, think about what kind of businessperson you want to be. Will you be someone who just puts in the hours and collects a paycheck? Or will you be someone who performs on a higher plane, someone who wants to make a meaningful contribution and be viewed as a true professional? **Professionalism** is the quality of performing at a high level and conducting oneself with purpose and pride. True professionals exhibit seven distinct traits: striving to excel, being dependable and accountable, being a team player, communicating effectively, demonstrating a sense of etiquette, making ethical decisions, and maintaining a positive outlook (see Exhibit 1.8 on the next page).

STRIVING TO EXCEL

Pros are good at what they do, and they never stop improving. No matter what your job might be at any given time—even if it is far from where you aspire to be—strive to perform at the highest possible level. Not only do you have an ethical obligation to give your employer and your customers your best effort, but excelling at each level in your career is the best way to keep climbing up to new positions of responsibility. Plus, being good at what you do delivers a sense of satisfaction that is hard to beat.

In many jobs and in many industries, performing at a high level requires a commitment to continuous learning and improvement. The nature of the work often changes as markets and technologies evolve, and expectations of quality tend to increase over time as well. View this constant change as a positive thing, as a way to avoid stagnation and boredom.

EXHIBIT 1.8 Elements of Professionalism

To develop a reputation as a true professional, develop these seven attributes—and keep improving all the way through your career.

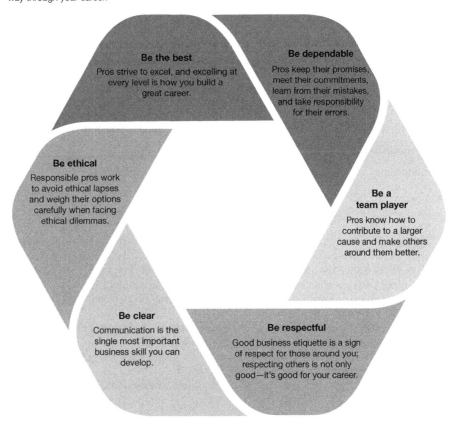

Be the best
Pros strive to excel, and excelling at every level is how you build a great career.

Be dependable
Pros keep their promises, meet their commitments, learn from their mistakes, and take responsibility for their errors.

Be ethical
Responsible pros work to avoid ethical lapses and weigh their options carefully when facing ethical dilemmas.

Be a team player
Pros know how to contribute to a larger cause and make others around them better.

Be clear
Communication is the single most important business skill you can develop.

Be respectful
Good business etiquette is a sign of respect for those around you; respecting others is not only good—it's good for your career.

BEING DEPENDABLE AND ACCOUNTABLE

Develop a reputation as somebody people can count on. This means meeting your commitments, including staying on schedule and staying within budgets. These are skills that take some time to develop as you gain experience with the amount of time and money required to accomplish various tasks and projects. With experience, you'll learn to be conservative with your commitments. You don't want to be known as someone who overpromises and underdelivers.

Being accountable also means owning up to your mistakes and learning from failure so that you can continue to improve. Pros don't make excuses or blame others. When they make mistakes—and everybody does—they face the situation head on, make amends, and move on.

BEING A TEAM PLAYER

Professionals know that they are contributors to a larger cause, that it's not all about them. Just as in athletics and other team efforts, being a team player in business is something of a balancing act. On the one hand, you need to pay enough attention to your own efforts and skills to make sure you're pulling your own weight. On the other hand, you need to pay attention to the overall team effort to make sure the team succeeds. Remember that if the team fails, you fail, too.

Great team players know how to make those around them more effective, whether it's lending a hand during crunch time, sharing resources, removing obstacles, making introductions, or offering expertise. In fact, the ability to help others improve their performance is one of the key attributes executives look for when they want to promote people into management.

Being a team player also means showing loyalty to your organization and protecting your employer's reputation—one of the most important assets any company has. Pros don't trash their employers in front of customers or in their personal blogs. When they have a problem, they solve it; they don't share it.

COMMUNICATING EFFECTIVELY

If you're looking for a surefire way to stand out from your competition and establish yourself as a competent professional, improving your communication skills may be the most important step you can take. Follow these guidelines to improve your effectiveness as a communicator:

- **Listen actively.** Active listening means making a conscious effort to turn off your own filters and biases to truly hear and understand what someone else is saying.
- **Provide practical information.** Give people useful information that is adapted to their specific needs.
- **Give facts rather than vague impressions.** Use concrete language, specific detail, and supporting information that is clear, convincing, accurate, and ethical.
- **Don't present opinions as facts.** If you are offering an opinion, make sure the audience understands that.
- **Present information in a concise, efficient manner.** Audiences appreciate—and respond more positively to—high-efficiency messages.
- **Clarify expectations and responsibilities.** Clearly state what you expect from your readers or listeners and what you can do for them.
- **Offer compelling, persuasive arguments and recommendations.** Make it clear to people how they will benefit from responding to your messages the way you want them to.

DEMONSTRATING ETIQUETTE

A vital element of professionalism is **etiquette**, the expected norms of behavior in any particular situation. The way you conduct yourself, interact with others, and handle conflict can have a profound influence on your company's success and on your career. Etiquette blunders can have serious financial costs through lower productivity and lost business opportunities.[18] When executives hire and promote you, they expect your behavior to protect the company's reputation. The more you understand such expectations, the better chance you have of avoiding career-damaging mistakes. Moreover, etiquette is an important way to show respect for others and contribute to a smooth-running workplace.

etiquette
The expected norms of behavior in any particular situation.

Long lists of etiquette "rules" can be overwhelming, and you'll never be able to memorize all of them. Fortunately, you can count on three principles to get you through any situation: respect, courtesy, and common sense. Moreover, following these principles will encourage forgiveness if you do happen to make a mistake. As you prepare to encounter new situations, take some time to learn the expectations of the other people involved. Travel guidebooks are a great source of information about norms and customs in other countries. Check to see if your library has online access to the CultureGrams database. Don't be afraid to ask questions, either. People will respect your concern and curiosity. You will gradually accumulate considerable knowledge, which will help you feel comfortable and be effective in a wide range of business situations.

MAKING ETHICAL DECISIONS

True professionals conduct themselves with a clear sense of right and wrong. They avoid committing *ethical lapses*, and they carefully weigh all the options when confronted with *ethical dilemmas*. Chapter 4 discusses these situations in more detail.

MAINTAINING A CONFIDENT, POSITIVE OUTLOOK

Spend a few minutes around successful people in any field, and chances are you'll notice how optimistic they are. They believe in what they're doing, and they believe in themselves and their ability to solve problems and overcome obstacles.

Being positive doesn't mean displaying mindless optimism or spewing happy talk all the time. It means acknowledging that things may be difficult but then buckling down and getting the job done anyway. It means no whining and no slacking off, even when the going gets tough. We live in an imperfect world, no question—jobs can be boring or difficult, customers can be unpleasant, and bosses can be unreasonable. But when you're a pro, you find a way to power through.

Your energy, positive or negative, is contagious. Both in person and online, you'll spend as much time with your colleagues as you spend with family and friends. Personal demeanor is therefore a vital element of workplace harmony. No one expects (or wants) you to be artificially upbeat and bubbly every second of the day, but one negative personality can make an entire office miserable and unproductive. Every person in a company has a responsibility to contribute to a positive, productive work environment.

For the latest information on developing a business mindset and becoming a successful professional, visit http://real-timeupdates.com/bia8 and click on Chapter 1.

 Checkpoint

LEARNING OBJECTIVE 6: Identify seven components of professionalism.

SUMMARY: Professionalism is the quality of performing at a high level and conducting yourself with purpose and pride. Seven key traits of professionalism are striving to excel, being dependable and accountable, being a team player, communicating effectively, demonstrating a sense of etiquette, making ethical decisions, and maintaining a positive outlook.

CRITICAL THINKING: (1) How much loyalty do employees owe to their employers? Explain your answer. (2) Would it be unethical to maintain a positive public persona if you have private doubts about the path your company is pursuing? Why or why not?

IT'S YOUR BUSINESS: (1) In what ways do you exhibit professionalism as a student? (2) You can see plenty of examples of unprofessional business behavior in the news media and in your own consumer and employee experiences. Why should you bother being professional yourself?

KEY TERMS TO KNOW: professionalism, etiquette

BEHIND THE SCENES
YOLANDA DIAZ GROWS MIRADOR ENTERPRISES INTO A MULTIMILLION-DOLLAR SUCCESS STORY

Like millions of people spending their days working for others, Yolanda Diaz of El Paso, Texas, had the dream of striking out on her own. Unlike many dreamers, however, Diaz took the risks and put in the hard work to make her dream a reality. Her company, Mirador Enterprises, provides facilities maintenance and management services to public-sector customers ranging from local school districts to the U.S. Army and the Department of Homeland Security. A cornerstone of her success is delivering solid value for customers by offering low-risk solutions to everything from routine maintenance to environmental compliance services to archeological site assessments.

As she built her company, Diaz demonstrated principles you read about in this chapter and will study in later chapters. She started with a customer-focused business model and a carefully thought-out business plan—a plan she still follows after more than a decade in business.

To translate those plans into action, she applied good old-fashioned hard work and a valuable combination of work experience and academic preparation. Her degree in accounting from the University of Texas at El Paso and 10 years of experience supervising accounting departments in several other companies taught her what it takes to achieve and maintain profitability. Those jobs also let her hone her management and leadership skills, essential traits for anyone who wants to grow a company.

On the subject of finances, Diaz has a passionate message for anyone who might want to start a company: Take care of your personal finances and your credit score. Banks, investors, strategic partners, suppliers, government agencies, and even customers will investigate your personal credit history to decide whether they want to do business with your company. Even as Mirador grew into a multimillion-dollar operation, banks still wanted evidence that Diaz could manage her personal finances responsibly, taking that as a sign that her business would be able to pay back loans and use lines of credit responsibly. Diaz is particularly keen to make sure college students grasp the importance of smart credit management, because this is the stage in life when many people develop destructive financial habits and set themselves up for years of painful compromises.

Another key message Diaz shares with aspiring entrepreneurs is that you don't have to go it alone. She had years of business experience when she launched Mirador, but she still sought advice and support all along the way, and she continues to network to make connections with potential customers and business partners. She makes a point to help others, too, sharing knowledge and advice with other business owners.

Diaz also took advantage of support offered by the U.S. Small Business Administration (SBA), particularly the SBA's business development assistance for small, disadvantaged businesses. As a minority- and woman-owned company, Mirador

qualified for a program that helps entrepreneurs secure contracts to provide goods and services to government agencies. (The SBA has a variety of services available to all entrepreneurs and small business owners. If you're thinking of starting a company, check out what the SBA has to offer at www.sba.gov.)

After more than a decade of growth, Diaz's company is well beyond the shaky start-up phase that many new businesses never get past. With several dozen full-time employees and annual revenues exceeding $5 million, Mirador is a testament to the success that hardworking entrepreneurs can achieve with a smart plan, a positive attitude, and the necessary help and resources. Other people think so, too: Diaz and her company have won multiple awards, including recognition from the SBA and the El Paso Hispanic Chamber of Commerce. Perhaps the most important evidence of her success is that most of Mirador's work is repeat business from existing customers—a sure sign that a company is delivering value on competitive terms.

Critical Thinking Questions

1-1. Would Yolanda Diaz have been as successful if she had started her company right out of college, rather than waiting until she'd had a decade of corporate experience? Why or why not?

1-2. If your personal credit is shaky at the moment and you don't have a lot of cash to invest in a new business, what steps could you take to get a new company going?

1-3. Are programs that help specific groups of entrepreneurs, such as the SBA program that helps minority- and woman-owned businesses, fair to those who don't qualify? Explain your answer. (You can read more about this particular program, the "8(a) Business Development Program," on the SBA website.)

LEARN MORE ONLINE

Explore Mirador's website at www.miradorenterprises.com. What steps does the company take to present its qualifications to potential customers? What is the purpose of the customer testimonial quotations featured on the website? If you were thinking of starting a business in any industry, what could you learn from Mirador's online presence?

KEY TERMS

barrier to entry
business
business mindset
business model
competitive advantage
economic environment
etiquette
goods-producing businesses
information technology
legal and regulatory
  environment

market environment
not-for-profit organizations
operations management
professionalism
profit
research and development (R&D)
revenue
service businesses
social environment
stakeholders
technological environment

TEST YOUR KNOWLEDGE

Questions for Review

1-4. What is a business model?

1-5. Give a few examples of risk.

1-6. What are four ways that business can benefit society?

1-7. Do all companies have an R&D function? Explain your answer.

1-8. How does the role of a financial manager differ from the role of an accountant?

1-9. What is revenue?

Questions for Analysis

⭐ **1-10.** Does a downturn in the economy hurt all companies equally? Provide several examples to support your answer.

1-11. Why is mobile connectivity considered a disruptive technology?

1-12. Ethical Considerations. Is managing a business in ways that reflect society's core values always ethical? Explain your answer.

1-13. How can business knowledge and skills help social entrepreneurs reach their goals?

Questions for Application

1-14. How will you be able to apply your experience as a consumer of educational services to the challenges you'll face in your career after graduation?

1-15. What are some of the ways a company in the health-care industry could improve its long-term planning by studying population trends?

⭐ **1-16.** Identify at least five ways in which your life would be different without digital technology. Would it be more or less enjoyable? More or less productive?

⭐ **1-17.** Identify three ways in which the principles of professionalism described in this chapter can make you a more successful student.

EXPAND YOUR KNOWLEDGE

Discovering Career Opportunities

There are now more ways to seek advice and access resources that can help you in finding your future career. Consider the different ways in which you might be able to find help in starting your career. Select one of these methods and create a poster that explains its uses and advantages.

Improving Your Tech Insights: Digital Products

The category of digital products encompasses an extremely broad range of product types, from e-books to music and movie files to software and instruction sets for automated machinery. Digital products are commonplace these days, but the ability to remotely deliver product value is quite a staggering concept when you think about it. (As just one example, consider that a single digital music player or smartphone can carry the equivalent of several thousand tapes or CDs.)

Supplying music over the Internet is amazing enough, but today even *tangible* products can be delivered electronically via three-dimensional (3D) printing: The technology that deposits layers of ink in inkjet printers is being adapted to deposit layers of other liquefied materials, including plastics and metals. 3D printers are already being used to "print" product prototypes, architectural models, and a variety of electronic and mechanical components. The price of the technology is dropping far enough that 3D printing is starting to become a possibility for hobbyists, independent inventors, and small businesses. Cubify, maker of the Cube 3D home printer, promotes the ability to make your own toys or jewelry and create parts to repair things around the house.[19]

Choose a category of products that has been changed dramatically by the ability to deliver value digitally. In a brief email message to your instructor, explain how digital technology revolutionized this market segment.

PRACTICE YOUR SKILLS

Sharpening Your Communication Skills

Identify a service-based business that you are familiar with and consider the following questions: What identifies this organization as a service provider? What role do the customers play? Why are they important to your chosen business? What could the company do to attract more customers? Present your ideas to the rest of the group.

Building Your Team Skills

In teams assigned by your instructor, each member should first identify one career path (such as marketing or accounting) that he or she might like to pursue and share that choice with the rest of the team. Each team member should then research the others' career options to find at least one significant factor, positive or negative, that could affect someone entering that career. For example, if there are four people on your team, you will research the three careers identified by your three teammates. After the research is complete, convene an in-person or online meeting to give each member of the team an informal career counseling session based on the research findings.

Developing Your Research Skills

Gaining a competitive advantage in today's marketplace is critical to a company's success. Research any company that sounds interesting to you and identify the steps it has taken to create competitive advantages for individual products or the company as a whole.

1-18. What goods or services does the company manufacture or sell?

1-19. How does the company set its goods or services apart from those of its competitors? Does the company compete on price, quality, service, innovation, or some other attribute?

1-20. How do the company's customer communication efforts convey those competitive advantages?

MyBizLab®

Go to the Assignments section of your MyLab to complete these writing exercises.

1-21. If individual accountability is an essential element of professionalism, why is it also important to be an effective team player? Explain your answer.

1-22. Do laws and regulations always restrict or impede the efforts of business professionals, or can they actually help businesses? Explain your answer.

ENDNOTES

1. Mirador Enterprises website, accessed 7 January 2015, www.miradorenterprises.com; "8(a) Business Development Program," U.S. Small Business Administration website, accessed 23 October 2013, www.sba.gov; "Contractor of Year: Mirador Enterprises," El Paso Times, 27 May 2010, www.elpasotimes.com; Chris Lechuga, "Entrepreneur Profile: Diaz Knows Hard Work Leads to Success," El Paso Times, 7 November 2010, www.elpasotimes.com.

2. "Employment by Major Industry Sector," U.S. Bureau of Labor Statistics, accessed 7 February 2015, www.bls.gov; "Value Added by Industry Group as a Percentage of GDP," accessed 7 February 2015, www.bea.gov.

3. "SOI Tax Stats—Integrated Business Data."

4. Cheryl Winokur Munk, "4 Generations," Community Banker, January 2009, 30–33.

5 "The Mobile Revolution Is Just Beginning," press release, World Economic Forum, 13 September 2013, www.weforum.org.

6. Maribel Lopez, "Three Trends That Change Business: Mobile, Social and Cloud," Forbes, 28 January 2012, www.forbes.com.

7. Kevin Custis, "Three Ways Business Can Be Successful on Mobile," Forbes, 15 November 2013, www.forbes.com; "IBM Survey: Speed and Analytics Key Drivers in Mobile Adoption for Organizations," press release, IBM, 19 November 2013, www.ibm.com.

8. "More Than Nine in 10 Internet Users Will Go Online via Phone," eMarketer, 6 January 2014, www.emarketer.com.

9. Christina "CK" Kerley, The Mobile Revolution & B2B, white paper, 2011, www.b2bmobilerevolution.com.

10. Jordie can Rijn, "The Ultimate Mobile Email Statistics Overview," Emailmonday.com, accessed 9 February 2014, www.emailmonday.com.

11. Jessica Lee, "46% of Searchers Now Use Mobile Exclusively to Research [Study]," Search Engine Watch, 1 May 2013, http://searchenginewatch.com.

12. Dennis McCafferty, "10 Awesome Facts About the Mobile Revolution," CIO Insight, 6 December 2013, www.cioinsight.com.

13. Nicco Mele, The End of Big: How the Internet Makes David the New Goliath (New York: St. Martin's Press: 2013), 1–2.

14. "JWT's 13 Mobile Trends for 2013 and Beyond," J. Walter Thompson website, 2 April 2013, www.jwt.com.

15. Career profiles in this section adapted from U.S. Bureau of Labor Statistics, Occupational Outlook Handbook, 2008–2009 Edition, www.bls.gov/oco.

16. Kris Dunn, "The Five Sweetest Jobs in HR and Talent Management," Workforce, July 2008, www.workforce.com.

17. Meredith Levinson, "Should You Get an MBA?" CIO, 5 July 2007, www.cio.com.

18. Susan G. Hauser, "The Degeneration of Decorum," Workforce Management, January 2011, 16–18, 20–21.

19. Cubify website, accessed 7 February 2015, http://cubify.com.

1

Only those who want to be managers need to take a course in management.

Anyone who works
in an organization
—not just managers—
can gain insight into how
organizations work and the
behaviors of their boss and
coworkers by taking a course
in management.

ASSUME

for a moment that it's your first day in an introductory physics class. Your instructor asks you to take out a piece of paper and "describe Newton's second law of motion." How would you react? I expect most students would respond with something like "How would I know? That's why I'm taking this course!"

Now let's change the situation to the first day in an introductory management class. Your instructor asks you to write an answer to the question: "What traits does one need to be an effective leader?" When we've done this on the first day, we find that students always have an answer. Everyone seems to think they know what makes a good leader.

This example illustrates a popular myth about the study of management: It's just common sense. Well, we can assure you . . . it's not! When it comes to managing, much of what passes for common sense is just plain wrong. You might be surprised to know that the *academic* study of management is filled with insights, based on extensive research, which often run counter to what seems to be common sense. That's why we decided to tackle head-on this common-sense perception by opening each chapter with a particular "management myth" and then "debunking" this myth by explaining how it *is* just a common-sense myth.

Take a minute to re-look at this chapter's "management myth" and "management myth debunked." This "debunked" myth often surprises students majoring in subjects like accounting, finance, statistics, information technology, or advertising. Since they don't expect to be managers, they see spending a semester studying management as a waste of time and irrelevant to their career goals. Later in this chapter, we'll explain why the study of management is valuable to *every* student, no matter what you're majoring in or whether you are a manager or aspire to be a manager. ●

Learning Outcomes

1-1 Tell who managers are and where they work. p. 27

1-2 Define management. p. 29

1-3 Describe what managers do. p. 31

1-4 Explain why it's important to study management. p. 36

1-5 Describe the factors that are reshaping and redefining management. p. 37

Although we'd like to think that all managers are good at what they do, you may have discovered through jobs you've had that managers can be good at what they do or maybe not so good, or even good one day and not so good the next! One thing you need to understand is that all managers—good or not so good—have important jobs to do. And this book is about the work managers do. In this chapter, we introduce you to managers and management: who they are, where they work, what management is, what they do, and why you should spend your time studying management. Finally, we'll wrap up the chapter by looking at some key factors reshaping and redefining organizations *and* the way managers manage.

Who Are Managers and Where Do They Work?

1-1 Tell who managers are and where they work.

There's no pattern or prototype or standard criteria as to who can be a manager. Managers today can be under age 18 or over age 80. They may be women as well as men, and they can be found in all industries and in all countries. They manage entrepreneurial businesses, large corporations, government agencies, hospitals, museums, schools, and not-for-profit enterprises. Some hold top-level management jobs while others are supervisors or team leaders. However, all managers share one common element: They work in an organizational setting. An **organization** is a deliberate arrangement of people brought together to accomplish some specific purpose. For instance, your college or university is an organization, as are the United Way, your neighborhood convenience store, the New Orleans Saints football team, fraternities and sororities, the Cleveland Clinic, and global companies such as Nestlé, Lego, and Samsung. These and all organizations share three common characteristics. (See Exhibit 1–1.)

organization
A systematic arrangement of people brought together to accomplish some specific purpose

What Three Characteristics Do All Organizations Share?

The *first* characteristic of an organization is that it has a distinct purpose, which is typically expressed as a goal or set of goals. For example, Bob Iger, Walt Disney Company's president and CEO, has said his company's goal is to create amazing family entertainment and to provide customers extraordinary experiences, which will lead to increasing shareholder value.[1] The *second* characteristic is that people in an organization work to achieve those goals. How? By making decisions and engaging in work activities to make the desired goal(s) a reality. For instance, at Disney, many employees work to create the content and experiences that are so important to the company's businesses. Others provide supporting services or interact with guests (customers) directly. Finally, the *third* characteristic is that an organization is structured in some way that defines and limits the behavior of its members. Disney, like most large organizations, has a fairly complex structure with different businesses, departments, and functional areas. Within that structure, rules, regulations, and policies might guide what people can or cannot do; some members will supervise other members; work teams might be formed or disbanded; or job descriptions might be created or changed so organizational members know what they're supposed to do. That structure is the setting within which managers manage.

Exhibit 1–1 Three Characteristics of Organizations

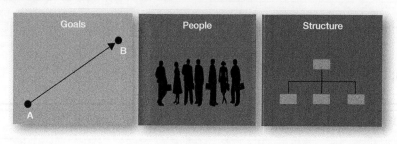

Exhibit 1–2 Management Levels

How Are Managers Different from Nonmanagerial Employees?

nonmanagerial employees
People who work directly on a job or task and have no responsibility for overseeing the work of others

managers
Individuals in an organization who direct the activities of others

top managers
Individuals who are responsible for making decisions about the direction of the organization and establishing policies that affect all organizational members

middle managers
Individuals who are typically responsible for translating goals set by top managers into specific details that lower-level managers will see get done

Although managers work in organizations, not everyone who works in an organization is a manager. For simplicity's sake, we'll divide organizational members into two categories: nonmanagerial employees and managers. **Nonmanagerial employees** are people who work directly on a job or task and have no responsibility for overseeing the work of others. The employees who ring up your sale at Home Depot, take your order at the Starbucks drive-through, or process your class registration forms are all nonmanagerial employees. These nonmanagerial employees may be called associates, team members, contributors, or even employee partners. **Managers**, on the other hand, are individuals in an organization who direct and oversee the activities of other people in the organization so organizational goals can be accomplished. A manager's job isn't about *personal* achievement—it's about helping *others* do their work. That may mean coordinating the work of a departmental group, leading an entire organization, or supervising a single person. It could involve coordinating the work activities of a team with people from different departments or even people outside the organization, such as temporary employees or individuals who work for the organization's suppliers. This distinction doesn't mean, however, that managers don't ever work directly on tasks. Some managers do have work duties not directly related to overseeing the activities of others. For example, an insurance claims supervisor might process claims in addition to coordinating the work activities of other claims employees.

Ajiti Banga is an associate product manager at Pocket Gems, a firm in San Francisco that makes and publishes mobile games such as Pet Tap Hotel and Paradise Cove. Collaborating with multiple teams of engineers and designers, she manages games from initial concept through development to product launch.

What Titles Do Managers Have?

Although they can have a variety of titles, identifying exactly who the managers are in an organization shouldn't be difficult. In a broad sense, managers can be classified as top, middle, first-line, or team leaders. (See Exhibit 1–2.) **Top managers** are those at or near the top of an organization. They're usually responsible for making decisions about the direction of the organization and defining policies and values that affect all organizational members. Top managers typically have titles such as vice president, president, chancellor, managing director, chief operating officer, chief executive officer, or chairperson of the board. **Middle managers** are those managers found between the lowest and top levels of the organization. These individuals often manage other managers and maybe some nonmanagerial employees and are typically responsible for translating the goals set by top managers

◄◄◄ From the Past to the Present ►►►

The terms *management* and *manager* are actually centuries old.[2] One source says that the word *manager* originated in 1588 to describe one who manages. The specific use of the word as a person who oversees a business or public organization is believed to have originated in the early part of the 18th century. However, used in the way we're defining it in terms of overseeing and directing organizational members, *management* and *manager* are more appropriate to the early-twentieth-century time period. The word *management* was first popularized by Frederick Winslow Taylor. Taylor is a "biggie" in management history, so let's look at his contributions to how management is practiced today.

- In 1911, Taylor's book *Principles of Scientific Management* took the business world by storm—his ideas spread in the United States and to other countries and inspired others.

- Why? His theory of **scientific management**: the use of scientific methods to define the *"one best way"* for a job to be done.

- Taylor, a mechanical engineer in Pennsylvania steel companies, observed workers and was continually shocked by how inefficient they were:

  — Employees used vastly different techniques to do the same job and often "took it easy" on the job.

  — Few, if any, work standards existed.

— Workers were placed in jobs with little or no concern for matching their abilities and aptitudes with the tasks they were required to do.

- The result was worker output only about *one-third* of what was possible.

- Taylor's remedy? Apply scientific management to these manual shop-floor jobs.

  - The result was phenomenal increases in worker output and efficiency—in the range of *200 percent or more!*

  - Because of his work, Taylor is known as the "father" of scientific management.

Management: Finding one best way to do a job?

Want to try your hand at using scientific management principles to be more efficient? Choose a task you do regularly (think…laundry, grocery shopping, studying for exams, cooking dinner, etc.). Analyze that task by writing down the steps involved in completing it. What activities could be combined or eliminated? Find the "one best way" to do this task. See if you can become more efficient—keeping in mind that changing habits isn't easy to do.

*If your professor has assigned this, go to the Assignments section of **mymanagementlab.com** to complete these discussion questions.*

✪ **Talk About It 1:** What would a "Taylor" workplace be like?

✪ **Talk About It 2:** How do Taylor's views contribute to how management is practiced today?

---

into specific details that lower-level managers will see get done. Middle managers may have such titles as department or agency head, project leader, unit chief, district manager, division manager, or store manager. **First-line managers** are those individuals responsible for directing the day-to-day activities of nonmanagerial employees. First-line managers are often called supervisors, shift managers, office managers, department managers, or unit coordinators. We want to point out a special type of manager that has become more common as organizations use employee work teams. These managers, or **team leaders**, are individuals who are responsible for managing and facilitating the activities of a work team.

What Is Management?

1-2 Define management.

Simply speaking, management is what managers do. But that simple statement doesn't tell us much. A better explanation is that **management** is the process of getting things done, effectively and efficiently, with and through other people. We need to look closer at some key words in this definition.

scientific management
The use of scientific methods to define the "one best way" for a job to be done

first-line managers
Supervisors responsible for directing the day-to-day activities of nonmanagerial employees

team leaders
Individuals who are responsible for managing and facilitating the activities of a work team

management
The process of getting things done, effectively and efficiently, through and with other people

efficiency
Doing things right, or getting the most output from the least amount of inputs

effectiveness
Doing the right things, or completing activities so that organizational goals are attained

A *process* refers to a set of ongoing and interrelated activities. In our definition of management, it refers to the primary activities or functions that managers perform—functions that we'll discuss in more detail in the next section.

Talk about new ways to be efficient!

ROWE—or results-only work environment—was a radical experiment tried at Best Buy headquarters. In this flexible work program, employees were judged only on tasks completed or results, not on how many hours they spent at work. Employees couldn't say whether they worked fewer hours because they stopped counting, BUT **employee productivity jumped 41 percent!**[3]

 Efficiency and effectiveness have to do with the work being done and how it's being done. **Efficiency** means doing a task correctly ("doing things right") and getting the most output from the least amount of inputs. Because managers deal with scarce inputs—including resources such as people, money, and equipment—they're concerned with the efficient use of those resources. Managers want to minimize resource usage and costs.

It's not enough, however, just to be efficient. Managers are also concerned with completing important activities. In management terms, we call this **effectiveness**. Effectiveness means "doing the right things" by doing those work tasks that help the organization reach its goals. Whereas efficiency is concerned with the *means* of getting things done, effectiveness is concerned with the *ends*, or attainment of organizational goals. (See Exhibit 1–3.)

A quick overview of managers and **efficiency & effectiveness**

* The concepts are different, but interrelated.
* It's easier to be effective if you ignore efficiency.
* Poor managers often allow
  — both inefficiency and ineffectiveness OR effectiveness achieved without regard for efficiency.
* Good managers are concerned with
  — both attaining goals (effectiveness) and doing so as efficiently as possible.

✪ **Write It!**
If your professor has assigned this, go to the Assignments section of **mymanagementlab.com** to complete *MGMT 1: Management Skills.*

Exhibit 1–3 Efficiency and Effectiveness

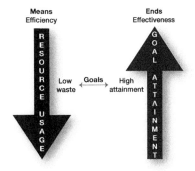

3 Ways to Look at What Managers Do

1-3 Describe what managers do.

NO TWO ORGANIZATIONS ARE ALIKE, and neither are managers' jobs. But their jobs do share some common elements, as you'll see in these three approaches to describing what managers do.

1

4 Functions Approach

- Says that managers perform certain activities, tasks, or functions as they direct and oversee others' work.

- WHAT Fayol said managers do: First person to identify five common activities managers engage in: plan, organize, command, coordinate, and control (POCCC).[4]

- Today, the management functions have been condensed to four: **planning**, **organizing**, **leading**, and **controlling**.

- See Exhibit 1–4 for what managers do when they P-O-L-C.

✪ Try It!
If your professor has assigned this, go to the Assignments section of **mymanagementlab.com** to complete the **Simulation: *What Is Management?***

Exhibit 1–4 Four Management Functions

PLANNING
Includes defining goals, establishing strategy, and developing plans to coordinate activities

ORGANIZING
Includes determining what tasks are to be done, who is to do them, how the tasks are to be grouped, who reports to whom, and who will make decisions

LEADING
Includes motivating employees, directing the activities of others, selecting the most effective communication channel, and resolving conflicts

CONTROLLING
Includes monitoring performance, comparing it with goals, and correcting any significant deviations

Achieving the organization's stated purpose

THEN | **P O C C C**
plan   organize   command   coordinate   control

NOW | **P O L C**
planning   organizing   leading   controlling

Who: Henri Fayol—an engineer/executive at a large French mining company
When: Early 1900s
How: Personal experience and observations.

planning
Defining goals, establishing strategy, and developing plans to coordinate activities

organizing
Determining what needs to be done, how it will be done, and who is to do it

leading
Directing and coordinating the work activities of an organization's people

controlling
Monitoring activities to ensure that they are accomplished as planned

2

Management Roles Approach

- Says that managers engage in certain "roles" as they manage others.
- WHAT Mintzberg said managers do: He identified and defined **managerial roles**—specific categories of managerial actions or behaviors expected of a manager. (Not sure what a "role" is? Think of the different roles you play—such as student, employee, volunteer, bowling team member, boyfriend/girlfriend, sibling, and so forth—and the different things you're expected to do in those roles.)
- Exhibit 1–5 shows Mintzberg's ten separate, but interrelated roles.

Exhibit 1–5 Mintzberg's Managerial Roles

Who: Henry Mintzberg
When: late 1960s
How: Empirical study of five chief executives at work.[5]

Source: Based on Mintzberg, Henry, *The Nature of Managerial Work*, 1st edition, © 1973.

Which Approach—Functions or Roles—Is Better at Defining What Managers Do?

— Both approaches appear to do a good job of describing what managers do.

— However, the *functions* approach stands out! It continues to be popular due to its clarity and simplicity.[6] But, don't disregard the roles approach; it offers another way to understand and appreciate what managers do.

managerial roles
Specific categories of managerial behavior; often grouped around interpersonal relationships, information transfer, and decision making

interpersonal roles
Involving people (subordinates and persons outside the organization) and other duties that are ceremonial and symbolic in nature

decisional roles
Entailing making decisions or choices

informational roles
Involving collecting, receiving, and disseminating information

3

Skills and Competencies

Source: Simon/Fotolia

- Says that managers need certain skills and competencies as they manage others.

- WHAT these researchers say managers do: Identified four general management skills including:[7]

  — **CONCEPTUAL SKILLS:** Analyzing and diagnosing complex situations to see how things fit together and to facilitate making good decisions.

  — **INTERPERSONAL SKILLS:** Working well with other people both individually and in groups by communicating, motivating, mentoring, delegating, etc.

  — **TECHNICAL SKILLS:** Job-specific knowledge, expertise, and techniques needed to perform work tasks. (For *top-level managers*—knowledge of the industry and a general understanding of the organization's processes and products; For *middle- and lower-level managers*—specialized knowledge required in the areas where they work—finance, human resources, marketing, computer systems, manufacturing, information technology.)

  — **POLITICAL SKILLS:** Building a power base and establishing the right connections to get needed resources for their groups. *Want to learn more?* Assess and develop *your* political skill by completing the PIA and the Management Skill Builder found at the end of the chapter on p. 42.

- Other important managerial competencies:[8] decision making, team building, decisiveness, assertiveness, politeness, personal responsibility, trustworthiness, loyalty, professionalism, tolerance, adaptability, creative thinking, resilience, listening, self-development.

Analyze and diagnose

Working well with others

Possessing expert job knowledge

Political adeptness

Who: Robert Katz and others
When: 1970s to present
How: Studies by various researchers

Is the Manager's Job Universal?

So far, we've discussed the manager's job as if it were a generic activity. If management is truly a generic discipline, then what a manager does should be the same whether he or she is a top-level executive or a first-line supervisor; in a business firm or a government agency; in a large corporation or a small business; or located in Paris, Texas, or Paris, France. Is that the case? Let's take a closer look.

> Is a manager **a manager no matter** where or what he or she manages?

LEVEL IN THE ORGANIZATION. Although a supervisor of the Genius Bar in an Apple Store may not do exactly the same things that Apple's CEO Tim Cook does, it doesn't mean that their jobs are inherently different. The differences are of degree and emphasis but not of activity.

As managers move up in the organization, they do more planning and less direct overseeing of others. (See Exhibit 1–6.) All managers, regardless of level, make decisions. They plan, organize, lead, and control, but the amount of time they spend on each activity is not

conceptual skills
A manager's ability to analyze and diagnose complex situations

interpersonal skills
A manager's ability to work with, understand, mentor, and motivate others, both individually and in groups

technical skills
Job-specific knowledge and techniques needed to perform work tasks

political skills
A manager's ability to build a power base and establish the right connections

Exhibit 1–6 Management Activities by Organizational Level

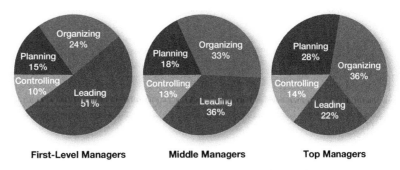

First-Level Managers   **Middle Managers**   **Top Managers**

Source: Based on T. A. Mahoney, T. H. Jerdee, and S. J. Carroll, "The Job(s) of Management," *Industrial Relations* 4, no. 2 (1965), p. 103.

small business
An independent business having fewer than 500 employees that doesn't necessarily engage in any new or innovative practices and has relatively little impact on its industry

This first-grader participates in a 10-week circus arts program offered by Marquis Studios, a not-for-profit group that offers arts-in-education services to New York City public schools. Managed in much the same way as for-profit firms, Marquis provides programs that encourage students to explore visual arts, theater, music, dance, architecture, circus arts, and puppetry.

necessarily constant. In addition, "what" they plan, organize, lead, and control changes with the manager's level. For example, as we'll demonstrate in Chapter 6, top managers are concerned with designing the overall organization's structure, whereas lower-level managers focus on designing the jobs of individuals and work groups.

PROFIT VERSUS NOT-FOR-PROFIT. Does a manager who works for the U.S. Postal Service, the Memorial Sloan-Kettering Cancer Center, or the Red Cross do the same things that a manager at Amazon or Symantec does? That is, is the manager's job the same in both profit and not-for-profit organizations? The answer, for the most part, is yes. All managers make decisions, set goals, create workable organization structures, hire and motivate employees, secure legitimacy for their organization's existence, and develop internal political support in order to implement programs. Of course, the most important difference between the two is how performance is measured. Profit—the "bottom line"—is an unambiguous measure of a business organization's effectiveness. Not-for-profit organizations don't have such a universal measure, which makes performance measurement more difficult. But don't think this means that managers in those organizations can ignore finances. Even not-for-profit organizations need to make money to continue operating. However, in not-for-profit organizations, "making a profit" for the "owners" is not the primary focus.

SIZE OF ORGANIZATION. Would you expect the job of a manager in a local FedEx store that employs 12 people to be different from that of a manager who runs the FedEx global distribution center in Memphis? This question is best answered by looking at the jobs of managers in small businesses and comparing them with our previous discussion of managerial roles. First, however, let's define a small business.

No commonly agreed-upon definition of a small business is available because different criteria are used to define *small*. For example, an organization can be classified as a small business using such criteria as number of employees, annual sales, or total assets. For our purposes, we'll describe a small business as an independent business having fewer than 500 employees that doesn't necessarily engage in any new or innovative practices and has relatively little impact on its industry.[9] So, *is* the job of managing a small business different from that of managing a large one? Yes, some

Exhibit 1–7 Managerial Roles in Small and Large Businesses

IMPORTANCE OF ROLES

Roles Played by Managers in Small Firms		Roles Played by Managers in Large Firms
	High	
Spokesperson		Resource allocator
Entrepreneur Figurehead Leader	Moderate	Liaison Monitor Disturbance handler Negotiator
Disseminator	Low	Entrepreneur

Source: Based on J. G. P. Paolillo, "The Manager's Self-Assessments of Managerial Roles: Small vs. Large Firms," *American Journal of Small Business* (January–March 1984), pp. 61–62.

differences appear to exist. As Exhibit 1–7 shows, the small business manager's most important role is that of spokesperson. He or she spends a great deal of time performing outwardly directed actions such as meeting with customers, arranging financing with bankers, searching for new opportunities, and stimulating change. In contrast, the most important concerns of a manager in a large organization are directed internally—deciding which organizational units get what available resources and how much of them. Accordingly, the entrepreneurial role—looking for business opportunities and planning activities for performance improvement—appears to be least important to managers in large firms, especially among first-level and middle managers.

Compared with a manager in a large organization, a small business manager is more likely to be a generalist. His or her job will combine the activities of a large corporation's chief executive with many of the day-to-day activities undertaken by a first-line supervisor. Moreover, the structure and formality that characterize a manager's job in a large organization tend to give way to informality in small firms. Planning is less likely to be a carefully orchestrated ritual. The organization's design will be less complex and structured, and control in the small business will rely more on direct observation than on sophisticated, computerized monitoring systems. Again, as with organizational level, we see differences in degree and emphasis but not in the activities that managers do. Managers in both small and large organizations perform essentially the same activities, but how they go about those activities and the proportion of time they spend on each are different. (You can find more information on managing small, entrepreneurial organizations in the Entrepreneurship Module at the end of the book.)

MANAGEMENT CONCEPTS AND NATIONAL BORDERS.   The last generic issue concerns whether management concepts are transferable across national borders. If managerial concepts were completely generic, they would also apply universally in any country in the world, regardless of economic, social, political, or cultural differences. Studies that have compared managerial practices among countries have not generally supported the universality of management concepts. In Chapter 3, we'll examine some specific differences between countries and describe their effect on managing. At this point, it's important for you to understand that most of the concepts discussed in the rest of the book primarily apply to the United States, Canada, Great Britain, Australia, and other English-speaking countries. Managers likely will have to modify these concepts if they want to apply them in India, China, Chile, or other countries whose economic, political, social, or cultural environments differ from that of the so-called free-market democracies.

Why Study Management?

1-4 Explain why it's important to study management.

Good managers are important because:

- Organizations need their skills and abilities, especially in today's uncertain, complex, and chaotic environment.
- They're critical to getting things done.
- They play a crucial role in employee satisfaction and engagement.

A Question of Ethics

▶ **26%** of new managers feel they're unprepared to transition into management roles.

▶ **58%** of new managers don't receive any training to help them make the transition.

▶ **48%** of first-time managers fail in that transition.

Moving to a management position isn't easy, as these statistics indicate.[10]

*If your professor has assigned this, go to the Assignments section of **mymanagementlab. com** to complete these discussion questions.*

⭐ **Talk About It 3:** Does an organization have an ethical responsibility to assist its new managers in their new positions? Why or why not?

⭐ **Talk About It 4:** What could organizations do to make this transition easier?

Well…we're finally at the point where we're going to address the chapter-opening myth! You may still be wondering *why* you need to take a management class. Especially if you're majoring in accounting or marketing or information technology and may not see how studying management is going to help you in your career. Let's look at some reasons why you may want to understand more about management.

Eighty-two percent of Millennials surveyed by a staffing firm expressed an interest in being a manager.[11]

First, all of us have a vested interest in improving the way organizations are managed. Why? Because we interact with them every day of our lives and an understanding of management offers insights into many organizational aspects. When you renew your driver's license or get your car tags, are you frustrated that a seemingly simple task takes so long? Were you surprised when well-known businesses you thought would never fail went bankrupt or were you angry when entire industries had to rely on government bailout money to survive declining economic conditions? Are you annoyed when you use a drive-through and get ready to enjoy your food or drink and realize something is missing or that it's not what you ordered? Such problems are mostly the result of managers doing a poor job of managing.

Organizations that are well managed—such as Apple, Tata, Starbucks, Nike, Singapore Airlines, and Google—develop a loyal following and find ways to prosper even when the economy stinks. Poorly managed organizations may find themselves with a declining customer base and reduced revenues and may have to file for bankruptcy protection even in a strong economy. For instance, Gimbel's, W. T. Grant, Hollywood Video, Dave & Barry's, Circuit City, Eastern Airlines, and Enron were once thriving corporations. They employed tens of thousands of people and provided goods and services on a daily basis to hundreds of thousands of customers. You may not recognize some of these names because these companies no longer exist. Poor management did them in. You can begin to recognize poor management and know what good managers should be doing by studying management.

What can a great boss do?

- Inspire you professionally *and* personally
- Energize you and your coworkers to do things together that you couldn't do alone
- Provide you feedback on how you're doing
- Provide coaching and guidance with problems
- Change your life[12]

The *second* reason for studying management is the *reality that for most of you, once you graduate from college and begin your career, you will either manage or be managed.* For those who plan to be managers, an understanding of management forms the foundation on which to build your own management skills and abilities. For those of you who don't see yourself managing, you're still likely to have to work with managers. Also, assuming that you'll have to work for a living and recognizing that you're likely to work in an organization, you're likely to have some managerial responsibilities even if you're not a manager. Our experience tells us that you can gain a great deal of insight into the way your boss (and coworkers) behave and how organizations function by studying management. Our point is that you don't have to aspire to be a manager to gain valuable information from a course in management.

What Factors Are Reshaping and Redefining Management?

1-5 Describe the factors that are reshaping and redefining management.

Welcome to the **new world of management!**

Changing Workplaces + Changing Workforce

* Not surprisingly, every business is now a technology business. Technology is changing the way we work *and* play.

* As mobile and social technologies continue to proliferate, more organizations are using apps and mobile-enhanced Web sites for managing their workforces and for other organizational work.
* Distributed labor companies like Uber, TaskRabbit, Gigwalk, and IAmExec are changing the face of temporary work.
* About 58 percent of workers ages 60 and older are currently delaying retirement.[13]
* Some 30 to 45 percent of employees work from home or are virtual employees.[14] The CEO of a New Jersey–based social media management company never sees her team members because they're part of a virtual workforce.[15]
* About 3 percent of U.S. businesses currently offer unlimited vacation time to employees—a percentage that's likely to grow.[16]

In today's world, managers are dealing with changing workplaces, a changing workforce, changing technology, and global uncertainties. For example, grocery stores continue to struggle to retain their customer base and to keep costs down. At Publix Super Markets, the large grocery chain in the southeastern United States, everyone, including managers, is looking for ways to better serve customers. The company's president, Todd Jones, who started his career bagging groceries at a Publix in New Smyrna Beach, Florida, is guiding the company through these challenges by keeping everyone's focus—from baggers to checkers to stockers—on exceptional customer service.[17] Or consider the management challenges faced by the *Seattle Post-Intelligencer* (P-I) when it, like many other newspapers, struggled to find a way to be successful in an industry that was losing readers and revenues at an alarming rate. Managers made the decision to go all-digital and the P-I became an Internet-only news source. Difficult actions followed as the news staff was reduced from 165 to less than 20 people. In its new "life" as a digital news source, the organization faces other challenges—challenges for the manager who needs to plan, organize, lead, and control in this changed environment.[18] Managers everywhere are likely to have to manage in changing circumstances, and the fact is that *how* managers manage is changing. Throughout the rest of this book, we'll be

Claire Hobean, operations manager for Re-Time Pty. Ltd., models the Australian firm's innovative Re-Timer glasses at a consumer electronics show. The medical device innovation uses bright light therapy to assist in the treatment of insomnia, jet lag, and Seasonal Affective Disorder by helping reset a person's natural body clock.

Steve Marcus/Reuters

discussing these changes and how they're affecting the way managers plan, organize, lead, and control. We want to highlight four specific changes that are increasingly important to organizations and managers everywhere: customers, innovation, social media, and sustainability.

Why Are Customers Important to the Manager's Job?

John Chambers, CEO of Cisco Systems, likes to listen to voice mails forwarded to him from dissatisfied customers because he wants to hear firsthand the emotions and frustrations they're experiencing. He can't get that type of insight by reading an e-mail.[19] This is a manager who understands the importance of customers. Organizations need customers. Without them, most organizations would cease to exist. Yet, focusing on the customer has long been thought by many managers to be the responsibility of the marketers. We're discovering, however, that employee attitudes and behaviors play a big role in customer satisfaction. Think of the times you've been treated poorly (or superbly) by an employee during a service encounter and how that affected the way you felt about the situation.

Managers are recognizing that delivering consistent high-quality customer service is essential for survival and success in today's competitive environment and that employees are an important part of that equation.[20] The implication is clear—they must create a customer-responsive organization where employees are friendly and courteous, accessible, knowledgeable, prompt in responding to customer needs, and willing to do what's necessary to please the customer.[21]

✪ **Watch It!**

If your professor has assigned this, go to the Assignments section of **mymanagementlab.com** to complete the video exercise titled *Zane's Cycles: The Management Environment*.

⠿ **Technology and the Manager's Job** ⠿
IS IT STILL MANAGING WHEN WHAT YOU'RE MANAGING ARE ROBOTS?

The office of tomorrow is likely to include workers that are faster, smarter, more responsible—and who just happen to be robots.[22] Surprised? Although robots have been used in factory and industrial settings for a long time, it's becoming more common to find robots in the office and it's bringing about new ways of looking at how work is done and at what and how managers manage. So what *would* a manager's job be like managing robots? And even more intriguing is how these "workers" might affect how human coworkers interact with them.

As machines have become smarter and smarter, researchers have been exploring the human-machine interaction and how people interact with the smart devices that are now such an integral part of our professional and personal lives. One insight is that people find it easy to bond with a robot, even one that doesn't look or sound anything like a real person. In a workplace setting, if a robot moves around in a "purposeful way," people tend to view it, in some ways, as a coworker. People name their robots and can even describe the robot's moods and tendencies. As telepresence robots become more common, the humanness becomes even more evident. For example, when Erwin Deininger, the electrical engineer at Reimers Electra Steam, a small company in Clear Brook, Virginia, moved to

the Dominican Republic when his wife's job transferred her there, he was able to still be "present" at the company via his VGo robot. Now "robot" Deininger moves easily around the office and shop floor, allowing the "real" Deininger to do his job just as if he were there in person. The company's president, satisfied with how the robot solution has worked out, has been surprised at how he acts around it, feeling at times that he's interacting with Deininger himself.

There's no doubt that robotic technology will continue to be incorporated into organizational settings. The manager's job will become even more exciting and challenging as humans and machines work together to accomplish the organization's goals.

*If your professor has assigned this, go to the Assignments section of **mymanagementlab.com** to complete these discussion questions.*

✪ **TALK ABOUT IT 5:** What's your response to the title of this box: *Is* it still managing when what you're managing are robots? Discuss.

✪ **TALK ABOUT IT 6:** If you had to manage people and robots, how do you think your job as manager might be different than what the chapter describes? (Think in terms of functions, roles, and skills/competencies.)

Why Is Innovation Important to the Manager's Job?

Success in business today demands innovation. Innovation means doing things differently, exploring new territory, and taking risks. And innovation isn't just for high-tech or other technologically sophisticated organizations; innovative efforts are needed in all types, all levels, all areas, and all sizes of organizations. You'd expect companies like Apple, Google, Toyota, and Instagram to be on a list of the world's 50 most innovative companies.[23] But what about the likes of Panera Bread? Here's a company that's using technology to improve everything it does. It's installing a new master system across its North American locations (over 1,800) that will provide customers with new ways to order their food (and even entertain themselves) and kitchen staff with capabilities to better handle custom orders. Or how about Kickstarter, which created the crowdfunding phenomenon? Now, it's looking at ways to better encourage creativity among potential projects and startups and is also expanding its business beyond fundraising into publishing and distribution. In today's challenging environment, innovation *is* critical and managers need to understand what, when, where, how, and why innovation can be fostered and encouraged throughout an organization. In a presentation a few years ago, a manager in charge of Walmart's global business explained his recipe for success (personal and organizational): continually look for new ways to do your job better; that is, be innovative. Managers not only need to be innovative personally, but also encourage their employees to be innovative. We'll share stories of innovative practices and approaches throughout the book.

social media
Forms of electronic communication through which users create online communities to share ideas, information, personal messages, and other content

Importance of Social Media to the Manager's Job

You probably can't imagine a time when employees did their work without e-mail or Internet access. Yet, some 20 years ago, as these communication tools were becoming more common in workplaces, managers struggled with the challenges of providing guidelines for using them. Today, it's all about social media, which are forms of electronic communication through which users create online communities to share ideas, information, personal messages, and other content. Social platforms such as Facebook, Twitter, LinkedIn, Tumblr, Instagram, and others are used by more than a billion people.[24] And employees don't just use these on their personal time, but also for work purposes. That's why managers again are struggling with guidelines for employee use as they attempt to navigate the power and peril of social media. For example, at grocery chain SuperValu, managers realized that keeping 135,000-plus employees connected and engaged was imperative to continued success.[25] They decided to adopt an internal social media tool to foster cooperation and collaboration among its 10 distinct store brands operating in 44 states. And they're not alone. More and more businesses are turning to social media not just as a way to connect with customers, but also as a way to manage their human resources and tap into their innovation and talent. That's the potential power of social media. But the potential peril is in how it's used. When the social media platform becomes a way for boastful employees to brag about their accomplishments, for managers to publish one-way messages to employees, or for employees to argue or gripe about something or someone they don't like at work, then it's lost its usefulness. To avoid this, managers need to remember that social media is a tool that needs to be managed to be beneficial. At SuperValu, about 9,000 store managers and assistant managers use the social media system. Although sources say it's too early to draw any conclusions, it appears that managers who actively make use of the system are having better store sales revenues than those who don't. In the remainder of

Managing in a sustainable way is important to Kim Marotta, Director of Sustainability at MillerCoors. As part of her role in achieving the company's water conservation goals, she manages initiatives to reduce water usage throughout MillerCoors' brewery processes and supply chain and to include water stewardship messages in the firm's marketing campaigns.

Milwaukee Journal Sentinel/MCT/Landov

the book, we'll look at how social media is impacting how managers manage, especially in the areas of human resource management, communication, teams, and strategy.

Importance of Sustainability to the Manager's Job

BMW is probably not a company that would come to mind in a section describing sustainability. Yet, BMW, the iconic German manufacturer of high-performance luxury autos, is making a huge bet on green, wired cars for those who reside in cities.[26] Its all-electric car, called the i3, is unlike anything that BMW or any other car manufacturer has made. The car's weight-saving, carbon-fiber body is layered with electronic services and smartphone apps ready to make life simpler and more efficient for the owner and better for the planet. Company executives recognized that it had to add products that would meet the challenges of a changing world. This corporate action by a well-known global company affirms that sustainability and green management have become mainstream issues for managers.

What's emerging in the twenty-first century is the concept of managing in a sustainable way, which has had the effect of widening corporate responsibility not only to managing in an efficient and effective way, but also to responding strategically to a wide range of environmental and societal challenges.[27] Although "sustainability" may mean different things to different people, the World Business Council for Sustainable Development describes a scenario where all earth's inhabitants can live well with adequate resources.[28] From a business perspective, **sustainability** has been defined as a company's ability to achieve its business goals and increase long-term shareholder value by integrating economic, environmental, and social opportunities into its business strategies.[29] Sustainability issues are now moving up the business agenda. Managers at BMW, Walmart, and other global businesses are discovering that running an organization in a more sustainable way will mean making informed business decisions based on (1) communicating openly with various stakeholders and understanding their requirements, and (2) factoring economic, environmental, and social aspects into how they pursue their business goals. Throughout the rest of the book, we'll explore sustainability as it relates to various aspects of managing. Just look for this 🌐 for those conversations.

Managers Matter!

Wrapping It Up...

As you can see, being a manager is both challenging and exciting! One thing we know for sure is that *managers do matter* to organizations. The Gallup Organization, which has polled millions of employees and tens of thousands of managers, has found that *the single most important variable in employee productivity and loyalty isn't pay or benefits or workplace environment; it's the quality of the relationship between employees and their direct supervisors.* Gallup also found that employees' relationship with their manager is the largest factor in **employee engagement**—which is when employees are connected to, satisfied with, and enthusiastic about their jobs—accounting for at least 70 percent of an employee's level of engagement.[30] And Gallup found that when companies increase their number of talented managers and double the rate of engaged employees, their EPS (earnings per share) is 147 percent higher than their competitors.[31] That's significant! This same research also showed that talented managers contribute about 48 percent higher profit to their companies than do average managers.[32] Finally, a different study found that when a poor manager was replaced with a great one, employee productivity increased by 12 percent.[33] What can we conclude from such reports? That talented managers *do* matter and will continue to matter to organizations!

sustainability
A company's ability to achieve its business goals and increase long-term shareholder value by integrating economic, environmental, and social opportunities into its business strategies

employee engagement
When employees are connected to, satisfied with, and enthusiastic about their jobs

MyManagementLab®

Go to **mymanagementlab.com** to complete the problems marked with this icon .

1 Review

CHAPTER SUMMARY

1-1 Tell who managers are and where they work.

Managers are individuals who work in an organization directing and overseeing the activities of other people. Managers are usually classified as top, middle, first-line, or team leader. Organizations, which are where managers work, have three characteristics: goals, people, and a deliberate structure.

1-2 Define management.

Management is the process of getting things done, effectively and efficiently, with and through other people. Efficiency means doing a task correctly ("doing things right") and getting the most output from the least amount of inputs. Effectiveness means "doing the right things" by doing those work tasks that help the organization reach its goals.

1-3 Describe what managers do.

What managers do can be described using three approaches: functions, roles, and skills/competencies. The functions approach says that managers perform four functions: planning, organizing, leading, and controlling. Mintzberg's roles approach says that what managers do is based on the 10 roles they use at work, which are grouped around interpersonal relationships, the transfer of information, and decision making. The skills/competencies approach looks at what managers do in terms of the skills and competencies they need and use. Four critical management skills are conceptual, interpersonal, technical, and

political. Additional managerial competencies include aspects such as dependability, personal orientation, emotional control, communication, and so forth. All managers plan, organize, lead, and control although how they do these activities and how often they do them may vary according to level in the organization, whether the organization is profit or not-for-profit, the size of the organization, and the geographic location of the organization.

1-4 Explain why it's important to study management.

One reason it's important to study management is that all of us interact with organizations daily so we have a vested interest in seeing that organizations are well managed. Another reason is the reality that in your career you will either manage or be managed. By studying management you can gain insights into the way your boss and fellow employees behave and how organizations function.

1-5 Describe the factors that are reshaping and redefining management.

In today's world, managers are dealing with changing workplaces, a changing workforce, global economic and political uncertainties, and changing technology. Four areas of critical importance to managers are delivering high-quality customer service, encouraging innovative efforts, using social media efficiently and effectively, and recognizing how sustainability contributes to an organization's effectiveness.

DISCUSSION QUESTIONS

1-1 What is an organization and what characteristics do organizations share?

1-2 Duties define the manager. Do you agree or disagree with this statement? Discuss the role of managers.

1-3 In today's environment, which is more important to organizations—efficiency or effectiveness? Explain your choice.

⭐ 1-4 Are there any differences between the managerial functions in a profit organization and a non-profit organization? Explain.

1-5 Using any of the popular business periodicals (such as *Bloomberg BusinessWeek, Fortune, Wall Street Journal, Fast Company*), find examples of managers doing

each of the four management functions. Write up a description and explain how these are examples of that function.

1-6 Consider your local greengrocer. Discuss how managers of such small businesses can adopt Mintzberg's ten managerial roles to run their business.

1-7 Business is changing over time, which requires management methods to evolve. What are the factors that contribute to management changes?

⭐ 1-8 Is there one best "style" of management? Why or why not?

1-9 In what ways can managers at each of the four levels of management contribute to efficiency and effectiveness?

MyManagementLab

Go to **mymanagementlab.com** for the following Assisted-graded writing questions.

1-10 Do all organizations need managers? Explain.

1-11 Explain how the 4 functions approach is better than the roles approach and the skills and competencies approach for describing what managers do.

1-12 MyManagementLab Only – comprehensive writing assignment for this chapter.

Management Skill Builder | BECOMING POLITICALLY ADEPT

Anyone who has had much work experience knows that organizational politics exists everywhere. That is, people try to influence the distribution of advantages and disadvantages within the organization in their favor. Those who understand organizational politics typically thrive. Those who don't, regardless of how good their actual job skills are, often suffer by receiving less positive performance reviews, fewer promotions, and smaller salary increases. If you want to succeed as a manager, it helps to be politically adept. Research has shown that people differ in their political skills.[34] Those who are politically skilled are more effective in their use of influence tactics. Political skill also appears to be more effective when the stakes are high. Finally, politically skilled individuals are able to exert their influence without others detecting it, which is important in being effective so that you're not labeled as playing politics. A person's political skill is determined by (1) his or her networking ability, (2) interpersonal influence, (3) social astuteness, and (4) apparent sincerity.

⭐ PERSONAL INVENTORY ASSESSMENT PERSONAL INVENTORY ASSESSMENT

Using Influence Strategies

Take a look at how well you use influence strategies. This PIA will help you determine how skillfully you do that and what you need to work on.

Skill Basics

Forget, for a moment, the ethics of politicking and any negative impressions you might have of people who engage in organizational politics. If you want to become more politically adept in your organization, follow these steps:

- *Develop your networking ability.* A good network can be a powerful tool. You can begin building a network by getting to know important people in your work area and the organization and then developing relationships with individuals in positions of power. Volunteer for committees or offer your help on projects that will be noticed by those in positions of power. Attend important organizational functions so that you can be seen as a team player and someone who's interested in the organization's success. Start a file list of individuals that you meet, even if for a brief moment. Then, when you need advice on work, use your connections and network with others throughout the organization.

- *Work on gaining interpersonal influence.* People will listen to you when they're comfortable and feel at ease around you. Work on your communication skills so that you can communicate easily and effectively with others. Work on developing a good rapport with people in all areas and at all levels of your organization. Be open, friendly, and willing to pitch in. The amount of interpersonal influence you have will be affected by how well people like you.

- *Develop your social astuteness.* Some people have an innate ability to understand people and sense what they're thinking. If you don't have that ability, you'll have to work at developing your social astuteness by doing things such as saying the right things at the right time, paying close attention to people's facial expressions, and trying to determine whether others have hidden agendas.

- *Be sincere.* Sincerity is important to getting people to want to associate with you. Be genuine in what you say and do. And show a genuine interest in others and their situations.

Practicing the Skill

Take each of the components of political skill and spend one week working on it as you navigate your school life and work life. Keep a brief set of notes describing your experiences—good and bad. Were you able to begin developing a network of people you could rely on or connect with for school or work commitments? How did you try to become better at influencing those around you? Did you work at communicating better or at developing a good rapport with coworkers or class project team members? Did you work at developing your social astuteness, maybe by starting to recognize and interpret people's facial expressions and the meaning behind those expressions? Did you make a conscious effort to be more sincere in your relationships with others, especially those that are not close friends? What could you have done differently to be more politically skilled? Once you begin to recognize what's involved with political skills, you should find yourself becoming more connected and better able to influence others—that is, more politically adept.

Experiential Exercise

Heartland's Traditional Fragrances

To: Eric Kim, Training Coordinator

From: Helen Merkin, Human Resources Director

Re: Supervisory Training and Management Certification Program

The good news: our sales numbers continue to grow. The bad news: it's putting a strain on our manufacturing supervisors. They're finding it difficult to keep our line employees motivated. We need to get some training in place to help them deal with this demanding pace or our line employees are likely to get even more stressed and we may see product quality go down.

I need you to look into two issues for me. One is a training program that focuses on important supervisory skills. Do some research and put together a list of the skills you think are most important for our supervisors to have, together with a justification for why you think these skills are important.

The second issue is how we could help our supervisors achieve certification that verifies their skills, knowledge, and professionalism. One certification program that I'm aware of is the Certified Professional Manager. Please research this program and prepare a brief (no more than half a page) bulleted list of what's involved. And get me the information as soon as possible. Thnx!

This fictionalized company and message were created for educational purposes only, and not meant to reflect positively or negatively on management practices by any company that may share this name.

CASE APPLICATION #1

Managing Without Managers

Spotify, a Swedish commercial music service, is synonymous with dramatically changing the way consumers access and use music on a day-to-day basis. They have succeeded in moving consumers away from buying music and, instead, moving them towards a model of renting the music they enjoy for a monthly fee. The Swedish music giant, launched in 2008, was developed into the business we know today by Swedish entrepreneur Daniel Ek, who was inspired to create a service that would be easier and more convenient for customers to use than the now-illegal file sharing websites that were popular at the time.[35]

Like many technology companies, Spotify has a flat organizational structure as opposed to complex hierarchies of management. For companies like Spotify it is imperative that they can work in a fast moving way that allows changes in content to get to the customer as quickly as possible. In order to work as efficiently as possible Spotify have adopted a management and organizational structure based upon squads, chapters, tribes, and guilds. Although you won't find theory talking about organizational tribes or chapters, it does provide a useful way for Spotify to organize their staff and reporting structures in an industry where many are trying to remove mangers entirely.[36]

'Squads' are the building blocks of organizational structure at Spotify. These small teams work in a way that is similar to a small start up business. These squads sit together

Spotify shows that it is possible to thrive without traditional managers!

in one shared space in order to work as effectively as possible on one long term mission; usually improving a specific area or part of the Spotify experience. Squads do not have a manager and instead work together to ensure the overall problem is solved. Each squad does however have a 'Product Owner', and it is their job to ensure that work is prioritized across the whole squad. Within each squad you will find employees with different skills that can contribute towards the squad achieving their goal.[37]

'Tribes' are groups of squads that work in similar areas. This means that all the squads who are working on web based services are part of the same tribe; and squads who work on the mobile Spotify application will be part of a different tribe. Each tribe, like the individual squads, is able to work autonomously with very little traditional management taking place. Within the Spotify offices the multiple squads that make up each tribe sit close together to allow collaboration between squads as needed, however the ethos of Spotify aims to discourage squads and tribes being dependent on one another so that change can happen as quickly as possible, something that is incredibly important in the ever changing technology markets.[38]

In order to be able to manage the staff and structure throughout the organization Spotify utilizes what they term 'Chapters'. These chapters are collections of people who have similar skills but who work in various squads; for example a chapter may be comprised of all of the programmers in the various squads within one tribe. It is within these chapters that we see more of a link to traditional management theory with clearer lines of management and responsibility for staff members, their development, pay and progression. The only time

people tend to work outside their tribe is when taking part in 'Guild' activities. The guilds are cross tribe groups of people who have similar interests but again do not have any formal management, and are instead autonomous and self managed, working on projects or problems that interest them.[39]

As a fast-moving technology company it is of course essential for Spotify to be able to react, change, and adapt their online content quickly.[40] In approaching management in a more traditional manner they have allowed individuals to be more creative whilst still meeting the overall goals of the business. There are however potential difficulties with adopting this more relaxed attitude to management, as there is an overall lack of control and there are opportunities for the freedom offered to staff to be misused. The increase in technology companies such as Spotify is changing the landscape of management, with many trying to avoid traditional management practices altogether. Spotify is somewhat unique in its field as they have recognized the need for management within the organization, however they have attempted to find a unique way of balancing the need for freedom and creativity in the workforce whilst still undertaking basic management activities. As Spotify grows in size they may need to reflect upon their approach to management.[41]

Discussion Questions

1-13 Who undertakes management at Spotify?

1-14 How could Spotify manage poor performing individuals or teams? Do you think this is a problem at Spotify? Why or why not?

1-15 Are there any similarities to traditional management at Spotify?

1-16 Do you think that this approach to management would be effective within another company?

CASE APPLICATION #2

Building a Better Boss

Google doesn't do anything halfway. So when it decided to "build a better boss," it did what it does best: look at data.[42] Using data from performance reviews, feedback surveys, and supporting papers turned in for individuals being nominated for top-manager awards, Google tried to find what a great boss is and does. The project, dubbed Project Oxygen, examined some 100 variables and ultimately identified eight characteristics or habits of Google's most effective managers. Here are the "big eight":

- Provide an unambiguous vision of the future;
- Help individuals to reach their long-term work goals;

- Express interest in employees' well-being;
- Ensure you have the necessary technical abilities to support employee efforts;
- Display effective communication skills, especially listening;
- Provide coaching support when needed;
- Focus on being productive and on end results; and
- Avoid over-managing; let your team be responsible.

At first glance, you're probably thinking that these eight attributes seem pretty simplistic and obvious and you may be wondering why Google spent all this time and effort to uncover these. Even Google's vice president for people operations,

Laszlo Bock, said, "My first reaction was, that's it?" Another writer described it as "reading like a whiteboard gag from an episode of *The Office*." But, as the old saying goes, there *was* more to this list than meets the eye.

When Bock and his team began looking closer and rank ordering the eight items by importance, Project Oxygen got interesting—a lot more interesting! And to understand this, you have to understand something about Google's approach to management since its founding in 1999. Plain and simple, managers were encouraged to "leave people alone. Let the engineers do their stuff. If they become stuck, they'll ask their bosses, whose deep technical expertise propelled them to management in the first place." It's not hard to see what Google wanted its managers to be—outstanding technical specialists. Mr. Bock explains, "In the Google context, we'd always believed that to be a manager, particularly on the engineering side, you need to be as deep or deeper a technical expert than the people who work for you." However, Project Oxygen revealed that technical expertise was ranked number eight (very last) on the list. So, here's the complete list from most important to least important, along with what each characteristic entails:

> ## Data cruncher **Google crunched data** to find out what being a great manager involves.

- *Provide coaching support when needed* (provide specific feedback and have regular one-on-one meetings with employees; offer solutions tailored to each employee's strengths)
- *Avoid over-managing; let your team be responsible* (give employees space to tackle problems themselves, but be available to offer advice)
- *Express interest in employees' well-being* (make new team members feel welcome and get to know your employees as people)
- *Focus on being productive and on end results* (focus on helping the team achieve its goals by prioritizing work and getting rid of obstacles)

- *Display good communication skills, especially listening* (learn to listen and to share information; encourage open dialogue and pay attention to the team's concerns)
- *Help individuals to reach their long-term work goals* (notice employees' efforts so they can see how their hard work is furthering their careers; appreciate employees' efforts and make that appreciation known)
- *Provide an unambiguous vision of the future* (lead the team but keep everyone involved in developing and working toward the team's vision)
- *Ensure you have the necessary technical abilities to support employee efforts* (understand the challenges facing the team and be able to help team members solve problems)

Now, managers at Google aren't just encouraged to be great managers, they know what being a great manager involves. And the company is doing its part, as well. Using the list, Google started training managers, as well as providing individual coaching and performance review sessions. You can say that Project Oxygen breathed new life into Google's managers. Bock says the company's efforts paid off quickly. "We were able to have a statistically significant improvement in manager quality for 75 percent of our worst-performing managers."

Discussion Questions

1-17 Describe the findings of Project Oxygen using the functions approach, Mintzberg's roles approach, and the skills approach.

1-18 Are you surprised at what Google found out about "building a better boss?" Explain your answer.

1-19 What's the difference between encouraging managers to be great managers and knowing what being a great manager involves?

1-20 What could other companies learn from Google's experiences?

1-21 Would you want to work for a company like Google? Why or why not?

CASE APPLICATION #3

Saving the World

You used to be able to tell who the bad guys were. But in our digital online world, those days are long gone.[43] Now, the bad guys are faceless and anonymous. And they can and do inflict all kinds of damage on individuals, businesses, governments, and other organizations. Surveys show that data breach attacks are happening with alarming regularity. And while your home and school PCs are hopefully well protected from data theft and viruses, don't think that you're in the clear. The newest targets for data thieves are smartphones and other mobile devices. However, the good guys are fighting back. For instance, security technology company Symantec Corporation set up a sting called Operation HoneyStick, in which it distributed 50 smartphones in Silicon Valley; Washington, DC; New York; Los Angeles; and Ottawa, Canada. The phones were loaded with a lot of important but fake data and left in locations where thieves would be tempted to pick them up, such as restaurants, elevators, convenience stores, and college student gathering places. Oh, and one other thing: the smartphones were equipped with monitoring software so the security experts could track where the devices were taken once found and what type of information was accessed by the finders. This is just one example of how Symantec's employees are trying to "save the world" one step at a time—not an easy thing to do.

"Imagine what life would be like if your product were never finished, if your work were never done, if your market shifted 30 times a day." Sounds pretty crazy, doesn't it? However, the computer-virus hunters and security experts at Symantec don't have to imagine—that's the reality of their daily work. For instance, at the company's well-obscured Dublin facility (one of three around the globe), operations manager Patrick Fitzgerald must keep his engineers and researchers focused 24/7 on identifying and combating what the bad guys are throwing out there. Right now, they're trying to stay ahead of a big virus threat, Stuxnet, which targets computer systems running the environmental controls in industrial facilities, such as temperature in power plants, pressure in pipelines, automated timing, and so forth. The consequences of someone intent on doing evil getting control over such critical functions could be disastrous.

Symantec, which designs content and network security software for both consumers and businesses, reflects the realities facing many organizations today—quickly shifting customer expectations and continuously emerging global competitors and global threats. Managing talented people in such an environment can be quite challenging.

Symantec's virus hunters around the world deal with some 20,000 virus samples each month, not all of which are unique, stand-alone viruses. To make the hunters' jobs even more interesting is that computer attacks are increasingly being spread by criminals around the world wanting to steal information, whether corporate data or personal user account information that can be used in fraud. Dealing with these critical and time-sensitive

issues requires special talents. The response-center team is a diverse group whose members weren't easy to find. "It's not as if colleges are creating thousands of anti-malware or security experts every year that we can hire. If you find them in any part of the world, you just go after them." The response-center team's makeup reflects that. For instance, one senior researcher is from Hungary; another is from Iceland; and another works out of her home in Melbourne, Florida. But they all share something in common: They're all motivated by solving problems.

The launch of the Blaster-B worm, a particularly nasty virus, in late summer 2003 changed the company's approach to dealing with viruses. The domino effect of Blaster-B and other viruses spawned by it meant that frontline software analysts were working around the clock for almost two weeks. The "employee burn-out" potential made the company realize that its virus-hunting team would now have to be much deeper talent-wise. Now, the response center's team numbers in the hundreds and managers can rotate people from the front lines—where they're responsible for responding to new security threats that crop up—into groups where they can help with new-product development. Others write internal research papers. Still others are assigned to develop new tools that will help their colleagues battle the next wave of threats. There's even an individual who tries to figure out what makes the virus writers tick—and the day never ends for these virus hunters. When Dublin's team finishes its day, colleagues in Santa Monica take over. When the U.S. team finishes its day, it hands off to the team in Tokyo, who then hands back to Dublin for the new day. It's a frenetic, chaotic, challenging work environment that spans the entire globe. But the goals for managing the virus hunters are to "try to take the chaos out, to make the exciting boring," to have a predictable and well-defined process for dealing with the virus threats, and to spread work evenly to the company's facilities around the world. It's a managerial challenge that company managers have embraced.

Managing talented people in a **work environment that's quickly shifting can be quite** challenging!

Discussion Questions

⭐ **1-22** Keeping professionals excited about work that is routine, standardized, *and* chaotic is a major challenge for Symantec's managers. How could they use technical, human, and conceptual skills to maintain an environment that encourages innovation and professionalism among the virus hunters?

⭐ **1-23** What managerial competencies might be important for these managers and why are these important?

★ **1-24** What management roles would operations manager Patrick Fitzgerald be playing as he (a) held weekly security briefing conference calls with coworkers around the globe, (b) assessed the feasibility of adding a new network security consulting service, and (c) kept employees focused on the company's commitments to customers?

1-25 Go to Symantec's Web site (www.symantec.com) and look up information about the company. What can you tell about its emphasis on customer service and innovation? In what ways does the organization support its employees in servicing customers and in being innovative?

Endnotes

1. The Walt Disney Company, Letter to Shareholders, *2012 Annual Report*, 1–3.
2. From the Past to the Present box based on Dictionary.com Unabridged, based on the Random House Dictionary, © Random House, Inc. 2009, http://dictionary.reference.com/browse/manage; Online Etymology Dictionary, www.etymonline.com (June 5, 2009); P. F. Drucker, *Management: Revised Edition* (New York: HarperCollins Publishers, 2008); and F. W. Taylor, *Principles of Scientific Management* (New York: Harper, 1911), 44. For other information on Taylor, see S. Wagner-Tsukamoto, "An Institutional Economic Reconstruction of Scientific Management: On the Lost Theoretical Logic of Taylorism," *Academy of Management Review*, January 2007, 105–17; R. Kanigel, *The One Best Way: Frederick Winslow Taylor and the Enigma of Efficiency* (New York: Viking, 1997); and M. Banta, *Taylored Lives: Narrative Productions in the Age of Taylor, Veblen, and Ford* (Chicago: University of Chicago Press, 1993).
3. S. Stevenson, "Don't Go to Work," http://www.slate.com/articles/business/psychology_of_management/2014/05/best_buy_s_rowe_experiment_can_results_only_work_environments_actually_be.html, May 11, 2014; S. Miller, "Study: Flexible Schedules Reduce Conflict, Lower Turnover," www.shrm.org, April 13, 2011; K. M. Butler, "We Can ROWE Our Way to a Better Work Environment," EBN.BenefitNews.com, April 1, 2011, p. 8; P. Moen, E. L. Kelly, and R. Hill, "Does Enhancing Work-Time Control and Flexibility Reduce Turnover? A Naturally Occurring Experiment," *Social Problems*, February 2011, 69–98; and R. J. Erickson, "Task, Not Time: Profile of a Gen Y Job," *Harvard Business Review*, February 2008, 19.
4. H. Fayol, *Industrial and General Administration* (Paris: Dunod, 1916).
5. H. Mintzberg, *The Nature of Managerial Work* (New York: Harper & Row, 1973).
6. S. J. Carroll and D. A. Gillen, "Are the Classical Management Functions Useful in Describing Managerial Work?" *Academy of Management Review*, January 1987, 48.
7. See, for example, J. G. Harris, D. W. DeLong, and A. Donnellon, "Do You Have What It Takes to Be an E-Manager?" *Strategy and Leadership* (August 2001): 10–14; C. Fletcher and C. Baldry, "A Study of Individual Differences and Self-Awareness in the Context of Multi-Source Feedback," *Journal of Occupational and Organizational Psychology* (September 2000): 303–19; and R. L. Katz, "Skills of an Effective Administrator," *Harvard Business Review*, September–October 1974, 90–102.
8. R. P. Tett, H. A. Guterman, A. Bleier, and P. J. Murphy, "Development and Content Validation of a 'Hyperdimensional' Taxonomy of Managerial Competence," *Human Performance* 13, no. 3 (2000): 205–51.
9. "Frequently Asked Questions," *U.S. Small Business Administration*, www.sba.gov/advo (September 2008); T. L. Hatten, *Small Business: Entrepreneurship and Beyond* (Upper Saddle River, NJ: Prentice Hall, 1997), 5; L. W. Busenitz, "Research on Entrepreneurial Alertness," *Journal of Small Business Management* (October 1996): 35–44; and J. W. Carland, F. Hoy, W. R. Boulton, and J. C. Carland, "Differentiating Entrepreneurs from Small Business Owners: A Conceptualization," *Academy of Management Review* 9, no. 2 (1984): 354–59.
10. A Question of Ethics box based on M. S. Plakhotnik and T. S. Rocco, "A Succession Plan for First-Time Managers," *T&D*, December 2011, 42–45; P. Brotherton, "New Managers Feeling Lost at Sea," *T&D*, June 2011, 25; and "How Do We Help a New Manager Manage?" *Workforce Management Online*, June 16, 2011.
11. "A New Millennium of Managers," *TD*, February 2015, 19.
12. J. Welch and S. Welch, "An Employee Bill of Rights," *Bloomberg BusinessWeek*, March 16, 2009, 72.
13. N. Hellmich, "Many Delay Retiring: Need More Money, Enjoy Their Jobs," http://www.usatoday.com/story/money/personalfinance/2014/02/27/delay-retirement-money/5785373/, February 27, 2014.
14. M. M. Biro, "Telecommuting Is the Future of Work," www.forbes.com, January 12, 2014.
15. L. Vankam, "Virtual Workforce Stands Ready," *USA Today*, January 8, 2013, 11A.
16. The Muse, "Could Unlimited Vacation Time Work for Your Company?" http://www.forbes.com/sites/dailymuse/2014/10/29/could-unlimited-vacation-time-work-for-your-company/, October 29, 2014.
17. T. W. Martin, "May I Help You?" *Wall Street Journal*, April 23, 2009, R4.
18. "Contact the Staff of seattlepi.com," http://www.seattlepi.com/pistaff/; and W. Yardley and R. Perez-Peña, "Seattle Paper Shifts Entirely to the Web," *New York Times Online* (March 17, 2009).
19. F. F. Reichheld, "Lead for Loyalty," *Harvard Business Review*, July–August 2001, 76.
20. See, for instance, H. Ernst, W. D. Hoyer, M. Krafft, and K. Krieger, "Customer Relationship Management and Company Performance—The Mediating Role of New Product Performance," *Journal of the Academy of Marketing Science* (April 2011): 290–306; J. P. Dotson and G. M. Allenby, "Investigating the Strategic Influence of Customer and Employee Satisfaction on Firm Financial Performance," *Marketing Science* (September–October 2010): 895–908; R. Grewal, M. Chandrashekaran, and A. V. Citrin, "Customer Satisfaction Heterogeneity and Shareholder Value," *Journal of Marketing Research* (August 2010): 612–26; M. Riemann, O. Schilke, and J. S. Thomas, "Customer Relationship Management and Firm Performance: The Mediating Role of Business Strategy," *Journal of the Academy of Marketing Science* (Summer 2010): 326–46; and K. A. Eddleston, D. L. Kidder, and B. E. Litzky, "Who's the Boss? Contending with Competing Expectations from Customers and Management," *Academy of Management Executive* (November 2002): 85–95.
21. See, for instance, C. B. Blocker, D. J. Flint, M. B. Myers, and S. F. Slater, "Proactive Customer Orientation and Its Role for Creating Customer Value in Global Markets," *Journal of the Academy of Marketing Science* (April 2011): 216–33; G. A. Gorry and R. A. Westbrook, "Once More, with Feeling: Empathy and Technology in Customer Care," *Business Horizons* (March–April 2011): 125–34; M. Dixon, K. Freeman, and N. Toman, "Stop Trying to Delight Your Customers," *Harvard Business Review*, July–August 2010, 116–22; D. M. Mayer, M. G. Ehrhart, and B. Schneider, "Service Attribute Boundary Conditions of the Service Climate-Customer Satisfaction Link," *Academy of Management Journal* (October 2009): 1034–50; B. A. Gutek, M. Groth, and B. Cherry, "Achieving Service Success Through Relationships and Enhanced Encounters," *Academy of Management Executive* (November 2002): 132–44; Eddleston, Kidder, and Litzky, "Who's the Boss? Contending with Competing Expectations from Customers and Management"; S. D. Pugh, J. Dietz, J. W. Wiley, and S. M. Brooks, "Driving Service Effectiveness Through Employee-Customer Linkages," *Academy of Management Executive* (November 2002): 73–84; S. D. Pugh, "Service with a Smile: Emotional Contagion in the Service Encounter," *Academy of Management Journal* (October 2001): 1018–27; W. C. Tsai, "Determinants and Consequences of Employee Displayed Positive Emotions," *Journal of Management* 27, no. 4 (2001): 497–512; Naumann and Jackson, Jr., "One More Time: How Do You Satisfy Customers?"; and M. D. Hartline and O. C. Ferrell, "The Management of Customer-Contact Service Employees: An Empirical Investigation," *Journal of Marketing* (October 1996): 52–70.
22. Technology and the Manager's Job box based on D. Bennett, "I'll Have My Robots Talk to Your Robots," *Bloomberg BusinessWeek*

(February 21–27, 2011): 52–62; E. Spitznagel, "The Robot Revolution Is Coming," *Bloomberg BusinessWeek,* January 17–23, 2011, 69–71; G. A. Fowler, "Holiday Hiring Call: People vs. Robots," *Wall Street Journal,* December 20, 2010, B1+; A. Schwartz, "Bring Your Robot to Work Day," *Fast Company.com* (November 2010): 72–74; and P. J. Hinds, T. L. Roberts, and H. Jones, "Whose Job Is It Anyway? A Study of Human-Robot Interaction in a Collaborative Task," *Human-Computer Interaction* (March 2004): 151–81.

23. *Fast Company Staff,* "World's 50 Most Innovative Companies," *Fast Company,* March 2015, 66+.

24. "Top 15 Most Popular Social Networking Sites," http://www.obimba.com/articles/social-networking-websites, February 2015; and "Social Media Update 2014," Pew Research Center, http://www.pewinternet.org/2015/01/09/social-media-update-2014/, January 9, 2015.

25. D. Ferris, "Social Studies: How to Use Social Media to Build a Better Organization," *Workforce Online,* February 12, 2012.

26. A. Taylor III, "BMW Gets Plugged In," *Fortune,* March 18, 2013, 150–56.

27. KPMG Global Sustainability Services, *Sustainability Insights,* October 2007.

28. *Vision 2050* Report, Overview, www.wbcsd.org/vision2050.aspx.

29. *Symposium on Sustainability—Profiles in Leadership,* New York, October 2001.

30. J. Harter and A. Adkins, "Employees Want a Lot More From Their Managers," www.gallup.com/businessjournal, April 8, 2015.

31. R. Beck and J. Harter, "Why Great Managers Are So Rare," www.gallup.com/businessjournal, March 26, 2014.

32. Ibid.

33. S. Bailey, "No Manager Left Behind," *Chief Learning Officer,* February 2015, 30.

34. S. Y. Todd, K. J. Harris, R. B. Harris, and A. R. Wheeler, "Career Success Implications of Political Skill," *Journal of Social Psychology,* June 2009, 179–204; G. R. Ferris, D. C. Treadway, P. L. Perrewé, R. L. Brouer, C. Douglas, and S. Lux, "Political Skill in Organizations," *Journal of Management,* June 2007, 290–329; K. J. Harris, K. M. Kacmar, S. Zivnuska, and J. D. Shaw, "The Impact of Political Skill on Impression Management Effectiveness," *Journal of Applied Psychology,* January 2007, 278–85; and G. R. Ferris, D. C. Treadway, R. W. Kolodinsky, W. A. Hochwarter, C. J. Kacmar, C. Douglas, and D. D. Frink, "Development and Validation of the Political Skill Inventory," *Journal of Management,* February 2005, 126–52.

35. H. Kniberg, (2014) "Spotify engineering culture (part 1)," www.labs.spotify.com/2014/03/27/spotify-engineering-culture-part-1/, March 27, 2014.

36. Kniberg, H. (2014). *Spotify engineering culture (part 2).* Available: https://labs.spotify.com/2014/09/20/spotify-engineering-culture-part-2/. Last accessed 21 October 2015.

37. Lynskey, D. (2013). *Is Daniel Ek, Spotify founder, going to save the music industry…or destroy it?.* Available: http://www.theguardian.com/technology/2013/nov/10/daniel-ek-spotify-streaming-music. Last accessed 21 October 2015.

38. D. Richards, "At Zappos, Culture Pays," www.strategy-business.com/article, August 24, 2010.

39. A. Groth, "Zappos Is Going Holacratic: No Job Titles, No Managers, No Hierarchy."

40. G. Anders, "No More Bosses for Zappos (A Cautionary Tale)."

41. R. E. Silverman, "At Zappos, Some Employees Find Offer to Leave Too Good to Refuse," *Wall Street Journal Online,* May 7, 2015.

42. R. D'Aprix, "A Simple Effective Formula for Leadership," *Strategic Communication Management,* May 2011, 14; R. Jaish, "Pieces of Eight," *e-learning age,* May 2011, 6; M. L. Stallard, "Google's Project Oxygen: A Case-Study in Connection Culture," www.humanresourcesiq.com, March 25, 2011; J. Aquino, "8 Traits of Stellar Managers, Defined by Googlers," www.businessinsider.com, March 15, 2011; and A. Bryant, "Google's Quest to Build a Better Boss," *New York Times Online,* March 12, 2011.

43. N. Perlroth, "Outmaneuvered at Their Own Game, Anti-Virus Makers Struggle to Adapt," *New York Times Online,* December 31, 2012; A. Vance, "Have You Seen This Android?" *Bloomberg BusinessWeek,* March 12–18, 2012, 37–38; "Are We Winning the Cybersecurity War?" www.networkworld.com, February 13, 2012, 19–20; "Symantec Corporation: Company Profile," *Datamonitor,* February 10, 2012; A. Greenberg, "As Hackers Leak Symantec's Source Code, Firm Says Cops Set Up Extortion Sting Operation," Forbes.com, February 7, 2012, 8; "Under Siege," *Best's Review,* January 2012, 77; E. Savits and A. K. Ghosh, "Cyber Spies Are Winning: Time to Reinvent Online Security," Forbes.com, November 18, 2011, 3; and "The Virus Hunters," *Management Today,* December 2010, 98.

History Module

A BRIEF HISTORY OF MANAGEMENT'S ROOTS

Henry Ford once said, "History is more or less bunk." Well...Henry Ford was wrong! History is important because it can put current activities in perspective. We propose that you need to know management history because it can help you understand what today's managers do. In this module, you'll find an annotated timeline that discusses key milestones in management theory. *Check out each chapter's "From the Past to the Present" box feature where we highlight a key person and his or her contributions or a key historical factor and its effect on contemporary management concepts.* We believe this approach will help you better understand the origins of many contemporary management concepts.

Early Management

Management has been practiced a long time. Organized endeavors directed by people responsible for planning, organizing, leading, and controlling activities have existed for thousands of years. Regardless of what these individuals were called, someone had to perform those functions.

● 3000 BCE–1776	1911–1947	Late 1700s–1950s	1940s–1950s	1960s–present
Early Management	Classical Approaches	Behavioral Approach	Quantitative Approach	Contemporary Approaches

Stephen Studd/Getty Images

3000–2500 BCE

The Egyptian pyramids are proof that projects of tremendous scope, employing tens of thousands of people, were completed in ancient times.[1] It took more than 100,000 workers some 20 years to construct a single pyramid. Someone had to plan what was to be done, organize people and materials to do it, make sure those workers got the work done, and impose some controls to ensure that everything was done as planned. That someone was managers.

Antonio Natale/Getty Images

1400s

At the arsenal of Venice, warships were floated along the canals, and at each stop, materials and riggings were added to the ship.[2] Sounds a lot like a car "floating" along an assembly line, doesn't it? In addition, the Venetians used warehouse and inventory systems to keep track of materials, human resource management functions to manage the labor force (including wine breaks), and an accounting system to keep track of revenues and costs.

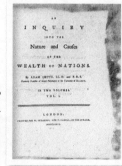

Fotosearch/Getty Images

1776

Although this is an important date in U.S. history, it's also important because it's the year Adam Smith's *Wealth of Nations* was published. In it, he argued the economic advantages of the **division of labor** (or **job specialization**)—that is, breaking down jobs into narrow, repetitive tasks. Using division of labor, individual productivity could be increased dramatically. Job specialization continues to be a popular way to determine how work gets done in organizations. As you'll see in Chapter 6, it does have its drawbacks.

Transcendental Graphics/Getty Images

1780s–Mid-1800s

The **Industrial Revolution** may be the most important pre-twentieth-century influence on management. Why? Because with the industrial age came the birth of the corporation. With large, efficient factories pumping out products, someone needed to forecast demand, make sure adequate supplies of materials were available, assign tasks to workers, and so forth. Again, that someone was managers! It was indeed a historic event for two reasons: (1) because of all the organizational aspects (hierarchy, control, job specialization, and so forth) that became a part of the way work was done, and (2) because management had become a necessary component to ensure the success of the enterprise.

Classical Approaches

Beginning around the turn of the twentieth century, the discipline of management began to evolve as a unified body of knowledge. Rules and principles were developed that could be taught and used in a variety of settings. These early management proponents were called classical theorists.

3000 BCE–1776	● 1911–1947	Late 1700s–1950s	1940s–1950s	1960s–present
Early Management	Classical Approaches	Behavioral Approach	Quantitative Approach	Contemporary Approaches

Bettmann/CORBIS

1911

That's the year Frederick W. Taylor's *Principles of Scientific Management* was published. His groundbreaking book described a theory of **scientific management**—the use of scientific methods to determine the "one best way" for a job to be done. His theories were widely accepted and used by managers around the world, and Taylor became known as the "father" of scientific management.[3] (Taylor's work is profiled in Chapter 1's "From the Past to the Present" box.) Other major contributors to scientific management were Frank and Lillian Gilbreth (early proponents of time-and-motion studies and parents of the large family described in the original book *Cheaper by the Dozen*) and Henry Gantt (whose work on scheduling charts was the foundation for today's project management).

Hulton Archive/Getty Images

1916–1947

Unlike Taylor, who focused on an individual production worker's job, Henri Fayol and Max Weber (depicted in the photo) looked at organizational practices by focusing on what managers do and what constituted good management. This approach is known as **general administrative theory**. Fayol was introduced in Chapter 1 as the person who first identified five management functions. He also identified 14 **principles of management**—fundamental rules of management that could be applied to all organizations.[4] (See Exhibit HM–1 for a list of these 14 principles.) Weber is known for his description and analysis of bureaucracy, which he believed was an ideal, rational form of organization structure, especially for large organizations. In Chapter 6, we elaborate on these two important management pioneers.

Exhibit HM–1 Fayol's 14 Principles of Management

1 **Division of Work.** This principle is the same as Adam Smith's "division of labor." Specialization increases output by making employees more efficient.

2 **Authority.** Managers must be able to give orders. Authority gives them this right. Along with authority, however, goes responsibility. Whenever authority is exercised, responsibility arises.

3 **Discipline.** Employees must obey and respect the rules that govern the organization. Good discipline is the result of effective leadership, a clear understanding between management and workers regarding the organization's rules, and the judicious use of penalties for infractions of the rules.

4 **Unity of Command.** Every employee should receive orders from only one superior.

5 **Unity of Direction.** Each group of organizational activities that have the same objective should be directed by one manager using one plan.

6 **Subordination of Individual Interests to the General Interest.** The interests of any one employee or group of employees should not take precedence over the interests of the organization as a whole.

7 **Remuneration.** Workers must be paid a fair wage for their services.

8 **Centralization.** Centralization refers to the degree to which subordinates are involved in decision making. Whether decision making is centralized (to management) or decentralized (to subordinates) is a question of proper proportion. The task is to find the optimum degree of centralization for each situation.

9 **Scalar Chain.** The line of authority from top management to the lowest ranks represents the scalar chain. Communications should follow this chain. However, if following the chain creates delays, cross-communications can be allowed if agreed to by all parties and if superiors are kept informed. Also called chain of command.

10 **Order.** People and materials should be in the right place at the right time.

11 **Equity.** Managers should be kind and fair to their subordinates.

12 **Stability of Tenure of Personnel.** High employee turnover is inefficient. Management should provide orderly personnel planning and ensure that replacements are available to fill vacancies.

13 **Initiative.** Employees who are allowed to originate and carry out plans will exert high levels of effort.

14 **Esprit de Corps.** Promoting team spirit will build harmony and unity within the organization.

Behavioral Approach

The behavioral approach to management focused on the actions of workers. How do you motivate and lead employees in order to get high levels of performance?

3000 BCE-1776	1911-1947	● Late 1700s-1950s	1940s-1950s	1960s-present
Early Management	Classical Approaches	Behavioral Approach	Quantitative Approach	Contemporary Approaches

Ken Welsh/Newscom

Late 1700s–Early 1900s

Managers get things done by working with people. Several early management writers recognized how important people are to an organization's success.[5] For instance, Robert Owen, who was concerned about deplorable working conditions, proposed an idealistic workplace. Hugo Munsterberg, a pioneer in the field of industrial psychology, suggested using psychological tests for employee selection, learning theory concepts for employee training, and studies of human behavior for employee motivation. Mary Parker Follett was one of the first to recognize that organizations could be viewed from both individual *and* group behavior. She thought that organizations should be based on a group ethic rather than on individualism.

Hawthorne Works Factory of Morton College

Relay Assembly Operation

1924–Mid-1930s

The **Hawthorne studies**, a series of studies that provided new insights into individual and group behavior, were without question the most important contribution to the behavioral approach to management.[6] Conducted at the Hawthorne (Cicero, Illinois) Works of the Western Electric Company, the studies were initially designed as a scientific management experiment. Company engineers wanted to see the effect of various lighting levels on worker productivity. Using control and experimental groups of workers, they expected to find that individual output in the experimental group would be directly related to the intensity of the light. However, much to their surprise, they found that productivity in both groups varied with the level of lighting. Not able to explain it, the engineers called in Harvard professor Elton Mayo. Thus began a relationship that lasted until 1932 and encompassed numerous experiments in the behavior of people at work. What were some of their conclusions? Group pressures can significantly affect individual productivity, and people behave differently when they're being observed. Scholars generally agree that the Hawthorne studies had a dramatic impact on management beliefs about the role of people in organizations and led to a new emphasis on the human behavior factor in managing organizations.

Self-Actualization

Esteem

Social

Safety

Physiological

1930s–1950s

The human relations movement is important to management history because its supporters never wavered from their commitment to making management practices more humane. Proponents of this movement uniformly believed in the importance of employee satisfaction—a satisfied worker was believed to be a productive worker.[7] So they offered suggestions like employee participation, praise, and being nice to people to increase employee satisfaction. For instance, Abraham Maslow, a humanistic psychologist, who's best known for his description of a hierarchy of five needs (a well-known theory of employee motivation), said that once a need was substantially satisfied, it no longer served to motivate behavior. Douglas McGregor developed Theory X and Theory Y assumptions, which related to a manager's beliefs about an employee's motivation to work. Even though both Maslow's and McGregor's theories were never fully supported by research, they're important because they represent the foundation from which contemporary motivation theories were developed. Both are described more fully in Chapter 11.

Monkey Business Images/Shutterstock

1960s–Today

An organization's people continue to be an important focus of management research. The field of study that researches the actions (behaviors) of people at work is called **organizational behavior (OB)**. OB researchers do empirical research on human behavior in organizations. Much of what managers do today when managing people—motivating, leading, building trust, working with a team, managing conflict, and so forth—has come out of OB research. These topics are explored in depth in Chapters 9–13.

Quantitative Approach

The quantitative approach, which focuses on the application of statistics, optimization models, information models, computer simulations, and other quantitative techniques to management activities, provided tools for managers to make their jobs easier.

3000 BCE–1776	1911–1947	Late 1700s–1950s	● 1940s–1950s	1960s–present
Early Management	Classical Approaches	Behavioral Approach	Quantitative Approach	Contemporary Approaches

Bert Hardy/Getty Images

1940s

The **quantitative approach** to management—which is the use of quantitative techniques to improve decision making—evolved from mathematical and statistical solutions developed for military problems during World War II. After the war was over, many of these techniques used for military problems were applied to businesses.[8] For instance, one group of military officers, dubbed the "Whiz Kids," joined Ford Motor Company in the mid-1940s and immediately began using statistical methods to improve decision making at Ford. You'll find more information on these quantitative applications in Chapter 15.

Richard Drew/AP Images

1950s

After World War II, Japanese organizations enthusiastically embraced the concepts espoused by a small group of quality experts, the most famous being W. Edwards Deming (photo below) and Joseph M. Juran. As these Japanese manufacturers began beating U.S. competitors in quality comparisons, Western managers soon took a more serious look at Deming's and Juran's ideas.[9] Their ideas became the basis for **total quality management (TQM)**, which is a management philosophy devoted to continual improvement and responding to customer needs and expectations. We'll look more closely at Deming and his beliefs about TQM in Chapter 15.

Contemporary Approaches

Most of the early approaches to management focused on managers' concerns inside the organization. Starting in the 1960s, management researchers began to look at what was happening in the external environment outside the organization.

3000 BCE–1776	1911–1947	Late 1700s–1950s	1940s–1950s	● 1960s–present
Early Management	Classical Approaches	Behavioral Approach	Quantitative Approach	Contemporary Approaches

Frederic J. Brown/Newscom

1960s

Although Chester Barnard, a telephone company executive, wrote in his 1938 book *The Functions of the Executive* that an organization functioned as a cooperative system, it wasn't until the 1960s that management researchers began to look more carefully at systems theory and how it related to organizations.[10] The idea of a system is a basic concept in the physical sciences. As related to organizations, the **systems approach** views systems as a set of interrelated and interdependent parts arranged in a manner that produces a unified whole. Organizations function as **open systems**, which means they are influenced by and interact with their environment. Exhibit HM–2 illustrates an organization as an open system. A manager has to efficiently and effectively manage all parts of the system in order to achieve established goals. See Chapter 2 for additional information on the external and internal factors that affect how organizations are managed.

Exhibit HM–2 Organization as an Open System

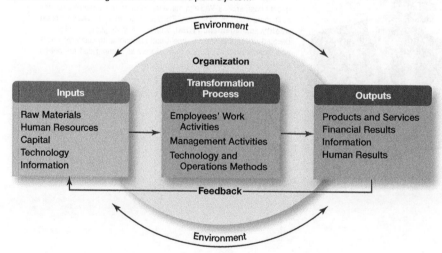

● Contemporary Approaches

1960s

Early management theorists proposed management principles that they generally assumed to be universally applicable. Later research found exceptions to many of these principles. The **contingency approach (or situational approach)** says that organizations, employees, and situations are different and require different ways of managing. A good way to describe contingency is "if...then." *If* this is the way my situation is, *then* this is the best way for me to manage in this situation. One of the earliest contingency studies was done by Fred Fiedler and looked at what style of leadership was most effective in what situation.[11] Popular contingency variables have been found to include organization size, the routineness of task technology, environmental uncertainty, and individual differences.

Image Source/Getty Images

1980s–Present

Although the dawn of the information age is said to have begun with Samuel Morse's telegraph in 1837, the most dramatic changes in information technology have occurred in the latter part of the twentieth century and have directly affected the manager's job.[12] Managers now may manage employees who are working from home or working halfway around the world. An organization's computing resources used to be mainframe computers locked away in temperature-controlled rooms and only accessed by the experts. Now, practically everyone in an organization is connected—wired or wireless—with devices no larger than the palm of the hand. Just like the impact of the Industrial Revolution in the 1700s on the emergence of management, the information age has brought dramatic changes that continue to influence the way organizations are managed. The impact of information technology on how managers do their work is so profound that we've included in several chapters a boxed feature on "Technology and the Manager's Job."

Industrial Revolution
The advent of machine power, mass production, and efficient transportation beginning in the late eighteenth century in Great Britain

division of labor (or job specialization)
The breakdown of jobs into narrow repetitive tasks

scientific management
The use of the scientific method to define the one best way for a job to be done

general administrative theory
Descriptions of what managers do and what constitutes good management practice

principles of management
Fayol's fundamental or universal principles of management practice

Hawthorne studies
Research done in the late 1920s and early 1930s devised by Western Electric industrial engineers to examine the effect of different work environment changes on worker productivity, which led to a new emphasis on the human factor in the functioning of organizations and the attainment of their goals

organizational behavior (OB)
The field of study that researches the actions (behaviors) of people at work

quantitative approach
The use of quantitative techniques to improve decision making

total quality management (TQM)
A managerial philosophy devoted to continual improvement and responding to customer needs and expectations

systems approach
An approach to management that views an organization as a system, which is a set of interrelated and interdependent parts arranged in a manner that produces a unified whole

open systems
Systems that dynamically interact with their environment

contingency approach (or situational approach)
An approach to management that says that individual organizations, employees, and situations are different and require different ways of managing

Endnotes

1. C. S. George, Jr., *The History of Management Thought,* 2d ed. (Upper Saddle River, NJ: Prentice Hall, 1972), p. 4.

2. Ibid., pp. 35–41.

3. F. W. Taylor, *Principles of Scientific Management* (New York: Harper, 1911), p. 44. For other information on Taylor, see S. Wagner-Tsukamoto, "An Institutional Economic Reconstruction of Scientific Management: On the Lost Theoretical Logic of Taylorism," *Academy of Management Review,* January 2007, pp. 105–117; R. Kanigel, *The One Best Way: Frederick Winslow Taylor and the Enigma of Efficiency* (New York: Viking, 1997); and M. Banta, *Taylored Lives: Narrative Productions in the Age of Taylor, Veblen, and Ford* (Chicago: University of Chicago Press, 1993).

4. H. Fayol, *Industrial and General Administration* (Paris: Dunod, 1916); M. Weber, *The Theory of Social and Economic Organizations,* ed. T. Parsons, trans. A. M. Henderson and T. Parsons (New York: Free Press, 1947); and M. Lounsbury and E. J. Carberry, "From King to Court Jester? Weber's Fall from Grace in Organizational Theory,"

Organization Studies, vol. 26, no. 4 (2005), pp. 501–525.

5. R. A. Owen, *A New View of Society* (New York: E. Bliss and White, 1825); H. Munsterberg, *Psychology and Industrial Efficiency* (Boston: Houghton Mifflin, 1913); and M. P. Follett, *The New State: Group Organization the Solution of Popular Government* (London: Longmans, Green, 1918).

6. E. Mayo, *The Human Problems of an Industrial Civilization* (New York: Macmillan, 1933); and F. J. Roethlisberger and W. J. Dickson, *Management and the Worker* (Cambridge, MA: Harvard University Press, 1939). Also see G. W. Yunker, "An Explanation of Positive and Negative Hawthorne Effects: Evidence from the Relay Assembly Test Room and Bank Wiring Observation Room Studies," paper presented, Academy of Management Annual Meeting, August 1993, Atlanta, Georgia; S. R. Jones, "Was There a Hawthorne Effect?" *American Sociological Review,* November 1992, pp. 451–468; and S. R. G. Jones, "Worker Interdependence and Output: The Hawthorne Studies Reevaluated," *American Sociologi-*

cal Review, April 1990, pp. 176–190; J. A. Sonnenfeld, "Shedding Light on the Hawthorne Studies," *Journal of Occupational Behavior* (April 1985), pp. 111–130; B. Rice, "The Hawthorne Defect: Persistence of a Flawed Theory," *Psychology Today,* February 1982, pp. 70–74; R. H. Franke and J. Kaul, "The Hawthorne Experiments: First Statistical Interpretations," *American Sociological Review,* October 1978, pp. 623–643; and A. Carey, "The Hawthorne Studies: A Radical Criticism," *American Sociological Review,* June 1967, pp. 403–416.

7. A. Maslow, "A Theory of Human Motivation," *Psychological Review,* July 1943, pp. 370–396; see also A. Maslow, *Motivation and Personality* (New York: Harper & Row, 1954); and D. McGregor, *The Human Side of Enterprise* (New York: McGraw-Hill, 1960).

8. P. Rosenzweig, "Robert S. McNamara and the Evolution of Management," *Harvard Business Review,* December 2010, pp. 86–93; and C. C. Holt, "Learning How to Plan Production, Inventories, and Work Force," *Operations Research,* January–February 2002, pp. 96–99.

9. T. A. Stewart, "A Conversation with Joseph Juran," *Fortune,* January 11, 1999, pp. 168–170; J. R. Hackman and R. Wageman, "Total Quality Management: Empirical, Conceptual, and Practical Issues," *Administrative Science Quarterly,* June 1995, pp. 309–342; B. Krone, "Total Quality Management: An American Odyssey," *The Bureaucrat,* Fall 1990, pp. 35–38; and A. Gabor, *The Man Who Discovered Quality* (New York: Random House, 1990).

10. C. I. Barnard, *The Functions of the Executive* (Cambridge: Harvard University Press, 1938); and K. B. DeGreene, *Sociotechnical Systems: Factors in Analysis, Design, and Management* (Upper Saddle River, NJ: Prentice Hall, 1973), p. 13.

11. F. E. Fiedler, *A Theory of Leadership Effectiveness* (New York: McGraw-Hill, 1967).

12. "Information Age: People, Information & Technology—An Exhibition at the National Museum of American History," *Smithsonian Institution,* http://photo2.si.edu/ infoage/infoage.html (June 11, 2009); and P. F. Drucker, *Management, Revised Edition* (New York: HarperCollins Publishers, 2008).

Chapter 2
External Environment and Economics

Understanding Basic Economics

1 Define *economics,* and explain why scarcity is central to economic decision making.

2 Differentiate among the major types of economic systems.

3 Explain the interaction between demand and supply.

4 Identify four macroeconomic issues that are essential to understanding the behavior of the economy.

5 Outline the debate over deregulation, and identify four key roles that governments play in the economy.

6 Identify the major ways of measuring economic activity.

BEHIND THE SCENES COULD YOU PREDICT SALES OF APPLE'S NEXT BESTSELLER?

David Paul Morris/Bloomberg/Getty Images

Apple's Jeff Williams oversees global operations for the company's popular iPod and iPhone product lines.

www.apple.com

Predicting demand for a new product or a new business is one of the toughest decisions managers and entrepreneurs need to make. How can you determine how many people are likely to buy a new car model, business service, industrial machine, or mobile phone? If you guess too high, you could end up losing money after investing in unwanted inventory, underused distribution channels, or overstaffed departments. If you guess too low, you could stress your supply chain and service delivery systems and annoy potential customers who want to buy from you but can't because you aren't prepared to meet demand, and these customers might jump to a competitor who can meet their needs.

Forecasting product demand accurately requires a combination of economic data analysis, experience-driven judgment, and plain old luck. However, even the data analysis component requires a heavy dose of judgment because you have to decide which economic variables are relevant and how to factor them into your forecasting. If you're trying to decide whether to open a coffee shop near campus, for example, and you see that unemployment has dropped in your city, will that mean more demand for your coffee because more people have disposable income or less demand because fewer people have time to hang out in coffee shops?

Now imagine you're in the shoes of Jeff Williams, the senior vice president in charge of operations at Apple. In this role, you oversee production of the company's wildly popular iPhones, and your job includes trying to align production resources with anticipated sales demand. You're responsible for both sides of the equation: Coming up with an accurate idea of demand and making sure the vast Apple supply and manufacturing chain can build enough products to meet that demand in a timely fashion.

Your latest supply-and-demand challenge is the iPhone6. Previous generations of the iPhone have sold many, many millions of units, and surveys indicate that consumer interest in the iPhone6 appears to be through the roof. However, you know from experience that the stated intent to buy a new product doesn't necessarily translate into actual purchases. How can you be sure you've read market demand accurately and lined up the necessary production resources?[1]

INTRODUCTION

From a local coffee shop to a global giant such as Apple (profiled in the chapter-opening Behind the Scenes) economic forces affect every aspect of business. This chapter offers a brief introduction to economics from a business professional's perspective, a high-level look at the study of economics, types of economic systems, and the interaction of supply and demand. Understanding basic economic principles is essential to successful business management, and this knowledge can make you a more satisfied consumer and a more successful investor as well.

What Is This Thing Called the Economy?

The **economy** is the sum total of all the economic activity within a given region, from a single city to a whole country to the entire world. The economy can be a difficult thing to get your mind wrapped around because it is so complex, constantly in motion, a subject of heated dispute, and at times hard to see—even though it's everywhere around us. People who devote their lives to studying it can have a hard time agreeing on how the economy works, when it might be "broken," or how to fix it if it is broken. However, business leaders need to understand and pay attention to some key principles.

Economics is the study of how a society uses its scarce resources to produce and distribute goods and services. Economics is roughly divided into a small-scale perspective and a large-scale perspective. The study of economic behavior among consumers, businesses, and industries that collectively determine the quantity of goods and services demanded and supplied at different prices is termed **microeconomics**. The study of a country's larger economic issues, such as how firms compete, the effect of government policies, and how an economy maintains and allocates its scarce resources, is termed **macroeconomics**.

Although microeconomics looks at the small picture and macroeconomics looks at the big picture, understanding the economy at either scale requires an understanding of how the small and large forces interact. For instance, numerous macro forces and policies determine whether homeowners can afford to install solar energy systems. In turn, the aggregate behavior of all those homeowners at the micro level affects the vitality and direction of the overall economy.

FACTORS OF PRODUCTION

Each society must decide how to use its economic resources, or *factors of production* (see Exhibit 2.1 on the next page). **Natural resources** are things that are useful in their natural state, such as land, forests, minerals, and water. **Human resources** are people and their individual talents and capacities. **Capital** includes money, machines, tools, and buildings that a business needs in order to produce goods and services. **Entrepreneurship** is the spirit of innovation, the initiative, and the willingness to take the risks involved in creating and operating businesses. **Knowledge** is the collective intelligence of an organization. *Knowledge workers*, employees whose primary contribution is the acquisition and application of business knowledge, are a key economic resource for businesses in today's economy.

Traditionally, a business or a country was considered to have an advantage if its location offered plentiful supplies of natural resources, human resources, capital, and entrepreneurs. In today's global marketplace, however, intellectual assets are often the key.

1 **LEARNING OBJECTIVE**

Define *economics*, and explain why scarcity is central to economic decision making.

economy
The sum total of all the economic activity within a given region.

economics
The study of how a society uses its scarce resources to produce and distribute goods and services.

microeconomics
The study of how consumers, businesses, and industries collectively determine the quantity of goods and services demanded and supplied at different prices.

macroeconomics
The study of "big-picture" issues in an economy, including competitive behavior among firms, the effect of government policies, and overall resource allocation issues.

natural resources
Land, forests, minerals, water, and other tangible assets usable in their natural state.

human resources
All the people who work in an organization or on its behalf.

capital
The funds that finance the operations of a business as well as the physical, human-made elements used to produce goods and services, such as factories and computers.

entrepreneurship
The combination of innovation, initiative, and willingness to take the risks required to create and operate new businesses.

knowledge
Expertise gained through experience or association.

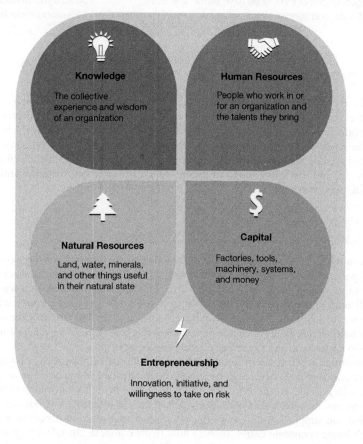

EXHIBIT 2.1   Factors of Production

Every good or service is created from some combination of these five factors of production.

Knowledge
The collective experience and wisdom of an organization

Human Resources
People who work in or for an organization and the talents they bring

Natural Resources
Land, water, minerals, and other things useful in their natural state

Capital
Factories, tools, machinery, systems, and money

Entrepreneurship
Innovation, initiative, and willingness to take on risk

Companies can easily obtain capital from one part of the world, purchase supplies from another, and locate production facilities in still another. They can relocate some of their operations to wherever they find a steady supply of affordable workers, or they can assemble virtual teams of knowledge workers from anywhere on the planet. Chapter 3 discusses this issue of economic globalization in more detail.

THE ECONOMIC IMPACT OF SCARCITY

scarcity
A condition of any productive resource that has finite supply.

The impact of **scarcity**, meaning that a given resource has a finite supply, is fundamental to understanding economics.[2] Looking back over the factors of production, you can see that the supply of all these resources is limited. Even entrepreneurial energy is limited in the sense that there are only so many entrepreneurs in the economy, and each entrepreneur can accomplish only so much during a given time span.

Scarcity has two powerful effects: It creates competition for resources, and it forces trade-offs on the part of every participant in the economy. First, at every stage of economic activity, people and organizations compete for the resources they need. Businesses and industries compete with each other for materials, employees, and customers. As a consumer, you compete with other consumers. If you were the only person in town who needed a loaf of bread, you would have tremendous power over the bakeries and grocery stores as the only customer. However, because you compete with thousands of other consumers for a limited supply of bread, you have far less control over the bread market.

Second, this universal scarcity of resources means that consumers, companies, and governments are constantly forced to make *trade-offs*, having to give up one thing to get something else. You have to decide how to spend the 24 hours you have every day, and every choice involves a trade-off: The more time you spend on one activity means less time for every other activity you could possibly pursue. Businesses must make similar trade-offs, such as deciding how much money to spend on advertising a new product versus how much to spend on the materials used to make it, or deciding how many employees to have in sales versus in customer support. Just like you, businesses never have enough time, money, and other resources to accomplish what they'd like to, so success in life and in business is largely a matter of making smart trade-offs.

By the way, economists have a name for the most-attractive option not selected when making a trade-off. **Opportunity cost** refers to the value of the most appealing alternative from all those that weren't chosen.[3] In other words, opportunity cost is a way to measure the value of what you gave up when you pursued a different opportunity.

opportunity cost
The value of the most appealing alternative not chosen.

 Checkpoint

Economic Systems

The roles that individuals, businesses, and the government play in allocating a society's resources depend on the society's **economic system**, the basic set of rules for allocating resources to satisfy its citizens' needs (see Exhibit 2.2 on the next page). Economic systems are generally categorized as either *free-market systems* or *planned systems*, although these are really theoretical extremes; every economy combines aspects of both approaches.

2 LEARNING OBJECTIVE

Differentiate among the major types of economic systems.

economic system
The policies that define a society's particular economic structure; the rules by which a society allocates economic resources.

FREE-MARKET SYSTEMS

In a **free-market system**, individuals and companies are largely free to decide what products to produce, how to produce them, whom to sell them to, and at what price to sell them. In other words, they have the chance to succeed—or fail—by their own efforts. **Capitalism** and *private enterprise* are the terms most often used to describe the free-market system, one in which private parties (individuals, partnerships, or corporations) own and operate the majority of businesses and where competition, supply, and demand determine which goods and services are produced.

free-market system
Economic system in which decisions about what to produce and in what quantities are decided by the market's buyers and sellers.

capitalism
Economic system based on economic freedom and competition.

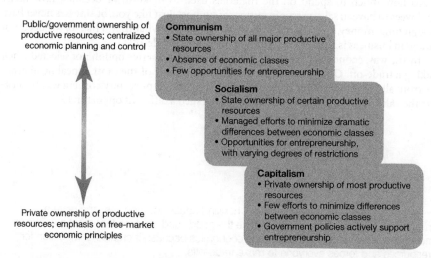

EXHIBIT 2.2   Economic Systems

All economic systems are based on certain fundamental principles about how a country should allocate its resources to satisfy the needs of its citizens. Except at the theoretical extremes, the distinctions between systems tend to be blurry, and arguments continue over the precise definition of each system. Most modern economies exhibit a combination of capitalism and socialism. Here are a few of the characteristics that distinguish the three major systems.

Public/government ownership of productive resources; centralized economic planning and control

Communism
- State ownership of all major productive resources
- Absence of economic classes
- Few opportunities for entrepreneurship

Socialism
- State ownership of certain productive resources
- Managed efforts to minimize dramatic differences between economic classes
- Opportunities for entrepreneurship, with varying degrees of restrictions

Capitalism
- Private ownership of most productive resources
- Few efforts to minimize differences between economic classes
- Government policies actively support entrepreneurship

Private ownership of productive resources; emphasis on free-market economic principles

In practice, however, no economy is truly "free" in the sense that anyone can do whatever he or she wants to do. Local, state, national, and even international governments such as the European Union intervene in the economy to accomplish goals that leaders deem socially or economically desirable. This practice of limited intervention is characteristic of a *mixed economy* or *mixed capitalism*, which is the economic system of the United States and most other countries. For example, government bodies intervene in the U.S. economy in a variety of ways, such as influencing particular allocations of resources through tax incentives, prohibiting or restricting the sale of certain goods and services, or setting *price controls*. Price controls can involve maximum allowable prices (such as limiting rent increases) and minimum allowable prices (such as supplementing the prices of agricultural goods to ensure producers a minimum level of income or establishing minimum wage levels).[4]

PLANNED SYSTEMS

planned system
Economic system in which the government controls most of the factors of production and regulates their allocation.

In a **planned system**, governments largely control the allocation of resources and limit freedom of choice in order to accomplish government goals. Because social equality is a major goal of planned systems, private enterprise and the pursuit of private gain are generally regarded as wasteful and exploitive. The planned system that allows individuals the least degree of economic freedom is *communism*, which still exists in a few countries, most notably North Korea and China. As an economic system, communism can't be regarded as anything but a dismal failure. In fact, even as its government remains strongly communist from a political perspective, China has embraced many concepts of capitalism in recent years and has become one of the world's most powerful and important economies as a result.

socialism
Economic system characterized by public ownership and operation of key industries combined with private ownership and operation of less-vital industries.

Socialism lies somewhere between capitalism and communism, with a fairly high degree of government planning and some government ownership of capital resources. However, government ownership tends to be focused on industries considered vital to the common welfare, such as transportation, health care, and communications. Private ownership is permitted in other industries.

Although "socialism" is sometimes used as a pejorative term in today's heated political and economic dialogues, and many people believe capitalism is inherently superior to socialism, that opinion is not universal. For example, many European countries, including economic heavyweights France and Germany, incorporate varying degrees of socialism.

Moreover, although free-market capitalism remains the foundation of the U.S. economy, some important elements of the U.S. economy are socialized and have been for many years. Public schools, much of the transportation infrastructure, various local and regional utilities, and several major health-care programs all fit the economic definition of socialism. Socialism and capitalism are competing philosophies, but they are not mutually exclusive, and each approach has strengths and weaknesses, which is why most modern economies combine aspects of both.

NATIONALIZATION AND PRIVATIZATION

The line between socialism and capitalism isn't always easy to define, and it doesn't always stay in the same place, either. Governments can change the structure of the economy by **nationalizing**—taking ownership of—selected companies or in extreme cases even entire industries. They can also move in the opposite direction, **privatizing** services once performed by the government by allowing private businesses to perform them instead.

In recent years, governments of various countries have done both, for different reasons and in different industries. For example, private companies now own or operate a number of highways, bridges, ports, prisons, and other infrastructure elements in the United States, providing services once provided by the government. The primary reason for this trend is the belief that private firms motivated by the profit incentive can do a more efficient job of running these facilities.[5]

nationalizing
A government's takeover of selected companies or industries.

privatizing
Turning over services once performed by the government to private businesses.

✓ **Checkpoint**

LEARNING OBJECTIVE 2: Differentiate among the major types of economic systems.

SUMMARY: The two basic types of economic systems are free-market systems, in which individuals and companies are largely free to make economic decisions, and planned systems, in which government administrators make all major decisions. The terms *capitalism* and *private enterprise* are often used to describe free-market systems. Communism is the most extreme type of planned system; socialism lies somewhere between capitalism and communism and generally refers to government ownership of fundamental services. The U.S. economy, like virtually all other economies, blends elements of free-market capitalism and government control.

CRITICAL THINKING: (1) Why are no economies truly free, in the sense of having no controls or restrictions? (2) What are some possible risks of privatizing basic services such as the transportation infrastructure?

IT'S YOUR BUSINESS: (1) What are your emotional reactions to the terms *capitalism* and *socialism*? Explain why you feel the way you do. (2) Would you rather pay lower taxes and accept the fact that you need to pay for many services such as health care and education or pay higher taxes with the assurance that the government will provide many basic services for you? Why?

KEY TERMS TO KNOW: economic system, free-market system, capitalism, planned system, socialism, nationalizing, privatizing

3 **LEARNING OBJECTIVE**

Explain the interaction between demand and supply.

demand
Buyers' willingness and ability to purchase products at various price points.

supply
A specific quantity of a product that the seller is able and willing to provide at various prices.

demand curve
A graph of the quantities of a product that buyers will purchase at various prices.

The Forces of Demand and Supply

At the heart of every business transaction is an exchange between a buyer and a seller. The buyer wants or needs a particular service or good and is willing to pay the seller in order to obtain it. The seller is willing to participate in the transaction because of the anticipated financial gains. In a free-market system, the marketplace (composed of individuals, firms, and industries) and the forces of demand and supply determine the quantity of goods and services produced and the prices at which they are sold. **Demand** refers to the amount of a good or service that customers will buy at a given time at various prices. **Supply** refers to the quantities of a good or service that producers will provide on a particular date at various prices. In other words, *demand* refers to the behavior of buyers, whereas *supply* refers to the behavior of sellers. The two forces work together to impose a kind of dynamic order on the free-market system.

UNDERSTANDING DEMAND

The airline industry offers a helpful demonstration of supply and demand. A **demand curve** is a graph that shows the amount of product that buyers will purchase at various prices, all other factors being equal. Demand curves typically slope downward, implying that as price drops, more people are willing to buy. The black line labeled *Initial demand* in Exhibit 2.3 shows a possible demand curve for the monthly number of economy tickets on one airline's Chicago-to-Denver route. You can see that as price decreases, demand increases, and vice versa. If demand is strong, airlines can keep their prices consistent or perhaps even raise them. If demand weakens, they can lower prices to stimulate more purchases. (Airlines use sophisticated *yield management* software to constantly adjust prices in order to keep average ticket prices as high as possible while also keeping their planes as full as possible.)

This movement up and down the demand curve is only part of the story, however. Demand at all price points can also increase or decrease in response to a variety of factors. If overall demand for air travel decreases, the entire demand curve moves to the left (the

---

EXHIBIT 2.3   Demand Curve

The demand curve (black line) for economy seats on one airline's Chicago-to-Denver route shows that the higher the ticket price, the smaller the quantity of seats demanded, and vice versa. Overall demand is rarely static; however, market conditions can shift the entire curve to the left (decreased demand at every price, red line) or to the right (increased demand at every price, green line).

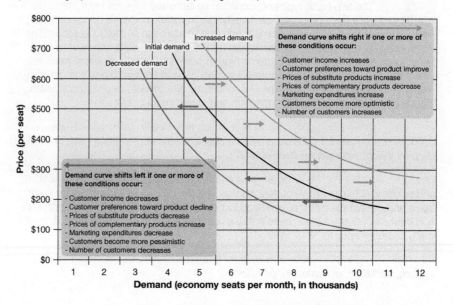

red line in Exhibit 2.3). If overall demand increases, the curve moves to the right (the green line). The bulleted lists in Exhibit 2.3 indicate the effects of some of the major factors that can cause overall demand to increase or decrease:

- Customer income
- Customer preferences toward the product (fears regarding airline safety, for example)
- The price of *substitute products* (products that can be purchased instead of air travel, including rail tickets, automobile travel, or web conferencing)
- The price of *complementary products* (such as hotel accommodations or restaurant dining for the airline industry)
- Marketing expenditures (for advertising and other promotional efforts)
- Customer expectations about future prices and their own financial well-being

For example, if the economy is down and businesses and consumers have less money to spend, overall demand for air travel is likely to shrink. Businesses will seek less-expensive substitutes, such as videoconferencing and online meetings, and consumers may vacation closer to home so they can travel by car. Conversely, if customers have more money to spend, more of them are likely to travel, thereby increasing overall demand.

UNDERSTANDING SUPPLY

Demand alone is not enough to explain how a company operating in a free-market system sets its prices or production levels. In general, a firm's willingness to produce and sell a product increases as the price it can charge and its profit potential per item increase. In other words, as the price goes up, the quantity supplied generally goes up. The depiction of the relationship between prices and quantities that sellers will offer for sale, regardless of demand, is called a **supply curve**.

Movement along the supply curve typically slopes upward: As prices rise, the quantity that sellers are willing to supply also rises. Similarly, as prices decline, the quantity that sellers are willing to supply declines. Exhibit 2.4 shows a possible supply curve for the

supply curve
A graph of the quantities of a product that sellers will offer for sale, regardless of demand, at various prices.

EXHIBIT 2.4	Supply Curve

This supply curve for economy seats on the Denver-to-Chicago route shows that the higher the price, the more tickets (seats) the airline would be willing to supply, all else being equal. As with demand, however, the entire supply curve can shift to the left (decreased supply) or the right (increased supply) as producers respond to internal and external forces.

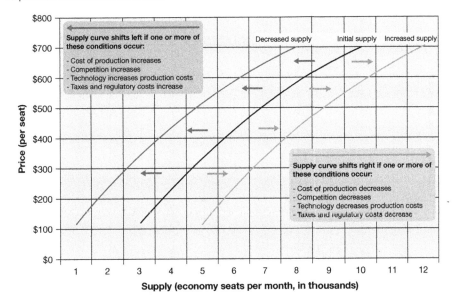

monthly number of economy tickets (seats) supplied on an airline's Chicago-to-Denver route at different prices. The graph shows that increasing prices for economy tickets on that route should increase the number of tickets (seats) an airline is willing to provide for that route, and vice versa.

As with demand, supply is dynamic and is affected by a variety of internal and external factors. They include the cost of inputs (such as wages, fuel, and airport gate fees for the airlines), the number of competitors in the marketplace, and advancements in technology that allow companies to operate more efficiently. A change in any of these variables can shift the entire supply curve, either increasing or decreasing the amount offered at various prices, as Exhibit 2.4 suggests.

UNDERSTANDING HOW DEMAND AND SUPPLY INTERACT

Buyers and sellers clearly have opposite goals: Buyers want to buy at the lowest possible price, and sellers want to sell at the highest possible price. Neither side can "win" this contest outright. Customers might want to pay $100 for a ticket from Chicago to Denver, but airlines aren't willing to sell many, if any, at that price. Conversely, the airlines might want to charge $1,000 for a ticket, but customers aren't willing to buy many, if any, at that price. So the market in effect arranges a compromise known as the **equilibrium point**, at which the demand and supply curves intersect (see Exhibit 2.5). At the equilibrium price point, customers are willing to buy as many tickets as the airline is willing to sell.

equilibrium point
The point at which quantity supplied equals quantity demanded.

Because the supply and demand curves are dynamic, so is the equilibrium point. As variables affecting supply and demand change, so will the equilibrium price. For example, increased concerns about airline safety could encourage some travelers to choose alternatives such as automobile travel or web conferencing, thus reducing the demand for air travel at every price and moving the equilibrium point as well. Suppliers might respond to such a reduction in demand by either cutting the number of flights offered or lowering ticket prices in order to restore the equilibrium level.

EXHIBIT 2.5   **The Relationship Between Supply and Demand**

The equilibrium price is established when the amount of a product that suppliers are willing to sell at a given price equals the amount that consumers are willing to buy at that price.

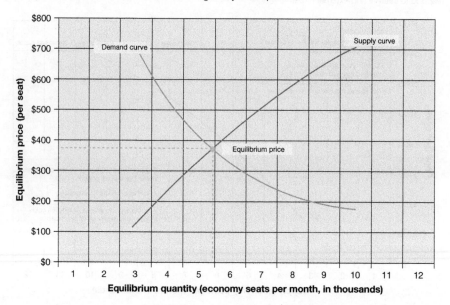

As the iPhone6 story at the beginning of the chapter pointed out, questions of supply, demand, and equilibrium pricing are among the toughest issues managers and entrepreneurs face. For example, imagine you're a concert promoter planning for next year's summer season. You have to balance the potential demand for each performer across a range of prices, in the hope of matching the supply you can deliver (the seating capacity of each venue and the number of shows). You have to make these predictions months in advance and make financial commitments based on your predictions. Predict well, and you'll make a tidy profit. Predict poorly, and you could lose a pile of money.

✓ Checkpoint

LEARNING OBJECTIVE 3: Explain the interaction between demand and supply.

SUMMARY: *Demand* is the amount of a good or service that customers will buy at a given time at various prices; it can be shown visually as a *demand curve*. The entire demand curve can shift as market conditions change. Similarly, *supply* is the amount of a good or service that producers will provide on a particular date at various prices; it can be shown with a *supply curve*, which can also shift in response to market forces. In the simplest sense, demand and supply affect price in the following manner: When the price goes up, the quantity demanded goes down, but the supplier's incentive to produce more goes up. When the price goes down, the quantity demanded increases, but the quantity supplied may (or may not) decline. The point at which the demand and supply curves intersect—the point at which demand and supply are equal—is the *equilibrium point*.

CRITICAL THINKING: (1) How does the interaction of demand and supply keep a market in balance, at least approximately and temporarily? (2) If the prices of complementary products for a given product go up, what effect is this increase likely to have on demand for that product?

IT'S YOUR BUSINESS: (1) Are there any products or brands you are so loyal to that you will purchase them at almost any price? Will you accept less-expensive substitutes? (2) Have you ever purchased something simply because it was on sale? Why or why not?

KEY TERMS TO KNOW: demand, supply, demand curve, supply curve, equilibrium point

The Macro View: Understanding How an Economy Operates

All the individual instances of supply and demand and all the thousands and millions of transactions that take place over time add up to the economy. This section explores four "big-picture" issues that are essential to understanding the overall behavior of the economy: competition in a free-market system, business cycles, unemployment, and inflation.

COMPETITION IN A FREE-MARKET SYSTEM

Competition is the situation in which two or more suppliers of a product are rivals in the pursuit of the same customers. The nature of competition varies widely by industry, product category, and geography (see Exhibit 2.6 on the next page). At one extreme is **pure competition**, in which no single firm becomes large enough to influence prices and thereby distort the workings of the free-market system. At the other extreme, in a **monopoly**, one supplier so thoroughly dominates a market that it can control prices and essentially shut out other competitors. Monopolies can happen "naturally," as companies innovate or markets evolve (a *pure monopoly*) or by government mandate (a *regulated monopoly*). However, the lack of competition in a monopoly situation is considered so detrimental

4 LEARNING OBJECTIVE

Identify four macroeconomic issues that are essential to understanding the behavior of the economy.

competition
Rivalry among businesses for the same customers.

pure competition
A situation in which so many buyers and sellers exist that no single buyer or seller can individually influence market prices.

monopoly
A situation in which one company dominates a market to the degree that it can control prices.

| EXHIBIT 2.6 | Categories of Competition |

EXHIBIT 2.6 Categories of Competition

Markets vary widely in the nature of competition they exhibit and the choices that buyers have. Here are five major categories of competition and the factors that distinguish them.

Pure Competition	Monopolistic Competition	Oligopoly	Pure Monopoly	Regulated Monopoly
Characteristics: • Many small suppliers • Virtually identical products • Low barriers to entry	**Characteristics:** • Can have few or many suppliers, of varying size • Products can be distinguished but are similar enough to be replacements • Variable barriers to entry but market open to all	**Characteristics:** • Small number of suppliers, even as few as just two (a *duopoly*) • Products can be distinguished in important ways, but replacements are still available • Barriers to entry tend to be high, making entering the market difficult	**Characteristics:** • Only one supplier in a given market • Monopoly achieved without government intervention, by innovation, specialization, exclusive contracts, or a simple lack of competitors • Products are unique, with no direct replacements available • Barriers to entry are extremely high, making entering the market difficult or impossible	**Characteristics:** • Only one supplier in a given market • Monopoly granted by government mandate, such as a license to provide cable TV and Internet service • No product competition is allowed • Barriers to entry are infinitely high; new competitors are not allowed
Price competition: • No single firm can grow large enough to influence prices across the market	**Price competition:** • Firms that excel in one or more aspects can gain some control over pricing	**Price competition:** • Individual firms can have considerable control over pricing	**Price competition:** • Suppliers can charge as much as they want, at least until people stop buying	**Price competition:** • Prices are set by government mandate
Buyers' choices: • Extensive	**Buyers' choices:** • Extensive	**Buyers' choices:** • Limited	**Buyers' choices:** • None	**Buyers' choices:** • None

monopolistic competition
A situation in which many sellers differentiate their products from those of competitors in at least some small way.

oligopoly
A market situation in which a small number of suppliers, sometimes only two, provide a particular good or service.

to a free-market economy that monopolies are often prohibited by law (see "Merger and Acquisition Approvals" on page 87).

Most of the competition in advanced free-market economies is **monopolistic competition**, in which numerous sellers offer products that can be distinguished from competing products in at least some small way. The risk/reward nature of capitalism promotes constant innovation in pursuit of competitive advantage, rewarding companies that do the best job of satisfying customers.

When the number of competitors in a market is quite small, a situation known as **oligopoly** is created. In an oligopoly, customers have some choice, unlike in a monopoly, but not as many choices as in monopolistic competition.

BUSINESS CYCLES

The economy is always in a state of change, expanding or contracting in response to the combined effects of factors such as technological breakthroughs, changes in investment patterns, shifts in consumer attitudes, world events, and basic economic forces. *Economic expansion* occurs when the economy is growing and consumers are spending more money, which stimulates higher employment and wages, which then stimulate more consumer purchases. *Economic contraction* occurs when such spending declines, employment drops, and the economy as a whole slows down.

If the period of downward swing is severe, the nation may enter into a **recession**, traditionally defined as two consecutive quarters of decline in the *gross domestic product* (see page 90), which is a basic measure of a country's economic output. A deep and prolonged recession can be considered a *depression*, which doesn't have an official definition but is generally considered to involve a catastrophic collapse of financial markets.

When a downward swing or recession is over, the economy enters into a period of recovery. These up-and-down swings are commonly known as **business cycles**, although this term is somewhat misleading because real economies do not expand and contract in regular and predictable "cycles." *Economic fluctuations* is a more accurate way to characterize the economy's real behavior (see Exhibit 2.7).[6]

recession
A period during which national income, employment, and production all fall; defined as at least six months of decline in the GDP.

business cycles
Fluctuations in the rate of growth that an economy experiences over a period of several years.

UNEMPLOYMENT

Unemployment is one of the most serious effects of economic contraction. It is traumatic at a personal level for idle workers and their families, and the decrease in the number of active workers affects the overall economy in terms of lost output.[7] Moreover, unemployed workers increase the financial burden on state governments when they collect unemployment benefit payments.

The **unemployment rate** indicates the percentage of the *labor force* currently without employment. The labor force consists of people ages 16 and older who are either working or looking for jobs.[8] Not all cases of unemployment are the same, however. As Exhibit 2.8 on the next page explains, each of the four types of unemployment—*frictional, structural, cyclical,* and *seasonal*—has unique implications for business and political leaders.

unemployment rate
The portion of the labor force (everyone over 16 who has or is looking for a job) currently without a job.

inflation
An economic condition in which prices rise steadily throughout the economy.

INFLATION

Like almost everything else in the economy, prices of goods and services rarely stay the same for very long. **Inflation** is a steady rise in the average prices of goods and services throughout the economy. **Deflation**, on the other hand, is a sustained fall in average prices. Inflation is a major concern for consumers, businesses, and government leaders

deflation
An economic condition in which prices fall steadily throughout the economy.

EXHIBIT 2.7   Fluctuations in the U.S. Economy

The U.S. economy has a long history of expansion and contraction. This chart shows the year-to-year change (as a percentage of the previous year) in *gross domestic product* (see page 90), a key measure of the country's overall economic output. (Note that because this chart shows *percentage changes*, not absolute output, all the bars above zero represent years of economic expansion, even though a bar might be smaller than the one preceding. All the bars below zero represent years of contraction.)

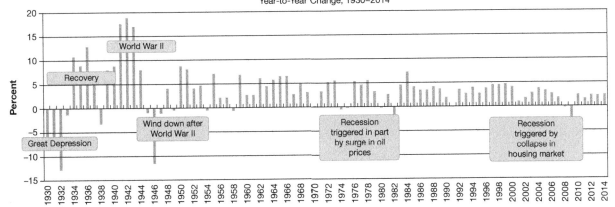

U.S. Gross Domestic Product
Year-to-Year Change, 1930–2014

Source: Data from U.S. Bureau of Economic Analysis, National Income and Product Accounts Tables, 27 February 2015, www.bea.gov.

EXHIBIT 2.8   Types of Unemployment

Economists identify four types of unemployment, each with unique causes and concerns.

 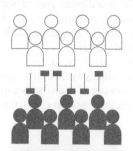 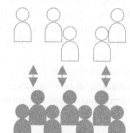 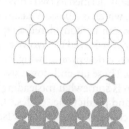

Frictional Unemployment	**Structural Unemployment**	**Cyclical Unemployment**	**Seasonal Unemployment**
• The "natural" flow of workers into and out of jobs, such as when a person leaves one job without first lining up a new job • Always some level of frictional unemployment in the economy	• A mismatch between workers' skills and current employer needs • Workers can't find jobs that match their qualifications, and employers can't find employees with the skills their job openings require • A never-ending concern as changes in the external environments of business make some skills obsolete and create demand for new skills	• Caused by economic fluctuations • Occurs when demand for goods and services drops, businesses reduce production, thereby requiring fewer workers • An increasing number of people who want to work can't find jobs • During catastrophic depressions, can run as high as 20 or 25 percent	• Predictable increases and decreases in the need for workers in industries with seasonal fluctuations in customer demand • Common in agriculture, leisure and entertainment, retailing, and accounting services

Source: Data from Roger LeRoy Miller, *Economics Today*, 15th ed. (Boston: Addison-Wesley, 2010), 164–165.

because of its effect on *purchasing power,* or the amount of a good or service you can buy for a given amount of money. When prices go up, purchasing power goes down. If wages keep pace with prices, inflation is less worrisome, but if prices rise faster than wages, consumers definitely feel the pinch.

 Checkpoint

LEARNING OBJECTIVE 4: **Identify four macroeconomic issues that are essential to understanding the behavior of the economy.**

SUMMARY: First, competition in a free-market system occurs on a spectrum from pure competition to monopolies; most competition in free-market economies is monopolistic competition, meaning that the number of sellers is large enough that none can dominate the market and products can be distinguished in at least some small way. Second, the economy expands and contracts, or fluctuates over time; this activity is commonly called the *business cycle*, although the fluctuations do not follow a regular cyclical pattern. Third, unemployment is a vitally important issue in economics because of the serious effects it has on individuals, families, communities, and the economy as a whole. The types of unemployment include cyclical (from reduced labor needs during an economic contraction), frictional (from the normal inflow and outflow of workers as people change jobs), structural (from the skills workers possess not aligning with the skills employers need), and seasonal (from the ebb and flow of labor demand in certain industries over the course of a year). Fourth, inflation affects every aspect of economic activity because of the effects it has on the prices of goods, services, and labor.

CRITICAL THINKING: (1) Are colleges and universities an example of pure competition or monopolistic competition? Why? (2) Are monopolies always harmful to consumers? Why or why not?

IT'S YOUR BUSINESS: (1) What state of the business cycle is the economy currently in? Is this influencing your career plans? (2) Have you ever been unemployed (at a time when you were actively looking for work)? Which of the four categories of unemployment would you have fallen under?

KEY TERMS TO KNOW: competition, pure competition, monopoly, monopolistic competition, oligopoly, recession, business cycles, unemployment rate, inflation, deflation

Government's Role in a Free-Market System

5 LEARNING OBJECTIVE

Outline the debate over deregulation, and identify four key roles that governments play in the economy.

For as long as the United States has been in existence, people have been arguing over just how free the free market should be. In the broader view, this argument springs from profound philosophical differences over the role government should play in society as a whole. More narrowly, even professional economists don't always agree on what role the government should play in the economy.

Much of the debate about the government's role can be framed as a question of **regulation** versus **deregulation**—having more rules in place to govern economic activity or having fewer rules in place and relying more on the market to prevent excesses and correct itself over time. Generally speaking, the argument for more regulation asserts that companies can't always be counted on to act in ways that protect stakeholder interests and that the market can't be relied on as a mechanism to prevent or punish abuses and failures. The argument for deregulation contends that government interference can stifle innovations that ultimately help everyone by boosting the entire economy and that some regulations burden individual companies and industries with unfair costs and limitations.

regulation
Relying more on laws and policies than on market forces to govern economic activity.

deregulation
Removing regulations to allow the market to prevent excesses and correct itself over time.

Four major areas in which the government plays a role in the economy are protecting stakeholders, fostering competition, encouraging innovation and economic development, and stabilizing and stimulating the economy.

PROTECTING STAKEHOLDERS

Chapter 1 points out that businesses have many stakeholders, including colleagues, employees, supervisors, investors, customers, suppliers, and society at large. In the course of serving one or more of these stakeholders, a business may sometimes neglect, or at least be accused of neglecting, the interests of other stakeholders in the process. For example, managers who are too narrowly focused on generating wealth for shareholders might not spend the funds necessary to create a safe work environment for employees or to minimize the business's impact on the community.

In an attempt to balance the interests of stakeholders and protect those who might be adversely affected by business, the U.S. federal government has established numerous regulatory agencies (see Exhibit 2.9 on the next page), and state and local governments have additional agencies as well. Chapter 4 takes a closer look at society's concerns for ethical and socially responsible behavior and the ongoing debate about business's role in society.

FOSTERING COMPETITION

Based on the belief that fair competition benefits the economy and society in general, governments intervene in markets to preserve competition and ensure that no single enterprise becomes too powerful. For instance, if a company has a monopoly, it can potentially harm customers by raising prices or stifling innovation and harm potential competitors by denying access to markets. Numerous laws and regulations have been established to

EXHIBIT 2.9	Major Government Agencies and What They Do

Government agencies protect stakeholders by developing and promoting standards, regulating and overseeing industries, and enforcing laws and regulations.

Government Agency or Commission	Major Areas of Responsibility
Consumer Financial Protection Bureau (CFPB)	Educates consumers about and supervises providers of consumer financial services
Consumer Product Safety Commission (CPSC)	Regulates and protects public from unreasonable risks of injury from consumer products
Environmental Protection Agency (EPA)	Develops and enforces standards to protect the environment
Equal Employment Opportunity Commission (EEOC)	Protects and resolves discriminatory employment practices
Federal Aviation Administration (FAA)	Sets rules for the commercial airline industry
Federal Communications Commission (FCC)	Oversees communication by telephone, telegraph, radio, and television
Federal Energy Regulatory Commission (FERC)	Regulates rates and sales of electric power and natural gas
Federal Highway Administration (FHA)	Regulates vehicle safety requirements
Federal Trade Commission (FTC)	Enforces laws and guidelines regarding unfair business practices and acts to stop false and deceptive advertising and labeling
Food and Drug Administration (FDA)	Enforces laws and regulations to prevent distribution of harmful foods, drugs, medical devices, and cosmetics
Interstate Commerce Commission (ICC)	Regulates and oversees carriers engaged in transportation between states: railroads, bus lines, trucking companies, oil pipelines, and waterways
Occupational Safety and Health Administration (OSHA)	Promotes worker safety and health
Securities and Exchange Commission (SEC)	Protects investors and maintains the integrity of the securities markets
Transportation Security Administration (TSA)	Protects the national transportation infrastructure

help prevent individual companies or groups of companies from taking control of markets or acting in other ways that restrain competition or harm consumers.

As the business environment evolves, legislators sometimes consider whether to adjust business regulations in order to maintain a level playing field. The disruptive technology of online commerce provides a good example. Currently, 45 U.S. states collect sales tax on purchases made in physical ("brick-and-mortar") stores, but until recently many of these states have not required online retailers to collect sales taxes from their customers. Combined state and local sales taxes can add anywhere from about 5 percent to nearly 10 percent to the purchase price, which can be a significant amount for major purchases. Brick-and-mortar retailers complain that these inconsistent regulations give online retailers an unfair competitive advantage. In response, about half the states that have sales taxes now require Amazon and other online retailers to collect sales tax.[9]

Antitrust Legislation

Antitrust laws limit what businesses can and cannot do, to ensure that all competitors have an equal chance of succeeding. Some of the earliest government moves in this arena produced such landmark pieces of legislation as the Sherman Antitrust Act, the Clayton Antitrust Act, and the Federal Trade Commission Act, which generally sought to rein in the power of a few huge companies that had financial and management control of a significant number of other companies in the same industry. Usually referred to as *trusts* (hence the label *antitrust legislation*), these huge companies controlled enough of the supply and distribution in their respective industries, such as Standard Oil in the petroleum industry, to muscle smaller competitors out of the way. More recently, government bodies in the United States and Europe have taken action against high-tech firms such as Microsoft and Intel to prevent unfair competitive practices.

Merger and Acquisition Approvals

To preserve competition and customer choice, governments occasionally prohibit companies from combining through mergers or acquisitions (see Chapter 5). In other cases, they may approve a combination but only with conditions, such as *divesting* (selling) some parts of the company or making other concessions.

ENCOURAGING INNOVATION AND ECONOMIC DEVELOPMENT

Governments can use their regulatory and policymaking powers to encourage specific types of economic activity. A good example is encouraging the development and adoption of innovations that governments consider beneficial in some way, such as promoting the growth of alternative energy sources through economic incentives for producers and customers. Governments can also encourage businesses to locate or expand in particular geographic areas by establishing *economic development zones*. These zones typically offer a variety of financial incentives such as tax credits, low-interest loans, and reduced utility rates to businesses that meet specific job-creation and local investment criteria.

STABILIZING AND STIMULATING THE ECONOMY

In addition to the specific areas of regulation and policy just discussed, governments have two sets of tools they can use to stabilize and stimulate the national economy: monetary policy and fiscal policy. **Monetary policy** involves adjusting the nation's *money supply*, the amount of "spendable" money in the economy at any given time, by increasing or decreasing interest rates. In the United States, monetary policy is controlled primarily by the Federal Reserve Board (often called "the Fed"), a group of government officials who oversee the country's central banking system. Chapter 20 discusses the objectives and activities of the Fed in more detail.

monetary policy
Government policy and actions taken by the Federal Reserve Board to regulate the nation's money supply.

Fiscal policy involves changes in the government's revenues and expenditures to stimulate a slow economy or dampen a growing economy that is in danger of overheating and causing inflation. On the revenue side, governments can adjust the revenue they bring in by changing tax rates and various fees collected from individuals and businesses (see Exhibit 2.10). When the federal government lowers the income tax rate, for instance, it does so with the hope that consumers and businesses will spend and invest the money they save from lower tax bills.

fiscal policy
Use of government revenue collection and spending to influence the business cycle.

On the expenditure side, local, state, and federal government bodies constitute a huge market for goods and services, with billions of dollars of collective buying power. Governments can stimulate the economy by increasing their purchases, sometimes even to the point of creating new programs or projects with the specific purpose of expanding employment opportunities and increasing demand for goods and services.

EXHIBIT 2.10   Major Types of Taxes

Running a government is an expensive affair. Here are the major types of taxes that national governments, states, counties, and cities collect to fund government operations and projects.

Type of Tax	Levied On
Income taxes	Income earned by individuals and businesses. Income taxes are the government's largest single source of revenue.
Real property taxes	Assessed value of the land and structures owned by businesses and individuals.
Sales taxes	Retail purchases made by customers. Sales taxes are collected by retail businesses at the time of the sale and then forwarded to state governments. Disputes continue over taxes e-commerce sales made across state lines.
Excise taxes	Selected items such as gasoline, tobacco, and liquor. Often referred to as "sin" taxes, excise taxes are implemented in part to help control potentially harmful practices.
Payroll taxes	Earnings of individuals to help fund Social Security, Medicare, and unemployment compensation. Corporations match employee contributions.

No instance of government spending in recent years has generated more heated controversy than the bailouts made during the financial crisis of 2008 and 2009. The federal government spent billions of dollars in investments and loans to troubled banks to encourage lending after the credit markets had dried up and to prevent several large financial companies from collapsing. The government also stepped in to help save the automakers General Motors and Chrysler during this period.

Debate continues on whether it was wise to intervene by rescuing these ailing companies or whether the government should have let market forces play out. Would the money invested in saving one large company have been better spent in helping a number of small, young companies get off the ground? In general, the rationale for stepping in to rescue any specific company is that its collapse would harm a significant portion of the economy as a whole. However, these decisions hit at the heart of an economic system because they determine how a society chooses to deploy its scarce resources.

 Checkpoint

LEARNING OBJECTIVE 5: Outline the debate over deregulation, and identify four key roles that governments play in the economy.

SUMMARY: Proponents of increased regulation assert that companies can't always be counted on to act in ways that protect stakeholder interests and that the market can't be relied on to prevent or punish abuses and failures. Proponents of deregulation contend that government interference can stifle innovations that ultimately help everyone by boosting the entire economy and that some regulations burden individual companies and industries with unfair costs. Four key roles the government plays in the economy are protecting stakeholders, fostering competition, encouraging innovation and economic development, and stabilizing and stimulating the economy.

CRITICAL THINKING: (1) Would it be wise for the government to put price controls on college tuition? Why or why not? (2) Under what conditions, if any, should the federal government step in to rescue failing companies?

IT'S YOUR BUSINESS: (1) How do you benefit from competition among the companies that supply you with the goods and services you need? (2) Does this competition have any negative impact on your life?

KEY TERMS TO KNOW: regulation, deregulation, monetary policy, fiscal policy

6   LEARNING OBJECTIVE

Identify the major ways of measuring economic activity.

economic indicators
Statistics that measure the performance of the economy.

Economic Measures and Monitors

Economic indicators are statistics such as interest rates, unemployment rates, housing data, and industrial productivity that let business and political leaders measure and monitor economic performance. *Leading indicators* suggest changes that may happen to the economy in the future and are therefore valuable for planning. In contrast, *lagging indicators* provide confirmation that something has occurred in the past.

Housing starts, for example, are a leading indicator showing where several industries are headed. When housing starts drop, the construction industry contracts, and the effect soon ripples through other sectors of the economy, from the manufacture of plumbing fixtures, carpet, and appliances to a variety of services, including furniture retailing, real estate sales, and other areas that are dependent on housing-related transactions.

Another key leading indicator is *durable-goods orders*, or orders for goods that typically last more than three years (which can mean everything from desk chairs to airplanes). A rise in durable-goods orders is a positive indicator that business spending is turning around. In addition to these indicators, economists closely monitor several *price indexes* and the nation's economic output to get a sense of how well the economy is working.

In contrast, corporate profits and unemployment are among the key lagging indicators.[10] For example, companies tend to reduce their workforces after the economy has slowed down and sales revenues have dropped. Although they don't have the predictive power of leading indicators, lagging indicators give policymakers insights into how the economy is functioning and whether corrective steps might be needed.

PRICE INDEXES

Price changes, especially price increases, are a significant economic indicator. Price indexes offer a way to monitor the inflation or deflation in various sectors of the economy. An index is simply a convenient way to compare numbers over time and is computed by dividing the current value of some quantity by a baseline historical value and then multiplying by 100. Rather than saying something has increased by 28 percent, for example, economists would say the index is at 128.

Government statisticians compute a huge variety of price indexes, each designed to monitor a particular aspect of economic activity. The best known of these, the **consumer price index (CPI)**, measures the rate of inflation by comparing the change in prices of a representative "basket" of consumer goods and services, such as clothing, food, housing, and transportation (see Exhibit 2.11). The CPI has always been a hot topic because the government uses it to adjust Social Security payments, businesses use it to calculate cost-of-living increases for employees, and many use it as a gauge of how well the government is keeping inflation under control.

consumer price index (CPI)
A monthly statistic that measures changes in the prices of a representative collective of consumer goods and services.

EXHIBIT 2.11 **Composition of the Consumer Price Index**

The U.S. Bureau of Labor Statistics computes a variety of consumer price indexes by tracking prices for a representative collection of goods and services, and it periodically adjusts the mix to reflect consumer buying patterns. The particular CPI shown here, often referred to as the "headline CPI" because it is the one usually mentioned in news reports, is officially called the "All Items CPI for All Urban Consumers." The "core CPI," in comparison, excludes the typically volatile categories of food and energy in an attempt to show long-term trends more accurately. The "market basket" of goods and services is adjusted from time to time; this chart reflects the CPI composition in December 2014.

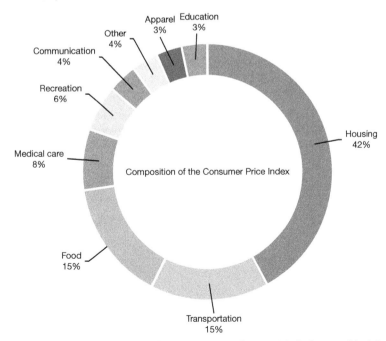

Composition of the Consumer Price Index

Apparel 3%
Education 3%
Other 4%
Communication 4%
Recreation 6%
Medical care 8%
Food 15%
Transportation 15%
Housing 42%

Source: Data from U.S. Bureau of Labor Statistics, "Relative Importance of Components in the Consumer Price Indexes: U.S. City Average," December 2014, www.bls.gov.

producer price index (PPI)
A statistical measure of price trends at the producer and wholesaler levels.

In contrast to the CPI, the **producer price index (PPI)** measures prices at the producer or wholesaler level, reflecting what businesses are paying for the products they need. (Like the CPI, the PPI is often referred to as a single index, but it is actually a family of more than 600 industry-specific indexes.) In addition to monitoring economic activity, PPIs have a number of managerial uses, from helping companies place an accurate value on inventories to protecting buyers and sellers with *price-escalation clauses* in long-term purchasing contracts.[11]

NATIONAL ECONOMIC OUTPUT

gross domestic product (GDP)
The value of all the final goods and services produced by businesses located within a nation's borders; excludes outputs from overseas operations of domestic companies.

The broadest measure of an economy's health is the **gross domestic product (GDP)**. The GDP measures a country's output—its production, distribution, and use of goods and services—by computing the sum of all goods and services produced for *final* use in a country during a specified period (usually a year). The products may be produced by either domestic or foreign companies as long as the production takes place within a nation's boundaries. Sales from a Honda assembly plant in California, for instance, would be included in the U.S. GDP, even though Honda is a Japanese company. Monitoring GDP helps a nation to evaluate its economic policies and compare current performance with prior periods or with the performance of other nations.

GDP has largely replaced a previous measure called the *gross national product (GNP)*, which excludes the value of production from foreign-owned businesses within a nation's boundaries and includes receipts from the overseas operations of domestic companies. GNP considers *who* is responsible for the production; GDP considers *where* the production occurs.

For the latest information on economic issues in business, visit http://real-timeupdates .com/bia8 and click on Chapter 2.

 Checkpoint

LEARNING OBJECTIVE 6: **Identify the major ways of measuring economic activity.**

SUMMARY: Economic activity is monitored and measured with statistics known as *economic indicators*; leading indicators help predict changes, and lagging indicators confirm changes that have already occurred. Two major indicators are *price indexes*, which track inflation or deflation over time for a fixed "basket" of goods and services, and *gross domestic product (GDP)*, the total value of the goods and services produced for final use in a country during a specified time period.

CRITICAL THINKING: (1) Why would anyone bother to monitor lagging indicators? (2) Why is GDP considered a more accurate measure of a country's economic health than GNP?

IT'S YOUR BUSINESS: (1) In your multiple economic roles as a consumer, employee, and investor, is inflation a good thing, a bad thing, or both? Explain your answer. (2) How have increases in college costs affected your educational plans?

KEY TERMS TO KNOW: economic indicators, consumer price index (CPI), producer price index (PPI), gross domestic product (GDP)

BEHIND THE SCENES
RACING TO SUPPLY ONE OF THE HOTTEST PRODUCTS IN HISTORY

As one of the major forces driving the mobile communications revolution, Apple's involvement in mobile phones has in many ways surpassed its initial identity as a computer company. Its iPhone product launches have almost become cultural events, with the news media covering them like Hollywood movie premiers and consumers lining up outside Apple stores to be the first to get their hands on the latest bit of gadgetry.

From a supply-and-demand perspective, Apple phone launches are massive undertakings, with hundreds of companies and hundreds of thousands of workers involved in producing tens of millions of phones. iPhones are assembled in gargantuan factories in China, primarily those owned by two Taiwanese companies, Foxconn and Pegatron. To give a sense of scale, Foxconn's factory in Zhengzhou employs 200,000 workers. In addition to the assembly factories, the iPhone supply chain involves a host of other companies around the world that provide electrical and mechanical components, from semiconductors to glass touchscreens. Completed products are sold through a global distribution network that includes e-commerce outlets, wireless carriers, and several hundred Apple retail stores.

In other words, estimating the demand for a new Apple product is a decision with far-reaching consequences. Apple and its hundreds of business partners need to figure out how many workers to hire, how many production lines to build or change over to the specific model, how many components to buy, how to structure wireless service contracts, and how many completed phones to have in inventory.

Predicting demand is never a sure thing, but Jeff Williams, Apple's senior vice president in charge of operations, did have one big advantage as Apple readied the iPhone6 for public launch. Unlike a situation with new companies or companies that are introducing an all-new type of product, Williams could analyze the sales histories of the previous generations of iPhones to get at least a pattern of how demand for the iPhone6 might shape up over time. In addition, market researchers cover the smartphone market closely, and buyers have shown a consistent pattern of interest in new iPhone models as each one nears introduction. Williams could also consider the various deals and contracts that wireless carriers would be offering to get a sense of how many current iPhone customers might want to upgrade to the new model and how soon they would be able to do so under their existing contracts.

Of course, even with deep insights into consumer behavior, no one can predict what buyers will do until they actually do it. Moreover, even if Apple can predict demand with great precision, that doesn't mean the company can produce that many phones as fast as consumers want them. Smartphones are amazing devices that incorporate multiple types of radio transceivers, motion sensors, cameras, microphones, special glass for touchscreens, and a powerful computing system. Each of these components has to be designed, manufactured, and delivered to the assembly factories on time for production to stay on schedule.

Perhaps no level of forecasting precision and no amount of planning, however, could've prepared Apple for the crush of demand for the iPhone6. Even before these models were released in the United States in September 2014, eager buyers had preordered 4 million units. By the third day after launch, the sales total hit 10 million, and by the end of the year, iPhone6 sales had topped 75 million.

Whether Apple underestimated demand or simply wasn't able to ramp up production enough to meet that demand isn't known, but it was clear the company had a huge hit on its hands—and a huge backlog. Not long after the launch, as some buyers were waiting up to a month to get their phones, CEO Tim Cook acknowledged that demand and supply were severely out of balance. "We're not close. We're not on the same planet."

By early 2015, supply finally caught up with demand, even as the number of smartphone buyers who said they planned to buy an iPhone6 stayed at a record level. Apple's customer loyalty is legendary, so it's hard to tell if the long wait times damaged the brand or prompted some impatient buyers to switch to Samsung or another competitor. Whatever the long-term outcome, the iPhone6 experience shows that even the world's top companies can struggle to manage the unpredictable nature of supply and demand in today's markets.[12]

Critical Thinking Questions

2-1. If consumers are willing to wait weeks or months for the latest iPhone, why does Apple need to worry about producing enough phones to meet immediate demand?

2-2. If Apply temporarily can't meet demand for a product, should it raise the price to bring supply and demand into balance? Why or why not?

2-3. Apple is famously secretive about the details of upcoming product launches, leaving consumers and industry insiders to speculate on the features and functions of new models. What effect might this have on demand?

Learn More Online

Depending on when you read this, rumors are likely to be swirling online about an upcoming Apple product launch, whether it's the iPhone7 or 8, a new generation of the Apple smartwatch, or another product. Choose one upcoming product and read several articles by industry observers to get a sense of consumer demand for the new product. What products from other companies will be competing with the new Apple product, and what effect will they have on consumer demand? Can you find any worries regarding supply issues? Overall, do you think the new Apple product will be a hit? If not, what factors will account for lower demand?

KEY TERMS

business cycles
capital
capitalism
competition
consumer price index (CPI)
deflation
demand
demand curve
deregulation
economic indicators
economic system
economics
economy
entrepreneurship
equilibrium point
fiscal policy
free-market system
gross domestic product (GDP)
human resources
inflation
knowledge

macroeconomics
microeconomics
monetary policy
monopolistic competition
monopoly
nationalizing
natural resources
oligopoly
opportunity cost
planned system
privatizing
producer price index (PPI)
pure competition
recession
regulation
scarcity
socialism
supply
supply curve
unemployment rate

MyBizLab
To complete the problems with the ⭐,
go to EOC Discussion Questions in the
MyLab.

TEST YOUR KNOWLEDGE

Questions for Review

2-4. Why is it important, especially for businesspeople, to understand economic issues at both micro and macro levels?

2-5. Give examples of various economic resources.

2-6. Does China have a purely planned economic system?

2-7. What is the argument for regulation and deregulation in an economic activity?

2-8. Why is it important for a government to stimulate its economy through an active fiscal policy?

Questions for Analysis

⭐ **2-9.** Why do governments intervene in free-market systems?

2-10. What would happen if scarcity did not exist in economies?

2-11. How does the inflation affect the economy of a country?

2-12. How do sellers in the monopolistic competition and monopoly competition compete?

⭐ **2-13. Ethical Considerations.** The risk of failure is an inherent part of free enterprise. Does society have an obligation to come to the aid of entrepreneurs who try but fail? Why or why not?

Questions for Application

2-14. How can the government accelerate the economic performance of its leading businesses or industries?

2-15. What would be the impact of introducing a minimum allowable price on a highly desirable product?

⭐ **2-16.** If you wanted to increase demand for your restaurant but are unable to lower prices or increase advertising, what steps might you take?

2-17. Concept Integration. What effect might the technological environment, discussed on page 11 in Chapter 1, have on the equilibrium point in a given market?

EXPAND YOUR KNOWLEDGE

Discovering Career Opportunities

Thinking about a career in economics? Find out what economists do by reviewing the *Occupational Outlook Handbook* in your library or online at www.bls.gov/oco. This is an authoritative resource for information about all kinds of occupations. Search for "economists" and then answer these questions:

2-18. Briefly describe what economists do and their typical working conditions.

2-19. What is the job outlook for economists? What is the average salary for starting economists?

2-20. What training and qualifications are required for a career as an economist? Are the qualifications different for jobs in the private sector than for those in the government?

Improving Your Tech Insights: Data Mining

To find a few ounces of precious gold, you dig through a mountain of earth. To find a few ounces of precious information, you dig through mountains of data, using *data mining*, a combination of technologies and techniques to extract important customer insights buried within thousands or millions of transaction records. (Data mining has many other uses as well, such as identifying which employees are most valuable to a firm. And a related technology, *text mining*, applies similar analysis tools to documents.)

Data mining is an essential part of business intelligence because it helps extract trends and insights from millions of pieces of individual data (including demographics, purchase histories, customer service records, and research results). Data mining helps marketers identify who their most profitable customers are, which goods and services are in highest demand in specific markets, how to structure promotional campaigns, where to target upcoming sales efforts, and which customers are likely to be high credit risks, among many other benefits. You may hear the terms *business analytics* and *predictive analytics* used in this context as well, to describe efforts to extract insights from databases.

Research one of the commercially available data-mining or business analytics systems. The list of member companies of the Data Mining Group (www.dmg.org) is a good place to start. In a brief email message to your instructor, describe how the system you've chosen can help companies market their goods and services more effectively.[13]

PRACTICE YOUR SKILLS

Sharpening Your Communication Skills

The economics of supply and demand can affect us every day, from the ever-changing prices of plane tickets to the depleted stock of the latest must-have products. In a brief paragraph (no more than 100 words), explain the impact and effect of supply and demand on the business world.

Building Your Team Skills

Economic indicators help businesses and governments determine where the economy is headed. As part of a team assigned by your instructor, analyze the following headlines for clues to the direction of the U.S. economy:

- "Housing Starts Lowest in Months"
- "Fed Lowers Discount Rate and Interest Rates Tumble"
- "Retail Sales Up 4 Percent Over Last Month"
- "Business Debt Down from Last Year"
- "More Manufacturers Showing Interest in Upgrading Production Equipment"

- "Local Economy Sinks as Area Unemployment Rate Climbs to 9.2 Percent"
- "Computer Networking Firm Reports 30-Day Backlog in Installing Business Systems"

Is each item good news or bad news for the economy? Why? What does each news item mean for large and small businesses? Report your team's findings to the class. Did all the teams come to the same conclusions about each headline? Why or why not? With your team, discuss how these different perspectives might influence the way you interpret economic news in the future.

Developing Your Research Skills

In small groups, research examples of privatization in different industries, such as energy and rail, around the world. Consider the following questions: What impact does privatization have on the industry and the economy? What are the kinds of difficulties that may exist when governments try to privatize industries? Write a one-page report summarizing your findings.

MyBizLab®

Go to the Assignments section of your MyLab to complete these writing exercises.

2-21. When the needs of various stakeholders conflict, how should legislators and regulators approach these dilemmas?

2-22. How might the word "free" affect public and political discussions of free-market systems?

ENDNOTES

1. Louis Bedigian, "iPhone 6 Demand Is Highest Ever 90 Days After Launch … Will This Impact Apple?" *Benzinga*, 27 January 2015, www.benzinga.com; Sam Oliver, "Apple Catches Up with iPhone 6 Demand, US Online Store Lists All Models 'In stock'," AppleInsider, 9 January 2015, http://appleinsider.com; Linda Federico-O'Murchu, "Why Can't Apple Meet Demand for the iPhone 6?" CNBC, 5 December 2014, www.cnbc.com; Jeff Williams executive biography, Apple, accessed 28 March 2015, www.apple.com; "Is Apple's Supply Chain Really the No. 1? A Case Study," Supplychain247, 2 September 2013, www.supplychain247.com; "How & Where iPhone Is Made: Comparison of Apple's Manufacturing Process," CompareCamp.com, 17 September 2014, http://comparecamp.com; Tom Warren, "Apple Sells 10 million iPhones in Opening Weekend Record," *The Verge*, 22 September 2014, www.theverge.com.

2. Roger LeRoy Miller, *Economics Today*, 15th ed. (Boston: Addison-Wesley, 2010), 28.

3. Miller, *Economics Today*, 31.

4. Ronald M. Ayers and Robert A. Collinge, *Economics: Explore and Apply* (Upper Saddle River, N.J.: Pearson Prentice Hall, 2005), 97–103.

5. Emily Thornton, "Roads to Riches," *BusinessWeek*, 7 May 2007, www.businessweek.com; Palash R. Ghosh, "Private Prisons Have a Lock on Growth," *BusinessWeek*, 6 July 2006, www.businessweek.com.

6. Miller, *Economics Today*, 174.

7. Miller, *Economics Today*, 160.

8. Miller, *Economics Today*, 160.

9. Adam Satariano, "Amazon Sales Take a Hit in States with Online Tax," *Bloomberg*, 21 April 2014, www.bloomberg.com; Kevin Drawbaugh, "Congress Expected to Reboot Internet Tax Issues in 2015," *Reuters*, 9 December 2014, www.reuters.com; Scott Drenkard, "State and Local Sales Tax Rates in 2014," Tax Foundation website, 18 March 2014, http://taxfoundation.org.

10. "Lagging Indicator," Investopedia, accessed 22 January 2014, www.investopedia.com.

11. U.S. Bureau of Labor Statistics, Producer Price Indexes; Program Overview, accessed 29 July 2011, www.bls.gov.

12. See Note 1.

13. Data Mining Group website, accessed 19 March 2015, www.dmg.org; James Kobielus, "The Forrester Wave: Predictive Analytics and Data Mining Solutions, Q1 2010," SAS website, accessed 1 August 2011, www.sas.com; Stephen Baker, "How Much Is That Worker Worth?" *BusinessWeek*, 23 March 2009, 46–48; Doug Henschen, "IDC Reports on BI Sales: Which Vendors Are Hot?" *Intelligent Enterprise*, 1 July 2007, www.intelligententerprise.com; Angoss website, accessed 21 May 2009, www.angoss.com.

1 Business organisations: the external environment

Ian Worthington

Business organisations differ in many ways, but they also have a common feature: the transformation of inputs into output. This transformation process takes place against a background of external influences which affect the firm and its activities. This external environment is complex, volatile and interactive, but it cannot be ignored in any meaningful analysis of business activity.

Learning outcomes

Having read this chapter you should be able to:

● indicate the basic features of business activity

● portray the business organisation as a system interacting with its environment

● demonstrate the range and complexity of the external influences on business activity

● identify the central themes inherent in the study of the business environment

Key terms

Environmental change	Immediate (or operational)	Outputs
External environment	environment	PESTLE analysis
General (or contextual)	Inputs	Transformation system
environment	Open system	

Introduction

Business activity is a fundamental and universal feature of human existence and yet the concept of 'business' is difficult to define with any degree of precision. Dictionary definitions tend to describe it as being concerned with buying and selling, or with trade and commerce, or the concern of profit-making organisations, and clearly all of these would come within the accepted view of business. Such a restricted view, however, would exclude large parts of the work of government and its agencies and the activities of non-profit-making organisations – a perspective it would be hard to sustain in a climate in which business methods, skills, attitudes and objectives are being increasingly adopted by these organisations. It is this broader view of business and its activities that is adopted below and that forms the focus of an investigation into the business environment.

The business organisation and its environment

A model of business activity

Most business activity takes place within an organisational context and even a cursory investigation of the business world reveals the wide variety of organisations involved, ranging from the small local supplier of a single good or service to the multi-billion-dollar international or multinational corporation producing and trading on a global scale. Given this rich organisational diversity, most observers of the business scene tend to differentiate between organisations in terms of their size, type of product and/or market, methods of finance, scale of operations, legal status and so on. Nissan, for example, would be characterised as a major multinational car producer and distributor trading on world markets, while a local builder is likely to be seen as a small business operating at a local level with a limited market and relatively restricted turnover.

Further information on Nissan is available at *www.nissan-global.com*
The Nissan UK website address is *www.nissan.co.uk*

While such distinctions are both legitimate and informative, they can conceal the fact that all business organisations are ultimately involved in the same basic activity, namely, the transformation of **inputs** (resources) into **outputs** (goods or services). This process is illustrated in Figure 1.1.

In essence, all organisations acquire resources – including labour, premises, technology, finance, materials – and transform these resources into the goods or services required by their customers. While the type, amount and combination of resources will vary according to the needs of each organisation and may also vary over time, the simple process described above is common to all types of business organisation and provides a useful starting point for investigating business activity and the environment in which it takes place.

A more detailed analysis of business resources and those internal aspects of organisations which help to transform inputs into output can be found in Chapters 2 and 7 below. The need, here, is simply to appreciate the idea of the firm as a **transformation system** and to recognise that in producing and selling output, most organisations hope

Figure 1.1   The business organisation as a transformation system

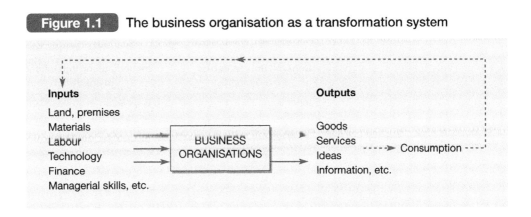

to earn sufficient revenue to allow them to maintain and replenish their resources, thus permitting them to produce further output which in turn produces further inputs. In short, inputs help to create output and output creates inputs. Moreover, the output of one organisation may represent an input for another, as in the case of the firm producing capital equipment or basic materials or information or ideas. This interrelationship between business organisations is just one example of the complex and integrated nature of business activity and it helps to highlight the fact that the fortunes of any single business organisation are invariably linked with those of another or others – a point clearly illustrated in many of the examples cited in the text.

The firm in its environment

The simple model of business activity described above is based on the systems approach to management (see Chapter 2). One of the benefits of this approach is that it stresses that organisations are entities made up of interrelated parts which are intertwined with the outside world – the **external environment** in systems language. This environment comprises a wide range of influences – economic, demographic, social, political, legal, technological, etc. – which affects business activity in a variety of ways and which can impinge not only on the transformation process itself but also on the process of resource acquisition and on the creation and consumption of output. This idea of the firm in its environment is illustrated in Figure 1.2.

Figure 1.2   The firm in its environment

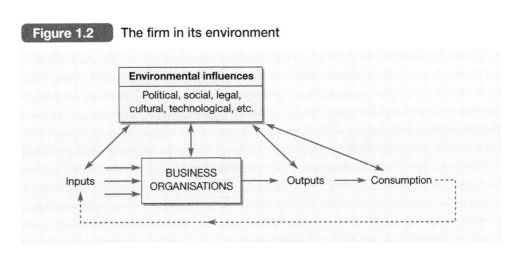

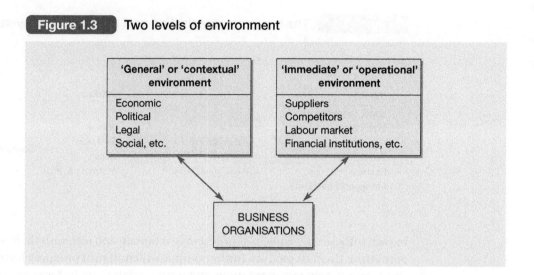

Figure 1.3 Two levels of environment

In examining the business environment, a useful distinction can be made between those external factors that tend to have a more immediate effect on the day-to-day operations of a firm and those that tend to have a more general influence. Figure 1.3 makes this distinction.

The **immediate** or **operational environment** for most firms includes suppliers, competitors, labour markets, financial institutions and customers, and may also include trade associations, trade unions and possibly a parent company. In contrast, the **general** or **contextual environment** comprises those macroenvironmental factors such as economic, political, socio-cultural, technological, legal and ethical influences on business which affect a wide variety of businesses and which can emanate not only from local and national sources but also from international and supranational developments.

This type of analysis can also be extended to the different functional areas of an organisation's activities such as marketing or personnel or production or finance, as illustrated in Figure 1.4. Such an analysis can be seen to be useful in at least two ways. First, it emphasises the influence of external factors on specific activities within the firm

Figure 1.4 Environmental influences on a firm's marketing system

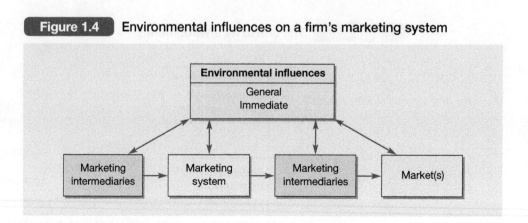

and in doing so underlines the importance of the interface between the internal and external environments. Second, by drawing attention to this interface, it highlights the fact that, while business organisations are often able to exercise some degree of control over their internal activities and processes, it is often very difficult, if not impossible, to control the external environment in which they operate.

The general or contextual environment

While the external factors referred to above form the subject matter of the rest of the book, it is useful at this point to gain an overview of the business environment by highlighting some of the key environmental influences on business activity. In keeping with the distinction made between general and more immediate influences, these are discussed separately below. In this section we examine what are frequently referred to as the 'PESTLE' factors (i.e. political, economic, socio-cultural, technological, legal and ethical influences). A **PESTLE** (or **PEST**) **analysis** can be used to analyse a firm's current and future environment as part of the strategic management process (see Chapter 18).

The political environment

A number of aspects of the political environment clearly impinge on business activity. These range from general questions concerning the nature of the political system and its institutions and processes (Chapter 4) to the more specific questions relating to government involvement in the working of the economy (Chapter 5) and its attempts to influence market structure and behaviour (Chapters 11, 15, 17). Government activities, both directly and indirectly, influence business activity and government can be seen as the biggest business enterprise at national or local level (Chapter 13). Given the trend towards the globalisation of markets (Chapters 3 and 16) and the existence of international trading organisations and blocs, international politico-economic influences on business activity represent one key feature of the business environment (Chapters 4, 7 and 16). Another is the influence of public, as well as political, opinion in areas such as environmental policy and corporate responsibility (Chapter 9).

The economic environment

The distinction made between the political and economic environment – and, for that matter, the legal environment – is somewhat arbitrary. Government, as indicated above, plays a major role in the economy at both national and local level (Chapters 5 and 13) and its activities help to influence both the demand and supply side (e.g. see Chapter 14). Nevertheless there are a number of other economic aspects related to business activity which are worthy of consideration. These include various structural aspects of both firms and markets (Chapters 10, 11, 12 and 15) and a comparison of economic theory and practice (e.g. Chapters 14, 15 and 16).

mini case   The impact of regional economic conditions

For a company that trades in different markets across the world, macroeconomic conditions (see Chapter 5) in a particular part of its overall market can play a key role in determining its corporate sales and profitability. French carmaker PSA Peugeot Citroën, for instance, experienced a significant decline in sales in 2012 as demand fell in southern Europe on the back of the recession in the Eurozone. In response to the problem, the company announced significant job cuts aimed at reducing costs and looked to the French government for a series of multi-billion-euro loans to keep it afloat until trading conditions improved.

Another company experiencing the impact of the recession in Europe was India's Tata Steel, which was affected by a downturn in the demand from the construction and carmaking industries, culminating in significant losses in the European

arm of its business in 2012–13. As with Peugeot Citroën, Tata announced steps to cut its costs and improve its efficiency via a programme of restructuring and redundancies, decisions which will clearly have an impact not only on employees but also on the communities in which they live and on other firms in Tata's supply chain.

Since market conditions can vary substantially in different locations, some businesses can experience significant variations in performance in different parts of their operations. US car giant Ford, for example, announced significant losses in Europe in 2012 alongside 'spectacular' results in its North American division. Like Chrysler and other competitors including GM, Ford was able to offset its European losses with stronger sales in the US. It also posted pre-tax profits in its South American and Asian markets.

web link

Further information on the organisations mentioned in this mini case is available at *www.psa-peugeot-citroen.com*; *www.tatasteel.com*; *www.ford.com*; *www.chrysler.com*; *www.gm.com*

The social, cultural and demographic environment

Both demand and supply are influenced by social, cultural and demographic factors. Cultural factors, for example, may affect the type of products being produced or sold, the markets they are sold in, the price at which they are sold and a range of other variables. People are a key organisational resource and a fundamental part of the market for goods and services. Accordingly, socio-cultural influences and developments have an important effect on business operations, as do demographic changes (Chapters 6 and 7).

The technological environment

Technology is both an input and an output of business organisations as well as being an environmental influence on them. Investment in technology and innovation is frequently seen as a key to the success of an enterprise and has been used to explain differences in the relative competitiveness of different countries (Chapter 7). It has also been responsible for significant developments in the internal organisation of businesses in the markets for economic resources.

The legal environment

Businesses operate within a framework of law, which has a significant impact on various aspects of their existence. Laws usually govern, among other things, the status of the organisation (Chapter 10), its relationship with its customers and suppliers and certain internal procedures and activities (Chapter 8). They may also influence market structures and behaviour (e.g. Chapters 15 and 17). Since laws emanate from government (including supranational governments) and from the judgments of the courts, some understanding of the relevant institutions and processes is desirable (e.g. Chapters 4 and 8).

The ethical and ecological environment

Ethical considerations have become an increasingly important influence on business behaviour, particularly among the larger, more high-profile companies. One area where this has been manifest is in the demand for firms to act in a more socially responsible way and to consider the impact they might have on people, their communities and the natural environment (Chapter 9).

The immediate or operational environment

Resources and resource markets

An organisation's need for resources makes it dependent to a large degree on the suppliers of those resources, some of which operate in markets that are structured to a considerable extent (e.g. Chapter 7). Some aspects of the operation of resource markets or indeed the activities of an individual supplier can have a fundamental impact on an organisation's success and on the way in which it structures its internal procedures and processes. By the same token, the success of suppliers is often intimately connected with the decisions and/or fortunes of their customers. While some organisations may seek to gain an advantage in price, quality or delivery by purchasing resources from overseas, such a decision can engender a degree of uncertainty, particularly where exchange rates are free rather than fixed (Chapter 16). Equally, organisations may face uncertainty and change in the domestic markets for resources as a result of factors as varied as technological change, government intervention or public opinion (e.g. conservation issues).

Customers

Customers are vital to all organisations and the ability both to identify and to meet consumer needs is seen as one of the keys to organisational survival and prosperity – a point not overlooked by politicians, who are increasingly using business techniques to attract the support of the electorate. This idea of consumer sovereignty – where resources are allocated to produce output to satisfy customer demands – is a central tenet of the market economy (Chapter 5) and is part of an ideology whose influence has become all-pervasive in recent years. Understanding the many factors affecting both individual and market demand, and the ways in which firms organise themselves to satisfy that demand, is a vital component of a business environment that is increasingly market led.

Competitors

Competition – both direct and indirect – is an important part of the context in which many firms operate and is a factor equally applicable to the input as well as the output side of business. The effects of competition, whether from domestic organisations or from overseas firms (see Chapter 16, for example), are significant at the macro as well as the micro level and its influence can be seen in the changing structures of many advanced industrial economies (Chapter 12). How firms respond to these competitive challenges (e.g. Chapter 11) and the attitudes of governments to anti-competitive practices (Chapter 17) is a legitimate area of concern for students of business.

Analysing the business environment

In a subject as all-encompassing as the business environment it is possible to identify numerous approaches to the organisation of the material. One obvious solution would be to examine the various factors mentioned above, devoting separate chapters to each of the environmental influences and discussing their impact on business organisations. While this solution has much to recommend it – not least of which is its simplicity – the approach adopted below is based on the grouping of environmental influences into three main areas, in the belief that this helps to focus attention on key aspects of the business world, notably contexts, firms and their markets.

mini case   Fresh but not so easy

A recurring theme in this and previous editions of the book is the need for businesses to monitor and, where necessary, respond to changes in the business environment. Equally important is the requirement for a firm to understand the needs of the customers in the markets in which it currently operates or in which it wishes to expand its operations as a means of growing the organisation. Even some of the world's largest and most sophisticated companies can sometimes get this wrong.

Take the case of Tesco PLC's foray into the US grocery retailing market with the launch of its

Fresh & Easy stores in 2007–8. Initially established in a number of states on the west coast of America, the experiment was aimed at providing a low-risk method of entry into a large and lucrative market, with the focus on providing fresh produce at low prices in competition with existing retailers such as Trader Joe's and Walmart. As a preliminary step, the company sent some of its senior executives to the US to live with American families for several months in order to understand their shopping habits and product preferences. It also ran a high-profile promotional campaign to support its plans to open up 1,000 stores in California and neighbouring states before launching the brand on the east coast.

Tesco's hope that it would be able to break even in two years quickly evaporated and the company was forced to pump hundreds of millions of pounds into the venture to keep it afloat. Apart from the rather unfortunate coincidence of the launch of its brand with the sub-prime crisis and subsequent recession in the US, retail analysts have pointed to some fundamental errors in understanding the preferences of US consumers. Mistakes are said to have included an unclear image; cold and antiseptic stores; the introduction of self-pay checkouts; using cling film on fresh products; an over-emphasis on ready meals; an unwillingness to embrace the 'coupon culture' that is an important part of the US shopping experience; and problems in ensuring high-quality produce. Some consumers also apparently complained that the name Fresh & Easy reminded them of a deodorant or a sanitary product.

By the time of its withdrawal from the market in 2013, Tesco had reputedly spent more than £1 billion on the venture and final losses are expected to be considerably higher. Efforts to break into a number of other overseas markets – particularly India and China – have also run into difficulty for a variety of reasons and underline the challenges that can face a business that embarks on a strategy of international expansion. On the positive side, the company learned in late December 2013 that India's foreign investment regulator had approved a multi-billion-pound investment plan which, if cleared by the Indian government, would allow Tesco to become the first foreign company to establish supermarkets in the country.

> **web link** Tesco's website address is: *www.tesco.com*

Following a basic introduction to the idea of the 'business environment', in Part Two consideration is given to the political, economic, social, cultural, demographic, legal, ethical and ecological contexts within which businesses function. In addition to examining the influence of political and economic systems, institutions and processes on the conduct of business, this section focuses on the macroeconomic environment and on those broad social influences that affect both consumers and organisations alike. The legal system and the influence of law in a number of critical areas of business activity are also a primary concern and one which has links with Part Three.

In Part Three, attention is focused on three central structural aspects: legal structure, size structure and industrial structure. The chapter on legal structure examines the impact of different legal definitions on a firm's operations and considers possible variations in organisational goals based on legal and other influences. The focus then shifts to how differences in size can affect the organisation (e.g. access to capital, economies of scale) and to an examination of how changes in scale and/or direction can occur, including the role of government in assisting small business development and growth. One of the consequences of changes in the component elements of the economy is the effect on the overall structure of industry and commerce – a subject which helps to highlight the impact of international competition on the economic structure of many advanced industrial economies. Since government is a key actor in the economy, the section concludes with an analysis of government involvement in business and in particular its influence on the supply as well as the demand side of the economy at both national and local levels.

In Part Four, the aim is to compare theory with practice by examining issues such as pricing, market structure and foreign trade. The analysis of price theory illustrates the degree to which the theoretical models of economists shed light on the operation of business in the 'real' world. Similarly, by analysing basic models of market structure, it is possible to gain an understanding of the effects of competition on a firm's behaviour and to appreciate the significance of both price and non-price decisions in the operation of markets.

The analysis continues with an examination of external markets and the role of government in influencing both the structure and the operation of the marketplace. The chapter on international markets looks at the theoretical basis of trade and the development of overseas markets in practice, particularly in the context of recent institutional, economic and financial developments (e.g. the Single Market, globalisation, the euro). The section concludes with an investigation of the rationale for government intervention in markets and a review of government action in three areas, namely, privatisation and deregulation, competition policy and the operation of the labour market.

To emphasise the international dimension of the study of the business environment, each of the four main parts of the book concludes with a section entitled 'International business in action', which draws together some of the key themes discussed in the previous chapters. By examining specific issues and/or organisations, the aim is to highlight linkages between the material discussed in the text and to provide an appreciation of some of the ways in which business activity reaches well beyond national boundaries.

The concluding chapter in the book stresses the continuing need for organisations to monitor change in the business environment and examines a number of frameworks through which such an analysis can take place. In seeking to make sense of their environment, businesses need access to a wide range of information, much of which is available from published material, including government sources. Some of the major types of information available to students of business and to business organisations – including statistical and other forms of information – are considered in the final part of this chapter.

Central themes

A number of themes run through the text and it is useful to draw attention to these at this point.

Interaction with the environment

Viewed as an **open system**, the business organisation is in constant interaction with its environment. Changes in the environment can cause changes in inputs, in the transformation process and in outputs, and these in turn may engender further changes in the organisation's environment. The internal and external environments should be seen as interrelated and interdependent, not as separate entities.

Interaction between environmental variables

In addition to the interaction between the internal and external environments, the various external influences affecting business organisations are frequently interrelated. Changes in interest rates, for example, may affect consumer confidence and this can have an important bearing on business activity. Subsequent attempts by government to influence the level of demand could exacerbate the situation and this may lead to changes in general economic conditions, causing further problems for firms. The combined effect of these factors could be to create a turbulent environment which could result in uncertainty in the minds of managers. Failure to respond to the challenges (or opportunities) presented by such changes could signal the demise of the organisation or at best a significant decline in its potential performance.

The complexity of the environment

The environmental factors identified above are only some of the potential variables faced by all organisations. These external influences are almost infinite in number and variety and no study could hope to consider them all. For students of business and for managers alike, the requirement is to recognise the complexity of the external environment and to pay greater attention to those influences which appear to be the most pertinent and pressing for the organisation in question, rather than to attempt to consider all possible contingencies.

Environmental volatility and change

The organisation's external environment is further complicated by the tendency towards **environmental change**. This volatility may be particularly prevalent in some areas (e.g. technology) or in some markets or in some types of industry or organisation. As indicated above, a highly volatile environment causes uncertainty for the organisation (or for its sub-units) and this makes decision-making more difficult.

Environmental uniqueness

Implicit in the remarks above is the notion that each organisation has to some degree a unique environment in which it operates and which will affect it in a unique way. Thus, while it is possible to make generalisations about the impact of the external environment on the firm, it is necessary to recognise the existence of this uniqueness and where appropriate to take into account exceptions to the general rule.

Different spatial levels of analysis

External influences operate at different spatial levels – local, regional, national, supranational, international/global – exemplified by the concept of LoNGPEST/LoNGPESTLE (see Chapter 18). There are few businesses, if any, today that could justifiably claim to be unaffected by influences outside their immediate market(s).

Two-way flow of influence

As a final point, it is important to recognise that the flow of influence between the organisation and its environment operates in both directions. The external environment influences firms, but by the same token firms can influence their environment, and this is an acceptable feature of business in a democratic society which is operating through a market-based economic system. This idea of democracy and its relationship with the market economy is considered in Chapters 4 and 5.

Synopsis

In the process of transforming inputs into output, business organisations operate in a multifaceted environment which affects and is affected by their activities. This environment tends to be complex and volatile and comprises influences which are of both a general and an immediate kind and which operate at different spatial levels. Understanding this environment and its effects on business operations is vital to the study and practice of business.

Summary of key points

- Business activity is essentially concerned with transforming inputs into outputs for consumption purposes.

- All businesses operate within an external environment that shapes their operations and decisions.

- This environment comprises influences that are both operational and general.

- The operational environment of business is concerned with such factors as customers, suppliers, creditors and competitors.

- The general environment focuses on what are known as the PESTLE factors.

- In analysing a firm's external environment attention needs to be paid to the interaction between the different environmental variables, environmental complexity, volatility and change, and to the spatial influences.

- While all firms are affected by the environment in which they exist and operate, at times they help to shape that environment by their activities and behaviour.

case study   Facing the unexpected

In previous editions of the book we have stressed how the business environment can sometimes change dramatically and unexpectedly for the worse, using the September 11 2001 attack on the World Trade Center in the US as an example of what is known as an exogenous shock to the economic system. Mercifully, events of this kind tend to be relatively rare, but when they occur they present a considerable challenge to the businesses and industries affected.

The same is true when natural disasters occur, as the following recent examples illustrate.

2010 – the eruption of an Icelandic volcano sent a cloud of volcanic ash over large parts of Europe, resulting in the grounding of planes and weeks of disruption of air travel. Airlines in particular were badly affected and faced additional costs because of stranded passengers and cancelled flights. Beneficiaries included hoteliers who had to accommodate people unable to travel and alternative transport businesses (e.g. ferry operators).

2011 – an earthquake in Chile devastated the Chilean wine industry by destroying storage tanks and infrastructure. Another earthquake and a tsunami in Japan destroyed a major nuclear facility and led to damage and the temporary closure of major factories, including those of Nissan and Toyota. The negative impact on the Japanese economy resulted in a reduction in oil imports as industrial production declined and shortages of electricity occurred. To support the economy the Japanese government pumped billions of yen into the economic system.

2013 – sudden and devastating storms in the Burgundy and Bordeaux regions of France destroyed swathes of the French wine industry, resulting in a loss of jobs and income in the affected local communities, with a knock-on impact on local businesses. In China, a heatwave across the central and eastern parts of the country badly affected the farming industry and tempted the government to

spend millions on artificial steps to trigger rain. In some areas power failures occurred as the demand for electricity soared as individuals and organisations turned on the air conditioning. Much warmer conditions were also experienced in parts of northern Europe, including the UK, resulting in increased sales of certain items (e.g. barbecues, sunscreen) and tempting many people to holiday at home. Other adverse natural events in 2013–14 included a super typhoon in the Philippines, extensive fires in parts of Australia, a major drought in California and severe storms and flooding in southern Britain, all of which had major effects on businesses and communities in the affected areas.

While there is little a business can do to protect itself totally against events of this kind, many larger firms, especially multinationals, tend to put in place contingency plans to manage unexpected crises, whether they are caused by human or natural events. A business continuity plan (BCP) can help an organisation to respond quickly and effectively to a negative situation and hopefully to survive the experience and learn from it. Smaller firms on the whole tend to lack the financial and human resources needed to adopt such resilience measures and some may not survive an adverse change in the external environment. For other organisations such a change may bring with it business opportunities, an unexpected though possibly welcome gain from an event that has a negative impact on other firms.

Case study questions

1 Can you think of any other examples of major unanticipated events in your own country (or areas of your own country) that have had a serious adverse effect on its firms and/or industries?

2 Can you think of any businesses that may have benefited commercially from this event or these events?

Review and discussion questions

1 In what senses could a college or university be described as a business organisation? How would you characterise its 'inputs' and 'outputs'?

2 Taking examples from a range of quality newspapers, illustrate ways in which business organisations are affected by their external environment.

3 Give examples of the ways in which business organisations can affect the external environment in which they operate.

Assignments

1 Assume you are a trainee in a firm of management consultants. As part of your induction process you have been asked to collect a file of information on an organisation of your choice. This file should contain information not only on the structure of the organisation and its products but also on the key external influences that have affected its operations in recent years.

2 For a firm or industry of your choice, undertake a PESTLE analysis indicating the likely major environmental influences to be faced by the firm/industry in the next five to ten years.

Further reading

Capon, C., *Understanding the Business Environment*, FT/Prentice Hall, 2009.

Daniels, J. D., Radebough, L. H. and Sullivan, D. P., *International Business: Environments and Operations*, 14th edition, Prentice Hall, 2012.

Fernando, A. C., *Business Environment*, Dorling Kindersley/Pearson Education India, 2011.

Steiner, G. A. and Steiner, J. F., *Business, Government and Society: A Managerial Perspective*, 13th edition, McGraw-Hill/Irwin, 2011.

Wetherly, P. and Otter, D. (eds) *The Business Environment: Themes and Issues*, Oxford University Press, 2011.

Worthington, I., Britton, C. and Rees, A., *Economics for Business: Blending Theory and Practice*, 2nd edition, Financial Times/Prentice Hall, 2005, Chapter 1.

Web links and further questions are available on the website at:
www.pearsoned.co.uk/worthington

Chapter 3
Industry Structure

15 Market structure

Chris Britton

All businesses operate in a market that will be peculiar to that industry. Each market will have its own particular characteristics which depend upon many factors, and although it is not possible to have a model that describes every market, there are some economic models that provide some guidance to the kinds of characteristics and behaviour that will be found in individual markets.

Learning outcomes

Having read this chapter you should be able to:

- explain the market structures of perfect competition, monopoly, oligopoly and monopolistic competition and indicate their implications for the behaviour of firms
- demonstrate the applicability of these predictions to the real world
- apply Porter's five-forces model to an analysis of the structure of industries
- understand the measurement of competition by concentration ratios
- survey differences in industrial concentration between industries, countries and over time
- indicate what determines market structure and what determines the behaviour of firms

Key terms

Abnormal profits	Interdependence	Perfect mobility
Average cost of production	Market structure	Price competition
	Minimum efficient scale of production (MES)	Price discrimination
Barriers to entry	Monopolistic competition	Price leadership
Barriers to exit	Monopoly	Price maker
Cartel	Monopsony	Price taker
Collusion	Natural monopoly	Price war
Concentration ratio	Non-price competition	Sticky prices
Contestable market	Normal profits	Structure–conduct–performance model
Differentiation	Oligopoly	
Economies of scale	Perfect competition	Transaction cost economics
Five-forces model	Perfect knowledge	
Homogeneous products		

Introduction

In economics the behaviour and the performance of firms in an industry are thought to depend upon some basic structural characteristics. This view is exemplified by the **structure–conduct–performance model**, where structure determines conduct, which in turn determines performance. The basic elements included under these headings are given in Table 15.1.

The structure–conduct–performance model provides a good framework for classifying and analysing an industry. A simple example of the process can be seen in the soap powder industry. Here the market is dominated by two large producers, Unilever and Procter & Gamble. This apparent lack of competition gives rise to certain behavioural characteristics, such as the massive amount of advertising, the existence of many brand names and fairly uniform prices. This process will be considered in more detail later in the chapter, but the example serves to indicate the relationship between the structure of the market and the behaviour and ultimately the performance of firms in an industry.

web link For more information on these companies see *www.unilever.com* and *www.pg.com*

Market structure refers to the amount of competition that exists in a market between producers. The degree of competition can be thought of as lying along a continuum with very competitive markets at one end and markets in which no competition exists at all at the other end. This chapter looks at the two extremes (perfect competition and monopoly), and the market structures that exist between. The theory predicts the effects of market structure on behaviour and performance in those markets. However, as with the working of the market mechanism, the real world is often different from the theory and therefore this chapter will look at real markets and the relevance of the theory to the real world. The structure–conduct–performance model is open to criticism[1] since it says little about what determines structure in the first place. It also tends to view the firm as passive in the face of market structure, accepting the implications for conduct and performance, rather than actively trying to change and mould market structure. Michael Porter's **five-forces model**[2] will be used to broaden out the analysis.

Table 15.1 Structure–conduct–performance model

Structural factors
    Amount of actual competition: (a) seller concentration and (b) buyer concentration
    Existence of potential competition
    Cost conditions
    Demand conditions
    Existence of barriers to entry
Conduct factors
    Pricing policy
    Amount of advertising
    Merger behaviour
    Product differentiation
Performance factors
    Profitability
    Technological innovation

Market structure is important not only because of the implications it has for conduct and performance but also because it has an impact upon the strategic possibilities that face the organisation, its ability to act strategically and the likely effects of such strategic behaviour (see Chapter 18).

In addition, this chapter will examine how the level of competition is measured in a market, how the level of competition varies between industries and countries, and how and why this has changed over time.

Market structures – in theory and practice

As mentioned above, market structures can be thought of as lying along a continuum with perfect competition at one end and monopoly at the other (see Figure 15.1). Both of these market structures are unrealistic representations of the real world, but are useful as benchmarks in assessing the degree of competition in a market. Between these two extremes lie other market structures, which are more realistic. Two will be described: oligopoly and monopolistic competition.

Perfect competition

This is the most competitive market structure. A number of conditions need to be fulfilled before **perfect competition** is said to exist. These conditions are as follows:

1 There are so many buyers and sellers in the market that no *one* of them can influence price through its activities.
2 The good being sold in the market is **homogeneous** (i.e. all units of the good are identical).
3 **Perfect knowledge** exists in the market. This means that producers have perfect knowledge of prices and costs of other producers and that consumers know the prices charged by all firms.
4 There exists **perfect mobility** of both the factors of production and consumers. This means that people, machines and land can be used for any purpose, and that consumers are free to purchase the good from any of the producers.
5 There are no **barriers to entry or exit** in the industry. There is nothing to prevent a new firm setting up production in the industry.

Figure 15.1   Market structures

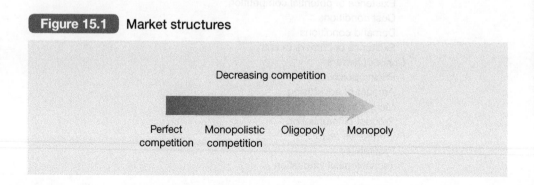

Decreasing competition

Perfect competition   Monopolistic competition   Oligopoly   Monopoly

Naturally, this is a highly theoretical model and these conditions are unlikely to be all met in reality, but if they were, and the theory was followed through, the conclusion is that there would be only one price in the market for the good being sold. For example, if one firm is charging a higher price for the good than other firms, everyone in the market will know (because of perfect knowledge), and because the good is homogeneous and because of perfect mobility on the part of consumers, consumers will simply purchase the good from another firm. The firm that was charging a higher price would be forced to reduce the price of the good in order to sell it, or face mounting stocks of the good. There is therefore only one price for the good and this will be determined by market demand and supply – that is, total demand and total supply, no one consumer or producer having enough market power to influence the price. Accordingly, the firm is said to be a **price taker**.

Price determination in perfect competition

Firms need to cover costs of production and to earn a certain level of profits in order to stay in business. This minimum level of profits is called **normal profit**, and profits over and above this level are called **abnormal profits**. If the firm is trying to maximise its profits it will decide what level of output to produce by setting the cost of producing the last unit of the good equal to the revenue gained from selling the last unit: in economic terminology, where marginal cost equals marginal revenue. Included in cost would be elements of wages, rent, rates, interest, raw materials and normal profits. If these costs are not being covered, the firm will be making a loss.

As there is only one price in perfect competition, the revenue derived from selling the last unit must be equal to its price. Therefore, the price of the good depends on the level of marginal cost.

In the short run, individual firms can earn abnormal profits, but these are not sustainable in the longer term. If one firm is earning abnormal profits, given the assumption of perfect knowledge, everyone will know and, since freedom of entry exists, other firms will enter the market in order to earn abnormal profits. This means that there is an increase in market supply and price will fall back to a level where abnormal profits have been competed away. Similarly, when losses are being made, freedom of exit means that supply will be reduced and price will rise again until normal profits have been regained.

The implications of perfect competition for market behaviour and performance are summarised in Table 15.2. Perfect competition involves very restrictive assumptions,

Table 15.2 Implications of perfect competition for conduct and performance of firms in an industry

Extent of market power	The firm has no market power at all.
Price	There will be only one price for the good. The firm will be a 'price taker'.
Advertising	There will be no advertising, as all units of the good are the same and everyone knows this.
Profitability	There can be no abnormal profits, except possibly in the very short run if a producer reduces price and captures a larger share of the market.

which will rarely be fulfilled in the real world. The usefulness of the model lies in its role as an *ideal market* in which competition is at a maximum, rather than in its applicability to the real world.

An example of perfect competition?

The nearest example to perfect competition is probably the fruit and vegetable market in the centre of a large town. The goods will be fairly homogeneous, with perhaps slight variation in the quality. Knowledge will be almost perfect with respect to prices charged, as consumers could quickly walk around the market and ascertain the price of tomatoes, for example. Mobility of consumers is also high because the sellers are located in the same place. Thus, the conditions for perfect competition nearly hold. The prediction is that there will be only one price for a particular good. Again this prediction is nearly fulfilled; the price of tomatoes tends to be rather similar across such a market, and when one trader reduces the price towards the end of the day, others tend to follow suit.

Another market that is said to be close to perfect competition is the stock exchange, although with the increasing use of computers this is less likely to be true in the future.

Monopoly

Monopoly lies at the opposite end of the spectrum to competition. In its purest form a monopolistic market is one in which there is no competition at all; there is a single producer supplying the whole market. The monopolist has considerable market power and can determine price or quantity sold, but not both because he or she cannot control demand. The power of the monopolist depends on the availability of substitutes, and on the existence and height of barriers to entry. If there are no close substitutes for the good being produced, or if there are high barriers to entry, the power of the monopolist will be high and abnormal profits can be earned in the long run.

A monopolist could also be a group of producers acting together to control supply to the market: for example, a **cartel** such as OPEC (Organization of the Petroleum Exporting Countries).

 For information on OPEC see *www.opec.org*

In monopolistic markets the producer might be able to charge different prices for the same good: for example, on an aeroplane it is quite likely that there will be passengers sitting in the same class of seat having paid very different prices, depending upon where and when the tickets were bought. Essentially they are paying different prices for the same service, and the producer is said to be exercising **price discrimination**. Why is this possible? There are certain conditions that must hold for this type of price discrimination to occur. First, the market must be monopolistic and the producer must be able to control supply. Second, there must be groups of consumers with different demand conditions. For example, the demand for train travel by the commuter who works in London will be more inelastic than the demand of a student going to London for the day, who could use alternative forms of transport or even not go. This means that the willingness to pay among consumers will vary. The final condition necessary is that it must be possible to separate these groups in some way. For example, telephone companies are able to separate markets by time so that it is cheaper to phone after a certain time; British Rail used to separate groups by age for certain of its railcards.

The monopolist will maximise its profits by charging different prices in different markets. Price discrimination is often thought of as a bad thing as the monopolist is exploiting the consumer by charging different prices for the same good. But there are some advantages, in that it makes for better use of resources if cheap airline tickets are offered to fill an aeroplane that otherwise would have flown half-full. It can also lead to a more equitable solution in that higher-income users pay a higher price than lower-income users. The main problems with the notion of price discrimination is not that it is always a bad thing, but that it is the monopolist who has the power to decide who is charged what price.

Again the effects of monopoly on the behaviour and performance of the firm can be predicted (see Table 15.3). Like perfect competition, this is a highly theoretical model and is mainly used as a comparison with perfect competition to show the effects of the lack of competition.

Table 15.3 Implications of monopoly for conduct and performance of firms in an industry

Extent of market power	The firm has absolute market power.
Price	There will only be one price for the good, except in the case of price discrimination. The firm is a '**price maker**'.
Advertising	There will be no need for advertising, as there is only one firm producing the good.
Profitability	Abnormal profits can exist in the long run as there is no competition that might erode them away.

A comparison of perfect competition and monopoly

- It would be expected that price would be higher under monopoly than under perfect competition because of the absence of competition in the monopolistic market. It is argued, for example, that the large telephone companies (including BT) are overcharging the consumer. The benefits of the considerable technological advances that have been made in this area have not been passed on fully to the consumer. This can be sustained only by virtue of the monopolistic power of the companies. But to counter this, it could be argued that a monopolist is in a better position to reap the benefits of economies of scale, therefore it is possible that price might be lower.
- There might be less choice under monopoly since firms do not have to continually update their products in order to stay in business. But it is also possible to think of examples where monopolies provide greater choice (e.g. in the case of radio stations), where under perfect competition all radio stations would cater for the biggest market, which would be for pop music. A monopolist, however, would be able to cover all tastes with a variety of stations.
- There is less incentive to innovate under monopoly, since the monopolist is subject to less competition. But, equally, a monopolist might have more incentive to innovate as it can reap the benefits in terms of higher profits. It may also have more resources to devote to innovation.

As we can see, there is not a clear set of arguments implying that perfect competition is better than monopoly, and, as we will see in Chapter 17, this is taken into account in UK competition policy.

An example of monopoly?

Although it is easy to think of examples of industries where the dominant firm has a great deal of monopoly power, there is no such thing as a pure monopoly, as substitutes exist for most goods. For example, British Rail used to have monopoly power in the market for rail travel, but there are many alternative forms of travel. This point highlights the difficulties of defining markets and industries discussed in Chapter 10. The nearest examples of monopolies are the old public utilities, such as gas, electricity, water and so on, which have been privatised.

The government, in determining whether monopoly power exists in a market, has a working definition of what constitutes a monopoly: it is when 25 per cent of the market is accounted for by one firm or firms acting together. This would form grounds for investigation by the Competition Commission. The process of UK competition policy is discussed in more detail in Chapter 17. The sources of monopoly power are the existence of barriers to entry and exit and the availability of substitutes (these will be discussed later in this chapter).

For information on the operation of the Competition Commission see
www.competition-commission.org.uk

Oligopoly

In both perfect competition and monopoly firms make independent decisions. In the case of monopoly there are no other firms in the industry to consider; in the case of perfect competition the firm has no power to affect the market at all. So for different reasons they act as though they have no rivals. This is not true in the case of oligopoly. **Oligopoly** is where a small number of producers supply a market in which the product is differentiated in some way (see Table 15.4). The characteristics of oligopoly are:

Table 15.4 Implications of oligopoly for conduct and performance of firms in an industry

Extent of market power	A great deal of market power.
Price	A stable price level. Prices set by price leadership or collusion.
Advertising	Much advertising and branding. Non-price competition is common.
Profitability	Abnormal profits can exist; their extent depends on the strength of competitors.

- a great deal of **interdependence** between the firms; each firm has to consider the likely actions of other firms when making its decisions;
- a lack of **price competition** in the market; firms are reluctant to increase their prices in case their competitors do not and they might lose market share. Firms are also reluctant to reduce their prices, in case other firms do the same and a price war

results that reduces prices but leaves market share unchanged and so everyone is left worse off;[3]

- this lack of price competition means that different forms of **non-price competition** take place, such as branding or advertising. Oligopolists will sell their products not by reducing the price but through heavy advertising, brand names or special offers. In the UK, Tesco has a reward scheme whereby customers accrue points on their grocery shopping and these can be used to get money off their next shop or can be doubled up to buy other products such as visits to theme parks or the cinema.

The way in which price is determined in an oligopolistic market is through either **price leadership** or some sort of **collusion**. Price leadership is where one firm takes the lead in setting prices and the others follow suit. The price leader is not necessarily the firm with the lowest cost, as it depends upon the power of the firm. So price could be set at a higher level than in a competitive market. Collusion is an explicit or implicit agreement between firms on price, which serves to reduce the amount of competition between firms. Collusion is illegal in most countries as it is seen as a form of restrictive practice, but this does not mean that collusion does not take place. A cartel is a form of collusion where firms come together to exercise joint market power. Cartels are outlawed in most states, but the most famous of all is OPEC, which has had a dramatic effect on the oil industry over the last 30 years. Collusive agreements, as well as possibly being harmful to the consumer, tend to be unstable as there is great temptation on the part of individual firms/countries to cheat. What is clear in the case of oligopoly is that once price is set, there is a reluctance to change it. Therefore price competition is replaced by non-price competition of the sort mentioned above.

The most often quoted examples of oligopoly are the markets for tobacco and soap powder, both of which are dominated by a very small number of producers and exhibit the predicted characteristics. There is little price competition and price is fairly uniform in both markets. There is a high degree of non-price competition in both markets – high advertising, strong brand names and images, and the use of special offers or gifts at times in order to sell the goods. Compared with monopoly and perfect competition, oligopoly is a much more realistic market structure, with many markets exhibiting the characteristics stated above. Table 15.5 gives a few examples.

Table 15.5 The top firms' share of the market in the UK (percentages)

Industry	Percentages
Cigarettes[a]	92*
Laundry detergents[b]	78**
Lager[b]	71*
Motor insurance[b]	60**
Greetings cards[b]	53***
Ice cream[b]	43*
Clothing retail[c]	29**

Note: *Top three firms in the industry; **Top five firms; ***Top two firms.
Source: [a] ASH.org.uk, 2012; [b] Mintel Reports, 2013; [c] Mintel Report, 2012.

For information and reports on specific industries see *www.mintel.co.uk* and *www.keynote.co.uk*

Monopolistic competition

Monopolistic competition exists when all of the conditions for perfect competition are met except for the existence of a homogeneous good, so that each firm has a monopoly over its own good but there is a great deal of competition in the market from other suppliers producing very similar products. In **monopolistic competition** the good is slightly **differentiated** in some way, either by advertising and branding or by local production. There does not have to be a technical difference between the two goods, which could be identical in composition, but there must be an 'economic difference' – that is, a difference in the way the goods are perceived by consumers. There is also some degree of consumer loyalty, so that if one firm reduces price, consumers might not necessarily move to that firm if they believe that the difference between the brands justifies the higher price. Abnormal profits can exist in the short run but cannot persist since new firms are free to enter the industry and compete away abnormal profit (see Table 15.6).

Table 15.6 Implications of monopolistic competition for conduct and performance of firms in an industry

Extent of market power	The firm has little market power.
Price	There will be small differences in price.
Advertising	There will be heavy advertising and branding.
Profitability	Small abnormal profits can exist in the short run but will be competed away in the longer run.

An example of monopolistic competition?

There are many examples of this type of industry: for example, the paint industry, where ICI is the only producer of Dulux, but there are many other types of paint on the market.

How accurate is the theory?

The implications of the theory of market structures for the behaviour and performance of firms are summarised in Table 15.7.

Table 15.7 Implications of theory for behaviour of firms

	Market power	Price	Advertising	Profitability
Perfect competition	None	One price	None	Only normal profits
Monopoly	Absolute	Price discrimination possible	None	Abnormal profits
Oligopoly	High	One price	High	Abnormal profits
Monopolistic competition	Little	Small differences in price	High	Only normal profits in long run

As argued above, both perfect competition and pure monopoly tend to be based on assumptions that are somewhat unrealistic and should be regarded as 'ideal types' of market structure, in the sense that they establish the boundaries within which true markets exist and operate, and against which they can be analysed. In contrast, oligopoly and monopolistic competition are much nearer to the types of market structure that can be found in the real world, and economic theory does appear to explain and predict behaviour in these markets to a certain extent. In oligopolistic markets, for example, price tends to be **sticky** and much of the competition between firms occurs in non-price ways, particularly branding, advertising and sales promotion (see Table 15.8). Occasionally, however, **price wars** do occur – as in the petrol market in the 1980s and more recently between the four biggest supermarkets in the UK.

Table 15.8 shows the top advertisers in the United Kingdom ranked for 2012; their ranks in 1994 are also given. The names in the list are familiar and largely expected from the predictions: for example, Procter & Gamble and Unilever account for around 90 per cent of the market for washing powder. A less familiar name is Reckitt Benckiser, which subsequently acquired Boots in 2007. It is interesting to note that many well-known brands do not appear in the top ten – Apple lies at number 54 (ad spend of £27.2 million) and Coca-Cola at number 24 (ad spend £44.1 million).

Table 15.8 Top advertisers in the UK, 2012

Rank			
2012	*1994*	*Advertiser*	*Total adspend (£mill)*
1	1	Procter & Gamble	203.9
2	48	British Sky Broadcasting	145.1
3	3	Unilever	125.5
4	19	Tesco	114.6
5	–	Asda	113.3
6	–	Central Office of Information Communication	105.4
7	–	DFS Furniture	94.3
8	32	Reckitt Benckiser	80.9
9	2	British Telecom	79.4
10	5	Kellogg's	76.9

Source: Adapted from *Advertising Statistics Yearbook*, 1995 and Adbrands.net 2012.

 For information on advertising see *www.adassoc.org.uk*

It is much more difficult to judge how accurate the behavioural implications are. Lack of data is one problem, as is the fact that only one structural characteristic has been considered here – the level of competition between producers. The other structural factors listed in Table 15.1 will also have an effect, such as the level of demand, the degree of competition between the buyers and the degree of potential competition. Profitability, price and advertising, for instance, will be affected by the level of demand in the market.

Porter's five-forces model

Porter's model[4] says that the structure of an industry and the ability of firms in that industry to act strategically depend upon the relative strengths of five forces: current competition, potential competition, the threat of substitute products, the power of buyers and the power of suppliers. Each of these five forces will be examined in turn. The case study at the end of this chapter uses this model to analyse the tobacco industry.

Current competition

Current competition has already been considered under the heading of market structure, but the important point to remember is that by acting strategically firms can change the structure of the industry. Firms in a highly competitive market might be unhappy with the lack of power they have over various factors such as pricing and may, through their strategic actions, try to change the situation. If they are successful there will be a change in the level of current competition and therefore in market structure.

Potential competition (or threat of new entry)

It has been shown that market structure or current competition affects the behaviour of firms in an industry. However, looking at the number of firms in an industry does not provide the whole picture. It is possible that firms in an oligopolistic market might act in a way consistent with perfect competition because of the threat of potential competition. This threat can affect the behaviour of firms even if it does not happen. The degree of potential competition depends upon the existence and height of barriers to entry and exit.

Barriers to entry

Barriers to entry are any barriers which prevent or inhibit the entry of firms into the industry. There are several sources of barriers to entry.

Some industries are what are called **natural monopolies** in that the production process is such that competition would be wasteful. The old public utilities are good examples of these, as it would be very wasteful for there to be two national grid systems in the electricity industry.

Some production processes are subject to **economies of scale**. As firms grow in size, or as the scale of production increases, certain economies occur that serve to reduce the **average cost of production**. The scale of production can be increased in many ways, for example by increasing the capacity of the existing plant, by increasing the number of plants or by increasing the product range. Figure 15.2 shows how the average *cost* of production changes as the *scale* of production changes.

| Figure 15.2 | A firm's average cost curve |

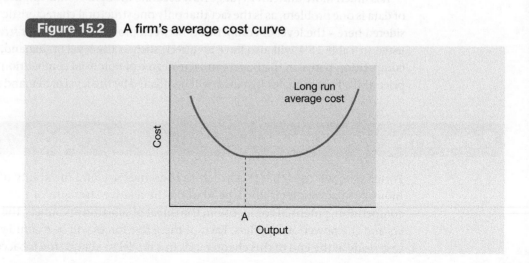

The downward-sloping part of the curve shows falling average cost or economies of scale. The upward-sloping part shows rising average cost or diseconomies of scale. Economies of scale reduce average cost and therefore benefit the producer and also the consumer if they are passed on in lower prices.

The sources of economies of scale are usually classified under three headings: technical; marketing; and financial.

- *Technical economies* come from increased specialisation and indivisibilities. The larger the scale of production, the more the production process can be broken down into its component parts and the greater the gain from specialisation. There are certain indivisibilities involved in production, which only large firms can benefit from. For example, a small firm cannot have half a production line as that is meaningless, but might not be big enough to use a whole production line. Another type of indivisibility is involved in the notion of fixed costs. Fixed costs like the cost of rates or the fees of an accountant, for example, remain the same irrespective of the level of production. Therefore the greater the level of production, the lower will be the average cost of items as it is being spread over a larger output.
- *Marketing economies* come from spreading marketing costs over a larger output, so that average costs will be lower. The company can also take advantage of bulk buying, and will probably have a specialised department devoted to marketing.
- *Financial* economies come from the fact that larger companies find it easier and often cheaper to borrow capital.

Added to these is *risk diversification*, which is possible with larger companies as they may well have interests in other industries. All of these economies of scale give rise to falling average cost and therefore explain the downward-sloping part of the cost curve in Figure 15.2. Economies of scale are a very effective barrier to entry. If the incumbent firm in an industry has lower average cost as a result of economies of scale, it will be hard for a newcomer to compete effectively at a smaller scale of production. Gas, electricity and water are examples of this. The production processes of these goods are subject to economies of scale and it is therefore difficult for others to come into the market in competition with established firms. This is why such industries are called 'natural monopolies'.

Barriers to entry can be legal ones, as in the case of patents and franchises, which serve to restrict competition and prevent new firms from entering an industry. Advertising and branding can also be barriers, in that industries where brand names are well established are difficult to enter without massive expenditure on advertising. Some industries require a high initial capital investment to enter, for example dry cleaning, where the machinery is very expensive. Switching costs can also be regarded as a barrier to entry. If the consumer has to bear a cost in switching from one good to another, that might be enough to deter the consumer from doing so and therefore serve as a barrier to entry. The recent practice of the building societies and banks of offering low fixed-rate mortgages with penalties for early withdrawal can be seen as an example of the introduction of switching costs into the market.

A **contestable market**[5] is one in which there are no barriers to entry or exit. This means that all firms (even potential entrants) have access to the same technology and there are therefore no cost barriers to entry. It also means that there are no sunk or unrecoverable costs that would prevent a firm leaving the industry. It follows that it is possible to ensure that firms behave in a competitive way, even if the market structure they operate in is imperfectly competitive, by ensuring that the market is contestable. What is regulating market behaviour, then, is not *actual* competition but *potential* competition.

mini case   Open Skies and contestability

The 'Open Skies' agreement between the USA and the EU, which was introduced in 2008, is a policy that was designed to make markets more contestable. It eased restrictions on air travel between the USA and the EU so that any airline could fly to US destinations and not necessarily from its home nation, as was previously the case. British Airways could now fly from Paris to New York, whereas previously it could only fly from London Heathrow to New York. Similarly, any US airline could do the same for European destinations. The second phase of this agreement was put into place in 2010.

This policy was not designed to break up existing companies or to introduce more competition into the market directly. It makes the market more contestable – it opens up the market for the possibility of competition. The stated aims are to increase free market competition, allow price to be determined by the market, allow fair and equal opportunity to compete, cooperative marketing arrangements and the provision of a mechanism for dispute resolution. The agreement has led to structural changes in the market. For example, as a direct result of this deal:

- British Airways launched a new airline called OpenSkies, which flew between Paris and Newark, New York. It has since been renamed Elysair.

- In December 2012 Delta Airlines purchased a 49 per cent stake in Virgin Atlantic in order to launch a joint venture in January 2014 – by March 2014 there should be daily flights between Seattle and London.

Theory predicts that more competition will lead to lower prices. Unfortunately this agreement came into force at a time of rapidly rising oil prices so this was unlikely to happen – Virgin Atlantic declared that prices could not be any lower. It is possible that lower prices will come in the future as Michael O'Leary of Ryanair has claimed that he could have $10 flights running from the UK to the USA by 2017. Whether this will happen or not will have to be seen. EU airlines also argue that the agreement is unbalanced: US airlines can fly between EU destinations (from Paris to London, for example) but EU airlines cannot do the same within the USA. In addition to this, US carriers are allowed to buy up their EU rivals but foreign ownership of US airlines is not allowed. The second stage of the agreement, which came into place in 2010, has done nothing to dispel this view as there was still no indication that European carriers would be allowed to carry inter-US routes and there was no further progress on ownership, only a 'commitment to engage in a process towards reforming airline ownership'. This, then, is not true contestability.

Barriers to exit

Exit barriers are those that prevent or deter exit from an industry; they are mainly related to the cost of leaving the industry. The cost of exit depends upon how industry-specific the assets of the firm are. If we take physical assets as an example, a printing press is highly specific to the printing industry and could not be used for anything other than printing. There will be a second-hand market for printing presses, but the press would probably have to be sold at a loss, therefore incurring a high cost. A van, however, would be different, as it is still a physical asset but one that would not be specific to a particular industry, therefore the loss involved in selling would be less. Generally speaking, the more industry-specific an asset is, the lower will be the second-hand value and the higher the cost of exit. An intangible asset such as knowledge of the market or expenditure on research and development cannot be resold and must be left in the market, and therefore is a sunk cost – a non-recoverable cost.

Barriers to entry and exit can be 'innocent' or can be deliberately erected. Economies of scale can be regarded as innocent barriers to entry since they are inherent in the production process. Advertising and branding can be thought of as deliberately erected barriers to entry since they increase the expense of any firm entering the market. Similarly, the introduction of penalty clauses on mortgages is a deliberately erected barrier since it incurs switching costs for the consumer.

Where innocent barriers to entry or exit are low, potential competition will be high and firms within such a market are faced with the choice of accepting the situation or deliberately erecting some barriers. This is an example of strategic behaviour on the part of firms; whether it is attempted or not depends on the likelihood of success and the relative costs and benefits. It is another area where game theory is used to formulate strategic possibilities.[6]

The threat of substitute products

The threat from substitute products largely depends upon the nature of the good being traded in the market and the extent of product differentiation. It has a clear impact upon market structure, because if there are no substitutes for a good the producer of that good will face little competition and have a great deal of market power. However, as we saw earlier, even industries that appear to be pure monopolies (the former British Rail, for instance) can face competition from substitutes since there are other ways to travel. Much of the expenditure by firms to differentiate their products is designed to reduce the threat from substitute products.

The power of buyers

So far this chapter has concentrated on the competition between producers in a market, but the amount of competition between buyers will also have an impact on an industry. Markets will range from those where there are many buyers, as in the case of retailing, through markets where there are a small number of buyers, as in the case of car and parts manufacturers, to markets where there is only one buyer. This latter type of market is called a **monopsony**, and it is the buyer who has a great deal of market power rather than the seller. An example of this is the coal industry, where the majority of output goes to the electricity producers. Increasingly in retailing the giant retailers are exerting a great deal of power over the manufacturers. TOYS 'R' US, the world's largest toy retailer, is involved very early on by manufacturers in the design process for new toys and as a result gets many exclusives that are not available in other toy shops.

The level of buyer power could be measured in the same way as seller power (see later in this chapter), but no data are collected centrally on the level of buyer concentration. It is clear, however, that there are many markets in which powerful buyers can and do exert a great deal of control over suppliers, and this power is an important source of marketing economies of scale. It is possible to put together the level of competition between producers and consumers in order to predict behaviour. For example, a market that consists of a single buyer and a single seller will have quite different characteristics from a market that has many buyers and sellers. The existence of strong buyers might have beneficial effects on the market as they could offset the power of strong producers or it could lead to higher seller concentration as sellers come together to counteract the power of the buyer.

In markets where there are strong sellers and weak buyers the producers' power can be offset by, for example, consumer advice centres or regulatory bodies, as in the case of the former public utilities.

A distinction can be made between existing and potential customers. Existing customers are particularly significant to firms in industries where repeat orders are important or where goods are supplied on a regular basis, as in grocery retailing. It is no surprise that the large grocery retailers are using loyalty cards to increase the loyalty of existing customers. The power of existing customers is much lower where the firm supplies goods on a one-off basis, although the firm cannot disregard existing customers as this will affect its reputation and the ability to attract potential customers. Potential customers might be new to the market or can be buying from an existing competitor at present.

The power of suppliers

The power of suppliers over the firm is likely to be extremely important in certain markets, depending upon the nature of the product being supplied. For example: is the product highly specialised? Is the same or similar product available from elsewhere? How important is the product in the production process? The importance of good and reliable supplies has assumed greater significance since firms have started to adopt just-in-time production methods. Reducing stock levels to reduce costs can be effective only if firms can depend upon their suppliers; hence there has been the development of partnership sourcing as firms nurture long-term relationships with their suppliers.

Another important factor here is whether or not the firm itself can produce the components it needs in the production process. If it can, the power of suppliers is greatly reduced. The decision as to whether to produce or to buy from a supplier is the subject of an interesting area of economics called **transaction cost economics**.[7]

Porter's five-forces model provides a good structure for looking at market structures. The case study at the end of the chapter uses the framework to analyse the market for cigarettes in the UK, while the mini case study on Prosecco uses Porter's model to identify which of the forces are important.

mini case   The success story of Prosecco

Wine sales in the UK have averaged a growth rate of around 3 per cent per annum since 2008. Sales were badly affected by the economic downturn – there was a fall in the sales of wine of 4 per cent in 2009, but there were big differences between market segments. The sales of still wine and Champagne both fell in 2009 by 3.8 per cent and 22 per cent respectively, while sales of non-Champagne sparkling wine rose by 11.3 per cent in 2009. As Figure 15.3 shows, annual sales of sparkling wine overtook Champagne in 2011,

and the trend is forecast to continue into the foreseeable future. According to Mintel, sales of Champagne in the UK are forecast to fall to £609 million by 2017, while sales of other sparkling wine are forecast to rise to £835 million.

In the non-Champagne sparkling wine market, Cava accounts for half of the market and Prosecco around one third, but sales of Prosecco have been growing fast. The Cooperative's own-brand Prosecco won a *Which?* best value award in 2013 and as a result the sales of this wine rose

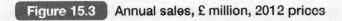

Figure 15.3   Annual sales, £ million, 2012 prices

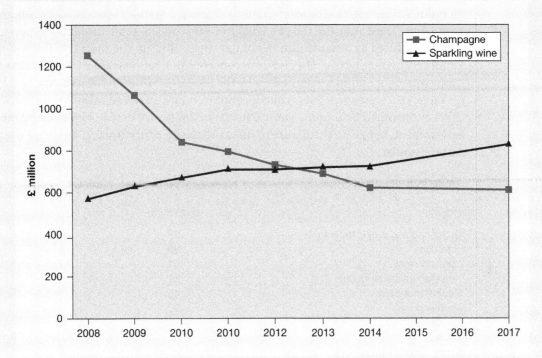

Source: Adapted from Figures 29 and 30, Mintel Report, Still, Sparkling and Fortified Wine, 2013.

by 875 per cent over the Christmas 2013 period. Similar success can be seen from other wine sellers: Sainsbury's own-brand Prosecco increased its sales by 41 per cent in volume between 18 and 31 December 2013, its Prosecco magnums rose in sales by 291 per cent; Prosecco was the fourth most popular wine at Majestic in 2013 and sales rose by 39 per cent in the summer of 2013. Majestic Wine has attributed at least part of a rise in profits for the second half of 2013 to sales of Prosecco.

Why has it been so successful? Clearly there is a price difference between Champagne and sparkling wine and in times of economic downturn, price will be very important. In addition to this there has been clever promotion – while Champagne is the drink of celebration and special occasions, Prosecco has been marketed and accepted as the drink of every day. The sales figures above show that Prosecco is seen as a drink for summer days as well as at Christmas time. In addition, Prosecco is scoring well on

flavour, it is much lighter than Champagne and often lower in alcohol, and this makes it popular among its demographic, which (according to Mintel) is female and aged between 18 and 35 years old. One limitation to this growth is that, under EU law, only wines produced in the Prosecco region of Italy (north of Venice), which includes Conegliano and Valdobbiadene, can use the name Prosecco, which limits the output. This means it might not be able to continue to grow at the present rate, but there are other sparkling wines waiting to fill any gaps in the market – English sparkling wines and wines from other parts of the world, including Chile and Australia.

From this brief analysis, it can be seen that of Porter's five forces, the most important one is buyer behaviour – the impact of economic downturn on demand and the characteristics of buyers. In addition, producers have cleverly marketed the wine as an everyday drink (current competition), although there may be limitations to the growth of the market (suppliers).

Measuring the degree of actual competition in the market

In industrial economics the level of competition in a market is measured by concentration ratios. These measure the percentage of value added, total output or employment that is produced by a stated number of the largest firms in the industry. The common numbers are three or five. The five-firm concentration ratio measures the percentage of employment or output accounted for by the five largest firms in the industry.

Table 15.9 shows the five-firm concentration ratios for a selection of industries in 2004 as measured by output. These data are no longer collected or collated by the UK government, but given the nature of these industries, concentration levels are likely to be very similar.

Table 15.9 Five-firm concentration ratios for selected industries in the UK, 2004

Industry	Output (%)
Sugar and sugar by-products	99
Tobacco	99
Iron and steel	61
Pharmaceutical products	57
Rubber products	45
Leather goods	30
Footwear	25
Legal service	9
Other business services	5

Source: Adapted from Appendix 1, 'Concentration ratios for businesses by industry in 2004', Sanjiv Mahajan, *Economic Trends*, ONS, October 2006.

Although Table 15.9 shows only a small selection of industries, it does illustrate that there is a wide variation in the degree of concentration across industries. Only two services industries are listed because there is a general lack of data on the service sector. Generally, services are less concentrated than manufacturing industries because of the nature of the production process and the fact there is less scope for economies of scale. The differences between the market shares of sugar and tobacco in Tables 15.5 and 15.9 are due to the fact that the large producers also produce the own-brand labels.

While it is relatively easy to compare the level of concentration in particular industries over time, it is more difficult to make any conclusion about the 'average' level of concentration (see mini case on concentration in last edition of this text). Table 15.10 gives an illustration of the percentage share of total employment and sales of the largest 100 private firms in the UK between 1979 and 1992. Although these are not concentration ratios as such, the data do provide an indication of how concentration has changed over time in aggregate. The change in the Standard Industrial Classification during this period has only a small impact on the figures. Note how the level of 'average' concentration decreased slightly during the first part of the period, reversing the trend of the first half of this century where industrial concentration increased. The reason for the decrease is largely the process of privatisation and the growth in the small-firm sector during the 1970s and 1980s. In the later part of the period concentration started to rise again, mainly due to the industrial restructuring taking place and the increased level of merger activity identified in Chapter 11. As the UK government ceased publication of these figures in 1992 it is difficult to assess what has happened to concentration more recently.

Table 15.10 100 largest private enterprise groups

Year	Percentage share of total Employment	Sales
SIC(68)		
1979	12	18
SIC(80)		
1980	13	15
1981	13	16
1982	12	15
1983	12	16
1984	15	19
1985	9.5	14
1986	9.7	15.4
1987	10.8	17.1
1988	9.8	17.6
1989	12.1	21.6
1990	14.6	23.6
1991	14.9	21.2
1992	16.9	24.9

Source: *Census of Production*, various. Crown copyright. Reproduced by permission of the Controller of HMSO and of the Office for National Statistics, UK.

Making comparisons between different countries tends to be difficult because of this problem of 'averaging' concentration and because of national differences in the way in which data are collected and reported. Moreover, official EU publications on industry have changed the way in which they report data, so comparisons over time are problematical. Despite the difficulties in comparing concentration ratios, the general view of industrial economists is that concentration is greater in the UK than in other member states.

Reasons for high concentration

Many industries in the United Kingdom are highly concentrated and it is believed that the UK has higher concentration ratios than other large industrial countries. Why are there different market structures between industries?

Referring back to Figure 15.2, the point at which the curve becomes horizontal (A in the figure) is called the **minimum efficient scale of production (MES)**. It is the point at which all economies of scale have been reaped by the firm, and the point at which firms that wish to maximise their efficiency must operate.

The higher the MES relative to the total output of the industry, the fewer will be the number of firms operating in an industry and therefore the higher will be the level of concentration. For example, if the MES in an industry is half of the industry output, the industry could support only two firms, as smaller firms could not achieve low enough costs to compete with the large firms.

As the scale of production continues to increase, average costs eventually start to rise. This is due to diseconomies of scale, which are mostly attributed to managerial inefficiencies. These are the difficulties faced by management in controlling, coordinating and communicating in a large organisation.

Firms in every industry will face differing average cost curves and therefore market structures will be different. In services, for example, because of the nature of the product, the scope for economies of scale is small and, accordingly, the MES is small relative to the size of the total market and the industries tend to be unconcentrated. The level of concentration in manufacturing tends to be much higher because of the nature of the production process and the scope for economies of scale.

The size of the MES is not the only explanation of why there are different market structures. If it was, one might expect that the same industry would have similar levels of concentration in different countries, but this is not the case, as indicated above. The strength of the five forces will differ greatly between industries and will therefore give many different structures. Obviously government policy can influence the type of market structure, and this will differ between countries. It is also true that the significance of barriers to entry varies between countries. Empirical results from Germany and the UK show that in both countries barriers to entry are high, but that in the UK advertising is the most important barrier, while in Germany it is economies of scale.

Synopsis

In this chapter, four different market structures were considered that embraced the whole spectrum of competition: perfect competition, monopoly, oligopoly and monopolistic competition. Each of these market structures gives predictions about the behaviour of firms in those markets. Generally, the more realistic of these market structures predict well what happens in the real world. This analysis was then incorporated into Porter's five-forces model, which includes further factors largely ignored by traditional economic theory. Nevertheless, these factors are particularly important in certain industries, like the power of the giant retailers as buyers and the importance of potential customers to industries where the level of repeat business is high.

The amount of competition in a market is measured using concentration ratios and evidence on concentration was examined both within the UK and between countries as far as that was possible.

Summary of key points

- There are four different market structures identified by business economists. These are (arranged with the most competitive first): perfect competition, monopolistic competition, oligopoly and monopoly.

- Perfect competition is a market structure which is very competitive and where the producers are 'price takers'.

- Pure monopoly is a market structure with a single producer that is a 'price maker'.

- Monopolistic competition is a market structure where there is a great deal of competition but where the product is slightly differentiated, so producers have a little market power.

- Oligopoly is a market structure where there is a small number of large producers, interdependent in their decision-making. This is a common market structure.

- The determinants of market structure include the existence and height of barriers to entry and exit and the existence of economies of scale.

- Knowledge of market structure gives some indication of likely behaviour of firms with respect to factors such as pricing and advertising.

case study
A Porter's five-forces analysis of the cigarette industry in the UK

Porter's five-forces model will be used to analyse the cigarette industry in the UK. Cigarette smoking has fallen since 1948, as Figure 15.4 shows, being 19.6 per cent of the adult population in 2012.

In 2012, smoking cigarettes was more prevalent among men (20 per cent) than women (19 per cent) and among manual workers (36 per cent) than non-manual workers (15 per cent).[8]

Figure 15.5 shows the age profile of smokers in the UK in 2012.

The UK government has specific objectives in place with respect to smoking – to reduce the total percentage among adults to 18.5 per cent by 2015, to reduce the percentage for the age group 16–19 years to 12 per cent and among pregnant women to 11 per cent by 2015. Although the percentage of smokers

Figure 15.4   Percentage of adult population who smoke, UK

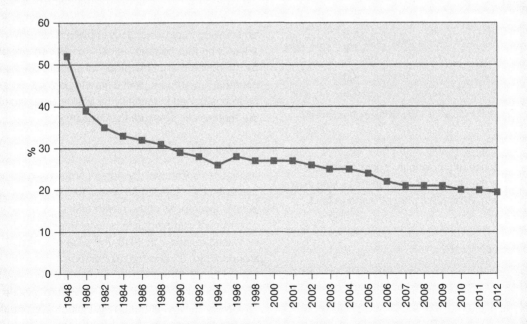

Source: Adapted from Table 2.1 Statistics on Smoking, NHS, *www.hscic.gov.uk*

Figure 15.5   Percentage of adult population who are smokers by age, UK

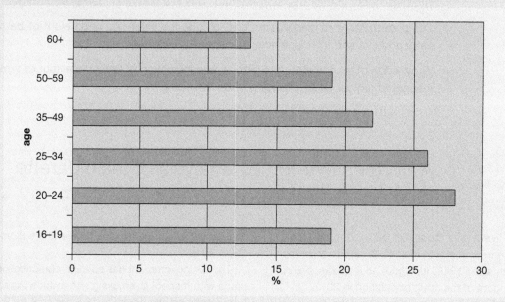

Source: Adapted from Table 2.1 Statistics on Smoking, NHS, *www.hscic.gov.uk*

has fallen, the expenditure on cigarettes in the UK has risen since 2008, as Table 15.11 Shows. This is because of tax and price increases.

Table 15.11 Percentage of total expenditure spent on cigarettes, UK

2008	1.8
2009	1.8
2010	1.9
2011	1.9
2012	1.9

Source: Adapted from Table 1.2, Keynote Report Cigarettes and Tobacco, 2013.

The incidence of smoking in other countries is much higher than in the UK, the top three are Greece (31.9 per cent), Chile (29.8 per cent) and Ireland (29 per cent).

Current competition

The cigarette market is an oligopoly both globally and in the UK. Worldwide, four firms account for 50 per cent of the market – Philip Morris International, British American Tobacco (BAT), Imperial Tobacco and Japan Tobacco International (JTI).[9] In the UK, Imperial

Tobacco accounts for 45 per cent of the market, JTI 39 per cent and BAT 8 per cent.[10]

The traditional tools available to firms to increase their market share, such as pricing and promotion, are severely curtailed in this industry by legislation. A large proportion (77 per cent) of the price of a packet of cigarettes is taxation and many countries have bans on smoking in public spaces in place. The extent of advertising that companies can do has been reduced by the government. The proposal (adopted in some countries) to enforce plain cigarette packaging has been postponed indefinitely by the UK government, but there is still pressure to introduce this.

Power of buyers

As Figure 15.4 shows, the rate of smoking in the UK has fallen over the last 50 years. This is mainly due to greater awareness of the health effects of smoking, government campaigns to reduce smoking and increased taxation. In 2013, the price of a packet was around £8 for 20 and the tax component of that was around £6.20. The demand for cigarettes is inelastic because it is habit forming and difficult to give up. This explains why, although the incidence of smoking has fallen, revenue to the tobacco companies has gone up. It would be expected that the economic downturn would have had a negative impact on the market for cigarettes in the UK as households tightened their belts; the inelastic nature of demand, however, would tend to negate this.

The availability of substitutes

Substitutes for cigarettes include hand-rolled tobacco, which is cheaper than ready-rolled. There is some evidence in the UK that substitution has taken place – in 2008, cigarettes made up 86.1 per cent of total spending on tobacco products; by 2013 this had gone down to 85.7 per cent.

A newer substitute is the electronic cigarette or e-cigarette. These enable smokers to consume nicotine but without the more harmful chemicals like carbon monoxide or tar. These were patented in 2003 and by 2013 more than 1 million people in the UK were using them.[10] There are some health issues with e-cigarettes: the World Health Organisation advised against them in 2013 because of the possibility of getting nicotine poisoning. In the UK, they will be licensed as a medicine by 2016. This means that they will be more controlled and could be prescribed by doctors.

The e-cigarette market is one that has seen rapid growth – the sales of e-cigarettes rose from £2.5 million in 2012 to £23.9 million in 2013. There are many brands of e-cigarettes that are widely available from supermarkets and online. Another substitute is e-shisha devices, which contain no nicotine. Although this is a competitive market at the moment, this is likely to change as the major cigarette producers are very active in the market. Imperial Tobacco bought Dragonite International in 2013, which produced the Ruyan brand, while BAT introduced its e-cigarette (Vype) in 2013 and JTI has diversified into shisha.

Potential competition

This industry is one with a small number of large producers globally and with high barriers to entry. It is also a declining market, so the level of potential competition is low. This is not true at present in the market for e-cigarettes, but this may change.

Power of suppliers

The main raw material needed for production of cigarettes is tobacco and the main sources of tobacco are Brazil and China. Tobacco is a product that can be stored for a considerable time, which gives the suppliers less power over the cigarette producers. Some cigarette producers have an involvement in tobacco growing to further protect themselves from seller power – BAT, for example – this is an example of vertical integration (see Chapter 11).

Case study questions

1 If e-cigarettes become licensed as a medicine, what is likely to be the impact on the market structure?

2 Given that cigarette smoking is a declining market which is predicted to continue to decline, use the life cycle model (in Chapter 12) to show how e-cigarettes can rejuvenate the market.

web link For information on smoking and e cigarettes, see *www.ash.org.uk*, *www.ecita.org.uk*; there was also a report on e-cigarettes due from Mintel in February 2014.

Review and discussion questions

1 Use Porter's five-forces model to analyse two industries of your choice. Try to choose industries which have contrasting market structures.

2 What economies of scale are likely to exist in retailing?

3 Think of examples of a market which is very competitive and a market which is not very competitive. Does the behaviour of the firms in these markets comply with the predictions in Table 15.7?

4 Why are goods such as washing powders and coffee advertised more heavily than goods like matches or bread?

Assignments

1 You are working in the strategic planning department of a large recorded music producer and have been asked to write a briefing document for a board meeting on the structure of the industry. Use either the structure–conduct–performance model or Porter's five-forces model as a framework for this briefing. (Sources of information: Competition Commission reports, the previous editions of this book, media and local libraries, Mintel and Key Note.)

2 You are working in the local consumer advice centre, which each week produces an information sheet giving the prices of a typical 'basket of goods' in local shops. Choose ten branded items (Nescafé, for example) to constitute your basket of goods and survey three types of retail outlet: a small corner shop, a mini-market on a local main road and a large supermarket. Design an information sheet and present the information you have gathered in the form of a table. Include a list of bullet points that might explain any differences in price.

Notes and references

1 See Hay, D. A. and Morris, D. J., *Industrial Economics: Theory and Evidence*, Oxford University Press, 1979, for a summary of the criticisms that are beyond the scope of this book.

2 Porter, M., *Competitive Strategy: Techniques for Analyzing Industries and Competitors*, The Free Press, 1980.

3 For a full discussion of this, see Begg, D., Fischer, S. and Dornbusch, R., *Economics*, 10th edition, McGraw-Hill, 2011.

4 Porter, *op. cit.*

5 Baumol, W. J., Panzar, J. C. and Willig, R. D., *Contestable Markets and the Theory of Industry Structure*, Harcourt Brace Jovanovich, 1988.

6 In this context students should note the use of game theory to model and predict the behaviour of firms in oligopolistic markets. For a simple introduction to this area, see Griffiths, A. and Wall, S., *Applied Economics: An Introductory Course*, 12th edition, Financial Times/Prentice Hall, 2011.

7 Williamson, O. E., 'The economics of organisation: the transaction cost approach', *American Journal of Sociology*, 87 (3), 1981, pp. 548–577.

8 See Statistics on Smoking, 2013, Health & Social Care Information Centre, *www.hscic.gov.uk*

9 The other 50 per cent of the global market is almost completely accounted for by the China National Tobacco Corporation.

10 See Economics of Tobacco, Action on Smoking Health, *www.ash.org.uk*

Further reading

Begg, D., Fischer, S. and Dornbusch, R., *Economics*, 10th edition, McGraw-Hill, 2011.

Griffiths, A. and Wall, S., *Applied Economics: An Introductory Course*, 12th edition, Financial Times/Prentice Hall, 2012.

Worthington, I., Britton, C. and Rees, A., *Economics for Business: Blending Theory and Practice*, 2nd edition, Financial Times/Prentice Hall, 2005.

Web links and further questions are available on the website at:
www.pearsoned.co.uk/worthington

Chapter 4
Social Environment and CSR

6 The demographic, social and cultural context of business

Ian Worthington

As an integral part of society, businesses are subject to a variety of social influences. These influences, which include demography, social class and culture, can change over time and affect both the demand and supply sides of the economy. Marketing organisations recognise and make use of these factors when segmenting markets for consumer goods and services.

Learning outcomes

Having read this chapter you should be able to:

- explain the notions of demography, social class, lifestyles, reference groups, culture and sub-culture
- identify key demographic and social trends that can affect organisations in the private, public and voluntary sectors
- provide examples of how demographic, social and cultural factors can influence both the demand and supply sides of the economy
- outline the concept of market segmentation and demonstrate how marketing organisations can use demographic and socio-cultural variables to segment consumer markets

Key terms

ACORN	Family life cycle	Psychographic
Ageing population	Geo-demographic	segmentation
Birth rate	segmentation	Reference group
Cultural diversity	Lifestyle	Secondary reference
Culture	Market segmentation	group
Death rate	MOSAIC	Social class
Demographic time-bomb	Natural population change	Social mobility
Demography	Net migration	Sub-culture
Dependent population	Primary reference group	VALS

Introduction

Previous chapters have demonstrated that human beings are a critical element of business activity, both in their role as producers (e.g. workers, managers, entrepreneurs) and as consumers of outputs provided by the private, public and voluntary sectors. Put simply, business activity ultimately takes place because of and for people, a point well illustrated by the concept of the circular flow of income (CFI) (Chapter 5) and by the systems model introduced in Chapter 1. In order to more fully understand the environment in which business organisations exist and operate, it is important to consider how broader 'social' influences affect business organisations by examining how they can impact upon both the demand and supply sides of the economy.

In this chapter we look at three such influences – demography, social aspects and the idea of culture – illustrating how these can affect both the amount and types of goods and services consumed within an economy and the different aspects of the production process. In the next chapter, on the resource context, we examine people as a key factor of production and look at a number of areas associated with the concept of the workforce.

As the CFI model clearly shows, the demand and supply sides of the economy are interrelated (e.g. consider the notion of 'derived demand'); the same is often true for demographic, social and cultural influences. In some countries, for example, changing attitudes to female participation in the workforce (a socio-cultural factor) have helped to influence family sizes (a demographic factor) and this in turn has had implications for the markets for goods and services and for human resources. To simplify the analysis, however, we have chosen to examine the different social influences and their impact on the economy separately, but would encourage you to think of the various ways in which the different factors can be interconnected, both in themselves and with other macroenvironmental variables (e.g. the political environment).

The examples provided below are by no means exhaustive and you might like to think of others based on your own interest and/or experience (e.g. public administration students should consider the impact of a changing demographic and socio-cultural environment on the supply of and demand for public sector services such as education, pensions and healthcare). Moreover, the analysis can also be applied across different countries and cultures and ideally should seek to demonstrate the impact of socio-cultural and demographic change on business activity in different national and cultural settings.

The demographic environment of business

Demography is the study of populations in terms of both their overall size and their structural characteristics. From a business point of view the key areas of interest include the age structure of a given population, its gender balance, its geographical distribution and the tendency for both the size and structure of the population to change over time. As noted above, demographic change can have important implications for both sides of the economy and hence for organisations of all types.

The size of the population

A country's population normally increases over time and will vary according to such factors as changes in the birth and death rates and in the rate of net migration. Take the UK population, which in 1971 was just under 56 million; by 2008 this had risen to 60 million. The most recent (2013) estimates suggest that over the next 25 years it will rise again, to 73.3 million, partly because of immigration and partly through natural change (see below). In comparison, Russia's current population of around 143 million is projected to fall by at least 25 million by 2050 as a result of a declining birth rate and a rising death rate in the wake of the country's economic collapse. If this occurs, the world's biggest country will have fewer people than countries such as Uganda and Egypt. It is worth remembering, however, that future population changes are only projections and that these can vary considerably over time as new data become available. For example, in late 2007 the UK's Office for National Statistics provided three projections for the UK population by 2081: 63 million (lowest estimate), 108.7 million (highest estimate), 85 million (most likely estimate). These estimates show considerable variation and indicate how future population changes are relatively unpredictable, which can make forward planning in areas such as education, housing and healthcare provision very difficult.

Table 6.1 indicates the wide variations that can occur in the size of national populations by examining a range of countries across the globe. Within the EU we can see that major member countries such as France, Germany, Italy and the UK all had populations over 50 million in 2012, while the majority of the new member states had populations below 10 million. These figures are dwarfed, however, by India and China, which had populations of around 1.24 billion and 1.35 billion respectively. Such differences in overall population size have important economic implications in areas such as potential market size, workforce availability, public expenditure, economic growth and international trade.

Table 6.1 Population size in selected countries, 2012

Country	Population (millions)
Germany	81.9
France	65.7
UK	63.2
Italy	60.9
The Netherlands	16.8
Greece	11.3
Poland	38.5
Hungary	9.9
Slovakia	5.4
Malta	0.4
USA	313.9
India	1236.7
China	1350.7

Source: Various (including World Bank).

The age and sex distribution of the population

In addition to examining the overall size of a country's population, demographers are interested in its structural characteristics, including the balance between males and females and the numbers of people in different age categories. Table 6.2 gives illustrative data for the UK population by age and gender for selected age groups and intervals over the period 1971–2021. As we can see from the figures in the right-hand column, women outnumber men in the UK population, despite the fact that the annual number of male births slightly exceeds that of female births. Moreover, the data clearly point to an **ageing population**, with an increasing percentage of the population in the over-65 group and a decreasing percentage in the under-16 category. Projections suggest that by 2061 the number of over-65s in the UK population will significantly exceed the number who are under 16, a trend which is sometimes described as the **demographic time-bomb**. This clearly has important implications for both the private and public sectors, not least in terms of the overall demand for goods and services, including 'public goods' such as education, healthcare, social services, state pensions and social security arrangements.

Table 6.2 Distribution of UK population by age and gender, 1971–2021, at selected intervals

	Under 16 (%)	35–44 (%)	55–64 (%)	Over 65 (%)	All ages (millions)
Males					
1971	27	12	11	10	27.2
2001	21	15	11	14	28.8
2021[1]	18	13	13	18	31.4
Females					
1971	24	11	12	16	28.8
2001	19	15	11	18	30.2
2021[1]	17	12	13	22	32.4

Note: [1] Projections.

Source: Adapted from *Social Trends*. Available via www.ons.gov.uk.

The UK's ageing population is a characteristic shared by many other countries, including those in the European Union. Data produced by Eurostat indicate similar trends in both the original EU-15 and in the new accession countries (Table 6.3). In comparison, both India and China have a much smaller percentage of the population

Table 6.3 Percentage of EU populations aged 65 and over for selected EU countries, 1970–2011

Country	1970	1991	2003	2011
Germany	13	15	17	21
Belgium	13	15	17	17
Spain	9	14	17	17
Finland	9	13	15	18
Denmark	12	16	15	17
Estonia	12	12	16	17
Lithuania	10	11	15	18
Czech Republic	12	13	14	16
Slovakia	9	10	12	13
EU-27 average	12	14	16	18

Source: Adapted from Eurostat available via epp.eurostat.ec.europa.eu/ © European Union, 1995–2014. Figures are rounded.

in the over-65 category, the figures being around 5 per cent and 9 per cent respectively for 2012.

Other structural characteristics

Populations can also be examined in a number of other ways, including their ethnicity and geographical distribution. For instance, in the 2001 population census in the UK, around 8 per cent of people surveyed described themselves as belonging to a minority ethnic group; a Leeds University study in 2010 predicts this will rise to 20 per cent by 2051. The census data show that, in general, minority ethnic groups in the UK have a younger age structure than those in the 'White Group' and tend to be highly concentrated in large urban centres, particularly London. For the UK population as a whole, the majority of people live in England, with significant concentrations in regions such as the south-east, the Midlands, the north-west and the north-east, a fact that has important economic, political and social ramifications. Moreover, inter-regional movements of population, together with other factors such as international migration and differential birth and death rates, can result in significant local and regional variations in population over time, with a knock-on effect for both the public and private sectors (for example, demand for housing and school places).

Population change

As the previous analysis indicates, populations can change in either size and/or structure, with important consequences for economic activity both within and between countries. The size and structure of a country's population depend on a number of variables, the most important of which are the birth rate, the death rate and the net migration rate.

The birth rate

Birth rates tend to be expressed as the number of live births per thousand of the population in a given year. In many countries this figure has been falling steadily over a long period of time for a number of reasons. These include:

- a trend towards smaller families as people become better off and health improves and death rates fall;
- the increased availability of contraception;
- the trend towards later marriages and later childbearing for social and/or economic reasons;
- declining fertility rates;
- changing attitudes towards women and work.

In some countries, governments have offered financial and other incentives to married couples to try to reduce the birth rate (e.g. China) as a means of controlling population growth. In others, incentives have been offered to try to reverse the actual or potential decline in the birth rate because of its economic consequences (e.g. France, Singapore). Changing birth rates are, of course, an important contributor to an ageing population, but they can also have other effects. For instance, a recent increase in the birth rate in the UK has led to a call by the Optimum Population Trust for British couples to restrict themselves to two children in order to reduce the impact of population growth on the natural environment.

The death rate

Like birth rates, death rates are usually measured per thousand of the population in a given year. For developed economies such as the UK this figure has tended to fall over time before reaching a plateau. Among the main contributors to this trend have been:

- rising living standards, including better housing, sanitation and nutrition;
- developments in medical technology and practice;
- better education;
- improved working conditions.

The difference between the birth rate and the death rate represents the **natural change** in the population (i.e. increase or decrease).

Net migration

Apart from the movement of population within a country (internal migration), people may move from one country to another for a variety of reasons. The balance between those leaving (emigrants) and those entering (immigrants) a country over a given period of time represents the rate of **net migration**. Along with changes in the birth and/or death rate, this can be a significant factor in population change and can have important consequences for the economy (e.g. the gain or loss of certain skills) and for the political system. In the UK, estimates by the Migration Observatory at Oxford University have suggested that around 50 per cent of the country's increase in population between 1991 and 2010 was due to the direct contribution of net migration, much of which was related to EU enlargement.

Influences on the rate of net migration include:

- legal barriers (e.g. immigration laws);
- economic migrancy;
- the numbers fleeing persecution;
- government policy;
- political developments.

Demographic change and business

Changes in the size and/or structure of a country's population can affect enterprises in all sectors, both in the short and the long term. Given increased globalisation and international trade, the impact of demographic change has an international as well as a national dimension for a growing number of trading organisations.

The following examples provide illustrations of how a changing demography can influence both the level and pattern of demand within an economy and in turn help to explain why changes can occur in a country's economic and industrial structure (see Chapter 12) and why some countries engage in international trade (see Chapter 16). Demographic change can also have important effects on the supply side of the economy. You should try to think of other examples.

- As populations grow in size, the demand for many types of goods and services also tends to grow (e.g. energy, consumer durables, food). A growing population also provides a larger workforce, other things being equal.
- An 'ageing population' increases the demand for a range of public, private and voluntary sector goods and services (e.g. healthcare, pensions, specialist holidays, sheltered housing). It also creates an increasingly **dependent population**. The Office for Budget Responsibility (OBR) in the UK has calculated that by 2018 the country's ageing population will be costing the Exchequer an additional £19 billion.
- A declining birth rate influences the demand for education, children's products, childcare, certain TV programmes, comics, toys, etc. It can also reduce the numbers of young people available to enter the workforce to replace those who retire.
- Changes in the ethnic make-up of the population can affect the demand for particular food products, clothing and media services and can place increased demands on public authorities (e.g. documents printed in different languages). Some researchers also argue that a more diverse workforce can improve an organisation's performance.
- The regional redistribution of the population will affect the consumption of a range of goods and services, including housing, education, healthcare, transport, energy and many day-to-day products. It can also affect prices (e.g. in the housing market) and the make-up of the local labour market.

On a more general level, it is also worth remembering that demographic change can impact on a country's social as well as its economic structure and that this can result in increased (or reduced) demands on a range of organisations, particularly those in the public sector. For example, the growing imbalance being experienced in many countries between an increasing and dependent elderly population and a diminishing population of working age touches on many areas of public policy, from healthcare and social provision on the one hand to pensions and fiscal policy on the other. Governmental responses to the consequences of demographic change can have both direct and indirect consequences for a wide variety of organisations across the economy.

The social context

Being part of society, organisations are subject to a variety of societal influences that operate at both a general and a specific level. In this section we consider some of the key factors within an organisation's social environment, starting with the concept of social class. The notion that organisations also have responsibilities to society is examined in Chapter 9.

Social class

Throughout history, all societies have normally exhibited a certain degree of social and economic inequality that has given rise to the tendency to classify individuals into different social categories. For example, in India the 'caste system' has been an important source of social differentiation and one that has exerted a key influence over the life and opportunities available to members of the different castes. In other countries, including the United Kingdom, the categorisation of individuals has often been based around notions of **social class**, the idea of grouping together people who share a similar social status which is related to certain common features such as educational background, income and occupation. Whereas in some types of social system, movement between groups is either very difficult or impossible (e.g. the caste system), in others **social mobility** is frequently observed, with some individuals able to move relatively quickly between the different social strata (e.g. upper class, middle class, working class) as their personal circumstances change.

The process of allocating individuals to a particular class category has generally been based on socio-economic criteria such as income, wealth and occupational status. Advertisers and market researchers – including the Institute of Practitioners in Advertising – have tended to favour a scheme known as 'ABC1' (see Table 6.4), which uses an individual's occupation as a basis for allocation, the assumption being that a person's job is closely linked to key aspects of her/his attitudes and behaviour, including their choice of car, clothes, home furnishings, holidays, reading material and so on. There is even evidence to suggest that class might be influential in an individual's choice of retail outlets (e.g. different UK supermarket chains appear to attract customers from different socio-economic groups).[1]

Table 6.4 The ABC1 system of social grading

Social grading	Social status	Occupation
A	Upper middle class	Higher managerial, administrative and professional
B	Middle class	Intermediate managerial, administrative and professional
C1	Lower middle class	Supervisory or clerical, junior managerial, administrative and professional
C2	Skilled working class	Skilled manual workers
D	Working class	Semi and unskilled manual workers
E	Lowest subsistence level	State pensioners or widows, casual workers, lowest grade workers

mini case   A new class structure?

According to the Great British Class Survey (2013) – a collaboration between the BBC and academics from six universities – the traditional three-class model (working, middle and upper) may no longer be sufficient to describe the British class structure. Using economic, social and cultural indicators to define a person's social class, the researchers suggested that the following seven categories of class now seemed more appropriate to modern Britain. These are presented in descending (sic) order:

1 *Elite* – individuals educated at top universities, with average savings of more than £140,000 and possessing extensive social contacts. Members of this class constitute about 6 per cent of the population.

2 *Established middle class* – comprising around 25 per cent of the population, this group scores highly on economic, social and cultural capital, has a household income of £47,000 and some 'highbrow' tastes.

3 *Technical middle class* – a small new group of prosperous individuals, but who score lowly on social and cultural capital.

4 *New affluent worker* – people with middling levels of economic capital and who are young and socially and culturally aware.

5 *Traditional working class* – making up around 14 per cent of the population, this group tends to be property owners, largely middle-aged and with low scores on all forms of capital.

6 *Emergent social worker* – with a mean age of 34 and a high proportion of ethnic minority members, this group is relatively poor but has high social and cultural capital.

7 *Precariat* – or precarious proletariat, this group comprises about 15 per cent of the total population. Members have average savings of £800, an after tax income of £8,000 and are unlikely to be university graduates.

As with any new system of classification of this kind, there are inevitably going to be criticisms. In a letter to *The Guardian* (6 April 2013), two leading UK academics pointed out that the current NS-SEC scheme used by the ONS, public organisations and researchers alike currently identifies eight social classes based on a wide range of socio-economic indicators. They also suggested that the authors seemed to have started by choosing a set of outcomes and then allocating individuals to different groups on this basis. In short, outcomes seemed to have been used to determine social class, rather than class determining outcomes, the latter being the approach normally used by social researchers.

Similar systems of classification have also been/are used for official purposes (e.g. the UK ten-year census of population). In the 1990s in the UK, government statistics used what was called the Registrar General's Social Scale – subsequently renamed 'Social Class based on Occupation' – to group the UK population into seven different categories according to their occupation (e.g. Group I was professional; Group II was managerial and technical; Group V was unskilled occupations). This system has now been replaced by NS-SEC (the National Statistics Socio-Economic Classifications), which again focuses on occupation as the key criterion for class allocation. An example of NS-SEC is shown in Table 6.5. The figures in the right-hand column represent the socio-economic classification of the UK population of working age in autumn 2005.[2] Current figures are difficult to obtain as some revision to the approach has taken place in recent years.

While it would be unwise to assume that a factor such as a person's social class will invariably affect their choice of goods and services, empirical evidence reveals some interesting variations in the levels of expenditure on particular products among different groups in the UK population, a fact not lost on marketing organisations, which often use socio-economic criteria as one way to segment a market (see below). According to data produced by the Office for National Statistics (see Table 6.6), total expenditure was highest among the large employer and higher managerial group and was more than three times that of people in the never worked/long-term unemployed category. Within this overall pattern of expenditure some interesting data emerge, particularly with regards to priorities, as indicated by expenditure on different items by the different social groupings. For instance, expenditure on restaurants and hotels and on recreation and culture was significantly higher among the large employer/higher managerial group than other groups, while spending on housing, fuel and power was similar across most categories. Note that spending by people in the never worked/long-term unemployed group shows clear evidence of the impact of the prolonged recession in the UK economy after 2008.

Table 6.5 National Statistics Socio-Economic Classifications (NS-SEC)

Category	Occupation	Estimated % of working population in 2005
1	Higher managerial and professional occupations	11.1
1.1	Employers and managers in larger organisations (e.g. company directors, senior managers, senior civil servants, senior police and armed forces officers)	
1.2	Higher professionals such as doctors, lawyers, teachers, social workers, clergy	
2	Lower managerial/professional occupations, including nurses, midwives, journalists, actors, musicians, prison officers, etc.	22.4
3	Intermediate occupations, for example clerks, secretaries, driving instructors	10.0
4	Small employers and own-account workers such as publicans, farmers, taxi drivers, window cleaners, painters and decorators	7.6
5	Lower supervisory, craft and related occupations, including plumbers, printers, train drivers and butchers	9.1
6	Semi-routine occupations, for example shop assistants, hairdressers, bus drivers, cooks	12.8
7	Routine occupations such as labourers, couriers, waiters, refuse collectors	9.3
8	People who have never had paid work or are long-term unemployed	3.8

Source: Office for National Statistics.

Table 6.6 Household expenditure (£/week) by socio-economic classification of household reference person, by selected categories, 2011

	Large employers and higher managerial	Intermediate occupations	Routine occupations	Never worked and long-term unemployed[1]
Transport	137.30	67.90	48.10	15.10
Recreation and culture	115.30	62.30	46.80	25.90
Food and non-alcoholic drink	69.90	56.30	53.50	42.60
Housing, fuel and power	74.50	67.60	73.00	44.70
Restaurant and hotels	83.20	43.20	32.00	18.30
Clothing and footwear	40.80	23.80	20.80	9.80
Alcohol, tobacco and narcotics	17.80	10.60	16.60	8.00
Communication	15.90	14.50	13.00	7.40
Education	14.80	4.70	[0.70]	[3.00]
Health	12.50	8.00	5.00	0.60
All expenditure groups	703.90	426.20	365.90	196.80

Note: [1] This category excludes students. Figures in brackets are based on very small samples.
Source: Adapted from ONS, Family Spending, 2011.

Lifestyles

Another factor that can clearly affect people's attitudes and behaviour is the **lifestyle** that they choose to adopt. Lifestyles are basically concerned with the way in which people live and how they spend their money, decisions which are not necessarily always linked to their socio-economic position. Two individuals with the same occupation – and nominally in the same social class – may have entirely different lifestyles, a point well illustrated by examining two university lecturers. My own lifestyle is highly sophisticated, environmentally sensitive, artistic and cosmopolitan; that of a colleague – who happens to teach marketing – is narrow, parochial, philistine and consumption-driven. Then, what would one expect?!

Joking apart, lifestyle analysis provides another way of seeking to categorise and explain human behaviour, based on factors such as an individual's interests, activities and opinions as well as on their demographic characteristics. The proposition is that by examining distinctive patterns of consumer response, a marketing organisation can build up a clearer picture of an individual's habits, preferences and behaviour and by doing so can design more effective and appealing products, marketing programmes and/or communications that can be aimed at specific lifestyle groups. Data collected from an individual's use of social networking sites and from their expenditure choices (e.g. their supermarket bills) are particularly useful in this regard.

While we should be cautious of over-generalising, the evidence suggests that in many countries the way in which people spend their time and money has changed considerably in recent decades as a result of changes in demography, working patterns, technology, income and a range of other factors. Once again we can illustrate this by looking at longitudinal data collected through the annual survey of social trends in the UK. These data show, for example, that between 1971 and 2009:

- household spending on communication (including mobile phones) increased more than eleven-fold. Within this period, ownership of mobile phone equipment and services rose from 27 per cent in the late 1990s to 79 per cent in 2008, internet access by households rising from 10 per cent to 66 per cent during the same period;
- there was an eight times increase in spending on recreation and culture and a five-fold rise in spending on overseas holidays. Alcoholic drinks and tobacco was the only category of expenditure that fell during the period.

Other social trends data indicate that:

- by 2009–10 40 per cent of household waste per person was being recycled, composted or reused compared with less than 1 per cent in 1983–4;
- domestic energy consumption in the UK increased by 18 per cent between 1970 and 2009;
- there were 1.8 billion transactions by cheque in 1985 compared with only 0.6 billion in 2009 as a result of a rapid growth in the use of electronic payment methods;
- almost all (98 per cent) single music tracks were purchased digitally in 2009, with digital sales increasing more than 90 per cent between 2007 and 2009;

- in 2009–10 UK adults (16 and over) spent an average of 3.5 hours watching TV, 2.5 hours using a computer and 1 hour listening to the radio;
- sales of books by UK publishers fell by almost 6 per cent between 2007 and 2009. This trend is particularly worrying!

If we take changing expenditure patterns in the UK as an indication of changes in lifestyles, then there has been a discernible shift in emphasis from essential products such as food, housing, water and fuel to the less essential items such as communications, and recreation and culture. This can be seen in Table 6.7, which highlights the changing volumes of household spending in particular categories of goods and services over a 38-year period.

Table 6.7 Volume of household expenditure on selected items, 1971–2009, expressed as index numbers (base year 1971)

Category of spending	1971	1991	2001	2009
Food and non-alcoholic drink	100	117	137	151
Alcohol and tobacco	100	92	88	90
Housing, water, fuel	100	139	152	160
Health	100	182	188	229
Communication	100	306	790	1126
Recreation and culture	100	279	545	869
Transport	100	181	246	273

Source: Adapted from ONS.

In light of the discussion on inflation in Chapter 5, it is worth noting that such changes in spending patterns over time are reflected in changes in the official 'basket of goods and services' used to calculate the Retail Prices Index (and the CPI) in the UK. The 1980s saw CDs, CD players and condoms added to the basket, with computers, camcorders and mobile phone charges added in the next decade. By 2004–5 dishwater tablets had replaced dishwasher powder, wooden garden furniture sets had replaced plastic sets and leather sofas had replaced ordinary ones. More bizarrely, hamsters and popcorn bought in cinemas had been added to the index, while baguettes, corned beef and writing paper were dropped (see, for example, *The Guardian*, 22 March 2005, p. 20). By 2007–8, the RPI contained fruit smoothies, USB sticks, peppers, muffins and small oranges and had discarded microwaves, TV repairs, washable carpets and 35mm camera films. In 2013 it included e-books, continental meats, blueberries, vegetable stir fry and kitchen wall units. What does this tell us about the changing lifestyles and spending habits of UK citizens; are people in the UK getting healthier? Judging by the current statistics on obesity and alcohol consumption, we should be cautious about drawing this conclusion.

Many of the trends referred to above are, of course, mirrored in consumer aspirations and behaviour in other countries, particularly in respect of issues such as healthier lifestyles, increased foreign travel, greater access to communications technology and more environmentally friendly products (though not necessarily rodent purchases!). Thus, while some firms have benefited from the changing trends (e.g. Facebook, Twitter, Apple, Google), others have experienced a decline in business as a result of factors such as changes in habits, in the law or in competition (e.g. France has experienced a substantial fall in the number of bistros and cafés over the last decade). Where change occurs, there will always be winners and losers.

Other social influences

While it is important to consider the influence of broad social factors such as class and lifestyles, it is also worth remembering that consumers are individuals and that they are subject to influences that operate at a personal level. Such influences include the wide variety of individuals and groups with whom we come into contact during our lifetime and who may influence our attitudes, values, opinions and/or behaviour. Primary among these are our interactions within the family, with friends or work colleagues, and through our involvement with sports and social clubs, religious organisations, trade unions and so on. Such groups are sometimes referred to as **reference groups**.

Groups that have a regular or direct (i.e. face-to-face) influence on us are known as **primary reference groups**, while those whose influence tends to be more indirect and formal are known as **secondary reference groups**. The former, in particular, can be very influential in shaping our attitudes and behaviour, including our decisions on consumption.

The importance of reference groups – especially family and friends – is recognised by both economists and marketers, with the former using the notion of 'households' (see Chapter 5) to indicate that the consumption of goods and services often takes place within a collective family framework, as in the case of groceries, holidays, vehicles and many other everyday products. Marketers use concepts such as the **family life cycle** to show changing patterns of consumption as the individual moves from being a child in a family to being a parent with different needs and responsibilities.

While it is difficult to be precise about when and how far an individual's demand is shaped by the family and other reference groups, it is not difficult to think of particular examples when this is likely to be the case. For many services such as builders, restaurants, hotels, hairdressers and car repairs, consumers often rely on the advice of a trusted friend or colleague and firms can gain new business through such word-of-mouth recommendations. Equally, through membership and/or support of a particular group or club, individuals may be tempted to purchase particular goods and/or services (e.g. football kit, trainers, a CD, tickets), especially those with a desirable 'brand name' and endorsed by a well-known personality (e.g. sportsperson, musician, singer, film star). In such cases, the demand for the product is often less price sensitive (see Chapter 14) since it is a 'must-have' product.

The cultural environment

Culture

The term **culture** generally refers to a complex set of values, norms, beliefs, attitudes, customs, systems and artefacts, handed down from generation to generation through the process of socialisation, and which influences how individuals see the world and how they behave in it. Defined in this way, culture can be seen to have at least three important features:

- it comprises both material (e.g. human artefacts such as buildings, literature, art, music) and abstract elements (e.g. rituals, symbols, values);
- it is socially learned and transmitted over time; and
- it influences human behaviour.

As a concept, 'culture' is often applied in a variety of circumstances at both the macro and the micro level: terms such as 'western culture', 'Asian culture', 'European culture', 'New York City culture', 'youth culture', 'pop culture', 'entrepreneurial culture' and 'research culture' are just some of the examples of its usage in the modern world. What they have in common is that they imply certain shared aspects of human belief, understanding and behaviour that link individuals into some form of definable group and/or range of activities.

In a business context, it can be easy to underestimate the degree to which a person's perceptions, attitudes and behaviour can be shaped by cultural influences, some of which may be relatively enduring (e.g. certain 'core' values and beliefs) while others may be more open to change (i.e. secondary beliefs and values). In the United States, for example, American citizens believe in the right of individuals to bear arms and this is enshrined in the US Constitution. The buying and selling of handguns and rifles is thus acceptable within American society, despite the fact that they are frequently used in violent crimes, including robbery and murder. In other countries, trade in such weapons tends to be seen as highly questionable by most people and is usually heavily regulated by the government to certain types of weapons for use in acceptable pursuits such as hunting or rifle shooting. Cultural differences such as this can, of course, apply not only to the kinds of goods and services that are consumed (e.g. eating horsemeat in France is acceptable but not in the UK) but also to other aspects of both the production and consumption process and this can have important implications for an organisation's behaviour.

Examples include:

- who decides what is bought, how it is bought or where it is bought (e.g. in some cultures women have predominantly been the purchasers of household products);
- what colours are acceptable (e.g. the colour associated with bereavement varies across cultures);
- how far harmonisation of products and marketing activities is feasible (e.g. the EU's perennial debates over what constitutes an acceptable definition of certain products such as sausages, feta cheese, chocolate);
- what factors can enhance the prospect of a sale (e.g. bribes are acceptable in some cultures);
- how business is conducted (e.g. the length of negotiations, the meaning of a handshake);
- the method of communicating with the target audience (e.g. in the UK a single shared language allows organisations to use national media);
- how customer enquiries/complaints are dealt with (e.g. UK businesses using call centres in India often give their operators British names and train them to talk about everyday British preoccupations such as the weather and sport).

Culture not only influences an individual's response to products and the nature of the buying and selling process, it also exercises a significant influence on the structure of consumption within a given society. For companies that can gain acceptability on a global scale, despite cultural differences between countries, the potential benefits are huge (e.g. global brands such as Coca-Cola, McDonald's, Nike).

While the so-called 'Americanisation' of consumption is not to everyone's taste, other forms of cultural exportation are often more acceptable and can prove highly lucrative for the country concerned, exemplified by the UK's overseas earnings from culture and arts-related tourism (see Chapter 16). Many other countries benefit in similar ways.

mini case   National cultures

Recognising and responding to cultural differences between countries can have an important impact on how successful organisations are in international trade. But is it possible to generalise about a country's culture?

One academic who has made a significant contribution in this area is Professor Geert Hofstede, who has developed a theory of culture that allows comparisons to be made between the main cultural characteristics in different countries. Hofstede's research is based on data collected from IBM employees across the world while he was working at the company as a psychologist. On the basis of his research Hofstede identified four cultural dimensions; later he added a fifth. These dimensions can be used to compare value systems at different levels, from the family through to the state.

The five cultural dimensions are as follows:

1 *Power distance* – this is concerned with the degree to which the members of a society accept an unequal or hierarchical power structure. In societies where the power distance is large, there is a perception that inequality exists and subordinates tend to be more dependent on their superiors. This can result in an autocratic or paternalistic style of management or governance (e.g. in some African countries), which can evoke either positive or negative reactions. Where the power distance is small, individuals tend to see themselves more as equals and management/governance styles tend to be more consultative and less hierarchical (e.g. in northern European countries).

2 *Uncertainty avoidance* – this focuses on how members of society cope with uncertainty in their lives. Where levels of anxiety are generally high, this results in high uncertainty avoidance and people in these cultures are deemed to be more expressive and emotional (e.g. Latin American countries) than in low uncertainty avoidance countries (e.g. many Asian countries).

3 *Individualism* – this refers to the extent to which individuals in society see themselves as independent and autonomous human beings or as part of a collectivity. High individualist countries tend to be those such as the USA, the UK, Canada and Australia; low individualism is said to be prevalent in Asian and Latin American countries.

4 *Masculinity* – this is concerned with how far a society is predisposed to aggressive and materialistic behaviour and is linked to gender role. Hofstede associates masculinity with toughness, assertiveness and materialism and with a predisposition to conflict and competition. Femininity, in contrast, is characterised as caring, sensitive and concerned with the quality of life; the result is a more accommodating style based on negotiation and compromise. Hofstede's analysis suggests the more masculine countries include Austria and Japan, while Scandinavian countries tend to be the most feminine.

5 *Long-term orientation* – this relates to the degree to which a society embraces a long-term view and respect for tradition. In societies with a short-term orientation, people tend to stress the 'here and now', typified by western countries. Eastern cultures, by comparison, are generally held to have a longer-term orientation that emphasises concern for the future and for tradition as well as for the present.

One of the benefits of Hofstede's research is that it reminds us that cultural differences can and do occur between states and, as a result, there is no 'one-size-fits-all' style of management or governance that would be suitable across all countries. For companies that are multinational organisations, management styles and approaches in the country of origin may not necessarily be suitable in other parts of the organisation for cultural reasons. Vive la différence!

Sub-culture

A society is rarely, if ever, culturally homogeneous. Within every culture **sub-cultures** usually exist, comprising groups of individuals with shared value systems based on common experiences, origins and/or situations. These identifiable sub-groups may be distinguished by nationality, race, ethnicity, religion, age, class, geographical location or some other factor and their attitudes, behaviour, customs, language and artefacts often reflect sub-cultural differences. At times such differences can be relatively easily accommodated and ultimately may become institutionalised through the legal and/or political process (e.g. the Scottish and Welsh Assemblies – see Chapter 4). At other times sub-cultural differences can be the source of a considerable degree of conflict between various sub-groups, resulting in serious divisions within a society and even in civil war and genocide.

The UK provides a good example of the notion of **cultural diversity** and can be used to illustrate how this can influence the demand for goods and services. In addition to nationality groups such as the Irish, Scots and Welsh, the country has provided a home for successive generations of immigrants from around the globe and this has created a rich mix of ethnic and other sub-groups, often concentrated in particular parts of the country and having their own language, traditions and lifestyles. In Leicester, for instance, where a significant proportion of the population is of Asian origin, there is a substantial Asian business community, part of which has developed to cater specifically for the local ethnic population (e.g. halal butchers, saree shops), as well as attracting custom from the wider community (e.g. Indian restaurants). Many Asian businesses in Leicester are small, family-owned enterprises, employing members of the extended family in keeping with cultural traditions. Aspects such as the organisation and financing of the business, its network of relationships and the working conditions for staff are also frequently influenced by cultural values, traditions and norms, although changes in these areas are becoming more apparent, especially among second- and third-generation Asian-owned enterprises.

Application: market segmentation

Marketers have long recognised the importance of demographic, social and cultural factors in shaping people's demand for goods and services. This is exemplified by the concept of **market segmentation**.

Market segmentation refers to the practice of dividing a market into distinct groups of buyers who share the same or similar attitudes and patterns of behaviour and who might require separate products or marketing to meet their particular needs. By segmenting a market into its broad component parts, businesses should be able to focus their marketing efforts more effectively and efficiently by developing product offerings and marketing programmes which meet the requirements of the different market segments.

Markets can be segmented in a variety of ways and this tends to differ between consumer markets and those which involve business-to-business transactions. Table 6.8 outlines some of the major variables used in segmenting consumer markets. As the table indicates, demographic, social and cultural factors provide a basis for identifying distinct market segments within the markets for consumer goods and services. In practice, of course, marketers may use either one (e.g. demography) or a combination (e.g. age, location and social class) of different variables to segment a market they are seeking to target.

Table 6.8 Methods of segmenting consumer markets

Type of segmentation	Key segmentation variables	Examples
Demographic	Age, gender, religion, ethnic group, family size, family life cycle stage	Children's products, ethnic foods, 18–30 holidays, retirement homes, cars
Socio-economic	Social class, income, occupation	Luxury products, convenience services, discount goods
Geographic	Country, region, urban/suburban/rural, town/city, climate	Country clothing, air conditioning, regional specialities
Geo-demographic	House type and location	Conservatories, lawnmowers
Psychographic	Lifestyles, values, personality	Health/healthier products, cosmetics, cigarettes
Mediagraphic	Media habits (e.g. papers read)	Specialist magazines, eco-friendly holidays
Behavioural	Behavioural characteristics including time/occasion of purchase, loyalty, user status, benefits sought, attitude to product, etc.	Mother's Day products, disposable cameras, toothpaste

A good example of combining the different variables is provided by the notion of **geo-demographic segmentation**, which focuses on the relationship between an individual's geographical location and her/his demographic characteristics, given that close links frequently exist between a person's place and type of residence and factors such as income, family size and attitudes. One well-known scheme of this type is **ACORN** (A Classification of Residential Neighbourhoods), which uses 40 variables from population census data to differentiate residential areas. Another is **MOSAIC**, developed by Experian, which draws on a variety of data sources (e.g. census data, financial data, property characteristics, demographic information) and uses a range of sophisticated analytical techniques to produce household profiles at full postcode level. Under the MOSAIC scheme, UK households are divided into 11 groups with names such as 'Symbols of Success', 'Suburban Comfort' and 'Grey Perspectives' and these are then further sub-divided into 61 types, again with interesting and evocative names, including 'Golden Empty Nesters', 'Sprawling Subtopia' and 'Childfree Serenity'. For a fuller description of MOSAIC and Experian's other products (e.g. commercial MOSAIC) and methodology you should access the company's website at **www.experian.co.uk** and follow the links.

With regard to factors such as social class and lifestyles, these tend to be grouped under the notion of **psychographic segmentation**, an approach that has attracted considerable attention in recent years given the reciprocal link between lifestyles and consumption indicated above. Lifestyle segments can be developed either as 'off-the-shelf' products by marketing agencies/management consultancies or can be customised for/by individual companies, although the latter often tend to be both complex and expensive to design. One established and popular example of the former is **VALS** (Values and Lifestyles) developed by SRI International. Under this model, individuals are allocated to different categories on the basis of a combination of demographic and lifestyle factors such as age, education, income and levels of self-confidence, and then these categories are grouped into a number of broader segments, which reflect a category's predominant orientations. Thus, under VALS 2, the three broad groups identified were (1) people who were *principle-orientated* (i.e. guided by their views of how the world should be); (2) people who were *status-orientated* (i.e. guided by the opinions and actions of others); (3) people who were *action-orientated* (i.e. guided by the desire for social and physical activity, variety in life and risk taking). Again you can gain further information on this scheme by visiting the SRI website at *www.sri.com/*.

Synopsis

All organisations are an integral part of the society in which they exist and carry out their activities and as a result are affected by a range of influences emanating from the demographic, social and cultural environment. These influences can change over time and help to shape both the demand and supply sides of business activity. Businesses and other organisations need to be aware of and respond to the process of societal change and to the opportunities and threats that such change can engender.

Summary of key points

- Organisations exist and operate within society and are subject to a variety of demographic and socio-cultural influences.

- Demography is concerned with population variables, including population size, structure and distribution.

- Changes in demography are primarily related to changes in birth and/or death and/or net migration rates.

- Demographic change can affect both the demand and supply sides of the economy.

- The social context of business includes factors such as social class, lifestyles and reference group influences. The consumption of goods and services in an economy can be linked to such factors.

- The cultural environment of business comprises those institutions and other forces that help to shape society's basic attitudes, values, perceptions, preferences and behaviour.

- Societies usually also contain sub-cultures, which can influence a person's beliefs, attitudes and actions.

- Like demography and social factors, cultural influences can change over time and can affect organisations. Businesses need to be sensitive to such change.

- The importance of demographic, social and cultural factors in business can be illustrated by the concept of market segmentation.

case study   An invitation to 'tweet'

The last decade has seen a remarkable explosion in the use of social media/social networking sites by individuals, groups and organisations. Facebook, Twitter, YouTube and others now attract hundreds of millions of users across the globe on a daily basis, a growing number of whom use smartphones and tablets to access these media services. Interacting with others and creating and sharing content through internet-based communities has become relatively commonplace, as has shopping for products on the internet and accessing online music, videos and sports content.

Where businesses are concerned, social networking sites appear to provide substantial marketing opportunities for firms of all sizes. Media can be used to build stronger relationships with existing customers, attract new consumers, inform users about current and future goods and services, generally promote the business and the firm's brand name(s), and find out what customers think about the organisation and its performance, including the issue of customer satisfaction. Most major firms now have a Facebook site and/or use Twitter to communicate with existing and potential consumers who are encouraged to 'follow' the business via the different media and to receive regular updates on its products and activities.

As a tool for marketing communication, social media sites have a number of important advantages. They are often free to businesses; they have a broad (often global) reach; they are fast and easy to access; they can be used to target specific groups of individuals; they allow an organisation to communicate with particular customers or groups on a personal basis at any point in time and wherever they may be. Far from replacing other forms of marketing communication and promotion, social media usage has become an additional weapon in the armoury of participating businesses; many firms have been quick to recognise that for a rapidly growing number of individuals, accessing the different networking sites is an essential part of their daily lives and hence a potentially lucrative marketing opportunity that can be exploited by suppliers of goods and services.

For organisations that choose to use social media to market their businesses, there can be risks involved, a point illustrated by the following example. In October 2013, Britain's largest energy company, British Gas, announced its intention of increasing energy prices by 10 per cent, which was around three times the level of inflation. Faced with a consumer and political backlash over its decision, the company decided to use Twitter[1] to try to head off criticism of its price hike by inviting questions from concerned customers. In the event, the organisation's attempts to pacify angry consumers proved to be a PR disaster,[2] with almost 16,000 Twitter comments – most of which were vitriolic – raining down on the company within a few hours of the invitation. To compound the problem, British Gas evidently failed to answer customers' tweets, choosing instead to use the networking site to explain to customers the reason for the decision to raise energy prices substantially, despite an earlier promise by the parent group, Centrica, to use windfall profits from the previous winter to keep prices down.

As this example illustrates, communicating with customers through social media needs to be undertaken with care and forethought; bad news can spread as rapidly as good news, even if only 140 characters are available. It doesn't take much to get things wrong, however genuine the intention.

Notes

1 Twitter – which was established in 2006 – is a 'micro-blogging' service which allows individuals and organisations to send and receive short messages about all kinds of issues and topics, including world events (e.g. the 'Arab Spring'). Popular with ordinary individuals, celebrities and companies alike, it currently attracts hundreds of millions of users worldwide, who send around 1 billion tweets every two and a half days. Like Facebook, Twitter has recently become a public company and derives most of its revenue from advertising. By 2015 it is estimated that its advertising revenue is likely to be in the region of $1 billion, or almost double its earnings in 2013.

▶

2 British Gas's experience is reminiscent of the wrath engendered by Starbucks' invitation to 'spread the cheer' via Twitter at Christmas time 2012. This prompted a plethora of angry tweets over the company's failure to pay UK corporation tax, which had received widespread media coverage.

Case study questions

1 What are the key advantages for firms of using social networking sites to market themselves and/or their products?

2 Is the use of social media by businesses size dependent, i.e. predominantly limited to larger firms?

Review and discussion questions

1 What is meant by an 'ageing' population? Examine some of the key ways in which an ageing population can affect the supply side of the economy.

2 In a country of your choice, identify some of the major social trends over the last decade. How are these trends reflected in changing patterns of consumption?

3 What is meant by the term 'culture'? To what extent do you agree with the proposition that globalisation could destroy local cultural diversity?

4 Why do marketers segment markets? Give examples of particular markets where demographic segmentation might be appropriate.

Assignments

1 Assume you work in the HR department of a large retail organisation that is seeking to replace staff who are about to retire. Because of demographic and other trends you anticipate problems in recruiting school leavers in sufficient numbers. Produce a report outlining the problem to senior executives and suggest possible solutions. Provide justifications for your recommendations.

2 Choose three countries from different continents. Produce data to show the age distribution of the population in each of the countries in a given year. Account for any differences in the age profile of the three countries and suggest ways in which these differences might affect their respective economies in both the short and the long term.

Notes and references

1 See, for example, Worthington, I., Britton, C. and Rees, A., *Economics for Business: Blending Theory and Practice*, 2nd edition, Financial Times/Prentice Hall, 2005, pp. 86–89.

2 The figure for long-term unemployment excludes students and others who are not officially in paid employment (e.g. housewives).

Further reading

Hofstede, G., *Culture's Consequences: Comparing Values, Behaviors, Institutions and Organizations Across Nations*, 2nd edition, Sage, 2003.

Hofstede, G., Hofstede, G. J. and Minkov, M., *Cultures and Organizations: Software of the Mind*, 3rd edition (Google eBook), McGraw-Hill Professional, 2010.

Kotler, P., Armstrong, G., Wong, V. and Saunders, J., *Principles of Marketing*, 5th European edition, Pearson Education, 2008.

Masterson, R. and Pickton, D., *Marketing: An Introduction*, 3rd edition, Sage, 2014.

Morrison, J., *The Global Business Environment: Meeting the Challenges*, 3rd edition, Palgrave Macmillan, 2011, Chapter 6.

Office for National Statistics, available free online (*www.statistics.gov.uk*).

Worthington, I., 'The social and economic context', in Rose, A. and Lawton, A., *Public Services Management*, Financial Times/Prentice Hall, 1999, pp. 26–43.

Web links and further questions are available on the website at:
www.pearsoned.co.uk/worthington

Business Ethics and Corporate Social Responsibility

4

1 Discuss what it means to practice good business ethics, and highlight three factors that influence ethical decision making.

2 Define *corporate social responsibility (CSR)*, and explain the difference between philanthropy and strategic CSR.

3 Distinguish among the four perspectives on corporate social responsibility.

4 Discuss the role of business in protecting the natural environment, and define *sustainable development*.

5 Identify four fundamental consumer rights and the responsibility of business to respect them.

6 Explain the responsibilities businesses have toward their employees.

BEHIND THE SCENES **NIKE'S GLOBAL PRESENCE PUTS IT ON THE FRONT LINES OF CORPORATE SOCIAL RESPONSIBILITY**

Nike has taken a leadership role in improving workplace conditions and environmental stewardship in factories around the globe.

www.nike.com

Imagine yourself in this dilemma. Much of the appeal of your products is based on their association with famous athletes, but paying these celebrities to endorse your products adds millions of dollars a year to the cost of doing business. You're also in a ferociously competitive, trend-driven industry, where you can drop off the public radar practically overnight if you don't invest heavily in constant promotion. Plus, many of your products are technically innovative, which requires ongoing research and development. Finally, consumers want to be able to buy your products from thousands of retail outlets, at a moment's notice, wherever they like to shop, so you must keep a vast distribution network supplied with inventory.

Add up all these costs, and you still haven't paid for somebody to actually *make* your products. You could make them in the United States, with its comparatively high labor costs, which would force you to raise prices in order to sustain the profit margin your investors expect in return for the money they have entrusted to you. Of course, if you raise prices too high, consumers will decide that, as cool as your products are, they can get a better deal from your competitors.

Or you could move production to a country with significantly lower labor costs, taking the pressure off your prices and profit margins and allowing you to maintain high levels of investments in other areas. Looks great on paper, but you know that every decision in business involves trade-offs. Moving production overseas and into the hands of other companies entails a significant loss of control over the manufacturing process, materials sourcing, and working conditions.

You can measure financial costs and product quality, providing clear feedback on some important performance parameters. But what about the way your production partners conduct business? Do they conduct themselves in a manner that is consistent with your values and your public image? Do they treat workers humanely? Do they steward shared natural resources in a responsible manner? Do they minimize negative impacts on their communities?

You don't have direct control over how these companies perform, and you don't always know what they're up to, but you know one thing for certain: People are going to hold you accountable for the performance and behavior of these business partners, even if they are independent companies operating in other countries. Big companies make big targets, and you've been the focus of a number of campaigns by advocacy groups and other nongovernmental organizations.

Welcome to a day in the life of Mark Parker, president and CEO of Nike, the athletic footwear and apparel giant based in Beaverton, Oregon. If you were in Parker's Nikes, how would you balance the competing demands of investors, employees, retailers, advocacy groups, and business partners? How would you keep Nike on its path of strong growth while also being a responsible corporate citizen in the more than 160 countries where it does business?[1]

INTRODUCTION

Like Nike's Mark Parker (profiled in the chapter-opening Behind the Scenes), managers in every industry today must balance the demands of running a profitable business with the expectations of running a socially responsible company. As a future business leader, you will face some of the challenges discussed in this chapter, and your choices won't always be easy. You may struggle to find ethical clarity in some situations or even to understand what your choices are and how each option might affect your company's various stakeholders. You may need to muster the courage to stand up to colleagues, bosses, or customers if you think ethical principles are being violated. Fortunately, by having a good understanding of what constitutes ethical behavior and what society expects from business today, you'll be better prepared to make these tough choices. This chapter explores the basic ideas of business ethics and corporate social responsibility and then takes a closer look at business's responsibility toward the natural environment, consumers, and employees.

1   **LEARNING OBJECTIVE**

Discuss what it means to practice good business ethics, and highlight three factors that influence ethical decision making.

Ethics in Contemporary Business

Assessing the ethics of contemporary business is no simple matter, partly because of disagreement over what constitutes ethical behavior and partly because the behavior of individual companies runs the gamut from positive to neutral to negative. However, it is safe to say that there is significant concern about the ethics of current (and future) business leaders. Harvard Business School professor Rakesh Khurana probably speaks for many when he says, "One way of looking at the problem with American business today is that it has succeeded in assuming many of the appearances and privileges of professionalism, while evading the attendant constraints and responsibilities."[2] By and large, the general public seems to agree (see Exhibit 4.1).

The news is not all bad, of course. Most businesses are run by ethical managers and staffed by ethical employees whose positive contributions to their communities are unfortunately overshadowed at times by headline-grabbing scandals. Companies around the world help their communities in countless ways, from sponsoring youth sports teams to raising millions of dollars to build hospitals.

Moreover, even when companies are simply engaged in the normal course of business—and do so ethically—they contribute to society by making useful products, providing employment, and paying taxes. Business catches a lot of flak these days, some of it deserved, but overall, its contributions to the health, happiness, and well-being of society are beyond measure.

REAL-TIME UPDATES
Learn More by Reading This Article

Which companies do U.S. consumers like and loathe the most?

Peruse this ranking of America's most- and least-liked corporations. Go to http://real-timeupdates.com/bia8 and click on Learn More in the Students section.

EXHIBIT 4.1   Public Perceptions of Business Ethics

One can argue whether public perceptions of business ethics accurately reflect the behavior of the entire community of business professionals or simply mirror the behavior of businesses and individuals who make headlines. However, there is no argument on this point: The general public doesn't think too highly of business. This graph shows the percentage of Americans who rate the honesty and ethics of a particular profession as either "high" or "very high." Several business professions are shown, with several nonbusiness professions for comparison.

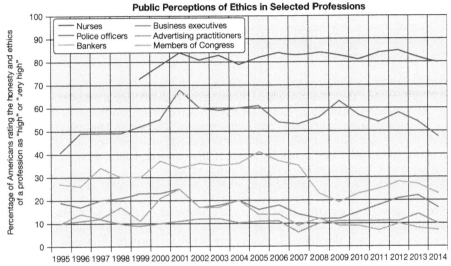

Public Perceptions of Ethics in Selected Professions

Source: Data from "USA Today/Gallup Poll, December 11–14, 2014—Final Topline," www.gallup.com.

WHAT IS ETHICAL BEHAVIOR?

Ethics are the principles and standards of moral behavior that are accepted by society as right and wrong. Practicing good business ethics involves, at a minimum, competing fairly and honestly, communicating truthfully, being transparent, and not causing harm to others:

- **Competing fairly and honestly.** Businesses are expected to compete fairly and honestly and to not knowingly deceive, intimidate, or misrepresent themselves to customers, competitors, clients, employees, the media, or government officials.
- **Communicating truthfully.** Communicating truthfully is a simple enough concept: Tell the truth, the whole truth, and nothing but the truth. However, matters sometimes aren't so clear. For instance, if you plan to introduce an improved version of a product next year, do you have an obligation to tell customers who are buying the existing product this year? Suppose you do tell them, and so many decide to delay their purchases that you end up with a cash flow problem that forces you to lay off several employees. Would that be fair for customers but unfair for your employees?
- **Being transparent.** Business communication ethics often involve the question of **transparency**, which can be defined as "the degree to which information flows freely within an organization, among managers and employees, and outward to stakeholders."[3]
- **Not causing harm to others.** All businesses have the capacity to cause harm to employees, customers, other companies, their communities, and investors. Problems can start when managers make decisions that put their personal interests above those of other stakeholders, underestimate the risks of failure, or neglect to consider potential effects on other people and organizations. For example, **insider trading**, in which company insiders use confidential information to gain an advantage in stock market trading, harms other investors. (Insider trading is illegal, in addition to being unethical.) Of course, harm can also result even when managers have acted ethically—but they are still responsible for these negative outcomes.

ethics
The rules or standards governing the conduct of a person or group.

transparency
The degree to which affected parties can observe relevant aspects of transactions or decisions.

insider trading
The use of unpublicized information that an individual gains from the course of his or her job to benefit from fluctuations in the stock market.

FACTORS INFLUENCING ETHICAL BEHAVIOR

Of the many factors that influence ethical behavior, three warrant particular attention: cultural differences, knowledge, and organizational behavior.

Cultural Differences

Chapter 3 points out that globalization exposes businesspeople to a variety of cultures and business practices. What does it mean for a business to do the right thing in Thailand? In Nigeria? In Norway? What may be considered unethical in one culture could be an accepted practice in another. Managers may need to consider a wide range of issues, including acceptable working conditions, minimum wage levels, product safety issues, and environmental protection. (See the Nike Behind the Scenes wrap-up on page 137 for more on this important topic.)

Knowledge

As a general rule, the more you know and the better you understand a situation, the better your chances of making an ethical decision. In the churn of daily business, though, it's easy to shut your eyes and ears to potential problems. However, as a business leader, you have the responsibility not only to pay attention but also to actively seek out information regarding potential ethical issues. Ignorance is never an acceptable defense in the eyes of the law, and it shouldn't be in questions of ethics, either.

Organizational Behavior

code of ethics
A written statement that sets forth the principles that guide an organization's decisions.

whistle-blowing
The disclosure of information by a company insider that exposes illegal or unethical behavior by others within the organization.

Companies with strong ethical practices create cultures that reward good behavior—and don't intentionally or unintentionally reward bad behavior.[4] At United Technologies (www.utc.com), a diversified manufacturer based in Hartford, Connecticut, ethical behavior starts at the top; executives are responsible for meeting clearly defined ethical standards, and their annual compensation is tied to how well they perform.[5] To help avoid ethical breaches, many companies develop programs to improve ethical conduct, typically combining training, communication, and a **code of ethics** that defines the values and principles that should be used to guide decisions.

Employees who observe unethical or illegal behavior within their companies and are unable to resolve the problems through normal channels may have no choice but to resort to **whistle-blowing**—expressing their concerns internally through formal reporting mechanisms or externally to the news media or government regulators. However, the decision to "blow the whistle" on one's own employer is rarely easy or without consequences. More than 80 percent of whistle-blowers in one survey said they were punished in some way for coming forward with their concerns.[6] In addition, the laws governing whistle-blowing are a complicated web of federal and state legislation that can be difficult for employees and employers to navigate.[7]

Although whistle-blowing is sometimes characterized as "ratting on" colleagues or managers, it has an essential function. According to international business expert Alex MacBeath, "Often whistle-blowing can be the only way that information about issues such as rule breaking, criminal activity, cover-ups, and fraud can be brought to management's attention before serious damage is suffered."[8]

ETHICAL DECISION MAKING

ethical lapse
A situation in which an individual or a group makes a decision that is morally wrong, illegal, or unethical.

ethical dilemma
A situation in which more than one side of an issue can be supported with valid arguments.

When the question of what is right and what is wrong is clear, ethical decisions are easy to make: You simply choose to do the right thing. (At least making the decision is simple; *implementing* the decision may be another story.) If you choose the wrong course, such as cheating on your taxes or stealing from your employer, you commit an **ethical lapse**. The choices were clear, and you made the wrong one.

However, you will encounter situations in which choices are not so clear. An **ethical dilemma** is a situation in which you must choose between conflicting but arguably valid options, or even situations in which all your options are unpleasant. As Exhibit 4.2 suggests, stakeholders' needs often conflict, requiring managers to make tough decisions about resource allocation.

EXHIBIT 4.2   Stakeholders' Rights: A Difficult Balancing Act

Balancing the individual needs and interests of a company's stakeholders is one of management's most difficult tasks. Consider how these three examples could affect each of five stakeholder groups in a different way. (Note that some people may fall into multiple groups. Employees, for example, are taxpayers and members of the local community, and they may also be shareholders. Also, these scenarios and outcomes offer a simplified view of what is likely to happen in each case, but they illustrate the mixed effects that can result from management decisions.)

Decision	Shareholders (entrust money to the company in anticipation of a positive return on their investment)	Employees (devote time, energy, and creativity to the company's success)	Customers (expect to receive quality products and maximum value for prices paid)	Local Community (can be affected both positively and negatively by the company's presence and actions)	Taxpayers (affected indirectly by the amount of tax revenue that local, state, and federal governments get from the company)
Company decides to *offshore* some of its production to another country with lower labor costs; lays off significant number of employees	Stand to benefit from lower production costs, which could increase sales, profits, or both, probably leading to increases in share price	Some employees lose their jobs; morale likely to suffer among those who keep theirs	Benefit from lower prices	Suffers from loss of spendable income in the local economy and taxes paid to local government; exodus of employees can drive down home values	Might be hurt or helped by the move, depending on whether loss of income tax paid by U.S. employees is offset by increased income tax paid by the company, for example
Company institutes a generous pay and benefits increase to improve employee morale	Might be hurt in the short term as the stock market punishes the company for increasing its cost structure and diverting funds away from development; could help over the long term if the moves boost employee productivity	Benefit from higher pay and more valuable benefits	Could be hurt by higher prices if prices are raised to cover the added costs; could benefit from higher levels of employee satisfaction, leading to improved customer service	Benefits from more spendable income in the local economy and taxes paid to local government; better employee benefits could also mean less drain on community resources such as health clinics	Benefit from more money paid into government treasuries through higher income taxes
Company installs a multimillion-dollar waste water recirculation system that surpasses regulatory requirements; system will pay for itself in lower water bills, but not for 10 years	Probably hurt as stock market punishes an investment with no immediate payback; increased goodwill and long-term cost savings help in years ahead	Probably hurt in the short term as less money is available for raises and benefits; likely to benefit in the long term as the costs are recovered	Hurt as higher costs are passed along as higher prices	Helped by the company's efforts to conserve a shared natural resource	Hurt as the company writes off the cost of the system, thereby lowering the taxes it pays to the government

Consider the following points to help find the right answer whenever you face an ethical dilemma:

- Make sure you frame the situation accurately, taking into account all relevant issues and questions.
- Identify all parties who might be affected by your decision, and consider the rights of everyone involved.

EXHIBIT 4.3 **Approaches to Resolving Ethical Dilemmas**

These approaches can help you resolve ethical dilemmas you may face on the job. Be aware that in some situations, different approaches can lead to different ethical conclusions.

Approach	Summary
Justice	Treat people equally or at least fairly in a way that makes rational and moral sense.
Utilitarianism	Choose the option that delivers the most good for the most people (or protects the most people from a negative outcome).
Individual rights	To the greatest possible extent, respect the rights of all individuals, particularly their right to control their own destinies.
Individual responsibilities	Focus on the ethical duties of the individuals involved in the situation.
The common good	Emphasize qualities and conditions that benefit the community as a whole, such as peace and public safety.
Virtue	Emphasize desirable character traits such as integrity and compassion.

Sources: Manuel Velasquez, Claire Andre, Thomas Shanks, S. J., and Michael J. Meyer, "Thinking Ethically: A Framework for Moral Decision Making," Markkula Center for Applied Ethics, Santa Clara University, accessed 3 June 2009, www.scu.edu; Ben Rogers, "John Rawls," *The Guardian*, 27 November 2002, www.guardian.co.uk; Irene Van Staveren, "Beyond Utilitarianism and Deontology: Ethics in Economics," *Review of Political Economy*, January 2007, 21–35.

- Be as objective as possible. Make sure you're not making a decision just to protect your own emotions, and don't automatically assume you're viewing a situation fairly and objectively.
- Don't assume that other people think the way you do. The time-honored "Golden Rule" of treating others the way you want to be treated can cause problems when others don't *want* to be treated the same way you do.
- Watch out for **conflicts of interest**, situations in which competing loyalties can lead to ethical lapses. For instance, if you are in charge of selecting an advertising agency to handle your company's next campaign, you would have an obvious conflict of interest if your spouse or partner works for one of the agencies under consideration.

conflicts of interest
Situations in which competing loyalties can lead to ethical lapses, such as when a business decision may be influenced by the potential for personal gain.

Exhibit 4.3 identifies six well-known approaches to resolving ethical dilemmas.

 Checkpoint

LEARNING OBJECTIVE 1: Discuss what it means to practice good business ethics, and highlight three factors that influence ethical decision making.

SUMMARY: Three essential components of good business ethics are competing fairly and honestly, communicating truthfully, and not causing harm to others. Three major influences on ethical decision making are culture, knowledge, and organizational behavior. When facing an ethical dilemma, you can often find clarity by starting with universal standards of justice, considering the rights of everyone involved, being as objective as possible, not assuming that other people think the way you do, and avoiding conflicts of interest.

CRITICAL THINKING: (1) If you go to work tomorrow morning and your boss asks you to do something you consider unethical, what factors will you take into consideration before responding? (2) How can you balance the business need to inspire employees to compete aggressively with the moral need to avoid competing unethically?

IT'S YOUR BUSINESS: (1) In your current job (or any previous job you've held), in what ways does your employer contribute to society? (2) Have you ever encountered an ethical dilemma in your work? If so, how did you resolve it?

KEY TERMS TO KNOW: ethics, transparency, insider trading, code of ethics, whistleblowing, ethical lapse, ethical dilemma, conflicts of interest.

Corporate Social Responsibility

Corporate social responsibility (CSR) is the notion that business has obligations to society beyond the pursuit of profits. There is a widespread assumption these days that CSR is both a moral imperative for business and a good thing for society, but the issues aren't quite as clear as they might seem at first glance.

THE RELATIONSHIP BETWEEN BUSINESS AND SOCIETY

What does business owe society, and what does society owe business? Any attempt to understand and shape this relationship needs to consider four essential truths:

- Consumers in contemporary societies enjoy and expect a wide range of benefits, from education and health care to credit and products that are safe to use. Most of these benefits share an important characteristic: They require money.
- Profit-seeking companies are the economic engine that powers modern society; they generate the vast majority of the money in a nation's economy, either directly (through their own taxes and purchases) or indirectly (through the taxes and purchases made by the employees they support).
- Much of what we consider when assessing a society's standard of living involves goods and services created by profit-seeking companies.
- Conversely, companies cannot hope to operate profitably without the many benefits provided by a stable, functioning society: talented and healthy employees, a legal framework in which to pursue commerce, a dependable transportation infrastructure, opportunities to raise money, and customers with the ability to pay for goods and services, to name just some of them.

Business and society clearly need each other—and each needs the other to be healthy and successful.

PHILANTHROPY VERSUS STRATEGIC CSR

Companies that engage in CSR activities can choose between two courses of action: general philanthropy or strategic CSR. **Philanthropy** involves donating money, employee time, or other resources to various causes without regard for any direct business benefits for the company. For instance, a company might support the arts in its hometown in the interest of enhancing the city's cultural richness. Through a combination of free products, employee time, use of company facilities, and cash contributions, U.S. companies donate billions of dollars to charity every year.[9]

In contrast to generic philanthropy, **strategic CSR** involves social contributions that are directly aligned with a company's overall business strategy. In other words, the company helps itself and society at the same time. This approach can be followed in a variety of ways. A company can help develop the workforce by supporting job training efforts or use volunteering programs to help train employees. For example, in UPS's Community Internship Program, management candidates volunteer in community programs to help them understand the needs and challenges of various population groups while developing essential skills.[10] A company can also make choices that address social concerns while giving it a competitive advantage. As you can read in the "Improving Your Tech Insights" activity on page 140, IBM and Microsoft are among the many companies that invest in *assistive technologies* that help people with disabilities while expanding market opportunities and access to employee talent.

Strategic CSR makes more sense than general philanthropy or an antagonistic business-versus-society mindset, for several reasons. First, because business and society are mutually dependent, choices that weaken one or the other will ultimately weaken both. Second, investments that benefit the company are more likely to be sustained over time. Third, making sizable investments in a few strategically focused areas will yield greater benefits to society than spreading smaller amounts of money around through generic philanthropy.[11]

2 LEARNING OBJECTIVE

Define *corporate social responsibility (CSR)*, and explain the difference between philanthropy and strategic CSR.

corporate social responsibility (CSR)
The idea that business has obligations to society beyond the pursuit of profits.

philanthropy
The donation of money, time, goods, or services to charitable, humanitarian, or educational institutions.

strategic CSR
Social contributions that are directly aligned with a company's overall business strategy.

Exactly how much can or should businesses contribute to social concerns? This is a difficult decision because all companies have limited resources that must be allocated to a number of goals, such as upgrading facilities and equipment, developing new products, marketing existing products, and rewarding employee efforts, in addition to contributing to social causes.

✓ Checkpoint

LEARNING OBJECTIVE 2: Define *corporate social responsibility (CSR)*, and explain the difference between philanthropy and strategic CSR.

SUMMARY: Corporate social responsibility (CSR) is the notion that business has obligations to society beyond the pursuit of profits. However, there is no general agreement over what those responsibilities are or which elements of society should determine those obligations or benefit from them. Philanthropy involves donating time, money, or other resources, without regard for any direct business benefits. In contrast, strategic CSR involves contributions that are aligned with the company's business needs and strategies.

CRITICAL THINKING: (1) Given that "society" is not an organized entity, how can society decide what the responsibilities of business are in a CSR context? (2) Is philanthropy morally superior to strategic CSR? Why or why not?

IT'S YOUR BUSINESS: (1) How do a company's philanthropic or CSR efforts influence your purchasing behavior? (2) Is it ethical for companies to invest in your college or university in exchange for publicity? Why or why not?

KEY TERMS TO KNOW: corporate social responsibility (CSR), philanthropy, strategic CSR

---

3   LEARNING OBJECTIVE

Distinguish among the four perspectives on corporate social responsibility.

Perspectives on Corporate Social Responsibility

To encourage ethical behavior and promote a mutually beneficial relationship between business and society, it is clearly necessary to establish expectations about how businesses should conduct themselves. However, both business and society are still grappling with exactly what those expectations should be. "Social responsibility" certainly sounds admirable, but it's not always clear which segments of society it involves or what those responsibilities are.[12] Approaches to CSR can be roughly categorized into four perspectives (see Exhibit 4.4), from minimalist through proactive.

MINIMALIST CSR

According to what might be termed the *minimalist view*, the only social responsibility of business is to pay taxes and obey the law. In a 1970 article that is still widely discussed today, Nobel Prize–winning economist Milton Friedman articulated this view by saying, "There is only one social responsibility of business: to use its resources and engage in activities designed to increase its profits so long as it stays within the rules of the game, which is to say, engages in open and free competition without deception or fraud."[13]

This view, which tends to reject the stakeholder concept described in Chapter 1, might seem selfish and even antisocial, but it raises a couple of important issues. First, any business that operates ethically and legally provides society with beneficial goods and services at fair prices. One can argue that doing so fulfills a company's primary obligation to society.

Second—and this is a vital point to consider even if you reject the minimalist view—should businesses be in the business of making social policy and spending the public's money? Proponents of the minimalist view claim that this is actually what happens when companies make tax-deductible contributions to social causes. For example, assume that

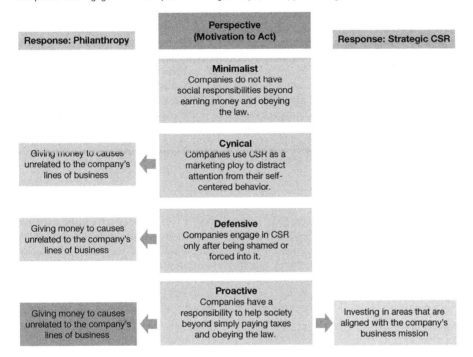

EXHIBIT 4.4   Perspectives on Corporate Social Responsibility

The perspectives on CSR can be roughly divided into four categories, from minimalist to proactive. Companies that engage in CSR can pursue either generic *philanthropy* or *strategic CSR*.

in response to pressure from activists, a company makes a sizable contribution that nets it a $1 million tax break. That's $1 million taken out of the public treasury, where voters and their elected representatives can control how money is spent, and put it into whatever social cause the company chooses to support. In effect, the corporation and the activists are spending the public's money, and the public has no say in how it is spent. Would it be better for society if companies paid full taxes and let the people (through their elected representatives) decide how their tax dollars are put to work?

REAL-TIME UPDATES
Learn More by Watching This Video

> **Are corporations putting too much emphasis on shareholder value?**
>
> Wharton professor Eric W. Orts discusses the potential harm of focusing too heavily on stock price. Go to http://real-timeupdates .com/bia8 and click on Learn More in the Students section.

DEFENSIVE CSR

Many companies today face pressure from a variety of activists and **nongovernmental organizations (NGOs)**, nonprofit groups that provide charitable services or that promote causes, from workers' rights to environmental protection. One possible response to this pressure is to engage in CSR activities as a way to avoid further criticism. In other words, the company may take positive steps to address a particular issue only because it has been embarrassed into action by negative publicity.

Note that companies can engage in proactive CSR and still receive criticism from advocacy groups. A company and an NGO might disagree about responsibilities or outcomes, or in some cases an NGO might target a company for a problem that the company has already been working on. In other words, it can't immediately be concluded that a company is simply being defensive when it engages in CSR while in the glare of public criticism. (For an example, see the Nike Behind the Scenes wrap-up at the end of the chapter.)

nongovernmental organizations (NGOs) Nonprofit groups that provide charitable services or promote social and environmental causes.

John Gress/Corbis

Major corporations are often the target of advocacy groups, and the pressure can influence their responses to various CSR issues.

CYNICAL CSR

Another possible approach to CSR is purely cynical, in which a company accused of irresponsible behavior promotes itself as being socially responsible without making substantial improvements in its business practices. For example, environmental activists use the term *greenwash* (a combination of *green* and *whitewash*, a term that suggests covering something up) as a label for publicity efforts that present companies as being environmentally friendly when their actions speak otherwise. Ironically, some of the most ardent anti-business activists and the staunchly pro-business advocates of the minimalist view tend to agree on one point: Many CSR efforts are disingenuous. Thirty-five years after his provocative article, Friedman said he believed that "most of the claims of social responsibility are pure public relations."[14]

PROACTIVE CSR

In the fourth approach, proactive CSR, company leaders believe they have responsibilities beyond making a profit, and they back up their beliefs and proclamations with actions taken on their own initiative. Laurie Erickson is the founder and CEO of The Finest Accessories, a North Bend, Washington, company that markets handmade barrettes and other hair accessories to high-end department stores. After a customer asked Erickson if she sold any products for women who had lost their hair to chemotherapy, Erickson not only created a fashionable scarf that fit the bill but also launched a program of offering a free scarf to any cancer patient who asks for one. The company has now given away thousands of scarves, each accompanied with a get-well card signed by every employee in the company.[15]

See Chapter 5 (page 106) for a discussion of a new type of corporate structure, the *benefit corporation*, which builds proactive CSR into a company's very foundation and legally obligates it to pursue a social or environmental goal.

REAL-TIME UPDATES
Learn More by Visiting This Website

Want to make an impact with your entrepreneurial efforts?

Impact Hub is a global community of local "hubs" that nurture social entrepreneurs. Go to http://real-timeupdates.com/bia8 and click on Learn More in the Students section.

RESOLVING THE CSR DILEMMA

So what's the right answer? Of the four perspectives on CSR, we can instantly eliminate the cynical approach simply because it is dishonest and therefore unethical. Beyond that, the debate is less clear, but the opinions are certainly strong. Some proponents of the minimalist view equate CSR with *collectivism*, a term that suggests socialism and even communism. Some consider CSR demands from activist groups and other outsiders to be little more than extortion.[16] At the other extreme, some critics of contemporary business seem convinced that corporations can never be trusted and that every CSR initiative is a cynical publicity stunt.

A two-tiered approach to CSR can yield a practical, ethical answer to this complex dilemma. At the first tier, companies must take responsibility for the consequences of their actions and limit the negative impact of their operations. This approach can be summarized as "do no harm," and it is not a matter of choice. Just as a society has a right to expect certain behavior from all citizens, it has a right to expect a basic level of responsible behavior from all businesses, including minimizing pollution and waste, minimizing the depletion of shared natural resources, being honest with all stakeholders, offering real value in exchange for prices asked, and avoiding exploitation of employees, customers, suppliers, communities, and investors. Some of these issues are covered by

REAL-TIME UPDATES
Learn More by Exploring This Interactive Website

See how one of the world's biggest energy consumers is reducing, reusing, and recycling

Explore Google's efforts to reduce its energy usage and minimize its impact on the environment. Go to http://real-timeupdates.com /bia8 and click on Learn More in the Students section.

laws, but others aren't, thereby creating the responsibility of ethical decision making by all employees and managers in a firm.

At the second tier, moving beyond "do no harm" becomes a matter of choice. Companies can choose to help in whatever way that investors, managers, and employees see fit, but the choices are up to the company and should not be the result of pressure from outside forces.

For the latest information on CSR, visit http://real-timeupdates.com/bia8 and click on Chapter 4.

Checkpoint

LEARNING OBJECTIVE 3: Distinguish among the four perspectives on corporate social responsibility.

SUMMARY: The spectrum of viewpoints on CSR can be roughly divided into minimalist (business's only obligation is to compete to the best of its abilities without deception or fraud), defensive (in which businesses engage in CSR efforts only in response to social pressure), cynical (in which businesses engage in CSR as a public relations ploy), and proactive (in which businesses contribute to society out of a belief that they have an obligation to do so).

CRITICAL THINKING: (1) Do you agree that giving companies tax breaks for charitable contributions distorts public spending by indirectly giving companies and activists control over how tax revenues are spent? Why or why not? (2) If Company A takes a cynical approach to CSR and Company B takes a proactive approach but they make identical contributions to society, is one company "better" than the other? Why or why not?

IT'S YOUR BUSINESS: (1) Have you ever suspected a company of engaging in greenwashing or other disingenuous CSR activities? How would you prove or disprove such a suspicion? (2) If you were the head of a small company and wanted to give back to society in some way, how would you select which organizations or causes to support?

KEY TERM TO KNOW: nongovernmental organizations (NGOs)

CSR: The Natural Environment

4 **LEARNING OBJECTIVE**

Discuss the role of business in protecting the natural environment, and define *sustainable development*.

In recent years, few issues in the public dialogue have become as politicized and polarized as pollution and resource depletion. Environmentalists and their political allies sometimes portray business leaders as heartless profiteers who would strip the Earth bare for a few bucks. Corporate leaders and their political allies, on the other hand, sometimes cast environmentalists as "tree huggers" who care more about bunnies and butterflies than about jobs and other human concerns. As is often the case, the shouting match between these extreme positions obscures real problems—and opportunities for real solutions.

To reach a clearer understanding of this situation, keep three important points in mind. First, the creation, delivery, use, and disposal of products that society values virtually always generate pollution and consume natural resources. For instance, it's tempting to assume that web-based businesses are "clean" because there is no visible pollution. However, the Internet and all the devices attached to it have a voracious appetite for electricity; Google is one of the largest users of electricity in the world, for example.[17] (See more about Google's energy consumption under "Efforts to Conserve Resources and Reduce Pollution.") Moreover, generation of electricity seriously affects the environment. Although the share of the electricity generated by renewable means in the United States is increasing, and solar is cost-competitive with coal in many locations, two-thirds of the country's electricity is still generated by burning coal, oil, or natural gas (see Exhibit 4.5 on the next page).[18]

| EXHIBIT 4.5 | Sources of Electrical Power in the United States |

Most of the electricity generated in the United States is produced by burning fossil fuels. Nuclear and hydroelectric power provide most of the rest. Renewable sources such as wind and solar have grown over the past decade, but they remain minor sources of electricity at this point.

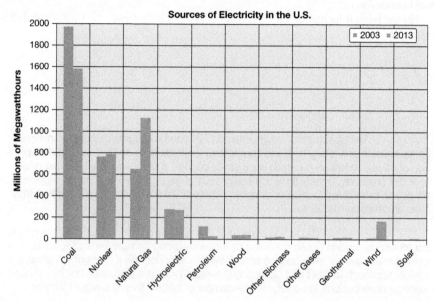

Source: Data from *Electric Power Annual*, 23 March 2015, U.S. Energy Information Administration, www.eia.gov.

Second, "environmental" issues are often as much about human health and safety as they are about forests, rivers, and wildlife. The availability of clean air, water, and soil affects everyone, not just people concerned with wild spaces.

Third, many of these issues are neither easy nor simple. They often require tough trade-offs, occasional sacrifice, disruptive change, and decision making in the face of uncertainty. Meeting these challenges will require people to be clear-headed, open-minded, adaptable, and courageous.

EFFORTS TO CONSERVE RESOURCES AND REDUCE POLLUTION

Concerns over pollution and resource depletion have been growing since the dawn of the Industrial Age in the 19th century. However, widespread concern for the environment really dates to the 1960s, when *ecology*, the study of the relationship between organisms and the natural environment, entered mainstream discussion. In 1963, federal, state, and local governments began enacting laws and regulations to reduce pollution (see Exhibit 4.6). Many states and cities have also passed their own tough clean-air laws.

You've no doubt heard the slogan "reduce, reuse, recycle" as advice for conserving resources and minimizing pollution. Google offers a great example of what businesses can do in this regard. As a major consumer of energy, the company is taking responsibility for that consumption in a number of significant ways, including reducing energy usage in its data centers (massive complexes that house the thousands of computers that make Google searches possible) by more than half, investing in renewable energy in ways that help this fledgling industry sector grow, *repurposing* hundreds of thousands of older computers for new uses, using

REAL-TIME UPDATES
Learn More by Exploring This Interactive Website

Create a more sustainable product with Nike's interactive tool

Nike's Environmental Design Tool measures the environmental impact of a manufactured product and helps design teams improve the sustainability of their products. You can plug in data from your own apparel to see how your clothing scores. Go to http://real-timeupdates.com/bia8 and click on Learn More in the Students section.

EXHIBIT 4.6	Major Federal Environmental Legislation

Since the early 1960s, major federal legislation aimed at the environment has focused on providing cleaner air and water and reducing toxic waste. (Many of these laws have been amended since their original passage dates.)

Legislation	Key Provisions
Clean Air Act (1963) Clean Air Act (1967) Clean Air Act (1970)	Assist states and localities in formulating control programs; set federal standards for auto-exhaust emissions; set maximum permissible pollution levels; authorize nationwide air-pollution standards and limitations to pollutant discharge; require scrubbers in new coal-fired power plants; direct the (Environmental Protection Agency [EPA]) to prevent deterioration of air quality in clean areas; set schedule and standards for cutting smog, acid rain, hazardous factory fumes, and ozone-depleting chemicals
Solid Waste Disposal Act (1965)	Authorizes research and assistance to state and local control programs; regulates treatment, storage, transportation, and disposal of hazardous waste
National Environmental Policy Act (1969)	Establishes a structure for coordinating all federal environmental programs
Resource Recovery Act (1970)	Subsidizes pilot recycling plants; authorizes nationwide control programs
Clean Water Act (1972) Clean Water Act (1977)	Authorizes grant to states for water-pollution control; give federal government limited authority to correct pollution problems; authorize EPA to set and enforce water-quality standards
Noise Control Act (1972)	Requires EPA to set standards for major sources of noise and to advise Federal Aviation Administration on standards for airplane noise
Endangered Species Act (1973)	Establishes protections for endangered and threatened plants and animals
Safe Drinking Water Act (1974)	Sets standards of drinking-water quality; requires municipal water systems to report on contaminant levels; establishes funding to upgrade water systems
Toxic Substances Control Act (1976)	Requires chemicals testing; authorizes EPA to restrict the use of harmful substances
Resource Conservation and Recovery Act (1976)	Gives the EPA authority to control hazardous waste
Comprehensive Environmental Response, Compensation, and Liability Act (1980)	Establishes the "Superfund" program to oversee the identification and cleanup of uncontrolled or abandoned hazardous-waste sites
Nuclear Waste Policy Act (1982)	Establishes procedures for creating geologic repositories of radioactive waste
Marine Protection, Research, and Sanctuaries Act (1988)	Prohibits ocean dumping that could threaten human health or the marine environment
Oil Pollution Act (1990)	Sets up liability trust fund; extends operations for preventing and containing oil pollution
Energy Independence and Security Act (2007)	Aims to reduce U.S. dependence on foreign energy sources by expanding energy production options and improving energy efficiency

Sources: U.S. Environmental Protection Agency website, accessed 23 March 2015, www.epa.gov; "Overview: Key Federal Environmental Laws," FindLaw, accessed 23 March 2015, www.findlaw.com.

its position as a major corporation to help shape energy policy and public awareness, and sharing the results of its considerable research efforts with other companies to help them reduce resource usage.[19]

In addition to technological efforts to reduce pollution and resource consumption, businesses, governments, and NGOs are pursuing a variety of political and economic solutions. For example, **cap and trade** programs try to balance free-market economics with government intervention. Lawmakers first establish a maximum allowable amount of a particular pollutant that a designated group of companies or industries is allowed to emit (the "cap") and then distribute individual emission allowances to all the companies in that group. If a company lowers its emissions enough to stay under its prescribed limit, it can sell, trade, or save leftover allowances (the "trade"). If a company exceeds its emission allowances, it must buy or trade for enough allowances to cover the excess emissions. In this way, companies can choose the lowest-cost means of taking responsibility for their emissions.[20] During the 1990s, a cap-and-trade program to reduce sulfur dioxide emissions from coal-burning power plants, a leading cause of acid rain, reduced emissions by 50 percent.[21]

cap and trade
A type of environmental policy that gives companies some freedom in addressing the environmental impact of specified pollutants, by either reducing emissions to meet a designated cap or buying allowances to offset excess emissions.

When you replaced your smartphone or laptop, where did the old one go?

REAL-TIME UPDATES
Learn More by Watching This Video

Hear what 1,000 global CEOs think about sustainability

Get the highlights of a comprehensive survey of executive perspectives on business and sustainability issues. Go to http://real-timeupdates.com/bia8 and click on Learn More in the Students section.

sustainable development
Operating business in a manner that minimizes pollution and resource depletion, ensuring that future generations will have vital resources.

THE TREND TOWARD SUSTAINABILITY

Efforts to minimize resource depletion and pollution are part of a broader effort known as *sustainability*, or **sustainable development**, which the United Nations has defined as development that "meets the needs of the present without compromising the ability of future generations to meet their own needs."[22] Notice how this idea expands the stakeholder concept from Chapter 1 by including stakeholders from the future, not just those with an immediate interest in what a company does.

Sustainable development can certainly require changes to the way companies conduct business, but paying attention to a broader scope of stakeholders and managing for the longer term doesn't automatically mean that companies have to take a financial hit to go "green." Many businesses are discovering that taking steps now to reduce consumption and pollution can end up saving money down the road by reducing everything from cleanup and litigation expenses to ongoing production costs. As Xerox CEO Ursula Burns puts it, "The greener we get, the more we can reduce costs and boost efficiency."[23]

In other words, in addition to better stewardship of shared natural resources, sustainable development is also a smart business strategy. By taking a broad and long-term view of their companies' impact on the environment and stakeholders throughout the world, managers can ensure the continued availability of the resources their organizations need and be better prepared for changes in government regulations and shifting social expectations. In fact, a majority of global CEOs now view sustainability as a business opportunity,[24] a viewpoint firmly in line with the concept of strategic CSR.

 Checkpoint

LEARNING OBJECTIVE 4: Discuss the role of business in protecting the natural environment, and define *sustainable development*.

SUMMARY: As major users of natural resources and generators of waste products, businesses play a huge role in conservation and pollution-reduction efforts. Many businesses are making an effort to reduce, reuse, and recycle, and governments are trying market-based approaches such as *cap and trade* to encourage businesses to reduce emissions. All these efforts are part of a trend toward *sustainable development*, which can be defined as meeting the needs of the present without compromising the ability of future generations to meet their own needs.

CRITICAL THINKING: (1) Should all industries be required to meet the same levels of pollution control? Why or why not? (2) How would you respond to critics who say that cap-and-trade programs allow polluters to buy their way out of the responsibility of cleaning up their operations?

IT'S YOUR BUSINESS: (1) In what ways could your employer (or your college, if you're not currently working) take steps to reduce resource depletion? (2) How did you dispose of the last electronic product you stopped using?

KEY TERMS TO KNOW: cap and trade, sustainable development

CSR: Consumers

The 1960s activism that awakened business to its environmental responsibilities also gave rise to **consumerism**, a movement that put pressure on businesses to consider consumer needs and interests. (Note that some people use *consumerism* in a negative sense, as a synonym for *materialism*.) Consumerism prompted many businesses to create consumer affairs departments to handle customer complaints. It also prompted state and local agencies to set up bureaus to offer consumer information and assistance. At the federal level, President John F. Kennedy announced a "bill of rights" for consumers, laying the foundation for a wave of consumer-oriented legislation (see Exhibit 4.7).

5 **LEARNING OBJECTIVE**

Identify four fundamental consumer rights and the responsibility of business to respect them.

consumerism
A movement that pressures businesses to consider consumer needs and interests.

THE RIGHT TO BUY SAFE PRODUCTS—AND TO BUY THEM SAFELY

As mentioned previously, doing no harm is one of the foundations of CSR. The United States and many other countries go to considerable lengths to ensure the safety of the products sold within their borders. The U.S. government imposes many safety standards that are enforced by the Consumer Product Safety Commission (CPSC), as well as by other

EXHIBIT 4.7   Major Federal Consumer Legislation

Major federal legislation aimed at consumer protection has focused on food and drugs, false advertising, product safety, and credit protection.

Legislation	Major Provisions
Food, Drug, and Cosmetic Act (1938)	Puts cosmetics, foods, drugs, and therapeutic products under Food and Drug Administration's jurisdiction; outlaws misleading labeling
Cigarette Labeling and Advertising Act (1965)	Mandates warnings on cigarette packages and in ads
Fair Packaging and Labeling Act (1966, 1972)	Requires honest, informative package labeling; labels must show origin of product, quantity of contents, uses or applications
Truth in Lending Act (Consumer Protection Credit Act) (1968)	Requires creditors to disclose finance charge and annual percentage rate; limits cardholder liability for unauthorized use
Fair Credit Reporting Act (1970)	Requires credit-reporting agencies to set process for assuring accuracy; requires creditors to explain credit denials
Consumer Product Safety Act (1972)	Creates Consumer Product Safety Commission
Magnuson-Moss Warranty Act (1975)	Requires complete written warranties in ordinary language; requires warranties to be available before purchase
Alcohol Beverage Labeling Act (1988)	Requires warning labels on alcohol products, saying that alcohol impairs abilities and that women shouldn't drink when pregnant
Children's Online Privacy Protection Act (1988)	Gives parents control over the collection or use of information that websites can collect about children
Nutrition Education and Labeling Act (1990)	Requires specific, uniform product labels detailing nutritional information on every food regulated by the Food and Drug Administration (FDA)
American Automobile Labeling Act (1992)	Requires carmakers to identify where cars are assembled and where their individual components are manufactured
Deceptive Mail Prevention and Enforcement Act (1999)	Establishes standards for sweepstakes mailings, skill contests, and facsimile checks to prevent fraud and exploitation
Controlling the Assault of Non-Solicited Pornography and Marketing Act (2003)	Known as CAN-SPAM, attempts to protect online consumers from unwanted and fraudulent email
Consumer Product Safety Improvement Act (2008)	Strengthens standards for lead in children's products; mandates safety testing for imported children's products; creates a searchable database for reporting accidents, injuries, and illnesses related to consumer products
Dodd-Frank Wall Street Reform and Consumer Protection Act (2010)	Amends a number of previous acts and regulations in an attempt to improve the stability of the banking and investment industries; establishes the Consumer Financial Protection Bureau

Sources: www.fda.gov; http://uscode.house.gov; www.ftc.gov; www.cpsc.com; www.ttb.gov; www.consumerfinance.gov.

federal and state agencies. Companies that don't comply with these rules are forced to take corrective action, and the threat of product-liability suits and declining sales motivates companies to meet safety standards.

Product safety concerns range from safe toys, food, and automobiles to less-tangible worries such as online privacy and **identity theft**, in which criminals steal personal information and use it to take out loans, request government documents and tax refunds, get expensive medical procedures, and commit other types of fraud. Companies play a vital role in fighting this crime because they frequently collect the information that identity thieves use to commit their fraud, including credit card and Social Security numbers. Any company that collects such information has a clear ethical obligation to keep it safe and secure, but the number of massive data-security breaches in recent years indicates how poorly many companies are meeting this obligation.

identity theft
A crime in which thieves steal personal information and use it to take out loans and commit other types of fraud.

THE RIGHT TO BE INFORMED

Consumers have a right to know what they're buying, how to use it, and whether it presents any risks to them. They also have a right to know the true price of goods or services and the details of purchase contracts. Accordingly, numerous government regulations have been put in place to make sure buyers get the information they need in order to make informed choices. Of course, buyers share the responsibility here, at least morally if not always legally. Not bothering to read labels or contracts or not asking for help if you don't understand them is no excuse for not being informed.

REAL-TIME UPDATES
Learn More by Visiting This Website

Know your rights as a consumer

Get advice on everything from filing a complaint to protecting yourself against fraud. Go to http://real-timeupdates.com/bia8 and click on Learn More in the Students section.

Fortunately, both consumers and businesses can turn to a wide range of information sources to learn more about the goods and services they purchase. The spread of social media and their use in *social commerce* (see page 346), in which buyers help educate one another, has helped shift power from sellers to buyers. For just about every purchase you can envision these days, you can find more information about it before you choose.

THE RIGHT TO CHOOSE WHICH PRODUCTS TO BUY

Especially in the United States, the number of products available to consumers is staggering, even sometimes overwhelming. But how far should the right to choose extend? Are we entitled to choose products that are potentially harmful, such as cigarettes, alcoholic beverages, guns, sugary soft drinks, or fatty fried foods? Should the government take measures to make such products illegal, or should consumers always be allowed to decide for themselves what to buy?

Consider cigarettes. Scientists determined long ago that the tar and nicotine in tobacco are harmful and addictive. In 1965, the Federal Cigarette Labeling and Advertising Act was passed, requiring all cigarette packs to carry the Surgeon General's warnings. Over the years, tobacco companies have spent billions of dollars to defend themselves in lawsuits brought by smokers suffering from cancer and respiratory diseases. Lawsuits and legislative activity surrounding tobacco products continue to this day—and are likely to continue for years. Meanwhile, consumers can still purchase cigarettes in the marketplace. As one tobacco company executive put it, "Behind all the allegations…is the simple truth that we sell a legal product."[25]

THE RIGHT TO BE HEARD

The final component of consumer rights is the right to be heard. As with the challenge of gathering information, social media give consumers numerous ways to ask questions, voice concerns, provide feedback, and—if necessary—demand attention. Savvy companies monitor Twitter, blogs, and other online venues to catch messages from dissatisfied customers. Companies that fail to respond or that respond in defensive, inward-looking ways are likely to lose business to competitors that embrace this new media environment and the power it gives today's consumers.

 Checkpoint

CSR: Employees

Explain the responsibilities businesses have toward their employees.

The past few decades have brought dramatic changes in the composition of the global workforce and in the attitudes of workers. These changes have forced businesses to modify their recruiting, training, and promotion practices, as well as their overall corporate values and behaviors. This section discusses some key responsibilities that employers have regarding employees.

THE PUSH FOR EQUALITY IN EMPLOYMENT

The United States has always stood for economic freedom and the individual's right to pursue opportunity. Unfortunately, in the past many people were targets of economic **discrimination**, being relegated to low-paying, menial jobs and prevented from taking advantage of many opportunities solely on the basis of their race, gender, disability, or religion.

The Civil Rights Act of 1964 established the Equal Employment Opportunity Commission (EEOC), the regulatory agency that addresses job discrimination. The EEOC is responsible for monitoring hiring practices and for investigating complaints of job-related discrimination. It has the power to file legal charges against companies that discriminate and to force them to compensate individuals or groups that have been victimized by unfair practices. The Civil Rights Act of 1991 amended the original act in response to a number of Supreme Court decisions that had taken place in the intervening quarter-century. Among its key provisions are limiting the amount of damage awards, making it easier to sue for discrimination, giving employees the right to have a trial by jury in discrimination cases, and extending protections to overseas employees of U.S. companies.[26]

discrimination
In a social and economic sense, denial of opportunities to individuals on the basis of some characteristic that has no bearing on their ability to perform in a job.

Affirmative Action

In the 1960s, **affirmative action** programs were developed to encourage organizations to recruit and promote members of groups whose past economic progress has been hindered through legal barriers or established practices. Affirmative action programs address a variety of situations, from college admissions to hiring to conducting business with government agencies. Note that although affirmative action programs address a range of

affirmative action
Activities undertaken by businesses to recruit and promote members of groups whose economic progress has been hindered through either legal barriers or established practices.

population segments, from military veterans with disabilities to specific ethnic groups, in popular usage, "affirmative action" usually refers to programs based on race.

Affirmative action remains a controversial and politicized issue, with opponents claiming that it creates a double standard and can encourage reverse discrimination against white males; proponents say that it remains a crucial part of the effort to ensure equal opportunities for all. One of the key points of contention is whether affirmative action programs are still needed, given the various antidiscrimination laws now in place. Opponents assert that everyone has an equal shot at success now, so the programs are unnecessary and, if anything, should be based on income, not race; proponents argue that laws can't remove every institutionalized barrier and that discrimination going back decades has left many families and communities at a long-term disadvantage.[27]

Policy debates aside, well-managed companies across the country are finding that embracing diversity in the richest sense is simply good business. You'll read more about *diversity initiatives* in Chapter 11.

People with Disabilities

In 1990, people with a wide range of physical and mental difficulties got a boost from the passage of the federal Americans with Disabilities Act (ADA), which guarantees equal opportunities in housing, transportation, education, employment, and other areas for the estimated 50 to 75 million people in the United States who have disabilities. As defined by the 1990 law, *disability* is a broad term that refers not only to those with physical handicaps but also those with cancer, heart disease, diabetes, epilepsy, HIV/AIDS, drug addiction, alcoholism, emotional illness, and other conditions. In most situations, employers cannot legally require job applicants to pass a physical examination as a condition of employment. Employers are also required to make reasonable accommodations to meet the needs of employees with disabilities, such as modifying workstations or schedules.[28]

OCCUPATIONAL SAFETY AND HEALTH

Every year several thousand U.S. workers lose their lives on the job and many thousands more are injured (see Exhibit 4.8).[29] During the 1960s, mounting concern about workplace hazards resulted in the passage of the Occupational Safety and Health Act of 1970, which set mandatory standards for safety and health and also established the Occupational Safety and Health Administration (OSHA) to enforce them. These standards govern everything from hazardous materials to *ergonomics*, the study of how people interact with computers and other machines.

EXHIBIT 4.8	Fatal Occupational Injuries

Transportation accidents are the leading cause of death on the job in the United States. Overall, U.S. workers suffer fatal on-the-job injuries at a rate of 3.2 deaths per 100,000 full-time employees per year.

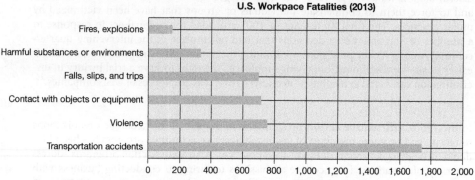

U.S. Workpace Fatalities (2013)

Source: "2013 Census of Fatal Occupational Injuries," U.S. Bureau of Labor Statistics, www.bls.gov.

Concerns for employee safety can extend beyond a company's own workforce, and this concern is particularly acute for the many U.S. companies that contract out production to factories in Asia, Latin America, and parts of the United States to make products under their brand names. Some of these companies have been criticized for doing business with so-called *sweatshops*, a disparaging term applied to production facilities that treat workers poorly. As discussed in the Behind the Scenes wrap-up, Nike is one of many companies taking positive steps to improve conditions in the factories that make its products. U.S. colleges have been influential in this effort, too. Nearly 200 schools have joined the Fair Labor Association (www.fairlabor.org) to help ensure that school-logo products are manufactured in an ethical manner.[30]

✓ Checkpoint

LEARNING OBJECTIVE 6: Explain the responsibilities businesses have toward their employees.

SUMMARY: In addition to the impact a company has on its external stakeholders, CSR applies within the company as well, to the way employees are treated. Major issues include the push for equal opportunity, which includes affirmative action programs and regulations to protect the rights of people with disabilities, and occupational safety and health.

CRITICAL THINKING: (1) Does affirmative action seem like a fair approach? Why or why not? (2) Should employees automatically get paid more to work in hazardous jobs? Why or why not?

IT'S YOUR BUSINESS: (1) Have you ever experienced or observed discrimination on the job? If so, how did you handle the situation? (2) Has this chapter changed your perspective about the relationship between business and society? Why or why not?

KEY TERMS TO KNOW: discrimination, affirmative action

BEHIND THE SCENES
NIKE BUILDS A SUSTAINABLE BUSINESS THROUGH SUSTAINABLE DESIGN AND MANUFACTURING

Nike CEO Mark Parker would surely agree that any examination of Nike's business–society relationship needs to include a look at the massive scale of the company's operations. With annual revenues climbing past $25 billion, a strong presence in every continent except Antarctica, and billions of products sold since its founding in the 1960s, Nike is one of the world's largest and most visible corporations. (Starting right now, see how long you can go without seeing a Nike logo.) In addition to the 40,000 employees who work directly for the company, another million work in hundreds of contract factories across nearly 50 countries that manufacture the company's products. With millions of shoes, garments, sporting goods, and other "Swoosh"-branded products rolling off those production lines every month, the company oversees a vast supply chain that sources a wide variety of natural and synthetic materials and uses almost every mode of transportation imaginable.

It's safe to say that Nike and the global community are stuck with each other—and Nike needs a vibrant, stable world

economy as much as the global community needs Nike to be a well-managed and well-behaved corporate citizen.

Workplace conditions and sustainable manufacturing are two issues in particular that highlight the impact Nike has on stakeholders and the considerable investments the company continues to make toward improving its entire "business ecosystem." In the matter of workplace conditions, the first wave of improvement efforts focused on building monitoring systems so that Nike and other companies could get a better sense of how workers were being treated in contract factories. Across a number of industries, some of these "sweatshop" factories had been accused of forcing employees to work 24 hours or more at a time, employing young children in unsafe conditions, or virtually imprisoning workers in conditions that have at times been compared to slavery. Mattel, Reebok, Patagonia, Liz Claiborne, and Gap are among the other industry leaders that have been working at improving monitoring of contract factories.

However, Nike began to realize that setting standards and monitoring operations weren't improving conditions in its contract factories sufficiently, and the company is now working closely with vendors to improve their operations and practices. As the company explains, "What we've learned, after nearly a decade, is that monitoring alone hasn't solved the problems. And many of the problems are recurring in the industry. Our focus now is getting to the root of the problems."

A key part of that effort is an in-depth auditing process conducted by Nike inspectors, who look for evidence of compliance with Nike's own environmental safety and health codes. Nike inspectors examine factory operations and interview supervisors as well as employees to make sure contract manufacturers are living up to the expectations outlined in Nike's *Code of Conduct*. Nike doesn't leave compliance to chance, either. The company's *Code Leadership Standards* is a comprehensive manual that describes exactly what a factory needs to do to meet Nike's standards. If a factory is out of compliance, Nike teams work with local management to help them figure where their processes are breaking down and how to improve.

Sustainable manufacturing has become a strategic imperative for the company, and Nike has sustainability experts working in such areas as reducing the environmental impact of various manufacturing processes and designing new products with more sustainable materials. For example, Nike has worked for years to analyze and document the environmental impact of a wide variety of garment and shoe materials, and its designers now have a handy software tool to help them choose fabrics and other components that maximize product performance and resource sustainability. After spending several million dollars developing it, Nike released this tool for free public use to help other companies improve their design practices. (You can try this software yourself, actually—it's the Environmental Design Tool featured in the Real-Time Updates Learn More item on page 130 in this chapter.)

Recycling is another area of concentration for the company. Nike collects and grinds up millions of pairs of worn-out sneakers every year to produce shock-absorbing materials that are used in running tracks, tennis courts, playgrounds, and other playing surfaces. Nike designers are also ramping up their use of recycled polyester from discarded plastic bottles, keeping hundreds of millions of them out of landfills.

Fabric manufacturing uses enormous volumes of water, and Nike has had a water stewardship program in place since 2001 to help factories minimize water usage and to do a more responsible job of "borrowing" water, as the company phrases it. Given the number of factories it works with worldwide, Nike figures its efforts to improve water stewardship influence the usage of more than 500 billion gallons of water a year.

Even with the considerable investments it has made and the measurable progress that has come from those efforts, the scale of its operations and the visibility of its brand ensure that Nike will continue to attract the attention of stakeholders and advocacy groups. For example, Greenpeace launched a "detox challenge" publicity campaign in which the environmental advocacy group challenged Nike and arch-rival Adidas to reduce the discharge of toxic fabric-treatment chemicals from contract factories in China.

Nike's response included a comprehensive report on its progress toward eliminating toxic chemicals from the manufacturing process—efforts that had been under way for more than a decade. These included the research and chemistry patents it has freely shared with other manufacturers through the GreenXchange intellectual property collaborative and an offer to work with Greenpeace and other NGOs on water usage issues.

Nike also exhibits a remarkable degree of transparency, such as issuing report cards on its progress toward its CSR goals and offering an extensive set of interactive online tools and downloadable files that cover everything from contract employee injury rates to waste management processes to the ethnic and gender composition of its workforce, executive ranks, and board of directors. You can view these files at **www.nikeresponsibility .com/report/downloads**.

Parker talks frankly of the lessons Nike has learned along the way. Reflecting on pressure the company received in the 1990s from worker rights groups, he says, "Our critics were smart (and right) to focus on the industry leader." After first defending conditions in the factories as just the way business was done in those countries, the company realized that change was needed, and it had to be fundamental change affecting every part of the company. Parker now welcomes collaboration with stakeholders and promotes the value of transparency, so that affected groups can see what the company is doing, and the company can learn from anybody who has great ideas to share. "For all the athletic and cultural and financial successes of the company," he says, "I believe our work in sustainable business and innovation has equal potential to shape our legacy."[31]

Critical Thinking Questions

4-1. This chapter covers three factors that influence ethical decisions: cultural differences, knowledge, and organizational behavior. How have these factors shaped Nike's CSR actions over the past two decades?

4-2. How does Mark Parker's phrase "sustainable business" relate to sustainable manufacturing?

4-3. Is it ethical for NGOs to put pressure on just one company in an industry when they are trying to effect change across the entire industry, given that responding to that pressure is likely to cost that company more than its competitors?

LEARN MORE ONLINE

Visit Nike's consumer-oriented website, **www.nike.com**, and its investor-oriented website, **http://investors.nike.com**. Study the messages presented on the two sites. How does Nike reach out to different stakeholder groups using these two separate sites? Read the "Letter to Shareholders" from Nike's latest annual report. How does Nike present itself to this vital stakeholder group? How does the company present its CSR efforts in a way that appeals to a reader whose primary interest is financial investment?

KEY TERMS

affirmative action
cap and trade
code of ethics
conflicts of interest
consumerism
corporate social responsibility (CSR)
discrimination
ethical dilemma
ethical lapse

ethics
identity theft
insider trading
nongovernmental organizations (NGOs)
philanthropy
strategic CSR
sustainable development
transparency
whistle-blowing

MyBizLab®

To complete the problems with the ⭐,
go to EOC Discussion Questions in the
MyLab.

TEST YOUR KNOWLEDGE

Questions for Review

4-4. How does ethics differ from corporate social responsibility?

4-5. What is whistle-blowing? Why would this be used?

4-6. What is the difference between defensive and proactive CSR?

4-7. How are businesses responding to the environmental issues facing society?

4-8. What is identity theft, and what responsibilities do businesses have to prevent it?

Questions for Analysis

4-9. Why can't legal considerations resolve every ethical question?

4-10. Why would a business choose to adopt practices and policies that encourage social responsibility?

4-11. Why is it important for a company to balance its social responsibility efforts with its need to generate profits?

⭐ **4-12. Ethical Considerations.** Is it ethical for companies to benefit from their efforts to practice CSR? Why or why not? How can anyone be sure that CSR efforts aren't just public relations ploys?

⭐ **4-13.** What effects have social media had on CSR?

⭐ **4-14.** Would it be ethical for U.S. consumers to boycott products made in exploitive, low-wage overseas factories if the employees in those factories are grateful to have their jobs? Why or why not?

Questions for Application

⭐ **4-15.** Based on what you've learned about CSR, what effect will CSR considerations have on your job search?

⭐ **4-16. Concept Integration.** Chapter 2 identified knowledge workers as a key economic resource of the 21st century. If an employee leaves a company to work for a competitor, what types of knowledge would be ethical for the employee to share with the new employer, and what types would be unethical to share?

⭐ **4-17. Concept Integration.** Is it ethical for state and city governments to entice specific businesses to relocate their operations to that state or city by offering them special tax breaks that are not extended to other businesses operating in that area?

EXPAND YOUR KNOWLEDGE

Discovering Career Opportunities

As businesses and consumers become more aware of ethics and social responsibility, employers have begun to offer more and more opportunities in this area. How can you learn more about these careers?

4-18. Using online resources available to you, either through your careers office or search engines, look for job roles and opportunities with a focus on ethics and corporate

social responsibility. Describe each one of the jobs you have found in no more than two lines.

4-19. Choose two of the jobs that you have found and compare them. What skills and qualifications are required for each? Are employers looking for any personality traits or characteristics? How do you think these roles fit in with the rest of the organization? Conducting additional Internet research, what information can you find on a typical working day in these roles?

4-20. If you were to apply for one of the roles you have found so far, what skills would you need to develop further in order to be successful? What skills do you already have which could be advantageous?

Improve Your Tech Insights: Assistive Technologies

There is a huge potential of using the technology that is out there in a different way for the differently abled people. SEDL, an affiliate of American Institutes for Research, has been activity promoting the rural students with disabilities through assistive technology http://www.sedl.org/rural/seeds/assistivetech/. When the engineers, designers and technology professionals at Microsoft found that the amyotrophic laterals sclerosis (ALS) patients and other individuals are more concerned about communicating with their loved ones, they worked with the people with disabilities to empower their daily lives https://news .microsoft.com/features/microsoft-ability-summit-aims -to-bring-next-wave-of-technology-to-empower-people -with-disabilities/. Recently, Google Foundation expressed its commitment to fund non-profits that use emerging technologies to help people living with a disability http://www.csmonitor .com/USA/USA-Update/2015/0527/Google-s-pioneering -20-million-bid-to-help-disabled-feel-empowered. These technology leaders are relentlessly pursuing historic partnership projects on assistive technologies in India to help others achieve economic and social goals http://www.indiapost.com/digital -india-great-vehicle-to-empower-the-disabled/. Research has shown that when adequate support is given to the groups with different disabilities, they can use the technologies very effectively to assist their work. Robin Christopherson, being a blind himself and leading UK inclusive technology expert at AbilityNet, concurred that he would challenge anyone who doubted the potential of technologies http://www.city.ac.uk/events/2015/november/ technological-empowerment-for-disabled-people. Technology companies had pledged their commitments to create a better hiring and recruitment program by empowering their recruitment directors or managers to hire more women and minorities http://digigrass.com/5-tech-companies-committed- to-improving-diversity-in-tech/. If you are hired by one of these corporations, how would you develop and promote assistive technologies for the employees and the public? How effective would that be?

Businesses have a social responsibility towards their employees' well-being. This article at Forbes http://www.forbes .com/sites/csr/2010/11/04/the-social-responsibility-to -generate-employee-happiness/ highlights the importance of the happiness of employees at successful corporations.

Watch the TED podcast on Chip Conley (CEO of Joie de Vivre hotels) which is available at the end of the article. Explore how Joie's inspirational story may empower companies to develop sustainability practices and policies for women, minority and employees with disabilities. What are the resources corporations may need to consider in order for these groups of employees to exude optimal performance and pursue desired career pathways horizontally and vertically in the organization?

Corporations are using the assistive technologies to create greater impact on the implementation of the occupational health and safety at workplace. Read the article on the commitment of corporations on the safety and health programs in 2010 http://www.ishn.com/articles/89771-100-committed -companies. To what extend do the corporations use various technologies to develop and promote safety and health programs for their employees and the public? How effective be that be?

PRACTICE YOUR SKILLS

Sharpening Your Communication Skills

Imagine you are working as part of a team in a large sales department. In recent weeks, you have become more and more concerned with the behavior of one of your more senior colleagues. You suspect that they are pressuring potential customers into signing up for expensive contracts that they cannot afford to pay. As you work in a high-pressure, target-driven department, jobs are at risk if people do not meet their targets. You do not feel like you can talk to your colleague about their unethical behavior, and think it best to discuss the matter with your manager instead. Draft an email to your manager outlining your concerns regarding the behavior of your colleague in an appropriate and professional manner. Ensure that you consider the tone, formality, and overall length of your email.

Building Your Team Skills

Every organization can benefit from having a code of ethics to guide decision making. But whom should a code of ethics protect, and what should it cover? In this exercise, you and the rest of your team are going to draft a code of ethics for your college or university.

Start by thinking about who will be protected by this code of ethics. What stakeholders should the school consider when making decisions? What negative effects might decisions have on these stakeholders? Then think about the kinds of situations you want your school's code of ethics to cover. One example might be employment decisions; another might be disclosure of confidential student information.

Next, draft your school's code of ethics. Start by identifying general principles and then provide specific guidelines. Write a general introduction explaining the purpose of the code and who is being protected. Next, write a positive statement to guide ethical decisions in each situation you identified previously in this exercise. Your statement about promotion decisions, for example, might read: "School officials will encourage equal access to job promotions for all qualified candidates, with every applicant receiving fair consideration."

Compare your code of ethics with the codes drafted by your classmates. Did all the codes seek to protect the same stakeholders? What differences and similarities do you see in the statements guiding ethical decisions?

Developing Your Research Skills

Articles on corporate ethics and social responsibility regularly appear in business journals and newspapers. Find one or more articles discussing one of the following ethics or social responsibility challenges faced by a business:

- Environmental issues, such as pollution, acid rain, and hazardous-waste disposal
- Employee or consumer safety measures
- Consumer information or education
- Employment discrimination or diversity initiatives
- Investment ethics
- Industrial spying and theft of trade secrets

- Fraud, bribery, and overcharging
- Company codes of ethics

4-21. What is the nature of the ethical challenge or social responsibility issue presented in the article? Does the article report any wrongdoing by a company or agency official? Was the action illegal, unethical, or questionable? What course of action would you recommend the company or agency take to correct or improve matters now?

4-22. What stakeholder group(s) is affected? What lasting effects will be felt by (a) the company and (b) this stakeholder group(s)?

4-23. Writing a letter to the editor is one way consumers can speak their mind. Review some of the letters to the editor in newspapers or journals. Why are letters to the editor an important feature for that publication?

MyBizLab®

Go to the Assignments section of your MyLab to complete these writing exercises.

4-24. What steps could a bookstore take to engage in strategic CSR?

4-25. Why would a company want to make it easy for its own employees to engage in whistle-blowing, even if doing so could subject the firm to legal penalties?

ENDNOTES

1. Nike website, accessed 23 March 2015, www.nikeinc.com; *Nike Sustainable Business Report*, accessed 23 March 2015, www.nikeresponsibility.com; "Nike, Inc.'s Response to Greenpeace Report," 18 July 2011, Nike website, www.nikebiz.com; *Nike 2011 Annual Report*, accessed 4 August 2011, www.nikebiz.com; "Detox Campaign," Greenpeace, accessed 4 August 2011, www.greenpeace.org; *Nike Code Leadership Standard*, Nike website, accessed 7 August 2011, www.nikebiz.com; GreenXchange, accessed 4 August 2011, www.greenxchange.cc; "Workers & Factories: Improving Conditions in Our Contract Factories," Nike website, accessed 4 August 2011, www.nike.com; Abigail Goldman, "Sweat, Fear, and Resignation Amid All the Toys," *Los Angeles Times*, 26 November 2004, A1, A30–A32; Edward Iwata, "How Barbie Is Making Business a Little Better," *USA Today*, 27 March 2006, B1–B2; "Nike Corporate Responsibility/Compliance ESH CLS Audit" worksheet, accessed 4 August 2011, www.nikebiz.com.
2. Rakesh Khurana, "The Future of Business School," *BusinessWeek*, 26 May 2009, www.businessweek.com.
3. James O'Toole and Warren Bennis, "What's Needed Next: A Culture of Candor," *Harvard Business Review*, June 2009, 54–61.
4. O'Toole and Bennis, "What's Needed Next: A Culture of Candor," 59.
5. "Ethics and Business Practices," United Technologies website, accessed 3 August 2011, www.utc.com.
6. Ben Levisohn, "Getting More Workers to Whistle," *BusinessWeek*, 28 January 2008, 18.
7. Alan D. Berkowitz, Claude M. Tusk, J. Ian Downes, and David S. Caroline, "Whistleblowing," *Employee Relations Law Journal*, Vol. 36, No. 4, Spring 2011, 15–32.
8. "Less Than Half of Privately Held Businesses Support Whistleblowing," Grant Thornton website, accessed 13 October 2008, www.internationalbusinessreport.com.
9. "Corporate Giving Restored Since Pre-Global Recession; Non-Cash Contributions Dominate," press release, 16 September 2013, The Conference Board, www.conferenceboard.org.
10. Susan Ladika, "The Responsible Way," *Workforce*, 16 July 2013, www.workforce.com.
11. Michael Porter and Mark Kramer, "Strategy & Society: The Link Between Competitive Advantage and Corporate Social Responsibility," *Harvard Business Review*, December 2006, 78–92.
12. Timothy M. Devinney, "Is the Socially Responsible Corporation a Myth? The Good, the Bad, and the Ugly of Corporate Social Responsibility," *Academy of Management Perspectives*, May 2009, 44–56.
13. Milton Friedman, "The Social Responsibility of Business Is to Increase Its Profits," *New York Times Magazine*, 13 September 1970, SM17.
14. "Social Responsibility: 'Fundamentally Subversive'?" Interview with Milton Friedman, *BusinessWeek*, 15 August 2005, www.businessweek.com.
15. Krisi Heim, "In Person: Laurie Erickson Is a 'Wrap' Star to Cancer Patients," *Seattle Times*, 24 April 2011, www.seattletimes.com.
16. Henry G. Manne, "Milton Friedman Was Right," *WSJ Opinion Journal*, 24 November 2006, www.opinionjournal.com.
17. Kas Thomas, "Google Uses More Electricity Than Most Countries on Earth," assertTrue() blog, 9 March 2009, http://asserttrue.blogspot.com; Rich Miller, "Google Data Center FAQ," Data Center Knowledge website, 26 August 2008, www.datacenterknowledge.com.
18. *Electric Power Annual*, 23 March 2015, U.S. Energy Information Administration, www.eia.gov; Daniel Gross, "Big Solar," *Slate*, 20 February 2015, www.slate.com.
19. Google Green website, accessed 16 October 2013, www.google.com/green; Urs Hölzle, "Energy and the Internet," The Official Google Blog, 11 May 2009, http://googleblog.blogspot.com; eSolar website, accessed 1 June 2009, www.esolar.com; "Google's Green PPAs: What, How, and Why," 29 April 2011, Google website, www.google.com; "Step 5: An Efficient and Clean Energy Future," Google website, accessed 1 June 2009, www.google.com; "Google Data Centers, Best Practices," Google website, accessed 3 August 2011, www.google.com.

20. "Cap and Trade 101," U.S. Environmental Protection Agency website, accessed 1 June 2009, www.epa.gov.

21. John M. Broder, "From a Theory to a Consensus on Emissions," *New York Times*, 16 May 2009, www.nytimes.com.

22. "Report of the World Commission on Environment and Development," United Nations General Assembly, 96th Plenary Meeting, 11 December 1987, www.un.org.

23. Ursula M. Burns, "Is the Green Movement a Passing Fancy?" *BusinessWeek*, 27 January 2009, www.businessweek.com.

24. Accenture and the United Nations Global Compact, "The UN Global Compact-Accenture CEO Study on Sustainability 2013," www.accenture.com.

25. Action on Smoking and Health website, accessed 15 March 2005, www.ash.org; Chris Burritt, "Fallout from the Tobacco Settlement," *Atlanta Journal and Constitution*, 22 June 1997, A14; Jolie Solomon, "Smoke Signals," *Newsweek*, 28 April 1997, 50–51; Marilyn Elias, "Mortality Rate Rose Through '80s," *USA Today*, 17 April 1997, B3; Mike France, Monica Larner, and Dave Lindorff, "The World War on Tobacco," *BusinessWeek*, 11 November 1996; Richard Lacayo, "Put Out the Butt, Junior," *Time*, 2 September 1996, 51; Elizabeth Gleick, "Smoking Guns," *Time*, 1 April 1996, 50.

26. "The Civil Rights Act of 1991," U.S. Equal Employment Opportunity Commission website, accessed 7 August 2011, www.eeoc.gov.

27. Lorraine Woellert, "Anger on the Right, Opportunity for Bush," *BusinessWeek*, 7 July 2003, www.businessweek.com; Roger O. Crockett, "The Great Race Divide," *BusinessWeek*, 14 July 2003, www.businessweek.com; Earl Graves, "Celebrating the Best and the Brightest," *Black Enterprise*, February 2005, 16.

28. "Disability Discrimination," Equal Employment Opportunity Commission website, accessed 12 June 2007, www.eeoc.gov.

29. "Injuries, Illnesses, and Fatalities," Bureau of Labor Statistics, accessed 31 May 2009, www.bls.gov/iif.

30. Fair Labor Association website, accessed 24 March 2015, www.fairlabor.org.

31. See note 1.

Chapter 5
Legal Framework

8 The legal environment

Martin Morgan-Taylor and Diane Belfitt

Businesses, like individuals, exist and carry on their activities within a framework of law which derives from custom and practice, from the judicial decisions of the courts and from statutes enacted by governments. This legal environment not only constrains and regulates a firm's operations, it also provides an enabling mechanism through which it is able to pursue its objectives, particularly the achievement of profits through entrepreneurial activity. Like the political and economic environment with which it is intertwined, the legal environment of business is a key influence on the business organisation and an important area of study for students of business. This can be demonstrated by an examination of a number of the fundamental areas in which the law impinges on the operations of an enterprise.

Learning outcomes

Having read this chapter you should be able to:

- understand the idea of 'law' and the sources from which laws are derived
- outline the court system, including the role of the European Court of Justice
- discuss the basic features of the laws of contract and agency
- analyse the reason for statutory intervention to protect the consumer and some of the principal pieces of legislation in this field

Key terms

Acceptance	Customs	Principal
Agent	Delegated legislation	Private law
Capacity	Intention to create legal	Public law
Case law	relations	Statute law
Codes of practice	Judicial precedent	Tort
Consideration	Legislation	Trust
Criminal law	Offer	

Introduction

It is almost universally accepted that for a society to exist and function in an ordered way, a set of rules is required to regulate human behaviour. Irrespective of whether these rules are laid down in custom or practice or in statute, they constitute a means of regulating and controlling the activities of individuals and groups, and of enforcing minimum standards of conduct – even though they may be ignored or flouted on occasions. This framework of rules and the institutions through which they are formulated and enforced represent what is normally understood as the 'law', which invariably evolves over time in response to changing social, economic and political circumstances (e.g. the influence of pressure groups). As one of the constraining (and enabling) influences on business organisations, this legal environment is an important area of study for students of business, hence the tendency for courses in business-related subjects to have specialist modules or units on different aspects of business law (e.g. contract, agency, property and so on).

The aim of this chapter is not to examine business law in detail or to provide a definitive insight into particular areas of the law as it relates to business organisations. Rather, it is to raise the reader's awareness of the legal context within which businesses function and to comment briefly on those aspects of law that regularly impinge on a firm's operations. Students wishing to examine business law in more detail should consult the many specialist texts in this field, some of which are listed at the end of this chapter.

Classification of law

Laws relating to both individuals and organisations can be classified in a number of ways: international and national, public and private, criminal and civil. In practice, there are no hard and fast rules to classification and some categories may overlap (e.g. where a person's behaviour is deemed to infringe different areas of law). Nevertheless, distinguishing laws in these terms serves as an aid to explanation and commentary, as well as helping to explain differences in liabilities and in legal remedies in England and Wales (e.g. a child under the age of ten cannot be held criminally liable).

Public and private law

Put simply, **public law** is the law that concerns the state, whether in international agreements or disputes or in the relationship between the state and the individual. Thus public law consists of international treaties and conventions, constitutional law, administrative law and criminal law. In contrast, **private law** is law governing the relationships between individuals and comprises laws in respect of contract, tort, property, trusts and the family.

Criminal law

Criminal law relates to a legal wrong (criminal offence) – a breach of a public duty, punishable by the state on behalf of society. Decisions on whether or not to bring a prosecution in a particular instance are taken by the Crown Prosecution Service (in England and Wales) and the matter may or may not involve trial by jury, according to the seriousness of the alleged offence and the plea of the defendant(s). In some cases, the consent of both magistrates and defendants is required for a case to remain in the magistrates' court, although this may change in the very near future. Moreover, while the criminal process may also arise from a private prosecution, such prosecutions are rare and, in these cases, the Attorney-General (the government's senior law officer) has the right to intervene if he or she sees fit.

Tort

A **tort** is a civil wrong other than a breach of contract or a breach of trust and is a duty fixed by law on all persons (e.g. road users have a duty in law not to act negligently). The law of tort, therefore, is concerned with those situations where the conduct of one party threatens or causes harm to the interests of another party and the aim of the law is to compensate for this harm. The most common torts are negligence, nuisance, defamation and trespass.

Trusts

A **trust** is generally defined as an 'equitable obligation imposing on one or more persons a duty of dealing with property, over which they have control, for the benefit of other persons who may enforce the obligation'. This property may be in the form of money or stocks and shares or in other types of asset, particularly land, where trusts have become a very common way of permitting persons who are forbidden to own legal estates in land to enjoy the equitable benefits of ownership. Partnerships, for example, cannot hold property as legal owners, so often several partners will act as trustees for all the partners (as a partnership has no separate corporate identity it cannot own property – see Chapter 10). Similarly, minors may not hold legal estates, so their interests must be protected by a trust, administered by an individual or an institution.

mini case   Banking on advice

Banks have duties as well as rights when dealing with the day-to-day affairs of their customers. Failure to discharge these duties, in some circumstances, may be deemed negligent behaviour.

In September 1995 the High Court ruled that Lloyds Bank had been negligent in lending money to two of its customers for use on a speculative property deal which had failed to come off because of a collapse in the property market in the late 1980s. In essence, the customers had claimed that the bank owed them a duty of care in advising them on the merits of a loan to invest in property speculation and that it had been in breach of its duty when agreeing to proceed with the loan. In effect, the claimants were arguing that they had

been badly advised and that this had resulted in a loss which was not only suffered but also reasonably foreseeable.

In finding for the claimants – who were suing Lloyds under the tort of negligence – the judge ruled that the bank manager was in breach of his duty of care in advising them to proceed and that the couple had relied on his advice, including claims made in the bank's promotional literature. While a ruling of this kind sent shock waves through the financial community, it is, as yet, uncertain whether it set a legal precedent. Certainly, this is likely to prove a far more significant question to Lloyds (and other financial institutions) than the £77,000 compensation awarded to the claimants by the High Court.

Sources of law

Laws invariably derive from a number of sources, including custom, judicial precedent, legislation and international and supranational bodies (e.g. the EU). All of these so-called legal sources of the law can be illustrated by reference to English law, which applies in England and Wales. Where laws made by Parliament are to apply only to Scotland or Northern Ireland, the legislation will state this. Similarly, any Act which is to apply to all four home countries will contain a statement to this effect.

Custom

Early societies developed particular forms of behaviour (or **customs**), which came to be accepted as social norms to be followed by the members of the community to which they applied. In England many of these customary rules ultimately became incorporated into a body of legal principles known as the common law. Today customs would be regarded as usage recognised by law, whether by judicial precedent (**case law**) or through statutory intervention, and hence they are largely of historical interest. Occasionally, however, they are recognised by the courts as being of local significance and may be enforced accordingly as exceptions to the general law (e.g. concerning land usage).

Judicial precedent

Much of English law is derived from **judicial precedent** (previous decisions of the courts). The present system of binding precedent, however, is of fairly recent origin, dating from the latter part of the nineteenth century, when advances in recording legal judgments and a reorganisation of the court structure facilitated its general acceptance.

In essence, judicial precedent is based on the rule that the previous decisions of a higher court must be followed by the lower courts – hence the significance of the court structure. In any judgment will be found a number of reasons, arguments, explanations and cases cited and these must all be considered carefully by judges to determine whether there are material differences in the case before the court and the earlier decision. To reach a decision, the court must find what is termed the *ratio decidendi* of the previous case. Put very simply, the *ratio* of a case is the essential steps in the legal reasoning which led the court to make that particular decision. Anything which cannot be regarded as a *rationes* is termed *obiter dicta* or 'things said by the way'. The whole of a dissenting judgment in a case is regarded as *obiter*. *Obiter dicta* are not binding but may be regarded as persuasive arguments if the facts of the case permit.

Clearly there are times when, perhaps because of the position of a court in the hierarchy, decisions are not to be regarded as binding precedent. However, if the judgment has been delivered by a jurisdiction that has a common law system (e.g. Canada, Australia) or, most importantly, by the Judicial Committee of the Privy Council, then those decisions will be regarded as being of persuasive precedent and may be used to help the court reach its own decision.

Legislation

A substantial proportion of current law – including laws governing the operations of business organisations – derives from **legislation** or **statutes**, enacted by the Queen (or King) giving Royal Assent in Parliament. As Chapter 4 indicated, the initiative in this sphere lies effectively with the government of the day, which can virtually guarantee a bill will become law, if it has a working majority in the House of Commons.

Apart from a limited number of bills proposed by backbench MPs (private members' bills), the vast majority of legislation emanates from government and takes the form of Acts of Parliament or delegated legislation. Acts of Parliament are those bills that have formally been enacted by Parliament and have received the Royal Assent and, except where overridden by EU law, they represent the supreme law of the land. In addition to creating new laws (e.g. to protect the consumer), statutes may be used to change or repeal existing laws. In some instances they may be designed to draw together all existing law (a consolidating Act) or to codify it or to grant authority to individuals or institutions to make regulations for specific purposes (an enabling Act). Under the Consumer Credit Act 1974, for instance, the Secretary of State for Trade and Industry is permitted to make regulations governing the form and content of credit agreements under delegated authority from Parliament.

As its name suggests, **delegated legislation** is law made by a body or person to which Parliament has given limited powers of law-making – as illustrated by the example above. More often than not, authority will be delegated to a Minister of the Crown, but it may also be conferred on local authorities or other public undertakings, either through the use of a statutory instrument or by some other means of delegation. Since Parliament remains sovereign, such legislation is required to receive parliamentary approval and scrutiny, but time tends to prevent anything other than a cursory glance at a limited proportion of the legislation of this kind. It does, however, remain subject to judicial control, in so far as the body granted authority may be challenged in the courts for exceeding its powers (*ultra vires*).

In addition to these two principal forms of domestic legislation, developments in the law emanate from Britain's membership of the European Union. Under the Union's main treaties – or those parts to which the British government has agreed – Union legislation becomes part of the law and takes precedence over domestic legislation, although the latter may sometimes be required to implement it. Accordingly, law that is inconsistent with Union law is repealed by implication and British citizens, like their counterparts elsewhere in the EU, become subject to the relevant Union laws (unless an 'opt-out' has been negotiated).[1]

Whereas the provisions of the main treaties represent primary legislation, the regulations, directives and decisions emanating from the Union's institutions are secondary (or subordinate) legislation, made under the authority conferred by the Treaty of Rome (1957) as amended by subsequent Treaties (e.g. the Maastricht Treaty 1992, the Amsterdam Treaty 1997, the Nice Treaty 2001 and the Lisbon Treaty 2007). As Chapter 4 indicated, regulations are of general application throughout the member states and confer individual rights and duties that must be recognised by the national courts. Their purpose is to achieve uniformity throughout the EU, as in the requirement for heavy goods vehicles to fit tachographs to control drivers' hours.

Directives, by contrast, are not directly applicable; they are addressed to member states and not individuals, although a directive may create rights enforceable by an individual citizen, as they become directly applicable if a member state fails to implement its provisions within the prescribed time limits. The aim of EU directives is to seek harmonisation or approximation between national laws rather than to achieve uniformity; hence the method of implementation is left to the discretion of the individual state, usually within a given time limit (e.g. the Companies Act of 1981 implemented the Union's fourth directive on company accounts by allowing small and medium-sized companies to reduce the amount of information provided to the Registrar of Companies).

Decisions, too, are binding, but only on the member state, organisation or individual to whom they are addressed and not on the population generally. In practice, EU decisions become effective from the date stated in the decision, which is generally the date of notification, and they are enforceable in national courts if they impose financial obligations.

The legal system: the courts

A country's legal system can be said to have two main functions: to provide an enabling mechanism within which individuals and organisations can exist and operate (e.g. companies are constituted by law) and to provide a means of resolving conflicts and of dealing with those who infringe the accepted standards of behaviour. These functions are carried out by a variety of institutions, including the government and the courts, and a detailed analysis of the legal system within a state would require consideration of the interrelationship between politics and law. Since the political system has been examined in Chapter 4, the focus here is on the courts as a central element of a country's legal system, with responsibility for interpreting the law and administering justice in democratic societies. It is worth remembering, however, that political and governmental activity takes place within a framework of law and that framework is itself a product of the political process at a variety of spatial levels.

The English legal system

Under the English legal system, a useful distinction can be made between courts on the basis of their status. The superior courts are the Supreme Court (formerly named the House of Lords), the Court of Appeal and the High Court. Law reports generally emanate from the higher courts – these cases involve a major point of law of general public interest (e.g. *R* v *R*, 1991). Inferior courts, in contrast, have limited jurisdiction and are subject to the supervisory jurisdiction of the High Court. The current hierarchy of courts is illustrated in Figure 8.1. For domestic purposes (i.e. not concerning EU legislation), the highest court is the Supreme Court, which is the final court of appeal for both civil and criminal cases. Decisions reached by the Court are binding on all other courts, though not necessarily on the Court's judges themselves.

Like the Supreme Court, the Court of Appeal has only appellate jurisdiction. In the case of the Civil Division of the court, its decisions bind all inferior courts and it is bound by its own previous decisions and by those of the Supreme Court. The Criminal Division similarly is bound by the decisions of the Law Lords, but not by the Court of

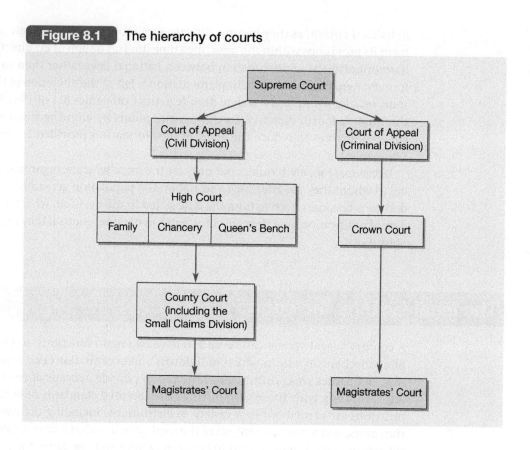

Figure 8.1   The hierarchy of courts

Appeal's Civil Division, nor is it bound by its own previous decisions where these were against a defendant, as exemplified in a number of celebrated cases in recent years.

The High Court is divided into three separate divisions – Chancery, Queen's Bench and Family – and has virtually unlimited original jurisdiction in civil matters, many of which are of direct relevance to business organisations. The Family court deals with such things as adoption, wardship and contested divorce cases, while the Chancery court deals with cases concerning trusts, property and taxation. Claims in contract and tort are the responsibility of the Queen's Bench division, which has two specialist courts to deal with commercial matters and with ships and aircraft. It also exercises the criminal jurisdiction of the High Court – the latter being entirely appellate in instances referred to it by the magistrates' courts or the Crown Court.

In criminal cases the Crown Court has exclusive original jurisdiction to try all indictable offences and can hear appeals against summary conviction or sentence from magistrates' courts. Broadly speaking, the latter largely deal with less serious offences (especially motoring offences), where trial by judge and jury is not permitted – an issue still under discussion following the publication of the Runciman Report (1993). Whereas magistrates' courts have both criminal and civil jurisdiction – with the emphasis towards the former – the jurisdiction of the county courts is entirely civil and derived solely from statute. Among the issues they deal with are conflicts between landlords and tenants and disputes involving small claims (e.g. concerning consumer matters) where a system of arbitration provides for a relatively inexpensive and quick method of resolving problems.

In disputes with a supranational dimension – involving EU member states, institutions, organisations, companies or individuals – ultimate jurisdiction rests with the European Court of Justice. Under Article 220 (ex 164) of the Treaty of Rome, the court is required to ensure that in the application and interpretation of the Treaty, the law is observed. As indicated elsewhere, in carrying out this function, the court has adopted a relatively flexible approach in order to take account of changing circumstances (see Chapter 4). Few would dispute that its judgments have had, and will continue to have, a considerable influence on the development of EU law.

---

mini case   Jean-Marc Bosman – a case of foul play?

An example of how EU law affects individuals and organisations in member states is provided by the case of Jean-Marc Bosman, a Belgian football player who successfully challenged the transfer fee system operated by Europe's football authorities in the mid-1990s.

Bosman, who had been under contract to the Belgian club Liège, had sought a transfer to a French team when his contract expired but had his ambitions thwarted when Liège demanded a very high transfer fee. In the judgment of the European Court of Justice, clubs could no longer demand a fee for players out of contract if the player was headed for another EU member state. According to the judges, the system allowing for a fee to be imposed violated the right enshrined in the Treaty of Rome that European citizens could go from one EU country to another in pursuit of work. They also held that the rule limiting the number of foreign players a club could field in European matches violated the principle of the free movement of workers. The impact of the Court's judgment continues down to the present day.

As a final comment, it is perhaps worth stating that while conflict remains an enduring feature of daily life, many disputes are settled without recourse to the courts, often through direct negotiation between the parties concerned. Moreover, even where negotiations fail or where one party declines to negotiate, a dispute will not necessarily result in court action but may be dealt with in other ways. Disputes over employment contracts, for example, tend to be dealt with by a specialist tribunal, set up by statute to exercise specific functions of a quasi-legal nature. Similarly, complaints concerning maladministration by public (and increasingly private) bodies are generally dealt with by a system of 'ombudsmen', covering areas as diverse as social security benefits and local authority services. Financial services such as banking and insurance are covered by the Financial Services Ombudsman.

Business organisations and the law

Business organisations have been described as transformers of inputs into output in the sense that they acquire and use resources to produce goods or services for consumption. As Table 8.1 illustrates, all aspects of this transformation process are influenced by the law.

It is important to emphasise from the outset that the law not only constrains business activity (e.g. by establishing minimum standards of health and safety at work which are enforceable by law), it also assists it (e.g. by providing a means by which a business unit can have an independent existence from its members), and in doing so helps an enterprise to achieve its commercial and other objectives. In short, the legal environment within which businesses operate is an enabling as well as a regulatory environment and one that provides a considerable degree of certainty and stability to the conduct of business both within and between democratic states.

Given the extensive influence of the law on business organisations, it is clearly impossible to examine all aspects of the legal context within which firms function. Accordingly, in the analysis below, attention is focused primarily on contract law, agency and some of the more important statutes enacted to protect the interests of the consumer, since these are areas fundamental to business operations. Laws relating to the establishment of an enterprise and to the operation of markets are discussed in Chapters 10 and 17 respectively.

Table 8.1 Law and the business organisation

Business activity	Examples of legal influences
Establishing the organisation	Company laws, partnerships, business names
Acquiring resources	Planning laws, property laws, contract, agency
Business operations	Employment laws, health and safety laws, contract, agency
Selling output for consumption	Consumer laws, contract, agency

Contract law: the essentials

All businesses enter into contracts, whether with suppliers or employees or financiers or customers, and these contracts will be important – and possibly crucial – to the firm's operations. Such contracts are essentially agreements (oral or written) between two or more persons that are legally enforceable, provided they comprise a number of essential elements. These elements are: **offer, acceptance, consideration, intention to create legal relations** and **capacity**.

Offer

An **offer** in law is a declaration by the offeror (offer maker) that they intend to be legally bound by the terms stated in the offer if it is accepted by the offeree (the person to whom the offer is made) – for example, to supply particular laptop computers, at a particular price within a specified time period. This declaration may be made orally or in writing or by conduct between the parties and must be clear and unambiguous. Simply writing 'offer for sale' is not in itself enough. Furthermore, it should not be confused with an 'invitation to treat', which is essentially an invitation to make an offer, and as such cannot be accepted. This is generally the case with advertisements, auctions and goods on display. Tenders are offers; a request for tenders is merely an invitation for offers to be made.

Termination of an offer can happen in several ways. Clearly an offer is ended when it is accepted, but that apart, an offer may be revoked at any time up to acceptance. It is of no consequence, legally, that an offer may be kept open for a certain time. It is only when some consideration is paid for 'buying the option' that the time factor is important and this 'buying the option' would generally be a separate contract in any case. If an offer is for a certain length of time, then later acceptance is ineffective, and even where there is no specified time limit, the courts will imply a reasonable time. Thus, in *Ramsgate Victoria Hotel* v *Montefiore* (1866), shares in the hotel were offered for sale. After several months the offer was 'accepted', but the court held that too much time had passed, bearing in mind that the purpose of the shares offer was to raise money.

Another way for an offer to come to an end is by the failure of a condition. Although a genuine offer is always held to be firm and certain, sometimes it may be conditional and not absolute. Thus, should A wish to buy a model car from B, B may agree but impose conditions on the deal, such as stating that A must collect at a specific time on a certain day at a particular place and must pay in cash. This is known as a 'condition precedent' and failure to complete the conditions will nullify the agreement. There is another type of condition, called a 'condition subsequent', where there is a perfectly good contract that runs until something happens. For instance, a garage may have a good contract with an oil company to buy petrol at £x per 1000 litres until the price of oil at Rotterdam reaches $x per barrel. It is only when oil reaches the stipulated price that the contract ends.

Acceptance

Just as an offer must be firm and certain, the **acceptance** of an offer by the person(s) to whom it was made must be unequivocal and must not contain any alterations or additions. Accordingly, any attempt to alter the terms of an offer is regarded as a counter-offer and thus a rejection of the original offer, leaving the original offeror free to accept or decline as he or she chooses.

While acceptance of an offer normally occurs either in writing or verbally, it may also be implied by conduct. In the case of *Brogden* v *Metropolitan Railways Co.* (1877), Mr Brogden had supplied the company for many years without formalities. It was then decided to regularise the position and a draft agreement was sent to him. He inserted a new term, marked the draft 'approved', and returned it to the company where it was placed in a drawer and forgotten about, although the parties traded with each other on the terms of the draft for more than two years. Following a dispute, Mr Brogden claimed there was no contract. The then House of Lords decided differently, saying that a contract had been created by conduct.

Inferring the acceptance of an offer by conduct is quite different from assuming that silence on the part of the offeree constitutes acceptance; silence cannot be construed as an acceptance. Equally, while the offeror may prescribe the method of acceptance (although this is regarded as permissive rather than directory), the offeree may not prescribe a method by which he or she will make acceptance. For instance, an offer may be made by fax, thus implying that a fast response is required; therefore a reply accepting the offer that is sent by second-class mail may well be treated as nugatory.

There are some rules about acceptance that are important. Postal acceptance, for example, is a good method of communication and one that is universally used by businesses, but to be valid for contractual purposes a communication must be properly addressed and stamped and then placed into the hands of the duly authorised person (i.e. the post box or over the counter). An acceptance sent to a home address may be nullified if there has been no indication that this is acceptable. Similarly, acceptance of the offer must be effectively received by the offeror where modern, instantaneous methods of communication are used. Thus, if a telephone call is muffled by extraneous sound, then the acceptance must be repeated so that the offeror hears it clearly.

Consideration

Together, offer and acceptance constitute the basis of an 'agreement' or meeting of minds, provided the parties are clear as to what they are agreeing about (i.e. a *consensus ad idem* exists). However, English courts will rarely enforce a 'naked promise'. As a result, a promise must have 'consideration'. Consideration has been defined as some right, interest, profit or benefit accruing to one party or some forbearance, detriment, loss or responsibility given, suffered or undertaken by the other. In commercial contracts, the consideration normally takes the form of a cash payment in return for the goods or services provided (i.e. the 'price' in a contract of sale). It does not need to be the full market value, but it must be something tangible. In contracts involving barter (exchange), however, which are sometimes used in international trade, goods are often exchanged for other goods or for some other form of non-pecuniary consideration (e.g. information or advice).

Intention to create legal relations

Not every agreement is intended to create a legally binding relationship. For example, most domestic agreements – such as the division of household chores – would not constitute a contract recognised in law. In commercial agreements, however, it is generally accepted that both parties intend to make a legally binding contract and therefore it is unnecessary to include terms to this effect. Should such a presumption be challenged, the burden of proof rests with the person who disputes the presumption.

Capacity

A contract may be valid, voidable or void and one of the factors that determines this is the contractual capacity of the respective parties to the agreement. Normally speaking, an adult may make a contract with another adult which, if entered into freely and without any defects, and which is not contrary to public policy, is binding upon them both (i.e. valid). However, the law provides protection for certain categories of persons deemed not to have full contractual capacity (e.g. minors, drunks and the mentally disordered); hence the practice by firms of excluding people under the age of 18 from offers of goods to be supplied on credit.

Concentrating on minors – those below voting age – the law prescribes that they can be bound by contracts only for 'necessaries' (e.g. food, clothing, lodging) and contracts of employment that are advantageous or beneficial, as in the case of a job which contains an element of training or education. In most other instances, contracts with minors are void or voidable and as such will be either unenforceable or capable of being repudiated by the minor.

In the case of business, legal capacity depends on the firm's legal status. Unincorporated bodies (e.g. sole traders, partnerships) do not have a distinct legal personality and hence the party to the agreement is liable for their part of the bargain. Limited companies, by contrast, have a separate legal identity from their members and hence contractual capacity rests with the company, within the limits laid down in the objects clause of its Memorandum of Association (see Chapter 10).

Other factors

To be enforceable at law a contract must be legal (i.e. not forbidden by law or contrary to public policy). Similarly, the agreement must have been reached voluntarily and result in a genuine meeting of minds. Consequently, contracts involving mistakes of fact, misrepresentation of the facts, or undue influence or duress may be void or voidable, depending on the circumstances. In insurance contracts, for instance, the insured is required to disclose all material facts to the insurer (e.g. health record, driving record), otherwise a policy may be invalidated. In this context a 'material fact' is one that would affect the mind of a prudent insurer, even though the materiality may not be appreciated by the insured.

Agency

As business activity has become more specialised and complex, firms have increasingly turned to other businesses to carry out specialist functions on their behalf, such as freight forwarding, the sale of goods, insurance broking and commercial letting. These parties (known as **agents**) are authorised by the individual or organisation hiring them (known as the **principal**) to act on their behalf, thus creating an agency relationship. As in other areas of commercial activity, special rules of law have evolved to regulate the behaviour of the parties involved in such a relationship.

In essence, the function of an agent is to act on behalf of a principal so as to effect a contract between the principal and a third party. The agent may be a 'servant' of the principal (i.e. under their control, as in the case of a sales representative) or an 'independent contractor' (i.e. their own master, as in the case of an estate agent) and will be operating with the consent of the principal, whether by contract or implication. Having established a contractual relationship between the principal and the third party, the agent generally leaves the picture and usually has no rights and duties under the contract thus made.

With regard to an agent's specific obligations under an agency agreement, these are normally expressly stated under the terms of the agreement, although some may also be implied. Traditionally, the common law of agency prescribes, however, that agents:

- *obey the lawful instruction of the principal,* otherwise they may be in breach of contract;
- *exercise due care and skill,* in order to produce a deal that is to the principal's best advantage;
- *act personally,* rather than delegate, unless expressly or implicitly authorised to do so;

- *act in good faith,* thus avoiding conflicts of interest or undisclosed profits and bribes;
- *keep proper accounts,* which separate the principal's funds from those that belong personally to the agent.

Moreover, in so far as an agent is acting under the principal's authority, the principal is bound to the third party only by acts that are within the agent's authority to make. Consequently, *ultra vires* acts affect the principal only if he or she adopts them by ratification and the agent may be liable for the breach of the implied warranty of authority to the third party.

In addition to these common law duties owed by the principal, the Commercial Agents (Council Directive) Regulations 1993 apply when an agent falls within the definition of a commercial agent (Reg. 2(1)). They apply to transactions involving the sale or purchase of goods and they bestow certain rights and obligations upon both the principal and the agent. It is clear that these duties overlap to some extent with the common law duties. Regulation 3 provides the agent's duties to their principal. A commercial agent must:

- look after the interests of her/his principal and act dutifully and in good faith;
- make proper efforts to negotiate and, where appropriate, conclude the transactions;
- communicate to their principal all the necessary information available to them;
- comply with reasonable instructions given by the principal.

Regulation 4 specifies the duties of the principal:

- to act dutifully and in good faith;
- to provide the commercial agent with the necessary documentation relating to the goods in question;
- to obtain necessary information for the agent. This is a higher standard, perhaps requiring searching for data, than under the common law, where all the principal needs to do is to disclose information in their possession;
- to notify the agent within a reasonable period of time if the usual volume of trade is likely to be significantly reduced;
- to inform the agent within a reasonable period of time of the principal's acceptance, refusal, or non-acceptance of a commercial transaction arranged by the agent.

Law and the consumer

Neo-classical economic theory tends to suggest that laws to protect the consumer are unnecessary. However, modern economists (in particular behavioural economists) have shown that the traditional assumption of working markets is not necessarily reliable, so regulation is sometimes required. If individuals were behaving rationally when consuming goods and services, they would arrange their consumption to maximise their satisfaction (or 'utility'), in the words of an economist. Products that because of poor quality or some other factor reduced a consumer's utility would be rejected in favour of those that proved a better alternative and this would act as an incentive to producers (and retailers) to provide the best products. In effect, market forces would ensure that the interest of the consumer was safeguarded as suppliers in a competitive market arranged their production to meet the needs and wants of rational consumers.

The 'ideal' view of how markets work is not always borne out in practice. Apart from the fact that consumers do not always act rationally, they often do not have access to information which might influence their choice of products; in some cases they may not even have a choice of products (e.g. where a monopoly exists), although this situation can change over time (e.g. through privatisation of state monopolies). Also, given the respective resources of producers and consumers, the balance of power in the trading relationship tends to favour producers who can influence consumer choices using a range of persuasive techniques, including advertising.

Taken together, these and other factors call into question the assumption that the consumer is 'sovereign' and hence the extent to which individuals have inherent protection in the marketplace from powerful (and, in some cases, unscrupulous) suppliers. It is in this context that the law is seen to be an important counterbalance in a contractual relationship where the consumer is, or may be, at a disadvantage, and this can be said to provide the basis of legal intervention in this area.

Existing laws to protect consumers come from both civil and criminal law. These rights, duties and liabilities have been created or imposed by common law (especially contract and tort) or by legislation. Significantly, as the examples below illustrate, a large element of current consumer law has resulted from statutory intervention, with much of it coming from the EU by way of directives. These laws – covering areas as diverse as commercial practices, the sale of goods and services, and consumer credit and product liability – indicate a growing willingness on the part of governments to respond to the complaints of consumers and their representative organisations and to use legislation to regulate the relationship between business organisations and their customers. Europe is keen to encourage consumers to take advantage of cross-border EU markets by harmonising consumer protection, as this boosts market access and consumer spending. To this end Europe has been adopting consumer protection directives, the most significant recent one being the Unfair Commercial Practices Directive, which has replaced a great deal of the pre-existing domestic law. However, major domestic law reform has been proposed with a Consumer Rights Bill, which was going through Parliament at the time of writing. This reform aims to consolidate the recent changes to consumer law.

> **web links**
>
> The Consumer Affairs Directorate in the Department of Business, Innovation and Skills is a useful source of reference on consumer law – see *www.gov. uk/consumer-protection-rights*

The Consumer Protection from Unfair Trading Regulations 2008

The Trade Descriptions Act 1968 was a mainstay of consumer protection before it was largely superseded by the Consumer Protection from Unfair Trading Regulations (2008). These Regulations implemented the Unfair Commercial Practices Directive 2005–29/EC, and extend criminal liability beyond simply misleading practices. These changes ban five categories of unfair practices, namely, a general prohibition on unfair practices, promoting unfair practices in codes of conduct, misleading actions and misleading omissions, aggressive commercial practices, and practices always deemed unfair under a 'banned list' of 31 practices. The Office of Fair Trading (OFT) (see Chapter 17), local authorities and the enforcement bodies also have powers to seek 'stop now' orders against such practices.

The Consumer Credit Acts 1974–2006

The Consumer Credit Act 1974, which became fully operational in May 1985, controls transactions between the credit industry and private individuals (including sole traders and business partnerships) up to a limit of £15,000. This statute has been updated since, especially so as to include EU directives, and it has recently been augmented by the Consumer Credit Act 2006. The Financial Conduct Authority took over regulation of consumer credit from the OFT on 1 April 2014. Under the legislation a consumer credit agreement is defined as a personal credit providing the debtor with credit up to the accepted limit. This credit may be in the form of a cash loan or some other type of financial accommodation (e.g. through the use of a credit card). The Act also covers hire purchase agreements (i.e. a contract of hire which gives the hirer the option to purchase the goods), conditional sale agreements for the sale of goods or land, and credit sale agreements, where the property passes to the buyer when the sale is effected.

The main aim of this consumer protection measure is to safeguard the public from trading malpractices where some form of credit is involved. To this end the Act provides, among other things, for a system of licensing controlled by the OFT, which must be satisfied that the person seeking a licence is a fit person and the name under which he or she intends to be licensed is neither misleading nor undesirable. Providing credit or acting as a credit broker without a licence is a criminal offence, as is supplying a minor with any document inviting them to borrow money or obtain goods on credit. The Consumer Credit Act 2006 created a Financial Services Ombudsman to settle disputes between consumers and their lenders. It has also created an unfair credit test that makes it easier for debtors to challenge excessive interest rates with the Ombudsman.

A further protection for the consumer comes from the requirements that the debtor be made fully aware of the nature and cost of the agreement and his or her rights and liabilities under it. The Act stipulates that prior to the contract being made the debtor must be supplied with certain information, including the full price of the credit agreement (i.e. the cost of the credit plus the capital sum), the annual rate of the total charge for credit expressed as a percentage (i.e. the annual percentage rate), and the amounts of payments due and to whom they are payable. In addition, the debtor must be informed of all the other terms of the agreement and of their right to cancel if this is applicable. In the case of the latter, this applies to credit agreements drawn up off business premises, and is designed to protect individuals from high-pressure doorstep sellers who offer credit as an incentive to purchase.

Sale of Goods Act 1979

Under the Sale of Goods Act 1979 (as amended), the Unfair Contract Terms Act 1977 and the Unfair Terms in Consumer Contracts Regulations 1999, consumers are essentially seen as individuals who purchase goods or services for their personal use from other individuals or organisations selling them in the course of business. A computer sold to a student, for example, is a consumer sale, while the same machine sold to a secretarial agency is not, since it has been acquired for business purposes. This legal definition of a consumer is important as some laws are designed specifically to provide consumers with extra protection, as in the case of the Sale of Goods Act. This statute governs agreements where a seller agrees to transfer ownership in goods to a buyer in return for a monetary consideration, known as the 'price'. Where such an agreement or contract is deemed to exist, the legislation provides all buyers with rights in respect of items that are faulty or that do not correspond with the description given to them, by identifying a number of implied conditions to the sale. However, consumer buyers are given extra remedies. In the case of contracts for the supply of services (e.g. repair work) or which involve the supply of goods and services (e.g. supplying units and fitting them in a bathroom or kitchen), almost identical rights are provided under the Supply of Goods and Services Act 1982 (as amended).

The three main implied conditions of the 1979 Act are relatively well known, namely, sale by description, satisfactory quality and fitness for purpose. The quality and fitness obligations are owed only when goods are sold in the course of a business, while section 13 applies to all sales. Under section 13, goods sold by description must match the description given to them, even if the buyer has selected the goods, for example, from a shop shelf. This description may be on the article itself or on the packaging or provided in some other way, and will include the price and possibly other information (e.g. washing instructions) which the buyer believes to be true. The description must describe the commercial characteristics and not be mere sales hype. A shirt described as 100 per cent cotton, for instance, must be just that, otherwise it fails to match the description given to it and the consumer is entitled to choose either a refund or an exchange.

The second condition relates to the quality of the goods provided. While this applies to all buyers, it applies only where goods are sold in the course of a business. So it will not apply to private sales. Under section 14(2) of the Act, goods had to be of 'merchantable quality', but 'merchantable quality' was a matter of some controversy, and so the phrase was amended to 'satisfactory quality' by section 1 of the Sale of Goods and Services Act 1994. The general expectation is that a product should be fit 'for all the purposes for which goods of the kind in question are commonly supplied', bearing in mind questions of age, price and any other relevant factors (e.g. brand name). A new top-of-the-range car should have no significant defects on purchase, whereas it would be unreasonable to expect the same from a high-mileage used car sold for a few hundred pounds. The quality expected of sale goods will normally be the same as the full-priced item. Thus, while the implied condition of 'satisfactory' applies to sale goods and used goods as well as to full-price purchases of new goods, it needs to be judged in light of the contract description and all the circumstances of a particular case, including the consumer's expectations.

The third implied condition derives from section 14(3) of the legislation, namely that goods are fit for a particular purpose (i.e. capable of performing the tasks indicated by the seller). Section 14(3) comes into its own when a use or range of uses is made known to the seller. Accordingly, section 14(3) will be breached if the seller, on request from the purchaser, confirms that goods are suitable for a particular purpose made known by the buyer and this proves not to be the case. Equally, if the product is unsuitable for its normal purposes, then section 14(2) would also be breached.

It is worth noting that 'satisfactory' and 'fitness for a purpose' are closely related and that a breach of one may include a breach of the other. By the same token, failure in a claim for a breach of section 14(2) is likely to mean that a claim for a breach of section 14(3) will also fail. Moreover, if, on request, a seller disclaims any knowledge of a product's suitability for a particular purpose and the consumer is willing to take a chance, any subsequent unsuitability cannot be regarded as a breach of section 14(3). The same applies if the buyer's reliance on the skill or judgement of the seller is deemed 'unreasonable'.

There are two sets of remedies available for breach of these implied terms, namely, rejection under a short-term right to reject, and/or damages. The time permitted to reject depends on the circumstances of the case, but usually it should at the very least be several weeks. The only exception to this has traditionally been that of durability, that is, where the goods have failed before goods of that type could reasonably be expected to fail. Durability has always been treated as a damages-only breach, so as to avoid over-compensating the buyer. These are the only remedies applicable to business buyers.

However, the Sale and Supply of Goods to Consumers Regulations 2002 have granted the consumer/buyer a choice, where they can use the traditional remedies (above) or additional remedies. The Regulations come from the European Consumer Guarantees Directive (1999–44/EC) and seek to continue the move towards harmonising the cross-border sale of consumer goods. The DTI (now BIS), keen not to reduce the pre-existing levels of consumer protection, added the new remedies to those already existing. The result is that the consumer retains the short-term right to reject the goods for non-conformity. However, if this remedy is lost due to lapse of time, or the consumer chooses not to use this remedy, the consumer now has four new paired remedies: repair or replace, price reduction or rescission. These are often called 'the four Rs' and are dealt with in more detail below, in the case study section. Until these Regulations the consumer had no right to require a repair or a replacement, and could sue for damages only.

Moreover, the Regulations now remove the problem of goods damaged in transit. Risk previously passed to the consumer/buyer once the goods had been handed over to a third-party carrier, the result being that the purchaser would find the carrier and the seller blaming one another for the loss. Ultimately, the consumer would go uncompensated unless they decided to sue both parties. The Regulations now require that goods must actually be received by the consumer/buyer in conformity with the contract, so risk passes later. Lastly, manufacturers must honour any guarantee that they provide, and bear the return cost for any defective goods under a manufacturer's guarantee.

These new remedies apply only to consumers/buyers of goods sold in the course of a business. Section 15A of the Sale of Goods Act applies to business-to-business sales where there is only a slight breach of an implied condition of description or quality. The provision seeks to prevent a business buyer from rejecting goods due to a minor technical breach, and imposes an award of damages only. As damages are based on loss, damages for a technical breach will probably be very low. As a result, businesses that find that they can get the goods cheaper elsewhere will be less tempted to try to seek to reject goods for minor breaches. This also recognises that rejection of goods is not the norm in business; normally a recalculation of the price or payment conditions takes place. Having theoretical rights is one thing, but in business one may need to trade with the other party again and it is wise to consider the impact of any decision taken.

As a final comment, under the Sale and Supply of Goods and Services Act 1982, section 3, there is an implied condition that a supplier acting in the course of business must carry out the service with reasonable care and skill and within a reasonable time, where a specific deadline is not stated in the contract. Reasonable care and skill tends to be seen as that which might be expected of an ordinary competent person performing the particular task, though this will, of course, depend on the particular circumstances of the case and the nature of the trade or profession. As in the case of the Sale of Goods Act, any attempt to deprive the consumer of any of the implied conditions represents a breach of both the Unfair Contract Terms Act 1977 and the Unfair Terms in Consumer Contracts Regulations 1999.

Exclusion or limitation clauses in consumer contracts are subject to the Unfair Contract Terms Act 1977 and the Unfair Terms in Consumer Contracts Regulations 1999, which currently operate as a dual regime, giving the consumer the choice of actions. Under the former, any clause seeking to exclude or limit liability for personal injury/death or the statutory implied terms against a consumer is void, while all other clauses are subject to the test of reasonableness. Under the latter regulations a term that has not been individually negotiated will be unfair if it is contrary to good faith by causing a significant imbalance between the parties. The situation is a little different in business deals, although personal injury/death still cannot be excluded. Thus, where a reference is made on a product or its container or in a related document to a consumer's rights under sections 13 to 15 of the Sale of Goods Act, there must be a clear and accessible notice informing consumers that their statutory rights are not affected when returning an item deemed unsatisfactory. It is an offence under the Fair Trading Act 1974 to display notices stating 'no refunds' or 'no refunds on sale goods'. The aim is to ensure that buyers are made fully aware of their legal rights and are not taken advantage of by unscrupulous traders who seek to deny them the protection afforded by the law.

The Consumer Protection Act 1987

The Consumer Protection Act 1987 came into force in March 1988 as a result of the government's obligation to implement EC Directive 85–374, which concerned product liability. In essence, the Act provides for a remedy in damages for any consumer who suffers personal injury or damage to property as a result of a defective product by imposing a 'strict' liability on the producers of defective goods (including substances, growing crops, ships, aircraft and vehicles). Naturally, the onus is on the complainant to prove that any loss was caused by the claimed defect and a claim can be made where damage to property, personal injury or death has occurred. In the case of the latter, for example, a relative or friend could pursue an action and, if American experience is anything to go by, could be awarded substantial damages if liability can be proven. As far as property is concerned, damage must be to private rather than commercial goods and property and the loss must exceed £275.

While the Act is, *inter alia,* intended to place liability on the producers of defective goods, this liability also extends to anyone putting a name or distinguishing mark on a product which holds that person out as being the producer (e.g. supermarkets' own-brand labels). Similarly, importers of products from outside the EU are also liable for any defects in imported goods, as may be firms involved in supplying components or parts of the process of manufacture of a product. To prevent a firm escaping its liability as a supplier claiming it is unable to identify its own suppliers, the legislation provides a remedy: any supplier unable or unwilling to identify the importing firm or previous supplier becomes liable itself for damages under the Act.

Firms seeking to avoid liability for any claim have a number of defences under section 4 of the Act. Specifically these are:

- that the defendant did not supply the product in question;
- that the product was not manufactured or supplied in the course of business;
- that the defect did not exist at the time the product was distributed;
- that where a product has a number of components, the defect is a defect of the finished product or due to compliance with any instructions issued by the manufacturer of the finished product;
- that the defect is attributable to the requirement to comply with existing laws;
- that the state of scientific and technical knowledge at the time the product was supplied was not sufficiently advanced for the defect to be recognised.

Of these, the last – the so-called development risks or 'state of the art' defence – is the most contentious, given that it applies largely to products such as new drugs and new technology where the implications of their usage may not be apparent for some years. As recent cases have shown, manufacturers faced with damages from claimants who appear to have suffered from the use of certain products often decide to settle out of court without accepting liability for their actions.

> **web link**
>
> The annual Report of the Office of Fair Trading contains useful commentary on consumer protection issues, including codes of practice and the powers of the OFT. See *www.oft.gov.uk*

Codes of practice

Alongside the protection provided by the law, consumers may be afforded a further measure of security when the organisation they are dealing with belongs to a trade association that is operating under a **code of practice** (e.g. the Association of British Travel Agents). In essence, codes of practice represent an attempt by trade associations to impose a measure of self-discipline on the behaviour of their members by establishing the standards of service customers should expect to receive and by encouraging acceptable business practices. In addition, such codes of conduct invariably identify how customer complaints should be handled and many offer low-cost or no-cost arbitration schemes to help settle disputes outside the more formal legal process.

While codes of practice do not in themselves have the force of law, they are normally seen as a useful mechanism for regulating the relationship between business organisations and their customers and accordingly they have the support of the Office of Fair Trading, which often advises trade associations on their content. Businesses, too, usually find them useful, particularly if through the establishment of a system of self-regulation they are able to avoid the introduction of restrictions imposed by the law.

Synopsis

All business activities, from the establishment of the organisation through to the sale of the product to the customer, are influenced by the law. This legal environment within which businesses exist and operate evolves over time and is a key influence on firms of all sizes and in all sectors, as illustrated by an examination of some of the main laws governing the relationship between a business and its customers. The majority of consumer laws are of relatively recent origin and derive from the attempts by successive governments to provide individuals with a measure of protection against a minority of firms that behave in ways deemed to be unacceptable. Concomitantly, they also provide reputable organisations with a framework within which to carry out their business and, as such, act as an incentive to entrepreneurial activity in market-based economies.

Summary of key points

- The legal rules within which businesses exist and operate are an important part of the external environment of business organisations.

- Laws affecting businesses derive from a variety of sources, including custom, the decisions of the courts and legislation.

- Laws are sometimes made at international and supranational level (including Europe).

- Contract, agency and consumer protection are three key areas governing the day-to-day work of businesses.

- Offer, acceptance, consideration, intention to create legal relations and capacity are central elements of contract law.

- Agency relationships are a common feature of business practice.

- The relationship between businesses and their customers is governed by a variety of laws, many of which derive from statute.

- In addition to the protection provided to consumers by the law, many organisations operate under agreed codes of conduct.

case study   The sale of goods on the internet

The sale of consumer goods on the internet (particularly those between European member states) raises a number of legal issues. First, there is the issue of trust, without which the consumer will not buy; they will need assurance that the seller is genuine, and that they will get the goods that they have ordered. Second, there is the issue of consumer rights with respect to the goods in question: what rights exist and do they vary across Europe? Last, the issue of enforcement: what happens should anything go wrong?

Information and trust

Europe recognises the problems of doing business across the internet or telephone and it has attempted to address the main stumbling blocks via directives which are incorporated into member states' own laws. The original Distance Selling Directive, implemented as the Consumer Protection (Distance Selling) Regulations 2000, was in the process of being replaced by the Consumer Rights Directive (2011–83/EU) at the time of going to press. The new directive is a 'maximum harmonisation' measure, meaning that the provisions are binding on, and cannot be modified by member states. Both directives attempt to address the issues of trust in distance sale. In short, the consumer who does not buy face to face may lack important information, which they may otherwise have easy access to if they were buying face to face.

Article 6 of the Consumer Rights Directive requires *inter alia* for the seller to identify themselves and an address must be provided if the goods are to be paid for in advance. Moreover, a full description of the goods and the final price (inclusive of any taxes) must also be provided. The new directive bans pre-ticked boxes (e.g. for insurance), and limits card transaction charges to those of the cost actually incurred by the trader. These provisions will help to cut hidden costs. The seller must also inform the buyer of the right of cancellation available under Article 9, where the buyer has a right to cancel the contract for 14 days starting on the day the consumer receives the goods or services (this was seven days under the

Distance Selling Directive). This 'cooling off' period is intended to place the consumer in the position as if they had seen the goods in store. Failure to inform the consumer of this right automatically extends the period to a year and 14 days. While the seller can place the cost of returning goods on the buyer, the seller must refund the standard rate outgoing postage. The seller is not entitled to deduct any costs as a restocking fee. All of this places a considerable obligation on the seller; however, such data should stem many misunderstandings and so boost cross-border trade by increasing consumer faith and confidence in non-face-to-face sales.

Another concern for the consumer is fraud. The consumer who has paid by credit card will be protected by section 83 of the Consumer Credit Act 1974, under which a consumer/purchaser is not liable for the debt incurred if it has been run up by a third party not acting as the agent of the buyer. The Distance Selling Regulations extended this to debit cards, and removed the ability of the card issuer to charge the consumer for the first £50 of loss. Moreover, section 75 of the Consumer Credit Act 1974 also gives the consumer/buyer a like claim against the credit card company for any misrepresentation or breach of contract by the seller. This is extremely important in a distance-selling transaction, where the seller may disappear.

What quality and what rights?

The next issue relates to the quality that may be expected from goods bought over the internet. Clearly, if goods have been bought from abroad, the levels of quality required in other jurisdictions may vary. It is for this reason that Europe has attempted to standardise the issue of quality and consumer remedies, with the Consumer Guarantees Directive (1999–44/EC), thus continuing the push to encourage cross-border consumer purchases. The Sale and Supply of Goods to Consumer Regulations 2002 came into force in 2003, which not only lay down minimum quality standards but also provide the series of consumer remedies (the four Rs) across

Europe. The Regulations further amend the Sale of Goods Act 1979. The former DTI (now BIS), whose job it was to incorporate the directive into domestic law (by way of delegated legislation), ensured that the pre-existing consumer rights were maintained, so as not to reduce the overall level of protection available to consumers.

The directive requires goods to be of 'normal' quality, or fit for any purpose made known by the seller. This has been taken to be the same as our pre-existing 'satisfactory quality' and 'fitness for purpose' obligations owed under sections 14(2) and 14(3) of the Sale of Goods Act 1979. Moreover, the pre-existing remedy of the short-term right to reject is also retained. This right provides the buyer a short period of time to discover whether the goods are in conformity with the contract. In practice, it is usually a matter of weeks. After that time has elapsed, the consumer has four new remedies that did not exist before, which are provided in two pairs. These are repair or replacement and price reduction or rescission. The pre-existing law only gave a right to damages, which would rarely be exercised in practice. (However, the Small Claims Court would ensure a speedy and cheap means of redress for almost all contract claims brought under £10,000.) Now there is a right to a repair or a replacement, so that the consumer is not left with an impractical action for damages over defective goods. The seller must also bear the cost of return of the goods for repair. So such costs must now be factored into any business sales plan.

If these remedies are not suitable, deproportionate or actioned within a 'reasonable period of time' then the consumer may rely on the second pair of remedies. Price reduction permits the consumer to claim back a segment of the purchase price if the goods are still useable. It is effectively a discount for defective goods. Rescission allows the consumer to reject the goods, but they do not get the full refund that they would under the short-term right to reject; here money is knocked off for 'beneficial use'. This is akin to the pre-existing treatment for breaches of durability, where goods have not lasted as long as goods of that type ought reasonably be expected to last. The level of payment would take account of the use that the consumer has (if any) been able to put the goods to and a deduction made off the return of the purchase price. However, the issue that must be addressed is the length of time that goods may be expected to last. A supplier may state the length of the guarantee period, so a £500 television set guaranteed for one year would have a life expectancy of one year. However, a consumer may expect a television set to last ten years. Clearly, if the set went wrong after six months, the consumer would get back only £250 if the retailer's figure was used, but would receive £475 if their own figure was used. It remains to be seen how this provision will work in practice.

One problem with distance sales has been that of liability for goods that arrive damaged. The pre-existing domestic law stated that risk would pass to the buyer once the goods were handed over to a third-party carrier. This had the major problem in practice of who would actually be liable for the damage. Carriers would blame the supplier and vice versa. The consumer would be able to sue for the loss, if they were able to determine which party was responsible. In practice, consumers usually went uncompensated and such a worry has deterred many consumers from buying goods over the internet. The Sale and Supply of Goods to Consumer Regulations 2003 also modify the transfer of risk, so that now the risk remains with a commercial seller of goods to a consumer, until actual delivery. This will clearly lead to a slight increase in the supply of goods to consumers, with the goods usually now being sent by insured delivery. However, this will avoid the problem of who is actually liable and should help to boost consumer confidence.

Enforcement

Enforcement for domestic sales is relatively straightforward. Small-scale consumer claims can be dealt with expeditiously and cheaply under the Small Claims Court. Here, claims under £10,000 for contract-based claims are brought in a special court intended to keep costs down by keeping the lawyers out of the court room, as a victorious party cannot claim for their lawyers' expenses. The judge will conduct the case in a more 'informal' manner, and will seek to discover the legal issues by questioning both parties, so no formal knowledge of the law is required. The total cost of such a case, even if it is lost, is the cost of issuing the proceedings (approximately 10 per cent of the value claimed) and the other side's 'reasonable expenses'. Expenses must be kept down, and a judge will not award value which has been deliberately run up, such as first-class rail travel and stays in five-star hotels. Such claims may now be made online via the internet (*www.courtservice.gov.uk* outlines the procedure for MCOL, or Money Claims Online). Cases will normally be held in the defendant's court, unless the complainant is a consumer and the defendant a business.

There is now a European-wide Small Claims Court dealing with transnational European transactions valued at less than €2,000. The case will be handled by member states' existing small claims courts.

Case study questions

1 Consider the checklist of data which a distance seller must provide to a consumer purchaser. Is this putting too heavy a burden on sellers?

2 Is a consumer distance buyer any better off after the European legislation?

3 Are there any remaining issues that must be tackled to increase European cross-border consumer trade?

Review and discussion questions

1 Why are laws to protect the consumer felt to be necessary? What other means do consumers have of protecting their interests in the marketplace?

2 To what extent does the supranational structure of European Union law infringe the principle of the supremacy of Parliament?

3 Do you think that tobacco companies should be made retrospectively liable for the safety of their product? Justify your answer.

4 Examine the case for and against increased government control over business practices.

Assignments

1 You are a trading standards officer in a local authority trading standards department. You have been asked to talk to a group of school sixth-form students on the Sale of Goods Act 1979. Prepare suitable PowerPoint slides outlining the following:

(a) The main provisions of the 1979 Act.
(b) The customer's rights in the event of a breach of the implied conditions.
(c) The sources of help and advice available to an individual with a consumer problem.

2 Imagine you work for a Citizens' Advice Bureau. A large part of your work involves offering advice to individuals with consumer problems. Design a simple leaflet indicating some of the principal pieces of legislation in the field of consumer protection and their main provisions. Your leaflet should also give guidance on further specialist sources of help and advice.

Notes and references

1 'Opt-outs' may sometimes be negotiated, however. Britain initially opted out of the Social Chapter of the Maastricht Treaty, which includes a provision for a 48-hour maximum working week. Within the Union an attempt was made to treat this issue as a health and safety measure, which could then be applicable to British firms by majority (not unanimous) vote of the member states. After the 1997 election, the government decided to 'opt in' to the Social Chapter. The 48-hour working restrictions are now causing concern in a number of areas, notably transport, deep sea fishing and the health service.

Further reading

Atiyah, P., *The Sale of Goods,* 12th edition, Longman/Pearson, 2010.

Furmston, M. and Chuah, J. (eds), *Commercial and Consumer Law,* 2nd edition, Pearson, 2013.

Marson, J., *Business Law,* 3rd edition, Oxford University Press, 2011.

Web links and further questions are available on the website at:

www.pearsoned.co.uk/worthington

Chapter 6
Organising for Success (Structure) and Technology

Information Technology (IT) for Business

chapter 14

incamerastock/Alamy

Engineers alone do not design new products.

Customers, marketers, financiers, production

managers,   and

purchasing employees use technology to

collaborate   in

ways that seemed impossible in the past.

Reported Web Forgery!

This web site at firstbanks.direct-updat...

...ery and has been blocked based...

...ed to trick...

Think Before
You Click

"Start a 'work-at-home' job as an 'international sales representative' or a 'shipping manager,' with excellent pay. Simply open a new bank account in your name, accept money transfers into the account, then forward the money to our customers at locations around the globe." For out-of-work computer users, this e-mail message can be quite appealing. In reality, the victim is tricked into becoming a "mule" in a money-laundering racket. The new "employee" provides anonymous racketeers a safe way to launder stolen or otherwise illegal money. As Internet money transfers arrive, the mule relays them (illegally) to a global network of recipient racketeers.

Clearly, the Internet creates infinite opportunities to research careers, search for jobs, and build a network. But the very nature of the Internet creates risks as well as opportunities. Perhaps you've posted a resume on a website such as LinkedIn or monster.com. Well, cybercriminals, as well as legitimate employers, may be after you. In an-all-too common scam, criminals posing as employers contact individuals who have posted their resumes online. They conduct an interview, often electronically, and make the job hunter the offer of a great job. All that's left is collecting a little information, such as the person's Social Security number. Unfortunately, there's really no company and no job, but your Social Security number, as well as other personal information can be used to apply for credit cards that will never get paid. Before you share information like your Social Security number, be sure to know who is at the other end of an e-mail. Do some research and make sure that the company is legitimate and that the person with whom you are exchanging e-mails is really an employee.

In one popular work-at-home scam, the unsuspecting victim (the new online "employee") cashes checks sent from the "employer" in a foreign country and gets to keep 10 percent of the cash as a payment for service. The remaining 90 percent is sent via Western Union back to the employer. Because the checks are bogus, they bounce, and the victim must repay the full amounts to the bank. Alerting the public to another scam, SC Johnson, the company that makes household products such as Raid, Windex, and Pledge furniture cleaner, warns of phony online job offers for work-at-home customer service jobs falsely using the Johnson name. The scammers say the job pays trainees $20 an hour initially, advancing to $25 after training, but employees must first buy some training software—which, of course, they pay for but never receive.

To protect yourself from cybercriminals when looking for a job, there are a couple of red flags that should alert you that something is not quite right. These cybercriminals are not

Andres Rodriguez/Fotolia

what's in it for me?

Protecting against cyber-attacks is an extreme example of the way the Internet and related technologies are reshaping the business landscape. But even the most traditional businesses must change with the times, whether those times are defined by paper and pencil, telephone and fax machine, or digital language translators and smartphones and smartwatches. Indeed, it may seem like the times are changing more rapidly with each passing year, and it is in this context that our discussion of the various kinds of information technology, their functions, and the benefits and risks associated with each assumes particular importance. By understanding the material in this chapter, you'll have a clearer picture of how technology is used by and affects business, and how you can use it to your best advantage—as an employee, investor, manager, or a business owner.

human resource professionals, so you may notice spelling or grammatical errors in e-mails. While mistakes can happen, this is a potential red flag that the communication is not legitimate. Similarly, if an offer **seems** too good to be true, it probably is. If you're offered a job, but required to pay money up front, there's a good chance that the offer is not legit. Finally, offers that are very time pressured are more likely to be fraudulent. Criminals don't want you to take the time to think through a bad deal and will encourage you to "act now" before this offer goes away.

Obviously, it's not just job-hunters who face risks. Text messages saying victims' credit cards have been deactivated lure bank customers into relaying account information to an unknown sender. Internet-based phone users receive fake caller IDs of real hospitals, government agencies, banks, and other businesses in a now-popular form of telephone phishing that talks victims into revealing personal information. Perhaps most impressive, cyber thieves are using marketing techniques—most notably "targeting"—to reach specific audiences. Also known as "spear phishing," with targeting, scammers do research to identify wealthy individuals, families, and professional money managers. Victims receive friendly sounding e-mails and social networking contacts containing contaminated attachments that, once opened, infect their computers, exposing bank account and other identity information to scammers. Although computer security devices—spam filters, data encryption, firewalls, and anti-virus software—catch a vast number of intrusions, the threat remains.[1]

Organizations, too, are victims of cyber invasions: Security consultants say that global cyber-attacks originating in China, and known as Night Dragon, have invaded computers of oil companies, stealing information on competitive bidding, financing, and operations practices. Some governments, to save money, are actively scamming others, using hackers to steal technology secrets for leading-edge military equipment, including defense systems of other countries. Organizations of all kinds are finding cyber security more difficult as more and more employees use their personal phones and computers for conducting business. Organizational information, then, is more widely dispersed and increasingly susceptible to intrusion via mobile-phone malware, virus-contaminated applications, and links containing spyware sent from text messages.[2] (After studying the content in this chapter, you should be able to answer a set of discussion questions found at the end of the chapter.)

Information Technology Impacts: A Driver of Changes for Business

OBJECTIVE 14-1
Discuss

the impacts information technology (IT) has had on the business world.

Information Technology (IT) *various appliances and devices for creating, storing, exchanging, and using information in diverse modes, including visual images, voice, multimedia, and business data*

The effect of **information technology (IT)** on business has been immeasurable. In fact, IT, the various appliances and devices for creating, storing, exchanging, and using information in diverse modes, including visual images, voice, multimedia, and business data, has altered the structure of business organizations, radically changing the way employees and customers interact. We see ads all the time for the latest cell phones, iPads, laptops, PDAs, tablets, and smartphones, and most of us connect daily to the Internet. E-mail has become a staple in business, and even such traditionally "low-tech" businesses as nail salons and garbage collection companies are dependent on the Internet, computers, and networks. As consumers, we interact with databases of IT networks every time we withdraw money from an ATM, order food at McDonald's, or check on the status of a package at UPS.com. Technology and its effects are evident everywhere.

E-commerce *use of the Internet and other electronic means for retailing and business-to-business transactions*

E-commerce (short for *electronic commerce*), the use of the Internet and other electronic means for retailing and business-to-business transactions, has created new market relationships around the globe. In this section, we'll look at how businesses are using IT to bolster productivity, improve operations and processes, create new opportunities, and communicate and work in ways not possible before.

Creating Portable Offices: Providing Remote Access to Instant Information

IT appliances such as Samsung mobile phones and Apple iPhones, along with IBM wireless Internet access and PC-style office applications, save businesses time and travel expenses by enabling employees, customers, and suppliers to communicate from any location. IT's mobile messaging capabilities mean that a geographic separation between the workplace and headquarters is more common. Employees no longer work only at the office or the factory, nor are all of a company's operations performed at one place; employees take the office with them. When using such devices, off-site employees have continuous access to information, instead of being forced to be at a desk to access their files and the Internet. Client project folders, e-mail, and voice messaging are accessible from any location. Such benefits currently attract 46 million enthusiastic subscribers worldwide to BlackBerry® smartphones and another 91 million users of Blackberry's messenger service.[3]

Looking to the future, a possible next step for office portability is Google's "Project Glass." This is a head-mounted, Internet-connected information display that may someday be blended into peoples' everyday eyeglasses. Using Google's *Android* system, it will respond to voice commands for rapid visual access to the Internet's vast ocean of digital information, all while on the move.[4]

Enabling Better Service by Coordinating Remote Deliveries

With access to the Internet, company activities may be geographically scattered but still remain coordinated through a networked system that provides better service for customers. Many businesses, for example, coordinate activities from one centralized location, but their deliveries flow from several remote locations, often at lower cost. When you order furniture—for example, a chair, a sofa, a table, and two lamps—from an Internet storefront, the chair may come from a warehouse in Philadelphia and the lamps from a manufacturer in California; the sofa and table may be shipped direct from different suppliers in North Carolina. Beginning with the customer's order, activities are coordinated through the company's network, as if the whole order were being processed at one place. This avoids the expensive in-between step of first shipping all the items to a central location.

Creating Leaner, More Efficient Organizations

Networks and technology are also leading to leaner companies with fewer employees and simpler structures. Because networks enable firms to maintain information linkages among both employees and customers, more work and customer satisfaction can be accomplished with fewer people. Bank customers connect into a 24-hour information system and monitor their accounts without employee assistance. Instructions that once were given to assembly workers by supervisors are now delivered to workstations electronically. IT communications provide better use of employee skills and greater efficiencies from physical resources. For example, truck drivers used to return to a shipping terminal to receive instructions from supervisors on reloading freight for the next delivery. Today, one dispatcher using IT has replaced several supervisors. Instructions to the fleet arrive on electronic screens in trucks on the road so drivers know in advance the next delivery schedule, and satellite navigation services, such as SiriusXM NavTraffic, alert drivers of traffic incidents ahead so they can reroute to avoid delivery delays.[5]

White House Photo/Alamy

Barack Obama's Blackberry uses an encrypted system for secure messaging with advisors and colleagues.

Enabling Increased Collaboration

Collaboration among internal units and with outside firms is greater when firms use collaboration (collaborative) software and other IT communications devices, which we'll discuss later in this chapter. Companies are learning that complex problems can be better solved through IT-supported collaboration, either with formal teams or spontaneous interaction among people and departments. The design of new products, for example, was once an engineering responsibility. Now it is a shared activity using information from customers, along with people in marketing, finance, production, engineering, and purchasing, who collectively determine the best design. For example, the design of Boeing's 787 Dreamliner aircraft is the result of collaboration, not just among engineers but also with passengers (who wanted electric outlets to recharge personal electronic devices), cabin crews (who wanted more bathrooms and wider aisles), and air-traffic controllers (who wanted larger, safer air brakes). Although the 787 suffered from some initial design flaws, solutions involved a worldwide network of technical collaboration among Boeing engineers, suppliers, customers, and NASA.[6]

This Boeing aircraft was the result of collaboration among Boeing engineers, suppliers, and customers.

dutchpilot22/Fotolia

Enabling Global Exchange

The global reach of IT enables business collaboration on a scale that was once unheard of. Consider Lockheed Martin's contract for designing and supplying thousands of Joint Strike Fighters in different versions for the United States, Britain, Italy, Denmark, Canada, and Norway. Lockheed can't do the job alone—over the project's 20-year life, more than 1,500 firms will supply everything from radar systems to engines to bolts. In just the start-up phase, Lockheed collaborated with Britain's BAE Systems along with more than 70 U.S. and 18 international subcontractors at some 190 locations, including an Australian manufacturer of aviation communications and a Turkish electronics supplier. In all, 40,000 remote computers are collaborating on the project using Lockheed's Internet-based system. Web collaboration on a massive scale is essential for coordinating design, testing, and construction while avoiding delays, holding down costs, and maintaining quality.[7]

Improving Management Processes

IT has also changed the nature of the management process. The activities and methods of today's manager differ significantly from those that were common just a few years ago. At one time, upper-level managers didn't concern themselves with all of the detailed information filtering upward from the workplace because it was expensive to gather, the collection and recording process was cumbersome, and information quickly became out of date. Workplace management was delegated to middle and first-line managers.

With electronic processing in digital databases, specialized software, and interactive networks, however, instantaneous information is accessible and useful to all levels of management. For example, consider *enterprise resource planning (ERP)*, which is an information system for organizing and managing a firm's activities across product lines, departments, and geographic locations. The ERP stores real-time information on work status and upcoming transactions and notifies employees when action is required if certain schedules are to be met. It coordinates internal operations with activities of outside suppliers and notifies customers of upcoming deliveries and billings. Consequently, more managers use it routinely for planning and controlling companywide operations. Today, a manager at Hershey Foods, for example, uses ERP to check on the current status of any customer order for Kisses or strawberry Twizzlers, inspect productivity statistics for each workstation, and analyze the delivery performance on any shipment. Managers can better coordinate companywide performance. They can identify departments that are working well together and those that are lagging behind schedule and creating bottlenecks.

Providing Flexibility for Customization

IT advances also create new manufacturing and service capabilities that enable businesses to offer customers greater variety, customizable options, and faster delivery cycles. Whether it's an iPhone app or a Rawlings baseball glove, today's design-it-yourself world is possible through fast, flexible manufacturing using IT networks. At Ponoko.com, you can design and make just about anything, from electronics to furniture. Buyers and materials suppliers, meeting electronically, have rapidly generated thousands of product designs online. The designs can be altered to suit each buyer's tastes. Similarly, at San Francisco–based Timbuk2's website, you can "build your own" custom messenger bag at different price levels with your choice of size, fabric, color combination, accessories, liner material, strap, and even left- or right-hand access.[8] This principle of **mass customization** allows companies to produce in large volumes, and IT allows each item to feature the unique options the customer prefers. With IT, the old standardized assembly line has become quickly adaptable because workers have instantaneous access to assembly instructions for all the product options, and equipment can be changed quickly for each customer's order.

Mass Customization *principle in which companies produce in large volumes, but each item features the unique options the customer prefers*

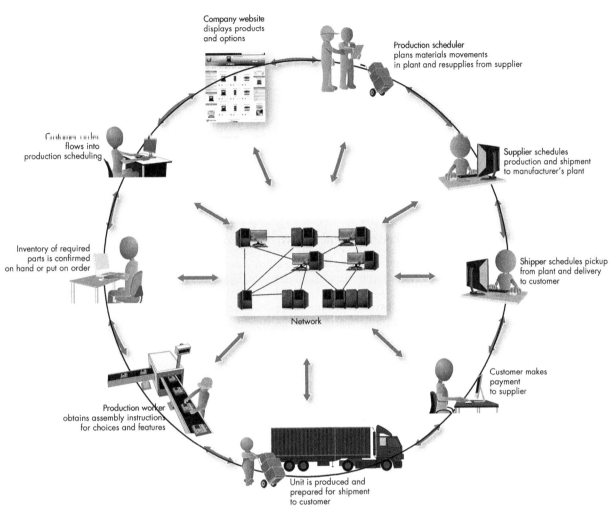

FIGURE 14.1 Networking for Mass Customization of a Physical Product

As shown in Figure 14.1, flexible production and speedy delivery depend on an integrated network of information to coordinate all the activities among customers, manufacturers, suppliers, and shippers.

Service industries, too, including health care, banking, and recreation, are emphasizing greater flexibility for meeting customers' needs. Personalized pet care at HappyPetCare.net, for example, relies on IT for scheduling customized activities—dog walking, pet boarding, pet sitting, house-sitting, pet taxis, and other services. In tourism, at OceaniaCruises.com, passengers have flexibility for selecting personalized onboard services for meals, recreation and entertainment activities, educational classes, and spa treatments. They also customize your air travel schedules along with personalized pre- and post-cruise land programs.

Providing New Business Opportunities

Not only is IT improving existing businesses, it also is creating entirely new businesses where none existed before. For big businesses, this means developing new products, offering new services, and reaching new clients. Only a few years ago, today's multibillion-dollar behemoth known as Google was a fledgling search engine. That company boasts not just a search engine but hundreds of services, including virtual maps, YouTube video, Twitter accounts, Facebook pages, instant messaging, Gmail (Google's e-mail service), and online voicemail and software services such as photo editing and document creation.

IT-based industries, including computer backup and identity-theft protection, offer valuable services for individuals and business customers. Online backup protects against data loss resulting from hard-drive crashes, fire, flood, and other causes. Carbonite.com and Backblaze.com, for example, provide automatic continuous backup so clients can recover lost data quickly. For guarding against identity theft, firms such as LifeLock.com and IdentityGuard.com protect personal information by alerting clients to various information-theft risks and sending advice on steps for avoiding identity theft.

The IT landscape has also presented home-based businesses with new e-business opportunities. Consider Richard Smith. His love for stamp collecting began at age seven. Now, some 50 years after saving that first stamp, he's turned his hobby into a profitable eBay business. Each day begins at the PC in his home office, scanning eBay's listings for items available and items wanted by sellers and buyers around the world. With more than 6,000 sales transactions to date, Richard maintains a perfect customer rating and has earned more than $4,000 on each of several eBay transactions. Today, thousands of online marketplaces allow entrepreneurs to sell directly to consumers, bypassing conventional retail outlets, and enable business-to-business (B2B) selling and trading with access to a worldwide customer base. To assist start-up businesses, eBay's services network is a ready-made online business model, not just an auction market. Services range from credit financing to protection from fraud and misrepresentation, information security, international currency exchanges, and postsales management. These features enable users to complete sales transactions, deliver merchandise, and get new merchandise for future resale, all from the comfort of their own homes. Many eBay users, like Richard Smith, have carved profitable new careers with the help of these systems.

Improving the World and Our Lives

Can advancements in IT really make the world a better place? Developments in smartphones, social networking, home entertainment, automobile safety, and other applications have certainly brought enjoyment and convenience to the everyday lives of millions of people around the globe. Extending technology beyond previous-model cell phones and PCs, new technologies provide access to endless

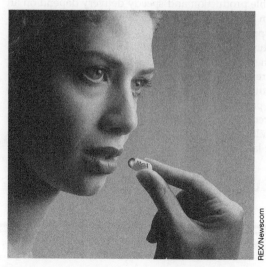

After this capsule is swallowed, the camera inside it can transmit almost 50,000 images during its eight-hour journey through the digestive tract.

REX/Newscom

choices of *apps* (shorthand for *application software*), allowing each user to "build it your way," depending on what you want your device to do and how and where you'll be using it. Apps for computers and smartphones include *programs* for learning languages, music, work, games, traveling, art, and almost any other area of interest. Just two years after its opening, Apple's App Store had supplied more than 40 billion app downloads worldwide to users of Macs, iPhones, iPads, and iPod Touches.

Social networking, a valuable service for individuals and organizations, is made possible by IT. The many forms of social media—blogs, chats, and networks such as LinkedIn, Twitter, and Facebook—are no longer just playthings for gossips and hobbyists. They're also active tools for getting a job. With the economic meltdown, millions of job seekers turned to online networking—tapping leads from friends, colleagues, and acquaintances—for contacts with companies that may be hiring. Peers and recruiters are networking using electronic discussion forums and bulletin boards at websites of professional associations and trade groups, technical schools, and alumni organizations. Some social sites provide occupation-specific career coaching and job tips: Scientists are connecting with Epernicus, top managers use Meet the Boss, and graduate students are connecting with Graduate Junction.[9]

Organizations, too, including hospitals and medical equipment companies, are embracing IT advancements to provide better services. For example, when treating combat injuries, surgeons at Walter Reed National Military Medical Center in Bethesda, Maryland, rely on high-tech imaging systems that convert two-dimensional photographs of their patients' anatomies into three-dimensional (3D) physical models for presurgical planning. These 3D mockups of shoulders, femurs, and facial bones give doctors the opportunity to see and feel the anatomy as it will be seen in the operating room, before they even use their scalpels. Meanwhile, pill-sized cameras that patients swallow are providing doctors with images of the insides of the human body, helping them make better diagnoses for such ailments as ulcers and cancer.[10]

IT Building Blocks: Business Resources

OBJECTIVE 14-2
Identify
the IT resources businesses have at their disposal and how these resources are used.

Businesses today have a wide variety of IT resources at their disposal. In addition to the Internet and e-mail, these include communications technologies, networks, hardware devices, and software, as shown at technology media sites such as Techweb.com.

The Internet and Other Communication Resources

Internet *gigantic system of interconnected computer networks linked together by voice, electronic, and wireless technologies*

Hypertext Transfer Protocol (HTTP) *communications protocol used for the World Wide Web, in which related pieces of information on separate Web pages are connected using hyperlinks*

World Wide Web *branch of the Internet consisting of interlinked hypertext documents, or Web pages*

The **Internet** is a gigantic global system of interconnected computer networks belonging to millions of collaborating organizations and agencies—government, business, academic, and public—linked together by voice, electronic, and wireless technologies.[11] Computers within the networks are connected by various communications protocols, or standardized coding systems, such as the **hypertext transfer protocol (HTTP)**, which is used for the **World Wide Web**, a branch of the Internet consisting of interlinked hypertext documents, or Web pages. Other protocols serve a variety of purposes, such as sending and receiving e-mail. The World Wide Web and its protocols provide the common language that allows information sharing on the Internet. For thousands of businesses, the Internet has replaced the telephone, fax machine, and standard mail as the primary communications tool. The Internet has also spawned a number of other business communications technologies, including *intranets, extranets, electronic conferencing*, and *VSAT satellite communications*.

In this map of the Internet, from The Opte Project, each line represents a connection between computers or other network devices.

Intranets Many companies have extended Internet technology by maintaining internal websites linked throughout the firm. These private networks, or **intranets**, are accessible only to employees (and others who may be granted access) and may contain confidential information on benefits programs, a learning library, production management tools, or product design resources. The Ford Motor Company's intranet is accessible to 200,000 people daily at workstations in Asia, Europe, and the United States. In addition to Ford employees, the intranet is accessible to Ford dealers and suppliers around the world. Sharing information on engineering, distribution, and marketing has reduced the lead time for getting new models into production and has shortened customer delivery times.[12]

Intranet *organization's private network of internally linked websites accessible only to employees*

Extranets **Extranets** allow outsiders limited access to a firm's internal information network. The most common application allows buyers to enter a system to see which products are available for sale and delivery, thus providing convenient product availability information. Industrial suppliers are often linked into customers' information networks so that they can see planned production schedules and prepare supplies for customers' upcoming operations. The extranet at Chaparral Steel Company, for example, lets customers shop electronically through its storage yards and gives them electronic access to Chaparral's planned inventory of industrial steel products. Service industries, too, allow customers access to supplies of available services. For example, tour providers such as Tauck, Globus, and Viking River Cruises rely on major airlines such as Delta to provide flights for tour customers. Tour companies, by connecting into Delta's future flight schedules, reserve blocks of flight seats to accommodate tourists.

Extranet *system that allows outsiders limited access to a firm's internal information network*

Electronic Conferencing **Electronic conferencing** allows groups of people to communicate simultaneously from various locations via e-mail, phone, or video, thereby eliminating travel time and providing immediate contact. One form, called *data conferencing*, allows people in remote locations to work simultaneously on one document. *Video conferencing* allows participants to see one another on video screens while the conference is in progress. For example, Lockheed Martin's Joint Strike Fighter project, discussed previously, uses Internet collaboration systems with both voice and

Electronic Conferencing *IT that allows groups of people to communicate simultaneously from various locations via e-mail, phone, or video*

video capabilities. Although separated by oceans, partners can communicate as if they were in the same room for redesigning components and production schedules. Electronic conferencing is attractive to many businesses because it eliminates travel and saves money.

VSAT Satellite Communications Another Internet technology businesses use to communicate is **VSAT satellite communications.** VSAT (short for *very small aperture terminal*) systems have a transmitter-receiver (*transceiver*) that sits outdoors with a direct line of sight to a satellite. The hub, a ground-station computer at the company's headquarters, sends signals to and receives signals from the satellite, exchanging voice, video, and data transmissions. An advantage of VSAT is privacy. A company that operates its own VSAT system has total control over communications among its facilities, no matter their location, without dependence on other companies. A firm might use VSAT to exchange sales and inventory information, advertising messages, and visual presentations between headquarters and store managers at remote sites. For example, stores in Minneapolis, London, and Boston might communicate with headquarters in New York, sending and receiving information via a satellite, as shown in Figure 14.2.

Networks: System Architecture

A **computer network** is a group of two or more computers linked together, either hardwired or wirelessly, to share data or resources, such as a printer. The most common type of network used in businesses is a **client-server network**. In client-server networks, *clients* are usually the laptop or desktop computers through

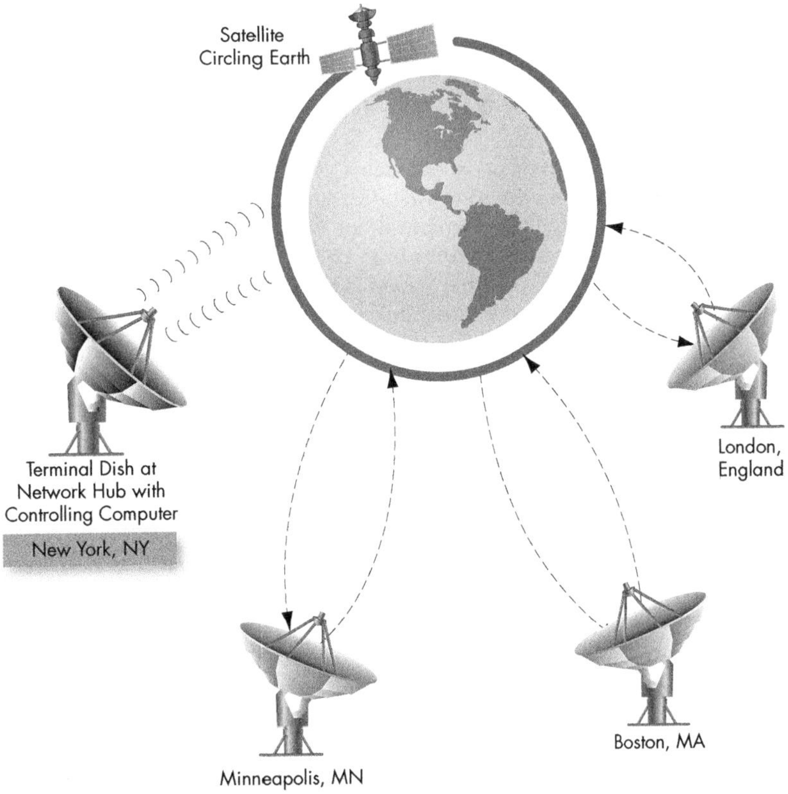

VSAT Satellite Communications *network of geographically dispersed transmitter receivers (transceivers) that send signals to and receive signals from a satellite, exchanging voice, video, and data transmissions*

Computer Network *group of two or more computers linked together by some form of cabling or by wireless technology to share data or resources, such as a printer*

Client-Server Network *common business network in which clients make requests for information or resources and servers provide the services*

FIGURE 14.2 A VSAT Satellite Communication Network

which users make requests for information or resources. *Servers* are the computers that provide the services shared by users. In big organizations, servers are usually assigned a specific task. For example, in a local university or college network, an *application server* stores the word-processing, spreadsheet, and other programs used by all computers connected to the network. A *print server* controls the printers, stores printing requests from client computers, and routes jobs as the printers become available. An *e-mail server* handles all incoming and outgoing e-mail. With a client-server system, users can share resources and Internet connections—and avoid costly duplication.

Cloud computing modifies traditional networks by adding an externally located component—the "cloud"—that replaces the functions previously performed by application servers. With a cloud, information resources are retrieved via the Internet from a remote storage service, instead of relying on network-connected user-shared servers for storing data and software packages in client-server systems. Data and software resources are accessible through Internet-based devices, including laptops, desktops, tablets, mobile phones, and other devices with access to the Web. The cloud enhances user flexibility, especially for employees working remotely because users can access e-mails and data files from any online location, rather than from one particular location.

Amazon's Simple Storage Service (S3) is an example of a *public* cloud that rents Internet storage space where users can store any amount of data and retrieve it at anytime from anywhere on the Web. S3 services have become cost savers for companies by eliminating the need for buying, installing, and maintaining in-house server computers, many of which have excessive unused storage capacity "just in case it's needed in the future." S3 allows you to store and manage your application data, search files online, upgrade software quickly, and then download and share data. In contrast with public clouds, *private* cloud services such as JustCloud and ZipCloud provide an added layer of security by surrounding the user-company's storage with a firewall to ensure against intrusion. Private clouds provide added flexibility for creating customized data storage, automated data integration, and integrated software applications to better meet users' needs. Networks can be classified according to geographic scope and means of connection (either wired or wireless).

Wide Area Networks (WANs)
Computers that are linked over long distances—statewide or even nationwide—through long-distance telephone wires, microwave signals, or satellite communications make up what are called **wide area networks (WANs)**. Firms can lease lines from communications vendors or maintain private WANs. Walmart, for example, depends heavily on a private satellite network that links thousands of U.S. and international retail stores to its Bentonville, Arkansas, headquarters.

Wide Area Network (WAN) *computers that are linked over long distances through telephone lines, microwave signals, or satellite communications*

Local Area Networks (LANs)
In **local area networks (LANs)**, computers are linked in a smaller area such as an office or a building, using telephone wires, fiber-optic, or coaxial cables. For example, a LAN unites hundreds of operators who enter call-in orders at TV's Home Shopping Network facility. The arrangement requires only one computer system with one database and one software system.

Local Area Network (LAN) *computers that are linked in a small area, such as all of a firm's computers within a single building*

Wireless Networks
Wireless networks use airborne electronic signals to link network computers and devices. Like wired networks, wireless networks can reach across long distances or exist within a single building or small area. For example, smartphone systems allow users to send and receive transmissions on the **wireless wide area networks (WWANs)** of hundreds of service providers service providers—such as Cellular One (United States), T-Mobile (United Kingdom and United States), and Vodafone Italia (Italy)—in more than 90 countries throughout the world. A *firewall* provides privacy protection. We'll discuss firewalls in more detail later in the chapter.

Wireless Wide Area Network (WWAN) *network that uses airborne electronic signals instead of wires to link computers and electronic devices over long distances*

Wi-Fi You probably use—or have at least heard of "hotspots"—millions of locations worldwide, such as coffee shops, hotels, airports, and cities, that provide wireless Internet connections for people on the go. Each hotspot, or **Wi-Fi** (a play on the audio recording term *Hi-Fi*) access point, uses its own small network, called a **wireless local area network (wireless LAN or WLAN)**. Although wireless service is free at some hotspots, others charge a fee—a daily or hourly rate—for the convenience of Wi-Fi service.

The benefit of Wi-Fi is that its millions of users are not tethered to a wire for accessing the Internet. Employees can wait for a delayed plane in the airport and still be connected to the Internet through their wireless-enabled laptops or other devices. However, as with every technology, Wi-Fi has limitations, including a short range of distance. This means that your laptop's Internet connection can be severed if you move farther than about 300 feet from the hotspot. In addition, thick walls, construction beams, and other obstacles can interfere with the signals sent out by the network. So, although a city may have hundreds of hotspots, your laptop must remain near one to stay connected. *WiMAX* (*Worldwide Interoperability for Microwave Access*), the next step in wireless advancements, improves this distance limitation with its wireless range of up to 30 miles.

Proposing a bolder approach for the future, the U.S. Federal Communications Commission in 2013 announced a proposed multiyear project for nationwide **"super Wi-Fi" networks** to be developed by the federal government. More powerful than today's networks, the super Wi-Fi would have farther reach, stretching across major metropolitan areas and covering much of the rural countryside as well. Super Wi-Fi's stronger signals will flow more freely, without obstruction, through concrete walls, steel beams, forests, and hills. The proposal would enable users to surf the Internet and make mobile phone calls without paying a monthly cell phone bill or Internet bill.[13] Scientists have also encouraged the government to use the bandwidth from old television frequencies to support super Wi-Fi.

Airlines, too, are expanding Wi-Fi service beyond just domestic flights by providing satellite-based Internet service on long-haul international flights. Japan Airlines offers Wi-Fi on routes between New York and Tokyo, in addition to flights between Tokyo and Los Angeles, Chicago, and Jakarta, Indonesia. Other airlines gearing up for Wi-Fi on long-haul flights include Air France, Delta, and United. Meanwhile, Qantas—the Australian airline—discontinued its trial program because of passenger disinterest in international Wi-Fi service.

Hardware and Software

Any computer network or system needs **hardware**, the physical components, such as keyboards, monitors, system units, and printers. In addition to the laptops and desktop computers, *handheld computers* and mobile devices are also used often in businesses. For example, Target employees roam the store aisles using handheld devices to identify, count, and order items; track deliveries; and update backup stock at distribution centers to keep store shelves replenished with merchandise.

The other essential in any computer system is **software**: programs that tell the computer how to function. Software includes *system software*, such as Microsoft Windows 8 for PCs, which tells the computer's hardware how to interact with the software, what resources to use, and how to use them. It also includes *application software* (apps) such as Microsoft Live Messenger and Photo Gallery, which are programs that meet the needs of specific users. Some application programs are used to address such common, long-standing needs as database management and inventory control, whereas others have been developed for a variety of specialized tasks ranging from mapping the oceans' depths to analyzing the anatomical structure of the human body. For example, IBM's Visualization Data Explorer software uses data from field samples to model the underground structure of an oil field. The imagery in the photo on the previous page, for example, provides engineers with better information on oil location and reduces the risk of their hitting less productive holes.

Wi-Fi *technology using a wireless local area network*

Wireless Local Area Network (Wireless LAN or WLAN) *local area network with wireless access points for PC users*

"Super Wi-Fi" Network *a powerful Wi-Fi network with extensive reach and strong signals that flow freely through physical objects such as walls*

Hardware *physical components of a computer network, such as keyboards, monitors, system units, and printers*

Software *programs that tell the computer how to function, what resources to use, how to use them, and application programs for specific activities*

entrepreneurship and new ventures

Speaking Loud and Clear: A New Voice Technology

IT users for years have sought a natural-sounding voice interface to enhance IT systems with vocal output, beyond traditional print or visual output. Vocal technologies, however, were less than effective until 2005, when Matthew Aylett and Nick Wright formed CereProc (short for Cerebral Processing) in Edinburgh, Scotland.[14] From the outset, the firm has been dedicated to creating better synthetic voices with character and emotion that stimulate listeners with natural-sounding messages. Before CereProc, these lofty goals were prohibitive. Speech experts couldn't create text-to-voice software that sounds realistically conversational, varying tone-of-voice and providing various vocal inflections for different situations. Previous software couldn't adapt incoming text (from word processing or from text messages) into natural voice formats. To attack these challenges, CereProc brought together a team of leading speech experts. It also partnered with leading universities and research programs in speech science technology and in developing new applications and markets for voice output.

The company's main product is CereVoice, an advanced text-to-voice technology available on mobile devices, PCs, servers, and headsets, and that has applications in most any company's products for better synthetic voices. Any computer's existing voice system can be replaced with more natural-sounding speech in a choice of accents, including Southern British English, Scottish, and American, that can be sampled with live voice demos at the firm's website.[15] Potential applications are endless—kitchen appliances, alarm systems, traffic controllers, automobile appliances, radio broadcasting, telephone messaging, and movies, to name a few. Although consumers may not see the CereVoice label, they will be hearing its various voices often in their everyday lives.

CereProc's Voice Creation service can create a synthesized imitation of a person's voice, including its tones and inflections. That's how noted film critic, the late Roger Ebert, got his voice back, four years after losing the ability to speak following cancer-related surgery. CereProc's voice engineers used recordings of Ebert's voice from 40 years of past television broadcasts, capturing individual sounds and identifying various voice characteristics. With meticulous care, specialists

C.M. Wiggins/AB5 WENN Photos/Newscom

then pieced them back together into software that mimicked the Pulitzer-Prize–winner's earlier voice. Ebert typed his comments into a computer that, in turn, converted the text into words that were spoken in his voice. This first-of-its-kind application made a memorable public appearance on the *Oprah* show, as Roger enthusiastically demonstrated his voice coming from the computer.[16] Beyond its technical success, this project vividly displays a compassionate side in CereProc's business.

While CereProc has clearly established a niche in the market, many other companies are working on similar technology. Since the introduction of Siri, Apple has used technology supplied by Nuance Communications for voice recognition. However, realizing that voice recognition has gone from being a gimmick to an essential technology, Apple is assembling an in-house team, headquartered in Cambridge, Massachusetts, to develop enhanced capabilities in this area. In June 2015, Apple announced that Siri now outperformed Google Now and Microsoft Cortana, with just a 5 percent error rate. Compare this to the 8 percent error rate proudly touted by Google just weeks earlier. Clearly, we are seeing that the future is now; voice recognition and voice creation have entered the mainstream of IT capabilities.[17]

Finally, *groupware*, software that connects group members for e-mail distribution, electronic meetings, message storing, appointments and schedules, and group writing, allows people to collaborate from their own desktop PCs, even if they're remotely located. It is especially useful when people work together regularly and rely heavily on information sharing. Groupware systems include IBM Lotus software and Novell GroupWise.

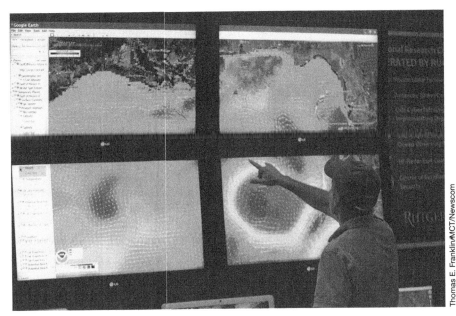

Thomas E. Franklin/MCT/Newscom

3-D computer modeling software gives engineers a better idea of where oil might be located.

Information Systems: Harnessing The Competitive Power of It

Describe

the role of information systems, the different types of information systems, and how businesses use such systems.

Information System (IS) *system that uses IT resources to convert data into information and to collect, process, and transmit that information for use in decision making*

Data *raw facts and figures that, by themselves, may not have much meaning*

Information *meaningful, useful interpretation of data*

Information Systems Managers *managers who are responsible for the systems used for gathering, organizing, and distributing information*

Business today relies on information management in ways that no one could foresee a decade ago. Managers now treat IT as a basic organizational resource for conducting daily business. At major firms, every activity—designing services, ensuring product delivery and cash flow, and evaluating personnel—is linked to *information systems*. An **information system (IS)** uses IT resources that enable managers to take **data**, raw facts and figures that, by themselves, may not have much meaning, and turn those data into **information**, the meaningful, useful interpretation of data. Information systems also enable managers to collect, process, and transmit that information for use in decision making.

Walmart is well known for its strategic use of information systems. The nerve center for company operations is a centralized IS in Bentonville, Arkansas. The IS drives costs down and raises efficiency because the same methods and systems are applied for all 11,000-plus stores in 27 countries. Data on the billions of sales transactions—time, date, and place—flow to Bentonville. The IS tracks millions of stock-keeping units (SKUs) weekly, enforces uniform reordering and delivery procedures on its more than 100,000 suppliers, including 20,000 in China, and regulates the flow of merchandise through its distribution centers and stores.

Beyond the firm's daily operations, information systems are also crucial in planning. Managers routinely use the IS to decide on products and markets for the next 5 to 10 years. The company's vast database enables marketing managers to analyze customer demographics for better marketing, and it is also used for financial planning, materials handling, and electronic funds transfers with suppliers and customers.

Walmart, like most businesses, regards its information as a private resource, an asset that's planned, developed, and protected. Therefore, it's not surprising that they have **information systems managers** who are responsible for the systems used for gathering, organizing, and distributing information, just as they have production, marketing, and finance managers. These managers use many of the IT resources we discussed previously—the Internet, communications technologies, networks, hardware, and software—to sift through information and apply it to their jobs.

Leveraging Information Resources: Data Warehousing and Data Mining

Almost everything you do leaves a trail of information about you. Your preferences in movie rentals, television viewing, Internet sites, and groceries; the destinations of your phone calls, your credit card charges, your financial status; personal information about age, gender, marital status, and even your health are just a few of the items about each of us that are stored in scattered databases. The behavior patterns of millions of users can be traced by analyzing files of information gathered over time from their Internet usage and in-store purchases.

The collection, storage, and retrieval of such data in electronic files is called **data warehousing**. For managers, the data warehouse can be a gold mine of information about their business. Indeed, Kroger Co., the Ohio-based grocery chain, collects data on customer shopping habits to find ways to gain greater customer loyalty. As part owner of a data-mining firm, Kroger accumulates information from its shopper cards, analyzes the data to uncover shopping patterns, and sends money-saving coupons to regular customers for the specific products they usually buy. Kroger's precision targeting pays off, especially in a sluggish economy. With a rate of coupon usage up to as much as 50 times the industry average, it's a money saver for Kroger customers and boosts the company's sales, too.[18] To help put this in context, coupons from Kroger's quarterly mailers, uniquely customized for each customer, have a 70 percent redemption rate within six weeks of delivery.

Data Warehousing *the collection, storage, and retrieval of data in electronic files*

Data Mining After collecting information, managers use **data mining**, the application of statistics and electronic technologies for searching, sifting, and reorganizing pools of data to uncover useful information. Data mining helps managers plan for new products, set prices, and identify trends and shopping patterns. By analyzing what consumers actually do, businesses can determine what subsequent purchases they are likely to make and then send them tailor-made ads. The *Washington Post*, for example, uses data-mining software to analyze census data and target households likely to respond to sales efforts.[19]

Data Mining *the application of electronic technologies for searching, sifting, and reorganizing pools of data to uncover useful information*

Frank van Delft/Cultura/Getty Images

Retailers such as Wal-Mart and Sam's Club rely on data warehousing and mining to keep shelves stocked with in-demand merchandise.

managing in turbulent times

Better Care, Lower Costs

Imagine that you are an emergency room doctor and a patient has just come in complaining of chest pains. You know that this could be serious—a heart attack, stroke, or aortic dissection—or perhaps something less dire, such as acid reflux or bruised or broken ribs. You have only minutes to make a quick assessment and connect the patient with the right resources. In addition to the physical exam, the patient's electronic medical record may provide key information to make a quick and accurate diagnosis and treatment plan. Perhaps the patient has had a prior admission for heart-related conditions, or they have been prescribed medication for high blood pressure. This information might point the ER team in the direction of quickly ordering tests to identify if a heart attack or other heart-related condition is occurring. On the other hand, if the patient has recently been in a car accident, physicians may try to rule out broken ribs before ordering expensive, and possibly invasive, heart-related testing. "The opportunity to integrate the data coming out of the electronic medical record into healthcare delivery is very exciting," according to Allen Kamer, Chief Commercial Officer for Analytics at Optum, a leader in healthcare IT services. On their website, they state their mission as follows: "We help deliver better outcomes for hospitals, doctors, pharmacies, health plans, governments, employers, and the millions of lives they touch."

The move to electronic health records is relatively recent, with many doctors and hospitals just moving to an IT solution in the past five years. As more data is collected into electronic health records, a wealth of predictive analytics is beginning to

Keith Brofsky/Getty Images

emerge. In the past, much of established practice came out of clinical trials with small samples of patients. However, with larger sample sizes, essentially 100 percent of all patients, health professionals can make better decisions, not only when the patient becomes ill but also before this ever happens. Data from the healthcare record allows insurance companies to proactively advise their members about their health risks and provide recommendations about lifestyle changes and preventive testing and procedures. These interventions have resulted in reduced hospital admissions for some of the most serious and expensive conditions, such as COPD and heart disease. Clearly, the use of healthcare analytics is a win-win—better patient care at lower costs.[20]

Information Linkages with Suppliers The top priority for Walmart's IS—improving in-stock reliability—requires integration of Walmart and suppliers' activities with store sales. That's why Procter & Gamble (P&G), Johnson & Johnson, and other suppliers connect into Walmart's information system to observe up-to-the-minute sales data on individual items, by store. They can use the system's computer-based tools—spreadsheets, sales forecasting, and weather information—to forecast sales demand and plan delivery schedules. Coordinated planning avoids excessive inventories, speeds up deliveries, and holds down costs throughout the supply chain while keeping shelves stocked for retail customers.

Types of Information Systems

Employees have a variety of responsibilities and decision-making needs, and a firm's IS may actually be a set of several systems that share information while serving different levels of the organization, different departments, or different operations. Because they work on different kinds of problems, managers and their employees have access to the specialized information systems that satisfy their different information needs.

In addition to different types of users, each business *function*—marketing, human resources, accounting, production, or finance—has special information needs, as do groups working on major projects. Each user group and department, therefore, may need a special IS.

DM7/Shutterstock

The 3-D computer model of this dinosaur is constructed from
digital scans of fossilized tissue.

Information Systems for Knowledge Workers

As we discussed in Chapter 10, *knowledge workers* are employees for whom information and knowledge are the raw materials of their work, such as engineers, scientists, and IT specialists who rely on IT to design new products or create new processes. These workers require **knowledge information systems**, which provide resources to create, store, use, and transmit new knowledge for useful applications—for instance, databases to organize and retrieve information, and computational power for data analysis.

Specialized support systems have also increased the productivity of knowledge workers. **Computer-aided design (CAD)** helps knowledge workers—and now ordinary people, too, as we saw with consumers designing customized products earlier in this chapter—design products ranging from cell phones to jewelry to auto parts by simulating them and displaying them in 3D graphics. In a more advanced version, known as *rapid prototyping*, the CAD system electronically transfers instructions to a computer-controlled machine that quickly builds a prototype—a physical model—of the newly designed product, such as a toy, an artificial limb for the disabled, or a solar panel. The older method—making handcrafted prototypes from wood, plastic, or clay—is replaced with faster, cheaper prototyping.

CAD is helping archaeological scientists uncover secrets hidden in fossils using 3D computer models of skeletons, organs, and tissues constructed with digital data from computed tomography (CT) scans of dinosaur fossils. From these models, scientists have learned, for example, that the giant apatosaurus's neck curved downward, instead of high in the air as once thought. By seeing how the animals' bones fit together with cartilage, ligaments, and vertebrae, scientists are discovering more about how these prehistoric creatures interacted with their environment.[21]

In a direct offshoot of computer-aided design, **computer-aided manufacturing (CAM)** uses computers to design and control the equipment needed in a manufacturing process. For example, CAM systems can produce digital instructions to control all the machines and robots on a production line, say, as an example, in making jewelry boxes. CAM-guided machines cut the materials, move them through the stages of production, and then assemble each stylish box without human physical involvement in production activities. CAD and CAM coupled together (CAD/CAM) are useful to engineers in a manufacturing environment for designing and testing new products and then designing the machines and tools to manufacture the new product.

Knowledge Information System *information system that supports knowledge workers by providing resources to create, store, use, and transmit new knowledge for useful applications*

Computer-Aided Design (CAD) *IS with software that helps knowledge workers design products by simulating them and displaying them in three-dimensional graphics*

Computer-Aided Manufacturing (CAM) *IS that uses computers to design and control equipment in a manufacturing process*

Information Systems for Managers Each manager's information activities and IS needs vary according to his or her functional area (accounting or human resources and so forth) and management level. The following are some popular information systems used by managers for different purposes.

Management Information System (MIS) *computer system that supports managers by providing information—reports, schedules, plans, and budgets—that can be used for making decisions*

MANAGEMENT INFORMATION SYSTEMS Management information systems (MIS) support managers by providing reports, schedules, plans, and budgets that can then be used for making both short- and long-term decisions. For example, at Walsworth Publishing Company, managers rely on detailed information—current customer orders, staffing schedules, employee attendance, production schedules, equipment status, and materials availability—for moment-to-moment decisions during the day. They require similar information to plan such midrange activities as personnel training, materials movements, and cash flows. They also need to anticipate the status of the jobs and projects assigned to their departments. Many MIS—cash flow, sales, production scheduling, and shipping—are indispensable for helping managers complete these tasks.

For longer-range decisions involving business strategy, Walsworth managers need information to analyze trends in the publishing industry and overall company performance. They need both external and internal information, current and future, to compare current performance data to data from previous years and to analyze consumer trends and economic forecasts.

Decision Support System (DSS) *interactive system that creates virtual business models for a particular kind of decision and tests them with different data to see how they respond*

DECISION SUPPORT SYSTEMS Managers who face a particular kind of decision repeatedly can get assistance from **decision support systems (DSS)**, interactive systems that create virtual business models and test them with different data to see how they respond. When faced with decisions on plant capacity, for example, Walsworth managers can use a capacity DSS. The manager inputs data on anticipated sales, working capital, and customer-delivery requirements. The data flow into the DSS processor, which then simulates the plant's performance under the proposed data conditions. A proposal to increase facility capacity by, say, 10 percent could be simulated to find costs of operation, percent of customer order fulfillments, and other performance measures that would result with the expanded capacity. After experimenting with various data conditions, the DSS makes recommendations on the best levels of plant capacity—those that result in best performance—for each future time period.

OBJECTIVE 14-4
Identify
the threats and risks information technology poses on businesses.

IT Risks and Threats

As with other technologies throughout history, IT continues to attract abusers set on doing mischief, with severity ranging from mere nuisance to outright destruction. Eager IT users everywhere are finding that even social networking and cell phones have a "dark side"—privacy invasion. Facebook postings of personal information about users have been intercepted and misused by intruders. Beacon, the former data-gathering service, caused a public uproar when it published peoples' online purchases publicly on their Facebook newsfeeds. And with cellular technology, some features of Bluetooth connections allow savvy intruders to read a victim's text messages, listen in on live conversations, and even view unwary users' photos.[22]

Businesses, too, are troubled with IT's dark side. Hackers break into computers, stealing personal information and company secrets, and launch attacks on other computers. Meanwhile, the ease of information sharing on the Internet has proven costly for companies who are having an increasingly difficult time protecting their intellectual property, and viruses that crash computers have cost companies many billions annually. In this section, we'll look at these and other IT risks. In the next section, we'll discuss ways in which businesses are protecting themselves from these risks.

Hackers

The term *breaking and entering* no longer refers merely to physical intrusion. Today, it applies to IT intrusions as well. **Hackers** are cybercriminals who gain unauthorized access to a computer or network, either to steal information, money, or property or to tamper with data. Twitter reported that hackers may have intercepted information—names, passwords, e-mail addresses—of some 250,000 of the social media's users. With different motives than the Twitter intruders, Chinese-based hackers, including the Chinese government, are suspected of continuing cyber-attacks into the computer systems of several newspapers, including *The New York Times, The Washington Post,* and *The Wall Street Journal.* China-based intruders have been accused of a multiyear campaign to illegally gain corporate secrets and confidential information that can be used to frighten critics from writing unfavorable articles, accusations that the Chinese government has denied.[23]

Another common hacker activity is to launch *denial of service (DoS) attacks.* DoS attacks flood networks or websites with bogus requests for information and resources, thereby overloading and shutting the networks or websites down, preventing legitimate users from accessing them.

Wireless mooching is a profitable industry for cybercriminals. In just five minutes, a *St. Petersburg Times* (Florida) reporter using a laptop found six unprotected wireless networks that were wide open to outside users.[24] Once inside an unsecured wireless network, hackers can use it to conduct illegal business, such as child pornography or money laundering. When police officers try to track down these criminals, they're long gone, leaving the innocent but naïve network host potentially exposed to criminal prosecution.

As we saw in this chapter's opening case, hackers, such as the Night Dragon, often break into company networks to steal company or trade secrets. But it's not just hackers who are doing the stealing. Because the chances of getting caught seem slim, home users continue, illegally, to download unpaid-for movies, music, and other resources from file-swapping networks. A recent study shows that sound piracy costs the United States $12.5 billion and 71,060 jobs annually. However, these losses also showcase what can happen to businesses that fail to adapt to changes in technology. Until recent years, the recording industry was reluctant to embrace the Internet as a path for distribution, preferring to prosecute pirates rather than offer them legal online alternatives. On the other hand, Apple has benefitted immensely from its online (download) distribution models, enabling it to become the world's most popular music vendor.[25]

Hacker *cybercriminal who gains unauthorized access to a computer or network, either to steal information, money, or property or to tamper with data*

Identity Theft

Once inside a computer network, hackers are able to commit **identity theft**, the unauthorized stealing of personal information (such as Social Security number and address) to get loans, credit cards, or other monetary benefits by impersonating the victim. Recent studies suggest that as many as 16.6 million victims fall prey to identify theft each year; identity theft is among the fastest-growing crimes in the United States.

Clever crooks get information on unsuspecting victims by digging in trash, stealing mail, or using *phishing* or *pharming* schemes to lure Internet users to bogus websites. For instance, a cybercriminal might send a PayPal user an e-mail notifying him or her of a billing problem with his or her account. When the customer clicks on the PayPal Billing Center link, he or she is transferred to a spoofed (falsified) Web page, modeled after PayPal's. The customer then submits the requested information—credit card number, Social Security number, and PIN—into the hands of the thief. The accounts are soon empty.

Identity Theft *unauthorized use of personal information (such as Social Security number and address) to get loans, credit cards, or other monetary benefits by impersonating the victim*

Intellectual Property Theft

Nearly every company faces the dilemma of protecting product plans, new inventions, industrial processes, and other **intellectual property**, something produced by the intellect or mind that has commercial value. Its ownership and right to its use

Intellectual Property *something produced by the intellect or mind that has commercial value*

may be protected by patent, copyright, trademark, and other means. But crooks may be able to steal information about intellectual property and create unauthorized duplications.

Computer Viruses, Worms, and Trojan Horses

Another IT risk facing businesses is rogue programmers who disrupt IT operations by contaminating and destroying software, hardware, or data files. *Viruses, worms, and Trojan horses* are three kinds of malicious programs that, once installed, can shut down any computer system. A *computer virus* exists in a file that attaches itself to a program and migrates from computer to computer as a shared program or as an e-mail attachment. It does not infect the system unless the user opens the contaminated file, and users typically are unaware they are spreading the virus by file sharing. It can, for example, quickly copy itself over and over again, using up all available memory and effectively shutting down the computer.

Worms are a particular kind of virus that travel from computer to computer within networked computer systems, without your needing to open any software to spread the contaminated file. In a matter of days, the notorious Blaster worm infected some 400,000 computer networks, destroying files and even allowing outsiders to take over computers remotely. The worm replicates itself rapidly, sending out thousands of copies to other computers in the network. Traveling through Internet connections and e-mail address books in the network's computers, it absorbs system memory and shuts down network servers, Web servers, and individual computers.

Unlike viruses, a *Trojan horse* does not replicate itself. Instead, it most often comes into the computer, at your request, masquerading as a harmless, legitimate software product or data file. Once installed, the damage begins. For instance, it may simply redesign desktop icons or, more maliciously, delete files and destroy information.

Spyware

Spyware *program unknowingly downloaded by users that monitors their computer activities, gathering e-mail addresses, credit card numbers, and other information that it transmits to someone outside the host system*

As if forced intrusion isn't bad enough, Internet users unwittingly invite spies—masquerading as a friendly file available as a giveaway or shared among individual users on their PCs. This so-called **spyware** is downloaded by users who are lured by "free" software. Once installed, it "crawls" around to monitor the host's computer activities, gathering e-mail addresses, credit card numbers, passwords, and other inside information that it transmits back to someone outside the host system. Spyware authors assemble incoming stolen information to create their own "intellectual property" that they then sell to other parties to use for marketing and advertising purposes or for identity theft.[26]

Spam

Spam *junk e-mail sent to a mailing list or a newsgroup*

Spam, junk e-mail sent to a mailing list or a newsgroup (an online discussion group), is a greater nuisance than postal junk mail because the Internet is open to the public, e-mail costs are negligible, and massive mailing lists are accessible through file sharing or by theft. Spam operators send unwanted messages ranging from explicit pornography to hate mail to advertisements, and even destructive computer viruses. In addition to wasting users' time, spam also consumes a network's bandwidth, thereby reducing the amount of data that can be transmitted in a fixed amount of time for useful purposes. U.S. industry experts estimate spam's annual damage in lost time and productivity at between $20 and $50 billion in the United States alone and that it could be as high as $575 billion globally.[27]

Although spammers sometimes gain significant incomes, they also risk anti-spanning prosecution that can be extremely costly. The judge in a lawsuit against Sanford Wallace, who proclaimed himself the "Spam King," issued a judgment for

$711 million against Wallace, one of the largest fines ever in an anti-spamming case. He was accused of sending 27 million spam mailings to Facebook, using phishing to get passwords from thousands of Facebook users, and then entering their accounts to post fraudulent information. He now faces criminal charges of electronic mail fraud, damage to protected computers, and criminal contempt.[28]

IT Protection Measures

OBJECTIVE 14-5
Describe
the ways in which businesses protect themselves from the threats and risks information technology poses.

Security measures against intrusion and viruses are a constant challenge. Most systems guard against unauthorized access by requiring users to have protected passwords. Other measures include firewalls, special software, and encryption.

Preventing Unauthorized Access: Firewalls

Firewalls are security systems with special software or hardware devices designed to keep computers safe from hackers. A firewall is located where two networks—for example, the Internet and a company's internal network—meet. It contains two components for filtering incoming data:

Firewall *security system with special software or hardware devices designed to keep computers safe from hackers*

- The company's *security policy*—Access rules that identify every type of data that the company doesn't want to pass through the firewall

- A *router*—A table of available routes or paths; a "traffic switch" that determines which route or path on the network to send each piece of data after it is tested against the security policy

Only the information that meets the conditions of the user's security policy is routed through the firewall and permitted to flow between the two networks. Data that fail the access test are blocked and cannot flow between the two networks.

Preventing Identity Theft

Although foolproof prevention is impossible, steps can be taken to avoid being victimized. A visit to the Identity Theft Resource Center (www.idtheftcenter.org) is a valuable first step to get information on everything from scam alerts to victim issues to legislation such as the Fair and Accurate Credit Transactions Act (FACTA). FACTA strengthens identity-theft protections by specifying how organizations must destroy information instead of dropping it in a dumpster. When a company disposes of documents that contain credit or Social Security information, they must be shredded, pulverized, or burned, and all electronic records (in computers and databases) must be permanently removed to keep them out of the hands of intruders.[29]

Preventing Infectious Intrusions: Anti-Virus Software

Combating viruses, worms, Trojan horses, and any other infectious software (collectively known as *malware*) has become a major industry for systems designers and software developers. Installation of any of hundreds of **anti-virus software** products protects systems by searching incoming e-mail and data files for "signatures" of known viruses and virus-like characteristics. Contaminated files are discarded or placed in quarantine for safekeeping. Many viruses take advantage of weaknesses in operating systems, such as Microsoft Windows, to spread and propagate. Network administrators must make sure that the computers on their systems are using the most up-to-date operating system that includes the latest security protection.

Anti-Virus Software *product that protects systems by searching incoming e-mails and data files for "signatures" of known viruses and virus-like characteristics*

Protecting Electronic Communications: Encryption Software

Security for electronic communications is another concern for businesses. Unprotected e-mail can be intercepted, diverted to unintended computers, and opened, revealing the contents to intruders. Protective software is available to guard against those intrusions, adding a layer of security by encoding e-mails so that only intended recipients can open them. An **encryption system** works by scrambling an e-mail message so that it looks like garbled nonsense to anyone who doesn't possess the "key," another part of the software that decodes encrypted e-mails.

Encryption System software that assigns an e-mail message to a unique code number (digital fingerprint) for each computer so only that computer, not others, can open and read the message

Avoiding Spam and Spyware

To help their employees avoid privacy invasion and to improve productivity, businesses often install anti-spyware and spam-filtering software on their systems. Although dozens of anti-spyware products provide protection—software such as Webroot Spy Sweeper and Microsoft Windows Defender—they can be continually updated to keep pace with new spyware techniques.

finding a better way

The Emerging Market for Cyber Insurance

If you are lucky enough to own a car, you probably have automobile insurance. Most states require drivers to be insured at a minimum level. In the event of an accident, automobile insurance may cover the direct costs to the vehicles involved, as well as medical bills and lost wages, in some cases. As you may read about in Appendix 1, an insurance policy is a formal agreement to pay the policyholder a specified amount in the event of certain losses. Insurance is available for almost any type of loss. Increasingly, businesses are turning to cyber insurance to protect themselves against losses associated with data breaches.

In recent years, hardly a month goes by without a high-profile data breach. Whether it's Target, T.J. Maxx, Heartland, or the U.S. government, data breaches result in millions of dollars in expenses. On top of the enormous damage to the organization's reputation, there are serious impacts on their bottom line as expenses pile up. In one of the more famous data breaches in recent years, Sony Pictures was hacked in November 2014. Hackers gained access to virtually everything stored on the company's network, including internal e-mails, personal information about employees, and unreleased movies. However, in spite of all the bad press, there was a silver lining to the cloud—Sony had purchased cyber insurance, which is expected to offset much of the cost, according to a statement by Sony CEO Michael Lynton.

Cyber insurance can cover a wide range of costs that result from data theft, data loss, computer malfunction, and malware. Companies can recover a wide range of costs, including fines and lost income, as well as public relations expenses associated with crisis management. While cyber insurance is just a small part of the general business insurance market, accounting for just 2 to 4 percent, the Sony breach has taught

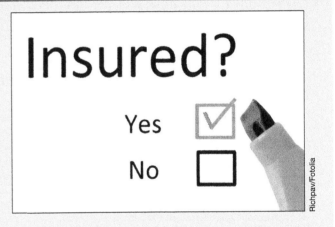

businesses around the globe that it is an important element of IT risk management.

There are, however, limitations. Cyber insurance cannot replace good security procedures. Although many of the costs may be reimbursed, it's very likely that the company's reputation may be damaged for some time. In addition, a data breach or loss can result in a loss in momentum on important projects because talent and energy are redirected to the immediate crisis. As with other types of insurance, it's important for IT and risk managers to look at the fine print to see exactly what is and isn't covered. Rates for cyber insurance are based on a variety of factors, but they will reflect the confidence or lack of confidence of the insurance company in the insured company's data security practices. In fact, according to Rick Dakin, CEO of Coalfire, a company specializing in security audits, companies providing cyber insurance may actually require the insured to contract for an independent security audit as a condition of insurance.[30]

The federal CAN-SPAM Act of 2003 requires the Federal Trade Commission to shield the public from falsified header information, sexually explicit e-mails that are not so labeled, Internet spoofing (using trickery to make a message appear as if it came from a trusted source), and hijacking of computers through worms or Trojan horses. Although it cannot be prevented entirely, spam is abated by many Internet service providers (ISPs) that ban the spamming of ISP subscribers. In a now-classic punishment, an ISP in Iowa was awarded $1 billion in a lawsuit against 300 spammers that jammed the ISP system with an astounding 10 million e-mails a day. Anti-spam groups, too, promote the public's awareness of known spammers. The Spamhaus Project (www.spamhaus.org), for example, maintains a list of "The 10 Worst Spammers," career spammers that are responsible for most of the world's spam traffic.

Ethical Concerns in IT

It is apparent that IT developments and usage are progressing faster than society's appreciation for the potential consequences, including new ethical concerns. Along with IT's many benefits, its usage is creating previously unanticipated problems for which solutions are needed, yet they don't exist. Ease of access to computers, mobile devices, and the Internet, together with messaging capabilities and social networking, promote widespread public exposure about people's private lives, including personal information about how they think and feel. Just how this information should be used, by whom, under what conditions, and with what restrictions, if any, are issues teeming with ethical considerations. Several real-life episodes with ethical implications are shown in Table 14.1. See if you can identify significant ethical issues among the episodes in the table.

table 14.1   Areas for Ethical Concerns in Information Technology and Its Uses

- In a now-classic case of cyberbullying, a 13-year-old girl hanged herself after being taunted by a hoax message on her MySpace page.
- Secret webcasts of other people's behavior have resulted in embarrassment and even death: A university student, leaving a final message on his Facebook page, jumped from a bridge to his death after other students covertly webcast his sexual activities with another student.
- IT is used increasingly for sending out cries for help. Many college students have posted public messages requesting physical and emotional support. Others, having read those messages, are unsure if they should respond, or not.
- Employers and employees struggle about the extent of personal use of the company's IT. Many employees admit they use social networking and personal e-mailing at work, but should they? Many companies say, "No," adding that employees should know that the company has access to all e-mails sent, received, and stored on its IT system.
- States are forming database pools, sharing information to check on suspicious prescription drug activities. Data are gathered on purchases at pharmacies, physicians' prescriptions, and police records to identify drug abuse by individuals and companies within states and are being shared across state lines.
- The Department of Homeland Security abandoned one of its major data-mining tools for combating terrorism after questions about its compliance with privacy rules. It was discovered that DHS had tested the data-mining program using information about real people, without ensuring the privacy of that information.
- To save money, IT users retrieve and share intellectual property—movies, articles, books, music, industrial information—with others, ignoring copyright, trademark, and patent protections. Written content is often taken from the Internet, inserted into the user's written work, and represented as the user's own original creation without citing its true source.
- Job seekers are being asked to answer unexpected questions by interviewers: "What is your Facebook username and password?" Some applicants are responding, "No, that's a terrible privacy invasion." Others are revealing the requested information to interviewers.

summary of learning objectives

Discuss the impacts information technology has had on the business world. (pp. 472–478)

The growth of IT—the various appliances and devices for creating, storing, exchanging, and using information in diverse modes, including visual images, voice, multimedia, and business data—has changed the very structure of business organizations. Its adoption provides new modes of communication, including portable offices using mobile messaging capabilities, resulting in the geographic separation of the workplace from headquarters for many employees. With access to the Internet, company activities may be geographically scattered but still remain coordinated through a networked system that provides better service for customers. Networks and technology are also leading to leaner companies with fewer employees and simpler structures. Because networks enable firms to maintain information linkages among employees and customers, more work and customer satisfaction can be accomplished with fewer people. IT also contributes to greater flexibility in serving customers and enables closer coordination with suppliers. Company activities may be geographically scattered but remain coordinated through a network system that provides better service for customers. Many businesses coordinate activities from one centralized location, but their deliveries flow from several remote locations, often at lower cost. IT's global reach facilitates project collaboration with remote business partners and the formation of new market relationships around the globe. Just as electronic collaboration has changed the way employees interact with each other, IT networks have created new manufacturing flexibility for mass customization, and Internet access has brought new opportunities for small businesses.

Identify the IT resources businesses have at their disposal and how these resources are used. (pp. 478–484)

The Internet and the World Wide Web serve computers with information and provide communication flows among networks around the world. For many businesses, the Internet has replaced the telephone, fax machine, and standard mail as the primary communications tool. To support internal communications, many companies maintain internal websites—*intranets*—accessible only to employees. Some firms give limited network access to outsiders via *extranets* allowing access to private information among businesses, customers, and suppliers for better planning and coordination of their activities. Electronic conferencing allows simultaneous communication globally among groups from various locations, saving travel time, time for information exchanges, and expenses. *VSAT satellite networks* provide private remote communications for voice, video, and data transmissions.

Computer networks, including wide area networks and local area networks, enable the sharing of information, hardware, software, and other resources over wired or wireless connections. *Wi-Fi* provides wireless Internet connections through laptops or other devices at "hotspots" or local access points. All computer networks or systems need hardware, the physical components such as keyboards, monitors, and printers. In addition, all systems require *software*, programs that tell the computer how to function. *Application software* includes programs to meet specific user needs, such as groupware with voice and video connections for remote collaboration.

Describe the role of information systems, the different types of information systems, and how businesses use such systems. (pp. 484–488)

An *information system (IS)* uses IT resources that enable users to create, process, and transmit information for use in decision making. An IS often includes *data warehousing*, a vast collection, storage, and retrieval system, which provides the data resources needed for creating information. The IS also includes *data mining* capabilities, the application of technologies for searching, sifting, and reorganizing data, to uncover useful information for planning new products, setting prices, and identifying trends.

The IS often is a set of several systems that share information while serving different levels of an organization, different departments, or different operations. *Knowledge information systems* support knowledge workers—engineers, scientists, and other specialists—by providing resources to create, store, use, and transmit new knowledge they use for specialty applications. Knowledge systems include *computer-aided design (CAD)*, software systems that receive engineering data and convert it into three-dimensional displays for rapid development of new products. *Computer-aided manufacturing (CAM)* uses computers to design and control the equipment needed in a manufacturing process. *Management information systems (MIS)* support managers by providing reports, schedules, plans, and budgets that can then be used for making decisions at all levels, ranging from detailed daily activities to long-range business strategies. The many uses of information systems include experimenting with *decision support systems (DSS)*, interactive systems that create business models and test them with different data to see how the models respond under diverse business conditions, to test the effectiveness of potential decisions.

OBJECTIVE 14-4

Identify the threats and risks information technology poses on businesses. (pp. 488–491)

IT has attracted abusers that do mischief, with severity ranging from mere nuisance to outright destruction, costing companies millions of dollars. Everything from Facebook postings to Bluetooth usage to private computer systems is subject to break-ins and destruction. *Hackers* break into computers, steal personal information and company secrets, tamper with data, and launch attacks on other computers. *Wireless moochers* use victims' networks for illegal activities, exposing the host to criminal prosecution. Once inside a computer network, hackers are able to commit *identity theft*, the unauthorized stealing of personal information to get loans, credit cards, or other monetary benefits by impersonating the victim. Even the ease of information sharing on the Internet poses a threat. It has proven costly for companies who are having a difficult time protecting their *intellectual property*, such as software products, movies, and music. Hackers break into company networks to steal anything of commercial value, including trade secrets, new inventions, and other valuable information that is protected by patent, copyright, or trademark. Another IT risk businesses face is system shutdown and destruction of software, hardware, or data files by *viruses, worms,* and *Trojan horses* that can shut down a computer system or otherwise disrupt IT operations by contaminating and destroying software, hardware, or data files. After invading a victim's computer, *spyware* gathers inside information and transmits it to outside spies. Masquerading as a friendly file available as a giveaway or shared among individual users on PCs and mobile devices, spyware is downloaded by unsuspecting users. Once installed, it monitors the host's electronic activities, gathers personal information, and transmits stolen information to an outside system. *Spam*, junk e-mail sent to a mailing list or news group, is costly in terms of lost time and productivity by overloading the network's capacity with massive mailings of unwanted messages.

OBJECTIVE 14-5

Describe the ways in which businesses protect themselves from the threats and risks information technology poses. (pp. 491–493)

Most systems guard against unauthorized access by requiring users to have protected passwords. In addition, many firms rely on *firewalls*, security systems with special software or hardware devices that intercept would-be intruders, so that only messages that meet the conditions of the company's security policy are permitted to flow through the network. Firms can protect against identity theft by using assistance from advisory sources, such as the Identity Theft Resource Center, and by implementing the identity-theft protection provisions of the federal FACTA rule for maintaining and destroying personal information records. To combat infectious intrusions by viruses, worms, and Trojan horses, *anti-virus software* products search incoming e-mail and data files for "signatures" of known viruses and virus-like characteristics.

Contaminated files are discarded or placed in quarantine for safekeeping. Additional intrusion protection is available by installing *anti-spyware* and *spam filtering software*. *Encryption* adds security by encoding, which is scrambling messages so they look like garbled nonsense to anyone who doesn't possess the key, so that the message can be read only by intended recipients. The federal *CAN-SPAM Act* requires the Federal Trade Commission to shield the public from falsified header information, sexually explicit e-mails that are not so labeled, Internet spoofing (using trickery to make a message appear as if it came from a trusted source), and hijacking of computers through worms or Trojan horses. Although it cannot be prevented entirely, *spam* is abated by many Internet service providers (ISPs) that ban the spamming of ISP subscribers

key terms

anti-virus software
client-server network
computer-aided design (CAD)
computer-aided manufacturing (CAM)
computer network
data
data mining
data warehousing
decision support system (DSS)
e-commerce
electronic conferencing
encryption system
extranet
firewall

hacker
hardware
hypertext transfer protocol (HTTP)
identity theft
information
information system (IS)
information systems managers
information technology (IT)
intellectual property
Internet
intranet
knowledge information system
local area network (LAN)

management information system (MIS)
mass customization
software
spam
spyware
"super Wi-Fi" network
VSAT satellite communications
wide area network (WAN)
Wi-Fi
wireless local area network (wireless LAN or WLAN)
wireless wide area network (WWAN)
World Wide Web

MyBizLab

To complete the problems with the ✪, go to EOC Discussion Questions in the MyLab.

questions & exercises

QUESTIONS FOR REVIEW

14-1. Explain how an organization can use mass customization.

✪ 14-2. What is ERP and how has the Internet and improved IT made it possible?

14-3. What use might an organization have for VSAT?

14-4. What can a Trojan horse do to a computer network?

14-5. What is the purpose of spyware and what information does it collect?

QUESTIONS FOR ANALYSIS

14-6. What does CAM do and how can an organization use this as the basis of its production processes?

✪ 14-7. How could an airline use data mining to make better business decisions?

✪ 14-8. How do your bank, employer, and e-mail provider protect your personal information from unauthorized use?

APPLICATION EXERCISES

14-9. Consider your daily activities—as a consumer, student, parent, friend, homeowner or renter, car driver, employee, and so forth—and think about the ways that you are involved with IT systems. Make a list of your recent IT encounters and then recall instances in those encounters that you revealed personal information that could be used to steal your identity. Are some encounters on your list riskier than others? Why or why not?

14-10. After reading the first section of this chapter, consider how IT has changed the business of higher education. Identify at least three functions, services, or activities that would not have been available 25 years ago. How do you think that colleges and universities will change in the future because of advances in IT?

building a business: continuing team exercise

Assignment

Meet with your team members to consider your new business venture and how it relates to the information technology topics in this chapter. Develop specific responses to the following:

14-11. In what ways do you expect IT will enable collaboration among your employees? Identify examples of occasions where IT will be useful for providing remote access between employees, and remote access between employees and company data files.

14-12. In what ways will IT be used for collaboration with external stakeholders, such as customers, suppliers, and other constituents? What types of remote interactions do you expect, and what kinds of IT equipment and installations will be needed for those interactions? Discuss how your team is going to identify the IT equipment requirements at this stage of development of your business.

14-13. At what stage of your company's development will you begin planning for its information system(s), if any?

Discuss the technical skills and information-management skills necessary for determining the kind(s) of information system(s) needed for your company's first two years of operation.

14-14. Based on your findings for Question 14-13, where will your company get the skills and resources for IS development and implementation? Have you included the anticipated costs for developing the information systems in your financial plan for year one, or will you do so? Explain why, or why not.

14-15. What measures, if any, will you take for protecting against intrusions into your company's IT system? What actions will be taken to prevent unauthorized access to information of customers, suppliers, and other external constituents? What security measures will be taken to protect non-IT information? Explain.

team exercise

NEW AGE HELP DESK

The Situation

You are a member of the technical support team for a rapidly growing start-up that provides data analysis and business consulting to private schools and daycare centers. The company began several years ago when four recent college graduates spotted an unfilled niche in the market and combined their business and technical skills to meet the need. The company quickly grew, adding more than 80 employees in just five years. While all of the employees are located in the Washington, DC, area, most of them work from home at least one day a week. Initially, there was no technical support team at the company. An informal network of experts made decisions about which computers to buy, the software they purchased, and their high-speed Internet in the office, and employees depended on friends, family members, or coworkers if they had trouble with their hardware or software. However, the company's rapid growth has strained this informal network and the partners have decided to hire several IT professionals for a technical support department, with the challenge being that many employees will be working remotely. As the members of this department, you have been asked to make recommendations about a variety of issues.

QUESTIONS FOR DISCUSSION:

14-16. Many of the company's employees work from home. What benefits can the company and employee expect from allowing employees to do so? Are there some jobs where working from home is not appropriate?

14-17. The company has not had a consistent policy about the technology for those working from home. Should the company provide employees with a computer to use in their home office, or is this a responsibility of the employee? What are the benefits and costs of each?

14-18. How will you provide technical support to employees working from home? Would this be easier if the company provided the employee with a computer? Why or why not?

14-19. Are there additional data security risks with employees working from home? Describe the potential risks or concerns and how they might be addressed.

14-20. Briefly outline the policies, procedures, and guidelines that your department should propose in your first year on the job.

exercising your ethics

UNAUTHORIZED ACCESS

The Situation

Security measures against intrusion and viruses are a constant challenge. Most systems guard against unauthorized access by requiring users to have protected passwords, but what happens when security is compromised by an employee? This

exercise illustrates how ethical issues may arise in tracking and using employee use of digital assets.

The Dilemma

"So what exactly is Admin access?" You ask the IT director. She has just called you into her office and expects you to explain how and why documents and assets related to your area of responsibility have been accessed and amended from a series of remote locations. In each case an unauthorized laptop has been used, often the access has been made using a public WI-FI network and in each case someone has used the Admin password. Only the network supervisor should have this password.

"Well it's written on a pad beside his workstation!" You explain. "I guess it must have been me, I've been working extra hours in the evenings and at the weekend to keep up with the workload. Besides, my password doesn't give me remote access."

"Very commendable," replies the IT director. "But you re alise that this is a gross breach of security and I'm going to ask HR to sack you."

cases

Think Before You Click

Continued from page 472

At the beginning of this chapter, you read about illicit activities of IT pirates and their methods for preying on victims, including both organizations and individuals around the globe. You saw that pirating aims to steal money and other resources by luring vulnerable potential victims with seemingly attractive offers of personal gain. Using the information presented in this chapter, you should now be able to answer the following questions.

QUESTIONS FOR DISCUSSION

14-24. Think about recent spam e-mails and text messages that you have received. What kinds of information were the intruders seeking?

14-25. Were you able to identify the e-mails and messages as "scams" before opening them, or did you discover their real contents after you opened them? What might have alerted you to the risks?

14-26. In what ways might the "opened" message from a scammer be harmful to you? To your IT devices and systems?

14-27. What steps can you take (or have you taken) to protect against such intrusions? What costs would be involved for gaining that protection?

14-28. Consider the various IT systems you use daily. What kinds of protection do they have to protect against invasion by cyber pirates?

Information Technology for Better Health Care

Going wireless to monitor a heart patient at home, a child's condition in an emergency department, an accident victim in an ambulance, and a patient's critical condition in a hospital room took a giant step forward after the Federal Communications Commission (FCC) authorized the use of Medical Body Area Network (MBAN) devices in 2012. MBAN is a wireless data system that transmits patients' conditions continuously so that changes can be detected quickly, and more serious problems can be detected before they fully develop. Small, lightweight, low-power sensors—much like Band-Aids in appearance—are attached to the patient's body to monitor vital signs that are transmitted over short distances to nearby "receiver devices" that, in turn, relay data over longer distances to nurse stations,

QUESTIONS TO ADDRESS

14-21. Given the factors in this situation, what, if any, ethical issues exist?

14-22. Do you think that the company is wise to monitor employees in this manner? Why or why not?

14-23. If you discovered that an employee accessing confidential or sensitive data outside the safety of the workplace what would your reaction be?

physicians' offices, and other staff locations for real-time non-invasive continuous observation. The FCC, which controls the allocation and use of U.S. wireless frequencies, has established a unique wireless spectrum that gives MBAN devices a protected transmission frequency. Accordingly, the wireless medical devices do not have to use Wi-Fi networks, with their risks of interference from the devices of many other Wi-Fi users. MBAN's uncontaminated transmissions provide more information faster, enabling better health care at lower cost, than is possible with onsite continuous observation by nurses, healthcare technicians, and physicians.

Although wireless monitoring is noninvasive, an emerging surgical technique uses snake robots (snake-bots) that slither through patients' bodies while assisting in surgeries on hearts, prostates, and other body organs. Surgeons at New York Presbyterian Hospital, Columbia University Medical Center, and Cornell University Medical Center, among other facilities, have been using robots as tools for years in thousands of surgeries. Snake-bots armed with miniature cameras, forceps, sensors, and scissors enable surgeons to see more and do more than previously possible. Instead of opening the chest cavity for heart surgery, a small incision provides an entry for the tiny snake that crawls to the location in need of repair. The surgeon, as if shrunken and placed inside the patient's heart, controls the snake's movements and activities while repairing the heart valve. The snake's small size is less damaging to the patient, enabling faster recovery than traditional surgery. Developers believe that, as the snakes become much smaller, the snake technology will eventually make intricate surgeries faster and easier, thus reducing costs.

Snake-bots are but one example of a broader class of robotic-assisted surgery. The Da Vinci Surgical System, for example, became the first robotic system approved by the U.S. Food and Drug Administration for use in a variety of surgical applications, including vaginal and hysterectomy repair, prostate cancer, and mitral valve (heart) repair. The Da Vinci System is used in more than 45,000 operations each year at more than 800 hospitals in Europe and the Americas. The system's three components are: (1) a 3D vision system, (2) a surgeon's workstation that translates hand movements into movements of surgical instruments, and (3) a patient-side station with robotic arms controlled by the surgeon. The robotic station's surgical actions are totally under the surgeon's control. Most intriguing, perhaps, is that the surgeon does not need to be at the patient's surgical platform, so long as assisting professionals are nearby. This makes it possible for a surgeon in New York to remotely perform mitral valve repair on a patient in Germany or elsewhere.[31]

QUESTIONS FOR DISCUSSION

14-29. In what ways are the IT developments for health care presented in this case changing the activities, services, and organizational practices of hospitals and clinics? Explain your responses and give examples.

14-30. In what ways are healthcare customers being affected by the IT developments presented in this case? Are all of these effects positive, or might some be negative? Explain your response.

14-31. How might doctors and hospitals change their marketing strategies as a result of these innovations?

14-32. Suppose you are in charge of security for a hospital using the IT systems discussed in this case. Identify the kinds of IT risks and threats that should be expected. Beyond your own ideas, be sure to indicate other sources you would consult to help identify the risks and threats.

14-33. What protection measures can be taken to reduce the risks of intrusions and threats for the hospital's IT systems (for the systems discussed in this case)? Describe how you would determine the costs for implementing those protection measures.

MyBizLab

Go to the Assignments section of your MyLab to complete these writing exercises.

14-34. How has information technology changed the way that organizations do business? In what ways has IT helped companies become more efficient and effective? What challenges are created by advances in IT?

14-35. Some of the risks with IT include intrusions and abuses by outsiders and the damages that can result from those activities. Organizations are continuously seeking ways to protect against those risks. (a) Why do companies try to protect against those risks? (b) Choose four major kinds of IT risks and explain the dangers they pose. (c) Identify and describe protection measures for guarding IT systems against cyber abuses.

end notes

[1] McQueen, M. P. "Cyber-Scams on the Uptick in Downturn," *The Wall Street Journal*, January 29, 2009, pp. D1, D4; Joseph De Avila, "Beware of Facebook 'Friends' Who May Trash Your Laptop," *The Wall Street Journal*, January 29, 2009, pp. D1, D4; Acohido, Byron, and Swartz, Jon. "Data Scams Have Kicked into High Gear as Markets Tumble," *USAToday*, January 28, 2009, at www.usatoday.com/tech/news/computersecurity/2009-01-28-hackers-data-scams_N.htm; Wragge, Chris. "FBI Warns of High-Tech Cyber ID Theft," *wcbstv.com*, April 8, 2009, at http://wcbstv.com/local/cyber.criminals.fbi.2.980245.html; Robertson, Jordan. "Bad Economy Helps Web Scammers Recruit 'Mules'," *ABC News*, December 9, 2008, at http://abcnews.go.com/print?id=6422327. All sources accessed on May 10, 2015.

[2] "Hackers in China Blamed for Cyber-Attacks," *Columbia Daily Tribune*, February 10, 2011, p. 5B, and at www.columbiatribune.com/news/2011/feb/10/hackers-in-china-blamed-for-cyber-attacks/?news; Milbourn, Mary Ann. "Beware of Fake Job Offers," *The Orange County Register*, October 12, 2010, at http://economy.ocregister.com/2010/10/12/beware-of-fake-job-offers/42194/; Eppstein, Richard. "Scammers Pop Up During Economic Downturns," *Toledo Biz Insider*, March 4, 2010, at www.toledoblade.com/article/20100304/BUSINESS11/100309863/-1/BUSINESS; Warman, Matt. "Viruses on Smart-Phones: Security's New Frontier," *The Telegraph*, February 8, 2011, at www.telegraph.co.uk/technology/news/8311214/Viruses-on-smartphones-securitys-new-frontier.html. Accessed on May 10, 2015.

[3] Goldstein, Phil. "RIM Unveils BlackBerry Z10 and Q10, but Pushes U.S. Launch to March," *FierceWireless*, January 30, 2013, at http://fiercewireless.com/story/rim-unveils-blackberry-z10-and-q10-pushes-us-launch-march/2013-01-30. Accessed on May 10, 2015.

[4] Stern, Joanna. "Google's Project Glass is Ready, but for Developers' Eyes Only," January 16, 2013, at http://abcnews.go.com/blogs/technology/2013/01/googles-glass-is-ready-but-for-developers-eyes-only/. Accessed on May 10, 2015.

[5] See www.siriusxm.com/navtraffic/

[6] "Appropriator Asks NASA to Help Boeing Fix Dreamliner Problems," January 13, 2013, at http://fattah.house.gov/latest-news/appropriator-asks-nasa-to-help-boeing-fix-dreamliner-problems/. Accessed on May 10, 2015.

[7] "Lockheed Martin Aeronautics: Siemens' PLM Software," *Siemens*, at www.plm.automation.siemans.com/en_us/about-us/success/case_s, accessed on June 16, 2009, and May 10, 2015.

[8] Northrup, Laura. "Timbuk2 Really, Really Wants You to Be Happy with Their Bags," *The Consumerist*, June 5, 2009, at www.consumerist.com/2009/06/timbuk2really-really-wants-you-to-be-happy-with-their-bags.html. Accessed on May 10, 2015.

[9] LaGesse, David. "How to Turn Social Networking into a Job Offer," *U.S. News & World Report*, May 11, 2009, at www.usnews.com/money/careers/articles/2009/05/11/how-to-turn-social-networking-into-a-job-offer.html. Accessed on May 10, 2015.

[10]3D Systems, "3D Systems Helps Walter Reed Army Medical Center Rebuild Lives," at www.3dsystems.com/apsolutions/casestudies/walter_reed.asp, accessed on June 15, 2009; Hickey, Hannah. "Camera in a Pill Offers Cheaper, Easier Window on Your Insides," UWNews.org (January 24, 2008), at http://uwnews.org/article.asp?articleid=39292. Accessed on May 10, 2015; see also www.wrnmmc.capmed.mil/SitePages/home.aspx

[11]See www.internetworldstats.com/stats.htm. Accessed on May 10, 2015.

[12]"BAN AMRO Mortgage Group Offers One Fee to Ford Motor Company Employees," *Mortgage Mag*, February 14, 2005, at www.mortgagemag.com/n/502_003.htm; "An Intranet's Life Cycle," *morebusiness.com* (June 16, 1999), at www.morebusiness.com/getting_started/website/d928247851.brc; Ahmed, Sally. "Ford Motor Company—Case Study," *Ezine Articles*, August 18, 2008, at http://ezinearticles.com/?Ford-Motor-Company—Case-Study&id=1420478. Accessed on May 10, 2015.

[13]"Companies Take Sides on Super Wi-Fi," *Columbia Daily Tribune*, February 4, 2013, p. 6B.

[14]Brizius, Glen. "CereProc: An Example of a Technology Finally Fulfilling Its Potential," *Associated Content in Technology*, March 16, 2010, at www.associatedcontent.com/article/2786052/cereproc_an_example_of_a_technology.html?cat=5. Accessed on May 10, 2015.

[15]www.cereproc.com/en/products

[16]Sheppard, Alyson. "Giving Roger Ebert a New Voice: Q&A With CereProc," *Popular Mechanics*, March 8, 2010, at www.popularmechanics.com/science/health/prosthetics/rogerebertvoicetech; Millar, Hayley. "New Voice for Film Critic," *BBC News*, March 3, 2010, at http://news.bbc.co.uk/2/hi/uk_news/scotland/edinburgh_and_east/8547645.stm. Accessed on May 10, 2015.

[17]Novet, Jordan. "Apple claims Siri's speech recognition tech is more accurate than Google's," *VentureBeat*, June 8, 2015, at http://venturebeat.com/2015/06/08/apple-claims-siris-speech-recognition-tech-is-more-accurate-than-googles/

[18]"Kroger Tailors Ads to Its Customers," *Columbia Daily Tribune*, January 12, 2009, 7B; Pletcher, Josh. "dunnhumby: Retailer's Secret Weapon," *Cincinnati.com*, January 31, 2013, at news.cincinnati.com/article/20130130/BIZ/301190100/dunnhumby-Retailers-secret-weapon?nclick_check=1. Accessed on May 10, 2015.

[19]"Data Mining Examples & Testimonials," at www.data-mining-software.com/data_mining_examples.htm, accessed February 24, 2011; Angwin, Julia, and Valentino-DeVries, Jennifer. "New Tracking Frontier: Your License Plates," *Wall Street Journal*, September 29–30, 2012, pp. A1, A13; Troianovski, Anton. "New Wi-Fi Pitch: Tracker," *Wall Street Journal*, June 19, 2012, p. B5. Accessed on May 10, 2015.

[20]Freedman, Lisa. "All Eyes on Predictive Analytics." *Business Week* no. 4423: S1–S4. *Business Source Premier*, EBSCOhost (accessed June 9, 2015).

[21]Marchant, Jo. "Virtual Fossils Reveal How Ancient Creatures Lived," *NewScientist*, May 27, 2009, at www.newscientist.com/article/mg20227103.500-virtual-fossils-reveal-how-ancient-creatures-lived.html. Accessed on May 10, 2015.

[22]Warman, Matt. "Viruses on Smartphones: Security's New Frontier," *The Telegraph*, February 8, 2011, at www.telegraph.co.uk/technology/news/8311214/

Viruses-on-smartphones-securitys-new-frontier.html; Cheng, Jacqui. "Canadian Group: Facebook 'A Minefield of Privacy Invasion'" May 30, 2008, at http://arstechnica.com/tech-policy/news/2008/05/canadian-group-files-complaint-over-facebook-privacy.ars; "Cell Phones a Much Bigger Privacy Risk Than Facebook," *Fox News*, February 20, 2009, at www.foxnews.com/printer_friendly_story/0,3566,497544,00.html. Accessed on May 10, 2015.

[23]Gorman, Siobhan, Barrett, Devlin, and Yadron, Danny. "China Hackers Hit U.S. Media," *Wall Street Journal*, February 1, 2013, pp. B1, B2; "Hackers Hit Twitter, Washington Post," *Columbia Daily Tribune*, February 4, 2013, p. 6B. Accessed on May 10, 2015.

[24]Leary, Alex. "Wi-Fi Cloaks a New Breed of Intruder," *St. Petersburg Times*, July 4, 2005, at www.sptimes.com/2005/07/04/State/Wi_Fi_cloaks_a_new_br.shtml. Accessed on May 10, 2015.

[25]Melanson, Donald. "Apple: 16 Billion iTunes Songs Downloaded, 300 Million iPods Sold," *Engadget*, October 4, 2011, at www.engadget.com/2011/10/04/apple-16-billion-itunes-songs-downloaded-300-million-ipods-sol/; Burgess, Christopher, and Power, Richard. "How to Avoid Intellectual Property Theft," *CIO*, July 10, 2006, at www.cio.com/article/22837; "For Students Doing Reports," *RIAA*, at www.riaa.com/faq.php, accessed on February 4, 2013; Sisario, Ben. "AC/DC Joins iTunes, as Spotify Emerges as Music's New Disrupter," *New York Times*, November 19, 2012, at mediadecoder.blogs.nytimes.com/2012/11/19/acdc-joins-itunes-as-spotify-emerges-as-musics-new-disrupter/. Accessed on May 10, 2015.

[26]See www.webopedia.com/TERM/S/spyware.html.

[27]Norman, Donald A. "Got Spam?" *MAPI: Manufacturers Alliance for Productivity and Innovation*, October 24, 2012, at www.mapi.net/blog/2012/10/got-spam. Accessed on May 10, 2015.

[28]"'Spam King' Faces Federal Fraud Charges," *Columbia Daily Tribune*, January 21, 2013, accessed at www.columbiatribune.com/wire/spam-king-faces-federal-fraud-charges/article_042ac575-7820-5bb4-bb17-3e425f2f24c0.html#.URE7hPKmFcI. Accessed on May 10, 2015.

[29]Carlson, Brad. "Organizations Face New Records-Destruction Rule," *Idaho Business Review*, July 25, 2005, at www.idahobusiness.net/archive.htm/2005/07/25/Organizations-face-new-recordsdestruction-rule. Accessed on May 10, 2015.

[30]Vijayan, Jaikumar. "5 Things You Should Know About Cyber Insurance." *Computerworld Digital Magazine*. 1 no. 11: 27–32. *Business Source Premier*, EBSCOhost (accessed June 9, 2015).

[31]Linebaugh, Kate. "Medical Devices in Hospitals to Go Wireless," *Wall Street Journal*, May 24, 2012, p. B8; "Tiny Snake Robots Aid Surgery," *Columbia Daily Tribune*, May 30, 2012, p. A2; Sandham, John. ""Robotic Assisted Surgery," *EBME Electrical and Biomedical Engineering*, December 2008, at www.ebme.co.uk/arts/robotic, accessed on May 11, 2013; iMedicalApps Team and Primosch, Robert D. "FCC Opens New Chapter in Wireless Medical Devices," *iMedicalApps*, June 6, 2012, at www.imedicalapps.com/2012/06/fcc-opens-chapter-wireless-medical-devices/. Accessed on May 10, 2015.

Organizing the Business

chapter 6

Shutterstock

The secret to success lies with the people behind

the products. The relationship between

managers and

employees can make or break

any company.

learning objectives

After reading this chapter, you should be able to:

6-1   **Discuss** the factors that influence a firm's organizational structure.

6-2   **Explain** specialization and departmentalization as two of the building blocks of organizational structure.

6-3   **Describe** centralization and decentralization, delegation, and authority as the key ingredients in establishing the decision-making hierarchy.

6-4   **Explain** the differences among functional, divisional, matrix, and international organizational structures and describe the most popular new forms of organizational design.

6-5   **Describe** the informal organization and discuss intrapreneuring.

Organizing for Success at South African Airways

South African Airways (SAA) celebrated its 80th anniversary in 2014. It is one of the oldest airlines in the world, and has won plaudits from numerous magazines and international organizations.

The airline has one of the most advanced aircraft fleets in the world. Its over-riding vision is to become the first African airline with a truly global reach. In order to achieve this, the airline places a great emphasis on safety, customer-focus, accountability, and integrity. Yet all of this is dependent on one thing: the ability to value its own people.

The airline has an international network that connects South Africa with every continent across the globe. SAA connects with 43 locations across Africa. It continues to refresh, improve, and expand its fleet. The airline is also instrumental in providing technical support for other African carriers.

In September 2013, after several years of government funding support, the airline announced that it would merge with regional operator SA Express and the low cost carrier Mango. This move is seen as a necessary step to ensure that SAA's business model was changed and that it could once again become self-funded.

For many years, deregulation and increased competition had eroded SAA's ability to fund its own operations without government support. The merger, designed to allow SAA to use their assets more efficiently, would also allow them to use their available capital in a better way. The new alliance would allow SAA to retain its position as a premium carrier. The role of SA Express would be that of a feeder airline, and Mango would offer customers a lower cost alternative. This model has worked successfully in Kenya and Ethiopia. In both countries, coordination between airlines has produced greater efficiency and savings in terms of fleet purchase, use of airports, and the right to operate on particular routes. The South African move is not seen as a short term fix, rather a medium to a long-term solution.

Interestingly, the merger will mean that three organizational structures will have to be dovetailed together to make a coherent entity. SAA had already begun a deep and fundamental restructuring process in 2007. It aimed to simplify the organization. In addition to this, SAA recognized the need to have the right size of management at various levels. A key part of the restructuring process was also to re-skill the workforce and provide incentives to employees and management.

When this initial restructuring plan was devised (in the financial year 2006-2007), many of the assumptions were based on the price of oil. Oil prices, and subsequently fuel

Radu Razvan/Fotolia

what's in it for me?

All managers need the assistance of others to succeed and so must trust the members of their team to do their jobs and carry out their responsibilities. The team members themselves need the support of their boss and a clear understanding of their role in the organization. The working relationship between managers and their subordinates is one of the most critical elements comprising an organization. As you will see in this chapter, managing the basic frameworks that organizations use to get their work done, *structure*, is a fundamental part of the management process.

Imagine asking a child to build a castle with a set of building blocks. She selects a few small blocks and other larger ones. She uses some square ones, some round ones, and some triangular ones. When she finishes, she has her own castle, unlike any other. Another child, presented with the same task, constructs a different castle. He selects different blocks, for example, and combines them in different ways. The children's activities, choosing certain combinations of blocks and then putting them together in unique ways, are in many ways analogous to the manager's job of organizing. Managers at similar companies competing in the same industries may create structures that are nearly identical to one another, completely different from one another, or somewhere in between.

Organizing is deciding how best to group organizational elements. Just as children select different kinds of building blocks, managers can choose a variety of structural possibilities. And just as the children can assemble the blocks in any number of ways, so, too, can managers put the organization together in many different ways. Understanding the nature of these building blocks and the different ways in which they can be configured can have a powerful impact on a firm's competitiveness.

By understanding the material in this chapter, you'll also be prepared to understand your "place" in the organization that employs you. Similarly, as a boss or owner, you'll be better equipped to create the optimal structure for your own organization. This chapter examines factors that influence a firm's organizational structure. We discuss the building blocks of organizational structure as well as the differences between decision making in different types of organizations. Along the way, we look at a variety of organizational structures and describe the most popular new forms of organizational design.

prices, determine the profitability and competitiveness of airlines, and at this point, the targets were based on the fact that oil was trading at US$50–60 a barrel. By the time that the restructuring had begun in 2007, oil was trading at more than twice that price. Clearly, this put tremendous pressure on the margins. SAA's response was to ground aircraft and focus on profitable routes. This was a short-term fix and not a long-term solution. Cost-cutting measures were implemented and determined efforts were made to streamline the organization and management of the business. As another result of cost cutting, the estimated restructuring costs was slashed to a third of the original estimated costs.

In 2005, SAA had suffered a ruinous labor dispute. The estimated cost of the strikes over pay increases had cost SAA at least 50 percent of its daily turnover. At the end of the dispute, SAA had to radically change its whole approach to labor relations. It recognized that it needed to build and sustain relationships with its workforce. This would encompass shared goals, knowledge and, above all, mutual respect.

This was the backdrop which had prompted the restructuring process. The new organization structure would have to incorporate ongoing communication (meaning that it had to be timely and frequent). At the same time, employees would need to feel that they had a stake and say in the decision making of SAA.

The airline industry represents a series of situations that require excellent planning, coordination, and cooperation. Teamwork across the organization is necessary to ensure that aircraft are turned around quickly. Flight departure times are very constrained and demand cooperation in order to be fulfilled.

After debuting their non-stop route to Beijing I early 2012, South African Airways lost around $72.6 million on the route. The non-stop flights to Beijing and Mumbai were terminated. Air China would take up the service to Beijing. At the same time, Etihad Airways would service the India route via Abu Dhabi. At a stroke, SAA managed to rid themselves of two loss making services. Until the deals were struck, the South African government had refused to give the airline permission to cut the services.

SAA will need to continue to streamline and reorganize in order to respond not only to the increased competition, but the opportunities that alliances will offer. Links to China, India, and Latin America could be very lucrative. First, however, and reflected in the merger with Mango and SA Express, is to capture the dominant share of the domestic market.

It would seem that SAA will follow the model of SA Express, which had already flattened its organizational structure and positively encouraged employee stake holders to take a more active role in decision making. Responsive, team orientated, and lean were the key elements of the independent SA Express organizational (After studying this chapter you should be able to answer the set of questions found at the end of the chapter.)

OBJECTIVE 6-1
Discuss

the factors that influence a firm's organizational structure.

Organizational Structure *specification of the jobs to be done within an organization and the ways in which they relate to one another*

What Is Organizational Structure?

One key decision that business owners and managers must address is how best to structure their organization. Stated differently, they must decide on an appropriate organizational structure. We can define **organizational structure** as the specification of the jobs to be done within an organization and the ways in which those jobs relate to one another.[1] Perhaps the easiest way to understand structure is in terms of an *organization chart*.

Organization Charts

Most small businesses prepare an **organization chart** to clarify structure and to show employees where they fit into a firm's operations. Figure 6.1 is an organization chart for Contemporary Landscape Services, a small but thriving business in a small Texas community. Each box in the chart represents a job. The solid lines define the *chain of command*. The **chain of command**, in turn, refers to *reporting relationships* within the company. In theory, such reporting relationships follow a "chain" from the highest level in the organization to the lowest. For example, the retail shop, nursery, and landscape operations managers all report to the owner and president. Within the landscape operation is one manager for residential accounts and another for commercial accounts. Similarly, there are other managers in the retail shop and the nursery.

The organization charts of large firms are far more complex and include individuals at many more levels than those shown in Figure 6.1. Size prevents many large firms from even having charts that include all their managers. Typically, they create one organization chart showing overall corporate structure, separate charts for each division, and even more charts for individual departments or units.

Recall our definition of organizational structure: the specification of the jobs to be done within an organization and the ways in which those jobs relate to one another. The boxes in the organization chart represent the jobs, and the lines connecting the boxes show how the jobs are related. As we will see, however, even though organizational structure can be broken down into a series of boxes and lines, virtually no two organizations will have the same structure. What works for Microsoft will not work for Google, Southwest Airlines, Shell Oil, Amazon, or the U.S. Department of Justice. Likewise, the structure of the American Red Cross will probably not work for Urban Outfitters, Walmart, Starbucks, or the University of Minnesota.

Determinants of Organizational Structure

How is an organization's structure determined? Ideally, managers carefully assess a variety of important factors as they plan for and then create an organizational structure that will allow their organization to function efficiently.

Many factors play a part in determining an organization's optimal structure. Chief among them are the organization's *mission* and *strategy*. A dynamic and rapidly growing business, for example, needs an organizational structure that allows it to be flexible, to respond to changes in its environment and strategy, and to grow. A stable organization with only modest growth goals and a more conservative strategy will most likely function best with a different organizational structure.

Size of the company and aspects of the organization's environment also affect organizational structure. As we saw in Chapter 5, organizing is a key part of the

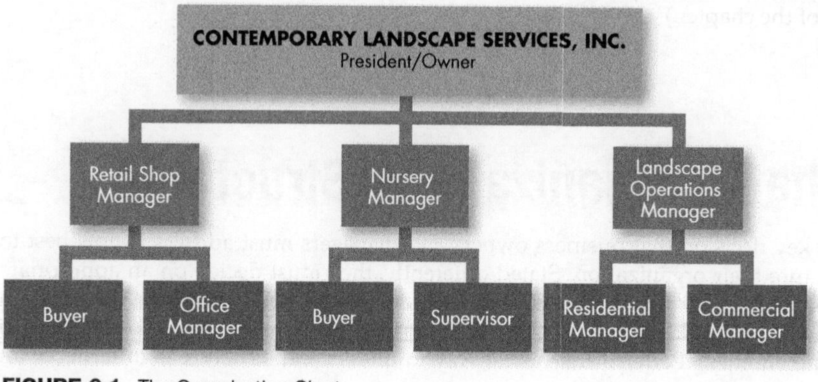

Organization Chart *diagram depicting a company's structure and showing employees where they fit into its operations*

Chain of Command *reporting relationships within a company*

FIGURE 6.1 The Organization Chart

management process. As such, it must be conducted with an equal awareness of both a firm's external and internal environments. A large services provider or manufacturer operating in a strongly competitive environment, such as Delta Airlines or Hewlett-Packard, requires a different organizational structure than a local barbershop or clothing boutique. Even after an organizational structure has been created, it is rarely free from tinkering—or even outright re-creation. Most organizations change their structures on an almost continuing basis.

Since it was first incorporated in 1903, Ford Motor Company has undergone literally dozens of major structural changes, hundreds of moderate changes, and thousands of minor changes. In the last 20 years alone, Ford has initiated several major structural changes. In 1995, for instance, the firm announced a major restructuring plan called Ford 2000, which was intended to integrate all of Ford's vast international operations into a single, unified structure by the year 2000.

By 1998, however, midway through implementation of the grand plan, top Ford executives announced major modifications, indicating that (1) additional changes would be made, (2) some previously planned changes would not be made, and (3) some recently realigned operations would be changed again. In early 1999, managers

entrepreneurship and new ventures

Organizing for Innovation

One of the key determinants of organizational structure is the mission and strategy of the business. Entrepreneurs must be particularly conscious as they begin to define an organizational structure that is appropriate to their goals and strategy. Henry Mintzberg identified five organizational structures and emphasizes that the most appropriate structure is dependent upon the business and its environment. In an entrepreneurial organization, simple, flat organizational structures with very few top managers are most appropriate. Unlike more complex structures, an entrepreneurial organization would ideally be relatively unstructured and informal. The advantage of this structure is that decisions can be made quickly and the structure is flexible enough to adapt to a rapidly changing market. However, with very few top managers, it's easy to become overwhelmed with decision-making.[2]

Perhaps one of the most iconic examples of a simple entrepreneurial structure is Valve Software, the company that created the Half-Life, Counter-Strike, and Portal video games series. While Valve has 300 employees, they have no managers – none. According to the employee handbook, "Of all the people at this company who aren't your boss, Gabe [the co-founder] is the MOST not your boss, if you get what we're saying." In an interview with Bloomberg Business, Newell explained it this way:

"When we started Valve [in 1996], we thought about what the company needed to be good at. We realized that here, our job was to create things that hadn't existed before. Managers are good at institutionalizing procedures, but in our line of work that's not always good. Sometimes the skills in one generation of product are irrelevant to the skills in another generation. Our industry is in such technological, design, and

Patrick Pleul/Picture Alliance/dpa/AP Images

artistic flux that we need somebody who can recognize that. It's pretty rare for someone to be in a lead role on two consecutive projects."

Employees at Valve move from project to project, often taking on different roles from one project to the next. A "group contributor" is responsible for helping others be more productive, although their ability to think creatively is often limited by this role. At other times, Valve employees may work on a more individual project, where they are allowed to work more independently.[3]

Valve is unique in other ways. It offers company massage rooms and free food and coffee for employees. Each employee is empowered to making hiring decisions, even though this can have serious consequences. Employees have desks on wheels, so they are free to roll their workstation to the project of their choice. And, just in case you're not convinced that this is a great place to work, the company takes all their employees on a tropical vacation once a year. [4]

announced another set of changes intended to eliminate corporate bureaucracy, speed decision making, and improve communication and working relationships among people at different levels of the organization. Early in 2001, Ford announced yet more sweeping changes intended to boost the firm's flagging bottom line and stem a decline in product quality. More significant changes followed in both 2003 and 2004, and in 2006, the firm announced several plant closings, resulting in even more changes. Not surprisingly, yet another major reorganization was announced in 2010 as the firm sought to deal with a global recession and a major slump in automobile sales.[5] In 2011 the firm announced even more restructuring to gain more international market share, and other changes were announced in 2015 as global auto sales began to increase and Ford needed additional manufacturing capacity.[6]

The Building Blocks of Organizational Structure

OBJECTIVE 6-2
Explain
specialization and departmentalization as two of the building blocks of organizational structure.

The first step in developing the structure of any business, large or small, involves three activities:

1 *Specialization.* Determining who will do what

2 *Departmentalization.* Determining how people performing certain tasks can best be grouped together

3 *Establishment of a Decision-Making Hierarchy.* Deciding who will be empowered to make which decisions and who will have authority over others

These three activities are the building blocks of all business organizations. In this section, we discuss specialization and departmentalization. Because the decision-making hierarchy actually includes several elements, we cover it in more detail in the next section.

Job Specialization

The process of identifying the specific jobs that need to be done and designating the people who will perform them leads to **job specialization**. In a sense, all organizations have only one major job, such as making cars (Ford), selling finished goods to consumers (Lenova), or providing telecommunications services (Verizon). Usually, that job is more complex in nature. For example, the job of Nucor Steel is converting scrap steel (such as wrecked automobiles) into finished steel products (such as beams and reinforcement bars). Similarly, the job of United Airlines is to transport passengers and their luggage from one airport to another.

Job Specialization *the process of identifying the specific jobs that need to be done and designating the people who will perform them*

To perform this one overall job, managers actually break it down, or specialize it, into several smaller jobs. Thus, some workers transport the scrap steel to the company's mills. Others operate shredding equipment before turning raw materials over to the workers who then melt them into liquid form. Other specialists oversee the flow of the liquid into molding equipment, where it is transformed into new products. Finally, other workers are responsible for moving finished products to a holding area before they are shipped out to customers. At United, some specialists schedule flights, others book passengers, others fly the planes, and still others deal with passenger luggage and other cargo. When the overall job of the organization is broken down like this, workers can develop real expertise in their jobs, and employees can better coordinate their work with that done by others.

In a small organization, the owner may perform every job. As the firm grows, however, so does the need to specialize jobs so that others can perform them. To see how specialization can evolve in an organization, consider the case of the Walt Disney Company. When Walt Disney first opened his animation studio, he and his brother Roy did everything. For example, when they created their first animated

When Walt Disney was just starting out, he did most of the work on his animated features all by himself. But today's features like *Cars*, *Planes*, *Up*, and *Finding Dory* all require the work of hundreds of people.

feature, *Steamboat Willy*, they wrote the story, drew the pictures, transferred the pictures to film, provided the voices, and went out and sold the cartoon to theater operators.

Today, however, a Disney animated feature is made possible only through the efforts of thousands of people. The job of one animator may be to create the face of a single character throughout an entire feature. Another artist may be charged with coloring background images in certain scenes. People other than artists are responsible for the subsequent operations that turn individual computer-generated images into a moving picture or for the marketing of the finished product.

Job specialization is a natural part of organizational growth. It also has certain advantages. For example, specialized jobs are learned more easily and can be performed more efficiently than nonspecialized jobs, and it is also easier to replace people who leave an organization if they have highly specialized jobs. However, jobs at lower levels of the organization are especially susceptible to overspecialization. If such jobs become too narrowly defined, employees may become bored and careless, derive less satisfaction from their jobs, and lose sight of their roles in the organization.

Departmentalization

After jobs are specialized, they must be grouped into logical units, which is the process of **departmentalization**. Departmentalized companies benefit from this division of activities; control and coordination are narrowed and made easier, and top managers can see more easily how various units are performing.

Departmentalization allows the firm to treat each department as a **profit center**, a separate company unit responsible for its own costs and profits. Thus, Macy's can calculate the profits it generates from men's clothing, home furnishings, cosmetics, women's shoes, and every other department within a given store separately. Managers can then use this information in making decisions about advertising and promotional events, space allocation adjustments, budgeting, and so forth.

Managers do not departmentalize jobs randomly, of course. They group them logically, according to some common thread or purpose. In general, departmentalization may occur along *functional, product, process, customer*, or *geographic* lines (or any combination of these).

Functional Departmentalization Many service and manufacturing companies, especially smaller ones just getting started, use **functional departmentalization**

Departmentalization *process of grouping jobs into logical units*

Profit Center *separate company unit responsible for its own costs and profits*

Functional Departmentalization *dividing an organization according to groups' functions or activities*

finding a better way

Blending the Old with the New

In 1883, the great composer and piano virtuoso Franz Liszt wrote Heinrich Steinway, founder of Steinway & Sons, to praise the Steinway grand piano. In particular, Liszt had good things to say about the tonal effect of the piano's *scale*, the arrangement of its strings. Thirty years earlier, Henry Steinway Jr., had patented a technique for scaling called *overstringing*: Instead of running them parallel to the piano's treble strings, he taught his workers to fan the bass strings above and diagonally to create a second tier of strings. As a result, he was able to improve the instrument's tone by using longer strings with superior vibratory quality.

Another feature developed by Steinway and his employees in the mid-nineteenth century made it possible to use strings that were also bigger—and thus louder. If you look under a piano, you'll see a cast-iron plate. This component was once made of wood fortified by metal braces, but Steinway had made the cast-iron plate a regular feature by the 1840s. The metal plate, of course, is much stronger and allowed the piano maker to apply much greater tension to the strings; in turn, the ability to increase string tension made it possible to tune the piano to more exacting standards of pitch.

Steinway was the first piano maker to combine the cast-iron plate with the technique of overstringing, and little has changed in the construction of a grand piano since these and a few other facets of traditional technology were first introduced. In effect, just as the job of a Disney animator has changed as the firm and its technology have changed, so too have the jobs at Steinway. Indeed, Steinway's workers still perform specialized jobs, but the jobs have also changed dramatically over the years. Take, for example, the soundboard, which you'll see if you open up a grand piano and look inside. A solid wooden "diaphragm" located between the strings and the metal plate, the *soundboard* is a marvel of deceptively simple design that vibrates to amplify the sound of the strings while withstanding the 1,000 pounds of pressure that they place on it. Because they're constructed by hand, no two soundboards are exactly the same size. Nor is any one piano *case*, the curved lateral surface that runs around the whole instrument, the same size as any other. The important thing is that the case is fitted—and fitted *precisely*—to a soundboard.

Because the soundboard is measured first and the case then fitted to it, there's only one case for each soundboard. To ensure a satisfactory fit between case and soundboard, the case must be *frazed*, sawed and planed to specification. Performed by hand, this task took 14 hours, but today it's done in 1 1/2 hours by a *computer numerically controlled* (CNC) milling machine, a system in which a computerized storage medium issues programmed commands to a variety of specialized tools. Steinway workers, then, must be masters of their craft to perform effectively.

Granted, CNC technology is fairly new at Steinway—the million-dollar milling machine and several other pieces of CNC

Ulrich Perrey/picture-alliance/dpa/dpaweb/Newscom

technology were introduced only in the last 10 years or so. Most of Steinway's CNC tools are highly specialized, and the company custom-built many of them. Obviously, such technology leads to a lot of labor savings, but Steinway officials are adamant about the role of technology in maintaining rather than supplanting Steinway tradition: Some people, says Director of Quality Robert Berger, "think that Steinway is automating to save on labor costs or improve productivity. But these investments are all about quality. We're making a few specific technology investments in areas where we can improve the quality of our product."[7]

Steinway has gone through many organizational changes over the past several decades. After going public in 1996, it struggled when the recession hit. However, the company has remained the brand of choice throughout this time and billionaire John Paulson purchased the company for over $500 million and took it private in 2013. As Paulson explains it, Steinway's legacy of high quality was the motivation behind his investment decision: "I've always been enamored with the product. You have Mercedes in cars and top brands in every other area. But no one has such a high share of the high end." The company sees great potential for international sales, with robust interest by cultural institutions in China. And, for Steinway, it's the people behind that product that make all the difference. According to *Forbes* magazine, it's an ideal export – "a luxury product produced with U.S. skilled labor, packed with prestige that can't be outsourced."[8]

to create departments according to a group's functions or activities. Most new start-up firms, for instance, use functional departmentalization. Such firms typically have production, marketing and sales, human resources, and accounting and finance departments. Departments may be further subdivided. For example, the marketing department might be divided into separate groups for market research, advertising, and sales promotions.

Product Departmentalization *dividing an organization according to specific products or services being created*

Product Departmentalization
Both manufacturers and service providers often opt for **product departmentalization**, dividing an organization according to the specific product or service being created. This becomes especially true when a firm grows and starts to offer multiple products or services. Kraft Foods uses this approach to divide departments. For example, the Oscar Mayer division focuses on hot dogs and lunch meats, the Kraft Cheese division focuses on cheese products, and the Maxwell House and Post division focus on coffee and breakfast cereal, respectively.[9] Because each division represents a defined group of products or services, managers at Kraft Foods are able—in theory—to focus on *specific* product lines in a clear and defined way.

Process Departmentalization *dividing an organization according to production processes used to create a good or service*

Process Departmentalization
Other manufacturers favor **process departmentalization**, in which the organization is divided according to production processes used to create a good or service. This principle is logical for Vlasic, which has three separate departments to transform cucumbers into either fresh-packed pickles, pickles cured in brine, or relishes. Cucumbers destined to become fresh-packed pickles must be packed into jars immediately, covered with a solution of water and vinegar, and prepared for sale. Those slated to be brined pickles must be aged in brine solution before packing. Relish cucumbers must be minced and combined with a host of other ingredients. Each process requires different equipment and worker skills, and different departments were created for each. Some service providers also use this approach as well. For instance, an insurance company might use one department to receive claims, another to review coverage, and another to issue payments.

Customer Departmentalization *dividing an organization to offer products and meet needs for identifiable customer groups*

Customer Departmentalization
Retail stores actually derive their generic name, department stores, from the manner in which they are structured—a men's department, a women's department, a luggage department, a lawn and garden department, and so on. Each department targets a specific customer category (men, women, people who want to buy luggage, people who want to buy a lawn mower) by using **customer departmentalization** to create departments that offer products, and meet the needs of, identifiable customer groups. Thus, a customer shopping for a baby's playpen at Target can bypass lawn and garden supplies and head straight for children's furniture. In general, the store is more efficient, and customers get better service because salespeople tend to specialize and gain expertise in their departments. Another illustration of customer departmentalization is reflected in most banks. An individual wanting a consumer loan goes to the retail banking office, whereas a small business owner goes to the commercial banking office and a farmer goes to the agricultural loan department.

Geographic Departmentalization *dividing an organization according to the areas of the country or the world served by a business*

Geographic Departmentalization
Geographic departmentalization divides firms according to the areas of the country or the world that they serve. Levi Strauss, for instance, has one division for North and South America; one for Europe, the Middle East, and North Africa; and one for the Asia Pacific region.[10] Within the United States, geographic departmentalization is common among utilities. For example, Southern Company organizes its power subsidiaries into four geographic departments—Alabama, Georgia, Gulf, and Mississippi Power.[11]

Multiple Forms of Departmentalization
Because different forms of departmentalization have different advantages, as firms grow in size they tend to adopt different types of departmentalization for various levels. The company illustrated in Figure 6.2 uses functional departmentalization at the top level. At the

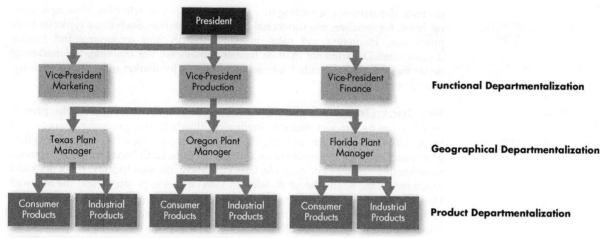

FIGURE 6.2 Multiple Forms of Departmentalization

middle level, production is divided along geographic lines. At a lower level, marketing is departmentalized by product group. Larger firms are certain to use all of these different forms of departmentalization in various areas.

Establishing the Decision-Making Hierarchy

The third major building block of organizational structure is the establishment of a decision-making hierarchy. This is usually done by formalizing reporting relationships. When the focus is on the reporting relationships among individual managers and the people who report to them, it is most commonly referred to as delegation. However, when the focus is on the overall organization, it becomes a question of decentralization versus *centralization*.

OBJECTIVE 6-3
Describe
centralization and decentralization, delegation, and authority as the key ingredients in establishing the decision-making hierarchy.

Distributing Authority: Centralization and Decentralization

Some managers make the conscious decision to retain as much decision-making authority as possible at the higher levels of the organizational structure; others decide to push authority as far down the hierarchy as possible. Although we can think of these two extremes as anchoring a continuum, most companies fall somewhere between the middle of such a continuum and one end point or the other.

Centralized Organizations
In a **centralized organization**, most decision-making authority is held by upper-level managers.[12] McDonald's practices centralization as a way to maintain standardization. All restaurants must follow precise steps in buying products and making and packaging menu items. Most advertising is handled at the corporate level, and any local advertising must be approved by a regional manager. Restaurants even have to follow prescribed schedules for facilities' maintenance and upgrades such as floor polishing and parking lot cleaning. Centralized authority is most commonly found in companies that face relatively stable and predictable environments and is also typical of small businesses.

Centralized Organization
organization in which most decision-making authority is held by upper-level management

Decentralized Organizations
As a company gets larger and more decisions must be made, the company tends to adopt **decentralized organization**, in

Decentralized Organization *organization in which a great deal of decision-making authority is delegated to levels of management at points below the top*

managing in turbulent times

Organized for Success

There's been quite a bit of news about the death of manufacturing jobs in the United States, but Illinois Tool Works, headquartered in Glenview, Illinois, is out to prove the critics wrong. Established in 1912 to manufacture metal cutting tools, the company has grown over the last century to more than 49,000 employees around the globe. Beginning in 1980, ITW grew through the acquisition of hundreds of smaller companies, acquiring their product lines and distinctive competencies. Today, the company is organized into seven segments or operating divisions: Automotive OEM; Test & Measurement and Electronics; Food Equipment; Polymers & Fluids; Welding; Construction Products; and Specialty Products. Their products and services are quite diverse—in their Automotive OEM division, they produce plastic and metal components for automobiles and light trucks, while their Polymers and Fluids division produces industrial adhesives, cleaning and lubrications fluids, and polymers and fillers for automotive repairs and maintenance.

ITW's structure is built around a highly decentralized philosophy. Each of the seven operating divisions is designed to operate as a smaller, more flexible and entrepreneurial organization, maintaining its own revenue and cost centers. Decision-making is highly decentralized, with most decisions about strategy made within the divisions. The company believes that this ITW Business Model not only responds effectively to customer needs, but also maximizes economic performance.

Another key to Illinois Tool Work's success is their 80/20 Business Process. This is an operating philosophy that states that 80% of their revenues and profits should come from just 20% of their customers. In a company where innovation is the key, this philosophy has helped ITW to focus their energies on product lines that will create the most synergy. ITW also emphasizes Customer Back Innovation, a term they use to

geogphotos/Alamy

describe that innovation is customer centered and focuses on the key needs of their most important constituents.

Illinois Tool Works has a strong global presence, operating in 57 countries, with major operations in Australia, Belgium, Brazil, Canada, China, Czech Republic, Denmark, France, Germany, Ireland, Italy, the Netherlands, Spain, Switzerland, and the United Kingdom. Though the United States is their biggest market, more than one-quarter of their revenues are in Europe and more than ten percent in Asia. This geographic diversification helps to mitigate the risk associated with the downturn in any regional economy.

These strategies have paid off for Illinois Tool Works. Like most companies, they were hit hard by the recession, but they have rebounded strongly. Their stock price nearly quadrupled in the seven years from 2008 to 2015. ITW's strategy and organizational structure have allowed the company to weather tough times and have positioned them for success in the future.[13]

which much decision-making authority is delegated to levels of management at various points below the top. Decentralization is typical in firms that have complex and dynamic environmental conditions. It is also common in businesses that specialize in customer services. Decentralization makes a company more responsive by allowing managers increased discretion to make quick decisions in their areas of responsibility. For example, Urban Outfitters practices relative decentralization in that it allows individual store managers considerable discretion over merchandising and product displays. Whole Foods Market takes things even further in its decentralization. Stores are broken up into small teams, which are responsible for making decisions on issues such as voting on which new staff members to hire and which products to carry based on local preferences. This practice taps into the idea that the people who will be most affected by decisions should be the ones making them.[14]

Flat Organizational Structure
characteristic of decentralized companies with relatively few layers of management

Tall Organizational Structures
characteristic of centralized companies with multiple layers of management

Tall and Flat Organizations Decentralized firms tend to have relatively fewer layers of management, resulting in a **flat organizational structure** like that of the hypothetical law firm shown in Figure 6.3(a). Centralized firms typically require multiple layers of management and thus **tall organizational structures**, as in the U.S.

Army example in Figure 6.3(b). Because information, whether upward or downward bound, must pass through so many organizational layers, tall structures are prone to delays in information flow.

As organizations grow in size, it is both normal and necessary that they become at least somewhat taller. For instance, a small firm with only an owner-manager and a few employees is likely to have two layers, the owner-manager and the employees who report to that person. As the firm grows, more layers will be needed. A manager must ensure that he or she has only the number of layers his or her firm needs. Too few layers can create chaos and inefficiency, whereas too many layers can create rigidity and bureaucracy.

Span of Control As you can see in Figure 6.3, the distribution of authority in an organization also affects the number of people who work for any individual manager. In a flat organizational structure, the number of people directly managed by one supervisor, the manager's **span of control**, is usually wide. In tall organizations, span of control tends to be narrower. Employees' abilities and the supervisor's managerial skills influence how wide or narrow the span of control should be, as do the similarity and simplicity of tasks and the extent to which they are interrelated.

Span of Control *number of people supervised by one manager*

If lower-level managers are given more decision-making authority, their supervisors will have fewer responsibilities and may then be able to take on a widened span of control. Similarly, when several employees perform either the same simple task or a group of interrelated tasks, a wide span of control is possible and often desirable.

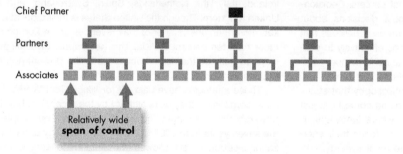

(a) FLAT ORGANIZATION: Typical Law Firm

Chief Partner

Partners

Associates

Relatively wide **span of control**

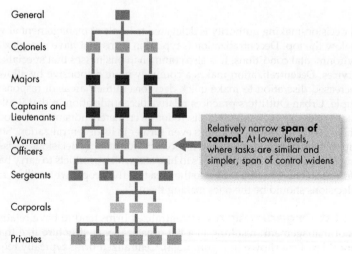

(b) TALL ORGANIZATION: U.S. Army

General

Colonels

Majors

Captains and Lieutenants

Warrant Officers

Sergeants

Corporals

Privates

Relatively narrow **span of control**. At lower levels, where tasks are similar and simpler, span of control widens

FIGURE 6.3 Organizational Structures and Span of Control

For instance, because of the routine and interdependent nature of jobs on an assembly line, one supervisor may well control the entire line.

In contrast, when jobs are more diversified or prone to change, a narrow span of control is preferable. Consider how Electronic Arts develops video games. Design, art, audio, and software development teams have specialized jobs whose products must come together in the end to create a coherent game. Although related, the complexities involved with and the advanced skills required by each job mean that one supervisor can oversee only a small number of employees.

The Delegation Process

Delegation is the process through which a manager allocates work to subordinates. In general, the delegation process involves:

Delegation *process through which a manager allocates work to subordinates*

1 Assigning **responsibility**, the duty to perform an assigned task

Responsibility *duty to perform an assigned task*

2 Granting **authority**, or the power to make the decisions necessary to complete the task.

Authority *power to make the decisions necessary to complete a task*

3 Creating **accountability**, the obligation employees have for the successful completion of the task

Accountability *obligation employees have to their manager for the successful completion of an assigned task*

For the delegation process to work smoothly, responsibility and authority must be equivalent. Table 6.1 lists some common obstacles that hinder the delegation process, along with strategies for overcoming them.

Three Forms of Authority

As individuals are delegated responsibility and authority, a complex web of interactions develops in the form of *line, staff,* and *committee and team* authorities.

Line Authority The type of authority that flows up and down the chain of command is **line authority**. Most companies rely heavily on **line departments** linked directly to the production and sales of specific products. For example, in the division of Clark Equipment that produces forklifts and small earthmovers, line departments include purchasing, materials handling, fabrication, painting, and assembly (all of which are directly linked to production) along with sales and distribution (both of which are directly linked to sales).

Line Authority *organizational structure in which authority flows in a direct chain of command from the top of the company to the bottom*

Line Department *department directly linked to the production and sales of a specific product*

As the doers and producers, each line department is essential to an organization's ability to sell and deliver finished goods. A bad decision by the manager in one

table 6.1   Learning to Delegate Effectively

I'm afraid to delegate because...	Solution
My team doesn't know how to get the job done.	If members of your team are exhibiting opportunities for improved performance, offer them the training necessary for them to become more effective at their jobs.
I like controlling as many things as possible.	Recognize that trying to accomplish everything yourself while your team does nothing only sets you up for burnout and failure. As you begin to relinquish control, you will come to trust your team more as you watch your team members succeed.
I don't want anyone on my team outperforming me.	High-performing team members are a reflection of your success as a manager. Encourage them to excel, praise them for it, and share the success of your team with the rest of the organization.
I don't know how to delegate tasks effectively.	Consider taking a management training course or reading some books on the topic of delegating effectively.

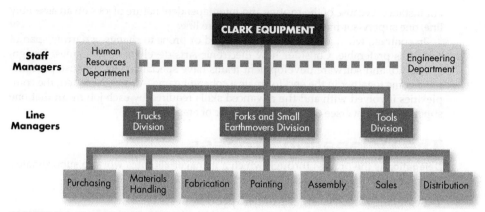

FIGURE 6.4 Line and Staff Organization

department can hold up production for an entire plant. For example, suppose the painting department manager at Clark Equipment changes a paint application on a batch of forklifts, which then show signs of peeling paint. The batch will have to be repainted (and perhaps partially reassembled) before the machines can be shipped.

Staff Authority   Some companies also rely on **staff authority**, which is based on special expertise and usually involves advising line managers in areas such as law, accounting, and human resources. A corporate attorney, for example, may advise the marketing department as it prepares a new contract with the firm's advertising agency, but will not typically make decisions that affect how the marketing department does its job. **Staff members** help line departments make decisions but do not usually have the authority to make final decisions.

Typically, the separation between line authority and staff responsibility is clearly delineated and is usually indicated in organization charts by solid lines (line authority) and dotted lines (staff responsibility), as shown in Figure 6.4. It may help to understand this separation by remembering that whereas *staff members* generally provide services to management, *line managers* are directly involved in producing the firm's products.

Committee and Team Authority   In recent times, many organizations have started to grant *committee and team authority* to groups that play central roles in daily operations. A committee, for example, may consist of top managers from several major areas. If the work of the committee is especially important and if the committee members will be working together for an extended time, the organization may grant it **committee and team authority**, special authority as a decision-making body beyond the individual authority possessed by each of its members.

At the operating level, many firms today use **work teams** that are empowered to plan, organize, and perform their work with minimal supervision and often with special authority as well. Most U.S. companies today use teams in at least some areas; some make widespread use of teams throughout every area of their operations.

Basic Forms of Organizational Structure

Organizations can structure themselves in an almost infinite number of ways; according to specialization, for example, or departmentalization, or the decision-making hierarchy. Nevertheless, it is possible to identify four basic forms of organizational structure that reflect the general trends followed by most firms: (1) *functional*, (2) *divisional*, (3) *matrix*, and (4) *international*.

Staff Authority *authority based on expertise that usually involves counseling and advising line managers*

Staff Members *advisers and counselors who help line departments in making decisions but who do not have the authority to make final decisions*

Committee and Team Authority *authority granted to committees or teams involved in a firm's daily operations*

Work Team *groups of operating employees who are empowered to plan and organize their own work and to perform that work with a minimum of supervision*

OBJECTIVE 6-4
Explain
the differences among functional, divisional, matrix, and international organizational structures and describe the most popular new forms of organizational design.

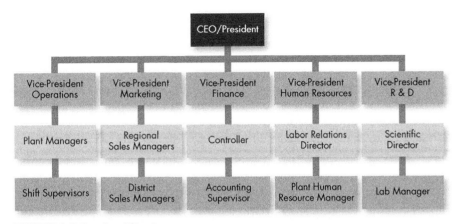

FIGURE 6.5 Functional Structure

Functional Structure

Under a **functional structure**, relationships between group functions and activities determine authority. Functional structure is used by most small to medium-sized firms, which are usually structured around basic business functions: a marketing department, an operations department, and a finance department. The benefits of this approach include specialization within functional areas and smoother coordination among them.

In large firms, coordination across functional departments becomes more complicated. Functional structure also fosters centralization (which can be desirable but is usually counter to the goals of larger businesses) and makes accountability more difficult. As organizations grow, they tend to shed this form and move toward one of the other three structures. Figure 6.5 illustrates a functional structure.

Divisional Structure

A **divisional structure** relies on product departmentalization. Organizations using this approach are typically structured around several product-based **divisions** that resemble separate businesses in that they produce and market their own products. The head of each division may be a corporate vice-president or, if the organization is large enough, a divisional president. In addition, each division usually has its own identity and operates as a relatively autonomous business under the larger corporate umbrella. Figure 6.6 illustrates a divisional structure.

Johnson & Johnson, one of the most recognizable names in healthcare products, organizes its company into three major divisions: consumer healthcare products, medical devices and diagnostics, and pharmaceuticals. Each major division is then

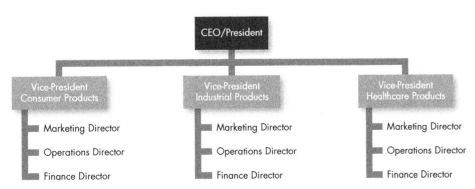

FIGURE 6.6 Divisional Structure

broken down further. The consumer healthcare products division relies on product departmentalization to separate baby care, skin and hair care, topical health care, oral health care, women's health, over-the-counter medicines, and nutritionals. These divisions reflect the diversity of the company, which can protect it during downturns, such as the recession in 2008–2010, which showed the slowest pharmaceutical growth in four decades. Because they are divided, the other divisions are protected from this decline and can carry the company through it.

Consider also that Johnson & Johnson's over-the-counter pain management medicines are essentially competition for their pain management pharmaceuticals. Divisions can maintain healthy competition among themselves by sponsoring separate advertising campaigns, fostering different corporate identities, and so forth. They can also share certain corporate-level resources (such as market research data). However, if too much control is delegated to divisional managers, corporate managers may lose touch with daily operations. Also, competition between divisions can become disruptive, and efforts in one division may duplicate those of another.[15]

Matrix Structure

Sometimes a **matrix structure**, a combination of two separate structures, works better than either simpler structure alone. This structure gets its matrix-like appearance, when shown in a diagram, by using one underlying "permanent" organizational structure (say, the divisional structure flowing up-and-down in the diagram), and then superimposing a different organizing framework on top of it (e.g., the functional form flowing side-to-side in the diagram). This highly flexible and readily adaptable structure was pioneered by NASA for use in developing specific space programs.

Matrix Structure *organizational structure created by superimposing one form of structure onto another*

Suppose a company using a functional structure wants to develop a new product as a one-time special project. A team might be created and given responsibility for that product. The project team may draw members from existing functional departments, such as finance and marketing, so that all viewpoints are represented as the new product is being developed; the marketing member may provide ongoing information about product packaging and pricing issues, for instance, and the finance member may have useful information about when funds will be available.

In some companies, the matrix organization is a temporary measure installed to complete a specific project and affecting only one part of the firm. In these firms, the end of the project usually means the end of the matrix—either a breakup of the team or a restructuring to fit it into the company's existing line-and-staff structure. Ford, for example, uses a matrix organization to design new models, such as the newest Mustang. A design team composed of people with engineering, marketing, operations, and finance expertise was created to design the new car. After its work was done, the team members moved back to their permanent functional jobs.[16]

In other settings, the matrix organization is a semipermanent fixture. Figure 6.7 shows how Martha Stewart Living Omnimedia has created a permanent matrix organization for its lifestyle business. As you can see, the company is organized broadly into media and merchandising groups, each of which has specific product and product groups. For instance, there is an Internet group housed within the media group. Layered on top of this structure are teams of lifestyle experts led by area specialists organized into groups, such as cooking, entertainment, weddings, crafts, and so forth. Although each group targets specific customer needs, they all work, as necessary, across all product groups. An area specialist in weddings, for example, might contribute to an article on wedding planning for an Omnimedia magazine, contribute a story idea for an Omnimedia cable television program, and supply content for an Omnimedia site. This same individual might also help select fabrics suitable for wedding gowns that are to be retailed.

International Structure

Several different **international organizational structures** are also common among firms that actively manufacture, purchase, and sell in global markets. These structures also evolve over time as a firm becomes more globalized. For example, when

International Organizational Structures *approaches to organizational structure developed in response to the need to manufacture, purchase, and sell in global markets*

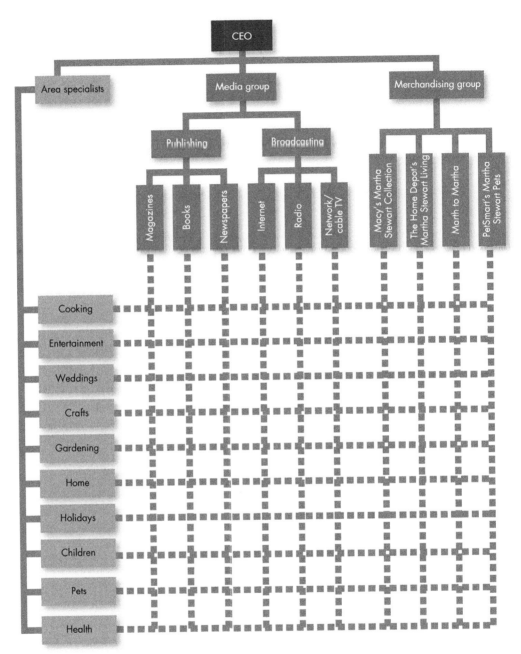

FIGURE 6.7 Matrix Organization of Martha Stewart Living Omnimedia

Walmart opened its first store outside the United States in 1992, it set up a special projects team. In the mid-1990s, the firm created a small international department to handle overseas expansion. By 1999 international sales and expansion had become such a major part of operations that a separate international division headed up by a senior vice-president was created. By 2002, international operations had become so important that the international division was further divided into geographic areas, such as Mexico and Europe. And as the firm expands into more foreign markets, such as Russia and India, new units are created to oversee those operations.[17]

Some companies adopt a truly global structure in which they acquire resources (including capital), produce goods and services, engage in research and development,

FIGURE 6.8 International Division Structure

and sell products in whatever local market is appropriate, without consideration of national boundaries. Until a few years ago, General Electric (GE) kept its international business operations as separate divisions, as illustrated in Figure 6.8. Now, however, the company functions as one integrated global organization. GE businesses around the world connect and interact with each other constantly, and managers freely move back and forth among them. This integration is also reflected in GE's executive team, which includes executives from Spain, Japan, Scotland, Ireland, and Italy.[18]

New Forms of Organizational Structure

As the world grows increasingly complex and fast-paced, organizations also continue to seek new forms of organization that permit them to compete effectively. Among the most popular of these new forms are the *team organization*, the *virtual organization*, and the *learning organization*.

Team Organization *Team organization* relies almost exclusively on project-type teams, with little or no underlying functional hierarchy. People float from project to project as dictated by their skills and the demands of those projects. As the term suggests, team authority is the underlying foundation of organizations that adopt this organizational structure.

Virtual Organization Closely related to the team organization is the *virtual organization*. A virtual organization has little or no formal structure. Typically, it has only a handful of permanent employees, a small staff, and a modest administrative facility. As the needs of the organization change, its managers bring in temporary workers, lease facilities, and outsource basic support services to meet the demands of each unique situation. As the situation changes, the temporary workforce changes in parallel, with some people leaving the organization and others entering. Facilities and the subcontracted services also change. In other words, the virtual organization exists only in response to its own needs.[19] This structure would be applicable to research or consulting firms that hire consultants based on the specific content knowledge required by each unique project. As the projects change, so too does the composition of the organization. Figure 6.9 illustrates a hypothetical virtual organization.

Learning Organization The so-called *learning organization* works to integrate continuous improvement with continuous employee learning and development. Specifically, a learning organization works to facilitate the lifelong learning and personal development of all of its employees while continually transforming itself to respond to changing demands and needs.

Although managers might approach the concept of a learning organization from a variety of perspectives, the most frequent goals are superior quality, continuous improvement, and performance measurement. The idea is that the most consistent and logical strategy for achieving continuous improvement is to constantly upgrade

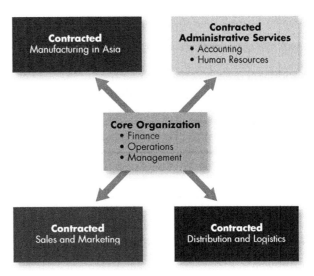

FIGURE 6.9 The Virtual Organization

employee talent, skill, and knowledge. For example, if each employee in an organization learns one new thing each day and can translate that knowledge into work-related practice, continuous improvement will logically follow. Indeed, organizations that wholeheartedly embrace this approach believe that only through constant employee learning can continuous improvement really occur. Shell Oil's Shell Learning Center boasts state-of-the-art classrooms and instructional technology, lodging facilities, a restaurant, and recreational amenities. Line managers rotate through the center to fulfill teaching assignments, and Shell employees routinely attend training programs, seminars, and related activities.

OBJECTIVE 6-5
Describe
the informal organization and discuss intrapreneuring.

Informal Organization *network, unrelated to the firm's formal authority structure, of everyday social interactions among company employees*

Informal Organization

The structure of a company, however, is by no means limited to the *formal organization* as represented by the organization chart and the formal assignment of authority. Frequently, the **informal organization**, everyday social interactions among employees that transcend formal jobs and job interrelationships, effectively alters a company's formal structure.[20] This level of organization is sometimes just as powerful—if not more powerful—than the formal structure. When Hewlett-Packard fired its CEO, Carly Fiorina, a few years ago, much of the discussion that led to her firing took place outside formal structural arrangements in the organization. Members of the board of directors, for example, held secret meetings and reached confidential agreements among themselves before Fiorina's future with the company was addressed in a formal manner.[21]

On the negative side, the informal organization can reinforce office politics that put the interests of individuals ahead of those of the firm and can disseminate distorted or inaccurate information. For example, if the informal organization is highlighting false information about impending layoffs, valuable employees may act quickly (and unnecessarily) to seek other employment.

Informal Groups

Informal groups are simply groups of people who decide to interact among themselves. They may be people who work together in a formal sense or who just get together for lunch, during breaks, or after work. They may talk about business, the boss, or nonwork-related topics such as families, movies, or sports. Their impact on the organization may be positive (if they work together to support the organization), negative (if they work together in ways that run counter to the organization's interests), or irrelevant (if what they do is unrelated to the organization).

Informal groups can be a powerful force that managers cannot ignore.[22] One writer described how a group of employees at a furniture factory subverted their boss's efforts to increase production. They tacitly agreed to produce a reasonable amount of work but not to work too hard. One man kept a stockpile of completed work hidden as a backup in case he got too far behind. In another example, auto workers described how they left out gaskets and seals and put soft-drink bottles inside doors to cause customer complaints.[23] Of course, informal groups can also be a positive force, as when people work together to help out a colleague who has suffered a personal tragedy. For example, several instances of this behavior were reported in the wake of the devastating tornadoes that swept through Alabama and Missouri in 2011, after hurricane Sandy devastated parts of the northeast in 2012, and during the Ebola virus outbreak in 2014–15.

In recent years the Internet has served as a platform for the emergence of more and different kinds of informal or interest groups. As one example, Yahoo! includes a wide array of interest groups that bring together people with common interests. And increasingly, workers who lose their jobs as a result of layoffs are banding together electronically to offer moral support to one another and to facilitate networking as they all look for new jobs.[24] Indeed, social media plays a major role in informal groups today.

Organizational Grapevine

The **grapevine** is an informal communication network that can permeate an entire organization. Grapevines are found in all organizations except the smallest, but they do not always follow the same patterns as, nor do they necessarily coincide with, formal channels of authority and communication. Research has identified two kinds of grapevines.[25] One such grapevine, the gossip chain, occurs when one person spreads the message to many other people. Each one, in turn, may either keep the information confidential or pass it on to others. The gossip chain is likely to carry personal information. The other common grapevine is the cluster chain, in which one person passes the information to a selected few individuals. Some of the receivers pass the information to a few other individuals; the rest keep it to themselves.

Grapevine *informal communication network that runs through an organization*

There is some disagreement about how accurate the information carried by the grapevine is, but research is increasingly finding it to be fairly accurate, especially when the information is based on fact rather than speculation. One study found that the grapevine may be between 75 percent and 95 percent accurate.[26] That same study also found that informal communication is increasing in many organizations for several basic reasons. One contributing factor is the recent increase in merger, acquisition, and takeover activity. Because such activity can greatly affect the people within an organization, it follows that they may spend more time talking about it.[27] The second contributing factor is that as more and more corporations move facilities from inner cities to suburbs, employees tend to talk less and less to others outside the organization and more and more to one another. Yet another contributing factor is simply the widespread availability of information technology that makes it easier than ever before for people to communicate quickly and easily. Much like in informal groups, social media plays a growing role in the grapevine.

More recently, another study looked at the effects of the recent recession and large-scale job losses on informal communication. More than half of the survey participants reported a sharp increase in gossip and rumors in their organizations. The same survey also reported an increase in the amount of eavesdropping in the most businesses.[28] Further, in another recent survey, 32 percent of people claimed to use their work e-mail inappropriately and 48 percent admitted gossiping with other employees through their e-mail.[29] In 2014, a poll found that 47 percent of those responding indicated that they gossiped at work and 18 agreed that no topics were "off-limits." And yet another study reported that 55 percent of conversations in the workplace between men and 67 percent of conversations among women involved at least some gossip.[30]

Attempts to eliminate the grapevine are fruitless, but fortunately the manager does have some control over it. By maintaining open channels of communication and responding vigorously to inaccurate information, the manager can minimize the damage the grapevine can do. The grapevine can actually be an asset. By learning who the key people in the grapevine are, for example, the manager can partially control the information they receive and use the grapevine to sound out employee reactions to new ideas, such as a change in human resource policies or benefit packages. The manager can also get valuable information from the grapevine and use it to improve decision making.[31]

Intrapreneuring

Good managers recognize that the informal organization exists whether they want it or not and can use it not only to reinforce the formal organization, but also to harness its energy to improve productivity.

Intrapreneuring *process of creating and maintaining the innovation and flexibility of a small-business environment within the confines of a large organization*

Many firms, including Rubbermaid, Dreamworks, 3M, and Xerox, support **intrapreneuring**, creating and maintaining the innovation and flexibility of a small-business environment within a large, bureaucratic structure. Historically, most innovations have come from individuals in small businesses. As businesses increase in size, however, innovation and creativity tend to become casualties in the battle for more sales and profits. In some large companies, new ideas are even discouraged, and champions of innovation have been stalled in midcareer. At Lockheed Martin, the Advanced Development Programs (ADP) encourages intrapreneurship in the tradition of Skunk Works, a legendary team developed in 1943 as engineer Kelly Johnson's response to Lockheed's need for a powerful jet fighter. Johnson's innovative organization approach broke all the rules, and not only did it work, but it also taught Lockheed the value of encouraging that kind of thinking.[32]

There are three intrapreneurial roles in large organizations.[33] To successfully use intrapreneurship to encourage creativity and innovation, the organization must find one or more individuals to perform these roles. The *inventor* is the person who actually conceives of and develops the new idea, product, or service by means of the creative process. Because the inventor may lack the expertise or motivation to oversee the transformation of the product or service from an idea into a marketable entity, however, a second role comes into play. A *product champion* is usually a middle manager who learns about the project and becomes committed to it. He or she helps overcome organizational resistance and convinces others to take the innovation seriously. The product champion may have only limited understanding of the technological aspects of the innovation. Nevertheless, product champions are skilled at knowing how the organization works, whose support is needed to push the project forward, and where to go to secure the resources necessary for successful development. A *sponsor* is a top-level manager who approves of and supports a project. This person may fight for the budget needed to develop an idea, overcome arguments against a project, and use organizational politics to ensure the project's survival. With a sponsor in place, the inventor's idea has a much better chance of being successfully developed.

summary of learning objectives

Discuss the factors that influence a firm's organizational structure. (pp. 204–207)

Each organization must develop an appropriate *organizational structure*—the specification of the jobs to be done and the ways in which those jobs relate to one another. Most organizations change structures almost continuously. Firms prepare *organization charts* to clarify structure and to show employees where they fit into a firm's operations. Each box represents a job, and solid lines define the *chain of command*, or *reporting relationships*. The charts of large firms are complex and include individuals at many levels. Because size prevents them from charting every manager, they may create single organization charts for overall corporate structure and separate charts for divisions. An organization's structure is determined by a variety of factors, including the organization's mission and strategy, size, environment, and history. Structure is not static but is changed and modified frequently.

Explain specialization and departmentalization as two of the building blocks of organizational structure. (pp. 207–211)

The process of identifying specific jobs and designating people to perform them leads to *job specialization*. After they're specialized, jobs are grouped into logical units—the process of *departmentalization*. Departmentalization follows one (or any combination) of five forms:

1 *functional departmentalization* based on functions or activities

2 *product departmentalization* based on products or services offered

3 *process departmentalization* based on production processes used to create goods and services

4 *customer departmentalization* based on customer types or customer groups

5 *geographic departmentalization* based on geographic areas

Larger companies may take advantage of different types of departmentalization for various levels.

Describe centralization and decentralization, delegation, and authority as the key ingredients in establishing the decision-making hierarchy. (pp. 211–215)

After jobs have been specialized and departmentalized, firms establish decision-making hierarchies. One major issue addressed through the creation of the decision-making hierarchy involves whether the firm will be relatively *centralized* or relatively *decentralized*. In a centralized organization, decision-making authority is retained at the top levels of the organization. Centralized authority systems typically require multiple layers of management and thus *tall organizational structures*. Conversely, in a decentralized organization, most decision-making authority is delegated to lower levels of management. A related concept is *span of control*, which refers to the number of people who report to a manager. Tall, centralized organizations tend to have a narrow span of control, whereas flat, centralized organizations tend to have wider spans of control.

Decentralized firms tend to have relatively fewer layers of management, resulting in a *flat organizational structure*. *Delegation* is the process through which a manager allocates work to subordinates. In general, the delegation process involves three steps:

1 the assignment of *responsibility*

2 the granting of *authority,*

3 the creation of *accountability.*

As individuals are delegated responsibility and authority in a firm, a complex web of interactions develops.

These interactions may take one of three forms of authority: line, staff, or committee and team. Line authority follows the chain of command, and staff authority relies on expertise in areas such as law, accounting, and human resources.

OBJECTIVE 6-4

Explain the differences among functional, divisional, matrix, and international organizational structures and describe the most popular new forms of organizational design. (pp. 215–220)

Most firms rely on one of four basic forms of organizational structure: (1) *functional*, (2) *divisional*, (3) *matrix*, or (4) *international*. A functional structure is based on organizational functions, such as marketing, finance, or operations. A divisional structure, in contrast, groups activities in terms of distinct product or service groups. A matrix structure, a combination of two structures, imposes one type of structure on top of another. Several different international organizational structures have emerged in response to the need to manufacture, purchase, and sell in global markets. A company may start with a small international department that may grow into an international division. As global competition becomes more complex, companies may experiment with ways to respond. Some adopt truly global structures, acquiring resources and producing and selling products in local markets without consideration of national boundaries.

Organizations also continue to seek new forms of organization that permit them to compete effectively. The most popular new forms include

1 *team organizations*, which rely almost exclusively on project-type teams with little or no underlying functional hierarchy.

2 *virtual organizations*, which have little or no formal structure and just a handful of employees.

3 *learning organizations*, which work to integrate continuous improvement with ongoing employee learning and development.

OBJECTIVE 6-5

Describe the informal organization and discuss intrapreneuring.
(pp. 220–222)

The *formal organization* is the part that can be represented in chart form. The *informal organization*, everyday social interactions among employees that transcend formal jobs and job interrelationships, may alter formal structure. There are two important elements in most informal organizations. *Informal groups* consist of people who decide to interact among themselves. Their impact on a firm may be positive, negative, or irrelevant. The *grapevine* is an informal communication network that can run through an entire organization. Because it can be harnessed to improve productivity, some organizations encourage the informal organization. Many firms also support *intrapreneuring*—creating and maintaining the innovation and flexibility of a small business within the confines of a large, bureaucratic structure. In large organizations, intrapreneurship requires the participation of individuals who will serve roles as inventors, product champions, and sponsors.

key terms

accountability
authority
centralized organization
chain of command
committee and team authority
customer departmentalization

decentralized organization
delegation
departmentalization
division
divisional structure
flat organizational structure

functional departmentalization
functional structure
geographic departmentalization
grapevine
informal organization
international organizational structures

intrapreneuring	organizational structure	staff authority
job specialization	process departmentalization	staff members
line authority	product departmentalization	tall organizational structure
line department	profit center	work team
matrix structure	responsibility	
organization chart	span of control	

MyBizLab

To complete the problems with the ✪, go to EOC Discussion Questions in the MyLab.

questions & exercises

QUESTIONS FOR REVIEW

6-1. What do the solid lines in an organization chart represent?

6-2. What does a manager's span of control suggest in terms of their workload?

6-3. If a manager believes that they cannot delegate because they like to control everything, what is the solution?

✪ 6-4. What are the significant differences between line authority and staff authority in an organization?

✪ 6-5. How can grapevines in organizations be both positive and negative?

QUESTIONS FOR ANALYSIS

6-6. What does the so-called learning organization aim to achieve?

6-7. Describe a hypothetical organizational structure for a small printing firm. Describe changes that might be necessary as the business grows.

✪ 6-8. Do you think that you would want to work in a matrix organization, such as Martha Stewart Living Omnimedia, where you were assigned simultaneously to multiple units or groups? Why or why not?

APPLICATION EXERCISES

6-9. Interview the manager of a local service business, such as a fast-food restaurant. What types of tasks does this manager typically delegate? Is the appropriate authority also delegated in each case?

6-10. Select a company where you would like to work one day. Using online research, determine if the company has a functional, divisional, matrix, international, team, virtual, or learning organization. Explain how you arrived at this conclusion. Do you believe that their organizational structure is consistent with the organization's mission?

building a business: continuing team exercise

Assignment

Meet with your team members and discuss your new business venture within the context of this chapter. Develop specific responses to the following:

6-11. Thinking ahead one year, how many employees do you expect that you will have in your business? How did you come to this conclusion?

6-12. Draw a sample organization chart for your business in one year. Although you won't know the names of all

your employees, your organization chart should include job titles.

6-13. Will decision-making in your business be centralized or decentralized? Be sure to support your conclusion.

6-14. How do you think that your organizational structure will change over time? Will it be the same in 10 years?

team exercise

TRUSTED FRIENDS

Background Information

You are the founder of a small but growing chain of coffee shops. You have eight shops and all of them are managed by

employees that have worked under your management in the original shop. You consider each of them to be friends and you trust all of them to follow your vision of how the shop should work. As the chain has grown you are spending less and less time in the coffee shops. You barely spend two or three days in the original coffee shop each month and with the prospect of opening three new shops in a city fifty miles away this is likely to be less in months to come.

Method

Working with three or four classmates, identify some ways in which specific organizational changes could mean that you were able to use similar techniques to train and choose potential managers even given the fact that you are too busy to devote much time yourself:

- *Delegation.* would it be possible to choose one of your current managers and give them the responsibility of choosing future managers for the new coffee shops? Is there one manager that you trust enough to take on your role? How might this work as an option?
- *Concentrated Training Programs.* another option could be to establish tri-annual training programs that you would lead. Other managers would choose candidates for the training.

- *Remote observation.* setting up cameras and watching the footage might be an option so you can see what is happening.
- *Shadowing.* perhaps good candidates could accompany you on your work so you can get to know them?

FOLLOW-UP QUESTIONS

6-15. What organizational changes are going to be necessary in order for you to continue to grow and select the right managers?

6-16. If you were the owner of the company, how would you choose the right coffee shop managers?

6-17. As the company founder, how willing would you be to make major organizational changes in light your increased and difficult workload?

exercising your ethics

I HEARD IT THROUGH THE GRAPEVINE

The Situation

Assume that you are a divisional manager at a large high-tech company. The company has just lost a large contract, and the human resources direction has just advised company executives that they must cut the workforce by 10 percent within three months to preserve their financial position. You are distressed at the prospect of losing long-time employees, especially those nearing retirement or with young families.

The Dilemma

As you ponder the situation, another regional member has brought up a potential solution that will spare you from actually

laying off employees. "The grapevine has worked against us in the past, so let's make it work for us this time. If we leak word that the company is planning to cut pay by 15 percent for most of the workforce as a result of the loss of this contract, people will get scared. They'll start looking for jobs or reevaluating retirement and the layoff will take care of itself. Once we've reached the desired level of resignations, we will reassure the remaining employees that their jobs are secure."

QUESTION TO ADDRESS

6-18. What are the ethical issues in this situation?

6-19. What do you think most people would do in this situation?

6-20. What would you do in this situation?

cases

Pushing the Product

Continued from page 204

In October 2015, SAA announced three additional weekly flights to Nigeria. It was hoped that this would help to encourage extra trade and mobility between the two countries. The expansion of operations was made possible by the successful introduction of SAA's West African service out of Accra in Ghana to Washington Dulles, USA in August 2015. SAA had cemented their turnaround and had begun their African growth strategy.

QUESTIONS FOR DISCUSSION

6-21. Identify as many examples that are closely related to organization structure as possible in this case.

6-22. In what ways does its structure help and hurt South African Airways?

6-23. If South African Airways wanted to change its structure, what structure would you suggest?

6-24. What aspects, if any, of virtual and learning organization structure do you see at South African Airways?

Heard it Through the Grapevine

When you think of the word "gossip," it's most likely that the term has negative connotations. Take it one step farther, into the workplace, and you almost certainly have concerns. However, there is considerable research to support the claim that gossip, or the grapevine, is an important part of organizational culture. According to Professor Kathleen Reardon of the USC Marshall School of Business, "We learn who we are through what people say to us and about us."[34] Managing the office grapevine and your role in this informal communication can be tricky.

Several guidelines can help you understand when to participate in gossip as a sender or receiver. First, you should understand the benefits of gossip. Gossip, or the office grapevine, may be the first place that you hear important information, such as a new job opening up or a major contract that the company is about to sign. However, as you pass along information, you must remember that what you say will reflect upon you. If you share negative information about a coworker, it is very likely that others may come to distrust you. In addition, you should carefully consider the people with whom you share gossip and information, making sure that they will keep confidential information private. Your supervisor may be particularly uncomfortable if you develop a reputation as a gossip, as your comments may be perceived as threatening. Finally, be very careful about the medium that you choose to share information. An email is never private and should not be used for any communication that you would not want shared publicly.[35]

As a manager, you may have a slightly different perspective on gossip or the office grapevine. You may be concerned that gossip limits your ability to control how information is shared and may limit your power. Holly Green, in an article in *Fortune* magazine, shares several suggestions about managing the office grapevine.[36] A vigorous grapevine is often the sign of boredom. Rather than having employees spend hours a week gossiping about others, find other outlets for their creative abilities. You should also realize that grapevines grow most quickly when information is scarce. Employees turn to the grapevine when they believe that they are not getting enough information from formal channels of communication. Therefore, to control rampant gossip, a manager should work towards intentionally sharing as much information as possible. Managers should also keep their ear to the grapevine, as it may convey important information,

such as manageable concerns of employees. Managed correctly, the grapevine can be a powerful tool for employees and managers.

QUESTIONS FOR DISCUSSION

6-25. Thinking about your office or college, what types of information are conveyed through the grapevine? How often is the information accurate?

6-26. Does a flat organization encourage or discourage office gossip? What leads you to this conclusion?

6-27. Do you think that the grapevine would be more or less active in a matrix organization? Why?

6-28. Many companies encourage their employees to form social relationships outside of work to build a sense of camaraderie. How would these informal groups feed or limit the grapevine?

6-29. Consider the following situation: You are the HR manager at a medium-sized business and the company's executives have decided that they must cut the workforce by 5%. You don't want to layoff anyone, so you "leak" information to a few people in the company that layoffs are imminent, hoping that this might motivate some employees to find jobs elsewhere. If people end up leaving on their own, you will not have to implement layoffs. Do you think that this is an ethical use of the grapevine? Why or why not?

MyBizLab

Go to the Assignments section of your MyLab to complete these writing exercises.

6-30. Each organization's structure is unique, but most structures can be grouped into four basic forms. There are advantages and disadvantages to each form of organization structure. Which of the four basic forms of organizational structure would you rather work in? Write an essay: (a) Explaining your choice, including the advantages and disadvantages of that form of organizational structure, and (b) Describing under what conditions that structure might work best.

6-31. How does an organization chart reflect the formal structure of an organization? Why is this important to managers and employees? Does organizational structure change over time? How does the informal organization differ from the formal structure? Which is more important and why?

end notes

[1]See Royston Greenwood and Danny Miller, "Tackling Design Anew: Getting Back to the Heart of Organizational Theory," *Academy of Management Perspectives*, November 2010, pp. 78–88.

[2]Henry Mintzberg, "Structure in 5's: A Synthesis of the Research on Organization Design," *Management Science*, March 1980, p. 322–341.

[3]Claire Suddath, "Why There are No Bosses at Valve," *Bloomberg Business*, April 27, 2012, at http://www.bloomberg.com/bw/articles/2012-04-27/why-there-are-no-bosses-at-valve#p1, accessed April 26, 2015.

[4]Claire Suddath, "What Makes Valve Software the Best Office Ever," *Bloomberg Business*, April 22, 2012, at http://www.bloomberg.com/bw/articles/2012-04-25/what-makes-valve-software-the-shangri-la-of-offices, accessed April 26, 2015.

[5]Joann S. Lublin, "Place vs. Product: It's Tough to Choose a Management Model," *Wall Street Journal*, June 27, 2001, A1, A4; Joann Muller, "Ford: Why It's Worse Than You Think," *BusinessWeek*, June 25, 2001, pp. 58–59; *Hoover's Handbook of American Business 2015*, (Austin, Texas: Hoover's Business Press, 2015), pp. 140–142.

[6]"How Mulally Helped Turn Ford Around," *USA Today*, July 18, 2011, p. 2B; http://corporate.ford.com/microsites/sustainability-report-2011-12/blueprint-strategy.

[7]Steinway & Sons, "Steinway History: Leadership Through Craftsmanship and Innovation," 2012, at www.steinway.com, accessed on April 11, 2013; Steinway & Sons, "Online Factory Tour," 2012, at http://archive.steinway.com, accessed on April 11, 2013; Victor Verney, "88 Keys: The Making of a Steinway Piano," *All About Jazz*, June 18, 2012, at www.allaboutjazz.com, accessed on April 11, 2013; WGBH (Boston), "*Note by Note*: The Making of Steinway L1037," 2010, at www.wgbh.org, accessed on April 11, 2013; M. Eric Johnson, Joseph Hall, and David Pyke, "Technology and Quality at Steinway & Sons," Tuck School of Business at Dartmouth, May 13, 2005, at http://mba.tuck.dartmouth.edu, accessed on April 11, 2013.

[8]O'Malley Greenburg, Zack. 2014. "Piano Forte: Inside Steinway's Century-Spanning Business." Forbes.Com 17. Business Source Premier, EBSCOhost (accessed April 27, 2015).

[9]AllBusiness.com, "Kraft Foods North America Announces New Management Structure," September 28, 2000 (March 5, 2011), at http://www.allbusiness.com/food-beverage/food-beverage-overview/6505848-1.html.

[10]See Levi Strauss & Co., at http://www.levistrauss.com/Company/WorldwideRegions.aspx.

[11]"Blowing Up Pepsi," *BusinessWeek*, April 27, 2009, pp. 32–36; *Hoover's Handbook of American Business 2015* (Austin, Texas: Hoover's Business Press, 2015), pp. 638–639.

[12]Michael E. Raynor and Joseph L. Bower, "Lead From the Center," *Harvard Business Review*, May 2001, 93–102.

[13]2014. "Illinois Tool Works Inc. SWOT Analysis." Illinois Tool Works, Inc. SWOT Analysis 1-8. Business Source Premier, EBSCOhost (accessed April 27, 2015).

[14]Gary Hamel, "What Google, Whole Foods Do Best," *Fortune*, September 27, 2007, p. 59.

[15]*Hoover's Handbook of American Business 2013* (Austin, Texas: Hoover's Business Press, 2013), pp. 58–60; Brian Dumaine, "How I Delivered the Goods," *Fortune Small Business*, October 2002, pp. 78–81; Charles Haddad, "FedEx: Gaining on the Ground," *BusinessWeek*, December 16, 2002, pp. 126–128; Claudia H. Deutsch, "FedEx Has Hit the Ground Running, but Will Its Legs Tire?" *New York Times*, October 13, 2002, p. BU7; http://www.Forbes.com/finance (February 16, 2006); PBS.org, "Who Made America" (June 19, 2008), at http://www.pbs.org/wgbh/theymadeamerica/whomade/fsmith_hi.html.

[16]phx.corporate-ir.net/phoenix.zhtml?c=96022&p=irol-newsArticle&ID=1489110&highlight=.

[17]"Wal-Mart Acquires Interspar," *Management Ventures* (July 20, 2001), at http://www.mvi-insights.com/Index.aspx; Kerry Capell et al., "Wal-Mart's Not-So-Secret British Weapon," *BusinessWeek Online* (July 20, 2001), at http://www.businessweek.com/2000/00_04/b3665095.htm; Brent Schlender, "Wal-Mart's $288 Billion Meeting," *Fortune*, April 18, 2005, pp. 90–106; see http://walmart-stores.com.

[18]Thomas A. Stewart, "See Jack. See Jack Run," *Fortune*, September 27, 1999, pp. 124–271; Jerry Useem, "America's Most Admired Companies," *Fortune*, March 7, 2005, pp. 67–82; see GE.com, "Executive Leaders," at http://www.ge.com/company/leadership/executives.html.

[19]Leslie P. Willcocks and Robert Plant, "Getting from Bricks to Clicks," *Sloan Management Review*, Spring 2001, pp. 50–60.

[20]"The Office Chart That Really Counts," *BusinessWeek*, February 27, 2006, pp. 48–49.

[21]Carol Loomis, "How the HP Board KO'd Carly," *Fortune*, March 7, 2005, pp. 99–102.

[22]Rob Cross, Nitin Nohria, and Andrew Parker, "Six Myths about Informal Networks—And How to Overcome Them," *Sloan Management Review*, Spring 2002, pp. 67–77.

[23]Robert Schrank, *Ten Thousand Working Days* (Cambridge, MA: MIT Press, 1978); Bill Watson, "Counter Planning on the Shop Floor," in Peter Frost, Vance Mitchell, and Walter Nord (eds.), *Organizational Reality*, 2nd ed. (Glenview, IL: Scott, Foresman, 1982), pp. 286–294.

[24]"After Layoffs, More Workers Band Together," *Wall Street Journal*, February 26, 2002, p. B1.

[25]Keith Davis, "Management Communication and the Grapevine," *Harvard Business Review*, September–October 1953, pp. 43–49.

[26]"Spread the Word: Gossip Is Good," *Wall Street Journal*, October 4, 1988, p. B1.

[27]See David M. Schweiger and Angelo S. DeNisi, "Communication with Employees Following a Merger: A Longitudinal Field Experiment," *Academy of Management Journal*, March 1991, pp. 110–135.

[28]"Job Fears Make Offices All Fears," *Wall Street Journal*, January 20, 2009, p. B7.

[29]Institute of Leadership and Management, "32% of People Making Inappropriate Use of Work Emails," April 20, 2011; accessed on April 12, 2013.

[30]www.valuewalk.com/2014/05/avoid-office-gossip/, accessed on February 10, 2015.

[31]Nancy B. Kurland and Lisa Hope Pelled, "Passing the Word: Toward a Model of Gossip and Power in the Workplace," *Academy of Management Review*, 2000, Vol. 25, No. 2, pp. 428–438.

[32]Lockheed Martin, "Skunk Works" (June 19, 2008), at http://www.lockheedmartin.com/aeronautics/skunkworks/index.html.

[33]See Gifford Pinchot III, *Intrapreneuring* (New York: Harper & Row, 1985).

[34]Gallo, Amy. "Go Ahead and Gossip." *Harvard Business Review*. N.p., 21 Mar. 2013. Web. 19 June 2013.

[35]Spiers, Carole. "Managing Office Gossip." Gulfnews.com. Al Nisr Publishing LLC, 7 Jan. 2013. Web. 19 June 2013

[36]Green, Holly. "How to Prune Your Organizational Grapevine." Forbes. *Forbes Magazine*, 22 May 2012. Web. 19 June 2013.

Chapter 7
Marketing

Marketing Processes and Consumer Behavior

chapter 11

As consumers, we are the forces that drive marketing.

But those same marketing campaigns push

us in directions

without   us   even   knowing   it.

After reading this chapter, you should be able to:

11-1   **Explain** the concept of marketing and identify the five forces that constitute the external marketing environment.

11-2   **Explain** the purpose of a marketing plan and identify its main components.

11-3   **Explain** market segmentation and how it is used in target marketing.

11-4   **Discuss** the purpose of marketing research and compare the four marketing research methods.

11-5   **Describe** the consumer buying process and the key factors that influence that process.

11-6   **Discuss** the four categories of organizational markets and the characteristics of business-to-business (B2B) buying behavior.

11-7   **Discuss** the marketing mix as it applies to small business.

Building a Brand With
Social Media

Perhaps you are one of the more than 7 million people who subscribe to Michelle Phan's YouTube Channel. Or maybe you know someone who has purchased products from her L'Oreal product line.

Even if you've never heard the name Michelle Phan, you'll find that she has an interesting story that highlights the importance of believing in yourself, identifying a target market, and building a brand.

While taking a college class, Phan was given the opportunity to use a MacBook Pro. Excited about the new technology, Phan started a blog about her life. Well, not exactly. The blog depicted the life that she dreamed of, one with money and a fantastic family, a life that was much more exciting and glamorous than her real-life experience. Phan's childhood was difficult. She grew up in Florida in a community with few Asian children, she was subject to ridicule, and she felt out of place because of her Vietnamese heritage. To make things worse, her father had gambling issues and the family moved from home to home. Eventually, her father left and her mother remarried, only to have that relationship end. By the age of 17, Phan was working as a hostess at a restaurant to supplement her mom's meager pay as a nail technician, just to put a roof over their heads; they couldn't even afford much furniture. It was the chance of a lifetime when Phan's extended family found the resources to send her to the Ringling College of Art and Design, where she received that MacBook Pro.

However, her blog was just the start. Several subscribers to her blog asked her to post a tutorial about how she did her makeup, so Phan created a short video tutorial about creating a "natural" look. She had expected that the audience for the video would be just the few people who read her blog, but she had 40,000 views in the first week. So, she created more videos on how to create different looks, from dark and stormy to soft hues appropriate for church. Phan established herself as an authority on beauty and she shared her expertise. "You need interesting content that entertains or informs—preferably both. You want people to look forward to your posts and come back for more. People want to follow you. They want to hear your words and see your vision." Her lack of money to buy makeup didn't limit her ability to create new videos—she scoured the bargain bins at stores, picking up many items for less than a dollar. Eventually, she was able to generate advertising revenue from her YouTube channel, allowing her to quit her job as a waitress.

Within four years, Phan had become a brand. The name Michelle Phan conveyed an image and position in the market. Google offered her $1 million to create 20 hours of content, and she began creating video content for high-end cosmetics line Lancome. A year later, L'Oreal offered Phan her

what's in it for me?

Businesses must adapt to their environment in many different ways. One common approach is to apply marketing basics in an innovative way to appeal to the forces of the external marketing environment. This chapter discusses these basics along with the marketing plan and components of the marketing mix, as well as target marketing and market segmentation. It also explores key factors that influence consumer and organizational buying processes. By grasping the marketing methods and ideas in this chapter, you will not only be better prepared as a marketing professional but you also will become a more informed consumer.

Auremar/Fotolia

own makeup line. At that moment, Phan realized she had made it—she called her mother and told her she'd just done her last pedicure. And she meant it.

Phan has expanded her presence in the market by creating Ipsy, a beauty sample service and community. Subscribers pay $10 a month to sample products selected especially for them and are able to view video content to optimize their experience. Phan is also a co-founder of Shift Music Group, a music publishing company, and is creating a premium lifestyle network called ICON, partnering with Endemol USA. While not yet 30, Phan has established herself as a powerhouse in the beauty and lifestyle industry. She carefully monitors trends in her environment and quickly spots new opportunities. At the same time, she's kept a keen eye on her target market and understands the consumer buying process.

While many might perceive YouTube as a difficult path to a successful career, Phan believes just the opposite. She explains, "You're in control of how people perceive you and see you. I can't say the same for traditional media because you have other people who are editing you—producers and other people who have the final say. Your YouTube channel is your own show. I think it's a wonderful platform for anyone who wants to have stronger creative control over their content, their message, their vision, and their branding."[1] (After studying the content in this chapter, you should be able to answer a set of discussion questions found at the end of the chapter.)

OBJECTIVE 11-1
Explain
the concept of marketing and identify the five forces that constitute the external marketing environment.

What Is Marketing?

As consumers, we are influenced by the marketing activities of people like Michelle Phan and companies like L'Oreal and Google that want us to buy their products rather than those of their competitors. Being consumers makes us the essential ingredients in the marketing process. Every day, we express needs for such essentials as food, clothing, and shelter and wants for such nonessentials as entertainment and leisure activities. Our needs and wants are major forces that drive marketing.

What comes to mind when you think of marketing? Most of us think of marketing as advertisements for detergents and soft drinks. Marketing, however, encompasses a much wider range of activities. The American Marketing Association defines **marketing** as "activities, a set of institutions, and processes for creating, communicating, delivering, and exchanging offerings that have value for customers, clients, partners, and society at large."[2] To see this definition in action, we'll continue this chapter by looking at some marketing basics, including the ways marketers build relationships with customers. We'll then examine forces that constitute the external marketing environment, followed by marketing strategy, the marketing plan, and the components of the marketing mix. We'll then discuss market segmentation and how it is used in target marketing. Next, we'll examine marketing research, followed by a look at key factors that influence the buying processes of consumers and industrial buyers. Finally, we'll consider the marketing mix for small business and then go beyond domestic borders to explore the international marketing mix.

Marketing *activities, a set of institutions, and processes for creating, communicating, delivering, and exchanging offerings that have value for customers, clients, partners, and society at large.*

Delivering Value

What attracts buyers to one product instead of another? Although our desires for the many available goods and services may be unbounded, limited financial resources force most of us to be selective. Accordingly, customers usually try to buy products that offer the best value when it comes to meeting their needs and wants.

Value *relative comparison of a product's benefits versus its costs*

Value and Benefits The **value** of a product compares its benefits with its costs. Benefits include not only the functions of the product but also the emotional satisfaction associated with owning, experiencing, or possessing it. But every product has costs, including sales price, the expenditure of the buyer's time, and even the emotional costs of making a purchase decision. A satisfied customer perceives the benefits derived from the purchase to be greater than its costs. Thus, the simple but important ratio for value is derived as follows:

$$\text{Value} = \frac{\text{Benefits}}{\text{Costs}}$$

The marketing strategies of leading firms focus on increasing value for customers. Marketing resources are deployed to add benefits and decrease costs of products to provide greater value. To satisfy customers, a company may do the following:

- Develop an entirely new product that performs better (provides greater performance benefits) than existing products.

- Keep a store open longer hours during a busy season (adding the benefit of greater shopping convenience).

- Offer price reductions (the benefit of lower costs).

- Offer information that explains how a product can be used in new ways (the benefit of new uses at no added cost).

Value and Utility To understand how marketing creates value for customers, we need to know the kind of benefits that buyers get from a firm's goods or services. As we discussed in Chapter 7, those benefits provide customers with **utility**, the ability of a product to satisfy a human want or need. Think about the competitive marketing efforts for Microsoft's Xbox series and those for Sony's competing PlayStation game consoles. In both companies, marketing strives to provide four kinds of utility in the following ways:

> **Utility** *ability of a product to satisfy a human want or need*

1 **Form utility**. Marketing has a voice in designing products with features that customers want. Microsoft's Xbox One features kineet technology (voice- and motion-detecting software) and can record a video of your game. Sony's newest PlayStation 4 (PS 4) touts a controller with a six-axis sensor.

> **Form Utility** *providing products with features that customers want*

2 **Time utility**. Marketing creates a time utility by providing products *when* customers will want them. Both Sony and Microsoft create Internet buzzes and rumors among gamers by hinting at upcoming release dates without mentioning specifics.

> **Time Utility** *providing products when customers will want them*

3 **Place utility**. Marketing creates a place utility by making products easily accessible—by making products available *where* customers will want them. Xbox One and PS 4 are available online at Amazon.com and at many brick-and-mortar retailers such as Best Buy and Target.

> **Place Utility** *providing products where customers will want them*

4 **Possession utility**. Marketing creates a possession utility by transferring product ownership to customers by setting selling prices, setting terms for customer credit payments, if needed, and providing ownership documents. Hints about prices from both companies have fueled rumors: Xbox One sells for around $350, while the PS 4 runs about $400.

> **Possession Utility** *transferring product ownership to customers by setting selling prices, setting terms for customer credit payments, and providing ownership documents*

As you can imagine, marketing responsibilities at Microsoft and Sony are extremely challenging in such a competitive arena, and the stakes are high. Because they determine product features, and the timing, place, and terms of sale that provide utility and add value for customers, marketers must understand customers' wants and needs. In today's fast-moving industries, those wants and needs must be determined quickly. Marketing methods for creating utility are described in this and the following two chapters.

Goods, Services, and Ideas

The marketing of tangible goods is obvious in everyday life. It applies to two types of customers: those who buy consumer goods and those who buy industrial goods. In a department store, an employee may ask if you'd like to try a new cologne. A pharmaceutical company proclaims the virtues of its new cold medicine. Your local auto dealer offers an economy car at an economy price. These products are all

Consumer Goods *physical products purchased by consumers for personal use*

Industrial Goods *physical products purchased by companies to produce other products*

Services *products having non-physical features, such as information, expertise, or an activity that can be purchased*

consumer goods, tangible goods that you, the consumer, may buy for personal use. Firms that sell goods to consumers for personal consumption are engaged in consumer marketing, also known as business-to-consumer (B2C) marketing.

Marketing also applies to **industrial goods**, physical items used by companies to produce other products. Surgical instruments and bulldozers are industrial goods, as are components and raw materials such as integrated circuits, steel, coffee beans, and plastic. Firms that sell goods to other companies are engaged in industrial marketing, also known as business-to-business (B2B) marketing.

But marketing techniques are also applied to **services**, products with intangible (nonphysical) features, such as professional advice, timely information for decisions, or arrangements for a vacation. Service marketing, the application of marketing for services, continues to be a major growth area in the United States. Insurance companies, airlines, public accountants, and health clinics all engage in service marketing, both to individuals (consumer markets) and to other companies (industrial markets). Thus, the terms *consumer marketing* and *industrial marketing* include services as well as goods.

Finally, marketers also promote ideas, such as "inspirational values" as seen in "Encouragement, Pass It On," on YouTube and in the popular television commercials. Ads in theaters warn us against copyright infringement and piracy. Other marketing campaigns may stress the advantages of avoiding fast foods, texting while driving, or quitting smoking, or they may promote a political party or candidate.

Relationship Marketing and Customer Relationship Management

Relationship Marketing *marketing strategy that emphasizes building lasting relationships with customers and suppliers*

Although marketing often focuses on single transactions for products, services, or ideas, marketers also take a longer-term perspective. Thus, **relationship marketing** is a type of marketing that emphasizes building lasting relationships with customers and suppliers. Stronger relationships, including stronger economic and social ties, can result in greater long-term satisfaction, customer loyalty, and customer retention.[3] Michelle Phan has used relationship marketing very successfully. Similarly, Starbucks's Card Rewards attracts return customers with free coffee refills and other extras. Commercial banks also offer economic incentives to encourage longer-lasting relationships. Longtime customers who purchase a certain number of the bank's products (for example, checking accounts, savings accounts, and loans) accumulate credits toward free or reduced-price products or services, such as free investment advice.

Customer Relationship Management (CRM) *organized methods that a firm uses to build better information connections with clients, so that stronger company-client relationships are developed*

Like many other marketing areas, the ways that marketers go about building relationships with customers have changed dramatically. **Customer relationship management (CRM)** is an organized method that an enterprise uses to build better information connections with clients, so that managers can develop stronger enterprise–client relationships.

The power of Internet communications coupled with the ability to gather and assemble information on customer preferences allows marketers to better predict what clients will want and buy. Viking River Cruises communicates with booked vacationers months in advance of departures, including e-mails with menus and recipes from countries that vacationers will be visiting. Viking also encourages social networking among booked passengers to establish prevoyage friendships, which can lead to faster face-to-face acquaintanceships once they board the riverboat.

Data Warehousing *the collection, storage, and retrieval of data in electronic files*

Data Mining *the application of electronic technologies for searching, sifting, and reorganizing pools of data to uncover useful information*

The compiling and storage of customers' data, known as **data warehousing**, provides the raw materials from which marketers can extract information that enables them to find new clients and identify their best customers. Marketers can then inform these priority clients about upcoming new products and postpurchase service reminders. **Data mining** automates the massive analysis of data by using computers to sift, sort, and search for previously undiscovered clues about what customers look at and react to and how they might be influenced. Marketers use these tools to get a clearer picture of how knowing a client's preferences can satisfy those particular needs, thereby building closer, stronger relationships with customers.[4]

Toronto-based Fairmont Resort Hotels, for example, first used data mining to re-build its customer-relations package by finding out what kinds of vacations their customers prefer and then placed ads where they were more likely to reach those customers. When data mining revealed the worldwide destinations of Fairmont cus-tomers, it helped determine Fairmont's decision to buy their customers' number-one preference, the Savoy in London.[5] Fairmont's enhanced CRM has attracted new guests and strengthened relationships and loyalty among existing clients through Web-based promotions and incentives. Using profiles of guest information, Fairmont identifies target traveler segments and supplies travelers with personalized price discounts and special hotel services.[6] We'll discuss data warehousing and data min-ing in more detail in Chapter 14.

The Marketing Environment

Marketing plans and strategies are not determined unilaterally by any business—rather, they are strongly influenced by powerful outside forces. As you see in Figure 11.1, every marketing program must recognize the factors in a company's *external environ-ment*, which is everything outside an organization's boundaries that might affect it. In this section, we'll discuss how these external forces affect the marketing environment in particular.

Political-Legal Environment The **political-legal environment**, both global and domestic, has profound effects on marketing. For example, environmental legis-lation has determined the destinies of entire industries. The political push for alter-native energy sources is creating new markets and products for emerging companies such as India's Suzlon Energy Limited (large wind turbines), wind-powered electric generators by Germany's Nordex AG, and wind farms and power plants by Spain's Gamesa Corporation. Marketing managers try to maintain favorable political and legal environments in several ways. To gain public support for products and activities, mar-keters use ad campaigns to raise public awareness of important issues. Companies contribute to political candidates and frequently support the activities of political ac-tion committees (PACs) maintained by their respective industries.

Political-Legal Environment *the relationship between business and government, usually in the form of government regulation of business*

Sociocultural Environment The **sociocultural environment** also impacts marketing. Changing social values force companies to develop and promote new products, such as poultry and meat without antibiotics and growth hormones, for both individual consumers and industrial customers. Just a few years ago, organic

Sociocultural Environment *the cus-toms, mores, values, and demographic characteristics of the society in which an organization functions*

FIGURE 11.1 The External Marketing Environment

foods were available only in specialty food stores such as Whole Foods. Today, in response to a growing demand for healthy foods, Target's Archer Farms product line brings affordable organic food to a much larger audience. Grocers like Kroger and HEB also have set aside large areas in their stores where consumers can find organic and/or natural products. In addition, new industrial products reflect changing social values: A growing number of wellness programs are available to companies for improving employees' health. Quest Diagnostics, for example, a B2B company, supplies a "Blueprint for Wellness" service that assesses employee healthcare risks in client companies and recommends programs for reducing those risks. This and other trends reflect the values, beliefs, and ideas that shape society. In similar fashion, businesses strive to distance themselves from people and products that are potentially offensive. For instance, when Donald Trump announced his bid for the presidency in 2015, he made several controversial remarks about illegal immigrants from Mexico. In quick response, NBC dropped plans to televise the Miss Universe pageant owned by Trump and Macy's discontinued its line of Trump-endorsed menswear.

Technological Environment *all the ways by which firms create value for their constituents*

Technological Environment
The **technological environment** creates new goods and services. New products make existing products obsolete, and many products change our values and lifestyles. In turn, lifestyle changes often stimulate new products not directly related to the new technologies themselves. Mobile devices, the availability of a vast array of apps, and social media, for example, facilitate business communication just as prepackaged meals provide convenience for busy household cooks. Both kinds of products also free up time for recreation and leisure.

Economic Environment *relevant conditions that exist in the economic system in which a company operates*

Economic Environment
Because economic conditions determine spending patterns by consumers, businesses, and governments, the **economic environment** influences marketing plans for product offerings, pricing, and promotional strategies. Marketers are concerned with such economic variables as inflation, interest rates, and recession. Thus, they monitor the general business cycle to anticipate trends in consumer and business spending.

Competitive Environment *the competitive system in which businesses compete*

Competitive Environment
In a **competitive environment**, marketers must convince buyers that they should purchase one company's products rather than another's. Because both consumers and commercial buyers have limited resources, every

John Locher/AP Images

Marketing strategies are strongly influenced by powerful outside forces. For example, new technologies create new products, such as the cell phone "gas station" shown here. These recharging stations enable customers to recharge their mobile devices just as they would refuel their cars. The screens at the stations also provide marketers with a new way to display ads to waiting customers.

managing in turbulent times

Feeling the Pressure for "Green"

Today's marketers are struggling with pressures from several outside forces: Changes in the political–legal, sociocultural, technological, and economic environments are changing the competitive landscape. Industries ranging from automobiles to energy to housing are grappling with a common environmental theme: *going green*. For example, public sentiment turned decidedly toward alternatives to gas-guzzling cars. Home buyers also want energy-efficient heating and cooling, such as geothermal heat, in their homes. Environmentalists are pushing for alternative energy sources, notably wind and solar power, to replace fossil fuels. Local utilities are offering incentives for construction using environmentally sensitive building designs to conserve energy. Purchases of tiny houses are growing. Solar-powered wells are replacing mechanical windmills on farms. In Washington, DC, the Barack Obama administration and Congress continue their struggle to create more jobs and reduce the national debt while also meeting commitments for a cleaner environment using energy-saving technologies.

David Koscheck/Shutterstock

These outside pressures present challenges for all areas of marketing—from identifying the new target markets to designing new products for those markets and, in some cases, finding technologies to make those products. Success depends on coordinating the various marketing activities and making them compatible with one another. Marketers need to present a convincing rationale for a product's pricing and demonstrate how the product provides the benefits sought by the target markets. Distribution methods, how companies deliver products and after-services to customers, have to match up with promises in the promotional message so that, together, the marketing activities provide a persuasive package that delivers the desired value and benefits. Further, this integrated marketing strategy must be coordinated with financial management and production operations to provide timely customer satisfaction.

The marketing blueprint for Toyota's Prius automobile used an integrated marketing mix for meeting the challenge of *going green*. While developing the fuel-efficient hybrid technology, Toyota identified niche target markets of users in some 40 countries and determined a price range compatible with the company's performance reliability and quality reputation. Promotion in the U.S. market started two years before the car was released so customers could view and purchase a Prius. In one prelaunch promotion, Toyota teamed up with the Sierra Club and lent the Prius to environmentally sensitive Hollywood superstars to provide exposure and allow car testing in the target market. The main ad campaign to general audiences emphasized that consumers can still have speed and comfort along with environmental friendliness. And preorders were delivered on time to buyers. As a result, the Prius became the most successful hybrid automobile in the United States and the rest of the world.

High fuel prices, as well as concern for the environment, were a major factor in the popularity of the Prius and other hybrid vehicles. However, falling fuel prices in 2014 affected the types of vehicles that consumers purchased. Sales of SUVs and trucks rose 10 percent in 2014 and sales of hybrid and electric vehicles slowed. With lower fuel prices, it could take five years or more to recover the additional cost associated with a hybrid from the fuel savings. However, as dealers find that they have excess inventory in hybrid cars, they have begun to cut prices, making the economic argument more compelling.

It's important to note that there's more to the story than fuel savings. Consumers are increasingly committed to lower emissions and a smaller carbon footprint. Interestingly, many hybrid owners consider their choice of a vehicle as an extension of their social identity. By September 2014, Prius dominated the market—accounting for more than half of all sales and seven times higher sales than the second-place vehicle, the Honda Civic. One explanation for this phenomenon relates directly to the buyer's social identity. Unlike the Civic, which is also available in a standard fuel option, the Prius is a hybrid-only model. Its distinctive appearance brands the owner as environmentally conscious, reinforcing the self-image of the owner.[7]

dollar spent on one product is no longer available for other purchases. Each marketing program, therefore, seeks to make its product the most attractive. Expressed in business terms, a failed program loses the buyer's dollar forever (or at least until it is time for the next purchase decision).

To promote products effectively, marketers must first understand which of three types of competition they face:

Substitute Product *product that is dissimilar from those of competitors, but that can fulfill the same need*

1 **Substitute products** may not look alike or they may seem different from one another, but they can fulfill the same need. For example, your cholesterol level may be controlled with either of two competing products: a physical fitness program or a drug regimen. The fitness program and the drugs compete as substitute products. Similarly, online video streaming services like Netflix provide substitute products for conventional television programming.

Brand Competition *competitive marketing that appeals to consumer perceptions of benefits of products offered by particular companies*

2 **Brand competition** occurs between similar products and is based on buyers' perceptions of the benefits of products offered by particular companies. For Internet searches, do you turn to Google, Bing, or Yahoo!? Brand competition is based on users' perceptions of the benefits offered by each product.

International Competition *competitive marketing of domestic products against foreign products*

3 **International competition** matches the products of domestic marketers against those of foreign competitors. The intensity of international competition has been heightened by the formation of alliances, such as the European Union and the North American Free Trade Agreement (NAFTA). The U.S. Air Force recently opened bidding to foreign manufacturers for three new planes to replace the existing Presidential Air Force One fleet (made by Boeing). If Europe's Airbus had won the contract, it would have been the first time a U.S. president has flown in a non-U.S.-made Air Force One.[8] Instead, however, Airbus withdrew from bidding, leaving Boeing the sole competitor. However, Airbus remains as a formidable competitor of Boeing in today's commercial aircraft industry.

Having identified the kind of competition, marketers can then develop a plan for attracting more customers.

OBJECTIVE 11-2
Explain
the purpose of a marketing plan and identify its main components.

Developing the Marketing Plan

A marketing manager at a major home appliance manufacturing company explains the concept of *developing the marketing plan* by using the analogy of planning for a trip as follows:

- "First, you decide where you want to go and what you want to happen when you get there. Why take this trip and not others, instead?"
  [Identify the *objective* or *goal* to be achieved.]

- "At some stage, you decide when the trip will happen and how you'll get to the destination."
  [*Plan* for *when* it will happen, and for the *paths* (or *routes*) that will be taken to get there.]

- "Every trip requires resources, so you identify those resource requirements and compare them against resources that are available."
  [*Evaluate resource* requirements and availabilities.]

- "If available resources are too expensive, then you adjust the trip so it becomes affordable."
  [*Adjust plans* as needed to become *realistic* and *feasible*.]

- "During and after the trip, you assess the successes (what went right) and the drawbacks (what went wrong) and remember them so you can make the next trip even better."
  [Keep notes and data about what happened because *learning* from this experience increases the chances for *greater success on the next*.]

As you will see, our discussion of the marketing plan contains many of the preceding elements. The **marketing plan** identifies the marketing objectives stating what marketing will accomplish in the future. It contains a strategy that identifies the specific activities and resources that will be used to meet the needs and desires of customers in the firm's chosen target markets, so as to accomplish the marketing objectives.

First and foremost, marketing plans are future-oriented, showing what will be happening with marketing's upcoming activities. Every well-founded marketing plan, as shown in Figure 11.2, begins with objectives or goals that set the stage for everything that follows. **Marketing objectives**, the goals the marketing plan intends to accomplish, are the foundation that guides all the detailed activities in the plan. The marketing objectives themselves, however, exist solely to support the company's overall business mission (at the top in Figure 11.2) and typically focus on maintaining or enhancing the organization's future competitive position in its chosen markets. Hypothetically, Starbucks's overall business mission could aim at being the world's leading retailer of specialty coffee. Two supporting marketing objectives, then, could be (1) a 5 percent increase in its worldwide market share by, say, 2018, and (2) be the leading retailer (in dollar sales) of specialty coffee in China by 2020.

Marketing Plan *detailed strategy for focusing marketing efforts on consumers' needs and wants*

Marketing Objectives *the things marketing intends to accomplish in its marketing plan*

Marketing Strategy: Planning the Marketing Mix

The marketing team can develop a strategy once they have clarified the marketing objectives. Specifically, **marketing strategy** identifies the planned marketing programs, all the marketing activities that a business will use to achieve its marketing goals, and when those activities will occur. If planned activities are not affordable, then marketers need to adjust the activities or goals until realistic plans emerge. Finally,

Marketing Strategy *all the marketing programs and activities that will be used to achieve the marketing goals*

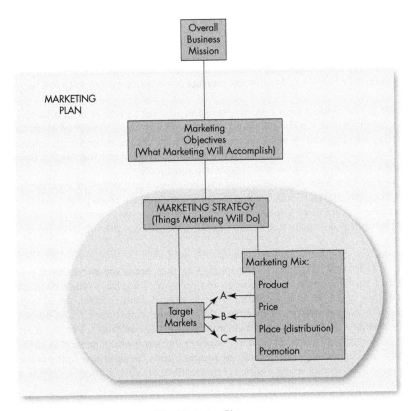

FIGURE 11.2 Components of the Marketing Plan

because marketing planning is an ongoing process—not just a one-time endeavor—it can be improved through experience by learning from past triumphs and mistakes.

Marketing Manager *manager who plans and implements the marketing activities that result in the transfer of products from producer to consumer*

Marketing managers are the people responsible for planning, organizing, leading, and controlling the organization's marketing resources toward supporting and accomplishing the organization's overall mission. To meet these responsibilities, marketing managers rely on mapping out a clear strategy for planning and implementing all the activities that result in the transfer of goods or services to customers. As you can see in Figure 11.2, the marketing strategy focuses on the needs and wants of customers in the company's chosen target markets. Marketing strategy also includes four basic components (often called the *Four Ps*) of the **marketing mix**—*product, pricing, place*, and *promotion*—that marketing managers use to satisfy customers in target markets. The specific activities for each of the Four Ps are designed differently to best meet the needs of each target market.

Marketing Mix *combination of product, pricing, promotion, and place (distribution) strategies used to market products*

Product *good, service, or idea that is marketed to fill consumers' needs and wants*

Product Differentiation *creation of a product feature or product image that differs enough from existing products to attract customers*

Product Marketing begins with a **product**, a good, a service, or an idea designed to fill a customer's need or want. Producers often promote particular features of products to distinguish them in the marketplace. **Product differentiation** is the creation of a feature or image that makes a product differ enough from existing products to attract customers. For example, in the years since Apple introduced the first iPhone, a succession of newer models evolved with faster, more powerful, and increasingly consumer-friendlier innovations. The iPhone's industry-leading features have attracted an enormous customer following that contributes substantially to Apple's booming financial success. The design for the iPhone 6, for example, offers more new features than previous models to keep on top in the increasingly competitive smartphone market. The phone is thinner and lighter, has a new Retina HD display, improved camera, and faster operating system.[9]

Meanwhile, Samsung surged onto the scene with its competitive Galaxy series, most recently the Galaxy S5, with equally attractive, distinct features. Compared with previous Galaxy models, the Galaxy S5 has a more powerful, removable battery, faster download and upload speeds, the popular Android operating system, and numerous additional features. The phone is also dustproof and water-resistant.[10]

So far, Samsung's smartphone features are attracting more customers, holding almost a 30 percent share of worldwide smartphone sales at the end of 2014, versus around 20 percent for second-place Apple. In the U.S. market, however, Apple has a larger share than Samsung. We discuss product development more fully in Chapter 12.

Pricing *process of determining the best price at which to sell a product*

Pricing The **pricing** of a product, selecting the best price at which to sell it, is often a balancing act. On the one hand, prices must support a variety of costs, such as operating, administrative, research, and marketing. On the other hand, prices can't be so high that customers turn to competitors. Successful pricing means finding a profitable middle ground between these two requirements.

Both low-and high-price strategies can be effective in different situations. Low prices, for example, generally lead to larger sales volumes. High prices usually limit market size but increase profits per unit. High prices may also attract customers by implying that a product is of high quality. We discuss pricing in more detail in Chapter 12.

Place (or Distribution) *part of the marketing mix concerned with getting products from producers to consumers*

Place (Distribution) In the marketing mix, **place (or distribution)** refers to *where* and *how* customers get access to the products they buy. When products are created, they must become available to customers at some *location* (*place*) such as a retail store, on the Internet, or by direct delivery to the customer. *Distribution* is the set of activities that moves products from producers to customers. Placing a product in the proper outlet, like a retail store, requires decisions about several activities, all of which are concerned with getting the product from the producer to the consumer. Decisions about warehousing and inventory control are distribution decisions, as are decisions about transportation options.

Firms must also make decisions about the *channels* through which they distribute products. Many manufacturers, for example, sell goods to other companies that, in

Weng lei/Imaginechina/AP Images

Rolex has had sustained success as a result of its well-conceived marketing mix. The Swiss company focuses exclusively on high-quality watches (product), sells them for thousands of dollars (price), uses an exclusive network of quality retailers (distribution), and advertises them in interesting ways (promotion).

turn, distribute them to retailers. Others sell directly to major retailers, such as Target and Sears. Still others sell directly to final consumers. We explain distribution decisions further in Chapter 13.

Promotion The most visible component of the marketing mix is no doubt **promotion**, which is a set of techniques for communicating information about products. The most important promotional tools include advertising, personal selling, sales promotions, publicity/public relations, and direct or interactive marketing. Promotion decisions are discussed further in Chapter 13. Here, we briefly describe four of the most important promotional tools.

ADVERTISING **Advertising** is any form of paid nonpersonal communication used by an identified sponsor to persuade or inform potential buyers about a product. For example, financial advisory companies that provide investment and securities products reach their customer audience by advertising in *Fortune* magazine and on the *Bloomberg* television network.

PERSONAL SELLING Many products (such as insurance, custom-designed clothing, and real estate) are best promoted through **personal selling**, person-to person sales. Industrial goods and services rely significantly on personal selling. When companies buy from other companies, purchasing agents and others who need technical and detailed information are often referred to the selling company's sales representatives.

SALES PROMOTIONS Historically, relatively inexpensive items have often been marketed through **sales promotions**, which involve one-time direct inducements to buyers. Premiums (usually free gifts), coupons, and package inserts are all sales promotions meant to tempt consumers to buy products. More recently, however, these promotions have expanded into B2B sales and to sales of larger items to consumers through Internet deals at sources such as Groupon.

PUBLIC RELATIONS **Public relations** includes all communication efforts directed at building goodwill. It seeks to build favorable attitudes in the minds of the public

Promotion *aspect of the marketing mix concerned with the most effective techniques for communicating information about products*

Advertising *any form of paid nonpersonal communication used by an identified sponsor to persuade or inform potential buyers about a product*

Personal Selling *person-to person sales*

Sales Promotion *direct inducements such as premiums, coupons, and package inserts to tempt consumers to buy products*

Public Relations *communication efforts directed at building goodwill and favorable attitudes in the minds of the public toward the organization and its products*

Urban Outfitters is a successful—but sometimes controversial—retailer. The company offers low-priced and unique products targeted at young, urban-oriented consumers. But the firm has also had some public relations problems due in part to some of its more offbeat products.

toward the organization and its products. The Ronald McDonald House Charities, and its association with McDonald's Corporation, is a well-known example of public relations.

Integrated Marketing Strategy *strategy that blends together the Four Ps of marketing to ensure their compatibility with one another and with the company's nonmarketing activities*

Blending It All Together: Integrated Strategy An **integrated marketing strategy** ensures that the Four Ps blend together so that they are compatible with one another and with the company's nonmarketing activities. As an example, Toyota has become the world's largest automaker. Its nearly 30-year auto superiority, even with its massive product recalls a few years ago, stems from a coherent marketing mix that is tightly integrated with its production strategy. Offering a relatively small number of different models, Toyota targets auto customers that want high quality, excellent performance reliability, and moderate prices (a good value for the price). With a smaller number of different models than U.S. automakers, fewer components and parts are needed, purchasing costs are lower, and less factory space is required for inventory and assembly in Toyota's lean production system. Lean production's assembly simplicity yields higher quality, the factory's cost savings lead to lower product prices, and speedy production gives shorter delivery times in Toyota's distribution system. Taken together, this integrated strategy is completed when Toyota's advertising communicates its message of industry-high customer satisfaction.[11]

Marketing Strategy: Target Marketing and Market Segmentation

OBJECTIVE 11-3
Explain
market segmentation and how it is used in target marketing.

Target Market *the particular group of people or organizations on which a firm's marketing efforts are focused*

Market Segmentation *process of dividing a market into categories of customer types, or "segments" having similar wants and needs and who can be expected to show interest in the same products*

Marketers have long known that products cannot be all things to all people. The emergence of the marketing concept and the recognition of customers' needs and wants led marketers to think in terms of **target markets**—the particular groups of people or organizations on which a firm's marketing efforts are focused. Selecting target markets is usually the first step in the marketing strategy.

Target marketing requires **market segmentation**, dividing a market into categories of customer types or "segments" having similar wants and needs and who can be expected to show interest in the same products. Once they have identified segments, companies may adopt a variety of strategies. Some firms market products by targeting more than one segment. General Motors, for example, once offered automobiles with various features and at various price levels. GM's past strategy was to provide an automobile for nearly every segment of the market. The financial crisis, however, forced GM's changeover to fewer target markets and associated brands by closing Saturn, phasing out Pontiac, and selling or shutting down Hummer and Saab.

In contrast, some businesses have always focused on a narrower range of products, such as Ferrari's high-priced sports cars, aiming at just one segment. Note that segmentation is a strategy for analyzing consumers, not products. Once marketers identify a target segment, they can begin marketing products for that segment. The process of fixing, adapting, and communicating the nature of the product itself is called **product positioning**.

Product Positioning *process of fixing, adapting, and communicating the nature of a product*

Identifying Market Segments

By definition, members of a market segment must share some common traits that affect their purchasing decisions. In identifying consumer segments, researchers look at several different influences on consumer behavior. Five of the most important variables are discussed next.

Geographic Segmentation

Many buying decisions are affected by the places people call home. Urban residents don't need agricultural equipment, and sailboats sell better along the coasts than on the Great Plains. **Geographic variables** are the geographic units, from countries to neighborhoods, that researchers consider in a strategy of **geographic segmentation**. McDonald's restaurants in Germany, in contrast to those in the United States, offer beer on the menu. Pharmacies in Jackson Hole, Wyoming, sell firearms that are forbidden in Chicago. Starbucks is currently focusing on the growing geographic segment in China.

Geographic Variables *geographic units that may be considered in developing a segmentation strategy*

Geographic Segmentation *geographic units, from countries to neighborhoods, that may be considered in identifying different market segments in a segmentation strategy*

Demographic Segmentation

Demographic segmentation is a strategy used to separate consumers by demographic variables. **Demographic variables** describe populations by identifying traits, such as age, income, gender, ethnic background, marital status, race, religion, and social class, as detailed in Table 11.1. Depending on the marketer's purpose, a demographic segment can be a single classification (for example, ages 20–34) or a combination of categories (ages 20–34, married without children, earning $25,000–$44,999 a year).

For example, Hot Topic started as a California-based chain specializing in clothes, accessories, and jewelry designed to appeal to Generation Y and Millennials, a demographic consisting of U.S. consumers born between the 1980s and 1990s. The theme was pop culture music because it was the biggest influence on the demographic's fashion tastes. More recently, Hot Topic has become a national retail chain for clothing, accessories, and entertainment products relating to today's pop culture.

Demographic Segmentation *a segmentation strategy that uses demographic characteristics to identify different market segments*

Demographic Variables *characteristics of populations that may be considered in developing a segmentation strategy*

table 11.1   Examples of Demographic Variables

Age	Under 5, 5–11, 12–19, 20–34, 35–49, 50–64, 65+
Education	Grade school or less, some high school, graduated high school, some college, college degree, advanced degree
Family Life Cycle	Young single, young married without children, young married with children, older married with children under 18, older married without children under 18, older single, other
Family Size	1, 2–3, 4–5, 6+
Income	Less than $15,000, $15,000–$24,999, $25,000–$50,000, $50,000–$100,000, $100,000–$200,000, more than $200,000
Nationality	African, American, Asian, British, Eastern European, French, German, Irish, Italian, Latin American, Middle Eastern, Scandinavian
Race	American Indian, Asian, African American, Caucasian
Religion	Buddhist, Catholic, Hindu, Jewish, Muslim, Protestant
Gender	Male, female

Geo-Demographic Segmentation

As the name implies, **geo-demographic segmentation** is a combination strategy. **Geo-demographic variables** are a combination of geographic and demographic traits and are becoming the most common segmentation tools. An example would be Female Young Urban Professionals, well-educated 25- to 54-year-olds with high-paying professional jobs living in the "downtown" zip codes of major cities. Chico's targets many women in this segment, offering stylish travel clothing well suited to the needs of this subset in the larger population. Segmentation is more effective because the greater number of variables defines the market more precisely.

Psychographic Segmentation

Markets can also be separated into a **psychographic segmentation** according to such **psychographic variables** as lifestyles, interests, personalities, and attitudes. For example, Burberry, promoted as "The Iconic British Luxury Brand" whose raincoats have been a symbol of British tradition since 1856, has repositioned itself as a global luxury brand, like Gucci and Louis Vuitton. The strategy calls for attracting a different type of customer—the top-of-the-line, fashion-conscious individual—who enjoys the prestige of shopping at stores like Neiman Marcus and Bergdorf Goodman. Psychographics are particularly important to marketers because, unlike demographics and geographics, they can be changed by marketing efforts. With the onset of global interdependence and open communications, marketing today is changing some traditional lifestyles and attitudes in nations around the globe. Polish companies, for example, have overcome consumer resistance by promoting the safety and desirability of using credit cards rather than depending on solely using cash.[12]

Behavioral Segmentation

Behavioral segmentation uses **behavioral variables** to market items, including such areas as heavy users (buy in bulk, the key to Sam's and Costco); situation buyers (Halloween is now the second-largest "holiday" in terms of spending); or specific purpose (All Free is a detergent for people who have skin reactions to additives in other detergents).

Marketing Research

Marketing decisions are seldom perfect, yet the consequences of a firm's choices of marketing mix and segmentation strategy can be long lasting. Effective decisions must be customer focused and based on timely information about marketplace trends. **Marketing research**, the study of what customers need and want and how best to meet those needs and wants, is a powerful tool for gaining decision-making information.

The relationship of research to the overall marketing process is shown in Figure 11.3. Ultimately, its role is to increase competitiveness by clarifying the interactions among a firm's stakeholders (including customers), marketing variables, environmental factors, and marketing decisions. Researchers use several methods to obtain, interpret, and apply information about customers. They determine the kinds of information needed for decisions on marketing strategy, goal setting, and target-market selection. In doing so, they may conduct studies on customer responses to proposed changes in the marketing mix. One researcher, for example, might study response to an experimental paint formula (new product). Another might explore the response to a price reduction (new price) on condominiums. Still a third might check responses to a proposed advertising campaign (new promotion). Marketers also try to learn whether customers will more likely purchase a product in a specialty shop or on the Internet (new place).

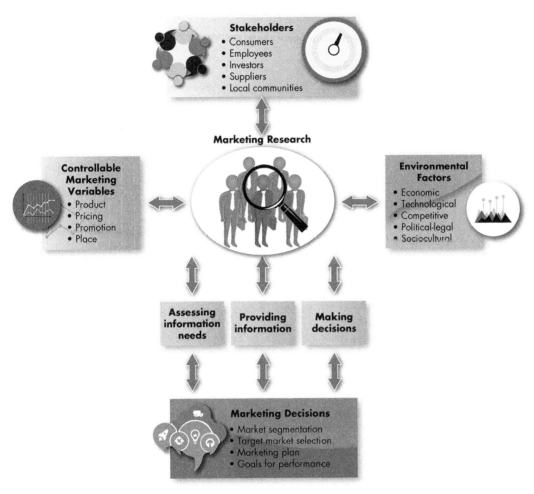

FIGURE 11.3 Market Research and the Marketing Process

The importance of selling products in international markets has expanded the role of marketing research. For example, when a company decides to sell goods or services globally, it must decide whether to standardize products or to specialize by offering different versions for each market. Accordingly, market research's orientation has become increasingly globalized.

The Research Process

Market research can occur at almost any point in a product's life cycle. Typically, however, it's used in developing new or altered products. Following are the five steps in performing market research:

1 ***Study the current situation.*** What is the need and what is being done to meet it? In the mid-1980s, Coca-Cola was alarmed by its declining market share. The company decided to undertake a now-famous market study to identify ways to recover its market position.

2 ***Select a research method.*** In choosing from a wide range of methods, marketers must consider the effectiveness and costs of different options. Coca-Cola's information suggested that the taste of Coke was the main source of the problem. Researchers decided to use taste tests for consumer opinions on a "New Coke" that was sweeter than original Coke.

Most companies undertake marketing research before launching new products. But even strong marketing research may prove to be inaccurate. For instance, when Google launched Google Glass in 2014 it anticipated huge demand. But slow sales caused the firm to stop distribution in early 2015.

Daniel Acker/Bloomberg/Getty Images

Secondary Data *data that are already available from previous research*

Primary Data *new data that are collected from newly performed research*

3   *Collect data.* We distinguish here two types of research data. **Secondary data** are already available from previous research. The *Statistical Abstract of the United States* offers data on geographic and demographic variables. Secondary data can save time, effort, and money. When secondary sources are unavailable or inadequate, researchers must obtain **primary data**, new data from newly performed research. In Coca-Cola's study, primary data were collected from some 200,000 tasters who compared the New Coke versus the taste of the original Coke and Pepsi.

4   *Analyze the data.* Data are of no use until organized into information. Analysis of data in the Coke research found that more than one-half of the tasters rated New Coke to be tastier than original Coke and Pepsi.

5   *Prepare a report.* This report should sum up the study's methodology and findings. It should also identify solutions and, where appropriate, make recommendations on a course of action. Coca-Cola's resulting recommendation—to replace original Coke with the New Coke—was implemented. The decision was a costly disaster that eventually resulted in restoring original Coke under a new name— Classic Coke—and then withdrawing New Coke from the market. Research flaws had biased the results: (1) test tasters were not told that if New Coke was launched, then original Coke would no longer be available, and (2) consumers' long-standing attachment to the original Coke brand would be lost when the product was withdrawn from the market.[13]

This Coca-Cola example was a costly learning experience, illustrating that even the most successful companies encounter occasional marketing mistakes. Although Coke's market research ultimately led them down the wrong path, many others, including Marriott Hotels and Resorts, Samsung Electronics, and Procter & Gamble personal care products, have conducted market research campaigns that led to increased market share and a better understanding of their markets.

Research Methods

The success of a research study often depends on the method a research team uses. Consider the following four basic methods of market research:

Observation *research method that obtains data by watching and recording consumer behavior*

1   **Observation** involves watching and recording consumer behavior. Today, information technology systems, including live camera feeds and computer recordings, allow marketers to observe consumer preferences rapidly and with great accuracy. Electronic scanners and data files at brick-and-mortar stores, along with data storage of television viewing, phone transactions, and website activity allow marketers to see each consumer's purchasing history—what products and brands that person prefers over a set period of time.

finding a better way

The Truth about Your Online Customer Service

As more and more retail purchases are being made online, the number of online merchandisers has exploded. You are probably pretty familiar with the stores in your area and the quality of service that they provide, but this is often not true for online sales. With thousands of sites from which to choose, it can be difficult for consumers to decide where to buy. Many retail sites feature comments from prior customers, but there is always a concern that these comments have been posted by the company itself. So, how good are a company's online customer services, especially when compared to its online competitors? StellaService Inc. answered that question by providing a better way to measure online service, enabling it to become a market winner for online shoppers and retailers alike.

Following its start-up in 2010, StellaService spent two years gathering data on customer satisfaction provided by thousands of online retailers, including such giants as Amazon.com and LLBean.com. Armed with results, co-founders Jordy Leister and John Ernsberger were able to raise $22 million in venture capital to expand their ability to develop powerful analytics. StellaService measures satisfaction in four service areas— phone support, e-mail support, delivery, returns and refunds— for each retailer. Each area includes from 9 to as many as 25 different measurements. Phone support, for example, considers speed of answering the call and respondent's knowledge of the product, among its nine measurements. Delivery measurements include delivery time and product accuracy. By combining the various measurements, consumers can find summary scores for each of the four service areas. Results provide rankings of competitors, from top to bottom, showing where each retailer currently stands relative to competitors in each of the four areas of service. In the category of Sporting Goods, for example, Stella's monthly report might show Phone Support rankings among such firms as BassPro.com, Cabelas.com, DicksSportingGoods.com, and so forth, along with rankings on Delivery, E-mail Support, and Returns and Refunds. Rankings allow period-to-period tracking, revealing trends for improvements (or erosions) in each of the areas across time for each company.

With these measurements, StellaServices hopes to better inform the consumer public on the range of customer service they can expect from online retailers. Knowing that success

hinges on the validity and believability of their methods, Stella uses an independent third-party rating system; "secret shoppers" (trained employees) use strict and controlled measurement methods as they engage online retailers via e-mails, phone calls, and live chats to purchase, await deliveries, or make returns for refunds. As added assurance for validity, Stella maintains a "Customer Service Measurement Process Audit" detailing its measurements, procedures for gathering and processing data, with specific steps to assure accuracy and validity. In 2012, KPMG, a Big Four auditing and CPA firm, stated in its Independent Auditing Report that, in its opinion, StellaService's methodologies are complying with Stella's stated policies.

It's not only consumers who are interested in the level of service that companies provide. KPMG's report was an important piece of marketing associated with the move to offering subscription services to retailers, which began in 2013. Subscribers, for the first time, can receive measured data showing their standing, along with competitors, on phone support, e-mail support, delivery, and returns and refunds. This service allows retailers to base decisions on objective and independent information about their online customer service.

Based on StellaService's ratings, shoppers can expect "elite" service from well-known retailers such as Nordstrom and Zappos. On average, e-mails from customers were handled within three to six hours and calls to customer service are answered in fewer than 90 seconds. High ratings may encourage customers to purchase from an online retailer, while low ratings may encourage consumers to consider more than low prices when making a purchase decision. In addition, data collected by StellaService helps companies identify where they excel as well as opportunities for improvement.[14]

---

2 Sometimes, marketers must go a step further and ask questions. One way to get useful information is by taking **surveys**, a method of collecting data in which the researcher interacts with people to gather facts, attitudes, or opinions, either by mailing or e-mailing questionnaires, by telephone calls, or by conducting face-to-face interviews. United Parcel Service (UPS) surveyed customers to find out how to improve service. Clients wanted more interaction with drivers

Survey *research method of collecting consumer data using questionnaires, telephone calls, and face-to-face interviews*

because they can offer practical advice on shipping. As a result, UPS added extra drivers, providing them with more time with customers. Most surveys today are conducted online.

3   In a **focus group**, participants are gathered in one place, presented with an issue, and asked to discuss it. The researcher takes notes and makes video recordings but provides only a minimal amount of structure. This technique allows researchers to explore issues too complex for questionnaires and can produce creative solutions.

4   **Experimentation** compares the responses of the same or similar people under different circumstances. For example, a firm trying to decide whether to include walnuts in a new candy bar probably wouldn't learn much by asking people what they thought of the idea. But if it asked some people to try bars with nuts and some without, the responses could be helpful.

Focus Group *research method using a group of people from a larger population who are asked their attitudes, opinions, and beliefs about a product in an open discussion*

Experimentation *research method using a sample of potential consumers to obtain reactions to test versions of new products or variations of existing products*

OBJECTIVE 11-5
Describe
the consumer buying process and the key factors that influence that process.

Understanding Consumer Behavior

Although marketing managers can tell us what features people want in a new refrigerator, they cannot tell us why they buy particular refrigerators. What desires are consumers fulfilling? Is there a psychological or sociological explanation for why they purchase one product and not another? These questions and many others are addressed in the study of **consumer behavior**, the decision process by which people buy and consume products.

Consumer Behavior *study of the decision process by which people buy and consume products*

Influences on Consumer Behavior

To understand consumer behavior, marketers draw heavily on such fields as psychology and sociology. The result is a focus on four major influences on consumer behavior: (1) *psychological*, (2) *personal*, (3) *social*, and (3) *cultural*. By identifying which influences are most active in certain circumstances, marketers try to explain consumer choices and predict future buying behavior.

Psychological Influences *include an individual's motivations, perceptions, ability to learn, and attitudes that marketers use to study buying behavior*

Personal Influences *include lifestyle, personality, and economic status that marketers use to study buying behavior*

Social Influences *include family, opinion leaders (people whose opinions are sought by others), and such reference groups as friends, coworkers, and professional associates that marketers use to study buying behavior*

Cultural Influences *include culture, subculture, and social class influences that marketers use to study buying behavior*

Brand Loyalty *pattern of repeated consumer purchasing based on satisfaction with a product's performance*

Psychological influences include an individual's motivations, perceptions, ability to learn, and attitudes.

Personal influences include lifestyle, personality, and economic status.

Social influences include family, opinion leaders (people whose opinions are sought by others), and such reference groups as friends, coworkers, and professional associates.

Cultural influences include culture (the way of living that distinguishes one large group from another), subculture (smaller groups with shared values), and social class (the cultural ranking of groups according to such criteria as background, occupation, and income).

Although these factors can have a strong impact on a consumer's choices, their effect on actual purchases is sometimes weak or negligible. Some consumers, for example, exhibit high **brand loyalty**; they regularly purchase products, such as McDonald's foods, because they are satisfied with their performance. Such people are less subject to influence and stick with preferred brands.[15] On the other hand, the clothes you wear, the social network you choose, and the way you decorate your room often reflect social and psychological influences on your consumer behavior.

The Consumer Buying Process

Students of consumer behavior have constructed various models to help show how consumers decide to buy products. Figure 11.4 presents one such model. At the core of this and similar models is an awareness of the many influences that

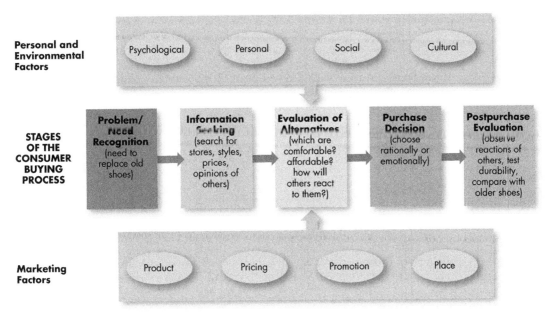

FIGURE 11.4 The Consumer Buying Process

lead to consumption. Ultimately, marketers use this information to develop marketing plans.

Problem or Need Recognition This process begins when the consumer recognizes a problem or need. Need recognition also occurs when you have a chance to change your buying habits. When you obtain your first job after graduation, your new income may enable you to buy things that were once too expensive for you. You may find that you need professional clothing, apartment furnishings, and a car. Bank of America and Citibank cater to such shifts in needs when they market credit cards to college students.

Information Seeking Having recognized a need, consumers often seek information. The search is not always extensive, but before making major purchases, most people seek information from personal sources, public sources, and experiences. Before joining a gym, you may read about your area gyms on yelp.com or you may visit several gyms in your neighborhood. From this information search, consumers develop an **evoked set (or consideration set)**, which is the group of products they will consider buying.

Evoked Set (Consideration Set) *group of products consumers will consider buying as a result of information search*

Evaluation of Alternatives If someone is in the market for skis, they probably have some idea of who makes skis and how they differ. By analyzing product attributes (price, prestige, quality) of the consideration set, consumers compare products before deciding which one best meets their needs.

Purchase Decision Ultimately, consumers make purchase decisions. "Buy" decisions are based on rational motives, emotional motives, or both. **Rational motives** involve the logical evaluation of product attributes: cost, quality, and usefulness. **Emotional motives** involve nonobjective factors and include sociability, imitation of others, and aesthetics. For example, you might buy the same brand of jeans as your friends to feel accepted in a certain group, not because your friends happen to have the good sense to prefer durable, reasonably priced jeans.

Rational Motives *reasons for purchasing a product that are based on a logical evaluation of product attributes*

Emotional Motives *reasons for purchasing a product that are based on nonobjective factors*

Postpurchase Evaluation Marketing does not stop with the sale of a product; what happens after the sale is also important. Marketers want consumers to be happy after buying products so that they are more likely to buy them again. Because consumers do not want to go through a complex decision process for every purchase, they often repurchase products they have used and liked. Not all consumers are satisfied with their purchases, of course. These buyers are not likely to purchase the same product(s) again and are much more apt to broadcast their experiences than are satisfied customers.

Organizational Marketing and Buying Behavior

OBJECTIVE 11-6
Discuss
the four categories of organizational markets and the characteristics of business-to-business (B2B) buying behavior.

In the consumer market, buying and selling transactions are visible to the public. Equally important, though far less visible, are organizational (or commercial) markets. Marketing to organizations that buy goods and services used in creating and delivering consumer products or public services involves various kinds of markets and buying behaviors different from those in consumer markets.

Business Marketing

Business marketing involves organizational or commercial markets that fall into four B2B categories: (1) services companies, (2) industrial, (4) reseller, and (4) government and institutional markets. Taken together, the B2B markets do more than $25 trillion in business annually—more than two times the amount of business conducted in the U.S. consumer market.[16]

Services Companies Market *firms engaged in the business of providing services to the purchasing public*

Services Market The **services companies market** encompasses the many firms that provide services to the purchasing public. Imagine, for example, the materials and supplies Disney World needs to provide exceptional experiences for visitors. Similar needs exist to operate United Airlines, MTV, and the accounting firm Ernst & Young. Everything from veterinary clinics to hospitality services providers to healthcare centers and nursery schools buy resources needed to provide services to customers.

Industrial Market *organizational market consisting of firms that buy goods that are either converted into products or used during production*

Industrial Market The **industrial market** includes businesses that buy goods to be converted into other products or that are used up during production. It includes farmers, manufacturers, and some retailers. For example, clock-making company Seth Thomas buys electronics, metal components, plastic, and glass from other companies to make clocks for the consumer market. The company also buys office supplies, tools, and factory equipment—items never seen by clock buyers—that are used during production.

Reseller Market *organizational market consisting of intermediaries that buy and resell finished goods*

Reseller Market Before products reach consumers, they pass through a **reseller market** consisting of intermediaries, including wholesalers and retailers, that buy and resell finished goods. For example, as a leading distributor of parts and accessories for the pleasure boat market, Coast Distribution System buys lights, steering wheels, and propellers and resells them to marinas and boat-repair shops.

Institutional Market *organizational market consisting of such nongovernmental buyers of goods and services as hospitals, churches, museums, and charitable organizations*

Government and Institutional Market In addition to federal and state governments, there are over 89,000 local governments in the United States. In 2014, state and local governments spent $3.1 trillion for durable goods, nondurables, services, and construction.[17] The **institutional market** consists of nongovernmental organizations, such as hospitals, churches, museums, and charities, that also use supplies and equipment as well as legal, accounting, and transportation services.

B2B Buying Behavior

In some respects, organizational buying behavior bears little resemblance to consumer buying practices. Differences include the buyers' purchasing skills and an emphasis on buyer–seller relationships.

Differences in Buyers Unlike most consumers, organizational buyers purchase in large quantities and are professional, specialized, and well informed. Additional characteristics of B2B buyers include the following:

- Industrial buyers usually *buy in bulk or large quantities*. Because of this fact, and with so much money at stake, buyers are often experts about the products they buy. On a regular basis, B2B buyers study competing products and alternative suppliers by attending trade shows, by networking with others electronically, by reading trade literature, and by conducting technical discussions with sellers' representatives.

- As professionals, B2B buyers *are trained in methods for negotiating purchase terms*. Once buyer–seller agreements have been reached, they also arrange formal contracts.

- As a rule, industrial buyers *are company specialists in a line of items and are often experts about the products they buy*. As one of several buyers for a large bakery, for example, you may specialize in food ingredients. Another buyer may specialize in baking equipment, whereas a third may buy office equipment and supplies.

Differences in the Buyer–Seller Relationship Consumer–seller relationships are often impersonal, short-lived, one-time interactions. In contrast, B2B situations often *involve frequent and enduring buyer–seller relationships*. The development of a long-term relationship provides each party with access to the technical strengths of the other as well as the security of knowing what future business to expect. Thus, a buyer and a supplier may form a design team to create products to benefit both parties. Accordingly, industrial sellers emphasize personal selling by trained representatives who understand the needs of each customer.

Social Media and Marketing

Social networking as used by marketers today refers to communications that flow among people and organizations interacting through an online platform that facilitates building social relations among its users. **Social networking media** are the websites or access channels, such as Facebook, Twitter, LinkedIn, and YouTube, to which millions of consumers go for information and discussions before making their purchase decisions.

Viral Marketing and Social Networking **Viral marketing** is a form of marketing that relies on social networking and the Internet to spread information like a "virus" from person to person. The marketing purpose may be to increase brand awareness, to promote new product ideas, or to foster excitement for stimulating sales. Messages about new cars, sports events, and numerous other goods and services flow via networks among potential customers who pass the information on to others. Using various social network formats—games, contests, chat rooms, blogs, and bulletin boards—marketers encourage potential customers to try out products and tell other people about them. For example, as Disney plans to launch new movies featuring characters from the *Star Wars* mythology and the Marvel universe, it often releases brief sample footage months—or even years—in advance. The hope is that viewers will like what they see and help build anticipation for the new movie well before it actually opens in theaters. Marketers, including such giants as Bank of America, McDonald's, eBay, and Cisco, are using **corporate blogs** increasingly for public relations, branding, and otherwise spreading messages that stimulate chat about products to target markets.[18]

Social Networking *network of communications that flow among people and organizations interacting through an online platform*

Social Networking Media *websites or access channels, such as Facebook, Twitter, LinkedIn, and YouTube, to which consumers go for information and discussions*

Viral Marketing *type of marketing that relies on the Internet to spread information like a "virus" from person to person about products and ideas*

Corporate Blogs *comments and opinions published on the Web by or for an organization to promote its activities*

Web-Driven Revenue with Social Networking Although many major consumer companies have their own Facebook page, small businesses also use social media channels to increase revenues by networking with customers in target markets. A2L Consulting, for example, offers services to law firms, such as jury consulting, pretrial services, courtroom technologies, and litigation graphics, among other litigation services. The company uses multiple social networks, including Google+, YouTube, Pinterest, LinkedIn, and Twitter to increase Web-driven revenue. With 12,000 website visits each month, A2L derives considerable revenue from Web traffic. Company representatives credited LinkedIn, from among the social-media networks used by A2L, as the most effective for connecting with this B2B target market.[19] LinkedIn itself now has 332 million users and adds two new members every second.

How effective can it be? Viral marketing and social networking can lead to consumer awareness faster and with wider reach than traditional media messages—and at a lower cost. Success of the movie *Avatar* is credited to 20th Century Fox's use of prerelease viral tactics for stimulating public awareness of the blockbuster movie. And A2L, the supplier of litigation services to law firms, credits social networking for increasing the firm's revenues. It works for two reasons. First, people rely on the Internet for information that they used to get from newspapers, magazines, and television. Equally important, however, is the interactive element; the customer becomes a participant in the process of spreading the word by forwarding information to and seeking information from other network users.

The continuing growth of social media is changing marketing practices of businesses and consumer behavior, too. Facebook has become the Internet's most-used social media site, with about 1.4 billion active users each month and more than 890 million users each day. Although Facebook is the leader, Twitter is another fast-growing network, ranking number two in size with more than 288 million active users and handling about 500 million tweets each day. These numbers reflect not only the huge size of the social media industry but also the enormous population of participants that influence and persuade one another to explore new ideas and products, thus becoming both consumers and sellers. The industry's growth is attributed especially to (1) increasing numbers of mobile device users, (2) more participants in the older-than-55 demographic who are using Twitter, and (3) greater global reach to more potential users. As companies gain experience, they are using social media in new ways. In addition to advertising promotions, Kellogg Company uses social media for consumer research and to get new product ideas. Procter & Gamble has learned that viral exposure on Facebook can generate more sales than TV advertising. eBay finds that its sellers and buyers use social media to guide other buyers and sellers to eBay's website. For students of marketing, the social media trend has two clear implications: (1) as consumers using social media, you will receive a growing number of tempting product exposures, and (2) as a user of social media who becomes familiar with its applications and technical operations, you will find a growing number of career opportunities in social media positions.[20]

The International Marketing Mix

Marketing internationally means mounting a strategy to support global business operations. Foreign customers differ from domestic buyers in language, customs, business practices, and consumer behavior. If they go global, marketers must reconsider each element of the marketing mix: product, pricing, place, and promotion.

International Products Some products can be sold abroad with virtually no changes. Coca-Cola and Marlboro are the same in Peoria, Illinois, and Paris, France. In other cases, U.S. firms have had to create products with built-in flexibility, like an electric shaver that is adaptable to either 120- or 230-volt outlets, so travelers can use it in both U.S. and European electrical outlets. Frequently, however, domestic products require a major redesign for buyers in foreign markets. To sell computers in Japan, for example, Apple had to develop a Japanese-language operating system.

International Pricing When pricing for international markets, marketers must consider the higher costs of transporting and selling products abroad. For example, because of the higher costs of buildings, rent, equipment, and imported meat, as well as differences in exchange rates, a McDonald's Big Mac that costs $4.80 in the United States has a price tag of $7.76 in Norway.

International Distribution In some industries, including consumer products and industrial equipment, delays in starting new international distribution networks can be costly, so companies with existing distribution systems often enjoy an advantage. Many companies have avoided time delays by buying existing businesses with already-established distribution and marketing networks. Procter & Gamble, for example, bought Revlon's Max Factor and Betrix cosmetics, both of which have distribution and marketing networks in foreign markets. Many times, distribution methods used in the United States don't fit in international markets. For example, in Europe, Breathe Right Nasal Strips are identified as "medicinal" and must be sold in pharmacies.

International Promotion Occasionally, a good ad campaign is a good campaign just about anywhere. Quite often, however, U.S. promotional tactics do not succeed in other countries. Many Europeans believe that a product must be inherently shoddy if a company resorts to any advertising, particularly the U.S. hard-sell variety.

International marketers are ever more aware of cultural differences that can cause negative reactions to improperly advertised products. Some Europeans, for example, are offended by TV commercials that show weapons or violence. On the other hand, some European advertising is more provocative and sexually explicit than would be accepted in some countries. Meanwhile, cigarette commercials that are banned from U.S. television thrive in many Asian and European markets. Managers must carefully match product promotions to local customs and cultural values to successfully promote sales and avoid offending customers.

Indranil Kishor/Photoshot

Before creating an international ad like this Chinese advertisement for Coca-Cola, it is crucial to research what disparities, such as meaning of words, traditions, and taboos, exist between different societies. For example, German manufacturers of backpacks label them as "body bags," not terribly enticing to the U.S. consumer. Can you guess why Gerber baby food is not sold in France? The French translation of Gerber is "to vomit"! Effective marketing does not just involve knowledge of culture abroad, but also requires a general sensitivity to social trends and language.

Because of the need to adjust the marketing mix, success in international markets is hard won. But whether a firm markets in domestic or international markets, the basic principles of marketing still apply; only their implementation changes.

OBJECTIVE 11-7
Discuss
the marketing mix as it applies
to small business.

Small Business and the Marketing Mix

Many of today's largest firms were yesterday's small businesses. Behind the success of many small firms lies a skillful application of the marketing concept and an understanding of each element in the marketing mix.

Small-Business Products

Some new products and firms are doomed at the start because few customers want or need what they have to offer. Many fail to estimate realistic market potential, and some offer new products before they have clear pictures of their target segments. In contrast, a thorough understanding of what customers want has paid off for many small firms. Take, for example, the case of Little Earth Productions, Inc., a company that makes fashion accessories, such as handbags. Originally, the company merely considered how consumers would use its handbags. But after examining shopping habits, Little Earth Productions redesigned for better in-store display. Because stores can give handbags better visibility by hanging them instead of placing them on floors or low countertops, Little Earth Productions added small handles specifically for that purpose, resulting in increased sales. More recently, Little Earth has been concentrating on accessories for sports fans such as logoed purses, headbands, wallets, and hair accessories.

Small-Business Pricing

Haphazard pricing can sink a firm with a good product. Small-business pricing errors usually result from a failure to estimate operating expenses accurately. The founder of Nomie Baby, makers of spill-proof removable car seat covers for infants, started by setting prices too low. Considering only manufacturing and materials costs, other costs—shipping, storage, designing—were mistakenly ignored and not covered by the original selling price. Thereafter, when start-up prices were increased to cover all costs, sales fortunately did not diminish. Owners, for fear of pricing too high, often tend to underprice, resulting in financial crisis. Failing businesses have often been heard to say, "I didn't realize how much it costs to run the business!" Sometimes, however, firms discover their prices are too low, even when they cover all costs. A computer error at Headsets.com once caused cost-only prices rather than retail prices to be posted for the company's products on the Internet. The CEO was surprised that the erroneous low prices did not create a surge in sales. Instead, steady consumer response indicated that the firm's products were not as price-sensitive as believed, so the company raised original prices once, by 8 percent. Revenue rose as sales continued with little or no change from previous levels.[21] When small businesses set prices by carefully assessing costs and understanding their competitive market, many earn satisfactory profits.

Small-Business Distribution

The ability of many small businesses to attract and retain customers depends partly on the choice of location, especially for new service businesses.

In distribution, as in other aspects of the marketing mix, however, smaller companies may have advantages over larger competitors. A smaller company may be able to address customers' needs more quickly and efficiently with an added personal

entrepreneurship and new ventures

Farming Your Niche

By all accounts, seven acres would be a very small farm. But, Rick Crofford, who is employed full-time as an environmental manager for the Virginia Department of Transportation, has a bustling farming operation on the seven acres of former cornfields that surround his Virginia home. His first foray into farming was blueberries—he has nearly 200 blueberry bushes that produce 10 to 15 pints of fruit each year. However, the blueberries are labor intensive during harvesting and he's had to install fencing to keep out the deer. He's expanded his berry operation to include 250 strawberry plants, as well, and three kinds of raspberries. Crofford has stretched his operation into other crops, including fingerling potatoes. A plot less than an acre yielded 1,000 pounds of four varieties, which average about $2 per pound. Garlic, hot peppers, and broccoli are all grown on the farm with the help of his four children and occasional temporary help. He's funneled all the profits into a college savings plan for his kids.

Not far away, Francis Ngoh grows mushrooms and other crops on his 39-acre farm. The West African native came to the United States to earn a degree in engineering at the University of Maryland. Although he held several corporate positions over the years, he has now focused his attention full-time on farming. His main crop is shitake mushrooms, harvesting 3,000 to 4,000 pounds per year, but he also grows asparagus, leeks, garlic, peppers, and greens. Although not yet a certified organic producer, Ngoh has embraced these standards and uses no chemicals. He's also catering to the local Muslim market with his livestock operation. He slaughters lambs on site according to Islamic tradition, with demand especially high on holy days.

Crofford and Ngoh have been supported in their efforts by finding the right distribution networks, as well as support from the Virginia Cooperative Extension Service. Crofford works extensively with produce wholesaler The Fresh Link. Co-founder Mollie Visosky helps local producers understand the needs of high-end restaurants in the DC area, explaining, "We get

zigzagmtart/Fotolia

together with the chefs in January to find out what produce they will want during the next growing season. Then we try to match our growers with crops that they can grow best and make a nice profit." On the other hand, Ngoh has been able to sell his mushrooms and other vegetables to Whole Foods stores as well as a number of other local buyers.

Both Crofford and Ngoh have worked with Jim Haskins from the Virginia Cooperative Extension Service, a program operated jointly by agents from Virginia State University and Virginia Tech. Haskins explains, "I try to identify small producers in our area and give them the technical support to be more successful." This support was key to Mr. Crofford's decision to plan fingerling potatoes, which have a much higher yield than traditional Irish potatoes. Grant funding also helped both farmers, providing them with free plants and seeds to get started. In fact, these two have become so successful that Haskins uses them to promote niche farming in the Fauquier County area. And it's likely that this symbiotic relationship is one of the keys to success. Haskins explains, "One of our goals is to increase farm income for small producers. Not only do we need to sustain the farm but we also need to sustain the farmer."[22]

touch. Everex Systems, Inc. of Fremont, California, designs and sells computers to wholesalers and dealers through a system that the company calls *zero response time*. Because Everex Systems is small and flexible, phone orders can be reviewed every two hours and factory assembly adjusted to match demand.

Small-Business Promotion

Successful small businesses plan for promotional expenses as part of start-up costs. Some hold down costs by using less expensive promotional methods, like publicity in local newspapers and online messaging. Other small businesses identify themselves and their products with associated groups, organizations, and events. Thus, a crafts gallery might partner with a local art league to organize public showings of their combined products.

summary of learning objectives

Explain the concept of marketing and identify the five forces that constitute the external marketing environment. (pp. 374–380)

Marketing is responsible for creating, communicating, and delivering value and satisfaction to customers. With limited financial resources, customers buy products that offer the best value, measured by the relationship between benefits and costs. Marketers must understand customers' wants and needs because they determine product features, and the timing, place, and terms of sale that provide utility and add value for customers. A product may be a tangible good, a service, or even an idea. In addition, products may be classified as either consumer products or industrial products when they are marketed to businesses or nonprofit organizations. Although marketing often focuses on single transactions for products, services, or ideas, marketers also take a longer-term perspective by managing customer relationships to benefit the organization and its stakeholders. Customer *relationship marketing* emphasizes building lasting relationships with customers and suppliers. Stronger relationships, including stronger economic and social ties, can result in greater long-term satisfaction, customer loyalty, and customer retention.

Five outside factors make up a company's external environment and influence its marketing programs: (1) the *political and legal environment* includes laws and regulations that may define or constrain business activities, (2) the *sociocultural environment* involves peoples' values, beliefs, and ideas that affect marketing decisions, (3) the *technological environment* includes new technologies that affect existing and new products, (4) the *economic environment* consists of conditions such as inflation, recession, and interest rates that influence organizational and individual spending patterns, and (5) the *competitive environment* is that in which marketers must persuade buyers to purchase their products rather than their competitors'.

Explain the purpose of a marketing plan and identify its main components. (pp. 380–384)

A *marketing plan* is a statement of all the future marketing activities and resources that will be used to meet the desires and needs of customers so that the firm's overall business mission will be accomplished. It begins with objectives or goals setting the stage for everything that follows. *Marketing objectives*—the things marketing intends to accomplish—are the foundation that guides all of the detailed activities in the marketing plan. The marketing objectives focus on maintaining or enhancing the organization's future competitive position in its chosen markets. A marketing strategy can be developed once the marketing objectives have been clarified. *Marketing strategy* identifies the planned marketing programs, including all the marketing activities that will be used for achieving the marketing goals, when those activities will occur, and the contents of its programs. If planned activities are not affordable—requiring more resources than are available—then activities, programs, or goals are adjusted until realistic plans emerge.

Marketing strategy includes four basic components (often called the "Four Ps") of the *marketing mix*—product, pricing, place (distribution), and promotion—that marketing managers use to satisfy customers in target markets. The specific activities for each of the Four Ps are designed differently to best meet the needs of each target market. Marketing begins with a *product*, a good, service, or idea designed to fill a customer's need or want. Conceiving and developing new products is a constant challenge for marketers who must always consider changing technology, consumer wants and needs, and economic conditions. Producers often promote particular features of products to distinguish them in the marketplace. *Product differentiation* is the creation of a feature or image that makes a product differ enough from existing products to attract consumers. The *pricing* of a product is often a balancing act. Prices must be high enough to support a variety of operating, administrative, research, and marketing costs, but low enough that consumers don't turn to competitors. In the marketing mix, *place* (or distribution) refers to where and how consumers get access to the products they buy. The most visible component of the marketing mix is *promotion*, a set of techniques for communicating information about products. The most important promotional tools include advertising, personal selling, sales promotions, publicity/public relations, and direct or interactive marketing.

OBJECTIVE 11-3

Explain market segmentation and how it is used in target marketing.
(pp. 384–386)

Marketers think in terms of *target markets*—particular groups of people or organizations on which a firm's marketing efforts are focused. Target marketing requires *market segmentation*—dividing a market into categories of customer types or "segments," such as age, geographic location, or level of income. Members of a market segment have similar wants and needs and share some common traits that influence purchasing decisions. Once they identify segments, companies adopt a variety of strategies for attracting customers in one or more of the chosen target segments. The following are five variables that are often used for segmentation: (1) *Geographic variables* are the geographical units that may be considered in developing a segmentation strategy. (2) *Demographic variables* describe populations by identifying such traits as age, income, gender, ethnic background, and marital status. (3) *Geo-demographic variables* combine demographic variables with geographic variables, such as an age category coupled with urban areas. (4) *Psychographic variables* include lifestyles, interests, and attitudes. (5) *Behavioral variables* include categories of behavioral patterns such as online consumers or large-volume buyers. Marketers search for segments showing promise for generating new sales if marketing efforts by other companies have overlooked or misjudged the segment's market potential. Such competitive weaknesses present marketing opportunities for other companies to enter into those segments. Desirable segments with market potential then become candidate target markets and, once chosen, they become part of the marketing strategy where its companion marketing mix is developed.

OBJECTIVE 11-4

Discuss the purpose of marketing research and compare the four marketing research methods. (pp. 386–390)

Effective marketing decisions should be customer based and focused on timely information about trends in the marketplace. *Marketing research* is a tool for gaining such information; it is the study of what customers want and how best to meet those needs. Researchers use several methods to obtain, interpret, and apply information about customers. They determine the kinds of information needed for marketing strategy, goal setting, target-market selection, and developing new or altered products for specific market segments. Marketing research's orientation has become increasingly globalized because of the increasing importance of selling products internationally.

Research success depends on which of four basic research methods is used: (1) *Observation* means watching and recording consumer preferences and behavior. By using live camera feeds, computer tracking, and other electronic technologies, marketers observe and record consumer preferences rapidly and with great accuracy. (2) The heart of any *survey* is a questionnaire on which participants record responses. Surveys can get responses to specific questions quickly and at relatively lower cost. (3) In a *focus group*, people are gathered in one place, presented with an issue or topic, and asked to discuss it. The researcher takes notes, makes video recordings, and encourages open discussion by providing only a minimal amount of structure for the group's discussion. This technique allows researchers to explore issues too complex for questionnaires; it can produce creative ideas and solutions. (4) *Experimentation* compares the responses and behaviors of the same or similar people under different conditions that are of interest to the researcher. Experimentation can be relatively expensive because of costs of obtaining the experimental setting, securing participants, paying participants, and paying those who administer the experiment.

OBJECTIVE 11-5

Describe the consumer buying process and the key factors that influence that process. (pp. 390–392)

In the study of *consumer behavior*, marketers evaluate the decision process by which people buy and consume products. There are four major influences on consumer behavior. (1) *Psychological influences* include an individual's motivations, perceptions, ability to learn, and attitudes. (2) *Personal influences* include lifestyle, personality, and economic status. (3) *Social influences* include family, opinion leaders, and reference groups such as friends, coworkers, and professional associates. (4) *Cultural influences* include culture, subculture, and social class. At times, these influences have a significant impact on buying decisions, although consumers demonstrate high *brand loyalty* at times, regularly purchasing the same products.

Observers of consumer behavior have constructed various models to help marketers understand how consumers decide to purchase products. One model considers five influences that lead to consumption: (**1**) *Problem or need recognition*: The buying process begins when the consumer recognizes a problem or need. (2) *Information seeking*: Having recognized a need, consumers seek information. The information search leads to an evoked set (or consideration set)—a group of products they will consider buying. (3) *Evaluation of alternatives*: By analyzing product attributes (price, prestige, quality) of the consideration set, consumers compare products to decide which product best meets their needs. (4) *Purchase decision*: "Buy" decisions are based on rational motives, emotional motives, or both. *Rational motives* involve the logical evaluation of product attributes, such as cost, quality, and usefulness. *Emotional motives* involve nonobjective factors and include sociability, imitation of others, and aesthetics. (5) *Postpurchase evaluations*: Consumers continue to form opinions after their purchase. Marketers want consumers to be happy after the consumption of products so that they are more likely to buy them again.

OBJECTIVE 11-6

Discuss the four categories of organizational markets and the characteristics of business-to-business (B2B) buying behavior. (pp. 392–396)

The various organizational markets exhibit different buying behaviors from those in consumer markets. Business marketing involves organizational or commercial markets that fall into four B2B categories. (1) The *services companies market* encompasses the many firms that provide services to the purchasing public. Every service company, from pet care to hospitality services to health care and nursery schools, airlines, and more, buys resources needed to provide services to customers. (2) The *industrial market* consists of businesses that buy goods to be converted into other products or that are used during production. It includes farmers, manufacturers, and some retailers. (3) Before some products reach consumers, they pass through a *reseller market* consisting of intermediaries—wholesalers and retailers—that buy finished goods and resell them. (4) The *government and institutional market* includes federal, state, and local governments and nongovernmental buyers—hospitals, churches, museums, and charities—that purchase goods and services needed for serving their clients. Taken together, these four organizational markets do more than two times the business annually than do the U.S. consumer markets.

Unlike most consumers, organizational buyers purchase in large quantities and are professional, specialized, and well informed. As professionals, they are trained in methods for negotiating purchase terms. Once buyer–seller agreements have been reached, they also arrange formal contracts. In contrast with consumer–seller relationships that are often one-time interactions, B2B situations involve frequent and enduring buyer–seller relationships that provide each party, buyer and seller, with access to the technical strengths of the other. Thus, a buyer and a supplier may form a design team to create products to benefit both parties. Accordingly, industrial sellers emphasize personal selling by trained representatives who understand the needs of each customer.

OBJECTIVE 11-7

Discuss the marketing mix as it applies to small business. (pp. 396–397)

Each element in the marketing mix can determine success or failure for any *small business*. Many *products* are failures because consumers don't need what they have to offer. A realistic market potential requires getting a clearer picture of what target segments want. Small-business *pricing* errors usually result from a failure to estimate start-up costs and operating expenses accurately. In addition to facilities construction or rental costs, shipping, storage, wages, taxes, utilities, and materials costs also must be considered. By carefully assessing costs, and by learning what customers are willing to pay, prices can be set to earn satisfactory profits. Perhaps the most crucial aspect of *place*, or distribution, is location, especially for services businesses, because locational convenience determines the ability to attract customers. Although *promotion* can be expensive and is essential for small businesses, costs can be reduced by using less expensive promotional methods. Local newspaper articles, online messaging, and television programming cover business events, thus providing free public exposure.

key terms

advertising
behavioral segmentation
behavioral variables
brand competition
brand loyalty
competitive environment
consumer behavior
consumer goods
corporate blogs
cultural influences
customer relationship management (CRM)
data mining
data warehousing
demographic segmentation
demographic variables
economic environment
emotional motives
evoked set (or consideration set)
experimentation
focus group
form utility
geographic segmentation
geographic variables
geo-demographic segmentation

geo-demographic variables
industrial goods
industrial market
institutional market
integrated marketing strategy
international competition
market segmentation
marketing
marketing manager
marketing mix
marketing objectives
marketing plan
marketing research
marketing strategy
observation
personal influences
personal selling
place (distribution)
place utility
political–legal environment
possession utility
pricing
primary data
product
product differentiation

product positioning
promotion
psychographic segmentation
psychographic variables
psychological influences
public relations
rational motives
relationship marketing
reseller market
sales promotion
secondary data
services
services companies market
social influences
social networking
social networking media
sociocultural environment
substitute product
surveys
target market
technological environment
time utility
utility
value
viral marketing

MyBizLab

To complete the problems with the ✪, go to EOC Discussion Questions in the MyLab.

questions & exercises

QUESTIONS FOR REVIEW

11-1. In order to promote products effectively, which three types of competition need to be identified?

11-2. How is the concept of product differentiation a vital one in order to ensure that a product stands out in the market?

11-3. What are psychographic variables and how are they used in target marketing?

✪ **11-4.** Why is post-purchase evaluation by customers important to marketers even though the sale has been made?

QUESTIONS FOR ANALYSIS

11-5. Select a technology product (cell phone, laptop, tablet, for example). Outline the four key areas of utility of that product. Explain how it addresses each of the four elements.

✪ **11-6.** There are four main influences on consumer behavior. Did these influences have a bearing on the decision you made about attending college? Why or why not?

11-7. Imagine being the marketing manager for a large U.S. hotel chain. How might the company have to adapt its marketing mix to move into foreign markets in South and Central America?

⭐ **11-8.** Choose an existing product that could benefit from viral marketing. Once you have identified the product, describe how you would use viral marketing to increase demand for the product.

APPLICATION EXERCISES

11-9. Identify a company with a product that interests you. Consider ways the company could use customer relationship management (CRM) to strengthen relationships with its target market. Specifically, explain your recommendations on how the company can use each of the four basic components of the marketing mix in its CRM efforts.

11-10. The U.S. Census collects an enormous amount of secondary data that is useful in marketing research. Go to the American Fact Finder home page at http://factfinder2.census.gov and collect data about people living in your zip code. Compare your zip code to your state as a whole in terms of factors such as age, race, household size, marital status, and educational attainment. Based on your data, what types of retail establishments would be specially appropriate to your area?

building a business: continuing team exercise

Assignment

Meet with your team members to consider your new business venture and how it relates to the marketing processes and consumer behavior topics in this chapter. Develop specific responses to the following:

11-11. Develop a "Statement of Marketing Objectives" for your company. Justify those marketing objectives by explaining how they contribute to the overall business mission of the company.

11-12. Identify the target market(s) for your business. Who are your customers? Describe the characteristics of customers in your target market(s).

11-13. Discuss how your team is going to identify the existing competitors in your chosen market. Based on the discussion, what are the key elements of your marketing plans that will give you a competitive edge over those competitors?

11-14. Consider, again, the customers in your target market(s). Are they individual consumers, organizations, or a mix of both consumers and organizations? Describe in detail the buying process(es) you expect them to use for purchasing your product(s). Discuss whether the customer buying process should or should not be a concern for your company.

11-15. Develop a preliminary design of the marketing mix for your target market(s). Retain the design for carryover and refinement in the following marketing chapters.

team exercise

WHO WOULD BUY FROM US?

You are the CEO of a medium-sized manufacturing company with three factory producing folding bicycles in China. Your bicycles are patented designs and your main target markets are commuters and students. Given the size and design of the bicycles, they are not endurance or long distance machines, more short-hop from railway station to office or campus. The USP is that the bicycles weight 10kg and can be unfolded and locked for use in less than 3 minutes.

Currently, you sell the product across Europe, in Turkey and Israel, in Canada and the USA and across the Far East with your biggest markets in Singapore and Japan. You are about to launch in South America and need to brief distributors that will handle the all-important launches in Brazil and Argentina, the two markets that market research has identified as the potentially most lucrative. The most important aspect is to identify the target markets and to build the marketing campaign from there.

TEAM ACTIVITY

11-16. As a group, describe the characteristics, wants, and needs of the target market.

11-17. Are there any other individuals or groups that might have an influence on the buying decision?

11-18. Identify the typical demographic variables of the target markets. Make sure that you cover age, education, family life cycle, family size, income, nationality, race, religion and gender. Does the group agree on the profiles?

11-19. Have each group member try to identify the key psychographic variables that the target market is likely to have.

11-20. Share your thoughts about the psychographic variables and develop a profile of the target market.

11-21. As a group, suggest how you would present the information to distributors and any advice you would give them about the marketing campaign.

exercising your ethics

WEIGHING THE ODDS

The Situation

You are the quality control manager for a major dietary supplement company. Because your products are sold over the counter as nutritional supplements rather than as medications, the supplements are not regulated by the Food and Drug Administration. Researchers have worked for years to develop a weight-loss product that is safe and effective. Several years ago, researchers identified a naturally occurring compound that was effective in appetite suppression. Your company has done several years of testing and you have found that 85 percent of people using the supplement were able to lose at least 20 pounds in the first year of use. In addition, those who continued to take the supplement were able to maintain their weight loss for an additional year. Company executives believe that this drug can bring billions of dollars in revenues in the first year of sales. Obesity has become an epidemic in the United States and much of the developed world and people who are obese are at a significantly greater risk of stroke, heart attack, and diabetes.

The Dilemma

You are reviewing the results of the clinical trials and are pleased to see that the product is effective. Just as you are ready to recommend that the company introduce the product to the market, you uncover some upsetting information. A small group of people who took the supplement during testing, actually less than 1 percent, developed a rare neurological disorder. It's not clear that the supplement is the cause of the disorder, but it was not observed in the control group that took a placebo. Because the risk is so small, the marketing manager is recommending that the company go ahead with introducing the supplement and monitor to see if consumers report a similar side effect. Commercialization of this product could make your company profitable and could potentially save thousands of lives by helping consumers lose weight, but you are unsure if this is the right thing to do.

QUESTIONS TO ADDRESS

11-22. How would you characterize the particular ethical issues in this situation?

11-23. From an ethical standpoint, what are the obligations of the quality control manager and the marketing manager regarding the introduction of the product in this situation?

11-24. If you were the quality control manager, how would you handle this matter?

cases

Building a Brand with Social Media

Continued from page 374

At the beginning of this chapter, you read about Michelle Phan and how she expanded a blog into a beauty and lifestyle empire. Using the information presented in this chapter, you should now be able to answer the following questions.

QUESTIONS FOR DISCUSSION

11-25. What forces in the external environment have created opportunities or challenges for Michelle Phan? Explain.

11-26. Who is Michelle Phan's target market?

11-27. Describe the consumer buying process for someone purchasing cosmetic products. Where would videos and a service like Ipsy fit into this process?

11-28. Go the website for Phan's beauty line with L'Oreal, www.emcosmetics.com. How does the product line appeal to Phan's target market?

Where Has All the Middle Gone?

Procter & Gamble (P&G), the iconic marketer of seemingly endless lines of household products since 1837, is confronted now with a puzzling marketing dilemma: "What's happening to the middle class in the United States? The number of mid-range shoppers is shrinking." With its lineup of popular brands such as Folgers, Clairol, Charmin, and Gillette, it is estimated that 98 percent of U.S. households are using at least one P&G product, a position that has grown largely by targeting middle-class consumers. Although its products are sold in more than 180 countries, U.S. consumers provide more than 35 percent of P&G sales and nearly 60 percent of annual profits.

The problem facing P&G is the shrinkage of middle-class purchasing power, a change that began with the 2008 recession and continues today. Many once-well-off middle-class families are pinched with rising prices for gasoline, food, education, and health care but little or no wage increases. The nation's economic condition, as a result, has been dubbed by Citigroup as the "Consumer Hourglass Theory." Advocates of the theory assert that purchasing power has shifted away from the once-massive middle and is concentrated now at the bottom and top. That's where consumer action is now, at the high-end market and the low-end market, and it will increase even more in those areas.[23]

On top of changing economics, preferences also are changing among consumers. Generation Y and Z buyers have been raised on premium brands. Rather than getting their clothes at bargain retailers, younger adults spent their teenage years in clothes from Hollister and Abercrombie & Fitch. As adults, they show a preference for premium brands, even when their incomes are solidly middle class. Will middle-class shrinkage continue, or is it a passing blip that will recover in the near future? Based on P&G's research, Melanie Healey, group president for P&G's North America business, expects middle-class downsizing will be a continuing trend. Accordingly, P&G and other companies are rethinking their target markets. Aiming at the high-end segment in 2009, the company introduced its more expensive Olay Pro-X skin-care product. Previously, P&G introduced Gain, the bargain-priced laundry detergent, which is aimed at the growing lower portion of the previous middle-class market following a dip in sales of the mid-priced Tide brand. Near the beginning of the recession, P&G's lower-priced Luvs diapers gained market share from the higher-priced Pampers brand. Following a path similar to that of P&G, H. J. Heinz has developed more food products for the lower-priced markets. Meanwhile, retailers focusing on lower-income consumers, such as Dollar General, are attracting customers from higher-priced Walmart and Target.[24]

Refocusing from the mainstream middle onto high- and low-end consumers is a new marketing experience at P&G. They have increased market research on lower-income households, often using face-to-face interviews to gain in-depth understanding of these consumers. So far, the low-end and the high-end segments each are generally smaller than the former massive middle-class market, which means P&G is splitting its marketing efforts, rather than having just a single larger thrust. As one company official noted, historically they have been good at doing things on a larger scale, but now they are learning how to deal with

smaller sales volumes for products in each of two segments. New product development is affected, too, because the high-end segment often involves fewer products with attractive extra features that will sell profitably at higher prices. P&G is betting that the Hourglass Theory has set the course for the company's future.

QUESTIONS FOR DISCUSSION

11-29. How would you best describe P&G's marketing strategy for the situation presented in this case? Explain why.

11-30. What elements of P&G's external marketing environment, if any, are influencing the company's marketing strategy? Explain your reasoning.

11-31. Why do you suppose P&G's marketing research includes face-to-face interviews for the situation described in this case? Would other forms of marketing research also be useful in this situation? Explain your reasoning.

11-32. Explain the roles of target marketing and market segmentation as they apply in this case.

11-33. In what ways are the components of P&G's marketing mix being affected by the situation described in this case? Give examples to illustrate.

MyBizLab

Go to the Assignments section of your MyLab to complete these writing exercises.

11-34. Marketing in every business must consider the firm's external environment and the environmental forces (or "marketing environments") that affect marketing decisions, successes, and failures. Recall and consider the major elements in the "marketing environment." Write an essay explaining how a firm's marketing strategy must consider each of those elements in the "marketing environment." In your discussion, give examples of how each element enters into the development of marketing strategy.

11-35. Describe the steps in the consumer buying process for someone purchasing a new automobile. What are the major influences on the consumer buying process? Explain how each might affect the decision made.

end notes

[1]Castillo, Michelle. 2014. "YouTube's Leading Ladies." *Adweek* 55, no. 41: 18–21. Business Source Premier, EBSCOhost (accessed May 29, 2015). "YouTube Makeup Guru Michelle Phan on Becoming a Beauty Superstar: 'My Only Goal Was to Help My Family.'" *Glamour*, September 2013. www.glamour.com/lipstick/2013/09/michelle-phan-youtube-beauty-glamour-october-2013. Stone, Madeline. "YouTube Superstar Michelle Phan Shares Her Tips for Building a Social Media Brand." *Business Insider*, November 2014. Accessed May 29, 2015. www.businessinsider.com/social-media-tips-from-youtube-star-michelle-phan-2014-11

[2]American Marketing Association, "Definition of Marketing," at www.marketingpower.com/aboutama/pages/definitionofmarketing.aspx, accessed on March 18, 2013.

[3]Kotler, Philip, and Armstrong, Gary. *Principles of Marketing*, 12th ed. (Upper Saddle River, NJ: Prentice Hall, 2008), 7.

[4]"CRM (customer relationship management)," *TechTarget.com*, at http://searchcrm.techtarget.com/definition/CRM,

accessed on December 8, 2010; "Customer Relationship Management," *Wikipedia*, at http://en.wikipedia.org/wiki/Customer_relationship_management, accessed on December 8, 2010.

[5]Khanna, Poonam. "Hotel Chain Gets Personal with Customers," *Computing Canada*, April 8, 2005, p. 18.

[6]"Fairmont Hotels & Resorts: Website Development and Enhanced CRM," *accenture*, at www.accenture.com/Global/Services/By_Industry/Travel/Client_Successes/FairmontCrm.htm, accessed on December 8, 2010.

[7]"Tiny House Purchases See Big Growth," *Columbia Daily Tribune*, December 4, 2010, p. 11; "Solar Wells Displace Windmills on Range," *Columbia Daily Tribune*, July 22, 2010, p. 8B; McCarthy, Shawn, and Keenan, Greg. "Ottawa Demands Lower Auto Worker Costs," *The Globe and Mail*, January 19, 2009, at http://v1business.theglobeandmail.com/servlet/story/RTGAM.20090119.wrautos19/BNStory/Business; Edmondson, Gail, Rowley, Ian, Lakshman,

Nandini, Welch, David, and Roberts, Dexter. "The Race to Build Really Cheap Cars," *BusinessWeek*, April 23, 2007, at www.businessweek.com/magazine/content/07_17/b4031064.htm; McClatchy Newspapers (Las Vegas), "Downsizing to 'Right-Sizing,'" *Columbia Daily Tribune: Saturday Business*, January 31, 2009, p. 10; Henry, Jim. "Prius Hybrid Aimed Small, Stood Tall," *Automotive News*, October 29, 2007, p. 150 (3 pages) at www.autonews.com/apps/pbcs.dll/article?AID=/20071029/ANA06/710290326/1078&Profile=1078#; Luce, Burrelles. "Hitting the Right Note: Best Practices for Corporate Social Responsibility (CSR) Marketing," *E-Newsletter*, July 2007, at http://luceonline.us/newsletter/default_july07.php; "Are Green Cars Still Worth the Money?" *Consumer Reports* 80, no. 4: 16. *Business Source Premier*, EBSCO*host* (accessed May 20, 2015); Champniss, Guy, Wilson, Hugh N., and Macdonald, Emma K. 2015. "Why Your Customers' Social Identities Matter." *Harvard Business Review* 93 no. 1/2: 88–96. *Business Source Premier*, EBSCO*host* (accessed May 20, 2015).

[8]McClatchy Newspapers, "Airbus to Be Allowed to Bid to Replace Air Force One," *Columbia Daily Tribune*, January 25, 2009, p. 4D.

[9]Stern, Joanna. "iPhone 5: The Best 5 New Features," *ABC News*, September 13, 2012, at http://abcnews.go.com/Technology/iphone-top-features/story?id=17228259#

[10]Barton, Seth. "Samsung Galaxy s4 Release Date, Price & Specs Unveiled," *Expert Reviews*, March 17, 2013, at http://www.expertreviews.co.uk/smartphones/1298554/samsung-galaxy-s4-release-date-price-specs-unveiled

[11]Schifferes, Steve. "The Triumph of Lean Production," *BBC News*, February 27, 2007, at http://news.bbc.co.uk/2/hi/business/6346315stm

[12]"Financial Cards in Poland," Euromonitor International, (May 2008), at http://www.euromonitor.com/Consumer_Finance_in_Poland

[13]Smith, Scott. "Coca-Cola Lost Millions Because of This Market Research Mistake," Qualtrics (Qualtrics Blog), January 21, 2013, at www.qualtrics.com/blog/coca-cola-market-research/

[14]"A World with Better Customer Service—Helping Consumers Find It, and Helping Businesses Achieve It," *StellaService*, at www.stellaservice.com/, accessed on March 25, 2013; Dana Mattioli, "Data Firm Attracts Funding," *Wall Street Journal*, February 28, 2013, p. B5; Davis, Don. "StellaService Raises $15 Million and Starts Charging for its e-Retail Data," *Internet Retailer*, February 28, 2013, at www.internetretailer.com/2013/02/28/stellaservice-raises-15-million-and-starts-charging-data; "Say Goodbye to Fake Reviews." *Inc.* 36, no. 3: 108–110. *Business Source Premier*, EBSCO*host* (accessed May 20, 2015).

[15]"2008 Brand Keys Customer Loyalty Engagement Index." (March 18, 2008), at www.brandkeys.com/awards/cli08.cfm

[16]"Lists and Structure of Governments," *United States Census Bureau, U.S. Department of Commerce*, at www.census.gov/govs/go, accessed on March 18, 2013.

[17]"Lists and Structure of Governments."

[18]Strauss, Judy, El-Ansary, Adel, and Frost, Raymond. *E-Marketing*, 5th ed. (Upper Saddle River, NJ: Prentice Hall, 2007); "Ten Corporate Blogs Worth Reading," February 19, 2009, at www.blogtrepreneuer.com/2009/02/19/ten-corporate-blogs-worth-reading/

[19]Maltby, Emily, and Ovide, Shira. "Which Social Media Work?" *Wall Street Journal*, January 31, 2013, p. B8; "A2L Consulting Offers Its Complex Civil Litigation E-Book as a Free Download to Litigators and Litigation Support Professionals," *A2L Consulting*, January 15, 2013, at www.marketwire.com/press-release/a2l-consulting-offers-its-complex-civil-litigation-e-book-as-free-download-litigators-1745621.htm

[20]Protalinski, Emil. "Facebook Passes 1.11 Billion Monthly Active Users, 751 Million Mobile Users, and 665 Mission Daily Users," *TNW: The Next Web*, May 1, 2013, at http://thenextweb.com/facebook/2013/05/01/facebook-passes-1-11-billion-monthly-active-users-751-million-mobile-users-and-665-million-daily-users/; Edwards, Jim. "Meet the 30 Biggest Social Media Advertisers of 2012 [Ranked]," *Business Insider*, September 27, 2012, at www.businessinsider.com/the-30-biggest-social-media-advertisers-of-2012-2012-9?op=1; McCue, T. J. "Twitter Ranked Fastest Growing Social Media Platform in the World," *Forbes*, January 29, 2013, at www.forbes.com/sites/tjmccue/2013/01/29/twitter-ranked-fastest-growing-social-platform-in-the-world/

[21]Zimmerman, Eilene. "Real-Life Lessons in the Delicate Art of Setting Prices," *New York Times*, April 20, 2011, at www.nytimes.com/2011/04/21/business/smallbusiness/21sbiz.html?pagewanted=all&_r=0

[22]Lyne, David. "Small Plots Produce Nice Profits for Niche Farmers." *Fauquier Now* (Warrenton, VA), September 23, 2012. Accessed May 26, 2015. www.fauquiernow.com/index.php/fauquier_news/article/small-plots-produce-nice-profits-for-niche-farmers

[23]Bhatnagar, Roshni. "Why Citi's Consumer Hourglass Theory Matters," *Northwestern Business Review*, January 3, 2012 at http://northwesternbusinessreview.org/why-citis-consumer-hourglass-theory-matters/

[24]Byron, Ellen. "As Middle Class Shrinks, P&G Aims High and Low," *Wall Street Journal*, September 12, 2011, pp. A1, A16; Groth, Aimee. "The Consumer Hourglass Theory: This Is Why P&G, Saks, and Heinz Are Ignoring the Middle Class," *Business Insider*, September 24, 2011 at www.businessinsider.com/hourglass-consumer-theory-pg-citigroup-2011-9

13 | The Art and Science of Marketing

LEARNING OBJECTIVES   After studying this chapter, you will be able to

1 Define *marketing*, and explain its role in society.

2 Identify three trends that help define contemporary marketing.

3 Differentiate between consumer buying behavior and organizational buying behavior.

4 Define *strategic marketing planning*, and identify the four basic options for pursuing new marketing opportunities.

5 Identify the four steps in crafting a marketing strategy.

6 Describe the four main components of the marketing mix.

BEHIND THE SCENES   RED ANTS PANTS GIVES WORKING WOMEN A CHOICE THAT FITS

Photo by Erik Peterson, Courtesy of Sarah Calhoun

Sarah Calhoun of Red Ants Pants crafted a successful marketing mix to fulfill her mission of providing hardwearing pants for hardworking women.

www.redantspants.com

Something doesn't add up here:

1. Thousands and thousands of women work in heavy labor jobs, from farming and ranching to welding, construction, and pile driving. In fact, a quarter of the workforce in the building trades, agriculture, fishing, and forestry consists of women.
2. The kind of work these women perform quickly shreds regular clothing. They need heavy-duty duds.
3. Carhartt and other work clothing suppliers sell heavy-duty pants that can stand up to the rigors of tough work, but when Sarah Calhoun surveyed the market, these suppliers focused on work pants made for men.
4. Women aren't shaped like men.

Calhoun wasn't a clothing designer, didn't work in the business, and wasn't chasing some lifelong entrepreneurial dream. But she was fed up—with men's work pants that didn't fit or women's regular pants that didn't hold up under the stress and strain of clearing trails, peeling logs, and doing the other sorts of work she took on in her adopted home state of Montana.

Tired of constantly putting down her tools so she could pull up her misfit britches, Calhoun decided to solve the problem herself. She launched Red Ants Pants with the single-minded goal of outfitting women who need rugged workwear.

Why "Red Ants Pants," by the way? In a conversation with a biologist about the social behaviors of ants, she learned that in red ant colonies, females do most of the work. In keeping with the cheeky style she adopted for all her company's communication, she uses the name as a salute to hardworking women everywhere.

Calhoun was convinced she had spotted a business opportunity, but what was the best way to pursue it? How could a total outsider—based in White Sulphur Springs, Montana, no less—break into the clothing industry? How could she design a product that would meet the needs of her target customers? How many choices should she offer in terms of colors, styles, and sizes? What could she do to craft a compelling message and get that message in front of the buying public? How should she price the high-quality product she had in mind? What about distribution and the rest of the marketing mix? If you were in Calhoun's position, how would you go about marketing Red Ants Pants?[1]

INTRODUCTION

Sarah Calhoun's experience in introducing the Red Ants Pants brand (profiled in the chapter-opening Behind the Scenes) illustrates the complex challenge of fashioning an appealing blend of products, prices, distribution methods, and customer communication efforts—the essential elements of marketing. This chapter introduces the basic concepts of marketing; products and pricing are addressed in Chapter 14, distribution and marketing logistics are the topics of Chapter 15, and customer communication is covered in Chapter 16.

Marketing in a Changing World

Marketing requires a wide range of skills, from research and analysis to strategic planning to persuasive communication. On the job and in the media, you will encounter many uses of the term *marketing,* from the broad and strategic to the narrow and tactical. However, noted marketing professors Philip Kotler and Gary Armstrong offer a definition that does a great job of highlighting the contemporary flavor of customer-focused marketing: **Marketing** is "the process by which companies create value for customers and build strong customer relationships in order to capture value from customers in return."[2] The ideas of *value,* the *exchange* of value, and lasting *relationships* are essential elements of successful marketing.

In addition to goods and services, marketing applies to not-for-profit organizations, people, places, and causes. Politicians and celebrities constantly market themselves. So do places that want to attract residents, tourists, and business investments. **Place marketing** describes efforts to market geographic areas ranging from neighborhoods to entire countries. **Cause-related marketing** promotes a cause or a social issue—such as physical fitness, cancer awareness, or environmental sustainability—while also promoting a company and its products.

THE ROLE OF MARKETING IN SOCIETY

Marketing plays an important role in society by helping people satisfy their needs and wants and by helping organizations determine what to produce.

Needs and Wants

Individuals and organizations have a wide variety of needs, from food and water necessary for survival to transaction-processing systems that make sure a retail store gets paid for all the credit card purchases it records. As a consumer, you experience needs any time differences or gaps exist between your actual state and your ideal state. You're hungry and you don't want to be hungry: You need to eat. **Needs** create the motivation to buy products and are, therefore, at the core of any discussion of marketing.

1   LEARNING OBJECTIVE

Define *marketing,* and explain its role in society.

marketing
The process of creating value for customers and building relationships with those customers in order to capture value back from them.

place marketing
Marketing efforts to attract people and organizations to a particular geographical area.

cause-related marketing
Identification and marketing of a social issue, cause, or idea to selected target markets.

needs
Differences between a person's actual state and his or her ideal state; they provide the basic motivation to make a purchase.

wants
Specific goods, services, experiences, or other entities that are desirable in light of a person's experiences, culture, and personality.

Your **wants** are based on your needs but are more specific. Producers do not create needs, but they do try to shape your wants by exposing you to attractive choices. For instance, when you *need* some food, you may *want* a Snickers bar, an orange, or a seven-course dinner at the swankiest restaurant in town. If you have the means, or *buying power*, to purchase the product you want, you create *demand* for that product.[3]

Exchanges and Transactions

exchange process
The act of obtaining a desired object or service from another party by offering something of value in return.

transaction
An exchange of value between parties.

When you participate in the **exchange process**, you trade something of value (usually money) for something else of value. When you make a purchase, you encourage the producer of that item to create or supply more of it. In this way, supply and demand tend toward balance, and society obtains the goods and services that are most satisfying. When the exchange actually occurs, it takes the form of a **transaction**. Party A gives Party B $1.29 and gets a medium Coke in return. A trade of values takes place.

Most transactions in today's society involve money, but money is not necessarily required. Bartering or trading, which predates the use of cash, is making a big comeback thanks to the Internet. Hundreds of online barter exchanges are now in operation in the United States alone. Intermediaries such as BizXchange (www.bizx.com) facilitate cashless trading among multiple members through a system of credits and debits. For instance, an advertising agency might trade services to a dairy farm, which then trades products to a catering company, which then trades services to the advertising agency. By eliminating the need for trading partners to have exactly complimentary needs at exactly the same time, these exchanges make it easy for companies to buy and sell without using cash.[4]

The Four Utilities

utility
The power of a good or service to satisfy a human need.

To encourage the exchange process, marketers enhance the appeal of their goods and services by adding **utility**, which is any attribute that increases the value that customers place on the product. When companies change raw materials into finished goods, they are creating *form utility* desired by consumers. When supermarkets provide fresh, ready-to-eat dishes as an alternative to food ingredients, they are creating form utility. In other cases, marketers try to make their products available when and where customers want to buy them, creating *time utility* and *place utility*. Overnight couriers such as FedEx and UPS create time utility, whereas coffee carts in office buildings and ATMs in shopping malls create place utility. Services such as Apple's iTunes create both time and place utility: You can purchase music any time and from just about anywhere. The final form of utility is *possession utility*—the satisfaction that buyers get when they actually possess a product, both legally and physically. Mortgage companies, for example, create possession utility by offering loans that allow people to buy homes they could otherwise not afford.

THE MARKETING CONCEPT

marketing concept
An approach to business management that stresses customer needs and wants, seeks long-term profitability, and integrates marketing with other functional units within the organization.

Business's view of the marketing function has evolved rather dramatically over the decades. In years past, many companies pursued what was known as the *product concept*, which was essentially to focus on the production of goods and count on customers to figure out which products they needed and to take the steps to find and purchase them. In other words, the product concept views the primary purpose of a business as making things, not satisfying customers. As markets evolved and competition heated up, the *selling concept* began to take over, which emphasizes building a business by generating as many sales transactions as possible. The customer features more prominently in the selling concept, but only as a target to be sold to, not as a partner in a mutually satisfying relationship.

In contrast, today's most successful companies tend to embrace the **marketing concept**, the idea that companies should respond to customers' needs and wants while seeking long-term profitability and coordinating their own marketing efforts to achieve the company's long-term goals (see Exhibit 13.1). These *customer-focused* companies build

EXHIBIT 13.1 **The Selling Concept Versus the Marketing Concept**

Firms that practice the selling concept sell what they make rather than making what the market wants. In contrast, firms that practice the marketing concept determine the needs and wants of a market and deliver the desired product or service more effectively and efficiently than competitors do.

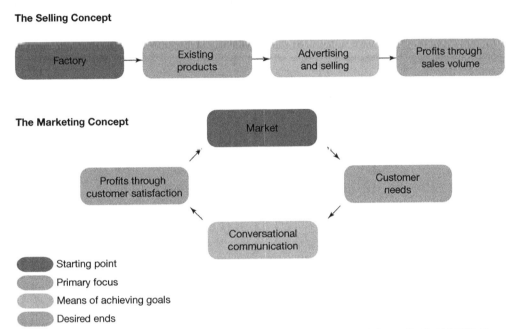

The Selling Concept

Factory → Existing products → Advertising and selling → Profits through sales volume

The Marketing Concept

Market → Customer needs → Conversational communication → Profits through customer satisfaction

- Starting point
- Primary focus
- Means of achieving goals
- Desired ends

Source: Based in part on Philip Kotler and Gary Armstrong, *Principles of Marketing*, 13th ed. (Upper Saddle River, N.J.: Pearson Prentice Hall, 2010), 10.

their marketing strategies around the goal of long-term relationships with satisfied customers.[5] The term **relationship marketing** is often applied to these efforts to distinguish them from efforts that emphasize production or sales transactions. One of the most significant goals of relationship marketing is **customer loyalty**, the degree to which customers continue to buy from a particular retailer or buy the products offered by a particular manufacturer. The payoff from becoming customer-focused can be considerable, but the process of transforming a product- or sales-driven company into one that embraces the marketing concept can take years and may involve changes to major systems and processes throughout the company, as well as the basic culture of the company.[6]

Why all the emphasis on customer service and customer satisfaction in the marketing concept? It's not just about being nice and helpful; satisfying customers is simply smart business. For one thing, keeping your existing customers is usually much cheaper and easier than finding new customers. For another, satisfied customers are the best promotion a company can hope for, particularly given the power of social media and social commerce.

relationship marketing
A focus on developing and maintaining long-term relationships with customers, suppliers, and distribution partners for mutual benefit.

customer loyalty
The degree to which customers continue to buy from a particular retailer or buy the products of a particular manufacturer or service provider.

✓ Checkpoint

LEARNING OBJECTIVE 1: Define *marketing*, and explain its role in society.

SUMMARY: Marketing can be defined as "the process by which companies create value for customers and build strong customer relationships in order to capture value from customers in return." The marketing function guides a company in selecting which products to offer, how much to charge for them, how to distribute them to customers, and how to promote them to potential buyers. Marketing plays an important role in society by helping people satisfy their needs and wants and by helping organizations determine what to produce.

2 LEARNING OBJECTIVE

Identify three trends that help define contemporary marketing.

Challenges in Contemporary Marketing

As business has progressed from the product concept to the selling concept to the market-ing concept—with the critical emergence of social commerce—the role of marketing has become increasingly complicated. You'll read about some specific challenges in this and the next three chapters, but here are three general issues that many marketing organiza-tions are wrestling with today: involving the customer in the marketing process, making data-driven decisions, and conducting marketing activities with greater concern for ethics and etiquette.

REAL-TIME UPDATES

Learn More by Visiting This Website

Marketing to the mobile buyer

The Mobile Marketing Association, whose members include many of the biggest consumer brands in the world, is helping refine the art and science of marketing to today's mobile buyers. Go to http://real-timeupdates.com/bia8 and click on Learn More in the Students section.

INVOLVING THE CUSTOMER IN THE MARKETING PROCESS

A central element in the marketing concept is involv-ing the customer as a partner in a mutually beneficial relationship rather than treating the customer as a pas-sive recipient of products and promotional messages. Involving the customer has always been relatively easy for small, local companies and for large companies with their major customers. For instance, a neighborhood bis-tro or coffee shop can prepare foods and drinks just the way its regular customers want, and satisfied customers are happy to tell friends and relatives about their favorite places to eat and drink. At the other extreme, a maker of jet engines such as Pratt & Whitney or Rolls-Royce works closely with its airplane manufacturing customers to create exactly the prod-ucts those customers want.

The challenge has been to replicate this level of intimacy on a broader scale, when a company has thousands of customers spread across the country or around the world. Two sets of technologies have helped foster communication and collaboration between com-panies and their customers. The first is **customer relationship management (CRM)** systems, which capture, organize, and capitalize on all the interactions that a company has with its customers, from marketing surveys and advertising through sales orders and customer support. A CRM system functions like an institutional memory for a com-pany, allowing it to record and act on the information that is pertinent to each customer relationship.

CRM can be a powerful means to foster relationships, but to a certain degree, con-ventional CRM simply computerizes an existing way of doing business. Companies can also enable **social commerce**, using social networks, *user-generated content* such as online reviews and videos, Twitter updates, and other social media technologies. These tools let customers communicate with companies, with each other, and with

customer relationship management (CRM)
A type of information system that captures, organizes, and capital-izes on all the interactions that a company has with its customers.

social commerce
The creation and sharing of product-related information among customers and potential customers.

EXHIBIT 13.2   The Social Element in Contemporary Marketing

Social media have dramatically reshaped the practice of marketing in recent years, giving buyers more influence over the success and failure of products and companies. For example, companies such as Indian Motorcycle use social media to build a sense of community among customers and potential customers, and these people help protect and promote the brand.

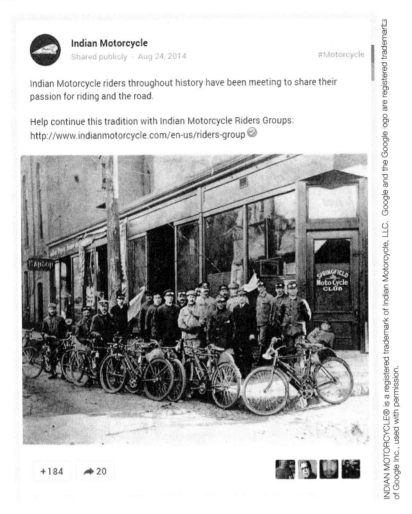

Indian Motorcycle
Shared publicly · Aug 24, 2014   #Motorcycle

Indian Motorcycle riders throughout history have been meeting to share their passion for riding and the road.

Help continue this tradition with Indian Motorcycle Riders Groups:
http://www.indianmotorcycle.com/en-us/riders-group

+184   20

INDIAN MOTORCYCLE® is a registered trademark of Indian Motorcycle, LLC. Google and the Google logo are registered trademarks of Google Inc., used with permission.

other influences in the marketplace such as prominent bloggers and journalists. For example, social networks such as Facebook have the potential to redefine advertising because consumers tend to view friends and peers as more reliable sources of product information than advertising (see Exhibit 13.2).[7]

As Chapter 16 explains, advertisers are learning to enable and participate in these online conversations, rather than blasting out messages to passive audiences as they did in the past. Another valuable use of social media is listening to feedback from customers.[8] Innovative companies are beginning to integrate these two relationship technologies, combining the data capture and retrieval of CRM with the interactivity of social media.[9]

REAL-TIME UPDATES
Learn More by Visiting This Website

New research into consumer-generated content marketing

From brief reviews to online videos, see how content from consumers is reshaping contemporary marketing. Go to http://real-timeupdates.com/bia8 and click on Learn More in the Students section.

MAKING DATA-DRIVEN MARKETING DECISIONS

Learning more about customers is one aspect of the larger challenge of collecting, analyzing, and using data to make marketing decisions. Marketers in every industry would like to have better insights for making decisions and better ways of measuring the results of every marketing initiative. Pioneering retailer John Wannamaker said 100 years ago that "half the money I spend on advertising is wasted. The trouble is, I don't know which half."[10] Actually, Wannamaker was probably overly optimistic. In one extensive study, advertising was found to increase revenue for slightly more than half of new products but for only one-third of existing products.[11] In other words, according to this research, the advertising campaigns for two-thirds of established products in the marketplace don't bring in more revenue.

REAL-TIME UPDATES
Learn More by Visiting This Website

Insights for marketing—and career building

Seth Godin is one of the most widely followed writers in contemporary business, with pithy advice for presenting your business and yourself to the world. Go to http://real-timeupdates.com/bia8 and click on Learn More in the Students section.

Understandably, top executives are demanding that marketing departments do a better job of justifying their budgets and finding the most effective ways of meeting marketing objectives. However, this accountability challenge is not a simple one, and the problem may never be completely solvable for many companies. With so many sources of information in the marketplace, particularly with the continuing growth of online and mobile marketing channels, identifying which sources influence which aspects of buyer behavior can be difficult.

To get a better idea of how well their marketing budgets are being spent, companies can use a class of tools and techniques called *marketing analytics*. For example, Google Analytics helps online advertisers measure the effectiveness of specific search-term keywords, track the behavior of website visitors from their initial landing on an e-commerce site on through to a purchase, and track the results of online videos and social networking efforts.[12] By integrating such tools into an overall measurement system that evaluates both online and offline marketing activities, a company can improve its decision making and focus its time and money in the most productive marketing efforts.

marketing research
The collection and analysis of information for making marketing decisions.

The process of gathering and analyzing *market intelligence* about customers, competitors, and related marketing issues through any combination of methods is known as **marketing research**. As markets grow increasingly dynamic and open to competition from all parts of the globe, today's companies realize that information is the key to successful action. Without it, they're forced to use guesswork, analogies from other markets that may or may not apply, or experience from the past that may not correspond to the future.[13]

At the same time, however, marketing research can't provide the answer to every strategic or tactical question. As a manager or an entrepreneur, you'll find yourself in situations that require creative thinking and careful judgment to make the leap beyond what the data alone can tell you. Research techniques range from the basic to the exotic, from simple surveys to advanced statistical techniques to neurological scanning that tries to discover how and why customers' brains respond to visual and verbal cues about products. You can see a sample of techniques in Exhibit 13.3.

MARKETING WITH GREATER CONCERN FOR ETHICS AND ETIQUETTE

Under pressure to reach and persuade buyers in a business environment that gets more fragmented and noisy all the time, marketers occasionally step over the line and engage in practices that are rude, manipulative, or even downright deceptive. The result is an increasing degree of skepticism of and hostility toward advertising and other marketing activities.[14]

EXHIBIT 13.3	Marketing Research Techniques

Marketers can use a wide variety of techniques to learn more about customers, competitors, and threats and opportunities in the marketplace.

Technique	Examples
Observation	Any in-person, mechanical, or electronic technique that monitors and records behavior, including website usage tracking and monitoring of blogs and social networking websites.
Surveys	Data collection efforts that measure responses from a representative subset of a larger group of people; can be conducted in person (when people with clipboards stop you in a mall, that's called a *mall intercept*), over the phone, by mail or email, or online. Designing and conducting a meaningful survey requires thorough knowledge of statistical techniques such as *sampling* to ensure valid results that truly represent the larger group. For this reason, many of the simple surveys that you see online these days do not produce statistically valid results.
Interviews and focus groups	One-on-one or group discussions that try to probe deeper into issues than a survey typically does. *Focus groups* involve a small number of people guided by a facilitator while being observed or recorded by researchers. Unlike surveys, interviews and focus groups are not designed to collect statistics that represent a larger group; their real value is in uncovering issues that might require further study.
Process data collection	Any method of collecting data during the course of other business tasks, including warranty registration cards, sales transaction records, gift and loyalty program card usage, and customer service interactions.
Experiments	Controlled scenarios in which researchers adjust one or more variables to measure the effect these changes have on customer behavior. For instance, separate groups of consumers can be exposed to different ads to see which ad is most effective. *Test marketing*, the launch of a product under real-world conditions but on a limited scale (such as in a single city), is a form of experimental research.
Ethnographic research	A branch of anthropology that studies people in their daily lives to learn about their needs, wants, and behaviors in real-life settings.
Neuromarketing studies	Research that measures brain activity while customers are viewing or interacting with products, websites, or other elements.

Sources: Ken Anderson, "Ethnographic Research: A Key to Strategy," *Harvard Business Review*, March 2009, 24; Emily R. Murphy, Judy Illes, and Peter B. Reiner, "Neuroethics of Neuromarketing," *Journal of Consumer Behaviour*, July–October 2008, 293–302; Dick Bucci, "Recording Systems Add More Depth When Capturing Answers," *Marketing News*, 1 March 2005, 50; Laurence Bernstein, "Enough Research Bashing!" *Marketing*, 24 January 2005, 10; Naresh K. Malhotra, *Basic Marketing Research* (Upper Saddle River, N.J.: Pearson Prentice Hall, 2002), 110–112, 208–212, 228–229.

To avoid intensifying the vicious circle in which marketers keep doing the same old things, only louder and longer—leading customers to get angrier and more defensive—some marketers are looking for a better way. Social commerce shows a lot of promise for redefining marketing communication from one-way promotion to two-way conversation. Another hopeful sign is **permission-based marketing**, in which marketers invite potential or current customers to receive information in areas that genuinely interest them. Many websites now take this approach, letting visitors sign up for specific content streams with the promise that they won't be bombarded with information they don't care about.

The widespread adoption of social media has also increased the attention given to transparency, which in this context refers to a sense of openness, of giving all participants in a conversation access to the information they need in order to accurately process the messages they are receiving. A major issue in business communication transparency is **stealth marketing**, which involves attempting to promote products and services to customers who don't know they're being marketed to. A common stealth marketing technique is rewarding someone for promoting products to his or her friends without telling them it's a form of advertising. Critics—including the U.S. Federal Trade Commission (FTC) and the Word of Mouth Marketing Association—assert that such techniques are deceptive because they don't give their targets the opportunity to raise their instinctive defenses against the persuasive powers of marketing messages.[15]

Aside from ethical concerns, trying to fool the public is simply bad for business. As LaSalle University professor Michael Smith puts it, "The public backlash can be long, deep, and damaging to a company's reputation."[16]

permission-based marketing
A marketing approach in which firms first ask permission to deliver messages to an audience and then promise to restrict their communication efforts to those subject areas in which audience members have expressed interest.

stealth marketing
The delivery of marketing messages to people who are not aware that they are being marketed to; these messages can be delivered by either acquaintances or strangers, depending on the technique.

3 LEARNING OBJECTIVE

Differentiate between consumer buying behavior and organizational buying behavior.

consumer market
Individuals or households that buy goods and services for personal use.

organizational market
Companies, government agencies, and other organizations that buy goods and services either to resell or to use in the creation of their own goods and services.

Understanding Today's Customers

To implement the marketing concept, companies must have good information about what customers want. Today's customers, both individual consumers and organizational buyers, are a diverse and demanding group, with little patience for marketers who do not understand them or will not adapt business practices to meet their needs. For instance, consumers faced with complex purchase decisions such as cars can now find extensive information online about products, prices, competitors, customer service rankings, safety issues, and other factors.

The first step toward understanding customers is recognizing the purchase and ownership habits of the **consumer market**, made up of individuals and families who buy for personal or household use, and the **organizational market**, composed of companies and a variety of noncommercial institutions, from local school districts to the federal government.

Exhibit 13.4 models two decision-making paths that buyers can take when they perceive the need to make a purchase, one for routine purchases and one for new, unusual, or highly significant purchases. Consumers and organizations can follow either path, depending on a specific purchase. Broadly speaking, however, organizational buyers tend to approach purchasing in a more rational, data-driven fashion, simply because organizational choices are nearly always about functional and financial value.

THE CONSUMER DECISION PROCESS

Think about several purchase decisions you've made recently. Classical economics suggests that your behavior would follow a rational process of first recognizing a need and then gathering information, identifying alternative solutions, and finally making

EXHIBIT 13.4	Buyer Decision Making

The steps buyers go through on the way to making a purchase vary widely, based on the magnitude of the purchase and the significance of the outcome. In general, businesses and other organizations use a more formal and more rational process than consumers, and nonroutine decisions in either sector require more time and energy than routine decisions. Defining routine is not a simple matter, however; a company might make huge resupply purchases automatically while a consumer spends days agonizing over a pair of jeans.

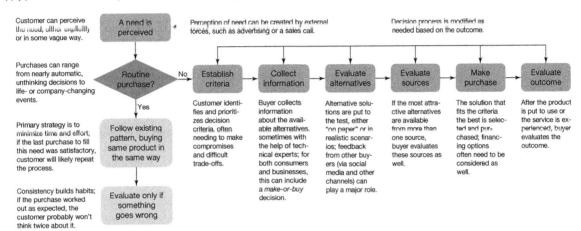

your choice from those alternatives. But how often do you really make decisions in this way? Researchers now understand that consumer behavior tends to be far less logical and far more complicated—and more interesting—than this model suggests. In fact, some research suggests that as much as 95 percent of the decision-making process is subconscious and that sensory cues can play a much larger role than objective information.[17] The emerging field of *behavioral economics* is starting to offer better insights into consumer behavior by incorporating a broader (and somewhat less-flattering) view of the way people really make decisions.[18]

Even in situations in which consumers gather lots of information and appear to be making a well-thought-out, rational decision, they often are acting more on gut feelings and emotional responses. For instance, you might see some jaw-dropping sports car glide past you on the street, and in that split second—before you even start "thinking" about it—you've already decided to buy one just like it. Sure, you'll gather brochures, do research on the Internet, test-drive other models, and so on, but chances are you're not really evaluating alternatives. Instead, your rational, conscious brain is just looking for evidence to support the decision that your emotional, semiconscious brain has already made.

Moreover, consumers make all kinds of decisions that are hard to explain by any rational means. We might spend two weeks gathering data on $200 music players but choose a college with a $20,000 annual tuition simply because a best friend is going there. Sometimes we buy things for no apparent reason other than the fact that we have money in our pockets. As a result, at one time or another, all consumers suffer from **cognitive dissonance**, which occurs when one's beliefs and behaviors don't match. A common form of this situation is *buyer's remorse*, in which one makes a purchase and then regrets doing so—sometimes immediately after the purchase.

REAL-TIME UPDATES
Learn More by Visiting This Website

What's hot in global consumer markets?

Follow Trendwatching.com's monthly reports on consumer trends around the world. Go to http://real-timeupdates.com/bia8 and click on Learn More in the Students section.

cognitive dissonance
Tension that exists when a person's beliefs don't match his or her behaviors; a common example is *buyer's remorse*, when someone regrets a purchase immediately after making it.

You can start to understand why so many decisions seem mysterious from a rational point of view if you consider all the influences that affect purchases:

- **Culture.** The cultures (and subgroups within cultures) that people belong to shape their values, attitudes, and beliefs and influence the way they respond to the world around them.
- **Socioeconomic level.** In addition to being members of a particular culture, people also perceive themselves as members of a certain social class—be it upper, middle, lower, or somewhere in between. In general, members of various classes pursue different activities, buy different goods, shop in different places, and react to different media—or at least like to believe they do.
- **Reference groups.** Individuals are influenced by *reference groups* that provide information about product choices and establish values that they perceive as important. Reference groups can be either *membership* or *aspirational*. As the name suggests, membership groups are those to which consumers actually belong, such as families, networks of friends, clubs, and work groups. In contrast, consumers are not members of aspirational reference groups but use them as role models for style, speech, opinions, and various other behaviors.[19] For instance, millions of consumers buy products that help them identify with popular musicians or professional athletes.
- **Situational factors.** These factors include events or circumstances in people's lives that are more circumstantial but that can influence buying patterns. Such factors can range from having a coupon to celebrating a holiday to being in a bad mood. If you've ever indulged in "retail therapy" to cheer yourself up, you know all about situational factors—and the buyer's remorse that often comes with it.
- **Self-image.** Many consumers tend to believe that "you are what you buy," so they make or avoid choices that support their desired self-images. Marketers capitalize on people's need to express their identity through their purchases by emphasizing the image value of goods and services.

THE ORGANIZATIONAL CUSTOMER DECISION PROCESS

The purchasing behavior of organizations is easier to understand than the purchasing behavior of consumers because it's more clearly driven by economics and influenced less by subconscious and emotional factors. Here are some of the significant ways in which organizational purchasing differs from consumer purchasing:[20]

- **An emphasis on economic payback and other rational factors.** Much more so than with consumer purchases, organizational purchases are carefully evaluated for financial impact, reliability, and other objective factors. Organizations don't always make the best choices, of course, but their choices are usually based on a more rational analysis of needs and alternatives. This isn't to say that emotions play little or no role in the purchase decision, however; organizations don't make decisions, people do. Fear of change, fear of failure, excitement about new technologies, and the pride of being associated with world-class suppliers are just a few of the emotional factors that can influence organizational purchases.
- **A formal buying process.** From office supplies to new factories, most organizational purchases follow a formal buying process, particularly in mid- to large-size companies.
- **Greater complexity in product usage.** Even for the same types of products, organizational buyers have to worry about factors that consumers may never consider, such as user training, compatibility with existing systems and procedures, established purchasing agreements, and compliance with government regulations. In addition, the *network effect*, in which the value of a product increases with the number of customers who use it, can be a key decision driver.[21] A major reason that other software providers have so much trouble putting a dent in Microsoft's dominance of the corporate market is that business users

need compatibility, so it is simpler to select the tools that more people already use. Also, organizations sometimes continue to use products long after better substitutes become available if the costs and complexity of updating outweigh the advantages of the newer solutions.

- **The participation and influence of multiple people.** Except in the very smallest businesses, the purchase process usually involves a group of people. This team can include end users, technical experts, the manager with ultimate purchasing authority, and a professional purchasing agent whose job includes researching suppliers, negotiating prices, and evaluating supplier performance. Multiple family members play a part in many consumer purchases, of course, but not with the formality apparent in organizational markets.

- **Close relationships between buyers and sellers.** Close relationships between buyers and sellers are common in organizational purchasing. In some cases, employees of the seller even have offices inside the buyer's facility to promote close interaction.

✓ Checkpoint

LEARNING OBJECTIVE 3: Differentiate between consumer buying behavior and organizational buying behavior.

SUMMARY: Classical economic theory suggests that consumers follow a largely rational process of recognizing a need, searching for information, evaluating alternatives, making a purchase, and evaluating the product after use or consumption. However, research into behavioral economics and consumer psychology suggests that many consumer purchases are far less rational. Much of this decision making happens subconsciously and is driven to a large degree by emotion, culture, and situational factors. Organizational buying behavior comes much closer to the rational model of classical economics because purchases are usually judged by their economic value to the organization. The most significant ways in which organizational purchasing differs from consumer purchasing are an emphasis on economic payback, a formal buying process, greater complexity in product usage, purchasing groups, and close relationships between buyers and sellers.

CRITICAL THINKING: (1) Can business-to-business marketers take advantage of new insights into consumer buying behavior? Why or why not? (2) How could families and individual consumers benefit from adopting some elements of organizational buying behavior?

IT'S YOUR BUSINESS: (1) Do you read product reviews online before making important purchases? Why or why not? Have you ever contributed to social commerce by posting your own reviews or product advice? (2) Why did you buy the clothes you are wearing at this very moment?

KEY TERMS TO KNOW: consumer market, organizational market, cognitive dissonance

Identifying Market Opportunities

With insights into your customers' needs and behaviors, you're ready to begin planning your marketing strategies. **Strategic marketing planning** is a process that involves three steps: (1) examining the current marketing situation, (2) assessing opportunities and setting objectives, and (3) crafting a marketing strategy to reach those objectives (see Exhibit 13.5 on the next page). Companies often record the results of their planning efforts in a formal *marketing plan*.

 4   **LEARNING OBJECTIVE**

Define *strategic marketing planning*, and identify the four basic options for pursuing new marketing opportunities.

strategic marketing planning
The process of examining an organization's current marketing situation, assessing opportunities and setting objectives, and then developing a marketing strategy to reach those objectives.

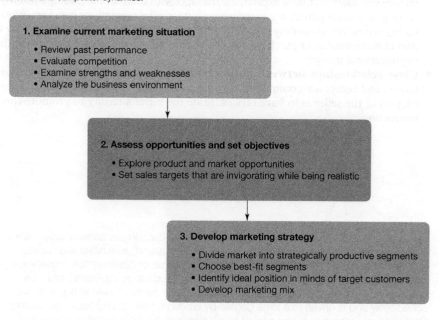

EXHIBIT 13.5 The Strategic Marketing Planning Process

Strategic marketing planning can involve a range of major decisions that fall into three general steps: (1) examining the current marketing situation, (2) assessing opportunities and setting objectives, and (3) developing a marketing strategy. The nature of these steps can vary widely depending on the products and markets involved; for example, emerging markets and mature markets have very different sets of customer and competitor dynamics.

1. Examine current marketing situation
- Review past performance
- Evaluate competition
- Examine strengths and weaknesses
- Analyze the business environment

2. Assess opportunities and set objectives
- Explore product and market opportunities
- Set sales targets that are invigorating while being realistic

3. Develop marketing strategy
- Divide market into strategically productive segments
- Choose best-fit segments
- Identify ideal position in minds of target customers
- Develop marketing mix

EXAMINING THE CURRENT MARKETING SITUATION

Examining your current marketing situation includes reviewing your past performance (how well each product is doing in each market where you sell it), evaluating your competition, examining your internal strengths and weaknesses, and analyzing the external environment.

Reviewing Performance

Unless you're starting a new business, your company has a history of marketing performance. Maybe sales have slowed in the past year, maybe you've had to cut prices so much that you're barely earning a profit, or maybe sales have been strong and you have money to invest in new marketing activities. Reviewing where you are and how you got there is critical because you want to learn from your mistakes and repeat your successes—without getting trapped in mindsets and practices that need to change for the future, even if they were successful in the past.

Evaluating Competition

In addition to reviewing past performance, you must evaluate your competition. If you own a Burger King franchise, for example, you need to watch what McDonald's and Wendy's are doing. You also have to keep an eye on Taco Bell, KFC, Pizza Hut, and other restaurants, as well as pay attention to any number of other ways your customers might satisfy their hunger—including fixing a sandwich at home. Furthermore, you need to watch the horizon for trends that could affect your business, such as consumer interest in organic foods or in locally produced ingredients.

Examining Internal Strengths and Weaknesses

Successful marketers try to identify sources of competitive advantage and areas that need improvement. They look at such factors as financial resources, production capabilities, distribution networks, brand awareness, business partnerships, managerial expertise, and promotional capabilities. (Recall the discussion of SWOT analysis on page 197.) On the basis of your internal analysis, you will be able to decide whether your business should (1) limit itself to those opportunities for which it possesses the required strengths or (2) challenge itself to reach higher goals by acquiring and developing new strengths.

Analyzing the External Environment

Marketers must also analyze trends and conditions in the business environment when planning their marketing strategies. For example, customer decisions are greatly affected by interest rates, inflation, unemployment, personal income, and savings rates. During recessions, consumers still aspire to enjoy the good life, but they are forced by circumstances to alter their spending patterns.[22] "Affordable luxuries" become particularly appealing during these times, for example. Recessions also create opportunities for agile and aggressive companies to take business away from companies weakened by poor sales and deteriorating finances.[23]

ASSESSING OPPORTUNITIES AND SETTING OBJECTIVES

After you've examined the current marketing situation, you're ready to assess your marketing opportunities and set your objectives. Successful companies are always on the lookout for new marketing opportunities, which can be classified into four options (see Exhibit 13.6).[24] **Market penetration** involves selling more of your existing products into the markets you already serve. **Product development** is creating new products for those current markets, and **market development** is selling your existing products to new markets. Finally, **diversification** involves creating new products for new markets.

Generally speaking, these four options are listed in order of increasing risk. Market penetration can be the least risky because your products already exist and the market has already demonstrated some level of demand for them. At the other extreme, creating new products for new markets is usually the riskiest choice of all because you encounter uncertainties in both dimensions (you may fail to create the product you need, and the market might not be interested in it).

After you've framed the opportunity you want to pursue, you are ready to set your marketing objectives. A common marketing objective is to achieve a certain level of **market share**, which is a firm's portion of the total sales within a market (market share can be defined by either number of units sold or by sales revenue).

market penetration
Selling more of a firm's existing products in the markets it already serves.

product development
Creating new products for a firm's current markets.

market development
Selling existing products to new markets.

diversification
Creating new products for new markets.

market share
A firm's portion of the total sales in a market.

EXHIBIT 13.6 **Pursuing Market Opportunities**

Every company has four basic options when it comes to pursuing market opportunities. The arrows show the increasing level of risk, from the lowest to the highest.

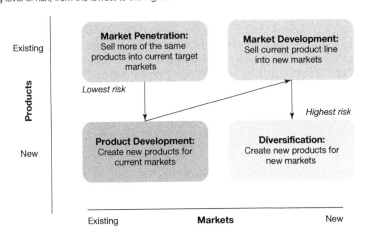

---

5 LEARNING OBJECTIVE

Describe the four main components of the marketing mix.

marketing strategy
An overall plan for marketing a product; includes the identification of target market segments, a positioning strategy, and a marketing mix.

market
A group of customers who need or want a particular product and have the money to buy it.

market segmentation
The division of a diverse market into smaller, relatively homogeneous groups with similar needs, wants, and purchase behaviors.

demographics
The study of the statistical characteristics of a population.

psychographics
Classification of customers on the basis of their psychological makeup, interests, and lifestyles.

Crafting a Marketing Strategy

Using the current marketing situation and your objectives as your guide, you're ready to develop a **marketing strategy**, which consists of dividing your market into *segments*, choosing your *target markets* and the *position* you'd like to establish in those markets, and then developing a *marketing mix* to help you get there.

DIVIDING MARKETS INTO SEGMENTS

A **market** contains all the customers who might be interested in a product and can pay for it. However, most markets contain subgroups of potential customers with different interests, values, and behaviors. To maximize their effectiveness in reaching these subgroups, many companies subdivide the total market through **market segmentation**, grouping customers with similar characteristics, behaviors, and needs. Each of these market segments can then be approached by offering products that are priced, distributed, and promoted in a unique way that is most likely to appeal to that segment. The overall goal of market segmentation is to understand why and how certain customers buy what they buy so that one's finite resources can be used to create and market products in the most efficient manner possible.[25]

Four fundamental factors marketers use to identify market segments are demographics, psychographics, geography, and behavior:

- **Demographics.** When you segment a market using **demographics**, the statistical analysis of a population, you subdivide your customers according to characteristics such as age, gender, income, race, occupation, and ethnic group.

- **Psychographics.** Whereas demographic segmentation is the study of people from the outside, **psychographics** is the analysis of people from the inside, focusing on their psychological makeup, including attitudes, interests, opinions, and lifestyles.

Psychographic analysis focuses on why people behave the way they do by examining such issues as brand preferences, media preferences, values, self-concept, and behavior.

- **Geography.** When differences in buying behavior are influenced by where people live, it makes sense to use **geographic segmentation**. Segmenting the market into geographic units such as regions, cities, counties, or neighborhoods allows companies to customize and sell products that meet the needs of specific markets and to organize their operations as needed.
- **Behavior. Behavioral segmentation** groups customers according to their relationship with products or response to product characteristics. To identify behavioral segments, marketers study such factors as the occasions that prompt people to buy certain products, the particular benefits they seek from a product, their habits and frequency of product usage, and the degree of loyalty they show toward a brand.[26]

geographic segmentation
Categorization of customers according to their geographical location.

behavioral segmentation
Categorization of customers according to their relationship with products or response to product characteristics.

Starting with these variables, researchers can also combine types of data to identify target segments with even greater precision, such as merging geographic, demographic, and behavioral data to define specific types of consumer neighborhoods.

CHOOSING YOUR TARGET MARKETS

After you have segmented your market, the next step is to find appropriate target segments, or **target markets**, on which to focus your efforts. Marketers use a variety of criteria to narrow their focus to a few suitable market segments, including the magnitude of potential sales within each segment, the cost of reaching those customers, the fit with a firm's core competencies, and any risks in the business environment.

target markets
Specific customer groups or segments to whom a company wants to sell a particular product.

Exhibit 13.7 diagrams four strategies for reaching target markets. Companies that practice *undifferentiated marketing* (also known as *mass marketing*) ignore differences among buyers and offer only one product or product line and present it with the same communication, pricing, and distribution strategies to all potential buyers. Undifferentiated marketing has the advantages of simplicity and economies of scale, but it can be less effective at reaching some portions of the market.

By contrast, companies that manufacture or sell a variety of products to several target customer groups practice *differentiated marketing*. This is Toyota's approach, for

EXHIBIT 13.7 Market-Coverage Strategies

Four alternative market-coverage strategies are undifferentiated marketing, differentiated marketing, concentrated marketing, and micromarketing.

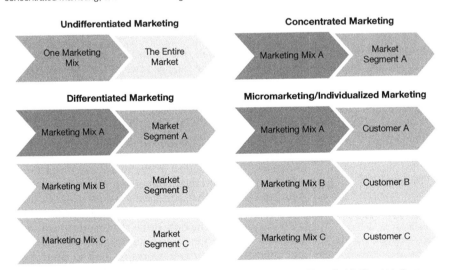

Source: Based on Philip Kotler and Gary Armstrong, *Principles of Marketing*, 13th ed. (Upper Saddle River, N.J.: Pearson Prentice Hall, 2010), 201–207.

example, aiming the Scion brand at young buyers, the Toyota brand at its core audience, and the Lexus brand at those wanting luxury cars. Differentiated marketing is a popular strategy, but it requires substantial resources because the company has to tailor products, prices, promotional efforts, and distribution arrangements for each customer group. The differentiation should be based on meaningful differences that don't alienate any audiences.

Concentrated marketing focuses on only a single market segment. With this approach, you acknowledge that various other market segments may exist but you choose to target just one. The biggest advantage of concentrated marketing is that it allows you to focus all your time and resources on a single type of customer (which is why this approach is usually the best option for start-up companies, by the way). The strategy can be risky, however, because you've staked your fortunes on just one segment.

Micromarketing, or *individualized marketing*, is the narrowest strategy of all, in which firms target a single location or even a single customer.[27] This approach can range from producing customizable products to creating *major accounts* sales teams that craft entire marketing programs for each of their largest customers.

REAL-TIME UPDATES
Learn More by Reading This Article

How established companies are trying to compete against "digital disrupters"

Highly focused start-ups often zero in on one piece of an established company's business or one key weakness. Go to http://real-timeupdates.com/bia8 and click on Learn More in the Students section.

Achieving success in any market segment can take time and significant investment, so embracing market segments for the long term is essential. In fact, many companies now think in terms of *customer lifetime value*: the total potential revenue from each customer over a certain time span minus the cost of attracting and keeping that customer. This approach lets companies focus on their most valuable customers while deciding what to do with their less-profitable customers (such as abandoning those customers or changing marketing strategies to make pursuing them more profitable).[28]

STAKING OUT A POSITION IN YOUR TARGET MARKETS

After you have decided which segments of the market to enter, your next step is to decide what *position* you want to occupy in those segments. **Positioning** is the process of designing a company's offerings, messages, and operating policies so that both the company and its products occupy distinct and desirable competitive positions in your target customers' minds. For instance, for every product category that you care about as a consumer, you have some ranking of desirability in your mind—you believe that certain colleges are more prestigious than others, that certain brands of shoes are more fashionable than others, that one video game system is better than the others, and so on. Successful marketers are careful to choose the position they'd like to occupy in buyers' minds.

positioning
Managing a business in a way designed to occupy a particular place in the minds of target customers.

In their attempts to secure favorable positions, marketers can emphasize such variables as product attributes, customer service, brand image (such as reliability or sophistication), price (such as low cost or premium), or category leadership (such as the leading online bookseller). For example, BMW and Porsche work to associate their products with performance, Mercedes Benz with luxury, and Volvo with safety.

A vital and often overlooked aspect of positioning is that although marketers take all kinds of steps to position their products, it is *customers* who ultimately decide on the positioning: They're the ones who interpret the many messages they encounter in the marketplace and decide what they think and feel about each product. For example, you can advertise that you have a luxury product, but if consumers aren't convinced, it's not really positioned as a luxury product. The only result that matters is what the customer believes. One auto industry marketing executive put it this way: "Everyone works so hard to control and define what their brand stands for, when they ought to just let the consumer do it."[29]

REAL-TIME UPDATES
Learn More by Reading This Article

Marketing a museum in the social media age

See how the venerated Tate collection of museums in the United Kingdom applies marketing concepts to attract visitors and enhance their museum experiences. Go to http://real-timeupdates.com/bia8 and click on Learn More in the Students section.

✓ **Checkpoint**

LEARNING OBJECTIVE 5: Identify the four steps in crafting a marketing strategy.

SUMMARY: Crafting a marketing strategy involves dividing your market into *segments*, choosing your *target markets* and the *position* you *marketing mix* to help you get there. Segmentation (using demographics, psychographics, geography, and behavior) allows a company to select parts of the market most likely to respond to specific marketing programs. Companies can use one of four approaches to selecting target markets: undifferentiated (mass) marketing, differentiated marketing (with a different marketing mix for each segment), concentrated marketing (focusing on a single market segment), and micromarketing or individualized marketing. A *position* refers to the position a company or brand occupies in the mind of the target market segments.

CRITICAL THINKING: (1) Would two companies interested in the same group of customers automatically use the same target market approach (such as differentiated or concentrated)? Why or why not? (2) Why aren't marketers ultimately in control of the positions their products achieve in the marketplace?

IT'S YOUR BUSINESS: (1) Think of three car brands or specific models. How are these products positioned in your mind? What terms do you use to describe them? (2) Given your transportation needs in the near future (assuming you will need a car), which model is the most desirable? The least desirable?

KEY TERMS TO KNOW: marketing strategy, market, market segmentation, demographics, psychographics, geographic segmentation, behavioral segmentation, target markets, positioning

The Marketing Mix

After you've segmented your market, selected your target market, and taken steps to position your product, your next task is to develop a marketing mix. A firm's **marketing mix** consists of product, price, distribution, and customer communication (see Exhibit 13.8). (You might also hear references to "the four Ps" of the marketing mix, which is short for products,

Describe the four main components of the marketing mix.

marketing mix
The four key elements of marketing strategy: product, price, distribution, and customer communication.

EXHIBIT 13.8   The Marketing Mix

The marketing mix consists of four key elements: the products a company offers to potential buyers, the price it asks in return, its methods of distributing those products to customers, and the various efforts it makes to communicate with customers before and after the sale.

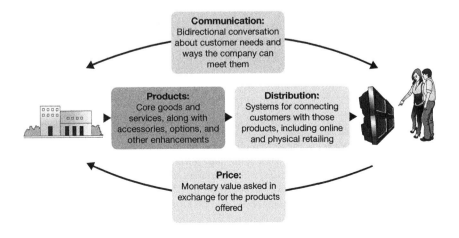

Communication: Bidirectional conversation about customer needs and ways the company can meet them

Products: Core goods and services, along with accessories, options, and other enhancements

Distribution: Systems for connecting customers with those products, including online and physical retailing

Price: Monetary value asked in exchange for the products offered

pricing, place or physical distribution, and promotion. However, with the advent of digital goods and services, distribution is no longer exclusively a physical concern. And many companies now view customer communication as a broader and more interactive activity than the functions implied by *promotion*.)

PRODUCTS

In common usage, *product* usually refers to a tangible good, whereas *service* refers to an intangible performance. However, for the purposes of studying marketing, it is helpful to define **product** as the bundle of value offered for the purpose of satisfying a want or a need in a marketing exchange. In this expanded definition, both tangible goods and intangible services are considered products. The reason for taking this broader view of *product* is that it encourages a more holistic look at the entire offering, which can include the brand name, design, packaging, support services, warranty, ownership experience, and other attributes.

For example, if you buy a pair of $200 Dolce & Gabbana sunglasses with the brand's prominent "DG" initials on the side, you are buying much more than a device that holds a couple of protective lenses in front of your eyes. You are buying a shopping and ownership experience that is distinctly different from that for buying a pair of $5 sunglasses from a discount drugstore. You are buying the opportunity to feel a particular way about yourself and to present a particular image to the world around you. You are buying the right to brand yourself with the Dolce & Gabbana brand and everything that brand means to you. All these elements constitute the Dolce & Gabbana product. You'll explore products in more detail in Chapter 14.

PRICING

Price, the amount of money customers pay for the product (including any discounts), is the second major component of a firm's marketing mix. Looking back at Kotler and Armstrong's definition of marketing, price is the *value captured* from customers in exchange for the value offered in the product. Setting and managing a product's price is one of the most critical decisions a company must make because price is the only element in a company's marketing mix that produces revenue; all other elements represent costs. Moreover, setting a product's price not only determines income but also can differentiate a product from the competition. Determining the right price is not an easy task, and marketers constantly worry whether they've turned away profitable customers by charging too much or "left money on the table" by charging too little.

A number of factors influence pricing decisions, including marketing objectives, government regulations, production costs, customer perceptions, competition, and customer demand. A company's costs establish the minimum amount it can charge, and the various external forces establish the maximum. Somewhere in between those two extremes lies an optimum price point. Products also exhibit different levels of *price elasticity*, which is a measure of how sensitive customers are to changes in price. If you don't have a smartphone yet and the price of such phones drops by 25 percent, you might well be tempted to buy one. In contrast, if the price of broccoli drops by 25 percent, chances are you won't eat more veggies as a result. You can read more about pricing in Chapter 14.

DISTRIBUTION

Distribution is the third marketing-mix element. It covers the organized network of firms and systems that move goods and services from the producer to the customer. This network is also known as *marketing channels, marketing intermediaries,* or **distribution channels**. As you can imagine, channel decisions are interdependent with virtually everything else in the marketing mix. Key factors in distribution planning include customer needs and expectations, market coverage, distribution costs, competition, positioning, customer support requirements, and sales support requirements. For example, when AstraZeneca introduced

---

product
A bundle of value that satisfies a customer need or want.

price
The amount of money charged for a product or service.

distribution channels
Systems for moving goods and services from producers to customers; also known as marketing channels.

a cancer drug with potentially significant side effects, it released the drug through a single specialty pharmacy so that it could manage pharmacist and doctor training more closely.[30]

Marketing intermediaries perform a variety of essential marketing functions, including providing information to customers, providing feedback to manufacturers, providing sales support, gathering assortments of goods from multiple producers to make shopping easier for customers, and transporting and storing goods. These intermediaries fall into two general categories: *wholesalers* and *retailers*. The basic distinction between them is that wholesalers sell to other companies whereas retailers sell to individual consumers. Across industries, you can find tremendous variety in the types of wholesalers and retailers, from independent representatives who sell products from several manufacturers to huge distribution companies with national or international scope to purely digital retailers such as Apple's iTunes service. You can read more about distribution in Chapter 15.

CUSTOMER COMMUNICATION

In traditional marketing thought, the fourth element of the marketing mix is **promotion**, all the activities a firm undertakes to promote its products to target customers. The goals of promotion include *informing, persuading,* and *reminding.* Among these activities are advertising in a variety of media, personal selling, public relations, and sales promotion. Promotion may take the form of direct, face-to-face communication or indirect communication through such media as television, radio, magazines, newspapers, direct mail, billboards, transit ads, social media, and other channels.

However, as "Involving the Customer in the Marketing Process" on page 346 points out, forward-thinking companies have moved beyond the unidirectional approach of promotion to interactive customer communication. By talking *with* their customers instead of *at* their customers, marketers get immediate feedback on everything from customer service problems to new product ideas. As you'll read in the Behind the Scenes at the end of the chapter, Sarah Calhoun and her company Red Ants Pants excel at authentic, engaging communication with customers and potential buyers.

Promotion is still a vital part of customer communication, but by encouraging two-way conversations, whether it's two people talking across a desk or an online network spread across the globe, marketers can also learn while they are informing, persuading, and reminding. Moreover, by replacing "sales pitches" with conversations and giving customers some control over the dialogue, marketers can also help break down some of the walls and filters that audiences have erected after years of conventional marketing promotion.[31] Chapter 16 offers a closer look at customer communication.

For the latest information on marketing principles, visit http://real-timeupdates .com/bia8 and click on Chapter 13.

promotion
A wide variety of persuasive techniques used by companies to communicate with their target markets and the general public.

✓ Checkpoint

LEARNING OBJECTIVE 7: Describe the four main components of the marketing mix.

SUMMARY: The four elements of the marketing mix are product, price, distribution, and customer communication. Products are goods, services, persons, places, ideas, organizations, or anything else offered for the purpose of satisfying a want or need in a marketing exchange. Price is the amount of money customers pay for the product. Distribution is the organized network of firms that move the goods and services from the producer to the customer. Customer communication involves the activities used to communicate with and promote products to target markets.

CRITICAL THINKING: (1) Why is price sometimes referred to as *captured value*? (2) Why do companies that embrace relationship marketing focus on "customer communication" rather than "promotion"?

BEHIND THE SCENES
AGGRAVATION LEADS TO INSPIRATION FOR SARAH CALHOUN OF RED ANTS PANTS

As with many other entrepreneurs, frustration was the source of inspiration for Sarah Calhoun. When she couldn't find rugged work pants designed for women, she decided to fill this unmet market need herself. A chance encounter in a coffee shop with an experienced apparel industry insider (who noticed she was reading *Starting a Business for Dummies*) convinced her that a real opportunity was there and waiting for someone to pursue it.

Calhoun based all three key elements of her marketing strategy—segmentation, target market selection, and positioning—on her mission of pursuing this opportunity. She founded Red Ants Pants with the singular focus on providing hardwearing pants for hardworking women, meeting the needs of customers whose work makes clothing a matter of practical utility and even on-the-job safety.

Red Ants Pants are made from tough, heavy cloth and in both "straight" and "curvy" styles to provide a better fit for more women. In addition, they come in two or three times as many waist/inseam combinations as typical pants, greatly increasing the chance that every woman will find exactly the size she needs.

In keeping with the capacity of a small business and the nature of her product offerings, simplicity is the key word in the product mix. Pants are available in exactly one color: chocolate brown. (It was only after buying $45,000 worth of the practical fabric that Calhoun learned "chocolate brown is the new black" in the fashion world.) A few years after introducing the pants, she expanded the product portfolio with a handful of complementary products, including shirts, hats, and belts.

Calhoun is adamant about keeping production in the United States, too, a rarity in the clothing business, where most production is outsourced to low-cost labor centers in other countries. Instead, she chose a mother/daughter-owned factory two states over, in Seattle, and she views supporting quality jobs in this country as "part of my responsibility as a business owner." Referring to her production partners, she says, "They have 23 employees who are treated well, paid well, and enjoy good working conditions."

At $129 a pair, the pants are not bargain-bin items, to be sure. However, like many purveyors of high-quality products, Calhoun emphasizes value, noting that customers would wear out several pairs of cheaper pants in the time they might wear out a single pair of Red Ants. Plus, the price reflects the structure she has chosen for her business: not offshoring in pursuit of the lowest possible production costs. At the rate her sales are growing, customers apparently agree that it's a fair price to pay for pants that keep them safe and comfortable on the job.

Distribution strategy was one of Calhoun's most important marketing and business decisions. Clothes in general and pants in particular are products for which individual fit and function can't be absolutely confirmed until the customer tries them on. Having her products available in hundreds of retail outlets would let more customers try them on—and give her tremendous visibility in the market. However, it would also put her at the mercy of retailers' demands regarding price and inventory. She opted to function as her own distribution channel, selling from her website, over the phone, and from her storefront operation in White Sulphur Springs, Montana. Having so many sizing options helps ensure that pants fit when customers receive them, but as with most online clothing retailers, she invites customers to exchange pants that don't fit.

Like millions of other small companies in recent years, Red Ants Pants has taken advantage of technology to overcome distribution hurdles. Calhoun explains, "The old quote of retail being location, location, location doesn't hold up as much. I have Internet and I have UPS and mail service, and that's all I need."

Customer communication is another aspect of the marketing mix in which Calhoun demonstrates both the greater flexibility that small companies often have compared to their larger, "more corporate" competitors—and the need to exercise creative brain power over brute-force budget power. Her communication style is more fun and more daring that the typical corporation would attempt, for example, and it seems to resonate with buyers. How many clothing companies would use photographs (discreetly staged, to be sure) to suggest that hardworking women would rather wear no pants than wear pants that don't fit?

Without a significant marketing budget, Calhoun looks for low-cost, high-visibility ways to reach customers. Her most unusual is hitting the highway in an ant-decorated Airstream travel trailer with her sales manager on trips they call the "Tour de Pants." They invite women to stage in-home gatherings, much like old-school Tupperware parties. Through visiting customers in their homes and hearing stories about women working in what are often male-dominated professions, Calhoun also gains invaluable marketing research insights.

Calhoun's most ambitious communication effort so far has been sponsoring the Red Ants Pants Music Festival, which has attracted such major Americana artists as Lyle Lovett and Guy Clark. All profits go to the Red Ants Pants Foundation, which she started to "support family farms and ranches, women in business, and rural initiatives."

The combination of meeting customer needs with quality products and a creative marketing effort is paying off. Red Ants Pants now has customers all across the country and around the world, from Europe to Australia, and even women working the research stations in Antarctica. Are customers satisfied with the product? "Putting on these pants was a religious experience," is how one phrased it.[32]

Critical Thinking Questions

13-1. How might Calhoun's decision to keep production in the United States help solidify her market position in the minds of her target customers?

13-2. If Red Ants Pants had investors looking for a quick return, how might that influence Calhoun's decision to continue functioning as her own retail channel, rather than going through established retailers?

13-3. How could meeting small groups of women in their homes to talk about pants possibly be an efficient communication strategy?

LEARN MORE ONLINE

Explore the Red Ants Pants website, at www.redantspants.com, and follow the links to the company's Facebook page, YouTube channel, and Twitter account. How are the various elements of the marketing mix represented? How does the style of communication help Red Ants Pants connect with customers? What sort of practical information is provided to help customers select and order products?

KEY TERMS

behavioral segmentation
cause-related marketing
cognitive dissonance
consumer market
customer loyalty
customer relationship management
demographics
distribution channels
diversification
exchange process
geographic segmentation
market
market development
market penetration
market segmentation
market share
marketing
marketing concept
marketing mix

marketing research
marketing strategy
needs
organizational market
permission-based marketing
place marketing
positioning
price
product
product development
promotion
psychographics
relationship marketing
social commerce
stealth marketing
strategic marketing planning
target markets
transaction
utility
wants

TEST YOUR KNOWLEDGE

Questions for Review

13-4. Why is cause-related marketing an influential form of marketing strategy?

13-5. Do organizational markets pose greater challenges than consumer markets?

13-6. What is strategic marketing planning, and what is its purpose?

13-7. What external environmental factors affect strategic marketing decisions?

13-8. What are the four basic components of the marketing mix?

Questions for Analysis

13-9. Why would consumers knowingly buy counterfeit luxury brands?

13-10. Should companies open themselves up to criticism by being active on social media? Why or why not?

13-11. Despite various debates and discussions surrounding the lack of nutrition facts in fast food products, consumers continue to buy them. Why?

13-12. Why do companies segment markets?

⭐ **13-13. Ethical Considerations.** Is it ethical to observe shoppers for the purposes of marketing research without their knowledge and permission? Why or why not?

Questions for Application

⭐ **13-14.** How might a retailer use relationship marketing to improve customer loyalty?

13-15. Suppose you are the marketing manager of the credit card department of a financial institution. After examining current market conditions, the objective is to support the company's growth through a market penetration strategy. How would you apply this strategy to increase the profitability of the credit card?

⭐ **13-16.** If you were launching a new manufacturing company, would you draft your marketing plan or design your production processes first? Why?

13-17. Concept Integration. How might the key economic indicators discussed in Chapter 2, including consumer price index, inflation, and unemployment, affect a company's marketing decisions?

EXPAND YOUR KNOWLEDGE

Discovering Career Opportunities

There are various organizations that recruit people in the area of marketing. Make an appointment with someone who is in the position you are interested in, such as a brand/product manager, customer relationship manager, or a marketing research manager. Relate to that person that you wish to do a 15-minute informational interview for your marketing class on a career in marketing.

13-18. At the end of the informational interview, list down the five most important job attributes/skills. Reflect on your personal strengths and weaknesses. Do you think you would be a good fit for this job?

13-19. In terms of job attribute/skill deficiencies, describe how you would go about closing the gap. What further academic qualifications or training would you seek to improve your career prospects? Would you accept a lower salary to improve your chances of securing a job?

13-20. Competing with hundreds of applicants for an interview to secure a marketing job can be stressful and frustrating. How do you personally cope with and overcome the continuous rejection and the prospect of being unemployed?

Improving Your Tech Insights: Search Engines

As most every web user knows, search engines identify individual webpages that contain specific words or phrases you've asked for. Search engines have the advantage of scanning millions of individual webpages, and they use powerful ranking algorithms to present the pages that are likely to be the most relevant to your search request. Because each engine uses a proprietary and secret algorithm to rank the displayed results, multiple engines can display different result sets for the same query.

To see how search engines can return markedly different results, search with the phrase "Apple market share" (use the quotation marks) using Google, Yahoo! and Bing. In a brief email message to your instructor, describe the differences and similarities among the three search results. If you were researching a report on Apple's financial prospects, which set of results would be most helpful? Did you see any search results that were more than a year out of date? Based on this one test, which of the three engines would you be most likely to use for your next research project?

PRACTICE YOUR SKILLS

Sharpening Your Communication Skills

In small groups, as assigned by your instructor, take turns interviewing each person in the group about a product that each person absolutely loves or detests. Try to probe for the real reasons behind the emotions, touching on all the issues you read about in this chapter, from self-image to reference groups. Do you see any trends in the group's collective answers? Do people learn anything about themselves when answering the group's questions? Does anyone get defensive about his or her reasons for loving or hating a product? Be prepared to share with the class at least two marketing insights you learned through this exercise.

Building Your Team Skills

In the course of planning a marketing strategy, marketers need to analyze the external environment to consider how forces outside the firm may create new opportunities and challenges. One important environmental factor for merchandise buyers at a retailer such as Target is weather conditions. For example, when merchandise buyers for lawn and garden products think about the assortment and number of products to purchase for the chain's stores, they don't place any orders without first poring over long-range weather forecasts for each market. In particular, temperature and precipitation predictions for the coming

12 months are critical to the company's marketing plan, because they offer clues to consumer demand for barbecues, lawn furniture, gardening tools, and other merchandise.

What other products would benefit from examining weather forecasts? With your team, brainstorm to identify at least three types of products (in addition to lawn and garden items) for which Target should examine the weather as part of its analysis of the external environment. Share your recommendations with the entire class. How many teams identified the same products your team did?

Developing Your Research Skills

Consumer decision-making is a five-step process that is used before a purchase is made. Look up the latest literature (from business journals) on the influence of cultural factors on the consumer decision-making process.

13-21. How are cultural values being transmitted today? How do values influence consumer decision-making on products and services?

13-22. How do marketers influence the purchasing behavior of family members?

13-23. What would you consider as your core values, and how does it influence your purchase decision?

MyBizLab®

Go to the Assignments section of your MyLab to complete these writing exercises.

13-24. If you have a product that appeals to the majority of consumers in a given market, would there be any value in segmenting the market before launching the product? Why or why not?

13-25. Is there still any need for traditional marketing techniques in a world of social commerce? Why or why not?

ENDNOTES

1. Red Ants Pants website, accessed 21 April 21, 2015, www.redantspants.com; Becky Warren, "Ants on the Pants," *Country Woman*, February–March 2011, www.countrywomanmagazine.com Dan Testa, "Red Ants Pants: By Working Women, for Working Women," *Flathead Beacon*, 4 March 2010, www.flatheadbeacon.com; Sammi Johnson, "Outdoor Woman: Red Ants Pants," *406 Woman*, April/May 2010, 52–53; Beth Judy, "Fit for Her," *Montana Magazine*, March–April 2010, 14–16; *Montana Quarterly*, Summer 2010, www.redantspants.com; Devan Grote, "Red Ants Pants," *Gettysburg*, Spring 2009, www.redantspants.com.

2. Philip Kotler and Gary Armstrong, *Principles of Marketing*, 13th ed. (Upper Saddle River, N.J.: Pearson Prentice Hall, 2010), 5.

3. Kotler and Armstrong, *Principles of Marketing*, 6.

4. BizXchange website, accessed 21 April 2015, www.bizx.com.

5. June Lee Risser, "Customers Come First," *Marketing Management*, November/December 2003, 22–26.

6. Ranjay Gulati and James B. Oldroyd, "The Quest for Customer Focus," *Harvard Business Review*, April 2005, 92–101.

7. Jonathan L. Yarmis, "How Facebook Will Upend Advertising," *BusinessWeek*, 28 May 2008, www.businessweek.com

8. Paul Gunning, "Social Media Reality Check," *Adweek*, 8 June 2008, 18.

9. Jeremiah Owyang, "When Social Media Marries CRM Systems," Web Strategy blog, 3 June 2008, www.web-strategist.com.

10. "Sorry, John," *Adweek*, 22 June 2009, 9.

11. Dominique M. Hanssens, Daniel Thorpe, and Carl Finkbeiner, "Marketing When Customer Equity Matters," *Harvard Business Review*, May 2008, 117–123.

12. Google Analytics, accessed 11 November 2013, www.google.com/analytics.

13. Eric Almquist, Martin Kon, and Wolfgang Bock, "The Science of Demand," *Marketing Management*, March/April 2004, 20–26; David C. Swaddling and Charles Miller, "From Understanding to Action," *Marketing Management*, July/August 2004, 31–35.

14. "Marketing Under Fire," *Marketing Management*, July/August 2004, 5.

15. Word of Mouth Marketing Association, "WOM 101," http://womma.org; Nate Anderson, "FTC Says Stealth Marketing Unethical," *Ars Technica*, 13 December 2006, http://arstechnica.com; "Undercover Marketing Uncovered," *CBSnews.com*, 25 July 2004, www.cbsnews.com; Stephanie Dunnewind, "Teen Recruits Create Word-of-Mouth 'Buzz' to Hook Peers on Products," *Seattle Times*, 20 November 2004, www.seattletimes.com.

16. Pophal, "Tweet Ethics: Trust and Transparency in a Web 2.0 World."

17. Dan Hill, "Why They Buy," *Across the Board*, November–December 2003, 27–32; Eric Roston, "The Why of Buy," *Time*, April 2004.

18. Dan Ariely, "The End of Rational Economics," *Harvard Business Review*, July/August 2009, 78–84.

19. Michael R. Solomon, *Consumer Behavior*, 6th ed. (Upper Saddle River, N.J.: Pearson Prentice Hall, 2004), 366–372.

20. Based in part on James C. Anderson and James A. Narus, *Business Market Management: Understanding, Creating, and Delivering Value,* 2nd ed. (Upper Saddle River, N.J.: Pearson Prentice Hall, 2004), 114–116.

21. Gerard J. Tellis, Eden Yin, and Rakesh Niraj, "Does Quality Win? Network Effects Versus Quality in High-Tech Markets," *Journal of Marketing Research*, May 2009, 135–149.

22. Eric Beinhocker, Ian Davis, and Lenny Mendonca, "The 10 Trends You Have to Watch," *Harvard Business Review*, July/August 2009, 55–60.

23. Beinhocker et al., "The 10 Trends You Have to Watch."

24. Kotler and Armstrong, *Principles of Marketing*, 43–46.

25. Gordon A. Wyner, "Pulling the Right Levers," *Marketing Management*, July/August 2004, 8–9.

26. Kotler and Armstrong, *Principles of Marketing*, 196–197.

27. Kotler and Armstrong, *Principles of Marketing*, 205–207.

28. Detlef Schoder, "The Flaw in Customer Lifetime Value," *Harvard Business Review*, December 2007, 26.

29. Mark Rechtin, "Scion's Dilemma," *AutoWeek*, 23 May 2006, www.autoweek.com.

30. Caprelsa website, accessed 11 November 2013, www.caprelsarems.com; Ben Comer, "AstraZeneca Signs Exclusive Distribution Deal for Vandetanib," *PharmExec.com*, 27 April 2011, http://blog.pharmexec.com.

31. Paul Gillin, *The New Influencers: A Marketer's Guide to the New Social Media* (Sanger, Calif.: Quill Driver Books, 2007), xi.

32. See Note 1.

Chapter 8
Operations Management

Production Systems

LEARNING OBJECTIVES   After studying this chapter, you will be able to

1 Explain the systems perspective, and identify seven principles of systems thinking that can improve your skills as a manager.

2 Describe the *value chain* and *value web* concepts, and discuss the controversy over offshoring.

3 Define *supply chain management*, and explain its strategic importance.

4 Identify the major planning decisions in production and operations management.

5 Explain the unique challenges of service delivery.

6 Define *quality*, explain the challenge of quality and product complexity, and identify four major tools and strategies for ensuring product quality.

BEHIND THE SCENES CUSTOMIZING DREAMS AT KIESEL GUITARS

Kiesel offers personalized guitars at affordable prices through a combination of sophisticated production systems and old-world handicraft.

Vasileios Karafillidis/Shutterstock

www.carvinguitars.com

After beginning guitarists have mastered the nuances of "Mary Had a Little Lamb" and set their sights on making serious music, they often encounter a serious equipment dilemma. Low-cost, beginner guitars lack the materials and workmanship needed to produce top-quality sounds. Some are difficult to keep in tune, and some cannot produce true notes all the way up and down the neck. Plus, they just aren't very cool. Nobody wants to jump on stage in front of 50,000 screaming fans with a guitar purchased at the local discount store.

And so the shopping begins, as the aspiring guitarist looks to find a better "axe." As with just about every product category these days, the array of choices is dizzying. For a few hundred dollars, budding musicians can choose from several imports that offer improved quality. Jumping up toward $1,000 to $2,000, they can enter the world of such classic American brands as Fender, Gibson, and Martin—a world that goes up to $10,000 and beyond for limited-edition models. Musicians with that much to spend and several months to wait can also hire skilled instrument builders known as *luthiers* to create custom guitars that reflect their individual personalities and playing styles. Luthiers can custom-craft just about any attribute a guitarist might want, from the types of wood for the body to the radius of the fingerboard.

But what if our superstar-in-training wants it all: world-class quality, the personalized touch of a custom guitar, and a midrange price tag, without the long delays associated with handcrafted instruments?

That "sweet spot" in the guitar market is the territory staked out by Kiesel Guitars, a San Diego company that has been in the instrument business for nearly 70 years. How can Kiesel profitably do business in this seemingly impossible market segment? How could the company quickly customize guitars and sell them in the $750–$1,500-range without compromising quality?[1]

INTRODUCTION

Kiesel Guitars (profiled in the chapter-opening Behind the Scenes) faced a classic systems challenge: how to design and operate business processes that would enable the company to deliver its unique value to customers. This chapter starts with an overview of systems concepts that every manager can use in any functional area; it then explores systems-related issues in the production function, including value chains and value webs, supply chain management, production and operations management, services delivery, and product and process quality.

The Systems View of Business

One of the most important skills you can develop as a manager is the ability to view business from a systems perspective. A **system** is an interconnected and coordinated set of *elements* and *processes* that convert *inputs* into desired *outputs*. A company is made up of numerous individual systems in the various functional areas, not only in manufacturing or operations but also in engineering, marketing, accounting, and other areas that together constitute the overall system that is the company itself. Each of these individual systems can also be thought of as a *subsystem* of the overall business.

1   **LEARNING OBJECTIVE**

Explain the systems perspective, and identify seven principles of systems thinking that can improve your skills as a manager.

system
An interconnected and coordinated set of *elements* and *processes* that converts *inputs* to desired *outputs*.

THINKING IN SYSTEMS

To grasp the power of systems thinking, consider a point, a line, and a circle (see Exhibit 9.1 on the next page). If you poked your head into a nearby office building, what would this snapshot tell you? You could see only one part of the entire operation—and only at this one moment in time. You might see people in the advertising department working on plans for a new ad campaign or people in the accounting department juggling numbers in spreadsheets, but neither view would tell you much about what it takes to complete these tasks or how that department interacts with the rest of the company.

If you stood and observed for several days, though, you could start to get a sense of how people do their jobs in a department. In the advertising department, for instance, you could watch as the staff transforms ideas, information, and goals into a plan that leads to the creation of a new online advertising campaign. Your "point" view would thereby extend into a "line" view, with multiple points connected in sequence. However, you still wouldn't have a complete picture of the entire process in action. Was the campaign successful? What did the marketing department learn from the campaign that could help it do even better next time? To see the process operate over and over, you need to connect the end of the line (the completion of this ad campaign) back to the beginning of the line (the start of the next ad campaign) to create a circle. Now you're beginning to form a systems view of what this department does and how its performance can be improved.

This circular view helps you understand the advertising system better, but it still isn't complete, because it doesn't show you how the advertising system affects the rest of the company and vice versa. For instance, did the finance department provide enough money to run the ad campaign? Was the information technology group prepared to handle the surge in website traffic? Was the manufacturing department ready with enough materials to build the product after customers started placing orders? Were the sales and customer service departments ready to handle the increase in their workloads? All of these subsystems connect to form the overall business system. Only by looking at the interconnected business system can you judge whether the ad campaign was a success for the company as a whole.

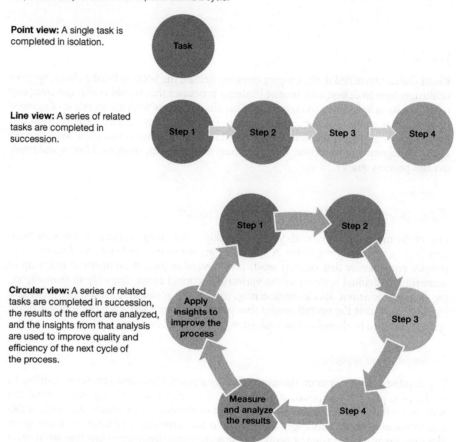

EXHIBIT 9.1   From Point to Line to Circle: The Systems View

The systems view considers all the steps in a process and "closes the loop" by providing feedback from the output of one cycle back to the input of the next cycle.

Point view: A single task is completed in isolation.

Task

Line view: A series of related tasks are completed in succession.

Step 1   Step 2   Step 3   Step 4

Circular view: A series of related tasks are completed in succession, the results of the effort are analyzed, and the insights from that analysis are used to improve quality and efficiency of the next cycle of the process.

Step 1   Step 2

Apply insights to improve the process

Step 3

Measure and analyze the results   Step 4

MANAGING SYSTEMS FOR PEAK PERFORMANCE

Much of the art and science of management involves understanding systems or creating new systems and figuring out ways to make them work more efficiently (using fewer resources) and more effectively (meeting goals more successfully). In some instances, systems analysts can run computer simulations to experiment with changes before making any resource decisions (see Exhibit 9.2). However, even without these formal techniques and tools, you can benefit from systems thinking by keeping these principles in mind:[2]

- **Help everyone see the big picture.** It's human nature for individual employees and departments to focus on their own goals and lose sight of what the company as a whole is trying to accomplish. Showing people how they contribute to the overall goal—and rewarding them for doing so—helps ensure that the entire system works efficiently.
- **Understand how individual systems really work and how they interact.** Managers need to avoid the temptation to jump in and try to fix systems without understanding how each one works and how they interact with one another. For instance, as a wholesaling distribution manager, you might notice that delivery drivers are spending more time at retail sites than deliveries really take, so you instruct drivers to reduce the amount of time they spend. However, it might be that drivers are spending that time gathering market intelligence that they turn over to the sales staff. If you're not careful, you might improve the distribution system but damage the sales system.

EXHIBIT 9.2   Systems Diagram and Simulation

Systems modeling software helps managers simulate complex processes in order to test the outcome of various decision possibilities. To find optimum staffing levels, for example, an organization can simulate different rates of hiring, promotion, and retirement to determine how many new people to bring on board.

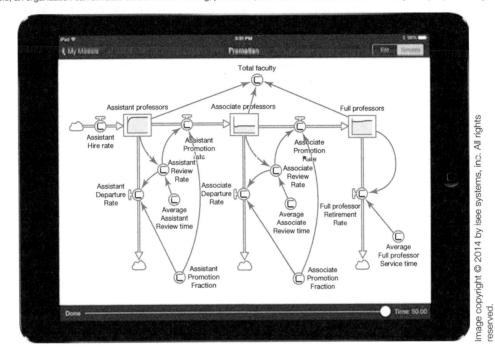

- **Understand problems before you try to fix them.** The most obvious answer is not always the right answer, and poorly conceived solutions often end up causing more harm than good. When you analyze system behavior and malfunctions, make sure you focus on things that are *meaningful*, not merely things that are *measurable*. For instance, it's easy to measure how many reports employees write every month, but that might not be the most meaningful gauge of how well a process is working.
- **Understand the potential impact of solutions before you implement them.** Let's say you manage the customer support department, and to encourage high productivity, you run a weekly contest to see who can handle the most calls. Trouble is, you're essentially rewarding people based on how quickly they can get the customer off the phone, not on how quickly they actually solve customer problems. Customers who aren't happy keep calling back—which adds to the department's workload and *decreases* overall productivity.
- **Don't just move problems around—solve them.** When one subsystem in a company is malfunctioning, its problems are sometimes just moved around from one subsystem to the next, without ever getting solved. For example, if the market research department does a poor job of understanding customers, this problem will get shifted to the engineering department, which is likely to design a product that doesn't meet customer needs. The problem will then get shifted to the advertising and sales departments, which will struggle to promote and sell the product. The engineering, advertising, and sales departments will all underperform, but the real problem is back in the market research department. Market research in this case is a *leverage point*, where a relatively small correction could make the entire company perform better.
- **Understand how feedback works in the system.** Systems respond to *feedback*, which is information from the output applied back to the input. In the case of an ad campaign, the response from target customers is a form of feedback that helps the

department understand whether the campaign is working. Feedback can work in unanticipated ways, too. A good example is managers sending mixed signals to their employees, such as telling them that customer satisfaction is the top priority but then criticizing anyone who spends too much time helping customers. Employees will respond to this feedback by spending less time with customers, leading to a decline in customer satisfaction.

- **Use mistakes as opportunities to learn and improve.** When mistakes occur, resist the temptation to just criticize or complain and then move on. Pull the team together and find out why the mistake occurred, and then identify ways to fix the system to eliminate mistakes in the future.

✓ Checkpoint

LEARNING OBJECTIVE 1: Explain the systems perspective, and identify seven principles of systems thinking that can improve your skills as a manager.

SUMMARY: The systems perspective involves looking at business as a series of interconnected and interdependent systems rather than as a lot of individual activities and events. Seven principles of systems thinking that can help every manager are (1) helping everyone see the big picture, (2) understanding how individual systems really work and how they interact, (3) understanding problems before you try to fix them, (4) understanding the potential impact of solutions before you implement them, (5) avoiding the temptation to just move problems from one subsystem to the next without fixing them, (6) understanding how feedback works in a system so that you can improve each process by learning from experience, and (7) using mistakes as opportunities to learn and improve a system.

CRITICAL THINKING: (1) Why are leverage points in a system so critical to understand? (2) Why should a manager in marketing care about systems in the finance or manufacturing departments?

IT'S YOUR BUSINESS: (1) How could a systems approach to thinking help you get up to speed quickly in your first job after graduation? (2) Think back to your experience of registering for this class. How might you improve that system?

KEY TERMS TO KNOW: system

---

2   **LEARNING OBJECTIVE**

Describe the *value chain* and *value web* concepts, and discuss the controversy over offshoring.

value chain
All the elements and processes that add value as raw materials are transformed into the final products made available to the ultimate customer.

outsourcing
Contracting out certain business functions or operations to other companies.

Value Chains and Value Webs

As Chapter 1 explains, the essential purpose of a business is adding value—transforming lower-value inputs into higher-value outputs. The details vary widely from industry to industry, but all businesses focus on some kind of transformation like this (see Exhibit 9.3). The **value chain** is a helpful way to consider all the elements and processes that add value as input materials are transformed into the final products made available to the ultimate customer.[3] Each industry has a value chain, and each company has its own value chain as well. (Exhibit 1.1 on page 49 is a simplified example of the value chain in the bread industry.)

REDEFINING ORGANIZATIONS WITH VALUE WEBS

In the decades since Michael Porter introduced the value chain concept, many companies have come to realize that doing everything themselves is not always the most efficient or most successful way to run a business. Many now opt to focus on their core competencies and let other companies handle the remaining business functions—a strategy known as **outsourcing**. Hiring other firms to handle some tasks is not a new concept, to be sure; advertising, public relations, and transportation are among the services that have a long

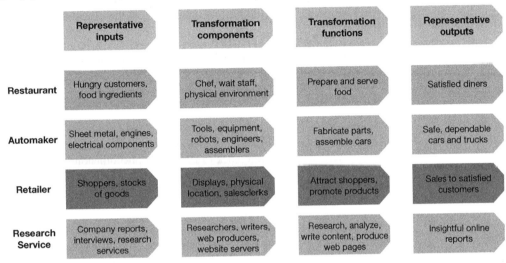

| EXHIBIT 9.3 | Business Transformation Systems |

All businesses engage in a transformation process of some kind, converting one type of value (inputs) to another type (outputs).

	Representative inputs	Transformation components	Transformation functions	Representative outputs
Restaurant	Hungry customers, food ingredients	Chef, wait staff, physical environment	Prepare and serve food	Satisfied diners
Automaker	Sheet metal, engines, electrical components	Tools, equipment, robots, engineers, assemblers	Fabricate parts, assemble cars	Safe, dependable cars and trucks
Retailer	Shoppers, stocks of goods	Displays, physical location, salesclerks	Attract shoppers, promote products	Sales to satisfied customers
Research Service	Company reports, interviews, research services	Researchers, writers, web producers, website servers	Research, analyze, write content, produce web pages	Insightful online reports

history of being handled by outside firms. The term *outsourcing* is usually applied when a firm decides to move a significant function that was previously done in house, such as information technology or manufacturing, to an outside vendor.

The combination of extensive globalization in many industries and the development of electronic networking has made it easy for companies to connect with partners around the world. Instead of the linear value chain, some businesses now think in terms of **value webs**, multidimensional networks of suppliers and outsourcing partners.[4] Value webs enable the virtual or network organization structures discussed in Chapter 8, and the *unstructured organizations* discussed in that chapter can be viewed as dynamic value webs that grow, shrink, or change as the company's needs change.

The outsourced, value web approach has several key advantages, including speed, flexibility, and the opportunity to access a wide range of talents and technologies that might be expensive or impossible to acquire otherwise. Established companies can narrow their focus to excel at their core competencies; entrepreneurs with product ideas can quickly assemble a team of designers, manufacturing plants, and distributors in far less time than it would take to build an entire company from scratch.

For all its potential advantages, outsourcing does carry some risks, particularly in terms of control. For example, to get its new 787 Dreamliner to market as quickly as possible, Boeing outsourced the manufacturing of many parts of the new plane to other manufacturers. Boeing managers initially decided not to impose the "Boeing way" on these suppliers, so it took a hands-off approach. However, the lack of control eventually came to haunt the company. Many suppliers missed target dates and quality standards, throwing the Dreamliner off schedule by at least three years and costing Boeing billions of dollars in extra work, canceled sales, and delivery penalties.[5]

value webs
Multidimensional networks of suppliers and outsourcing partners.

THE OFFSHORING CONTROVERSY

When companies outsource any function in the value chain, they usually eliminate many of the jobs associated with that function as well. In many cases, those jobs don't go across the street to another local company but rather around the world in pursuit of lower labor costs, a variation on outsourcing known as **offshoring**. (Offshoring can shift jobs to another company or to an overseas division of the same company.)

offshoring
Transferring a part or all of a business function to a facility (a different part of the company or another company entirely) in another country.

Offshoring has been going on for decades, but it began to be a major issue for U.S. manufacturing in the 1980s and then for information technology in the 1990s. Today, offshoring is affecting jobs in science, engineering, law, finance, banking, and other professional areas.[6] The offshoring debate is a great example of conflicting priorities in the stakeholder model; see Exhibit 9.4 for a summary of the key arguments for and against offshoring.

Measuring the impact of offshoring on the U.S. economy is difficult because isolating the effect of a single variable in such a complex system is not easy. For example, economists often struggle to identify the specific reasons one country gains jobs or another loses them. The emergence of new technology, phasing out of old technology, shifts in consumer tastes, changes in business strategies, and other factors can all create and destroy jobs.

As the offshoring debate rages on, the nature of offshoring is changing. The complexities and rising costs of long-distance manufacturing have prompted some U.S. companies to move their production back to U.S. soil, a phenomenon known as *reshoring*. For example, as manufacturing wages in China continue to rise—they increased by more than 70 percent from 2008 to 2013—and the demand for skilled workers outpaces supply, the U.S. states with lowest labor costs are starting to become cost-competitive with China when the total costs of offshoring are taken into account.[7]

Changes in global product demand are also influencing manufacturing location decisions. As developing economies generate more demand for products, some manufacturers are establishing production facilities in or near those markets, a strategy known as *near-shoring*.[8]

REAL-TIME UPDATES
Learn More by Visiting This Website

The effort to bring manufacturing activities back to the United States

See what the Reshoring Initiative is doing to encourage American companies to bring manufacturing back to the United States. Go to http://real-timeupdates.com/bia8 and click on Learn More in the Students section.

Although reshoring might reduce the amount of offshoring done by U.S. companies, globalized manufacturing is here to stay, so it's in everyone's best interest to make it work as well as possible for as many stakeholders as possible. For example, how should U.S. companies be taxed when they have operations all over the world? Also, should unions and regulatory agencies make it more difficult for companies to move jobs overseas, or would it be more beneficial in the long run to let companies compete as vigorously as possible and focus on retraining U.S. workers for new jobs here? These issues are not simple, and you can expect this debate to continue.

 Checkpoint

LEARNING OBJECTIVE 2: Describe the *value chain* and *value web* concepts, and discuss the controversy over offshoring.

SUMMARY: The *value chain* includes all the elements and processes that add value as input materials are transformed into the final products made available to the ultimate customer. The *value web* concept expands this linear model to a multi-dimensional network of suppliers and outsourcing partners. In the complex argument over *offshoring*—the transfer of business functions to entities in other countries in pursuit of lower costs—proponents claim that (a) companies have a responsibility to shareholder interests to pursue the lowest cost of production, (b) offshoring benefits U.S. consumers through lower prices, (c) many companies don't have a choice once their competitors move offshore, (d) some companies need to offshore in order to support customers around the world, and (e) offshoring helps U.S. companies be more competitive. Those who question the value or wisdom of offshoring raise points about (a) the future of good jobs in the United States, (b) hidden costs and risks, (c) diminished responsiveness, (d) knowledge transfer and theft issues, (e) product safety issues, and (f) national security and public health concerns.

EXHIBIT 9.4	The Offshoring Controversy

Offshoring, or shifting jobs performed by U.S. employees to countries with lower labor costs, is a complex controversy that pits some stakeholders against others. Here are the major arguments for and against the practice, along with some of the key stakeholder groups affected.

Arguments for Offshoring		Arguments Against or Concerns About Offshoring	
Argument	**Stakeholders who benefit**	**Argument/Concern**	**Stakeholders who suffer**
Responsibility to shareholder interests: Companies that engage in offshoring say they have a duty to manage shareholder investments for maximum gain, so it would be irresponsible not to explore cost-saving opportunities such as offshoring.	Shareholders	**Loss of well-paid U.S. jobs:** Opponents of offshoring say that companies are selling out the U.S. middle class in pursuit of profits and pushing a trend that can only harm the country.	Workers
Lower prices for U.S. consumers: For goods in which labor represents a significant portion of production costs, dramatically lowering labor costs lets a company lower its prices to consumers.	Consumers	**Hidden costs and risks:** Says J. Paul Dittman of the University of Tennessee, "Many firms are rethinking the mad rush to outsource . . . the long supply lines, incredibly volatile fuel costs, exchange rates, the geopolitical risks have all come home to roost."	Shareholders
Lack of choice in competitive industries: Given the pricing advantage that offshoring can give U.S. companies, as soon as one company in an industry does it, the others are put under pressure to lower their prices—and offshoring might be the only way for some to lower costs enough to do so.	Shareholders	**Business agility and responsiveness:** When companies rely on operations halfway around the world, they can be slow to respond to marketplace shifts and customer service issues.	Shareholders
Support for local customers around the world: Some companies say that as they expand into other countries, they have no choice but to hire overseas employees in order to support local customers.	Shareholders	**Knowledge transfer and theft risk:** By hiring other companies to perform technical and professional services, U.S. companies transfer important knowledge to these other countries—making them more competitive and depleting the pools of expertise in the United States. Offshoring can also increase the risks of product piracy and theft of intellectual property.	Shareholders, U.S. economy
U.S. competitiveness: Proponents say offshoring is crucial to the survival of many U.S. companies and that it saves other U.S. jobs by making U.S. companies more competitive in the global marketplace.	U.S. economy	**Product safety issues:** Moving more production beyond U.S. borders increases concerns about the ability of regulators to oversee vital health and safety issues.	Consumers
		National security and public health concerns: The weapons and systems used for national defense require lots of steel, semiconductors, and other manufactured materials, and the health-care industry requires a vast supply of materials. What if the United States comes to rely too heavily on other countries for things it needs to protect its borders and its people?	United States, Consumers

Sources: J. Paul Dittmann, "*WT100* and the University of Tennessee Supply Chain Survey," *World Trade 100*, July 2011, 42; Hayden Bush, "Reliance on Overseas Manufacturers Worries Supply Chain Experts," *Hospitals & Health Networks*, July 2011, 13; William T. Dickens and Stephen J. Rose, "Blinder Baloney," *The International Economy*, Fall 2007, 18+; "Supply Chain News: The Seven Timeless Challenges of Supply Chain Management," *SupplyChainDigest*, 2 June 2009, www.scdigest.com; Phil Fersht, Dana Stiffler, and Kevin O'Marah, "The Ins and Outs of Offshoring," *Supply Chain Management Review*, March 2009, 10–11; Ajay K. Goel, Nazgol Moussavi, and Vats N. Srivatsan, "Time to Rethink Offshoring?" *McKinsey Quarterly*, 2008 Issue 4, 108–111; Anita Hawser, "Offshoring Industry Faces New Opponent: Its Clients," *Global Finance*, November 2007, 6; Alan S. Brown, "A Shift in Engineering Offshore," *Mechanical Engineering*, March 2009, 24–29; John Ferreira and Len Prokopets, "Does Offshoring Still Make Sense?" *Supply Chain Management Review*, January/February 2009, 20–27; Dan Gilmore, "Can—and Should—Western Manufacturing Be Saved?" *SupplyChainDigest*, 28 May 2009, www.scdigest.com; Geri Smith and Justin Bachman, "The Offshoring of Airplane Care," *BusinessWeek*, 10 April 2008, www.businessweek.com; Susan Carey and Alex Frangos, "Airlines, Facing Cost Pressure, Outsource Crucial Safety Tasks," *Wall Street Journal*, 21 January 2005, A1, A5.

CRITICAL THINKING: (1) Do U.S. companies have an obligation to keep jobs in the United States? Why or why not? (2) Will global labor markets eventually balance out, with workers in comparable positions all over the world making roughly the same wages? Explain your answer.

IT'S YOUR BUSINESS: (1) How vulnerable are your target professions to offshoring? (2) Should such concerns affect your career planning?

KEY TERMS TO KNOW: value chain, outsourcing, value webs, offshoring

---

Define *supply chain management*, and explain its strategic importance.

supply chain
A set of connected systems that coordinate the flow of goods and materials from suppliers all the way through to final customers.

supply chain management (SCM)
The business procedures, policies, and computer systems that integrate the various elements of the supply chain into a cohesive system.

Supply Chain Management

Regardless of how and where it is structured, the lifeblood of every production operation is the **supply chain**, a set of connected systems that coordinate the flow of goods and materials from suppliers all the way through to final customers. Companies with multiple customer bases can also develop a distinct supply chain to serve each segment.[9]

Supply chain management (SCM) combines business procedures and policies with information systems that integrate the various elements of the supply chain into a cohesive system. As companies rely more on outsourcing partners, SCM has grown far beyond the simple procurement of supplies to become a strategic management function that means the difference between success and failure. Successful implementation of SCM can have a profound strategic impact on companies and the broader economy, in several important ways:[10]

- **Managing risks.** SCM can help companies manage the complex risks involved in a supply chain, risks that include everything from cost and availability to health and safety issues.
- **Managing relationships.** SCM can coordinate the numerous relationships in the supply chain and help managers focus their attention on the most important company-to-company relationships.
- **Managing trade-offs.** SCM helps managers address the many trade-offs in the supply chain. These trade-offs can be a source of conflict within the company, and SCM helps balance the competing interests of the various functional areas. This holistic view helps managers balance both capacity and capability along the entire chain.
- **Promoting sustainability.** As the part of business that moves raw materials and finished goods around the world, supply chains have an enormous effect on resource usage, waste, and environmental impact. A major effort is under way in the field of SCM to develop greener supply chains. A key player in this effort is the giant retailer Walmart, which buys products from more than 100,000 suppliers and has tremendous influence on global supply chains. The company now works with its suppliers to help them meet sustainability targets in the areas of energy and climate, material efficiency, natural resources, and people and community.[11]

SUPPLY CHAINS VERSUS VALUE CHAINS

The terms *supply chain* and *value chain* are sometimes used interchangeably, and the distinction between them isn't always clear in everyday usage. One helpful way to distinguish between the two is to view the **supply chain** as the part of the overall value chain that acquires and manages the goods and services needed to produce whatever it is the company produces and then deliver it to the final customer. Everyone in the company is part of the value chain, but not everyone is involved in the supply chain.[12]

Another way to distinguish the two is that the supply chain focuses on the "upstream" part of the process, collecting the necessary materials and supplies with an emphasis on

REAL-TIME UPDATES
Learn More by Visiting This Website

Sustainability at Walmart

As the world's largest retailer, Walmart is using its considerable influence to increase sustainability in the global supply chain. Go to http://real-timeupdates.com/bia8 and click on Learn More in the Students section.

reducing waste and inefficiency. The value chain focuses on the "downstream" part of the process and on adding value in the eyes of customers.[13]

Yet a third way that has recently emerged is talking about value chains as a strategic win-win business partnership rather than the more tactical, deal-driven arrangement of a supply chain. In this usage, "value" also encompasses *values*, including sustainability practices that make products more worthy and appealing in the eyes of customers.[14]

SUPPLY CHAIN SYSTEMS AND TECHNIQUES

The core focus of supply chain management is getting the right materials at the right price in the right place at the right time for successful production. Unfortunately, you can't just pile up huge quantities of everything you might eventually need, because **inventory**, the goods and materials kept in stock for production or sale, costs money to purchase and to store. On the other hand, not having an adequate supply of inventory can result in expensive delays. This balancing act is the job of **inventory control**, which tries to determine the right quantities of supplies and products to have on hand and then tracks where those items are. One of the most important technologies to emerge in inventory control in recent years is *radio frequency identification (RFID)*. RFID uses small antenna tags attached to products or shipping containers; special sensors detect the presence of the tags and can track the flow of goods through the supply chain.

Procurement, or *purchasing*, is the acquisition of the raw materials, parts, components, supplies, and finished products required to produce goods and services. The goal of purchasing is to make sure that the company has all the materials it needs, when it needs them, at the lowest possible cost. A company must always have enough supplies on hand to cover a product's *lead time*—the period that elapses between placing the supply order and receiving materials.

To accomplish these goals, operations specialists have developed a variety of systems and techniques over the years:

- **Material requirements planning (MRP).** MRP helps a manufacturer get the correct materials where they are needed, when they are needed, without unnecessary stockpiling. Managers use MRP software to calculate when certain materials will be required, when they should be ordered, and when they should be delivered so that storage costs will be minimal. These systems are so effective at reducing inventory levels that they are used almost universally in both large and small manufacturing firms.
- **Manufacturing resource planning (MRP II).** MRP II expands MRP with links to a company's financial systems and other processes. For instance, in addition to managing inventory levels successfully, an MRP II system can help ensure that material costs adhere to target budgets.[15] Because it draws together all departments, an MRP II system produces a companywide game plan that allows everyone to work with the same numbers. Moreover, the system can track each step of production, allowing managers throughout the company to consult other managers' inventories, schedules, and plans.
- **Enterprise resource planning (ERP).** ERP extends the scope of resource planning and management even further to encompass the entire organization. ERP software programs are typically made up of modules that address the needs of the various functional areas, from manufacturing to sales to human resources. Some companies deploy ERP on a global scale, with a single centralized system connecting all their operations worldwide.[16]

inventory
Goods and materials kept in stock for production or sale.

inventory control
Determining the right quantities of supplies and products to have on hand and tracking where those items are.

procurement
The acquisition of the raw materials, parts, components, supplies, and finished products required to produce goods and services.

Benjamin Haas/Shutterstock

Tracking and managing inventory levels are essential tasks for ensuring smooth, profitable operations.

REAL-TIME UPDATES
Learn More by Visiting This Website

Interested in a career in supply chain management?

The Council of Supply Chain Management Professionals offers advice on how to launch a career in this important field. Go to http://real-timeupdates.com/bia8 and click on Learn More in the Students section.

Checkpoint

LEARNING OBJECTIVE 3: Define *supply chain management*, and explain its strategic importance.

SUMMARY: Supply chain management (SCM) combines business procedures and policies with information systems that integrate the various elements of the supply chain into a cohesive system. SCM helps companies manage risks, relationships, and trade-offs throughout their supply chains, building partnerships that help everyone in the supply chain succeed.

CRITICAL THINKING: (1) Why can't companies just stockpile huge inventories of all the parts and materials they need rather than carefully manage supply from one day to the next? (2) Why would a company invest time and money in helping its suppliers improve their business practices? Why not just dump underperformers and get better suppliers?

IT'S YOUR BUSINESS: (1) In any current or previous job, what steps have supervisors taken to help you understand your role in the supply chain? (2) Is it dehumanizing to your colleagues and business partners to be participants in a supply chain? Why or why not?

KEY TERMS TO KNOW: supply chain, supply chain management (SCM), inventory, inventory control, procurement

---

4   LEARNING OBJECTIVE

Identify the major planning decisions in production and operations management.

production and operations management
Overseeing all the activities involved in producing goods and services.

productivity
The efficiency with which an organization can convert inputs to outputs.

lean systems
Systems (in manufacturing and other functional areas) that maximize productivity by reducing waste and delays.

Production and Operations Management

The term *production* suggests factories, machines, and assembly lines making automobiles, computers, furniture, motorcycles, or other tangible goods. With the growth in the number of service-based businesses and their increasing importance to the economy, however, the term *production* is now used to describe the transformation of resources into both goods and services. The broader term **production and operations management**, or simply *operations management*, refers to overseeing all the activities involved in producing goods and services. Operations managers are involved in a wide range of strategic and tactical decisions, from high-level design of the production system to forecasting and scheduling.

LEAN SYSTEMS

Throughout all the activities in the production process, operations managers pay close attention to **productivity**, or the efficiency with which they can convert inputs to outputs. (Put another way, productivity is equal to the value of the outputs divided by the value of the inputs.) Productivity is one of the most vital responsibilities in operations management because it is a key factor in determining the company's competitiveness and profitability. Companies that can produce similar goods or services with fewer resources have a distinct advantage over their competitors. Moreover, high productivity in the fullest sense also requires low waste, whether it's left-over materials, shoddy products that must be scrapped, or excess energy usage. Consequently, productivity improvements and sustainability improvements often complement each other.

    Lean systems, which maximize productivity by reducing waste and delays, are at the heart of many productivity improvement efforts. Many lean systems borrow techniques from Toyota; the *Toyota Production System* is world

REAL-TIME UPDATES
Learn More by Exploring This Interactive Website

Watch lean manufacturing in action

See how the Toyota Production System works from customer order to customer delivery. Go to http://real-timeupdates.com/bia8 and click on Learn More in the Students section.

renowned for its ability to continually improve both productivity and quality (see Exhibit 9.5).[17] Central to the notion of lean systems is **just-in-time (JIT)** inventory management, in which goods and materials are delivered throughout the production process right before they are needed rather than being stockpiled in inventories. Reducing stocks to immediate needs reduces waste and forces factories to keep production flowing smoothly.

just-in-time (JIT)
Inventory management in which goods and materials are delivered throughout the production process right before they are needed.

EXHIBIT 9.5   Conceptual Diagram of the Toyota Production System

The Toyota Production System, one of the most influential production strategies in modern business history, has been studied, duplicated, and adapted by companies in a variety of industries around the world. Toyota refined the system over decades, but it has always been based on the two fundamental principles of just-in-time inventory management, so that expensive inventory doesn't pile up when it isn't being used, and *jidoka*, or "automation with a human touch," whereby the highly automated process can be stopped by any worker any time a problem appears, to avoid making more defective parts or cars. However, as page 261 explains, for all its abilities to reduce manufacturing defects, the system has not been able to prevent all failures particularly now that cars are vast software systems as well as mechanical systems.

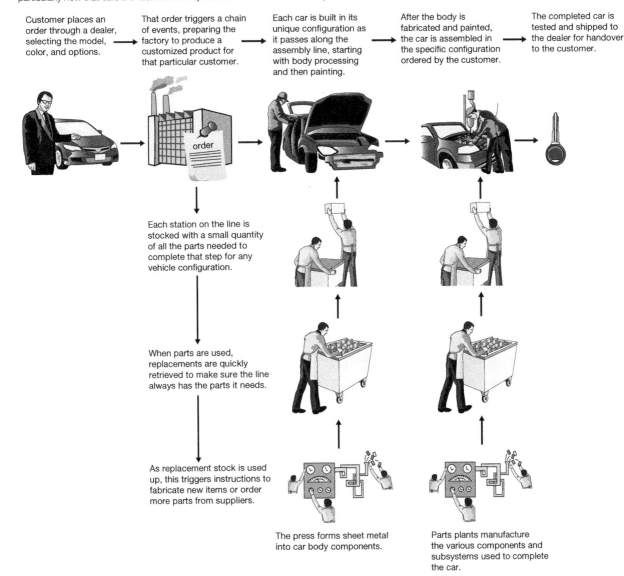

Customer places an order through a dealer, selecting the model, color, and options. → That order triggers a chain of events, preparing the factory to produce a customized product for that particular customer. → Each car is built in its unique configuration as it passes along the assembly line, starting with body processing and then painting. → After the body is fabricated and painted, the car is assembled in the specific configuration ordered by the customer. → The completed car is tested and shipped to the dealer for handover to the customer.

Each station on the line is stocked with a small quantity of all the parts needed to complete that step for any vehicle configuration.

When parts are used, replacements are quickly retrieved to make sure the line always has the parts it needs.

As replacement stock is used up, this triggers instructions to fabricate new items or order more parts from suppliers.

The press forms sheet metal into car body components.

Parts plants manufacture the various components and subsystems used to complete the car.

Source: Data from "Toyota Production System," Toyota Global website, accessed 4 November 2013, www.toyota-global.com.

Achieving such benefits requires constant attention to quality and teamwork because with no spare inventory, there is no room for delays or errors.[18] Without stockpiles of extra parts and materials, each stage in the production process goes idle if the stages before it have not delivered on time.

MASS PRODUCTION, CUSTOMIZED PRODUCTION, AND MASS CUSTOMIZATION

Goods and services can be created through *mass production, customized production*, or *mass customization*, depending on the nature of the product and the desires of target customers. In **mass production**, identical goods or services are created, usually in large quantities, such as when Apple churns out a million identical iPhones. Although not normally associated with services, mass production is also what American Airlines is doing when it offers hundreds of opportunities for passengers to fly from, say, Dallas to Chicago every day: Every customer on these flights gets the same service at the same time.

At the other extreme is **customized production**, sometimes called *batch-of-one production* in manufacturing, in which the producer creates a unique good or service for each customer. If you order a piece of furniture from a local craftsperson, for instance, you can specify everything from the size and shape to the types of wood and fabric used. Or you can hire a charter pilot to fly you wherever you want, whenever you want. Both products are customized to your unique requirements.

Mass production has the advantage of economies of scale, but it can't deliver many of the unique goods and services that today's customers demand. On the other hand, fully customized production can offer uniqueness but usually at a much higher price. An attractive compromise in many cases is **mass customization**, in which part of the product is mass produced and then the remaining features are customized for each buyer. With design and production technologies getting ever more flexible, the opportunities for customization continue to grow. As you'll read at the end of the chapter, this is the approach Kiesel has taken: Customers get the same basic guitar bodies but with their own individual combinations of woods, fingerboard styles, finishes, and electronic components.

mass production
The creation of identical goods or services, usually in large quantities.

customized production
The creation of a unique good or service for each customer.

mass customization
A manufacturing approach in which part of the product is mass produced and the remaining features are customized for each buyer.

FACILITIES LOCATION AND DESIGN

Choosing the location of production facilities is a complex decision that must consider such factors as land, construction, availability of talent, taxes, energy, living standards, transportation, and proximity to customers and business partners. Support from local communities and governments often plays a key role in location decisions as well. To provide jobs and expand their income and sales tax bases, local, state, and national governments often compete to attract companies by offering generous financial incentives such as tax reductions.

After a site has been selected, managers turn their attention to *facility layout*, the arrangement of production work centers and other elements (such as materials, equipment, and support departments) needed to process goods and services. Layout planning includes such decisions as how many steps are needed in the process, the amount and type of equipment and workers needed for each step, how each step should be configured, and where the steps should be located relative to one another.[19]

Well-designed facilities help companies operate more productively by reducing wasted time and wasted materials, but that is far from the only benefit. Smart layouts support close communication and collaboration among employees and help ensure their safety, both of which are important for employee satisfaction and motivation. In the delivery of services, facility layout can be a major influence on customer satisfaction because it affects the overall service experience.[20]

Tyler Olson/Shutterstock

With customized production, such as tailor-made or *bespoke* clothing, each product is created to meet the needs of an individual buyer.

FORECASTING AND CAPACITY PLANNING

Using customer feedback, sales orders, market research, past sales figures, industry analyses, and educated guesses about the future behavior of customers and competitors, operations managers prepare *production forecasts*—estimates of future demand for the company's products. After product demand has been estimated, management must balance that with the company's capacity to produce the goods or services. The term *capacity* refers to the volume of manufacturing or service capability that an organization can handle. **Capacity planning** is the collection of long-term strategic decisions that establish the overall level of resources needed to meet customer demand. When managers at Boeing plan for the production of an airliner, they have to consider not only the staffing of thousands of people but also massive factory spaces, material flows from hundreds of suppliers around the world, internal deliveries, cash flow, tools and equipment, and dozens of other factors. Because of the potential impact on finances, customers, and employees—and the difficulty of reversing major decisions—capacity choices are among the most important decisions that top-level managers make.[21]

capacity planning
Establishing the overall level of resources needed to meet customer demand.

SCHEDULING

In any production process, managers must do *scheduling*—determining how long each operation takes and deciding which tasks are done in which order. Manufacturing facilities often use a *master production schedule (MPS)* to coordinate production of all the goods the company makes. Service businesses use a variety of scheduling techniques as well, from simple appointment calendars for a small business to the comprehensive online systems that airlines and other large service providers use.

To plan and track projects of all kinds, managers throughout a company can use a *Gantt chart*, a special type of bar chart that shows the progress of all the tasks needed to complete a project (see Exhibit 9.6). For more complex projects, the *program evaluation and review technique (PERT)* is useful. PERT helps managers identify the optimal sequencing of activities, the expected time for project completion, and the best use of resources. To use PERT, managers map out all the activities in a network diagram (see Exhibit 9.7 on the next page). The longest path through the network is known as the **critical path** because it represents the minimum amount of time needed to complete the project. Tasks in the critical path usually receive special attention because they determine when the project can be completed.[22] (If anyone ever says *you* are in the critical path, make sure you stay on schedule!)

critical path
In a PERT network diagram, the sequence of operations that requires the longest time to complete.

EXHIBIT 9.6   Gantt Chart

A Gantt chart is a handy tool in project and production management because it shows the order in which tasks must be completed and which tasks are dependent on other tasks. For the new product launch shown here, for example, the analysis task is dependent on all three tasks before it, which means those tasks must be completed before analysis can begin. With periodic updates, it's also easy to show a team exactly where the project stands at any particular moment.

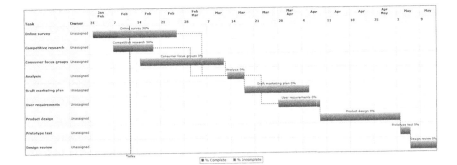

Simplified PERT Diagram for a Store Opening

This PERT diagram shows a subset of the many tasks involved in opening a new retail store. The tasks involved in staffing are on the critical path because they take the longest time to complete (51 days), whereas the promotion tasks can be completed in 38 days, and the merchandise tasks can be completed in 39 days. In other words, some delay can be tolerated in the promotion or merchandise tasks, but any delay in any of the staffing tasks will delay the store's opening day.

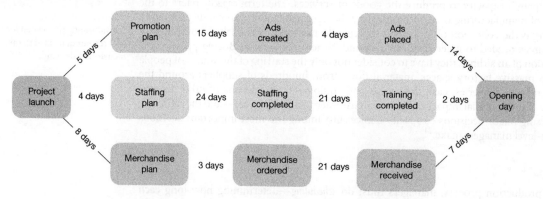

✓ Checkpoint

LEARNING OBJECTIVE 4: Identify the major planning decisions in production and operations management.

SUMMARY: The major decisions in operations management include (1) facilities location and design; (2) forecasting and capacity planning to match resources with demand; (3) scheduling; (4) lean system design to reduce waste and delays; and (5) the choice of mass production, customized production, or mass customization.

CRITICAL THINKING: (1) Why is it essential to identify tasks in the critical path of a project? (2) How does mass customization help a company balance productivity and customer satisfaction?

IT'S YOUR BUSINESS: (1) The phrase "lean and mean" is sometimes used to describe lean systems. What are the risks of using such language? (2) Is this course an example of mass production, customization, or mass customization? Explain.

KEY TERMS TO KNOW: production and operations management, productivity, lean systems, just-in-time (JIT), mass production, customized production, mass customization, capacity planning, critical path

---

5 **LEARNING OBJECTIVE**

Explain the unique challenges of service delivery.

The Unique Challenges of Service Delivery

With the majority of workers in the United States now involved in the service sector, managers in thousands of companies need to pay close attention to the unique challenges of delivering services: perishability, location constraints, scalability challenges, performance variability and perceptions of quality, and customer involvement and service provider interaction.

PERISHABILITY

Most services are *perishable*, meaning that they are consumed at the same time they are produced and cannot exist before or after that time. For example, if a 200-seat airliner takes off half-empty, those 100 sales opportunities are lost forever. The airline can't create these products ahead of time and store them in inventory until somebody is ready to buy. Similarly, restaurants can seat only so many people every night, so empty tables represent revenue lost forever. This perishability can have a profound impact on the way service businesses are managed, from staffing (making sure enough people are on hand to help with peak demands) to pricing (using discounts to encourage people to buy services when they are available).

LOCATION CONSTRAINTS

Perishability also means that for many services, customers and providers need to be in the same place at the same time. The equipment and food ingredients used in a restaurant can be produced just about anywhere, but the restaurant itself needs to be located close to customers. One of the most significant commercial advantages of the Internet is the way it has enabled many service businesses to get around this constraint. Online retailers, information providers, and other e-businesses can locate virtually anywhere on the planet.

SCALABILITY CHALLENGES AND OPPORTUNITIES

Any business that wants to grow must consider the issue of **scalability**, the potential to increase production by expanding or replicating its initial production capacity. Scaling up always creates some challenges, but service businesses that depend on the skills of specific professionals can be particularly difficult to scale. Examples range from chefs and interior designers to business consultants and graphic designers, particularly when the business is built around the reputation of a single person.

scalability
The potential to increase production by expanding or replicating its initial production capacity.

Of course, many goods businesses also rely on highly skilled production workers, but the potential to mechanize goods production can make it easier to scale up manufacturing in some cases. For example, by using computer-controlled routers to carve the bodies of its guitars, Kiesel frees itself from the constraint of hiring enough skilled carvers to do it all by hand.

PERFORMANCE VARIABILITY AND PERCEPTIONS OF QUALITY

For many types of services, the quality of performance can vary from one instance to the next—and that quality is in the eye of the beholder and often can't be judged until after the service has been performed. If you manufacture scissors, you can specify a certain grade of steel from your suppliers and use automated machinery to produce thousands of identical pairs of scissors of identical quality. Many key attributes such as the size and strength of the scissors are *objective* and measurable, and customers can experience the *subjective* variables such as the feel and action before they buy. In other words, there is little mystery and little room for surprise in the purchase.

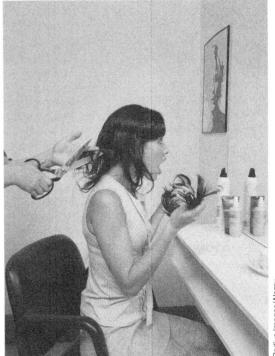

However, if you create a haircut using a pair of those scissors, perceptions of quality become almost entirely subjective *and* impossible to judge until after the service is complete. Plus, hair styling is a good example of a service in which *quality of experience* is an important part of customer perceptions as well, which is why, for instance, most salons pay a lot of attention to architecture, interior design, lighting, music, robes, refreshments, and other amenities that have nothing to do with the actual haircut itself.

CUSTOMER INVOLVEMENT AND PROVIDER INTERACTION

Finally, one of the biggest differences between goods and services production is the fact that customers are often involved in—and thereby can affect the quality of—the service delivery. For instance, personal trainers can instruct clients in the proper way to exercise, but if the clients don't follow directions, the result will be unsatisfactory. Similarly, a business consultant relies on accurate

One of the many challenges of providing services is that the evaluation of quality is often subjective.

information from managers in a client organization; lacking that, he or she will be unable to craft the most effective advice.

When customers and service providers interact, the quality of the interpersonal experience also affects customer perceptions of quality. In this sense, service delivery is something of a performance that needs to instill confidence in the client. Weak communication skills or poor etiquette can create dissatisfaction with a service that is satisfactory or even exceptional in all other respects.

✓ **Checkpoint**

LEARNING OBJECTIVE 5: Explain the unique challenges of service delivery.

SUMMARY: The delivery of services presents a number of unique challenges, including (1) perishability, which means that services are consumed at the same time they are produced; (2) location constraints, which often require that customers and service providers be in the same place at the same time; (3) scalability challenges, which can make some types of service businesses more difficult to expand; (4) performance variability and perceptions of quality, which heighten the challenge of delivering consistent quality and increase the subjectivity of the customer experience; and (5) customer involvement and service provider interaction, which can put some of the responsibility for service quality on the customer's shoulders and increase the importance of good interpersonal skills.

CRITICAL THINKING: (1) How can technology help some service businesses address the challenge of scalability? (2) If customers are paying for a service, why should they ever have to share in the responsibility of ensuring quality results?

IT'S YOUR BUSINESS: (1) Do you think you have a natural personality for working in a service business? Why or why not? (2) If you're not a "natural," what steps could you take to succeed in a service job anyway?

KEY TERMS TO KNOW: scalability

Product and Process Quality

6 LEARNING OBJECTIVE

Define *quality*, explain the challenge of quality and product complexity, and identify four major tools and strategies for ensuring product quality.

quality
The degree to which a product or process meets reasonable or agreed-on expectations.

The term *quality* is often used in a vague sense of "goodness" or "excellence," but to be meaningful from a managerial standpoint, it needs to be defined in context. Hyundai and Aston Martin both make quality automobiles, but quality means dramatically different things to the makers and buyers of these two car brands. People who spend $15,000 or $20,000 on a Hyundai are likely to be satisfied with the quality they receive in return, but people who spend 10 times that much on an Aston Martin have vastly different expectations, even if the two cars are equally safe and reliable. Accordingly, **quality** is best defined as the degree to which a product or process meets reasonable or agreed-on expectations. Within the framework of this general definition, a specific set of parameters can be identified that define quality in each situation.

Defining those expectations of quality and then organizing the resources and systems needed to achieve that level are vital responsibilities in today's competitive, resource-constrained environment. With numerous choices available in most product categories, consumers and business buyers alike tend to avoid or abandon products and companies that can't meet their expectations. Moreover, poor quality wastes time and money, squanders resources, frustrates customers and employees, erodes confidence in companies and their products, and can even put people in danger.

QUALITY AND COMPLEXITY

As many products become increasingly complex, defining and maintaining quality becomes an ever greater challenge. For example, even identical, mass-produced computers immediately become unique when their new owners start adding software, downloading files, and connecting to printers and other devices, each of which is a complex hardware/software system in its own right. All these changes and connections increase the chances that something will go wrong and thereby lower the functional quality of the product. In other words, even though the company verified the quality of the products before they left the factory, it could have thousands of quality issues on its hands over time.

Meeting expectations of quality in complicated, real-world operating conditions over time can present a sizable challenge but one that must be met to ensure buyer satisfaction. Dell, for example, has dozens of customer service specialists who monitor social media conversations for signs of discontent over its products. When they hear complaints, they jump in with advice and offers to help. The team logs more than 25,000 online conversations a day. This effort improves customer satisfaction and creates opportunities to sell additional goods and services—the company figures the program has generated more than $1 billion in additional sales—but it also gives Dell engineers valuable insights into how quality plays out in the messy real world outside the factory.[23]

Even the frequently copied Toyota Production System has proved fallible at times, with several notable safety-related recalls in recent years. According to engineering professor Jeffrey Liker, who has researched and written extensively about Toyota, none of the recalls could be traced to production defects.[24] To improve the design process, though, the company did respond to the criticism that senior engineers in charge of design were isolated at company headquarters in Japan and too insulated from real-world feedback. In response, the company announced that North American engineering teams were being given more control over the development of vehicles designed for the North American market.[25]

REAL-TIME UPDATES
Learn More by Watching This Video

Watch robots build a Tesla electric car

The Tesla factory is as technologically advanced as the electric cars it produces. Go to http://real-timeupdates.com/bia8 and click on Learn More in the Students section.

STRATEGIES FOR ENSURING PRODUCT QUALITY

The traditional means of maintaining quality is called **quality control**—measuring quality against established standards after the good or service has been produced and weeding out any defects. A more comprehensive and proactive approach is **quality assurance**, a holistic system of integrated policies, practices, and procedures designed to ensure that every product meets preset quality standards. Quality assurance includes quality control as well as doing the job right the first time by designing tools and machinery properly, demanding quality parts from suppliers, encouraging customer feedback, training and empowering employees, and encouraging employees to take pride in their work.

Companies can use a variety of tools and strategies to help ensure quality; four of the most significant are continuous improvement, statistical process control, Six Sigma, and ISO 9000.

Continuous Improvement

Delivering quality goods and services is as much a mindset as it is a technical challenge. Companies that excel tend to empower their employees to continuously improve the quality of goods production or service delivery, a strategy often expressed through the Japanese word *kaizen*. By making quality everyone's responsibility, the kaizen approach encourages all workers to look for quality problems, halt production when necessary, generate ideas for improvement, and adjust work routines as needed.[26]

Statistical Process Control

Any quality control or improvement effort depends on reliable feedback that tells workers and managers how well products and processes are performing. Quality assurance often includes the use of **statistical process control (SPC)**, which involves taking samples from the process periodically and analyzing these data points to look for trends and anomalies. One of the most important SPC tools is the *control chart*, which plots measured data over time and helps identify performance that is outside the normal range of operating conditions and therefore in need of investigation.[27]

quality control
Measuring quality against established standards after the good or service has been produced and weeding out any defective products.

quality assurance
A more comprehensive approach of companywide policies, practices, and procedures to ensure that every product meets quality standards.

statistical process control (SPC)
The use of random sampling and tools such as control charts to monitor the production process.

Six Sigma
A rigorous quality management program that strives to eliminate deviations between the actual and desired performance of a business system.

Six Sigma

Whereas *kaizen* is more of a general mindset and SPC is a set of analytical tools, **Six Sigma** is a comprehensive approach that encompasses a philosophy of striving toward perfection, a rigorous methodology for measuring and improving quality, and specific tools such as SPC to track progress.[28] (The term *six sigma* is used in statistics to indicate 3.4 defects per 1 million opportunities—near perfection, in other words.) Six Sigma is a highly disciplined, systematic approach to reducing the deviation from desired goals in virtually any business process, whether it's eliminating defects in the creation of a product or improving a company's cash flow.[29] Six Sigma efforts typically follow a five-step approach, known as DMAIC for short (see Exhibit 9.8).[30]

Many companies now marry the concepts of lean production and Six Sigma, seeking to reduce waste and defects simultaneously. And moving beyond operations, this hybrid approach of *Lean Six Sigma* is also being applied at a strategic level to help identify opportunities in the marketplace and align the resources needed to pursue them.[31]

ISO 9000

ISO 9000
A globally recognized family of standards for quality management systems.

Buyers and business partners often want reassurance that the companies they do business with take quality seriously and have practices and policies in place to ensure quality outputs. **ISO 9000** is a globally recognized family of standards for quality management systems, administered by the International Organization for Standardization (ISO). ISO 9000 is based on eight quality management principles, including customer focus, a systems approach to management, and fact-based decision making.[32]

Hundreds of thousands of organizations around the world have implemented ISO standards, making it a universally recognized indicator of compliance. Achieving ISO certification sends a reassuring signal to other companies that your internal processes meet these widely accepted standards, and many organizations now require that their supplies meet ISO standards. Even without the need to meet this requirement, ISO 9000 provides companies with a "tried and tested framework for taking a systematic approach to managing the organization's processes so that they consistently turn out products that satisfy customers' expectations."[33]

For the latest information on production systems, visit http://real-timeupdates .com/bia8 and click on Chapter 9.

EXHIBIT 9.8   The DMAIC Process in Six Sigma Quality Management

The five-step process of *define, measure, analyze, improve,* and *control* (DMAIC) is at the heart of Six Sigma quality management efforts. Notice how this is a specific implementation of the control cycle described on page 207.

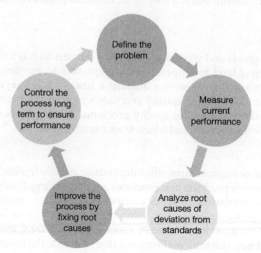

Source: Based on Kelly D. Sloan, "The Path to a Sustainable Playbook," *Industrial Engineer*, April 2011, 41–46.

✓ Checkpoint

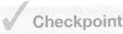

LEARNING OBJECTIVE 6: Define *quality*, explain the challenge of quality and product complexity, and identify four major tools and strategies for ensuring product quality.

SUMMARY: Quality is the degree to which a product or process meets reasonable or agreed-on expectations. As products become more complex, the challenges of defining what quality means, ensuring quality production or service performance, and ensuring quality once the product is out in the field all increase. Four major tools and strategies for ensuring product quality are (1) continuous process improvement, enabling employees to search for and correct quality problems; (2) statistical process control (SPC), the use of random sampling and tools such as control charts to monitor the production process; (3) Six Sigma, a rigorous quality management program that strives to eliminate deviations between the actual and desired performance of a business system; and (4) ISO 9000, a globally recognized family of standards for quality management systems.

CRITICAL THINKING: (1) How significant is the role of software in product quality today? (2) How can process simplicity contribute to quality?

IT'S YOUR BUSINESS: (1) Are the grades you get in your various classes an example of quality control or of quality assurance? Explain your answer. (2) Have you ever tried anything like the Six Sigma DMAIC process in your own life, even partially or informally?

KEY TERMS TO KNOW: quality, quality control, quality assurance, statistical process control (SPC), Six Sigma, ISO 9000

BEHIND THE SCENES
KIESEL'S PRODUCTION SYSTEM SATISFIES DEMANDING GUITARISTS

In 1946, Lowell Kiesel founded L. C. Kiesel to manufacture sound pickups for electric guitars, which were gaining popularity in jazz and blues. His timing couldn't have been better as the young company grew, when the new sound of rock and roll in the 1950s set off a tsunami of demand for amplified guitars. Along the way, the company branched out to building its own guitars and over the decades, made a name for itself among serious guitarists by filling the gap between mass-produced and fully custom guitars. (In 1949, the company changed its name to Carvin, but changed back to Kiesel in 2015. It continues to make guitars under both the Kiesel and Carvin brand names.)

The company's secret has been perfecting the art and science of *mass customization*, the ability to adapt standardized products to the tastes of individual customers. In four to six weeks, and for roughly $700 to $1,500, Kiesel can customize one of several dozen models of guitars and basses. All are available in a wide variety of woods, paints, stains, finishes, electronics, and even the slight curvature in the fingerboard; there are so many choices that online discussion boards buzz with debates about which combinations are best for specific styles of music.

Kiesel's factory combines old-world craftsmanship with new-world technologies. Because the custom guitars are built on a standard set of body shapes and styles, Kiesel can use computer-controlled cutting and milling machines that cut and shape the bodies and necks quickly and precisely. A diamond-surface finishing machine mills fingerboards to tolerances of a thousandth of an inch. A dehumidification chamber removes internal stresses from the wood used in the guitar necks to minimize the chance of warping years down the road. Experienced craftspeople with sensitive eyes and ears take over from there, performing such tasks as matching veneer pieces on guitar tops (veneers are thin sheets of wood, often exotic or expensive species), adjusting the action (the feel of the strings against the frets), and listening to the tone quality of finished instruments.

With this blend of automation and human touch, Kiesel produces thousands of instruments a year that win rave reviews from appreciative customers. "Nothing can touch it in terms of sound quality and workmanship" and "I haven't seen anything close to this price that can outperform it" are typical of the comments that Kiesel customers post online. Upon hearing a salesperson in another music store speak disparagingly of the brand, one indignant Kiesel owner retrieved his guitar from his car and put on an impromptu concert for the store's sales staff to demonstrate just how good the Kiesel product sounded. With a proven manufacturing approach and customer loyalty like that, Kiesel will be fulfilling the musical dreams of guitarists for years to come.[34]

Critical Thinking Questions

9-1. If Kiesel experienced an increase in orders from its website over a period of two weeks, should it expand its production capacity to make sure it can handle increased demand in the future? Why or why not?

9-2. Watch some of the video on Kiesel's YouTube channel at www.youtube.com/user/carvinguitars. How might this information help convince potential buyers to consider Kiesel or Carvin guitars?

9-3. Wooden musical instruments have been carved by hand for hundreds of years. Why wouldn't Kiesel want to continue this tradition?

LEARN MORE ONLINE

Visit the Kiesel website at www.carvinguitars.com (the URL may be changed by the time you read this as the company transitions its branding) and study how the company promotes its customized products. Pretend you're in the market and step through the process of customizing a guitar or bass. Would you feel comfortable purchasing a musical instrument in this manner? Review comments on www.facebook.com/kieselguitars. What are employees and customers talking about these days?

KEY TERMS

capacity planning
critical path
customized production
inventory
inventory control
ISO 9000
just-in-time
lean systems
mass customization
mass production
offshoring
outsourcing
procurement
production and operations management

productivity
quality
quality assurance
quality control
scalability
Six Sigma
statistical process control
supply chain
supply chain management
system
value chain
value webs

MyBizLab

To complete the problems with the ⭐, go to EOC Discussion Questions in the MyLab.

TEST YOUR KNOWLEDGE

Questions for Review

9-4. What role does feedback play in a system?

9-5. Why is offshoring controversial?

9-6. Define supply chain management.

9-7. What is a value chain?

9-8. What is scalability, in the context of managing a service business?

Questions for Analysis

9-9. Why is it important to monitor performance variables that are the most meaningful, not those that are the most easily measurable?

9-10. What are the challenges of delivering services as opposed to traditionally manufactured products?

9-11. How can supply chain management (SCM) help a company establish a competitive advantage?

9-12. Why is a good quality management system important to businesses?

⭐ **9-13. Ethical Considerations.** How does society's concern for the environment affect a company's decisions about facility location and layout?

Questions for Application

9-14. Business is booming. Sales last month were 50 percent higher than the month before, and so far, this month is looking even better than last month. Should you hire more people to accommodate the increase? Explain your answer.

⭐ **9-15.** If 30 percent of the patrons eating at your restaurant say they won't eat there again, what steps would you take to define the problem(s) that needs to be solved, measure the relevant performance variables, and then analyze the root cause of the problems(s)?

⭐ **9-16.** You've developed a reputation as an outstanding math tutor, and you want to turn your talent into a full-time business after graduation. How will you address the challenge of scalability in your new venture?

9-17. Concept Integration. How might supply chain management issues influence your decision on how to expand your vitamin and nutritional supplements company internationally?

EXPAND YOUR KNOWLEDGE

Discovering Career Opportunities

You stumbled on the website on careers in operations management http://www.careers-in-business.com/om.htm.

9-18. If you were offered an internship position at a local or international manufacturers or producers in the home country, would you consider it?

9-19. What is the career prospect in the production and operations management profession in your home country? You may consider the newspapers (print or online editions) to explore the trends or growth of the local and global production and operations management businesses in the domestic environment.

9-20. After reading the articles at Forbes http://www.forbes .com/sites/billconerly/2015/05/11/add-financial -modeling-to-your-operational-planning/ and http:// www.forbes.com/sites/freekvermeulen/2014/04/29/ the-two-questions-that-help-you-to-produce-both -cheaper-and-better/ what are the additional skills you should consider improving on before working in a production-related job?

Improving Your Tech Insights: Nanotechnology

Think small. Really small. Think about manufacturing products a molecule or even a single atom at a time. That's the scale of *nanotechnology*, a rather vague term that covers research and engineering done at nanoscale, or roughly 1/100,000 the width of a human hair.

The potential uses of nanotechnology range from the practical—smart materials that can change shape and heal themselves, more efficient energy generation and transmission, superstrong and superlight materials for airplanes, better cosmetics, smart medical implants, safer food containers, and ultrasmall computers—to the somewhat wilder: food-growing machines and microscopic robots that could travel throughout your body to cure diseases and fix injuries. (Like any new technology with lots of promise, nanotechnology also suffers from lots of hype.)

More than 1,000 nanotechnology-enabled products have hit the market in a number of industries, from automotive materials to medicine to consumer products. Also, although they're slightly larger than the generally accepted scale of nanotechnology, *microelectromechanical systems* (MEMS) are having a major impact in some industries. These tiny machines (pumps, valves, and so on), some no bigger than a grain of pollen, are used in the nozzles of ink-jet printers, air bag sensors, and ultraprecise miniature laboratory devices.[35]

Conduct research to identify a product currently on the market that uses nanotechnology in some fashion. In an email message to your instructor, describe the product, its target market, the role nanotechnology plays in the product's design, and any known safety concerns regarding the use of nanotechnology in this or similar products.

PRACTICE YOUR SKILLS

Sharpening Your Communication Skills

Communication is vital throughout a supply chain. Without clear communication, the supply chain would not be able to meet key targets or objectives. With this in mind, imagine you are working for a small firm that regularly supplies a large manufacturing company. In recent months, order levels from your customers have been erratic, resulting in employees working overtime significantly to fulfill orders. You feel that the problem lies in poor communication along the supply chain. In a short, one-page report to your line manager, outline potential areas for poor communication and give suggestions for improving communication along the supply chain.

Building Your Team Skills

In small teams, research the supply chain for a product of your choice. You should consider and discuss any areas where issues might occur. Make sure you also consider particular areas of strength along with scope for future development. In undertaking this task, ensure that you link your discussions as a group specifically to the product you have chosen. Prepare a short presentation for the benefit of the other groups, allowing time for questions and debate in the class.

Developing Your Research Skills

Seeking increased efficiency and productivity, growing numbers of producers of goods and services are applying technology to improve the production process. Find an article in a business journal or newspaper that discusses how one company used computer-aided design (CAD), computer-aided engineering (CAE), computer-integrated manufacturing (CIM), robots, or other technological innovations to refit or reorganize its production operations.

9-21. What problems led the company to rethink its production process? What kind of technology did it choose to address these problems? What goals did the company set for applying technology in this way?

9-22. Before adding the new technology, what did the company do to analyze its existing production process? What changes, if any, were made as a result of this analysis?

9-23. How did technology-enhanced production help the company achieve its goals for financial performance? For customer service? For growth or expansion?

MyBizLab®

Go to the Assignments section of your MyLab to complete these writing exercises.

9-24. How does the offshoring controversy reflect the larger question of balancing the competing demands of stakeholder groups?

9-25. Why might a service business be more selective than a goods-producing business regarding the customers it pursues or accepts?

ENDNOTES

1. Kiesel Carvin Guitars website, accessed 6 April 6, 2015, www.carvinguitars.com; Carvin Facebook page, accessed 6 April 6, 2015, www.facebook.com/Kieselguitars; Kiesel YouTube channel, accessed 6 April 6, 2015, www.youtube.com/user/carvinguitars; Max Mobley, "Builder Profile: Carvin," *PremierGuitar*, 9 August 2011, www.premierguitar.com; "Carvin AW175" (product reviews), Harmony Central website, accessed 18 March 2005, www.harmonycentral.com; "Carvin CT6M California Carved Top," *Guitar Player*, December 2004, www.guitarplayer.com; Rich Krechel, "Some Custom-Made Guitars Can Cost $4,000 to $8,000," *St. Louis Post Dispatch*, 27 September 2001, 16.

2. Based in part on Russell L. Ackoff, "Why Few Organizations Adopt Systems Thinking," Ackoff Center Weblog, 7 March 2007, http://ackoffcenter.blogs.com; Daniel Aronson, "Introduction to Systems Thinking," The Thinking Page website, accessed 21 June 2007, www.thinking.net; "What Is Systems Thinking?" The Systems Thinker website, accessed 21 June 2007, www.thesystemsthinker.com; Peter Senge, *The Fifth Discipline: The Art and Practice of the Learning Organization* (New York: Doubleday, 1994), 57–67.

3. Stephen P. Robbins and David A. DeCenzo, *Fundamentals of Management*, 4th ed. (Upper Saddle River, N.J.: Pearson Prentice Hall, 2004), 405.

4. Peter Fingar and Ronald Aronica, "Value Chain Optimization: The New Way of Competing," *Supply Chain Management Review*, September–October 2001, 82–85.

5. John Gillie, "Boeing Says Dreamliner Testing on Schedule for Third Quarter Delivery," *News Tribune* (Tacoma, Wash.), 25 February 2011, www.thenewstribune.com; Jeffrey Rothfeder, "Bumpy Ride," *Portfolio*, May 2009, www.portfolio.com.

6. Toni Waterman, "Big Name US Firms 'Reshoring' from China," *Channel NewsAsia*, 2 November 2013, www.channelnewsasia.com; Alan S. Brown, "A Shift in Engineering Offshore," *Mechanical Engineering*, March 2009, 24–29.

7. Lisa Harrington, "Is U.S. Manufacturing Coming Back?" *Inbound Logistics*, August 2011, www.inboundlogistics.com.

8. Katy George, "Next-Shoring: A CEO's Guide," *McKinsey Quarterly*, January 2014, www.mckinsey.com.

9. Bruce Constantine, Brian Ruwadi, and Josh Wine, "Management Practices That Drive Supply Chain Success," *McKinsey Quarterly*, no. 2 (2009): 24–26.

10. Tim Laseter and Keith Oliver, "When Will Supply Chain Management Grow Up?" *Strategy + Business*, Fall 2003, 32–36; Robert J. Trent, "What Everyone Needs to Know About SCM," *Supply Chain Management Review*, 1 March 2004, www.manufacturing.net.

11. Ayse Bayat, Sekar Sundararajan, H. Robert Gustafson Jr., and Emory W. Zimmers Jr., "Sustainably Driven Supply Chains," *Industrial Engineer*, August 2011, 26–31; "Sustainability Index," Walmart, accessed 26 August 2011, http://walmartstores.com.

12. Trent, "What Everyone Needs to Know About SCM."

13. Andrew Feller, Dan Shunk, and Tom Callarman, "Value Chains Versus Supply Chains," *BPTrends*, March 2006, www.bptrends.com.

14. Patty Cantrell, "Sysco's Journey from Supply Chain to Value Chain," The Wallace Center, August 2009, www.ngfn.org.

15. Lee J. Krajewski and Larry P. Ritzman, *Operations Management: Processes and Value Chains*, 7th ed. (Upper Saddle River, N.J.: Pearson Prentice Hall, 2005), 744.

16. Malcolm Wheatley and Kevin Parker, "Rise in Global Enterprise Deployments Seen as Response to Far-Flung Supply Networks," *Manufacturing Business Technology*, May 2007, 26–27.

17. Krajewski and Ritzman, *Operations Management: Processes and Value Chains*, 482–483.

18. Roberta A. Russell and Bernard W. Taylor III, *Operations Management: Focusing on Quality and Competitiveness*, 2d ed. (Upper Saddle River, N.J.: Prentice Hall, 1998), 511.

19. Krajewski and Ritzman, *Operations Management*, 299–300.

20. Russell and Taylor, *Operations Management*, 161.

21. Krajewski and Ritzman, *Operations Management*, 244–245.
22. Robert Kreitner, *Management*, 9th ed. (Boston: Houghton Mifflin, 2004), 202–203.
23. "Dell on Social Media,' Dell website, accessed 8 April 2015, www.dell.com; Malcolm Wheatley, "Learning from Failure," *Engineering & Technology*, 11 September–24 September 2010, 56–58.
24. Jeffrey K. Liker, "The Way Back for Toyota," *Industrial Engineer*, May 2010, 28–33; Wheatley, "Learning from Failure."
25. Mark Rechtin, "Toyota Gives Development Clout to N A ," *Automotive News*, 30 May 2011, 1, 23.
26. Russell and Taylor, *Operations Management*, 131.
27. Keith M. Bower, "Statistical Process Control," *ASQ*, accessed 27 August 2011, http://asq.org.
28. Donald W. Benbow and T. M. Kubiak, "Six Sigma," *ASQ*, accessed 27 August 2011, http://asq.org.
29. Steven Minter, "Six Sigma's Growing Pains," *IndustryWeek*, May 2009, 34–36; Tom McCarty, "Six Sigma at Motorola," *European CEO*, September–October 2004, www.motorola.com.
30. McCarty, "Six Sigma at Motorola"; General Electric, "What Is Six Sigma?" GE website, accessed 21 March 2005, www.ge.com.
31. George Byrne, Dave Lubowe, and Amy Blitz, "Driving Operational Innovation Using Lean Six Sigma," IBM, accessed 27 August 2011, www.ibm.com.
32. Quality Management Principles, *International Organization for Standardization*, 2012, www.iso.org.
33. "ISO 9000 Essentials," International Organization for Standardization website, accessed 27 August 2011, www.iso.org.
34. See note 1.
35. Project on Emerging Nanotechnologies website, accessed 11 April 2015, www.nanotechproject.org; National Nanotechnology Initiative website, accessed 11 April 2015, www.nano.gov; Barnaby J. Feder, "Technology: Bashful vs. Brash in the New Field of Nanotech," *New York Times*, 15 March 2004, www.nytimes.com; "Nanotechnology Basics," Nanotechnology Now website, accessed 16 April 2004, www.nanotech-now.com; Center for Responsible Nanotechnology website, accessed 16 April 2004, www.crnano.org; Gary Stix, "Little Big Science," *Scientific American*, 16 September 2001, www.sciam.com; Tim Harper, "Small Wonders," *Business 2.0*, July 2002, www.business2.com; Erick Schonfeld, "A Peek at IBM's Nanotech Research," *Business 2.0*, 5 December 2003, www.business2.com; David Pescovitz, "The Best New Technologies of 2003," *Business 2.0*, November 2003, 109–116.

Chapter 9
HRM

10 Employee Motivation

LEARNING OBJECTIVES   After studying this chapter, you will be able to

1. Define *motivation*, and identify the classical motivation theories.

2. Explain why many consider expectancy theory to be the best current explanation of employee motivation.

3. Identify the strengths and weaknesses of goal-setting theory.

4. Describe the *job characteristics model*, and explain how it helps predict motivation and performance.

5. Define *reinforcement theory*, and differentiate between positive and negative reinforcement.

6. List five managerial strategies that are vital to maintaining a motivated workforce.

BEHIND THE SCENES   TAKING A SECOND LOOK AT THE CAREER LADDER

Peter Dasilva/The New York Times/Redux

Having followed an unconventional career path herself, Cathy Benko helped redefine career options for Deloitte's employees.

www.deloitte.com

The notion of a business career being a straight vertical ascent from the bottom to the top is so embedded in our thinking that it has its own well-used metaphor: *climbing the corporate ladder.* The basic idea is that you join the workforce after college, you work hard for 30, 40, or 50 years, and you are rewarded along the way with positions of increasing responsibility and reward.

There's just one small problem with this whole ladder idea: It has never been true for millions of business professionals, and it often doesn't work out even for those who believe in the promise of continuous career progress. Simple arithmetic will tell you that the continuous climb simply can't work for most people—there just aren't enough high-level jobs, and the number shrinks dramatically with each step up the ladder. A major corporation with, say, 50,000 employees might have 100 executive positions from the vice president level up to the CEO. Even if only 10 percent of these employees (5,000) aspire to reach the upper levels, 4,900 of them aren't going to make it.

The numbers don't tell the whole story, either. Many employees have other priorities and demands in life, from raising families and dealing with health issues to continuing their education and exploring different career specialties along the way. In other words, millions of employees are unwilling or unable to maintain a straight climb up the ladder, and reward systems built on a steady climb aren't going to do much to motivate these people. As consultant Bruce Tulgan puts it, "Paying your dues, moving up slowly and getting the corner office—that's going away. In 10 years, it will be gone."

Cathy Benko is one of many executives who have been pondering this dilemma. As vice chairman and managing principal of Deloitte LLP, a diversified accounting, consulting, and financial advisory firm, Benko guides company strategy for attracting, developing, and motivating a highly skilled workforce. She realizes that the ladder metaphor has never quite fit many employees and that recent trends make it even less applicable to an ever-growing segment of the workforce. She knows the workplace needs to change to give employees a more satisfying, energizing, and motivating career path.

If you were Benko, what steps would you take to align the workplace with the changing workforce and make sure that every employee, on any career path, has a shot at success?[1]

INTRODUCTION

Deloitte's Cathy Benko (profiled in the chapter-opening Behind the Scenes) knows that a one-size-fits-all approach to managing and motivating employees has never been entirely satisfactory, and it is growing less effective every year as the workplace and the workforce continue to change. She could also tell you that although studying motivation is important, the task is challenging because no single theory or model can explain every motivational situation. The forces that affect motivation can vary widely from person to person and from situation to situation, and some managers and researchers continue to "rely on obsolete and discredited theories."[2] The various theories and models in this chapter each provide some insight into the complicated question of employee motivation, and taken as a whole, they provide an overall picture of the challenges and rewards of motivating employees to higher performance.

What Motivates Employees to Peak Performance?

1   LEARNING OBJECTIVE

Define *motivation*, and identify the classical motivation theories.

Motivating employees is one of the most important challenges every manager faces. No matter how skillful employees may be and how supportive the work environment is, without the motivation to excel, they won't perform at a high level. This section digs into the meaning of motivation and then explores some of the early attempts to provide practical models for motivating employees.

WHAT IS MOTIVATION?

Motivation is a complex subject that defies easy explanation, and some of the brightest minds in the field of management have been working for decades to understand this mysterious force. For one example, things that motivate you might have no effect on other people—or may even *demotivate* them. For another, some of the forces that motivate your behavior stem from deep within your subconscious mind, which means you might be driven by forces that you don't understand and can't even identify.

Starting with a basic definition, **motivation** is the combination of forces that drive individuals to take certain actions and avoid others in pursuit of individual objectives. Pay close attention to *drive* and *actions* in this definition; they are key to understanding motivation.

In a workplace setting, motivation can be assessed by measuring four indicators: *engagement, satisfaction, commitment,* and *rootedness* (see Exhibit 10.1 on the next page).[3] First, **engagement** reflects the degree of energy, enthusiasm, and effort each employee brings to his or her work. If you're "just not into it," chances are you won't perform at your best. Second, *satisfaction* indicates how happy employees are with the experience of work and the way they are treated. Third, *commitment* suggests the degree to which employees support the company and its mission. Fourth,

motivation
The combination of forces that move individuals to take certain actions and avoid other actions.

engagement
An employee's rational and emotional commitment to his or her work.

REAL-TIME UPDATES
Learn More by Reading This Article

Givers, takers, and matchers: How giving can be a source of motivation

Professor Adam Grant explains why being a giver rather than a taker can help your career and your motivation. Go to http://real-time updates.com/bia8 and click on Learn More in the Students section.

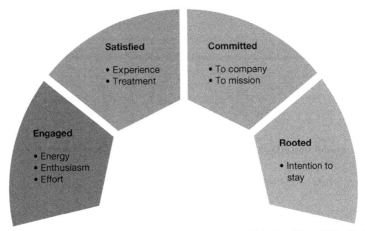

EXHIBIT 10.1   Four Indicators of Motivation

Employees can be said to be fully motivated when they are *engaged*, *satisfied*, *committed*, and *rooted* (meaning they have little or no intention to leave).

Satisfied
• Experience
• Treatment

Committed
• To company
• To mission

Engaged
• Energy
• Enthusiasm
• Effort

Rooted
• Intention to stay

Source: Based on Nitin Nohria, Boris Groysberg, and Linda-Eling Lee, "Employee Motivation: A Powerful New Model," *Harvard Business Review*, July–August 2008, 78–84.

rootedness (or its opposite, the intention to quit) predicts the likelihood that employees will stay or leave their jobs. A person who is engaged, satisfied, and committed and who has no intention of quitting can be safely said to be *motivated*.

These four indicators can identify who is motivated and who isn't, but they don't explain why. For that, it's necessary to dig deeper, looking into what drives people to choose certain actions and avoid others. Contemporary research suggests that motivation stems from four fundamental drives:[4]

- **The drive to acquire.** This includes fulfilling the need for not only physical goods such as food and clothing but also for enjoyable experiences and "psychological goods" such as prestige. Importantly, this drive is relative: Individuals want to know how well they're doing compared to others around them.
- **The drive to bond.** Humans are social creatures, and the need to feel a part of something larger is a vital aspect of employee motivation. This drive can be helpful, such as when it inspires employees to contribute to common goals, but it can also be harmful, such as when it pits groups of employees against one another in an "us-versus-them" mentality.
- **The drive to comprehend.** Learning, growing, meeting tough challenges, making sense of things—these are satisfying outcomes based on the drive to understand the world around us.
- **The drive to defend.** An instinct to protect and a sense of justice can lead human beings to vigorously defend the people, ideas, and organizations they hold dear. This drive is beneficial when it motivates people to fight for what is right, but it can be harmful as well, such as when it motivates people to resist change.

According to Harvard Business School's Nitin Nohria and his colleagues, who helped identify and explain these four drives, satisfying all four is essential to being motivated. When a need goes unsatisfied—or even worse, is betrayed, such as when employees believe an organization they've supported and defended no longer cares about them—poor motivation is the result.[5]

REAL-TIME UPDATES
Learn More by Watching This Presentation

Satisfying the four fundamental drives of employee behavior

Identify techniques that help satisfy the four fundamental drives in any workplace. Go to http://real-timeupdates.com/bia8 and click on Learn More in the Students section.

CLASSICAL THEORIES OF MOTIVATION

The quest to understand employee motivation has occupied researchers for more than a century. This section offers a brief overview of some of the important early theories that helped shape ideas about motivation. Although subsequent research has identified short-comings in all these theories, each contributed to our current understanding of motivation, and each continues to influence managerial practice.

Taylor's Scientific Management

One of the earliest motivational researchers, Frederick W. Taylor, a machinist and engineer from Philadelphia, studied employee efficiency and motivation in the late 19th and early 20th centuries. He is credited with developing **scientific management**, an approach that sought to improve employee efficiency through the scientific study of work. In addition to analyzing work and business processes in order to develop better methods, Taylor popularized financial incentives for good performance. His work truly revolutionized business and had a direct influence on the rise of the United States as a global industrial power in the first half of the 20th century.[6]

scientific management
A management approach designed to improve employees' efficiency by scientifically studying their work.

Although money proved to be a significant motivator for workers under scientific management, this approach didn't consider other motivational elements, such as opportunities for personal satisfaction. For instance, scientific management can't explain why a successful executive will take a hefty pay cut to serve in government or a nonprofit organization. Therefore, other researchers have looked beyond money to discover what else motivates people.

The Hawthorne Studies and the "Hawthorne Effect"

Between 1924 and 1932, a series of pioneering studies in employee motivation and productivity were conducted at the Hawthorne Works of the Western Electric Company in Chicago. The Hawthorne studies are intriguing both for what they uncovered and as an example of how management ideas can get oversimplified and misunderstood over the course of time. The research began as an experiment in scientific management: testing the effect of various levels of electric lighting on worker productivity. The researchers varied the lighting level for one group of workers (the experimental group) and kept it the same for a second group (the control group). Both groups were engaged in the tedious and exacting task of wrapping wire to make telephone coils, so lighting presumably played a key role in eye strain and other factors influencing productivity.[7]

Whatever the researchers expected to find, they surely didn't expect to see productivity increase in *both* groups as the lighting level was increased for the experimental group—and productivity kept increasing in both groups even when the lighting level was then lowered for the experimental group. In other words, no correlation between the level of lighting and the level of productivity was observed, and productivity increased among the control group workers even though their environment hadn't changed at all. This perplexing outcome was followed by a range of tests on other variables in the work environment and in employee rewards. The research team eventually concluded that group norms (see page 229) affected individual performance more than any other factor and that to understand employee performance one needed to understand an employee's total emotional and cultural makeup, on and off the job.[8]

By themselves, these conclusions are important, and the Hawthorne studies helped launch the entire field of industrial psychology and began to enlighten the practice of management in general.[9] Then a couple of decades later, a researcher not connected with the studies suggested the phenomenon of the **Hawthorne effect**, in which the behavior of the Western Electric workers changed because they were being observed and given special treatment as research subjects. In the years that followed, the concept of the Hawthorne effect took on a life of its own and became widely assumed across many fields of research, from management to medicine, even though the original research never reached this conclusion. Moreover, the phenomenon has come to be defined in so many ways that the use of the term could obscure more than it explains. The outcome of the Hawthorne studies has too often been reduced to this oversimplified and uncertain

Hawthorne effect
A supposed effect of organizational research, in which employees change their behavior because they are being studied and given special treatment.

conclusion about the behavior of research subjects; the real and lasting contribution of the studies was to open a lot of eyes about the benefits of understanding human behavior in organizational settings.[10]

Maslow's Hierarchy of Needs

In 1943, psychologist Abraham Maslow hypothesized that behavior is determined by a variety of needs, which he organized into categories arranged in a hierarchy. As Exhibit 10.2 shows, the most basic needs are at the bottom of this hierarchy, while the more advanced needs are toward the top. In **Maslow's hierarchy** all of the requirements for basic survival—food, clothing, shelter, and the like—fall into the category of *physiological needs*. These basic needs must be satisfied before the person can consider higher-level needs such as *safety needs*, *social needs* (the need to give and receive love and to feel a sense of belonging), and *esteem needs* (the need for a sense of self-worth and integrity).[11]

At the top of Maslow's hierarchy is *self-actualization*—the need to become everything one can be. This need is also the most difficult to fulfill—and even to identify in many cases. Employees who reach this point work not just because they want to make money or impress others but because they feel their work is worthwhile and satisfying in itself.

Maslow's hierarchy is a convenient and logical tool for classifying human needs, and many people continue to use it to explain behavior. However, other researchers have not been able to experimentally verify that this is how motivation actually works.[12]

Theory X and Theory Y

In the 1960s, psychologist Douglas McGregor proposed two radically different sets of assumptions that underlie most management thinking, which he classified as *Theory X* and *Theory Y*. According to McGregor, **Theory X**–oriented managers believe that employees dislike work and can be motivated only by the fear of losing their jobs or by *extrinsic rewards*—those given by other people, such as money and promotions. In contrast, **Theory Y**–oriented managers believe that employees like to work and can be motivated by working for goals that promote creativity or for causes they believe in. Consequently, Theory Y–oriented managers seek to motivate employees through *intrinsic rewards*—which employees essentially give to themselves.[13] As with Maslow's hierarchy, *Theory X* and *Theory Y* seem to have a permanent place in the management vocabulary, but they suffer from the same lack of empirical

Maslow's hierarchy
A model in which human needs are arranged in a hierarchy, with the most basic needs at the bottom and the more advanced needs toward the top.

Theory X
A managerial assumption that employees are irresponsible, are unambitious, and dislike work and that managers must use force, control, or threats to motivate them.

Theory Y
A managerial assumption that employees enjoy meaningful work, are naturally committed to certain goals, are capable of creativity, and seek out responsibility under the right conditions.

EXHIBIT 10.2   Maslow's Hierarchy of Needs

Abraham Maslow suggested that needs on the lower levels of the hierarchy must be satisfied before higher-level needs can be addressed (examples are shown to the right). This model offers a convenient way to categorize needs, but it lacks empirical validation.

Source: Based on Andrew J. DuBrin, *Applying Psychology: Individual & Organizational Effectiveness*, 6th ed. (Upper Saddle River, N.J.: Pearson Prentice Hall, 2004), 122–124.

evidence.[14] (However, the distinction between intrinsic and extrinsic rewards remains a valid and essential aspect of many theories of motivation.)

Herzberg's Two Factors

Also in the 1960s, Frederick Herzberg and his associates explored the aspects of jobs that make employees feel satisfied or dissatisfied. The researchers found that two entirely different sets of factors were associated with dissatisfying and satisfying work experiences. In **Herzberg's two-factor theory** (see Exhibit 10.3), so-called *hygiene factors* are associated with dissatisfying experiences, and *motivators* are associated with satisfying experiences. Hygiene factors are mostly extrinsic and include working conditions, company policies, pay, and job security. Motivators tend to be intrinsic and include achievement, recognition, responsibility, and other personally rewarding factors.[15] According to Herzberg's model, managers need to remove dissatisfying elements *and* add satisfying elements—doing one or the other is not enough.[16]

Like Maslow's hierarchy and Theory X/Theory Y, the two-factor theory seems logical and helps explain part of the motivation puzzle. However, it has been criticized because of the methodology used in the original research and the inability of subsequent research to validate the model. Also, although there is a strong causal link between customer satisfaction and profitability, it is far less clear whether satisfied *employees* automatically lead to satisfied *customers*.[17]

Herzberg's two-factor theory A model that divides motivational forces into satisfiers ("motivators") and dissatisfiers ("hygiene factors").

McClelland's Three Needs

The last of the classical theories to consider is the **three-needs theory** developed by David McClelland. McClelland's model highlights the *need for power* (having—and demonstrating—control over others), the *need for affiliation* (being accepted by others and having opportunities for social interaction), and the *need for achievement* (attaining personally meaningful goals).[18] Unlike with the other classical theories, there is a lot of research

three-needs theory David McClelland's model of motivation that highlights the needs for power, affiliation, and achievement.

EXHIBIT 10.3   Herzberg's Two-Factor Theory

According to Herzberg, *hygiene factors* such as working conditions and company policies can influence employee dissatisfaction. On the other hand, *motivators* such as opportunities for achievement and recognition can influence employee satisfaction.

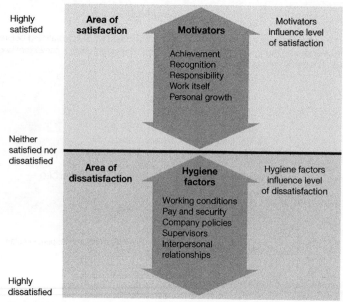

to validate McClelland's ideas and to explain particular outcomes in the workplace. For example, those with a high need for achievement tend to make successful entrepreneurs, but this focus on personal achievement can actually get in the way of managerial effectiveness, which relies on the ability to influence others toward shared goals.[19]

Conversely, managers who are most successful in a conventional organizational structure tend to have a higher need for power and relatively little need for affiliation. They are less concerned with achieving personal goals or being well liked than they are with building up the influence needed to get things done through other people.[20]

Although it helps explain motivation in various contexts, the biggest drawback to McClelland's approach is its limited practicality in terms of identifying needs and crafting motivational programs to harness them in beneficial directions. The three needs are subconscious, according to McClelland, and trained experts are required to help identify them in each individual.[21]

 Checkpoint

LEARNING OBJECTIVE 1: Define *motivation*, and identify the classical motivation theories.

SUMMARY: Motivation is the combination of forces that prompt individuals to take certain actions and avoid others in pursuit of individual objectives. Research suggests that four drives underlie all motivation: the drive to acquire tangible and intangible rewards, the drive to bond with others, the drive to comprehend, and the drive to defend. The classical motivation theories and research that helped shape today's thinking include Taylor's scientific management, the Hawthorne studies, Maslow's hierarchy of needs, McGregor's Theory X and Theory Y, Herzberg's two factors, and McClelland's three needs.

CRITICAL THINKING: (1) How could a manager tap into the drive to defend as a way to help rally employees? (2) Could Herzberg's hygiene factors help explain the significant problem of employee theft and embezzlement? Why or why not?

IT'S YOUR BUSINESS: (1) If you are a typical college student who doesn't have much financial security at the moment but is also trying to fulfill higher-order needs such as social interaction and self-actualization through your education, would it make more sense, according to Maslow, to drop out of college and work seven days a week so you could help ensure that your physiological and safety needs are met? (2) Do you think today's college students more closely match the descriptions of Theory X employees or Theory Y employees? What evidence can you provide to support your conclusion?

KEY TERMS TO KNOW: motivation, engagement, scientific management, Hawthorne effect, Maslow's hierarchy, Theory X, Theory Y, Herzberg's two-factor theory, three-needs theory

2 LEARNING OBJECTIVE

Explain why many consider expectancy theory to be the best current explanation of employee motivation.

expectancy theory
The idea that the effort employees put into their work depends on expectations about their own ability to perform, expectations about likely rewards, and the attractiveness of those rewards.

Explaining Employee Choices

The classical theories of motivation contributed in important ways to both managerial practices and the ongoing research into employee motivation, but each has been found wanting in some way or another. Starting with more contemporary theories, two models, known as expectancy theory and equity theory, help explain the choices that employees make.

EXPECTANCY THEORY

Expectancy theory, considered by some experts to offer the best available explanation of employee motivation, connects an employee's efforts to the outcome he or she expects from those efforts. Expectancy theory focuses less on the specific forces that motivate

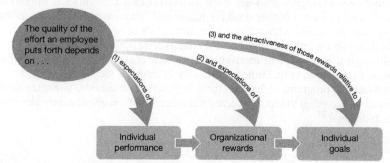

EXHIBIT 10.4   Expectancy Theory

Expectancy theory suggests that employees base their efforts on expectations of their own performance, expectations of rewards for that performance, and the value of those rewards.

The quality of the effort an employee puts forth depends on . . .

(1) expectations of

(2) and expectations of

(3) and the attractiveness of those rewards relative to

Individual performance → Organizational rewards → Individual goals

Source: Based on Stephen P. Robbins and David A. DeCenzo, *Fundamentals of Management,* 4th ed. (Upper Saddle River, N.J.: Pearson Prentice Hall, 2004), 289.

employees and more on the process they follow to seek satisfaction in their jobs. As shown in Exhibit 10.4, the effort employees will put forth depends on (1) their expectations regarding the level of performance they will be able to achieve, (2) their beliefs regarding the rewards that the organization will give in response to that performance, and (3) the attractiveness of those rewards relative to their individual goals.[22]

Exploring these connections from both an employee's and a manager's perspective will give you an idea of how the expectancy model can explain employee behavior and prescribe managerial tactics to help motivate employees. First, as an employee, if you don't believe that the amount of effort you are willing or able to apply to a task will result in an acceptable level of performance, a natural response will be to say, "Well, why bother?" This uncertainty could come from many sources, such as doubts about your skills, confusion about the task, or a belief that "the system" is so broken that no matter how hard you try you can't succeed. Belief in your ability to complete a task is known as *self-efficacy,* and it can be increased by gaining experience, mimicking successful role models, getting encouragement from others, and sometimes even "psyching yourself up."[23] As a manager, your challenges would be to ensure that employees have the skills and confidence they need, that tasks are clearly defined, and that company policies and processes are functional.

Your second concern as an employee is whether the organization will recognize and reward your performance. Knowing you've done great work is its own reward, of course, but for many employees, this isn't enough. As a manager, your challenges include establishing reward systems and expectations to minimize employee uncertainty and taking time from the daily chaos to acknowledge the efforts your employees make.

Finally, if you're confident in your performance and the organization's response, your third concern is whether the promised reward is something you value. What if you are offered a raise but what you really want is for your boss to acknowledge how important your contributions have been to the company? As a manager, aligning rewards with employee priorities is an ongoing challenge; see "Reinforcing High-Performance Behavior" on page 283.

EQUITY THEORY

If you work side by side with someone, doing the same job and giving the same amount of effort, only to learn that your colleague earns more money, will you be satisfied in your work and motivated to continue working hard? Chances are, you will perceive a state of *inequity,* and you probably won't be happy with the situation. **Equity theory** suggests that employee satisfaction depends on the perceived ratio of inputs to outputs. To remedy a

equity theory
The idea that employees base their level of satisfaction on the ratio of their inputs to the job to the outputs or rewards they receive from it.

perception of inequity, you might ask for a raise, decide not to work as hard, try to change perceptions of your efforts or their outcomes, or simply quit and find a new job. Any one of these steps has the potential to bring your perceived input-to-output ratio back into balance.[24] Some of the choices employees can make to address perceived inequity are obviously not desirable from an employer's point of view, so it's important to understand why employees might feel they aren't getting a fair shake.

Equity issues can show up in a number of areas, such as in complaints about gender pay fairness and executive compensation (see page 308) and in many unionizing efforts, whenever employees feel they aren't getting a fair share of corporate profits or are being asked to shoulder more than their fair share of hardships.

Research into equity theory has led to thinking about the broader concept of *organizational justice*, or perceptions of fairness in the workplace. These perceptions relate to outcomes, the processes used to generate those outcomes, and the way employees are treated during the process.[25] No reasonable employee expects to make as much as the CEO, for example, but as long as the process seems fair (both the employee's and the CEO's pay are related to performance, for example), most employees will be satisfied, and the disparity won't affect their motivation. In fact, perceptions of fairness can have as much impact on overall employee satisfaction as satisfaction with pay itself.[26]

 Checkpoint

LEARNING OBJECTIVE 2: Explain why many consider expectancy theory to be the best current explanation of employee motivation.

SUMMARY: Expectancy theory suggests that the effort employees put into their work depends on expectations about their own ability to perform, expectations about the rewards the organization will give in response to that performance, and the attractiveness of those rewards relative to their individual goals. This theory is thought to be a good model because it considers the links between effort and outcome. For instance, if employees think a link is "broken," such as having doubts that their efforts will yield acceptable performance or worries that they will perform well but no one will notice, they're likely to put less effort into their work.

CRITICAL THINKING: (1) What steps could managers take to alleviate the self-doubt employees often feel when they join a company or move into a new position? (2) If you were a human resources manager in a large corporation, how might you respond to employees who complain that the CEO makes two or three hundred times more than they make?

IT'S YOUR BUSINESS: (1) Have you ever given less than your best effort in a college course because you didn't believe you were capable of excelling in the course? (2) Was the outcome satisfying? Would you handle a similar situation the same way in the future?

KEY TERMS TO KNOW: expectancy theory, equity theory

---

 3 | **LEARNING OBJECTIVE**

Identify the strengths and weaknesses of goal-setting theory.

goal-setting theory
A motivational theory suggesting that setting goals can be an effective way to motivate employees.

Motivating with Challenging Goals

With the expectancy and equity theories offering some insight into why employees make the choices they do, the next step in understanding motivation is to explore specific leadership strategies that motivate employees. **Goal-setting theory**, the idea that carefully designed goals can motivate employees to higher performance, is one of the most important contemporary theories of motivation. It is both widely used and strongly supported by experimental research.[27] (However, as "Risks and Limitations of Goal-Setting Theory" on page 280 explains, some researchers assert that the benefits of goal setting have been overstated and the risks have been understated, partly because some research studies fail to measure the full consequences of goal-driven behaviors.)

For goals to function as effective motivators, a number of criteria must be met. These criteria include[28]

- Goals that are specific enough to give employees clarity and focus
- Goals that are difficult enough to inspire energetic and committed effort
- Clear "ownership" of goals so that accountability can be established
- Timely feedback that lets people know if they're progressing toward their goals and, if not, how to change course
- Individuals' belief in their ability to meet their goals
- Cultural support for the individual achievement and independence needed to reach the goals

As today's companies face the twin challenges of increasing global competition and a slow economy, goal setting could play an even more important role than it already does.

MANAGEMENT BY OBJECTIVES

Goal-setting theory is frequently implemented through a technique known as **management by objectives (MBO)**, a companywide process that empowers employees and involves them in goal setting and decision making. This process consists of four steps: setting goals, planning actions to meet those goals, implementing the plans, and reviewing performance (see Exhibit 10.5). Because employees at all levels are involved in all four steps, they learn more about company objectives and feel that they are an important part of the companywide team. Furthermore, they understand how their individual job functions contribute to the organization's long-term success.

management by objectives (MBO)
A motivational approach in which managers and employees work together to structure personal goals and objectives for every individual, department, and project to mesh with the organization's goals.

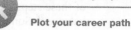

REAL-TIME UPDATES
Learn More by Exploring This Interactive Website

Plot your career path

See whether you've been on a straight path up the career ladder or have been moving around a career lattice. Go to http://real-time updates.com/bia8 and click on Learn More in the Students section.

EXHIBIT 10.5	Management by Objectives

The four steps of the MBO cycle are refined and repeated as managers and employees at all levels work toward establishing goals and objectives, thereby accomplishing the organization's strategic goals.

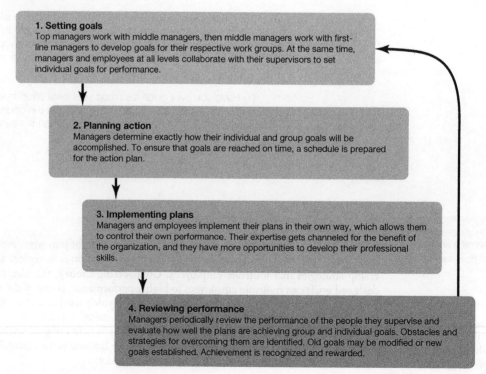

1. Setting goals
Top managers work with middle managers, then middle managers work with first-line managers to develop goals for their respective work groups. At the same time, managers and employees at all levels collaborate with their supervisors to set individual goals for performance.

2. Planning action
Managers determine exactly how their individual and group goals will be accomplished. To ensure that goals are reached on time, a schedule is prepared for the action plan.

3. Implementing plans
Managers and employees implement their plans in their own way, which allows them to control their own performance. Their expertise gets channeled for the benefit of the organization, and they have more opportunities to develop their professional skills.

4. Reviewing performance
Managers periodically review the performance of the people they supervise and evaluate how well the plans are achieving group and individual goals. Obstacles and strategies for overcoming them are identified. Old goals may be modified or new goals established. Achievement is recognized and rewarded.

One of the key elements of MBO is the collaborative goal-setting process. Together, a manager and an employee define the employee's goals, the responsibilities for achieving those goals, and the means of evaluating individual and group performance so that the employee's activities are directly linked to achieving the organization's long-term goals. Jointly setting clear and challenging but achievable goals can encourage employees to reach higher levels of performance, although participation alone is no guarantee of higher performance.[29]

RISKS AND LIMITATIONS OF GOAL-SETTING THEORY

As powerful as goal setting can be, it can misfire in a variety of ways, with results ranging from employee frustration to systematic underperformance to serious ethical and legal problems:[30]

- **Overly narrow goals.** When goals are too narrow, people can miss or intentionally ignore vital aspects of the bigger picture. Salespeople trying to meet their quotas, for example, might be tempted to offer huge discounts or extend credit to customers who can't make the payments.
- **Overly challenging goals.** Lofty goals can inspire great performance, but they can also lead to risky behavior, belligerent negotiating tactics, and ethical lapses as employees cut corners to reach targets.
- **Inappropriate time horizons.** Too much emphasis on short-term performance can degrade long-term performance. A good example is the unhealthy focus that a publicly traded company can place on quarterly performance in order to meet the stock market's expectations. This distorted focus can lead to decisions such as downsizing or cutting back on research that might help the bottom line in the short term but ultimately limit the company's ability to compete and grow.
- **Unintentional performance limitations.** Goals can limit performance potential when employees reach their targets and then stop trying, even though they could go beyond that level if reaching the goal didn't signal that it was acceptable to stop there.
- **Missed learning opportunities.** Employees can get so focused on meeting deadlines and other goals that they overlook opportunities to learn, whether to improve their own skills, fix process problems, or adapt to changes in the business environment—all of which could benefit the company more than meeting the original goal.[31]
- **Unhealthy internal competition.** Goals can pit groups within a company against each other, which can be beneficial if the competition is healthy but ultimately harmful if it is not. For example, healthy competitions among sales regions can be a great motivator, but what if several regions refuse to cooperate to help land a big national client?
- **Decreased intrinsic motivation.** Relying too heavily on exterior goals and their extrinsic rewards can eventually dull the intrinsic motivation to do well for the sake of the work itself—one of the most powerful and sustainable motivators.

As you ponder these limitations of goal-setting theory, you can start to sense how important it is to set goals carefully and only after considering the potential consequences.

 **Checkpoint**

LEARNING OBJECTIVE 3: Identify the strengths and weaknesses of goal-setting theory.

SUMMARY: Setting challenging goals has proven to be a dependable way to inspire employees to high levels of performance; goal setting is the foundation of a popular management system known as management by objectives (MBO). In addition to being widely used, goal-setting theory is strongly supported by experimental research. The weaknesses of goal setting generally lie in ways that the pursuit of goals can distort behavior. Potential problems include overly narrow or overly challenging goals, inappropriate time horizons, unintentional performance limitations, missed learning opportunities, unhealthy internal competition, and decreased intrinsic motivation.

CRITICAL THINKING: (1) Why is collaboration between employee and manager essential to goal setting in MBO? (2) How can overly narrow goals and overly challenging goals contribute to ethical lapses?

IT'S YOUR BUSINESS: (1) Do goals motivate you? Why or why not? (2) Does the motivation depend on whether the goals are your own or imposed by someone else?

KEY TERMS TO KNOW: goal-setting theory, management by objectives (MBO)

Redesigning Jobs to Stimulate Performance

4 | **LEARNING OBJECTIVE**

Describe the *job characteristics model*, and explain how it helps predict motivation and performance.

Along with setting challenging goals, many companies are exploring ways to redesign the work itself to improve employee satisfaction and motivation.

THE JOB CHARACTERISTICS MODEL

Using the **job characteristics model** proposed by Richard Hackman and Greg Oldman has proven to be a reliable way to predict the effects of five *core job dimensions* on employee motivation and other positive outcomes:[32]

job characteristics model
A model suggesting that five core job dimensions influence three critical psychological states that determine motivation, performance, and other outcomes.

- **Skill variety**—the range of skills and talents needed to accomplish the responsibilities associated with the job. The broader the range of skills required, the more meaningful the work is likely to be to the employee.
- **Task identity**—the degree to which the employee has responsibility for completing an entire task. Greater task identity contributes to the sense of meaning in work.
- **Task significance**—the employee's perception of the impact the job has on the lives of other people.
- **Autonomy**—the degree of independence the employee has in carrying out the job.
- **Feedback**—timely information that tells employees how well they're doing in their jobs.

You can see that some of these dimensions relate to the nature of the work itself and others relate more to management decisions and leadership styles. All of them contribute in one way or another to three *critical psychological states:*

- **Experienced meaningfulness of the work**—a measure of how much employees care about the jobs they are doing.
- **Experienced responsibility for results**—the sense each employee has that his or her efforts contribute to the outcome.
- **Knowledge of actual results**—employees' awareness of the real-life results of their efforts.

As these psychological states increase in intensity, they lead to improvements in motivation, performance, job satisfaction, absenteeism (the amount of time employees miss work), and turnover (the rate at which employees leave their jobs). In other words, if employees believe their work is meaningful, believe their individual efforts are responsible at least in large part for the outcome of that work, and can see evidence of the results of their efforts, they are likely to be more motivated than they would otherwise. It's not hard to see that the reverse is also true. Employees who believe their work is meaningless, who don't feel much responsibility for the outcome, or who never get to see the results of their efforts aren't likely to be terribly motivated or satisfied.

One final aspect of job characteristics research explores how various types of employees respond to changes in the

Companies can boost performance by designing jobs so that employees feel the meaning in their work and a sense of responsibility for results.

core job dimensions. Employees with strong *growth needs*, meaning they feel a strong need to increase self-esteem and self-actualization, respond more dramatically to improvements in job dimensions—and improvements in the critical psychological states will lead to greater increases in their motivation and the other positive outcomes.[33] Conversely, employees who feel little intrinsic need to grow can be among the most difficult to motivate, no matter what steps managers take.

The job characteristics model continues to offer helpful guidance as companies grapple with the challenges in today's work environment. For instance, as more companies increasingly rely on temporary workers to control costs or acquire skills that are needed only for specific projects, managers need to think carefully about the ways they supervise permanent versus temporary employees. As two examples, temporary workers may need to be assigned more discrete tasks that have enough task identity and autonomy to provide a sense of ownership and control, and managers need to make sure they don't take permanent employees for granted and fail to give them adequate feedback about their efforts.[34]

APPROACHES TO MODIFYING CORE JOB DIMENSIONS

The job characteristics model identifies the generic aspects of a job that can be adjusted to improve motivation, but it's up to individual companies and departments to identify and make the specific changes that are relevant to each job in the organization. Three popular approaches are job enrichment, job enlargement, and cross-training:

job enrichment
Making jobs more challenging and interesting by expanding the range of skills required.

- **Job enrichment.** The strategy behind **job enrichment** is to make jobs more challenging and interesting by expanding the range of skills required—typically by expanding upward, giving employees some of the responsibilities previously held by their managers.[35] For example, an employee who had been preparing presentations for his or her boss to give to customers could be asked to give the presentations as well. Job enrichment needs to be approached carefully, however. Some employees respond well, but for others, the increased responsibility is more a source of stress than of inspiration.[36]
- **Job enlargement.** Whereas job enrichment expands vertically, *job enlargement* is more of a horizontal expansion, adding tasks that aren't necessarily any more challenging. If it simply gives workers more to do, job enlargement won't do much to motivate and will more likely demotivate. However, if jobs are enlarged in ways that increase worker knowledge, expansion can improve job satisfaction.[37]

cross-training
Training workers to perform multiple jobs and rotating them through these various jobs to combat boredom or burnout.

- **Cross-training.** Job enrichment and job enlargement expand the scope of an individual job, whereas **cross-training**, or *job rotation*, involves training workers to perform multiple jobs and rotating them through these various jobs to combat boredom or burnout. Cross-training is also valuable in lean manufacturing (see page 254) because it lets companies keep staffs as small as possible and assign people wherever they are needed to handle fluctuations in workflow. And in a tight economy, cross-training helps companies address task needs without adding new staff.[38]

Not all the steps companies can take to improve motivation involve restructuring jobs, providing additional training, or making other explicit changes. Improvements can also come from making changes in management attitudes and practices, such as giving employees more control over their work and providing timely feedback. The best solution is usually a combination of changes that accommodate the nature of the work and the abilities and interests of individual employees and managers.

✓ Checkpoint

LEARNING OBJECTIVE 4: Describe the *job characteristics model*, and explain how it helps predict motivation and performance.

SUMMARY: The job characteristics model identifies five core job dimensions (skill variety, task identity, task significance, autonomy, and feedback) that create three critical psychological states (experienced meaningfulness of the work, experienced responsibility for results, and knowledge of actual results). Achieving these three states leads to improvements in motivation, job satisfaction, performance, absenteeism, and turnover.

CRITICAL THINKING: (1) Can the job characteristics model be used to motivate employees in such positions as janitors or security guards in a factory? How? (2) Is modifying the five core job dimensions likely to motivate employees who have low growth needs? Why or why not?

IT'S YOUR BUSINESS: (1) Has the requirement of working in teams ever lowered your motivation or satisfaction on a school project? If so, how does the job characteristics model explain this? (2) How does taking elective courses improve your experience of meaningfulness in your college "work"?

KEY TERMS TO KNOW: job characteristics model, job enrichment, cross-training

Reinforcing High-Performance Behavior

Challenging goals and creative job designs can motivate employees to higher levels of performance, but managers also need to make sure that performance can be sustained over time. Employees in the workplace, like people in all other aspects of life, tend to repeat behaviors that create positive outcomes for themselves and to avoid or abandon behaviors that bring negative outcomes. **Reinforcement theory** suggests that managers can motivate employees by shaping their actions through *behavior modification*. Using reinforcement theory, managers try to systematically encourage those actions considered beneficial to the company. Reinforcement is a valuable motivational tool, but it has broad application whenever managers want to shape employee behavior.

TYPES OF REINFORCEMENT

Reinforcement can be either *positive* or *negative*. In casual speech, the two terms are usually equated with praise for desirable behavior and criticism or punishment for undesirable behavior, respectively, but they have different and specific meanings in psychological terminology (see Exhibit 10.6). Both positive and negative reinforcement encourage behaviors to be repeated; the difference is in how they do it.

Positive reinforcement offers pleasant consequences for particular actions or behaviors, increasing the likelihood that the behaviors will be repeated. For example, even a simple but sincere "thank you" provides emotional reward and encourages employees

5 **LEARNING OBJECTIVE**

Define *reinforcement theory*, and differentiate between positive and negative reinforcement.

reinforcement theory
A motivational approach based on the idea that managers can motivate employees by influencing their behaviors with positive and negative reinforcement.

positive reinforcement
Encouraging desired behaviors by offering pleasant consequences for completing or repeating those behaviors.

EXHIBIT 10.6   **Reinforcement and Punishment**

The terminology of reinforcement theory can be confusing because the terms are used differently in everyday speech than in psychology. Three points will help you keep the terms straight in your mind. First, both positive and negative reinforcement encourage a behavior to be repeated—they *reinforce* it, in order words. The difference is in how they work. Second, punishment (not negative reinforcement) is the opposite of positive reinforcement. Third, positive reinforcement can encourage undesirable behaviors, so it isn't necessarily a good thing, despite the "positive" label.

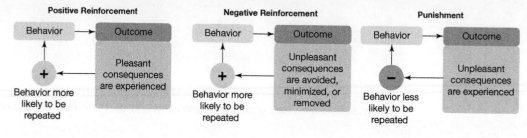

incentives
Monetary payments and other rewards of value used for positive reinforcement.

negative reinforcement
Encouraging the repetition of a particular behavior (desirable or not) by removing unpleasant consequences for the behavior.

to repeat whatever behavior elicited the praise.[39] Positive reinforcement can also have a multiplier effect, in which employees who receive positive reinforcement for one type of behavior are motivated to perform well in other areas, a process known as *chaining*.[40]

Many companies use some form of **incentives**, either monetary payments or other rewards of value, as positive reinforcement to motivate employees to achieve specific performance targets. Like praise and public recognition, incentive programs can become particularly important during economic slowdowns, when many employers can't afford to give big salary increases and companies aren't growing fast enough to create opportunities for career advancement.[41]

Again, don't be misled by the label "positive." Positive reinforcement can encourage bad behavior, so it isn't necessarily good. If an employee gets a compliment after taking credit for someone else's work, this positive feedback might encourage him or her to act unethically again the next time the opportunity arises.

Negative reinforcement also encourages a particular behavior to be repeated, but it does so through the reduction, removal, or absence of an unpleasant outcome. For example, if you initially received some complaints about publicly humiliating your employees after taking over as department manager, but those complaints dwindled over time as people gave up and accepted your poor behavior, their silence would encourage you to continue being a bully. Many people mistakenly use the term *negative reinforcement* when they are actually talking about *punishment*, which refers to actions used to diminish the repetition of unwanted behaviors by adding unpleasant outcomes.[42]

Of these three possibilities, you can see how positive reinforcement is the only one that injects positive energy into the situation. Fear can certainly be a powerful motivator, but it also adds stress and anxiety that can eventually lead to burnout and attrition as employees decide they don't want to deal with the constant pressure. And although punishment can be effective as a way to discourage particular behaviors, the effect isn't always permanent, and it can create serious morale problems.[43]

UNINTENDED CONSEQUENCES OF REINFORCEMENT

Reinforcement sounds like a simple enough concept, but the mechanisms of reinforcement can be subtle and the effects unexpected. Managers must be on constant alert for unintended consequences of incentives and other reinforcement efforts. For example, because they often focus on a single variable, incentive programs can distort performance by encouraging employees to focus on that variable to the detriment of other responsibilities.[44] If your salespeople get a bonus every time they land a new client but receive no penalties whenever an unhappy client leaves for a competitor, sales staffers will naturally tend to focus more on acquiring new clients than on making sure existing clients are satisfied.

Reinforcement doesn't have to involve explicit monetary incentives to distort behavior, either. For instance, imagine that a manager offers enthusiastic praise whenever employees suggest new ideas during meetings but never follows up to see whether those employees actually do any work to implement their great ideas. He or she can be encouraging empty "happy talk" through both positive reinforcement (there are pleasant consequences for spouting out ideas during meetings) *and* negative reinforcement (there are no unpleasant consequences for not doing any of the work, so employees will continue to not do it).

 Checkpoint

LEARNING OBJECTIVE 5: Define *reinforcement theory*, and differentiate between positive and negative reinforcement.

SUMMARY: Reinforcement theory suggests that managers can motivate employees by systematically encouraging actions that are beneficial to the company. Positive and negative reinforcement both tend to increase the specific behavior in question, but positive reinforcement does so by providing pleasant consequences for engaging in the behavior, whereas negative reinforcement does so by removing unpleasant consequences. The term *negative reinforcement* is sometimes used in casual speech when people are really talking about *punishment,* which is discouraging a particular behavior by offering unpleasant consequences for it.

CRITICAL THINKING: (1) Is demoting an employee for failing to finish a project an attempt at negative reinforcement or punishment? Why? (2) In what ways is reinforcement theory similar to goal-setting theory?

IT'S YOUR BUSINESS: (1) How does your instructor in this course use positive reinforcement to motivate students to higher levels of performance? (2) If you study diligently to avoid being embarrassed when a professor calls on you in class, is this positive or negative reinforcement in action? Why?

KEY TERMS TO KNOW: reinforcement theory, positive reinforcement, incentives, negative reinforcement

Motivational Strategies

Regardless of the specific motivational theories that a company chooses to implement in its management policies and reward systems, managers can improve their ability to motivate employees by providing timely and frequent feedback, personalizing motivational efforts, adapting to circumstances and special needs, tackling workplace problems before they have a chance to destroy morale, and being inspirational leaders.

6 | LEARNING OBJECTIVE

List five managerial strategies that are vital to maintaining a motivated workforce.

PROVIDING TIMELY AND FREQUENT FEEDBACK

Imagine how you'd feel if you worked for weeks on a complex project for one of your classes, turned it in on time, and then heard … nothing. As days passed with no feedback, doubts would begin to creep in. Was your work so good that your professor is passing it around to other faculty members in sheer astonishment? Was it so bad that your professor is still searching for the words to describe it? Was your project simply lost in the shuffle, and no one cares enough to find it?

No matter which theory of motivation an organization or a manager subscribes to, providing timely and frequent feedback is essential. From the perspective of reinforcement theory, for example, feedback is the mechanism that shapes employee behavior. Without it, opportunities for reinforcement will be missed, and the effort put forth by employees will eventually wane because they'll see little reason to continue.

Feedback "closes the loop" in two important ways: It give employees the information they need in order to assess their own performance and make improvements if necessary, and it serves the emotional purpose of reassuring employees that someone is paying attention. Even if the feedback is constructive criticism, it lets employees know that what they do is important enough to be done correctly.

MAKING IT PERSONAL

A recurring theme in just about every attempt to explain motivation is that motivation is a deeply personal phenomenon. Rewards and feedback that stimulate one employee to higher achievement can have no effect on a second employee and may demotivate a third. As you'll see in Behind the Scenes at the end of the chapter, customizing career paths is an essential aspect of how Cathy Benko and her colleagues at Deloitte help to personalize motivation and rewards.

In an ideal world, managers would be able to personalize motivational efforts completely, giving each employee

REAL-TIME UPDATES

Learn More by Exploring This Interactive Website

Quick summaries of key motivational concepts

These charts offer bite-sized wisdom about what works and what doesn't when it comes to employee motivation. Go to http://real-timeupdates.com/bia8 and click on Learn More in the Students section.

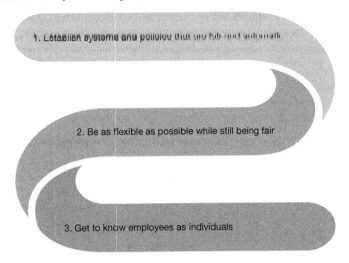

EXHIBIT 10.7   Personalizing Motivation

Gearing motivational efforts to the individual makes them more effective, but this approach must be conducted in a way that is fair for everyone. Achieving a balance is not always easy, because various employees are motivated by different things.

1. Establish systems and policies that are fair and automatic

2. Be as flexible as possible while still being fair

3. Get to know employees as individuals

the rewards and feedback that spur him or her to peak achievement. However, the need for fairness and the demands on a manager's time place practical limits on the degree to which motivational efforts can be individualized. The situation calls for a three-pronged approach (see Exhibit 10.7). First, establish systems and policies that are as equitable and as automatic as possible, and explain to employees why they are fair. Second, build in as much flexibility as you can, such as offering employees the cash equivalent of paid time off if they prefer money over time. Third, get to know employees as individuals in order to understand what is important to each person. For example, research suggests that younger employees are more likely to be demotivated by uninteresting work than their older counterparts.[45] (Another possible explanation is that older workers have learned to accept the fact that work can't always be exciting and are more willing to do whatever needs to be done.) If one person craves intellectual challenges, give him or her the tough problems to solve. If another thrives on recognition, give that employee the chance to give presentations to upper management.

Of course, managers need to give everyone an equal shot at opportunities, but as much as possible, they should let employees choose which opportunities and rewards they want to pursue. Employees understand that their managers can't always change "the system," but they do expect their managers to exercise some individual control over how policies are implemented and rewards are given.[46]

GAMIFYING FOR HEALTHY COMPETITION

gamification
Applying game principles such as scorekeeping to various business processes.

One of the newest motivational strategies is **gamification**, applying game principles to various business processes. Importantly, gamification isn't about "playing games" in a business context, but rather applying the motivational power of scorekeeping, competition, and other game-playing mechanics to existing business activities.[47] Companies are now gamifying processes ranging from sales and customer service to employee recruiting, training, and health and fitness. Encouraging participation in and contribution to social networks and other communities is a good example of how gamification can motivate employees and other stakeholders. Depending on the system, members can earn points, badges, and other rewards for anrs.[48]

ADAPTING TO CIRCUMSTANCES AND SPECIAL NEEDS

Just as the dynamics of motivation vary from person to person, they can vary from one situation to the next. For example, a slow economy and rising unemployment introduce a number of stresses into the workplace that need to be considered from a motivational perspective. Employers have less to spend on factors that can help avert employee dissatisfaction (salary, for example) or that can spur motivation (such as bonuses and other incentives). As a result, satisfaction and motivation are in danger of slipping, but employees have fewer options for finding new jobs if they aren't happy. The big exceptions are a company's top performers. When unemployment is rising and money is tight, high performers in any industry can often find new opportunities where average performers cannot. In other words, when companies are struggling, their best employees—the ones they need the most—are the ones most likely to leave. Consequently, managers need to work extra hard to keep these top performers happy and motivated.[49]

The threat of layoffs can motivate some employees but demoralize others. Some will work harder, in the hopes of minimizing their chances of being let go. Others, however, will wonder if there's any point in working hard if the economy is going to wipe out their jobs anyway. If layoffs are already starting to hit, survivors can be demoralized even further if they think the company is treating laid-off employees disrespectfully or unfairly.[50] Clearly, tough economic times put a huge motivational burden on managers, but those who treat employees with honesty and compassion stand the best chance of retaining the best people and keeping them motivated.

When the economy heats up again and unemployment drops, the balance of power shifts back toward workers. Employers who may have counted on job-loss fear as a motivator during the tough times will need to adjust strategies when employees have more options.[51]

ADDRESSING WORKPLACE NEGATIVITY

No workplace is immune to problems and conflicts, but negativity is an emotional "virus" that can infect an entire organization. Just as with physical health, in the workplace managers must address problems and conflicts quickly, before they multiply and erode employee morale. Left to fester long enough, these problems can destroy the sense of community in a company and leave employees feeling hopeless about the future.[52] Jumping on a problem quickly can have a double positive impact: It solves the problem, and it demonstrates to everyone that managers care about the emotional health of the workforce.

REAL-TIME UPDATES
Learn More by Reading This Article

Eight mistakes that demotivate employees

Leaders need to make sure these motivation poisons don't infect their workplaces. Go to http://real-timeupdates.com/bia8 and click on Learn More in the Students section.

BEING AN INSPIRING LEADER

Theories and systems aside, inspired motivation in a business enterprise requires inspired leadership. To a large degree, good employees come to work already motivated—that's part of what makes them good employees. One of your jobs as a manager is to make sure you don't *demotivate* them. For example, in one survey of U.S. workers, more than one-third of respondents said their supervisors' habits of **micromanaging**—overseeing every small detail of employees' work and refusing to give them freedom or autonomy—were destroying their initiative.[53] Managers with low emotional intelligence (see page 202) can create toxic work environments that demotivate even the most driven employees, so it is essential for managers to understand the effect that their behaviors and attitudes have on employees.

micromanaging
Overseeing every small detail of employees' work and refusing to give them freedom or autonomy.

MOTIVATING YOURSELF

This chapter has focused on systems that organizations can put in place and various steps managers can take to motivate employees. However, this emphasis shouldn't obscure the role and responsibility of employees themselves. Every employee has an ethical obligation to find the motivation to accomplish the tasks for which he or she is getting paid. Managers can foster motivation (and they can certainly diminish it through clumsy leadership), but the motivation has to originate from within each employee.

For the latest information on motivation, visit http://real-timeupdates.com/bia8 and click on Chapter 10.

 Checkpoint

LEARNING OBJECTIVE 6: List five managerial strategies that are vital to maintaining a motivated workforce.

SUMMARY: No matter which motivational theories a company chooses to implement in its management policies and reward systems, managers can motivate employees more effectively by (1) providing timely and frequent feedback, (2) personalizing motivational efforts as much as possible while still being fair to all employees, (3) adapting motivational tactics to circumstances and special needs, (4) addressing workplace negativity before it has a chance to destroy morale, and (5) being inspirational leaders.

CRITICAL THINKING: (1) Referring to the job characteristics model, how does micromanaging destroy motivation? (2) Annual performance reviews are common in many companies; how might they fail to motivate employees?

IT'S YOUR BUSINESS: (1) If you are motivated more by the love of learning than the promised rewards of a grade, how can you motivate yourself when grades play a key role in your success as others perceive it? (2) At work or in academic situations, how do you prevent someone else's negative attitude and behavior from dragging down your own performance?

KEY TERMS TO KNOW: gamification, micromanaging

BEHIND THE SCENES
MOTIVATING INDIVIDUALS BY PERSONALIZING CAREERS AT DELOITTE

As the chief talent officer for a company brimming with talent, Deloitte's Cathy Benko knows how challenging it can be to create stimulating environments and opportunities to motivate a diverse workforce. And having traveled an unconventional path herself ("lots of zigs and zags" is how she describes it), she knows that a relentless 30- or 40-year climb up the corporate ladder is not for everyone.

The conventional ladder concept has never been right for many employees, and it is less appealing to a growing portion of the population. Benko explains that in the time span of just two generations, society and the workforce have been transformed to such an extent that the old ways of work don't work anymore. In studying this lack of fit between workplace and workforce, Benko and her colleagues identified five key issues:

- **A looming talent shortage.** Talk of not enough people to fill jobs might be difficult to fathom in the aftermath of a deep recession and continuing high unemployment in some sectors of the economy, but the long-term trend is unmistakable. By 2025, the shortage of knowledge workers could be as high as 35 million people.

- **A vastly different society.** The corporate ladder—and with it the idea of devoting one's working life to a single company in order to climb one's way to the top—was conceived back in a time when two-thirds of U.S. households consisted of married couples in which one spouse (usually the husband) went to work and the other (usually the wife) stayed home. In a sense, this family structure helped support the corporate ladder by "freeing" the husband to devote himself to his company and career. Today, however, only about 15 percent of households fit that mold, and the old workplace ideals clearly don't fit them.

- **Expanded professional roles for women.** After years of gender imbalance in the workplace, women now hold more than half of all management jobs (although the ratio at the top of the ladder still leans heavily toward men). Plus, women now earn nearly 60 percent of bachelor's and master's degrees, so the presence of women in professional positions is only going to expand.

- **Different desires and expectations from men.** Growing numbers of men are ready to explore a more balanced life with more flexibility and personal time than the constant ladder climb typically offers.

- **A dramatic shift in generational attitudes.** To a large degree, the Baby Boom generation (those born between 1946 and 1964) defined itself by work, and the more of it the better, it seemed for many. However, the two generations that came after, Generation X and Generation Y, have different outlooks, with a much stronger desire to adapt their work to their lives rather than the other way around.

After pondering these tectonic shifts across the social landscape, Benko and Deloitte chose a new metaphor. Instead of a ladder, with its implication of a single path from bottom to top, they now speak in terms of a *lattice*, a crosshatch of horizontal and vertical lines. Just as a rosebush on a garden lattice can grow sideways and even downward for a while if upward isn't the best choice at the moment, a career lattice offers employees much the same flexibility.

Deloitte calls the model "mass career customization," and it mimics the idea of mass customized production described in Chapter 9 (page 256). Employees define where they've been, where they are, and where they'd like to go next, based on four variables: *pace* (from decelerated to accelerated), *workload* (reduced to full), *location/schedule* (restricted to not restricted), and *role* (individual contributor to leader). For example, to take time to have children or go back to college, a manager could

step into a nonmanagerial individual contributor role with a reduced workload and less travel. "Our goal is to offer people options to keep their work and personal lives in sync," Benko explains, "and to give employers the loyalty of their best and brightest people. It ends up being a perfect fit."[54]

Critical Thinking Questions

10-1. How might Deloitte's lattice approach help motivate employees and improve job satisfaction and performance?

10-2. How can managers determine whether a Deloitte employee is working at a decelerated pace in the career customization model or simply isn't working very hard?

10-3. What are the potential disadvantages, from the company's point of view, of giving employees this much flexibility?

LEARN MORE ONLINE

Visit the Corporate Lattice/Mass Career Customization website at **www.latticemcc.com**, which offers more information about the Deloitte lattice model. Read "Mass Career Customization at a Glance" and then try the "Interactive Career Exercise," where you can chart your own career (real or imaginary). You can also download two minibooks, *The Corporate Lattice* and *Mass Career Customization*. Does the lattice model sound appealing to you?

KEY TERMS

cross-training
engagement
equity theory
expectancy theory
gamification
goal-setting theory
Hawthorne effect
Herzberg's two-factor theory
incentives
job characteristics model
job enrichment

management by objectives
Maslow's hierarchy
micromanaging
motivation
negative reinforcement
positive reinforcement
reinforcement theory
scientific management
Theory X
Theory Y
three-needs theory

MyBizLab®
To complete the problems with the ★, go to EOC Discussion Questions in the MyLab

TEST YOUR KNOWLEDGE

Questions for Review

10-4. What is motivation?
10-5. What is scientific management?

10-6. What is management by objectives?
10-7. Research suggests that motivation stems from four fundamental drives. Describe them.
10-8. Explain the Hawthorne effect.

Questions for Analysis

10-9. Compare any two of the classical motivation theories. Are there any similarities?

10-10. How might a deadline that is too easy to meet cause someone to work more slowly than he or she might otherwise work?

⭐ **10-11.** What effect will job enhancement likely have on someone with low growth needs? Why?

10-12. Why do managers often find it difficult to motivate employees who remain after downsizing? Explain your answer in terms of one or more motivational theories discussed in the chapter.

10-13. Ethical Considerations. Motivational strategies that reward employees for meeting specific performance targets can encourage them to work hard—sometimes too hard. Overwork can contribute to mental and physical health problems as well as interfere with other aspects of employees' lives. As a manager, how do you determine how much work is too much for your employees?

Questions for Application

⭐ **10-14.** You manage the customer service department for an online clothing retailer. Customers tend to call or email with the same types of complaints and problems, day after day, and your employees are getting bored and listless. Some are starting to miss more days of work than usual, and several have quit recently. A few customers have called you directly to complain about poor treatment from your staff. Use the job characteristics model to identify several ways you could improve motivation, job satisfaction, and performance.

⭐ **10-15.** How do you motivate yourself when faced with school assignments or projects that are difficult or tedious? Do you ever try to relate these tasks to your overall career goals? Are you more motivated by doing your personal best or by outperforming other students?

10-16. Imagine yourself in one of the jobs you would like to land after graduation. Thinking about the importance of personalizing motivational tactics whenever possible, identify several steps your manager could take to make sure you stay motivated. Would these steps be fair to other employees as well?

10-17. Concept Integration. Chapter 7 discusses several styles of leadership, including autocratic, democratic, and laissez-faire. How do each of these styles relate to Theory X and Theory Y assumptions about workers?

EXPAND YOUR KNOWLEDGE

Discovering Career Opportunities

Working in a job role where you feel valued and motivated can make a huge difference in terms of satisfaction and productivity. What motivates one person may be very different from what motivates another. Make a list outlining the things you think motivates you at work. Explain each item on the list and then try to look for a job advertisement that meets as many of your motivators as possible. Would you be interested in this role? Why? Use examples.

Improving Your Tech Insights: Blogging and Microblogging

Blogging and microblogging (of which Twitter is the best-known example) have revolutionized business communication in recent years. Far more than just another communication medium, blogging and microblogging help change the relationship between companies and their stakeholders by transforming communication from the formal mindset of "we talk, you listen" to an informal and interactive conversational mindset.

Identify a company in which one or more managers are regular bloggers or Twitter users. In a brief email to your instructor, explain how the company uses blogging to build relationships with customers and potential customers, employees and potential employees, and other stakeholder groups.

PRACTICE YOUR SKILLS

Sharpening Your Communication Skills

For this task, you need to think carefully about what motivates you to attend your college or university and complete your course. In a blog post, explain what motivates you and how your motivations link to some of the theories discussed in this chapter. Use examples to illustrate your ideas.

Building Your Team Skills

With your teammates, explore the careers sections of the websites of six companies in different industries. Look for descriptions of the work environment, incentive plans, career paths, and other information about how the company develops, motivates, and supports its employees. After you've compiled notes about each company, vote on the most appealing company to work for. Next, review the notes for this company and identify all the theories of motivation described in this chapter that the company appears to be using, based on the information on its website.

Developing Your Research Skills

Various periodicals and websites feature "best companies to work for" lists. Locate one of these lists and find a company that

does a great job of attracting and motivating high performers. Learn as much as you can about the company's management philosophies. Which of the motivation theories does the company appear to be using? Summarize your findings in a brief email message to your instructor.

MyBizLab®

Go to the Assignments section of your MyLab to complete these writing exercises.

10-18. If a manager does nothing in response to a particular type of employee behavior that the company wants to encourage, is this an instance of reinforcement? Why or why not?

10-19. Do you have an ethical responsibility to motivate yourself at work, no matter the circumstances? Why or why not?

ENDNOTES

1. Cathy Benko profile, LinkedIn, accessed 12 April 2015, www.linkedin.com; Cathy Benko, "Up the Ladder? How Dated, How Linear," *New York Times*, 9 November 2008, www.deloitteandtouche.org; The Corporate Lattice/Mass Career Customization website, accessed 12 April 2015, www.latticemcc.com; Anne Fisher, "When Gen X Runs the Show," *Time*, 25 May 2009, 48–49; Lisa Takeuchi Cullen, "Flex Work Is Not the Answer," Work in Progress blog, 10 October 2007, http://workinprogress.blogs.time.com; Laura Fitzpatrick, "We're Getting Off the Ladder," *Time*, 5 May 2009, 45; "Customizing Your Career," Deloitte website, accessed 17 June 2009, http://careers.deloitte.com; "Mass Career Customization," PBWC Connections website, accessed 17 June 2009, http://www.pbwcconnections.com.

2. Piers Steel and Cornelius J. König, "Integrating Theories of Motivation," *Academy of Management Review*, 31, No. 4, 2006, 889–913.

3. Nitin Nohria, Boris Groysberg, and Linda-Eling Lee, "Employee Motivation: A Powerful New Model," *Harvard Business Review*, July–August 2008, 78–84.

4. Nohria, Groysberg, and Lee, "Employee Motivation."

5. Nohria, Groysberg, and Lee, "Employee Motivation."

6. Stephen P. Robbins and David A. DeCenzo, *Fundamentals of Management*, 4th ed. (Upper Saddle River, N.J.: Prentice-Hall, 2004), 27–29.

7. Augustine Brannigan and William Zwerman, "The Real 'Hawthorne Effect,'" *Society*, January/February 2001, 55–60; Stephen P. Robbins and Mary Coulter, *Management*, 10th ed. (Upper Saddle River, N.J.: Pearson Prentice Hall, 2009), 34.

8. Brannigan and Zwerman, "The Real 'Hawthorne Effect'"; Robbins and Coulter, *Management*, 34.

9. Frank Merrett, "Reflections on the Hawthorne Effect," *Educational Psychology*, February 2006, 143–146; Brannigan and Zwerman, "The Real 'Hawthorne Effect.'"

10. Mecca Chiesa and Sandy Hobbs, "Making Sense of Social Research: How Useful Is the Hawthorne Effect?" *European Journal of Social Psychology*, 38, 2008, 67–74; Brannigan and Zwerman, "The Real 'Hawthorne Effect'"; Robbins and Coulter, *Management*, 34.

11. Andrew J. DuBrin, *Applying Psychology: Individual & Organizational Effectiveness*, 6th ed. (Upper Saddle River, N.J.: Pearson Prentice Hall, 2004), 122–124.

12. Robbins and Coulter, *Management*, 342.

13. Richard L. Daft, *Management*, 6th ed. (Mason, Ohio: Thomson South-Western, 2003), 547; Robbins and DeCenzo, *Fundamentals of Management*, 283–284; DuBrin, *Applying Psychology: Individual & Organizational Effectiveness*, 15–16.

14. Stephen P. Robbins and Timothy A. Judge, *Essentials of Organizational Behavior*, 10th ed. (Upper Saddle River, N.J.: Pearson Prentice Hall, 2010), 64.

15. Daft, *Management*, 552–553.

16. Robbins and Judge, *Essentials of Organizational Behavior*, 66.

17. Rosa Chun and Gary Davies, "Employee Happiness Isn't Enough to Satisfy Customers," *Harvard Business Review*, April 2009, 19; Robbins and Judge, *Essentials of Organizational Behavior*, 66.

18. Saundra K. Ciccarelli and Glenn E. Meyer, *Psychology* (Upper Saddle River, N.J.: Prentice Hall, 2006), 339–340.

19. "Seeking to Hire Strong Leaders? Buyer Beware!" *Compensation & Benefits for Law Offices*, September 2006, 11+.

20. David C. McClelland and David H. Burnham, "Power Is the Great Motivator," *Harvard Business Review*, January 2003, 117–126; Robbins and Judge, *Essentials of Organizational Behavior*, 66–67.

21. Robbins and Judge, *Essentials of Organizational Behavior*, 67.

22. Robbins and DeCenzo, *Fundamentals of Management*, 289.

23. Robbins and Judge, *Essentials of Organizational Behavior*, 72.

24. Daft, *Management*, 554–555.

25. Robbins and Judge, *Essentials of Organizational Behavior*, 75.

26. Deborah Archambeault, Christopher M. Burgess, and Stan Davis, "Is Something Missing from Your Company's Satisfaction Package?" *CMA Management*, May 2009, 20–23.

27. Robbins and Coulter, *Management*, 346.

28. Bill Lycette and John Herniman, "New Goal-Setting Theory," *Industrial Management*, September 2008, 25–30; Robbins and Coulter, *Management*, 346–347.

29. Robbins and Coulter, *Management*, 346.

30. Lisa Ordóñez, Maurice Schweitzer, Adam Galinsky, and Max Bazerman, "Goals Gone Wild: The Systematic Side Effects of Overprescribing Goal Setting," *Academy of Management Perspectives*, February 2009, 6–16.

31. Robert D. Ramsey, "Why Deadlines and Quotas Don't Always Work," *Supervision*, October 2008, 3–5.

32. Richard J. Hackman and Greg R. Oldman, "Motivation Through the Design of Work: Test of a Theory," *Organizational Behavior & Human Performance*, August 1976, 250–279; Robbins and Judge, *Essentials of Organizational Behavior*, 81–82; Jed DeVaro, Robert Li, and Dana Brookshire, "Analysing the Job Characteristics Model: New Support from a Cross-Section of Establishments," *International Journal of Human Resource Management*, June 2007, 986–1003.

33. Robbins and Judge, *Essentials of Organizational Behavior*, 82.

34. Stuart D. Galup, Gary Klein, and James J. Jiang, "The Impacts of Job Characteristics on IS Employee Satisfaction: A Comparison Between Permanent and Temporary Employees," *Journal of Computer Information Systems*, Summer 2008, 58–68.

35. Robbins and Coulter, *Management*, 348.

36. Scott Lazenby, "How to Motivate Employees: What Research Is Telling Us," *Public Management*, September 2008, 22–25.

37. Robbins and Coulter, *Management*, 348.

38. "Caution Urged in Expanding Cross-Training of CU Staff," *Credit Union Journal*, 5 January 2009, 18.

39. Debi O'Donovan, "Motivation Is Key in a Crisis and Words Can Be the Best Reward," *Employee Benefits*, April 2009, 5.

40. Timothy R. Hinkin and Chester A. Schriesheim, "Performance Incentives for Tough Times," *Harvard Business Review*, March 2009, 26.

41. Tom Washington, "Incentives Play Big Part in Motivation During Recession," *Employee Benefits*, April 2009, 14.

42. Ciccarelli and Meyer, *Psychology*, 179.

43. Robbins and Coulter, *Management*, 348.

44. Dan Heath and Chip Heath, "The Curse of Incentives," *Fast Company*, February 2009, 48–49.

45. "Tailor Motivation Techniques to the Worker," *Teller Vision*, March 2009, 5–6.

46. Nohria, Groysberg, and Lee, "Employee Motivation: A Powerful New Model."

47. "What Is Gamification?" Bunchball, accessed 12 April 2015, www.bunchball.com

48. Robert Stanley, "Top 25 Best Examples of Gamification in Business," Clickipedia, 24 March 2014, http://blogs.clicksoftware.com; Brian Burke, "The Gamification of Business," *Forbes*, 21 January 2013, www.forbes.com.

49. Edward E. Lawler III, "Value-Based Motivation," *BusinessWeek*, 27 April 2009, 22.

50. Joan Lloyd, "Threat of Layoffs Demoralizes Employees," *Receivables Report for America's Health Care Financial Managers*, May 2009, 10–11.

51. Lawler, "Value-Based Motivation."

52. Betty MacLaughlin Frandsen, "Overcoming Workplace Negativity," *Long-Term Living: For the Continuing Care Professional*, March 2009, 26–27.

53. "Don't Be a Drag," *CA Magazine*, January–February 2009, 9.

54. See Note 1.

Human Resources Management

11

LEARNING OBJECTIVES   After studying this chapter, you will be able to

1 Identify four contemporary staffing challenges, and explain the process of planning for a company's staffing needs.

2 Discuss the challenges and advantages of a diverse workforce, and identify five major dimensions of workforce diversity.

3 Describe the three phases involved in managing the employment life cycle.

4 Explain the steps used to develop and evaluate employees.

5 Describe the major elements of employee compensation.

6 Identify the most significant categories of employee benefits and services.

BEHIND THE SCENES AN UNCONVENTIONAL APPROACH TO FINDING UNCONVENTIONAL EMPLOYEES

Zappos CEO Tony Hsieh makes sure the company's interviewing process finds the candidates who are compatible with an offbeat customer- and colleague-focused culture.

David Becker/UPI/Newscom

www.zappos.com

When a company communicates its core values with the help of a cartoon amphibian named Core Values Frog, you can guess the company doesn't quite fit the stuffy corporate stereotype. While it is passionately serious about customer satisfaction and employee engagement, the Las Vegas–based online shoe and clothing retailer Zappos doesn't take itself too seriously. In fact, one of the 10 values the frog promotes is "Create fun and a little weirdness."

Fun and a little weirdness can make a workplace more enjoyable, but CEO Tony Hsieh's commitment to employees runs much deeper than that. The company makes frequent reference to "the Zappos Family," and it embraces the ideals of taking care of one another and enjoying time spent together. These activities can range from parades in the workplace and other goofy events to the Wishez program, in which employees can ask one another to fulfill personal wishes, from lighthearted desires such as getting backstage access at concerts to serious matters such as getting help during tough financial times.

Corporate recruiting processes, particularly in this age of *applicant tracking systems*, are often obsessed with facts and figures—of applying standardized templates in an effort find the "ideal" employee. With a focus on measurable line items on a résumé and a risk-averse mindset, these automated systems and the recruiters who rely on them can overlook curiosity, passion, commitment, and other attributes that *really* define a successful employee.

If you were Hsieh, how would you make sure Zappos attracts the kind of employees who can contribute to and excel in the company's unique culture? Would you follow the same strategies that most companies use, or would you carve your own path—even if that means inventing an entirely new way of recruiting employees?[1]

INTRODUCTION

Zappos' Tony Hsieh (profiled in the chapter-opening Behind the Scenes) knows that hiring the right people to help a company reach its goals and then overseeing their training and development, motivation, evaluation, and compensation are critical to a company's success. This chapter explores the many steps companies take to build productive workforces, including solving staffing challenges, addressing workforce diversity, managing the employment life cycle, developing employees, and providing compensation and benefits.

Keeping Pace with Today's Workforce

Identify four contemporary staffing challenges, and explain the process of planning for a company's staffing needs.

human resources (HR) management
The specialized function of planning how to obtain employees, oversee their training, evaluate them, and compensate them.

The field of **human resources (HR) management** encompasses all the tasks involved in attracting, developing, and supporting an organization's staff, as well as maintaining a safe working environment that meets legal requirements and ethical expectations.[2] You may not pursue a career in HR specifically, but understanding the challenges and responsibilities of the HR function will improve your success as a manager.

CONTEMPORARY STAFFING CHALLENGES

Managers in every organization face an ongoing array of staffing challenges, including aligning the workforce with organizational needs, fostering employee loyalty, adjusting workloads and monitoring for employee burnout, and helping employees balance their work and personal lives:

- **Aligning the workforce.** Matching the right employees to the right jobs at the right time is a constant challenge. Externally, changes in market needs, moves by competition, advances in technology, and new regulations can all affect the ideal size and composition of the workforce. Internally, shifts in strategy, technological changes, and growing or declining product sales can force managers to realign their workforces.
- **Fostering employee loyalty.** Most companies can't guarantee long-term employment, but they want employees to commit themselves to the company. With the increasing number of temporary employees and independent contractors, this challenge will continue to grow.
- **Monitoring workloads and avoiding employee burnout.** As companies try to beat competitors and keep workforce costs to a minimum, managers need to be on guard for *employee burnout*, a state of physical and emotional exhaustion that can result from constant exposure to stress over a long period of time. One of the downsides of nonstop electronic connectivity is that many employees struggle to separate work life from personal life, which can create a feeling that work never ends.

work–life balance
Efforts to help employees balance the competing demands of their personal and professional lives.

quality of work life (QWL)
An overall environment that results from job and work conditions.

- **Managing work–life balance.** The concern over workloads is one of the factors behind the growing interest in **work–life balance**, the idea that employees, managers, and entrepreneurs need to balance the competing demands of their professional and personal lives. Many companies are trying to make it easier for employees to juggle multiple responsibilities with on-site day-care facilities, flexible work schedules, and other options designed to improve **quality of work life (QWL)**. Companies such as Zappos also take steps to make the workplace as enjoyable as possible as a way to minimize stress and relieve the monotony of repetitive business tasks.

PLANNING FOR A COMPANY'S STAFFING NEEDS

Planning for staffing needs is a delicate balancing act. Hire too few employees, and you can't keep pace with the competition or satisfy customers. Hire too many, and you raise fixed costs above a level that revenues can sustain. To avoid either problem, HR managers work carefully to evaluate the requirements of every job in the company and to forecast the supply and demand for all types of talent (see Exhibit 11.1). Many companies now rely on **workforce analytics**, a computer-based statistical approach to analyzing and planning for workforce needs.

Evaluating Job Requirements

Through the process of *job analysis*, employers try to identify the nature and demands of each position within the firm as well as the optimal employee profile to fill each position.[3] Once job analysis has been completed, the HR staff develops a **job description**, a formal statement summarizing the tasks involved in the job and the conditions under which the employee will work. In most cases, the staff will also develop a **job specification**, which identifies the type of personnel a job requires, including the skills, education, experience, and personal attributes that candidates need to possess[4] (see Exhibit 11.2 on the next page).

Forecasting Supply and Demand

To forecast demand for the numbers and types of employees who will be needed at various times, HR managers weigh (1) forecasted sales revenues; (2) the expected **turnover rate**, the percentage of the workforce that leaves every year; (3) the current workforce's skill level, relative to the company's future needs; (4) impending strategic decisions; (5) changes in technology or other business factors that could affect the number and type of workers needed; and (6) the company's current and projected financial status.[5]

In addition to overall workforce levels, every company has a number of employees and managers who are considered so critical to the company's ongoing operations that HR managers work with top executives to identify potential replacements in the event of the loss of any of these people, a process known as **succession planning**.[6] A *replacement chart* identifies these key employees and lists potential replacements.

With some idea of future workforce demands, the HR staff then tries to estimate the *supply* of available employees. To ensure a steady supply of experienced employees for new opportunities and to maintain existing operations, successful companies focus heavily on **employee retention**.

If existing employees cannot be tapped for new positions, the HR team looks outside the company for people to join as either permanent employees or **contingent employees** who fulfill many of the responsibilities of regular employees but on a temporary basis. Roughly a third of the U.S. workers fall in this broad category of contractors and freelancers, and all signs are that this portion will continue to grow.[7]

workforce analytics
Computer-based statistical approach to analyzing and planning for workforce needs.

job description
A statement of the tasks involved in a given job and the conditions under which the holder of a job will work.

job specification
A statement describing the kind of person who would be best for a given job—including the skills, education, and previous experience that the job requires.

turnover rate
The percentage of the workforce that leaves every year.

succession planning
Workforce planning efforts that identify possible replacements for specific employees, usually senior executives.

employee retention
Efforts to keep current employees.

contingent employees
Nonpermanent employees, including temporary workers, independent contractors, and full-time employees hired on a probationary basis.

EXHIBIT 11.1   Steps in Human Resources Planning

Careful attention to each phase of this sequence helps ensure that a company will have the right mix of talent and experience to meets its business goals.

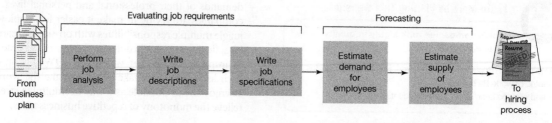

EXHIBIT 11.2   Job Description and Specification

A well-written job description and specification tells potential applicants what to expect from the job and what employers will expect from them.

Job Title
Director of E-Marketing

Location
Denver, CO

Reports to
Vice President of Marketing

Job Detail
Soccer Scope is a leading retailer of soccer equipment, apparel, and accessories based in Denver, Colorado, with retail locations in 23 states. We seek to expand our online presence under the guidance of a director of e-marketing, a new managerial position to be based in our Denver headquarters. The candidate who fills this position will be responsible for all nonstore aspects of our retailing efforts, including Soccer Scope's primary U.S. website and our country and region websites around the world, search-related advertising strategies, search engine optimization strategies, social media strategy and campaigns, email marketing campaigns, clicks-and-bricks integration strategy, affiliate marketing campaigns, customer retention efforts, and all aspects of online marketing research. The director of e-marketing will also work closely with the director of information technology to ensure the successful deployment of e-marketing platforms and with the director of retail operations to ensure a smooth clicks-and-bricks integration of offline and online retailing operations.

In addition to developing e-marketing strategies and directing e-marketing operations, the director is also responsible for leading a team of marketing and technical specialists who will implement and manage various programs.

Responsibilities
- Develop e-marketing strategies and plans consistent with Soccer Scope's overall business strategy and brand imperatives
- Integrate all outbound and inbound media streams to ensure seamless customer contact
- Establish and achieve aggressive customer acquisition and retention goals
- Coordinate efforts with technology and retailing counterparts to ensure successfully integrated online and offline marketing operations
- Assemble, lead, and develop an effective team of e-marketing professionals

Skills and Experience
- BA or BS in business, advertising, marketing, or related discipline required; MBA preferred
- Minimum 8 years of marketing experience, with at least 3 years in e-commerce and social media
- Current and thorough understanding of e-marketing strategies
- Demonstrated proficiency in developing and executing marketing strategies
- Excellent communication skills in all media

ALTERNATIVE WORK ARRANGEMENTS

To meet today's staffing and demographic challenges, many companies are adopting alternative work arrangements to better accommodate the needs of employees—and to reduce costs in many cases. Four of the most popular arrangements are flextime, telecommuting, job sharing, and flexible career paths:

- *Flextime* is a scheduling system that allows employees to choose their own hours, within certain limits. Of course, the feasibility of flextime differs from industry to industry and from position to position within individual companies.
- *Telecommuting*—working from home or another location using electronic communications to stay in touch with colleagues, suppliers, and customers—helps employees balance their professional and personal commitments because they can spend less time in transit between home and work. Telecommuting also plays an important role in efforts to reduce energy use, traffic, and mass transit overload. Telecommuting isn't appropriate for every job, and not every executive believes it is a workable solution, however. Yahoo! and HP, for example, severely curtailed their telecommunicating programs in order to foster better collaboration among workers (and, in Yahoo!'s case, reportedly, to monitor workers more closely).[8]

- *Job sharing*, which lets two employees share a single full-time job and split the salary and benefits, can be an attractive alternative for people who want part-time hours in situations normally reserved for full-time employees.
- Perhaps the most challenging of all alternative work arrangements are situations in which employees want to limit their work time or leave the workforce entirely for an extended period to raise children, attend school, volunteer, or pursue other personal interests. Programs such as Deloitte's mass career customization (see page 288) give employees more freedom in designing their own career paths.

✓ Checkpoint

LEARNING OBJECTIVE 1: Identify four contemporary staffing challenges, and explain the process of planning for a company's staffing needs.

SUMMARY: Four challenges that every HR department wrestles with are aligning the workforce with changing job requirements, fostering employee loyalty, monitoring workloads and avoiding employee burnout, and managing work–life balance. The process of planning for a company's staffing needs includes evaluating job requirements to develop *job descriptions* and *job specifications* and then forecasting the supply of and demand for various types of talent to ensure that the company has the right people in the right positions.

CRITICAL THINKING: (1) How can alternative work arrangements help companies reduce costs and their impact on the environment? (2) How can electronic communication technologies contribute to employee burnout?

IT'S YOUR BUSINESS: (1) Would you prefer to work as an independent contractor or as a permanent employee? What do you see as the advantages and disadvantages of each mode of work? (2) Would you function well as a full-time telecommuter? Why or why not?

KEY TERMS TO KNOW: human resources (HR) management, work–life balance, quality of work life (QWL), workforce analytics, job description, job specification, turnover rate, succession planning, employee retention, contingent employees

Managing a Diverse Workforce

2 LEARNING OBJECTIVE

Discuss the challenges and advantages of a diverse workforce, and identify five major dimensions of workforce diversity.

The companies that are most successful at managing and motivating their employees take great care to understand the diversity of their workforces and establish programs and policies that embrace that diversity and take full advantage of diversity's benefits.

DIMENSIONS OF WORKFORCE DIVERSITY

Although the concept is often framed in terms of ethnic background, a broader and more useful definition of *diversity* includes "all the characteristics and experiences that define each of us as individuals."[9] As one example, the pharmaceutical company Merck identifies 19 separate dimensions in its discussions of workforce diversity, including race, age, military experience, parental status, marital status, and thinking style.[10] Over the past few decades, many innovative companies have changed the way they approach workforce diversity, from seeing it as a legal matter to seeing it as a strategic opportunity to connect with customers and take advantage of the broadest possible pool of talent.[11] Smart business leaders such as Ron Glover, IBM's vice president of global workforce diversity, recognize the competitive advantages of a diverse workforce that offers a broader spectrum of viewpoints and ideas, helps companies understand and identify with diverse markets, and enables companies to benefit from a wider range of employee talents. According to Glover, more-diverse teams tend to be more innovative in the long term than more-homogeneous teams.[12]

Differences enrich the workplace but can create managerial challenges. A diverse workforce brings with it a wide range of skills, traditions, backgrounds, experiences, outlooks, and attitudes toward work—all of which can affect employee behavior on the job. Supervisors face the challenge of communicating with these diverse employees, motivating them, and fostering cooperation and harmony among them. Teams face the challenge of working together closely, and companies are challenged to coexist peacefully with business partners and with the community as a whole. Some of the most important diversity issues today include age, gender, race and ethnicity, religion, and ability.

Age

In U.S. culture, youth is often associated with strength, energy, possibilities, and freedom. In contrast, age is often associated with declining powers and a loss of respect and authority. However, older workers can offer broader experience, the benefits of important business relationships nurtured over many years, and high degrees of "practical intelligence," the ability to solve complex, poorly defined problems.[13]

In contrast, in cultures that value age and seniority, longevity earns respect and increasing power and freedom. For instance, in many Asian societies, the oldest employees hold the most powerful jobs, the most impressive titles, and the greatest degrees of freedom and decision-making authority. If a younger employee disagrees with one of these senior executives, the discussion is never conducted in public. The notion of "saving face"—that is, avoiding public embarrassment—is too strong. Instead, if a senior person seems to be in error about something, other employees will find a quiet, private way to communicate whatever information they feel is necessary.[14]

In addition to cultural values associated with various life stages, the multiple generations within a culture present another dimension of diversity (see Exhibit 11.3). Each of these generations has been shaped by dramatically different world events and social trends, and people's priorities often shift as they grow older, so it is not surprising that they often have different values, expectations, and communication habits.

Gender

Perceptions, roles, and treatment of men and women in the workplace has been a complex and at times contentious issue. The Equal Pay Act of 1963 mandated equal pay for comparable work, and the Civil Rights Act of 1964 made it illegal for employers to practice **sexism**, or discrimination on the basis of gender. The United States has made important strides toward gender equity since then, but significant issues remain. For example, the Equal Employment Opportunity Commission (EEOC) fields 25,000 to 30,000 complaints a year regarding gender discrimination.[15]

sexism
Discrimination on the basis of gender.

Another significant issue is access to opportunities. Although women now hold half of all managerial positions, that ratio shrinks dramatically the higher you look in an organization. For example, among the corporations that make up the S&P 500 stock market index, fewer than 5 percent have women as CEOs.[16] A lack of opportunities to advance into the top ranks is often referred to as the **glass ceiling**, implying that one can see the top but can't get there. The glass ceiling is an important issue for both women and minorities.

glass ceiling
An invisible barrier attributable to subtle discrimination that keeps women and minorities out of the top positions in business.

One of the most complicated issues of all is the *gender pay gap*, the difference between what women and men earn. Women in the United States earn, on average, about 75 to 80 percent of what men do.[17] While this appears on the surface to be a blatant case of simple discrimination, a closer look at the data reveals a more nuanced picture that requires lots of digging to figure out how much of that 20–25 percent gap is a result of discriminatory practices on the part of employers and how much is attributable to the choices made by individual employees or to subtle but pervasive social forces.

For example, a higher percentage of men choose careers in the lucrative fields of engineering and computer science, whereas a higher percentage of women choose careers in teaching, which pays considerably less. Tellingly, men dominate the ten most-lucrative careers, and women dominate the ten least-lucrative careers.[18]

These numbers help explain the pay gap, but they don't tell the whole story. Within the same profession, men often earn more than women—even in professions such

EXHIBIT 11.3 Generations in the Workplace

Lumping people into generations is an imprecise science at best, but it helps to know the labels commonly applied to various age groups and to have some idea of their broad characteristics. (Note that these labels are not official, and there is no general agreement on when some generations start and end.)

Common Label	Range of Birth Years	Some Workforce Implications
Radio Generation	1925–1945	People in this group are beyond what was once considered the traditional retirement age of 65, but many want or need to continue working.
Baby Boomers	1946–1964	This large segment of the workforce, which now occupies many mid- and upper-level managerial positions, got its name from the population boom in the years following World War II. The older members of this generation are now past traditional retirement age, but many will continue to work—meaning that younger workers waiting for some of these management spots to open up might have to wait a while longer.
Generation X	1965–1980	This relatively smaller "MTV generation" is responsible for many of the innovations that have shaped today's communication and business habits but sometimes feels caught between the large mass of Baby Boomers ahead of them and the younger Generation Y employees behind them in the workforce. As Generation X takes the reins of corporate leadership, it is overseeing in a vastly different business landscape, one in which virtual and networked organizations replace much of the hierarchy inherited from the Baby Boomers.
Generation Y	1981–1995	Often known as *millennials*, this generation has been noted for its technology-centric approach to communication, impatience with corporate hierarchy, and the desire for a meaningful and personalized work experience. Many in this generation are now managers with power to reshape organizational cultures. New research suggests, however, that millennials aren't dramatically different from their predecessors and generally value the same rewards and express the same career concerns.
Generation Z	1996–	Generation Z, also known as *Generation I* (for Internet) or the *Net Generation*, is the first full generation to be born after the World Wide Web was invented. With a global, socially aware outlook shaped by lifelong networking and media usage, this diverse group appears to be highly entrepreneurial and interested in new ways of approaching business.

Sources: Alexandra Levit, "Make Way for Generation Z," *New York Times*, 28 March 2015, www.nytimes.com; "Workforce 2020: A Millennial Misunderstanding," *SuccessFactors*, accessed 18 April 2015, www.successfactors.com; "How to Manage the Millennials," PwC.com, accessed 7 November 2013; Anne Fisher, "When Gen X Runs the Show," *Time*, 14 May 2009, www.time.com; Deloitte, "Generation Y: Powerhouse of the Global Economy," research report, 2009, www.deloitte.com; "Generation Y," Nightly Business Report website, 30 June 2010, www.pbs.org; Sherry Posnick-Goodwin, "Meet Generation Z," *California Educator*, February 2010, www.cta.org.

as nursing and teaching, where women outnumber men.[19] Several other factors that researchers have found add nuance to the picture. On average, men work more hours per week, take less time off to raise children, and are more likely to try to negotiate pay raises. According to an in-depth statistical analysis released by the U.S. Department of Labor, when adjusted for individual choices, the average pay gap is roughly 5 to 7 percent.[20]

However, even a rigorous statistical investigation doesn't provide all the insights needed to right the imbalance, whatever that figure might be. Important issues that need to be considered include whether girls and young women are being subtly steered away from engineering, computer science, and other lucrative fields, why pay varies so much across different professions, the degree to which the glass ceiling is keeping women out of higher-paying positions, whether women have access to equal work opportunities even when they have the same job titles as men, and how companies should accommodate parents who want or need to step away from work to care for children.[21]

As just one example, consider a case in which a working couple with a newborn child decides that one of them should stay home with the baby for several months. If the mother's employer offers paid maternity leave for new mothers, but the father's employer doesn't offer paid paternity leave for new fathers, the couple will likely make the economic decision for the woman to take time off and the man to continue working. Even if a company's managers make a concerted effort not to penalize employees who take time off for family, extended time away from work can make it difficult for employees

REAL-TIME UPDATES
Learn More by Visiting This Website

Get the facts on gender gaps in corporation leadership

The nonprofit organization Catalyst conducts extensive research around the world to identify and understand opportunities to improve gender inclusivity in business management. Go to http://real-time updates.com/bia8 and click on Learn More in the Students section.

to maintain their skill sets, customer relationships, networking contacts, and other attributes that lead to promotions and pay raises.

Beyond pay and promotional opportunities, many working women also have to deal with **sexual harassment**, defined as either an obvious request for sexual favors with an implicit reward or punishment related to work, or the more subtle creation of a sexist environment in which employees are made to feel uncomfortable by lewd jokes, remarks, or gestures. Even though male employees may also be targets of sexual harassment and both male and female employees may experience same-sex harassment, sexual harassment of female employees by male colleagues or superiors continues to make up the majority of reported cases.[22] Most corporations now publish strict policies prohibiting harassment, both to protect their employees and to protect themselves from lawsuits.[23]

sexual harassment
Unwelcome sexual advance, request for sexual favors, or other verbal or physical conduct of a sexual nature within the workplace.

Managers have the responsibility to educate their employees on the definition and consequences of sexual harassment.

Tom McCarthy/PhotoEdit

Race and Ethnicity

In many respects, the element of race and ethnicity in the diversity picture involves the same concerns as gender: equal pay for equal work, access to promotional opportunities, and ways to break through the glass ceiling. However, whereas the ratio of men and women in the workforce remains fairly stable year to year, the ethnic composition of the United States has been on a long-term trend of greater and greater diversity.

Grasping this changing situation can be complicated by confusion about the terms *race, ethnicity,* and *minority*. Ethnicity is a broader concept than race, incorporating both the genetic background of race and cultural issues such as language and national origin. Neither term is absolute or precise; millions of people have mixed racial heritage, and ethnicity doesn't always have fixed boundaries that clearly distinguish one group from another. *Minority* is a term often used to designate any race or ethnic segment other than white Americans of European descent. Aside from the negative connotations of *minority,* the term makes less and less sense every year. Caucasian Americans make up less than half the population in a growing number of cities and counties, and in two or three decades will make up less than half of the overall U.S. population.[24]

Labels aside, race remains an important issue in the workforce. The EEOC receives even more complaints about racial discrimination than about gender discrimination.[25] And as with average wages between women and men, disparity still exists along racial lines. Averaging across the entire workforce, Asian Americans earn the most, followed by Caucasian Americans, African Americans, and Hispanic Americans.[26] But as with gender, these aggregate figures need to be viewed in the context of individual decisions and opportunities for advancement.

Religion

The effort to accommodate employees' life interests on a broader scale has led a number of companies to address the issue of religion in the workplace. As one of the most personal aspects of life, of course, religion does bring potential for controversy in a work setting. On the one hand, some employees feel they should be able to express their beliefs in the workplace and not be forced to "check their faith at the door" when they come to work. On the other hand, companies want to avoid situations in which openly expressed religious differences might cause friction between employees or distract employees from their responsibilities.

Religion in the workplace is a complex and contentious issue—and it's getting more so every year, at least as measured by a significant rise in the number of religious discrimination lawsuits.[27] Beyond accommodating individual beliefs to a reasonable degree, as required by U.S. law, companies occasionally need to resolve situations that pit one group of employees against another or against the company's policies.[28] As more companies work to establish inclusive workplaces, and as more employees seek to integrate religious convictions into their daily work, you can expect to see this issue being discussed at many companies in the coming years.

REAL-TIME UPDATES
Learn More by Exploring This Interactive Website

Take a closer look at how the United States is changing

The U.S. population is aging and becoming more diverse; dive into the details with this interactive presentation. Go to http://real-timeupdates .com/bia8 and click on Learn More in the Students section.

Ability

People whose hearing, vision, cognitive ability, or physical ability to operate equipment is impaired can be at a significant disadvantage in the workplace. As with other elements of diversity, success starts with respect for individuals and sensitivity to differences. Employers can also invest in a variety of *assistive technologies* (see page 140 for more information) that help people with disabilities perform activities that might otherwise be difficult or impossible. These technologies include devices and systems that help people communicate orally and visually, interact with computers and other equipment, and enjoy greater mobility in the workplace. For example, designers can emphasize *web accessibility*, taking steps to make websites more accessible to people whose vision is limited. Assistive technologies create a vital link for employees with disabilities, giving them opportunities to pursue a greater range of career paths and giving employers access to a broader base of talent.

Diversity Initiatives

To respond to the many challenges—and to capitalize on the business opportunities offered by both diverse marketplaces and diverse workforces—companies across the country are finding that embracing diversity in the richest sense is simply good business. In response, thousands of U.S. companies have established **diversity initiatives**, which can include such steps as contracting with more suppliers owned by women and minorities, targeting a more diverse customer base, and supporting the needs and interests of a diverse workforce. For example, IBM established executive-led task forces to represent women, Asian Americans, African Americans, Hispanic Americans, Native Americans, people with disabilities, and individuals who are gay, lesbian, bisexual, and transgender. As the company puts it, "Our diversity is a competitive advantage and consciously building diverse teams helps us drive the best results for our clients." For instance, women and minorities are a significant presence in the small-business marketplace, and having women and minorities on product development and marketing teams helps IBM understand the needs of these customers.[29]

diversity initiatives
Programs and policies that help companies support diverse workforces and markets.

REAL-TIME UPDATES
Learn More by Watching These Videos

See what Google employees have to say about diversity

The search giant's YouTube channel features employees talking about their experiences working at Google. Go to http://real-timeupdates.com/bia8 and click on Learn More in the Students section.

✓ Checkpoint

LEARNING OBJECTIVE 2: Discuss the challenges and advantages of a diverse workforce, and identify five major dimensions of workforce diversity.

SUMMARY: Differences in everything from religion to ethnic heritage to military experience enrich the workplace and give employers a competitive advantage by offering better insights into a diverse marketplace. A diverse workforce brings with it a wide range of skills, traditions, backgrounds, experiences, outlooks, and attitudes toward work—all of which can affect employee behaviors, relationships, and communication habits. Five major dimensions of workforce diversity addressed in this chapter are age, gender, race, religion, and ability.

CRITICAL THINKING: (1) How could a company benefit by investing in assistive technologies for its workers? (2) How might socioeconomic diversity in a company's workforce create both challenges and opportunities for the company?

IT'S YOUR BUSINESS: (1) What general opinions do you have of the generation that is older than you and the generation that is younger than you? What experiences and observations shaped these opinions? (2) Do you believe that any aspect of your background or heritage has held you back in any way in college or at work? If so, why?

KEY TERMS TO KNOW: sexism, glass ceiling, sexual harassment, diversity initiatives

Managing the Employment Life Cycle

3 LEARNING OBJECTIVE

Describe the three phases involved in managing the employment life cycle.

HR managers oversee employment-related activities from recruiting and hiring through termination and retirement.

HIRING EMPLOYEES

recruiting
The process of attracting appropriate applicants for an organization's jobs.

The employment life cycle starts with **recruiting**, the process of attracting suitable candidates for an organization's jobs. The recruiting function is often judged by a combination of criteria known as *quality of hire*, which measures how closely incoming employees meet the company's needs.[30] Recruiters use a variety of resources, including internal searches, advertising, union hiring halls, college campuses and career offices, trade shows, *headhunters* (outside agencies that specialize in finding and placing employees), and social networking technologies. Exhibit 11.4 illustrates the general process that companies go through to hire new employees.

Federal and state laws and regulations govern many aspects of the hiring process. (See Exhibit 11.5 for a list of some of the most important employment-related laws.) In particular, employers must respect the privacy of applicants and avoid discrimination. For instance, any form or test that can be construed as a preemployment medical examination is prohibited by the Americans with Disabilities Act.[31]

TERMINATING EMPLOYEES

termination
The process of getting rid of an employee through layoff or firing.

layoffs
Termination of employees for economic or business reasons.

HR managers have the unpleasant responsibility of **termination**—permanently laying off employees because of cutbacks or firing employees for poor performance or other reasons. **Layoffs** are the termination of employees for economic or business reasons unrelated to employee performance. *Rightsizing* is a euphemism used to suggest that an organization is making changes in the workforce to match its business needs more

---

EXHIBIT 11.4   The Recruiting Process

This general model of the recruiting process shows the steps most companies go through to select the best employee for each position.

Step 1: Assemble candidate pool	Step 2: Screen candidates	Step 3: Interview candidates	Step 4: Compare candidates	Step 5: Investigate candidates	Step 6: Make an offer
• Recruiters select a small number of qualified candidates from all the internal and external applicants. • Many organizations now use computer-based applicant tracking systems to manage the hiring process.	• Recruiters then screen candidates, typically through phone interviews, online tests, or on-campus interviews. • Interviews at this stage are usually fairly structured, with applicants asked the same questions so that recruiters can easily compare responses.	• Candidates who make it through screening are invited to visit the company for another round of interviews. • This stage usually involves several interviews with a mix of colleagues, HR specialists, and managers.	• The interview team compares notes and assesses the remaining candidates. • Team members sometimes lobby for or against individual candidates based on what they've seen and heard during interviews.	• Recruiters talk to references, conduct background checks, scan social media postings, and in many cases subject applicants to preemployment tests. • Given the financial and legal risks associated with bad hiring decisions, smart employers research candidates carefully and thoroughly.	• With all this information in hand, the hiring manager selects the most suitable person for the job and makes a job offer.

EXHIBIT 11.5	Major Employment Legislation

Here are some of the most significant sets of laws that affect employer–employee relations in the United States.

Category	Legislation	Highlights
Labor and unionization	National Labor Relations Act, also known as the Wagner Act	Establishes the right of employees to form, join, and assist unions and the right to strike; prohibits employers from interfering in union activities
	Labor-Management Relations Act, also known as the Taft-Hartley Act	Expands union member rights; gives employers free speech rights to oppose unions; restricts union's strike options; gives the president the authority to impose injunctions against strikes
	Labor-Management Reporting and Disclosure Act, also known as the Landrum-Griffin Act	Gives union members the right to nominate and vote for union leadership candidates; combats financial fraud within unions
	State right-to-work laws	Give individual employees the right to choose not to join a union
	Fair Labor Standards Act	Establishes minimum wage and overtime pay for nonexempt workers; sets strict guidelines for child labor
	Immigration Reform and Control Act	Prohibits employers from hiring illegal immigrants
Workplace safety	State workers' compensation acts	Require employers (in most states) to carry either private or government sponsored insurance that provides income to injured workers
	Occupational Health and Safety Act	Empowers the Occupational Safety and Health Administration (OSHA) to establish, monitor, and enforce standards for workplace safety
Compensation and benefits	Employee Retirement Income Security Act	Governs the establishment and operation of private pension programs
	Consolidated Omnibus Budget Reconciliation Act (usually known by the acronym COBRA)	Requires employers to let employees or their beneficiaries buy continued health insurance coverage after employment ends
	Federal Unemployment Tax Act and similar state laws	Requires employers to fund programs that provide income for qualified unemployed persons
	Social Security Act	Provides a level of retirement, disability, and medical coverage for employees and their dependents; jointly funded by employers and employees
	Lilly Ledbetter Fair Pay Act	Amends and modifies several pieces of earlier legislation to make it easier for employees to file lawsuits over pay and benefit discrimination
	Patient Protection and Affordable Care Act	Requires companies with more than 50 full-time employees to offer health insurance coverage for employees

Sources: Henry J. Kaiser Family Foundation, *Focus on Health Reform: Summary of the Affordable Care Act*, 23 April 2013; U.S. Department of Labor website, accessed 7 November 2013, www.dol.gov; Henry R. Cheeseman, *Contemporary Business and E-Commerce Law*, 7th ed. (Upper Saddle River, N.J.: Pearson Prentice Hall, 2010), 487–495; "The Lilly Ledbetter Fair Pay Act of 2009," U.S. White House website, accessed 23 June 2009, www.whitehouse.gov.

precisely. Although rightsizing usually involves *downsizing* the workforce, companies sometimes add workers in some areas while eliminating jobs in others.

To help ease the pain of layoffs, many companies provide laid-off employees with job-hunting assistance. *Outplacement* services such as résumé-writing courses, career counseling, office space, and secretarial help are offered to laid-off executives and blue-collar employees alike.

With many companies trimming workforces during a recession, managers need to take care not to discriminate against any segment of the workforce. Older workers appear to be a particularly vulnerable group because they usually have higher salaries and more expensive benefits, making them an inviting target for cost cutting. Age discrimination complaints related to layoffs have been at all-time highs in recent years.[32]

Terminating employment by firing is a complex subject with many legal ramifications, and the line between a layoff and a firing can be blurry. For instance, every state except Montana supports the concept of *at-will employment*, meaning that companies are free to fire nearly anyone they choose. State laws vary, but in general, employers cannot discriminate in firing, nor can they fire employees for whistle-blowing, for filing a worker's compensation claim, or for testifying against the employer in harassment or discrimination lawsuits.[33] If a terminated employee believes any of these principles have been violated, he or she can file a *wrongful discharge* lawsuit against the employer. In addition, employers must abide by the terms of an employment contract, if one has been entered into with the employee (these are much more common for executives than for lower-level employees). Some employers offer written assurances that they will terminate employees only *for cause*, which usually includes such actions as committing crimes or violating company policy.

REPLACING RETIRING EMPLOYEES

worker buyouts
Distributions of financial incentives to employees who voluntarily depart; usually undertaken in order to reduce the payroll.

mandatory retirement
Required dismissal of an employee who reaches a certain age.

Companies can face two dramatically different challenges regarding retiring employees. For companies that are short-handed, the challenge is to persuade older employees to delay retirement. Conversely, companies with too many employees may induce employees to depart ahead of scheduled retirement by offering them *early retirement*, using financial incentives known as **worker buyouts**.

In the past, **mandatory retirement** policies forced people to quit working as soon as they turned a certain age. However, the Age Discrimination in Employment Act now outlaws mandatory retirement based on age alone, unless an employer can demonstrate that age is a valid qualification for "normal operation of the particular business."[34]

 Checkpoint

LEARNING OBJECTIVE 3: Describe the three phases involved in managing the employment life cycle.

SUMMARY: The three phases of managing the employment life cycle are hiring, termination, and retirement. The hiring phase typically involves six steps: selecting a small number of qualified candidates from all of the applications received, screening those candidates to identify the most attractive prospects, interviewing those prospects in depth to learn more about them and their potential to contribute to the company, evaluating and comparing interview results, conducting background checks and pre-employment tests, and then selecting the best candidate for each position and making job offers. Termination can involve firing employees for poor performance or other reasons or laying off employees for financial reasons. Retirement offers a variety of challenges depending on the industry and the company's situation; overstaffed companies may induce some employees to retire early through buyouts, whereas others that face talent shortages may try to induce retirement-age employees to delay retirement.

CRITICAL THINKING: (1) Why would a company spend money on outplacement counseling and other services for laid-off employees? (2) Why would a company spend money to induce retirement-age employees to stay on board for a while, rather than simply hiring younger employees to take their place?

IT'S YOUR BUSINESS: (1) What impression would a potential employer get from studying your current online presence? (2) Have you ever been interviewed over the phone or via computer? If so, did you feel you were able to present yourself effectively without face-to-face contact?

KEY TERMS TO KNOW: recruiting, termination, layoffs, worker buyouts, mandatory retirement

Developing and Evaluating Employees

4   LEARNING OBJECTIVE

Explain the steps used to
develop and evaluate employees.

Another major contribution that HR makes is helping managers throughout the company align employee skill sets with the evolving requirements of each position. This effort includes appraising employee performance, managing training and development programs, and promoting and reassigning employees.

APPRAISING EMPLOYEE PERFORMANCE

How do employees (and their managers) know whether they are doing a good job? How can they improve their performance? What new skills should they learn? Managers attempt to answer these questions by conducting **performance appraisals**, or *performance reviews*, to objectively evaluate employees according to set criteria. The ultimate goal of performance appraisals is not to judge employees but rather to guide them in improving their performance.

performance appraisals
Periodic evaluations of employees'
work according to specific criteria.

The worst possible outcome in an annual review is a negative surprise, such as when an employee has been working toward different goals than the manager expects or has been underperforming throughout the year but didn't receive any feedback or improvement coaching along the way.[35] In some instances, failing to confront performance problems in a timely fashion can make a company vulnerable to lawsuits.[36]

To avoid negative surprises, managers should meet with employees to agree on clear goals for the upcoming year and provide regular feedback and coaching as needed throughout the year if employee performance falls below expectations. Ideally, the annual review is more of a confirmation of the past year's performance and a planning session for the next year.

The specific measures of employee performance vary widely by job, company, and industry; Exhibit 11.6 on the next page shows one example of a performance appraisal form. Most jobs are evaluated in several areas, including tasks specific to the position, contribution to the company's overall success, and interaction with colleagues and customers. For example, a production manager might be evaluated on the basis of communication skills, people management, leadership, teamwork, recruiting and employee development, delegation, financial management, planning, and organizational skills.[37]

Many performance appraisals require the employee to be rated by several people (including more than one supervisor and perhaps several coworkers). This practice further promotes fairness by correcting for possible biases. The ultimate in multidimensional reviews is the **360-degree review**[38], in which a person is given feedback from subordinates (if the employee has supervisory responsibility), peers, superiors, and possibly customers or outside business partners. The multiple viewpoints can uncover weaknesses that employees and even their direct managers might not be aware of, as well as contributions and achievements that might have been overlooked in normal reviews.

360-degree review
A multidimensional review in
which a person is given feedback
from subordinates, peers, superiors, and possibly outside stakeholders such as customers and
business partners.

In addition to formal, periodic performance evaluations, many companies evaluate some workers' performance continuously, using **electronic performance monitoring (EPM)**, sometimes called *computer activity monitoring*. For instance, customer service and telephone sales representatives are often evaluated by the number of calls they complete per hour and other variables. Newer software products extend this monitoring capability, from measuring data input accuracy to scanning for suspicious words in employee emails. As you can imagine, EPM efforts can generate controversy in the workplace, elevating employee stress levels and raising concerns about invasion of privacy.[39] Using EPM as a development tool, rather than a disciplinary tool, helps employees accept the practice.[40]

**electronic performance
monitoring (EPM)**
Real-time, computer-based evaluation of employee performance.

TRAINING AND DEVELOPING EMPLOYEES

With the pace of change in everything from government regulations to consumer tastes to technology, employee knowledge and skills need to be constantly updated. Consequently, most successful companies place heavy emphasis on employee training and development efforts, for everyone from entry-level workers to the CEO.

Training usually begins with **orientation programs** designed to ease the new hire's transition into the company and to impart vital knowledge about the organization and its rules, procedures, and expectations. Effective orientation programs help employees

orientation programs
Sessions or procedures for
acclimating new employees
to the organization.

EXHIBIT 11.6   Sample Performance Appraisal Form

This sample form suggests the range of performance variables on which companies typically evaluate their employees.

| Name _____ Title _____ Service Date _____ Date _____ |
| Location _____ Division _____ Department _____ |
| Length of Time in Present Position   Period of Review   Appraised by _____ |
| From: _____ To: _____   Title of Appraisor _____ |

Area of Performance	Comment	Rating
Job Knowledge and Skill Understands responsibilities and uses background for job. Adapts to new methods/techniques. Plans and organizes work. Recognizes errors and problems.		5 4 3 2 1
Volume of Work Amount of work output. Adherence to standards and schedules. Effective use of time.		5 4 3 2 1
Quality of Work Degree of accuracy—lack of errors. Thoroughness of work. Ability to exercise good judgment.		5 4 3 2 1
Initiative and Creativity Self-motivation in seeking responsibility and work that needs to be done. Ability to apply original ideas and concepts.		5 4 3 2 1
Communication Ability to exchange thoughts or information in a clear, concise manner. Ability to deal with different organizational levels of clientele.		5 4 3 2 1
Dependability Ability to follow instructions and directions correctly. Performs under pressure. Reliable work habits.		5 4 3 2 1
Leadership Ability/Potential Ability to guide others to the successful accomplishment of a given task. Potential for developing subordinate employees.		5 4 3 2 1

5. Outstanding	Employee who consistently exceeds established standards and expectations of the job.
4. Above Average	Employee who consistently meets established standards and expectations of the job. Often exceeds and rarely falls short of desired results.
3. Satisfactory	Generally qualified employee who meets job standards and expectations. Sometimes exceeds and may occasionally fall short of desired expectations. Performs duties in a normally expected manner.
2. Improvement Needed	Not quite meeting standards and expectations. An employee at this level of performance is not quite meeting all the standard job requirements.
1. Unsatisfactory	Employee who fails to meet the minimum standards and expectations of the job.

I have had the opportunity to read this performance appraisal.	How long has this employee been under your supervision?
Signature Date	Signature of Supervisor Date

skills inventory
A list of the skills a company needs from its workforce, along with the specific skills that individual employees currently possess.

become more productive in less time, help eliminate confusion and mistakes, and can significantly increase employee retention rates.[41] Training and other forms of employee development continue throughout the employee's career in most cases. Many HR departments maintain a **skills inventory**, which identifies both the current skill levels of all the employees and the skills the company needs in order to succeed. (If your employer doesn't maintain one for you, be sure to maintain your own skills inventory so you can stay on top of developments and expectations in your field.)

PROMOTING AND REASSIGNING EMPLOYEES

Many companies prefer to look within the organization to fill job vacancies. In part, this promote-from-within policy allows a company to benefit from the training and experience of its own workforce. This policy also rewards employees who have worked hard and demonstrated the ability to handle more challenging tasks. In addition, morale is usually better when a company promotes from within because other employees see the possibility of advancement. For example, Enterprise Holdings (the parent company of Enterprise Rent-a-Car, Alamo, and National Car Rental) highlights its promote-from-within philosophy and the opportunity to move into managerial responsibilities.[42]

However, a possible pitfall of internal promotion is that a person may be given a job beyond his or her competence. The best salesperson in the company is not necessarily a good candidate for sales manager, because managing requires a different set of skills. If the promotion is a mistake, the company not only loses its sales leader but also risks demoralizing the sales staff. Companies can reduce such risks through careful promotion policies and by providing support and training to help newly promoted employees perform well.

 Checkpoint

LEARNING OBJECTIVE 4: **Explain the steps used to develop and evaluate employees.**

SUMMARY: The effort to develop and evaluate employees includes providing performance appraisals, managing training and development programs, and promoting and reassigning employees. Managers use performance appraisals to give employees feedback and develop plans to improve performance shortcomings. In a 360-degree review, an employee is evaluated by subordinates (if applicable), peers, and superiors. Training and development efforts begin with orientation for new hires and continue throughout a person's career in many cases. When employees have reached sufficient skill levels to take on new challenges, they may be considered for promotion into positions of more responsibility.

CRITICAL THINKING: (1) How can employers balance the need to provide objective appraisals that can be compared across the company's entire workforce with the desire to evaluate each employee on an individual basis? (2) Beyond increasing their skill and knowledge levels, how can training improve employees' motivation and job satisfaction? (Review Chapter 10 if you need to.)

IT'S YOUR BUSINESS: (1) Have you ever had a performance appraisal that you felt was inaccurate or unfair? How would you change the process as a result? (2) Do the methods your college or university uses to evaluate your performance as student accurately reflect your progress? What changes would you make to the evaluation process?

KEY TERMS TO KNOW: performance appraisals, 360-degree review, electronic performance monitoring (EPM), orientation programs, skills inventory

Administering Employee Compensation

Pay and benefits are of vital interest to all employees, of course, and these subjects also consume considerable time and attention in HR departments. For many companies, payroll is the single biggest expense, and the cost of benefits, particularly health care, continues to climb. Consequently, **compensation**, the combination of direct payments such as wages or salary and indirect payments through employee benefits, is one of the HR manager's most significant responsibilities.

 5 LEARNING OBJECTIVE

Describe the major elements of employee compensation.

compensation
Money, benefits, and services paid to employees for their work.

SALARIES AND WAGES

salary
Fixed cash compensation for work, usually by a yearly amount; independent of the number of hours worked.

wages
Cash payment based on the number of hours an employee has worked or the number of units an employee has produced.

Most employees receive the bulk of their compensation in the form of a **salary**, if they receive a fixed amount per year, or **wages**, if they are paid by the unit of time (hourly, daily, or weekly) or by the unit of output (often called "getting paid by the piece" or "piecework"). The Fair Labor Standards Act, introduced in 1938 and amended many times since then, sets specific guidelines that employers must follow when administering salaries and wages, including setting a minimum wage and paying overtime for time worked beyond 40 hours a week. However, most professional and managerial employees are considered exempt from these regulations, meaning, for instance, their employers don't have to pay them for overtime. The distinction between *exempt employees* and *nonexempt employees* is based on job responsibilities and pay level. In general, salaried employees are exempt, although there are many exceptions.[43]

REAL-TIME UPDATES
Learn More by Exploring This Interactive Website

Explore the salary potential for virtually any business career

Curious about salary potential in various business jobs? This free salary wizard has the answers. Go to http://real-timeupdates.com/bia8 and click on Learn More in the Students section.

Defining compensation levels for employees up and down the organization chart is a complex challenge. Companies need to manage compensation in a way that allows them to simultaneously earn a profit, create appealing goods and services, and compete with other companies for the same employees. A firm could attract most of the talent it needs by paying huge salaries, but that probably wouldn't be profitable. Conversely, it could keep salaries low to hold down costs, but then it couldn't attract the talent it needs to be competitive, so it might not generate enough revenue to turn a profit anyway.

In the broadest terms, compensation is dictated by prevailing conditions in the job market and the value each employee brings to the organization. Such variables as geography (locations with higher living expenses tend to have higher salaries), industry, and company size (larger companies tend to pay more) can also factor into the equation. Although it seems like going around in circles to base compensation on prevailing market rates when all the other companies in the market are doing the same thing, the market is the best quasi-independent arbiter available. As executive compensation consultant Russell Miller puts it, "If we don't look to the market to determine if we're paying competitively, where else should we look?"[44]

Judging an employee's worth to an organization is no simple matter, either. Few jobs—sales is a notable exception—have an immediate and measurable impact on revenue, which makes it difficult to say how much most employees are worth to the company. For most positions, companies tend to establish a salary range for each position, trying to balance what it can afford to pay with prevailing market rates. Each employee's salary is then set within that range based on performance evaluations, with higher-performing employees deemed more valuable to the company and therefore deserving of higher pay.

Not surprisingly, people expect to get paid what they believe they are worth—particularly relative to what other people are making. Recall from the discussion of equity theory (page 277) that most employees don't expect to make as much as the CEO, but they do expect the ratio of value provided to rewards gained to be at least reasonable. In the 1950s, CEOs made roughly 20 times more than the average worker pay in their companies, and the ratio has been steadily climbing. Depending on the survey methodology, CEO pay in major corporations is now roughly 200 to 300 times the average employee's.[45] Although it's not really possible to identify exactly how much more valuable a CEO is than an average employee, it is reasonable to ask if today's CEOs are 10 or 15 times more valuable than CEOs were in years past.

INCENTIVE PROGRAMS

As Chapter 10 mentions, many companies provide managers and employees with *incentives* to encourage productivity, innovation, and commitment to work. Incentives are typically cash payments linked to specific goals for individual, group, or companywide performance. In other words, achievements, not just activities, are made the basis for payment.

The success of these programs often depends on how closely incentives are linked to actions within the employee's control:

- For both salaried and wage-earning employees, one type of incentive compensation is a **bonus**, a payment in addition to the regular wage or salary. Paying performance-based bonuses has become an increasingly popular approach to compensation as more companies shift away from automatic annual pay increases.[46]

- In contrast to bonuses, **commissions** are a form of compensation that pays employees in sales positions based on the level of sales they make within a given time frame.

- Employees may be rewarded for staying with a company and encouraged to work harder through **profit sharing**, a system in which employees receive a portion of the company's profits.

Sales professionals usually earn at least part of their income through commissions; the more they sell, the more they earn.

- Similar to profit sharing, **gain sharing** ties rewards to profits (or cost savings) achieved by meeting specific goals such as quality and productivity improvement.

- A variation of gain sharing, **pay for performance** requires employees to accept a lower base pay but rewards them with bonuses, commissions, or stock options if they reach agreed-on goals. To be successful, this method needs to be complemented with effective feedback systems that let employees know how they are performing throughout the year.[47]

- Another approach to compensation being explored by some companies is **knowledge-based pay**, also known as *competency-based pay* or *skill-based pay*, which is tied to employees' knowledge and abilities rather than to their job per se. More than half of all large U.S. companies now use some variation on this incentive.[48]

bonus
A cash payment, in addition to regular wage or salary, that serves as a reward for achievement.

commissions
Employee compensation based on a percentage of sales made.

profit sharing
The distribution of a portion of the company's profits to employees.

gain sharing
Tying rewards to profits or cost savings achieved by meeting specific goals.

pay for performance
An incentive program that rewards employees for meeting specific, individual goals.

knowledge-based pay
Pay tied to an employee's acquisition of knowledge or skills; also called competency-based pay or skill-based pay.

✓ Checkpoint

LEARNING OBJECTIVE 5: Describe the major elements of employee compensation.

SUMMARY: For most employees, the bulk of their compensation comes in the form of a *salary*, if they receive a fixed amount per year, or *wages*, if they are paid by the unit of time or unit of output. In addition to their base salary or wages, some employees are eligible for a variety of incentive programs, including bonuses, commissions, profit sharing, and gain sharing. In some cases, employers offer pay-for-performance plans that have a lower base salary but allow employees to earn more by hitting specific performance goals. Some companies are also exploring knowledge-based pay, which rewards employees for acquiring information or developing skills related to their jobs.

CRITICAL THINKING: (1) What are some potential risks or limitations of performance-based pay systems? (2) How does equity theory (see Chapter 10) explain the anger some employees feel about the compensation packages their company CEOs receive?

IT'S YOUR BUSINESS: (1) If you worked for a large corporation, would a profit-sharing plan motivate you? Why or why not? (2) What questions would you ask before you accepted a sales position in which most of your compensation would be based on commissions, rather than base salary?

KEY TERMS TO KNOW: compensation, salary, wages, bonus, commissions, profit sharing, gain sharing, pay for performance, knowledge-based pay

6 **LEARNING OBJECTIVE**

Identify the most significant categories of employee benefits and services.

employee benefits
Compensation other than wages, salaries, and incentive programs.

cafeteria plans
Flexible benefit programs that let employees personalize their benefits packages.

Employee Benefits and Services

Companies regularly provide **employee benefits**—elements of compensation other than wages, salaries, and incentives. These benefits may be offered as either a preset package—that is, the employee gets whatever insurance, paid holidays, pension plan, and other benefits the company sets up—or as flexible plans, sometimes known as **cafeteria plans** (so called because of the similarity to choosing items in a cafeteria). The benefits most commonly provided by employers are insurance, retirement benefits, employee stock-ownership plans, stock options, and family benefits.

INSURANCE

Employers can offer a range of insurance plans to their employees, including life, health, dental, vision, disability, and long-term care insurance. Perhaps no other issue illustrates the challenging economics of business today better than health-care costs in general and health insurance in particular. With medical costs rising much faster than inflation in general, companies are taking a variety of steps to manage the financial impact, including forcing employees to pick up more of the cost, reducing or eliminating coverage for retired employees, auditing employees' health claims, monitoring employees' health and habits, dropping spouses from insurance plans, or even firing employees who are so sick or disabled that they are no longer able to work. The situation is particularly acute for small businesses, which don't have the purchasing power of large corporations.[49]

With health-care costs on an unsustainable upward spiral, health-care reform has been a hot political topic in recent years. In aggregate, the United States spends enough to provide adequate care for everyone, but the health-care sector is plagued by waste, inefficiency, and imbalance. Per capita, the United States spends more on health care than any other country, but according to a number of key measures, the quality of care is lower in the United States than in many other countries.[50]

The Affordable Care Act (ACA) of 2010, often referred to informally as Obamacare, sought to tackle one of the thorniest issues in U.S. healthcare: the millions of residents who lacked health insurance. Among other elements in this complex and controversial piece of legislation, the ACA requires that companies with more than 50 workers provide health insurance benefits for the employees, and that people who don't get insurance through work buy individual policies. Millions of previously uninsured people now have coverage, but the ACA also resulted in higher premiums for millions of people who had been buying their own insurance.[51]

retirement plans
Company-sponsored programs for providing retirees with income.

pension plans
Generally refers to traditional, defined-benefit retirement plans.

401(k) plan
A defined contribution retirement plan in which employers often match the amount employees invest.

employee stock-ownership plan (ESOP)
A program that enables employees to become partial owners of a company.

RETIREMENT BENEFITS

Many employers offer **retirement plans**, which are designed to provide continuing income after an employee retires. Company-sponsored retirement plans can be categorized as either *defined-benefit plans*, in which companies specify how much they will pay employees on retirement, or *defined-contribution plans*, in which companies specify how much they will put into the retirement fund (by matching employee contributions, for instance), without guaranteeing specific payout levels during retirement. Although both types are technically **pension plans**, when most people speak of pension plans, they are referring to traditional defined-benefit plans, which are far less common than they were in years past.[52]

Defined-contribution plans are similar to savings plans; they provide a future benefit based on annual employer contributions, voluntary employee matching contributions, and accumulated investment earnings. Employers can choose from several types of defined contribution plans, the most common being the **401(k) plan** (see Exhibit 11.7).

More than 10 million U.S. employees are now enrolled in an **employee stock-ownership plan (ESOP)**, in which a company places some or all of its stock in trust, with each eligible employee entitled to a certain portion. (Most ESOPs are in closely held corporations whose stock isn't available for sale to the public.) Many companies report that ESOPs help boost employee productivity because workers perceive a direct correlation between their efforts and the value of the company stock price.[53]

EXHIBIT 11.7	The Basics of a 401(k) Plan

The 401(k) plan is one of the most popular employer-sponsored retirement benefits.

Funding mechanism	• Defined-contribution plan (rather than defined-benefit) • Employees can invest a percentage of their pretax income, up to the amount allowed by law (currently $17,500 with an additional $5,500 allowed for people over 50) • Employers may choose to match some or all of the employee's contributions • Employees make their own investment choices from the mutual funds and other options available in the employer's plan
Advantages for employees	• Potential to significantly increase retirement investment if employer chooses to match employee contributions • Opportunity to reduce immediate tax burden (by reducing taxable income by the amount invested) • Automatic contribution feature makes it a forced savings plan • If the specific employer plan allows it, employees can borrow up to 50 percent of the balance in their plans before reaching retirement age • Plan is portable; employees can take it with them if they leave the company (*vesting* rules apply to any employer matching funds; if employee leaves before matching funds are fully invested, he or she forfeits a portion of those funds)
Potential risks and disadvantages for employees	• As a defined-contribution plan, does not guarantee a specific level of income in retirement • Employer's matching contribution might be in company stock, which might not be a good investment • Account balance vulnerable to changes in stock prices • Can be subject to high and sometimes hidden fees • Investment opportunities under a specific plan may not be desirable or appropriate for every employee • Except for special circumstances, employees cannot begin withdrawing funds until age 59.5 without incurring a penalty

Sources: Mark P. Cussen, "The Basics of a 401(k) Retirement Plan," *Forbes*, 30 July 2013, www.forbes.com; "401(k)s & Company Plans," *CNNMoney*, accessed 7 November 2013, http://money.cnn.com.

STOCK OPTIONS

One method for tying employee compensation to company performance is the stock option plan. **Stock options** grant employees the right to purchase a set number of shares of the employer's stock at a specific price, called the *grant* or *exercise price,* during a certain time period. Options typically *vest* over a number of years, meaning that employees can purchase a prorated portion of the shares every year until the vesting period is over (at which time they can purchase all the shares they are entitled to). The major attractions of stock options from an employer's point of view are that they provide a means of compensation that doesn't require any cash outlay and a means of motivating employees to work hard to make sure the stock price increases.

The popularity of stock options has waned somewhat in recent years, following a change in accounting rules that forced companies to account for the value of outstanding options in their annual financial reports. Before that change, investors and regulators argued that companies were hiding the true costs of options and thereby reporting inflated earnings.[54]

Stock options also figure into the controversy about executive compensation, for a couple of reasons. First, from the recipient's point of view, there is no real risk associated with stock options. Second, this lack of risk exposure can lead to riskier decision making. In fact, research suggests that CEOs who are compensated primarily through stock options tend to make poorer decisions regarding acquisitions, and their companies are more likely to experience accounting irregularities.[55]

stock options
A contract that allows the holder to purchase or sell a certain number of shares of a particular stock at a given price by a certain date.

OTHER EMPLOYEE BENEFITS

Employers offer a variety of other benefits in addition to those just discussed. Some of them are mandated by government regulation and some are offered voluntarily to attract and support employees. Here are some of the most common benefits:

• **Paid vacations and sick leave.** Some companies offer separate vacation and sick days; others combine the paid time off in a single "bucket" and let employees choose how to use the time.
• **Family and medical leave.** The Family Medical Leave Act (FMLA) of 1993 requires employers with 50 or more workers to provide up to 12 weeks of unpaid leave per

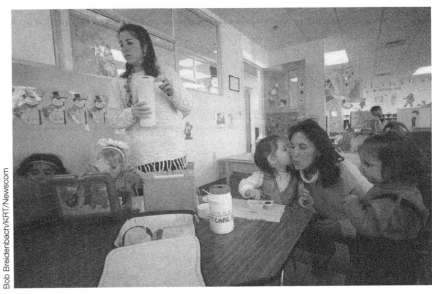

Trust Insurance employee Kathy Hatfield gets to spend time with her daughters at the company's on-site day-care center. Such centers reduce costs and stress for employees who have children.

employee assistance program (EAP)
A company-sponsored counseling or referral plan for employees with personal problems.

year for childbirth, adoption, or the care of oneself, a child, a spouse, or a parent with a serious illness.[56]

- **Child-care assistance.** Many companies offer child-care assistance, such as discounted rates at nearby child-care centers or on-site day-care centers.[57]
- **Elder-care assistance.** Many employers offer some form of elder-care assistance to help employees with the responsibility of caring for aging parents.
- **Tuition loans and reimbursements.** U.S. companies contribute billions of dollars every year to continuing education for their employees.[58]
- **Employee assistance programs.** One of the most cost-effective benefits employers can establish is an **employee assistance program (EAP)**, which offers private and confidential counseling to employees who need help with issues related to substance abuse, domestic violence, finances, stress, family issues, and other personal problems.[59]

For the latest information on employee benefits and other human resources topics, visit http://real-timeupdates.com/bia8 and click on Chapter 11.

✓ **Checkpoint**

LEARNING OBJECTIVE 6: Identify the most significant categories of employee benefits and services.

SUMMARY: The major types of employee benefits are insurance and retirement benefits. Companies may help employees with the cost of many types of insurance, including life, health, dental, vision, disability, and long-term care. Retirement programs fall into two basic categories: defined-benefit programs, which promise a specific amount per month after retirement, and defined-contribution programs, in which the company contributes a certain amount per month or year to an investment account but doesn't guarantee payment levels after retirement. Other important benefits are paid vacations and sick leave, family and medical leave, child- and elder-care assistance, tuition reimbursements or loans, and employee assistance programs that deal with personal matters such as substance abuse or domestic violence.

CRITICAL THINKING: (1) Why are stock options a controversial employee benefit, particularly for top executives? (2) What are the risks of investing in an ESOP?

BEHIND THE SCENES
FOR ZAPPOS, FINDING THE RIGHT EMPLOYEES MEANS REJECTING THE OLD WAY OF DOING BUSINESS

To a large degree, contemporary employee recruiting practices are all about conformity: identifying the measurable attributes of the ideal employee (education and training, years of experience, technical specialties, job titles, and facts and figures) and then using this template to filter out anyone who isn't a perfect match.

To the dismay of many job seekers, in fact, this is precisely what applicant tracking systems usually do. Candidates who could've turned out to be solid or even superstar employees may never get past this automated screening process if their résumés aren't worded in precisely the way the system expects or they happen to be missing one particular skill they could easily develop on the job if given the chance. People whose résumés aren't "perfect" or who could really shine in an interview may never get the chance to get in front of an interviewer. Moreover, the vigorous screening process offers little opportunity for hiring managers to assess curiosity, passion, and other intangibles that top performers have—or the negative attributes that can make someone a toxic presence in the workplace.

Those positive intangibles are vital to maintaining the upbeat, service-driven culture that Tony Hsieh and his colleagues have fostered. To attract the Zappos kind of candidate, a strict reliance on a facts-and-figures screening simply wouldn't work because it would filter out people with unconventional back-grounds while also passing through people who look good on paper but don't have what it takes to succeed at Zappos.

To find employees who will thrive in and protect the uncon-ventional Zappos culture, the company takes an unorthodox path when it comes to recruiting and interviewing. For example, many companies refuse to look at videos of job candidates early in the recruiting process out of fear of getting slapped with employment discrimination lawsuits appearance, age, race, and other visible factors. In sharp contrast, Zappos encourages applicants to send videos of themselves. And in perhaps its boldest recruiting move yet, the company no longer posts job openings. Instead, it now requires would-be employees to join a customized social network called Inside Zappos. The network lets candidates learn more about what it's like to work at Zappos, and it lets the company learn more about the candidates—including how they interact with other people.

The Zappos interviewing process is designed to find passionate, free-thinking candidates who fit the culture, from the offbeat antics to the serious commitment to customers and fellow employees. Some of the questions interviewees can expect to encounter include "What was the best mistake you made on the job?" and "On a scale of 1 to 10, how weird are you?"

Speaking of offbeat interviews, the company recently screened software engineering candidates using 30-minute coding challenges, in which the first programmer to solve the problem was "fast-tracked to Vegas" for the next round of interviews. Coding contests are not all that unusual for recruiting programmers, but it's unlikely that many feature an open bar, as the Zappos competition did.

A strong customer- and employee-focused culture, a strong commitment to maintaining that culture, and a recruiting strategy that finds the right people for that culture—this relentless focus on doing business the Zappos way keeps paying off. The company continues to grow and to be ranked as one of the best places to work in the United States.[60]

Critical Thinking Questions

11-1. Not all potentially good employees have a bubbly, goofy personality of the type that Zappos likes to attract. Would it be wise for the company to reject a candidate solely on the basis of a shy, introverted personality? Would it be discriminatory to do so?

11-2. What are the potential risks of emphasizing personality, particularly offbeat personality, in the recruiting process?

11-3. How should a positive, upbeat culture handle the inevitable disappointments and tragedies that happen in any company, from the need to terminate low performers to the death of an employee.

LEARN MORE ONLINE

Visit Inside Zappos (http://jobs.zappos.com), the careers portion of the Zappos website and read the various depart-ment descriptions in the Choose Your Team section. How do these descriptions and the profiles of various team members appeal to potential employees? Could they potentially turn off some job seekers? If so, would this necessarily be a bad thing? Which of the Zappos teams would you choose if you were applying at the company?

KEY TERMS

bonus
cafeteria plans
commissions
compensation
contingent employees
diversity initiatives
electronic performance monitoring (EPM)
employee assistance program (EAP)
employee benefits
employee retention
employee stock-ownership plan (ESOP)
401(k) plan
gain sharing
glass ceiling
human resources (HR) management
job description
job specification
knowledge-based pay
layoffs
mandatory retirement
orientation programs

pay for performance
pension plans
performance appraisals
profit sharing
quality of work life (QWL)
recruiting
retirement plans
salary
sexism
sexual harassment
skills inventory
stock options
succession planning
termination
360-degree review
turnover rate
wages
work–life balance
worker buyouts
workforce analytics

MyBizLab

To complete the problems with the ⭐,
go to EOC Discussion Questions in the
MyLab.

TEST YOUR KNOWLEDGE

Questions for Review

11-4. Give examples of possible employee benefits.

11-5. What are some strategic staffing alternatives that organizations use to avoid overstaffing and understaffing?

11-6. What is the purpose of conducting a job analysis? What are some of the techniques used for gathering information?

11-7. How do defined-benefit plans differ from defined contribution plans?

11-8. What is a job specification?

Questions for Analysis

11-9. What benefits could helping employees balance their work and personal lives have on the overall business?

11-10. Why do some employers offer comprehensive benefits even though the costs of doing so have risen significantly in recent years?

11-11. Why would HR managers be concerned with employee retention? Use examples.

⭐ 11-12. Why is it in a company's best interests to break down the glass ceiling?

⭐ 11-13. **Ethical Considerations.** Corporate headhunters have been known to raid other companies of their top talent to fill vacant or new positions for their clients. Is it ethical to contact the CEO of one company and lure him or her to join the management team of another company?

Questions for Application

11-14. Assume that you are the manager of human resources at a manufacturing company that employs about 500 people. A recent cyclical downturn in your industry has led to financial losses, and top management is talking about laying off workers. Several supervisors have come to you with creative ways of keeping employees on the payroll, such as sharing workers with other local companies. Why might you want to consider this option? What other options exist besides layoffs?

11-15. When you begin interviewing as you approach graduation, you will need to analyze job offers that include a number of financial and nonfinancial elements. Which of these aspects of employment are your top three priorities: a good base wage, bonus or commission opportunities, profit-sharing potential, rapid advancement opportunities, flexible work arrangements, good health-care insurance coverage, or a strong retirement program? Which of these elements would you be willing to forgo in order to get your top three?

11-16. What steps could you take as the owner of a small software company to foster "temporary loyalty" from the independent programmers you frequently hire for short durations (one to six months)?

11-17. Concept Integration. Of the five levels in Maslow's hierarchy of needs, which is satisfied by offering salary? By offering health-care benefits? By offering training opportunities? By developing flexible job descriptions?

EXPAND YOUR KNOWLEDGE

Discovering Career Opportunities

If you pursue a career in human resources, you'll be deeply involved in helping organizations find, select, train, evaluate, and retain employees. You have to like people and be a good communicator to succeed in HR. Is this field for you? Find ads seeking applicants for positions in the field of human resources, and then answer the following questions.

11-18. What educational qualifications, technical knowledge, or specialized skills are applicants for these jobs expected to have? How do these requirements fit with your background and educational plans?

11-19. Next, look at the duties mentioned in the ad for each job. What do you think you would be doing on an average day in these jobs? Does the work in each job sound interesting and challenging?

11-20. Now think about how you might fit into one of these positions. Do you prefer to work alone, or do you enjoy teamwork? How much paperwork are you willing to do? Do you communicate better in person, on paper, or by phone? Considering your answers to these questions, which of the HR jobs seems to be the closest match for your personal style?

Improving Your Tech Insights: Telecommuting Technologies

Thanks to mobile communications and cloud computing, working without going to the office is easier than ever before.

When they're used successfully, telecommuting technologies can reduce facility costs, put employees closer to customers, reduce traffic and air pollution, give companies access to a wide range of independent talent, and let employees work in higher-salary jobs while living in lower-cost areas of the country. In the future, these technologies have the potential to change business so radically that they could even influence the design of entire cities. With less need to pull millions of workers into central business districts, business executives, urban planners, and political leaders have the opportunity to explore such new ideas as *telecities*—virtual cities populated by people and organizations connected technologically rather than physically.

Telecommuting offers compelling benefits, but it must be planned and managed carefully. Conduct some online research to find out what experts believe are the keys to success. Start with the Telework Coalition, www.telcoa.org. You can also find numerous articles in business publications (search for both "telecommuting" and "telework"). In a brief email message to your instructor, provide four or five important tips for ensuring successful telecommuting work arrangements.[61]

PRACTICE YOUR SKILLS

Sharpening Your Communication Skills

Public companies occasionally need to issue news releases to announce or explain downturns in sales, profits, demand, or other business factors. Search the web to locate a company that has issued a press release that recently reported lower earnings or other bad news and access the news release on the firm's website. You can also search for press releases at www.prnewswire.com or www.businesswire.com. How does the headline relate to the main message of the release? Does the company come right out and deliver the bad news, or build up to it by explaining the circumstances behind it first? What does the company do to present the bad news in a favorable light, if applicable—and does this effort seem sincere and ethical to you? In a brief message to your instructor, give your assessment of how well the press release conveys the bad news without being overly negative or falsely positive.

Building Your Team Skills

Appraisals or performance monitoring is an important part of employment. With this in mind, work in pairs to conduct an appraisal of your efforts so far at college or university. Take turns to apprise the class of each other's efforts so far. As part of the appraisal or performance monitoring process, you should also look to build a personal development plan based on the findings from your appraisal session.

Developing Your Research Skills

Locate the 5 best companies in 2015 at Forbes (print or online editions) at http://www.forbes.com/sites/kathryndill/

2014/12/10/the-best-places-to-work-in-2015/.   Various policies implemented had resulted in high engagements and satisfaction among different generations in the workplace. These innovative companies are actively pursuing workforce diversity initiatives as a strategic opportunity. Equal gender opportunities in recruiting, promotion, returning women at the workforce, higher women representation at the board will remain one of the key interests for the management to retain local talents.

11-21. What are the workforce initiatives that are implemented that enable the companies to emerge as the best companies in 2015? Compare the rankings in 2014. Were there any significant changes on the workforce diversity initiatives? In what way(s) had the initiatives differed?

11-22. What would be the main constraint(s) of the small-medium size (SME) companies to achieve high engagements of workforce diversity at work place? How important are these initiatives to SMEs as opposed to global companies?

11-23. Locate the 5 best local companies in your home country in the newspapers (print or online editions). In what ways are the changes in the workforce differs? Do you think the leaders of the company will promote or discourage workforce diversity at workplace? Why?

MyBizLab®

Go to the Assignments section of your MyLab to complete these writing exercises.

11-24. How is management likely to change as companies increasingly use contingent workers instead of full-time employees?

11-25. What are some ways that pay-for-performance schemes could backfire if a company doesn't set them up carefully or effectively manage the factors that affect employee performance?

ENDNOTES

1. Zappos Inside Zappos page, accessed 8 August 2014, https://jobs.zappos.com; Blair Hanley Frank, "Zappos Ditches Job Posts, replaces Them with a Social Network," *GeekWire*, 27 May 2014, www.geekwire.com. "Wishez Is Live," Zappos Family blog, 17 November 2010, http://blogs.zappos.com; Tony Hsieh, "Amazon & Zappos, 1 Year Later," Zappos CEO & COO blog, 22 July 2010, http://blogs.zappos.com; Todd Raphael, "7 Interview Questions from Zappos," Todd Raphael's World of Talent blog, 22 July 2010, http://community.ere.net; Jeffrey M. O'Brien, "Zappos Knows How to Kick It," *Fortune*, 22 January 2009, http://about.zappos.com/ press-center; "Zappos Family Seattle Coding Challenge and Tech Tweet Up," Zappos Family blog, 22 March 2011, http://blogs.zappos.com.

2. Gary Dessler, *A Framework for Human Resource Management*, 3rd ed. (Upper Saddle River, N.J.: Pearson Prentice Hall, 2004), 2.

3. Dessler, *A Framework for Human Resource Management*, 66.

4. Dessler, *A Framework for Human Resource Management*, 72.

5. Dessler, *A Framework for Human Resource Management*, 74–75.

6. Shari Randall, "Succession Planning Is More Than a Game of Chance," *Workforce Management*, accessed 1 May 2004, www.workforce.com.

7. Bruce Morton, "Hello New Frontier: The Growing Contingent Workforce," *Allegis Group Services*, 26 March 2013, www.allegisgroupservices.com.

8. Arik Hesseldahl, "Yahoo Redux: HP Says 'All Hands on Deck' Needed, Requiring Most Employees to Work at the Office (Memo)," *AllThingsD*, 8 October 2013, http://allthingsd.com; Ted Samson, "Can a VPN Log Really Point to Employee Slacking?" *InfoWorld*, 5 March 2013, www.infoworld.com.

9. Michael R. Carrell, Everett F. Mann, and Tracey Honeycutt Sigler, "Defining Workforce Diversity Programs and Practices in Organizations: A Longitudinal Study," *Labor Law Journal*, Spring 2006, 5–12.

10. "Dimensions of Diversity—Workforce," Merck website, accessed 4 January 2011, www.merck.com.

11. Nancy R. Lockwood, "Workplace Diversity: Leveraging the Power of Difference for Competitive Advantage," *HR Magazine*, June 2005, special section 1–10.

12. Podcast interview with Ron Glover, *IBM* website, accessed 17 August, 2008, www.ibm.com.

13. Peter Coy, "Old. Smart. Productive." *BusinessWeek*, 27 June 2005, www.businessweek.com; Iris Beamer and Linda Varner, *Intercultural Communication in the Global Workplace*, 3rd ed. (Columbus, Ohio: McGraw-Hill/Irwin, 2004), 107–108.

14. Beamer and Varner, *Intercultural Communication in the Global Workplace*, 107–108.

15. "Sex-Based Charges: FY 1997–FY 2012," EEOC website, accessed 7 November 2013, www.eeoc.gov.

16. "Women CEOs of the S&P 500," Catalyst, 3 April 2015, www.catalyst.org.

17. *Women in America: Indicators of Social and Economic Well Being*, White House Council on Women and Girls, March 2011, iii; *An Analysis of Reasons for the Disparity in Wages Between Men and Women*, U.S. Department of Labor Employment Standards Administration, 12 January 2009, 1.

18. Christina Hoff Sommers, "No, Women Don't Make Less Money Than Men," *The Daily Beast*, 1 February 2014, www.thedailybeast.com.

19. Lydia Dishman, "The Other Wage Gap: Why Men in Female-Dominated Industries Still Earn More," *Fast Company*, 8 April 2015, www.fastcompany.com.

20. *An Analysis of Reasons for the Disparity in Wages Between Men and Women*, 1.

21. Hanna Rosin, "The Gender Wage Gap Lie," *Slate*, 30 August 2013, www.slate.com.

22. "Sexual Harassment Charges: EEOC & FEPAs Combined: FY 1997–FY 2006," EEOC website, accessed 13 August 2007, www.eeoc.gov.

23. Robert Kreitner, *Management*, 9th ed. (Boston: Houghton Mifflin, 2004), 375–377; "One-Fifth of Women Are Harassed Sexually," *HR Focus*, April 2002, 2.

24. Paul Taylor, "The Next America," Pew Research Center, 10 April 2014, www.pewressarch.com; "More Than 300 Counties Now 'Majority–Minority,'" press release, U.S. Census Bureau website, 9 August 2007, www.census.gov; Robert Kreitner, *Management*, 9th ed. (Boston: Houghton Mifflin, 2004), 84.

25. "Race-Based Charges: FY 1997–FY 2012," EEOC website, accessed 7 November 2013, www.eeoc.gov.

26. "Usual Weekly Earnings of Wage and Salary Workers: Third Quarter 2013," U.S. Bureau of Labor Statistics, 7 November 2013, www.bls.gov.

27. Mark D. Downey, "Keeping the Faith," HR Magazine, January 2008, 85–88.

28. Vadim Liberman, "What Happens When an Employee's Freedom of Religion Crosses Paths with a Company's Interests?" Conference Board Review, September/October 2007, 42–48.

29. "Diversity 3.0," IBM website, accessed 21 June 2009, www.ibm.com; Wendy Harris, "Out of the Corporate Closet," Black Enterprise, accessed 13 August 2007, http://integrate.factivia.com; May 2007, David A. Thomas, "Diversity as Strategy," Harvard Business Review, September 2004, 98–108; Joe Mullich, "Hiring Without Limits," Workforce Management, June 2004, 53–58; Mike France and William G. Symonds, "Diversity Is About to Get More Elusive, Not Less," BusinessWeek, 7 July 2003, www.businessweek.com; Anne Papmehl, "Diversity in Workforce Paying Off, IBM Finds," Toronto Star, 7 October 2002, www.elibrary.com.

30. Samuel Greengard, "Quality of Hire: How Companies Are Crunching the Numbers," Workforce Management, July 2004, www.workforce.com.

31. Steven Mitchell Sack, "The Working Woman's Legal Survival Guide: Testing," FindLaw.com, accessed 22 February 2004, www.findlaw.com; David W. Arnold and John W. Jones, "Who the Devil's Applying Now?" Security Management, March 2002, 85–88.

32. "Age Discrimination in Employment Act: FY 1997–FY 2010," EEOC website, accessed 30 August 2011, www.eeoc.gov; Russ Banham, "Age Bias Claims Rise," Treasury & Risk, May 2009, 14–15.

33. John Jude Moran, Employment Law: New Challenges in the Business Environment, 2nd ed. (Upper Saddle River, N.J.: Pearson Prentice Hall, 2002), 127; Dan Seligman, "The Right to Fire," Forbes, 10 November 2003, 126–128.

34. "The Age Discrimination in Employment Act of 1967," U.S. Equal Employment Opportunity Commission website, accessed 10 July 2009, www.eeoc.gov; Henry R. Cheeseman, Contemporary Business and E-Commerce Law, 7th ed. (Upper Saddle River, N.J.: Pearson Prentice Hall, 2010), 522–523.

35. Kelly Spors, "Why Performance Reviews Don't Work—And What You Can Do About It," Independent Street blog, Wall Street Journal, 21 October 2008, http://blogs.wsj.com.

36. Carrie Brodzinski, "Avoiding Wrongful Termination Suits," National Underwriter Property & Casualty—Risk & Benefits Management, 13 October 2003, www.elibrary.com.

37. PerformanceNow.com website, accessed 2 May 2004, www.performancenow.com; Dessler, A Framework for Human Resource Management, 199.

38. Amy Gallow, "Bouncing Back from a Negative 360-Degree Review," Harvard Business Review blogs, 29 July 2010, http://blogs.hbr.org; Tracy Gallagher, "360-Degree Performance Reviews Offer Valuable Perspectives," Financial Executive, December 2008, 61.

39. Jeff St. John, "Kennewick, Wash., 'Snoop' Software Maker Also Protects Privacy," (Kennewick, Wash.) Tri-City Herald, 17 April 2004, www.highbeam.com; Dessler, A Framework for Human Resource Management, 204–205.

40. Laurel A. McNall and Sylvia G. Roch, "A Social Exchange Model of Employee Reactions to Electronic Performance Monitoring," Human Performance, 22, 2009, 204–224.

41. Carol A. Hacker, "New Employee Orientation: Make It Pay Dividends for Years to Come," Information Systems Management, Winter 2004, 89–92.

42. "Enterprise Management Training Program," Enterprise Holdings website, accessed 19 April 2015, http://go.enterpriseholdings.com.

43. Dessler, A Framework for Human Resource Management, 223–225.

44. Vadim Liberman, "What About the Rest of Us?" Conference Board Review, Summer 2011, 40–47.

45. "Executive Paywatch," AFL-CIO website, accessed 19 April 2015, www.aflcio.org; Elliot Blair Smith & Phil Kuntz, "CEO Pay 1,795-to-1 Multiple of Wages Skirts U.S. Law," Bloomberg, 29 April 2013, www.bloomberg.com.

46. Jeff D. Opdyke, "Getting a Bonus Instead of a Raise," Wall Street Journal, 29 December 2004, D1–D2.

47. Paul Loucks, "Creating a Performance-Based Culture," Benefits & Compensation Digest, July 2007, 36–39.

48. Dessler, A Framework for Human Resource Management, 231–232.

49. Gregory Lopes, "Firms Dock Pay of Obese, Smokers," Washington Times, 13 August 2007, www.washingtontimes.com; Joseph Weber, "Health Insurance: Small Biz Is in a Bind," BusinessWeek, 27 September 2004, 47–48; Joseph Pereira, "Parting Shot: To Save on Health-Care Costs, Firms Fire Disabled Workers," Wall Street Journal, 14 July 2003, A1, A7; Timothy Aeppel, "Ill Will: Skyrocketing Health Costs Start to Pit Worker vs. Worker," Wall Street Journal, 17 July 2003, A1, A6; Vanessa Furhmans, "To Stem Abuses, Employers Audit Workers' Health Claims," Wall Street Journal, 31 March 2004, B1, B7; Milt Freudenheim, "Employees Paying Ever-Bigger Share for Health Care," New York Times, A1, C2; Julie Appleby, "Employers Get Nosy About Workers' Health," USA Today, 6 March 2003, B1–B2; Ellen E. Schultz and Theo Francis, "Employers' Caps Raise Retirees' Health-Care Costs," Wall Street Journal, 25 November 2003, B1, B11; Vanessa Furhmans, "Company Health Plans Try to Drop Spouses," Wall Street Journal, 9 September 2003, D1, D2.

50. "Global Health-Care Snapshot," Wall Street Journal MarketWatch, accessed 2 December 2011, www.marketwatch.com; Victoria Colliver, "We Spend More, but U.S. Health Care Quality Falls Behind," San Francisco Chronicle, 10 July 2007, www.scrippsnews.com; Steve Lohr, "The Disparate Consensus on Health Care for All," New York Times, 6 December 2004, C16; Sara Schaefer and Laurie McGinley, "Census Sees a Surge in Americans Without Insurance," Wall Street Journal, 30 September 2003, B1, B6; "Half of Health Care Spending Is Wasted, Study Finds," Detroit News, 10 February 2005, www.detnews.com.

51. Avik Roy, "3,137-County Analysis: Obamacare Increased 2014 Individual-Market Premiums By Average Of 49%," Forbes, 18 June 2014, www.forbes.com.

52. "Choosing a Retirement Plan: Defined Benefit Plan," U.S. Internal Revenue Service, accessed 31 August 2011, www.irs.gov; U.S. Pension Benefit Guaranty Corporation, accessed 31 August 2011, www.pbgc.gov; James H. Dulebohn, Brian Murray, and Minghe Sun, "Selection Among Employer-Sponsored Pension Plans: The Role of Individual Differences," Personal Psychology, Summer 2000, 405–432.

53. The ESOP Association website, accessed 19 April 2015, www.esopassociation.org; Dessler, A Framework for Human Resource Management, 282.

54. Michelle Kessler, "Fears Subside over Accounting for Stock Options," USA Today, 1 January 2006, www.usatoday.com; Robert A. Guth and Joann S. Lublin, "Tarnished Gold: Microsoft Users Out Era of Options," Wall Street Journal, 9 July 2003, A1, A9; John Markoff and David Leonhardt, "Microsoft Will Award Stock, Not Options, to Employees," New York Times, 9 July 2003, A1, C4.

55. Sydney Finkelstein, "Rethinking CEO Stock Options," BusinessWeek, 20 April 2009, 23.

56. Cheeseman, Contemporary Business and E-Commerce Law, 626.

57. Patrick J. Kiger, "Child-Care Models," Workforce Management, April 2004, 38.

58. Andy Meisler, "A Matter of Degrees," Workforce Management, May 2004, 32–38; Stephanie Armour, "More Firms Help Workers Find Home Sweet Home," USA Today, 30 August 2004, C1–C2.

59. William Atkinson, "Wellness, Employee Assistance Programs: Investments, Not Costs," *Bobbin*, May 2000, 42; Kevin Dobbs, Jack Gordon, and David Stamps, "EAPs Cheap but Popular Perk," *Training*, February 2000, 26.

60. See Note 1.

61. TelCoa website, accessed 19 April 2015, www.telcoa.org; "Benchmarking Study Finds 'Telework' Has Evolved into a Main-stream Way of Working; Now, 'It's Just Work,'" press release, *TelCoa*, 9 March 2006, www.telcoa.org; Rich Karlgaard, "Outsource Yourself," *Forbes*, 19 April 2004, www.highbeam .com; David Kirkpatrick, "Big-League R&D Gets Its Own eBay," *Fortune*, 3 May 2004, www.highbeam.com; Joseph N. Pelton, "The Rise of Telecities: Decentralizing the Global Society," *The Futurist*, 1 January 2004, www.highbeam.com.

Chapter 10
Finance and
Accounting

17 Financial Information and Accounting Concepts

BEHIND THE SCENES REALITY COMES KNOCKING AT THE GOOGLEPLEX

Google's chief financial officer Ruth Porat oversees the company's financial planning and management activities.

www.google.com

You may have received some nice employee benefits somewhere along the line, but did an armored truck ever back up to your company's front door to hand out $1,000 to every employee at Christmas time?

As Google's dominance in the profitable search engine market grew in recent years and its stock price soared, the company looked like it just might end up with all the cash in the world. To create one of the world's best places to work, the Mountain View, California, Internet giant sometimes spent money as if it had unlimited cash, too. Employee perks ranged from a companywide ski trip and an annual cash bonus—which really was delivered by armored truck—to free meals cooked by gourmet chefs and on-site doctors, massages, and car service.

Beyond these mere amenities, Google created one of the most interesting and stimulating workplaces imaginable. Engineers were allowed to spend up to 20 percent of their time exploring whatever fascinated them, even if those adventures weren't directly related to the company's current business efforts. Those explorations often did lead to new products and features, though, as Google's product line expanded far beyond its original search engine.

As it launched new projects and business initiatives right and left, Google kept hiring the best and the brightest; by 2008, the company had 20,000 employees and another 10,000 contractors. It had also acquired more than 50 other companies, paying from a few million dollars to get small niche companies on up to $1.65 billion to buy YouTube and $3.1 billion to buy the online advertising company DoubleClick.

Cash was flowing in, cash was flowing out, and all was good in the Googleplex, as the company's headquarters complex is known. But reality has a way of catching up to even the highest-flying companies, and Google would prove no exception. Internally, after a decade of rampant growth, expenses were eating up an ever-larger share of revenue. Externally, the global economy was cooling off quickly, and one company after another began trimming advertising budgets. Despite its many product innovations and explorations, Google still depended on search engine advertising for nearly all its revenue. Online advertising wasn't getting chopped quite as severely as ads for television and other traditional media, but the spending reductions were serious enough to slow Google's sales growth. With expenses growing faster than revenue, something had to give.

If you were in charge of Google's finances, how would you bring spending under control without alienating a workforce that has come to expect a certain level of pampering—and without stifling innovation, the engine behind the company's spectacular growth?[1]

INTRODUCTION

As the chief financial officer of Google (profiled in the chapter-opening Behind the Scenes), Ruth Porat could surely tell you how vital it is to have accurate, up-to-date accounting information. After providing an introduction to what accountants do and the rules they are expected to follow, this chapter explains the fundamental concepts of the accounting equation and double-entry bookkeeping. It then explores the primary "report cards" used in accounting: the balance sheet, income statement, and statement of cash flows. The chapter wraps up with a look at trend analysis and ratio analysis, the tools that managers, lenders, and investors use to predict a company's ongoing health.

Understanding Accounting

Accounting is the system a business uses to identify, measure, and communicate financial information to others, inside and outside the organization. Accurate and timely financial information is important to businesses such as Google for two reasons: First, it helps managers and owners plan and control a company's operations and make informed business decisions. Second, it helps outsiders evaluate a business. Suppliers, banks, and other parties want to know whether a business is creditworthy; shareholders and other investors are concerned with its profit potential; government agencies are interested in its tax accounting.

Because outsiders and insiders use accounting information for different purposes, accounting has two distinct facets. **Financial accounting** is concerned with preparing financial statements and other information for outsiders such as stockholders and *creditors* (people or organizations that have lent a company money or have extended its credit); **management accounting** is concerned with preparing cost analyses, profitability reports, budgets, and other information for insiders such as management and other company decision makers. To be useful, all accounting information must be accurate, objective, consistent over time, and comparable to information supplied by other companies.

WHAT ACCOUNTANTS DO

The work accountants do is sometimes confused with **bookkeeping**, which is the clerical function of recording the economic activities of a business. Although some accountants do perform bookkeeping functions, their work generally goes well beyond the scope of this activity. Accountants prepare financial statements, analyze and interpret financial information, prepare financial forecasts and budgets, and prepare tax returns. Some accountants specialize in certain areas of accounting, such as *cost accounting* (computing and analyzing production and operating costs), *tax accounting* (preparing tax returns and interpreting tax law), *financial analysis* (evaluating a company's performance and the financial implications of strategic decisions such as product pricing, employee benefits, and business acquisitions), or *forensic accounting* (combining accounting and investigating skills to assist in legal and criminal matters).

---

1 | **LEARNING OBJECTIVE**

Define *accounting*, and describe the roles of private and public accountants.

accounting
Measuring, interpreting, and communicating financial information to support internal and external decision making.

financial accounting
The area of accounting concerned with preparing financial information for users outside the organization.

management accounting
The area of accounting concerned with preparing data for use by managers within the organization.

bookkeeping
Recordkeeping; the clerical aspect of accounting.

In addition to traditional accounting work, accountants may also help clients improve business processes, plan for the future, evaluate product performance, analyze profitability by customer and product groups, and design and install new computer systems; assist companies with decision making; and provide a variety of other management consulting services. Performing these functions requires a strong business background and a variety of business skills beyond accounting.

PRIVATE ACCOUNTANTS

private accountants
In-house accountants employed by organizations and businesses other than a public accounting firm; also called *corporate accountants*.

Private accountants work for corporations, government agencies, and not-for-profit organizations. Their titles vary by function and include *corporate accountant, managerial accountant,* and *cost accountant.*[2] Private accountants generally work together as a team under the supervision of the organization's **controller**, who reports to the vice president of finance or the chief financial officer (CFO). Exhibit 17.1 shows the typical finance department of a large company. In smaller organizations, the controller may be in charge of the company's entire finance operation and report directly to the president.

controller
The highest-ranking accountant in a company, responsible for overseeing all accounting functions.

Although certification is not required of private accountants, many are licensed **certified public accountants (CPAs)**. Specific requirements vary by state, but to receive a CPA license, an individual must complete a certain number of hours of college-level coursework, have a minimum number of years of work experience in the accounting field, and pass the Uniform CPA Exam.[3] Growing numbers of private accountants are becoming *certified management accountants (CMAs)*; to do so, they must pass an intensive exam sponsored by the Institute of Management Accountants.[4]

certified public accountants (CPAs)
Professionally licensed accountants who meet certain requirements for education and experience and who pass a comprehensive examination.

PUBLIC ACCOUNTANTS

public accountants
Professionals who provide accounting services to other businesses and individuals for a fee.

In contrast to private accountants, **public accountants** are independent of the businesses, organizations, and individuals they serve. Most public accountants are employed by public accounting firms that provide a variety of accounting and consulting

---

EXHIBIT 17.1	Typical Finance Department

Here is a typical finance department of a large company. In smaller companies, the controller may be the highest-ranking accountant and report directly to the president. The top executive in charge of finance is often called the chief financial officer (CFO).

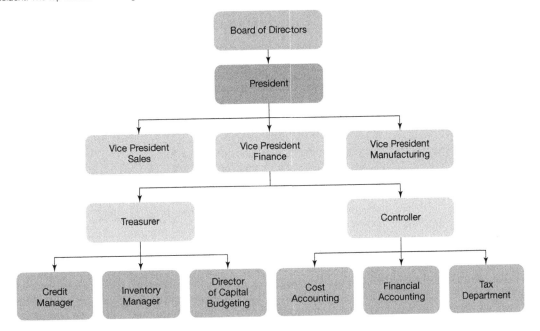

services to their clients. The largest of these, four international networks known as the "Big Four," are Deloitte Touche Tohmatsu (www.deloitte.com), Ernst & Young (www.ey.com), KPMG (www.kpmg.com), and PricewaterhouseCoopers, or PwC (www.pwc.com). Whether they belong to one of these giant networks (each of which employs more than 100,000 people) or to a smaller independent firm, public accountants generally are CPAs and must obtain CPA and state licensing certifications before they are eligible to conduct an **audit**—a formal evaluation of a company's accounting records and processes to ensure the integrity and reliability of a company's financial statements.

audit
Formal evaluation of the fairness and reliability of a client's financial statements.

By the way, if you've shied away from accounting as a career choice because of popular stereotypes about it being a dull job fit only for "bean counters," it's time to take another look. Partly as a consequence of financial scandals in recent years and the growing complexity of accounting regulations, accounting specialists are now in demand in many industries. Employment is growing faster than average for all accounting occupations, while salaries and benefits are increasing as everybody from the Big Four to the Federal Bureau of Investigation (FBI) to corporations both large and small actively recruit accountants to help navigate the challenging landscape of contemporary business finance.[5]

REAL-TIME UPDATES
Learn More by Visiting This Website

Considering a career in accounting?

This comprehensive directory can help you explore the profession and find potential employers. Go to http://real-timeupdates.com/bia8 and click on Learn More in the Students section.

✓ Checkpoint

LEARNING OBJECTIVE 1: Define *accounting*, and describe the roles of private and public accountants.

SUMMARY: Accounting is the system a business uses to identify, measure, and communicate financial information to others, inside and outside the organization. Accountants perform a wide variety of tasks, including preparing financial statements, analyzing and interpreting financial information, preparing financial forecasts and budgets, preparing tax returns, interpreting tax law, computing and analyzing production costs, evaluating a company's performance, and analyzing the financial implications of business decisions. Private accountants work for corporations, government agencies, and not-for-profit organizations, performing various accounting functions for their employers. Public accountants, in contrast, sell their services to individuals and organizations. One of the most important functions of public accountants is performing audits, a formal evaluation of a company's accounting records and processes.

CRITICAL THINKING: (1) Why would a private accountant bother with becoming a CPA? (2) What effect can unreliable or uncertain accounting have on the economy?

IT'S YOUR BUSINESS: (1) How rigorous are your personal bookkeeping and accounting efforts? Do you keep accurate records, analyze spending, and set budgets? (2) If you don't really account for your personal finances, how might doing so help you, now and in the future?

KEY TERMS TO KNOW: accounting, financial accounting, management accounting, bookkeeping, private accountants, controller, certified public accountants (CPAs), public accountants, audit

Major Accounting Rules

In order to make informed decisions, investors, bankers, suppliers, and other parties need some means to verify the quality of the financial information that companies release to the public. They also need some way to compare information from one company to the

2 LEARNING OBJECTIVE

Explain the impact of accounting standards such as GAAP and the Sarbanes-Oxley Act on corporate accounting.

next. To accommodate these needs, financial accountants are expected to follow a number of rules, some of which are voluntary and some of which are required by law.

GENERALLY ACCEPTED ACCOUNTING PRINCIPLES (GAAP)

Accounting is based on numbers, so it might seem like a straightforward task to tally up a company's revenues and costs to determine its net profits. However, accounting is often anything but simple. For instance, *revenue recognition*, how and when a company records incoming revenue, is a particularly complex topic.[6] As just one example, should a company record revenue (a) when it ships products to or performs services for customers, (b) when it bills customers, (c) when customers actually pay, or (d) after everyone has paid and any products that are going to be returned for refunds have been returned (because refunds reduce revenue)? If customers are in financial trouble and taking a long time to pay or are not paying at all, or if a poorly designed product is generating a lot of returns, the differences can be substantial.

From booking revenues and expenses to placing a value on assets and liabilities, these decisions affect just about every aspect of a company's stated financial picture. That picture in turn affects how much tax the company has to pay, how attractive it is as an investment opportunity, how creditworthy it is from a lender's point of view, and other significant outcomes.

GAAP (generally accepted accounting principles)
Standards and practices used by publicly held corporations in the United States and a few other countries in the preparation of financial statements.

To help ensure consistent financial reporting so that all stakeholders understand what they're looking at, over the years regulators, auditors, and company representatives have agreed on a series of accounting standards and procedures. **GAAP (generally accepted accounting principles)**, overseen in the United States by the Financial Accounting Standards Board (FASB), aims to give a fair and true picture of a company's financial position and to enable outsiders to make confident analyses and comparisons. GAAP can't prevent every reporting abuse, but it does make distorting financial results in order to fool outsiders more difficult.[7]

external auditors
Independent accounting firms that provide auditing services for public companies.

As Chapter 18 notes, companies whose stock is publicly traded in the United States are required to file audited financial statements with the Securities and Exchange Commission (SEC). During an audit, CPAs who work for an independent accounting firm, also known as **external auditors**, review a client's financial records to determine whether the statements that summarize these records have been prepared in accordance with GAAP. The auditors then summarize their findings in a report attached to the client's published financial statements. Sometimes these reports disclose information that might materially affect the client's financial position, such as the bankruptcy of a major supplier, a large obsolete inventory, costly environmental problems, or questionable accounting practices. A clean audit report means that to the best of the auditors' knowledge a company's financial statements are accurate.

To assist with the auditing process, many large organizations use *internal auditors*—employees who investigate and evaluate the organization's internal operations and data to determine whether they are accurate and whether they comply with GAAP, federal laws, and industry regulations. Although this self-checking process is vital to an organization's financial health, an internal audit is not a substitute for having an independent auditor look things over and render an unbiased opinion.

Non-GAAP Metrics

U.S. public companies are required to report financial results that meet GAAP standards, but they can also publish "non-GAAP" results. These metrics can range from the number of new customers during a particular period to the widely used but still non-GAAP measure known as EBITDA (see the discussion on page 456). This is typically done when executives believe non-GAAP metrics provide a more compelling or complete picture of the company's performance and prospects. However, the practice is controversial, with some accountants and investors wary that companies really use non-GAAP metrics to obscure poor performance rather than to highlight areas of good performance. Moreover, because the definitions of these measurements are not standardized, companies can change them over time, potentially to make performance look better.[8] In any event, companies must label these figures as non-GAAP data in their financial reports, and securities regulators can ask companies to remove or modify the presentation of non-GAAP data if these figures might mislead investors.[9]

Global Reporting Standards

GAAP has helped standardize accounting and financial reporting for companies in the United States, but the situation is more complex at the international level because GAAP standards are not used in most other countries. The lack of global standardization creates extra work for U.S. multinationals, essentially forcing them to keep two sets of books.[10] In addition, it complicates cross-border transactions, mergers, and investments because companies don't have a single set of tools to compute assets, liabilities, and other vital quantities.

Companies and investors have to deal with different reporting standards in financial markets around the world (*pictured*: the Hong Kong Stock Exchange).

Most other countries use **international financial reporting standards (IFRS)** maintained by the London-based International Accounting Standards Board. After a decade-long effort to harmonize the GAAP and IFRS, the two systems are closer in some respects but still different in some significant ways. In fact, there was a lot of momentum over the years to converge the two systems into a single, global set of standards. However, that convergence effort now appears to be stalled.[11] If the SEC ever does make the switch to IFRS, it could bring extensive changes to the accounting profession, financial management, information systems, stock-based compensation and bonuses, and other aspects of managing a public corporation.[12]

international financial reporting standards (IFRS)
Accounting standards and practices used in many countries outside the United States.

SARBANES-OXLEY

The need for and complexity of financial reporting standards is highlighted in the story of **Sarbanes-Oxley**, the informal name of the Public Company Accounting Reform and Investor Protection Act. (You'll hear it referred to as "Sox" or "Sarbox" as well.) Passed in 2002 in the wake of several cases of massive accounting fraud, most notably involving the energy company Enron and the telecom company WorldCom, Sarbanes-Oxley changed public company accounting in the United States in a number of important ways. Its major provisions include[13]

Sarbanes-Oxley
The informal name of comprehensive legislation designed to improve the integrity and accountability of financial information.

- Outlawing most loans by corporations to their own directors and executives
- Creating the Public Company Accounting Oversight Board (PCAOB) to oversee external auditors, rather than letting the industry regulate itself
- Requiring corporate lawyers to report evidence of financial wrongdoing
- Prohibiting external auditors from providing certain nonaudit services
- Requiring that audit committees on the board of directors have at least one financial expert and that the majority of board members be independent (not employed by the company in an executive position)
- Prohibiting investment bankers from influencing stock analysts
- Requiring CEOs and CFOs to sign statements attesting to the accuracy of their financial statements
- Requiring companies to document and test their internal financial controls and processes

Sarbox generated a lot of criticism initially, particularly from the amount of work involved in documenting internal financial controls. However, after a lot of initial criticism about the costs of compliance and a shift in the PCAOB's stance to let companies focus on monitoring the riskiest financial decisions instead of every mundane transaction, complaints about Sarbox have leveled off in recent years.[14] Opinions vary on whether some aspects went too far or didn't go far enough, but a decade after its implementation, the consensus seems to be that, by and large, the law has improved the quality of financial reporting, increased protections for shareholders, and increased the emphasis on legal compliance and ethical decision making.[15]

Checkpoint

3 **LEARNING OBJECTIVE**

Describe the accounting equation, and explain the purpose of double-entry bookkeeping and the matching principle.

Fundamental Accounting Concepts

In their work with financial data, accountants are guided by three basic concepts: the *fundamental accounting equation, double-entry bookkeeping,* and the *matching principle.* Here is a closer look at each of these essential ideas.

THE ACCOUNTING EQUATION

assets
Any things of value owned or leased by a business.

liabilities
Claims against a firm's assets by creditors.

owners' equity
The portion of a company's assets that belongs to the owners after obligations to all creditors have been met.

For thousands of years, businesses and governments have kept records of their **assets**— valuable items they own or lease, such as equipment, cash, land, buildings, inventory, and investments. Claims against those assets are **liabilities**, or what the business owes to its creditors—such as lenders and suppliers. For example, when a company borrows money to purchase a building, the lender has a claim against the company's assets. What remains after liabilities have been deducted from assets is **owners' equity**:

$$\text{Owners' equity} = \text{Assets} - \text{Liabilities}$$

As a simple example, if your company has $1,000,000 in assets and $800,000 in liabilities, your equity would be $200,000:

$$\$200,000 = \$1,000,000 - 800,000$$

accounting equation
The equation stating that assets equal liabilities plus owners' equity.

Using the principles of algebra, this equation can be restated in a variety of formats. The most common is the simple **accounting equation**, which serves as the framework for the entire accounting process:

$$\text{Assets} = \text{Liabilities} + \text{Owners' equity}$$
$$\$1,000,000 = \$800,000 + 200,000$$

This equation suggests that either creditors or owners provide all the assets in a corporation. Think of it this way: If you were starting a new business, you could contribute cash to the company to buy the assets you needed to run your business or you could borrow money from a bank (the creditor) or you could do both. The company's liabilities are placed before owners' equity in the accounting equation because creditors get paid first. After liabilities have been paid, anything left over belongs to the owners. As a business engages in economic activity, the dollar amounts and composition of its assets, liabilities, and owners' equity change. However, the equation must always be in balance; in other words, one side of the equation must always equal the other side.

REAL-TIME UPDATES
Learn More by Reading This Article

Introduction to the accounting equation

Get a better feel for the accounting equation with these practical examples. Go to http://real-timeupdates.com/bia8 and click on Learn More in the Students section.

DOUBLE-ENTRY BOOKKEEPING AND THE MATCHING PRINCIPLE

To keep the accounting equation in balance, most companies use a **double-entry bookkeeping** system that records every transaction affecting assets, liabilities, or owners' equity. Each transaction is entered twice, once as a *debit* and once as a *credit*, and they must offset each other to keep the accounting equation in balance. The double-entry method predates computers by hundreds of years and was originally created to minimize errors caused by entering and adding figures by hand; accounting software now typically handles all this behind the scenes.

The **matching principle** requires that expenses incurred in producing revenues be deducted from the revenue they generated during the same accounting period. This matching of expenses and revenue is necessary for the company's financial statements to present an accurate picture of the profitability of a business. Accountants match revenue to expenses by adopting the **accrual basis** of accounting, which states that revenue is recognized when you make a sale or provide a service, not when you get paid. Similarly, your expenses are recorded when you receive the benefit of a service or when you use an asset to produce revenue—not when you pay for it.

Accrual accounting focuses on the economic substance of an event rather than on the movement of cash. It's a way of recognizing that revenue can be earned either before or after cash is received and that expenses can be incurred when a company receives a benefit (such as a shipment of supplies) either before or after the benefit is paid for.

If a business runs on a **cash basis**, the company records revenue only when money from the sale is actually received. Your checking account is a simple cash-based accounting system: You record checks, debit card charges, and ATM withdrawals at the time of purchase and record deposits at the time of receipt. Cash-based accounting is simple, but it can be misleading. It's easy to inflate the appearance of income, for example, by delaying the payment of bills. For that reason, public companies are required to keep their books on an accrual basis.

Depreciation, or the allocation of the cost of a tangible long-term asset over a period of time, is another way that companies match expenses with revenue. (For intangible assets, this allocation over time is known as *amortization*.) When Google buys a piece of real estate, instead of deducting the entire cost of the item at the time of purchase, the company *depreciates* it, or spreads the cost over a certain number of years as specified by tax regulations because the asset will likely generate income for many years. If the company were to expense long-term assets at the time of purchase, its apparent financial performance would be distorted negatively in the year of purchase and positively in all future years when these assets generate revenue.

double-entry bookkeeping
A method of recording financial transactions that requires a debit entry and credit entry for each transaction to ensure that the accounting equation is always kept in balance.

matching principle
The fundamental principle requiring that expenses incurred in producing revenue be deducted from the revenues they generate during an accounting period.

accrual basis
An accounting method in which revenue is recorded when a sale is made and an expense is recorded when it is incurred.

cash basis
An accounting method in which revenue is recorded when payment is received and an expense is recorded when cash is paid.

depreciation
An accounting procedure for systematically spreading the cost of a tangible asset over its estimated useful life.

✓ **Checkpoint**

LEARNING OBJECTIVE 3: Describe the accounting equation, and explain the purpose of double-entry bookkeeping and the matching principle.

SUMMARY: The basic accounting equation is Assets = Liabilities + Owners' equity. Double-entry bookkeeping is a system of recording every financial transaction as two counterbalancing entries in order to keep the accounting equation in balance. The matching principle makes sure that expenses incurred in producing revenues are deducted from the revenue they generated during the same accounting period.

CRITICAL THINKING: (1) How does double-entry bookkeeping help eliminate errors? (2) Why is accrual-based accounting considered more fraud-proof than cash-based accounting?

IT'S YOUR BUSINESS: (1) Does looking at the accounting equation make you reconsider your personal spending habits? (Think about taking on liabilities that don't create any long-term assets, for example.) (2) How would accrual basis accounting give you better insights into your personal finances?

KEY TERMS TO KNOW: assets, liabilities, owners' equity, accounting equation, double-entry bookkeeping, matching principle, accrual basis, cash basis, depreciation

Using Financial Statements: The Balance Sheet

4 LEARNING OBJECTIVE

Identify the major financial statements, and explain how to read a balance sheet.

closing the books
Transferring net revenue and expense account balances to retained earnings for the period.

As a company conducts business day after day, sales, purchases, and other transactions are recorded and classified into individual accounts. After these individual transactions are recorded and then summarized, accountants must review the resulting summaries and adjust or correct all errors or discrepancies before **closing the books**, or transferring net revenue and expense items to *retained earnings*. Exhibit 17.2 illustrates the *accounting cycle* that companies go through during a given accounting period, such as a month.

In a way, this is what you do every month when you get your bank statement. You might think you have $50 left in your account but then see your statement and realize with delight that you forgot to record depositing the $100 check your grandmother sent you, and your true balance is $150. Or you might realize with dismay that you forgot to record the $300 ATM withdrawal you made on spring break, and your true balance is –$250. Before you know how much money you'll have available to spend next month—your retained earnings—you have to accurately close the books on this month.

UNDERSTANDING FINANCIAL STATEMENTS

Financial statements consist of three separate but interrelated reports: the *balance sheet*, the *income statement*, and the *statement of cash flows*. These statements are required by law for all publicly traded companies, but they are vital management tools for every company, no matter how large or small. Together, these statements provide information about an organization's financial strength and ability to meet current obligations, the effectiveness of its sales and collection efforts, and its effectiveness in managing its assets. Organizations and individuals use financial statements to spot opportunities and problems, to make business decisions, and to evaluate a company's past performance, present condition, and future prospects.

The following sections examine the financial statements of the hypothetical company Computer Central Services. In the past year, the company shipped more than 2.3 million orders, amounting to more than $1.7 billion in sales—a 35 percent increase in sales over the prior year. The company's daily sales volume has grown considerably over the last decade—from $232,000 to $6.8 million. Because of this tremendous growth and the increasing demand for new computer products, the company recently purchased a new headquarters building.

BALANCE SHEET

balance sheet
A statement of a firm's financial position on a particular date; also known as a *statement of financial position*.

The **balance sheet**, also known as the *statement of financial position*, is a snapshot of a company's financial position on a particular date (see Exhibit 17.3 on page 452). In effect, it freezes all business actions and provides a baseline from which a company can measure

EXHIBIT 17.2	The Accounting Cycle

Here are the general steps in the accounting process, or *accounting cycle*, from recording transactions to making sure the books are in balance to closing the books for a particular accounting period (usually a month). Steps 1 through 3 are done as transactions occur; steps 4 through 8 are usually performed at the end of the accounting period.

1. Perform *transactions*
A transaction is any relevant accounting event, including making a sale, making a purchase, or making a debt payment.

2. Analyze and record transactions in a *journal*
Journalizing means analyzing the *source document* (e.g., a sales receipt or a customer invoice) for each transaction, then separating the transaction into its debit and credit components and recording these chronologically in a journal.

3. *Post* journal entries to the *ledger*
Entries from the chronological journals are moved to the account-based ledger. Over the course of the month or other accounting period, each account (e.g., sales revenue or expenses) in the ledger fills up with the various transaction records posted from the journals. These accounts are considered temporary because they are closed out at the end of the accounting period (see step 8).

4. Prepare a *trial balance*
At the end of the accounting period, the debits and credits in the ledger are totaled, and then the two amounts are compared. If they aren't equal, one or more errors have crept in somewhere in the previous three steps and need to be found and corrected.

5. Make *adjusting entries*, as needed
Not all relevant changes are generated by transaction records during the accounting period, so accountants enter items such as asset depreciation or transactions whose revenues or expenses occur before or after the accounting period.

6. Prepare an adjusted trial balance
This is the same procedure as in step 4 but includes the adjusting entries made in step 5. Again, if the debits total and the credits total don't match, the error needs to be investigated and corrected.

7. Prepare *financial statements*
With the accounts adjusted and in balance for the accounting period, various managerial and government compliance reports can now be generated.

8. *Close the books* for the accounting period
Transfer the balances from temporary ledger accounts to the permanent balance sheet and income statement. Record *reversing entries* as needed to start fresh temporary accounts at the beginning of the next period.

Sources: Jeffery Slater, *College Accounting: A Practical Approach*, 11th ed. (Upper Saddle River, N.J.: Pearson Prentice Hall, 2010), 78, 104, 148; "The Accounting Process," NetMBA, www.netmba.com; Bob Schneider, "Accounting Basics: The Accounting Process," *Investopedia.com*, www.investopedia.com.

change from that point forward. This statement is called a balance sheet because it includes all elements in the accounting equation and shows the balance between assets on one side of the equation and liabilities and owners' equity on the other side.

Every company prepares a balance sheet at least once a year, most often at the end of the **calendar year**, covering January 1 to December 31. However, many business

calendar year
A 12-month accounting period that begins on January 1 and ends on December 31.

EXHIBIT 17.3   Balance Sheet for Computer Central Services

The categories used on the year-end balance sheet for Computer Central Services are typical.

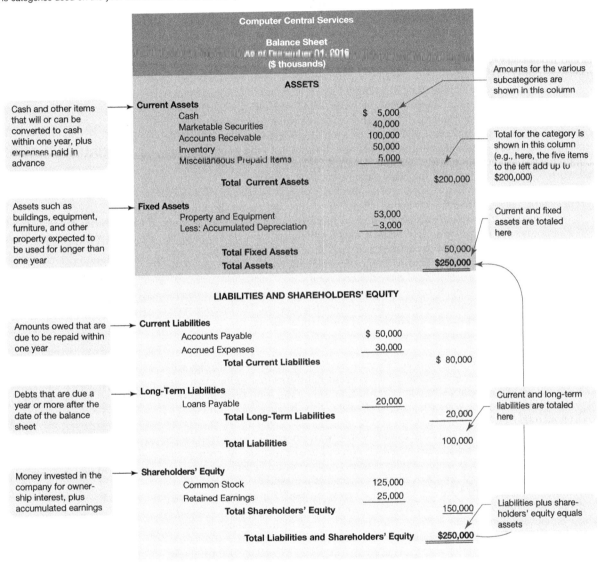

Cash and other items that will or can be converted to cash within one year, plus expenses paid in advance

Assets such as buildings, equipment, furniture, and other property expected to be used for longer than one year

Amounts owed that are due to be repaid within one year

Debts that are due a year or more after the date of the balance sheet

Money invested in the company for owner-ship interest, plus accumulated earnings

Computer Central Services

Balance Sheet

As of December 31, 2016

($ thousands)

ASSETS

Amounts for the various subcategories are shown in this column

Current Assets		
Cash	$ 5,000	
Marketable Securities	40,000	
Accounts Receivable	100,000	
Inventory	50,000	
Miscellaneous Prepaid Items	5,000	
Total Current Assets		$200,000

Total for the category is shown in this column (e.g., here, the five items to the left add up to $200,000)

Fixed Assets		
Property and Equipment	53,000	
Less: Accumulated Depreciation	−3,000	
Total Fixed Assets		50,000
Total Assets		**$250,000**

Current and fixed assets are totaled here

LIABILITIES AND SHAREHOLDERS' EQUITY

Current Liabilities		
Accounts Payable	$ 50,000	
Accrued Expenses	30,000	
Total Current Liabilities		$ 80,000

Long-Term Liabilities		
Loans Payable	20,000	
Total Long-Term Liabilities		20,000
Total Liabilities		100,000

Current and long-term liabilities are totaled here

Shareholders' Equity		
Common Stock	125,000	
Retained Earnings	25,000	
Total Shareholders' Equity		150,000
Total Liabilities and Shareholders' Equity		**$250,000**

Liabilities plus share-holders' equity equals assets

fiscal year
Any 12 consecutive months used as an accounting period.

and government bodies use a **fiscal year**, which may be any 12 consecutive months. Some companies prepare a balance sheet more often than once a year, such as at the end of each month or quarter. Every balance sheet is dated to show the exact date when the financial snapshot was taken.

By reading a company's balance sheet, you should be able to determine the size of the company, the major assets owned, any asset changes that occurred in recent periods, how the company's assets are financed, and any major changes that have occurred in the company's debt and equity in recent periods.

Assets

As discussed previously in the chapter, an asset is something owned by a company with the intent to generate income. Assets can be *tangible* or *intangible*. Tangible assets include land, buildings, and equipment. Intangible assets include intellectual property (such as patents and business methods), *goodwill* (which includes company reputation), brand awareness and recognition, workforce skills, management talent, and even customer relationships.[16]

As you might expect, assigning value to intangible assets is not an easy task (and incidentally is one of the major points of difference between GAAP and IFRS), but these assets make up an increasingly important part of the value of many contemporary companies.[17] For instance, much of the real value of a company such as Google is not in its tangible assets but in its search engine algorithms, its software designs, its brand awareness, and the brainpower of its workforce. For example, a recent balance sheet for the company listed nearly $20 billion in goodwill and other intangibles.[18]

The asset section of the balance sheet is often divided into *current assets* and *fixed assets*. **Current assets** include cash and other items that will or can become cash within the following year, such as short-term investments such as money-market funds and *accounts receivable* (amounts due from customers). **Fixed assets** (sometimes referred to as *property, plant, and equipment*) are long-term investments in buildings, equipment, furniture and fixtures, transportation equipment, land, and other tangible property used in running the business. Fixed assets have a useful life of more than one year.

Assets are listed in descending order by *liquidity*, or the ease with which they can be converted into cash. Thus, current assets are listed before fixed assets. The balance sheet gives a subtotal for each type of asset and then a grand total for all assets.

Liabilities

Liabilities may be current or long term, and they are listed in the order in which they will come due. The balance sheet gives subtotals for **current liabilities** (obligations that will have to be met within one year of the date of the balance sheet) and **long-term liabilities** (obligations that are due one year or more after the date of the balance sheet), and then it gives a grand total for all liabilities.

Current liabilities include accounts payable, short-term financing (you'll read more about this in Chapter 18), and accrued expenses. *Accounts payable* include the money the company owes its suppliers as well as money it owes vendors for miscellaneous services (such as electricity and telephone charges). *Accrued expenses* are expenses that have been incurred but for which bills have not yet been received or paid. For example, because salespeople at Computer Central Services earn commissions, the company has a liability to those employees after the sale is made. If such expenses and their associated liabilities were not recorded, the company's financial statements would be misleading and would violate the matching principle because the commission expenses earned at the time of sale would not be matched to the revenue generated from the sale.

Long-term liabilities include loans, leases, and bonds. A borrower makes principal and interest payments to the lender over the term of the loan, and its obligation is limited to these payments (see the section "Debt Financing Versus Equity Financing" in Chapter 18 on page 475). Rather than borrowing money to make purchases, a firm may enter into a *lease*, under which the owner of an item allows another party to use it in exchange for regular payments. Bonds are certificates that obligate the company to repay a certain sum, plus interest, to the bondholder on a specific date. Bonds are traded on organized securities exchanges and are discussed in detail in Chapter 19.

Owners' Equity

The owners' investment in a business is listed on the balance sheet under owners' equity (or *shareholders' equity* or *stockholders' equity* for corporations). Sole proprietorships list owner's equity under the owner's name with the amount (assets minus liabilities). Small

current assets
Cash and items that can be turned into cash within one year.

fixed assets
Assets retained for long-term use, such as land, buildings, machinery, and equipment; also referred to as *property, plant, and equipment*.

current liabilities
Obligations that must be met within a year.

long-term liabilities
Obligations that fall due more than a year from the date of the balance sheet.

retained earnings
The portion of shareholders' equity earned by the company but not distributed to its owners in the form of dividends.

partnerships list each partner's share of the business separately, and large partnerships list the total of all partners' shares. In a corporation, the shareholders' total investment value is the sum of two amounts: the total value of the all the shares currently held, plus **retained earnings**—cash that is kept by the company rather than distributed to shareholders in the form of dividends. As Exhibit 17.3 shows, Computer Central Services has retained earnings of $25 million. The company doesn't pay dividends—many small and growing corporations don't—but rather builds its cash reserves to fund expansion in the future. (Shareholders' equity can be slightly more complicated than this, depending on how the company's shares were first created, but this summary gives you the basic idea of how the assets portion of the balance sheet works.)

 Checkpoint

LEARNING OBJECTIVE 4: Identify the major financial statements, and explain how to read a balance sheet.

SUMMARY: The three major financial statements are the balance sheet, the income statement, and the statement of cash flows. The balance sheet provides a snapshot of the business at a particular point in time. It shows the size of the company, the major assets owned, the ways the assets are financed, and the amount of owners' investment in the business. Its three main sections are assets, liabilities, and owners' equity.

CRITICAL THINKING: (1) Why do analysts need to consider different factors when evaluating a company's ability to repay short-term versus long-term debt? (2) Would the current amount of the owners' equity be a reasonable price to pay for a company? Why or why not?

IT'S YOUR BUSINESS: (1) What are your current and long-term financial liabilities? Are these liabilities restricting your flexibility as a student or consumer? (2) As a potential employee, what intangible assets can you offer a company?

KEY TERMS TO KNOW: closing the books, balance sheet, calendar year, fiscal year, current assets, fixed assets, current liabilities, long-term liabilities, retained earnings

5 LEARNING OBJECTIVE

Explain the purpose of the income statement and the statement of cash flows.

Using Financial Statements: Income and Cash Flow Statements

In addition to the balance sheet, the two other fundamentally important financial statements are the income statement and the statement of cash flows.

INCOME STATEMENT

income statement
A financial record of a company's revenues, expenses, and profits over a given period of time; also known as a *profit-and-loss statement*.

expenses
Costs created in the process of generating revenues.

net income
Profit earned or loss incurred by a firm, determined by subtracting expenses from revenues; casually referred to as the *bottom line*.

If the balance sheet is a snapshot, the income statement is a movie. The **income statement**, or *profit-and-loss statement* or simply "P&L," shows an organization's profit performance over a period of time, typically one year. It summarizes revenue from all sources as well as all **expenses**, the costs that have arisen in generating revenues. Expenses and income taxes are then subtracted from revenues to show the actual profit or loss of a company, a figure known as **net income**—also called *profit* or, informally, the *bottom line*. By briefly reviewing a company's income statements, you should have a general sense of the company's size, its trend in sales, its major expenses, and the resulting net income or loss. Owners, creditors, and investors can evaluate the company's past performance and future prospects by comparing net income for one year with net income for previous years. Exhibit 17.4 shows the income statement for Computer Central Services.

Expenses include both the direct costs associated with creating or purchasing products for sale and the indirect costs associated with operating the business. If a company manufactures or purchases inventory, the cost of storing the product for sale (such as

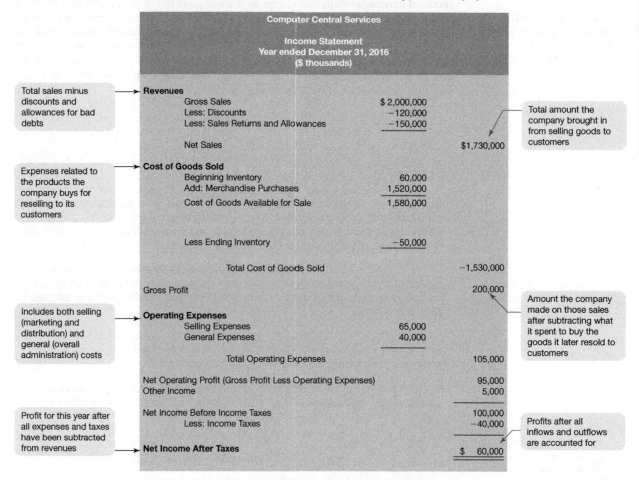

EXHIBIT 17.4   Income Statement for Computer Central Services

An income statement summarizes the company's financial operations over a particular accounting period, usually a year.

Computer Central Services
Income Statement
Year ended December 31, 2016
($ thousands)

Revenues		
Gross Sales	$ 2,000,000	
Less: Discounts	−120,000	
Less: Sales Returns and Allowances	−150,000	
Net Sales		$1,730,000
Cost of Goods Sold		
Beginning Inventory	60,000	
Add: Merchandise Purchases	1,520,000	
Cost of Goods Available for Sale	1,580,000	
Less Ending Inventory	−50,000	
Total Cost of Goods Sold		−1,530,000
Gross Profit		200,000
Operating Expenses		
Selling Expenses	65,000	
General Expenses	40,000	
Total Operating Expenses		105,000
Net Operating Profit (Gross Profit Less Operating Expenses)		95,000
Other Income		5,000
Net Income Before Income Taxes		100,000
Less: Income Taxes		−40,000
Net Income After Taxes		$ 60,000

Callouts:
- Total sales minus discounts and allowances for bad debts
- Expenses related to the products the company buys for reselling to its customers
- Includes both selling (marketing and distribution) and general (overall administration) costs
- Profit for this year after all expenses and taxes have been subtracted from revenues
- Total amount the company brought in from selling goods to customers
- Amount the company made on those sales after subtracting what it spent to buy the goods it later resold to customers
- Profits after all inflows and outflows are accounted for

heating the warehouse, paying the rent, and buying insurance on the storage facility) is added to the difference between the cost of the beginning inventory and the cost of the ending inventory in order to compute the actual cost of items that were sold during a period—or the **cost of goods sold**. The computation can be summarized as follows:

Cost of goods sold = Beginning inventory + Net purchases − Ending inventory

As shown in Exhibit 17.4, cost of goods sold is deducted from sales to obtain a company's **gross profit**—a key figure used in financial statement analysis. In addition to the costs directly associated with producing goods, companies deduct **operating expenses**, which include both *selling expenses* and *general expenses*, to compute a firm's *net operating income*. Net operating income is often a better indicator of financial health because it gives an idea of how much cash the company is able to generate. For instance, a company with a sizable gross profit level can actually be losing money if its operating expenses are out of control—and if it doesn't have enough cash on hand to cover the shortfall, it could soon find itself bankrupt.[19]

Selling expenses are operating expenses incurred through marketing and distributing the product (such as wages or salaries of salespeople, advertising, supplies, insurance for the sales operation, depreciation for the store and sales equipment, and other sales

cost of goods sold
The cost of producing or acquiring a company's products for sale during a given period.

gross profit
The amount remaining when the cost of goods sold is deducted from net sales; also known as *gross margin*.

operating expenses
All costs of operation that are not included under cost of goods sold.

department expenses such as telephone charges). *General expenses* are operating expenses incurred in the overall administration of a business. They include such items as professional services (such as accounting and legal fees), office salaries, depreciation of office equipment, insurance for office operations, and supplies.

A firm's net operating income is then adjusted by the amount of any nonoperating income or expense items such as the gain or loss on the sale of a building. The result is the net income or loss before income taxes (losses are shown in parentheses), a key figure used in budgeting, cash flow analysis, and a variety of other financial computations. Finally, income taxes are deducted to compute the company's after-tax net income or loss for the period.

An alternative—and controversial—measure of profitability is *earnings before interest, taxes, depreciation, and amortization,* or **EBITDA**. Because it doesn't include various items such as the interest payments on loans or the effects of depreciating expensive capital equipment, EBITDA is viewed by some investors as a "purer" measure of profitability and an easier way to compare financial performance across companies or industries. And even though it is a non-GAAP indicator and must be labeled as such, many public companies publish EBITDA because it can suggest greater profitability than the standard operating profit number. However, for those same reasons, EBITDA is also criticized because it doesn't reflect costs that every company has and could mask serious financial concerns. As an extreme example, in a recent year in which Twitter reported EBITDA earnings of $301 million, the company actually *lost* $578 million by conventional accounting measures.[20]

EBITDA
Earnings before interest, taxes, depreciation, and amortization.

STATEMENT OF CASH FLOWS

statement of cash flows
A statement of a firm's cash receipts and cash payments that presents information on its sources and uses of cash.

In addition to preparing a balance sheet and an income statement, all public companies and many privately owned companies prepare a **statement of cash flows**, or *cash flow statement,* to show how much cash the company generated over time and where it went (see Exhibit 17.5). The statement of cash flows tracks the cash coming into and flowing out of a company's bank accounts. It reveals the increase or decrease in the company's cash for the period and summarizes (by category) the sources of that change. From a brief review of this statement, you should have a general sense of the amount of cash created or consumed by daily operations, the amount of cash invested in fixed or other assets, the amount of debt borrowed or repaid, and the proceeds from the sale of stock or payments for dividends. In addition, an analysis of cash flows provides a good idea of a company's ability to pay its short-term obligations when they become due.

 **Checkpoint**

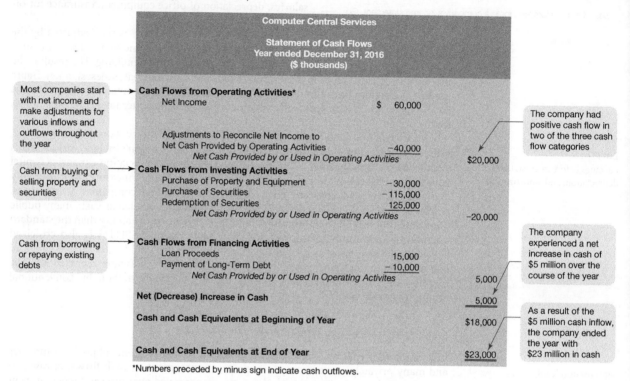

EXHIBIT 17.5 Statement of Cash Flows for Computer Central Services

A statement of cash flows shows a firm's cash receipts and cash payments as a result of three main activities—operating, investing, and financing—for an identified period of time (such as the year indicated here).

Computer Central Services

Statement of Cash Flows
Year ended December 31, 2016
($ thousands)

Most companies start with net income and make adjustments for various inflows and outflows throughout the year

Cash Flows from Operating Activities*
Net Income ... $ 60,000

Adjustments to Reconcile Net Income to
Net Cash Provided by Operating Activities ... −40,000
Net Cash Provided by or Used in Operating Activities ... $20,000

The company had positive cash flow in two of the three cash flow categories

Cash from buying or selling property and securities

Cash Flows from Investing Activities
Purchase of Property and Equipment ... −30,000
Purchase of Securities ... −115,000
Redemption of Securities ... 125,000
Net Cash Provided by or Used in Operating Activities ... −20,000

Cash from borrowing or repaying existing debts

Cash Flows from Financing Activities
Loan Proceeds ... 15,000
Payment of Long-Term Debt ... −10,000
Net Cash Provided by or Used in Operating Activites ... 5,000

The company experienced a net increase in cash of $5 million over the course of the year

Net (Decrease) Increase in Cash ... 5,000

Cash and Cash Equivalents at Beginning of Year ... $18,000

Cash and Cash Equivalents at End of Year ... $23,000

As a result of the $5 million cash inflow, the company ended the year with $23 million in cash

*Numbers preceded by minus sign indicate cash outflows.

IT'S YOUR BUSINESS: (1) What would your personal income statement look like today? Are you operating "at a profit" or "at a loss"? (2) What steps could you take to reduce your "operating expenses"?

KEY TERMS TO KNOW: income statement, expenses, net income, cost of goods sold, gross profit, operating expenses, EBITDA, statement of cash flows

Analyzing Financial Statements

After financial statements have been prepared, managers, investors, and lenders use them to evaluate the financial health of the organization, make business decisions, and spot opportunities for improvements by looking at the company's current performance in relation to its past performance, the economy as a whole, and the performance of competitors.

6 | LEARNING OBJECTIVE

Explain the purpose of ratio analysis, and list the four main categories of financial ratios.

TREND ANALYSIS

The process of comparing financial data from year to year is known as *trend analysis*. You can use trend analysis to uncover shifts in the nature of a business over time. Of course, when you are comparing one period with another, it's important to take into account the effects of extraordinary or unusual items such as the sale of major assets, the purchase of a new line of products from another company, weather, or economic conditions that may have affected the company in one period but not the next. These extraordinary items are usually disclosed in the text portion of a company's annual report or in the notes to the financial statements.

RATIO ANALYSIS

Unlike trend analysis, which tracks *absolute* numbers from one year to the next, ratio analysis creates *relative* numbers by comparing sets of figures from a single year's performance. By using ratios rather than absolute amounts, analysts can more easily assess a company's performance from one year to the next or compare it with other companies. A variety of commonly used ratios help companies understand their current operations and answer some key questions: Is inventory too large? Are credit customers paying too slowly? Can the company pay its bills? Ratios also allow comparison with other companies within an industry, which helps gauge how well a company is doing relative to its competitors. Every industry tends to have its own "normal" ratios, which act as yardsticks for individual companies.

TYPES OF FINANCIAL RATIOS

Financial ratios can be organized into the following groups, as Exhibit 17.6 shows: profitability, liquidity, activity, and leverage (or debt).

Profitability Ratios

You can analyze how well a company is conducting its ongoing operations by computing *profitability ratios*, which show the state of the company's financial performance or how well it's generating profits. Three of the most common profitability ratios are **return on sales**, or *profit margin* (the net income a business makes per unit of sales); **return on equity** (net income divided by owners' equity); and **earnings per share** (the profit earned for each share of stock outstanding). Exhibit 17.6 shows how to compute these profitability ratios by using the financial information from Computer Central Services.

Liquidity Ratios

Liquidity ratios measure a firm's ability to pay its short-term obligations. As you might expect, lenders and creditors are keenly interested in liquidity measures. A company's **working capital** (current assets minus current liabilities) is an indicator of liquidity because it represents current assets remaining after the payment of all current liabilities. The dollar amount of working capital can be misleading, however. For example, it may include the value of slow-moving inventory items that cannot be used to help pay a company's short-term debts.

A different picture of the company's liquidity is provided by the **current ratio**—current assets divided by current liabilities. This figure compares the current debt owed with the current assets available to pay that debt. The **quick ratio**, also called the *acid-test ratio*, is computed by subtracting inventory from current assets and then dividing the result by current liabilities. This ratio is often a better indicator of a firm's ability to pay creditors than the current ratio because the quick ratio leaves out inventories, which can take a long time to convert to cash. A quick ratio below 1.0 is a sign that the company could struggle to meet its near-time financial obligations and therefore might not be a safe credit risk, a good investment, or possibly a smart place to accept a job. Exhibit 17.6 shows that both the current and quick ratios of Computer Central Services are well above these benchmarks and industry averages.

Activity Ratios

Activity ratios analyze how well a company is managing and making use of its assets. For companies that maintain inventories, the most common activity ratio is the **inventory turnover ratio**, which measures how fast a company's inventory is turned into sales. Inventory is a constant balancing act—hold too little, and you risk being out of stock when orders arrive; hold too much, and you raise your costs. When inventory sits on the shelf, money is tied up without earning interest; furthermore, the company incurs expenses for its storage, handling, insurance, and taxes. In addition, there is often a risk that the inventory will become obsolete or go out of style before it can be converted into finished goods and sold. Car dealers, for example, face the never-ending challenge of

return on sales
The ratio between net income after taxes and net sales; also known as the *profit margin*.

return on equity
The ratio between net income after taxes and total owners' equity.

earnings per share
A measure of a firm's profitability for each share of outstanding stock, calculated by dividing net income after taxes by the average number of shares of common stock outstanding.

working capital
Current assets minus current liabilities.

current ratio
A measure of a firm's short-term liquidity, calculated by dividing current assets by current liabilities.

quick ratio
A measure of a firm's short-term liquidity, calculated by adding cash, marketable securities, and receivables, then dividing that sum by current liabilities; also known as the *acid-test ratio*.

inventory turnover ratio
A measure of the time a company takes to turn its inventory into sales, calculated by dividing cost of goods sold by the average value of inventory for a period.

EXHIBIT 17.6 How Well Does This Company Stack Up?

Financial ratios offer a quick and convenient way to evaluate how well a company is performing in relation to prior performance, the economy as a whole, and the company's competitors.

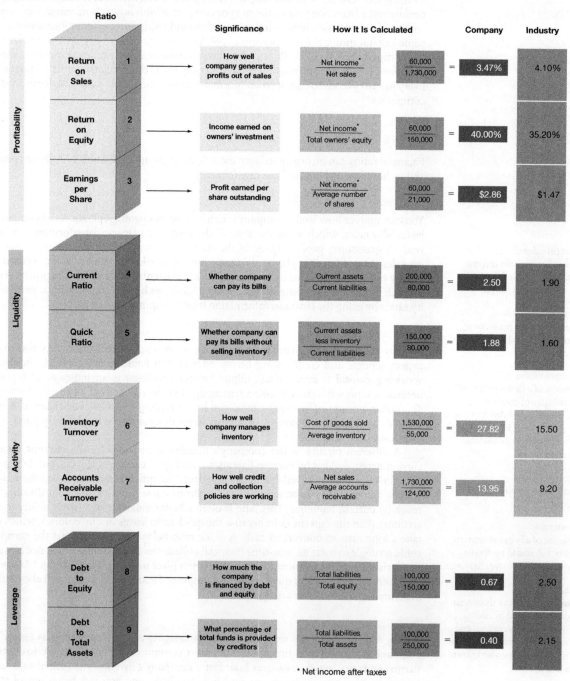

	Ratio		Significance	How It Is Calculated			Company	Industry
Profitability	Return on Sales	1	How well company generates profits out of sales	Net income* / Net sales	60,000 / 1,730,000	=	3.47%	4.10%
	Return on Equity	2	Income earned on owners' investment	Net income* / Total owners' equity	60,000 / 150,000	=	40.00%	35.20%
	Earnings per Share	3	Profit earned per share outstanding	Net income* / Average number of shares	60,000 / 21,000	=	$2.86	$1.47
Liquidity	Current Ratio	4	Whether company can pay its bills	Current assets / Current liabilities	200,000 / 80,000	=	2.50	1.90
	Quick Ratio	5	Whether company can pay its bills without selling inventory	Current assets less inventory / Current liabilities	150,000 / 80,000	=	1.88	1.60
Activity	Inventory Turnover	6	How well company manages inventory	Cost of goods sold / Average inventory	1,530,000 / 55,000	=	27.82	15.50
	Accounts Receivable Turnover	7	How well credit and collection policies are working	Net sales / Average accounts receivable	1,730,000 / 124,000	=	13.95	9.20
Leverage	Debt to Equity	8	How much the company is financed by debt and equity	Total liabilities / Total equity	100,000 / 150,000	=	0.67	2.50
	Debt to Total Assets	9	What percentage of total funds is provided by creditors	Total liabilities / Total assets	100,000 / 250,000	=	0.40	2.15

* Net income after taxes

selling this year's models before next year's arrive. Newer models usually make the older models a lot less attractive in buyers' eyes, often requiring dealers to resort to steep discounts just to get rid of aging inventory.[21]

A recent study of U.S. manufacturers found wide disparities in inventory turnover, with the best performers moving their inventory four or five times faster than lower performers.[22] As with all ratios, however, it's important to dig below the surface after making an initial comparison. For instance, a decline in a manufacturer's inventory turnover ratio could indicate that sales are slowing down, or it could mean sales are steady but the company made some forecasting errors and as a result produced more goods than it needed. Conversely, a company with a high ratio could be discounting heavily and not making as much money as it could by raising prices and lowering its sales volume.

Another useful activity ratio is the **accounts receivable turnover ratio**, which measures how well a company's credit and collection policies are working by indicating how frequently accounts receivable are converted to cash. The volume of receivables outstanding depends on the financial manager's decisions regarding several issues, such as who qualifies for credit and who does not, how long customers are given to pay their bills, and how aggressive the firm is in collecting its late payments. Be careful here as well. If the ratio is going up, you need to determine whether the company is doing a better job of collecting or if sales are rising. If the ratio is going down, it may be because sales are decreasing or because collection efforts are lagging.

accounts receivable turnover ratio
A measure of the time a company takes to turn its accounts receivable into cash, calculated by dividing sales by the average value of accounts receivable for a period.

Leverage, or Debt, Ratios

A company's ability to pay its long-term debts is reflected in its *leverage ratios*, also known as *debt ratios*. Both lenders and investors use these ratios to judge a company's risk and growth potential. The **debt-to-equity ratio** (total liabilities divided by total equity) indicates the extent to which a business is financed by debt as opposed to invested capital (equity). From a lender's standpoint, the higher this ratio is, the riskier the loan, because the company must devote more of its cash to debt payments. From an investor's standpoint, a higher ratio indicates that the company is spending more of its cash on interest payments than on investing in activities that will help raise the stock price.[23] Chapter 18 compares the advantages and disadvantages of debt and equity financing.

debt-to-equity ratio
A measure of the extent to which a business is financed by debt as opposed to invested capital, calculated by dividing the company's total liabilities by owners' equity.

The **debt-to-assets ratio** (total liabilities divided by total assets) indicates how much of the company's assets are financed by creditors. As with the debt-to-equity ratio, the higher this ratio gets, the riskier the company looks to a lender. From an investor's perspective, though, a high level of debt relative to assets could indicate that a company is making aggressive moves to grow without diluting the value of existing shares by offering more shares for sale.[24] However, having a high level of debt to assets, or being *highly leveraged*, puts a company at risk. Those assets may not be able to generate enough cash to pay back the debt, or lenders and suppliers might cut off the company's credit.

debt-to-assets ratio
A measure of a firm's ability to carry long-term debt, calculated by dividing total liabilities by total assets.

Again, you can use every ratio as a helpful initial indicator, but be sure to dig below the surface to see what the number really means.

For the latest information on accounting practices and financial reporting, visit http://real-timeupdates.com/bia8 and click on Chapter 17.

 Checkpoint

LEARNING OBJECTIVE 6: Explain the purpose of ratio analysis, and list the four main categories of financial ratios.

SUMMARY: Financial ratios provide information for analyzing the health and future prospects of a business. Ratios facilitate financial comparisons among different-size companies and between a company and industry averages. Most of the important ratios fall into one of four categories: profitability ratios, which show how well the company generates profits; liquidity ratios, which measure the company's ability to pay its short-term obligations; activity ratios, which analyze how well a company is managing its assets; and debt ratios, which measure a company's ability to pay its long-term debt.

CRITICAL THINKING: (1) Why is it so important to be aware of extraordinary items when analyzing a company's finances? (2) Why is the quick ratio frequently a better indicator than the current ratio of a firm's ability to pay its bills?

IT'S YOUR BUSINESS: (1) Assume that you are about to make a significant consumer purchase, and the product is available at two local stores, one with high inventory turnover and one with low. Which store would you choose based on this information? Why? (2) If you were applying for a home mortgage loan today, would a lender view your debt-to-assets ratio favorably? Why or why not?

KEY TERMS TO KNOW: return on sales, return on equity, earnings per share, working capital, current ratio, quick ratio, inventory turnover ratio, accounts receivable turnover ratio, debt-to-equity ratio, debt-to-assets ratio

BEHIND THE SCENES
GOOGLE THIS: "COST CONTROL"

By just about any measure you can think of, Google is one of the most spectacular success stories in the history of business. However, even a company as wealthy as Google has to control its spending.

Google's case is unusual in the sense of its sheer scale, but the story is not unique. When a young company is growing quickly and money is pouring in from sales or from investors, the natural tendency is to focus on building the business and capturing market opportunities. The less exciting—but ultimately no less important—task of creating a sustainable cost structure with rigorous expense management often doesn't get as much attention in the early years.

In some companies, rapid growth in a hot economy can mask serious underlying problems that threaten the long-term viability of the enterprise. In the dot-com boom of the late 1990s, for instance, more than a few high-flying companies fell to earth when investors who had enjoyed a rocket ride in the stock market realized the companies didn't have workable business models.

During the mid-2000s, Google's revenue had been increasing at a spectacular pace, from $10.6 billion in 2006, to $16.6 billion in 2007, to $21.8 billion in 2008. However, expenses were growing at an even faster rate. As a result, the company's profit margin dropped from 29 percent in 2006 to around 19 percent in 2008 (still 5 percentage points better than the industry average); 2008 ended with the first-ever drop in quarterly profits in the company's history.

The cooling economy and slowing profits didn't expose any fatal flaws in the Google business model, but the drop certainly was a wake-up call that emphasized the need to transition to the next stage of organizational development. It was time for the accounting and financial management functions to play a more prominent role and to transform a wild and wooly entrepreneurial success story into a major corporation with stable finances.

Back in 2001, Google cofounders Larry Page and Sergey Brin brought in Eric Schmidt, a seasoned technology industry executive, to guide the company's growth beyond its initial start-up stage. Under Schmidt's leadership, Google expanded from 200 employees to more than 20,000 and secured its place as one of the world's most influential companies. Facing the need for a more methodical approach to accounting and financial management, Schmidt brought in another executive with a proven track record in corporate leadership. Patrick Pichette made his name helping Bell Canada reduce operating expenses by $2 billion, and his proven ability to bring expenses in line with revenue was just what Google needed.

Pichette and other executives tackled expenses at three levels: employee perks, staffing, and project investment. Employee benefits have been trimmed and adjusted over time, although it's safe to say they are still better than you'll find just about anywhere, from on-site physicians and nurses and help with medical issues to extra time off and spending money for new parents, tuition reimbursement, and free legal advice. The company's position on benefits now appears to be less about adding fun and possibly frivolous perks and more about "removing barriers so Googlers can focus on the things they love, both inside and outside of work."

At the staffing level, Google began taking a much harder look at hiring practices to better align staffing with project needs. Tellingly, the first layoffs in the company's history, in January

2009, involved 100 recruiters whose services were no longer needed because Google's hiring rate had slowed so dramatically. Thousands of contract workers were let go as well. The vaunted "20 percent time" was adjusted, too, with the company aiming to focus engineers' time more directly on core projects. In some cases, staffers get access to data and computing resources in order to explore new ideas but don't necessarily get the free time during work hours.

At the project and program levels, Google now scrutinizes its investments more carefully and pulls the plug on less-promising activities. Some of the higher-profile shutdowns in the past few years include the Google Buzz social networking capability, the Google Wave collaboration platform, the iGoogle personalizable news page, and Google Reader, one of the most popular RSS newsfeed readers. "More wood behind fewer arrows" is how Google describes its new emphasis on putting its resources into the projects most likely to have sizable long-term success.

Pichette's efforts to install a more sustainable accounting and cost-control system yielded impressive results. After the economy emerged from its deep slump, Google had stockpiled some $50 billion in cash. $50 billion in cash as the economy pulled out of its slump. (Once asked why the company was sitting on so much cash, Pichette explained that in the fast-changing world of search and other digital services, Google might need to jump on an acquisition almost overnight, with potentially billions of dollars of cash in hand.)

Just as with personal finances, however, companies need to stay vigilant year in year out to make sure old habits don't come back. By 2015, Google was once again feeling the pinch after going on a hiring spree to staff up new projects, some of them in such wildly diverse areas as medical research and self-driving cars. Many investors had grown wary of the company's stock after earnings repeatedly failed to meet analysts' quarterly expectations.

Pichette retired in early 2015 and was replaced by Ruth Porat, a widely respected banking executive with a reputation for prudent financial management. As soon as she came on board, she announced her intention to get Google's expenses back under control. Investors apparently liked what they heard, as the company's stock took a healthy jump after the first quarterly earnings report under Porat's leadership. Now come the challenge of keeping history from repeating itself.[25]

Critical Thinking Questions

17-1. Given the eventual need for rigorous financial management, should every company have extensive cost controls in place from the first moment of operation? Explain your answer.

17-2. Google recently had a debt-to-equity ratio of 0.04. Microsoft, one of its key competitors, had a debt-to-equity ratio of 0.15. From a bank's point of view, which of the two companies is a more attractive loan candidate, based on this ratio? Why?

17-3. Over the course of a recent six-month period, Google's current ratio increased from 8.77 to 11.91. Does this make Google more or less of a credit risk in the eyes of potential lenders? Why?

LEARN MORE ONLINE

Visit Google's "Investor Relations" section, at http://investor.google.com. Peruse the latest financial news. How does the company's financial health look at present? What do the trends for revenue, expenses, and income look like? Does the company report both GAAP and non-GAAP financial results? Why would Google report non-GAAP figures?

KEY TERMS

accounting
accounting equation
accounts receivable turnover ratio
accrual basis
assets
audit
balance sheet
bookkeeping
calendar year
cash basis
certified public accountants (CPAs)
closing the books
controller
cost of goods sold
current assets
current liabilities
current ratio
debt-to-assets ratio

debt-to-equity ratio
depreciation
double-entry bookkeeping
earnings per share
EBITDA
expenses
external auditors
financial accounting
fiscal year
fixed assets
GAAP (generally accepted accounting principles)
gross profit
income statement
international financial reporting standards (IFRS)
inventory turnover ratio
liabilities
long-term liabilities

management accounting
matching principle
net income
operating expenses
owners' equity
private accountants
public accountants

quick ratio
retained earnings
return on equity
return on sales
Sarbanes-Oxley
statement of cash flows
working capital

MyBizLab®
To complete the problems with the ⭐,
go to EOC Discussion Questions in the
MyLab.

TEST YOUR KNOWLEDGE

Questions for Review

17-4. What is Sarbanes-Oxley?

17-5. What is an audit, and why are audits performed?

17-6. What is the matching principle?

17-7. What are the two methods used by companies to analyze financial statements?

17-8. What is the value of an income statement?

Questions for Analysis

17-9. Why were efforts made to converge the GAAP and IFRS standards?

17-10. Why would a company bother with double-entry bookkeeping?

17-11. Why are the costs of fixed assets depreciated?

17-12. Is it advisable for investors to make decisions solely based the company's EBITDA? Why?

17-13. **Ethical Considerations.** In the process of closing the company books, you encounter a problematic transaction. One of the company's customers was invoiced twice for the same project materials, resulting in a $1,000 overcharge. You immediately notify the controller, whose response is, "Let it go, it happens often. It'll probably balance out on some future transaction." What should you do now?

Questions for Application

⭐ **17-14.** The senior partner of an accounting firm is looking for ways to increase the firm's business. What other services besides traditional accounting can the firm offer to its clients? What new challenges might this additional work create?

17-15. Select a public company of your choice and download the company's latest annual report. Calculate the profitability ratios and analyze its financial performance. Identify some of the problem areas. Would you invest in the company? Why or why not?

⭐ **17-16.** If you were asked to lend money to your cousin's clothing store to help her through a slow sales period, would you be more interested in looking at the current ratio or the quick ratio as a measure of liquidity? Why?

⭐ **17-17.** **Concept Integration.** Your appliance manufacturing company recently implemented a just-in-time inventory system (see Chapter 9) for all parts used in the manufacturing process. How might you expect this move to affect the company's inventory turnover rate, current ratio, and quick ratio?

EXPAND YOUR KNOWLEDGE

Discovering Career Opportunities

The field of accounting is challenging yet highly rewarding. People interested in this field can choose from a wide variety of career pathways. For this exercise, visit the page on accountants and auditors at www.bls.gov/ooh/business-and-financial/accountants-and-auditors.htm to read more.

17-18. Based on the website, what are the differences between the job scope of a public accountant and an internal auditor?

17-19. What are the common challenges faced by accountants and auditors while performing their duties? Which skills should they acquire to help them overcome these challenges?

17-20. Assume you have just graduated and are offered a job in a large and reputable accounting firm. What is the average salary that you think you should be offered? Besides pay, what are your other considerations before accepting the job offer?

Improving Your Tech Insights: GRC Software

The Sarbanes-Oxley Act's requirement that publicly traded companies regularly verify their internal accounting controls spurred the development of software tools to help companies flag and fix problems in their financial systems. In the past few years, some software vendors have gone beyond Sarbox compliance to integrate the monitoring of a wide range of legal and financial issues that require management attention. This new category of software is generally known as *governance, risk, and compliance (GRC) software*. GRC capabilities can either be built into other software packages (such as accounting and finance software, process management software, or business intelligence software) or be offered as stand-alone compliance programs. Vendors that offer GRC capabilities include Oracle (www.oracle.com), SAP (www.sap.com), and IBM (www.ibm.com), among many others [26]

Explore one GRC software solution. In a brief email message to your instructor, describe the benefits of using this particular software package.

PRACTICE YOUR SKILLS

Sharpening Your Communication Skills

Obtain a copy of the annual report of a business and examine what the report shows about finances and current operations.

17-21. Consider the statements made by the CEO regarding the past year: Did the company do well, or are changes in operations necessary to its future well-being? What are the projections for future growth in sales and profits?

17-22. Examine the financial summaries for information about the fiscal condition of the company: Did the company show a profit?

17-23. Obtain a copy of the company's annual report from the previous year and compare it with the current report to determine whether past projections were accurate.

17-24. Prepare a brief written summary of your conclusions.

Building Your Team Skills

Divide into small groups and compute the following financial ratios for Entech Manufacturing using the company's balance sheet and income statement. Compare your answers to those of your classmates.

- Profitability ratios: return on sales; return on equity; earning per share
- Liquidity ratios: current ratio; quick ratio
- Activity ratios: inventory turnover; accounts receivable turnover
- Leverage ratios: debt to equity; debt to total assets

ENTECH MANUFACTURING INCOME STATEMENT YEAR ENDED DECEMBER 31, 2014

Sales	$24,000
Less: Cost of Goods Sold	20,000
Gross Profit	$ 4,000
Less: Total Operating Expenses	1,650
Net Operating Income Before Income Taxes	2,350
Less: Income Taxes	350
Net Income After Income Taxes	$ 2,000

ENTECH MANUFACTURING BALANCE SHEET DECEMBER 31, 2014

ASSETS		
Cash	$ 10,000	
Accounts Receivable (beginning balance $4,500)	5,000	
Inventory (beginning balance $2,000)	2,500	
Current Assets	7,500	
Fixed Assets	5,000	
Total Assets		$30,000
LIABILITIES AND SHAREHOLDERS' EQUITY		
Current Liabilities (beginning balance $5,000)	$6,000	
Long-Term Debts	1,000	
Shareholders' Equity (500 common shares outstanding valued at $15 each)	5,000	
Total Liabilities and Shareholders' Equity		$12,000

Developing Your Research Skills

Select an article from a business journal or newspaper (print or online edition) that discusses the quarterly or year-end performance of a company that industry analysts consider notable for either positive or negative reasons.

17-25. Did the company report a profit or a loss for this accounting period? What other performance indicators were reported? Is the company's performance improving or declining?

17-26. Did the company's performance match industry analysts' expectations, or was it a surprise? How did analysts or other experts respond to the firm's actual quarterly or year-end results?

17-27. What reasons were given for the company's improvement or decline in performance?

MyBizLab®

Go to the Assignments section of your MyLab to complete these writing exercises.

17-28. Should public companies be allowed to publish any non-GAAP performance metrics? Why or why not?

17-29. How could you apply the concept of a balance sheet to your personal financial planning?

ENDNOTES

1. Michael Liedtke, "New CFO Reins in Google Excess, Stock Soars," *Seattle Times*, 16 July 2015, www.seattletimes.com; Antoine Gara, "New Google CFO Ruth Porat Will Get A Massive Raise For Leaving Morgan Stanley," *Forbes*, 26 March 2015, www.forbes.com; Ryan Tate, "Google Couldn't Kill 20 Percent Time Even If It Wanted To," *Wired*, 21 August 2013, www.wired.com; James Manyika, "Google's CFO on Growth, Capital Structure, and Leadership," *McKinsey Quarterly*, August 2011, www.mckinsey quarterly.com; Google financial profile on Trefis, accessed 18 November 2013, www.trefis.com; Bill Coughran, "More Wood Behind Fewer Arrows," Google blog, 20 July 2011, http://google blog.blogspot.com; Julianne Pepitone, "Google Beats Profit Estimates," *CNNMoney.com*, 16 April 2009, http://money.cnn .com; "Frugal Google," *Fortune*, 22 January 2009, http://money .cnn.com/magazines/fortune; Miguel Helft, "Google's Profit Surges in Quarter," *New York Times*, 16 July 2009, www.nytimes. com; Catherine Clifford, "Layoffs Hit Google: 200 Jobs Cut," *CNNMoney.com*, 26 March 2009, http://money.cnn.com; Adam Lashinsky, "Belt-Tightening at Google," *Fortune*, 22 January 2009, http://money.cnn.com/magazines/fortune; Adam Lashinsky, "The Axman Comes to Google," *Fortune*, 23 March 2009, http:// money.cnn.com/magazines/fortune; Google website, accessed 18 November 2013, www.google.com; Jessica E. Vascellaro and Scott Morrison, "Google Gears Down for Tougher Times," *Wall Street Journal*, 3 December 2008, http://online.wsj.com; Abbey Klaassen, "A Maturing Google Buckles Down and Searches for Cost Savings," *Advertising Age*, 1 December 2008, 3, 29.
2. "Accountants and Auditors," *Occupational Outlook Handbook, 2010–11 Edition*, U.S. Bureau of Labor Statistics website, www .bls.gov.
3. "Frequently Asked Questions," American Institute of Certified Public Accountants website, accessed 19 August 2009, www .aicpa.org.
4. "CMA: The Essential Credential," Institute of Management Accountants, accessed 10 September 2011, www.imanet.org.
5. Danielle Lee, "Hiring, Salaries Up for Accounting Graduates," *Accounting Today*, 30 April 2013, www.accountingtoday.com; "Accountants and Auditors," *Occupational Outlook Handbook, 2010–11 Edition*, www.bls.gov/oco/; Nanette Byrnes, "Green Eyeshades Never Looked So Sexy," *BusinessWeek*, 10 January 2005, 44; "Rules Make Accountants Newly Hot Commodity," *Oregonian*, 13 April 2005, www.ebsco.com.
6. Sarah Johnson, "Goodbye GAAP," *CFO*, 1 April 2008, www.cfo .com.
7. "Detecting Two Tricks of the Trade," *Investopedia.com*, accessed 19 August 2009, www.investopedia.com.
8. "Earnings Before Interest, Taxes, Depreciation and Amortization—EBITDA," *Investopedia.com*, accessed 18 November 2013, www.investopedia.com; Jonathan Weil, "Readjusting Black Box's Earnings Adjustments (Adjusted)," *Bloomberg*, 30 January 2013, www.bloomberg.com; Anthony Catanach, "Non-GAAP Metrics: Is It Time to Toss Out the SEC's Reg G?" Grumpy Old Accountants blog, 20 June 2013, http://grumpyoldaccountants .com.
9. Emily Chasan, "New Benchmarks Crop Up in Companies' Financial Reports," *Wall Street Journal*, 13 November 2012, http:// online.wsj.com.
10. Johnson, "Goodbye GAAP."
11. Vincent Ryan, "Former SEC Chair Cox Declares IFRS "Bereft of Life," *CFO*, 10 June 2014, www.cfo.com; Paul Pacter, "What Have IASB and FASB Convergence Efforts Achieved?" *Journal of Accountancy*, February 2013, www.journalofaccountancy.com; Tammy Whitehouse, "FASB Looks Inward at Improving GAAP," *Compliance Week*, 1 November 2013, www.complianceweek .com; Anthony Catanach, "The Great IFRS Swindle: Accountants Scamming Accountants" Grumpy Old Accountants blog, 10 November 2013, http://grumpyoldaccountants.com.
12. American Institute of CPAs, "International Financial Reporting Standards (IFRS): An AICPA Backgrounder," 2011, www.ifrs .com; PricewaterhouseCoopers, "IFRS and US GAAP: Similarities and Differences," September 2010, www.pwc.com; KPMG, "IFRS Compared to US GAAP: An Overview," September 2010, www .kpmg.com.
13. "Summary of SEC Actions and SEC Related Provisions Pursuant to the Sarbanes-Oxley Act of 2002," SEC website, accessed 9 May 2004, www.sec.gov; "Sarbanes-Oxley Act's Progress," *USA Today*, 26 December 2002, www.highbeam.com.
14. Sarah Johnson, "PCAOB Chairman Mark Olson to Retire," *CFO*, 9 June 2009, www.cfo.com.
15. "Building Value in Your Sox Compliance Program: Highlights from Protiviti's 2013 Sarbanes-Oxley Compliance Survey," Protiviti, www.protiviti.com; Michael W. Peregrine, "The Law That Changed Corporate America," *New York Times*, 25 July 2012, www.nytimes.com; Kayla Gillan, "It Enhanced Investor Protection," *New York Times*, 25 July 2012, www. nytimes.com.
16. Thayne Forbes, "Valuing Customers," *Journal of Database Marketing & Customer Strategy Management*, October 2007, 4–10.
17. Baruch Lev, "Sharpening the Intangibles Edge," *Harvard Business Review*, June 2004, 109–116.
18. "Google Inc. Financial," Google Finance, accessed 18 November 2013, www.google.com/finance.
19. "How to Spot Trouble in Your Financials," *Inc.*, October 2004, 96.
20. Timothy Green, "How Twitter Tried to Convince Us That It's Doing Really Well," *Money*, 1 May 2015, http://time.com/ money; Ben McClure, "A Clear Look at EBITDA," *Investopedia.com*, 17 April 2010, www.investopedia.com; "Bobbie Gossage," Cranking Up the Earnings," *Inc.*, October 2004, 54; Lisa Smith, "EBITDA: Challenging the Calculation," *Investopedia.com*, 20 November 2009, www.investopedia.com.

21. Amy Wilson, "Old Vehicles Clog Dealer Lots," *Automotive News*, 11 May 2009, 4.

22. "Inventory Turnover," *Controller's Report*, October 2008, 13–14.

23. Jeffery Slater, *College Accounting: A Practical Approach*, 11th ed. (Upper Saddle River N.J.: Pearson Prentice Hall, 2010), 741.

24. Slater, *College Accounting: A Practical Approach*, 735.

25. See note 1.

26. Mary Hayes Weier, "Companies Look to Contain Risk with GRC Software," *InformationWeek*, 5 April 2008, www.informationweek.com; SAP website, accessed 19 June 2015, www.sap.com; IBM website, accessed 19 June 2015, www.ibm.com; Oracle website, accessed 19 June 2015, www.oracle.com; GRC Software Seems to Be Rising," *FierceComplianceIT*, 12 March 2007, www.fiercecomplianceit.com; James Kobielus, "Compliance-Enabling Technologies via SOA on the Rise," *ITWorldCanada*, 8 March 2007, www.itworldcanada.com.

Section Two

Chapter 11
International Business

The Global Marketplace

LEARNING OBJECTIVES After studying this chapter, you will be able to

1. Explain why nations trade, and describe how international trade is measured.

2. Discuss the nature of conflicts in global business, including free trade and government interventions into international trade.

3. Identify the major organizations that facilitate international trade and the major trading blocs around the world.

4. Discuss the importance of understanding cultural and legal differences in the global business environment.

5. Define the major forms of international business activity.

6. Discuss the strategic choices that must be considered before entering international markets.

BEHIND THE SCENES H&M: FIRST SWEDEN, THEN THE WORLD

PSL Images/Alamy

As it continues to expand from its home base in Stockholm, Sweden, the fashion retailer H&M has to decide how much to adapt to local markets and how much to maintain a consistent global strategy.

www.hm.com

If you have an eye for fashion and a good sense of value, chances are you already know about H&M. The Swedish company has grown to be the world's second-largest apparel company by pursuing a balance of cutting-edge style, quality, and attractive prices.

H&M started in 1947 as a women's clothing store in Västerås, Sweden. International expansion came slowly at first, with stores in Norway in 1964, Denmark in 1967, and the United Kingdom in 1976. The product range expanded as well, with the addition of men's and children's lines and eventually cosmetics and items for the home. Germany, currently the company's largest market, followed in 1980. The pace accelerated through the 1990s, and by 2013 the company boasted 3,000 stores in more than 50 countries. Even with so many stores in operation, H&M still aims to expand by 10 to 15 percent every year.

To be sure, H&M's global expansion has not gone uncontested. Its biggest competitor overall—and the world's largest clothing retailer—is the multibrand Spanish company Inditex. Inditex's biggest chain, Zara, is still relatively unknown in the United States but has a huge presence in Europe and other markets. Zara is highly regarded as the innovator of "fast fashion," in which high-speed design, production, and distribution systems can jump on trend shifts and get new styles into retail shops in as little as two or three weeks. Inditex isn't sitting still either, with plans to open 1,000 new stores in the next few years.

Imagine you are Karl-Johan Persson, H&M's managing director and chief executive officer. How would you plot the company's continuing global expansion? Would you use the same business strategies in every country or adapt to local markets? Would you present H&M as a consistent global brand or modify the presentation for each country? How would you keep growing when you're already the world's second-largest apparel retailer?[1]

INTRODUCTION

The experience of H&M (profiled in the chapter-opening Behind the Scenes) is a great example of the opportunities and challenges of taking a business international. As you'll read in this chapter, international business has grown dramatically in recent years, and it's no stretch to say this growth affects virtually every company, even those that never reach beyond their own borders. Studying international business is essential to your career, too. The future professionals and managers from Asia and Europe—people you'll be competing with for jobs in the global employment market—take international business seriously.[2]

1 LEARNING OBJECTIVE

Explain why nations trade, and describe how international trade is measured.

Fundamentals of International Trade

Wherever you're reading this, stop and look around for a minute. You might see cars that were made in Japan running on gasoline from Russia or Saudi Arabia, mobile phones made in South Korea, food grown in Canada or Mexico or Chile, a digital music player made in China, clothing from Vietnam or Italy, industrial equipment made in Germany—and dozens of other products from every corner of the globe. Conversely, if you or a family member works for a midsize or large company, chances are it gets a significant slice of its revenue from sales to other countries. In short, we live and work in a global marketplace. Moreover, although the United States remains one of the world's most competitive countries, dozens of other countries now compete for the same employees, customers, and investments (see Exhibit 3.1).

EXHIBIT 3.1   The World's Most Competitive Economies

According to the World Economic Forum (WEF), these are the 10 most competitive economies in the world, based on their ability to sustain economic growth. (Hong Kong, a Special Administrative Region of the People's Republic of China, is evaluated separately by the WEF.)

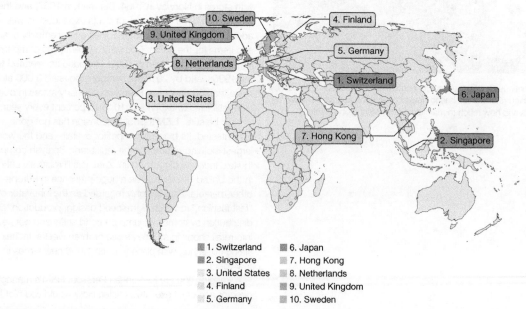

■ 1. Switzerland	■ 6. Japan
■ 2. Singapore	■ 7. Hong Kong
■ 3. United States	■ 8. Netherlands
■ 4. Finland	■ 9. United Kingdom
■ 5. Germany	■ 10. Sweden

Source: Data from Klaus Schwab, *The Global Competitiveness Report 2014–2015,* World Economic Forum, www.weforum.org.

WHY NATIONS TRADE

Commerce across borders has been going on for thousands of years, but the volume of international business has roughly tripled in the past 30 years.[3] One significant result is **economic globalization**, the increasing integration and interdependence of national economies around the world. Six reasons help explain why countries and companies trade internationally:

- **Focusing on relative strengths.** The classic theory of *comparative advantage* suggests that each country should specialize in those areas where it can produce more efficiently than other countries, and it should trade for goods and services that it can't produce as economically. The basic argument is that such specialization and exchange will increase a country's total output and allow both trading partners to enjoy a higher standard of living.

- **Expanding markets.** Many companies have ambitions too large for their own backyards. Well-known U.S. companies such as Microsoft and Boeing would be a fraction of their current size if they were limited to the U.S. marketplace. Similarly, companies based in other countries, from giants such as Toyota, Shell, and Nestlé to thousands of smaller but equally ambitious firms, view the U.S. consumer and business markets as a vast opportunity.

- **Pursuing economies of scale.** All this international activity involves more than just sales growth, of course. By expanding their markets, companies can benefit from **economies of scale**, which enable them to produce goods and services at lower costs by purchasing, manufacturing, and distributing higher quantities.[4]

- **Acquiring materials, goods, and services.** No country can produce everything its citizens want or need at prices they're willing to pay. China's rapidly growing middle class has a voracious appetite for consumer products, but the country has a relatively low concentration of brick-and-mortar stores to meet their needs, and some consumers voice concerns about the quality of locally produced goods. As a result, millions of Chinese shoppers now embrace online retailing—often buying from U.S. companies that are racing to expand their online presence in that country.[5]

- **Keeping up with customers.** In some cases, companies have to expand in order to keep or attract multinational customers. For example, suppose a retailer with stores in 20 countries wants to hire a single advertising agency to manage all its ad campaigns. Any agency vying for the account might need to open offices in all 20 countries in order to be considered.

- **Keeping up with competitors.** Companies are sometimes forced to engage on a global scale simply because their competitors are doing so. Failing to respond can allow a competitor to increase its financial resources and become a greater threat everywhere the companies compete, even on home turf.[6]

These motivations have provided the energy behind the rapid growth in global business, but the level of growth would not have been possible without two key enablers. First, the world's borders are much more open to trade than they were just a few decades ago, thanks to the advent of international trade organizations (see page 102) and a growing awareness by most governments that healthy trade can help their economies. Second, advances in communication and transportation technologies have made global trade safer, easier, and more profitable.[7]

economic globalization
The increasing integration and interdependence of national economies around the world.

economies of scale
Savings from buying parts and materials, manufacturing, or marketing in large quantities.

REAL-TIME UPDATES
Learn More by Exploring This Interactive Website

Do a deep dive into balance of trade data

Explore the overall U.S. balance of trade for any time period and compare trade balances with any other country. Go to http://real-timeupdates.com/bia8 and click on Learn More in the Students section.

HOW INTERNATIONAL TRADE IS MEASURED

Chapter 2 discusses how economists monitor certain key economic indicators to evaluate how well a country's economic system is performing, and several of these indicators measure international trade. As Exhibit 3.2 on the next page illustrates, the United States imports more goods than it exports, but it exports more services than it imports.

EXHIBIT 3.2   U.S. Exports and Imports Since 1990

The U.S. trade deficit has been growing dramatically in recent years. Although the United States maintains a trade surplus in services (middle graph), the international market for services isn't nearly as large as the market for goods. Consequently, the trade deficit in goods (*top graph*) far outweighs the trade surplus in services, resulting in an overall trade deficit (*bottom graph*).

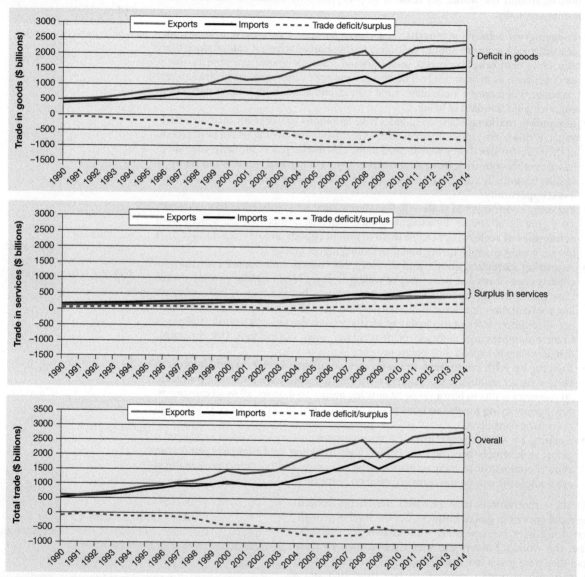

Source: Data from "U.S. International Trade Data," U.S. Census Bureau, 6 March 2015, www.census.gov.

balance of trade
Total value of the products a nation exports minus the total value of the products it imports, over some period of time.

trade surplus
A favorable trade balance created when a country exports more than it imports.

Two key measurements of a nation's level of international trade are the *balance of trade* and the *balance of payments.* The total value of a country's exports *minus* the total value of its imports, over some period of time, determines its **balance of trade**. In years when the value of goods and services exported by a country exceeds the value of goods and services it imports, the country has a positive balance of trade, or a **trade surplus**. The opposite is a **trade deficit**, when a country imports more than it exports.

The **balance of payments** is the broadest indicator of international trade. It is the total flow of money into the country *minus* the total flow of money out of the country over some period of time. The balance of payments includes the balance of trade plus the net dollars received and spent on foreign investment, military expenditures, tourism, foreign aid, and other international transactions. For example, when a U.S. company buys all or part of a company based in another country, that investment is counted in the balance of payments but not in the balance of trade. Similarly, when a foreign company buys a U.S. company or purchases U.S. stocks, bonds, or real estate, those transactions are part of the balance of payments.

FOREIGN EXCHANGE RATES AND CURRENCY VALUATIONS

When companies buy and sell goods and services in the global marketplace, they complete the transaction by exchanging currencies. The process is called *foreign exchange*, the conversion of one currency into an equivalent amount of another currency. The number of units of one currency that must be exchanged for a unit of the second currency is known as the **exchange rate** between the currencies.

Most international currencies operate under a *floating exchange rate system*, meaning that a currency's value or price fluctuates in response to the forces of global supply and demand. The supply and demand of a country's currency are determined in part by what is happening in the country's own economy. Moreover, because supply and demand for a currency are always changing, the rate at which it is exchanged for other currencies may change a little each day.

A currency is called *strong* relative to another when its exchange rate is higher than what is considered normal and called *weak* when its rate is lower than normal ("normal" is a relative term here). Note that "strong" isn't necessarily good, and "weak" isn't necessarily bad when it comes to currencies, as Exhibit 3.3 illustrates. Exchange rates can dramatically affect a company's financial results by raising or lowering the cost of supplies it imports and raising or lowering the price of goods it exports.

trade deficit
An unfavorable trade balance created when a country imports more than it exports.

balance of payments
The sum of all payments one nation receives from other nations minus the sum of all payments it makes to other nations, over some specified period of time.

exchange rate
The rate at which the money of one country is traded for the money of another.

EXHIBIT 3.3   Strong and Weak Currencies: Who Gains, Who Loses?

A strong dollar and a weak dollar aren't necessarily good or bad; each condition helps some people and hurts others.

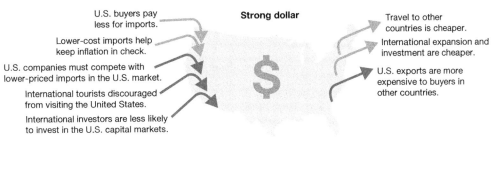

Strong dollar

U.S. buyers pay less for imports.
Lower-cost imports help keep inflation in check.
U.S. companies must compete with lower-priced imports in the U.S. market.
International tourists discouraged from visiting the United States.
International investors are less likely to invest in the U.S. capital markets.

Travel to other countries is cheaper.
International expansion and investment are cheaper.
U.S. exports are more expensive to buyers in other countries.

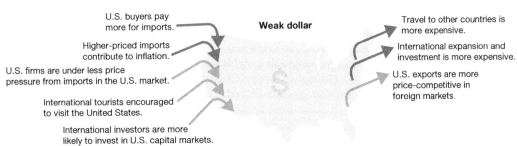

Weak dollar

U.S. buyers pay more for imports.
Higher-priced imports contribute to inflation.
U.S. firms are under less price pressure from imports in the U.S. market.
International tourists encouraged to visit the United States.
International investors are more likely to invest in U.S. capital markets.

Travel to other countries is more expensive.
International expansion and investment is more expensive.
U.S. exports are more price-competitive in foreign markets.

Source: Based on "Strong Dollar, Weak Dollar: Foreign Exchange Rates and the U.S. Economy," Federal Reserve Bank of Chicago website, accessed 29 January 2005, www.chicagofed.org.

✓ **Checkpoint**

LEARNING OBJECTIVE 1: Explain why nations trade, and describe how international trade is measured.

SUMMARY: Nations and companies trade internationally for any of six reasons: focusing on their relative strengths (producing the goods and services in which they excel and trading for other products they need); expanding into new markets to increase sales revenues; pursuing economies of scale to achieve lower production costs; acquiring materials, goods, and services not available at home; tending to the needs of multinational customers; and keeping up with competitors that are expanding internationally. Two primary measures of a country's international trade are its *balance of trade*, which is exports minus imports, and its *balance of payments*, a broader measure that includes all incoming payments minus all outgoing payments.

CRITICAL THINKING: (1) Would it be wise for an advertising agency to open offices in Europe and Asia to service a single multinational client? Why or why not? (2) If IBM invests $40 million in a joint venture in China, would that amount be counted in the U.S. balance of trade or the balance of payments?

IT'S YOUR BUSINESS: (1) In the last major purchase you made, did you take into consideration whether the product was made in the United States or another country? (2) Does country of origin matter to you when you shop?

KEY TERMS TO KNOW: economic globalization, economies of scale, balance of trade, trade surplus, trade deficit, balance of payments, exchange rate

2 LEARNING OBJECTIVE

Discuss the nature of conflicts in global business, including free trade and government interventions into international trade.

Conflicts in International Trade

Just as employees compete with one another for jobs and companies compete for customers, countries compete with one another for both. Naturally, the U.S. government promotes and protects the interests of U.S. companies, workers, and consumers. Other countries are trying to do the same thing for their stakeholders. As a consequence, international trade is a never-ending tug of war.

FREE TRADE

The benefits of the comparative advantage model are based on the assumption that nations don't take artificial steps to minimize their own weaknesses or to blunt the natural advantages of other countries. For example, if a country cannot produce a particular good at a cost that is competitive on the global market, its government might choose to *subsidize* exporters of this good with financial supports that allow them to charge lower prices than their business operations can naturally support. Trade that takes place without these interferences is known as **free trade**. (Like free-market capitalism, no trade is completely free in the sense that it takes place without regulations of any kind. Instead, international trade should be viewed along a continuum from "more free" to "less free.")

free trade
International trade unencumbered by restrictive measures.

Free trade is not a universally welcomed concept, despite the positive connotation of the word *free*. Supporters claim that it is the best way to ensure prosperity for everyone, and an overwhelming majority of U.S. economists say that the United States should eliminate barriers to trade.[8] Supporters of free trade generally acknowledge that it produces winners and losers but that the winners gain more than the losers lose, so the net effect is positive.[9]

Detractors call free trade unfair to too many people and a threat to the middle class.[10] In addition, some critics argue that free trade makes it too easy for companies to exploit workers around the world by pitting them against one another in a "race to the bottom," in which production moves to whichever country has the lowest wages and fewest restrictions regarding worker safety and environmental protection.[11] This complaint has been at the heart of recent protests over free trade and economic globalization in general. However, some researchers rebut this criticism by saying that companies prefer to do business in countries with stable, democratic governments. Consequently, this camp says, less-developed nations are motivated to improve their economic and social policies, which not only helps business but can raise the standard of living.[12] As one example, from 1981 to 2005, a period during which China became much more actively involved in free-market capitalism and global trade, the country's poverty rate dropped by 68 percent.[13] Of course, such progress might be little comfort to workers in other countries who've lost jobs as the global labor market evolves in the direction of parity.

Free trade agreements are often controversial, with various parties concerned about the effects on jobs, the environment, and other issues.

GOVERNMENT INTERVENTION IN INTERNATIONAL TRADE

When a government believes that free trade is not in the best interests of its national security, domestic industries, workforce, or consumers, it can intervene in a number of ways. Some of these methods are collectively known as **protectionism** because they seek to protect a specific industry or groups of workers. Although they can help some parties in the short term, many protectionist measures actually end up hurting the groups they were intended to help. When an industry is isolated from real-life competition for too long, it can fail to develop and become strong enough to compete efficiently.[14]

The following are the most commonly used ways to intervene in international trade:

- **Tariffs.** Taxes, surcharges, or duties levied against imported goods are known as **tariffs**. Tariffs can be levied to generate revenue, to restrict trade, or to punish other countries for disobeying international trade laws.
- **Quotas. Import quotas** limit the amount of particular goods that countries allow to be imported during a given year.
- **Embargoes.** An **embargo** is a complete ban on the import or export of certain products or even all trade between certain countries.
- **Restrictive import standards.** Countries can assist their domestic producers by establishing restrictive import standards, such as requiring special licenses for doing certain kinds of business and then making it difficult or expensive for foreign companies to obtain such licenses.[15]
- **Export subsidies.** In addition to intervening on imported goods, countries can also intervene to help domestic industries export their products to other countries. **Export subsidies** are a form of financial assistance in which producers receive enough money from the government to allow them to lower their prices in order to compete more effectively in the world market.
- **Antidumping measures.** The practice of selling large quantities of a product at a price lower than the cost of production or below what the company would charge in its home market is called **dumping**. This tactic is most often used to try to win foreign customers or to reduce product surpluses. If a domestic producer can demonstrate that the low-cost imports are damaging its business, most governments will seek redress on their behalf through international trade organizations. Dumping is often a tricky situation to resolve, however; buyers of a product that is being dumped benefit from the lower prices, and proving what constitutes a fair price in the country of origin can be difficult.[16]
- **Sanctions.** Sanctions are politically motivated embargoes that revoke a country's normal trade relations status; they are often used as forceful alternatives short of war. Sanctions can include arms embargoes, foreign-assistance reductions and cutoffs, trade limitations, tariff increases, import-quota decreases, visa denials, air-link cancellations, and more.

protectionism
Government policies aimed at shielding a country's industries from foreign competition.

tariffs
Taxes levied on imports.

import quotas
Limits placed on the quantity of imports a nation will allow for a specific product.

embargo
A total ban on trade with a particular nation (a sanction) or of a particular product.

export subsidies
A form of financial assistance in which producers receive enough money from the government to allow them to lower their prices in order to compete more effectively in the global market.

dumping
Charging less than the actual cost or less than the home-country price for goods sold in other countries.

3 LEARNING OBJECTIVE

Identify the major organizations that facilitate international trade and the major trading blocs around the world.

International Trade Organizations

With international trade such a huge part of the world's economies, organizations that establish trading rules, resolve disputes, and promote trade play an important role in global business.

ORGANIZATIONS FACILITATING INTERNATIONAL TRADE

In an effort to ensure equitable trading practices and to iron out the inevitable disagreements over what is fair and what isn't, governments around the world have established a number of important agreements and organizations that address trading issues, including the WTO, IMF, and World Bank.

The World Trade Organization

The World Trade Organization (WTO), www.wto.org, is a permanent forum for negotiating, implementing, and monitoring international trade procedures and for mediating trade disputes among its 160 member countries. The organization's work is guided by five principles: preventing discriminatory policies that favor some trading partners over others or a country's own products over those of other countries; reducing trade barriers between countries; making trade policies more predictable and less arbitrary; discouraging unfair practices; and promoting economic progress in the world's less-developed countries.[17]

Critics of globalization often direct their ire at the WTO, but the organization says these criticisms are unjustified and based on misunderstandings of the WTO's missions and methods. For example, the WTO asserts that contrary to claims by some critics, it does not dictate policies to national governments, does not ignore the special circumstances faced by the world's poorest countries, and does not ignore health and environmental concerns when trying to mediate commercial disputes.[18] One point everyone seems to agree on is that the WTO's work is exceedingly complex and therefore excruciatingly slow. Reaching agreement to eventually eliminate agricultural export subsidies, in which government payments to farmers allowed them to set artificially low prices on the world market, took several decades.[19]

The International Monetary Fund

The International Monetary Fund (IMF), www.imf.org, was established in 1945 to foster international financial cooperation and increase the stability of the international economy. Now with 188 member countries, the IMF's primary functions are monitoring global financial developments, offering technical advice and training to help countries manage their economies more effectively, and providing short-term loans to member countries. These loans can be made for a variety of reasons, from helping a country deal with a natural disaster to stabilizing a country's economy to limit the spread of a financial crisis beyond its borders.[20]

The World Bank

The World Bank (www.worldbank.org) is a group of five financial institutions whose primary goals are eradicating the most extreme levels of poverty around the world and raising the income of the poorest people in every country as a way to foster shared prosperity for everyone. Although it is not as directly involved in international trade and finance on the same scale as the WTO and IMF, the World Bank does indirectly contribute to trade by working to improve economic conditions by investing in education, health care, and other concerns in developing countries.[21]

TRADING BLOCS

Trading blocs, or *common markets*, are regional organizations that promote trade among member nations (see Exhibit 3.4 on the next page). Although specific rules vary from group to group, their primary objective is to ensure the economic growth and benefit of members. As such, trading blocs generally promote trade inside the region while creating uniform barriers against goods and services entering the region from nonmember countries.

trading blocs
Organizations of nations that remove barriers to trade among their members and that establish uniform barriers to trade with nonmember nations.

North American Free Trade Agreement

In 1994, the United States, Canada, and Mexico formed the North American Free Trade Agreement (NAFTA), paving the way for the free flow of goods, services, and capital within the bloc through the phased elimination of tariffs and quotas.[22] NAFTA was controversial when first implemented, and it has remained controversial ever since.[23] Assessing the treaty's full impact is difficult because so many economic factors are involved, and a variety of other forces have affected all three countries' economies over the past two decades.

To a large degree, judging the success of NAFTA depends on what you are trying to measure. Trade between the three nations has increased dramatically in the two decades since NAFTA was instituted, and companies in all three countries have benefitted from easier access to markets. Mexican exports are up dramatically, and U.S. and other foreign companies have invested billions of dollars in Mexico. Some Mexican companies are thriving, thanks to those export opportunities, whereas others, particularly in agriculture, have been hurt severely by low-cost imports from the United States. Many of the manufacturing jobs Mexico hoped to attract wound up in China and other countries instead. In the United States, critics claim that much of the promised benefits of lower consumer prices and steady export markets for small farmers didn't materialize, that benefits of NAFTA have gone mostly to huge agribusiness corporations, and that contrary to promises of job creation in the United States, NAFTA has destroyed many U.S. jobs.[24]

NAFTA illustrates the challenge of analyzing international economic activity and linking measurable effects to specific causes. And, as is often the case with economic change, gains for some groups come at the expense of losses for other groups. The authors of a congressional report issued on NAFTA's 20th anniversary in 2014 summarized its

EXHIBIT 3.4   Members of Major Trading Blocs

As the economies of the world become increasingly linked, many countries have formed powerful regional trading blocs that trade freely with one another but place restrictions on trade with other countries and blocs.

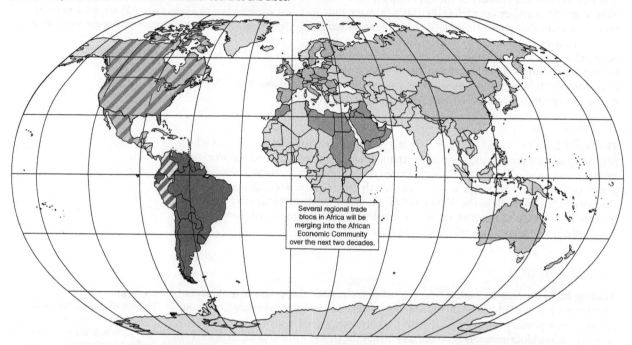

Several regional trade blocs in Africa will be merging into the African Economic Community over the next two decades.

European Union (EU)	North American Free Trade Agreement (NAFTA)	Association of Southeast Asian Nations (ASEAN)	Union of South American Nations	Asia-Pacific Economic Cooperation (APEC)	Greater Arab Free Trade Area (GAFTA)
Austria	Canada	Brunei Darussalam	Argentina	Australia	Bahrain
Belgium	Mexico	Cambodia	Bolivia	Brunei Darussalam	Egypt
Bulgaria	United States	Indonesia	Brazil	Canada	Iraq
Croatia		Laos	Chile	Chile	Jordan
Cyprus		Malaysia	Colombia	China	Kuwait
Czech Republic		Myanmar	Ecuador	Hong Kong	Lebanon
Denmark		Philippines	Guyana	Indonesia	Libya
Estonia		Singapore	Paraguay	Japan	Morocco
Finland		Thailand	Peru	Republic of Korea	Oman
France		Vietnam	Suriname	Malaysia	Palestine
Germany			Uruguay	Mexico	Qatar
Greece			Venezuela	New Zealand	Saudi Arabia
Hungary				Papua New Guinea	Sudan
Ireland				Peru	Syria
Italy				Philippines	Tunisia
Latvia				Russia	United Arab Emirates
Lithuania				Singapore	Yemen
Luxembourg				Chinese Taipei	
Malta				Thailand	
Netherlands				United States	
Poland				Vietnam	
Portugal					
Romania					
Slovakia					
Slovenia					
Spain					
Sweden					
United Kingdom					

Source: Member lists as of 20 March 2015: http://europa.eu; www.asean.org; www.unasursg.org; www.apec.org; www.economy.gov.lb.

overall impact this way. "NAFTA did not cause the huge job losses feared by the critics or the large economic gains predicted by supporters."[25]

The European Union

One of the largest trading blocs is the European Union (EU), http://europa.eu, whose membership now encompasses more than two dozen countries and a half billion people. Viewed as a whole, the EU now constitutes the world's largest economy. EU nations have eliminated hundreds of local regulations, variations in product standards, and protectionist measures that once limited trade among member countries. Trade now flows among member countries in much the same way it does among states in the United States. And the EU's reach extends far beyond the borders of Europe; to simplify design and manufacturing for world markets, many companies now create their products to meet EU specifications. If you've seen the "CE" marking on any products you may own, that stands for Conformité Européene and indicates that the product has met EU standards for safety, health, and environmental responsibility.[26]

REAL-TIME UPDATES
Learn More by Exploring This Interactive Website

Explore the latest data on Europe's financial health

This interactive guide shows employment, debt, and other key figures. Go to http://real-timeupdates.com/bia8 and click on Learn More in the Students section.

The EU has taken a significant step beyond all other trading blocs in the area of money by creating its own currency, the *euro*, which has been adopted by more than half the member states of the EU. By switching to a common currency, these countries have made financial transactions simpler and less expensive. According to EU leadership, the euro has simplified commerce for consumers and businesses, lowered inflation and interest rates, improved transparency in pricing, provided a more stable currency, and given the EU a stronger presence in global financial markets.[27] However, with widespread trade imbalances and ongoing financial crises in Greece, Italy, and several other nations weighing down the economies of all Eurozone members, some observers now question whether the currency bloc can continue in its current configuration.

The Asia-Pacific Economic Cooperation

The Asia-Pacific Economic Cooperation (APEC), www.apec.org, is an organization of 21 countries working to liberalize trade in the Pacific Rim (the land areas that surround the Pacific Ocean). Member nations represent 40 percent of the world's population and more than 50 percent of the world's gross domestic product. Like other trade blocs, APEC has a long-term goal of liberalizing and simplifying trade and investment among member countries and helping the region as a whole achieve sustainable economic growth. Since APEC's establishment in 1989, trade among member nations has increased sevenfold.[28]

The Trans-Pacific Partnership

The Trans-Pacific Partnership (TPP) is a potentially major trade agreement involving about a dozen countries around the Pacific Rim. After a decade of negotiations, the TPP may be finalized in the near future. Supporters say the TPP is vital to promoting U.S. economic interests in fast-growing countries, but detractors fear it would undermine U.S. laws while giving tremendous legal power to multinational corporations.[29]

 **Checkpoint**

LEARNING OBJECTIVE 3: Identify the major organizations that facilitate international trade and the major trading blocs around the world.

SUMMARY: Major organizations that facilitate trade include the World Trade Organization (WTO), the International Monetary Fund (IMF), and, at least indirectly, the World Bank. Major regional trading blocs include NAFTA (Canada, Mexico, and the United States), the European Union (more than two dozen countries across Europe), and APEC (21 countries around the Pacific Rim).

4 | **LEARNING OBJECTIVE**

Discuss the importance of understanding cultural and legal differences in the global business environment.

The Global Business Environment

Doing business internationally can be a boon for many companies, but it also presents many challenges. Every country has unique laws, customs, consumer preferences, ethical standards, labor skills, and political and economic forces. Understanding cultural and legal differences is an essential first step for any business contemplating international operations.

CULTURAL DIFFERENCES IN THE GLOBAL BUSINESS ENVIRONMENT

culture
A shared system of symbols, beliefs, attitudes, values, expectations, and norms for behavior.

Culture is a shared system of symbols, beliefs, attitudes, values, expectations, and norms for behavior. Your cultural background influences the way you prioritize what is important in life, helps define your attitude toward what is appropriate in a situation, and establishes rules of behavior.[30] Successful global business leaders recognize and respect differences in language, social values, ideas of status, decision-making habits, attitudes toward time, use of space, body language, manners, religions, and ethical standards. Ignorance of or indifference toward cultural differences is a common cause of communication breakdowns in international affairs. Above all else, businesspeople dealing with other cultures must avoid the twin traps of **stereotyping**, assigning a wide range of generalized (and often superficial or even false) attributes to an individual on the basis of membership in a particular culture or social group, and **ethnocentrism**, the tendency to judge all other groups according to one's own group's standards, behaviors, and customs.

stereotyping
Assigning a wide range of generalized attributes, which are often superficial or even false, to an individual based on his or her membership in a particular culture or social group.

ethnocentrism
Judging all other groups according to the standards, behaviors, and customs of one's own group.

Education and an open mind are the best ways to prepare yourself for doing business with people from another culture. Numerous books and websites offer advice on traveling to and working in specific countries. It is also helpful to sample newspapers, magazines, and even the music and movies of another country. For instance, a movie can demonstrate nonverbal customs even if you don't grasp the language. Learn everything you can about the culture's history, religion, politics, and customs—especially its business customs. Who makes decisions? How are negotiations usually conducted? Is gift giving expected? What is the proper attire for a business meeting? In addition to the suggestion that you learn about the culture, seasoned international businesspeople offer the following tips for improving communication with a person from another culture:

- **Be alert to the other person's customs.** Expect the other person to have values, beliefs, expectations, and mannerisms that may differ from yours.
- **Deal with the individual.** Don't stereotype the other person or react with preconceived ideas. Regard the person as an individual first, not as a representative of another culture.
- **Clarify your intent and meaning.** The other person's body language may not mean what you think, and the person may read unintentional meanings into your message. Clarify your true intent by repetition and examples. Ask questions and listen carefully.

- **Adapt your style to the other person's.** If the other person appears to be direct and straightforward, follow suit. If not, adjust your behavior to match.
- **Show respect.** Learn how respect is communicated in various cultures through gestures, eye contact, social customs, and other actions.

These are just a few tips for doing business in the global marketplace. Successful international businesses learn as much as they can about political issues, cultural factors, and the economic environment before investing time and money in new markets. Exhibit 3.5 can guide you in your efforts to learn more about a country's culture before doing business there.

LEGAL DIFFERENCES IN THE GLOBAL BUSINESS ENVIRONMENT

Differences in national legal systems may not be as immediately obvious as cultural differences, but they can have a profound effect on international business efforts. For instance, the legal systems in the United States and the United Kingdom are based on *common law*,

---

EXHIBIT 3.5   Checklist for Doing Business Abroad

Use this checklist as a starting point when planning business activity in another country.

Action	Details to Consider
Understand social customs	• How do people react to strangers? Are they friendly? Hostile? Reserved? • How do people greet each other? Should you bow? Nod? Shake hands? • How do you express appreciation for an invitation to lunch, dinner, or someone's home? Should you bring a gift? Send flowers? Write a thank-you note? • Are any phrases, facial expressions, or hand gestures considered rude? • How do you attract the attention of a waiter? Do you tip the waiter? • When is it rude to refuse an invitation? How do you refuse politely? • What topics may or may not be discussed in a social setting? In a business setting? • How do social customs dictate interaction between men and women? Between younger people and older people?
Learn about clothing and food preferences	• What occasions require special attire? • What colors are associated with mourning? Love? Joy? • Are some types of clothing considered taboo for one gender or the other? • How many times a day do people eat? • How are hands or utensils used when eating? • Where is the seat of honor at a table?
Assess political patterns	• How stable is the political situation? • Does the political situation affect businesses in and out of the country? • Is it appropriate to talk politics in social or business situations?
Understand religious and social beliefs	• To which religious groups do people belong? • Which places, objects, actions, and events are sacred? • Do religious beliefs affect communication between men and women or between any other groups? • Is there a tolerance for minority religions? • How do religious holidays affect business and government activities? • Does religion require or prohibit eating specific foods? At specific times?
Learn about economic and business institutions	• Is the society homogeneous or heterogeneous? • What languages are spoken? • What are the primary resources and principal products? • Are businesses generally large? Family controlled? Government controlled? • What are the generally accepted working hours? • How do people view scheduled appointments? • Are people expected to socialize before conducting business?
Appraise the nature of ethics, values, and laws	• Is money or a gift expected in exchange for arranging business transactions? • Do people value competitiveness or cooperation? • What are the attitudes toward work? Toward money? • Is politeness more important than factual honesty?

tax haven
A country whose favorable banking laws and low tax rates give companies the opportunity to shield some of their income from higher tax rates in their home countries or other countries where they do business.

in which tradition, custom, and judicial interpretation play important roles. In contrast, the system in countries such as France and Germany is based on *civil law*, in which legal parameters are specified in detailed legal codes. A third type of legal system, *theocratic law*, or law based on religious principles, predominates in countries such as Iran and Pakistan. Beyond the differences in legal philosophies, the business of contracts, copyrights, and other legal matters can vary considerably from one country to another.

Tax havens and bribery are two serious issues that highlight the challenges and complexities of international business law. A **tax haven** is a country whose favorable banking laws and low tax rates give companies the opportunity to shield some of their income from higher tax rates in their home countries or other countries where they do business.

Although a vast amount of criminal money moves through or is sheltered in certain tax havens, using tax havens isn't necessarily illegal. However, it can be a highly controversial practice, particularly in the case of multinational corporations that use internal transfers or other processes to lower their tax burdens.

For example, Microsoft, Google, and Amazon have lowered their tax burdens in the United Kingdom by recording UK sales through subsidiaries in Ireland or Luxembourg, whose corporate tax rates are much lower than those in the United Kingdom. Similarly, Starbucks has a third of the coffeeshop market in the United Kingdom but in a recent 15-year span avoided paying corporation taxes in 14 of those years through internal transfers that effectively erased the taxable income of its UK stores. Local UK companies complain that they have to pay full UK taxes and are therefore at a competitive disadvantage. Moreover, a rising tide of criticism over the loss of revenue to fund public services is spurring changes in international tax laws that will make it more difficult to avoid taxes through these internal maneuvers. In response to these criticisms and recent moves by government regulators, all three companies have begun changing their accounting practices in ways that will increase the local taxes they pay.[31]

Perhaps no issue in international business law generates as much confusion and consternation as bribery. In some countries, payments to government and business officials are so common that some businesspeople consider them to be standard operating practice—and companies sometimes fear they won't be able to compete if they don't play along. These payments are used to facilitate a variety of actions, from winning contracts for public works projects (such as roads or power plants) to securing routine government services (such as customs inspections) to getting preferential treatment (such as the approval to raise prices).[32]

These payment systems discourage much-needed investment in developing countries, undermine democratic processes and weaken trust in government, raise prices for consumers by inflating business costs, and can even present security risks by essentially putting officials' actions up for the highest bid. Some businesspeople have argued that critics of such payoffs are trying to impose U.S. values on other cultures, but Transparency International, a watchdog group that works to reduce business–government corruption around the world, discredits this argument by saying that "the abuse of power for personal gain—the siphoning off of public or common resources into private pockets—is unacceptable in all cultures and societies."[33]

All U.S. companies operating in other countries and foreign companies doing business in the United States are bound by the Foreign Corrupt Practices Act (FCPA), which outlaws payments with the intent of getting government officials to break the laws of their own countries or to secure "improper advantage" in gaining or retaining sales.[34] The FCPA does allow payments to expedite routine actions such as setting up utilities for a new facility, even though the U.S. and other governments discourage such payments. In addition to banning outright cash payments, the FCPA also forbids indirect means of influence such as expensive gifts, charitable contributions intended to influence government officials, and travel opportunities (such as company-hosted training seminars) that have little or no legitimate business purpose.[35]

Following the FCPA, the Organisation for Economic Co-Operation and Development (OECD), an international body dedicated to fostering economic prosperity and combating poverty, made bribery of foreign officials a criminal offense for its member nations as well.[36]

 Checkpoint

LEARNING OBJECTIVE 4: Discuss the importance of understanding cultural and legal differences in the global business environment.

SUMMARY: Elements of culture include language, social values, ideas of status, decision-making habits, attitudes toward time, use of space, body language, manners, religions, and ethical standards. Awareness of and respect for cultural differences is essential to avoiding communication breakdowns and fostering positive working relationships. Understanding differences in legal systems and specific laws and regulations in other countries is another vital aspect of successful international business. One of the most confusing and frustrating aspects of international trade law is the issue of bribery.

CRITICAL THINKING: (1) What steps could you take to help someone from another country adapt to U.S. business culture? (2) How can you convey respect for another person's culture even if you don't agree with it or even understand it?

IT'S YOUR BUSINESS: (1) When you encounter someone whose native language is different from yours, what steps do you take to make sure communication is successful? (2) How does another person's "foreignness" influence your perceptions of his or her abilities?

KEY TERMS TO KNOW: culture, stereotyping, ethnocentrism, tax haven

Forms of International Business Activity

5 **LEARNING OBJECTIVE**

Define the major forms of international business activity.

Beyond cultural and legal concerns, companies that plan to go international also need to think carefully about the right organizational approach to support these activities. The five common forms of international business are importing and exporting, licensing, franchising, strategic alliances and joint ventures, and foreign direct investment; each has varying degrees of ownership, financial commitment, and risk (see Exhibit 3.6 on the next page).

IMPORTING AND EXPORTING

Importing, the buying of goods or services from a supplier in another country, and **exporting**, the selling of products outside the country in which they are produced, have existed for centuries. Exporting is one of the least risky forms of international business activity. It allows a firm to enter a foreign market gradually, assess local conditions, and then fine-tune its product offerings to meet the needs of local markets. In most cases, the firm's financial exposure is limited to the costs of researching the market, advertising, and either establishing a direct sales and distribution system or hiring intermediaries. Moreover, a variety of intermediaries exist to help companies, even the smallest businesses, get started with exporting.

importing
Purchasing goods or services from another country and bringing them into one's own country.

exporting
Selling and shipping goods or services to another country.

Many countries now have foreign trade offices to help importers and exporters interested in doing business within their borders. Other helpful resources include professional agents, local businesspeople, and the International Trade Administration of the U.S. Department of Commerce (http://export.gov), which offers several services, including political and credit-risk analysis, advice on entering foreign markets, and financing tips.[37]

EXHIBIT 3.6   Forms of International Business Activity

Depending on their goals and resources and the opportunities available, companies can choose from five different ways to conduct business internationally.

Importing and exporting	**International licensing**	**International franchising**
Buying and selling goods and services across national borders, without establishing a physical or legal business presence in other countries	Licensing intellectual property such as a design patent to a company in another country, which then produces the product and sells it locally	Selling the rights to use an entire business system, such as a fast-food restaurant, including the brand name and internal processes

International strategic alliances and joint ventures	**Foreign direct investment**
Forming a long-term business partnership with a local company in a new market or creating a new company with a local partner	Buying an established company or launching a new company in another country

INTERNATIONAL LICENSING

licensing
Agreement to produce and market another company's product in exchange for a royalty or fee.

Licensing is another popular approach to international business. License agreements entitle one company to use some or all of another firm's intellectual property (patents, trademarks, brand names, copyrights, or trade secrets) in return for a royalty payment.

Low up-front costs are an attractive aspect of international licensing. Pharmaceutical firms such as Germany's Boehringer Ingelheim routinely use licensing to enter foreign markets.[38] After a pharmaceutical company has developed and patented a new drug, it is often more efficient to grant existing local firms the right to manufacture and distribute the patented drug in return for royalty payments. (Licensing agreements are not restricted to international business, of course; a company can also license its products or technology to other companies in its domestic market.)

INTERNATIONAL FRANCHISING

Some companies choose to expand into foreign markets by *franchising* their operations. Chapter 6 discusses franchising in more detail, but briefly, franchising involves selling the right to use a *business system*, including brand names, business processes, trade secrets, and other assets. For instance, there are more than 18,000 McDonald's restaurants in more than 100 countries outside the United States, and the vast majority of them are run by independent franchisees.[39] Franchising is an attractive option for many companies because it reduces the costs and risks of expanding internationally while leveraging their investments in branding and business processes.

INTERNATIONAL STRATEGIC ALLIANCES AND JOINT VENTURES

Strategic alliances (discussed in Chapter 5), which are long-term partnerships between two or more companies to jointly develop, produce, or sell products, are another important way to reach the global marketplace. Alliance partners typically share ideas, expertise, resources, technologies, investment costs, risks, management, and profits. In some cases, a strategic alliance might be the only way to gain access to a market.

A *joint venture*, in which two or more firms join together to create a new business entity that is legally separate and distinct from its parents, is an alternative to a strategic alliance. In some countries, foreign companies are prohibited from owning facilities outright or from investing in local business, so establishing a joint venture with a local partner may be the only way to do business in that country.

REAL-TIME UPDATES
Learn More by Visiting This Website

Ready to take a business international?

Export.gov can help you at every step, including finding out if your company has what it takes to be a successful exporter. Go to http://real-timeupdates.com/bia8 and click on Learn More in the Students section.

FOREIGN DIRECT INVESTMENT

Many firms prefer to enter international markets through partial or whole ownership and control of assets in foreign countries, an approach known as **foreign direct investment (FDI)**. Some facilities are set up through FDI to exploit the availability of raw materials; others take advantage of low wage rates, whereas still others minimize transportation costs by choosing locations that give them direct access to markets in other countries. Companies that establish a physical presence in multiple countries through FDI are called **multinational corporations (MNCs)**. MNCs can approach international markets in a variety of ways; see "Organizational Strategies for International Expansion" in the next section.

FDI typically gives companies greater control, but it carries much greater economic and political risk and is more complex than any other form of entry in the global marketplace. Consequently, most FDI takes place between the industrialized nations with large, stable economies such as the United States, Canada, Japan, and most countries in Europe, which tend to offer greater protection for foreign investors.[40]

foreign direct investment (FDI)
Investment of money by foreign companies in domestic business enterprises.

multinational corporations (MNCs)
Companies with operations in more than one country.

 Checkpoint

LEARNING OBJECTIVE 5: Define the major forms of international business activity.

SUMMARY: The major forms of international business activity are importing and exporting (buying and selling across national boundaries), licensing (conferring the rights to create a product), franchising (selling the rights to use an entire business system and brand identity), strategic alliances and joint ventures (forming partnerships with other companies), and foreign direct investment (buying companies or building facilities in another country).

CRITICAL THINKING: (1) Can a company successfully export to other countries without having staff and facilities in those countries? Why or why not? (2) Why does so much foreign direct investment take place between the industrialized nations?

IT'S YOUR BUSINESS: (1) What connotations does the word "imported" have for you? (2) On what do you base your reaction?

KEY TERMS TO KNOW: importing, exporting, licensing, foreign direct investment (FDI), multinational corporations (MNCs)

Strategic Approaches to International Markets

6 LEARNING OBJECTIVE
Discuss the strategic choices that must be considered before entering international markets.

Expanding internationally is obviously not a decision any business can take lightly. The rewards can be considerable, but the costs and risks must be analyzed carefully during the planning stage. This section offers a brief look at overall organizational strategies for international expansion, followed by strategic questions in the various functional areas of the business.

ORGANIZATIONAL STRATEGIES FOR INTERNATIONAL EXPANSION

When a firm decides to establish a presence in another country, it needs to consider its long-term objectives, the nature of its products, the characteristics of the markets into which it plans to expand, and the management team's ability to oversee a geographically dispersed operation. These considerations can lead to one of several high-level strategies:[41]

multidomestic strategy
A decentralized approach to international expansion in which a company creates highly independent operating units in each new country.

- In the **multidomestic strategy**, a company creates highly independent operating units in each new country, giving local managers a great deal of freedom to run their operations almost as though they are independent companies. Although this strategy can help a company respond more quickly and effectively to local market needs, it doesn't deliver the economy-of-scale advantages that other strategies can bring. In addition, the lack of centralized control can lead to situations in which local managers act in ways contrary to corporate strategy or guidelines. For example, when the French grocery retailer Carrefour learned that some of its local store managers in China were luring customers with low advertised prices but then charging more in their stores, the company clamped down on the practice, even though it is apparently widespread in Chinese retailing (despite being illegal).[42]

global strategy
A highly centralized approach to international expansion, with headquarters in the home country making all major decisions.

- In the **global strategy**, a company embraces the notion of economic globalization by viewing the world as a single integrated market. This is essentially the opposite of the multidomestic strategy. Managerial control in the global strategy is highly centralized, with headquarters in the home country making all major decisions.

transnational strategy
A hybrid approach that attempts to reap the benefits of international scale while being responsive to local market dynamics.

- In the **transnational strategy**, a company uses a hybrid approach as it attempts to reap the benefits of international scale while being responsive to local market dynamics. This is the essence of the often-heard advice to "think globally, act locally." With this approach, major strategic decisions and business systems such as accounting and purchasing are often centralized, but local business units are given the freedom to make "on-the-ground" decisions that are most appropriate for local markets.

FUNCTIONAL STRATEGIES FOR INTERNATIONAL EXPANSION

Choosing the right form of business to pursue is the first of many decisions that companies need to make when moving into other countries. Virtually everything you learn about in this course, from human resources to marketing to financial management, needs to be reconsidered carefully when going international. Some of the most important decisions involve products, customer support, pricing, promotion, and staffing:

Patrizia Wyss/Alamy

Product branding and packaging are key decisions for international marketers. Notice how Coca-Cola maintains the look of its packaging while translating the product name.

- **Products.** You face two primary questions regarding products. First, which products should you try to sell in each market? Second, should you *standardize* your products, selling the same product everywhere in the world, or *customize* your products to accommodate the lifestyles and habits of local target markets? Customization seems like an obvious choice, but it can increase costs and operational complexity, so the decision to customize is not automatic. As you'll read at the end of the chapter, for example, H&M follows a strategy of standardized product lines. The degree of customization can also vary. A company may change only a product's name or packaging, or it can modify a product's components, size, and functions. Understanding a country's regulations, culture, and local competition is essential to making smart product design and branding decisions.
- **Customer support.** Cars, computers, and other products that require some degree of customer support add another layer of complexity to international business. Many customers are reluctant to buy foreign products that don't offer some form of local support, whether it's a local dealer, a manufacturer's branch office, or a third-party organization that offers support under contract to the manufacturer.
- **Promotion.** Advertising, public relations, and other promotional efforts also present the dilemma of standardization versus customization. In addition to language differences, companies need to consider nonverbal symbols (the significance of colors and hand gestures, for example), local competition, and a variety of cultural differences.
- **Pricing.** Even a standardized strategy adds to the cost of doing business, from transportation to communication, and customized international strategies add even more. Before moving into other countries, businesses need to make sure they can cover all these costs and still be able to offer competitive prices.

- **Staffing.** Depending on the form of business a company decides to pursue in international markets, staffing questions can be major considerations. Many companies find that a combination of U.S. and local personnel works best, mixing company experience with local connections and lifelong knowledge of the working culture. Staffing strategies can evolve over time, too, as conditions change in various countries. In recent years, for example, U.S. and European countries with operations in China have begun filling more middle- and upper-management positions with local talent, rather than relocating managers from headquarters. The costs of hiring locally are often considerably lower, and there is less risk of a foreign manager failing to adapt to working and living in China.[43] When transferring managers to foreign posts, some U.S. companies have experienced failure rates as high as 50 percent.[44]

Given the number and complexity of the decisions to be made, you can see why successful companies plan international expansion with great care—and adapt quickly if their strategies and tactics aren't working. The consequences of not planning carefully or adapting quickly to missteps can be high. Recognizing the number of Canadian shoppers who crossed the border to shop at its U.S. stores, Target decided to enter the Canadian market to serve these customers on their home turf. The idea seemed to make solid business sense: If people are willing to drive some distance and put up with the hassles of border crossings just to shop at your stores, imagine how much more you could sell to them and their neighbors if you were right down the street.

Target jumped in with both feet, quickly opening more than 100 stores in its first expansion outside the United States. However, after only two years, it shut them all down and left the country. The company admits it tried too much too soon, and shoppers and retailing experts pointed to multiple blunders, including underestimating the strong local competition, opening stores in unappealing locations, setting prices too high, and failing to keep stores stocked with adequate inventory. It was an expensive mistake that cost the company billions of dollars.[45]

For the latest information on internal business, visit http://real-timeupdates.com /bia8 and click on Chapter 3.

✓ Checkpoint

BEHIND THE SCENES
H&M EXPANDS IT GLOBAL FOOTPRINT, BUT NOT WITHOUT COMPETITION AND CHALLENGES

From its humble start in 1947 as a single store in Västerås, Sweden, H&M has grown into a global brand recognized on main streets and in shopping malls around the world. The several brands that make up the H&M family now boast a combined 3,000 stores in more than 50 countries, with the flagship H&M store the leading presence.

Because H&M designs its own clothing lines, manages their production (via outsourcing partners), and retails them in its own branded stores, the company's international expansion strategy is more complicated than it would be for a business that operates strictly on the production side or strictly on the retailing side. However, H&M management has put a lot of thought into its supply chain, creating a system that is both cost-effective and flexible to respond quickly to shifts in consumer demand.

The process starts with the 160 designers and 100 pattern makers who work in the company's Stockholm headquarters. These specialists are members of teams with autonomous responsibility for keeping a finger on the pulse of fashion trends in art, cinema, music, and other cultural influences. When new designs are ready, they are sent to production partners in Europe or Asia, then the finished products are shipped to regional H&M distribution centers for final delivery to stores or e-commerce customers.

With a well-established global network in place, expanding its retail presence is easier than it would be for a younger or smaller company. That retail presence is primarily through company-managed sites, but H&M also works with franchising partners in selected markets such as Indonesia and the Middle East. With its global organizational strategy (see page 102), the company establishes guidelines for merchandising displays, which it develops in a "test store" near company headquarters in Stockholm. Stores themselves are uniquely adapted to local settings and leasing opportunities, but they maintain a consistent and recognizable brand presentation and shopping experience.

H&M's product strategy is fairly consistent worldwide as well, with the same styles generally rolled out on a global scale. The product mix does get adapted to local needs to a degree, such as not selling winter coats in locales that do not experience cold winter temperatures. However, the overall sense of style is consistent all around the globe.

Customer communication is localized to varying degrees. For example, website content is translated into local languages in major markets such as France, Germany, the United States, and Italy. In countries where the company currently has a smaller presence, the websites tend to be in English, with price in the local currency and store-location search engines sometimes presented in the local language. Graphic design and product photography are fairly consistent from country to country, however.

H&M's global expansion strategy has served it well so far, but the company does face serious challenges from two directions. On the one hand, it generally can't beat Zara when it comes to fast turnaround times of new designs, particularly in Europe, because Zara's production facilities are closer to retail outlets. Consequently, H&M can't always present the most cutting-edge fashions to consumers who simply must have the latest styles and are willing to pay for the pleasure. On the other hand, H&M's prices aren't low enough to compete with low-price chains such as Primark in Great Britain or Forever 21 in the United States.

From its position between these two market layers, H&M appears to be pushing both upward and downward. It has opened a small number of stores under the more high-end & Other Stories brand, and it continues to expand its offerings aimed at eco-conscious consumers (such as clothes made of organic cotton). And two other company brands, Monki and Cheap Monday, are aimed at more casual and cost-conscious buyers.

As it expands its brand portfolio, the company shows no intention to ease off from its aggressive global growth, with the aim of increasing the number of stores by 10 to 15 percent every year. Two key markets for near-term expansion are China and the United States, so if you haven't bumped into an H&M store yet, chances are you will soon.

Critical Thinking Questions

3-1. Some companies play up their home-country roots as they expand internationally, such as the way BMW and Mercedes emphasize their German engineering. Should H&M promote some aspect of its "Swedishness"? Why or why not?

3-2. Would H&M have been able to succeed with its consistent global style strategy in the days before mass media and digital communications? Explain your answer.

3-3. H&M's growth, including its international expansion, is entirely self-funded (meaning it doesn't borrow money to launch new stores). How might this influence the company's decision-making and expansion efforts?

LEARN MORE ONLINE

Visit **www.hm.com** and select three of H&M's country websites. How are these sites similar and how are they different? Are the sites translated into the local language for each country? Are the imagery, messaging, and product promotion consistent across all three sites? What does this tell you about H&M's global product strategy?

KEY TERMS

balance of payments
balance of trade
culture
dumping
economic globalization
economies of scale
embargo
ethnocentrism
exchange rate
export subsidies
exporting
foreign direct investment (FDI)
free trade
global strategy

import quotas
importing
licensing
multidomestic strategy
multinational corporations (MNCs)
protectionism
stereotyping
tariffs
tax haven
trade deficit
trade surplus
trading blocs
transnational strategy

MyBizLab®
To complete the problems with the ⭐,
go to EOC Discussion Questions in the
MyLab.

TEST YOUR KNOWLEDGE

Questions for Review

3-4. How can a company use a licensing agreement to enter world markets?

3-5. What two fundamental product strategies do companies choose between when selling their products in the global marketplace?

3-6. What is the balance of trade, and how is it related to the balance of payments?

3-7. What are tariffs?

3-8. How can international trade be measured?

Questions for Analysis

3-9. Why would a company choose to work through intermediaries when selling products in a foreign country?

3-10. How do companies benefit from forming international joint ventures and strategic alliances?

3-11. How can governments intervene in international trade? Is this considered a positive action?

3-12. What benefits can trading internationally have on small businesses?

⭐ 3-13. **Ethical Considerations.** Is it unethical for a U.S. company to choose export markets specifically for their less stringent consumer protection standards? Why or why not?

Questions for Application

3-14. You own health and wellness distribution networks in China and Korea. You have been exporting your products there and are currently enjoying brisk sales in the two countries. You are planning to open a new distribution network in the United Kingdom and are aware that the legal system in the United Kingdom is stronger. What steps should you take to enhance your learning on the legal elements in the United Kingdom?

3-15. Who are the local companies that have successfully expanded abroad? Why do the two companies trade internationally? You may retrieve information from the newspaper (prints or online editions) to provide support to your interpretations.

⭐ 3-16. Would a major shopping mall developer with experience all across Europe be a good strategic alliance partner for your fast-food chain's first overseas expansion effort? Why or why not?

⭐ 3-17. **Concept Integration.** You just received notice that a large shipment of manufacturing supplies that one of your factories in another country has been waiting for has been stuck in customs for two weeks. A local business associate in that country tells you that you are expected to give customs agents some "incentive money" to see that everything clears easily. How will you handle this situation? Evaluate the ethical merits of your decision by considering the approaches listed in Exhibit 4.3 on page 124.

EXPAND YOUR KNOWLEDGE

Discovering Career Opportunities

The thought of your company with international trade with governments and trading partners excites you. You begin to consider education qualifications and professional skills that will enable you to undertake trade assignments. To perform successful trade assignments, you had been advised by the trade experts to appreciate current trading issues at major regional trading blocs.

3-18. If the company of your choice is a member in one of the regional trading blocs, how would you prepare to succeed in your new role as an international trade development? You may choose any two products or services that are governed by the trade member agreements in the newspapers (prints/online editions).

3-19. If the company of your choice is not a member in any of the regional trading blocs, would you think you will be able to succeed in your new role as an international trade development? You may choose any two services of the non-trade members. You may refer to the newspapers (prints/online editions).

3-20. How important would the specialist knowledge skills be in this new role?

Improving Your Tech Insights: Telepresence

Telepresence systems start with the basic idea of videoconferencing but go far beyond, with imagery so real that colleagues thousands of miles apart virtually appear to be in the same room together. The interaction feels so lifelike that participants can forget that the person "sitting" on the other side of the table is actually in another city or even another country. The ability to convey nonverbal subtleties such as facial expressions and hand gestures makes these systems particularly good for negotiations, collaborative problem solving, and other complex discussions. How do you think businesses can use the technology of *telepresence?* What are the benefits of adopting such a technology? What are its drawbacks?

PRACTICE YOUR SKILLS

Sharpening Your Communication Skills

Languages never translate on a word-for-word basis. When doing business in the global marketplace, choose words that communicate a single idea clearly. Avoid using slang or idioms (words that can have meanings far different from their individual components when translated literally). For example, if a U.S. executive tells an Egyptian executive that a change in plans "really threw us a curve ball," chances are that communication will fail.

Team up with two other students and list 10 examples of slang (in your native language) that would probably be misinterpreted or misunderstood during a business conversation with someone from another culture. Next to each example, suggest other words you might use to convey the same message. Make sure the alternatives mean exactly the same as the original slang or idiom. Compare your list with those of your classmates.

Building Your Team Skills

In 2009, eight U.S. steel companies and the United Steelworkers union accused Chinese pipe manufacturers of dumping $2.7 billion worth of a particular type of stainless steel pipe on the U.S. market the previous year. (Specifically, the type of pipe is called "oil country tubular goods" and is used in oil and gas wells.) In a petition to the U.S. International Trade Commission (ITC) and the U.S. Department of Justice (DOJ), the group said 2,000 U.S. employees had lost their jobs as a result of the unfairly priced Chinese imports. The petition asked for tariffs of up to 99 percent on the Chinese steel.[46]

With your team, research the outcome of the steel industry's petition. Did the ITC and DOJ enact tariffs on Chinese steel?

After you have discovered the outcome of the petition, analyze the potential effect of the government's position on the following stakeholders:

- U.S. businesses that buy this type of steel
- U.S. steel manufacturers
- Employees of U.S. steel manufacturers
- The United Steelworkers union
- Chinese steel manufacturers

Present your analysis to the class and compare your conclusions with those reached by other teams.

Developing Your Research Skills

In today's global environment, businesses both small and large have to be aware of the global marketplace and the demands within it. With more and more businesses choosing to trade and compete internationally, trading in only one nation can be considered a risk to many businesses. Research examples of companies that trade internationally, and consider the questions below:

3-21. When undertaking your research, what examples did you find of trade occurring within a trading block? Considering one of your company examples, explain the benefits of doing so.

3-22. Based on your research, what risks might a business be exposed to if it chooses not to trade internationally? Use specific examples to illustrate your answer.

3-23. List some of the other examples you have found of companies that trade internationally. What strategies for international trade have these companies adopted? What risks might be seen in adopting one?

MyBizLab®

Go to the Assignments section of your MyLab to complete these writing exercises.

3-24. How does free trade create situations in which companies can pit the workers of one country against the workers of another?

0-25. Should the U.S. government promote trade policies that benefit some companies or industries while potentially harming others? Why or why not?

ENDNOTES

1. H&M website, accessed 22 March 2015, www.hm.com; Inditex website, accessed 28 October 2013, www.inditex.com; Lydia Dishman, "H&M's Competitive Advantage: Expansion in India," *Forbes*, 29 April 2013, www.forbes.com; John Lynch, "How Fashion Giant Inditex Bucked Trend to Notch €16bn Sales," *Irish Independent*, 28 October 2013, www.independent.ie; "H&M Struggles to Compete in High-Street Fashion," MarketWatch, 15 March 2013, www.marketwatch.com.
2. Ricky W. Griffin and Michael W. Pustay, *International Business*, 6th ed. (Upper Saddle River, N.J.: Pearson Prentice Hall, 2010), 6.
3. Griffin and Pustay, *International Business*, 12.
4. Holley H. Ulbrich and Mellie L. Warner, *Managerial Economics* (New York: Barron's Educational Series, 1990), 190.
5. Janet I. Tu, Seattle-Area Businesses Plug into China's Love of Online Shopping, *Seattle Times*, 2 January 2015, www.seattletimes.com.
6. Griffin and Pustay, *International Business*, 13.
7. Griffin and Pustay, *International Business*, 14.
8. Robert Whaples, "The Policy Views of American Economic Association Members: The Results of a New Survey," *Econ Journal Watch*, September 2009, 337–348.
9. Uwe E. Reinhardt, "How Convincing Is the Case for Free Trade?" blog post, 18 February 2011, *New York Times*, www.nytimes.com.
10. "President Bush's Statement on Open Economies," FDCH Regulatory Intelligence Database, 10 May 2007, www.ebsco.com; Vladimir Masch, "A Radical Plan to Manage Globalization," *BusinessWeek*, 24 February 2007, 11; Philip Levy, "Trade Truths for Turbulent Times," *BusinessWeek*, 24 February 2007, 9.
11. "Twelve Myths About Hunger," Institute for Food and Development Policy website, accessed 27 January 2005, www.foodfirst.com.
12. Peter Davis, "Investment and the Development Theory Myth," *Ethical Corporation*, October 2006, 29–30.
13. Moisés Naim, "Globalization," *Foreign Policy*, March–April 2009, 28–34.
14. "Protectionism Fades, So EU Carmakers Must Fight," *Automotive News Europe*, 11 June 2007, 10.
15. "Common Trade Concerns and Problems Experienced by U.S. Textile/Apparel/Footwear/Travel Goods Exporters," U.S. Department of Commerce, International Trade Administration, Office of Textiles and Apparel website, accessed 1 August 2011, http://web.ita.doc.gov.
16. John D. Daniels, Lee H. Radebaugh, and Daniel P. Sullivan, *International Business*, 10th ed. (Upper Saddle River, N.J.: Pearson Prentice Hall, 2004), 182.
17. World Trade Organization website, accessed 22 March 2015, www.wto.org.
18. "10 Common Misunderstandings About the WTO," World Trade Organization website, accessed 6 October 2013, www.wto.org.
19. Joe Chidley, "The WTO at the Brink," *Canadian Business*, 10 April 2009, 35–39.
20. International Monetary Fund website, accessed 22 March 2015, www.imf.org.
21. World Bank Group website, accessed 22 March 2015, www.worldbank.org.
22. "North American Free Trade Agreement (NAFTA)," USDA Foreign Agricultural Service website, accessed 29 June 2007, www.fas.usda.gov.
23. Julián Aguilar, "Twenty Years Later, NAFTA Remains a Source of Tension," *New York Times*, 7 December 2012, www.nytimes.com.
24. Armand de Mestral, "NAFTA: The Unfulfilled Promise of the FTA," *European Law Journal*, Vol. 17, No. 5, September 2011, 649–666; "Fool Me Twice? Chamber of Commerce Distorts NAFTA Record, Hides CAFTA Costs," *Public Citizen*, March 2005, www.citizen.org; "North American Free Trade Agreement (NAFTA)," Public Citizen website, accessed 28 January 2005, www.citizen.org; Debra Beachy, "A Decade of NAFTA," *Hispanic Business*, July/August 2004, 24–25; Geri Smith and Cristina Lindblad, "Mexico: Was NAFTA Worth It?" *BusinessWeek*, 22 December 2003, 66–72; Charles J. Walen, "NAFTA's Scorecard: So Far, So Good," *BusinessWeek*, 9 July 2001, 54–56.
25. M. Angeles Villarreal and Ian F. Fergusson, "NAFTA at 20: Overview and Trade Effects," *Congressional Research Service*, 28 April 2014, www.crs.gov.
26. European Community website, accessed 22 March 2015, http://europa.eu.
27. "The Euro," European Community website, accessed 6 October 2013, http://europa.eu.
28. "About APEC," APEC website, accessed 22 March 2015, www.apec.org.
29. "Trans-Pacific Partnership (TPP): Job Loss, Lower Wages and Higher Drug Prices," *Public Citizen*, accessed 22 March 2015, www.citizen.org; "Trans-Pacific Partnership Agreement," Electronic Frontier Foundation, accessed 22 March 2015, www.eff.org; Everett Rosenfeld, "Major Asia-Pacific Trade Pact Enters Final Stages," CNBC, 20 March 2015, www.cnbc.com; "Trans-Pacific Partnership," Office of the United States Trade Representative, accessed 22 March 2015, http://ustr.gov.
30. Linda Beamer and Iris Varner, *Intercultural Communication in the Workplace*, 2nd ed. (New York: McGraw-Hill Irwin, 2001), 3.
31. Mathew Ingram, "Amazon to Start Paying More EU Taxes After Pressure from Regulators," *Fortune*, 25 May 2015, www.fortune.com; Peter Campbell and Jay Akbar, "Embarrassment for EU Chief Juncker as Sweetheart Tax Deal Between Amazon and Luxembourg Made When He Was Nation's PM Is Declared Illegal," *Daily Mail*, 16 January 2015, www.dailymail.co.uk; Simon Bowers and Patrick Wintour, "Amazon Told: Time Is Up for Tax Avoidance," *Guardian*, 19 July 2013, www.theguardian.com; Kiran Stacey, Jim Pickard, and Vanessa Houlder, "Coalition Hardens Stance Over Tax," *Financial Times*, 12 February 2013, www.ft.com; "Starbucks Pays UK Corporation Tax for First Time Since 2009," BBC News, 23 June 2013, www.bbc.co.uk; Matt Warman, "Google's UK Division Paid £12m in Corporation Tax in 2012," *Telegraph*, 29 September 2013, www.telegraph.co.uk.
32. Daniels, et al., *International Business*, 335.

33. "FAQs on Corruption," *Transparency International,* accessed 8 October 2013, www.transparency.org.

34. "Foreign Corrupt Practices Act," U.S. Department of Justice website, accessed 8 October 2013, www.justice.gov.

35. *A Resource Guide to the U.S. Foreign Corrupt Practices Act,* Criminal Division of the U.S. Department of Justice and the Enforcement Division of the U.S. Securities and Exchange Commission, 2012, 15–17, 25.

36. Organisation for Economic Co-Operation and Development website, accessed 1 August 2011, www.oecd.org.

37. Export.gov, accessed 1 August 2011, http://export.gov.

38. "Partnering for Success," Boehringer Ingelheim, accessed 23 May 2009, www.boehringer-ingelheim.com.

39. Hoovers, accessed 1 August 2011, www.hoovers.com.

40. U.S. Census Bureau, "U.S. Businesses Acquired or Established by Foreign Direct Investors—Investment Outlays by Industry of U.S. Business Enterprise and Country of Ultimate Beneficial Owner," accessed 1 August 2011, www.census.gov; Griffin and Pustay, *International Business,* 170.

41. Griffin and Pustay, *International Business,* 310–311.

42. "Carrefour in China: When the Price Isn't Right," Knowledge @ Wharton, 16 March 2011, www.knowledgeatwharton.com.

43. Griffin and Pustay, *International Business,* 555.

44. Griffin and Pustay, *International Business,* 559.

45. Jordan Weissmann, "Target Is Closing All of Its Stores in Canada. These Pictures Show Why They Were Such a Failure." *Slate,* 15 January 2015, www.slate.com; Anne D'innocenzio and Michelle Chapman, "Litany of Problems Pushes Target into Giving Up on Canada," *Seattle Times,* 16 January 2015, www .seattletimes.com.

46. Beth Murtagh, "U.S. Steel Files Trade Complaint Against China for Steel Dumping," *Pittsburgh Business Times,* 11 May 2009, www .bizjournals.com.

3 The global context of business

Chris Britton

Businesses of all sizes operate in international markets – products are sold across borders; the resources used in production can come from anywhere in the world; communication is instantaneous; and financial markets are inextricably linked, as the events of 2013/14 demonstrate. Individual businesses operate across borders in a variety of ways – they can do this directly, through the formation of strategic alliances, or through merger and takeover. It is clear then that businesses need to be aware of the global context of their markets.

Learning outcomes

Having read this chapter you should be able to:

- understand the difference between globalisation and internationalisation
- outline the main elements of globalisation
- illustrate the role of the multinational enterprise
- introduce the implications of globalisation for business

Key terms

Capital market flows	Free trade area	Multinational enterprises (MNEs)
Consortium	Globalisation	Regional trade agreements (RTAs)
Cross-subsidisation	Hyperglobalisation	Regionalism
Customs union	International trade	Strategic alliance
Emerging economies	Internationalisation	Transfer pricing
Foreign direct investment (FDI)	Joint venture	Transformationalism
Franchising	Licensing	

Introduction

Businesses operate in a global context: even if they do not trade directly with other countries, they might be affected by a domestic shortage of skilled labour or may be subject to developments on the global financial markets. There is a difference between globalisation and internationalisation in the business literature but both result in increased exposure to global forces. This means that businesses need an understanding of the process of globalisation. The nature of globalisation is changing; it used to mean the westernisation of the developing world, but the newly emerging economies such as Brazil, China and India are redefining processes and institutions. In 1980 the share of the developing countries in world exports was 34 per cent; by 2011 it was 47 per cent and share of world imports had gone up from 29 per cent to 42 per cent in the same period. Globalisation is here to stay and the World Bank forecasts that the share of global gross domestic product (GDP) for developing countries will rise from 29 per cent (2010) to 39 per cent (2030).

Globalisation versus internationalisation

These terms are often used interchangeably but they refer to different processes. Although there is not a single accepted definition of **globalisation**, it is a term used to describe the process of integration on a worldwide scale of markets and production. The world is moving away from a system of national markets isolated from each other by trade barriers, distance or culture. Advances in technology and mass communications have made it possible for people in one part of the world to watch happenings in far-off places on television or via the internet. So, for globalisation, national boundaries are not important economically; free trade and movement of labour and other resources result in the breakdown of these boundaries and one big global marketplace. **Internationalisation**, meanwhile, refers to the increased links between nation states with respect to trade and the movement of resources. The relevant thing here is that the nation state is still important; it is participating and cooperating with other nation states to a common end.

Regionalism and regional trade agreements are also important in this process, the European Union (EU) being an example. The main difference is that with internationalisation, the nation state remains important whereas the process of globalisation breaks down the barriers between nation states. An extreme view of this process is called **hyperglobalisation**, where the world market is seen as a borderless global marketplace consisting of powerless nation states and powerful multinational corporations.[1] The more generally accepted view is called **transformationalism**, which sees the process of globalisation as bringing about changes both in the power of countries and companies and in national characteristics and culture.[2] Any differences do not disappear but are maintained, albeit in changed forms. The population in India might drink Coca-Cola and listen to western music, but this does not mean that they hold the same views and values as the west. Similarly, even within the EU national differences remain important (especially in times of crisis).

Although these definitions are important theoretically, they are difficult to apply in practice, so here the term globalisation is used to mean the process of integration of markets, however that happens. Until recently globalisation meant the westernisation (or Americanisation) of markets, but the world has started to change. Companies from **emerging economies** have started to compete with the older **multinational enterprises (MNEs)** and the nature of the MNE is being redefined. Globalisation has taken place because of closer economic ties between countries and because of developments in mass communications, transportation, electronics and the greater mobility of labour. A heated debate has taken place over the past decade between the pro- and the anti-globalisation lobbies.

The arguments put forward by the proponents of globalisation stem from the benefits brought about by increased **international trade** and specialisation (see Chapter 16 for a discussion). They argue that all countries open to international trade have benefited – only those that are closed to international trade (some African countries, for example) have become poorer. In the case of China, the opening up to world trade in 1978 has led to increases in GDP per capita, up from $1460 per head in 1980 to $6188 per head in 2013. The pro-globalisation arguments can be summarised as follows:

- Increased globalisation leads to greater specialisation so that all countries involved benefit from the increased international trade.
- Countries that are open to international trade have experienced much faster growth than countries that are not.
- Barriers to trade encourage industries to be inefficient and uncompetitive.
- It is not just the large multinationals that benefit from globalisation – small and medium-sized companies are also engaged in global production and marketing.

The arguments against globalisation are just as strong. It is claimed that the benefits of higher world output and growth brought about through globalisation have not been shared equally by all countries. The main beneficiaries have been the large multinationals rather than individual countries or people. It is suggested that the international organisations that promote free trade should pay more attention to the issues of equity, human rights and the natural environment rather than focusing simply on trade. It is also argued that increased globalisation leads to economic instability. The anti-globalisation arguments can be summarised thus:

- The benefits of globalisation have not been shared equitably throughout the world.
- Globalisation undermines the power of nation states – it empowers the large multinationals at the expense of governments, many multinationals being financially bigger than nation states.
- The large organisations that promote free trade (such as the WTO and the IMF) are not democratically elected and their decisions are not made in the public eye.
- The policies of these organisations are aimed at trade only – human rights and environmental concerns are often ignored.

The main international organisations concerned with globalisation are discussed in more detail in Chapter 5. They are the World Trade Organisation (WTO), the International Monetary Fund (IMF), the World Bank and the Organisation for Economic Co-operation and Development (OECD). In addition to these there is the United Nations Conference on Trade and Development (UNCTAD), which is a permanent intergovernmental body of the United Nations that aims to maximise investment to the developing nations and to help them in their integration into the world economy.

There are several key elements of economic globalisation: international trade, **foreign direct investment (FDI)** and capital market flows. The OECD categorises members into three bands – high-income countries, which includes the EU, North America and Australasia; middle-income countries, which includes East Asia and the Pacific Rim; and low-income countries, which includes South Asia and Africa.

International trade

The share of international trade in goods as a percentage of GDP increased between 1990 and 2011 for all income groups and particularly for the low-income group (see Table 3.1). The same is true for services. Thus there is evidence of increased globalisation. Note that there are differences within each group – in the low-income group, for example, although the share has increased overall, there are countries that have experienced negative growth (Botswana and Togo for instance, both of which are open to international trade). Although the share of developing countries has increased over time, world markets are still dominated by the developed world, especially in high-value, high-tech products. It is also true that increased trade does not automatically lead to increased development, as in parts of sub-Saharan Africa where the products sold are basic primary products.

Table 3.1 Elements of economic globalisation

	Trade in goods as a % of GDP		Gross private capital flows as a % of GDP*		Gross FDI as a % of GDP	
	1990	2011	1990	2005	1990	2011
Low income	23.6	58.1	2.4	6.7	0.4	3.8
Middle income	32.5	53.0	6.6	13.3	0.9	2.7
High income	32.3	53.0	11.0	37.2	1.0	2.7

*Not available after 2005.
Source: Adapted from Table 6.1, *World Development Indicators,* 2013, and the Little Data Book 2013, both World Bank.

Capital market flows

This refers to the flows of money from private savers wishing to include foreign assets in their portfolios. This also increased in all income bands between 1990 and 2005 (Table 3.1) – later figures are not available. The overall figures hide a greater volatility than in international trade or foreign direct investment and the fact that the flows have been largely restricted to emerging economies in East Asia. **Capital market flows** occur because investors want to diversify their portfolios to include foreign assets; it is therefore aimed at bringing about short-term capital gains. Unlike FDI, there is no long-term involvement on the part of the investor.

Foreign direct investment

This refers to the establishment of production facilities in overseas countries and therefore represents a more direct involvement in the local economy (than capital market flows) and a longer-term relationship. Between 1990 and 2000, the value of FDI worldwide more than doubled; since then FDI has moved in line with world economic conditions (see case study on FDI at the end of the chapter). FDI represents the largest form of private capital inflow into the developing countries. Each of the three elements of economic globalisation has a different effect and carries different consequences for countries. Capital market flows are much more volatile and therefore carry higher risk – these flows introduce the possibility of 'boom and bust' for countries where capital market flows are important. The financial crisis in the emerging countries in 2013–14 had a lot to do with these capital flows. Openness to trade and FDI are less volatile and it is these that are favoured by the international organisations such as the World Bank and the WTO. It is also true that the benefits of globalisation have not been shared equally between those taking part – the developed nations have reaped more benefit than the poorer nations.

The role of multinational enterprises

Substantial amounts of foreign trade and hence movements of currency result from the activities of very large multinational companies or enterprises. Multinational enterprises/companies (MNEs/MNCs), strictly defined, are enterprises operating in a number of countries and having production or service facilities outside the country of their origin. These multinationals usually have their headquarters in a developed country, but this is beginning to change. At one time globalisation meant that businesses were expanding from developed to developing economies. The world is a different place now – business flows in the opposite direction and often between developing countries. One indication of this is the number of companies from the emerging nations that appear in the Global 500 list of the world's biggest companies. In 1980, 23 (5 per cent) came from emerging countries; in 2010, the number had gone up to 85 (17 per cent) and of these 54 were Chinese, including Lenovo, a Chinese computer manufacturer which bought IBM's personal computer business in 2005.

Multinationals can diversify their operations across different countries and many are well-known household names (see Table 3.2). The footloose nature of such companies brings with it certain benefits.

Table 3.2 The world's ten largest non-financial MNEs, ranked by foreign assets, 2012

Rank	Company	Home economy	Transnationality index %*
1	General Electric	United States	23
2	Royal Dutch Shell plc	UK/Netherlands	77
3	BP	United Kingdom	84
4	Toyota Motor Corporation	Japan	55
5	Total SA	France	79
6	Exxon Mobil Corporation	United States	65
7	Vodafone Group plc	United Kingdom	90
8	GDF Suez	France	59
9	Chevron Corporation	United States	60
10	Volkswagen Group	Germany	58

Note: *Measured as the average of three ratios: foreign assets to total assets, foreign sales to total sales, and foreign employment to total employment.
Source: Adapted from Annex Table 28, *World Investment Report,* UNCTAD, 2013.

1 MNEs can locate their activities in the countries that are best suited for them. For example, production planning can be carried out in the parent country, and the production itself can be carried out in one of the newly industrialised countries where labour is relatively cheap and marketing can be done in the parent country where such activities are well developed. The relocation of production may go some way to explaining the decline in the manufacturing sector in the developed nations.

2 An MNE can cross-subsidise its operations. Profits from one market can be used to support operations in another one. The **cross-subsidisation** could take the form of price cutting, increasing productive capacity or heavy advertising.

3 The risk involved in production is spread not just over different markets but also over different countries.

4 MNEs can avoid tax by negotiating special tax arrangements in one of their host countries (tax holidays) or through careful use of **transfer pricing**. Transfer prices are the prices at which internal transactions take place. These can be altered so that high profits can be shown in countries where the tax rate is lower. The principle in place is that the transfer price should represent what an 'arm's length' customer would pay or an 'arm's length' supplier would charge. In 2019, Shell India was sold to its parent company for the price of Rs 8,000 crore but the Indian tax department valued the sale as Rs 80,000 crore. The Indian government is trying to tax the difference of Rs 72,000 crore (see mini case study on transfer pricing).

5 MNEs can take advantage of subsidies and tax exemptions offered by governments to encourage start-ups in their country.

The very size of MNEs gives rise to concern as their operations can have a substantial impact upon the economy. For example, the activities of MNEs will affect the labour markets of host countries and the balance of payments. If a subsidiary is started in one country there will be an inflow of capital to that country. Once it is up and running, however, there will be outflows of dividends and profits that will affect the invisible balance. Also, there will be flows of goods within the company, and therefore between countries, in the form of semi-finished goods and raw materials. These movements will affect the exchange rate as well as the balance of payments and it is likely that the effects will be greater for developing countries than for developed countries.

mini case Transfer pricing

Although transfer pricing has always been a feature of the operation of multinationals, it became a huge public issue in 2013 and very unpopular. A survey by the Institute of Business Ethics in the UK found that tax avoidance had replaced remuneration as the issue that most concerned them about corporate behaviour.[3] In times of austerity, cutbacks in government spending and falls in real wages, anything that reduces the tax liability of large companies is seen as bad. There were many reports of the small amount of tax paid by multinationals such as Google, Starbucks and Amazon in countries where they do large amounts of business. In 2011, in the UK Amazon had sales of £3.35 billion but reported a tax expense of £1.8 million, while Google paid the UK government £6 million on a turnover of £395 million. Neither of these is illegal, both companies were operating within the law – it is tax avoidance, not tax evasion (see, for example, Chapter 9). This is an issue that affects all countries, rich and poor alike – according to Christian Aid, poor countries lose an estimated $160 billion per year from tax avoidance by multinational companies.

The problem with multinationals is that they can use tax loopholes such as transfer pricing to pay tax in the country where the tax rate is lower and as tax rates are largely under the control of individual countries, there is little that one country can do alone. There are international controls over transfer pricing which have been in place for some time. The European Commission, for instance, has had a Joint Transfer Pricing Forum since 2002, and the OECD issued guidelines in 1979 which were updated in 2010.[4]

The greater public awareness and the outcry the issue has created has increased the calls for more controls, both nationally and internationally. In 2013 the Global Alliance for Tax Justice was formed, made up of tax campaigners from many different countries, with the aim of increasing the pressure on international organisations. There is agreement in the OECD and the EU that multinational companies must reveal more information about their activities on a country-by-country basis, which would make action possible. Also, there are moves towards greater transparency; some tax havens (countries where tax rates are low) have agreed to start sharing information about bank accounts.

As well as government action on tax laws and increased transparency at national and international levels, there has been the 'naming and shaming' of the companies avoiding tax. This may have several effects on a company. First, the information could encourage customers to boycott the company – there have been such campaigns against Amazon and Google. Second, there will be reputational effects on the companies involved, and this could damage their claims to act with corporate responsibility. Third, as in the case of Starbucks in the UK, it could result in the payment of tax to the government. There has been direct action against these companies around the world, including sit-down protests and occupations which have sometimes caused stores to close. Social media has increased the velocity of these protests. It is difficult to assess the impact of naming and shaming – information on the extent of any boycott or its financial impact is impossible to come by. What is true is that with continued austerity there will be continued public pressure on governments and international organisations and that the campaign will continue.

There is also the possibility of exploitation of less developed countries, and it is debatable whether such footloose industries form a viable basis for economic development. Added to this, MNEs take their decisions in terms of their overall operations rather than with any consideration of their effects on the host economy. There is therefore a loss of economic sovereignty for national governments.

The main problem with multinationals is the lack of control that can be exerted by national governments. As the mini case study shows, there are increased calls from around the world for more transparency, monitoring and control of their activities. In 2011 the OECD updated its *Guidelines for Multinational Enterprises,* which are not legally binding but are promoted by OECD member governments. These seek to provide a balanced framework for international investment that clarifies both the rights and responsibilities of the business community. The publication contains guidelines on business ethics, employment relations, information disclosure and taxation, among other things. Against all this is the fact that without the presence of MNEs, output in host countries would be lower, and there is evidence that on labour market issues the multinationals do not perform badly.

Transnationality

The transnationality index gives a measure of an MNE's involvement abroad by looking at three ratios – foreign assets/total assets, foreign sales/total sales and foreign employment/total employment. As such it captures the importance of foreign activities in its overall activities. In Table 3.2 Vodafone Group plc has the highest index – this is because in all three ratios it has a high proportion of foreign involvement. Since 1990 the average index of transnationality for the top 100 MNEs has increased from 51 per cent to 54.4 per cent.

These multinationals are huge organisations and their market values often exceed the gross national product (GNP) of many of the countries in which they operate. There are more than 60,000 MNEs around the world and they are estimated to account for a quarter of the world's output. The growth in MNEs is due to relaxation of exchange controls, making it easier to move money between countries, and the improvements in communication, which make it possible to run a worldwide business from one country. The importance of multinationals varies from country to country, as Table 3.3 shows.

Table 3.3 Share of foreign affiliates in manufacturing production and employment, 2010

Country	% share of foreign affiliates in manufacturing production	% share of foreign affiliates in manufacturing employment
Ireland	83	48
Hungary	63	46
Czech Republic	59	41
Great Britain	40	31
Netherlands	41	30
Luxembourg	34	25
Germany	27	16
Finland	24	19
Italy	18	11

Source: Adapted from OECD (2013), Foreign affiliates, in OECD Science, Technology and Industry Scoreboard 2013: Innovation for Growth, OECD Publishing. http://dx.doi.org/10.1787/sti_scoreboard-2013-64-en.

As we can see, foreign affiliates are very important for some countries and not so important for others; in the case of Italy the level of foreign presence is low. For all of the countries, foreign affiliates have a bigger impact on production than employment.

Globalisation and business

Businesses of all sizes need to have an awareness of their international context. As noted above, even if they are not directly involved in international trade, firms will be affected by international forces that lie largely outside their control. Globalisation has meant that the financial crisis of 2008, for instance, affected virtually the whole world. Some of the issues facing businesses are discussed below in brief; many of them are discussed later in the book in more detail.

Markets

Globalisation means that firms are faced with bigger markets for their products. Many of these markets are covered by **regional trade agreements (RTAs)**, which are groupings of countries set up to facilitate world trade. All such agreements have to be notified to the World Trade Organisation and they can take a variety of forms. The most basic relationship and the most common is a **free trade area**, where trade barriers between members are abolished but where each member maintains its own national barriers with non-members. An example of this is the North American Free Trade Agreement

(NAFTA). Agreements can also take the form of a **customs union** or common market, where members abolish trade barriers among themselves and adopt a common external tariff which is applied to non-members, as in the EU. All of these agreements increase the size of the marketplace for producers in the member countries and the enlargement of these agreements (the EU, for example) means that markets are increasing all the time.

In addition to these trade agreements, the opening up of the emerging economies (e.g. China and India) to international trade, their high growth rates and the corresponding increase in per capita income mean that there has been a huge increase in the demand for goods and services. The population in India is 1237 million, income per head has doubled since 2000 and GDP growth rate was 9.3 per cent between 2010 and 2011. The Chinese population stood at 1351 million in 2012, income per head has doubled since 2000 and the growth rate in 2012 was 7.8 per cent. Many believe that China's high growth rate has been fuelled by exports, but recent research shows that demand is more consumption driven than previously thought. It also shows that consumer demand has changed in favour of products that have a higher imported content. This is good news for the rest of the world.

Labour markets

It has been estimated that the global integration of emerging markets has doubled the supply of labour for the global production of goods. The OECD estimates that the percentage of the world population living outside their country of birth doubled between 1985 and 2010. About half of this is between the developed countries, the other half from developing to developed countries. The impact of migration is considered in more detail in the international case study at the end of Part Two ('Contexts').

International labour mobility can be used by businesses for hard-to-fill vacancies. Typically these are at the low-skill, high-risk and low-paid end of the spectrum and at the high-skill, high-paid end. Legal labour migration can be permanent (where migrants settle permanently) or temporary (where migrants eventually return home). The regulations pertaining to these will differ. In addition to international labour migration there are three other alternatives: outsourcing (for example, the location of US call centres in India involves the movement of jobs rather than people); cross-border commuting (for example, the commuting of Poles into western Europe); or the use of internet trade (where the work could take place anywhere).

For businesses wishing to recruit internationally, there are practical problems including locating the necessary people and dealing with the rules and regulations involved in employing migrants, such as work permits and visas. These requirements will vary from one country to another.

Other resources

As well as labour, businesses have to source and purchase other resources such as raw materials and energy. Natural resources are differentially distributed around the world and therefore they require international trade to take place if firms are to acquire these inputs. The market for energy, for example, is a global market, with attendant concerns about the environmental impact of the methods used for its generation. The issue of resources is further discussed in Chapter 7.

mini case   Currency crisis in emerging markets

Since the start of the global financial crisis in 2008, the emerging economies have done well out of international capital flows. Low interest rates in the developed nations (designed to stimulate the economies) made international capital look for higher rates of return and the emerging economies with their high growth rates were the recipients. It is estimated that $4 trillion has flowed into the emerging economies since 2008. This is speculative money looking for high rates of return. The tapering of quantitative easing (QE) in the USA in 2014 has made it a more attractive place to invest and there are worries that the emerging economies may face a sudden stop to these capital flows (see the case study on QE at the end of Chapter 5).

How did this happen? Since 2008 there have been four rounds of quantitative easing in the USA where the Federal Reserve Bank pledged to buy up bank debt, Treasury bonds and longer-term bonds. This has the effect of increasing liquidity in the economy – like 'printing money' – in the hope that this will stimulate economic growth. It also has the effect of reducing the rate of interest, which is good for borrowers and business but bad for savers and investors. Speculators want to maximise their rate of return and if the rate of interest in the USA (and other developed nations) is too low, they look to other places to put their money. The emerging nations, including India, Turkey and South Africa, had high growth rates and were the recipients of these speculative flows.

With improvements in the state of the US economy, a tapering of QE was signalled by the Federal Reserve Bank in May 2013 and announced formally in December. The tapering off of the purchase of bonds will continue at a measured rate until the end of 2014 and the expectation is that it will have finished by spring 2015. This announcement had a significant effect on the emerging countries – there were dramatic falls in their exchange rates (the Turkish lira lost 10 per

cent of its value between December 2013 and January 2014 and smaller falls have occurred in South Africa, Argentina, Brazil, India and Chile). Five countries have been identified as 'fragile' as they have large balance-of-payments deficits that need financing – these are Turkey, India, South Africa, Brazil and Indonesia. Hours before the December announcement, the Turkish central bank increased the benchmark interest rate from 4.5 per cent to 10 per cent. In South Africa the rate of interest went up to 5.5 per cent and in India it was 8 per cent. These interest rate rises attempt to stop the flow of international capital away from the country and to prop up their currencies, but of course have undesirable effects on other economic variables. It reduces the level of demand in the economy; it causes inflation through the higher price of imports; it means that the countries cannot service their external debts so there may be political repercussions; it affects their ability to finance their large balance-of-payments deficits. In 2001, in similar circumstances, Argentina defaulted on its external debts and the repercussions of that are still being felt.

It is not clear where this will end; the measures introduced in Turkey to support its currency have not worked and the pressure is still on all of these countries. Of course, this crisis is not only about US monetary policy, there are factors specific to each country, such as a major corruption scandal in Turkey and political unrest in the Ukraine. But many argue that the Federal Reserve is, in effect, the banker to the whole world and should consider other economies and not just the American one when deciding on policy.

This mini case shows how interrelated global markets are and how quickly measures announced in one part of the world can affect others. By the same argument, the repercussions of tapering of QE in the USA will find its way back to the USA. Globalisation is contagious.

Financial markets

Businesses need to raise capital to be able to produce, trade and invest. Although much of this takes place domestically, banks operate internationally and so businesses are exposed to global forces. Never has this been seen more vividly than in the events of recent years.

Globalisation and the small and medium-sized firm

There are problems for small and medium-sized enterprises (SMEs) wishing to trade internationally. They will not have the same access to resources, finance or markets as the large multinationals or even the large national companies which could either trade directly or expand internationally through mergers and takeovers. SMEs, however, have a number of options, which are outlined briefly below as they are discussed more fully in later chapters of the book.

- A **strategic alliance** is a collaborative agreement between firms to achieve a common aim, in this context a presence in other markets. These agreements can take many forms.
- **Franchising** is an arrangement where one party (the franchiser) sells the rights to another party (the franchisee) to market its product or service. There are different types of franchise relationship (see Chapter 10) and this is a possibility for international expansion. It is an attractive option for companies seeking international expansion without having to undertake substantial direct investments.
- **Licensing** is where a company (the licensor) authorises a company in another country (the licensee) to use its intellectual property in return for certain considerations, usually royalties. Licensors are usually multinationals located in developed countries (see Chapter 10).
- A **joint venture** is usually a jointly owned and independently incorporated business venture involving two or more organisations. This is a popular method of expanding abroad as each party can diversify, with the benefit of the experience of the others involved in the venture and a reduction in the level of risk. Where a large number of members are involved in such an arrangement, this is called a **consortium**.

Synopsis

This chapter has looked at the global context of business. No business is immune from international forces, no matter what it is producing or how small its markets are. The whole concept of globalisation has been discussed, along with the claimed costs and benefits. The elements of globalisation have been outlined together with the impact of globalisation on businesses.

Summary of key points

- There is a difference between globalisation and internationalisation that centres on the role of national boundaries.

- There are costs and benefits associated with the process of globalisation.

- There are three main elements of globalisation – international trade, capital market flows and foreign direct investment.

- Multinational enterprises are very important in the process of globalisation.

- With the arrival of the emerging economies in the global marketplace, some changes in the nature and the process of globalisation are evident.

- Globalisation affects all firms in one way or another – either through markets, access to resources or finance.

- There are several different possibilities for small and medium-sized businesses wishing to expand internationally.

case study   FDI flows

Foreign direct investment is an important element in the process of globalisation and economic integration as it creates long-term links between economies. Unlike capital market flows, it carries a long-term interest in an economy and it is a source of investment funds, it promotes sharing of ideas between countries and can be an important tool in development. Inward flows are all direct investment in a country by non-residents; outflows represent direct investment by residents in other countries. FDI can take the form of the opening of new factories or subsidiaries, or mergers and acquisitions, and as would be expected multinational enterprises are very active in the process. FDI flows since 2000 have been mixed and volatile. There have been record flows of FDI and great variability in the performance of countries and groupings of countries. Tables 3.4 and 3.5 show changes in inflows and outflows between 2001 and 2012 for selected groupings of countries.

Most of the groupings are well known but the one that might be less so is the 'Next 11' or N11.[5] This term was coined by Jim O'Neill of Goldman Sachs

Table 3.4 Change in FDI inflows for selected groupings of countries 2001–12 (%)

	2001–2	2003–4	2005–7	2008–12
G8	−26	+31	+73	−40
EU27	−18	−30	+71	−53
Developed	−26	+9	+112	−45
Developing	−25	+44	+76	+5
Emerging	−30	+57	+88	+48
N11				−25

Source: adapted from *unctadstat.unctad.org*

Table 3.5 Change in FDI outflows for selected groupings of countries 2001–12 (%)

	2001–2	2003–4	2005–7	2008–12
G8	−18	+79	+220	−27
EU27	−39	+27	+108	−66
Developed	−28	+53	+154	−43
Developing	−49	+110	+136	+24
Emerging	−60	+127	+164	+60
N11				+110

Source: adapted from *unctadstat.unctad.org*

International Bank and it includes 11 countries that have good prospects for growth and openness to trade. Many commentators argue that the N11, along with the BRIC countries, are the ones that will push forward the global engine of growth. In 2012 it was forecast that the BRIC economies would be larger than the USA by 2015 and the G7 by 2032 and the N11 would be larger than the USA and twice the size of the EU by 2050.

These tables show great variability between the groupings and within each grouping there is even greater variability. The reasons put forward for the dramatic decline in total FDI flows in the early 2000s were the sluggishness of the global economy, some uncertainty over monetary policy in some countries and, most significantly, increasing international political instability and insecurity. The reasons put forward for the recovery in FDI flows between 2003 and 2008 were the relative decline in the value of the US dollar and large-value mergers and acquisitions during the period. The fall in flows from 2008 onwards was due to the global financial crisis, which has been well documented elsewhere in this book.

What is most interesting about Table 3.4 is the differences in performance between the groupings. In the period 2003–4, FDI inflows fell for the EU while there was growth for all other groupings. The main reasons for this were the continuing effects of the recession and the expansion of the EU that occurred in 2004. The rapid growth in the 2005–7 period was universal, even if the growth was variable. In the last time period, 2008–12, the only groupings where flows increased were for the developing and emerging countries. The fall in inflows for the N11 countries was mainly due to political factors in individual countries – Egypt experienced a big reduction due to the repercussions of the 'Arab Spring', Turkey experienced a fall mainly due to corruption allegations against the government. By 2012 both FDI inflows and outflows for many countries and groupings had started to recover. The OECD compiles the FDI Regulatory Restrictiveness Index each year, which measures the restrictions to FDI according to four factors: limitations on foreign equity, screening mechanisms, restrictions of foreign employment and operational restrictions. The index can take any value between 0 – completely open – and 1 – completely closed. There does not seem to be very much correlation between the level of FDI flows and the FDI index. The three biggest recipients of FDI inflows in 2012 were (FDI index shown in brackets) USA (0.09), China (0.4) and Belgium (0.04). The biggest source of FDI outflows were USA, Japan (0.3) and the UK (0.06). The OECD calculates that the FDI index is higher in the service sector and that manufacturing is the most open sector for FDI.

As a growing number of countries have emerged from the financial crisis, the global landscape is changing. After 2008, the highly indebted developed nations were in trouble and the emerging economies showed the most resilience and growth potential. But this was before the currency crisis of 2013–14 (see mini case study). At the time of writing it is unclear how this will end, but it does seem that the well-known developed economies may be resuming their position in the global economy. The USA, Canada and Japan are returning to slow growth, while in the EU the position is mixed and still uncertain. But the USA did not fall off a 'fiscal cliff',[6] the Japanese tsunami did not return Japan to low growth, and the EU did not break up, even though there are still problems in these countries. As the case study shows, things change very quickly in such an interrelated world.

Case study questions

1 Why are FDI flows cyclical in nature?

2 How might a country make itself more attractive to inward FDI?

Review and discussion questions

1 What role does the advancement of ICT have in the process of globalisation?

2 What are the arguments for and against foreign ownership of strategic industries such as energy?

3 How are multinationals changing?

4 For a business considering expansion into another country, what methods of expansion are available? What are the advantages and disadvantages of each?

5 What has been the impact of the financial crisis in 2008 on the process of globalisation?

Assignments

1 You work in a local office of a multinational enterprise and your line manager has been invited to take part in a discussion arranged by the local newspaper on the pros and cons of globalisation. You have been asked to provide a briefing paper outlining the arguments for your line manager.

2 You have been asked to give a presentation on regional trade agreements to students of business at a local college. Research which regional trade agreements your country is a member of and what effects membership has on labour mobility. Prepare PowerPoint slides together with notes to accompany each slide.

Notes and references

1 See Gray, J., *False Dawn: The Delusions of Global Capitalism,* Granta Books, 1998.

2 See Held, D., McGrew, A., Goldblatt, D. and Perraton, J., *Global Transformations: Politics, Economics and Culture,* Polity Press, 1999.

3 http://www.ibe.org.uk/userfiles/pressreleases/attitudes2013.pdf

4 Transfer Pricing Guidelines for MNE and Tax Administrations, OECD, 2010.

5 N11: Bangladesh, Egypt, Indonesia, Iran, South Korea, Mexico, Nigeria, Pakistan, the Philippines, Turkey and Vietnam.

Emerging economies: (UNCTAD) Argentina, Brazil, Chile, Mexico, Peru, China, South Korea, Malaysia, Singapore and Thailand.

There is some overlap between these two groupings.

6 In 2013 the USA faced a 'fiscal cliff' where attempts by President Obama to increase the debt ceiling to deal with the huge public sector budget deficit were rejected by the Republican House of Representatives. A stalemate ensued and public buildings were closed and public employees sent home. Eventually the crisis was averted when the House of Representatives agreed a compromise. The roots of the fiscal cliff go right back to 2001. For a further discussion see the mini case in Chapter 4, 'The power of the purse'.

Further reading

Daniels, J. D., Radebaugh, L. and Sullivan, D., *International Business: Environments and Operations,* 13th edition, Prentice Hall, 2010.

Griffiths, A. and Wall, S., *Applied Economics,* 12th edition, Financial Times/Prentice Hall, 2011.

Worthington, I., Britton, C. and Rees, A., *Business Economics: Blending Theory and Practice,* 2nd edition, Financial Times/Prentice Hall, 2005.

Web links and further questions are available on the website at:
www.pearsoned.co.uk/worthington

Chapter 12
Leadership and Strategy

Foundations of Decision Making

4

A good decision should be defined by its outcome.

lenetstan/Shutterstock

465

A good decision should be judged by the process used, not the results achieved. In some cases, a good decision results in an undesirable outcome. As a decision maker, you can control the process. But in the real world, factors outside your control can adversely affect the outcome. Using the right process may not always result in a desirable outcome, but it increases the probability!

MANAGERS

at all organizational levels and in all areas make a lot of decisions—routine and non-routine; minor and major. The overall quality of those decisions goes a long way in determining an organization's success or failure. To be a successful manager—and to be a valued employee—you need to know about decision making. In this chapter, we'll look at types of decisions and how decisions should be made. But we'll also consider some common biases and errors that can undermine the quality of decisions and discuss contemporary issues facing managerial decision makers. ●

Learning Outcomes

How Do Managers Make Decisions?

4-1 Describe the decision-making process.

How do businesses put new ideas into action? Through lots of decisions, that's how. When Bertucci's, a shopping-mall restaurant chain in New England and the mid-Atlantic region, wanted to create a spin-off chain with a more contemporary, "hipper" appeal, managers had lots of decisions to make over a nine-month period from concept to opening. Managers hope, of course, that those decisions prove to be good ones.[1]

decision-making process
A set of eight steps that includes identifying a problem, selecting a solution, and evaluating the effectiveness of the solution

problem
A discrepancy between an existing and a desired state of affairs

---

Forty hours a week: how often companies expect people to be strong decision makers.[2]

Decision making is typically described as choosing among alternatives, but this view is overly simplistic. Why? Because decision making is a process, not a simple act of choosing among alternatives. Exhibit 4–1 illustrates the **decision-making process** as a set of eight steps that begins with identifying a problem; it moves through selecting an alternative that can alleviate the problem and concludes with evaluating the decision's effectiveness. This process is as applicable to your decision about what you're going to do on spring break as it is to the decisions UPS executives are making as they deal with issues that could affect the organization's future profitability (see Case Application #1 on p. 136). The process can also be used to describe both individual and group decisions. Let's take a closer look at the process in order to understand what each step entails by using a simple example most of us can relate to—the decision to buy a car.

What Defines a Decision Problem?

Step 1. The decision-making process begins with the identification of a **problem** or, more specifically, a discrepancy between an existing and a desired state of affairs.[3] Take the case of a sales manager for Pfizer. The manager is on the road a lot and spent nearly $6,000 on auto repairs over the past few years. Now her car has a blown engine and cost estimates indicate it's not economical to repair. Furthermore, convenient public transportation is unavailable. So, we have a problem—a discrepancy between the manager's need to have a car that works and the fact that her current one doesn't.

Identifying problems is **IMPORTANT . . . and CHALLENGING!**[4]

In our example, a blown engine is a clear signal to the manager that she needs a new car, but few problems are that obvious. In the real world, most problems don't come with neon signs identifying them as such. And problem identification is subjective. A manager who mistakenly solves the wrong problem perfectly is just as likely to perform poorly as the manager

Exhibit 4–1 The Decision-Making Process

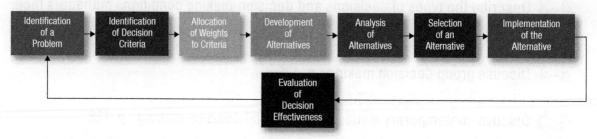

The steps involved in buying a vehicle provide a good example of the decision-making process. For this young woman, the process starts with the first step of identifying the problem of needing a car so she can drive to her new job and ends with the last step in the process of evaluating the results of her decision.

who fails to identify the right problem and does nothing. So, how do managers become aware they have a problem? They have to make a comparison between current reality and some standard, which can be (1) past performance, (2) previously set goals, or (3) the performance of some other unit within the organization or in other organizations. In our car-buying example, the standard is past performance—a car that runs.

What Is Relevant in the Decision-Making Process?

Step 2. Once a manager has identified a problem that needs attention, the **decision criteria** that will be important in solving the problem must be identified. In our vehicle-buying example, the sales manager assesses the factors that are relevant in her decision, which might include criteria such as price, model (two-door or four-door), size (compact or intermediate), manufacturer (French, Japanese, South Korean, German, American), optional equipment (navigation system, side-impact protection, leather interior), and repair records. These criteria reflect what she thinks is relevant in her decision. Every decision maker has criteria—whether explicitly stated or not—that guide his or her decision making. Note that in this step in the decision-making process, what's not identified can be as important as what is because it's still guiding the decision. For instance, although the sales manager didn't consider fuel economy to be a criterion and won't use it to influence her choice of car, she had to assess that criteria before choosing to include or not include it in her relevant criteria.

How Does the Decision Maker Weight the Criteria and Analyze Alternatives?

Steps 3, 4, and 5. In many decision-making situations, the criteria are not all equally important.[5] So, the decision maker has to allocate weights to the items listed in step 2 in order to give them their relative priority in the decision (step 3). A simple approach is to give the most important criterion a weight of 10 and then assign weights to the rest against that standard. Thus, in contrast to a criterion that you gave a 5, the highest-rated factor is twice as important. The idea is to use your personal preferences to assign priorities to the relevant criteria in your decision and indicate their degree of importance by assigning a weight to each. Exhibit 4–2 lists the criteria and weights that our manager developed for her vehicle replacement decision. What is the most important criterion in her decision? Price. What has low importance? Performance and handling.

decision criteria
Factors that are relevant in a decision

Exhibit 4–2 Important Criteria and Weights in a Car-Buying Decision

CRITERION	WEIGHT
Price	10
Interior comfort	8
Durability	5
Repair record	5
Performance	3
Handling	1

Exhibit 4–3 Assessment of Possible Car Alternatives

ALTERNATIVES	INITIAL PRICE	INTERIOR COMFORT	DURABILITY	REPAIR RECORD	PERFORMANCE	HANDLING	TOTAL
Jeep Compass	2	10	8	7	5	5	37
Ford Focus	9	6	5	6	8	6	40
Hyundai Elantra	8	5	6	6	4	6	35
Ford Fiesta SES	9	5	6	7	6	5	38
Volkswagen Golf	5	6	9	10	7	7	44
Toyota Prius	10	5	6	4	3	3	31
Mazda 3 MT	4	8	7	6	8	9	42
Kia Soul	7	6	8	6	5	6	38
BMW i3	9	7	6	4	4	7	37
Nissan Cube	5	8	5	4	10	10	42
Toyota Camry	6	5	10	10	6	6	43
Honda Fit Sport MT	8	6	6	5	7	8	40

Then the decision maker lists the alternatives that could successfully resolve the problem (step 4). No attempt is made in this step to evaluate these alternatives, only to list them.[6] Let's assume that our manager identifies 12 cars as viable choices: Jeep Compass, Ford Focus, Hyundai Elantra, Ford Fiesta SES, Volkswagen Golf, Toyota Prius, Mazda 3 MT, Kia Soul, BMW i3, Nissan Cube, Toyota Camry, and Honda Fit Sport MT.

Once the alternatives have been identified, the decision maker critically analyzes each one (step 5). How? By evaluating it against the criteria. The strengths and weaknesses of each alternative become evident as they're compared with the criteria and weights established in steps 2 and 3. Exhibit 4–3 shows the assessed values that the manager assigned each of her 12 alternatives after she had test-driven each car. Keep in mind that the ratings shown in Exhibit 4–3 are based on the assessment made by the sales manager. Again, we're using a scale of 1 to 10. Some assessments can be achieved in a relatively objective fashion. For instance, the purchase price represents the best price the manager can get online or from local dealers, and consumer magazines report data from owners on frequency of repairs. Others, like how well the car handles, are clearly personal judgments.

Most decisions involve **judgments**.

Personal judgments by a decision maker are reflected in (1) the criteria chosen in step 2, (2) the weights given to the criteria, and (3) the evaluation of alternatives. The influence of personal judgment explains why two car buyers with the same amount of money may look at two totally distinct sets of alternatives or even look at the same alternatives and rate them differently.

Exhibit 4–3 shows only an assessment of the 12 alternatives against the decision criteria; it does not reflect the weighting done in step 3. If one choice had scored 10 on every criterion, obviously you wouldn't need to consider the weights. Similarly, if all the weights were equal—that is, all the criteria were equally important to you—each alternative would be evaluated merely by summing up the appropriate lines in Exhibit 4–3. For instance, the Ford Fiesta SES would have a score of 38, and the Toyota Camry a score of 43. But if you multiply each alternative assessment against its weight, you get the figures in Exhibit 4–4. For instance, the Kia Soul scored a 40 on durability, which was determined by multiplying the weight given to durability [5] by the manager's appraisal of the car on this criterion [8]. The sum of these scores represents an evaluation of each alternative against the previously established criteria and weights. Notice that the weighting of the criteria has changed the ranking of alternatives in

Exhibit 4–4 Evaluation of Car Alternatives: Assessment Criteria ✕ Criteria Weight

ALTERNATIVES	INITIAL PRICE [10]		INTERIOR COMFORT [8]		DURABILITY [5]		REPAIR RECORD [5]		PERFORMANCE [3]		HANDLING [1]		TOTAL
Jeep Compass	2	20	10	80	8	40	7	35	5	15	5	5	195
Ford Focus	9	90	6	48	5	25	6	30	8	24	6	6	223
Hyundai Elantra	8	80	5	40	6	30	6	30	4	12	6	6	198
Ford Fiesta SES	9	90	5	40	6	30	7	35	6	18	5	5	218
Volkswagen Golf	5	50	6	48	9	45	10	50	7	21	7	7	221
Toyota Prius	10	100	5	40	6	30	4	20	3	9	3	3	202
Mazda 3 MT	4	40	8	64	7	35	6	30	8	24	9	9	202
Kia Soul	7	70	6	48	8	40	6	30	5	15	6	6	209
BMW i3	9	90	7	56	6	30	4	20	4	12	7	7	215
Nissan Cube	5	50	8	64	5	25	4	20	10	30	10	10	199
Toyota Camry	6	60	5	40	10	50	10	50	6	18	6	6	224
Honda Fit Sport MT	8	80	6	48	6	30	5	25	7	21	8	8	212

our example. The Volkswagen Golf, for example, has gone from first to third. Looking at the analysis, both initial price and interior comfort worked against the Volkswagen.

What Determines the Best Choice?

Step 6. Now it's time to choose the best alternative from among those assessed. Because we determined all the pertinent factors in the decision, weighted them appropriately, and identified and assessed the viable alternatives, this step is fairly simple. We merely choose the alternative that generated the highest score in step 5. In our vehicle example (Exhibit 4–4), the manager would choose the Toyota Camry. On the basis of the criteria identified, the weights given to the criteria, and her assessment of each car on the criteria, the Toyota scored highest [224 points] and, thus, became the best alternative.

What Happens in Decision Implementation?

Step 7. Although the choice process is completed in the previous step, the decision may still fail if it's not implemented properly (step 7). Therefore, this step, **decision implementation**, involves putting the decision into action. If others will be affected by the decision, implementation also includes conveying the decision to those affected and getting their commitment to it.[7] *Want people to be committed to a decision?* Let them participate in the decision-making process. We'll discuss later in the chapter how groups can help a manager do this.

What Is the Last Step in the Decision Process?

Step 8. In the last step in the decision-making process, managers appraise the outcome of the decision to see *whether the problem was resolved*. Did the alternative chosen in step 6 and implemented in step 7 accomplish the desired result? For our sales manager, that means does she have a car that reliably works? Evaluating the results of a decision is part of the managerial control process, which we'll discuss in Chapter 14.

What Common Errors Are Committed in the Decision-Making Process?

decision implementation
Putting a decision into action

heuristics
Judgmental shortcuts or "rules of thumb" used to simplify decision making

When managers make decisions, they use their own particular style, and may use "rules of thumb," or **heuristics**, to simplify their decision making.[8] Rules of thumb can be useful because they help make sense of complex, uncertain, and ambiguous information. However, even though

Exhibit 4–5 Common Decision-Making Errors and Biases

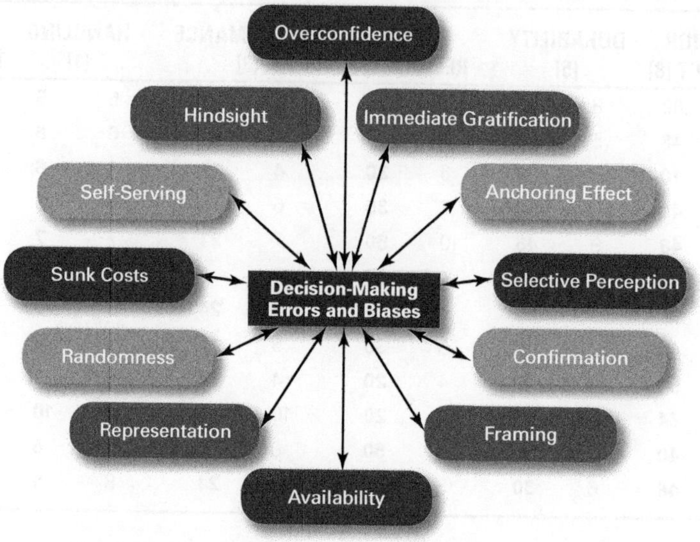

managers may use rules of thumb, that doesn't mean those rules are reliable. Why? Because they may lead to errors and biases in processing and evaluating information. Exhibit 4–5 identifies 12 common decision errors and biases that managers make. Let's look briefly at each.[9]

Which of these **are YOU guilty** of when making decisions?

When decision makers tend to think they know more than they do or hold unrealistically positive views of themselves and their performance, they're exhibiting the *over-confidence bias*. The *immediate gratification bias* describes decision makers who tend to want immediate rewards and to avoid immediate costs. For these individuals, decision choices that provide quick payoffs are more appealing than those in the future. The *anchoring effect* describes when decision makers fixate on initial information as a starting point and then, once set, fail to adequately adjust for subsequent information. First impressions, ideas, prices, and estimates carry unwarranted weight relative to information received later. When decision makers selectively organize and interpret events based on their biased perceptions, they're using the *selective perception bias*. This influences the information they pay attention to, the problems they identify, and the alternatives they develop. Decision makers who seek out information that reaffirms their past choices and discount information that contradicts past judgments exhibit the *confirmation bias*. These people tend to accept at face value information that confirms their preconceived views and are critical and skeptical of information that challenges these views. The *framing bias* happens when decision makers select and highlight certain aspects of a situation while excluding others. By drawing attention to specific aspects of a situation and highlighting them, while at the same time downplaying or omitting other aspects, they distort what they see and create incorrect reference points. The *availability bias* occurs when decision makers tend to remember events that are the most recent and vivid in their memory. The result? It distorts their ability to recall events in an objective manner and results in

(*continues on p. 122*)

✪ Watch It 1!

If your professor has assigned this, go to the Assignments section of **mymanagementlab.com** to complete the video exercise titled *Rudi's Bakery: Decision Making*.

What Are the **3** Approaches Managers Can Use to Make Decisions?

4-2 Explain the three approaches managers can use to make decisions.

Decision making is the essence of management.[10]

- Everyone in an organization makes decisions, *but* it's particularly important to managers.
- Managers *make decisions*—mostly routine ones like which employee will work what shift, what information to include in a report, how to resolve a customer's complaint, etc.—as they **plan, organize, lead**, and **control**. See Exhibit 4–6.

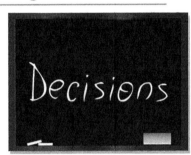
© mihaela1975/0405/Fotolia

Exhibit 4–6 Decisions Managers May Make

Planning	Leading
What are the organization's long-term objectives?	How do I handle unmotivated employees?
What strategies will best achieve those objectives?	What is the most effective leadership style in a given situation?
What should the organization's short-term objectives be?	How will a specific change affect worker productivity?
How difficult should individual goals be?	When is the right time to stimulate conflict?

Organizing	Controlling
How many employees should I have report directly to me?	What activities in the organization need to be controlled?
How much centralization should there be in an organization?	How should those activities be controlled?
How should jobs be designed?	When is a performance deviation significant?
When should the organization implement a different structure?	What type of management information system should the organization have?

Source: Robbins, Stephen P., Coulter, Mary, *Management*, 13th Ed., © 2016, p. 45. Reprinted and electronically reproduced by permission of Pearson Education, Inc., New York, NY.

McCarony/Fotolia

- Managers *want to be good decision makers* and *exhibit good decision-making behaviors* so they appear **competent** and **intelligent** to their boss, employees, and coworkers.

1 Rational Model

- This approach assumes: Decision makers MUST ACT RATIONALLY.[11]
  How? Use **rational decision making**; that is, make logical and consistent choices to maximize value.[12]

> **rational decision making**
> Describes choices that are consistent and value-maximizing within specified constraints

(Check out the two decision-making tools described in the Technology and the Manager's Job box on p. 121.)

- A "rational" decision maker...

Should Be:	Can Ever Be?
Fully objective and logical ┈┈┈┈▸	Can we ever be fully objective and logical?
Problem is clear and ┈┈┈┈┈▸ unambiguous	Can problems ever be totally clear and unambiguous?
Clear and specific goal ┈┈┈┈▸ regarding decision	Can a goal ever be made that clear and specific?
All possible alternatives ┈┈┈┈▸ and consequences known	Can all possible alternatives and consequences ever be known?
Alternative selected maximizes ┈┈┈▸ likelihood of achieving goal	Can any alternative ever really do that?
Organization's best interests ┈┈┈▸ are considered	Managers should do this but may face factors beyond their control.

Rationality is not a very realistic approach.

2 Bounded Rationality
"A. More. Realistic. Approach."

- **Bounded rationality:** Managers make rational decisions, but are limited (bounded) by their ability to process information.[13]
- Most decisions managers make don't fit the assumption of perfect rationality.
- No one can possibly analyze _all_ information on _all_ alternatives so they...
- **satisfice**—that is, accept solutions that are "good enough," rather than spend time and other resources trying to maximize. *(See From Past to Present box on p. 120.)*

(See From Past to Present box on p. 120.)

Example: As a newly graduated finance major, you look for a job as a financial planner—minimum salary of $55k, and within 100 miles of your hometown. After searching several different options, you accept a job as a business credit analyst at a bank 50 miles away at a starting salary of $52k. HOORAY! If, however, you'd *maximized*—that is, continued to search all possible alternatives—you'd have eventually found this financial planning job at a trust company 25 miles away with a starting salary of $57k. However, the first job offer was *satisfactory*—"good enough"—and you took it! Your decision making was still rational...but within the bounds of your abilities to process information!

iConcept/Fotolia

bounded rationality
Making decisions that are rational within the limits of a manager's ability to process information

satisfice
Accepting solutions that are "good enough"

◀◀◀ From the Past to the Present ▶▶▶

Who: Bounded rationality and satisficing are the work of Herbert A. Simon, who won a Nobel Prize in economics for his work on decision making.

What: His primary concern was how people use logic and psychology to make choices and proposed that individuals were limited in their ability to "grasp the present and anticipate the future." This bounded rationality made it difficult for them to "achieve the best possible decisions," but they made "good enough" or "satisficing" choices.[14]

How: Simon's important contributions to management thinking stemmed from his belief that understanding organizations meant studying the complex network of decisional processes that were inherent.

> When faced with too many choices, we **SATISFICE**!

Why: His work in bounded rationality helps us make sense of how managers can behave rationally and still make satisfactory decisions, even given the limits of their capacity to process information.

If your professor has assigned this, go to the Assignments section of **mymanagementlab.com** *to complete these discussion questions.*

✪ **Talk About It 1:** Is satisficing settling for second best? Discuss.

✪ **Talk About It 2:** How does knowing about bounded rationality help managers be better decision makers?

- Most managerial decisions don't fit the assumptions of perfect rationality, but can still be influenced by (1) the organization's culture, (2) internal politics, (3) power considerations, and (4) a phenomenon called:

escalation of commitment An increased commitment to a previous decision despite evidence that it may have been wrong.[15]

- *Why* would anyone—especially managers—escalate commitment to a bad decision?
  - Hate to admit that initial decision may have been flawed.
  - Don't want to search for new alternatives.

---

3 Intuition and Managerial Decision Making

When deciding yay or nay on new shoe styles, Diego Della Valle, chairman of Tod's luxury shoe empire, doesn't use common decision-making tools like focus groups or poll testing. Nope...he wears the shoes for a few days. If they're not to his liking, his verdict: No! **His intuitive decision approach has helped make Tod's a successful multinational company.**[16]

Smalik/Fotolia

- **Intuitive decision making**—making decisions on the basis of experience, feelings, and accumulated judgment
  - Described as "unconscious reasoning."[17]
  - Five different aspects of intuition: *See Exhibit 4–7.*[18]

Almost **half of managers rely on intuition** more often than formal analysis **to make decisions** about their companies.[19]

Exhibit 4–7 What Is Intuition?

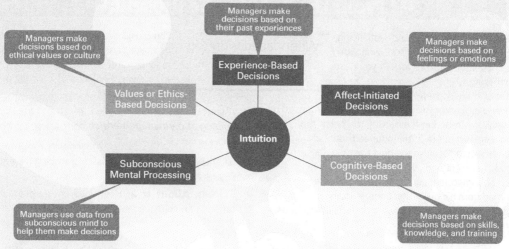

Sources: Based on J. Evans, "Intuition and Reasoning: A Dual-Process Perspective," *Psychological Inquiry,* October–December 2010, pp. 313–326; T. Betsch and A. Blockner, "Intuition in Judgment and Decision Making: Extensive Thinking Without Effort," *Psychological Inquiry,* October–December 2010, pp. 279–294; R. Lange and J. Houran, "A Transliminal View of Intuitions in the Workplace," *North American Journal of Psychology,* 12, no. 3 (2010), pp. 501–516; E. Dane and M. G. Pratt, "Exploring Intuition and Its Role in Managerial Decision Making," *Academy of Management Review,* January 2007, pp. 33–54; M. H. Bazerman and D. Chugh, "Decisions Without Blinders," *Harvard Business Review,* January 2006, pp. 88–97; C. C. Miller and R. D. Ireland, "Intuition in Strategic Decision Making: Friend or Foe in the Fast-Paced 21st Century," *Academy of Management Executive,* February 2005, pp. 19–30; E. Sadler-Smith and E. Shefy, "The Intuitive Executive: Understanding and Applying 'Gut Feel' in Decision-Making," *Academy of Management Executive,* November 2004, pp. 76–91; and L. A. Burke and M. K. Miller, "Taking the Mystery Out of Intuitive Decision Making," *Academy of Management Executive,* October 1999, pp. 91–99.

- Suggestions for using intuitive decision making:
  - Use it to complement, not replace, other decision-making approaches.[20]
  - Look to act quickly with limited information because of past experience with a similar problem.
  - Pay attention to the intense feelings and emotions experienced when making decisions.

    The payoff? Better decisions![21]

::::: Technology and the Manager's Job :::::
MAKING BETTER DECISIONS WITH TECHNOLOGY

Information technology is providing managers with a wealth of decision-making support.[22] Two decision-making tools include: *Expert systems* and *Neural networks.*

EXPERT SYSTEMS:

- Encode relevant expert experience using software programs.
- Act as that expert in analyzing and solving unstructured problems.
- Guide users through problems by asking sequential questions about the situation and drawing conclusions based on answers given.
- Make decisions easier for users through programmed rules modeled on actual reasoning processes of experts.
- Allow employees and lower-level managers to make high-quality decisions normally made only by upper-level managers.

NEURAL NETWORKS:

- Use computer software to imitate the structure of brain cells and connections among them.

- Can distinguish patterns and trends too subtle or complex for human beings.
- Can perceive correlations among hundreds of variables, unlike our limited human brain capacity, which can only easily assimilate no more than two or three variables at once.
- Can perform many operations simultaneously, recognizing patterns, making associations, generalizing about problems not exposed to before, and learning through experience.
- Example: banks using neural network systems to catch fraudulent credit card activities in a matter of hours, not days.

If your professor has assigned this, go to the Assignments section of **mymanagementlab.com** *to complete these discussion questions.*

☼ TALK ABOUT IT 3: Can a manager ever have too much data when making decisions? Explain.

☼ TALK ABOUT IT 4: How can technology help managers make better decisions?

escalation of commitment
An increased commitment to a previous decision despite evidence that it may have been a poor decision

intuitive decision making
Making decisions on the basis of experience, feelings, and accumulated judgment

distorted judgments and probability estimates. When decision makers assess the likelihood of an event based on how closely it resembles other events or sets of events, that's the *representation bias*. Managers exhibiting this bias draw analogies and see identical situations where they don't exist. The *randomness bias* describes when decision makers try to create meaning out of random events. They do this because most decision makers have difficulty dealing with chance even though random events happen to everyone and there's nothing that can be done to predict them. The *sunk costs error* takes place when decision makers forget that current choices can't correct the past. They incorrectly fixate on past expenditures of time, money, or effort in assessing choices rather than on future consequences. Instead of ignoring sunk costs, they can't forget them. Decision makers who are quick to take credit for their successes and to blame failure on outside factors are exhibiting the *self-serving bias*. Finally, the *hindsight bias* is the tendency for decision makers to falsely believe that they would have accurately predicted the outcome of an event once that outcome is actually known.

How can managers avoid the negative effects of these decision errors and biases? ❶ Be aware of them and then don't use them! ❷ Pay attention to "how" decisions are made, try to identify heuristics being used, and critically evaluate how appropriate those are. ❸ Ask colleagues to help identify weaknesses in decision-making style and then work on improving those weaknesses.

✪ Watch It 2!

If your professor has assigned this, go to the Assignments section of **mymanagementlab.com** to complete the video exercise titled *CH2MHill: Decision Making*.

What Types of Decisions and Decision-Making Conditions Do Managers Face?

4-3 Describe the types of decisions and decision-making conditions managers face.

Laura Ipsen is a senior vice president and general manager at Smart Grid, a business unit of Cisco Systems, which is working on helping utility companies find ways to build open, interconnected systems. She describes her job as "like having to put together a 1,000-piece puzzle, but with no box top with the picture of what it looks like and with some pieces missing."[23] Decision making in that type of environment is quite different from decision making done by a manager of a local Gap store.

The types of problems managers face in decision-making situations often determine how it's handled. In this section, we describe a categorization scheme for problems and types of decisions and then show how the type of decision making a manager uses should reflect the characteristics of the problem.

How Do Problems Differ?

Some problems are straightforward. The goal of the decision maker is clear, the problem familiar, and information about the problem easily defined and complete. Examples might include a supplier who is late with an important delivery, a customer who wants to return an Internet purchase, a TV news team that has to respond to an unexpected and fast-breaking event, or a university that must help a student who is applying for financial aid. Such situations are called **structured problems**.

structured problem
A straightforward, familiar, and easily defined problem

unstructured problem
A problem that is new or unusual for which information is ambiguous or incomplete

Many situations faced by managers, however, are **unstructured problems**. They are new or unusual. Information about such problems is ambiguous or incomplete. Examples of unstructured problems include the decision to enter a new market segment, to hire an architect to design a new office park, or to merge two organizations. So, too, is the decision to invest in a new, unproven technology. For instance, when Takeshi Idezawa founded his mobile messaging app LINE, he faced a situation best described as an unstructured problem.[24]

How Does a Manager Make Programmed Decisions?

Decisions are also divided into two categories: programmed and nonprogrammed (described in the next section). **Programmed,** or routine, **decisions** are the most efficient way to handle structured problems.

An auto mechanic damages a customer's rim while changing a tire. What does the shop manager do? Because the company probably has a standardized method for handling this type of problem, it's considered a programmed decision. For example, the manager may replace the rim at the company's expense. *Decisions are programmed* to the extent that (1) they are repetitive and routine and (2) a specific approach has been worked out for handling them. Because the problem is well structured, the manager does not have to go to the trouble and expense of an involved decision process. Programmed decision making is relatively simple and tends to rely heavily on previous solutions. The develop-the-alternatives stage in the decision-making process is either nonexistent or given little attention. Why? Because once the structured problem is defined, its solution is usually self-evident or at least reduced to only a few alternatives that are familiar and that have proved successful in the past. In many cases, programmed decision making becomes decision making by precedent. Managers simply do what they and others have done previously in the same situation. The damaged rim does not require the manager to identify and weight decision criteria or develop a long list of possible solutions.

For structured problems, use: — Procedures
— Rules
— Policies

PROCEDURES. A **procedure** is a series of interrelated sequential steps that a manager can use when responding to a well-structured problem. The only real difficulty is identifying the problem. Once the problem is clear, so is the procedure. For instance, a purchasing manager receives a request from computing services for licensing arrangements to install 250 copies of Norton Antivirus Software. The purchasing manager knows that a definite procedure is in place for handling this decision. Has the requisition been properly filled out and approved? If not, he can send the requisition back with a note explaining what is deficient. If the request is complete, the approximate costs are estimated. If the total exceeds $8,500, three bids must be obtained. If the total is $8,500 or less, only one vendor need be identified and the order placed. The decision-making process is merely executing a simple series of sequential steps.

RULES. A **rule** is an explicit statement that tells a manager what he or she must—or must not—do. Rules are frequently used by managers who confront a structured problem because they're simple to follow and ensure consistency. In the preceding example, the $8,500 cutoff rule simplifies the purchasing manager's decision about when to use multiple bids.

POLICIES. A third guide for making programmed decisions is a **policy**. It provides guidelines to channel a manager's thinking in

Thad ALLTON/AP Images

programmed decision
A repetitive decision that can be handled using a routine approach

procedure
A series of interrelated, sequential steps used to respond to a structured problem

rule
An explicit statement that tells employees what can or cannot be done

policy
A guideline for making decisions

Top managers of Mars Chocolate North America decided to build a new plant for making its M&M brand and other candy in Topeka, Kansas, the first new chocolate facility built by Mars in 35 years. The nonprogrammed decision involved gathering and analyzing demographic and other data for 82 possible locations in 13 states.

a specific direction. The statement that "we promote from within, whenever possible" is an example of a policy. In contrast to a rule, a policy establishes parameters for the decision maker rather than specifically stating what should or should not be done. Policies often leave interpretation up to the decision maker. It's in such instances that ethical standards may come into play.

How Do Nonprogrammed Decisions Differ from Programmed Decisions?

When problems are unstructured, managers must rely on **nonprogrammed decisions** in order to develop unique solutions. Examples of nonprogrammed decisions include deciding whether to acquire another organization, deciding which global markets offer the most potential, or deciding whether to sell off an unprofitable division. Such decisions are unique and nonrecurring. When a manager confronts an unstructured problem, no cut-and-dried solution is available. A custom-made, nonprogrammed response is required.

The creation of a new organizational strategy is a nonprogrammed decision. This decision is different from previous organizational decisions because the issue is new, a different set of environmental factors exists, and other conditions have changed. For example, Amazon's strategy to "get big fast" helped the company grow tremendously. But this strategy came at a cost—perennial financial losses. To turn a profit, CEO Jeff Bezos made decisions regarding how to organize orders, anticipate demand, ship more efficiently, establish foreign partnerships, and create a marketplace for other sellers to sell their books on Amazon. As a result, Amazon has moved towards profitability.[25]

How Are Problems, Types of Decisions, and Organizational Level Integrated?

Exhibit 4–8 describes the relationship among types of problems, types of decisions, and level in the organization. Structured problems? Use programmed decision making. Unstructured problems? Use nonprogrammed decision making. Lower-level managers essentially confront familiar and repetitive problems so they most typically rely on programmed decisions such as standard operating procedures. However, as managers move up the organizational hierarchy, the problems they confront are likely to become less structured. Why? Because lower-level managers handle the routine decisions themselves and only pass upward decisions that they find unique or difficult. Similarly, managers pass down routine decisions to their employees so they can spend their time on more problematic issues.

MANAGERIAL DECISIONS: **Real World—Real Advice**

* Few managerial decisions are either fully programmed or fully nonprogrammed. Most fall somewhere in between.
* At the top level, most problems that managers face *are* unique—that is, nonprogrammed.
* Programmed routines may help even in situations requiring a nonprogrammed decision.
* Top-level managers often create policies, standard operating procedures, and rules—that is, programmed decision making—for lower-level managers in order to control costs and other variables.
* Programmed decision making can facilitate organizational efficiency—maybe that's why it's so popular!
* Programmed decisions minimize the need for managers to exercise discretion.
* Discretion—the ability to make sound judgments—costs money because it's an uncommon and valuable quality and managers who have it are paid more.
* Even in some programmed decisions, individual judgment may be needed.

Exhibit 4–8 Types of Problems, Types of Decisions, and Organizational Level

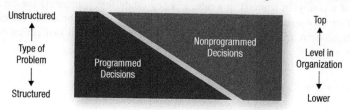

What Decision-Making Conditions Do Managers Face?

When making decisions, managers face three different conditions: certainty, risk, and uncertainty. Let's look at each.

The ideal situation for making decisions is one of **certainty**, which is a situation where a manager can make accurate decisions because the outcome of every alternative is known. For example, when South Dakota's state treasurer decides where to deposit excess state funds, he knows exactly the interest rate being offered by each bank and the amount that will be earned on the funds. He is certain about the outcomes of each alternative. As you might expect, most managerial decisions aren't like this.

Far more common is a situation of **risk**, conditions in which the decision maker is able to estimate the likelihood of certain outcomes. Under risk, managers have historical data from past personal experiences or secondary information that lets them assign probabilities to different alternatives.

What happens if you face a decision where you're not certain about the outcomes and can't even make reasonable probability estimates? We call this condition **uncertainty**. Managers do face decision-making situations of uncertainty. Under these conditions, the choice of alternative is influenced by the limited amount of available information and by the psychological orientation of the decision maker.

certainty
A situation in which a decision maker can make accurate decisions because all outcomes are known

risk
A situation in which a decision maker is able to estimate the likelihood of certain outcomes

uncertainty
A situation in which a decision maker has neither certainty nor reasonable probability estimates available

---

✪ Write It!

If your professor has assigned this, go to the Assignments section of **mymanagementlab.com** to complete *MGMT 8: Decision Making*.

How Do Groups Make Decisions?

4-4 Discuss group decision making.

Work teams are common at Amazon. Jeff Bezos, founder and CEO, uses a **"two-pizza" philosophy**—that is, a team should be small enough that it can be fed with two pizzas.[26]

Do managers make a lot of decisions in groups? You bet they do! Many decisions in organizations, especially important decisions that have far-reaching effects on organizational activities and people, are typically made in groups. It's a rare organization that doesn't at some time use committees, task forces, review panels, work teams, or similar groups as vehicles for making decisions. Why? In many cases, these groups represent the people who will be most affected by the decisions being made. Because of their expertise, these people are often best qualified to make decisions that affect them.

Studies tell us that managers spend a significant portion of their time in meetings. Undoubtedly, a large portion of that time is involved with defining problems, arriving at solutions to those problems, and determining the means for implementing the solutions. It's possible, in fact, for groups to be assigned any of the eight steps in the decision-making process.

What Are the Advantages and Disadvantages of Group Decision Making?

Decisions can be made by individuals or by groups—each approach has its own set of strengths and neither is ideal for all situations.

Advantages of Group Decisions

- *More complete information.*[27]
- *Diversity of experiences and perspectives* brought to the decision process.[28]
- *More alternatives generated* due to greater quantity and diversity of information, especially when group members represent different specialties.
- *Increased acceptance of a solution* by having people who will be affected by a certain solution and who will help implement it participate in the decision.[29]
- *Increased legitimacy* because the group decision-making process is consistent with democratic ideals, and decisions made by groups may be perceived as more legitimate than those made by a single person, which can appear autocratic and arbitrary.

Disadvantages of Group Decisions

- *Time-consuming*—assembling the group, getting decisions made.
- *Minority domination* can unduly influence final decision because group members are never perfectly equal—they differ in rank, experience, knowledge about the problem, influence on other members, verbal skills, assertiveness, etc.[30]
- *Ambiguous responsibility.* Group members share responsibility, BUT who is actually responsible for final outcome?[31] Individual decision—it's clear. Group decision—it's not.
- *Pressures to conform.* Have you ever been in a group where your views didn't match the group's consensus views and you remained silent? Maybe others felt the same way and also remained silent. This is what Irving Janis called **groupthink**, a form of conformity in which group members withhold deviant, minority, or unpopular views in order to give the *appearance of agreement*.[32]

The Tragedy of Groupthink

What It Does

Hinders decision making, possibly jeopardizing the quality of the decision by:

- Undermining critical thinking in the group.
- Affecting a group's ability to objectively appraise alternatives.
- Deterring individuals from critically appraising unusual, minority, or unpopular views.

How Does It Occur? Here are some things to watch out for:

- Group members rationalize resistance to assumptions.
- Members directly pressure those who express doubts or question the majority's views and arguments.
- Members who have doubts or differing points of view avoid deviating from what appears to be group consensus.
- An illusion of unanimity prevails. Full agreement is *assumed* if no one speaks up.

groupthink
When a group exerts extensive pressure on an individual to withhold his or her different views in order to appear to be in agreement

<u>What Can Be Done to Minimize Groupthink?</u>

- Encourage cohesiveness.
- Foster open discussion.
- Have an impartial leader who seeks input from all members.[33]

When Are Groups Most Effective?

Well, that depends on the *criteria you use for defining effectiveness*, such as accuracy, speed, creativity, and acceptance. Group decisions tend to be more accurate. On average, groups tend to make better decisions than individuals, although groupthink may occur.[34] However, if decision effectiveness is defined in terms of speed, individuals are superior. If creativity is important, groups tend to be more effective than individuals. And if effectiveness means the degree of acceptance the final solution achieves, the nod again goes to the group.

The *effectiveness* of group decision making is *also influenced by the size of the group*. The larger the group, the greater the opportunity for heterogeneous representation. On the other hand, a larger group requires more coordination and more time to allow all members to contribute. This means that groups probably shouldn't be too large: A minimum of five to a maximum of about fifteen members is best. Groups of five to seven individuals appear to be the most effective (remember Amazon's "two-pizza" rule!). Because five and seven are odd numbers, decision deadlocks are avoided. You can't consider effectiveness without also assessing efficiency. Groups almost always stack up as a poor second in efficiency to the individual decision maker. Yet, with few exceptions, group decision making consumes more work hours than does individual decision making.

Bottom Line on Groups or Individuals: Do **increases in effectiveness offset losses in efficiency?**

How Can You Improve Group Decision Making?

Use these techniques to make group decisions more creative: (1) brainstorming, (2) the nominal group technique, and (3) electronic meetings.

WHAT IS BRAINSTORMING?   **Brainstorming** is a relatively simple idea-generating process that specifically encourages any and all alternatives while withholding criticism of those alternatives.[36] In a typical brainstorming session, a half-dozen to a dozen people sit around a table. Of course, technology is changing where that "table" is. The group leader states the problem in a clear manner that is understood by all participants. Members then shout out, offer up, fire off, "freewheel" as many alternatives as they can in a given time. No criticism is allowed, and all the alternatives are recorded for later discussion and analysis.[37]

HOW DOES THE NOMINAL GROUP TECHNIQUE WORK?   The **nominal group technique** helps groups arrive at a preferred solution by restricting discussion during the decision-making process.[38] Group members must be present, as in a traditional committee meeting, but they're required to operate independently. They secretly write a list of general problem areas or potential solutions to a problem. The chief advantage of this technique is that it permits the group to meet formally but does not restrict independent thinking or lead to groupthink, as can often happen in a traditional interacting group.[39]

brainstorming
An idea-generating process that encourages alternatives while withholding criticism

nominal group technique
A decision-making technique in which group members are physically present but operate independently

Bloomberg/Getty Images

Brainstorming is an important way of improving group decision making at SAP AG, a provider of enterprise software. Employees working at SAP headquarters in Walldorf, Germany, use white boards during a brainstorming session to develop product and service innovations following the company's decision to target the growing online software market.

HOW CAN ELECTRONIC MEETINGS ENHANCE GROUP DECISION MAKING? Another approach to group decision making blends the nominal group technique with information technology and is called the **electronic meeting**.

Once the technology is in place, the concept is simple. Numerous people sit around a table with laptops or tablets. Participants are presented issues and type their responses onto their computers. Individual comments, as well as aggregate votes, are displayed on a projection screen in the room.

The major advantages of electronic meetings are anonymity, honesty, and speed.[40] Participants can anonymously type any message they want, and it will flash on the screen for all to see with a keystroke. It allows people to be brutally honest with no penalty. And it's fast—chitchat is eliminated, discussions do not digress, and many participants can "talk" at once without interrupting the others.

Electronic meetings *are* significantly faster and much cheaper than traditional face-to-face meetings.[41] Nestlé, for instance, uses the approach for many of its meetings, especially globally focused meetings.[42] However, as with all other forms of group activities, electronic meetings have some drawbacks. Those who type quickly can outshine those who may be verbally eloquent but lousy typists; those with the best ideas don't get credit for them; and the process lacks the informational richness of face-to-face oral communication. However, group decision making is likely to include extensive usage of electronic meetings.[43]

A variation of the electronic meeting is the videoconference. Using technology to link different locations, people can have face-to-face meetings even when they're thousands of miles apart. This capability has enhanced feedback among the members, saved countless hours of business travel, and ultimately saved companies such as Nestlé and Logitech hundreds of thousands of dollars, especially during the recent global recession. As a result, they're more effective in their meetings and have increased the efficiency with which decisions are made.[44]

What Contemporary Decision-Making Issues Do Managers Face?

4-5 Discuss contemporary issues in managerial decision making.

> ## Bad decisions can cost millions.

Today's business world revolves around making decisions, often risky ones, usually with incomplete or inadequate information, and under intense time pressure. Most managers make one decision after another; and as if that weren't challenging enough, more is at stake than ever before since bad decisions can cost millions. We're going to look at three important issues—**1** national culture, **2** creativity and design thinking, and **3** big data—that managers face in today's fast-moving and global world.

How Does National Culture Affect Managers' Decision Making?

Research shows that, to some extent, decision-making practices differ from country to country.[45] The way decisions are made—whether by group, by team members, participatively, or autocratically by an individual manager—and the degree of risk a decision maker is willing to take are just two examples of decision variables that reflect a country's cultural environment.

electronic meeting
A type of nominal group technique in which participants are linked by computer

For example, in India, power distance and uncertainty avoidance (see Chapter 3) are high. There, only very senior-level managers make decisions, and they're likely to make safe decisions. In contrast, in Sweden, power distance and uncertainty avoidance are low. Swedish managers are not afraid to make risky decisions. Senior managers in Sweden also push decisions down to lower levels. They encourage lower-level managers and employees to take part in decisions that affect them. In countries such as Egypt, where time pressures are low, managers make decisions at a slower and more deliberate pace than managers do in the United States. And in Italy, where history and traditions are valued, managers tend to rely on tried and proven alternatives to resolve problems.

Decision making in Japan is much more group oriented than in the United States.[46] The Japanese value conformity and cooperation. Before making decisions, Japanese CEOs collect a large amount of information, which is then used in consensus-forming group decisions called **ringisei**. Because employees in Japanese organizations have high job security, managerial decisions take a long-term perspective rather than focusing on short-term profits, as is often the practice in the United States.

Senior managers in France and Germany also adapt their decision styles to their countries' cultures. In France, for instance, autocratic decision making is widely practiced, and managers avoid risks. Managerial styles in Germany reflect the German culture's concern for structure and order. Consequently, German organizations generally operate under extensive rules and regulations. Managers have well-defined responsibilities and accept that decisions must go through channels.

As managers deal with employees from diverse cultures, they need to recognize common and accepted behavior when asking them to make decisions. Some individuals may not be as comfortable as others with being closely involved in decision making, or they may not be willing to experiment with something radically different. *Managers who accommodate the diversity in decision-making philosophies and practices can expect a high payoff if they capture the perspectives and strengths that a diverse workforce offers.*

Bloomberg/Getty Images

These senior managers of Mitsubishi Motors, a multinational automaker based in Tokyo, Japan, take a long-term perspective in making decisions rather than focusing on short-term results. In Japan, where conformity and cooperation are valued, managers adapt their decisions to their country's group-oriented culture.

Why Are Creativity and Design Thinking Important in Decision Making?

How do most of you take and save photos today? It's highly unlikely that you've ever had to insert film into a camera, shoot the photos you wanted while hoping you "got the shot," remove the film from the camera, take the film to be processed, and then pick up your photos later. When Apple, Facebook, and Instagram wanted to make this process easier and better, someone making decisions about future products had to *be creative* and they had to *use design thinking*. Both are important to decision makers today.

UNDERSTANDING CREATIVITY. A decision maker needs **creativity**: the ability to produce novel and useful ideas. These ideas are different from what's been done before but are also appropriate to the problem or opportunity presented. Why is creativity important to decision making? It allows the decision maker to appraise and understand the problem more fully, including "seeing" problems others can't see. However, creativity's most obvious value is in helping the decision maker identify all viable alternatives.

ringisei
Japanese consensus-forming group decisions

creativity
The ability to produce novel and useful ideas

Most people have creative potential that they can use when confronted with a decision-making problem. But to unleash that potential, they have to get out of the psychological ruts most of us get into and learn how to think about a problem in divergent ways.

Learn to **unleash YOUR** creativity.

We can start with the obvious. People differ in their inherent creativity. Einstein, Edison, Dali, and Mozart were individuals of exceptional creativity. Not surprisingly, exceptional creativity is scarce.

A study of lifetime creativity of 461 men and women found that:

- Fewer than 1 percent were exceptionally creative
- 10 percent were highly creative
- About 60 percent were somewhat creative.

These findings suggest that most of us have some creative potential, *if* we can learn to unleash it.

Given that most people have the capacity to be at least moderately creative, what can individuals and organizations do to stimulate employee creativity? The best answer to this question lies in the three-component model of creativity based on an extensive body of research.[47] This model proposes that individual creativity essentially requires ❶ expertise, ❷ creative-thinking skills, and ❸ intrinsic task motivation. Studies confirm that the higher the level of each of these three components, the higher the creativity.

Expertise is the foundation of all creative work. Dali's understanding of art and Einstein's knowledge of physics were necessary conditions for them to be able to make creative contributions to their fields. And you wouldn't expect someone with a minimal knowledge of programming to be highly creative as a software engineer. The potential for creativity is enhanced when individuals have abilities, knowledge, proficiencies, and similar expertise in their fields of endeavor.

The second component is *creative-thinking skills*. It encompasses personality characteristics associated with creativity, the ability to use analogies, as well as the talent to see the familiar in a different light. For instance, the following individual traits have been found to be associated with the development of creative ideas: intelligence, independence, self-confidence, risk taking, internal locus of control, tolerance for ambiguity, and perseverance in the face of frustration. The effective use of analogies allows decision makers to apply an idea from one context to another. One of the most famous examples in which analogy resulted in a creative breakthrough was Alexander Graham Bell's observation that it might be possible to take concepts that operate in the ear and apply them to his "talking box." He noticed that the bones in the ear are operated by a delicate, thin membrane. He wondered why, then, a thicker and stronger piece of membrane shouldn't be able to move a piece of steel. Out of that analogy the telephone was conceived. Of course, some people have developed their skill at being able to see problems in a new way. They're able to make the strange familiar and the familiar strange. For instance, most of us think of hens laying eggs. But how many of us have considered that a hen is only an egg's way of making another egg?

The final component in our model is *intrinsic task motivation*—the desire to work on something because it's interesting, involving, exciting, satisfying, or personally challenging. This motivational component is what turns creative *potential* into *actual* creative ideas. It determines the extent to which individuals fully engage their expertise and creative skills. So creative people often love their work, to the point of seeming obsessed. Importantly, an individual's work environment and the organization's culture (which we discussed in Chapter 2) can have a significant effect on intrinsic motivation. Five organizational factors have been found that can impede your creativity:

- expected evaluation—focusing on how your work is going to be evaluated
- surveillance—being watched while you're working
- external motivators—emphasizing external, tangible rewards
- competition—facing win–lose situations with your peers
- constrained choices—being given limits on how you can do your work.

Prisma Bildagentur AG/Alamy

⭐ **Try It!**

If your professor has assigned this, go to the Assignments section of **mymanagementlab.com** to complete the **Simulation:** *Decision Making*.

design thinking
Approaching management problems as designers approach design problems

Apple—a great example of how **design thinking benefits** an organization.

UNDERSTANDING DESIGN THINKING.   The way managers approach decision making—using a rational and analytical mindset in identifying problems, coming up with alternatives, evaluating alternatives, and choosing one of those alternatives—may not be the best and certainly not the only choice in today's environment. That's where design thinking comes in. **Design thinking** has been described as "approaching management problems as designers approach design problems."[48] More organizations are beginning to recognize how design thinking can benefit them.[49] For instance, Apple has long been celebrated for its design thinking. The company's lead designer, Jonathan "Jony" Ive (who was behind some of Apple's most successful products including the iPod and iPhone) had this to say about Apple's design approach, "We try to develop products that seem somehow inevitable. That leave you with the sense that that's the only possible solution that makes sense."[50]

While many managers don't deal specifically with product or process design decisions, they still make decisions about work issues that arise, and design thinking can help them be better decision makers. What can the design thinking approach teach managers about making better decisions? Well, it begins with (1) the first step in the decision-making process of identifying problems. Design thinking says that managers should look at problem identification collaboratively and integratively with the goal of gaining a deep understanding of the situation. They should look not only at the rational aspects, but also at the emotional elements. Then invariably, of course, design thinking would (2) influence how managers identify and evaluate alternatives—steps 2 through 5 in the decision-making process. A traditional manager (educated in a business school, of course) would look at the alternatives, rationally evaluate them, and select the one with the highest payoff. However, using design thinking, a manager would say, "What is something completely new that would be lovely if it existed but doesn't now?"[51] Design thinking means opening up your perspective and gaining insights by using observation and inquiry skills, and not relying simply on rational analysis. We're not saying that rational analysis isn't needed; we are saying that there's more needed in making effective decisions, especially in today's world.

Design thinking leads the strategic decisions of Jack Dorsey, co-founder of Twitter and CEO of Square, a mobile payments processor for smartphones and tablets. Dorsey used observation and inquiry in deciding to start a company based on the idea that people needed an easy way to make payments in person.

Big data is **changing the way** managers make decisions.

Big Data Understood.

- Amazon.com, Earth's biggest online retailer, earns billions of dollars of revenue each year—estimated at one-third of sales—from its "personalization technologies" such as product recommendations and computer-generated e-mails.[52]
- At AutoZone, decision makers are using new software that gleans information from a variety of databases and allows its 5,000-plus local stores to target deals and hopefully reduce the chance that customers will walk away without making a purchase. AutoZone's chief information officer says, "We think this is the direction of the future."[53]

Bloomberg/Getty Images

big data
The vast amount of quantifiable information that can be analyzed by highly sophisticated data processing

- It's not just businesses that are exploiting big data. A team of San Francisco researchers was able to predict the magnitude of a disease outbreak halfway around the world by analyzing phone patterns from mobile phone usage.[54]

Yes, there's a ton of information out there—100 petabytes here in the decade of the 2010s, according to experts. (In bytes, that translates to 1 plus 17 zeroes, in case you were wondering!)[55] And businesses—and other organizations—are finally figuring out how to use it. So what is **big data**? It's the vast amount of quantifiable information that can be analyzed by highly sophisticated data processing. One IT expert described big data with "3V's: high volume, high velocity, and/or high variety information assets."[56]

What does big data have to do with decision making? A lot, as you can imagine. With this type of data at hand, decision makers have very powerful tools to help them make decisions. However, experts caution that collecting and analyzing data for data's sake is wasted effort. Goals are needed when collecting and using this type of information. As one individual said, "Big data is a descendant of Taylor's 'scientific management' of more than a century ago."[57] While Taylor used a stopwatch to time and monitor a worker's every movement, big data is using math modeling, predictive algorithms, and artificial intelligence software to measure and monitor people and machines like never before. (See Case Applications #2 and #3 on pp. 137 and 138.) But managers need to really examine and evaluate how big data might contribute to their decision making before jumping in with both feet.

MyManagementLab®

Go to **mymanagementlab.com** to complete the problems marked with this icon .

4 Review

CHAPTER SUMMARY

4-1 Describe the decision-making process.

The decision-making process consists of eight steps: (1) identify a problem, (2) identify decision criteria, (3) weight the criteria, (4) develop alternatives, (5) analyze alternatives, (6) select alternative, (7) implement alternative, and (8) evaluate decision effectiveness. As managers make decisions, they may use heuristics to simplify the process, which can lead to errors and biases in their decision making. The 12 common decision-making errors and biases include overconfidence, immediate gratification, anchoring, selective perception, confirmation, framing, availability, representation, randomness, sunk costs, self-serving bias, and hindsight.

4-2 Explain the three approaches managers can use to make decisions.

The first approach is the rational model. The assumptions of rationality are as follows: the problem is clear and unambiguous; a single, well-defined goal is to be achieved; all alternatives and consequences are known; and the final choice will maximize the payoff. The second approach, bounded rationality, says that managers make rational decisions but are bounded (limited) by their ability to process information. In this approach, managers satisfice, which is when decision makers accept solutions that are good enough. Finally, intuitive decision making is making decisions on the basis of experience, feelings, and accumulated judgment.

4-3 Describe the types of decisions and decision-making conditions managers face.

Programmed decisions are repetitive decisions that can be handled by a routine approach and are used when the problem being resolved is straightforward, familiar, and easily defined (structured). Nonprogrammed decisions are unique decisions that require a custom-made solution and are used when the problems are new or unusual (unstructured) and for which information is ambiguous or incomplete. Certainty involves a situation in which a manager can make accurate decisions because all outcomes are known. With risk, a manager can estimate the likelihood of certain outcomes in a situation. Uncertainty is a situation in which a manager is not certain about the outcomes and can't even make reasonable probability estimates.

4-4 Discuss group decision making.

Groups offer certain advantages when making decisions—more complete information, more alternatives, increased acceptance of a solution, and greater legitimacy. On the other hand, groups are time-consuming, can be dominated by a minority, create pressures to conform, and cloud responsibility. Three ways of improving group decision making are brainstorming (utilizing an idea-generating process that specifically encourages any and all alternatives while withholding any criticism of those alternatives), the nominal group technique (a technique that restricts discussion during the decision-making process), and electronic meetings (the most recent approach to group decision making, which blends the nominal group technique with sophisticated computer technology).

4-5 Discuss contemporary issues in managerial decision making.

As managers deal with employees from diverse cultures, they need to recognize common and accepted behavior when asking them to make decisions. Some individuals may not be as comfortable as others with being closely involved in decision making, or they may not be willing to experiment with something radically different. Also, managers need to be creative in their decision making because creativity allows them to appraise and understand the problem more fully, including "seeing" problems that others can't see. Design thinking also influences the way that managers approach decision making, especially in terms of identifying problems and how they identify and evaluate alternatives. Finally, big data is changing what and how decisions are made, but managers need to evaluate how big data might contribute to their decision making.

DISCUSSION QUESTIONS

⭐ 4-1 Why is decision making often described as the essence of a manager's job?

4-2 Provide an eight-step illustration of any decision-making process undertaken by you.

4-3 Since decision making is personalized, do you think bias plays an important role for a CEO or a first-line manager in a developing country? Explain the potential daily bias that managers may encounter.

4-4 Managers make decisions by planning, organizing, leading, and controlling. Which of these skills is more important for a manager to master in order to be a competent manager?

4-5 What is intuitive decision making? In your opinion, when is this method best used? What are the major drawbacks of this managerial decision-making style?

4-6 Herbert A. Simon started work on bounded rationality and satisficing because of his hypothesis, which indicated that people had limited ability to grasp the present and anticipate the future. Discuss the problems associated with making decisions using the rational model.

4-7 Explain how a manager might deal with making decisions under conditions of uncertainty.

⭐ 4-8 Why do companies invest in nurturing group decision making rather than individual decision making? Explain the advantages and disadvantages of both techniques.

4-9 Find two examples each of procedures, rules, and policies. Bring your examples to class and be prepared to share them.

4-10 Do a Web search on the phrase "dumbest moments in business" and get the most current version of this list. Choose three of the examples and describe what happened. What's your reaction to each example? How could the managers in each have made better decisions?

MyManagementLab

Go to **mymanagementlab.com** for the following Assisted-graded writing questions:

4-11 Today's world is chaotic and fast-paced. How does time pressure affect managerial decision making? What can managers do to still be good decision makers under such conditions?

4-12 Discuss the pros and cons of managers using technology to help make decisions.

4-13 MyManagementLab Only – comprehensive writing assignment for this chapter.

Management Skill Builder | BEING A CREATIVE DECISION MAKER

Many decisions that managers make are routine, so they can fall back on experience and "what's worked in the past." But other decisions—especially those made by upper-level managers—are unique and haven't been confronted before. The uniqueness and variety of problems that managers face demand creativity—the ability to produce novel and useful ideas. If managers are to successfully progress upward in an organization, they'll find an increasing need to develop creative decisions. Creativity is partly a frame of mind. You need to expand your mind's capabilities—that is, open yourself up to new ideas. Every individual has the ability to improve his or her creativity, but many people simply don't try to develop that ability.

✪ PERSONAL INVENTORY ASSESSMENT

Problem Solving, Creativity, and Innovation

Making decisions is all about solving problems. Do this PIA and find out about your level of creativity and innovation in problem solving.

Skill Basics

Creativity is a skill you can develop. Here are some suggestions on how you can do this:

- *Think of yourself as creative.* Research shows that if you think you can't be creative, you won't be. Believing in your ability to be creative is the first step in becoming more creative.

- *Pay attention to your intuition.* Every individual has a subconscious mind that works well. Sometimes answers will come to you when you least expect them. Listen to that "inner voice." In fact, most creative people will keep a notepad near their bed and write down ideas when the thoughts come to them.

- *Move away from your comfort zone.* Every individual has a comfort zone in which certainty exists. But creativity and the known often do not mix. To be creative, you need to move away from the status quo and focus your mind on something new.

- *Determine what you want to do.* This includes such things as taking time to understand a problem before beginning to try to resolve it, getting all the facts in mind, and trying to identify the most important facts.

- *Think outside the box.* Use analogies whenever possible (for example, could you approach your problem like a fish out of water and look at what the fish does to cope? Or can you use the things you have to do to find your way when it's foggy to help you solve your problem?). Use different problem-solving strategies such as verbal, visual, mathematical, or theatrical. Look at your problem from a different perspective or ask yourself what someone else, like your grandmother, might do if faced with the same situation.

- *Look for ways to do things better.* This may involve trying consciously to be original, not worrying about looking foolish, keeping an open mind, being alert to odd or puzzling facts, thinking of unconventional ways to use objects and the environment, discarding usual or habitual ways of doing things, and striving for objectivity by being as critical of your own ideas as you would those of someone else.

- *Find several right answers.* Being creative means continuing to look for other solutions even when you think you have solved the problem. A better, more creative solution just might be found.

- *Believe in finding a workable solution.* Like believing in yourself, you also need to believe in your ideas. If you don't think you can find a solution, you probably won't.

- *Brainstorm with others.* Creativity is not an isolated activity. Bouncing ideas off of others creates a synergistic effect.

- *Turn creative ideas into action.* Coming up with creative ideas is only part of the process. Once the ideas are generated, they must be implemented. Keeping great ideas in your mind, or on papers that no one will read, does little to expand your creative abilities.

Based on J. V. Anderson, "Mind Mapping: A Tool for Creative Thinking," *Business Horizons*, January–February 1993, 42–46; and T. Proctor, *Creative Problem Solving for Managers* (New York: Routledge, 2005).

Practicing the Skill

Read through this scenario and follow the directions at the end of it:

Every time the phone rings, your stomach clenches and your palms start to sweat. And it's no wonder! As sales manager for Brinkers, a machine tool parts manufacturer, you're besieged by calls from customers who are upset about late deliveries. Your boss, Carter Hererra, acts as both production manager and scheduler. Every time your sales representatives negotiate a sale, it's up to Carter to determine whether production can actually meet the delivery date the customer specifies. And Carter invariably says, "No problem." The good thing about this is that you make a lot of initial sales. The bad news is that production hardly ever meets the shipment dates that Carter authorizes. And he doesn't seem to be all that concerned about the aftermath of late deliveries. He says, "Our customers know they're getting outstanding quality at a great price. Just let them try to match that anywhere. It can't be done. So even if they have to wait a couple of extra days or weeks, they're still getting the best deal they can." Somehow the customers don't see it that way. And they let you know about their unhappiness. Then it's up to you to try to soothe the relationship. You know this problem has to be taken care of, but what possible solutions are there? After all, how are you going to keep from making your manager mad or making the customers mad?

Break into groups of three. Assume you're the sales manager. What creative solutions can your group come up with to deal with this problem?

Magic Carpet Software

To: Rajiv Dutta, Research Manager

From: Amanda Schrenk, Vice President of Operations

Re: Software Design Decisions

Rajiv, we have a problem in our software design unit. Our diverse pool of extremely talented and skilled designers is, undoubtedly, one of our company's most important assets. However, I'm concerned that our designers' emotional attachment to the software they've created overshadows other important factors that should be considered in the decision whether to proceed with the new product design. At this point, I'm not sure how to approach this issue. The last thing I want to do is stifle their creativity. But I'm afraid if we don't come up with an action plan soon, the problem may get worse.

I need you to research the role of emotions in decision making. What do the "experts" say? Is it even an issue that we need to be concerned about? What's the best way to deal with it? Please provide me with a one-page bulleted list of the important points you find from your research. And be sure to cite your sources in case I need to do some follow-up.

This fictionalized company and message were created for educational purposes only, and not meant to reflect positively or negatively on management practices by any company that may share this name.

CASE APPLICATION #1

 Big Brown Numbers

It's the world's largest package delivery company with the instantly recognizable trucks.[58] Every day, United Parcel Service (UPS) transports more than 18 million packages and documents throughout the United States and to more than 220 countries and territories, including every address in North America and Europe. (Total worldwide delivery volume was 4.6 billion packages and documents in 2014.) Delivering those packages efficiently and on time is what UPS gets paid to do, and that takes a massive effort in helping drivers to make decisions about the best routes to follow.

Efficiency and uniformity have always been important to UPS. The importance of work rules, procedures, and analytic tools are continually stressed to drivers through training and retraining. For instance, drivers are taught to hold their keys on a pinky finger so they don't waste time fumbling in their pockets for the keys. And for safety reasons, they're taught no-left turns and no backing up. Now, however, the company has been testing and rolling out a quantum leap in its long-used business model of uniformity and efficiency. It goes by the name ORION, which stands for On-Road Integrated Optimization and Navigation. What it boils down to is helping UPS drivers shave millions of miles off their delivery routes using decision algorithms built by a team of mathematicians.

Consider that each UPS driver makes an average of 120 stops per day. The efficiency challenge is deciding the best order to make all those stops (6,689,502,913,449,135 + 183 zeroes of possible alternatives)—taking into consideration "variables such as special delivery times, road regulations, and the existence of private roads that don't appear on a map?"[59] Another description of the logistics decision challenge: There are more ways to deliver packages along an average driver's route "than there are nanoseconds that Earth has existed."[60] Any way you look at it, that's a lot of alternatives. The human mind can't even begin to figure it out. But the ORION algorithm, which has taken 10 years and an estimated hundreds of millions of dollars to build, is the next best thing. IT experts have described ORION as the largest investment in operations research ever by any company.

> UPS has been described as an **EFFICIENCY FREAK**.

So what does ORION do? Instead of searching for the one best answer, ORION is designed to refine itself over time, leading to a balance between an optimum result and consistency to help drivers make the best possible decisions about route delivery. And considering how many miles UPS drivers travel every day, saving a dollar or two here and there can add up quickly. When a driver "logs on" his delivery information acquisition device (DIAD) at the beginning of his shift each workday, what comes up are two possible ways to make the day's package deliveries: one that uses ORION and one that uses the "old" method. The driver can choose to use either one but if ORION is not chosen, the driver is asked to explain the decision. The roll-out of ORION hasn't been without challenges. Some drivers have been reluctant to give up autonomy; others have had trouble understanding ORION's logic—why deliver a package in one neighborhood in the morning and come back to the same neighborhood later in the day. But despite the challenges, the company is committed to ORION, saying that "a driver together with ORION is better than each alone."[61]

Discussion Questions

⭐ 4-14 Why is efficiency and safety so important to UPS?

⭐ 4-15 Would you characterize a driver's route decisions as structured or unstructured problems? Programmed or nonprogrammed decisions? Explain.

⭐ 4-16 How would ORION technology help drivers make better decisions? (Think of the steps in the decision-making process.)

4-17 How is UPS being a sustainable corporation?

CASE APPLICATION #2

Galloping to the Right Decision

Horseracing has rich traditions dating back to the first races in 4500 BC and the early civilizations of Central Asia, the Mediterranean, and Europe.[62] Once considered the "Sport of Kings", today's horse racing has evolved in to multi-billion dollar entertainment industry. Owners, jockeys, trainers, and horses travel the globe in search for a win. Crossing the finish line in one of the top three places can produce significant earnings from the modest racing circuits in small cities to the extravagant payouts of the most prestigious venues. In the Hong Kong circuit alone, winning owners can earn up to 60% of prize money ranging from $100,000 to over $3 million per weekly race over a season. A winning jockey and trainer can easily earn 10% each from an owner's winnings.

Fans from all walks of life share in the enthusiasm as they fill massive grand stands and hotel rooms. Hong Kong's world class Happy Valley Racecourse can draw up to 55,000 spectators on any given night. The Dubai Cup with the largest purse in all of horseracing at a $10,000,000 attracts not only the top horses in the world but entices tourists to visit the United Arab Emirates eager to experience the spectacular Meydon Hotel overlooking the Dubai racecourse. And the Kentucky Derby continues to draw record-breaking crowds to the U.S. city of Louisville where ticket prices for this spectacle can range from $43 for general admission tickets to $11,000 for an upper clubhouse seat.

As the big business of horse racing continues to grow, risk and uncertainty in this high stakes affair looms heavy for its decision makers. Each decision can be the difference between winning and losing. Not just a sport for pleasure, owners with small and large pocketbooks seek returns on their investment. And a jockey's livelihood for the month can be decided in a matter of seconds.

An owner must assess whether to invest in the potential of young colt or buy an experienced mare. Pedigree, age, and past performance are just a few factors alongside sentiment. Tradition can influence a buyer to seek a thoroughbred from England's hallowed breeding grounds in Newmarket or to lean toward the bloodline of an Arabian. Evaluating the return on investment must be weighed against the cost of ownership including training and boarding fees.

Managing HORSE RACING... Numbers or Emotion, Which Works Better?

Decisions do not just rest in ownership. A jockey makes split second decisions during a race while galloping at speeds exceeding 35mph. Not knowing a horse's tendencies or using the wrong race strategy could lead to life threatening injury to horse or rider. A well prepared jockey studies course dimensions and the patterns of competitors. Horse preparation relies on the daily decision of trainer who must decide optimal diets and appropriate equipment such as proper fitting horseshoes. This extends to exercise routines monitored by data collected via smartphone apps and tracking of graphical data.

The rationality of science continues to permeate the sport. Race teams seek competitive advantage via genetic testing and aerobic measurements. Yet, at the end of the day, many decisions are still made by one's love and feel for the horse.

Discussion Questions

⭐ **4-18** What are some examples of rational and intuitive decision making that you may see in horse racing?

4-19 A jockey from Melbourne, Australia is swayed by a friend to race at the last minute in Happy Valley, Hong Kong without a track preview. How would bounded rationality affect the jockey who normally races in Australia?

⭐ **4-20** What decision-making approaches could an owner use to help decide what type of horse to buy?

⭐ **4-21** Suppose some trainers meet at a conference and view a presentation about an organic new feed that naturally improves muscle development in race horses. A trainer who did not attend the presentation hears each trainer who left the presentation signed up for a month's supply. Then the trainer decides to follow suit without gathering any evidence. What type of decision bias would you consider this to be?

CASE APPLICATION #3

Tasting Success

The Coca-Cola Company (Coke) is in a league by itself.[63] As the world's largest and number one nonalcoholic beverage company, Coke makes or licenses more than 3,500 drinks in more than 200 countries. Coke has built 15 billion-dollar brands and also claims four of the top five soft-drink brands (Coke, Diet Coke, Fanta, and Sprite). Each year since 2001, global brand consulting firm Interbrand, in conjunction with *Bloomberg BusinessWeek,* has identified Coke as the number one best global brand. Coke's executives and managers are focusing on ambitious, long-term growth for the company—doubling Coke's business by 2020. A big part of achieving this goal is building up its Simply Orange juice business into a powerful global juice brand. Decision making is playing a crucial role as managers try to beat rival PepsiCo, which has a 40 percent market share in the not-from-concentrate juice category compared to Coke's 28 percent share. And those managers aren't leaving anything to chance in this hot—umm, cold—pursuit!

Orange Juice and the **1 Quintillion Decisions** needed to deliver it!

You'd think that making orange juice (OJ) would be relatively simple—pick, squeeze, pour. While that would probably be the case in your own kitchen, in Coke's case, that glass of 100 percent OJ is possible only through the use of satellite images, complex mathematical algorithms, and a pipeline solely for the purpose of transporting juice. The purchasing director for Coke's massive Florida juice packaging facility says that when you're dealing with "Mother Nature," standardization is a huge problem. Yet, standardization is what it takes for Coke to make this work profitably. And producing a juice beverage is far more complicated than bottling soda.

Using what it calls its "Black Book model," Coke wants to ensure that customers have consistently fresh, tasty OJ 12 months a year despite a peak growing season that's only three months long. To help in this, Coke relies on a consultant experienced with revenue analytics, who has described OJ as "one of the most complex applications of business analytics." How complex? To consistently deliver an optimal blend given the challenges of nature requires some 1 quintillion (that's 1 followed by 18 zeroes) decisions!

There's no secret formula to Black Book, it's simply an algorithm. It includes detailed data about the more than 600 different flavors that make up an orange and about customer preferences. This data is correlated to a profile of each batch of raw juice. The algorithm then determines how to blend batches to match a certain taste and consistency. At the juice bottling plant, "blend technicians" carefully follow the Black Book instructions before beginning the bottling process. The weekly OJ recipe they use is "tweaked" constantly. Black Book also includes data on external factors such as weather patterns, crop yields, and other cost pressures. This is useful for Coke's decision makers as they ensure they'll have enough supplies for at least 15 months. One Coke executive says the company's mathematical modeling means that if a weather catastrophe (hurricane or hard freeze) hits, the business can quickly regroup and replan in a very short time frame: as little as 5 or 10 minutes.

Discussion Questions

⭐ **4-22** Which decisions in this story could be considered unstructured problems? Structured problems?

⭐ **4-23** How does the Black Book help Coke's managers and other employees in decision making?

⭐ **4-24** What does Coke's big data have to do with its goals?

4-25 Do some research on revenue analytics. What is it? How can it help managers make better decisions?

Endnotes

1. J. Zucker, "Proof in the Eating," *Fast Company*, March 2013, 34+.

2. A. Blackman, "Inside the Executive Brain," *Wall Street Journal*, April 28, 2014, R1.

3. See, for example, A. Nagurney, J. Dong, and P. L. Mokhtarian, "Multicriteria Network Equilibrium Modeling with Variable Weights for Decision-Making in the Information Age with Applications to the Telecommuting and Teleshopping," *Journal of Economic Dynamics and Control* (August 2002): 1629–50.

4. J. Flinchbaugh, "Surfacing Problems Daily: Advice for Building a Problem-Solving Culture," *Industry Week*, April 2011, 12; "Business Analysis Training Helps Leaders Achieve an Enterprise-Wide Perspective," *Leader to Leader*, Fall 2010, 63–65; D. Okes, "Common Problems with Basic Problem Solving," *Quality*, September 2010, 36–40; J. Sawyer, "Problem-Solving Success Tips," *Business and Economic Review*, April–June 2002, 23–24.

5. See J. Figueira and B. Ray, "Determining the Weights of Criteria in the Electre Type of Methods with a Revised Simons' Procedure," *European Journal of Operational Research*, June 1, 2002, 317–26.

6. For instance, see M. Elliott, "Breakthrough Thinking," *IIE Solution*, October 2001, 22–25; and B. Fazlollahi and R. Vahidov, "A Method for Generation of Alternatives by Decision Support Systems," *Journal of Management Information Systems* (Fall 2001): 229–50.

7. D. Miller, Q. Hope, R. Eisenstat, N. Foote, and J. Galbraith, "The Problem of Solutions: Balancing Clients and Capabilities," *Business Horizons*, March–April 2002, 3–12.

8. E. Teach, "Avoiding Decision Traps," *CFO*, June 2004, 97–99; and D. Kahneman and A. Tversky, "Judgment Under Uncertainty: Heuristics and Biases," *Science* 185 (1974): 1124–31.

9. Information for this section taken from S. P. Robbins, *Decide & Conquer* (Upper Saddle River, NJ: Financial Times/Prentice Hall, 2004).

10. T. A. Stewart, "Did You Ever Have to Make Up Your Mind?" *Harvard Business Review*, January 2006, 12; and E. Pooley, "Editor's Desk," *Fortune*, June 27, 2005, 16.

11. J. G. March, "Decision-Making Perspective: Decisions in Organizations and Theories of Choice," in A. H. Van de Ven and W. F. Joyce (eds.), *Perspectives on Organization Design and Behavior* (New York: Wiley-Interscience, 1981), 232–33.

12. See T. Shavit and A. M. Adam, "A Preliminary Exploration of the Effects of Rational Factors and Behavioral Biases on the Managerial Choice to Invest in Corporate Responsibility," *Managerial and Decision Economics*, April 2011, 205–13; A. Langley, "In Search of Rationality: The Purposes Behind the Use of Formal Analysis in Organizations," *Administrative Science Quarterly*, December 1989, 598–631; and H. A. Simon, "Rationality in Psychology and Economics," *Journal of Business* (October 1986), 209–24.

13. See D. R. A. Skidd, "Revisiting Bounded Rationality," *Journal of Management Inquiry* (December 1992): 343–47; B. E. Kaufman, "A New Theory of Satisficing," *Journal of Behavioral Economics* (Spring 1990): 35–51; and N. McK. Agnew and J. L. Brown, "Bounded Rationality: Fallible Decisions in Unbounded Decision Space," *Behavioral Science*, July 1986, 148–61.

14. From the Past to the Present box based on M. Ibrahim, "Theory of Bounded Rationality," *Public Management*, June 2009, 3–5; D. A. Wren, *The Evolution of Management Thought*, Fourth Edition (New York: John Wiley & Sons, Inc., 1994), 291; and H. A. Simon, *Administrative Behavior* (New York: Macmillan Company, 1945).

15. See, for example, G. McNamara, H. Moon, and P. Bromiley, "Banking on Commitment: Intended and Unintended Consequences of an Organization's Attempt to Attenuate Escalation of Commitment," *Academy of Management Journal* (April 2002): 443–52; V. S. Rao and A. Monk, "The Effects of Individual Differences and Anonymity on Commitment to Decisions," *Journal of Social Psychology* (August 1999): 496–515; C. F. Camerer and R. A. Weber, "The Econometrics and Behavioral Economics of Escalation of Commitment: A Re-examination of Staw's Theory," *Journal of Economic Behavior and Organization* (May 1999): 59–82; D. R. Bobocel and J. P. Meyer, "Escalating Commitment to a Failing Course of Action: Separating the Roles of Choice and Justification," *Journal of Applied Psychology* (June 1994): 360–63; and B. M. Staw, "The Escalation of Commitment to a Course of Action," *Academy of Management Review*, October 1981, 577–87.

16. L. Alderman, "A Shoemaker That Walks but Never Runs," *New York Times Online*, October 8, 2010.

17. C. Flora, "When to Go with Your Gut," *Women's Health*, June 2009, 68–70.

18. See J. Evans, "Intuition and Reasoning: A Dual-Process Perspective," *Psychological Inquiry*, October–December 2010, 313–26; T. Betsch and A. Blockner, "Intuition in Judgment and Decision Making: Extensive Thinking without Effort," *Psychological Inquiry*, October–December 2010, 279–94; R. Lange and J. Houran, "A Transliminal View of Intuitions in the Workplace," *North American Journal of Psychology* 12, no. 3 (2010): 501–16; E. Dane and M. G. Pratt, "Exploring Intuition and Its Role in Managerial Decision Making," *Academy of Management Review*, January 2007, 33–54; M. H. Bazerman and D. Chugh, "Decisions without Blinders," *Harvard Business Review*, January 2006, 88–97; C. C. Miller and R. D. Ireland, "Intuition in Strategic Decision Making: Friend or Foe in the Fast-Paced 21st Century," *Academy of Management Executive*, February 2005, 19–30; E. Sadler-Smith and E. Shefy, "The Intuitive Executive: Understanding and Applying 'Gut Feel' in Decision-Making," *Academy of Management Executive*, November 2004, 76–91; and L. A. Burke and M. K. Miller, "Taking the Mystery Out of Intuitive Decision Making," *Academy of Management Executive*, October 1999, 91–99.

19. C. C. Miller and R. D. Ireland, "Intuition in Strategic Decision Making: Friend or Foe," 20.

20. E. Sadler-Smith and E. Shefy, "Developing Intuitive Awareness in Management Education," *Academy of Management Learning & Education*, June 2007, 186–205.

21. M. G. Seo and L. Feldman Barrett, "Being Emotional During Decision Making—Good or Bad? An Empirical Investigation," *Academy of Management Journal* (August 2007): 923–40.

22. Technology and the Manager's Job box based on M. Xu, V. Ong, Y. Duan, and B. Mathews, "Intelligent Agent Systems for Executive Information Scanning, Filtering, and Interpretation: Perceptions and Challenges," *Information Processing & Management*, March 2011, 186–201; J. P. Kallunki, E. K. Laitinen, and H. Silvola, "Impact of Enterprise Resource Planning Systems on Management Control Systems and Firm Performance," *International Journal of Accounting Information Systems* (March 2011), 20–39; H. W. K. Chia, C. L. Tan, and S. Y. Sung, "Enhancing Knowledge Discovery via Association-Based Evolution of Neural Logic Networks," *IEEE Transactions on Knowledge and Data Engineering* (July 2006): 889–901; F. Harvey, "A Key Role in Detecting Fraud Patterns: Neural Networks," *Financial Times*, January 23, 2002, 3; D. Mitchell and R. Pavur, "Using Modular Neural Networks for Business Decisions," *Management Decision*, January–February 2002, 58–64; B. L. Killingsworth, M. B. Hayden, and R. Schellenberger, "A Network Expert System Management System of Multiple Domains," *Journal of Information Science* (March–April 2001): 81; and S. Balakrishnan, N. Popplewell, and M. Thomlinson, "Intelligent Robotic Assembly," *Computers & Industrial Engineering*, December 2000, 467.

23. "Next: Big Idea," *Fast Company*, December 2010–January 2011, 39–40.

24. H. McCracken, "50 Most Innovative Companies: LINE," *Fast Company*, March 2015, 84+.

25. And the Survey Says box based on D. Kahneman, D. Lovallo, and O. Siboney, "Before You Make That Big Decision," *Harvard Business Review*, June 2011, 50–60; P. Wang, "To Make Better Choices, Choose Less," *Money*, June 2010, 111–14; B. Dumaine, "The Trouble with Teams," *Fortune*, September 5, 1994, 86–92; A. S. Wellner, "A Perfect Brainstorm," *Inc.*, October 2003, 31–35; "The Poll," *BusinessWeek*, August 21–28, 2006, 44; "Hurry Up and Decide," *BusinessWeek*, May 14, 2001, 16; J. MacIntyre, "Bosses and Bureaucracy," *Springfield, Missouri Business Journal*, August 1–7, 2005, 29; J. Crick, and "On the Road to Invention," *Fast Company*, February 2005, 16.

26. A. Deutschman, "Inside the Mind of Jeff Bezos," *Fast Company*, August 2004, 50–58.

27. See, for instance, S. Schulz-Hardt, A. Mojzisch, F. C. Brodbeck, R. Kerschreiter, and D. Frey, "Group Decision Making in Hidden Profile Situations: Dissent as a Facilitator for Decision Quality," *Journal of Personality and Social Psychology* (December 2006), 1080–83; and C. K. W. DeDreu and M. A. West, "Minority Dissent and Team Innovation: The Importance of Participation in Decision Making," *Journal of Applied Psychology* (December 2001): 1191–1201.

28. S. Mohammed, "Toward an Understanding of Cognitive Consensus in a Group Decision-Making Context," *Journal of Applied Behavioral Science* (December 2001): 408.

29. M. J. Fambrough and S. A. Comerford, "The Changing Epistemological Assumptions of Group Theory," *Journal of Applied Behavioral Science* (September 2006): 330–49.

30. R. A. Meyers, D. E. Brashers, and J. Hanner, "Majority-Minority Influence: Identifying Argumentative Patterns and Predicting Argument-Outcome Links," *Journal of Communication* (Autumn 2000): 3–30.

31. See, for instance, T. Horton, "Groupthink in the Boardroom,"

Directors and Boards, Winter 2002, 9.

32. I. L. Janis, *Groupthink* (Boston: Houghton Mifflin, 1982). See also J. Chapman, "Anxiety and Defective Decision Making: An Elaboration of the Groupthink Mode," *Management Decision*, October 2006, 1391–1404.

33. See, for example, T. W. Costello and S. S. Zalkind, eds., *Psychology in Administration: A Research Orientation* (Upper Saddle River, NJ: Prentice Hall, 1963), 429–30; R. A. Cooke and J. A. Kernaghan, "Estimating the Difference between Group versus Individual Performance on Problem Solving Tasks," *Group and Organization Studies*, September 1987, 319–42; and L. K. Michaelsen, W. E. Watson, and R. H. Black, "A Realistic Test of Individual versus Group Consensus Decision Making," *Journal of Applied Psychology* (October 1989): 834–39. See also J. Hollenbeck, D. R. Ilgen, J. A. Colquitt, and A. Ellis, "Gender Composition, Situational Strength, and Team Decision-Making Accuracy: A Criterion Decomposition Approach," *Organizational Behavior and Human Decision Processes*, May 2002, 445–75.

34. See, for example, L. K. Michaelsen, W. E. Watson, and R. H. Black, "A Realistic Test of Individual versus Group Consensus Decision Making," *Journal of Applied Psychology* (October 1989): 834–39; and P. W. Pease, M. Beiser, and M. E. Tubbs, "Framing Effects and Choice Shifts in Group Decision Making," *Organizational Behavior and Human Decision Processes*, October 1993, 149–65.

35. M. Strachan, "NCAA Schools Can Absolutely Afford to Pay College Athletes, Economists Say," http://www.huffingtonpost.com/2015/03/27/ncaa-pay-student-athletes_n_6940836.html, March 27, 2015; A. Zimbalist, "Paying College Athletes: Take Two," http://www.huffingtonpost.com/andrew-zimbalist/paying-college-athletes-take-two_b_6961314.html, March 28, 2015; S. Terlep,

"NCAA Reaches $20 Million Settlement with Ex-Players over Videogames," *Wall Street Journal*, http://www.wsj.com/articles/ncaa-unveils-20-million-settlement-with-ex-players-over-videogames-1402330931, June 9, 2014; and C. Smith, "The Most Valuable Conferences in College Sports 2014," www.forbes.com, April 15, 2014.

36. J. Wagstaff, "Brainstorming Requires Drinks," *Far Eastern Economic Review*, May 2, 2002, 34.

37. T. Kelley, "Six Ways to Kill a Brainstormer," *Across the Board*, March–April 2002, 12.

38. K. L. Dowling and R. D. St. Louis, "Asynchronous Implementation of the Nominal Group Technique: Is It Effective," *Decision Support Systems*, October 2000, 229–48.

39. See also B. Andersen and T. Fagerhaug, "The Nominal Group Technique," *Quality Progress*, February 2000, 144.

40. J. Burdett, "Changing Channels: Using the Electronic Meeting System to Increase Equity in Decision Making," *Information Technology, Learning, and Performance Journal* (Fall 2000): 3–12.

41. "Fear of Flying," *Business Europe*, October 3, 2001, 2.

42. "VC at Nestlé," *Business Europe*, October 3, 2001, 3.

43. M. Roberti, "Meet Me on the Web," *Fortune: Tech Supplement*, Winter 2002, 10.

44. See also, J. A. Hoxmeier and K. A. Kozar, "Electronic Meetings and Subsequent Meeting Behavior: Systems as Agents of Change," *Journal of Applied Management Studies* (December 2000): 177–95.

45. See, for instance, P. Berthon, L. F. Pitt, and M. T. Ewing, "Corollaries of the Collective: The Influence of Organizational Culture and Memory Development on Perceived Decision-Making Context," *Academy of Marketing Science Journal* (Spring 2001): 135–50.

46. J. de Haan, M. Yamamoto, and G. Lovink, "Production Planning in Japan: Rediscovering Lost Experiences or New Insights,"

International Journal of Production Economics (May 6, 2001): 101–09.

47. T. M. Amabile, "Motivating Creativity in Organizations," *California Management Review* (Fall 1997): 39–58.

48. D. Dunne and R. Martin, "Design Thinking and How It Will Change Management Education: An Interview and Discussion," *Academy of Management Learning & Education*, December 2006, 512.

49. M. Korn and R. E. Silverman, "Forget B-School, D-School Is Hot," *Wall Street Journal*, June 7, 2012, B1+; R. Martin and J. Euchner, "Design Thinking," *Research Technology Management*, May/June 2012, 10–14; T. Larsen and T. Fisher, "Design Thinking: A Solution to Fracture-Critical Systems," *DMI News & Views*, May 2012, 31; T. Berno, "Design Thinking versus Creative Intelligence," *DMI News & Views*, May 2012, 28; J. Liedtka and Tim Ogilvie, "Helping Business Managers Discover Their Appetite for Design Thinking," *Design Management Review*, Issue 1, 2012, 6–13; and T. Brown, "Strategy by Design," *Fast Company*, June 2005, 52–54.

50. C. Guglielmo, "Apple Loop: The Week in Review," *Forbes.com*, May 25, 2012, 2.

51. D. Dunne and R. Martin, "Design Thinking and How It Will Change Management Education: An Interview and Discussion," 514.

52. K. Cukier and V. Mayer-Schönberger, "The Financial Bonanza of Big Data," *Wall Street Journal*, March 8, 2013, A15.

53. R. King and S. Rosenbush, "Big Data Broadens Its Range," *Wall Street Journal*, March 14, 2013, B5.

54. "Big Data, Big Impact: New Possibilities for International Development," *World Economic Forum*, weforum.org, 2012.

55. M. Kassel, "From a Molehill to a Mountain," *Wall Street Journal*, March 11, 2013, R1.

56. D. Laney, "The Importance of 'Big Data': A Definition," www.gartner.com/it-glossary/big-data/, March 22, 2013.

57. S. Lohr, "Sure, Big Data Is Great. But So Is Intuition," *New York Times Online*, December 29, 2012.

58. S. Rosenbush and L. Stevens, "At UPS, the Algorithm Is the Driver," *Wall Street Journal*, February 17, 2015, B1+; D. Zax, "Brown Down: UPS Drivers vs. the UPS Algorithm," http://www.fastcompany.com/3004319/brown-down-ups-drivers-vs-ups-algorithm, January 3, 2013; T. Bingham and P. Galagan, "Delivering 'On Time, Every Time' Knowledge and Skills to a World of Employees," *T&D*, July 2012, 32–37; J. Levitz, "UPS Thinks Outside the Box on Driver Training," *Wall Street Journal*, April 6, 2010, B1+; and K. Kingsbury, "Road to Recovery," *Time*, March 8, 2010, Global 14–Global 16.

59. Rosenbush and Stevens, "At UPS, the Algorithm Is the Driver."

60. Zax, "Brown Down: UPS Drivers vs. the UPS Algorithm."

61. Rosenbush and Laura Stevens, "At UPS, the Algorithm Is the Driver."

62. Hong Kong Jockey Club WebSite; P. Catton and C. Herrings, "Do Horses Really Need Jockeys?" *The Wall Street Journal*, www.wsj.com, May 3, 2012; McKenzie, "Space-age skyscrapers and sheiks: Racing's new world order," *CNN* Website, http://edition.cnn.com/2013/03/29/sport/dubai-world-cup-horse-racing/, March 29, 2013; C. Galofaro, "The Latest: Keep black cats away from Baffert," *Associated Press*, http://bigstory.ap.org/article/7c6d91b3926346b9b8989426a666044e/latest-fans-stream-churchill-downs-derby-day, May 3, 2015; A. Waller, J. Daniels, N. Weaver, P. Robinson, 2000. "Jockey injuries in the United States," Journal of the American Medical Association, 283(10), 1326–28; J. Roach, "The Science of Horse Racing," www.nbcnews.com, 2013.

63. D. D. Stanford, "Coke Has a Secret Formula for Orange Juice, Too," *Bloomberg Businessweek*, February 4–10, 2013, 19–20; P. Sellers, "The New Coke," *Fortune*, May 21, 2012, 138–44; and Adi Ignatious, "Shaking Things Up at Coca-Cola," *Harvard Business Review*, October 2011, 94–99.

Not all managers are leaders. But if an organization

can develop capable managers who are

also leaders, they

will be formidable competitors in any market.

learning objectives

After reading this chapter, you should be able to:

9-1   **Define** *leadership* and distinguish it from management.

9-2   **Summarize** early approaches to the study of leadership.

9-3   **Discuss** the concept of situational approaches to leadership.

9-4   **Describe** transformational and charismatic perspectives on leadership.

9-5   **Identify** and discuss leadership substitutes and neutralizers.

9-6   **Discuss** leaders as coaches and examine gender and cross-cultural issues in leadership.

9-7   **Describe** strategic leadership, ethical leadership, and virtual leadership.

9-8   **Relate** leadership to decision making and discuss both rational and behavioral perspectives on decision making.

Cinna-Yum

Perhaps you've been lucky enough to visit a Cinnabon bakery—the creator of a cinnamon bun on steroids. Cinnabon's signature product has been labelled a "gut bomb" by the *Dallas Observer*, but it's hard to deny the appeal. From the tender pastry, to their proprietary Indonesian korintje cinnamon and brown sugar mix, to the cream cheese topping, a Cinnabon is an indulgence that everyone should taste at least once. A Cinnabon fan described their appeal in a recent tweet, "Just ate a Cinnabon while staring through a window of a gym while watching people work out. This is what heroin must be like."

At the helm of Cinnabon is Kat Cole, the president since 2010. Kat's career path has been less than conventional. At 17, she took a job as a hostess at a Hooters restaurant in Jacksonville, Florida, becoming a waitress when she turned 18. Shortly after this, an impromptu strike by kitchen employees inspired Kat to exercise her leadership skills when she convinced several coworkers to join her in the kitchen. She explains, "If the food didn't get made, it wouldn't get delivered, and I wouldn't get paid, and I couldn't pay my bills. I did it because I wanted to be helpful. But I also did it because I was curious to see if I could do it." Cole continued to step up—she filled in when a bartender left early to pick up her child and when a manager was late and needed someone to open the restaurant. She quickly gained the eye of management, although she certainly didn't see Hooters as a career. She was working there to pay her bills while her goal was to complete a degree in engineering at the University of North Florida. It wasn't long, however, before Hooters recruited her to act as a trainer for other franchises and moved her into a regional manager position.

At the young age of 19, Cole was contacted by the corporate office—they wanted her to join a team opening the first Hooters franchise in Australia. "I had never been on a plane. I didn't have a passport, I had never been out of the country, and I had only been out of the state two times in my life for cheerleading competitions on a school bus. But despite all that, I still said yes." She returned from Australia and went on to assignments in Mexico City and Buenos Aires. By this time, Cole was just 20, but she realized that she would not be able to complete her undergraduate degree in engineering while pursuing this unexpected career. She bravely dropped out of college, moving full steam ahead with her prestigious, but lower-paying job. Fortunately, the move from the restaurant to the corporate office paid off and she was vice president by age 26.

Along the way, Cole broadened her knowledge base by networking. She joined the Women's Foodservice Forum and began to see that it was possible for a woman to become a CEO. She volunteered on committees and nurtured relationships with people she

Chunumunu/Fotolia

what's in it for me?

Is your boss a manager? A leader? What does she or he do to inspire you to work harder? Do you aspire to be a manager or a leader? When you have a leadership position, what will you do to inspire your employees to work harder? Do you think management and leadership are the same thing? These are some of the issues we'll explore in this chapter. In Chapter 8, we described the primary determinants of employee behavior and noted that managers can influence the behavior and enhance the motivation of employees. Now it's time to examine in detail how leaders—who may or may not also be managers such as Kat Cole—actually go about influencing employee behavior and motivating employee performance. We will place these strategies and tactics in the context of various approaches to leadership through the years, including the situational perspective accepted today. Understanding these concepts will help you function more effectively as a leader and give you more insight into how your manager or boss strives to motivate you through his or her own leadership.

We start this chapter by taking a look at the nature of leadership. We then describe early approaches to leadership, as well as the situational perspective accepted today. Next, we examine leadership through the eyes of followers as well as alternatives to leadership. The changing nature of leadership and emerging issues in leadership are discussed next. Finally, we describe the important related concept of decision making.

met. While her involvement in the WFF was voluntary and unpaid, she sees it as a key to her success. "Because I was being curious and helpful ... I amassed a resume of leadership skills that I never would have gotten that fast if I only worked one job." She also was the cofounder of Changers for Commerce, "a group of leaders that identify with mixing money and meaning and making as much of a difference in the world as they make a profit." These experiences help to shape Cole at a young age. She explains to *Real Simple* magazine, "I always had a bit of insecurity because I had dropped out of college, so as I moved up, I would get every certification I could. And I started volunteering in industry groups. I ended up getting on boards of directors of nonprofits at a very young age. That gave me leadership experience and it helped me build relationships."

By 2010, Hooters was being sold and Cole was approached by a number of organizations, in spite of the fact that she had not yet completed her MBA. Ultimately, she decided to take a position as Group President for Cinnabon, which has more than 1,000 stores in 35 countries. Cinnabon is just one of the brands behind Atlanta-based FOCUS brands. In addition to Cinnabon, FOCUS operates Carvel, Scholotzsky's, Moe's Southwest Grill, Auntie Anne's, and McAlister's Deli.

Cole provides keen insight into what it takes to be a leader. Throughout her career, Cole has demonstrated her leadership skills by focusing on meeting the needs of customers and employees rather than trying to impress her boss. In a post to the Leadership Online community, she explains, "Your boss wants to see results, the right relationships being built, and an approach that is complementary to the company's culture. Be clear on any early objectives and align your time and focus with those. And one more thing: If results are one of the most important drivers for perceived success, it's typically your team and your customers that help you deliver results much more so than your boss—don't ever forget that." In addition, Cole encourages leaders to be careful how they measure success. "Rarely do people question success in the same way they do failure. That's a mistake. When you fail, the lessons smack you in the face. But you might misdiagnose the things that drive success. I learned that in restaurants. People would say, 'That manager is so great. His restaurant is up 50 percent,' when he's a really bad manager and they're just located on a street with a new strip mall. You can reward the wrong behaviors and duplicate the wrong things if you don't dig deep behind success."[1] (After studying the content of this chapter, you should be able to answer the set of discussion questions found at the end of the chapter.)

Define

leadership and distinguish it from management.

Leadership *the processes and behaviors used by someone, such as a manager, to motivate, inspire, and influence the behaviors of others*

The Nature of Leadership

Because *leadership* is a term that is often used in everyday conversation, you might assume that it has a common and accepted meaning. It is also, however, a word that is often misused. We define **leadership** as the processes and behaviors used by someone, such as a manager, to motivate, inspire, and influence the behaviors of others.

Leadership and Management

One of the biggest errors people make is assuming that leadership and management mean the same thing when they are really different concepts. A person can be a manager, a leader, both, or neither.[2] Some of the basic distinctions between the two are summarized in Figure 9.1. As illustrated in the circle on the left, management (as discussed in Chapter 5) focuses primarily on the activities of planning, organizing, leading, and controlling. Leadership, in contrast, is much more closely related to activities such as agenda setting, aligning, inspiring, and monitoring. As also illustrated in the figure, management and leadership may occasionally overlap but each

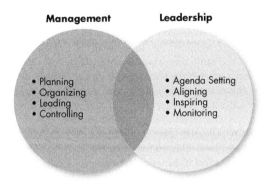

Management   **Leadership**

- Planning
- Organizing
- Leading
- Controlling

- Agenda Setting
- Aligning
- Inspiring
- Monitoring

FIGURE 9.1 Distinctions between Management and Leadership

is also a discrete and separate set of activities. Hence, a person may be a manager (but not a leader), a leader (but not a manager), or both a manager and a leader.

Consider the various roles of managers and leaders in a hospital setting. The chief of staff (chief physician) of a large hospital, though clearly a manager by virtue of his position, may not be respected or trusted by others and may have to rely solely on the authority vested in the position to get people to do things. On the other hand, a nurse in the emergency department with no formal authority may be quite effective at taking charge of a chaotic situation and directing others in dealing with specific patient problems. The chief of staff is a manager but not really a leader, whereas the nurse is a leader but not really a manager.

Finally, the head of pediatrics, supervising a staff of 20 other doctors, nurses, and attendants, may also enjoy the staff's complete respect, confidence, and trust. They readily take her advice, follow directives without question, and often go far beyond what is necessary to help carry out the unit's mission. Thus, the head of pediatrics is both a manager (by virtue of the position she occupies) and a leader (by virtue of the respect she commands from others and their willingness to follow her direction).

Organizations need both management and leadership if they are to be effective. Management in conjunction with leadership can help achieve planned orderly change, and leadership in conjunction with management can keep the organization properly aligned with its environment.

Leadership and Power

To fully understand leadership, it is also necessary to understand *power*. **Power** is the ability to affect the behavior of others. Of course, one can have power without actually using it. For example, a football coach has the power to bench a player who is not performing up to par. The coach seldom has to use this power because players recognize that the power exists and work hard to keep their starting positions. In organizational settings, there are usually five kinds of power: legitimate, reward, coercive, referent, and expert power.[3]

Legitimate power is power granted through the organizational hierarchy; it is the power defined by the organization to be accorded to people occupying a particular position. A manager can assign tasks to a subordinate, and a subordinate who refuses to do them can be reprimanded or even fired. Such outcomes stem from the manager's legitimate power as defined and vested in her or him by the organization. Legitimate power, then, is authority. All managers have legitimate power over their subordinates. The mere possession of legitimate power, however, does not by itself make someone a leader. Some subordinates follow only orders that are strictly within the letter of organizational rules and policies. If asked to do something not in their job descriptions, they refuse or do a poor job. The manager of such employees is exercising authority but not leadership.

Power the ability to affect the behavior of others

Legitimate Power power granted through the organizational hierarchy

Reward Power *the power to give or withhold rewards*

Reward power is the power to give or withhold rewards. Rewards that a manager may control include salary increases, bonuses, promotion recommendations, praise, recognition, and interesting job assignments. In general, the greater the number of rewards a manager controls and the more important the rewards are to subordinates, the greater is the manager's reward power. If the subordinate values only the formal organizational rewards provided by the manager, then the manager is not a leader. If the subordinate also wants and appreciates the manager's informal rewards, such as praise, gratitude, and recognition, however, then the manager is also exercising leadership.

Coercive Power *the power to force compliance by means of psychological, emotional, or physical threat*

Coercive power is the power to force compliance by means of psychological, emotional, or physical threat. Physical coercion in organizations was once relatively common. In most organizations today, however, coercion is limited to verbal reprimands, written reprimands, disciplinary layoffs, fines, demotion, and termination. Some managers occasionally go so far as to use verbal abuse, humiliation, and psychological coercion in an attempt to manipulate subordinates. (Of course, most people agree that these are not appropriate managerial behaviors.) James Dutt, a "legendary" former CEO of a major company, once told a subordinate that if his wife and family got in the way of his working a 24-hour day seven days a week, he should get rid of them.[4] More recently, Charlie Ergen, founder and Chairman of the Board of Dish Network, has a reputation for yelling at employees, belittling managers in front of their peers, and imposing harsh penalties on those who disagree with him.[5] The more punitive the elements under a manager's control and the more important they are to subordinates, the more coercive power the manager possesses. On the other hand, the more a manager uses coercive power, the more likely he is to provoke resentment and hostility and the less likely he is to be seen as a leader.[6]

Referent Power *power based on identification, imitation, loyalty, or charisma*

Compared with legitimate, reward, and coercive power, which are relatively concrete and grounded in objective facets of organizational life, **referent power** is abstract. It is based on identification, imitation, loyalty, or charisma. Followers may react favorably because they identify in some way with a leader, who may be like them in personality, background, or attitudes. In other situations, followers might choose to imitate a leader with referent power by wearing the same kind of clothes, working the same hours, or espousing the same management philosophy. Referent power may also take the form of charisma, an intangible attribute of the leader that inspires loyalty and enthusiasm. Thus, a manager might have referent power, but it is more likely to be associated with leadership.

Expert Power *power derived from information or expertise*

Expert power is derived from information or expertise. A manager who knows how to interact with an eccentric but important customer, a scientist who is capable of achieving an important technical breakthrough that no other company has dreamed of, and an administrative assistant who knows how to unravel bureaucratic red tape all have expert power over anyone who needs that information. The more important the information and the fewer the people who have access to it, the greater is the degree of expert power possessed by any one individual. In general, people who are both leaders and managers tend to have a large amount of expert power.

OBJECTIVE 9-2
Summarize

early approaches to the study of leadership.

Early Approaches to Leadership

Although leaders and leadership have profoundly influenced history, careful scientific study of them began only about a century ago. Early studies focused on the *traits*, or personal characteristics, of leaders. Later research shifted to examine actual leader *behaviors*.

Trait Approaches to Leadership

Trait Approach to Leadership *focused on identifying the essential traits that distinguished leaders*

Early researchers believed that notable leaders had some unique set of qualities or traits that distinguished them from their peers and endured throughout history. This **trait approach to leadership** led researchers to focus on identifying the essential leadership traits, including intelligence, dominance, self-confidence, energy, activity

Bettmann/Corbis

MPVHistory/Alamy

GL Archive/Alamy

Dinodia Photo/AGE Fotostock

When asked to identify important leaders, people often mention influential historical figures such as Winston Churchill, Abraham Lincoln, Martin Luther King, Jr., and Mother Teresa.

(versus passivity), and knowledge about the job. Unfortunately, the list of potential leadership traits quickly became so long that it lost any practical value. In addition, the results of many studies were inconsistent. For example, one argument stated that the most effective leaders were tall, like Abraham Lincoln. But critics were quick to point out that neither Napoleon Bonaparte nor Adolf Hitler was tall, but both were effective leaders in their own way.

Although the trait approach was all but abandoned several decades ago, in recent years, it has resurfaced. For example, some researchers have again started to focus on a limited set of traits. These traits include emotional intelligence, mental intelligence, drive, motivation, honesty and integrity, self-confidence, knowledge of the business, and charisma. Some people even believe that biological factors, such as appearance or height, may play a role in leadership. However, it is too early to know whether these traits really do relate to leadership.

Behavioral Approaches to Leadership

In the late 1940s, most researchers began to shift away from the trait approach and to look at leadership as a set of actual behaviors. The goal of the **behavioral approach to leadership** was to determine what *behaviors* were employed by effective leaders. These researchers assumed that the behaviors of effective leaders differed somehow from the behaviors of less effective leaders, and that the behaviors of effective leaders would be the same across all situations.

This research led to the identification of two basic forms of leader behavior. Although different researchers applied different names, the following are the basic leader behaviors identified during this period:

- **Task-focused leader behavior:** Task-focused leader behavior occurs when a leader focuses on how tasks should be performed to meet certain goals and to achieve certain performance standards.

- **Employee-focused leader behavior:** Employee-focused leader behavior occurs when a leader focuses on the satisfaction, motivation, and well-being of his or her employees.

During this period, people believed that leaders should always try to engage in a healthy dose of both behaviors, one to increase performance and the other to increase job satisfaction and motivation. Experts also began to realize that they could train

Behavioral Approach to Leadership *focused on determining what behaviors are employed by leaders*

Task-Focused Leader Behavior *leader behavior focusing on how tasks should be performed to meet certain goals and to achieve certain performance standards*

Employee-Focused Leader Behavior *leader behavior focusing on satisfaction, motivation, and well-being of employees*

managers to engage in these behaviors in a systematic manner. But they also discovered that other leader behaviors needed to be considered, and that, in some circumstances, different combinations of leader behaviors might be more effective than other combinations.

For instance, suppose a new manager takes over a work site that is plagued by low productivity and whose workers, although perhaps satisfied, are not motivated to work hard. The leader should most likely emphasize task-focused behaviors to improve lagging productivity. But suppose the situation is different—productivity is high, but workers are stressed out about their jobs and have low levels of job satisfaction. In this instance, the manager should most likely concentrate on employee-focused behaviors to help improve job satisfaction. This line of thinking led to the development of *situational theories*.

The Situational Approach to Leadership

OBJECTIVE 9-3
Discuss
the concept of situational approaches to leadership.

Situational Approach to Leadership *assumes that appropriate leader behavior varies from one situation to another*

The **situational approach to leadership** assumes that appropriate leader behavior varies from one situation to another, as shown in Figure 9.2. The trait and behavioral approaches to leadership were both universal in nature. They attempted to prescribe leader behaviors that would lead to a set of universal set of outcomes and consequences. For instance, proponents of these universal perspectives might argue that tall and intelligent people or people who are consistently employee-focused will always be good leaders. In reality, though, research has found this simply is not true. So, the situational approach to leadership attempts to identify various forms of leader behavior that result in contingent outcomes and consequences. By contingent, we mean that they depend on elements of the situation and characteristics of both the leader and followers.

Consider, for example, how Jeff Smisek, CEO of United Airlines, has to vary his leadership style when he is interacting with different kinds of people. When he is dealing with investors, he has to convey an impression of confidence about the company's financial picture. When he interacts with union officials, he needs to take a firm stand on cost control combined with collaboration. Smisek often speaks to leaders at other

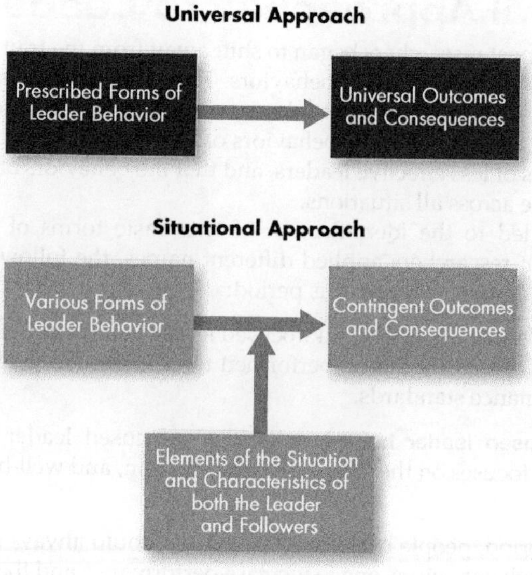

FIGURE 9.2 The Situational Approach to Leadership

airlines and has to balance their mutual interests against United's own competitive situation. And when dealing with customers, he has to be charming and respectful.

Leadership characteristics include the manager's value system, confidence in subordinates, personal inclinations, feelings of security, and actual behaviors. Subordinate characteristics include the subordinates' need for independence, readiness to assume responsibility, tolerance for ambiguity, interest in the problem, understanding of goals, knowledge, experience, and expectations. Situational characteristics that affect decision making include the type of organization, group effectiveness, the problem itself, and time pressures. Three important situational approaches to leadership are (1) the *path–goal theory*, (2) the *decision tree approach*, and (3) the *leader–member exchange model*.

The **path–goal theory** of leadership is a direct extension of the expectancy theory of motivation discussed in Chapter 8.[7] Recall that the primary components of expectancy theory include the likelihood of attaining various outcomes and the value associated with those outcomes. The path–goal theory of leadership suggests that the primary functions of a leader are to make valued or desired rewards available in the workplace and to clarify for the subordinate the kinds of behavior that will lead to goal accomplishment and valued rewards. The leader should clarify the paths to goal attainment.

> **Path–Goal Theory** *theory of leadership that is a direct extension of the expectancy theory of motivation*

Path–goal theory identifies four kinds of behaviors that leaders can use, depending on the situation. *Directive leader behavior* lets subordinates know what is expected of them, gives guidance and direction, and schedules work. *Supportive leader behavior* is being friendly and approachable, showing concern for subordinates' welfare, and treating members as equals. *Participative leader behavior* includes consulting with subordinates, soliciting suggestions, and allowing participation in decision making. *Achievement-oriented leader behavior* sets challenging goals, expects subordinates to perform at high levels, encourages subordinates, and shows confidence in subordinates' abilities.

Another major contemporary approach to leadership is the **decision tree approach**. Like the path–goal theory, this approach attempts to prescribe a leadership style appropriate to a given situation. It also assumes that the same leader may display different leadership styles. But the decision tree approach concerns itself with only a single aspect of leader behavior: subordinate participation in decision making. The decision tree approach assumes that the degree to which subordinates should be encouraged to participate in decision making depends on the characteristics of the situation. In other words, no one decision-making process is best for all situations. After evaluating a variety of problem attributes (characteristics of the problem or decision), the leader determines an appropriate decision style that specifies the amount of subordinate participation.

> **Decision Tree Approach** *approach to leadership that provides decision rules for deciding how much participation to allow*

The **leader–member exchange (LMX) model** stresses the importance of variable relationships between supervisors and each of their subordinates.[8] Each superior-subordinate pair represents a "vertical dyad." The model differs from previous approaches in that it focuses on the differential relationship leaders often establish with different subordinates. This model suggests that supervisors establish a special relationship with a small number of trusted subordinates, referred to as "the in-group." The in-group usually receives special duties requiring responsibility and autonomy; they may also receive special privileges. Subordinates who are not a part of this group are called "the out-group," and they receive less of the supervisor's time and attention. However, the key element of this theory is the concept of individual vertical dyads and how leaders have different relationships with each of their subordinates.

> **Leader–Member Exchange (LMX) Model** *approach to leadership that stresses the importance of variable relationships between supervisors and each of their subordinates*

Leadership Through the Eyes of Followers

Another recent perspective that has been adopted by some leadership experts focuses on how leaders are seen through the eyes of their followers. The two primary approaches to leadership through the eyes of followers are *transformational leadership*

OBJECTIVE 9-4
Describe
transformational and charismatic perspectives on leadership.

and *charismatic leadership*. Barack Obama's successful bid for the U.S. presidency was fueled in part by many people's perceptions that he was both a transformational and charismatic leader. Indeed, during both of his campaigns, he frequently talked about the need to transform the way the United States addressed issues such as health care, education, and foreign policy. His personal charisma undoubtedly attracted support from many people as well.

Transformational Leadership

Transformational leadership focuses on the importance of leading for change (as opposed to leading during a period of stability). According to this view, much of what a leader does involves carrying out what might be thought of as basic management "transactions," such as assigning work, evaluating performance, and making decisions. Occasionally, however, the leader has to engage in transformational leadership to initiate and manage major change, such as managing a merger, creating a new work team, or redefining the organization's culture.

Transformational Leadership *the set of abilities that allows a leader to recognize the need for change, to create a vision to guide that change, and to execute the change effectively*

Transactional Leadership *comparable to management, it involves routine, regimented activities*

Thus, **transformational leadership** is the set of abilities that allows a leader to recognize the need for change, to create a vision to guide that change, and to execute the change effectively. Some experts believe that change is such a vital organizational function that even successful firms need to change regularly to avoid becoming complacent and stagnant. In contrast, **transactional leadership** is essentially the same as management in that it involves routine, regimented activities. Only a leader with tremendous influence can hope to perform both functions successfully. Accordingly, leadership for change is extremely important.

Some leaders are able to adopt either transformational or transactional perspectives, depending on their circumstances. For instance, when Jeff Bezos started Amazon.com, his strategy was to simply sell books through an online "store." When Amazon developed sustainable revenues, he used transactional leadership to slowly grow the business and build cash reserves. Bezos then adopted a transformational style as he led the company to become a major online "retailer" of thousands of different products. He then reverted to a transactional approach to again let the business entrench itself. More recently, Bezos has again been using transformational leadership as Amazon develops new methods for product distribution, explores new product lines and extensions, and tries to position itself as a competitor for Apple and Google.

Charismatic Leadership

Charismatic Leadership *type of influence based on the leader's personal charisma*

Charismatic leadership is a type of influence based on the leader's charisma, a form of interpersonal attraction that inspires support and acceptance. Charismatic leaders are likely to have a lot of confidence in their beliefs and ideals and a strong need to influence people. They also tend to communicate high expectations about follower performance and to express confidence in their followers. Many of the most influential leaders in history have been extremely charismatic, including entrepreneurs Mary Kay Ash, Steve Jobs, and Ted Turner; civil rights leader Martin Luther King, Jr.; and Pope John Paul II. Unfortunately, charisma can also empower leaders in other directions. Adolf Hitler, for instance, had strong charismatic qualities.

Most experts today acknowledge three crucial elements of charismatic leadership:[9]

1 Charismatic leaders envision likely future trends and patterns, set high expectations for themselves and for others, and behave in ways that meet or exceed those expectations.

2 Charismatic leaders energize others by demonstrating personal excitement, personal confidence, and consistent patterns of success.

3 Charismatic leaders enable others by supporting them, empathizing with them, and expressing confidence in them.

entrepreneurship and new ventures

"Success Unshared Is Failure"

John Paul DeJoria is the charismatic leader behind John Paul Mitchell Systems, which produces and distributes Paul Mitchell hair care products, and the Patron Spirits Company. His net worth has been estimated at more than $4 billion. However, unlike many of those on the Forbes 400 list of wealthiest Americans, DeJoria did not inherit wealth or privilege. He grew up in a working-class neighborhood and had his first job selling Christmas cards door-to-door at age 9. After graduating from high school and serving in the Navy, DeJoria began selling encyclopedias and quickly moved through ten jobs in just a couple of years. Eventually, he moved into sales in the beauty industry and quickly found his niche. However, after nine years of success in the industry, he lost his job when his commissions began to exceed the pay of the owner of the company.

In 1980, DeJoria was homeless, living in an old Rolls Royce in LA. He had just invested all of his savings—amounting to just $700—in Paul Mitchell, which he cofounded with the company's namesake. With a bare-bones budget, they sold their products door-to-door in hair salons. While others might have given up, DeJoria believed in their products and was persistent. In a 2013 interview with *Forbes* magazine, he advises, "Be prepared for the rejection. No matter how bad it is, don't let it overcome you and influence you—keep on going towards what you want to do—no matter what. You need to be as enthusiastic about door number one hundred as door number one." While the first two years were difficult, they had almost $1 million in annual sales in their third year of operation. Today, the company's products are sold in more than 150,000 beauty salons in 87 countries.

DeJoria is a serial entrepreneur, having started more than a dozen businesses, including House of Blues, DeJoria Diamonds, and Gustin Energy Company. Although he started Patron Spirits in 1989 as a hobby with friend Martin Crowley, the business quickly got more serious. They wanted to create a market for high-end tequila and selected a hand-blown bottle and expensive blue agave as the base. Building on DeJoria's connections, Patron quickly became a well-recognized brand. DeJoria's good friend Clint Eastwood put Patron in his movie *In the Line of Fire,* and chef Wolfgang Puck began touting it to his friends and business contacts.

In each of his businesses, DeJoria makes high quality and sustainability a priority. In his interview with *Fortune* magazine, he explains, "A lot of people make things to sell. But when the product is old, the consumer tosses it out and buys something else. If you make things with the highest quality, you'll be in the reorder business, which keeps the sales growing." Sustainability is a common thread, from his investment in environmentally responsible oil and gas exploration with Gustin Energy Company to sales of conflict-free

Nicholas Kamm/Staff/Getty Images

diamonds through DeJoria Diamonds. This theme is also a big part of the Paul Mitchell product line, "We looked at costs in our warehouse system—everything from what doors we can shut to what lights we can change. We found ways to create a 25 percent savings in our power costs. We plant trees to offset our Tea Tree shampoo line to make up for the carbon that we use. It's good for the world and good for business."

While much of DeJoria's success can be attributed to hard work, his charisma and message inspire others. One of his mottos is "Success unshared is failure." He is committed to giving back through organizations such as Habitat for Humanity and Food4Africa. He is also the founder of Grow Appalachia, an organization that helps those in rural areas to overcome food insecurity by growing their own food. Not surprisingly, DeJoria signed Warren Buffett and Bill Gates' Giving Pledge, through which the world's wealthiest citizens commit to giving most of their wealth to philanthropy.[10]

Charismatic leadership ideas are quite popular among managers today and are the subject of numerous books and articles.[11] Unfortunately, few studies have specifically attempted to test the meaning and impact of charismatic leadership. Lingering ethical concerns about charismatic leadership also trouble some people. They stem from the fact that some charismatic leaders inspire such blind faith in their followers that they may engage in inappropriate, unethical, or even illegal behaviors just because the leader instructed them to do so. This tendency likely played a role in the unwinding of both Enron and Arthur Andersen because people followed orders from their charismatic bosses to hide information, shred documents, and mislead investigators.

Taking over a leadership role from someone with substantial personal charisma is also a challenge. For instance, the immediate successors to successful and charismatic athletic coaches such as Vince Lombardi (Green Bay Packers) and Phil Jackson (Chicago Bulls) each failed to measure up to their predecessors' legacies and were subsequently fired.

OBJECTIVE 9-5
Identify
and discuss leadership
substitutes and neutralizers.

Special Issues in Leadership

Another interesting perspective on leadership focuses on *alternatives* to leadership. In some cases, certain factors may actually *substitute* for leadership, making actual leadership unnecessary or irrelevant. In other cases, factors may exist that *neutralize* or negate the influence of a leader even when that individual is attempting to exercise leadership.

Leadership Substitutes

Leadership Substitutes *individual, task, and organizational characteristics that tend to outweigh the need for a leader to initiate or direct employee performance*

Leadership substitutes are individual, task, and organizational characteristics that tend to outweigh the need for a leader to initiate or direct employee performance. In other words, if certain factors are present, the employee will perform his or her job capably, without the direction of a leader. Table 9.1 identifies several basic leadership substitutes.

Consider, for example, what happens when an ambulance with a critically injured victim screeches to the door of a hospital emergency department. Do the emergency department employees stand around waiting for someone to take control and instruct

table 9.1 Leadership Substitutes and Neutralizers

Individual factors	• Individual professionalism • Individual ability, knowledge, and motivation • Individual experience and training • Indifference to rewards
Job factors	• Structured/automated • Highly controlled • Intrinsically satisfying • Embedded feedback
Organization factors	• Explicit plans and goals • Rigid rules and procedures • Rigid reward system not tied to performance • Physical distance between supervisor and subordinate
Group factors	• Group performance norms • High level of group cohesiveness • Group interdependence

them on what to do? The answer is no: They are highly trained, well-prepared professionals who know how to respond and work together as a team without someone playing the role of leader. When a U.S. Airways flight crashed into the Hudson River in 2009, all members of the flight crew knew exactly what to do, without waiting for orders. As a result of their effective and prompt actions, a disaster was averted, and all passengers on the plane were quickly rescued.

Leadership Neutralizers

In other situations, even if a leader is present and attempts to engage in various leadership behaviors, those behaviors may be rendered ineffective—or neutralized—by various factors that can be called **leadership neutralizers**. Suppose, for example, that a relatively new and inexperienced leader is assigned to a work group composed of experienced employees with long-standing performance norms and a high level of group cohesiveness. The norms and cohesiveness of the group may be so strong that there is nothing the new leader can do to change things.

Leadership Neutralizers *factors that may render leader behaviors ineffective*

In addition to group factors, elements of the job itself may also limit a leader's ability to "make a difference." Consider, for example, employees working on a moving assembly line. Employees may only be able to work at the pace of the moving line, so performance quantity and quality are constrained by the speed of the line and simplicity of each individual task.

Finally, organizational factors can also neutralize at least some forms of leader behavior. Suppose a new leader is accustomed to using merit pay increases as a way to motivate people. But in his or her new job, pay increases are dictated by union contracts and are based primarily on employee seniority and cost of living. The leader's previous approach to motivating people would be neutralized, and new approaches would have to be identified.

The Changing Nature of Leadership

OBJECTIVE 9-6
Discuss
leaders as coaches and examine gender and cross-cultural issues in leadership.

Various alternatives to leadership aside, many settings still call for at least some degree of leadership, although the nature of that leadership continues to evolve. Among the recent changes in leadership that managers should recognize are the increasing role of *leaders as coaches* as well as *gender and cross-cultural patterns* of leader behavior.

Leaders as Coaches

We noted in Chapter 6 that many organizations today are using teams. Many other organizations are attempting to become less hierarchical by eliminating the old-fashioned command-and-control mentality often inherent in bureaucratic organizations and motivating and empowering individuals to work independently. In each case, the role of leaders is also changing. Whereas leaders were once expected to control situations, direct work, supervise people, closely monitor performance, make decisions, and structure activities, many leaders today are being asked to change how they manage people. Perhaps the best description of this new role is for the leader to become a *coach* instead of an *overseer*.[12]

From the standpoint of a business leader, a coaching perspective would call for the leader to help select and train team members and other new employees, to provide some general direction, and to help the team get the information and other resources it needs. Coaches from different teams may play important roles in linking the activities and functions of their respective teams. Some leaders may function as *mentors*, helping less experienced employees learn the ropes and better preparing them to advance within the organization; they may also help resolve conflicts among team members and mediate other disputes that arise. But beyond these activities, the leader keeps a low profile and lets the group get its work done with little or no direct oversight, just as during a game, an athletic coach trusts his or her players to execute the plays successfully.

Jeff Bezos, founder and CEO of Amazon.com, often plays the role of coach. He likes to focus on long-term, strategic issues and leave the daily management of Amazon.com to senior managers. But their decisions must also be consistent with his vision for the firm. As a result, he works with them on a regular basis to help them develop their decision-making skills and to equip them with the information they need to help lead the firm in the directions he has set.

Gender and Leadership

Another factor that is clearly altering the face of leadership is the growing number of women advancing to higher levels in organizations. Given that most leadership theories and research studies have focused on male leaders, developing a better understanding of how women lead is clearly an important next step. Some early observers, for instance, predicted that (consistent with prevailing stereotypes) female leaders would be relatively warm, supportive, and nurturing as compared to their male counterparts. But research suggests that female leaders are not necessarily more nurturing or supportive than male leaders. Likewise, male leaders are not systematically harsher, more controlling, or more task focused than female leaders.

The one difference that has arisen in some cases is that women may be slightly more democratic in making decisions, whereas men have a tendency to be more autocratic.[13] However, much more work needs to be done to better understand the

finding a better way

Leading Like a Woman

In a workforce that has been historically dominated by men, much of the research of leadership has focused on men and the ways in which they lead. As more women entered the workforce, research began to evolve and turned to evaluating the differences between men and women as leaders. Unfortunately, many of the conclusions were focused on ways that women could adapt their innate style to be more like men. Ruzwana Bashir, cofounder of the travel site Peek and former Goldman Sachs employee, would beg to differ. As she began her career in the financial services industry, she felt pressure to act more like her male counterparts. At the Forbes Under 30 summit, she explains, "In that environment as a woman, you can feel crowd-forced to conform." While earning her MBA at Harvard's Business School as a Fulbright Scholar, she realized that traditionally feminine attributes can be an advantage. "Those 'female' traits of empathy and compassion—of being collaborate—are true business strengths."

Bashir has made a huge mark at an early age. Born in Pakistan, she was educated in the United Kingdom and studied at Oxford University. At Oxford, she became president of the Oxford Union, a debating society famed for hosting speakers as famous as Senator John McCain and fashion designer Tom Ford. In 2012, she and cofounder Oskar Bruening launched Peek.com. Although there are already several travel websites, Peek occupies a unique space in the market. Peek

David Hartley/REX/Newscom

helps travelers to plan the perfect trip, including itineraries for a "Perfect Day" in your destination.

At Peek.com, the company has maintained a staffing mix of 50 percent men and 50 percent women, with considerable ethnic diversity. Bashir encourages female employees and introduces them to mentors. She also practices what she preaches—allowing herself to show vulnerability rather than presenting the traditionally male decisive and authoritative style. Embracing her femininity as an asset even extends to her appearance, as Bashir explains, "Don't wear that boxy trouser suit because you feel like you have to. Wear whatever you want."[14]

dynamics of gender and leadership. In the meantime, high-profile and successful female leaders, such as Indra Nooyi (CEO of PepsiCo), Sherilyn McCoy (CEO of Avon Products), and Angela Merkel (chancellor of Germany), continue to demonstrate the effectiveness with which women can be exceptional leaders.

Cross-Cultural Leadership

Another changing perspective on leadership relates to cross-cultural issues. In this context, *culture* is used as a broad concept to encompass both international differences and diversity-based differences within one culture. For instance, Japan is generally characterized by *collectivism* (group before individual), whereas the United States is based more on *individualism* (individual before group). So when a Japanese firm sends an executive to head up the firm's operation in the United States, that person will likely find it necessary to recognize the importance of individual contributions and rewards and the differences in individual and group roles that exist in Japanese and U.S. businesses.

For instance, Carlos Ghosn runs both Renault (an Italian car company) and Nissan (a Japanese car company). Ghosn knows that cultural differences cause his European managers to expect him to lead in certain ways, whereas his Japanese managers expect him to lead in slightly different ways. More specifically, in Europe, leaders must often be aggressive, and meetings are often characterized by loud verbal exchanges and arguments. In Japan, though, more emphasis is put on consensus building and polite exchanges of dialogue.

Similarly, cross-cultural factors also play a growing role in organizations as their workforces become more diverse. As African Americans, Asian Americans, Hispanics, and members of other ethnic groups achieve leadership positions, it may be necessary to reassess how applicable current theories and models of leadership are when applied to an increasingly diverse pool of leaders.

Emerging Issues in Leadership

OBJECTIVE 9-7
Describe
strategic leadership, ethical leadership, and virtual leadership.

Finally, three emerging issues in leadership warrant discussion. These issues are *strategic leadership*, *ethical leadership*, and *virtual leadership*.

Strategic Leadership

Strategic leadership is a new concept that explicitly relates leadership to the role of top management. **Strategic leadership** is a leader's ability to understand the complexities of both the organization and its environment and to lead change in the organization so as to enhance its competitiveness. Howard Schutz, CEO of Starbucks, is recognized as a strong strategic leader. Not content to continue functioning as "simply" a coffee retailer, Schutz is always on the lookout for new opportunities and how Starbucks can effectively exploit those opportunities.

Strategic Leadership *leader's ability to understand the complexities of both the organization and its environment and to lead change in the organization so as to enhance its competitiveness*

To be effective as a strategic leader, a manager needs to have a thorough and complete understanding of the organization—its history, its culture, its strengths, and its weaknesses. In addition, the leader needs a firm grasp of the organization's external environment. This understanding needs to include current business and economic conditions and circumstances as well as significant trends and issues on the horizon. The strategic leader also needs to recognize the firm's current strategic advantages and shortcomings.

Ethical Leadership

Most people have long assumed that business leaders are ethical people. But in the wake of corporate scandals at firms such as Enron, Boeing, and AIG, faith in business leaders has been shaken. Perhaps now more than ever, high standards of ethical conduct are being held up as a prerequisite for effective leadership. More specifically, business leaders are being called on to maintain high ethical standards for their own conduct, to unfailingly exhibit ethical behavior, and to hold others in their organizations to the same standards—in short, to practice **ethical leadership**.

Ethical Leadership *leader behaviors that reflect high ethical standards*

The behaviors of top leaders are being scrutinized more than ever, and those responsible for hiring new leaders for a business are looking more closely at the backgrounds of those being considered. The emerging pressures for stronger corporate governance models are likely to further increase the commitment to select only those individuals with high ethical standards for leadership positions in business and to hold them more accountable than in the past for both their actions and the consequences of those actions.

managing in turbulent times

Leading in a Virtual World

One of the most important challenges facing managers today is their ability to lead in a virtual world. Toward this end, the Association for Talent Development (ASTD) explored the challenges facing leaders in a workshop for members in India. Virtual work environments can take many forms—from employees telecommuting on a part-time or full-time basis to a geographically dispersed workforce that crosses cultures and time zones.

In a survey conducted for the purposes of this workshop, ASTD conducted a survey to determine the most important leadership skills for a "co-located environment." The top responses included the ability to do the following:

- Set clear goals and measurements for projects.

- Provide a consistent focus on the big picture.

- Operate in a highly complex environment.

- Promote and stimulate organizational commitment.

Some of the challenges facing virtual leaders include the potential feelings of isolation for remote workers. Lack of face-to-face contact can limit the clarity of communication and also can act as a barrier to organizational commitment. Isolation becomes even more of an issue when employees are spread across multiple time zones, challenging the ability of a work team to collaborate effectively.

In spite of the special challenges associated with virtual leadership, some things remain the same. One interviewee for the ASTD study made this clear, stating, "Leadership is leadership. Being authentic, connecting with others, promoting inclusiveness, networking, and all of the interpersonal skills that build relationships and trust are always important." Leaders cannot rely upon frequent, casual contact to build a shared vision in a virtual environment. Instead, leaders must be planned, disciplined, deliberate, and intentional about reaching out to employees on a regular basis.

The ASTD concluded that several best practices are associated with virtual leadership. First, and most important,

Syda Productions/Fotolia

effective communication is essential. Virtual leaders must learn to use multiple channels to communicate, including phone, e-mail, instant messaging, and video conferencing, and must appropriately match the media channel to the message. In addition, communication must be part of a two-way process that includes active listening. The second-best practice identified by ASTD was team building. When your team is geographically dispersed, it's essential that leaders plan intentional team-building activities, including structured work-related events as well as more casual social events, if possible. Finally, leaders must establish the ground rules for their organizations. The unwritten rules of corporate culture are harder to communicate in the virtual world, so it's important to be clear about work-hour expectations as well as risk tolerance. The authors of the ASTD 2013 report arrive at a very important conclusion: "While at first glance it may seem that all the same leadership skills are needed, it may be that leaders in a virtual environment need just a little more of everything: more knowledge of technology, more knowledge on how to work with team dynamics, stronger communication skills, and, of course, a little more patience."[15]

Virtual Leadership

Finally, **virtual leadership** is also emerging as an important issue for organizations. In previous times, leaders and their employees worked together in the same physical location and engaged in face-to-face interactions on a regular basis. But in today's world, both leaders and their employees may work in locations that are far from one another. Such arrangements might include people telecommuting from a home office one or two days a week to people actually living and working far from company headquarters.

Increasingly, then, communication between leaders and their subordinates happens largely by telephone and e-mail. One implication may be that leaders in these situations must work harder at creating and maintaining relationships with their employees that go beyond words on a computer screen. Although nonverbal communication, such as smiles and handshakes, may not be possible online, managers can instead make a point of adding a few personal words in an e-mail (whenever appropriate) to convey appreciation, reinforcement, or constructive feedback.

Virtual Leadership leadership in settings where leaders and followers interact electronically rather than in face-to-face settings

Leadership, Management, and Decision Making

OBJECTIVE 9-8
Relate leadership to decision making and discuss both rational and behavioral perspectives on decision making.

We noted previously the differences and similarities between managing and leading. *Decision making* is another important related concept. Indeed, decision making is a fundamental component of both leadership and management—managers and leaders must frequently make decisions.

The Nature of Decision Making

Decision making can refer to either a specific act or a general process. **Decision making** is the act of choosing one alternative from among a set of alternatives. The decision-making process, however, is much more than this. One step of the process, for example, is that the person making the decision must both recognize that a decision is necessary and identify the set of feasible alternatives before selecting one. Hence, the **decision-making process** includes recognizing and defining the nature of a decision situation, identifying alternatives, choosing the "best" alternative, and putting it into practice.[16]

Decision Making choosing one alternative from among several options

Decision-Making Process recognizing and defining the nature of a decision situation, identifying alternatives, choosing the "best" alternative, and putting it into practice

The word *best* implies effectiveness. Effective decision making requires that the decision maker understand the situation driving the decision. Most people would consider an effective decision to be one that optimizes some set of factors, such as profits, sales, employee welfare, and market share. In some situations, though, an effective decision may be one that minimizes losses, expenses, or employee turnover. It may even mean selecting the best method for going out of business, laying off employees, or terminating a strategic alliance.

We should also note that managers make decisions about both problems and opportunities. For example, making decisions about how to cut costs by 10 percent reflects a problem—an undesirable situation that requires a solution. But decisions are also necessary in situations of opportunity. Learning that the firm is earning higher-than-projected profits, for example, requires a subsequent decision. Should the extra funds be used to increase shareholder dividends, reinvest in current operations, or expand into new markets? Of course, it may take a long time before a manager can know if the right decision was made.

Types of Decisions Managers must make many different types of decisions. In general, however, most decisions fall into one of two categories: *programmed* and *nonprogrammed*.[17] A **programmed decision** is one that is relatively structured or recurs with some frequency (or both). Starbucks uses programmed

Programmed Decision decision that is relatively structured or recurs with some frequency (or both)

decisions to purchase new supplies of coffee beans, cups, and napkins, and Starbucks employees are trained in exact procedures for brewing coffee. Likewise, the College Station Ford dealer made a decision that he will sponsor a youth soccer team each year. Thus, when the soccer club president calls, the dealer already knows what he will do. Many decisions regarding basic operating systems and procedures and standard organizational transactions are of this variety and can therefore be programmed.[18]

Nonprogrammed Decision *decision that is relatively unstructured and that occurs with low frequency*

Nonprogrammed decisions, on the other hand, are relatively unstructured and occur much less often. Disney's decision to buy the *Stars Wars* properties from George Lucas was a nonprogrammed decision. Managers faced with such decisions must treat each one as unique, investing enormous amounts of time, energy, and resources into exploring the situation from all perspectives. Intuition and experience are major factors in nonprogrammed decisions. Most of the decisions made by top managers involving strategy (including mergers, acquisitions, and takeovers) and organization design are nonprogrammed. Nonprogrammed decisions also include those concerning new facilities, new products, labor contracts, and legal issues.

Decision-Making Conditions

Just as there are different kinds of decisions, the conditions in which decisions must be made also are different. Managers sometimes have an almost perfect understanding of conditions surrounding a decision, but at other times they have few clues about those conditions. In general, the circumstances that exist for the decision maker are conditions of certainty, risk, or uncertainty.[19]

State of Certainty *when the decision maker knows with reasonable certainty what the alternatives are and what conditions are associated with each alternative*

CERTAINTY When the decision maker knows with reasonable certainty what the alternatives are and what conditions are associated with each alternative, a **state of certainty** exists. Suppose, for example, that managers at Singapore Airlines make a decision to buy five new jumbo jets. Their next decision is from whom to buy them. Because only two companies in the world make jumbo jets, Boeing and Airbus, Singapore Airlines knows its options exactly. Each has proven products and will guarantee prices and delivery dates. The airline thus knows the alternative conditions associated with each. There is little ambiguity and relatively little chance of making a bad decision.

Few organizational decisions, however, are made under conditions of true certainty. The complexity and turbulence of the contemporary business world make such situations rare. Even the airplane purchase decision we just considered has less certainty than it appears. The aircraft companies may not be able to guarantee delivery dates, so they may write cost-increase or inflation clauses into contracts. Thus, the airline may be only partially certain of the conditions surrounding each alternative.

State of Risk *when the availability of each alternative and its potential payoffs and costs are all associated with probability estimates*

RISK A more common decision-making condition is a state of risk. Under a **state of risk**, the availability of each alternative and its potential payoffs and costs are all associated with probability estimates.[20] Suppose, for example, that a labor contract negotiator for a company receives a "final" offer from the union right before a strike deadline. The negotiator has two alternatives: to accept or to reject the offer. The risk centers on whether the union representatives are bluffing. If the company negotiator accepts the offer, he or she avoids a strike but commits to a relatively costly labor contract. If he or she rejects the contract, he or she may get a more favorable contract if the union is bluffing, but he or she may provoke a strike if it is not.

On the basis of past experience, relevant information, the advice of others, and his or her own judgment, he or she may conclude that there is about a 75 percent chance that union representatives are bluffing and about a 25 percent chance that they will back up their threats. Thus, he or she can base a calculated decision on the two alternatives (accept or reject the contract demands) and the probable consequences of each. When making decisions under a state of risk, managers must reasonably estimate the probabilities associated with each alternative. For example, if the union negotiators are committed to a strike if their demands are not met, and the company negotiator rejects their demands because he or she guesses they will not strike, the miscalculation will prove costly. Decision making under conditions of risk is accompanied by moderate ambiguity and chances of a bad decision.

UNCERTAINTY Most of the major decision making in contemporary organizations is done under a **state of uncertainty**. The decision maker does not know all the alternatives, the risks associated with each, or the likely consequences of each alternative. This uncertainty stems from the complexity and dynamism of contemporary organizations and their environments. The emergence of the Internet as a significant force in today's competitive environment has served to increase both revenue potential and uncertainty for most managers.

State of Uncertainty *when the decision maker does not know all the alternatives, the risks associated with each, or the likely consequences of each alternative*

To make effective decisions in these circumstances, managers must acquire as much relevant information as possible and approach the situation from a logical and rational perspective. Intuition, judgment, and experience always play major roles in the decision-making process under conditions of uncertainty. Even so, uncertainty is the most ambiguous condition for managers and the one most prone to error.[21] Lorraine Brennan O'Neil is the founder and CEO of 10 Minute Manicure, a quick-service salon located in airports. The company found quick success and experienced rapid growth from its inception. However, the Great Recession required O'Neil to rethink her plans in an attempt to stay afloat through a rocky and unknown future. Knowing that the company no longer had the time to wait and monitor new stores' success, she opted to focus solely on existing stores with profits, shutting down those with losses. Aside from this, she restructured her business plan, seeking nontraditional locations, reducing corporate overhead, cutting products, and developing an online product line as a second source of income.[22]

Rational Decision Making

Managers and leaders should strive to be rational in making decisions. Figure 9.3 shows the steps in the rational decision-making process.

Recognizing and Defining the Decision Situation
The first step in rational decision making is recognizing that a decision is necessary; some stimulus or spark must initiate the process. The stimulus for a decision may be either positive or negative. Managers who must decide how to invest surplus funds, for example, face a positive decision situation. A negative financial stimulus could involve having to trim budgets because of cost overruns.

Inherent in making such a decision is the need to precisely define the problem. Consider the situation currently being faced in the international air travel industry. Because of the growth of international travel related to business, education, and tourism, global carriers need to increase their capacity. Because most major international airports are already operating at or near capacity, adding a significant number of new flights to existing schedules is not feasible. As a result, the most logical alternative is to increase capacity on existing flights. Thus, Boeing and Airbus, the world's biggest manufacturers of large commercial aircraft, recognized an important opportunity and defined their decision situations as how best to respond to the need for increased global travel capacity.[23]

Identifying Alternatives
Once the decision situation has been recognized and defined, the second step is to identify alternative courses of effective action. Developing both obvious, standard alternatives and creative, innovative alternatives is useful. In general, the more important the decision, the more attention is directed to developing alternatives. Although managers should seek creative solutions, they must also recognize that various constraints often limit their alternatives. Common constraints include legal restrictions, moral and ethical norms, and constraints imposed by the power and authority of the manager, available technology, economic considerations, and unofficial social norms. After assessing the question of how to increase international airline capacity, Boeing and Airbus identified three different alternatives: They could independently develop new large planes, they could

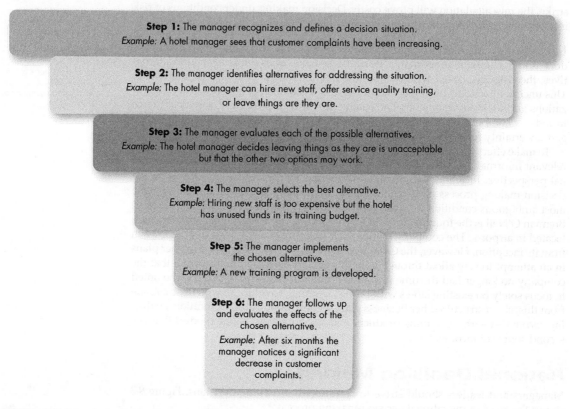

FIGURE 9.3 Steps in the Rational Decision-Making Process
Source: Based on Griffin, *Management* 8e. © 2005 South-Western, a part of Cengage Learning, Inc. Reproduced by permission.
www.cengage.com/permissions. Courtesy of Ronald Ebert.

collaborate in a joint venture to create a single new large plane, or they could modify their largest existing planes to increase their capacity.

Evaluating Alternatives The third step in the decision-making process is evaluating each of the alternatives. Some alternatives may not be feasible because of legal or financial barriers. Limited human, material, and information resources may make other alternatives impractical. Managers must thoroughly evaluate all the alternatives to increase the chances that the alternative finally chosen will be successful. For example, Airbus felt it would be at a disadvantage if it tried simply to enlarge its existing planes because the Boeing 747 was at the time already the largest aircraft being made and could readily be expanded to remain the largest. Boeing, meanwhile, was seriously concerned about the risk inherent in building a new and even larger plane, even if it shared the risk with Airbus as a joint venture partner.

Selecting the Best Alternative Choosing the best available alternative is the real crux of decision making. Even though many situations do not lend themselves to objective, mathematical analysis, managers and leaders can often develop subjective estimates and weights for choosing an alternative. Decision makers should also remember that finding multiple acceptable alternatives may be possible; selecting just one alternative and rejecting all the others might not be necessary. For example, Airbus proposed a joint venture with Boeing. Boeing, meanwhile, decided that its best course of action was to modify its existing 747 to increase its capacity. As a result, Airbus decided to proceed on its own to develop and manufacture a new jumbo jet. Boeing then decided that in addition to modifying its 747, it would develop a new plane to offer as an alternative, albeit one not as large as the 747 or the proposed Airbus plane.

Implementing the Chosen Alternative After an alternative has been selected, managers and leaders must put it into effect. Boeing set its engineers to work expanding the capacity of its 747 by adding 30 feet to the plane's body; the firm also began developing another plane intended for international travel, the 787. Airbus engineers, meanwhile, developed design concepts for a new jumbo jet equipped with escalators and elevators and capable of carrying 655 passengers. Airbus's development costs alone were estimated to exceed $12 billion.

Managers must also consider people's resistance to change when implementing decisions. The reasons for such resistance include insecurity, inconvenience, and fear of the unknown. Managers should anticipate potential resistance at various stages of the implementation process. However, even when all alternatives have been evaluated as precisely as possible and the consequences of each alternative have been weighed, unanticipated consequences are still likely. Employees may resist or protest change; they may even quit rather than agree to it. Other factors, such as unexpected cost increases, a less-than-perfect fit with existing organizational subsystems, or unpredicted effects on cash flow or operating expenses, could develop after implementation has begun. Both Boeing and Airbus were plagued by production delays that pushed back delivery of their respective aircrafts by years and ended up costing each company billions of dollars. Airbus got its plane to market first (it began flying in late 2007), but profits have been pushed far into the future because the global recession caused many airlines to cancel or delay orders for several years.

Following Up and Evaluating the Results The final step in the decision-making process requires that managers and leaders evaluate the effectiveness of their decision. They should make sure that the chosen alternative has served its original purpose. If an implemented alternative appears not to be working, they can respond in several ways. Another previously identified alternative (the original second or third choice, for instance) could be adopted. Or they might recognize that the situation was not correctly defined to begin with and start the process all over again. Finally, managers and leaders might decide that the original alternative is in fact appropriate but either has not yet had time to work or should be implemented in a different way.

At this point, both Boeing and Airbus are nearing the crucial period when they will learn whether they made good decisions. Airbus's A380 made its first commercial flight in 2007, though delays continue to push back its production schedule. The plane has also been hampered by technical problems. Meanwhile, Boeing's 787 faced numerous delays, and widespread use of the plane continues to be delayed by technical issues.[24] The expanded 747 was launched on schedule, however, and was in service in 2011. Most airlines have been willing to wait patiently for the 787s, which are designed to be much more fuel efficient than other international airplanes. Given the dramatic surge in fuel costs in recent years, a fuel-efficient option like the 787 could be an enormous success. Indeed, Airbus has begun developing its own fuel-efficient jet, the A350.[25] Qatar Airways took delivery of the first A350 in December 2014.

Behavioral Aspects of Decision Making

If all decision situations were approached as logically as described in the previous section, more decisions would prove successful. Yet decisions are often made with little consideration for logic and rationality. Some experts have estimated that U.S. companies use rational decision-making techniques less than 20 percent of the time. Of course, even when organizations try to be logical, they sometimes fail. For example, when Starbucks opened its first coffee shops in New York, it relied on scientific marketing research, taste tests, and rational deliberation in making a decision to emphasize drip over espresso coffee. However, that decision proved wrong because it became clear that New Yorkers strongly preferred the same espresso-style coffees that were Starbucks mainstays in the West. Hence, the firm had to reconfigure its stores hastily to meet customer preferences.

On the other hand, sometimes a decision made with little regard for logic can still turn out to be correct.[26] Important ingredients in how these forces work are behavioral aspects of decision making. These include *political forces, intuition, escalation of commitment*, and *risk propensity*.

Political Forces in Decision Making Political forces contribute to the behavioral nature of decision making. One major element of politics, *coalitions*, is especially relevant to decision making. A **coalition** is an informal alliance of individuals or groups formed to achieve a common goal. This common goal is often a preferred decision alternative. For example, coalitions of stockholders frequently band together to force a board of directors to make a certain decision.

Coalition *an informal alliance of individuals or groups formed to achieve a common goal*

The New York Yankees once contacted three major sneaker manufacturers, Nike, Reebok, and Adidas, and informed them that they were looking to make a sponsorship deal. While Nike and Reebok were carefully and rationally assessing the possibilities, managers at Adidas quickly realized that a partnership with the Yankees made a lot of sense for them. They responded quickly to the idea and ended up hammering out a contract while the competitors were still analyzing details.[27]

When these coalitions enter the political arena and attempt to persuade lawmakers to make decisions favorable to their interests, they are called *lobbyists*. Lobbyists may also donate money to help elect a candidate who is more likely to pursue their agendas. A recurring theme in U.S. politics is the damaging influence these special interest groups have on politicians, who may feel unduly obligated to favor campaign donors when making decisions.

Intuition *an innate belief about something, often without conscious consideration*

Intuition Intuition is an innate belief about something, often without conscious consideration. Managers sometimes decide to do something because it "feels right" or they have a hunch. This feeling is usually not arbitrary, however. Rather, it is based on years of experience and practice in making decisions in similar situations. Such an inner sense may help managers make an occasional decision without going through a full-blown rational sequence of steps. That said, all managers, but most especially inexperienced ones, should be careful not to rely too heavily on intuition. If rationality and logic are continually flouted for "what feels right," the odds are that disaster will strike one day.

Escalation of Commitment
condition in which a decision maker becomes so committed to a course of action that she or he stays with it even when it appears to have been wrong

Escalation of Commitment Another important behavioral process that influences decision making is **escalation of commitment** to a chosen course of action. In particular, decision makers sometimes make decisions and then become so committed to the course of action suggested by that decision that they stay with it, even when it appears to have been wrong.[28] For example, when people buy stock in a company, they sometimes refuse to sell it even after repeated drops in price. They choose a course of action, buying the stock in anticipation of making a profit, and then stay with it even in the face of increasing losses. Moreover, after the value drops, they may rationalize that they can't sell at such a low price because they will lose money.

Risk Propensity *extent to which a decision maker is willing to gamble when making a decision*

Risk Propensity and Decision Making The behavioral element of **risk propensity** is the extent to which a decision maker is willing to gamble when making a decision. Some managers are cautious about every decision they make. They try to adhere to the rational model and are extremely conservative in what they do. Such managers are more likely to avoid mistakes, and they infrequently make decisions that lead to big losses. Others are extremely aggressive in making decisions and willing to take risks.[29] They rely heavily on intuition, reach decisions quickly, and often risk big investments on their decisions. As in gambling, these managers are more likely than their conservative counterparts to achieve big successes with their decisions; they are also more likely to incur greater losses.[30] The organization's culture is a prime ingredient in fostering different levels of risk propensity.

summary of learning objectives

Define *leadership* and distinguish it from management. (pp. 308–310)

Leadership refers to the processes and behaviors used by someone to motivate, inspire, and influence the behaviors of others. Although leadership and management are often related, they are not the same thing. Leadership involves such things as developing a vision, communicating that vision, and directing change. Management, meanwhile, focuses more on outlining procedures, monitoring results, and working toward outcomes.

Power is the ability to affect the behavior of others. In organizational settings, there are usually five kinds of power: (1) legitimate, (2) reward, (3) coercive, (4) referent, and (5) expert power. *Legitimate power* is power granted through the organizational hierarchy; it is the power defined by the organization to be accorded to people occupying a particular position. *Reward power* is the power to give or withhold rewards. *Coercive power* is the power to force compliance by means of psychological, emotional, or physical threat. *Referent power* is based on identification, imitation, loyalty, or charisma. *Expert power* is derived from information or expertise.

Summarize early approaches to the study of leadership. (pp. 310–312)

The *trait approach to leadership* focused on identifying the traits of successful leaders. The earliest researchers believed that important leadership traits included intelligence, dominance, self-confidence, energy, activity (versus passivity), and knowledge about the job. However, this research did not produce conclusive results. More recent researchers have started to focus on traits such as emotional and mental intelligence, drive, motivation, honesty and integrity, self-confidence, knowledge of the business, and charisma.

The *behavioral approach* to leadership sought to determine what behaviors were employed by effective leaders. Research identified two basic and common leader behaviors: *task-focused* and *employee-focused* leader behaviors. It is thought that leaders should engage in both behaviors to increase performance and motivation.

Discuss the concept of situational approaches to leadership. (pp. 312–313)

The *situational approach to leadership* proposes that there is no single best approach to leadership. Instead, situational factors influence the approach to leadership that is most effective. This approach was proposed as a continuum of leadership behavior, ranging from having the leader make decisions alone to having employees make decisions with minimal guidance from the leader. Each point on the continuum is influenced by *characteristics of the leader, his or her subordinates*, and the *situation*.

The path–goal theory of leadership is a direct extension of the expectancy theory of motivation. It suggests that the primary functions of a leader are to make valued or desired rewards available in the workplace and to clarify for the subordinate the kinds of behavior that will lead to goal accomplishment and valued rewards. The leader should clarify the paths to goal attainment. Path–goal theory identifies four kinds of behaviors that leaders can use, depending on the situation: (1) *directive leader behavior*, (2) *supportive leader behavior*, (3) *participative leader behavior*, and (4) *achievement-oriented leader behavior*.

The decision tree approach attempts to prescribe a leadership style appropriate to a given situation. The decision tree approach assumes that the degree to which subordinates should be encouraged to participate in decision making depends on the characteristics of the situation. After evaluating a variety of problem attributes (characteristics of the problem or decision), the leader determines an appropriate decision style that specifies the amount of subordinate participation.

The *leader-member exchange (LMX) model of leadership* stresses the importance of variable relationships between supervisors and each of their subordinates. Each superior–subordinate pair represents a "vertical dyad." The model differs from previous approaches in that it focuses on the differential relationship leaders often establish with different subordinates.

OBJECTIVE 9-4

Describe transformational and charismatic perspectives on leadership. (pp. 313–316)

Transformational leadership (as distinguished from *transactional leadership*) focuses on the set of abilities that allows a leader to recognize the need for change, to create a vision to guide that change, and to execute the change effectively. *Charismatic leadership* is influence based on the leader's personal charisma. The basic concept of charisma suggests that charismatic leaders are likely to have self-confidence, confidence in their beliefs and ideals, and a need to influence people. They also tend to communicate high expectations about follower performance and to express confidence in their followers.

OBJECTIVE 9-5

Identify and discuss leadership substitutes and neutralizers. (pp. 316–317)

Leadership substitutes are individual, task, and organizational factors that tend to outweigh the need for a leader to initiate or direct employee performance. In other words, if certain factors are present, the employee will perform his or her job without the direction of a leader. Examples of leadership substitutes include individual professionalism, highly structured jobs, explicit plans and goals, and group performance norms. Even if a leader attempts to engage in leadership behaviors, *leadership neutralizers* may render the leader's efforts ineffective. Such neutralizers include group cohesiveness as well as elements of the job itself.

OBJECTIVE 9-6

Discuss leaders as coaches and examine gender and cross-cultural issues in leadership. (pp. 317–319)

Many organizations expect their leaders to play the role of *coach*—to select team members, provide direction, train, and develop—but otherwise allow the group to function autonomously. Some leaders may function as mentors, helping less experienced employees learn the ropes and better preparing them to advance in an organization.

Another factor that is altering the face of leadership is the number of women advancing to higher levels. Although there appear to be few differences between men and women leaders, the growing number of women leaders suggests a need for more study. Some evidence indicates that women are more democratic in decision making and have the potential to be excellent leaders, as shown by a number of high-profile, successful women leaders.

Another changing perspective on leadership relates to cross-cultural issues. In this context, *culture* encompasses international differences and diversity-based differences within one culture. For example, the level of collectivism or individualism can affect a manager's leadership style.

OBJECTIVE 9-7

Describe strategic leadership, ethical leadership, and virtual leadership. (pp. 319–321)

Strategic leadership is the leader's ability to lead change in the organization so as to enhance its competitiveness. To be effective as a strategic leader, a manager needs to have a thorough and complete understanding of the organization's history, culture, strengths, and weaknesses. Business leaders are also being called on to practice *ethical leadership*—that is, to maintain high ethical standards for their own conduct, and to hold others in their organizations to the same standards. As more leaders and employees work in different settings, a better understanding of *virtual leadership* is also becoming more important.

OBJECTIVE 9-8

Relate leadership to decision making and discuss both rational and behavioral perspectives on decision making. (pp. 321–326)

Decision making—choosing one alternative from among several options—is a critical management and leadership skill. Decision making can refer to either a specific act or a general process. Most decisions fall into one of two categories: programmed and nonprogrammed. A programmed decision is one that is relatively structured or recurs with some frequency (or both). Nonprogrammed decisions are relatively unstructured and occur much less often. There are three different conditions in which decisions must be made. These are conditions of certainty, risk, or uncertainty. When the decision maker knows what the alternatives are and the likely outcomes, a *state of certainty* exists. Under a *state of risk*, the availability of each alternative and its payoffs and costs are not clear. Finally, in a *state of uncertainty*, the decision maker does not know all the alternatives, risks, or consequences.

The *rational perspective* prescribes a logical process for making decisions. It involves six steps: (1) recognizing and defining the decision situation, (2) identifying alternatives, (3) evaluating alternatives, (4) selecting the best alternative, (5) implementing the chosen alternative, and (6) following up and evaluating the results. The *behavioral perspective* acknowledges that things such as *political forces, intuition, escalation of commitment*, and *risk propensity* are also important aspects of decision making.

key terms

behavioral approach to leadership
charismatic leadership
coalition
coercive power
decision making
decision-making process
decision tree approach
employee-focused leader behavior
escalation of commitment
ethical leadership
expert power
intuition

leader-member exchange (LMX)
   model
leadership
leadership neutralizers
leadership substitutes
legitimate power
nonprogrammed decision
path–goal theory
power
programmed decision
referent power
reward power

risk propensity
situational approach to leadership
state of certainty
state of risk
state of uncertainty
strategic leadership
task-focused leader behavior
trait approach to leadership
transactional leadership
transformational leadership
virtual leadership

MyBizLab

To complete the problems with the ✪, go to EOC Discussion Questions in the MyLab.

questions & exercises

QUESTIONS FOR REVIEW

✪ **9-1.** How do you distinguish between reward and coercive power?

9-2. Outline the main differences between a task-focussed and an employee-focussed leader.

9-3. In leadership substitutes and neutralizers, what are organizational factors?

9-4. What is expert power? Give an example of it in action.

QUESTIONS FOR ANALYSIS

✪ **9-5.** Why might it be the case that a school teacher might choose to use reward power to influence her students?

9-6. In terms of cross-cultural leadership, how would you characterize the key cultural differences between countries like the US and Japan?

9-7. The impact of virtual leadership is likely to grow in the future. As a potential "follower" in a virtual leadership situation, what issues would be of most concern to you? What would the issues be from the perspective of the "leader" role in such a situation?

⭐ 9-8. Identify a leader who you believe exhibits charismatic leadership and explain the behaviors that support this conclusion.

APPLICATION EXERCISES

9-9. Overwhelmingly, the CEOs of the largest companies in the United States are white males, but women and minorities are making inroads. Identify a leader who is a member of a minority group and describe the challenges that he or she faced and overcame.

9-10. In 2012, Marrisa Mayer was appointed president and CEO of Yahoo!. In her tenure with Yahoo!, she has made a number of bold decisions, not all of which were popular. Research Mayer's career, especially at Yahoo!. What type of leader is Mayer? How would you describe her leadership style? Do you think she is effective?

building a business: continuing team exercise

Assignment

Meet with your team members to consider your new business venture and how it relates to the leadership topics in this chapter. Develop specific responses to the following:

9-11. How will you select a leader for your organization? What traits or characteristics will be most important to you when selecting a leader?

9-12. Which types of power will be most important to the leader of your business venture?

9-13. What leadership substitutes could support your business venture as you get started?

9-14. Are there any leadership neutralizers that could derail your new effort?

9-15. As your business venture gets off the ground, you will have to make many important decisions. Will you rely more heavily on rational decision making or intuition? Why?

team exercise

EXCITING FUTURE

The Situation

WHC Solutions are CEO head-hunting recruitment specialists based in Dubai. They have offices in nine capital cities and earn commission by identifying and securing the services of some of the best talent in the world to run major organizations. After several years of organic growth, the three original partners in the company have decided to accept an offer of a major investment company to help them expand. The partners have asked you to come in as a consultant and explain to representatives of the investment company how WHC Solutions use leadership theory to help them identify ideal characteristics of future CEOs. WHC Solutions want you to lead the research and presentation as an objective outsider to ensure that the investment company is not swamped with jargon and understands what is involved.

Team Activity

Assemble a group of four students and assign each group member to one of the following approaches to leadership:

- leader-member exchange (LMX) model
- path—goal theory
- task-focused leader
- employee-focused leader

ACTION STEPS

9-16. What are the most important aspects of the leadership approach? How can it be used to identify outstanding leaders capable of becoming CEOs?

9-17. Assemble your group and share your assignment perspectives.

9-18. As a group, develop a list of advantages and disadvantages of each approach.

9-19. Select the most appropriate leadership style and develop a justification for your decision.

exercising your ethics

LEADING THE WAY

The Situation

You are the marketing director for a solar panel manufacturer and installer based in Abu Dhabi. Your production facilities are in India, but the majority of the sales are in the Middle East and Africa. Recently, having pressurized your production people to expand their factory near Kolkata, quality issues have resulted in nearly 20 percent of panels being returned to factory for replacement or repair within three months of installation. This has seriously impacted on the company's reputation. The director of sales, relatively newly appointed is furious and is already using it as an excuse for not hitting his first year sales targets. The CEO wants solutions not excuses. The company is seriously considering closing the Kolkata facility and contracting the production out to Chinese manufacturers. Ten years ago, the company made solemn and binding promises to create 1,000 permanent jobs in Kolkata. You have been given a marketing budget to deal with any fall-out.

The Dilemma

After considerable debate, the CEO is backing the sales director's suggestion to close the factory in Kolkata. You will have to try to come up with a positive spin, at least to placate the city's officials who authorized grants and tax breaks to the company in order to attract the firm to the city. Unfortunately, the timing is not great; the incentives are due to run out in five months' time. This is almost exactly the estimated time-frame to run down the factory and dispose of assets in India. It is going to be very difficult to claim that the two things are not connected. According to the CEO, out of the Indian workforce and management, there are just twelve people that will retain their jobs, four are experienced buyers, seven are expert installers and repairers and the final one is the production manager who will be expected to move to China. The other retained employees will operate from Abu Dhabi and have agreed to relocate. The changes will impact on all areas of the business; all of the marketing materials will have to be reworked as will the website. The biggest problem is the company's USP has disappeared overnight.

QUESTIONS TO ADDRESS

9-20. What are the ethical issues in this situation?

9-21. What do you think most managers would do in this situation?

9-22. What would you do?

cases

Cinna-Yum

Continued from page 308

At the beginning of this chapter, you read about Kat Cole's unexpected career path from being a hostess at Hooters to group president at Cinnabon. Using the information presented in this chapter, you should now be able to respond to these questions.

QUESTIONS FOR DISCUSSION

9-23. What personal traits does Kat Cole possess that aid her as a leader?

9-24. How would you describe Kat Cole's leadership style?

9-25. Do you believe that Kat Cole's gender affects her leadership style? Why or why not?

9-26. What are three important lessons from Kat Cole's career path?

The Man Behind the Genius

There is no doubt that Steve Jobs, cofounder of Apple, was a one-of-a-kind leader. In many ways, Jobs was defined by his passion for innovation and willingness to take risks. As the leader of a company that created the iMac, iPhone, iPod, and iPad, Jobs demonstrated that he could see beyond the present and motivate his employees by sharing his vision clearly and compellingly. According to Apple's current CEO, "Even though he was running a large company, he kept making bold moves that I don't think that anyone else would have done."[31]

The challenge, however, for Jobs and Apple was this same vision and passion. A visionary leader's strength is their ability to mobilize their employees to work toward a goal at superhuman speed. Yet, when the vision is flawed, the employees demonstrate the same commitment and move quickly, and even dangerously, in the wrong direction.[32] Often, these visionary leaders effectively screen out negative chatter, but this is not always positive, particularly when employees discover a fatal flaw.

Jobs had a unique managerial style. According to Joe Nocera of *The New York Times*, he "violated every rule of management. He was not a consensus builder but a dictator who listened mainly to his own intuition. He was a maniacal micromanager. He had an astonishing aesthetic sense, which businesspeople almost always lack.... He never mellowed, never let up on Apple employees, never stopped relying on his singular instincts in making decisions about how Apple products should look and how they should work."[33]

Although inspiring thousands of employees and millions of customers, Jobs could be brutal when dealing with employees who failed to successfully implement his vision. Despite many successes, Apple had its failures. One of the most notable was the MobileMe e-mail system. Jobs was so disappointed by flaws in the system that he fired the employee leading the MobileMe effort in front of a crowd of employees.

Jobs's passion was at the core of his being. When Jobs had a liver transplant in 2009, he found himself in the hospital with an oxygen mask. He pulled off the mask and told the pulmonologist that he was unwilling to suffer through the poor design, though barely able to speak. Ultimately, Jobs succumbed to pancreatic cancer in 2011, but he left an indelible mark on the world.

QUESTIONS FOR DISCUSSION

9-27. Do you think Steve Jobs was a charismatic leader? What leads you to this conclusion?

9-28. Jobs enjoyed almost cult-like loyalty among his employees. Why do you think people clamored to work for Apple under Jobs's leadership?

9-29. What challenges face employees working for a leader such as Jobs?

9-30. Describe Jobs with respect to intuition, escalation of commitment, and risk propensity.

9-31. Do you think that you would have enjoyed working for Apple during Jobs's leadership? Why or why not?

9-32. How does a leader differ from a manager? Describe the situational approach to leadership and three major theories within this category. How would the path–goal theory help you identify the most appropriate leadership style in a situation?

MyBizLab

Go to the Assignments section of your MyLab to complete these writing exercises.

9-33. Many followers prefer to have transformational or charismatic leaders. Do you think that a transformational focus and charisma are guarantees for success? Does being a transformational or charismatic leader indicate successful management? Are there situations where charisma can mislead followers about a leader's ability? Support your answers.

9-34. How does a leader differ from a manager? Describe the situational approach to leadership and three major theories within this category. How would the path-goal theory help you to identify the most appropriate leadership style in a situation?

end notes

[1] Ruggless, Ron. 2015. "KAT COLE." *Nation's Restaurant News* 49, no. 1: 26. Business Source Premier, EBSCOhost (accessed May 9, 2015); Alter, Charlotte. 2014. "How to Run a Billion Dollar Company Before You're 35." Time. Com N.PAG. Business Source Premier, EBSCOhost (accessed May 9, 2015); Cole, Kat. 2015. "Advice for new employees: Stop trying to impress your boss." Fortune. Com N.PAG. Business Source Premier, EBSCOhost (accessed May 9, 2015); Stanford, Duane. 2013. "Cinnabon President Kat Cole: Hustling the Gut Bomb." Businessweek.Com 78.0. Business Source Premier, EBSCOhost (accessed May 9, 2015); Porter, Jane. "From Hooters Waitress to CEO of a Billion-Dollar Company: Smart Advice From the President of Cinnabon." *Real Simple.* Accessed May 9, 2015. http://www.real-simple.com/work-life/life-strategies/job-career/brilliant-career-strategies-from-kat-cole

[2] See John Kotter, "What Leaders Really Do," *Harvard Business Review*, December 2001, 85–94.

[3] French, John R. P., and Raven, Bertram. "The Bases of Social Power," in Cartwright, Dorwin, (ed.), *Studies in Social Power* (Ann Arbor, MI: University of Michigan Press, 1959), pp. 150–167.

[4] Menzies, Hugh D. "The Ten Toughest Bosses," *Fortune*, April 21, 1980, pp. 62–73.

[5] "Management Secrets from the Meanest Company in America," *Bloomberg BusinessWeek*, January 2, 2013, pp. 46–51.

[6] "Bad Bosses Can Be Bad for Your Health," *USA Today*, August 8, 2012, p. 5B; Tepper, Bennett J. "Abusive Supervision in Work Organizations: Review, Synthesis, and Research Agenda," *Journal of Management*, 2007, Vol. 33, No. 3, pp. 261–289.

[7] Evans, Martin G. "The Effects of Supervisory Behavior on the Path–Goal Relationship," *Organizational Behavior and Human Performance*, May 1970, pp. 277–298; House, Robert J., and Mitchell, Terence R. "Path-Goal Theory of Leadership," *Journal of Contemporary Business*, Autumn 1974, pp. 81–98; see also Yukl, Gary. *Leadership in Organizations* 8th ed. (Upper Saddle River: Prentice-Hall, 2013).

[8] Graen, George, and Cashman, J. F. "A Role-Making Model of Leadership in Formal Organizations: A Developmental Approach," in Hunt, J. G., and Larson L. L., (eds.), *Leadership Frontiers* (Kent, OH: Kent State University Press, 1975), pp. 143–165; Dansereau, Fred, Graen, George, and Haga, W. J. "A Vertical Dyad Linkage Approach to Leadership Within Formal Organizations: A

Longitudinal Investigation of the Role-Making Process," *Organizational Behavior and Human Performance*, 1975, Vol. 15, pp. 46–78.

[9]Waldman, David A., and Yammarino, Francis J. "CEO Charismatic Leadership: Levels-of-Management and Levels-of-Analysis Effects," *Academy of Management Review*, 1999, vol. 24, no. 2, pp. 266–285.

[10]Canal, Emily. 2014. "FORBES 400: Meet The American Billionaires Attending The Forbes Under 30 Summit." *Forbes.Com* 1. *Business Source Premier*, EBSCOhost (accessed May 13, 2015); Eng, Dinah. 2012. "Adventures of a Serial Entrepreneur." *Fortune* 165, no. 6: 23–26; *Business Source Premier*, EBSCOhost (accessed May 13, 2015); Peterson-Withorn, Chase. 2014. "After Building Two Billion-Dollar Brands, John Paul DeJoria Shares His Success." Forbes.Com 1. Business Source Premier, EBSCOhost (accessed May 13, 2015).

[11]Howell, Jane, and Shamir, Boas. "The Role of Followers in the Charismatic Leadership Process: Relationships and Their Consequences," *Academy of Management Review*, January 2005, pp. 96–112.

[12]Hackman, J. Richard, and Wageman, Ruth. "A Theory of Team Coaching," *Academy of Management Review*, April 2005, pp. 269–287.

[13]"How Women Lead," *Newsweek*, October 24, 2005, pp. 46–70.

[14]O'Connor, Clare. 2014. "Don't Try To Be a Man, And More Honest Tips From Highly Successful Women." Forbes.Com 7. Business Source Premier, EBSCOhost (accessed May 11, 2015); Barret, Victoria. 2012. "New Travel Startup Peek Helps You Once You Get There." Forbes.Com 18. Business Source Premier, EBSCOhost (accessed May 12, 2015).

[15]Dennis, Donna J., Meola, Deborah, and Hall, M. J. 2013. "Effective Leadership in a Virtual Workforce." T+D 67, no. 2: 46-51. Business Source Premier, EBSCOhost (accessed May 13, 2015).

[16]For a review of decision making, see E. Frank Harrison, *The Managerial Decision Making Process*, 5th ed. (Boston: Houghton Mifflin, 1999). See also Weber, Elke U., and Johnson, Eric J. "Mindful Judgment and Decision Making," in Fiske, Susan T., Schacter, Daniel L., and Sternberg, Robert (eds.), *Annual Review of Psychology 2009* (Palo Alto, CA: Annual Reviews, 2009), pp. 53–86; Gigerenzer, Gerd, and Gaissmaier, Wolfgang. "Heuristic Decision Making," in Fiske, Susan T., Schacter, Daniel L., and and Taylor, Shelley (eds.), *Annual Review of Psychology 2011* (Palo Alto, CA: Annual Reviews, 2011), pp. 451–482.

[17]Huber, George P. *Managerial Decision Making* (Glenview, IL: Scott, Foresman, 1980).

[18]For an example, see Paul D. Collins, Lori V. Ryan, and Sharon F. Matusik, "Programmable Automation and the Locus of Decision-Making Power," *Journal of Management*, 1999, Vol. 25, pp. 29–53.

[19]Huber, George. *Managerial Decision Making*. See also David W. Miller and Martin K. Starr, *The Structure of Human Decisions* (Englewood Cliffs, NJ: Prentice-Hall, 1976); Elbing, Alvar. *Behavioral Decisions in Organizations*, 2nd ed. (Glenview, IL: Scott, Foresman, 1978).

[20]Stulz, Rene M. "Six Ways Companies Mismanage Risk," *Harvard Business Review*, March 2009, pp. 86–94.

[21]Hodgkinson, Gerard P., Bown, Nicola J., Maule, A. John, Glaister, Keith W., and Pearman, Alan D. "Breaking the Frame: An Analysis of Strategic Cognition and Decision Making under Uncertainty," *Strategic Management Journal*, 1999, Vol. 20, pp. 977–985.

[22]"Using Intuition in Your Business Plan," *Forbes*, September 20, 2010, pp. 34–36.

[23]Useem, Jerry. "Boeing vs. Boeing," *Fortune*, October 2, 2000, pp. 148–160; "Airbus Prepares to 'Bet the Company' As It Builds a Huge New Jet," *Wall Street Journal*, November 3, 1999, pp. A1, A10.

[24]"Dreamliner Reliability in Doubt After Failures," *USA Today*, January 9, 2013, pp. 1A, 5A.

[25]"Accommodating the A380," *Wall Street Journal*, November 29, 2005, B1; "Boeing Roars Ahead," *BusinessWeek*, November 7, 2005, pp. 44–45; "Boeing's New Tailwind," *Newsweek*, December 5, 2005, p. 45; Crown, Judith. "Even More Boeing 787 Delays?" *BusinessWeek*, April 4, 2008 (May 27, 2008), at http://www.businessweek.com/bwdaily/dnflash/content/apr2008/db2008043_948354.htm?campaign_id=rss_daily; Aaron Karp, *ATW Daily News*, April 9, 2008 (May 27, 2008), at http://www.atwonline.com/news/story.html?storyID=12338; "Airbus: New Delays for A380 Deliveries," CNNMoney.com, May 13, 2008 (May 27, 2008), at http://money.cnn.com/2008/05/13/news/international/airbus_delay.ap/index.htm?postversion=2008051304; "Airbus A380 Delays Not Disclosed for Months," MSNBC.com, May 29, 2007 (May 27, 2008), at http://www.msnbc.msn.com/id/18918869/

[26]"Making Decisions in Real Time," *Fortune*, June 26, 2000, 332–334; see also Gladwell, Malcolm. *Blink* (New York: Little, Brown, 2005).

[27]Wallace, Charles P. "Adidas—Back in the Game," *Fortune*, August 18, 1997, pp. 176–182.

[28]Staw, Barry M., and Ross, Jerry. "Good Money After Bad," *Psychology Today*, February 1988, pp. 30–33; Bobocel, D. Ramona, and Meyer, John. "Escalating Commitment to a Failing Course of Action: Separating the Roles of Choice and Justification," *Journal of Applied Psychology*, vol. 79, 1994, pp. 360–363.

[29]McNamara, Gerry, and Bromiley, Philip. "Risk and Return in Organizational Decision Making," *Academy of Management Journal*, vol. 42, 1999, pp. 330–339.

[30]See Brian O'Reilly, "What It Takes to Start a Startup," *Fortune*, June 7, 1999, pp. 135–140, for an example.

[31]Caulfield, Brian. "Steve Jobs Bio: Neither Insane Nor Great." *Forbes. Forbes Magazine*, October 26, 2011, at http://www.forbes.com/sites/briancaulfield/2011/10/26/steve-jobs-bio-neither-insane-nor-great/, accessed on June 28 2013.

[32]Sherman, Erik. "The Problem with Charismatic Leaders." *Inc.com.* May 6, 2013, at http://www.inc.com/erik-sherman/the-problem-with-charismatic-leaders.html, accessed on June 28, 2013.

[33]Allen, Frederick E. "Steve Jobs Broke Every Leadership Rule. Don't Try It Yourself." *Forbes. Forbes Magazine*, August 27, 2011, at http://www.forbes.com/sites/frederickallen/2011/08/27/steve-jobs-broke-every-leadership-rule-dont-try-that-yourself/, accessed on June 28, 2013.

Chapter 13
Managing Change

8

Management Myth **Myth** Myth

There's nothing managers can do to reduce the stress inherent in today's jobs.

Management **DEBUNKED?** Myth

It's an unusual employee today who isn't dealing with stress. Cutbacks, increased workloads, open workspace designs, work/life conflicts, and 24/7 communication access are just a few of the things that have increased job stress. However, organizations are not ignoring this problem. Smart managers are redesigning jobs, realigning schedules, and introducing employee assistance programs to help employees cope with the increasing stresses in their work and in balancing their work and personal lives.

STRESS

can be an unfortunate consequence of change and anxiety, both at work and personally. However, change is a constant for organizations and thus for managers and for employees. Large companies, small businesses, entrepreneurial startups, universities, hospitals, and even the military are changing the way they do things. Although change has always been part of a manager's job, it's become even more so in recent years. And because change can't be eliminated, managers must learn how to manage it successfully. In this chapter, we're going to look at organizational change efforts and how to manage those, the ways that managers can deal with the stress that exists in organizations, and how managers can stimulate innovation in their organizations. ●

Learning Outcomes

8-1 Define organizational change and compare and contrast views on the change process. p. 261

8-2 Explain how to manage resistance to change. p. 266

8-3 Describe what managers need to know about employee stress. p. 268

8-4 Discuss techniques for stimulating innovation. p. 272

What Is Change and How Do Managers Deal with It?

8-1 Define organizational change and compare and contrast views on the change process.

> If it weren't for change, a **manager's job** would be relatively easy.

When John Lechleiter assumed the CEO's job at Eli Lilly, he sent each of his senior executives a clock ticking down the hours, minutes, and seconds until the day when one of the company's premier cash-generating drugs went off patent. It was a visual reminder of some major changes the executives had better be prepared for. By the end of 2016, Lilly was losing $10 billion in annual revenues as patents on three of its key drugs expired. Needless to say, the company has had to make some organizational changes as it picked up the pace of drug development.[1] Lilly's managers are doing what managers everywhere must do—implement change!

Change makes a manager's job more challenging. Without it, managing would be relatively easy. Planning would be easier because tomorrow would be no different from today. The issue of organization design would be solved because the environment would be free from uncertainty and there would be no need to adapt. Similarly, decision making would be dramatically simplified because the outcome of each alternative could be predicted with near pinpoint accuracy. It would also simplify the manager's job if competitors never introduced new products or services, if customers didn't make new demands, if government regulations were never modified, if technology never advanced, or if employees' needs always remained the same. But that's not the way it is.

Change is an organizational reality. Most managers, at one point or another, will have to change some things in their workplace. We call these changes **organizational change**, which is any alteration or adaptation of an organization's structure, technology, or people. (See Exhibit 8–1.) Let's look more closely at each.

1. **Changing *structure*:** Includes any change in authority relationships, coordination mechanisms, degree of centralization, job design, or similar organization structure variables. Examples might be restructuring work units, empowering employees, decentralizing, widening spans of control, reducing work specialization, or creating work teams. All of these may involve some type of structural change.
2. **Changing *technology*:** Encompasses modifications in the way work is done or the methods and equipment used. Examples might be computerizing work processes and procedures, adding robotics to work areas, installing energy usage monitors, equipping employees with mobile communication tools, implementing social media tools, or installing a new computer operating system.
3. **Changing *people*:** Refers to changes in employee attitudes, expectations, perceptions, or behaviors. Examples might be changing employee attitudes and behaviors to better support a new customer service strategy, using team building efforts to make a team more innovative, or training employees to adopt a "safety-first" focus.

organizational change
Any alteration of an organization's people, structure, or technology

Exhibit 8–1 Categories of Organizational Change

Structure	Technology	People
Authority relationships	Work processes	Attitudes
Coordinating mechanisms	Work methods	Expectations
Job redesign	Equipment	Perceptions
Spans of control		Behavior

Why Do Organizations Need to Change?

In Chapter 2 we pointed out that both external and internal forces constrain managers. These same forces also bring about the need for change. Let's briefly review these factors.

WHAT EXTERNAL FORCES CREATE A NEED TO CHANGE?   The external forces that create the need for organizational change come from various sources. In recent years, the *marketplace* has affected firms such as AT&T and Lowe's because of new competition. AT&T, for example, faces competition from local cable companies and from Internet services such as Hulu and Skype. Lowe's, too, must now contend with a host of aggressive competitors such as Home Depot and Menard's. *Government laws and regulations* are also an impetus for change. For example, when the Patient Protection and Affordable Care Act was signed into law, thousands of businesses were faced with decisions on how best to offer employees health insurance, revamp benefit reporting, and educate employees on the new provisions. Even today, organizations continue to deal with the requirements of improving health insurance accessibility.

Technology also creates the need for organizational change. The Internet has changed pretty much everything—the way we get information, how we buy products, and how we get our work done. Technological advancements have created significant economies of scale for many organizations. For instance, technology allows Scottrade to offer its clients the opportunity to make online trades without a broker. The assembly line in many industries has also undergone dramatic change as employers replace human labor with technologically advanced mechanical robots. Also, the fluctuation in *labor markets* forces managers to initiate changes. For example, the shortage of registered nurses in the United States has led many hospital administrators to redesign nursing jobs and to alter their rewards and benefits packages for nurses, as well as join forces with local universities to address the nursing shortage.

As the news headlines remind us, *economic* changes affect almost all organizations. For instance, prior to the mortgage market meltdown, low interest rates led to significant growth in the housing market. This growth meant more jobs, more employees hired, and significant increases in sales in other businesses that supported the building industry. However, as the economy soured, it had the opposite effect on the housing industry and other industries as credit markets dried up and businesses found it difficult to get the capital they needed to operate.

WHAT INTERNAL FORCES CREATE A NEED TO CHANGE?   Internal forces can also create the need for organizational change. These internal forces tend to originate primarily from the internal operations of the organization or from the impact of external changes. (It's also important to recognize that such changes are a normal part of the organizational life cycle.)[2]

When managers redefine or modify an organization's *strategy*, that action often introduces a host of changes. For example, Nokia bringing in new equipment is an internal force for change. Because of this action, employees may face job redesign, undergo training to operate the new equipment, or be required to establish new interaction patterns within their work groups. Another internal force for change is that the *composition of an organization's workforce* changes in terms of age, education, gender, nationality, and so forth. A stable organization in

Challenged by changed consumer preferences, increased competition, and declining revenues, McDonald's has named internal manager Steve Easterbrook as its new CEO. As a change agent, Easterbrook's goal is to revitalize McDonald's "as a modern and progressive burger company delivering a contemporary customer experience."

Hannelore Foerster/Getty Images

which managers have been in their positions for years might need to restructure jobs in order to retain more ambitious employees by affording them some upward mobility. The compensation and benefits systems might also need to be reworked to reflect the needs of a diverse workforce and market forces in which certain skills are in short supply. *Employee attitudes*, such as increased job dissatisfaction, may lead to increased absenteeism, resignations, and even strikes. Such events will, in turn, often lead to changes in organizational policies and practices.

Who Initiates Organizational Change?

Organizational changes need a **catalyst.**

People who act as catalysts and assume the responsibility for managing the change process are called **change agents**.[3] WHO can be a change agent?

- Any *manager* can. We assume organizational change is initiated and carried out by a manager within the organization.
- OR any *nonmanager*—for example, an *internal staff specialist* or an *outside consultant* whose expertise is in change implementation—can.

For major systemwide changes, an organization will often hire outside consultants for advice and assistance. Because these consultants come from the outside, they offer an objective perspective that insiders usually lack. However, the problem is that outside consultants may not understand the organization's history, culture, operating procedures, and personnel. They're also prone to initiating more drastic changes than insiders—which can be either a benefit or a disadvantage—because they don't have to live with the repercussions after the change is implemented. In contrast, internal managers who act as change agents may be more thoughtful (and possibly more cautious) because they must live with the consequences of their actions.

> ⭐ **Watch It 1!**
>
> If your professor has assigned this, go to the Assignments section of **mymanagementlab.com** to complete the video exercise titled *Rudi's Bakery: Organizational Change and Development*.

How Does Organizational Change Happen?

We often use two metaphors in describing the change process.[4] These two metaphors represent distinctly different approaches to understanding and responding to change. Let's take a closer look at each one.

1 WHAT IS THE "CALM WATERS" METAPHOR?   The **"calm waters" metaphor** envisions the organization as a large ship crossing a calm sea. The ship's captain and crew know exactly where they're going because they've made the trip many times before. Change appears as the occasional storm, a brief distraction in an otherwise calm and predictable trip. Until recently, the "calm waters" metaphor dominated the thinking of practicing managers and academics. The prevailing model for handling change in such circumstances is best illustrated in Kurt Lewin's three-step description of the change process.[5] (See Exhibit 8–2.)

According to Lewin, successful change requires unfreezing the status quo, changing to a new state, and freezing the new change to make it permanent. The status quo can be considered an equilibrium state. Unfreezing is necessary to move from this equilibrium. It can be achieved in one of three ways:

- Increase the driving forces, which direct behavior away from the status quo.
- Decrease the restraining forces, which hinder movement from the existing equilibrium.
- Do both.

change agents
People who act as change catalysts and assume the responsibility for managing the change process

"calm waters" metaphor
A description of organizational change that likens that change to a large ship making a predictable trip across a calm sea and experiencing an occasional storm

Exhibit 8–2 The Three-Step Change Process

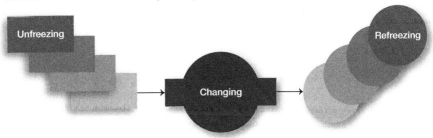

Once the situation has been "unfrozen," the change itself can be implemented. However, just introducing change doesn't mean it's going to take hold. The new situation needs to be "frozen" so that it can be sustained over time. Unless this last step is done, the change is likely to be short-lived, with employees reverting to the previous equilibrium state. The objective, then, is to freeze at the new equilibrium state and stabilize the new situation by balancing the driving and restraining forces. (Read more about Lewin and his organizational research in the From the Past to the Present box.)

Note how Lewin's three-step process treats change as a break in the organization's equilibrium state.[6] The status quo has been disturbed, and change is necessary to establish a new equilibrium state. Although this view might have been appropriate to the relatively calm environment faced by most organizations during the twentieth century, it's increasingly obsolete as a description of the kinds of "seas" that current managers have to navigate.

◄◄◄ From the Past to the Present ►►►

Who Is Kurt Lewin?

- German-American psychologist, known for his research on group dynamics
- Often called the father of modern social psychology (an academic field of study that uses scientific methods to "understand and explain how the thought, feeling, and behavior of individuals are influenced by the actual, imagined, or implied presence of other human beings")[7]

What Did He Do?

- Described group behavior as an intricate set of symbolic interactions and forces that affect group structure and also modify individual behavior.
- One particular study that looked at modifying family food habits during World War II provided new and important insights into how best to introduce change.

Major Lessons from His Work:

- Change is more easily introduced *through group decision making* than through lectures and individual appeals

- Change is more readily accepted *when people feel they have an opportunity to be involved in the change* rather than being simply asked or told to change
- Use force field analysis to *look at the factors (forces) that influence* a change situation
    - Forces either *drive* or *block* movement toward a goal
    - Make change work and overcome resistance by *increasing the driving forces, decreasing the blocking forces,* or *doing both*

Lewin's ideas have helped us better understand **ORGANIZATIONAL CHANGE.**

If your professor has assigned this, go to the Assignments section of **mymanagementlab.com** *to complete these discussion questions.*

✪ **Talk About It 1:** Explain force field analysis and how it can be used in organizational change.

✪ **Talk About It 2:** What advice do you see in this information about Lewin's ideas that managers might use?

2 WHAT IS THE "WHITE-WATER RAPIDS" METAPHOR? As former chair of Nielsen Media Research (the company best known for its TV ratings, which are frequently used to determine how much advertisers pay for TV commercials), Susan Whiting had to tackle significant industry changes. Video-on-demand services, streaming technologies, smartphones, tablet computers, and other changing technologies have made data collection much more challenging for the media research business. Here's what she had to say about the business environment: "If you look at a typical week I have, it's a combination of trying to *lead a company in change in an industry in change.*"[8] That's a pretty accurate description of what change is like in our second change metaphor—white-water rapids. It's also consistent with a world that's increasingly dominated by information, ideas, and knowledge.[9]

In the **"white-water rapids" metaphor**, the organization is seen as a small raft navigating a raging river with uninterrupted white-water rapids. Aboard the raft are half a dozen people who have never worked together before, who are totally unfamiliar with the river, who are unsure of their eventual destination, and who, as if things weren't bad enough, are traveling at night. In the white-water rapids metaphor, change is the status quo and managing change is a continual process.

To get a feeling of what managing change might be like in a white-water rapids environment, consider attending a college that had the following rules: Courses vary in length. When you sign up, you don't know how long a course will run; it might go for 2 weeks or 30 weeks. Furthermore, the instructor can end a course at any time with no prior warning. If that isn't challenging enough, the length of the class changes each time it meets: Sometimes the class lasts 20 minutes; other times it runs for 3 hours. And the time of the next class meeting is set by the instructor during this class. There's one more thing. All exams are unannounced, so you have to be ready for a test at any time. To succeed in this type of environment, you'd have to respond quickly to changing conditions. Students who were overly structured or uncomfortable with change wouldn't succeed.

DOES EVERY MANAGER FACE A WORLD OF CONSTANT AND CHAOTIC CHANGE? Well, not *every* manager, but it *is* becoming more the norm. The stability and predictability of the calm waters metaphor don't exist. Disruptions in the status quo are not occasional and temporary, and they're not followed by a return to calm waters. Many managers never get out of the rapids. Like Susan Whiting, just described, they face constant forces in the environment (external *and* internal) that bring about the need for planned organizational change.

Most organizational **changes don't happen** by chance.

HOW DO ORGANIZATIONS IMPLEMENT PLANNED CHANGES? At the Wyndham Peachtree Conference Center in Georgia, businesses bring groups of employees to try their hand at the ancient Chinese water sport of dragon boat racing. Although the physical exercise is an added benefit, it's the team-building exercise in which participants learn about communication, collaboration, and commitment that's meant to be the longest-lasting benefit.[10]

Most organizational changes don't happen by chance. Often managers make a concerted effort to alter some aspect of the organization. Whatever happens—especially in terms of structure or technology—ultimately affects the organization's people. Efforts to assist organizational members with a planned change are referred to as **organization development (OD)**.

Kiyoshi Ota/Bloomberg/Getty Images

As president and CEO of DeNA Company, a Japanese Internet firm, Isao Moriyasu manages in a white-water rapids environment where change is the status quo and managing change is a continual process. Moriyasu is rapidly acquiring firms and developing new services as DeNA expands from its base in Japan to countries worldwide.

In facilitating long-term, organization-wide changes, managers use OD to constructively change the attitudes and values of organization members so they can more readily adapt to and be more effective in achieving the new directions of the organization.[11] When OD efforts are planned, organization leaders are, in essence, attempting to change the organization's culture.[12] However, a fundamental issue of OD is its reliance on employee participation to foster an environment in which open communication and trust exist.[13] Persons involved in OD efforts acknowledge that change can create stress for employees. Therefore, OD attempts to involve organizational members in changes that will affect their jobs and seeks their input about how the change is affecting them (just as Lewin suggested).

Any organizational activity that assists with implementing planned change can be viewed as an OD technique. The more popular OD efforts in organizations rely heavily on group interactions and cooperation and include:

survey feedback
A method of assessing employees' attitudes toward and perceptions of a change

process consultation
Using outside consultants to assess organizational processes such as workflow, informal intra-unit relationships, and formal communication channels

team-building
Using activities to help work groups set goals, develop positive interpersonal relationships, and clarify the roles and responsibilities of each team member

intergroup development
Activities that attempt to make several work groups more cohesive

1. **Survey feedback.** Employees are asked their attitudes about and perceptions of the change they're encountering. Employees are generally asked to respond to a set of specific questions regarding how they view such organizational aspects as decision making, leadership, communication effectiveness, and satisfaction with their jobs, coworkers, and management.[14] The data that a change agent obtains are used to clarify problems that employees may be facing. As a result of this information, the change agent takes some action to remedy the problems.

2. **Process consultation.** Outside consultants help managers perceive, understand, and act on organizational processes they're facing.[15] These elements might include, for example, workflow, informal relationships among unit members, and formal communications channels. Consultants give managers insight into what is going on. It's important to recognize that consultants are not there to solve these problems. Rather, they act as coaches to help managers diagnose the interpersonal processes that need improvement. If managers, with the consultants' help, cannot solve the problem, the consultants will often help managers find experts who can.

3. **Team-building.** In organizations made up of individuals working together to achieve goals, OD helps them become a team. How? By helping them set goals, develop positive interpersonal relationships, and clarify the roles and responsibilities of each team member. It's not always necessary to address each area because the group may be in agreement and understand what's expected. The *primary* focus of team-building is to increase members' trust and openness toward one another.[16]

4. **Intergroup development.** Different groups focus on becoming more cohesive. That is, intergroup development attempts to change attitudes, stereotypes, and perceptions that one group may have toward another group. The goal? Better coordination among the various groups.

How Do Managers Manage Resistance to Change?

8-2 Explain how to manage resistance to change.

We know that it's better for us to eat healthy and to be physically active, yet few of us actually follow that advice consistently and continually. We resist making lifestyle changes. Volkswagen Sweden and ad agency DDB Stockholm did an experiment to see if they could get people to change their behavior and take the healthier option of using the stairs instead of riding an escalator.[17] How? They put a working piano keyboard on stairs in a Stockholm subway station (you can see a video of it on YouTube) to see if commuters would use it. The experiment was a resounding success as stair traffic rose 66 percent. The lesson: People *can change* if you make the change appealing!

Managers should be motivated to initiate change because they're concerned with improving their organization's effectiveness. But change isn't easy in any organization. It can be disruptive and scary. And people and organizations can build up inertia and not want to change.

People resist change even if **it might be beneficial!**

Let's look at why people in organizations resist change and what can be done to lessen that resistance.

Why Do People Resist Organizational Change?

It's often said that most people hate any change that doesn't jingle in their pockets. Resistance to change is well documented.[18] Why *do* people resist organizational change? The main reasons include:[19]

1. UNCERTAINTY. *Change replaces the known with uncertainty and we don't like uncertainty.* No matter how much you may dislike attending college (or certain classes), at least you know what's expected of you. When you leave college for the world of full-time employment, you'll trade the known for the unknown. Employees in organizations are faced with similar uncertainty. For example, when quality control methods based on statistical models are introduced into manufacturing plants, many quality control inspectors have to learn the new methods. Some may fear that they'll be unable to do so and may develop a negative attitude toward the change or behave poorly if required to use them.

2. HABIT. *We do things out of habit.* Every day when you go to school or work you probably get there the same way, if you're like most people. We're creatures of habit. Life is complex enough—we don't want to have to consider the full range of options for the hundreds of decisions we make every day. To cope with this complexity, we rely on habits or programmed responses. But when confronted with change, our tendency to respond in our accustomed ways becomes a source of resistance.

3. CONCERN OVER PERSONAL LOSS. *We fear losing something already possessed.* Change threatens the investment you've already made in the status quo. The more that people have invested in the current system, the more they resist change. Why? They fear losing status, money, authority, friendships, personal convenience, or other economic benefits that they value. This helps explain why older workers tend to resist change more than younger workers, since they generally have more invested in the current system and more to lose by changing.

4. CHANGE IS NOT IN ORGANIZATION'S BEST INTERESTS. *We believe that the change is incompatible with the goals and interests of the organization.* For instance, an employee who believes that a proposed new job procedure will reduce product quality can be expected to resist the change. Actually, this type of resistance can be beneficial to the organization if expressed in a positive way.

What Are Some Techniques for Reducing Resistance to Organizational Change?

At an annual 401(k) enrollment meeting, the CEO of North American Tool, frustrated at his employees' disinterest in maxing out their investments, brought in a big bag, unzipped it, and upended it over a table.[20] Cash poured out—$9,832 to be exact—the amount employees had failed to claim the prior year. He gestured at the money and said, "This is your money. It should be in your pocket. Next year, do you want it on the table or in your pocket?" When the 401(k) enrollment forms were distributed, several individuals signed up. Sometimes to get people to change, *you first have to get their attention.*

When managers see resistance to change as dysfunctional, what can they do? Several strategies have been suggested in dealing with resistance to change. These approaches include education and communication, participation, facilitation and support, negotiation, manipulation and co-optation, and coercion. These tactics are summarized here and described in Exhibit 8–4. Managers should view these techniques as tools and use the most appropriate one depending on the type and source of the resistance.

- *Education and communication* can help reduce resistance to change by helping employees see the logic of the change effort. This technique, of course, assumes that much of the resistance lies in misinformation or poor communication.

(*list continues on p. 272*)

What Reaction Do Employees Have to Organizational Change?

8-3 Describe what managers need to know about employee stress.

Yuri Arcurs/Alamy

Change often creates stress for employees!

Employee Stress Levels in Six Major Economies[21]	
United Kingdom	**35%** of employees
Brazil	**34%** of employees
Germany	**33%** of employees
United States	**32%** of employees
GLOBAL AVERAGE	**29%** of employees
China	**17%** of employees
India	**17%** of employees

What Is **Stress**?

- **Stress**—response to anxiety over intense demands, constraints, or opportunities.[22, 23]
- Not always bad; can be positive, especially when there's potential gain.
  - **Functional stress**—allows a person to perform at his or her highest level at crucial times.
- Often associated with **constraints** *(an obstacle that prevents you from doing what you desire)*, **demands** *(the loss of something desired)*, and **opportunities** *(the possibility of something new, something never done)*.
  Examples: Taking a test or having your annual work performance review.

- Although conditions may be right for stress to surface that doesn't mean it will.

stress
Response to anxiety over intense demands, constraints, or opportunities

For **potential stress** to become **actual stress**: • there is uncertainty over the outcome • the outcome is important.

What Are the **Symptoms of Stress?**

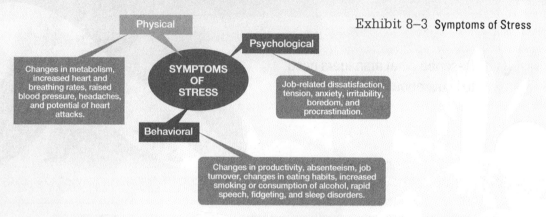

Exhibit 8–3 Symptoms of Stress

Too much stress can also have tragic consequences. In Japan, there's a stress phenomenon called **karoshi** (pronounced kah-roe-she), which is translated as death from overwork.

karoshi
A Japanese term that refers to a sudden death caused by overworking

2

What Causes Stress? **Stressors**
Job-related factors:

- Examples: Pressures to avoid errors or complete tasks in a limited time period; changes in the way reports are filed; a demanding supervisor; unpleasant coworkers

  1 **Task demands:** Stress due to an employee's job—job design (autonomy, task variety, degree of automation); working conditions (temperature, noise, etc.); physical work layout (overcrowded or in visible location with constant interruptions; work quotas, especially when excessive;[25] high level of task interdependence with others. (FYI: Autonomy lessens stress.)

  2 **Role demands:** Stress due to employee's particular role.

  - **Role conflicts:** expectations that may be hard to reconcile or satisfy.
  - **Role overload:** created when employee is expected to do more than time permits.
  - **Role ambiguity:** created when role expectations are not clearly understood—employee not sure what he or she is to do.

52%
of employees say: Colleagues are a stressful part of their jobs.[24]

stressors
Factors that cause stress

role conflicts
Work expectations that are hard to satisfy

role overload
Having more work to accomplish than time permits

role ambiguity
When role expectations are not clearly understood

③ Interpersonal demands: Stress due to other employees—little or no social support from colleagues; poor interpersonal relationships.

④ Organization structure: Stress due to excessive rules; no opportunity to participate in decisions that affect an employee.

⑤ Organizational leadership: Stress due to managers' supervisory style in a culture of tension, fear, anxiety, unrealistic pressures to perform in the short run, excessively tight controls, and routine firing of employees who don't measure up.

Personal factors:
Life demands, constraints, opportunities of any kind

1 Family issues, personal economic problems, and so forth.
- Can't just ignore! Managers need to be understanding of these personal factors.[26]

2 Employees' personalities —Type A or Type B.
- **Type A personality**—chronic sense of time urgency, excessive competitive drive, and difficulty accepting and enjoying leisure time; more likely to shows symptoms of stress.
- **Type B personality**—little to no sense of time urgency or impatience.
- Stress comes from the hostility and anger associated with Type A behavior. Surprisingly, Type Bs are just as susceptible.

A Question of Ethics

One in five companies offers some form of stress management program.[27] Although such programs are available, many employees may choose not to participate. They may be reluctant to ask for help, especially if a major source of that stress is job insecurity. After all, there's still a stigma associated with stress. Employees don't want to be perceived as being unable to handle the demands of their job. Although they may need stress management now more than ever, few employees want to admit that they're stressed.

*If your professor has assigned this, go to the Assignments section of **mymanagementlab.com** to complete these discussion questions.*

⭐ **Talk About It 3:** What can be done about this paradox?

⭐ **Talk About It 4:** Do organizations even have an ethical responsibility to help employees deal with stress?

Type A personality
People who have a chronic sense of urgency and an excessive competitive drive

Type B personality
People who are relaxed and easygoing and accept change easily

Beyond Fotomedia GmbH/Alamy

How Can Stress Be Reduced?

1 **General guidelines:**

- Not all stress is dysfunctional.
- Stress can never be totally eliminated!
- Reduce dysfunctional stress by controlling job-related factors and offering help for personal stress.

2 **Job-related factors:**

- **Employee selection**—provide a realistic job preview and make sure an employee's abilities match the job requirements.
- **On-the-job**—improve organizational communications to minimize ambiguity; use a performance planning program such as MBO to clarify job responsibilities, provide clear performance goals, and reduce ambiguity through feedback; redesign job, if possible, especially if stress can be traced to boredom (increase challenge) or to work overload (reduce the workload); allow employees to participate in decisions and to gain social support, which also lessen stress.[28]

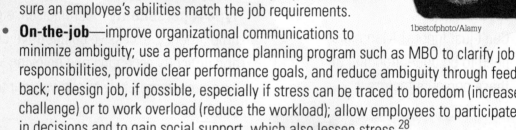
1bestofphoto/Alamy

3 **Personal factors:**

- Not easy for manager to control directly
- Ethical considerations

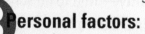

Does a manager have the **right to intrude**— even subtly—**in an employee's personal life**?

- If the manager believes it's ethical and the employee is receptive, consider employee assistance and wellness programs,[29] which are designed to assist employees in areas where they might be having difficulties (financial planning, legal matters, health, fitness, or stress).[30]

  - **Employee assistance programs (EAPs)**[31]— the rationale is to get a productive employee back on the job as quickly as possible.

  - **Wellness programs**—the rationale is to keep employees healthy.

Samantha Craddock/Alamy

employee assistance programs (EAPs)
Programs offered by organizations to help employees overcome personal and health-related problems

wellness programs
Programs offered by organizations to help employees prevent health problems

Exhibit 8–4 Techniques for Reducing Resistance to Change

TECHNIQUE	WHEN USED	ADVANTAGE	DISADVANTAGE
Education and communication	When resistance is due to misinformation	Clear up misunderstandings	May not work when mutual trust and credibility are lacking
Participation	When resisters have the expertise to make a contribution	Increase involvement and acceptance	Time-consuming; has potential for a poor solution
Facilitation and support	When resisters are fearful and anxiety-ridden	Can facilitate needed adjustments	Expensive; no guarantee of success
Negotiation	When resistance comes from a powerful group	Can "buy" commitment	Potentially high cost; opens doors for others to apply pressure too
Manipulation and co optation	When a powerful group's endorsement is needed	Inexpensive, easy way to gain support	Can backfire, causing change agent to lose credibility
Coercion	When a powerful group's endorsement is needed	Inexpensive, easy way to gain support	May be illegal; may undermine change agent's credibility

- *Participation* involves bringing those individuals directly affected by the proposed change into the decision-making process. Their participation allows these individuals to express their feelings, increase the quality of the process, and increase employee commitment to the final decision.
- *Facilitation and support* involve helping employees deal with the fear and anxiety associated with the change effort. This help may include employee counseling, therapy, new skills training, or a short paid leave of absence.
- *Negotiation* involves exchanging something of value for an agreement to lessen the resistance to the change effort. This resistance technique may be quite useful when the resistance comes from a powerful source.
- *Manipulation and co-optation* refer to covert attempts to influence others about the change. They may involve twisting or distorting facts to make the change appear more attractive.
- *Coercion* involves the use of direct threats or force against those resisting the change.

✪ Try It!
If your professor has assigned this, go to the Assignments section of **mymanagementlab.com** to complete the **Simulation: *Change***.

Chapter 14
Entrepreneurship

Entrepreneurship and Small-Business Ownership

6

LEARNING OBJECTIVES After studying this chapter, you will be able to

1. Highlight the contributions small businesses make to the U.S. economy.
2. List the most common reasons people start their own companies, and identify the common traits of successful entrepreneurs.
3. Explain the importance of planning a new business, and outline the key elements in a business plan.
4. Identify the major causes of business failures, and identify sources of advice and support for struggling business owners.
5. Discuss the principal sources of small-business private financing.
6. Explain the advantages and disadvantages of franchising.

BEHIND THE SCENES BRINGING TRADITIONAL HEALING WISDOM TO MODERN CONSUMERS AT SISTER SKY

Image copyright © 2015 by Sister Sky. All rights reserved.

Monica Simeon and Marina TurningRobe, the sisters behind Sister Sky bath and body products, have turned their business dreams into reality but still face some important challenges as they continue to grow.

www.sistersky.com

For entrepreneurial inspiration, Monica Simeon didn't have to look far. She learned how to run a business by helping her father operate one of the first Native American casinos. She got the inspiration for her business while preparing batches of skin lotions based on traditional herbal remedies after commercial products didn't help with her son's severe eczema. And the opportunity to form a business partnership was as close as her sister, Marina TurningRobe.

Thus was born Sister Sky, which makes natural bath and body products based on recipes and natural plant knowledge handed down from generation to generation. The company is based on the Spokane Indian Reservation in northeast Washington state, where the sisters grew up—and grew into their entrepreneurial lifestyle.

As with many other entrepreneurs, the sisters' vision is much broader than simply earning a living. They emphasize purity and authenticity in their products, whether that means using more-expensive distilled water to avoid risks of contamination, shunning the cheaper petroleum-based ingredients used in many mass-produced bath and body products, or staying true to the wisdom they have inherited from their ancestors. In addition, the sisters believe they have a duty to "promote cultural sharing in a positive way by educating consumers about the indigenous essence and spirit of the plant botanicals contained in our products." Finally, Simeon says, "One of our main goals is to improve the tribal economy by expanding opportunities for jobs beyond the casino."

If you were Simeon or TurningRobe, what steps would you take to make sure your young business made it through the launch stage and onto a path of sustainable growth and profitability? Where might you turn for advice and support if you needed it? How would you stay true to your vision of authentic and purposeful products while pursuing the goal of providing job opportunities—and still meet the unrelenting demands of managing a business in a highly competitive industry?[1]

INTRODUCTION

Because you're studying business, chances are you've already had an idea or two for a new business. Are you ready to commit yourself fully to a business idea, as Monica Simeon and Marina TurningRobe (profiled in the chapter-opening Behind the Scenes) have done? Are you ready to make sacrifices and do whatever it takes to get your company off the ground? Should you start something from scratch or buy an existing business? Being an entrepreneur is one of the most exciting and important roles in business, but it requires high energy and some tough decision making, as you'll discover in this chapter.

1 LEARNING OBJECTIVE

Highlight the contributions small businesses make to the U.S. economy.

The Big World of Small Business

Many businesses start out the way Sister Sky did: with an entrepreneur (or two, in this case), a compelling idea, and the drive to succeed. Small-business ownership gives people like Monica Simeon and Marina TurningRobe the opportunity to pursue their dreams while making lasting and important contributions to their communities. Entrepreneurship also provides the platform for launching companies that grow to be quite large. With the exception of operations spun off from existing companies, even the biggest corporations begin life as small businesses.

Defining just what constitutes a small business is surprisingly tricky, but it is vitally important because billions of dollars are at stake when it comes to such things as employment regulations—from which the smallest companies are often exempt—and government contracts reserved for small businesses.[2] Roughly speaking, a **small business** is an independently owned and operated company that employs fewer than 500 people and "is not dominant in its field of operation," in the words of the U.S. Small Business Administration (SBA). Beyond that general starting point, the SBA defines the maximum size of "small" through either annual revenue or number of employees. The limits vary by industry and are occasionally adjusted to reflect industry changes or inflation.[3]

small business
A company that is independently owned and operated, is not dominant in its field, and employs fewer than 500 people (although this number varies by industry).

ECONOMIC ROLES OF SMALL BUSINESSES

From employing millions of people to creating essential products, small businesses play a vital role in the U.S. economy. Here are some of the major contributions small firms make (see Exhibit 6.1):

- **They provide jobs.** Although most small businesses have no employees, those that do employ about half of the private-sector workforce in this country and create roughly two thirds of all new jobs.[4]
- **They introduce new products.** The freedom to innovate that is characteristic of many small firms continues to yield countless advances: Among all firms that apply for U.S. patents on new inventions, small businesses receive 16 times more patents per employee than larger firms.[5]
- **They meet the needs of larger organizations.** Many small businesses act as distributors, servicing agents, and suppliers to larger corporations and to numerous government agencies (which often reserve a certain percentage of their purchasing contracts for small businesses).
- **They inject a considerable amount of money into the economy.** Small businesses pay nearly half the private-sector payroll in the United States and produce half the country's gross domestic product.[6]

EXHIBIT 6.1 The Economic Impact of Small Businesses in the United States

As these selected statistics show, small businesses are a major force in employment, economic activity, and global exports.

The U.S. Economy:
The Impact of Small Business

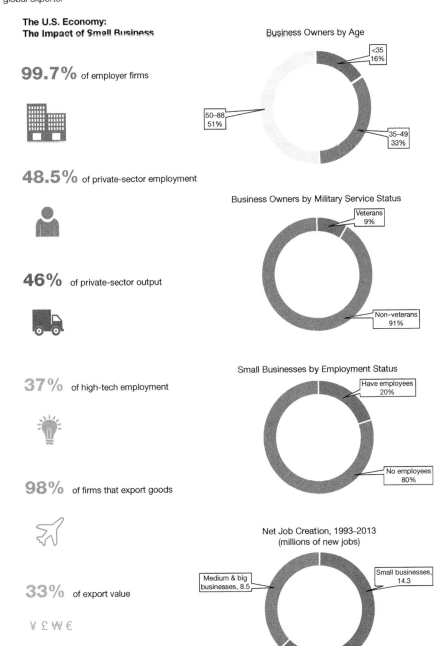

99.7% of employer firms

48.5% of private-sector employment

46% of private-sector output

37% of high-tech employment

98% of firms that export goods

33% of export value

¥ £ ₩ €

Business Owners by Age
- <35 16%
- 35–49 33%
- 50–88 51%

Business Owners by Military Service Status
- Veterans 9%
- Non–veterans 91%

Small Businesses by Employment Status
- Have employees 20%
- No employees 80%

Net Job Creation, 1993–2013 (millions of new jobs)
- Medium & big businesses, 8.5
- Small businesses, 14.3

Source: Frequently Asked Questions: Advocacy the Voice of Small Business in Government, U.S. Small Business Administration, March 2014, www.sba.gov.

- **They take risks that larger companies sometimes avoid.** Entrepreneurs play a significant role in the economy as risk takers—people willing to try new and unproven ideas.
- **They provide specialized goods and services.** Small businesses frequently spring up to fill niches that aren't being served by existing companies.

CHARACTERISTICS OF SMALL BUSINESSES

The majority of small businesses are modest operations with little growth potential, although some have attractive income potential for the solo businessperson. Small businesses such as a self-employed consultant, a local florist, or a small e-commerce venture are sometimes called *lifestyle businesses* because they are built around the personal and financial needs of an individual or a family. In contrast, other firms are small simply because they are young, but they have ambitious plans to grow. These *high-growth ventures* are usually run by a team rather than by one individual, and they expand rapidly by obtaining a sizable supply of investment capital and by introducing new products or services to a large market.

Regardless of their primary objectives, small companies tend to differ from large ones in a variety of important ways. First, most small firms have a narrow focus, offering fewer goods and services to fewer market segments. Second, unless they are launched with generous financial backing, which is rare, small businesses have to get by with limited resources. Third, smaller businesses often have more freedom to innovate and move quickly. As they grow larger, companies tend to get slower and more bureaucratic. In contrast, entrepreneurial firms usually find it easier to operate "on the fly," making decisions quickly and reacting to changes in the marketplace.

FACTORS CONTRIBUTING TO THE INCREASE IN THE NUMBER OF SMALL BUSINESSES

Three factors are contributing to the increase in the number of small businesses today: e-commerce, social media, and other technological advances; the growing diversity in entrepreneurship; and corporate downsizing and outsourcing.

E-Commerce, Social Media, and Other Technologies

Technology has always played a major role in business formation, but the rapid growth of e-commerce and social media in recent years has revolutionized the way many businesses operate. Companies such as Pandora and Facebook couldn't exist without web technologies, of course, because their connection to customers happens entirely online. In other instances, technology enables innovation in one or more functional areas. For example, thousands of companies use the web to replace physical retail stores while continuing to use conventional production and distribution systems in the physical world. Online technology also allows an operation such as handcrafts marketplace Etsy (www.etsy.com) to give "very-very small businesses" a unified presence online, as well as making it easier for shoppers to find products of interest.[7] In fact, avoiding the high cost of establishing a physical presence while being able to market to the entire world is one of the most significant and lasting changes that technology has brought to small business.

Similarly, social media have dramatically changed the marketing and selling functions for many companies. Although Facebook, YouTube, and other online media tools are used by companies of every size, these sites are particularly vital to small companies whose minuscule marketing budgets prohibit them from doing much advertising or other traditional promotional activities.

Growing Diversity in Entrepreneurship

Small-business growth is being fueled in part by women, minorities, immigrants, military veterans who want to apply their leadership skills, older workers who can't find employment to fit their interests or skills, and young people who want alternatives to traditional employment. It's never too early to start. Facebook, Google, and Dell are just a few of the significant companies started by college students. In the words of Joseph Keeley, who formed College Nannies and Tutors when he was a freshman at the University of St. Thomas, "As a young entrepreneur, the risk is relatively low. If you have a well-thought-out plan, don't be afraid to execute it. The risk only gets higher as you get older."[8]

REAL-TIME UPDATES
Learn More by Watching This Video

Young entrepreneurs changing the world

Get insights and inspiration from *Forbes* Under 30 Summit presenters. Go to http://real-timeupdates.com/bia8 and click on Learn More in the Students section.

Downsizing and Outsourcing

Business start-ups often soar when the economy sours. During hard times, many companies downsize or lay off talented employees, who then have little to lose by pursuing self-employment. Tech titans William Hewlett and David Packard joined forces in Silicon Valley in 1938 during the Great Depression, and Microsoft launched amidst the 1975 recession.[9] During the recent global recession, another wave of entrepreneurs took their turn. As companies were trimming staff, Mark Cannice, who runs the entrepreneurship program at the University of San Francisco, said, "If there is a silver lining, the large-scale downsizing from major companies will release a lot of new entrepreneurial talent and ideas—scientists, engineers, business folks now looking to do other things."[10]

Outsourcing, the practice of engaging outside firms to handle either individual projects or entire business functions (page 248), also creates numerous opportunities for small businesses and entrepreneurs. Some companies subcontract special projects and secondary business functions to experts outside the organization, whereas others turn to outsourcing as a way to permanently eliminate entire departments, and some laid-off employees even become entrepreneurs and sell services to their former employers.

 Checkpoint

LEARNING OBJECTIVE 1: Highlight the contributions small businesses make to the U.S. economy.

SUMMARY: Small businesses provide jobs, employing about half the private-sector workforce. They introduce new and innovative products, they supply many of the needs of larger organizations, they inject considerable amounts of money into the economy, they often take risks that larger organizations avoid, and they provide many specialized goods and services.

CRITICAL THINKING: (1) Why do you think many companies grow more risk averse as they grow larger? (2) If they wanted to, could large businesses take the place of small businesses in the U.S. economy? For instance, could someone build a nationwide landscaping company? Why or why not?

IT'S YOUR BUSINESS: If you can't land the right job soon after graduation, would you consider starting a business? Why or why not?

KEY TERMS TO KNOW: small business

The Entrepreneurial Spirit

2 **LEARNING OBJECTIVE**

List the most common reasons people start their own companies, and identify the common traits of successful entrepreneurs.

entrepreneurial spirit
The positive, forward-thinking desire to create profitable, sustainable business enterprises.

To some people, working for themselves or starting a company seems a perfectly natural way to earn a living. To others, the thought of working outside the structure of a regular company might seem too scary to even contemplate. However, every professional should understand the **entrepreneurial spirit**—the positive, forward-thinking desire to create profitable, sustainable business enterprises—and the role it can play in *every* company, not just small or new firms. The entrepreneurial spirit is vital to the health of the economy and to everyone's standard of living, and it can help even the largest and oldest companies become profitable and competitive.

Frustrated in a tough job market, Alex Andon used his expertise in biology and aquarium design to launch Jellyfish Art. The company specializes in the unique and demanding field of aquariums for jellyfish.

WHY PEOPLE START THEIR OWN COMPANIES

Starting a company is nearly always a difficult, risky, exhausting endeavor that requires significant sacrifice. Why do people do it? Some want more control over their future; others are simply tired of working for someone else. Some, such as Monica Simeon and Marina TurningRobe of Sister Sky, have new product ideas that they believe in with such passion that they're willing to risk everything on a start-up enterprise. Some start companies to pursue business goals that are important to them on a personal level. Jennie Baird, cofounder of Generation Grownup, which publishes parenting-related websites, had two important reasons—reasons shared by Simeon, TurningRobe, and many others: "I wanted to take the opportunity to be the one in control of innovation and work on something that I believe in."[11]

Another reason, one that becomes more common during tough job markets, is the inability to find attractive employment anywhere else. Alex Andon searched for months after being laid off from his job in the biotech industry. Out of frustration as much as anything else ("I hate looking for work," he explained), he became an entrepreneur, putting his biology background to work launching Jellyfish Art (www.jellyfishart.com) to create and sell jellyfish aquariums.[12]

QUALITIES OF SUCCESSFUL ENTREPRENEURS

Although it's impossible to lump millions of people into a single category, successful entrepreneurs tend to share a number of characteristics (see Exhibit 6.2). If you have many of these traits, successful entrepreneurship could be in your future, too—if you're not already a hard-working entrepreneur.

INNOVATING WITHOUT LEAVING: INTRAPRENEURSHIP

The entrepreneur's innovative spirit is so compelling that many large companies and individuals within companies now try to express it through *intrapreneurship*, a term coined by business consultant Gifford Pinchot to designate entrepreneurial efforts within a larger organization.[13]

However, innovating within a larger organization is often much easier said than done, because companies tend to become more analytical, more deliberate, more structured, and more careful as they mature. Mechanisms put in place to prevent mistakes can also hamper innovative thinking by restricting people to tried-and-true methods. Organizations can develop habits based on behaviors and decisions that made sense in the past but that no longer make sense as the business environment changes. Injecting the entrepreneurial spirit sometimes means going against the accepted wisdom.[14] In other words, it can be risky behavior that may or may not be rewarded. Companies sometimes need to take special steps to encourage, protect, and reward the entrepreneurial spirit.

REAL-TIME UPDATES
Learn More by Reading This Article

The innovation advantage of intrapreneurs

Get advice for entrepreneurs who want to hire game-changing innovators. Go to http://real-timeupdates.com/bia8 and click on Learn More in the Students section.

 Checkpoint

LEARNING OBJECTIVE 2: List the most common reasons people start their own companies, and identify the common traits of successful entrepreneurs.

SUMMARY: People start businesses for a variety of reasons, including gaining more control over their futures, wanting to avoid working for someone else, having

EXHIBIT 6.2 Qualities Shared by Successful Entrepreneurs

Although no single personality profile fits all successful entrepreneurs, here are the qualities that entrepreneurs tend to have.

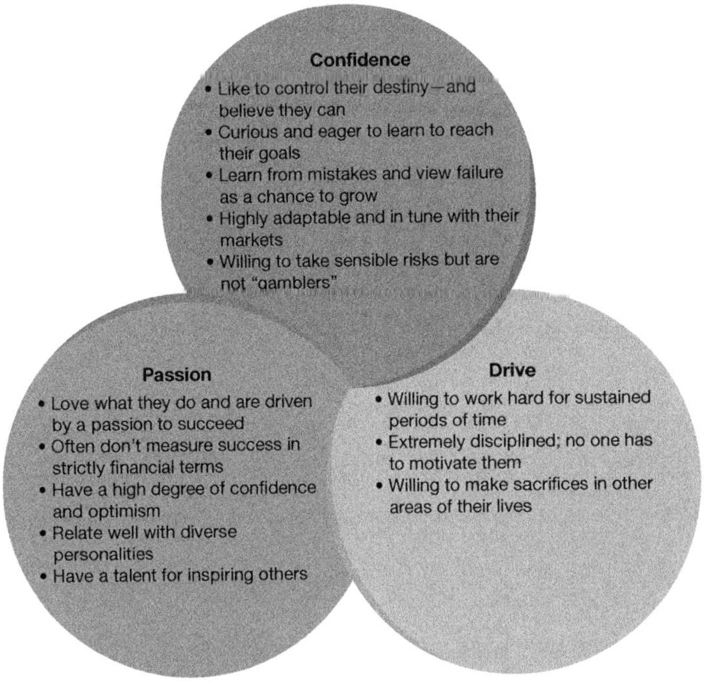

Confidence
- Like to control their destiny—and believe they can
- Curious and eager to learn to reach their goals
- Learn from mistakes and view failure as a chance to grow
- Highly adaptable and in tune with their markets
- Willing to take sensible risks but are not "gamblers"

Passion
- Love what they do and are driven by a passion to succeed
- Often don't measure success in strictly financial terms
- Have a high degree of confidence and optimism
- Relate well with diverse personalities
- Have a talent for inspiring others

Drive
- Willing to work hard for sustained periods of time
- Extremely disciplined; no one has to motivate them
- Willing to make sacrifices in other areas of their lives

Sources: "Thinking About Starting a Business?," U.S. Small Business Administration website, accessed 2 November 2013, www.sba.gov; Kelly K. Spors, "So, You Want to Be an Entrepreneur," *Wall Street Journal*, 23 February 2009, http://online .wsj.com; Marshall Goldsmith, "Demonstrating the Entrepreneurial Spirit," *BusinessWeek*, 26 August 2008, www.businessweek .com; Sarah Pierce, "Spirit of the Entrepreneur," *Entrepreneur*, 28 February 2008, www.entrepreneur.com; Norman M. Scarborough and Thomas W. Zimmerer, *Effective Small Business Management*, 7th ed. (Upper Saddle River, N.J.: Prentice Hall, 2003), 4.

new product ideas that they are deeply passionate about, pursuing business goals that are important to them on a personal level, or seeking income alternatives during tough employment markets. The entrepreneurial spirit, the positive, forward-thinking desire to create profitable, sustainable business enterprises, is a good way to summarize the entrepreneurial personality. Specifically, successful entrepreneurs tend to love what they do and are driven by a passion to succeed at it, they are disciplined and willing to work hard, they are confident and optimistic, and they like to control their own destiny. Moreover, they relate well to others and have the ability to inspire others, are curious, learn from their mistakes without letting failure drag them down, are adaptable and tuned into their environments, and are moderate but careful risk takers.

CRITICAL THINKING: (1) Would someone who excels at independent entrepreneurship automatically excel at an intrapreneurial effort? Why or why not? (2) Does the inability or unwillingness to work within the constraints of a typical corporation mean someone is naturally suited to entrepreneurship? Why or why not?

IT'S YOUR BUSINESS: (1) If you had to start a business right now and generate profit as quickly as possible, what kind of business would you start? Explain your answer. (2) How would you describe your level of entrepreneurial spirit?

KEY TERMS TO KNOW: entrepreneurial spirit

3   LEARNING OBJECTIVE

Explain the importance of
planning a new business, and
outline the key elements in a
business plan.

The Start-Up Phase: Planning and Launching a New Business

The start-up phase is an exciting time because entrepreneurs and small-business owners love to roll up their sleeves and get to work, but it's also an exhausting time because a lot of work must be done. Focusing that start-up energy and making sure essential tasks get completed calls for careful decision making and planning, starting with choosing the best ownership option and creating an effective business plan.

SMALL-BUSINESS OWNERSHIP OPTIONS

People who have an entrepreneurial urge sometimes jump to the conclusion that starting a new company is the best choice, but it's definitely not the only choice—and not always the right choice. Before you decide, consider all three options: creating a new business, buying an existing business, or buying a franchise. Creating a new business has many advantages, but it can also be the most difficult option (see Exhibit 6.3).

EXHIBIT 6.3   Business Start-Up Options

Creating an all-new, independent business can be an exciting prospect, but this brief comparison highlights how much work it requires and how many risks are involved. (You can read more about franchising on page 184.)

Start-Up Strategy	Financial Outlay at Start-Up	Possibilities for Borrowing Start-Up Capital or Getting Investors	Owner's Freedom and Flexibility	Business Processes and Systems	Support Networks	Workforce	Customer Base, Brand Recognition, and Sales
Create a new, independent business	Some businesses can be started with very little cash; others, particularly in manufacturing, may require a lot of capital	Usually very limited; most lenders and many investors want evidence that the business can generate revenue before they'll offer funds; venture capitalists invest in new firms, but only in a few industries	Very high, particularly during early phases, although low capital can severely restrict the owner's ability to maneuver	Must be designed and created from scratch, which can be time-consuming and expensive	Suppliers, bankers, and other elements of the network must be selected; the good news is that the owner can select and recruit ones that he or she specifically wants	Must be hired and trained at the owner's expense	None; must be built from the ground up, which can put serious strain on company finances until sales volume builds
Buy an existing independent business	Can be considerable; some companies sell for multiples of their annual revenue, for example	Banks are more willing to lend to "going concerns," and investors are more likely to invest in them	Less than when creating a new business because facilities, workforce, and other assets are already in place—more than when buying a franchise	Already in place, which can be a plus or minus, depending on how well they work	Already in place; may need to be upgraded	Already in place, which could a positive or a negative, but at least there are staff to operate the business	Assuming that the business is at least somewhat successful, it has a customer base with ongoing sales and some brand reputation (which could be positive or negative)
Buy into a franchise system	Varies widely, from a few thousand to several hundred thousand dollars	Varies, but many franchisors do not allow franchisees to buy a franchise with borrowed funds, so they must have their own capital	Low to very low; most franchisors require rigid adherence to company policies and processes	One of the key advantages of buying a franchise is that it comes with an established business system	Varies; some franchise companies specify which suppliers a franchisee can use	Must be hired and trained, but a franchisor usually provides training or training support	Customer base and repeat sales must be built up, but one of the major advantages of a franchise is established brand recognition

Compared to starting a new business, buying an existing business can involve less work and less risk—provided, of course, that you check out the company carefully. When you buy a healthy business, you generally purchase an established customer base, functioning business systems, proven products or services, and a known location. In addition, financing an existing business is often much easier because lenders are reassured by the company's history and existing assets and customer base.

Still, buying an existing business is not without disadvantages and risks. You may need a considerable amount of financing to buy a fully functioning company, for example, and you will inherit any problems the company has, from unhappy employees to obsolete equipment to customers with overdue accounts. Thorough research is a must.[15]

The third option, buying a franchise (see page 184), combines many of the benefits of independent business ownership with the support that comes with being part of a larger organization.

BLUEPRINT FOR AN EFFECTIVE BUSINESS PLAN

Although some successful entrepreneurs claim to have done little formal planning, they all have at least *some* intuitive idea of what they're trying to accomplish and how they hope to do it. In other words, even if they haven't produced a formal printed document, chances are they've thought through the big questions, which is just as important. As FedEx founder Fred Smith put it, "Being entrepreneurial doesn't mean [you] jump off a ledge and figure out how to make a parachute on the way down."[16]

A **business plan** summarizes a proposed business venture, communicates the company's goals, highlights how management intends to achieve those goals, and shows how customers will benefit from the company's goods or services. Preparing a business plan serves three important functions. First, it guides the company operations and outlines a strategy for turning an idea into reality. Second, it helps persuade lenders and investors to finance your business if outside money is required. Third, it can provide a reality check in case an idea just isn't feasible.

business plan
A document that summarizes a proposed business venture, its goals, and plans for achieving those goals.

Business plans can be written before the company is launched, when the founders are defining their vision of what the company will be, when the company is seeking funding, and after the company is up and running, when the plan serves as a monitor-and-control mechanism to make sure operations are staying on track. At any stage, a business plan forces you to think about personnel, marketing, facilities, suppliers, distribution, and a host of other issues vital to a company's success. The specific elements to include in a business plan can vary based on the situation; here are the sections typically included in a plan written to attract outside investors:[17]

- **Summary.** In one or two paragraphs, summarize your business concept, particularly the *business model*, which defines how the company will generate revenue and produce a profit. The summary must be compelling, catching the investor's attention and giving him or her reasons to keep reading. Describe your product or service and its market potential. Highlight some things about your company and its leaders that will distinguish your firm from the competition. Summarize your financial projections and indicate how much money you will need from investors or lenders and where it will be spent.
- **Mission and objectives.** Explain the purpose of your business and what you hope to accomplish.
- **Company overview.** Give full background information on the origins and structure of your venture.
- **Products or services.** Concisely describe your products or services, focusing on their unique attributes and their appeal to customers.
- **Management and key personnel.** Summarize the background and qualifications of the people most responsible for the company's success.

Whenever you seek outside funding, investors and lenders will demand to know how they will be repaid and will expect to find this information in your business plan.

68/attrendo images/Ocean/Corbis

- **Target market.** Provide data that will persuade an investor that you understand your target market. Be sure to identify the strengths and weaknesses of your competitors.
- **Marketing strategy.** Provide projections of sales volume and market share; outline a strategy for identifying and reaching potential customers, setting prices, providing customer support, and physically delivering your products or services. Whenever possible, include evidence of customer acceptance, such as advance product orders.
- **Design and development plans.** If your products require design or development, describe the nature and extent of what needs to be done, including costs and possible problems.
- **Operations plan.** Provide information on facilities, equipment, and personnel requirements.
- **Start-up schedule.** Forecast development of the company in terms of completion dates for major aspects of the business plan.
- **Major risk factors.** Identify all potentially negative factors and discuss them honestly.
- **Financial projections and requirements.** Include a detailed budget of start-up and operating costs, as well as projections for income, expenses, and cash flow for the first three years of business. Identify the company's financing needs and potential sources.
- **Exit strategy.** Explain how investors will be able to cash out or sell their investment, such as through a public stock offering, sale of the company, or a buyback of the investors' interest.

REAL-TIME UPDATES
Learn More by Reading This PDF

Want to pitch to investors? Learn from the pros first

Guy Kawasaki and his partners at Garage Technology Ventures offer invaluable advice on presenting a business idea to potential investors. Go to http://real-timeupdates.com/bia8 and click on Learn More in the Students section.

Veteran Silicon Valley entrepreneur and investor Guy Kawasaki advises entrepreneurs to create a concise *executive summary* of their business plan to use when presenting their ideas to investors for the first time. Entrepreneurs often have as little as 20 minutes (and sometimes even less) to make these pitches, so a compelling presentation backed up by an executive summary no longer than 20 pages is ideal. The most important part of the entire package is "the grab," a compelling one- or two-sentence statement that gets an investor's attention. If an investor is intrigued, he or she can then read the executive summary to get a better sense of the opportunity and then review the full business plan before making a decision to provide funds.[18]

Be aware that not all start-up veterans and investors believe in the value of a conventional business plan, at least in a company's early stages. Reasons for the skepticism include the amount of time and energy required to research and write a plan, the reluctance of many target readers to read such lengthy documents, the uncertainty of whether a new product or company idea will even work, and the difficulty of correctly anticipating all the circumstances and obstacles that a young company will encounter. Particularly for companies that are developing new products or new business models before they can launch, some experts recommend that entrepreneurs devote most of their energy to getting a working product or service model in front of potential customers as quickly as possible so they can verify and fine-tune it before proceeding to extensive business planning. Two popular alternatives to conventional business plans are high-level overviews known as the Business Model Canvas and the Lean Canvas. They are essentially one-page business plans that present only the essential ideas that make up an intended business model.[19]

✓ **Checkpoint**

LEARNING OBJECTIVE 3: Explain the importance of planning a new business, and outline the key elements in a business plan.

SUMMARY: Planning is essential because it forces you to consider the best ownership strategy for your needs and circumstances (creating a new company, buying an existing company, or buying a franchise), and it forces you to think through the factors that will lead to success. An effective business plan should include your mission and objectives, company overview, management, target market, marketing strategy, design and development plans, operations plan, start-up schedule, major risk factors, and financial projections and requirements.

CRITICAL THINKING: (1) Why is it important to identify critical risks and problems in a business plan? (2) Many experts suggest that you write the business plan yourself, rather than hiring a consultant to write it for you. Why is this a good idea?

IT'S YOUR BUSINESS: (1) Think of several of the most innovative or unusual products you currently own or have recently used (don't forget about services as well). Were these products created by small companies or large ones? (2) Optimism and perseverance are two of the most important qualities for entrepreneurs. On a scale of 1 (lowest) to 10 (highest), how would you rate yourself on these two qualities? How would your best friend rate you?

KEY TERM TO KNOW: business plan

The Growth Phase: Nurturing and Sustaining a Young Business

Identify the major causes of business failures, and identify sources of advice and support for struggling business owners.

So far, so good. You've done your planning and launched your new enterprise. Now the challenge is to keep going and keep growing toward your goals. To ensure a long and healthy life for your business, start by understanding the reasons new businesses can fail.

THE NEW BUSINESS FAILURE RATE

You may have heard some frightening "statistics" about the failure rate of new businesses, with various sources saying that 70, 80, or even 90 percent of new business ventures fail. Unfortunately, calculating a precise figure that represents all types of businesses across all industries is probably impossible. First, the definition of "failure" can be hard to pin down and varies from one business owner to the next. For example, business owners may retire, return to the corporate workforce to get away from the grind of running a business alone, or simply decide to pursue a different path in life. All of these closures would count as failures in a typical survey, but they wouldn't count as failures to the business owners themselves. Second, establishing a time frame is essential for a failure rate to have any meaning. For example, ill-conceived or undercapitalized businesses often don't survive the first year, so the early failure rate is quite high. However, after the bad ideas collide with reality and disappear, the rate of failure slows down, and the companies that fail do so for a wide variety of reasons, some internal and some external. Third, structural changes in the economy or in a particular industry can cause business closures that don't reflect a general pattern applicable to all companies. For example, since the advent of the online travel shopping, the number of traditional, in-person travel agencies in the United States has plummeted by roughly two-thirds.[20] The fact that so many companies, including many long-established ones, went out of business is the more the result of this structural change in the industry than of some "new business failure" phenomenon.

In other words, view every failure statistic with skepticism unless you can find out how it was calculated. For instance, in the notoriously difficult restaurant industry, "90 percent of new restaurants fail" is repeated so often that many people assume that it must be true. However, one in-depth study showed the rate to be only 60 percent after four years—still a serious number, but considerably less than the near-certain failure rate of 90 percent.[21]

REAL-TIME UPDATES
Learn More by Reading This Article

Learn from the failure of other entrepreneurs

The lessons of failure are just as important as the lessons of success. Go to http://real-timeupdates.com/bia8 and click on Learn More in the Students section.

EXHIBIT 6.4	Why New Businesses Fail

These 12 blunders are among the most common reasons for the failure of new businesses.

Leadership Issues	Marketing and Sales Issues	Financial Issues	Systems and Facilities Issues
Managerial incompetence: Owner doesn't know how to plan, lead, control, or organize.	**Ineffective marketing:** Small companies—especially *new* small companies—face a tremendous challenge getting recognition in crowded markets.	**Inadequate financing:** Being undercapitalized can prevent a company from building the scale required to be successful or sustaining operations until sales revenues increase enough for the firm to be self-funding.	**Poor location:** Being in the wrong place will doom a retail operation and can raise costs for other types of business as well.
Lack of strategic planning: Owner didn't think through all the variables needed to craft a viable business strategy.	**Uncontrolled growth:** Company may add customers faster than it can handle them, leading to chaos, or may even "grow its way into bankruptcy" if it spends wildly to capture and support customers.	**Poor cash management:** A company may spend too much on nonessentials, fail to balance expenditures with incoming revenues, fail to use loan or investment funds wisely, or fail to budget enough to pay its bills.	**Poor inventory control:** Company may produce or buy too much inventory, raising costs too high—or it may do the opposite and be unable to satisfy demand.
Lack of relevant experience: Owner may be experienced in business but not in the particular markets or technologies that are vital to the new firm's success.	**Overreliance on a single customer:** One huge customer can disappear overnight, leaving the company in dire straits.	**Too much overhead:** Company creates too many fixed expenses that aren't directly related to creating or selling products, leaving it vulnerable to any slowdown in the economy.	
Inability to make the transition from corporate employee to entrepreneur: Owner can't juggle the multiple and diverse responsibilities or survive the lack of support that comes with going solo.			

Sources: Brian Hamilton, "The 7 Biggest Financial Mistakes Businesses Make," *Inc.*, 9 August 2011, www.inc.com; Norman M. Scarborough and Thomas W. Zimmerer, *Effective Small Business Management*, 7th ed. (Upper Saddle River, N.J.: Prentice Hall, 2003), 27–29.

Another study—this one a comprehensive analysis using data from the U.S. Census Bureau—found that 50 percent of all new employer firms (those that hire employees) were still in business after four years, and another 17 percent were no longer in operation but had closed "successfully," meaning that the owner retired, sold the company, or otherwise ended the enterprise on a positive note. In other words, averaged across all industries, only 33 percent actually "failed" during this time frame.[22]

Although the statistics may not be quite as gloomy as many people think, even a 33 percent failure rate should demand the careful entrepreneur's attention. To help make sure you don't become a statistic, start by understanding why businesses tend to fail (see Exhibit 6.4) and figure out how to avoid making the same mistakes.

Perhaps one of the most important reasons companies fail is something that doesn't always show up in surveys. It's a simple matter of "motivational collapse," when the would-be entrepreneur encounters one too many setbacks and simply doesn't have the drive to keep going.[23] A truly committed entrepreneur, in contrast, keeps pushing onward, experimenting, making adjustments, and keeping his or her enthusiasm level high until things start to click. One would be hard-pressed to improve on the insight and advice offered by Marina TurningRobe of Sister Sky: "In business, you must have the courage and honesty to admit when you fall short. This helps you refine, reformulate, redesign and come back stronger and better. If you can't admit your shortcomings you will become stagnant, irrelevant, or just plain arrogant. In a competitive business environment, being any of these will be your demise."[24]

ADVICE AND SUPPORT FOR BUSINESS OWNERS

Keeping a business going is no simple task, to be sure. Fortunately, entrepreneurs can get advice and support from a wide variety of sources.

Government Agencies and Not-for-Profit Organizations

Numerous city, state, and federal government agencies offer business owners advice, assistance, and even financing in some cases. For instance, many cities and states have an office of economic development chartered with helping companies prosper so that they might contribute to the local or regional economy. At the federal level, small businesses can apply for loans backed by the Small Business Administration (SBA), get management and financing advice, and learn about selling to the federal government at www.sba.gov. The Minority Business Development Agency (www.mbda.gov) offers advice and programs to minority-owned businesses. Many state agencies also have offices to help small firms compete.

Some of the best advice available to small businesses is delivered by thousands of volunteers from the Service Corps of Retired Executives (SCORE), a resource partner of the SBA. These experienced business professionals offer free advice and one-to-one counseling to entrepreneurs. You can learn more at www.score.org.

Many colleges and universities also offer entrepreneurship and small-business programs. Check with your college's business school to see whether resources are available to help you launch or expand a company. The U.S. Chamber of Commerce (www.uschamber.com) and its many local chambers offer advice and special programs for small businesses as well.

Business Partners

Banks, credit card companies, software companies, and other firms you do business with can also be a source of advice and support. For example, the Open Forum, hosted by American Express, offers a variety of videos, articles, and online network tools to help small-business owners, as well as online tutorials and forums where business owners can post questions.[25] As you might expect, the free resources from these companies are part of their marketing strategies and so include a certain amount of self-promotion, but don't let that stop you from taking advantage of all the free advice you can get.

Mentors and Advisory Boards

Many entrepreneurs and business owners take advantage of individual mentors and advisory boards. Mentoring can happen through both formal programs such as SCORE and informal relationships developed in person or online. In either case, the advice of a mentor who has been down the road before can be priceless.

An **advisory board** is a form of "group mentoring" in which you assemble a team of people with subject-area expertise or vital contacts to help review plans and decisions. Unlike a corporate board of directors, an advisory board does not have legal responsibilities, and you don't have to incorporate to establish an advisory board. In some cases, advisors will agree to help for no financial compensation. In other cases, particularly for growth companies that want high-profile experts, advisors agree to serve in exchange for either a fee or a small portion of the company's stock (up to 3 percent is standard).[26]

advisory board
A team of people with subject-area expertise or vital contacts who help a business owner review plans and decisions.

Print and Online Media

Your local library and the Internet offer information to help any small-business owner face just about every challenge imaginable. For instance, blogs written by business owners, investors, and functional specialists such as marketing consultants can offer valuable insights. Websites such as www.entrepreneurship.org provide free advice on every aspect of managing an entrepreneurial organization. Also, the websites affiliated with these well-known business magazines should be considered for every small-business owner's regular reading list:

- *Inc.* (www.inc.com)
- *Bloomberg Businessweek* (www.businessweek.com/small-business)
- *Fortune* and *Money* (http://money.cnn.com/smallbusiness/)
- *Harvard Business Review* (https://hbr.org/topic/entrepreneurship)
- *Forbes* (www.forbes.com/entrepreneurs/)
- *Entrepreneur* (www.entrepreneur.com/)
- *Fast Company* (www.fastcompany.com/)

Networks and Support Groups

No matter what industry you're in or what stage your business is in, you can probably find a local or an online network of people with similar interests. Many cities across the

EXHIBIT 6.5	Social Networking for Entrepreneurs

Here are just a few of the many online networks that provide advice and vital connections for entrepreneurs. Some of these are not specific to small business, but they've become major resources for business owners. Some also feature public and private groups that focus on specific business issues.

Network	Special Features	URL
StartupNation	Provides articles, forums, blogs, seminars, and podcasts	www.startupnation.com
LinkedIn	So many business professionals and corporate managers are members of this popular network that most entrepreneurs should have a presence as well	www.linkedin.com
Xing	Similar to LinkedIn, with a European focus	www.xing.com
Facebook	Not specifically for entrepreneurs or small business owners but has become a major marketing platform for many small businesses	www.facebook.com
The Funded	Lets entrepreneurs share information on venture capitalists and angel investors, including the amounts and terms they've been offered	http://thefunded.com
Young Entrepreneur	For active entrepreneurs and those considering entrepreneurship	www.facebook.com/YoungEntrepreneurs
Twitter	Not specifically for entrepreneurs or small business owners, but many use it to build connections and conduct research	https://twitter.com
Pinterest	Many consumers use Pinterest to search for product ideas, so it can be a great promotional platform for businesses	www.pinterest.com

country have local networks; search online for "entrepreneur network." Some entrepreneurs meet regularly in small groups to analyze each other's progress month by month. Being forced to articulate your plans and decisions to peers—and to be held accountable for results—can be an invaluable reality check. Some groups focus on helping entrepreneurs hone their presentations to potential investors. In addition to local in-person groups, social networking technology gives entrepreneurs an endless array of opportunities to connect online (see Exhibit 6.5).

Business Incubators

business incubators
Facilities that house small businesses and provide support services during the company's early growth phases.

Business incubators are centers that provide "newborn" businesses with various combinations of advice, financial support, access to industry insiders and connections, facilities, and other services a company needs to get started. Some incubators are not-for-profit organizations affiliated with the economic development agencies of local or state governments or universities, some are for-profit enterprises, some are run by venture capitalists, and some companies have internal incubators to encourage new ventures.

One of the best-known incubators, Y Combinator (http://ycombinator.com), has helped to fund and nurture hundreds of companies in digital media and related industries. In exchange for a small share of ownership, it makes small investments in companies; more important, it helps founders refine their ideas, develop products, polish their pitches to investors, connect with industry experts, handle incorporation issues to avoid legal trouble later on, hire the right kind of employees, and even mediate disputes between company founders. If all this help sounds priceless, Y Combinator would certainly agree with you: "The kind of

REAL-TIME UPDATES
Learn More by Visiting This Website

Find an incubator to nurture your new venture

The National Business Incubation Association has information about incubators and links to one in your area. Go to http://real-time updates.com/bia8 and click on Learn More in the Students section.

advice we give literally can't be bought, because anyone qualified to give it is already rich. You can only get it from investors."[27]

Checkpoint

LEARNING OBJECTIVE 4: Identify the major causes of business failures, and identify sources of advice and support for struggling business owners.

SUMMARY: Ten common reasons for failure are managerial incompetence, inexperience, inadequate financing, poor cash management, lack of strategy planning, ineffective marketing, uncontrolled growth, poor location, poor inventory control, and the inability to make the transition from corporate employee to independent entrepreneur. Another factor that can contribute to any of these explicit reasons is motivational collapse, when the entrepreneur simply gives up. For help and advice, business owners can turn to a variety of government agencies, not-for-profit organizations, business partners, mentors and advisory boards, print and online media, networks and support groups, and business incubators.

CRITICAL THINKING: (1) Why would a state or local government invest taxpayer dollars in a business incubator? (2) Can you think of any risks of getting advice from other entrepreneurs?

IT'S YOUR BUSINESS: (1) Have you ever shopped at a store or eaten in a restaurant and said to yourself, "This place isn't going to make it"? What factors caused you to reach that conclusion? (2) Does your college have an entrepreneur program or participate in a business incubator? If you wanted to start a business, how might such services help you?

KEY TERMS TO KNOW: advisory board, business incubators

Financing Options for Small Businesses

5 LEARNING OBJECTIVE
Discuss the principal sources of small-business private financing.

Figuring out *how much* you'll need in order to start a business requires good insights into the particular industry you plan to enter. Figuring out *where* to get the money is a creative challenge no matter which industry you're in. Financing a business enterprise is a complex undertaking, and chances are you'll need to piece together funds from multiple sources, possibly using a combination of *equity* (in which you give investors a share of the business in exchange for their money) and *debt* (in which you borrow money that must be repaid). You'll read more about equity and debt financing in Chapter 18. Exhibit 6.6 on the next page identifies, in broad terms, the major types of financing available to businesses at various stages in their life cycle.

PRIVATE FINANCING

Private financing covers every source of funding except selling stocks and bonds. Nearly all companies start with private financing, even those that eventually "go public." The range of private financing options is diverse, from personal savings to investment funds set up by large corporations looking for entrepreneurial innovations. Many firms get **seed money**, their first infusion of capital, through family loans. If you go this route, be sure to make the process as formal as a bank loan would be, complete with a specified repayment plan. Otherwise, problems with the loan can cause problems in the family.[28]

seed money
The first infusion of capital used to get a business started.

Four common categories of private financing are banks and microlenders, venture capitalists, angel investors, and personal credit cards and lines of credit.

Banks and Microlenders

Bank loans are one of the most important sources of financing for small business, but there's an important catch: In most cases, banks won't lend money to a start-up that hasn't

EXHIBIT 6.6	Financing Possibilities over the Life of a Small Business

The potential funding sources available to a business owner vary widely, depending on where the business is in its life cycle. Note that this is a general map and covers only the most common funding sources. Individual lending opportunities depend on the specific business owner(s), the state of the economy, and the type of business and its potential for growth. For example, venture capital is available only to firms with the potential to grow rapidly and only in a few industries.

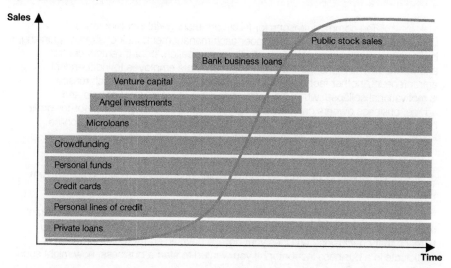

established a successful track record.[29] As your company grows, a bank will usually be a good long-term partner, helping you finance expansions and other major expenses. However, just about your only chance of getting a bank loan is by putting up marketable collateral, such as buildings or equipment, to back the loan.[30]

In response to the needs of entrepreneurs who don't qualify for standard bank loans or who don't need the amount of a regular loan, hundreds of organizations now serve as **microlenders**, offering loans up to $35,000 or so. You can learn more at the Association for Enterprise Opportunity website, at **www.microenterpriseworks.org**.[31]

Venture Capitalists

At the other end of the funding scale are **venture capitalists (VCs)**, investment specialists who raise pools of capital from large private and institutional sources (such as pension funds) to finance ventures that have high growth potential and need large amounts of capital. VC funding provides a crucial stimulus to the economy by making risky, early-stage investments in firms that are likely to become major employers if their products succeed in the marketplace. Because one-third of VC-funded start-ups don't succeed, those that do succeed need to really pay off to compensate. VCs are therefore extremely focused and selective; they invest in only a few thousand companies in the United States every year.[32]

Given the amounts of money involved and the expectations of sizable returns, VCs usually invest in high-potential areas such as information technology, energy, biotechnology, and digital media. Unlike banks or most other financing sources, VCs do more than simply provide money. They also provide management expertise in return for a sizable ownership interest in the business. Once the business becomes profitable, VCs reap the reward by selling their interest to long-term investors, usually after the company goes public.

Angel Investors

Start-up companies that can't attract VC investment (perhaps because they are too early in their product development) often look for **angel investors**, private individuals who put their own money into start-ups, with the goal of eventually selling their interest for a profit.

microlenders
Organizations, often not-for-profit, that lend smaller amounts of money to business owners who might not qualify for conventional bank loans.

venture capitalists (VCs)
Investors who provide money to finance new businesses or turnarounds in exchange for a portion of ownership, with the objective of reselling the business at a profit.

angel investors
Private individuals who invest money in start-ups, usually earlier in a business's life and in smaller amounts than VCs are willing to invest or banks are willing to lend.

These individuals are willing to invest smaller amounts than VCs and often stay involved with the company for a longer period of time. Many of these investors join *angel networks* or *angel groups* that invest together in chosen companies. Angel investing tends to have a more local focus than venture capitalism, so you can search for angels through local business contacts and organizations.

Credit Cards and Personal Lines of Credit

Although they tend to be one of the most expensive forms of financing, credit cards are also widely available and sometimes the only source of funding an entrepreneur has. Consequently, roughly half of all entrepreneurs and small-business owners use their cards to get cash for start-up or ongoing expenses.[33]

Funding a business with credit cards or a personal line of credit might be the only option for many people, but it is extremely risky. Unfortunately, there is no simple answer about whether to use credit cards; some entrepreneurs have used them to launch successful, multimillion-dollar businesses, whereas others have destroyed their credit ratings and racked up debts that take years to pay off.

Small Business Administration Assistance

The SBA offers a number of financing options for small businesses. To get an SBA-backed loan, you apply to a regular bank or credit union, which actually provides the money. The SBA guarantees to repay most of the loan amount (the percentage varies by program) if you fail to do so. In addition to operating its primary loan guarantee program, the SBA also manages a microloan program in conjunction with nonprofit, community-based lenders.[34]

Another option for raising money is the Small Business Investment Companies (SBICs) created by the SBA. These investment firms offer loans, venture capital, and management assistance, although they tend to make smaller investments and are willing to consider businesses that VCs or angel investors may not want to finance. The SBIC program has helped fund some of the best-known companies in the United States, including Apple, FedEx, Jenny Craig, and Outback Steakhouse.[35]

PUBLIC FINANCING

Companies with solid growth potential may also seek funding from the public at large, although only a small fraction of the companies in the United States are publicly traded. Whenever a corporation offers its shares of ownership to the public for the first time, the company is said to be *going public*. The shares offered for sale at this point are the company's **initial public offering (IPO)**. Going public is an effective method of raising needed capital, but it can be an expensive and time-consuming process with no guarantee of raising the amount of money needed. Public companies must meet a variety of regulatory requirements, as you'll explore in more detail in Chapter 18.

initial public offering (IPO)
A corporation's first offering of shares to the public.

CROWDFUNDING

Crowdfunding is an intriguing twist to funding that combines elements of public and private financing. Kickstarter is perhaps the best known of these web services that provide a way for people and organizations to seek money from the public. Crowdfunding services fall into two general categories. Kickstarter and a number of other sites focus on individual projects or charitable endeavors, and people provide money in exchange for the product being created or simply to help people and causes they believe in. In contrast, services such as Crowdfunder (www.crowdfunder.com) and Indiegogo (www.indiegogo.com) help business owners raise money to launch or expand companies, and the people who provide money are investing in or lending to the company. Government regulations regarding investment crowdfunding are still being finalized, but these services have the potential to give entrepreneurs some potent new ways to get their companies off the ground.[36]

crowdfunding
Soliciting project funds, business investment, or business loans from members of the public.

Checkpoint

LEARNING OBJECTIVE 5: Discuss the principal sources of small-business private financing.

SUMMARY: Sources of *private financing* for small businesses include banks and microlenders, venture capitalists, angel investors, credit cards and personal lines of credit, and loan programs from the Small Business Administration. Companies that reach sufficient size with continued growth potential have the additional option of seeking *public financing* by selling shares.

CRITICAL THINKING: (1) Would a profitable small business with only moderate growth potential be a good candidate for venture capitalist funding? Why or why not? (2) Why would angel investors help finance companies privately, rather than buying shares of publicly traded companies?

IT'S YOUR BUSINESS: (1) Would you be willing to take on credit card debt in order to start a company? Why or why not? (2) What would it take to convince you to invest in or contribute to a crowdsourced startup?

KEY TERMS TO KNOW: seed money, microlenders, venture capitalists (VCs), angel investors, initial public offering (IPO), crowdfunding

---

6 | LEARNING OBJECTIVE

Explain the advantages and disadvantages of franchising.

franchise
A business arrangement in which one company (the franchisee) obtains the rights to sell the products and use various elements of a business system of another company (the franchisor).

franchisee
A business owner who pays for the rights to sell the products and use the business system of a franchisor.

franchisor
A company that licenses elements of its business system to other companies (franchisees).

The Franchise Alternative

An alternative to creating or buying an independent company is to buy a **franchise**, which enables the buyer to use a larger company's trade name and sell its goods or services in a specific territory. In exchange for this right, the **franchisee** (the small-business owner who contracts to sell the goods or services) pays the **franchisor** (the supplier) an initial start-up fee, then monthly royalties based on sales volume. Franchises are a large and growing presence in the U.S. economy, accounting for roughly 10 percent of all employer businesses (those that hire employees).[37]

TYPES OF FRANCHISES

Franchises are of three basic types. A *product franchise* gives you the right to sell trademarked goods, which are purchased from the franchisor and resold. Car dealers and gasoline stations fall into this category. A *manufacturing franchise,* such as a soft-drink bottling plant, gives you the right to produce and distribute the manufacturer's products, using supplies purchased from the franchisor. A *business-format franchise* gives you the right to open a business using a franchisor's name and format for doing business. This format includes many well-known chains, including Taco Bell, Pizza Hut, The UPS Store, and Curves fitness centers.

ADVANTAGES OF FRANCHISING

Franchising is a popular option for many people because it combines at least some of the freedom of working for yourself with many of the advantages of being part of a larger, established organization. You can be your own boss, hire your own employees, and benefit directly from your hard work. If you invest in a successful franchise, you know you are getting a viable business model, one that has worked many times before. If the franchise system is well managed, you get the added benefit of instant name recognition, national advertising programs, standardized quality of goods and services, and a proven formula for success. Buying a franchise also gives you access to a support network and in many cases a ready-made blueprint for building a business. Depending on the system, your initial investment provides you with such services as site-location studies, market research, training, and technical assistance, as well as assistance with building or leasing your structure, decorating the building, purchasing supplies, and operating the business during your initial ownership phase.

DISADVANTAGES OF FRANCHISING

Although franchising offers many advantages, it is not the ideal vehicle for everyone. Perhaps the biggest disadvantage is the relative lack of control, at several levels. First, when you buy into a franchise system, you typically agree to follow the business format, and franchisors can prescribe virtually every aspect of the business, from the color of the walls to the products you can carry. In fact, if your primary purpose in owning a business is the freedom to be your own boss, franchising probably isn't the best choice because you don't have a great deal of freedom in many systems. Second, as a franchisee, you usually have little control over decisions the franchisor makes that affect the entire system. Disagreements and even lawsuits have erupted in recent years over actions taken by franchisors regarding product supplies, advertising, and pricing.[38] Third, if the fundamental business model of the franchise system no longer works—or never worked well in the first place—or if customer demand for the goods and services you sell declines, you don't have the option of independently changing your business in response.

In addition, buying a franchise involves both initial costs associated with buying into a franchise system and regular payments after that, based on a percentage of sales revenue. These costs vary widely, based on the complexity and popularity of the franchise. Many systems require a minimum level of liquid assets (spendable cash, essentially) and personal net worth, in addition to the out-of-pocket costs you'll have. The start-up costs for a simple home-based franchise can be less than $10,000, but a popular fast-food franchise can run from $250,000 to $2 million, and luxury hotels can top $5 million. Most franchises, however, have initial costs in the $50,000 to $200,000 range.[39]

Buying a new or existing franchise is an attractive alternative for many people who want some of the freedoms of entrepreneurship without all the risks.

REAL-TIME UPDATES
Learn More by Reading This PDF

Don't sign that franchise agreement before you read this

Before you commit to a franchise, consult "Buying a Franchise: A Consumer Guide," a free publication from the FTC. Go to http://real-timeupdates.com/bia8 and click on Learn More in the Students section.

HOW TO EVALUATE A FRANCHISING OPPORTUNITY

With so much at stake, researching a franchising opportunity carefully is vital (see Exhibit 6.7). The Federal Trade Commission (FTC) requires franchisors to disclose extensive information about their operations to prospective franchisees, including background information on the company and its executives, the company's financial status, the history of any litigation involving other franchisees, initial and ongoing costs, all restrictions put on franchisees, the availability and cost of training, procedures for ending the franchise agreement, earnings projections, and the names of current and former franchise owners. Study all this information and talk to as many current and former franchise owners as you can before taking the plunge.[40]

 **Checkpoint**

LEARNING OBJECTIVE 6: Explain the advantages and disadvantages of franchising.

SUMMARY: Franchising appeals to many because it combines some of the advantages of independent business ownership with the resources and support of a larger organization. It can also be less risky than starting or buying an independent business

| EXHIBIT 6.7 | Key Questions to Ask Before Signing a Franchise Agreement |

A franchise agreement is a legally binding contract that defines the relationship between a franchisee and a franchisor. Before signing a franchise agreement, be sure to read the disclosure document and consult an attorney.

1. What are the total start-up costs? What does the initial franchise fee cover? Does it include a starting inventory of supplies and products?
2. Who pays for employee training?
3. How are the periodic royalties calculated, and when must they be paid?
4. Who provides and pays for advertising and promotional items? Do you have to contribute to an advertising fund?
5. Are all trademarks and names legally protected?
6. Who selects or approves the location of the business?
7. Are you restricted to selling certain goods and services?
8. Are you allowed to sell online?
9. How much control will you have over the daily operation of the business?
10. Is the franchise assigned an exclusive territory?
11. If the territory is not exclusive, does the franchisee have the right of first refusal on additional franchises established in nearby locations?
12. Is the franchisee required to purchase equipment and supplies from the franchisor or other suppliers?
13. Under what conditions can the franchisor or the franchisee terminate the franchise agreement?
14. Can the franchise be assigned to heirs?

Source: "Buying a Franchise: A Consumer Guide," U.S. Federal Trade Commission website, accessed 31 March 31, 2015, www.ftc.gov.

because you have some evidence that the business model works. The primary disadvantages are the lack of control and the costs, both the initial start-up costs and the monthly payments based on a percentage of sales.

CRITICAL THINKING: (1) Why might a business owner with a successful concept decide to sell franchises rather than expand the company under his or her own control? (2) Why might someone with strong entrepreneurial spirit be dissatisfied with franchise ownership?

IT'S YOUR BUSINESS: (1) Are you a good candidate for owning and operating a franchise? Why or not? (2) Think about a small-business idea you've had or one of the small businesses you patronize frequently. Could this business be expanded into a national or international chain? Why or why not?

KEY TERMS TO KNOW: franchise, franchisee, franchisor

BEHIND THE SCENES
BUILDING AN AUTHENTIC AND PURPOSEFUL BUSINESS AT SISTER SKY

Sisters Monica Simeon and Marina TurningRobe have committed themselves to making products that are both authentic and purposeful and in doing so have created a company that shares those same attributes. Of course, like just about every other small business, Sister Sky has required intense dedication and many, many long days.

After Simeon and TurningRobe decided to turn their first homemade lotions into a real business, they started in a leased manufacturing space in Spokane, Washington. Both of their families would pitch in for 12-hour days, seven days a week—mixing, bottling, and boxing. When sales began to take off, they built their own manufacturing facility on the Spokane Indian

Reservation, as part of their commitment to help reservation economies diversify beyond gaming. Putting their houses up for collateral, they installed a $100,000 automated manufacturing system to replace much of the manual labor and expand their production volume. Beyond employing and mentoring fellow tribal members, including offering job-readiness training for tribal youth, the sisters also made a point of buying goods and services from other Native American–owned companies and serving as entrepreneurial role models in Native American communities.

In addition to scaling up manufacturing, Simeon and TurningRobe had to adjust their original marketing strategy. They initially focused on the general gift market but found that they were a tiny player in a vast market. Realizing that the cultural heritage of their product line gave them a unique advantage, they refocused on hotels and resorts, particularly those with luxury spa services. They also now offer spa consulting services, helping property owners create culturally authentic environments and experiences for their guests.

As is often the case, the challenges don't stop as a business grows, and Simeon and TurningRobe faced several classic small-business dilemmas, including time management. Simeon's husband joined the company as production manager, which freed up the sisters' time for selling, but as Simeon said recently, "We're so busy selling, we have no time to step back and strategize." A consultant who worked with them during a "business makeover" sponsored by *Fortune Small Business* magazine stressed that they really have no choice on this: They simply have to make time for strategizing, forcing themselves to step away from marketing and sales activities every quarter to review and adjust their business plan.

One of the key strategic decisions Simeon and TurningRobe must make is where to expand next. They've already moved beyond spa sales to high-end boutiques and gift shops, where their unique product concept appeals to consumers looking for something out of the ordinary. Being active in social media is helping them make connections with customers and potential business partners, too. Also, having received Minority Business Enterprise (MBE) certification from the National Minority Supplier Development Council, the company has made its first inroads into having its products used by Wyndham and other major hotel and resort chains. Sister Sky's MBE status helps these large customers meet supplier diversity goals.

After more than a decade into their entrepreneurial adventure, the sisters and their company are going strong with expanding sales but also with rewards that go beyond their own business objectives. By employing fellow tribe members and offering both inspiration and practical training, TurningRobe and Simeon are fulfilling their larger purpose, too. "Wealth building in our tribal communities through entrepreneurship is critical if we are going to improve our conditions and solve our own problems," Simeon explains. TurningRobe also speaks for many passionate entrepreneurs when she says, "If you love what you do and strive to create meaning to what you sell or create, and do it on a professional level, then I think you have found your purpose."[41]

Critical Thinking Questions

6-1. Which of the qualities of successful entrepreneurs have Simeon and TurningRobe demonstrated?

6-2. Should Simeon and TurningRobe consider lowering their ingredient costs by switching to petroleum-based ingredients or stopping their use of pure distilled water? Why or why not?

6-3. Would opening their own retail stores be a risky decision for Sister Sky? How would this change the company's business model?

LEARN MORE ONLINE

Explore the Sister Sky website at www.sistersky.com and find the company on Facebook and Twitter. How well does the company's online presence reflect its values? Does the information you find encourage you to learn more about the company's products? How could all entrepreneurs, regardless of market niche or company style, learn from Sister Sky's online presence?

KEY TERMS

advisory board
angel investors
business incubators
business plan
crowdfunding
entrepreneurial spirit
franchise
franchisee

franchisor
initial public offering (IPO)
microlenders
seed money
small business
venture capitalists (VCs)

MyBizLab®
To complete the problems with the ⭐,
go to EOC Discussion Questions in the
MyLab.

TEST YOUR KNOWLEDGE

Questions for Review

6-4. What contributions do small businesses make to our society?

6-5. What are the advantages of buying a business rather than starting one from scratch?

6-6. What are the advantages and disadvantages of owning a franchise?

6-7. What are the key reasons for most small-business failures?

6-8. What is a business plan?

Questions for Analysis

⭐ **6-9.** Why is the entrepreneurial spirit vital to the health of the nation's economy?

6-10. Do you expect that the number of entrepreneurs in the United States will grow in the next 10 years? Why or why not?

6-11. Could writing a conventional business plan every cause more harm than good? Explain your answer?

6-12. What are the financing options for entrepreneurs looking to start their own business?

⭐ **6-13.** **Ethical Considerations.** You're thinking about starting your own chain of upscale, drive-through espresso stands. You have several ideal sites in mind, and you've analyzed the industry and all the important statistics. You have financial backing, and you really understand the coffee market. In fact, you've become a regular at a competitor's operation for over a month. The owner thinks you're his best customer. But you're not there because you love the espresso. No, you're actually spying. You're learning everything you can about the competition so you can outsmart them. Is this behavior ethical? Explain your answer.

Questions for Application

6-14. Briefly describe an incident in your life in which you failed to achieve a goal you set for yourself. What did you learn from this experience? How could you apply this lesson to a future experience as an entrepreneur?

6-15. Based on your total life experience up to this point—as a student, consumer, employee, parent, and any other role you've played—what sort of business would you be best at running? Why?

⭐ **6-16.** **Concept Integration.** Entrepreneurship is one of the five factors of production, as discussed in Chapter 2 (page 27). Review that material and explain why entrepreneurs are an important factor for economic success.

6-17. **Concept Integration.** Pick a local small business or franchise that you visit frequently and discuss whether that business competes on price, speed, innovation, convenience, quality, or any combination of those factors. Be sure to provide some examples.

EXPAND YOUR KNOWLEDGE

Discovering Career Opportunities

Do you aspire to be an entrepreneur? You are inspired by Brian and Joe, the co-founders of AirBnB. Starting a company is not easy, yet you are determined to own and operate your own business. Being the youngest and only son in a family of five, you think this chapter will be the turning point in your life.

6-18. On the enterprise website, read the Forbes articles on AirBnB at http://www.forbes.com/search/?q=Airbnb. You assumed Brian and Jo as your mentors. How had their business failures motivated you in your personal and professional networks? Besides Brian and Jo, what were the other business and social supports that you could possibly benefit from? You are also keen to reach out to the local entrepreneurial support groups, who are they and in what ways could these entrepreneurial support groups offer sound advice?

6-19. Give a few names of successful entrepreneurs. Which of the entrepreneurial characteristics determine their success? Which one entrepreneurial characteristic will you be able to unleash?

6-20. Read the tech startup articles on http://techcrunch.com/startups/. Choose one entrepreneur of your choice. List the efforts that the entrepreneur has done for the business. How will you be preparing for your own business in order to achieve sustainability?

Improving Your Tech Insights: Social Networking Technology

One of the biggest challenges small-business owners face is finding the right people and making those connections, whether they're looking for a new employee, an investor, a potential customer, or anyone else who might be important to the future of the business. Using social networking, businesspeople can reach more people than they could ever hope to reach via traditional, in-person networking. In a brief email message to your instructor, describe how you could use social networking to locate potential candidates to serve on the advisory board of your small business. (Make up any details you need about your company.)

PRACTICE YOUR SKILLS

Sharpening Your Communication Skills

In order to receive support both financially and non-financially, entrepreneurs need to be able to communicate their plan, vision, and ideas to others. Imagine that you want to start your own business.

For this task, come up with an idea for a business either in small groups or individually and devise a business plan that can be shown to potential investors. Make sure to include a clear vision for the business as well as projected financial estimates. Use specific examples.

Building Your Team Skills

The questions shown in Exhibit 6.7 cover major legal issues you should explore before investing money in a franchise. In addition, however, there are many more questions you should ask in the process of deciding whether to buy a particular franchise.

With your team, think about how to investigate the possibility of buying a Burger King franchise. Go to www.bk.com/franchising/home and explore the information the company provides about franchising opportunities.

Next, brainstorm a plan to learn more about the potential positives and negatives of buying a Burger King franchise. Then generate a list of at least 10 questions an interested buyer should ask about this potential business opportunity.

Choose a spokesperson to present your team's ideas to the class. After all the teams have reported, hold a class discussion to analyze the lists of questions generated by all the teams. Which questions were on most teams' lists? Why do you think those questions are so important? Can your class think of any additional questions that were not on any team's list but seem important?

Developing Your Research Skills

There are a number of opportunities for individuals to gain support and funding for their business ideas. In order to complete this task, research the different sources of funding and support that would be available to you when starting your own business.

6-21. As a university student, what opportunities have you found so far for your business idea? Discuss the different sources of support that may be available to you.

6-22. Compare two of the sources of support. What do they offer? Why would each be beneficial to your idea?

6-23. Why might now be a good time to start your own business? Use examples.

MyBizLab®

Go to the Assignments section of your MyLab to complete these writing exercises.

6-24. Given the risks involved in starting any company, should an aspiring entrepreneur investigate all possible failure scenarios and develop action plans to avoid these potential outcomes? Explain your answer.

6-25. Is "I don't like having a boss tell me what to do" a good reason to start your own company? Explain your answer.

ENDNOTES

1. Sister Sky website, accessed 28 March 2015, www.sistersky .com; Sister Sky Facebook page, accessed 28 March 2015, www .facebook.com/pages/Sister-Sky/230340194280; "MBDA Helps Sister Sky Tap into a Legacy of Entrepreneurism," *MBDA.gov Newsletter*, March 2011, U.S. Department of Commerce Minority Business Development Agency, accessed 8 August 2011, www .mbda.gov; Patricia Gray, "Conditioning a Firm for Growth," *Fortune Small Business*, 3 December 2007; "Necessity Inspires This Mother's Invention: New Body Lotion Is Nature-Based Eczema Treatment," press release, 2 July 2007, www.theproductrocket .com; A. J. Naff, "Sister Sky: A Perfect Blend of Entrepreneurship and Native Wisdom," *Indian Gaming*, June 2008, 32–33.
2. Bernard Stamler, "Redefinition of Small Leads to a Huge Brawl," *New York Times*, 21 September 2004, G8.
3. "Small Business Size Standards," U.S. Small Business Administration, accessed 31 March 2015, www.sba.gov; "Table

of Small Business Size Standards Matched to North American Industry Classification System Codes," U.S. Small Business Administration, effective 14 July 2014, www.sba.gov.
4. "How Important Are Small Businesses to the U.S. Economy?" U.S. Small Business Administration, accessed 30 March 2009, www.sba.gov; Malik Singleton, "Same Markets, New Marketplaces," *Black Enterprise*, September 2004, 34; Edmund L. Andrews, "Where Do the Jobs Come From?" *New York Times*, 21 September 2004, E1, E11.
5. U.S. Small Business Administration, *Frequently Asked Questions: Advocacy the Voice of Small Business in Government*, September 2012.
6. *Frequently Asked Questions: Advocacy the Voice of Small Business in Government*.
7. "About Etsy," Etsy, accessed 11 August 2011, www.etsy.com.
8. College Nannies & Tutors, accessed 2 November 2013, www .collegenanniesandtutors.com; Stacy Perman, "The Startup Bug

Strikes Earlier," *BusinessWeek*, 31 October 2005, www.business week.com.

9. Jim Hopkins, "Bad Times Spawn Great Start-Ups," *USA Today*, 18 December 2001, 1B; Alan Cohen, "Your Next Business," *FSB*, February 2002, 33–40.

10. Matt Richtel and Jenna Wortham, "Weary of Looking for Work, Some Create Their Own," *New York Times*, 13 March 2009, www .nytimes.com.

11. Heather Green, "Self-Help for Startups," *BusinessWeek*, 5 February 2009, www.businessweek.com.

12. Richtel and Wortham, "Weary of Looking for Work, Some Create Their Own."

13. Intrapreneur, accessed 31 March 2009, www.intrapreneur.com.

14. Jeffrey Bussgang, "Think Like a VC, Act Like an Entrepreneur," *BusinessWeek*, 14 August 2008, www.businessweek.com.

15. "Buy a Business," U.S. Small Business Administration, accessed 3 July 2007, www.sba.gov.

16. Joshua Hyatt, "The Real Secrets of Entrepreneurs," *Fortune*, 15 November 2004, 185–202.

17. Heidi Brown, "How to Write a Winning Business Plan," *Forbes*, 18 June 2010, www.forbes.com; Michael Gerber, "The Business Plan That Always Works," *Her Business*, May/June 2004, 23–25; J. Tol Broome, Jr., "How to Write a Business Plan," *Nation's Business*, February 1993, 29–30; Albert Richards, "The Ernst & Young Business Plan Guide," *R & D Management*, April 1995, 253; David Lanchner, "How Chitchat Became a Valuable Business Plan," *Global Finance*, February 1995, 54–56; Marguerita Ashby-Berger, "My Business Plan—And What Really Happened," *Small Business Forum*, Winter 1994–1995, 24–35; Stanley R. Rich and David E. Gumpert, *Business Plans That Win $$$* (New York: Harper & Row, 1985).

18. "Writing a Compelling Executive Summary," Garage Technology Ventures, accessed 9 March 2011, www.garage.com; "Crafting Your Wow! Statement," Garage Technology Ventures, accessed 9 March 2011, www.garage.com; Guy Kawasaki website, accessed 9 March 2011, www.guykawasaki.com.

19. Strategyzer website, accessed 1 March 2015, www.business modelgeneration.com; Ash Maurya, "Why Lean Canvas vs Business Model Canvas?" Practice Trumps Theory blog, 27 February 2012, http://practicetrumpstheory.com

20. Rebecca L. Weber, "The Travel Agent Is Dying, But It's Not Yet Dead," *CNN*, 10 October 2013, www.cnn.com.

21. Kerry Miller, "The Restaurant-Failure Myth," *BusinessWeek*, 16 April 2007, 19.

22. Brian Headd, "Redefining Business Success: Distinguishing Between Closure and Failure," *Small Business Economics* 21, 51–61, 2003.

23. Joel Spolsky, "Start-Up Static," *Inc.*, March 2009, 33–34.

24. "MBDA Helps Sister Sky Tap into a Legacy of Entrepreneurism."

25. OPEN Forum, accessed 2 November 2013, https://www.open forum.com/explore/.

26. Christine Comaford-Lynch, "Don't Go It Alone: Create an Advisory Board," *BusinessWeek*, 1 February 2007, www.business week.com.

27. "About Y Combinator," Y Combinator, accessed 31 March 2015, http://ycombinator.com.

28. Paulette Thomas, "It's All Relative," *Wall Street Journal*, 29 November 2004, R4, R8.

29. Reed Albergotti, "Long Shot," *Wall Street Journal*, 29 November 2004, R4; Norman Scarborough and Thomas Zimmerer, *Effective Small Business Management* (Upper Saddle River, N.J.: Pearson Prentice Hall, 2002), 439.

30. Bob Zider, "How Venture Capital Works," *Harvard Business Review*, November/December 1998, 131–139.

31. Association for Enterprise Opportunity website, accessed 11 August 2011, www.microenterpriseworks.org.

32. National Venture Capital Association website, accessed 11 August 2011, www.nvca.org.

33. David Port, "APR Hikes Ambush Biz Owners," *Entrepreneur*, 16 March 2009, www.entrepreneur.com; Bobbie Gossage, "Charging Ahead," *Inc.*, January 2004, www.inc.com.

34. U.S. Small Business Administration website, accessed 11 August 2011, www.sba.gov.

35. U.S. Small Business Administration website, accessed 11 August 2011, www.sba.gov.

36. SoMoLend website, accessed 3 November 2013, www.somolend .com; Crowdfunder website, accessed 3 November 2013, http://crowdfunder.com; Steven M. Davidoff, "Trepidation and Restrictions Leave Crowdfunding Rules Weak," *New York Times*, 29 October 2013, www.nytimes.com; Chance Barnettt, "Top 10 Crowdfunding Sites for Fundraising," *Forbes*, 8 May 2013, www .forbes.com.

37. U.S. Census Bureau, "Census Bureau's First Release of Comprehensive Franchise Data Shows Franchises Make Up More Than 10 Percent of Employer Businesses," 14 September 2010, www.census.gov.

38. Douglas MacMillan, "Franchise Owners Go to Court," *BusinessWeek*, 29 January 2007, www.businessweek.com; Jill Lerner, "UPS Store Dispute Escalating," *Atlanta Business Chronicle*, 24 February 2006, www.bizjournals.com.

39. Eddy Goldberg, "The Costs Involved in Opening a Franchise," Franchising.com, accessed 31 March 2015, www.franchising .com; "U.S. Franchising," McDonald's website, accessed 31 March 2015, www.aboutmcdonalds.com; Hayley Peterson, "Here's How Much It Costs to Open Different Fast Food Franchises in the U.S.," *Business Insider*, 4 November 2014. www.businessinsider .com.

40. *Buying a Franchise: A Consumer Guide*, U.S. Federal Trade Commission, accessed 12 August 2011, www.ftc.gov.

41. See Note 1.

Entrepreneurship Module
MANAGING ENTREPRENEURIAL VENTURES

Russell Simmons is an entrepreneur. He co-founded Def Jam Records because the emerging group of New York hip-hop artists needed a record company, and the big record companies refused to take a chance on unknown artists. Def Jam was just one piece of Simmons's corporation, Rush Communications, which also included a management company; a clothing company called Phat Farm; a movie production house; television shows; a magazine; and an advertising agency. In 1999, Simmons sold his stake in Def Jam to Universal Music Group, and in 2004, he sold Phat Farm. Today, Simmons is involved in UniRush, a Cincinnati company that sells a prepaid Visa debit card, and Russell Simmons ArgyleCulture, a clothing line. He also launched an advertising venture described as a digital solutions company, set up to work for ad agencies, not to be one. And in his latest announced venture, Simmons is bringing rap to Broadway. His show "The Scenario" is a musical featuring songs from more than 30 years of rap hits. *USA Today* named Simmons one of the top 25 Influential People, while *Inc.* magazine named him one of America's 25 Most Fascinating Entrepreneurs.

In this appendix, we're going to look at the activities engaged in by entrepreneurs like Russell Simmons. We'll start by looking at the context of entrepreneurship and then examining entrepreneurship from the perspective of the four managerial functions: planning, organizing, leading, and controlling.

What Is Entrepreneurship?

Entrepreneurship is the process of starting new businesses, generally in response to opportunities. For instance, Fred Carl, founder of the Viking Range Corporation, saw an opportunity to create an appliance that combined the best features of commercial and residential ranges.

Many people think that entrepreneurial ventures and small businesses are the same, but they're not. Entrepreneurs create **entrepreneurial ventures**—organizations that pursue opportunities, are characterized by innovative practices, and have growth and profitability as their main goals. On the other hand, a **small business** is an independent business having fewer than 500 employees that doesn't necessarily engage in any new or innovative practices and that has relatively little impact on its industry. A small business isn't necessarily entrepreneurial because it's small. To be entrepreneurial means that the business is innovative and seeking out new opportunities. Even though entrepreneurial ventures may start small, they pursue growth. Some new small firms may grow, but many remain small businesses, by choice or by default.

Who's Starting Entrepreneurial Ventures?

Call them accidental entrepreneurs, unintended entrepreneurs, or forced entrepreneurs: As the unemployment rate hovers around double digits, many corporate "refugees" are becoming entrepreneurs. These individuals are looking to entrepreneurship, not because they sense some great opportunity, but because there are no jobs. The Index of Entrepreneurial Activity by the Kauffman Foundation showed the rate at which new businesses formed in 2010 remained high, representing the "highest level of entrepreneurship over the past decade and a half." The report found that "the patterns provided some early evidence that 'necessity' entrepreneurship is increasing and 'opportunity' entrepreneurship is decreasing." But "accidental or by design," entrepreneurship is on the rise again.

entrepreneurship
The process of starting new businesses, generally in response to opportunities

entrepreneurial ventures
Organizations that pursue opportunities, are characterized by innovative practices, and have growth and profitability as their main goals

small business
An independent business having fewer than 500 employees that doesn't necessarily engage in any new or innovative practices and that has relatively little impact on its industry

As many entrepreneurs (successful and not-so-successful) would attest to, being an entrepreneur isn't easy. According to the Small Business Administration, only two-thirds of new businesses survive at least two years. The survival rate falls to 44 percent at four years, and to 31 percent at seven. But the interesting thing is that entrepreneurial venture survival rates are about the same in economic expansions and recessions.

What Do Entrepreneurs Do?

Describing what entrepreneurs do isn't an easy or simple task! No two entrepreneurs' work activities are exactly alike. In a general sense, entrepreneurs create something new, something different. They search for change, respond to it, and exploit it.

Initially, an entrepreneur is engaged in assessing the potential for the entrepreneurial venture and then dealing with startup issues. In exploring the entrepreneurial context, entrepreneurs gather information, identify potential opportunities, and pinpoint possible competitive advantage(s). Then, armed with this information, an entrepreneur researches the venture's feasibility—uncovering business ideas, looking at competitors, and exploring financing options.

After looking at the potential of the proposed venture and assessing the likelihood of pursuing it successfully, an entrepreneur proceeds to plan the venture. This process includes such activities as developing a viable organizational mission, exploring organizational culture issues, and creating a well-thought-out business plan. Once these planning issues have been resolved, the entrepreneur must look at organizing the venture, which involves choosing a legal form of business organization, addressing other legal issues such as patent or copyright searches, and coming up with an appropriate organizational design for structuring how work is going to be done.

Only after these startup activities have been completed is the entrepreneur ready to actually launch the venture. A launch involves setting goals and strategies, and establishing the technology-operations methods, marketing plans, information systems, financial-accounting systems, and cash flow management systems.

Once the entrepreneurial venture is up and running, the entrepreneur's attention switches to managing it. What's involved with actually managing the entrepreneurial venture? An important activity is managing the various processes that are part of every business: making decisions, establishing action plans, analyzing external and internal environments, measuring and evaluating performance, and making needed changes. Also, the entrepreneur must perform activities associated with managing people, including selecting and hiring, appraising and training, motivating, managing conflict, delegating tasks, and being an effective leader. Finally, the entrepreneur must manage the venture's growth, including such activities as developing and designing growth strategies, dealing with crises, exploring various avenues for financing growth, placing a value on the venture, and perhaps even eventually exiting the venture.

What Planning Do Entrepreneurs Need to Do?

Planning is important to entrepreneurial ventures. Once a venture's feasibility has been thoroughly researched, an entrepreneur then must look at planning the venture. The most important thing that an entrepreneur does in planning the venture is developing a **business plan**—a written document that summarizes a business opportunity and defines and articulates how the identified opportunity is to be seized and exploited. A written business plan can range from basic to thorough. The most basic type of business plan would simply include an *executive summary,* sort of a mini-business plan that's no longer than two pages. A *synopsis* type plan is a little more involved. It's been described as an "executive summary on steroids." In addition to the executive summary, it includes a business proposal that explains why the idea is relevant to potential investors. A *summary business plan* includes an executive summary and a page or so of explanation of each of the key components of a business plan. A *full business plan* is the traditional business plan, which we describe fully next. Finally, an *operational business plan* is the most detailed (50 or more pages) and is used by ventures already operating with an

business plan
A written document that summarizes a business opportunity and defines and articulates how the identified opportunity is to be seized and exploited

existing strategy. It's often used to "plan the business" but also can be used to raise additional money or to attract potential acquirers. It's important for entrepreneurs to know which type of business plan they need for their purposes.

What's in a Full Business Plan?

For many would-be entrepreneurs, developing and writing a business plan seems like a daunting task. However, a good business plan is valuable. It pulls together all the elements of the entrepreneur's vision into a single coherent document. The business plan requires careful planning and creative thinking. But if done well, it can be a convincing document that serves many functions. It serves as a blueprint and road map for operating the business. And the business plan is a "living" document, guiding organizational decisions and actions throughout the life of the business, not just in the startup stage.

If an entrepreneur has completed a feasibility study, much of the information included in it becomes the basis for the business plan. A good business plan covers six major areas: executive summary, analysis of opportunity, analysis of the context, description of the business, financial data and projections, and supporting documentation.

Executive summary. The executive summary summarizes the key points that the entrepreneur wants to make about the proposed entrepreneurial venture. These might include a brief mission statement; primary goals; brief history of the entrepreneurial venture, maybe in the form of a timeline; key people involved in the venture; nature of the business; concise product or service descriptions; brief explanations of market niche, competitors, and competitive advantage; proposed strategies; and selected key financial information.

Analysis of opportunity. In this section of the business plan, an entrepreneur presents the details of the perceived opportunity, which essentially includes (1) sizing up the market by describing the demographics of the target market; (2) describing and evaluating industry trends; and (3) identifying and evaluating competitors.

Analysis of the context. Whereas the opportunity analysis focuses on the opportunity in a specific industry and market, the context analysis takes a much broader perspective. Here, the entrepreneur describes the broad external changes and trends taking place in the economic, political-legal, technological, and global environments.

Description of the business. In this section, an entrepreneur describes how the entrepreneurial venture is going to be organized, launched, and managed. It includes a thorough description of the mission statement; a description of the desired organizational culture; marketing plans including overall marketing strategy, pricing, sales tactics, service-warranty policies, and advertising and promotion tactics; product development plans such as an explanation of development status, tasks, difficulties and risks, and anticipated costs; operational plans, including a description of proposed geographic location, facilities and needed improvements, equipment, and work flow; human resource plans, including a description of key management persons, composition of board of directors including their background experience and skills, current and future staffing needs, compensation and benefits, and training needs; and an overall schedule and timetable of events.

Financial data and projections. Every effective business plan contains financial data and projections. Although the calculations and interpretation may be difficult, they are absolutely critical. No business plan is complete without financial information. Financial plans should cover at least three years and contain projected income statements, pro forma cash flow analysis (monthly for the first year and quarterly for the next two), pro forma balance sheets, breakeven analysis, and cost controls. If major equipment or other capital purchases are expected, the items, costs, and available collateral should be listed. All financial projections and analyses should include explanatory notes, especially where the data seem contradictory or questionable.

Supporting documentation. This *is* an important component of an effective business plan. The entrepreneur should back up his or her descriptions with charts, graphs, tables, photographs, or other visual tools. In addition, it might be important to include information (personal and work-related) about the key participants in the entrepreneurial venture.

Just as the idea for an entrepreneurial venture takes time to germinate, so does the writing of a good business plan. It's important for an entrepreneur to put serious thought and consideration into the plan. It's not an easy thing to do. However, the resulting document should be valuable in current and future planning efforts.

What Issues Are Involved in Organizing an Entrepreneurial Venture?

Once the startup and planning issues for the entrepreneurial venture have been addressed, the entrepreneur is ready to begin organizing the entrepreneurial venture. The main organizing issues an entrepreneur must address include the legal forms of organization, organizational design and structure, and human resource management.

What Are the Legal Forms of Organization for Entrepreneurial Ventures?

The first organizing decision that an entrepreneur must make is a critical one. It's the form of legal ownership for the venture. The two primary factors affecting this decision are taxes and legal liability. An entrepreneur wants to minimize the impact of both of these factors. The right choice can protect the entrepreneur from legal liability as well as save tax dollars, in both the short run and the long run.

The three basic ways to organize an entrepreneurial venture are sole proprietorship, partnership, and corporation. However, when you include the variations of these basic organizational alternatives, you end up with six possible choices, each with its own tax consequences, liability issues, and pros and cons. These six choices are sole proprietorship, general partnership, limited liability partnership (LLP), C corporation, S corporation, and limited liability company (LLC).

The decision regarding the legal form of organization is important because it has significant tax and liability consequences. Although the legal form of organization can be changed, it's not easy to do. An entrepreneur needs to think carefully about what's important, especially in the areas of flexibility, taxes, and amount of personal liability, in choosing the best form of organization.

What Type of Organizational Structure Should Entrepreneurial Ventures Use?

The choice of an appropriate organizational structure is also an important decision when organizing an entrepreneurial venture. At some point, successful entrepreneurs find that they can't do everything. They need people. The entrepreneur must then decide on the most appropriate structural arrangement for effectively and efficiently carrying out the organization's activities. Without a suitable type of organizational structure, an entrepreneurial venture may soon find itself in a chaotic situation.

In many small firms, the organizational structure tends to evolve with very little intentional and deliberate planning by the entrepreneur. For the most part, the structure may be very simple—one person does whatever is needed. As an entrepreneurial venture grows and the entrepreneur finds it increasingly difficult to go it alone, employees are brought on board to perform certain functions or duties that the entrepreneur can't handle. As the company continues to grow, these individuals tend to perform those same functions. Soon, each functional area may require managers and employees.

As the venture evolves to a more deliberate structure, an entrepreneur faces a whole new set of challenges. All of a sudden, he or she must share decision making and operating responsibilities, which are typically the most difficult things for an entrepreneur to do—letting go and allowing someone else to make decisions. *After all*, he or she reasons, *how can anyone know this business as well as I do?* Also, what might have been a fairly informal, loose, and flexible atmosphere that worked well when the organization was small may no longer be effective. Many entrepreneurs are greatly concerned about keeping that "small company" atmosphere alive even as the venture grows and evolves into a more structured arrangement. But having a structured organization doesn't necessarily mean giving up flexibility, adaptability, and freedom. In fact, the structural design may be as fluid as the entrepreneur feels comfortable with and yet still have the rigidity it needs to operate efficiently.

Organizational design decisions in entrepreneurial ventures also revolve around the six elements of organizational structure discussed in Chapter 6: work specialization, departmentalization, chain of command, span of control, amount of centralization-decentralization, and amount of formalization. Decisions about these six elements will determine whether an entrepreneur designs a more mechanistic or organic organizational structure. When would each be preferable? A mechanistic structure would be preferable when cost efficiencies are critical to the venture's competitive advantage; when more control over employees' work activities is important; if the venture produces standardized products in a routine fashion; and when the external environment is relatively stable and certain. An organic structure would be most appropriate when innovation is critical to the organization's competitive advantage; for smaller organizations where rigid approaches to dividing and coordinating work aren't necessary; if the organization produces customized products in a flexible setting; and where the external environment is dynamic, complex, and uncertain.

What Human Resource Management (HRM) Issues Do Entrepreneurs Face?

As an entrepreneurial venture grows, additional employees must be hired to perform the increased workload. As employees are brought on board, two HRM issues of particular importance are employee recruitment and employee retention.

An entrepreneur wants to ensure that the venture has the people to do the required work. Recruiting new employees is one of the biggest challenges that entrepreneurs face. In fact, the ability of small firms to successfully recruit appropriate employees is consistently rated as one of the most important factors influencing organizational success.

Entrepreneurs, particularly, look for high-potential people who can perform multiple roles during various stages of venture growth. They look for individuals who "buy into" the venture's entrepreneurial culture—individuals who have a passion for the business. Unlike their corporate counterparts who often focus on filling a job by matching a person to the job requirements, entrepreneurs look to fill in critical skills gaps. They're looking for people who are exceptionally capable and self-motivated, flexible, multiskilled, and who can help grow the entrepreneurial venture. While corporate managers tend to focus on using traditional HRM practices and techniques, entrepreneurs are more concerned with matching characteristics of the person to the values and culture of the organization; that is, they focus on matching the person to the organization.

Getting competent and qualified people into the venture is just the first step in effectively managing the human resources. An entrepreneur wants to keep the people he or she has hired and trained. A unique and important employee retention issue entrepreneurs must deal with is compensation. Whereas traditional organizations are more likely to view compensation from the perspective of monetary rewards (base pay, benefits, and incentives), smaller entrepreneurial firms are more likely to view compensation from a total rewards perspective. For these firms, compensation encompasses psychological rewards, learning opportunities, and recognition in addition to monetary rewards (base pay and incentives).

What Issues Do Entrepreneurs Face in Leading an Entrepreneurial Venture?

Leading is an important function of entrepreneurs. As an entrepreneurial venture grows and people are brought on board, an entrepreneur takes on a new role—that of a leader. In this section, we want to look at what's involved with that. First, we're going to look at the unique personality characteristics of entrepreneurs. Then we're going to discuss the important role entrepreneurs play in motivating employees through empowerment and leading the venture and employee teams.

What Type of Personality Do Entrepreneurs Have?

Think of someone you know who is an entrepreneur. Maybe it's someone you personally know or maybe it's someone you've read about, like Bill Gates of Microsoft. How would you describe this person's personality? One of the most researched areas of entrepreneurship has been the search to determine what—if any—psychological characteristics entrepreneurs have in common; what types of personality traits entrepreneurs have that might distinguish them from nonentrepreneurs; and what traits entrepreneurs have that might predict who will be a successful entrepreneur.

Is there a classic "entrepreneurial personality"? Although trying to pinpoint specific personality characteristics that all entrepreneurs share has the same problem as identifying the trait theories of leadership—that is, being able to identify specific personality traits that *all* entrepreneurs share—this hasn't stopped entrepreneurship researchers from listing common traits. For instance, one list of personality characteristics included the following: high level of motivation, abundance of self-confidence, ability to be involved for the long term, high energy level, persistent problem solver, high degree of initiative, ability to set goals, and moderate risk-taker. Another list of characteristics of "successful" entrepreneurs included high energy level, great persistence, resourcefulness, the desire and ability to be self-directed, and relatively high need for autonomy.

Another development in defining entrepreneurial personality characteristics was the proactive personality scale to predict an individual's likelihood of pursuing entrepreneurial ventures. The **proactive personality** is a personality trait describing those individuals who are more prone to take actions to influence their environment—that is, they're more proactive. Obviously, an entrepreneur is likely to exhibit proactivity as he or she searches for opportunities and acts to take advantage of those opportunities. Various items on the proactive personality scale were found to be good indicators of a person's likelihood of becoming an entrepreneur, including gender, education, having an entrepreneurial parent, and possessing a proactive personality. In addition, studies have shown that entrepreneurs have greater risk propensity than do managers. However, this propensity is moderated by the entrepreneur's primary goal. Risk propensity is greater for entrepreneurs whose primary goal is growth versus those whose focus is on producing family income.

How Can Entrepreneurs Motivate Employees?

When you're motivated to do something, don't you find yourself energized and willing to work hard at doing whatever it is you're excited about? Wouldn't it be great if all of a venture's employees were energized, excited, and willing to work hard at their jobs? Having motivated employees is an important goal for any entrepreneur, and employee empowerment is an important motivational tool entrepreneurs can use.

Although it's not easy for entrepreneurs to do, employee empowerment—giving employees the power to make decisions and take actions on their own—is an important motivational approach. Why? Because successful entrepreneurial ventures must be quick and nimble, ready to pursue opportunities and go off in new directions. Empowered employees can provide that flexibility and speed. When employees are empowered, they often display stronger work motivation, better work quality, higher job satisfaction, and lower turnover.

Empowerment is a philosophical concept that entrepreneurs have to "buy into." It doesn't come easily. In fact, it's hard for many entrepreneurs to do. Their life is tied up in the business. They've built it from the ground up. But continuing to grow the entrepreneurial venture is eventually going to require handing over more responsibilities to employees. How can entrepreneurs empower employees? For many entrepreneurs, it's a gradual process.

proactive personality
A personality trait describing those individuals who are more prone to take actions to influence their environment

Entrepreneurs can begin by using participative decision making, in which employees provide input into decisions. Although getting employees to participate in decisions isn't quite taking the full plunge into employee empowerment, at least it's a way to begin tapping into the collective array of employees' talents, skills, knowledge, and abilities.

Another way to empower employees is through delegation—the process of assigning certain decisions or specific job duties to employees. By delegating decisions and duties, the entrepreneur is turning over the responsibility for carrying them out.

When an entrepreneur is finally comfortable with the idea of employee empowerment, fully empowering employees means redesigning their jobs so they have discretion over the way they do their work. It's allowing employees to do their work effectively and efficiently by using their creativity, imagination, knowledge, and skills.

If an entrepreneur implements employee empowerment properly—that is, with complete and total commitment to the program and with appropriate employee training—results can be impressive for the entrepreneurial venture and for the empowered employees. The business can enjoy significant productivity gains, quality improvements, more satisfied customers, increased employee motivation, and improved morale. Employees can enjoy the opportunities to do a greater variety of work that is more interesting and challenging.

How Can Entrepreneurs Be Leaders?

The last topic we want to discuss in this section is the role of an entrepreneur as a leader. In this role, the entrepreneur has certain leadership responsibilities in leading the venture and in leading employee work teams.

Today's successful entrepreneur must be like the leader of a jazz ensemble known for its improvisation, innovation, and creativity. Max DePree, former head of Herman Miller, Inc., a leading office furniture manufacturer known for its innovative leadership approaches, said it best in his book, *Leadership Jazz*, "Jazz band leaders must choose the music, find the right musicians, and perform—in public. But the effect of the performance depends on so many things—the environment, the volunteers playing the band, the need for everybody to perform as individuals and as a group, the absolute dependence of the leader on the members of the band, the need for the followers to play well.... The leader of the jazz band has the beautiful opportunity to draw the best out of the other musicians. We have much to learn from jazz band leaders, for jazz, like leadership, combines the unpredictability of the future with the gifts of individuals."

The way an entrepreneur leads the venture should be much like the jazz leader—drawing the best out of other individuals, even given the unpredictability of the situation. One way an entrepreneur does this is through the vision he or she creates for the organization. In fact, the driving force through the early stages of the entrepreneurial venture is often the visionary leadership of the entrepreneur. The entrepreneur's ability to articulate a coherent, inspiring, and attractive vision of the future is a key test of his or her leadership. But if an entrepreneur can do this, the results can be worthwhile. A study contrasting visionary and nonvisionary companies showed that visionary companies outperformed the nonvisionary ones by six times on standard financial criteria, and their stocks outperformed the general market by 15 times.

As we know from Chapter 6, many organizations—entrepreneurial and otherwise—are using employee work teams to perform organizational tasks, create new ideas, and resolve problems. The three most common types of employee work teams in entrepreneurial ventures are empowered teams (teams that have the authority to plan and implement process improvements), self-directed teams (teams that are nearly autonomous and responsible for many managerial activities), and cross-functional teams (work teams composed of individuals from various specialties who work together on various tasks).

Developing and using teams is necessary because technology and market demands are forcing entrepreneurial ventures to make products faster, cheaper, and better. Tapping into the collective wisdom of a venture's employees and empowering them to make decisions just may be one of the best ways to adapt to change. In addition, a team culture can improve the overall workplace environment and morale. For team efforts to work, however, entrepreneurs must shift from the traditional command-and-control style to a coach-and-collaboration style.

What Controlling Issues Do Entrepreneurs Face?

Entrepreneurs must look at controlling their venture's operations in order to survive and prosper in both the short run and long run. The unique control issues that face entrepreneurs include managing growth, managing downturns, exiting the venture, and managing personal life choices and challenges.

How Is Growth Managed?

Growth is a natural and desirable outcome for entrepreneurial ventures. Growth is what distinguishes an entrepreneurial venture. Entrepreneurial ventures pursue growth. Growing slowly can be successful, but so can rapid growth.

Growing successfully doesn't occur randomly or by luck. Successfully pursuing growth typically requires an entrepreneur to manage all the challenges associated with growing, which entails planning, organizing, and controlling for growth.

How Are Downturns Managed?

Although organizational growth is a desirable and important goal for entrepreneurial ventures, what happens when things don't go as planned—when the growth strategies don't result in the intended outcomes and, in fact, result in a decline in performance? There are challenges, as well, in managing the downturns.

Nobody likes to fail, especially entrepreneurs. However, when an entrepreneurial venture faces times of trouble, what can be done? How can downturns be managed successfully? The first step is recognizing that a crisis is brewing. An entrepreneur should be alert to the warning signs of a business in trouble. Some signals of potential performance decline include inadequate or negative cash flow, excess number of employees, unnecessary and cumbersome administrative procedures, fear of conflict and taking risks, tolerance of work incompetence, lack of a clear mission or goals, and ineffective or poor communication within the organization.

Although an entrepreneur hopes to never have to deal with organizational downturns, declines, or crises, these situations do occur. After all, nobody likes to think about things going bad or taking a turn for the worse. But that's exactly what the entrepreneur should do—think about it *before* it happens (remember feedforward control from Chapter 14). It's important to have an up-to-date plan for covering crises. It's like mapping exit routes from your home in case of a fire. An entrepreneur wants to be prepared before an emergency hits. This plan should focus on providing specific details for controlling the most fundamental and critical aspects of running the venture—cash flow, accounts receivable, costs, and debt. Beyond having a plan for controlling the venture's critical inflows and outflows, other actions would involve identifying specific strategies for cutting costs and restructuring the venture.

What's Involved with Exiting the Venture?

Getting out of an entrepreneurial venture may seem to be a strange thing for entrepreneurs to do. However, the entrepreneur may come to a point at which he or she decides it's time to move on. That decision may be based on the fact that the entrepreneur hopes to capitalize financially on the investment in the venture—called **harvesting**—or that the entrepreneur is facing serious organizational performance problems and wants to get out, or even on the entrepreneur's desire to focus on other pursuits (personal or business). The issues involved with exiting the venture include choosing a proper business valuation method and knowing what's involved in the process of selling a business.

Although the hardest part of preparing to exit a venture may involve valuing it, other factors are also important. These include being prepared, deciding who will sell the business, considering the tax implications, screening potential buyers, and deciding whether to tell employees before or after the sale. The process of exiting the entrepreneurial venture

harvesting
Exiting a venture when an entrepreneur hopes to capitalize financially on the investment in the venture

should be approached as carefully as the process of launching it. If the entrepreneur is selling the venture on a positive note, he or she wants to realize the value built up in the business. If the venture is being exited because of declining performance, the entrepreneur wants to maximize the potential return.

Why Is It Important to Think About Managing Personal Challenges as an Entrepreneur?

Being an entrepreneur is extremely exciting and fulfilling, yet extremely demanding. It involves long hours, difficult demands, and high stress. Yet, many rewards can come with being an entrepreneur as well. In this section, we want to look at how entrepreneurs can make it work—that is, how can they be successful and effectively balance the demands of their work and personal lives?

Entrepreneurs are a special group. They're focused, persistent, hardworking, and intelligent. Because they put so much of themselves into launching and growing their entrepreneurial ventures, many may neglect their personal lives. Entrepreneurs often have to make sacrifices to pursue their entrepreneurial dreams. However, they can make it work. They can balance their work and personal lives. But how?

One of the most important things an entrepreneur can do is *become a good time manager*. Prioritize what needs to be done. Use a planner (daily, weekly, monthly) to help schedule priorities. Some entrepreneurs don't like taking the time to plan or prioritize, or they think it's a ridiculous waste of time. Yet identifying the important duties and distinguishing them from those that aren't so important actually makes an entrepreneur more efficient and effective. In addition, part of being a good time manager is delegating those decisions and actions the entrepreneur doesn't have to be personally involved in to trusted employees. Although it may be hard to let go of some of the things they've always done, entrepreneurs who delegate effectively will see their personal productivity levels rise.

Another suggestion for finding that balance is to *seek professional advice* in those areas of business where it's needed. Although entrepreneurs may be reluctant to spend scarce cash, the time and energy saved and potential problems avoided in the long run are well worth the investment. Competent professional advisors can provide entrepreneurs with information to make more intelligent decisions. Also, it's important to *deal with conflicts* as they arise—both workplace and family conflicts. If an entrepreneur doesn't deal with conflicts, negative feelings are likely to crop up and lead to communication breakdowns. When communication falls apart, vital information may get lost, and people (employees *and* family members) may start to assume the worst. It can turn into a nightmare situation that feeds on itself. The best strategy is to deal with conflicts as they come up. Talk, discuss, argue (if you must), but an entrepreneur shouldn't avoid the conflict or pretend it doesn't exist.

Another suggestion for achieving that balance between work and personal life is to *develop a network of trusted friends and peers*. Having a group of people to talk with is a good way for an entrepreneur to think through problems and issues. The support and encouragement offered by these people can be an invaluable source of strength for an entrepreneur.

Finally, *recognize when your stress levels are too high*. Entrepreneurs *are* achievers. They like to make things happen. They thrive on working hard. Yet, too much stress can lead to significant physical and emotional problems (as we discussed in Chapter 8). Entrepreneurs have to learn when stress is overwhelming them and to do something about it. After all, what's the point of growing and building a thriving entrepreneurial venture if you're not around to enjoy it?

Endnotes

1. Entrepreneurship Module based on J. Newman, "Russell Simmons Is Ready to Bring Rap to Broadway," http://www.rollingstone.com/music/features/russell-simmons-is-ready-to-bring-rap-to-broadway-scenario-20150323, March 23, 2015; "Russell Simmons' New Venture Digital Marketing Launches 'Digital-Solutions' Shop Called Narrative," adage.com, April 10, 2013; T. Padgett, "Russell Simmons: Getting Rich Is So Simple," *CNNMoney.com*, April 29, 2011; R. Schmidt and P. O'Connor, "Def Jam's Founder Out-Lobbies Big Banks," *Bloomberg BusinessWeek*, June 28, 2010, 21–22; R. A. Smith, "From Phat to Skinny," *Wall Street Journal*, May 1, 2010, W7; J. Dean, "The Endless Flow of Russell Simmons," *Entrepreneur*, September 2009, 24–28; S. Page, "Top 25 Influential People," *USA Today*, September 4, 2007, A10;

S. Berfield, "Hip-Hop Nation," *BusinessWeek*, June 13, 2005, 12; R. Kurtz, "Russell Simmons, Rush Communications," *Inc.*, April 2004, 137; J. Reingold, "Rush Hour," *Fast Company*, November 2003, 68–80; S. Berfield, "The CEO of Hip Hop," *BusinessWeek*, October 27, 2003, 90–98; J. L. Roberts, "Beyond Definition," *Newsweek*, July 28, 2003, 40–43; C. Dugas, "Hip-Hop Legend Far Surpassed Financial Goals," *USA Today*, May 15, 2003, 6B; "Jobless Entrepreneurship Tarnishes Steady Rate of U.S. Startup Activity, Kauffman Study Shows," www.kauffman.org/newsroom/ (March 7, 2011); "Frequently Asked Questions," *U.S. Small Business Administration*, www.sba.gov/advo (September 2008); D. E. Gumpert, "The Right Business Plan for the Job," *BusinessWeek Online*, January 7, 2008; W. H. Stewart, "Risk Propensity

Differences between Entrepreneurs and Managers: A Meta-Analytic Review," *Journal of Applied Psychology* (February 2001): 145–53; I. O. Williamson, "Employer Legitimacy and Recruitment Success in Small Businesses," *Entrepreneurship Theory and Practice*, Fall 2000, 27–42; R. L. Heneman, J. W. Tansky, and S. M. Camp, "Human Resource Management Practices in Small and Medium-Sized Enterprises: Unanswered Questions and Future Research Perspectives," *Entrepreneurship Theory and Practice*, Fall 2000, 11–26; T. L. Hatten, *Small Business: Entrepreneurship and Beyond* (Upper Saddle River, NJ: Prentice Hall, 1997), 5; L. W. Busenitz, "Research on Entrepreneurial Alertness," *Journal of Small Business Management* (October 1996): 35–44; J. M. Crant, "The Proactive Personality Scale as Predictor

of Entrepreneurial Intentions," *Journal of Small Business Management* (July 1996): 42–49; J. C. Collins and J. I. Porras, *Built to Last: Successful Habits of Visionary Companies* (New York: Harper Business, 1994); Max Depree, *Leadership Jazz: The Essential Elements of a Great Leader*, Dell.; P. B. Robinson, D. V. Simpson, J. C. Huefner, and H. K. Hunt, "An Attitude Approach to the Prediction of Entrepreneurship," *Entrepreneurship Theory and Practice*, Summer 1991, 13–31; P. F. Drucker, *Innovation and Entrepreneurship: Practice and Principles* (New York: Harper & Row, 1985); and J. W. Carland, F. Hoy, W. R. Boulton, and J. C. Carland, "Differentiating Entrepreneurs from Small Business Owners: A Conceptualization," *Academy of Management Review* 9, no. 2 (1984): 354–59.

Chapter 15
Innovation and Sustainability

How Can Managers Encourage Innovation in an Organization?

8-4 Discuss techniques for stimulating innovation.

"Innovation is the **key to continued** success."

"We innovate today to **secure the future**."

These two quotes (the first by Ajay Banga, the CEO of MasterCard, and the second by Sophie Vandebroek, chief technology officer of Xerox Innovation Group) reflect how important innovation is to organizations.[32] SUCCESS IN BUSINESS TODAY DEMANDS INNOVATION. In the dynamic, chaotic world of global competition, organizations must create new products and services and adopt state-of-the-art technology if they're going to compete successfully.[33]

K.C. Alfred/U-T San Diego/ZUMAPRESS/Alamy

Entrepreneur Nick Woodman channeled his creativity into a useful product. As founder of GoPro, Inc., Woodman designed a compact wearable camera that surfers, skydivers, and other sports enthusiasts can use to take high-quality photographs and videos. Woodman is shown here taking a photo of students with his wrist-strap GoPro during a college alumni event.

What companies come to mind when you think of successful innovators? Maybe Apple with all its cool work and entertainment gadgets. Maybe Facebook for its 1 billion-plus users. Maybe Nissan for creating the Leaf, the first mass-market all-electric car. Or even maybe Foursquare, a startup that revved up the social-local-mobile trend by having users "check in" at locations, unlocking quirky badges and special offers from merchants.[34] What's the secret to the success of these innovator champions? What can other managers do to make their organizations more innovative? In the following pages, we'll try to answer those questions as we discuss the factors behind innovation.

How Are Creativity and Innovation Related?

- **Creativity** refers to the ability to combine ideas in a unique way or to make unusual associations between ideas.[35] A creative organization develops unique ways of working or novel solutions to problems. For instance, at Mattel, company officials introduced "Project Platypus," a special group that brings people from all disciplines—engineering, marketing, design, and sales—and tries to get them to "think outside the box" in order to "understand the sociology and psychology behind children's play patterns." To help make this kind of thinking happen, team members embarked on such activities as imagination exercises, group crying, and stuffed-bunny throwing. What does throwing stuffed bunnies have to do with creativity? It's part of a juggling lesson where team members tried to learn to juggle two balls and a stuffed bunny. Most people can easily learn to juggle two balls but can't let go of that third object. Creativity, like juggling, is learning to let go—that is, to "throw the bunny."[36] Creativity by itself isn't enough, though.
- The outcomes of the creative process need to be turned into useful products or work methods, which is defined as **innovation**. Thus, the *innovative organization is characterized by its ability to channel creativity into useful outcomes.* When managers talk about changing an organization to make it more creative, they usually mean they want to stimulate and nurture innovation.

What's Involved in Innovation?

Some people believe that creativity is inborn; others believe that with training, anyone can be creative. The latter group views creativity as a fourfold process.[37]

1. *Perception* involves the way you see things. Being creative means seeing things from a unique perspective. One person may see solutions to a problem that others cannot or will not see at all. The movement from perception to reality, however, doesn't occur instantaneously.

2. Instead, ideas go through a process of *incubation*. Sometimes employees need to sit on their ideas, which doesn't mean sitting and doing nothing. Rather, during this incubation period, employees should collect massive amounts of data that are stored, retrieved, studied, reshaped, and finally molded into something new. During this period, it's common for years to pass. Think for a moment about a time you struggled for an answer on a test. Although you tried hard to jog your memory, nothing worked. Then suddenly, like a flash of light, the answer popped into your head. You found it!

creativity
The ability to produce novel and useful ideas

innovation
The process of taking a creative idea and turning it into a useful product, service, or method of operation

---

Technology and the Manager's Job
HELPING INNOVATION FLOURISH

When employees are busy doing their regular job tasks, how can innovation ever flourish? When job performance is evaluated by what you get done, how you get it done, and when you get it done, how can innovation ever happen? This has been a real challenge facing organizations wanting to be more innovative. One solution has been to give employees mandated time to experiment with their own ideas on company-related projects.[38] For instance, Google has its "20% Time" initiative, which encourages employees to spend 20 percent of their time at work on projects not related to their job descriptions. Other companies—Facebook, Apple, LinkedIn, 3M, Hewlett-Packard, among others—have similar initiatives. Hmmm...so having essentially one day a week to work on company-related ideas you have almost seems too good to be true. But, more importantly, does it really spark innovation? Well, it can. At Google, it led to the auto-complete system, Google News, Gmail, and Adsense. However, such "company" initiatives do face tremendous obstacles, despite how good they sound on paper. These challenges include:

- Strict employee monitoring in terms of time and resources leading to a reluctance to use this time since most employees have enough to do just keeping up with their regular tasks.
- When bonuses/incentives are based on goals achieved, employees soon figure out what to spend their time on.

- What happens to the ideas that employees do have?
- Unsupportive managers and coworkers who may view this as a "goof-around-for-free-day."
- Obstacles in the corporate bureaucracy.

So, how can companies make it work? Suggestions include: top managers need to support the initiatives/projects and make that support known; managers need to support employees who have that personal passion and drive, that creative spark—clear a path for them to pursue their ideas; perhaps allow employees more of an incentive to innovate (rights to design, etc.); and last, but not least, don't institutionalize it. Creativity and innovation, by their very nature, involve risk and reward. Give creative individuals the space to try and to fail and to try and to fail as needed.

*If your professor has assigned this, go to the Assignments section of **mymanagementlab.com** to complete these discussion questions.*

✪ **TALK ABOUT IT 5:** What benefits do you see with such mandated experiment time for (a) organizations? (b) individuals?

✪ **TALK ABOUT IT 6:** What obstacles do these initiatives face and how can managers overcome those obstacles?

---

3. *Inspiration* in the creative process is similar. Inspiration is the moment when all your efforts successfully come together. Although inspiration leads to euphoria, the creative work isn't complete. It requires an innovative effort.

4. *Innovation* involves taking that inspiration and turning it into a useful product, service, or way of doing things. Thomas Edison is often credited with saying that "Creativity is 1 percent inspiration and 99 percent perspiration." That 99 percent, or the innovation,

involves testing, evaluating, and retesting what the inspiration found. It's usually at this stage that an individual involves others more in what he or she has been working on. Such involvement is critical because even the greatest invention may be delayed, or lost, if an individual cannot effectively deal with others in communicating and achieving what the creative idea is supposed to do.

How Can a Manager Foster Innovation?

The systems model (inputs → transformation process → outputs) can help us understand how organizations become more innovative.[39] If an organization wants innovative products and work methods (*outputs*), it has to take its *inputs* and *transform* them into those outputs. Those *inputs* include creative people and groups within the organization. But as we said earlier, having creative people isn't enough. The *transformation process* requires having the right environment to turn those inputs into innovative products or work methods. This "right" environment—that is, an environment that stimulates innovation— includes three variables: the organization's structure, culture, and human resource practices. (See Exhibit 8–5.)

Exhibit 8–5 Innovation Variables

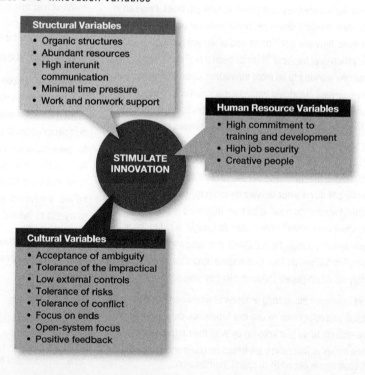

Structural Variables
- Organic structures
- Abundant resources
- High interunit communication
- Minimal time pressure
- Work and nonwork support

Human Resource Variables
- High commitment to training and development
- High job security
- Creative people

STIMULATE INNOVATION

Cultural Variables
- Acceptance of ambiguity
- Tolerance of the impractical
- Low external controls
- Tolerance of risks
- Tolerance of conflict
- Focus on ends
- Open-system focus
- Positive feedback

⊙ **Watch It 2!**

If your professor has assigned this, go to the Assignments section of **mymanagementlab.com** to complete the video exercise titled *CH2MHill: Innovation*.

HOW DO STRUCTURAL VARIABLES AFFECT INNOVATION?   Research into the effect of structural variables on innovation shows five things.[40]

1. An organic-type structure positively influences innovation. Because this structure is low in formalization, centralization, and work specialization, it facilitates the flexibility and sharing of ideas that are critical to innovation.

2. The availability of plentiful resources provides a key building block for innovation. With an abundance of resources, managers can afford to purchase innovations, can afford the cost of instituting innovations, and can absorb failures.

3. Frequent communication between organizational units helps break down barriers to innovation.[41] Cross-functional teams, task forces, and other such organizational designs facilitate interaction across departmental lines and are widely used in innovative organizations.

4. Extreme time pressures on creative activities are minimized despite the demands of white-water-rapids-type environments. Although time pressures may spur people to work harder and may make them feel more creative, studies show that it actually causes them to be less creative.[42]

5. When an organization's structure explicitly supports creativity, employees' creative performance can be enhanced. Beneficial kinds of support include encouragement, open communication, readiness to listen, and useful feedback.[43]

HOW DOES AN ORGANIZATION'S CULTURE AFFECT INNOVATION? Innovative organizations tend to have similar cultures.[44] They encourage experimentation; reward both successes and failures; and celebrate mistakes. An innovative organization is likely to have the following characteristics.

idea champions
Individuals who actively and enthusiastically support new ideas, build support for, overcome resistance to, and ensure that innovations are implemented

- *Accepts ambiguity.* Too much emphasis on objectivity and specificity constrains creativity.
- *Tolerates the impractical.* Individuals who offer impractical, even foolish, answers to what-if questions are not stifled. What at first seems impractical might lead to innovative solutions.
- *Keeps external controls minimal.* Rules, regulations, policies, and similar organizational controls are kept to a minimum.
- *Tolerates risk.* Employees are encouraged to experiment without fear of consequences should they fail. Mistakes are treated as learning opportunities.
- *Tolerates conflict.* Diversity of opinions is encouraged. Harmony and agreement between individuals or units are *not* assumed to be evidence of high performance.
- *Focuses on ends rather than means.* Goals are made clear, and individuals are encouraged to consider alternative routes toward meeting the goals. Focusing on ends suggests that there might be several right answers to any given problem.
- *Uses an open-system focus.* Managers closely monitor the environment and respond to changes as they occur. For example, at Starbucks, product development depends on "inspiration field trips to view customers and trends." When Michelle Gass (now Kohl's Corporation's chief customer officer) was in charge of Starbucks marketing, she had her team travel to several trendy global cities to visit local Starbucks and other dining establishments to "get a better sense of local cultures, behaviors, and fashions."[45] Her rationale? Seeing and experiencing firsthand different ideas and different ways to think about things can be so much more valuable than reading about them.
- *Provides positive feedback.* Managers provide positive feedback, encouragement, and support so employees feel that their creative ideas receive attention. For instance, Mike Lazaridis, co-founder of Blackberry maker Research in Motion, said "I think we have a culture of innovation here, and [engineers] have absolute access to me. I live a life that tries to promote innovation."[46]

Netflix founder and CEO Reed Hastings has created a culture of innovation that encourages employees to become idea champions. Netflix gives employees the freedom to come up with new ideas and the responsibility to implement them by engaging employees from different departments and by forming groups to "socialize" their ideas.

WHAT HUMAN RESOURCE VARIABLES AFFECT INNOVATION? In this category, we find that innovative organizations (1) actively promote the training and development of their members so their knowledge remains current, (2) offer their employees high job security to reduce the fear of getting fired for making mistakes, and (3) encourage individuals to become **idea champions,** actively and enthusiastically supporting new ideas, building support, overcoming resistance, and ensuring that innovations are implemented. Research finds that idea champions have common personality characteristics: extremely

high self-confidence, persistence, energy, and a tendency toward risk taking. They also display characteristics associated with dynamic leadership. They inspire and energize others with their vision of the potential of an innovation and through their strong personal conviction in their mission. They're also good at gaining the commitment of others to support their mission. In addition, idea champions have jobs that provide considerable decision-making discretion. This autonomy helps them introduce and implement innovations in organizations.[47]

How Does Design Thinking Influence Innovation?

We introduced you to the concept of design thinking in a previous chapter. Well, undoubtedly, there's a strong connection between design thinking and innovation. "Design thinking can do for innovation what TQM did for quality."[48] Just as TQM provides a process for improving quality throughout an organization, design thinking can provide a process for coming up with things that don't exist. When a business approaches innovation with a design thinking mentality, the emphasis is on getting a deeper understanding of what customers need and want. It entails knowing customers as real people with real problems—not just as sales targets or demographic statistics. But it also entails being able to convert those customer insights into real and usable products. For instance, at Intuit, the company behind TurboTax software, founder Scott Cook felt the company was "lagging behind in innovation."[49] So he decided to apply design thinking. He called the initiative "Design for Delight," and it involved customer field research to understand their "pain points"—that is, what most frustrated them as they worked in the office and at home. Then, Intuit staffers brainstormed (they nicknamed it "pain-storm") a wide array of possible ideas to address customer problems, which they would then try out with customers to find ones that worked best. For example, one pain point uncovered by an Intuit team was how customers could take pictures of tax forms to reduce typing errors. Some younger customers, used to taking photos with their smartphones, were frustrated that they couldn't just complete their taxes on their mobiles. To address this, Intuit developed a mobile app called SnapTax, which the company says has been downloaded more than a million times since it was introduced in 2010. That's how design thinking works in innovation.

MyManagementLab®

Go to **mymanagementlab.com** to complete the problems marked with this icon .

9 The ethical and ecological environment

Ian Worthington

There is a growing body of opinion that businesses have a duty to fulfil objectives that stretch beyond the simple well-being of the organisation and its owners to the promotion of greater corporate social responsibility, particularly with regard to the natural environment. This chapter looks at the emergence of this perspective and analyses why and how a firm may seek to improve on its environmental performance.

Learning outcomes

Having read this chapter you should be able to:

- define the concepts of business ethics and corporate social responsibility
- discuss the emergence of corporate environmentalism as a business issue
- differentiate between the drivers of, and motivations for, green behaviour by businesses
- analyse the reasons why a firm might seek to improve on its environmental performance and what forms this could take
- illustrate how firms both affect and are affected by the natural environment

Key terms

Business ethics
Circular economy
Competitive advantage
Corporate social
  responsibility
Cradle-to-cradle™ (C2C)
Eco-efficiency
Eco-label
Eco-Management
  and Audit Scheme
  (EMAS)
Environmental
  champions

Environmental
  management system
  (EMS)
Environmental subsidies
Environmental taxes
European Emissions
  Trading Scheme (ETS)
Gold plating
Inside-out view
Market niche
Negative externalities
Outside-in view
Polluter pays principle

Public voluntary
  programmes
Resource-based view
Stakeholders
Sustainable development
Tradeable (or marketable)
  pollution permits
Unilateral commitments
Unlevel playing field
Voluntary approach (VA)
Win-win philosophy

Introduction

In May 1999 the largest ever survey of global public opinion took place on the changing expectations of businesses in the twenty-first century. Twenty-five thousand people in 23 countries on 6 continents were interviewed about their perceptions of the roles and responsibilities of business organisations in the social and environmental as well as the economic spheres. This worldwide survey – known as the Millennium Poll on Corporate Social Responsibility (CSR) – confirmed what many business researchers and corporate leaders had come to recognise over the course of the previous decade or so. Namely, that a firm's social and environmental performance was no less important to the general public (and, therefore, customers) than its traditional roles of making profits, paying taxes and complying with the law. While there were differences in the strengths of opinions expressed in the countries surveyed, the overall message of the poll was clear: consumers believe that business organisations should behave in a socially and environmentally responsible way and should be held accountable for their actions across a range of areas, from protecting the health and safety of their employees, through avoiding unethical business practices, to protecting the natural environment. This remains a common perception.

In the analysis below, we discuss how ethical and ecological issues in business have become an increasingly important aspect of a firm's macroenvironmental context. This development can be illustrated in a number of ways. Many larger organisations now publish annual social and environmental reports, which are designed to highlight improvements in the firm's performance on a range of indicators (e.g. employee training, charitable donations, reduction in carbon emissions) to a variety of stakeholder groups (see below). To achieve these claimed improvements, a growing number of firms have appointed senior executives and managers with responsibility for directing, monitoring and auditing the social and environmental performance of the business and for communicating this both internally and externally to the various interested parties.

In the lexicon of business, concepts such as **corporate social responsibility**, social responsiveness, corporate social performance, corporate citizenship and corporate sustainability have become relatively commonplace, as have notions such as supply chain ethics, green marketing and triple bottom line accounting. Parallel developments have also taken place in the academic world as a growing number of business and management programmes now incorporate the study of **business ethics**, CSR and sustainable development into the curriculum, supported by a burgeoning literature in these fields and an expanding group of international journals focusing on the ethical and environmental aspects of business (e.g. *Journal of Business Ethics, Journal of Environmental Management, Business Strategy and the Environment*).

To provide an insight into how businesses can be affected by ethical and ecological pressures, the chapter begins with a general discussion of the notions of business ethics and corporate social responsibility before moving on to a more detailed examination of the very topical issue of environmental management in business. For students wishing to investigate these subjects in more detail, we have recommended some useful sources in the 'Further reading' section at the end of the chapter. You could also consult the websites of leading multinational corporations and bodies such as business representative organisations (e.g. Confederation of British Industry, Institute of Directors, Chambers of

Commerce), environmental NGOs (e.g. Greenpeace, Friends of the Earth, Forum for the Future), advocacy groups (e.g. Business in the Community) and the various international groups/agencies whose work includes consideration of ethical and environmental issues in business (e.g. the UN, World Bank).

Ethics and business

As we saw in the previous chapter, business organisations exist and function within a framework of law emanating from various sources, including government. In many areas of life, laws essentially direct what individuals and/or organisations can or cannot do and set minimum standards of behaviour based on underlying ethical principles. Not all ethical aspects of business, however, are covered by government legislation or the common law, as in the case of selling weapons to overseas governments or paying low wages to workers producing a product in other countries. By the same token, not all laws governing individual or organisational behaviour raise what would be regarded as important ethical issues.

As Crane and Matten (2004) suggest, business ethics is basically concerned with those issues in business that are not covered by law or where there is no definite consensus on what is 'right' or 'wrong' behaviour. Accordingly, they define business ethics as 'the study of business situations, activities and decisions where issues of right and wrong are addressed', stressing quite rightly that in terms of organisational behaviour right and wrong should be seen in a moral sense, not from a financial or strategic point of view. It might make financial sense, for instance, for an organisation to exploit cheap labour or flush its waste products into a river at no cost to the business, and it might not be illegal, but is it ethical? As the Millennium Poll (Available via www.ipsos-mori.com) and other surveys have illustrated, a firm's stance on ethical issues in business are an important aspect of its external environment and one that applies to enterprises of all kinds, in all sectors, and across different national jurisdictions.

While it is beyond the scope of this chapter to discuss all the potential ethical dilemmas faced by modern business organisations, it is worth noting that these have tended to intensify and broaden as business activity has become more globalised and as technological transformation has given rise to the globalisation of communications and the 24-hour instant news culture. Multinational corporations in particular are facing much closer scrutiny by different groups of stakeholders which are increasingly willing to pressurise larger businesses to behave in a more ethically and ecologically sustainable way. Allegations that some high-profile western companies are (sometimes unwittingly) exploiting child labour in the developing world or are involved in ethically questionable commercial practices (e.g. bribery, price fixing) or in environmentally damaging activities (e.g. illegal logging, oil exploration in unspoiled natural environments) inevitably attract media attention and can result in significant damage to a firm's reputation and, potentially, its bottom line. By the same token, firms recognised for having a good ethical stance may find favour with the different stakeholder interests and this could bring organisational benefits of various kinds, including increased sales, access to new customers/markets, improvements in labour recruitment and retention, lower insurance premiums and less scrutiny by governments and/or NGOs.

mini case   Illegal or unethical?

While definitions of business ethics focus on issues of right and wrong that are not covered by the law, the dividing line between behaviour that is evidently illegal and that which is unethical can sometimes be difficult to draw. Take the following recent cases of alleged and controversial business practices. Where would you draw the line?

1 Major banks – including UBS, Barclays, Standard Chartered, HSBC, RBS, J.P. Morgan and Lloyds – have been accused of, and sometimes fined for, a series of misdemeanours. These have included mis-selling of payment protection insurance; manipulating the key London inter-bank interest rate (LIBOR); breaches of money laundering rules and sanctions busting; selling of sub-prime mortgages; being involved in businesses that speculate on world food prices; manipulation of exchange rates. Not all of the above named banks have been accused of every one of these practices and some allegations are still being investigated.

2 Major international companies (e.g. Starbucks, Vodafone, Amazon, Apple, Facebook, Google) have been criticised for arranging their business affairs so as to minimise the tax paid to host governments.

3 GSK has been accused of paying bribes to win business in China. Rolls-Royce is facing similar allegations relating to past contracts in both Indonesia and China.

4 A number of major retailers – including Primark, Marks and Spencer, H&M, New Look – have come under pressure to investigate more fully the conditions in overseas factories supplying their garments following a fatal fire in a Bangladeshi supplier's premises. Most major retailers have now signed up to a UN-sponsored, legally binding agreement on worker safety and building regulations.

5 Some major food and drink firms have been exhorted to provide more accurate product labelling, particularly salt, sugar and calorie content, because of concerns over diabetes and obesity. Critics have accused some of the major companies in the food industry of providing unclear information and guidance to consumers.

As the above examples illustrate, there may be cases where a certain business practice may be judged to be both illegal and unethical in the moral sense of the word. Where businesses fail to provide an adequate system of corporate governance to address ethically questionable behaviour by their employees, governments are sometimes forced to intervene through the law. This is not necessarily easy, particularly if the issue is a cross-national problem (e.g. tax avoidance) requiring a coordinated approach by different national governments.

Whether 'good ethics' and 'good business' are always complementary has been the subject of considerable debate in both practitioner and academic circles and is one that is far from resolved.[1] That said, what is clear is that the question of ethics in business and the related concept of corporate social responsibility are no longer peripheral issues and have been rapidly moving up the corporate agenda in most large business organisations in recent years. If firms are to avoid the potential risks posed by a poor ethical performance (e.g. Enron) and/or exploit the anticipated opportunities offered by a positive ethical stance (e.g. The Body Shop), they need to put in place appropriate mechanisms for managing the ethical issues they face (e.g. values statements, codes of ethics, robust systems of corporate governance, accredited auditing and reporting systems). They also need to think more broadly about society's expectations of corporate behaviour and of their obligations and responsibilities beyond those to the immediate owners of the business. This notion of a firm's social responsibilities is the issue to which we now turn.

Corporate social responsibility (CSR)

The idea of CSR essentially means that business organisations have responsibilities that go beyond mere profit-making and encompass voluntary activities and actions that affect people, their communities and the natural environment. The question of whether, and how far, a firm should engage in such activities if they might adversely affect profitability remains a contested arena. A central theme in this debate has been the issue of the central purpose of the business organisation and the knowledge, abilities and responsibilities of those that run profit-seeking enterprises. Under the neo-classical view of the firm, private sector businesses exist to make profits for the owners (e.g. shareholders) and the responsibility of the firm's managers is to act in a way that enhances the position of the providers of capital, by maximising profits and/ or shareholder value. Writing in *The New York Times* in 1970, the economist Milton Friedman basically echoed this perspective when he argued that the social responsibility of a business was to increase its profits so long as it obeyed the law and operated ethically.[2] In Friedman's opinion, a firm's directors were not only ill-equipped to make decisions on social and environmental matters but, as agents for the firm's owners (the principals), they also had a fiduciary responsibility to the shareholders, not to some broader conception of the social good. Under this interpretation, allocating some of the firm's resources to the pursuit of socially responsible objectives could effectively be construed as unethical since it involves spending money that belongs to other individuals.

This conventional view of the role of business in society has been challenged on a number of grounds and to many observers of the business scene now seems outdated, narrow and arguably naïve. As Chapter 1 has shown, businesses exist within and draw their resources from the broader society and therefore could be said to have a moral obligation to take account of their social and environmental performance. Added to this, shareholders are only one of the groups with which the firm interacts and consequently there are other stakeholder interests to which a business has responsibilities and obligations when carrying out its activities (see, for example, Chapter 10). Such **stakeholders** are both internal (e.g. employees) and external (e.g. customers) to the organisation and under the stakeholder view of the firm (see, for example, Freeman, 1984) businesses have a social responsibility to take into account the interests of all parties affected by their actions and decisions, not just the owners of the business. In contrast to the neo-classical view of the firm, the stakeholder approach stresses the necessity for managers to try to operate the business to the benefit of all stakeholder groups and to seek to gain an effective balance between the different interested parties. Using some of the firm's profits to achieve such an outcome is not necessarily detrimental to the firm's owners and indeed may ultimately help to enhance shareholder value, particularly over the longer term.

More recent discussions of why businesses should take account of their social and environmental responsibilities have tended to focus on the strategic benefits of CSR, how acting 'responsibly' can generate advantages for the business on both the demand and the supply sides (see, for example, McWilliams *et al.*, 2006). Writers such as Porter and Kramer (2002) have argued that a firm can gain a **competitive advantage** by investing in CSR, particularly if its actions in this area become an intrinsic part of its business and corporate differentiation strategies. One important element in this debate has been the application of a **resource-based view (RBV)** of the firm in which social and environmental responsibility are portrayed as an organisational resource/capability that can lead to sustained competitive advantage.[3] The claim is that engaging in CSR has the potential to enhance a firm's reputation with key stakeholder groups and this could give it an advantage over its rivals that is both valuable and potentially difficult to imitate. One arena where this might be particularly important is with regard to an organisation's environmental performance, given the growing international concerns over the impact of business activity on the natural environment. This is the subject we now investigate in more detail.

The 'environment' as a business issue: the emergence of corporate environmentalism

In Chapter 1 we portrayed goods and services as the outputs of business activity, the end result of transforming inputs into products to meet the needs and demands of individuals, organisations and governments. While such economic activity undoubtedly gives rise to significant individual and societal benefits, these desirable aspects of business come at a price; production generates 'bads' as well as 'goods', including damage to the natural environment and resource depletion. Hawken (1996) has suggested that the business community contributes to environmental degradation in three main ways – by what it takes, by what it makes and by what it wastes. This bad face of business is found at all stages of the transformation process (see, for example, Worthington, 2013) and involves environmental problems across all spatial levels from the local (e.g. litter) to the global (e.g. climate change).

Pressure on firms to accept responsibility for the negative impacts they have on the natural environment can be seen as part of the broader debate on corporate social responsibility. Worthington (2013) has argued that growing levels of corporate environmental awareness began to emerge in the closing decades of the twentieth century and can be linked to several key factors, including the publication of a number of influential books (e.g. Rachel Carson's *Silent Spring* in 1962), a series of high-profile ecological disasters (e.g. the chemical release at the Union Carbide plant in Bhopal in the 1980s), scientific discoveries (e.g. ozone depletion) and global media coverage of major environmental concerns (e.g. climate change). In helping to place the environment on both the public and political agendas, developments such as these helped to spawn a growing environmental movement and to encourage action at governmental and intergovernmental levels, both of which have had important implications for the business community and for the debate over how to reconcile the widespread demand for economic growth with the need for greater environmental protection.

As far as the latter question was concerned, what emerged from a lengthy and complex process of debate and discussion at an international level was the notion of **sustainable development**, the idea that when making choices designed to increase well-being today, countries should ensure that future generations are left no worse off than their current counterparts. In environmental terms, this implied, *inter alia,* the need to take steps to limit environmental damage and degradation, conserve the world's natural capital, preserve essential ecosystem functions and aim for qualitative rather than simply quantitative improvements over time. From a business point of view, this philosophical stance appeared to run counter to the traditional notion of 'business as usual', with its emphasis on year-on-year growth and unfettered access to the world's natural resources and environmental services.

The late twentieth century debate over sustainable development clearly poses an important question for the business community: how far should a firm be prepared to incorporate concern for the environment into its strategic decisions and day-to-day operations? Should environmental protection be seen as an inevitable additional cost to the business, or could it be leveraged for competitive advantage? As with CSR generally, opinions have tended to vary on this question, the latter view eventually gaining traction with business leaders of major international companies as the new millennium approached.

While it is impossible to pinpoint an exact time or event which helped to place the environment on corporate agendas, the available evidence indicates that its emergence as an important business issue has been gradual and largely incremental and has been shaped by a combination of pressures emanating from the regulatory, market and social domains of business. What these pressures have been and how and why firms have responded in different ways are the focus of the subsequent sections of this chapter.

Drivers of 'green' business

Academic researchers have long been interested in the factors that predispose businesses to engage in different forms of socially responsible behaviour (see, for example, Burke and Logsdon, 1996; McWilliams *et al.*, 2006). With regard to a firm's 'green' responses, these have been linked to four major influences: governmental action, other stakeholder pressures, economic opportunities and ethical considerations. We discuss each of these in turn.

Government action

As we saw in Chapters 4 and 5, government is a key actor and stakeholder in a firm's external environment. Its actions and decisions can play a formative role in promoting more sustainable forms of development and in encouraging businesses to improve on their environmental performance; to address, in effect, imperfections in the market system, including the existence of **negative externalities** such as pollution (for a discussion see Worthington, 2013).

Where environmental protection is concerned, three main approaches have been used: legislation and regulation, market-based instruments and voluntary agreements.

With regard to legal instruments, this basically involves the establishment of a system of direct control over organisations and their activities via the adoption of laws and other forms of regulatory measure, including the use of directives, permits, licences, and the creation of regulatory, inspection and enforcement regimes, backed by the application of sanctions in the event of non-compliance. Examples of environmental laws and regulations can be found in most, if not all, countries, and action may also be taken at an intergovernmental level, as in the case of the European Union.

While governments can and do use legislation/regulation to shape the environmental behaviour of firms, in practice instruments of this kind can vary substantially in style, content and degree of application; they are also aimed at a range of environmental problems from pollution control to resource management. Regulatory intervention can be used *inter alia* to outlaw or ban certain activities, apply particular standards, specify the characteristics required of certain products, determine the inputs to be used, mandate the techniques and/or technology a firm must apply, and identify its obligations regarding issues such as recycling and information disclosure. In short, they are generally imposed by a governing authority to produce outcomes that might otherwise not occur if decisions are left entirely to market forces. The evidence suggests that in this respect they have probably been the key driver of firm-level environmental behaviour (see, for example, Bansal and Roth, 2000; Etzion, 2007).

It is worth remembering that while governments are ultimately responsible for environmental laws and regulations, these are frequently shaped by different stakeholder interests, including the business community and its representative organisations. It is not uncommon for firms to lobby against proposed environmental legislation on the grounds that it will increase business costs and/or reduce international competitiveness, particularly if there are disparities in regulatory requirements between countries. Complaints that there is frequently an **unlevel playing field** or that **gold plating** of standards can occur are often used in this sphere; some businesses may even threaten to move their operations to locations (i.e. other countries) where environmental demands are less stringent, though it is unlikely that this consideration alone will be the determinant of such a strategic decision.

Turning to market-based or economic instruments, these involve the use of financial (or other) incentives or disincentives aimed at shaping business behaviour, **environmental taxes/subsidies** and **tradeable pollution permits** being two major examples. In simple terms, an environmental tax or charge seeks to take account of the negative environmental impact of business activity (e.g. pollution) by imposing a cost on firms that are responsible for the problem. Action taken by a business to reduce its environmental impact is rewarded by the reduction or removal of the financial penalty. Alternatively the organisation may be granted a financial gain in the form of an environmental subsidy or other type of fiscal reward (e.g. a reduction in corporate tax).

At the heart of this approach lies the use of the price mechanism to shape the behaviour of economic actors; to correct the market for negative externalities by endorsing the **polluter pays principle**. Whereas regulation basically involves government in deciding on the best course of action to address environmental problems, so-called green taxes and subsidies essentially leave businesses free to respond to certain stimuli in ways they themselves decide are most beneficial to the organisation, such as through investment in pollution reduction measures/technology or in changes in inputs or production or distribution methods. In this regard, taxes and subsidies can be said to work with the grain of the market and to act as a spur to innovation and investment. On the downside, they often tend to be viewed by firms as a revenue-raising exercise, can be difficult to design and implement and can, in some cases, have an adverse effect on firm, industry and national competitiveness.

Whereas environmental taxes and subsidies work by creating a price where none previously existed or by modifying an existing price, **tradeable** or **marketable pollution** permits are an example of market creation. Government establishes, in effect, a system of tradeable pollution rights, issues quotas, allowances or permits up to an agreed level and then allows the holders of those rights to trade them like any other commodity. The trading of rights (e.g. relating to greenhouse gas emissions) usually takes place under prescribed rules and may be external (e.g. between different enterprises or countries) or internal (e.g. between different plants within the same firm), within a free or controlled permit market. Gunningham and Grabosky (1998) have described this approach as a hybrid between direct regulations and free market environmentalism in that governments decide on the overall quantity of pollution permissible, while market forces determine the eventual distribution of rights between participating firms or countries.

As with green taxes/subsidies, a tradeable permit system – exemplified by the **European Emissions Trading Scheme (ETS)** – has both benefits and drawbacks. On the positive side, it offers firms a degree of flexibility in their responses and acts as an inducement to reducing their emissions, not least since any unused permits can be sold to businesses which have exceeded their quota. On the negative side, the system can be extremely bureaucratic and can be difficult to implement; there are also questions over its effectiveness and its impact on poorer nations.

Alongside regulation and market-based instruments, governments also use **voluntary approaches (VAs)** in an attempt to improve the environmental performance of firms beyond existing legal requirements. The three main types of instrument employed are:

- **public voluntary programmes** – which involve commitments devised by an environment agency and in which individual firms are invited to participate, the EU's **Eco-Management and Audit Scheme (EMAS)** being a prime example;
- **negotiated agreements** – which are initiatives that result from a process of bargaining between a public authority (e.g. national government) and an industry or industry sector, exemplified by the covenants that form part of the Netherlands National Environment Policy Plan;
- **unilateral commitments** – which are environmental programmes set up by firms independently of any public authority, but which may be aimed at forestalling government regulation, hence their inclusion here. An example of this form of self-regulation is the Chemical Manufacturers' Association Responsible Care Programme.

Since this approach to environmental protection provides firms with a substantial degree of flexibility regarding how far and in what ways they respond, it tends to be popular with the business community; it also has the potential to enhance stakeholder relationships (e.g. by improving the firm's image with customers) and possibly increase participants' competitiveness.

Other stakeholder pressures

In addition to the legislative, regulatory and fiscal demands imposed by governments, firms face pressures to reduce their environmental impact from other constituencies. Customers, competitors, suppliers, creditors, investors, shareholders, employees, civil society organisations and the media can all be instrumental in inducing a green response in businesses. Consumers, for instance, may actively seek out goods with a higher level of environmental performance or may boycott products deemed to have an adverse effect on the natural environment. Other examples include pressure exerted through the supply chain and/or by major investors, shareholder activism, adverse media publicity, lobbying by environmental NGOs and withdrawal by a public authority of a licence to operate. The extent to which stakeholder pressures are likely to prove effective in shaping firm-level behaviour is normally related to their impact on an organisation's bottom line, either directly or indirectly.

Economic opportunities

Organisations may also seek to improve on their environmental performance as a means of gaining an economic and commercial benefit, with opportunities potentially available on both sides of business. Gains could be generated by:

- reducing waste and generally increasing the efficiency of factor inputs, as highlighted by the concepts of **eco-efficiency** and acronyms such as Pollution Prevention Pays (PPP) and Waste Reduction Always Pays (WRAP);
- creating revenue-raising opportunities by developing green products and processes which may allow the firm to create a **market niche** by differentiating its offering to consumers who may be willing to pay a premium price;
- enhancing the organisation's resources and capabilities, including its corporate reputation with external stakeholders and its capacity to innovate;
- managing current and future environmental (e.g. accidents) and regulatory (e.g. stricter laws) risks with their associated costs.

As with CSR generally, the claim that environmental responsibility can pay remains hotly contested (see, for example, Worthington, 2013, Chapter 6).

Ethical considerations

A firm's green behaviour can also be driven by influences emanating from within the business itself, most notably the belief by organisational decision-makers that 'it is the right thing to do'. Initiatives may come from an organisation's owners and/or senior management team or from **environmental champions**, or the workforce generally. In some cases, the organisation's culture and values may be largely or wholly attuned to an ecologically responsible approach (e.g. environmental NGOs such as Greenpeace).

Why and how firms become more environmentally responsible

Whereas a discussion of the 'drivers' of corporate greening focuses on the factors that push a firm towards pro-environmental responses, examining its motivations for going in this direction raises a related, though slightly different, question: What is the underlying rationale for its behaviour?

In broad terms, the academic literature suggests three main reasons: it provides benefits or creates opportunities for the organisation; it reduces threats or risks to the enterprise; it accords with the firm's ethical stance. In practice, of course, an organisation's actions could reflect any or all of these motivations, each of which can be expressed in several ways.

Benefit-focused or opportunity-focused explanations link a firm's responses to the various strategic advantages thought to derive from a green response. These include meeting stakeholder or societal expectations, achieving market-related benefits through product differentiation, exploiting a green market niche, making cost savings or eco-efficiencies, and enhancing the organisation's image and/or corporate reputation. To what extent these claimed advantages represent *ex ante* explanations for a firm's actions or are *ex post* rationales aimed at persuading key stakeholders that there is a sound business case for investing in proactive green behaviour is not always clear.

Risk-focused or threat-focused arguments centre around the idea that corporate environmentalism is a way of protecting the organisation from adverse stakeholder reactions and/or the consequences of a negative or limited response to external pressures for change. Reduced current and future liabilities and risk – including fines, adverse publicity, loss of business, the danger of legislative sanctions and retrospective liabilities – may all be reasons why a firm might engage in pro-environmental behaviour. While this perspective suggests a predominantly defensive rationale, it is not always easy to separate risk-based explanations from the more proactive, opportunity-related motivations, given that investments in green responses may simultaneously reduce risks and create organisational benefits.

Whereas the two above explanations suggest that organisations are motivated primarily by economic and commercial considerations, some firms may believe that they have a moral obligation to protect the natural environment and this could explain their behaviour. As discussed previously, ethical explanations reflect the view that a business has obligations to the wider society not just to narrow, stakeholder interests such as shareholders or other investors. That said, as with other forms of corporate social responsibility, a firm's ethical stance could help it to gain a strategic advantage over its rivals, particularly if its actions are seen as an important aspect of doing business by powerful and influential stakeholder groups (see, for example, Porter and Kramer, 2002).

Turning to the question of what steps a firm may take to demonstrate its green credentials, these can range from relatively simple initiatives such as recycling or energy-saving measures to more complex practices and processes, including greening the supply chain, investing in new technology and developing an **environmental management system (EMS)**, the latter being a multi-stage process aimed at identifying, measuring and controlling a firm's environmental impact. Some businesses may also seek external recognition for their actions and decisions, whether by engaging in a strategic alliance with an environmental NGO (e.g. McDonald's and the Environmental Defense Fund), seeking certification for their products by a recognised and reputable body (e.g. the Forest Stewardship Council), or qualifying for the display of an **eco-label**, which certifies that a given product is environmentally safe or friendly (e.g. Germany's Blue Angel, Japan's Eco-Mark, the EU's European Eco-Label).

mini case — Going round in circles: Desso Carpets

Linear models of business activity – such as the systems approach presented in Chapter 1 – are essentially based on notions of 'take, make and dispose'. Inputs are acquired, a production process occurs, the product is consumed and then disposed of at the end of its life. Despite some opportunities for recycling, reclamation and re-use of materials and components, products produced in this way generate considerable levels of waste and pollution and consume large quantities of energy and raw materials, including non-renewables.

An alternative philosophy – currently exciting a degree of interest among forward-looking businesses (see below) – is the notion of the **circular economy**, a concept that focuses on waste eradication, rebuilding natural and social capital and adopting a renewable approach. Advocates of what is sometimes called the **cradle-to-cradle™ (C2C)** stance conceive of manufacturers continuing to own their own products, the use of which they sell to customers. These products are designed in a way that eliminates waste and involves manufacturing

and distribution systems based around renewable sources of energy.

The Dutch company Desso is one of Europe's largest producers of commercial-grade carpet and carpet tiles used in a wide range of domestic and commercial situations. In 2007 the firm announced its intention of designing by 2020 a fully closed-loop system for all its products based on C2C principles. The company aims to produce products that are entirely biodegradable or are capable of being recycled to produce new goods. This will involve designing systems and processes that will allow the firm to purchase appropriate materials, use waste to provide a source of energy, reduce energy consumption, provide facilities for recycling, product take-back and composting, and completely modify the way it does business (e.g. renting rather than selling products). To achieve its ambitious aims, the firm is working in partnership with the Environmental Protection Encouragement Agency (EPEA), which has its headquarters in Hamburg.

web link   See, for example, *www.desso.com/c2c-corporate-responsibility*

On the whole, it tends to be the case that smaller firms are more limited in their responses than their larger counterparts, given that they tend to lack the knowledge, resources and capabilities needed to invest in more advanced forms of environmental behaviour. Schemes such as General Electric's (GE) Ecomagination initiative and Marks and Spencer's Plan A (see the case study) are clearly beyond the reach of smaller businesses, many of which face substantial barriers to improved environmental performance and remain to be convinced that they have a negative impact on the natural environment or that they can benefit from investment in environmental protection measures.

Another perspective: the 'outside-in' view

In examining the interaction between firms and the natural environment, much of the focus has been on the pressures exerted on business to address the negative impacts that result from their activities, what might be called an **inside-out** view from the firm to the environment. It is important to recognise, however, that the natural environment also provides critical economic functions for the business community: it is a provider of inputs (e.g. raw materials), an assimilator of waste products (e.g. pollution) and a source of amenity value for individuals and organisations (e.g. landscape). When viewed in this way (i.e. the **outside-in** perspective), it is clear that economic activity and organisational competitiveness, both now and in the future, are intrinsically linked with the well-being of the natural environment (see, for example, Porter and Reinhardt, 2007). In 2006, for example, the Stern Report estimated that failure to tackle climate change could result in an up to 20 per cent decline in the size of the global economy and a plethora of recent authoritative reports by both national and international bodies paint a picture of how environmental problems – caused in part by business activity – can impact adversely on the business community.

To repeat the assertion made in Chapter 1, the business/environment relationship flows in both directions and is complex, interactive and dynamic, varying both between places and over time. In short, organisations not only affect the natural environment, they are affected by it and by what services it can provide. Protecting the environment may equally be a matter of self-interest, rather than simply a question of corporate social responsibility or inter-generational equity and social justice.

Synopsis Summary of key points

- Business ethics is concerned with issues of 'right' and 'wrong' behaviour in a business context.

- Corporate social responsibility (CSR) is the idea that organisations should be held accountable for the effects of their actions on people, their communities and the environment.

- CSR has become an important consideration for modern businesses, alongside traditional concerns with profitability and growth.

- Being socially responsible as a business does not preclude being profitable.

- Increasingly, business organisations have to take account of the views of their stakeholders on questions of social and environmental responsibility.

- One area where this has become particularly significant is with regard to the impact of business operations and decisions on the natural environment.

- The key 'drivers' of corporate environmental responsiveness are government intervention, other stakeholder pressures, economic opportunities and ethical considerations.

- Firms that implement environmental policies tend to be motivated by questions of organisational benefit or risk avoidance.

- Different businesses respond in different ways, ranging from reactive stances through to more proactive environmental approaches, which go beyond compliance with regulatory demands.

- Firms not only affect the natural environment, they are affected by it in a variety of ways.

case study

Doing well by doing good

As consumers have become increasingly aware of environmental issues, many organisations have felt compelled to demonstrate their commitment to a greener approach by announcing a range of high-profile environmental initiatives and programmes. This case study looks at two examples: GE's Ecomagination initiative and Marks and Spencer's Plan A.

GE's Ecomagination initiative

Launched in 2005, General Electric's Ecomagination initiative is an environmentally focused business strategy aimed at producing profitable growth by providing solutions to environmental problems such as the demand for cleaner sources of energy, reduced carbon emissions and access to cleaner water. Backed by a multi-million-dollar advertising campaign, the initiative emphasised that being 'good' and being commercially successful were complementary, what has been called a **win-win** situation, where both the environment and the firm benefit.

To qualify for inclusion in the firm's Ecomagination portfolio, a product or service must be able to demonstrate significant and measurable improvement in operational and environmental performance or in value proposition, additional value being provided for both investors and customers. Since the initiative began, products meeting these criteria have ranged from electric vehicles and aircraft engines to energy-efficient light bulbs and water-purification technologies.

During the first five years of the initiative it is estimated that Ecomagination products and services generated $85 billion for the business; there also appears to have been a number of less tangible benefits, such as creating customer trust in GE's brands and helping the business to attract and retain high-quality employees (see, for example, Esty and Winston, 2006; Laszlo and Zhexembayeva, 2011). The company has also been able to significantly reduce its environmental footprint during this period and it aims to achieve further reductions in environmental impact in the future and to increase its investment in clean technology research and development.

Marks and Spencer's 'Plan A'

M&S's Plan A was announced in early 2007 by the then chief executive Stuart Rose, who claimed that the initiative was so named because there was no Plan B. Under the new scheme the company committed itself to spending several hundred million pounds to reduce its environmental impact and to put social and environmental commitment at the heart of its commercial activities. Key aspects of the plan included reducing waste, saving energy, promoting animal welfare and trading fairly, goals which required it to consider a wide range of aspects of the business, including its logistics and retail operations, its relationship with suppliers and its sourcing policies. As the plan has been rolled out and incorporated into the fabric of the Marks and Spencer brand, additional aspects have been added or developed more fully, community engagement being one example.

According to a report in *The Guardian* on 8 July 2013, M&S had saved around £135 million through Plan A in the previous year alone and has evidently cut carbon emissions by 23 per cent since 2006, reduced waste by 28 per cent and made substantial savings in its use of glass. On the downside, the use of disposable plastic bags has been rising year-on-year and the company has had difficulties in reducing food packaging and in meeting its targets for converting to the use of Fairtrade cotton and for supplying more organic food and free-range products. There are also doubts as to whether it will reach its highly ambitious target of 20 million items of recycled clothing by 2015 through its Shwopping initiative.

For further information on these two companies and their social and environmental initiatives go to *www.ge.com* and *www.marksandspencer.com* and follow the links.

Case study questions

1 What do you think have been the key drivers of the two initiatives mentioned in this case study?

2 Will investors in these organisations benefit from or be disadvantaged by the two schemes?

Review and discussion questions

1 To what extent are governments responsible for establishing the parameters by which organisations conduct business? Should a business be free to decide its own level of corporate responsibility?

2 How can governments influence the environmental behaviour of firms?

3 Writers have argued that the only objective of business is to make profit, within the boundaries established by government. Do you agree?

Assignments

1 As a group, select an environmental issue (e.g. business or natural feature) and write a report to the leader of a local pressure group which details an environmental impact assessment of the issue. The report should make clear reference to:

    (a) a cost-benefit analysis, carried out by the group, of the salient factors;

    (b) any legislation/regulation that concerns the case; and

    (c) the provision of a stakeholder map that illustrates who the stakeholders are, their importance to the case and their ability to affect future decisions.

2 As a newly appointed trainee manager you have been asked to look afresh at the business, with particular reference to the implementation of an environmental management system. Your immediate superior has asked you to write a report. Accordingly, you are required to:

    (a) consult the available literature and identify what you consider to be the necessary processes and procedures that would comprise an environmental management system;

    (b) indicate the areas within the organisation that need to be addressed; and

    (c) explain how such a policy should be implemented within the organisation.

Notes and references

1 For a discussion see, for example, Vogel (2005).

2 Friedman, M., 'The social responsibility of business is to increase its profits', *New York Times Magazine,* 13 September 1970, pp. 7–13.

3 See, for example, Hart, S., 'A natural resource-based view of the firm', *Academy of Management Review,* 20, 1995, pp. 986–1014.

Further reading

Bansal, P. and Roth, K., 'Why companies go green: a model of ecological responsiveness', *Academy of Management Journal,* 43 (4), 2000, pp. 717–736.

Burke, L. and Logsdon, J. M., 'How corporate social responsibility pays off', *Long Range Planning,* 29 (4), 1996, pp. 495–502.

Cairncross, F., *Green Inc: A Guide to Business and the Environment,* Earthscan Publications, 1995.

Crane, A. and Matten, D., *Business Ethics,* Oxford University Press, 2004. A third edition was published in 2010.

Esty, D. C. and Winston, A. S., *Green to Gold: How Smart Companies Use Environmental Strategy to Innovate, Create Value and Build Competitive Advantage,* Yale University Press, 2006.

Etzion, D., 'Research on organizations and the natural environment, 1992–Present: a review', *Journal of Management,* 33 (4), 2007, pp. 637–664.

Frederick, W. C., Post, J. E. and Davis, K., *Business and Society: Corporate Strategy, Public Policy, Ethics,* 8th edition, McGraw-Hill, 1996.

Freeman, R. E., *Strategic Management: A Stakeholder Perspective,* Prentice Hall, 1984.

Gunningham, N. and Grabosky, P., *Smart Regulation: Designing Environmental Policy,* Clarendon Press, 1998.

Hawken, P., 'A teasing irony', in Welford, R. and Starkey, R. (eds), *Business and the Environment,* Earthscan, 1996, pp. 5–16.

Kolk, A., *Economics of Environmental Management,* Financial Times/Prentice Hall, 2000.

Laszlo, C. and Zhexembayeva, N. *Embedded Sustainability: The Next big Competitive Advantage,* 2011, Greenleaf Publishing.

McWilliams, A., Siegel, D. S. and Wright, P. M., 'Corporate social responsibility: strategic implications', *Journal of Management Studies,* 43 (1), 2006, pp. 1–18.

Pearce, D. and Barbier, E., *Blueprint for a Sustainable Economy,* Earthscan Publications, 2000.

Porter, M. E. and Kramer, M. R., 'The competitive advantage of corporate philanthropy', *Harvard Business Review,* 80 (12), 2002, pp. 56–69.

Porter, M. E. and Reinhardt, F. L., 'A strategic approach to climate change', *Harvard Business Review,* 85 (10), 2007, pp. 22–26.

Vogel, D., *The Market for Virtue: The Potential and Limits of Corporate Social Responsibility,* Brookings Institution, 2005.

Welford, R. and Gouldson, A., *Environmental Management and Business Strategy,* Pitman Publishing, 1993.

Worthington, I., *Greening Business: Research, Theory & Practice,* Oxford University Press, 2013.

Worthington, I., Britton, C. and Rees, A., *Economics for Business: Blending Theory and Practice,* 2nd edition, Financial Times/Prentice Hall, 2005, Chapter 14.

web link

Web links and further questions are available on the website at:
www.pearsoned.co.uk/worthington

Chapter 16
E Business

CHAPTER 1

Introduction to E-commerce

LEARNING OBJECTIVES

After reading this chapter, you will be able to:

- Define e-commerce and describe how it differs from e-business.
- Identify and describe the unique features of e-commerce technology and discuss their business significance.
- Describe the major types of e-commerce.
- Understand the evolution of e-commerce from its early years to today.
- Describe the major themes underlying the study of e-commerce.
- Identify the major academic disciplines contributing to e-commerce.

The Uber-ization of Everything

I f you were trying to pick iconic examples of e-commerce in the two decades since it began in 1995, it is likely that companies such as Amazon, eBay, Google, Apple, and Facebook would be high on the list. Today, there's a new company that may become the face of e-commerce as it enters its third decade: Uber. Uber and other firms with similar business models, such as Lyft (a ride service similar to Uber's), Airbnb (rooms for rent), Heal (doctor home visits), Handy and Homejoy (part-time household helpers), Instacart (grocery shopping), Washio (laundry service), and BloomThat

© Lenscap/Alamy

(flower delivery), are the pioneers of a new on-demand service e-commerce business model that is sweeping up billions of investment dollars in 2015 and disrupting major industries from transportation to hotels, real estate, house cleaning, maintenance, and grocery shopping. On-demand service firms have collected over $26 billion in venture capital funding over the last five years, making this the hottest business model in e-commerce for 2015.

Uber provides two major services: UberTaxi (also called UberX), which provides taxi service, and UberBlack, which provides a higher-priced town car service for business executives. UberPool is a ride-sharing service that allows users to share a ride with another person who happens to be going to same place. Google is working with Uber on developing this new service. In several cities, Uber is developing UberEats, a food delivery service; UberRush, a same-day delivery service; and UberCargo, a trucking service.

Uber was founded in 2009 by Travis Kalanick and Garrett Camp, and has grown explosively since then to over 300 cities and 60 countries. Drivers are signing up at an exponential rate, doubling every year; as of the beginning of 2015, there were over 160,000. According to an Uber-sponsored survey, over 44% of Uber drivers have college degrees (compared to 15% of taxi drivers), 71% say they have boosted their income and financial security by driving for Uber, and 73% say they prefer a job where they choose their hours rather than a 9-to-5 job. In 2015, Uber's revenue is estimated to be $10 billion, with profits (after paying its drivers) of $2 billion. This is five times as much as it made in 2014, when net revenue was about $400 million, which itself is about four times as much as its net revenue in 2013. Uber appears to be growing at

300% a year! As a result, in 2015, Uber is the most richly valued start-up in history and is currently valued at more than $50 billion.

Uber has a compelling value proposition for both customers and drivers. Customers can sign up for free, request and pay for a ride (at a cost Uber claims is 40% less than a traditional taxi) using a smartphone and credit card, and get picked up within a few minutes. No need to stand on a street corner frantically waving, competing with others, or waiting and waiting for an available cab to drive by without knowing when that might happen. Instead, customers can use the Uber app to secure a ride, and they know just how long it will take for the ride to arrive and how much it will cost. With UberPool, the cost of a ride drops by 50%, making it cost-competitive with owning a car in an urban area, according to Uber. For drivers, Uber's value proposition is: set your own hours, work when you like, and put your own car to use generating revenue.

Uber is the current poster child for "digital disruption." It is easy see to why Uber has ignited a firestorm of opposition from existing taxi services around the world. Who can compete in a market where a new upstart firm offers a 50% price reduction? If you've paid €240,000 for a license to drive a taxi in Paris, what is it worth now that Uber has arrived? Even governments find Uber to be a disruptive threat. Cities and states do not want to give up regulatory control over passenger safety, driver training, or the healthy revenue stream generated by charging taxi firms for a taxi license and sales taxes.

Uber's business model differs from traditional retail e-commerce. Uber doesn't sell goods. Instead, it has created a smartphone-based platform that enables people who want a service—like a taxi—to find a provider with the resources, such as a personal automobile that spends much of its time parked and a driver with available time, to fill the demand. It's important to understand that although Uber and similar firms were initially called "sharing economy" companies, this is a misnomer. Uber drivers are selling their services as drivers and the temporary use of their car. Uber the company is not in the sharing business either: it charges a hefty fee for every transaction on its platform. Uber is not an example of "peer-to-peer" e-commerce because Uber transactions involve an online intermediary: a third party that takes a cut of all transactions and arranges for the marketplace to exist in the first place.

Uber has disrupted the traditional taxi business model because it offers a superior, fast, convenient taxi-hailing service when compared to traditional taxi companies that rely on the telephone, a central dispatcher using antiquated radio communications to direct cabs, or, as in many urban areas, customers standing on street corners frantically waving their hands. With traditional taxi services, there is no guarantee you will find a cab or that a cab will arrive when you really need one. Customers have no way of knowing how long a traditional taxi will take to arrive. Uber reduces that uncertainty: using a smartphone, the customer enters a request for pickup, and nearly instantly (under the best of circumstances) a provider will be found by Uber and the estimated time of arrival established along with the price. Riders can accept the price or find an alternative.

Uber's business model is much more efficient than a traditional taxi firm. Uber does not own taxis and has no maintenance or financing costs. It does not have employees but instead calls its drivers "independent contractors." Uber is not encumbered with the costs for workers compensation, minimum wage requirements, background checks on drivers, driver training, health insurance, or commercial licensing.

Quality control would seem to be a nightmare with over 160,000 contract drivers. But Uber relies on user reviews of drivers and the ride experience to identify problematic drivers, and driver reviews of customers to identify problematic passengers. It also sets standards for cleanliness. The reviews can be used to discipline drivers: drivers are evaluated by riders on a 5-point scale, and if drivers fall below 4.5, they are warned and may be dropped if they don't improve. Anything less than a 5 is a sign to the company that something was not right about the ride experience. Customers are also rated with a 5-point system. Drivers can refuse to pick up troublesome customers, and the Uber server can delay service to problematic people with low ratings or ban them entirely. Uber does not publicly report on how many poorly rated drivers or passengers there are in its system. Academic articles have found that in similar on-demand companies, such as Airbnb, there's a built-in bias for both sellers and buyers to give good reviews regardless of the actual experience. If you routinely give low reviews to sellers (drivers), they will think you are too demanding and not service you in the future. If a driver gives low reviews to passengers, they might not rate you highly in return.

Rather than having a dispatcher in every city, Uber has an Internet-based app service running on cloud servers located throughout the world. It does not provide radios to its drivers, who instead must use their own smartphones and cell service, which the drivers pay for. It does not provide insurance or maintenance for its drivers' cars. Uber has shifted the costs of running a taxi service entirely to the drivers. Uber charges prices that vary dynamically with demand: the higher the demand, the greater the price of a ride. Therefore, it is impossible using public information to know if Uber's prices are lower than traditional taxis. Clearly, in high-demand situations they are higher, sometimes ten times higher, than a regulated taxi. There is no regulatory taxi commission setting uniform per mile fares. Consumers do face some traditional uncertainties regarding availability: during a rain storm, a convention, or a sports event, when demand peaks, not enough drivers may be available at any price.

What could be wrong with Uber's apparent over-the-top success? It is digitally disrupting a staid, highly regulated, and decidedly non-digital industry that employs over 200,000 people, most of whom are full-time employees, and who have a median pay of $22,820 per year, or about $11 an hour. In the not-so-distant future, Uber's part-time drivers will likely outnumber full-time taxi drivers worldwide.

If Uber is the poster child for the new on-demand service economy, it's also the iconic example of the social costs and conflicts associated with this new kind of e-commerce. Uber has been accused by attorney generals in many countries of misclassifying its drivers as contractors as opposed to employees, thereby denying the drivers the benefits of employee status, such as minimum wages, social security, workers compensation, and health insurance.

Uber has also been accused of violating public transportation laws and regulations throughout the world; abusing the personal information it has collected on users of the service; seeking to use personal information to intimidate journalists; failing to protect

SOURCES: "Uber CEO Travis Kalanick: 30% of Our Trips Take Place in China," by Douglas MacMillan, *Wall Street Journal,* October 20, 2015; "Uber vs GrabCar: Who's Speeding Ahead in Southeast Asia?," by Nadine Freischlad, Techinasia.com, October 17, 2015; "Spanish Uber Rival Cabify Seeks to Expand in Latin America after Rakuten-led Funding Round," by Robert Schoon, Latinpost.com, October 12, 2015; "Uber Faces New Threat in London," by Amir Mizroch, Bdlive.co.za, October 1, 2015; "Uber Under Fire in Europe... Again," by Alanna Petroff, Cnnmoney.com, September 30, 2015; "Twisting Words to Make 'Sharing' Apps Seem Selfless," by Natasha Singer, *New York Times,* August 9, 2015; "Uber Valued at More Than $50 Billion," by Douglas Macmillan and Telis Demos, *Wall Street Journal,* July 31, 2015; "Uber to Fight EU Rules in Europe's Top Court," by Sam Schechner, *Wall Street Journal,* July 20, 2015; "Uber Dealt Setback on Labor Rules," by Lauren Weber, *Wall Street Journal,* June 18, 2015; "The $50 Billion Question: Can Uber Deliver?," by Douglas Macmillan, *Wall Street Journal,* June 15, 2015; "George Zimmer Starts an 'Uber for Tailors,'" by David Gelles, *New York Times,* May 31, 2015; "Coming Next: The On-Demand Sales Force," by Christopher Mims, *Wall Street Journal,* May 31, 2015; "How Everyone Misjudges the Sharing Economy," by Christopher Mims, *Wall Street Journal,* May 25, 2015; "Icahn Puts Big Wager on Uber Rival Lyft," by Douglas Macmillan, *Wall Street Journal,* May 16, 2015; "An Uber for Doctor Housecalls," by Jennifer Jolly, *New York Times,* May 5, 2015; "Uber Expands Funding Round as Revenue Growth Accelerates," by Douglas Macmillan, *Wall Street Journal,* February 18, 2015; "The On-Demand Economy Is Reshaping Companies and Careers," *The Economist,* January 4, 2015; "The On-Demand Economy: Workers on Tap," *The Economist,* January 3, 2015.

public safety by refusing to do adequate criminal, medical, and financial background checks on its drivers; taking clandestine actions against its chief competitor Lyft in order to disrupt its business; and being tone-deaf to the complaints of its own drivers against the firm's efforts to reduce driver fees in 2015. Uber has met with heavy resistance in Europe's largest cities in 2015. In London, regulators hope to impose a mandatory five-minute wait before passengers can begin a ride as a protection for traditional taxicab drivers. In Paris, Uber executives appeared in court to stand trial for running an illegal taxi service, and the company was forced to shut down service in Paris due to "violent attacks" during protests against Uber following similar shutdowns of Uber service in Germany and Italy. In Amsterdam, law enforcement has searched Uber offices for evidence of transport law infractions. The EU's most powerful court, the European Court of Justice, is likely to rule on whether Uber is a transportation service that violates the existing laws in many countries or an "information society service" that requires more flexible rules and regulations.

Critics also fear that on-demand firms will create a society of part-time, low-paid temp work, displacing traditionally full-time, secure jobs—the so-called Uber-ization of work. As one critic put it, Uber is not the Uber for rides so much as it is the Uber for low-paid jobs. Uber responds to this fear by claiming that it is lowering the cost of transportation, making better use of spare human and financial resources, expanding the demand for ride services, and expanding opportunities for car drivers, whose pay is about the same as other taxi drivers. In reality, the point is moot: on-demand service companies will continue to grow explosively until the supply of part-time workers is exhausted. This means, inevitably, the continued growth of a part-time work economy, and growing political pressure to bring benefits to these workers.

Does Uber have a sustainable business model? Is the company really worth over $50 billion based on $2 billion in net revenue a year? If the company continues to triple its net revenue every year, the answer is yes. But Uber does have a few competitors already, such as Lyft in the United States, GrabTaxi in Southeast Asia, Cabify in Spain and Latin America, and a host of local firms around the world. Lyft is currently about one-tenth the size of Uber but growing rapidly, thanks to the support of Alibaba and several prominent venture capitalists. Uber faces a bevy of new, smaller competing firms, including Sidecar, Via, Tripda, and Shuddle, all of whom offer app-based hailing services. Many of these firms prioritize following the law and local regulations, which dramatically reduces expenses compared to Uber's growth-at-any-cost approach and its attendant legal fees. China has its own cab hailing services, Kuaidi Dache and Didi Dache, although Uber reports that 30% of its rides take place in China. Uber may find that its strong brand may be its most important asset going forward.

In 1994, e-commerce as we now know it did not exist. In 2015, just 21 years later, around 1.4 billion consumers worldwide are expected to spend about €1.96 trillion, and businesses around €14.2 trillion, purchasing goods, services, and digital content online or via a mobile device. And in this short period of time, e-commerce has been reinvented not just once, but twice.

The early years of e-commerce, during the late 1990s, were a period of business vision, inspiration, and experimentation. It soon became apparent, however, that establishing a successful business model based on those visions would not be easy. There followed a period of retrenchment and reevaluation, which led to the stock market crash of 2000–2001, with the value of e-commerce, telecommunications, and other technology stocks plummeting. After the bubble burst, many people were quick to write off e-commerce. But they were wrong. The surviving firms refined and honed their business models, and the technology became more powerful and less expensive, ultimately leading to business firms that actually produced profits. Between 2002–2008, retail e-commerce grew at more than 25% per year.

Today, we are in the middle of yet another transition. Social networks such as Facebook, Twitter, YouTube, Pinterest, and Tumblr, which enable users to distribute their own content (such as videos, music, photos, personal information, commentary, blogs, and more), have rocketed to prominence. Never before in the history of media have such large audiences been aggregated and made so accessible. Businesses are grappling with how best to approach this audience from a marketing, advertising, and sales perspective. At the same time, the traditional desktop platform and Web browser that most consumers have used to access the Internet in the past is being augmented by mobile devices such as smartphones and tablet computers, and mobile apps. Facilitated by technologies such as cloud computing, mobile devices have become advertising, shopping, reading, and media viewing machines, and in the process, consumer behavior is being transformed yet again. Mobile, social, and local have become driving forces in e-commerce. The mobile platform infrastructure is also giving birth to yet another e-commerce innovation: on-demand services that are local and personal. From hailing a taxi, to shopping, to washing your clothes, these new businesses are creating a marketspace where owners of resources such as cars, spare bedrooms, and spare time can find a market of eager consumers looking to buy a service in a few minutes using their smartphones. The opening case on Uber is a leading example of these new on-demand service firms that are disrupting traditional business models.

1.1 E-COMMERCE: THE REVOLUTION IS JUST BEGINNING

Table 1.1 describes the major trends in e-commerce in 2015–2016. The mobile platform based on smartphones and tablet computers has finally arrived with a bang, making true mobile e-commerce a reality. Social networks are enabling social e-commerce by providing search, advertising, and payment services to vendors and customers. More

TABLE 1.1	MAJOR TRENDS IN E-COMMERCE 2015–2016

BUSINESS

- Retail e-commerce continuesto grow worldwide, with a global growth rate of almost 25%, and even higher in emerging markets such as China, India, and Brazil.
- Mobile retail e-commerce explodes and in the United Kingdom now accounts for over 30% of total U.K retail e-commerce, totaling an estimated £19 billion in 2015.
- The mobile app ecosystem continues to grow, with around 2 billion people using mobile apps worldwide.
- Social e-commerce, based on social networks and supported by advertising, emerges and grows by 25% from 2013 to 2014, generating over $3.3 billion in revenue for the top 500 social media retailers in the United States.
- Local e-commerce, the third dimension of the mobile, social, local e-commerce wave, also is growing, fueled by an explosion of interest in on-demand services such as Uber.
- On-demand service firms like Uber and Airbnb attract billions in capital, garner multi-billion dollar valuations, and show explosive growth.
- Mobile and social advertising platforms show strong growth and begin to challenge search engine marketing.
- Small businesses and entrepreneurs continue to flood into the e-commerce marketplace, often riding on the infrastructures created by industry giants such as Apple, Facebook, Amazon, Google, and eBay.
- B2B e-commerce worldwide continues to strengthen and grow to €14.2 trillion.

TECHNOLOGY

- A mobile computing and communications platform based on smartphones, tablet computers, and mobile apps becomes a reality, rivaling the PC platform and creating an alternative platform for online transactions, marketing, advertising, and media viewing. Mobile messaging services like WhatsApp and Snapchat are used by 40% of smartphone users.
- Cloud computing completes the transformation of the mobile platform by storing consumer content and software on Internet servers and making it available to any consumer-connected device from the desktop to a smartphone.
- Computing and networking component prices continue to fall dramatically.
- As firms track the trillions of online interactions that occur each day, a flood of data, typically referred to as Big Data, is being produced.
- In order to make sense out of Big Data, firms turn to sophisticated software called business analytics (or Web analytics) that can identify purchase patterns as well as consumer interests and intentions in milliseconds.

SOCIETY

- User-generated content, published online as social network posts, tweets, blogs, and pins, as well as video and photo-sharing, continues to grow and provides a method of self-publishing that engages millions.
- Social networks encourage self-revelation, while threatening privacy.
- Participation by adults in social networks increases; Facebook becomes ever more popular in all demographic categories.
- Conflicts over copyright management and control continue, but there is substantial agreement among online distributors and copyright owners that they need one another.
- Taxation of online sales poses challenges for governments.
- Surveillance of online communications by both repressive regimes and Western democracies grows.
- Concerns over commercial and governmental privacy invasion increase.
- Online security continues to decline as major sites are hacked and lose control over customer information.
- Spam remains a significant problem.
- On-demand service e-commerce produces a flood of temporary, poorly paid jobs without benefits.

and more people and businesses are using the Internet and mobile devices to conduct commerce; smaller, local firms are taking advantage of the Internet and mobile platform as e-commerce technologies become less and less expensive. New e-commerce brands have emerged while traditional retail brands such as Tesco and Carrefour are further extending their omnichannel strategies and retaining their dominant retail positions by strengthening their e-commerce operations. At the societal level, other trends are apparent. The Internet and mobile platform provide an environment that allows millions of people to create and share content, establish new social bonds, and strengthen existing ones through social network, photo- and video-posting, and blogging sites and apps, while at the same time creating significant privacy issues. The major digital copyright owners have increased their pursuit of online file-sharing services with mixed success, while reaching broad agreements with the big technology players like Apple, Amazon, and Google to protect intellectual property rights. Taxation of online sales continues to pose challenges for governments. Sovereign nations have expanded their surveillance of, and control over, online communications and content as a part of their anti-terrorist activities and their traditional interest in snooping on citizens. Privacy seems to have lost some of its meaning in an age when millions create public online personal profiles.

THE FIRST 30 SECONDS

It is important to realize that the rapid growth and change that has occurred in the first 21 years of e-commerce represents just the beginning—what could be called the first 30 seconds of the e-commerce revolution. Technology continues to evolve at exponential rates. This underlying ferment presents entrepreneurs with new opportunities to both create new businesses and new business models in traditional industries, and also to destroy old businesses. Business change becomes disruptive, rapid, and even destructive, while offering entrepreneurs new opportunities and resources for investment. For instance, on-demand service firms such as Uber and Airbnb threaten the traditional taxi and low-cost hotel industries.

Improvements in underlying information technologies and continuing entrepreneurial innovation in business and marketing promise as much change in the next decade as was seen in the previous decade. The twenty-first century will be the age of a digitally enabled social and commercial life, the outlines of which we can barely perceive at this time. Analysts estimate that by 2019, U.S. consumers will be spending over $775 billion and businesses over $8.5 trillion in digital transactions. It appears likely that e-commerce will eventually impact nearly all commerce, and that most commerce will be e-commerce by the year 2050.

Can e-commerce continue to grow indefinitely? It's possible that at some point, e-commerce growth may slow simply as a result of overload: people may just not have the time to watch yet another online video, open another e-mail, or read another blog, tweet, or Facebook update. However, currently, there is no foreseeable limit to the continued rapid development of e-commerce technology, or limits on the inventiveness of entrepreneurs to develop new uses for the technology. Therefore, for now at least, it is likely that the disruptive process will continue.

Business fortunes are made—and lost—in periods of extraordinary change such as this. The next five years hold out exciting opportunities—as well as risks—for new and traditional businesses to exploit digital technology for market advantage. For society as a whole, the next few decades offer the possibility of extraordinary gains in social wealth as the digital revolution works its way through larger and larger segments of the world's economy, offering the possibility of high rates of productivity and income growth in an inflation-free environment.

As a business or technology student, this book will help you perceive and understand the opportunities and risks that lie ahead. By the time you finish, you will be able to identify the technological, business, and social forces that have shaped, and continue to shape, the growth of e-commerce, and ready to participate in, and ultimately guide, discussions of e-commerce in the firms where you work.

WHAT IS E-COMMERCE?

e-commerce
the use of the Internet, the Web, and mobile apps and browsers running on mobile devices to transact business. More formally, digitally enabled commercial transactions between and among organizations and individuals

Our focus in this book is **e-commerce**—the use of the Internet, the World Wide Web (Web), and mobile apps and browsers running on mobile devices to transact business. Although the terms Internet and Web are often used interchangeably, they are actually two very different things. The *Internet* is a worldwide network of computer networks, and the *Web* is one of the Internet's most popular services, providing access to billions of Web pages. An *app* (short-hand for application) is a software application. The term is typically used when referring to mobile applications, although it is also sometimes used to refer to desktop computer applications as well. A *mobile browser* is a version of Web browser software accessed via a mobile device. (We describe the Internet, Web, and mobile platform more fully later in this chapter and in Chapters 2 and 3.) More formally, we focus on digitally enabled commercial transactions between and among organizations and individuals. Each of these components of our working definition of e-commerce is important. *Digitally enabled transactions* include all transactions mediated by digital technology. For the most part, this means transactions that occur over the Internet, the Web, and/or via mobile devices. *Commercial transactions* involve the exchange of value (e.g., money) across organizational or individual boundaries in return for products and services. Exchange of value is important for understanding the limits of e-commerce. Without an exchange of value, no commerce occurs.

The professional literature sometimes refers to e-commerce as digital commerce. For our purposes, we consider e-commerce and digital commerce to be synonymous.

THE DIFFERENCE BETWEEN E-COMMERCE AND E-BUSINESS

There is a debate about the meaning and limitations of both e-commerce and e-business. Some argue that e-commerce encompasses the entire world of electronically based organizational activities that support a firm's market exchanges—including a firm's entire information system's infrastructure (Rayport and Jaworski, 2003). Others argue, on the other hand, that e-business encompasses the entire world of internal and external electronically based activities, including e-commerce (Kalakota and Robinson, 2003).

We think it is important to make a working distinction between e-commerce and e-business because we believe they refer to different phenomena. E-commerce is not

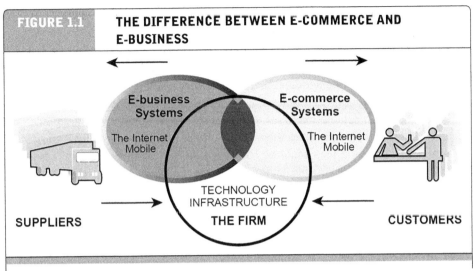

FIGURE 1.1 — THE DIFFERENCE BETWEEN E-COMMERCE AND E-BUSINESS

E-commerce primarily involves transactions that cross firm boundaries. E-business primarily involves the application of digital technologies to business processes within the firm.

"anything digital" that a firm does. For purposes of this text, we will use the term **e-business** to refer primarily to the digital enabling of transactions and processes *within* a firm, involving information systems under the control of the firm. For the most part, in our view, e-business does not include commercial transactions involving an exchange of value across organizational boundaries. For example, a company's online inventory control mechanisms are a component of e-business, but such internal processes do not directly generate revenue for the firm from outside businesses or consumers, as e-commerce, by definition, does. It is true, however, that a firm's e-business infrastructure provides support for online e-commerce exchanges; the same infrastructure and skill sets are involved in both e-business and e-commerce. E-commerce and e-business systems blur together at the business firm boundary, at the point where internal business systems link up with suppliers or customers (see **Figure 1.1**). E-business applications turn into e-commerce precisely when an exchange of value occurs (see Mesenbourg, U.S. Department of Commerce, 2001, for a similar view). We will examine this intersection further in Chapter 12.

e-business
the digital enabling of transactions and processes within a firm, involving information systems under the control of the firm

WHY STUDY E-COMMERCE?

Why are there college courses and textbooks on e-commerce when there are no courses or textbooks on "TV Commerce," "Radio Commerce," "Railroad Commerce," or "Highway Commerce," even though these technologies had profound impacts on commerce in the twentieth century and account for far more commerce than e-commerce?

The reason for the interest specifically in e-commerce is that e-commerce technology (discussed in detail in Chapters 2 and 3) is different and more powerful than any of the other technologies we have seen in the past century. E-commerce technologies—and the digital markets that result—have brought about some fundamental, unprecedented shifts in commerce. While these other technologies transformed economic life in the twentieth century, the evolving Internet and other information technologies are shaping the twenty-first century.

Prior to the development of e-commerce, the marketing and sale of goods was a mass-marketing and sales force–driven process. Marketers viewed consumers as passive targets of advertising campaigns and branding "blitzes" intended to influence their long-term product perceptions and immediate purchasing behavior. Companies sold their products via well-insulated channels. Consumers were trapped by geographical and social boundaries, unable to search widely for the best price and quality. Information about prices, costs, and fees could be hidden from the consumer, creating profitable information asymmetries for the selling firm. **Information asymmetry** refers to any disparity in relevant market information among parties in a transaction. It was so expensive to change national or regional prices in traditional retailing (what are called *menu costs*) that one national price was the norm, and dynamic pricing to the marketplace let alone to individuals in the marketplace—changing prices in real time—was unheard of. In this environment, manufacturers prospered by relying on huge production runs of products that could not be customized or personalized. One of the shifts that e-commerce is bringing about is a reduction in information asymmetry among market participants (consumers and merchants). Preventing consumers from learning about costs, price discrimination strategies, and profits from sales becomes more difficult with e-commerce, and the entire marketplace potentially becomes highly price competitive. At the same time, online merchants gain considerable market power over consumers by using consumer personal information in ways inconceivable 10 years ago to maximize their revenues.

information asymmetry

any disparity in relevant market information among parties in a transaction

EIGHT UNIQUE FEATURES OF E-COMMERCE TECHNOLOGY

Figure 1.2 illustrates eight unique features of e-commerce technology that both challenge traditional business thinking and explain why we have so much interest in e-commerce. These unique dimensions of e-commerce technologies suggest many new possibilities for marketing and selling—a powerful set of interactive, personalized, and rich messages are available for delivery to segmented, targeted audiences. E-commerce technologies make it possible for merchants to know much more about consumers and to be able to use this information more effectively than was ever true in the past. Online merchants can use this new information to develop new information asymmetries, enhance their ability to brand products, charge premium prices for high-quality service, and segment the market into an endless number of subgroups, each receiving a different price. To complicate matters further, these same technologies make it possible for merchants to know more about other merchants than was ever true in the past. This presents the possibility that merchants might collude on prices rather than compete and drive overall average prices up. This strategy works especially well when there are just a few suppliers (Varian, 2000a). We examine these different visions of e-commerce further in Section 1.2 and throughout the book.

Each of the dimensions of e-commerce technology illustrated in Figure 1.2 deserves a brief exploration, as well as a comparison to both traditional commerce and other forms of technology-enabled commerce.

FIGURE 1.2   EIGHT UNIQUE FEATURES OF E-COMMERCE TECHNOLOGY

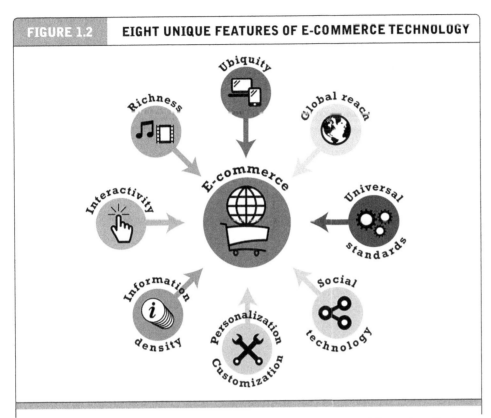

E-commerce technologies provide a number of unique features that have impacted the conduct of business.

Ubiquity

In traditional commerce, a **marketplace** is a physical place you visit in order to transact. For example, television and radio typically motivate the consumer to go someplace to make a purchase. E-commerce, in contrast, is characterized by its **ubiquity**: it is available just about everywhere, at all times. It liberates the market from being restricted to a physical space and makes it possible to shop from your desktop, at home, at work, or even from your car, using mobile e-commerce. The result is called a **marketspace**—a marketplace extended beyond traditional boundaries and removed from a temporal and geographic location. From a consumer point of view, ubiquity reduces *transaction costs*—the costs of participating in a market. To transact, it is no longer necessary that you spend time and money traveling to a market. At a broader level, the ubiquity of e-commerce lowers the cognitive energy required to transact in a marketspace. *Cognitive energy* refers to the mental effort required to complete a task. Humans generally seek to reduce cognitive energy outlays. When given a choice, humans will choose the path requiring the least effort—the most convenient path (Shapiro and Varian, 1999; Tversky and Kahneman, 1981).

marketplace
physical space you visit in order to transact

ubiquity
available just about everywhere, at all times

marketspace
marketplace extended beyond traditional boundaries and removed from a temporal and geographic location

Global Reach

E-commerce technology permits commercial transactions to cross cultural, regional, and national boundaries far more conveniently and cost-effectively than is true in traditional commerce. As a result, the potential market size for e-commerce merchants is roughly equal to the size of the world's online population (an estimated 3.1 billion in 2015) (eMarketer, Inc., 2015a). More realistically, the Internet makes it much easier for start-up e-commerce merchants within a single country to achieve a national audience than was ever possible in the past. The total number of users or customers an e-commerce business can obtain is a measure of its **reach** (Evans and Wurster, 1997).

In contrast, most traditional commerce is local or regional—it involves local merchants or national merchants with local outlets. Television and radio stations, and newspapers, for instance, are primarily local and regional institutions with limited but powerful national networks that can attract a national audience. In contrast to e-commerce technology, these older commerce technologies do not easily cross national boundaries to a global audience.

reach
the total number of users or customers an e-commerce business can obtain

Universal Standards

One strikingly unusual feature of e-commerce technologies is that the technical standards of the Internet, and therefore the technical standards for conducting e-commerce, are **universal standards**—they are shared by all nations around the world. In contrast, most traditional commerce technologies differ from one nation to the next. For instance, television and radio standards differ around the world, as does cell phone technology. The universal technical standards of e-commerce greatly lower *market entry costs*—the cost merchants must pay just to bring their goods to market. At the same time, for consumers, universal standards reduce *search costs*—the effort required to find suitable products. And by creating a single, one-world marketspace, where prices and product descriptions can be inexpensively displayed for all to see, *price discovery* becomes simpler, faster, and more accurate (Banerjee et al., 2005; Bakos, 1997; Kambil, 1997). Users, both businesses and individuals, also experience *network externalities*—benefits that arise because everyone uses the same technology. With e-commerce technologies, it is possible for the first time in history to easily find many of the suppliers, prices, and delivery terms of a specific product anywhere in the world, and to view them in a coherent, comparative environment. Although this is not necessarily realistic today for all or even most products, it is a potential that will be exploited in the future.

universal standards
standards that are shared by all nations around the world

Richness

Information **richness** refers to the complexity and content of a message (Evans and Wurster, 1999). Traditional markets, national sales forces, and small retail stores have great richness: they are able to provide personal, face-to-face service using aural and visual cues when making a sale. The richness of traditional markets makes them a powerful selling or commercial environment. Prior to the development of the Web,

richness
the complexity and content of a message

there was a trade-off between richness and reach: the larger the audience reached, the less rich the message. E-commerce technologies have the potential for offering considerably more information richness than traditional media such as printing presses, radio, and television because they are interactive and can adjust the message to individual users. Chatting with an online sales person, for instance, comes very close to the customer experience in a small retail shop. The richness enabled by e-commerce technologies allows retail and service merchants to market and sell "complex" goods and services that heretofore required a face-to-face presentation by a sales force to a much larger audience.

Interactivity

Unlike any of the commercial technologies of the twentieth century, with the possible exception of the telephone, e-commerce technologies allow for **interactivity**, meaning they enable two-way communication between merchant and consumer and among consumers. Traditional television, for instance, cannot ask viewers questions or enter into conversations with them, or request that customer information be entered into a form. In contrast, all of these activities are possible on an e-commerce site and are now commonplace with smartphones, social networks, and Twitter. Interactivity allows an online merchant to engage a consumer in ways similar to a face-to-face experience.

interactivity
technology that allows for two-way communication between merchant and consumer

Information Density

E-commerce technologies vastly increase **information density**—the total amount and quality of information available to all market participants, consumers, and merchants alike. E-commerce technologies reduce information collection, storage, processing, and communication costs. At the same time, these technologies greatly increase the currency, accuracy, and timeliness of information—making information more useful and important than ever. As a result, information becomes more plentiful, less expensive, and of higher quality.

information density
the total amount and quality of information available to all market participants

A number of business consequences result from the growth in information density. In e-commerce markets, prices and costs become more transparent. *Price transparency* refers to the ease with which consumers can find out the variety of prices in a market; *cost transparency* refers to the ability of consumers to discover the actual costs merchants pay for products (Sinha, 2000). But there are advantages for merchants as well. Online merchants can discover much more about consumers; this allows merchants to segment the market into groups willing to pay different prices and permits them to engage in *price discrimination*—selling the same goods, or nearly the same goods, to different targeted groups at different prices. For instance, an online merchant can discover a consumer's avid interest in expensive exotic vacations, and then pitch expensive exotic vacation plans to that consumer at a premium price, knowing this person is willing to pay extra for such a vacation. At the same time, the online merchant can pitch the same vacation plan at a lower price to more price-sensitive consumers. Merchants also have enhanced abilities to differentiate their products in terms of cost, brand, and quality.

Personalization/Customization

E-commerce technologies permit **personalization**: merchants can target their marketing messages to specific individuals by adjusting the message to a person's name, interests, and past purchases. Today this is achieved in a few milliseconds and followed by an advertisement based on the consumer's profile. The technology also permits **customization**—changing the delivered product or service based on a user's preferences or prior behavior. Given the interactive nature of e-commerce technology, much information about the consumer can be gathered in the marketplace at the moment of purchase. With the increase in information density, a great deal of information about the consumer's past purchases and behavior can be stored and used by online merchants. The result is a level of personalization and customization unthinkable with traditional commerce technologies. For instance, you may be able to shape what you see on television by selecting a channel, but you cannot change the contents of the channel you have chosen. In contrast, the online version of the *Financial Times* allows you to select the type of news stories you want to see first, and gives you the opportunity to be alerted when certain events happen. Personalization and customization allow firms to precisely identify market segments and adjust their messages accordingly.

Social Technology: User-Generated Content and Social Networks

In a way quite different from all previous technologies, e-commerce technologies have evolved to be much more social by allowing users to create and share content with a worldwide community. Using these forms of communication, users are able to create new social networks and strengthen existing ones. All previous mass media in modern history, including the printing press, used a broadcast model (one-to-many) where content is created in a central location by experts (professional writers, editors, directors, actors, and producers) and audiences are concentrated in huge aggregates to consume a standardized product. The telephone would appear to be an exception but it is not a mass communication technology. Instead the telephone is a one-to-one technology. E-commerce technologies have the potential to invert this standard media model by giving users the power to create and distribute content on a large scale, and permit users to program their own content consumption. E-commerce technologies provide a unique, many-to-many model of mass communication.

Table 1.2 provides a summary of each of the unique features of e-commerce technology and their business significance.

TYPES OF E-COMMERCE

There are several different types of e-commerce and many different ways to characterize them. **Table 1.3** on page 58 lists the major types of e-commerce discussed in this book.[1] For the most part, we distinguish different types of e-commerce by the nature of

---

[1] For the purposes of this text, we subsume business-to-government (B2G) e-commerce within B2B e-commerce, viewing the government as simply a form of business when it acts as a procurer of goods and/or services.

TABLE 1.2	BUSINESS SIGNIFICANCE OF THE EIGHT UNIQUE FEATURES OF E-COMMERCE TECHNOLOGY
E-COMMERCE TECHNOLOGY DIMENSION	BUSINESS SIGNIFICANCE
Ubiquity—E-commerce technology is available everywhere: at work, at home, and elsewhere via mobile devices, anytime.	The marketplace is extended beyond traditional boundaries and is removed from a temporal and geographic location. "Marketspace" is created; shopping can take place anywhere. Customer convenience is enhanced, and shopping costs are reduced.
Global reach—The technology reaches across national boundaries, around the earth.	Commerce is enabled across cultural and national boundaries seamlessly and without modification. "Marketspace" includes potentially billions of consumers and millions of businesses worldwide.
Universal standards—There is one set of technology standards.	There is a common, inexpensive, global technology foundation for businesses to use.
Richness—Video, audio, and text messages are possible.	Video, audio, and text marketing messages are integrated into a single marketing message and consuming experience.
Interactivity—The technology works through interaction with the user.	Consumers are engaged in a dialog that dynamically adjusts the experience to the individual, and makes the consumer a co-participant in the process of delivering goods to the market.
Information density—The technology reduces information costs and raises quality.	Information processing, storage, and communication costs drop dramatically, while currency, accuracy, and timeliness improve greatly. Information becomes plentiful, cheap, and accurate.
Personalization/Customization—The technology allows personalized messages to be delivered to individuals as well as groups.	Personalization of marketing messages and customization of products and services are based on individual characteristics.
Social technology—User-generated content and social networks.	New online social and business models enable user content creation and distribution, and support social networks.

the market relationship—who is selling to whom. Mobile, social, and local e-commerce can be looked at as subsets of these types of e-commerce.

Business-to-Consumer (B2C) E-commerce

The most commonly discussed type of e-commerce is **business-to-consumer (B2C) e-commerce**, in which online businesses attempt to reach individual consumers. B2C commerce includes purchases of retail goods, travel services, and online content. B2C has grown exponentially since 1995, and is the type of e-commerce that most

business-to-consumer (B2C) e-commerce
online businesses selling to individual consumers

TABLE 1.3	MAJOR TYPES OF E-COMMERCE
TYPE OF E-COMMERCE	**EXAMPLE**
B2C—business-to-consumer	Amazon is a general merchandiser that sells consumer products to retail consumers.
B2B—business-to-business	Go2Paper is an independent third-party marketplace that serves the paper industry.
C2C—consumer-to-consumer	Auction sites such as eBay, and listing sites such as Craigslist, enable consumers to auction or sell goods directly to other consumers. Airbnb and Uber provide similar platforms for services such as room rental and transportation.
M-commerce—mobile e-commerce	Mobile devices such as tablet computers and smartphones can be used to conduct commercial transactions.
Social e-commerce	Facebook is both the leading social network and social e-commerce site.
Local e-commerce	Groupon offers subscribers daily deals from local businesses in the form of Groupons, discount coupons that take effect once enough subscribers have agreed to purchase.

consumers are likely to encounter (see **Figure 1.3**). Within the B2C category, there are many different types of business models. Chapter 5 has a detailed discussion of seven different B2C business models: portals, online retailers, content providers, transaction brokers, market creators, service providers, and community providers.

Business-to-Business (B2B) E-commerce

business-to-business (B2B) e-commerce
online businesses selling to other businesses

Business-to-business (B2B) e-commerce, in which businesses focus on selling to other businesses, is the largest form of e-commerce, with around $6.3 trillion in transactions in the United States in 2015 (see **Figure 1.4** on page 60) and about €14.2 trillion worldwide. This is a small portion of total B2B commerce (which remains largely non-automated), suggesting that B2B e-commerce has significant growth potential. The ultimate size of B2B e-commerce is potentially huge. There are two primary business models used within the B2B arena: Net marketplaces, which include e-distributors, e-procurement companies, exchanges and industry consortia, and private industrial networks.

Consumer-to-Consumer (C2C) E-commerce

consumer-to-consumer (C2C) e-commerce
consumers selling to other consumers

Consumer-to-consumer (C2C) e-commerce provides a way for consumers to sell to each other, with the help of an online market maker (also called a platform provider) such as eBay or Etsy, the classifieds site Craigslist, or on-demand service companies such as Airbnb and Uber. Given that in 2014, eBay by itself generated around €76 billion in gross merchandise volume around the world, it is probably safe to estimate that the size of the global C2C market in 2015 is more than €92 billion (eBay, 2015). In C2C e-commerce, the consumer prepares the product for market, places the product for auction or sale, and relies on the market maker to provide catalog, search engine, and transaction-clearing capabilities so that products can be easily displayed, discovered, and paid for.

Mobile E-commerce (M-commerce)

Mobile e-commerce, or m-commerce, refers to the use of mobile devices to enable online transactions. Described more fully in Chapter 2, m-commerce involves the use of cellular and wireless networks to connect laptops, smartphones such as the iPhone and Android phones, and tablet computers such as the iPad to the Internet. Once connected, mobile consumers can conduct transactions, including stock trades, in-store price comparisons, banking, travel reservations, and more. M-commerce purchases are expected to reach around £19 billion in 2015 in the United Kingdom, for instance, and to grow rapidly over the next five years (eMarketer, Inc., 2015b).

mobile e-commerce (m-commerce)
use of mobile devices to enable online transactions

Social E-commerce

Social e-commerce is e-commerce that is enabled by social networks and online social relationships. It is sometimes also referred to as Facebook commerce, but in actuality is a much larger phenomenon that extends beyond just Facebook. The growth

social e-commerce
e-commerce enabled by social networks and online social relationships

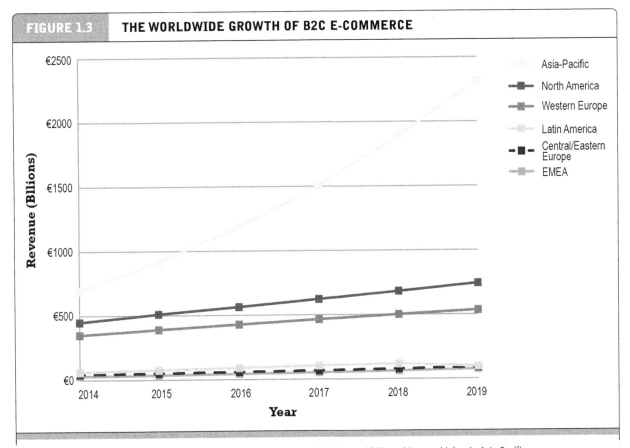

FIGURE 1.3   THE WORLDWIDE GROWTH OF B2C E-COMMERCE

B2C e-commerce is growing rapidly in all regions. Overall global growth is about 25%, and is even higher in Asia-Pacific.

SOURCES: Based on data from eMarketer, Inc., 2015c, 2015d; authors' estimates.

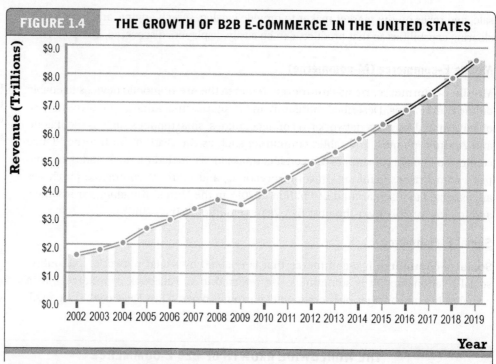

FIGURE 1.4   **THE GROWTH OF B2B E-COMMERCE IN THE UNITED STATES**

B2B e-commerce in the United States is about 10 times the size of B2C e-commerce. In 2019, B2B e-commerce is projected to be over $8.5 trillion. (Note: Does not include EDI transactions.)

SOURCES: Based on data from U.S. Census Bureau, 2015; authors' estimates.

of social e-commerce is being driven by a number of factors, including the increasing popularity of social sign-on (signing onto Web sites using your Facebook or other social network ID), network notification (the sharing of approval or disapproval of products, services, and content via Facebook's Like button or Twitter tweets), online collaborative shopping tools, and social search (recommendations from online trusted friends). Social e-commerce is still in its infancy, but in 2014, the top 500 retailers in Internet Retailer's Social Media 500 earned about $3.3 billion from social commerce, a 25% increase over 2013, and shoppers clicking from social networks to Social Media 500 retailers' Web sites accounted for about 5.8% of all traffic to those Web sites in 2014, up from about 5.4% in the previous year (Zaroban, 2015).

Local E-commerce

local e-commerce
e-commerce that is focused on engaging the consumer based on his or her current geographic location

Local e-commerce, as its name suggests, is a form of e-commerce that is focused on engaging the consumer based on his or her current geographic location. Local merchants use a variety of online marketing techniques to drive consumers to their stores. Local e-commerce is the third prong of the mobile, social, local e-commerce wave, and fueled by an explosion of interest in local on-demand services such as Uber, is expected to grow in the United States to over $25 billion in 2015.

    Figure 1.5 illustrates the relative size of all of the various types of e-commerce.

GROWTH OF THE INTERNET, WEB, AND MOBILE PLATFORM

The technology juggernauts behind e-commerce are the Internet, the Web, and increasingly, the mobile platform. We describe the Internet, Web, and mobile platform in some detail in Chapter 2. The **Internet** is a worldwide network of computer networks built on common standards. Created in the late 1960s to connect a small number of mainframe computers and their users, the Internet has since grown into the world's largest network. It is impossible to say with certainty exactly how many computers and other wireless access devices such as smartphones are connected to the Internet worldwide at any one time, but the number is clearly more than 1 billion. The Internet links businesses, educational institutions, government agencies, and individuals together, and provides users with services such as e-mail, document transfer, shopping, research, instant messaging, music, videos, and news.

One way to measure the growth of the Internet is by looking at the number of Internet hosts with domain names. (An *Internet host* is defined by the Internet Systems Consortium as any IP address that returns a domain name in the in-addr.arpa

Internet
worldwide network of computer networks built on common standards

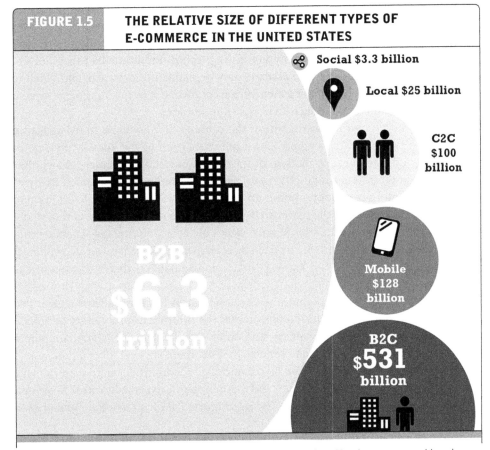

| FIGURE 1.5 | THE RELATIVE SIZE OF DIFFERENT TYPES OF E-COMMERCE IN THE UNITED STATES |

B2B e-commerce dwarfs all other forms of e-commerce; mobile, social, and local e-commerce, although growing rapidly, are still relatively small in comparison to "traditional" e-commerce.

domain, which is a special part of the DNS namespace that resolves IP addresses into domain names.) In July 2015, there were more than 1 billion Internet hosts in over 245 countries, up from just 70 million in 2000 (Internet Systems Consortium, 2015).

The Internet has shown extraordinary growth patterns when compared to other electronic technologies of the past. It took radio 38 years to achieve a 30% share of U.S. households. It took television 17 years to achieve a 30% share. It took only 10 years for the Internet/Web to achieve a 53% share of U.S. households once a graphical user interface was invented for the Web in 1993.

World Wide Web (the Web)
provides access to billions of Web pages

The **World Wide Web (the Web)** is one of the most popular services that runs on the Internet infrastructure. The Web was the original "killer app" that made the Internet commercially interesting and extraordinarily popular. The Web was developed in the early 1990s and hence is of much more recent vintage than the Internet. We describe the Web in some detail in Chapter 2. The Web provides access to billions of Web pages indexed by Google and other search engines. These pages are created in a language called *HTML (HyperText Markup Language)*. HTML pages can contain text, graphics, animations, and other objects. You can find an exceptionally wide range of information on Web pages, ranging from the entire collection of public records from the Securities and Exchange Commission, to the card catalog of your local library, to millions of music tracks and videos. The Internet prior to the Web was primarily used for text communications, file transfers, and remote computing. The Web introduced far more powerful and commercially interesting, colorful multimedia capabilities of direct relevance to commerce. In essence, the Web added color, voice, and video to the Internet, creating a communications infrastructure and information storage system that rivals television, radio, magazines, and even libraries.

There is no precise measurement of the number of Web pages in existence, in part because today's search engines index only a portion of the known universe of Web pages, and also because the size of the Web universe is unknown. Google has identified over 60 trillion unique URLs, up from 1 trillion in 2008, although many of these pages do not necessarily contain unique content (Google, 2014). In addition to this "surface" or "visible" Web, there is also the so-called deep Web that is reportedly 500 to 1,000 times greater than the surface Web. The deep Web contains databases and other content that is not routinely indexed by search engines such as Google. Although the total size of the Web is not known, what is indisputable is that Web content has grown exponentially since 1993.

mobile platform
provides the ability to access the Internet from a variety of highly mobile devices such as smartphones, tablets, and other ultra-lightweight laptop computers

The mobile platform is the newest development in Internet infrastructure. The **mobile platform** provides the ability to access the Internet from a variety of mobile devices such as smartphones, tablets, and other ultra-lightweight laptop computers via wireless networks or cell phone service. In 2015, there are over 350 million mobile devices in the United States that can be connected to the Internet (more than 1 device for each person in the United States), and that number is expected to grow to around 370 million by 2019 (eMarketer, Inc., 2015e). **Figure 1.6** illustrates the rapid growth of mobile Internet access.

Read *Insight on Technology: Will Apps Make the Web Irrelevant?* for a look at the challenge that apps and the mobile platform pose to the Web's dominance of the Internet ecosphere.

FIGURE 1.6   MOBILE INTERNET ACCESS IN THE UNITED STATES

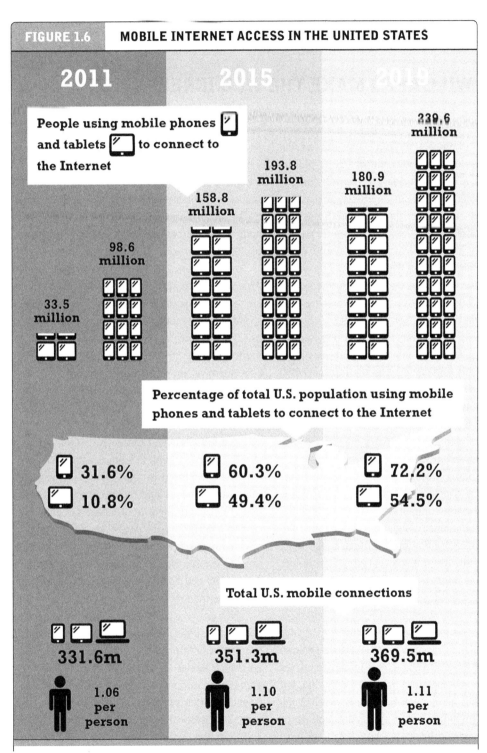

Continued growth in the number of people using mobile phones and tablets to connect to the Internet will provide a significant stimulus to m-commerce.

SOURCES: Based on data from eMarketer, Inc., 2013a, 2013b, 2013c, 2015e, 2015f, 2015g.

INSIGHT ON TECHNOLOGY

WILL APPS MAKE THE WEB IRRELEVANT?

Nowadays, it's hard to recall a time before the Web. How did we get along without the ability to pull up a Web browser and search for any item, learn about any topic, or play just about any type of game? Though the Web has come a remarkably long way from its humble beginnings, many experts claim that the Web's best days are behind it, and that there's a new player on the field: apps. Opinions vary widely over the future role of the Web in a world where apps have become an ever larger portion of the Internet marketspace. In 10 years, will Web browsers be forgotten relics, as we rely entirely on apps to do both our work and our play on the Internet? Will the Web and apps coexist peacefully as vital cogs in the Internet ecosystem? Or will the app craze eventually die down as tech users gravitate back toward the Web as the primary way to perform Internet-related tasks?

Apps have grown into a disruptive force ever since Apple launched its App Store in 2008. The list of industries apps have disrupted is wide-ranging: communications, media and entertainment, logistics, education, healthcare, and most recently, with Uber, the taxi industry. Despite not even existing prior to 2008, in 2015, sales of apps are expected to account for well over $30 billion in revenues worldwide, and the app economy is continuing to show robust growth, with estimates of $70 billion in revenue by 2017. More of those revenues are likely to come from in-app purchases than from paid app downloads. Not only that, but the growth is not coming from more users trying the same small number of apps. Although usage of apps tends to be highly concentrated, with nearly 80% of smartphone app minutes spent on an individual's top 3 apps, consumers are trying new apps all the time and visit about 25 apps per month, leaving plenty of room for new app

developers to innovate and create best-selling apps. In fact, according to mobile advertising company Flurry, 280 million people worldwide qualify as mobile addicts, which they define as someone who launches a smartphone app more than 60 times a day. According to Flurry, the number of such addicts has increased by about 350% from 2013 to 2015.

In January 2014, for the first time ever, Americans used apps more than desktop computers to access the Internet. The time U.S. adults are spending using mobile apps has exploded, growing by 90% over the past two years, and now accounting for 53.8% of total digital media time spent; time spent on the desktop now accounts for just 38%, and mobile browsers just 8.2%. U.S. adults are spending 68 hours a month (over 2 hours a day) within apps on their smartphones, while young adults between the ages of 18–24 spend over 90 hours a month (3+ hours a day). Consumers have gravitated to apps for several reasons. First, smartphones and tablet computers enable users to use apps anywhere, instead of being tethered to a desktop or having to lug a heavy laptop around. Of course, smartphones and tablets enable users to use the Web too, but apps are often more convenient and boast more streamlined, elegant interfaces than mobile Web browsers.

Not only are apps more appealing in certain ways to consumers, they are much more appealing to content creators and media companies. Apps are much easier to control and monetize than Web sites, not to mention they can't be crawled by Google or other services. On the Web, the average price of ads per thousand impressions is falling, and after twenty years, many content providers are still mostly struggling to turn the Internet into a profitable content delivery platform. Much of software and media companies' focus has shifted to developing mobile apps for this reason.

These trends are why some pundits boldly proclaim that the Web is dead, and that the shift from the Web to apps has only just started. These analysts believe that the Internet will be used to transport data, but individual app interfaces will replace the Web browser as the most common way to access and display content. Even the creator of the Web, Tim Berners-Lee, feels that the Web as we know it is being threatened. That's not a good sign.

But there is no predictive consensus about the role of the Web in our lives in the next decade and beyond. Many analysts believe the demise of the Web has been greatly exaggerated, and that the Web boasts many advantages over today's apps that users will be unwilling to relinquish. Although apps may be more convenient than the Web in many respects, the depth of the Web browsing experience trumps that of apps. The Web is a vibrant, diverse array of sites, and browsers have an openness and flexibility that apps lack. The connections between Web sites enhance their usefulness and value to users, and apps that instead seek to lock users in cannot offer the same experience.

Other analysts who are more optimistic about the Web's chances to remain relevant in an increasingly app-driven online marketplace feel this way because of the emergence of HTML5. HTML5 is a new markup language that will enable more dynamic Web content and allow for browser-accessible Web apps that are as appealing as device-specific apps. In fact, there is another group of analysts who believe that apps and the Web are going to come together, with HTML5 bringing the best of the app experience to the Web, and with apps developing new Web-like capabilities. Already, work is underway to create more "smart" apps that handle a wider array of tasks than today's apps can handle, such as apps with Siri integration.

A shift towards apps and away from the Web could have a ripple effect on e-commerce firms. As the pioneer of apps and the market leader in apps, smartphones, and tablet computers, Apple stands to gain from a shift towards apps, and although it will also face increasing opposition from other companies, including Google, the established success of the App Store will make it next to impossible to dethrone Apple. While Google's Google Play store has dwarfed the App Store in downloads in 2015, Apple nevertheless maintains a strong lead in app revenues. Google's search business is likely to suffer from all of the "walled garden" apps that it cannot access, but it also has a major stake in the world of smartphones, tablets, and apps itself with its Android operating system, which is used by over 80% of smartphones worldwide. Facebook has already seen its members make the transition from using its site on the Web to using its mobile app and has made, and continues to make, significant investments in standalone apps, such as Instagram and WhatsApp. Web-based companies that fail to find an answer to the growth of the mobile platform may eventually fall by the wayside.

SOURCES: "Smartphone OS Market Share, 2015 Q2," Idc.com, accessed September 24, 2015; "The 2015 U.S. Mobile App Report," by comScore, September 2015; "Mobile Addicts Multiply Across the Globe," by Simon Khalaf, Flurrymobile.tumblr.com, July 15, 2015; "App Annie Report: Google Play's Downloads Dwarf the App Store as Apple Retains Revenue Lead," by Jackie Dove, Thenextweb.com, July 15, 2015; "Mobile Apps Poised to Hit $70B in Revenues by 2017," by Per Petterson, Impactradius.com, December 3, 2014; "More People Are Opening More Mobile Apps Every Day," by Ewan Spence, Forbes.com, April 24, 2014; "The Rise of the Mobile Addict," by Simon Khalaf, Flurry.com, April 22, 2014; "How Apps Won the Mobile Web," by Thomas Claburn, Informationweek.com, April 3, 2014; "Apps Solidify Leadership Six Years into the Mobile Revolution," by Simon Khalaf, Flurry.com, April 1, 2014; "Mobile Apps Overtake PC Internet Usage in U.S.," by James O'Toole, Money.cnn.com, February 28, 2014; "Convergence of User Experiences," Savas.me, April 4, 2013; "Flurry Five-Year Report: It's an App World. The Web Just Lives in It," by Simon Khalaf, Flurry.com, April 3, 2013; "Here's Why Google and Facebook Might Completely Disappear in the Next 5 Years," by Eric Jackson, Forbes.com, April 30, 2012; "Is The Web Dead In the Face of Native Apps? Not Likely, But Some Think So," by Gabe Knuth, Brianmadden.com, March 28, 2012; "Imagining the Internet," by Janna Quitney Anderson and Lee Rainie, Pew Internet and American Life Project, March 23, 2012; "The Web Is Dead. Long Live the Internet," by Chris Anderson and Michael Wolff, Wired.com, August 17, 2010; "The Web Is Dead? A Debate," by Chris Anderson, Wired.com, August 17, 2010.

ORIGINS AND GROWTH OF E-COMMERCE

It is difficult to pinpoint just when e-commerce began. There were several precursors to e-commerce. In the late 1970s, a pharmaceutical firm named Baxter Healthcare initiated a primitive form of B2B e-commerce by using a telephone-based modem that permitted hospitals to reorder supplies from Baxter. This system was later expanded during the 1980s into a PC-based remote order entry system and was widely copied throughout the United States long before the Internet became a commercial environment. The 1980s saw the development of Electronic Data Interchange (EDI) standards that permitted firms to exchange commercial documents and conduct digital commercial transactions across private networks.

In the B2C arena, the first truly large-scale digitally enabled transaction system was deployed in France in 1981. The Minitel was a French videotext system that combined a telephone with an 8-inch screen. By the mid-1980s, more than 3 million Minitels were deployed, and more than 13,000 different services were available, including ticket agencies, travel services, retail products, and online banking. The Minitel service continued in existence until December 31, 2006, when it was finally discontinued by its owner, France Telecom.

However, none of these precursor systems had the functionality of the Internet. Generally, when we think of e-commerce today, it is inextricably linked to the Internet. For our purposes, we will say e-commerce begins in 1995, following the appearance of the first banner advertisements placed by AT&T, Volvo, Sprint, and others on Hotwired in late October 1994, and the first sales of banner ad space by Netscape and Infoseek in early 1995. Since then, e-commerce has been the fastest growing form of commerce in the United States.

The data suggests that, over the next five years, global retail e-commerce will grow by over 20% annually, much faster than traditional retail sales (which are growing at only about 6% a year). There is tremendous upside potential. Today, for instance, retail e-commerce is still a very small part (around 7%) of the overall €21 trillion retail market, and under current projections, in 2019, will still only be about 12% of total retail sales. There is obviously much room to grow (see **Figure 1.7**). However, it's not likely that retail e-commerce revenues will continue to expand forever at double-digit rates. As online sales become a larger percentage of all sales, online sales growth will likely eventually decline to that growth level. This point still appears to be a long way off. Online content sales, everything from music, to video, medical information, games, and entertainment, have an even longer period to grow before they hit any ceiling effects.

1.2   E-COMMERCE: A BRIEF HISTORY

Although e-commerce is not very old, it already has a tumultuous history. The history of e-commerce can be usefully divided into three periods: 1995–2000, the period of invention; 2001–2006, the period of consolidation; and 2007–present, a period of

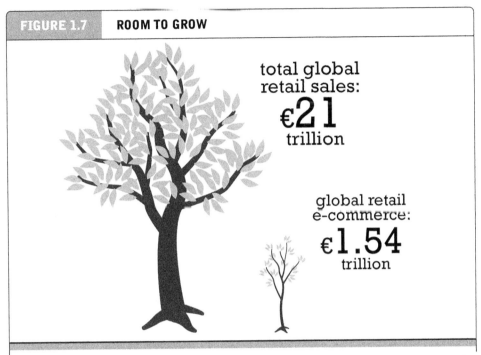

FIGURE 1.7   **ROOM TO GROW**

total global
retail sales:
€21
trillion

global retail
e-commerce:
€1.54
trillion

E-commerce retail is still just a small part of the overall global retail market, but with much room to grow in the future.

reinvention with social, mobile, and local expansion. The following examines each of these periods briefly, while **Figure 1.8** places them in context along a timeline.

E-COMMERCE 1995–2000: INVENTION

The early years of e-commerce were a period of explosive growth and extraordinary innovation, beginning in 1995 with the first widespread use of the Web to advertise products. During this Invention period, e-commerce meant selling retail goods, usually quite simple goods, on the Internet. There simply was not enough bandwidth for more complex products. Marketing was limited to unsophisticated static display ads and not very powerful search engines. The Web policy of most large firms, if they had one at all, was to have a basic static Web site depicting their brands. The rapid growth in e-commerce was fueled by over $125 billion in U.S. venture capital. This period of e-commerce came to a close in 2000 when stock market valuations plunged, with thousands of companies disappearing (the "dot-com crash").

The early years of e-commerce were also one of the most euphoric of times in commercial history. It was also a time when key e-commerce concepts were developed. For computer scientists and information technologists, the early success of e-commerce was a powerful vindication of a set of information technologies that had developed over a period of 40 years—extending from the development of the early Internet, to the PC, to local area networks. The vision was of a universal

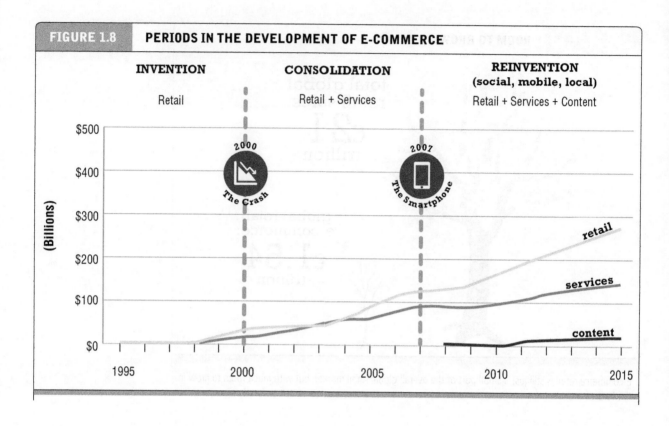

FIGURE 1.8

PERIODS IN THE DEVELOPMENT OF E-COMMERCE

communications and computing environment that everyone on Earth could access with cheap, inexpensive computers—a worldwide universe of knowledge stored on HTML pages created by hundreds of millions of individuals and thousands of libraries, governments, and scientific institutes. Technologists celebrated the fact that the Internet was not controlled by anyone or any nation, but was free to all. They believed the Internet—and the e-commerce that rose on this infrastructure—should remain a self-governed, self-regulated environment.

For economists, the early years of e-commerce raised the realistic prospect of a nearly perfect competitive market: where price, cost, and quality information are equally distributed, a nearly infinite set of suppliers compete against one another, and customers have access to all relevant market information worldwide. The Internet would spawn digital markets where information would be nearly perfect—something that is rarely true in other real-world markets. Merchants in turn would have equal direct access to hundreds of millions of customers. In this near-perfect information marketspace, transaction costs would plummet because search costs—the cost of searching for prices, product descriptions, payment settlement, and order fulfillment—would all fall drastically (Bakos, 1997). For merchants, the cost of searching for customers would also fall, reducing the need for wasteful advertising. At the same time, advertisements could be personalized to the needs of every customer. Prices and even costs would be increasingly transparent to the consumer, who could now know exactly and instantly the worldwide best price, quality, and availability of most products. Information asymmetry would be greatly reduced. Given the instant nature of Internet communications, the availability of powerful sales information systems, and the low cost involved in changing prices on a Web site (low menu costs), producers could dynamically price their products to reflect actual demand, ending the idea of one national price, or one suggested manufacturer's list price. In turn, market middlemen — the distributors and wholesalers who are intermediaries between producers and consumers, each demanding a payment and raising costs while adding little value—would disappear (**disintermediation**). Manufacturers and content originators would develop direct market relationships with their customers. The resulting intense competition, the decline of intermediaries, and the lower transaction costs would eliminate product brands, and along with these, the possibility of *monopoly profits* based on brands, geography, or special access to factors of production. Prices for products and services would fall to the point where prices covered costs of production plus a fair, "market rate" of return on capital, plus additional small payments for entrepreneurial effort (that would not last long). Unfair competitive advantages (which occur when one competitor has an advantage others cannot purchase) would be reduced, as would extraordinary returns on invested capital. This vision was called **friction-free commerce** (Smith et al., 2000).

For real-world entrepreneurs, their financial backers, and marketing professionals, e-commerce represented an extraordinary opportunity to earn far above normal returns on investment. This is just the opposite of what economists hoped for. The e-commerce marketspace represented access to millions of consumers worldwide who used the Internet and a set of marketing communications technologies (e-mail and Web pages) that was universal, inexpensive, and powerful. These new technologies would permit marketers to practice what they always had done—segmenting the market into groups with different needs and price sensitivity, targeting the segments with branding and promotional messages, and positioning the product and pricing for each group—but with even more precision. In this new marketspace, extraordinary profits would go to **first movers**—those firms who were first to market in a particular area and who moved quickly to gather market share. In a "winner take all" market, first movers could establish a large customer base quickly, build brand name recognition early, create an entirely new distribution channel, and then inhibit competitors (new entrants) by building in *switching costs* for their customers through proprietary interface designs and features available only at one site. The idea for entrepreneurs was to create near monopolies online based on size, convenience, selection, and brand. Online businesses using the new technology could create informative, community-like features unavailable to traditional merchants. These "communities of consumption" also would add value and be difficult for traditional merchants to imitate. The thinking was that once customers became accustomed to using a company's unique Web interface and feature set, they could not easily be switched to competitors. In the best case, the entrepreneurial firm would invent proprietary technologies and techniques that almost everyone adopted, creating a network effect. A **network effect** occurs where all participants receive value from the fact that everyone else uses the same tool or product (for example, a common operating system, telephone system, or software application such as a proprietary instant

disintermediation
displacement of market middlemen who traditionally are intermediaries between producers and consumers by a new direct relationship between producers and consumers

friction-free commerce
a vision of commerce in which information is equally distributed, transaction costs are low, prices can be dynamically adjusted to reflect actual demand, intermediaries decline, and unfair competitive advantages are eliminated

first mover
a firm that is first to market in a particular area and that moves quickly to gather market share

network effect
occurs where users receive value from the fact that everyone else uses the same tool or product

messaging standard or an operating system such as Windows), all of which increase in value as more people adopt them.[2]

To initiate this process, entrepreneurs argued that prices would have to be very low to attract customers and fend off potential competitors. E-commerce was, after all, a totally new way of shopping that would have to offer some immediate cost benefits to consumers. However, because doing business on the Web was supposedly so much more efficient when compared to traditional "bricks-and-mortar" businesses (even when compared to the direct mail catalog business) and because the costs of customer acquisition and retention would supposedly be so much lower, profits would inevitably materialize out of these efficiencies. Given these dynamics, market share, the number of visitors to a site ("eyeballs"), and gross revenue became far more important in the earlier stages of an online firm than earnings or profits. Entrepreneurs and their financial backers in the early years of e-commerce expected that extraordinary profitability would come, but only after several years of losses.

Thus, the early years of e-commerce were driven largely by visions of profiting from new technology, with the emphasis on quickly achieving very high market visibility. The source of financing was venture capital funds. The ideology of the period emphasized the ungoverned "Wild West" character of the Web and the feeling that governments and courts could not possibly limit or regulate the Internet; there was a general belief that traditional corporations were too slow and bureaucratic, too stuck in the old ways of doing business, to "get it"—to be competitive in e-commerce. Young entrepreneurs were therefore the driving force behind e-commerce, backed by huge amounts of money invested by venture capitalists. The emphasis was on *disrupting* (destroying) traditional distribution channels and disintermediating existing channels, using new pure online companies who aimed to achieve impregnable first-mover advantages. Overall, this period of e-commerce was characterized by experimentation, capitalization, and hypercompetition (Varian, 2000b).

E-COMMERCE 2001–2006: CONSOLIDATION

In the second period of e-commerce, from 2000 to 2006, a sobering period of reassessment of e-commerce occurred, with many critics doubting its long-term prospects. Emphasis shifted to a more "business-driven" approach rather than being technology driven; large traditional firms learned how to use the Web to strengthen their market positions; brand extension and strengthening became more important than creating new brands; financing shrunk as capital markets shunned start-up firms; and traditional bank financing based on profitability returned.

During this period of consolidation, e-commerce changed to include not just retail products but also more complex services such as travel and financial services. This period was enabled by widespread adoption of broadband networks in American homes and businesses, coupled with the growing power and lower prices of personal

---

[2] The network effect is quantified by Metcalfe's Law, which argues that the value of a network grows by the square of the number of participants.

computers that were the primary means of accessing the Internet, usually from work or home. Marketing on the Internet increasingly meant using search engine advertising targeted to user queries, rich media and video ads, and behavioral targeting of marketing messages based on ad networks and auction markets. The Web policy of both large and small firms expanded to include a broader "Web presence" that included not just Web sites, but also e-mail, display, and search engine campaigns; multiple Web sites for each product; and the building of some limited community feedback facilities. E-commerce in this period was growing again by more than 10% a year.

E-COMMERCE 2007–PRESENT: REINVENTION

Beginning in 2007 with the introduction of the iPhone, to the present day, e-commerce has been transformed yet again by the rapid growth of **Web 2.0** (a set of applications and technologies that enable user-generated content, such as online social networks, blogs, video and photo sharing sites, and wikis), widespread adoption of consumer mobile devices such as smartphones and tablet computers, the expansion of e-commerce to include local goods and services, and the emergence of an on-demand service economy enabled by millions of apps on mobile devices and cloud computing. This period can be seen as both a sociological, as well as a technological and business, phenomenon.

Web 2.0

set of applications and technologies that enable user-generated content

The defining characteristics of this period are often characterized as the "social, mobile, local" online world. Entertainment content has developed as a major source of e-commerce revenues and mobile devices have become entertainment centers, as well as on-the-go shopping devices for retail goods and services. Marketing has been transformed by the increasing use of social networks, word-of-mouth, viral marketing, and much more powerful data repositories and analytic tools for truly personal marketing. Firms have greatly expanded their online presence by moving beyond static Web pages to social networks such as Facebook, Twitter, Pinterest, and Instagram in an attempt to surround the online consumer with coordinated marketing messages. These social networks share many common characteristics. First, they rely on user-generated content. "Regular" people (not just experts or professionals) are creating, sharing, and broadcasting content to huge audiences. They are inherently highly interactive, creating new opportunities for people to socially connect to others. They attract extremely large audiences (about 1.5 billion monthly active users worldwide as of June 2015 in the case of Facebook). These audiences present marketers with extraordinary opportunities for targeted marketing and advertising.

More recently, the re-invention of the Web and e-commerce has resulted in a new set of on-demand, personal service businesses such as Uber, Airbnb, Instacart, Handy, and Homejoy. These businesses have been able to tap into a large reservoir of unused assets (cars, spare rooms, and personal spare time) and to create lucrative markets based on the mobile platform infrastructure. The *Insight on Business* case, *Rocket Internet,* takes a look at Rocket Internet, which has mentored a number of these new social, mobile, and local e-commerce ventures.

Table 1.4 on page 74 summarizes e-commerce in each of these three periods.

INSIGHT ON BUSINESS

ROCKET INTERNET

By now we've all heard the story of code written by Mark Zuckerberg in a Harvard dorm room blossoming into a multi-billion dollar business. These days, it's harder than ever to keep track of all the tech startups being bought for millions and even billions of euros, often even without any revenue to show for themselves. Many of them have something in common—they have been nurtured, and in some cases, whipped into shape, with the help of an "incubator."

Incubators have come to occupy a vital role in tech, helping new businesses move from little more than a great idea to an established, vibrant business. Rocket Internet is one such incubator. Founded in 2007 by German entrepreneurs Alexander, Oliver, and Marc Samwer, Rocket Internet launches e-commerce and other Internet start-ups in emerging markets, with the goal of becoming the world's largest Internet platform outside the United States and China. Headquartered in Berlin and with 25 international offices, Rocket Internet has over 75 independent companies active in 110 countries in its portfolio In 2014, Rocket went public on the Frankfurt Stock Exchange, in the largest German technology IPO in the past decade. The initial pricing valued the company at around €6.5 billion. In the previous two years, the company had raised nearly €3.2 billion from investors. In 2015, the share price dropped steeply for much of the year, but made a late rebound to approximately €30 per share.

Rocket bills itself as more than a venture capital firm or typical incubator. Rocket has a variety of teams that work closely with each of its ventures, including teams focused on engineering and product development, online marketing, CRM, business intelligence, operations, HR, and finance. Rocket also helps its start-ups by providing access to centralized logistics and other back-office functions to help them cut down on operational costs. The growing network of Rocket Internet companies is also a valuable resource. In many emerging markets, the most talented workers end up in established industries, but Rocket is ensuring that e-commerce also captures top talent in those regions. Prominent companies launched via Rocket Internet include Germany's Zalando, India's Jabong, Russia's Lamoda, Australia's The Iconic and Zanui, Pakistan's Azmalo (now Kaymu) and Daraz, and Southeast Asia's Zalora.

Former Rocket Internet employees also have a strong track record with their own independent start-ups once they've left the parent company. These employees note that their experience at Rocket has made the prospect of starting new businesses seem less intimidating. They also praise Oliver Samwer's attention to detail and emphasis on making decisions using data. Rocket Internet start-ups collect and analyze as much data as possible on their markets and customers. They also report that their association with Rocket Internet gives them more credibility with major investors.

Rocket Internet has yet to launch many new businesses in the United States, where the competitive environment is much more difficult than in emerging markets and even Europe. In 2015, Rocket Internet began the process of selling its holdings in India, including Jabong and on-demand food delivery company Foodpanda, due to increasingly heavy competition from India's booming startup environment. Many of Rocket's ventures focus on emerging markets because the profit margins are higher although the markets are smaller. This is in contrast to Amazon, for example, which has razor-thin margins but enormous scope and market reach. Critics of Rocket Internet claim that the company is less concerned with innovation than it is with launching clones of successful United States-based businesses in other markets.

For instance, in 2014, Rocket launched Zipjet, an on-demand laundry service modeled after U.S. counterpart Washio, and ShopWings, an online supermarket resembling Instacart, a similar service launched in major U.S. cities. Oliver Samwer counters talk of clones, noting that for the majority of these types of businesses, truly disruptive innovation is rare, and the business succeeds or not based on the efficiency of its business processes. Marc Samwer adds that Rocket Internet takes the best ideas and improves on them by localizing them to better fit specific areas. Investors are also concerned about the profitability of Rocket's portfolio. Many of Rocket's companies have market leader status in their respective areas, but hardly any of them are currently profitable. Rocket contends that by focusing on growth in emerging markets first, profits will come in time, but in 2015 Rocket amassed more than €46 million in yearly losses by the end of October, despite posting 142% revenue growth in its subset of "proven winner" businesses, nearly all of which are still unprofitable themselves.

Nevertheless, Rocket has captured significant market share in many industries by launching companies modeled after established businesses in emerging markets, and then selling these ventures to those established businesses when they're looking to expand into those markets. eBay's acquisition of Germany's leading auction site, Alando, where the Samwers got their start, is an example. Amazon was rumored to be interested in Jabong, though those talks were abandoned in 2015, and Africa-based Jumia and Southeast Asia-based Lazada, also modeled after Amazon, could conceivably be additional targets for Amazon. Payleven is a European mobile payment company modeled after Square and Paypal. Increasingly, however, Rocket is looking to create sustainable companies who are focused less on their eventual sale to bigger companies and more on their own growth. Oliver Samwer believes that in the past, it may have sold some businesses, such as Alando, too early, but that it was necessary in order for Rocket to build a track record. Now that it has one, it can afford to take a longer-term view.

Startupbootcamp is another start-up accelerator based in Europe that selects 10 start-ups from a pool of hundreds of applicants and provides cutting-edge training and a network of professionals to help them go from an idea to a thriving business. Applicants receive coaching from a network of volunteer mentors from successful tech companies as well as significant stipends for living expenses and partner deals. After 3 months, start-ups pitch their businesses to venture capitalists and investors. Established companies also have made deals with Startupbootcamp to mentor specific types of businesses, such as AVG Technologies' agreement to invest in Startupbootcamp's NFC and Contactless division. Though Internet start-ups have boomed, busted, and are now booming again, as the global economy continues to rely more on the Internet and Internet-based services, incubators and accelerators like Rocket Internet and Startupbootcamp are here to stay.

SOURCES: "About Startupbootcamp," Startupbootcamp.org, accessed November 30, 2015; "Rocket Internet: Waiting for Lift-Off," by Sarah Gordon and Dan McCrum, *Financial Times*, October 19, 2015; "Revenue Jumps at Rocket Internet's Top Start-ups," by Emma Thomason, Reuters.com, September 30, 2015; "Rocket Internet Plans to Sell Its Top Companies in India," by Biswarup Gooptu and Krithika Krishnamurthy, *Economic Times*, September 22, 2015; "Amazon-Jabong Call Off Talks for a Potential $1.2B Buyout Deal," by Priyanka Sahay, VCCircle.com, April 2, 2015; "Fear and Laundry in London as Rocket Internet's ZipJet Launches in the U.K. Capital City," by Steve O'Hear, Techcrunch.com, November 3, 2014; "With ShopWings, Instacart Gets a Wink and a Clone from Rocket Internet," by Ingrid Lunden, Techcrunch.com, October 13, 2014; "Rocket Internet — First Mover in Asia?" by Susan Cunningham, *Forbes*, October 5, 2014; "Rocket Internet Drops 13% in Debut," by Chase Gummer, *Wall Street Journal*, October 2, 2014; "Rocket Internet's Marc Samwer on Cloning: We Make Business Models Better Because We Localize," by Leena Rao, Techcrunch.com, October 28, 2013; "5 Reasons Why Rocket Internet Graduates Become Good Entrepreneurs," Ventureburn.com, October 17, 2013; "AVG Invests in Startupbootcamp NFC & Contactless Program in Amsterdam," *Wall Street Journal*, September 26, 2013; "Rocket Internet Raises $500M from Kinnevik and Access, Plans More E-Commerce in Emerging Markets," by Ingrid Lunden, TechCrunch.com, July 16, 2013; "Rocket Internet Raises $500M to Be the Biggest e Commerce Incubator on Earth," by Sean Ludwig, VentureBeat.com, July 16, 2013; "eBay Acquires Germany's Leading Onine Person-to-Person Trading Site — Alando.de AG," Prnewswire.com, June 22, 2013; "Payleven, the Samwer's Square/PayPal Rival, Ramps Up Security with FSA Authorization, MasterCard mPOS Scheme," by Ingrid Lunden, TechCrunch.com, March 27, 2013; "Rocket Internet's New Site Reveals a Huge Global Cloning Operation in Full Flow," by Mike Butcher, TechCrunch.com, July 20, 2012.

TABLE 1.4	EVOLUTION OF E-COMMERCE	
1995–2000 INVENTION	2001–2006 CONSOLIDATION	2007–PRESENT REINVENTION
Technology driven	Business driven	Mobile technology enables social, local, and mobile e-commerce
Revenue growth emphasis	Earnings and profits emphasis	Audience and social network connections emphasis
Venture capital financing	Traditional financing	Return of venture capital financing; buy-outs of start-ups by large firms
Ungoverned	Stronger regulation and governance	Extensive government surveillance
Entrepreneurial	Large traditional firms	Entrepreneurial social, mobile, and local firms
Disintermediation	Strengthening intermediaries	Proliferation of small online intermediaries renting business processes of larger firms
Perfect markets	Imperfect markets, brands, and network effects	Continuation of online market imperfections; commodity competition in select markets
Pure online strategies	Mixed "bricks-and-clicks" strategies	Return of pure online strategies in new markets; extension of bricks-and-clicks in traditional retail markets
First-mover advantages	Strategic-follower strength; complementary assets	First-mover advantages return in new markets as traditional Web players catch up
Low-complexity retail products	High-complexity retail products and services	Retail, services, and content

ASSESSING E-COMMERCE: SUCCESSES, SURPRISES, AND FAILURES

Looking back at the evolution of e-commerce, it is apparent that e-commerce has been a stunning technological success as the Internet and the Web ramped up from a few thousand to billions of e-commerce transactions per year, and this year will generate an estimated €1.96 trillion in total B2C revenues and around €14.2 trillion in B2B revenues, with around 1.4 billion online buyers in the United States. With enhancements and strengthening, described in later chapters, it is clear that e-commerce's digital infrastructure is solid enough to sustain significant growth in e-commerce during the next decade. The Internet scales well. The "e" in e-commerce has been an overwhelming success.

From a business perspective, though, the early years of e-commerce were a mixed success, and offered many surprises. Only about 10% of dot-coms formed since 1995 have survived as independent companies in 2015. Only a very tiny percentage of these survivors are profitable. Yet online B2C sales of goods and services are still growing very rapidly. Contrary to economists' hopes, online sales are increasingly concentrated in the top ten retailers who account for over 50% of all online retail sales (Internet Retailer, 2015). So thousands of firms have failed, and those few that have survived dominate the market. The idea of thousands of suppliers competing on price has been replaced by a market dominated by giant firms. Consumers have learned to use the Web as a powerful source of information about products they actually purchase through other channels, such as at a traditional bricks-and-mortar store. For instance, a 2014 study found that almost 90% of those surveyed "webroomed" (researched a product online before purchasing at a physical store) (Interactions Consumer Experience Marketing, Inc., 2014). This is especially true of expensive consumer durables such as appliances, automobiles, and electronics. This offline "Internet-influenced" commerce is very difficult to estimate, but is believed to be somewhere around $1.5 trillion in 2015 (Forrester Research, 2014). Altogether then, B2C retail e-commerce (actual online purchases) and purchases influenced by online shopping but actually buying in a store (Internet-influenced commerce) are expected to amount to almost $1.9 trillion in 2015, or almost 40% of total retail sales in the United States. The "commerce" in e-commerce is basically very sound, at least in the sense of attracting a growing number of customers and generating revenues and profits for large e-commerce players.

Although e-commerce has grown at an extremely rapid pace in customers and revenues, it is clear that many of the visions, predictions, and assertions about e-commerce developed in the early years have not have been fulfilled. For instance, economists' visions of "friction-free" commerce have not been entirely realized. Prices are sometimes lower online, but the low prices are sometimes a function of entrepreneurs selling products below their costs. In some cases, online prices are higher than those of local merchants, as consumers are willing to pay a small premium for the convenience of buying online. Consumers are less price sensitive than expected; surprisingly, the Web sites with the highest revenue often have the highest prices. There remains considerable persistent and even increasing price dispersion: online competition has lowered prices, but price dispersion remains pervasive in many markets despite lower search costs (Levin, 2011; Ghose and Yao, 2010). In a study of 50,000 goods in the United Kingdom and the United States, researchers found Internet prices were sticky even in the face of large changes in demand, online merchants did not alter prices significantly more than offline merchants, and price dispersion across online sellers was somewhat greater than traditional brick and mortar stores (Gorodnichenko, et al., 2014). The concept of one world, one market, one price has not occurred in reality as entrepreneurs discover new ways to differentiate their products and services. While for the most part Internet prices save consumers about 20% on average when compared to in-store prices, sometimes online prices are higher than for similar products purchased offline, especially if shipping costs are considered. For instance, prices on books and CDs vary by as much as 50%, and prices for airline tickets as much as 20% (Alessandria, 2009; Aguiar and Hurst, 2008; Baye, 2004; Baye et al., 2004; Brynjolfsson and Smith, 2000; Bailey, 1998a, b). Merchants have adjusted to the competitive Internet environment by engaging in "hit-and-run pricing" or changing prices every day or hour (using "flash pricing" or "flash sales") so competitors never know what they are charging (neither do customers); by making their prices hard to discover and sowing confusion among consumers by "baiting and switching" customers from low-margin products to high-margin products with supposedly "higher quality." Finally, brands remain very important in e-commerce—consumers trust some firms more than others to deliver a high-quality product on time and they are willing to pay for it (Rosso and Jansen, 2010).

The "perfect competition" model of extreme market efficiency has not come to pass. Merchants and marketers are continually introducing information asymmetries. Search costs have fallen overall, but the overall transaction cost of actually completing a purchase in e-commerce remains high because users have a bewildering number of new questions to consider: Will the merchant actually deliver? What is the time frame of delivery? Does the merchant really stock this item? How do I fill out this form? Many potential e-commerce purchases are terminated in the shopping cart stage because of these consumer uncertainties. Some people still find it easier to call a trusted catalog merchant on the telephone than to order on a Web site. Finally, intermediaries have not disappeared as predicted. Most manufacturers, for instance, have not adopted the manufacturer-direct sales model of online sales, and some that had, such as Sony, have returned to an intermediary model. Dell, one of the pioneers of online manufacturer-direct sales, has moved toward a mixed model heavily reliant on in-store sales where customers can "kick the tires;" Apple's physical stores are among the most successful stores in the world. People still like to shop in a physical store.

If anything, e-commerce has created many opportunities for middlemen to aggregate content, products, and services and thereby introduce themselves as the "new" intermediaries. Third-party travel sites such as Travelocity, Orbitz, and Expedia are an example of this kind of intermediary. E-commerce has not driven existing retail chains and catalog merchants out of business, although it has created opportunities for entrepreneurial online-only firms to succeed.

The visions of many entrepreneurs and venture capitalists for e-commerce have not materialized exactly as predicted either. First-mover advantage appears to have succeeded only for a very small group of companies, albeit some of them extremely well-known, such as Google, Facebook, Amazon, and others. Getting big fast sometimes works, but often not. Historically, first movers have been long-term losers, with the early-to-market innovators usually being displaced by established "fast-follower" firms with the right complement of financial, marketing, legal, and production assets needed to develop mature markets, and this has proved true for e-commerce as well. Many e-commerce first movers, such as eToys, FogDog (sporting goods), Webvan (groceries), and Eve.com (beauty products), failed. Customer acquisition and retention costs during the early years of e-commerce were extraordinarily high, with some firms, such as E*Trade and other financial service firms, paying up to $400 to acquire a new customer. The overall costs of doing business online—including the costs of technology, site design and maintenance, and warehouses for fulfillment—are often no lower than the costs faced by the most efficient bricks-and-mortar stores. A large warehouse costs tens of millions of dollars regardless of a firm's online presence. The knowledge of how to run the warehouse is priceless, and not easily moved. The start-up costs can be staggering. Attempting to achieve or enhance profitability by raising prices has often led to large customer defections. From the e-commerce merchant's perspective, the "e" in e-commerce does not stand for "easy."

On the other hand, there have been some extraordinary, and unanticipated surprises in the evolution of e-commerce. Few predicted the impact of the mobile platform. Few anticipated the rapid growth of social networks or their growing success as advertising platforms based on a more detailed understanding of personal behavior than even Google has achieved. And few, if any, anticipated the emergence of on-demand e-commerce, which enables people to use their mobile devices to order up everything from taxis, to groceries, to laundry service.

1.3   UNDERSTANDING E-COMMERCE: ORGANIZING THEMES

Understanding e-commerce in its totality is a difficult task for students and instructors because there are so many facets to the phenomenon. No single academic discipline is prepared to encompass all of e-commerce. After teaching the e-commerce course for several years and writing this book, we have come to realize just how difficult it is to "understand" e-commerce. We have found it useful to think about e-commerce as involving three broad interrelated themes: technology, business, and society. We do not mean to imply any ordering of importance here because this book and our thinking freely range over these themes as appropriate to the problem we are trying to understand and describe. Nevertheless, as in previous technologically driven commercial revolutions, there is a historic progression. Technologies develop first, and then those developments are exploited commercially. Once commercial exploitation of the technology becomes widespread, a host of social, cultural, and political issues arise, and society is forced to respond to them.

TECHNOLOGY: INFRASTRUCTURE

The development and mastery of digital computing and communications technology is at the heart of the newly emerging global digital economy we call e-commerce. To understand the likely future of e-commerce, you need a basic understanding of the information technologies upon which it is built. E-commerce is above all else a technologically driven phenomenon that relies on a host of information technologies as well as fundamental concepts from computer science developed over a 50-year period. At the core of e-commerce are the Internet and the Web, which we describe in detail in Chapter 2. Underlying these technologies are a host of complementary technologies: cloud computing, desktop computers, smartphones, tablet computers, local area networks, relational and non-relational databases, client/server computing, data mining, and fiber-optic switches, to name just a few. These technologies lie at the heart of sophisticated business computing applications such as enterprise-wide information systems, supply chain management systems, manufacturing resource planning systems, and customer relationship management systems. E-commerce relies on all these basic technologies—not just the Internet. The Internet, while representing a sharp break from prior corporate computing and communications technologies, is nevertheless just the latest development in the evolution of corporate computing and part of the continuing chain of computer-based innovations in business. **Figure 1.9** illustrates the major stages in the development of corporate computing and indicates how the Internet and the Web fit into this development trajectory.

To truly understand e-commerce, you will need to know something about packet-switched communications, protocols such as TCP/IP, client/server and cloud computing, mobile digital platforms, Web servers, HTML5, CSS, and software programming tools such as Flash and JavaScript on the client side, and Java, PHP, Ruby on Rails, and ColdFusion on the server side. All of these topics are described fully in Chapters 2 and 3.

BUSINESS: BASIC CONCEPTS

While technology provides the infrastructure, it is the business applications—the potential for extraordinary returns on investment—that create the interest and excitement in e-commerce. New technologies present businesses and entrepreneurs with new ways of organizing production and transacting business. New technologies change the strategies and plans of existing firms: old strategies are made obsolete and new ones need to be invented. New technologies are the birthing grounds where thousands of new companies spring up with new products and services. New technologies are the graveyard of many traditional businesses. To truly understand e-commerce, you will need to be familiar with some key business concepts, such as the nature of digital markets, digital goods, business models, firm and industry value chains, value webs, industry structure, digital disruption, and consumer behavior in digital markets, as well as basic concepts of financial analysis. We'll examine these concepts further in Chapters 5 through 12.

SOCIETY: TAMING THE JUGGERNAUT

With 3.1 billion people now using the Internet worldwide, the impact of the Internet and e-commerce on society is significant and global. Increasingly, e-commerce is subject to the laws of nations and global entities. You will need to understand the pressures that global e-commerce places on contemporary society in order to conduct a successful

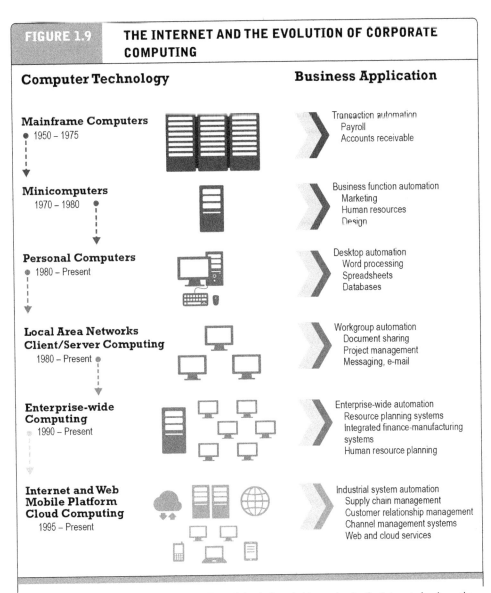

| FIGURE 1.9 | THE INTERNET AND THE EVOLUTION OF CORPORATE COMPUTING |

Computer Technology   **Business Application**

Mainframe Computers
● 1950 – 1975

> Transaction automation
>   Payroll
>   Accounts receivable

Minicomputers
1970 – 1980 ●

> Business function automation
>   Marketing
>   Human resources
>   Design

Personal Computers
● 1980 – Present

> Desktop automation
>   Word processing
>   Spreadsheets
>   Databases

Local Area Networks Client/Server Computing
1980 – Present ●

> Workgroup automation
>   Document sharing
>   Project management
>   Messaging, e-mail

Enterprise-wide Computing
1990 – Present

> Enterprise-wide automation
>   Resource planning systems
>   Integrated finance-manufacturing systems
>   Human resource planning

Internet and Web Mobile Platform Cloud Computing
1995 – Present

> Industrial system automation
>   Supply chain management
>   Customer relationship management
>   Channel management systems
>   Web and cloud services

The Internet and Web, and the emergence of a mobile platform held together by the Internet cloud, are the latest in a chain of evolving technologies and related business applications, each of which builds on its predecessors.

e-commerce business or understand the e-commerce phenomenon. The primary societal issues we discuss in this book are individual privacy, intellectual property, and public welfare policy.

Because the Internet and the Web are exceptionally adept at tracking the identity and behavior of individuals online, e-commerce raises difficulties for preserving privacy—the ability of individuals to place limits on the type and amount of information collected about them, and to control the uses of their personal information. Read the *Insight on Society* case, *Facebook and the Age of Privacy*, to get a view of some of the ways e-commerce sites use personal information.

Because the cost of distributing digital copies of copyrighted intellectual property—tangible works of the mind such as music, books, and videos—is nearly zero on the Internet, e-commerce poses special challenges to the various methods societies have used in the past to protect intellectual property rights.

The global nature of e-commerce also poses public policy issues of equity, equal access, content regulation, and taxation. For instance, in the United States, public telephone utilities are required under public utility and public accommodation laws to make basic service available at affordable rates so everyone can have telephone service. Should these laws be extended to the Internet and the Web? If goods are purchased by a New York State resident from a Web site in California, shipped from a center in Illinois, and delivered to New York, what state has the right to collect a sales tax? Should some heavy Internet users who consume extraordinary amounts of bandwidth by streaming endless movies be charged extra for service, or should the Internet be neutral with respect to usage? What rights do nation-states and their citizens have with respect to the Internet, the Web, and e-commerce? We address issues such as these in Chapter 8, and also throughout the text.

ACADEMIC DISCIPLINES CONCERNED WITH E-COMMERCE

The phenomenon of e-commerce is so broad that a multidisciplinary perspective is required. There are two primary approaches to e-commerce: technical and behavioral.

Technical Approaches

Computer scientists are interested in e-commerce as an exemplary application of Internet technology. They are concerned with the development of computer hardware, software, and telecommunications systems, as well as standards, encryption, and database design and operation. Operations management scientists are primarily interested in building mathematical models of business processes and optimizing these processes. They are interested in e-commerce as an opportunity to study how business firms can exploit the Internet to achieve more efficient business operations. The information systems discipline spans the technical and behavioral approaches. Technical groups within the information systems specialty focus on data mining, search engine design, and artificial intelligence.

Behavioral Approaches

From a behavioral perspective, information systems researchers are primarily interested in e-commerce because of its implications for firm and industry value chains, industry structure, and corporate strategy. Economists have focused on online consumer behavior, pricing of digital goods, and on the unique features of digital electronic markets. The marketing profession is interested in marketing, brand development and extension, online consumer behavior, and the ability of e-commerce technologies to

FACEBOOK AND THE AGE OF PRIVACY

In a January 2010 interview, Mark Zuckerberg, the founder of Facebook, proclaimed that the age of privacy had to come to an end. According to Zuckerberg, people were no longer worried about sharing their personal information with friends, friends of friends, or even the entire Web. Supporters of Zuckerberg's viewpoint believe the twenty-first century is a new era of openness and transparency. If true, this is good news for Facebook because its business model is based on selling access to a database of personal information.

However, not everyone is a true believer. Privacy—limitations on what personal information government and private institutions can collect and use—is a founding principle of democracies. A decade's worth of privacy surveys in the United States show that well over 80% of the American public fear the Internet is a threat to their privacy.

With about 1.5 billion monthly users worldwide, and around 165 million in North America, Facebook's privacy policies are going to shape privacy standards on the Internet for years to come. The economic stakes in the privacy debate are quite high, involving billions in advertising and transaction dollars. Facebook's business model is based on building a database of billions of users who are encouraged, or even perhaps deceived, into relinquishing control over personal information, which is then sold to advertisers and other third parties. The less privacy Facebook's users want or have, the more Facebook profits. Eliminating personal information privacy is built into Facebook's DNA.

Facebook's current privacy policies are quite a flip-flop from its original policy in 2004, which promised users near complete control over who could see their personal profile. However,

every year since 2004, Facebook has attempted to extend its control over user information and content, often without notice. For instance, in 2007, Facebook introduced the Beacon program, which was designed to broadcast users' activities on participating Web sites to their friends. After a public outcry, Facebook terminated the Beacon program, and paid $9.5 million to settle a host of class action lawsuits. In 2009, undeterred by the Beacon fiasco, Facebook unilaterally decided that it would publish users' basic personal information on the public Internet, and announced that whatever content users had contributed belonged to Facebook, and that its ownership of that information never terminated. However, as with the Beacon program, Facebook's efforts to take permanent control of user information resulted in users joining online resistance groups and it was ultimately forced to withdraw this policy as well.

In 2011, Facebook began publicizing users' "likes" of various advertisers in Sponsored Stories (i.e., advertisements) that included the users' names and profile pictures without their explicit consent, without paying them, and without giving them a way to opt out. This resulted in yet another class action lawsuit, which Facebook settled for $20 million in June 2012. (Facebook dropped Sponsored Stories in April 2014.) In 2011, Facebook enrolled all Facebook subscribers into its facial recognition program without notice. This too raised the privacy alarm, forcing Facebook to make it easier for users to opt out.

In May 2012, Facebook went public, creating even more pressure to increase revenues and profits to justify its stock market value. Shortly thereafter, Facebook announced that it was launching a mobile advertising product that pushes ads to the mobile news feeds of

(continued)

users based on the apps they use through the Facebook Connect feature, without explicit permission from the user to do so. It also announced Facebook Exchange, a program that allows advertisers to serve ads to Facebook users based on their browsing activity while not on Facebook. Privacy advocates raised the alarm yet again and more lawsuits were filed by users. In 2013, Facebook agreed to partner with several data marketing companies that deliver targeted ads based on offline data. The firms provide customer data to Facebook, which then allows Facebook advertisers to target their ads to those users based on that data.

In December 2013, another class action lawsuit was filed against Facebook by users alleging that it violated their privacy by scanning users' private Facebook messages and mining them for data such as references to URLs that Facebook could then sell to advertisers. In May 2014, an enhancement to Facebook's mobile app that allows the app to recognize the music, television show, or movie playing in the background when a user makes a status update raised a new privacy alarm. In 2015, Facebook implemented a "new" privacy policy that allows it to share user personal data across partner sites and apps, including WhatsApp and Instagram. Also in 2015, Facebook admitted that its Facebook Messenger app collected and shared user geolocation as the default setting. After negative publicity, it changed the default to "do not share."

After all these lawsuits and online public protests, one might think that Facebook's privacy policy would improve. But an academic analysis of Facebook's privacy policies from 2008 to 2015 found that on most measures of privacy protection, Facebook's policies have worsened. Since 2008, Facebook has made it more difficult for users to find out what information is being shared with whom, how it builds profiles, or how to change privacy settings. Its privacy policies have become less readable, even inscrutable, according to the researchers.

Facebook is certainly aware of consumer suspicion of its privacy policies, and it changes its policies almost yearly in response to criticism. But the response is often not helpful for users, and typically extends the company's claims to do whatever it wants with personal information. Its latest privacy policy, implemented in 2015, claims to switch its default privacy settings for new users from Public to Friends, provide a Privacy Checkup tool for users, and give users the ability to see the data it keeps on their likes and interests, and enable users to change, delete, or add to that data. Facebook argues this new policy gives users more control of the ads they are shown. Analysts point out, however, that using these new features requires users to navigate a maze of check boxes and menus that are difficult to understand even for expert Facebook users. Facebook's growth in North America has steadily declined in part because users have come to realize that everything they post or say on Facebook will be given over to advertisers. There is no privacy on Facebook. People who are concerned about their privacy, analysts have concluded, should delete their Facebook accounts.

▬▬ **SOURCES:** "Facebook Rescinds Internship to Harvard Student Who Exposed a Privacy Flaw in Messenger," by Robert Gabelhoff, *Washington Post,* August 14, 2015; "Did You Really Agree to That? The Evolution of Facebook's Privacy Policy," by Jennifer Shore and Jill Steinman, *Technology Science,* August 11, 2015; "Facebook's Privacy Incident Response: A Study of Geolocation Sharing on Facebook Messenger," by Aran Khanna, *Technology Science,* August 11, 2015; "Sharing Data, but Not Happily," by Natasha Singer, *New York Times,* June 4, 2015; "How Your Facebook Likes Could Cost You a Job," by Anna North, *New York Times,* January 20, 2015; "Facebook Stops Irresponsibly Defaulting Privacy of New Users' Posts to 'Public,' Changes to 'Friends,'" by Josh Constine, Techcrunch.com, May 22, 2014; "Facebook Users Revolt Over Privacy Feature—Enables Microphone in Apps," by Jan Willem Aldershoff, Myce.com, June 9, 2014; "Didn't Read Those Terms of Service? Here's What You Agreed to Give Up," by Natasha Singer, *New York Times,* April 28, 2014; "Facebook Eliminates Sponsored Stories—Will It Matter to Advertisers?," by Amy Durbin, Mediapost.com, February 25, 2014; "Facebook Sued for Allegedly Intercepting Private Messages," by Jennifer Van Grove, Cnet.com, January 2, 2014; "Facebook to Partner with Data Brokers," by Bob Sullivan, Redtape.nbcnews.com, February 26, 2013; "Facebook Exchange Ads Raise Privacy Concerns," by Mikal E. Belicove, Cnbc.com, June 21, 2012; "Facebook Suit Over Subscriber Tracking Seeks \$15 Billion," by Kit Chellel and Jeremy Hodges, Bloomberg.com, May 19, 2012; "How Facebook Pulled a Privacy Bait and Switch," by Dan Tynan, *PC World,* May 2010.

segment and target consumer groups, and differentiate products. Economists share an interest with marketing scholars who have focused on e-commerce consumer response to marketing and advertising campaigns, and the ability of firms to brand, segment markets, target audiences, and position products to achieve above-normal returns on investment.

Management scholars have focused on entrepreneurial behavior and the challenges faced by young firms who are required to develop organizational structures in short time spans. Finance and accounting scholars have focused on e-commerce firm valuation and accounting practices. Sociologists—and to a lesser extent, psychologists—have focused on general population studies of Internet usage, the role of social inequality in skewing Internet benefits, and the use of the Web as a social network and group communications tool. Legal scholars are interested in issues such as preserving intellectual property, privacy, and content regulation.

No one perspective dominates research about e-commerce. The challenge is to learn enough about a variety of academic disciplines so that you can grasp the significance of e-commerce in its entirety.

CASE STUDY

Puma
Goes Omni

When Puma, one of the world's top sports footwear, apparel, and accessories brands, conceived its Love=Football campaign in 2010, the goal was to create a memorable tagline in a language that would be understood the world over—pictures. In the process, the company stumbled upon the power of social marketing. Puma's ad agency, Droga5, filmed a light-hearted commercial featuring scruffy everyday men in a Tottenham pub singing love songs to their Valentines. The video went viral, garnering more than 130 million impressions and spawning hundreds of homemade response videos. In 2015, Puma launched an ad campaign called Forever Faster, featuring videos of celebrities and professional athletes training to meet their goals, including sprinter Usain Bolt and pop star Rihanna, whom the company also named its women's creative director. The campaign has been another major success, driving sales of Puma's Ignite XT shoe and further rejuvenating its brand.

Puma maintains an extensive presence on Facebook, Twitter, Instagram, Pinterest, and YouTube and closely integrates its social strategy with its other marketing channels

© ngaga35/Fotolia.com

with an eye towards driving the conversation and deepening its engagement with consumers. It uses social media in part to better understand the different regional and sub-brand audiences within more than 120 countries in which it operates. Not all content is suitable for every one of its 14+ million global Facebook fans. Dedicated sport, country, region, and product category pages were created for each social network. For several years, Puma took a trial-and-error approach, focusing on building its follower base. Today, Puma uses a data-driven approach, geo-targeting posts at the appropriate times of day to maximize fan engagement and generate the right mix of online content to best drive sales. A tab for its iPhone app sends followers directly to Apple's App Store, substantially boosting sales. This integration of channels into a cohesive customer acquisition strategy is in fact a key element of the emerging world of omni-channel retailing.

The advent of the term omni-channel signals the evolution of multi-channel or cross-channel retailing to encompass all digital and social technologies. The idea is that customers can examine, access, purchase, and return goods from any channel, and even change channels during the process, and receive timely and relevant product information at each step along the way and in each channel. The rise of social networks and the personalized retail it engenders is a primary driver of omni-channel—the complete integration of the shopping and brand experience. Marketing efforts must be unified undertakings combining offline events and sales and online promotions and brand building that not only employ all available channels but provide multiple opportunities for customer involvement. For a company like Puma, with e-commerce sites in the United States, Russia, Canada, China, India, Switzerland, Germany, France, the United Kingdom, and a European site that serves multiple countries in multiple languages, this presents quite a challenge.

Puma's Global Head of E-Commerce, Tom Davis, has overseen a major restructuring of its e-commerce business. Puma was not fully prepared to compete with Adidas, Nike, and other sports apparel companies in a global market that was rapidly shifting away from mature Western markets and desktop commerce. To coordinate market rollouts and ensure a unified brand image, Puma's regional e-commerce teams needed oversight. A command center took over brand strategy and investment decisions, leaving daily operational and locality-based decision-making to the regional teams. Unified content and product strategies were developed in addition to a centralized product database. One central Web site replaced multiple e-commerce sites on different platforms. Demandware, Puma's main e-commerce platform, was used to simplify managing global e-commerce operations from a central digital platform, though several other e-commerce platforms are still used. The goal was to achieve a consistent and cohesive brand building strategy so that the teams would all be on the same page and decisions could be more quickly reached. Yet local customization of the message and ensuring that globally produced goods meet local requirements would still be most efficiently handled.

Puma assigned the overhaul of its Web site to Viget, a Web design firm. It created templates to unite several Puma sites into one and unify the look across numerous categories and content types. A dozen category sites now complement Puma.com, with a custom-built content management system (CMS) ensuring that consistent Puma branding and navigation are maintained across all sub-sites and pages. Category managers can customize home pages outside of the template layout. The flexibility to roll out local, regional, or global campaigns is thus built into the Web site design. What's more, the CMS integrates with a language translation tool, a Storefinder tool that helps visitors locate Puma stores, and Puma's product inventory manager. The design changes have improved site visualization and navigation, prompting customers to spend twice as much time on the site and raising the order rate by 7.1%.

The Viget team then turned to the mobile site, first incorporating Storefinder into the interface. Using the GPS capability of the mobile device, Puma stores nearest to the user can be located, along with address and contact information. Users experience the same content and appearance as Puma.com and each of the category sites, managed by the same CMS. Puma's mobile site has also been rebuilt using responsive design features. Puma also incorporated mobile into its omni-channel marketing strategy. The Puma Joy Pad—32 synchronized iPads mounted on a wall—allows shoppers at its flagship Paris store and other select locations to play games and experiment with Web apps. In the near future, shoppers will be able to generate content that they can share with their social networks, and walls will be connected so that customers in stores around the globe will be able to share their shopping experiences. On Black Friday 2014, 3.4% of mobile visitors to Puma's site made a purchase, compared to just 1.6% the previous year. In 2013, Puma released PUMATRAC, an iPhone app that automatically analyzes environmental conditions to give runners feedback on how these variables impact their performance. The app offers multiple options to share statistics and routes with other runners.

In 2014, Puma focused on unifying its branding efforts and e-commerce Web sites within one centralized site. The company has also solidified its worldwide e-commerce teams. In the past, Puma maintained nine independent e-commerce teams on five continents. Currently, it is working towards teams divided into the three major segments that comprise the majority of its sales—North America, Europe, and Asia-Pacific—as well as a global unit that operates at a level above these regional segments. The goal is to centralize Puma's e-commerce business both at one e-commerce site as well as internally within the company. At the same time, the company hopes to pursue a strategy that is flexible and focused more on the precise local needs in individual markets. These changes have already reaped rewards, improving conversion rates from 10% to 20% and boosting average order value by 12%. Centralizing its e-commerce operations under a single site also helps Puma better collect customer data to personalize marketing and develop more appealing products.

Although over the past three years Puma has gained invaluable omni-channel experience, racked up social marketing accomplishments, and laid the groundwork for resurgent e-commerce success, implementing a successful omni-channel strategy is a monumental task. In 2013 and 2014, Puma's profits sagged, and the company claimed its increased marketing budget was the reason while insisting that their strategy would pay dividends in the future. Puma knows it cannot compete on price with mass merchandisers such as Amazon and Zappos, and it cannot control Puma product presentation in those venues.

SOURCES: "Puma's Sales Start Seeing Boost from Marketing Spend," Reuters.com, July 24, 2015; "Puma Share Price up, States Narrower Loss on 'Forever Faster,'" Binarytribune.com, February 20, 2015; "Puma Boss: Our Future Is Female," by Shona Ghosh, Marketingmagazine.co.uk, February 18, 2015; "Inside Puma's Branded Content Strategy," by Lucia Moses, Digiday.com, December 15, 2014; "The Case of Puma: Can Tmall and In-House E-Store Co-Exist in China?" by Gelati Ting, Fashionbi.com, June 26, 2014; "Puma Understands the Importance of Local Needs in a Global E-commerce Rollout," by Derek Du Preez, Diginomica.com, June 24, 2014; "Puma and Newegg Discuss Their Entry Into the China E-commerce Market," Cdnetworks.com, June 3, 2014; "How Puma Is Improving Sales Operations Through E-commerce," by Paul Demery, Internetretailer. com, May 20, 2014; "Clients: Puma," Demandware.com, accessed October 20, 2013; "Droga5 Case Studies: The HardChorus," Droga5.com, accessed October 20, 2013; "Puma Launches Innovative New Running App," News.puma.com, October 2, 2013; "Puma's Unified Approach to Global E-commerce," Ecommercefacts.com, August 5, 2013; "Puma's Head of E-Commerce: Changes and Challenges of Customization in the Apparel Industry," Masscustomiza- tion.de, July 16, 2013; "Puma Tries Out Mobile Photo-sharing with Rewards-based Campaign," by Lauren Johnson, Mobilemarketer. com, June 21, 2013; "PUMA: Challenges in an Omni-channel World," Embodee.com, May 3, 2013; "Puma Goes Mobile to Create Urban Playgrounds in Asia,"

External loss of brand control necessitates superior product content, product information management, and shopping experience internally, precisely the skills it has been nurturing. Puma's ability to adapt its strategy to individual areas is also likely to help the company advance into China, a growing market where Puma has traditionally had minimal presence. This flexibility allowed Puma to adapt to Chinese e-commerce giant Alibaba's Tmall platform, where it holds a strong brand score. In 2015, Puma finally began to see results from its innovative advertising, product development, and centralization efforts as its earnings rebounded to beat analysts' estimates, growing by 18% over its second quarter from 2014. Puma CEO Bjorn Gulden believes that 2014 and 2015 represent a turning point for the Puma brand back to profitability.

by Adaline Lau, Clickz.com, November 23, 2012; "Puma Embraces Mobile, Fun Tech to Attract Buyers," by Mark Walsh, Mediapost.com, November 14, 2012; "The 10 Best-Branded Companies on Instagram," by Allyson Galle, Blog.hubspot.com, May 18, 2012; "3 Shoe Brands Kicking Butt with Social Media," by Lauren Indvik, Mashable.com, February 6, 2012; "Why Brands Like Puma and GE Are Flocking to Instagram," by Cotton Delo, Adage.com, January 17, 2012.

Case Study Questions

1. What is the purpose of Puma's content management system?

2. Why did Puma build a single centralized Web site rather than continue with multiple Web sites serving different countries and regions?

3. What social media sites does Puma use, and what do they contribute to Puma's marketing effort?

1.5   REVIEW

KEY CONCEPTS

■ Define e-commerce and describe how it differs from e-business.

- E-commerce involves digitally enabled commercial transactions between and among organizations and individuals. Digitally enabled transactions include all those mediated by digital technology, meaning, for the most part, transactions that occur over the Internet, the Web, and/or via mobile devices. Commercial transactions involve the exchange of value (e.g., money) across organizational or individual boundaries in return for products or services.

- E-business refers primarily to the digital enabling of transactions and processes within a firm, involving information systems under the control of the firm. For the most part, e-business does not involve commercial transactions across organizational boundaries where value is exchanged.

■ Identify and describe the unique features of e-commerce technology and discuss their business significance.

There are eight features of e-commerce technology that are unique to this medium:

- *Ubiquity*—available just about everywhere, at all times, making it possible to shop from your desktop, at home, at work, or even from your car.
- *Global reach*—permits commercial transactions to cross cultural and national boundaries far more conveniently and cost-effectively than is true in traditional commerce.

- *Universal standards*—shared by all nations around the world, in contrast to most traditional commerce technologies, which differ from one nation to the next.
- *Richness*—enables an online merchant to deliver marketing messages in a way not possible with traditional commerce technologies.
- *Interactivity*—allows for two-way communication between merchant and consumer and enables the merchant to engage a consumer in ways similar to a face-to-face experience, but on a much more massive, global scale.
- *Information density*—is the total amount and quality of information available to all market participants. The Internet reduces information collection, storage, processing, and communication costs while increasing the currency, accuracy, and timeliness of information.
- *Personalization* and *customization*—the increase in information density allows merchants to target their marketing messages to specific individuals and results in a level of personalization and customization unthinkable with previously existing commerce technologies.
- *Social technology*—provides a many-to-many model of mass communications. Millions of users are able to generate content consumed by millions of other users. The result is the formation of social networks on a wide scale and the aggregation of large audiences on social network platforms.

■ Describe the major types of e-commerce.

There are six major types of e-commerce:
- *B2C e-commerce* involves businesses selling to consumers and is the type of e-commerce that most consumers are likely to encounter.
- *B2B e-commerce* involves businesses selling to other businesses and is the largest form of e-commerce.
- *C2C e-commerce* is a means for consumers to sell to each other. In C2C e-commerce, the consumer prepares the product for market, places the product for auction or sale, and relies on the market maker to provide catalog, search engine, and transaction clearing capabilities so that products can be easily displayed, discovered, and paid for.
- *Social e-commerce* is e-commerce that is enabled by social networks and online social relationships.
- *M-commerce* involves the use of wireless digital devices to enable online transactions.
- *Local e-commerce* is a form of e-commerce that is focused on engaging the consumer based on his or her current geographic location.

■ Understand the evolution of e-commerce from its early years to today.

E-commerce has gone through three stages: innovation, consolidation, and reinvention.
- The early years of e-commerce were a technological success, with the digital infrastructure created during the period solid enough to sustain significant growth in e-commerce during the next decade, and a mixed business success, with significant revenue growth and customer usage, but low profit margins.
- E-commerce entered a period of consolidation beginning in 2001 and extending into 2006.
- E-commerce entered a period of reinvention in 2007 with the emergence of the mobile digital platform, social networks, and Web 2.0 applications that attracted huge audiences in a very short time span.

■ Describe the major themes underlying the study of e-commerce.

E-commerce involves three broad interrelated themes:
- *Technology*—To understand e-commerce, you need a basic understanding of the information technologies upon which it is built, including the Internet, the Web, and mobile platform, and a host of complementary technologies—cloud computing, desktop computers, smartphones, tablet computers, local area networks, client/server computing, packet-switched communications, protocols such as TCP/IP, Web servers, HTML, and relational and non-relational databases, among others.

- *Business*—While technology provides the infrastructure, it is the business applications—the potential for extraordinary returns on investment—that create the interest and excitement in e-commerce. Therefore, you also need to understand some key business concepts such as electronic markets, information goods, business models, firm and industry value chains, industry structure, and consumer behavior in digital markets.
- *Society*—Understanding the pressures that global e-commerce places on contemporary society is critical to being successful in the e-commerce marketplace. The primary societal issues are intellectual property, individual privacy, and public policy.

■ Identify the major academic disciplines contributing to e-commerce.

There are two primary approaches to e-commerce: technical and behavioral. Each of these approaches is represented by several academic disciplines. On the technical side, this includes computer science, operations management, and information systems. On the behavioral side, it includes information systems as well as sociology, economics, finance and accounting, management, and marketing.

QUESTIONS

1. What does omni-channel mean in terms of e-commerce presence?
2. What is information asymmetry?
3. What are some of the unique features of e-commerce technology?
4. What are some of the factors driving the growth of social e-commerce?
5. What are three benefits of universal standards?
6. How does the ubiquity of e-commerce impact consumers?
7. Name three of the business consequences that can result from growth in information density.
8. What difficulties are presented in trying to measure the number of Web pages in existence?
9. Give examples of B2C, B2B, C2C, and social, mobile, and local e-commerce besides those listed in the chapter.
10. How are e-commerce technologies similar to or different from other technologies that have changed commerce in the past?
11. Describe the three different stages in the evolution of e-commerce.
12. Define disintermediation and explain the benefits to Internet users of such a phenomenon. How does disintermediation impact friction-free commerce?
13. What are some of the major advantages and disadvantages of being a first mover?
14. What is a network effect, and why is it valuable?
15. Discuss the ways in which the early years of e-commerce can be considered both a success and a failure.
16. What are five of the major differences between the early years of e-commerce and today's e-commerce?
17. Why is a multidisciplinary approach necessary if one hopes to understand e-commerce?
18. Why is the term "sharing economy" a misnomer?
19. What are those who take a behavioral approach to studying e-commerce interested in?
20. Why has Rocket Internet been criticized, and how do the Samwer brothers respond to that criticism?

PROJECTS

1. Choose an e-commerce company and assess it in terms of the eight unique features of e-commerce technology described in Table 1.2. In your opinion, which of the features does the company implement well, and which features poorly? Prepare a short memo to the president of the company you have chosen detailing your findings and any suggestions for improvement you may have.

2. Search the Web for an example of each of the major types of e-commerce described in Section 1.1 and listed in Table 1.3. Create a presentation or written report describing each company (take a screenshot of each, if possible), and explain why it fits into the category of e-commerce to which you have assigned it.

3. Given the development and history of e-commerce in the years from 1995–2015, what do you predict we will see during the next five years of e-commerce? Describe some of the technological, business, and societal shifts that may occur as the Internet continues to grow and expand. Prepare a brief presentation or written report to explain your vision of what e-commerce will look like in 2019.

4. Prepare a brief report or presentation on how companies are using Instagram or another company of your choosing as a social e-commerce platform.

5. Follow up on events at Uber since October 2015 (when the opening case was prepared). Prepare a short report on your findings.

REFERENCES

Aguiar, Mark and Erik Hurst. "Life-Cycle Prices and Production." *American Economic Review* 97:5, 1533–1559. (January 1, 2008).

Alessandria, George. "Consumer Search, Price Dispersion, and International Relative Price Fluctuations." *International Economic Review* 50:3, 803–829 (September 1, 2009).

Bailey, Joseph P. *Intermediation and Electronic Markets: Aggregation and Pricing in Internet Commerce*. Ph.D., Technology, Management and Policy, Massachusetts Institute of Technology (1998a).

Bakos, Yannis. "Reducing Buyer Search Costs: Implications for Electronic Marketplaces." *Management Science* (December 1997).

Banerjee, Suman and Chakravarty, Amiya. "Price Setting and Price Discovery Strategies with a Mix of Frequent and Infrequent Internet Users." (April 15, 2005). SSRN: http://ssrn.com/abstract=650706.

Baye, Michael R. "Price Dispersion in the Lab and on the Internet: Theory and Evidence." *Rand Journal of Economics* (2004).

Baye, Michael R., John Morgan, and Patrick Scholten. "Temporal Price Dispersion: Evidence from an Online Consumer Electronics Market." *Journal of Interactive Marketing* (January 2004).

Brynjolfsson, Erik, and Michael Smith. "Frictionless Commerce? A Comparison of Internet and Conventional Retailers." *Management Science* (April 2000).

eBay, Inc. "eBay Inc. Reports Fourth Quarter and Full Year Results." (January 21, 2015).

eMarketer, Inc. "Internet Users and Penetration, 2013–2019." (April 2015a).

eMarketer, Inc. (Yory Wurmser). "UK Retail Mcommerce Trends." (March 2015b).

eMarketer, Inc. (Cindy Liu). "Worldwide Retail Ecommerce: The eMarketer Forecast for 2015." (July 2015c).

eMarketer, Inc. (Cindy Liu). "Worldwide Digital Travel Sales: The eMarketer Forecast for 2015." (July 2015d).

eMarketer, Inc. "US Mobile Connections, 2013–2019." (February 2015e)."

eMarketer, Inc. "US Mobile Phone Internet Users and Penetration, 2013–2019." (February 2015f).

eMarketer, Inc. "US Tablet Users and Penetration, 2013–2019." (February 2015g).

eMarketer, Inc. "US Mobile Connections, 2011–2017." (March 2013a).

eMarketer, Inc. "US Mobile Phone Internet Users and Penetration, 2011–2017." (March 2013b).

eMarketer, Inc. "US Tablet Users and Penetration, 2011–2017." (March 2013c).

Evans, Philip, and Thomas S. Wurster. "Getting Real About Virtual Commerce." *Harvard Business Review* (November-December 1999).

Evans, Philip, and Thomas S. Wurster. "Strategy and the New Economics of Information." *Harvard Business Review* (September-October 1997).

Forrester Research. "U.S. Cross-Channel Retail Forecast, 2012 to 2017." (March 27, 2014).

Ghose, Anindya, and Yuliang Yao. "Using Transaction Prices to Re-Examine Price Dispersion in Electronic Markets." *Information Systems Research*, Vol. 22 No. 2. (June 2011).

Google. "How Search Works: From Algorithms to Answers." (accessed June 17, 2014).

Gorodnichenko, Yuriy, et al. "Price Setting in Online Markets: Does IT Click?" NBER Working Paper No. 20819 (December 2014).

Interactions Consumer Experience Marketing, Inc., "The Rise of Webrooming." (May 2014).

Internet Retailer. "Top 500 Guide 2015 Edition." (2015).

Internet Systems Consortium, Inc. "ISC Internet Domain Survey." (July 2015).

Kalakota, Ravi, and Marcia Robinson. *e-Business 2.0: Roadmap for Success, 2nd edition*. Reading, MA: Addison Wesley (2003).

Kambil, Ajit. "Doing Business in the Wired World." *IEEE Computer* (May 1997).

Levin, Jonathon. "The Economics of Internet Markets." Stanford University, Draft, February 18, 2011.

Mesenbourg, Thomas L. "Measuring Electronic Business: Definitions, Underlying Concepts, and Measurement Plans." U. S. Department of Commerce Bureau of the Census (August 2001).

Rayport, Jeffrey F., and Bernard J. Jaworski. *Introduction to E-commerce, 2nd edition*. New York: McGraw-Hill (2003).

Rosso, Mark and Bernard Jansen. "Smart Marketing or Bait & Switch: Competitors' Brands as Keywords in Online Advertising." Proceedings of the 4th Workshop on Information Credibility. ACM (2010).

Shapiro, Carl, and Hal R Varian. *Information Rules. A Strategic Guide to the Network Economy*. Cambridge, MA: Harvard Business School Press (1999).

Sinha, Indrajit. "Cost Transparency: The Net's Threat to Prices and Brands." *Harvard Business Review* (March-April 2000).

Smith, Michael, Joseph Bailey, and Erik Brynjolfsson. "Understanding Digital Markets: Review and Assessment." In Erik Brynjolfsson and Brian Kahin (eds.), *Understanding the Digital Economy*. Cambridge, MA: MIT Press (2000).

Tversky, A., and D. Kahneman. "The Framing of Decisions and the Psychology of Choice." *Science* (January 1981).

U.S. Census Bureau. "E-Stats." (May 28, 2015).

Varian, Hal R. "When Commerce Moves On, Competition Can Work in Strange Ways." *New York Times* (August 24, 2000a).

Varian, Hal R. "5 Habits of Highly Effective Revolution." *Forbes ASAP* (February 21, 2000b).

Zaroban, Stefany. "Social Networks Deliver for Retailers, But at a Price." Internetretailer.com (January 13, 2015).

Chapter 17
E Marketing

CHAPTER **6**

E-commerce Marketing and Advertising

After reading this chapter, you will be able to:

- Understand the key features of the Internet audience, the basic concepts of consumer behavior and purchasing, and how consumers behave online.
- Identify and describe the basic digital commerce marketing and advertising strategies and tools.
- Identify and describe the main technologies that support online marketing.
- Understand the costs and benefits of online marketing communications.

InMobi's

Global Mobile Ad Network

Watch out tech titans! InMobi, an innovative startup based in Bangalore, India, is making some serious waves in the global mobile advertising network marketplace currently dominated by Google, Facebook, and Twitter. InMobi was founded in early 2007 by four graduates of the Indian Institute of Technology, including Naveen Tewari. After unsuccessful attempts at SMS-based mobile search and a mobile-based deals company specifically for Mumbai, Tewari and his co-founders scrambled to come up with a new idea. With the last of their personal funds, they honed in on mobile advertising. Apple had just introduced the iPhone in

© fotografiedk/Fotolia.com

early 2007, and few companies were focusing yet on the cellphone as a mobile advertising platform. This new idea proved to be the company's golden ticket, and in 2008, Tewari convinced venture firms Kleiner Perkins Caufield & Byers and Sherpalo Investments to make an $8 million investment in the company. They then moved to Bangalore, deeming it a better location from which to attract talent, and later changed the name of the company to InMobi.

InMobi bills itself as a mobile advertising platform and solutions provider. It acts as an intermediary between companies that want to advertise and content owners/publishers that offer mobile content, often in the form of apps. For instance, if you've seen the advertisements that appear when you play the Angry Birds games on an Android smartphone, you've seen InMobi's mobile ad platform at work. InMobi serves almost 138 billion mobile ads a month to over 1 billion consumers in over 200 countries. There are over 30,000 apps and mobile sites on the inMobi network, and the company tracks over two billion app downloads on its platform. Although it is a private company, InMobi's revenues in 2014 are believed to have been over $250 million, and showed a profit for the first time in the last quarter of 2014. It makes money by keeping a percentage of the revenue per ad, typically 30–40%. Increasingly, InMobi has focused on native advertising as the marketplace abandons banner ads and moves towards more creative and interactive formats. Native advertising appears seamlessly within an app and often appears as if it were a post from a friend. InMobi's customers include Unilever, Samsung, Microsoft, Adidas, and a rapidly growing number of other prominent companies and brands.

SOURCES: "InMobi Vouches 100% Viewability on Mobile Ads," by Dhanya Ann Thoppil, Livemint.com, November 20, 2015; "InMobi Guarantees 100% In-App Mobile Ad Viewability," Prnewswire.com, November 18, 2015; "InMobi and Taboola Partner to Engage over One Billion Mobile Consumers Through Content Discovery on Native Platform," Prnewswire.com, October 29, 2015; "India's Global Ad Giant Taking on Google and Facebook," by Kinjal Pandya-Wagh, Bbc.com, October 20, 2015; "With $100 Million, InMobi Raises the Banner for the Future," by Pankaj Mishra, *Economic Times*, September 29, 2015; "India's InMobi Ties Up with China's APUS to Take On Google," Cnbc.com, September 16, 2015; "Dell, InMobi Forge Alliance for E-Commerce Platform," by Anirban Sen, *Economic Times*, September 14, 2015; "Why InMobi May Be India's Most Innovative Company," by Malini Goyal, *Economic Times*,

August 2, 2015; "InMobi, Google & Facebook Mobile Ad Rival, Puts Personalized Discovery Feature into Mobile Ads," by Saritha Rai, Forbes.com, July 15, 2015; "How a Monkey Will Help You Go Beyond Ads on InMobi Ad Network," by Barry Levine, Venturebeat.com, July 15, 2015; "Meet Miip, the Ad Monkey in Your App," by Vindu Goel, New York Times, July 14, 2015; "InMobi Plans to Stay Independent, Dismissing Rumors of Talks with Google," by Vindu Goel, New York Times, March 11, 2015; "InMobi in Numbers: Close to 138B Ad Impressions, Reaching 872M Users a Month," by Anand Rai, Techcircle.in, November 10, 2014; "InMobi Claims That It Reaches 872 Million Active Unique Users," by Aparajita Saxena, Medianama.com, November 7, 2014; "Think They're Tracking You Now? Wait till InMobi's Unveiling Next Month," by Richard Byrne Reilly, Venturebeat.com, October 16, 2014; "InMobi Takes a Bold Stand: But How Much Can They Really Guarantee?" by Michael Essany, Mobilemarketing-watch.com, October 14, 2014; "InMobi Has Positioned Itself as the Go-To Company In Mobile Advertising," by Deepak Ajwani, Forbes India, October 10, 2014; "InMobi and Rubicon Project Unveil Exchange for Mobile Native Ads," by Lauren Johnson, AdWeek, May 29, 2014; "InMobi Decoded: How Bangalore-based Firm Is Taking On Google and Facebook," by Peerzada Abrar and Krithika Krishnamurthy, The Economic Times, March 7, 2014; "The Next Infosys - Tapping the Mobile Entertainment Space - InMobi," by Anirban Sen, LiveMint.com, January 10, 2014; "inMobi Launches New AppGalleries, a White Label Web App Store for Publishers to Curate Apps, and Boost Mobile Ads," by Ingrid Lunden, Techcrunch.com, October 22, 2013; "InMobi and Mindshare Win Top Awards for Innovation and In-App Advertising," inMobi, October 14, 2013; "InMobi Claims New IAB Ad Formats Prompt Tenfold Spike to Interactions," by Zen Terrelonge, mobile-ent.biz, September 23, 2013; "InMobi Australia's Latest Mobile Insights Report for Q2 Reveals Mobile

From the very beginning, CEO Tewari and his co-founders knew that they wanted to have a global presence. It used a "reverse market strategy," establishing leadership positions in Asia and Africa first and then tackling the European Union and U.S. markets. Today it employs over 900 people and has offices around the world, including in India, Asia (China, Singapore, Malaysia, South Korea, Taiwan, and Japan), Australia, the European Union (Germany, the United Kingdom, Spain, France, and Sweden), the Middle East (UAE), and the United States (San Francisco). Fueled in part by a $200 million investment from Japanese media and telecommunications giant Softbank, which valued InMobi at over $1 billion, InMobi is currently focusing on growth in the United States and plans to focus next on Russia and Latin America, where growth in mobile users is expected to rise the fastest. InMobi has also used funds to make some strategic purchases, including MMTG Labs, a developer of an application market for Facebook pages, Appstores.com, and Overlay Media, which helps to deliver more highly targeted and context-sensitive ads.

Can InMobi truly hope to challenge Google, which is currently the dominant leader in market share? Its $250 million in revenues still trails behind Google's $1.5 billion in revenue from mobile display advertising. Nonetheless, Tewari thinks so, claiming that InMobi is currently second, with a market share of more than 10%, and that the company is on a trajectory to become one of the top 10 Internet companies by 2020. InMobi has modeled itself after Google and other tech titans in its hiring and employee policies, which allow employees the latitude and support to come up with the next big, disruptive idea. InMobi boasts a growing number of partnerships with other tech firms, including Amobee, which services a large portfolio of Fortune 500 brands that will now be using InMobi's ad network, as well as payment processing firm Stripe; Chinese tech firm APUS, which will broaden InMobi's reach to over 500 million Chinese users in 2016; and Dell Inc., with whom InMobi will team up to build an e-commerce platform for Dell products. Tewari also points to InMobi's primary focus on mobile, compared to Google, which is involved in many different areas. InMobi also claims that its technology is superior and that its data on customers is richer and more granular. In 2015, InMobi backed up its claims when it became one of the first mobile advertising companies to offer a 100% viewability guarantee, a rarity in the modern landscape of ad blockers and ad fraud. As more advertisers gravitate to the mobile platform, an emphasis on ensuring that ads are viewable will help InMobi differentiate itself from the pack.

Tewari also claims that inMobi understands user behavior better than most of the other large players in the mobile advertising market. His confidence stems from InMobi's appographic targeting system, which uses algorithms and data on how users interact with apps to determine very precise trends and preferences of those users. To develop the system, InMobi studied over 100,000 apps and how different types of consumers used them. The result is a system so accurate that InMobi has guaranteed 2–3% increases in engagement by app developers using InMobi's services. In 2014, InMobi continued to innovate, honing the Geo Context Targeting system used in its Smart Ads, which it says generate ten times the interaction compared to traditional ads, and more than three times the conversion rate of traditional ads. SmartAds support rich media and are tailored based on users' personal details and geographic conditions in the area, such as location and nearby weather. For example, if you're strolling city streets on a hot summer afternoon, you'll be given advertisements for cold beverages from nearby food chains. InMobi's emphasis on data drives its product offerings, prompting Tewari to describe InMobi as "a data company," not an advertising company.

In 2015, InMobi launched its Miip personalized discovery tool, which is a monkey character that persists throughout multiple apps and offers users options for different types of content, including product feeds and other apps. Over time, Miip improves its accuracy, offering only the most relevant and thematically consistent products to users, such as workout wear in a fitness app and fashion tips in a dating app, while also providing direct links to purchase products or download apps. Tewari asserts that Miip is an advertising feature that actually includes the user, making it much more engaging and persuasive, and InMobi believes Miip will generate $1 billion by 2017. InMobi has also partnered with Taboola, the largest global content discovery platform, to provide more personalized recommendations and content natively on iOS and Android.

InMobi also launched several new advertising platforms in 2014, including an interactive video ad platform as well as a native ad exchange, to help advertisers boost their sales on mobile beyond Facebook and Google. InMobi's video ad platform focuses on contextualized mobile video ads using its advanced targeting system. Developed in tandem with programmatic advertising service provider Rubicon Project, InMobi's native ad exchange is the first that allows buying and selling of mobile native advertising on a global scale.

Tewari realizes that the competition is about to get a lot tougher, but believes his company is well-positioned, particularly due to its global scope. Although InMobi is at a disadvantage because Google, Facebook, and Twitter have major social media platforms and services with which they can provide mobile advertising, the market for independent native ad networks that are not affiliated with these companies is estimated to be between $8 and $10 billion annually. For many advertisers, advertising with InMobi may be more cost effective than developing individual advertisements for Google, Facebook, Twitter, and other services of sufficient size. On the other hand, users spend much more time on these bigger sites than they do anywhere else, which complicates things for inMobi. The mobile advertising marketplace is expected to become so large (it is estimated that over $500 billion will be spent by mobile advertisers over the next 10 years) that there is plenty of room for more than just one company to benefit. InMobi also claims that its margins are a whopping 40% compared to just 5–10% in the TV and print advertising industry, and when asked whether users are tired of all the advertising, Tewari counters that users are tired of irrelevant ads, not advertising in general. Many analysts believe that InMobi is close to launching an IPO as the global mobile advertising market continues to grow rapidly and InMobi's future prospects get brighter. Perhaps sensing an eventual threat, rumors swirled in 2015 that Google was preparing an offer to acquire InMobi for over $2 billion, but InMobi is determined to go its own way and beat the giants at their own game.

Advertising Has Doubled," campaignbrief.com, August 15, 2013; "InMobi in the IPO Wings," Sramanamitra.com, August 2nd, 2013; "How inMobil Grew from a Startup to a Giant Mobile Ad Network," by Willis Wee, Techinasia.com, May 16, 2013; "InMobi Now Serves Ads to 691m Unique Users a Month," by Zen Terrelonge, mobile-ent.biz, May 1, 2013; "InMobi Named to MIT Technology Review's 2013 50 Disruptive Companies List Recognizing World's Most Innovative Companies," InMobi.com, February 20, 2013; "InMobi Acquires Overlay Media," InMobi, January 8, 2013; "Desi Software Product Company Takes Global Tech Giants Head-on," by Bibhu Ranjan Mishra, Business-standard.com, November 19, 2012; "InMobi Names Ex-Google Exec as North America Head," by Mark Walsh, Mediapost.com, October 30, 2012; "Softbank-backed Mobile Ad Giant InMobi Pulls Out of Africa and Russia over Its Poor Performance," by Jon Russell, Thenextweb.com, October 30, 2012; "Smart Mobile Ads 'Turn to the Sun' by Tracking Conversions," Marketingmag.com/au, October 23, 2012; "InMobi Wins Three Smartie Awards for Excellence in Mobile Advertising," InMobi, October 16, 2012; "InMobi Voted Number One Mobile Advertising Network in Malaysia," InMobi, October 11, 2012; "Make Your Dream a Success," InMobi, September 3, 2012; "Mobile Ad Network InMobi Continues Buying Spree, Picks Up Metaflow Solutions for App Distribution," by Ingrid Lunden, Techcrunch.con, July 31, 2012; "The New Poster Boys of Start-Ups," by Kushan Mitra, *Business Today*, November 1, 2011; "Softbank Invests $200M in InMobi," by Jamie Yap, ZDnet.com, September 15, 2011; "InMobi Raises Massive $200M to Overtake Google in Mobile Ads," by Matt Marshall, Venturebeat.com, September 15, 2011; "HTML Ad Builder Sprout Acquired by InMobi," by Jason Kincaid, Techcrunch.com, August 2, 2011; "InMobi Signs "Multi-million Dollar" Mobile Ad Partnership with Amobee," by Steve O'Hear, Techcrunch.com, May 11, 2011.

Perhaps no area of business has been more affected by Internet and mobile platform technologies than marketing and marketing communications. As a communications tool, the Internet affords marketers new ways of contacting millions of potential customers at costs far lower than traditional media. The Internet also provides new ways—often instantaneous and spontaneous—to gather information from customers, adjust product offerings, and increase customer value. The Internet has spawned entirely new ways to identify and communicate with customers, including search engine marketing, social marketing, behavioral targeting, and targeted e-mail, among others. And the Internet was just the first transformation. Today, the mobile platform based on smartphones and tablet computers is transforming online marketing and communications yet again. **Table 6.1** summarizes some of the significant new developments in online marketing and advertising for 2015–2016.

The subject of online marketing, branding, and market communications is very broad and deep. We have created two chapters to cover the material. In this chapter, we begin by examining consumer behavior on the Web, the major types of online marketing and branding, and the technologies that support advances in online marketing. We then focus on understanding the costs and benefits of online marketing communications. In Chapter 7, we focus on the social, mobile, and local marketing phenomenon in greater depth.

6.1 CONSUMERS ONLINE: THE INTERNET AUDIENCE AND CONSUMER BEHAVIOR

Before firms can begin to sell their products online, they must first understand what kinds of people they will find online and how those people behave in the online marketplace. In this section, we focus primarily on individual consumers in the business-to-consumer (B2C) arena. However, many of the factors discussed apply to the B2B arena as well, insofar as purchasing decisions by firms are made by individuals. For readers who have no background in marketing, we have created an online Learning Track, Learning Track 6.1, that discusses basic marketing and branding concepts.

INTERNET TRAFFIC PATTERNS: THE ONLINE CONSUMER PROFILE

We will start with an analysis of some basic background demographics of Web consumers. The first principle of marketing and sales is "know thy customer." Who is online, who shops online and why, and what do they buy? In 2015, around 3.1 billion people of all ages had access to the Internet. About 670 million households worldwide (almost 32% of all households) have broadband access to the Internet.

Although the number of new online users increased at a rate of 30% a year or higher in the early 2000s, over the last several years, this growth rate has slowed in most parts of the world. E-commerce businesses can no longer count on a double-digit

TABLE 6.1	WHAT'S NEW IN ONLINE MARKETING AND ADVERTISING 2015–2016

BUSINESS

- Online marketing and advertising spending continues to increase worldwide (by over 15% in 2015), compared to only about 6% for traditional media marketing and advertising.
- Video advertising continues to be one of the fastest growing formats.
- Search engine marketing and advertising continues in importance, but its rate of growth is slowing somewhat compared to other formats.
- Mobile, social, and local marketing spending all continue to rapidly expand.
- Viewability issues and ad fraud raise increasing concerns for marketers.
- Native advertising and other forms of content marketing rise.

TECHNOLOGY

- Ad blocking software usage increases, creating concern for both online publishers and advertisers.
- Big Data: online tracking produces oceans of data, challenging business analytics programs.
- Cloud computing makes rich marketing content and multi-channel, cross-platform marketing a reality.
- Programmatic advertising (automated, technology-driven method of buying and selling display and video ads) takes off.

SOCIETY

- Targeted advertising based on behavioral tracking leads to growing privacy awareness and fears.

growth rate in the online population to fuel their revenues. The days of extremely rapid growth in the Internet population are over.

Intensity and Scope of Usage

The slowing rate of growth in the Internet population is compensated for, in part, by an increasing intensity and scope of use. In the United States, 71% of all adults report logging on on a typical day (Pew Research Center, 2014). Internet use by U.S. teens is even more pervasive, with over 90% saying they go online daily, and about 25% reporting that they use the Internet almost constantly (Pew Research Center, 2015a). Several studies also show that a greater amount of time is being spent online—over 4.5 hours a day by U.K. adults, for instance. In 2015, mobile smartphones and tablets are major access points to the Internet and online commerce. About 2.25 billion people, about 72% of all Internet users worldwide, access the Internet using a mobile phone. Owners of mobile devices in the United Kingdom spend about 2.5 hours a day using them for nontelephone activities such as playing games, viewing videos, and visiting social networks (eMarketer, Inc., 2015a). Engaging in such activities is widespread—in the U.S. in 2015, for instance, around 165 million mobile users played games, about 107 million watched videos, 151 million visited a social network, and millions of others listened to music or shopped (eMarketer, Inc., 2015b). The more time users spend online, becoming more comfortable and familiar with Internet features and services, the more services they are likely to explore, according to the Pew Research Center.

Demographics and Access

In the United States, the demographic profile of the Internet—and e-commerce—has changed greatly since 1995. Up until 2000, single, white, young, college-educated males with high incomes dominated the Internet. This inequality in access and usage led to concerns about a possible "digital divide." However, in recent years, there has been a marked increase in Internet usage by females, minorities, seniors, and families with modest incomes, resulting in a notable decrease—but not elimination—in the earlier inequality of access and usage.

A roughly equal percentage of men (85%) and women (84%) use the Internet in the U.S. today. Young adults (18–29) form the age group with the highest percentage of Internet use, at 96%. Adults in the 30–49 group (93%) are also strongly represented. Another fast-growing group online is the 65 and over segment, 58% of whom now use the Internet. Teens (12–17) also have a very high percentage of their age group online (97%). The percentage of very young children (0–11 years) online has also spurted, to 50% of that age group. eMarketer predicts that future Internet user growth in the United States will come predominantly from those aged 55 and older and from children in the 0–11 age bracket (eMarketer, Inc., 2015b). Variation across ethnic groups is not as wide as across age groups. Ten years ago, there were significant differences among ethnic groups, but this has receded. In 2015, user participation by whites is 85%, Hispanics, 81%, and African-Americans, 78%.

About 97% of U.S. households with income levels above $75,000 have Internet access, compared to only 74% of households earning less than $30,000. Over time, income differences have declined but they remain significant with a 23% gap between the highest category of household income and the lowest. Amount of education also makes a significant difference when it comes to online access. Of those individuals with less than a high school education, only 66% were online in 2015, compared to 95% of individuals with a college degree or more. Even some college education boosted Internet usage, with that segment reaching 90% (Pew Research Center, 2015b).

Overall, the so-called "digital divide" has indeed moderated, but it still persists along income, education, age, and ethnic dimensions. Gender, income, education, age, and ethnicity also impact online behavior. According to the Pew Research Center, U.S. adults over the age of 65, those who have not completed high school, those who make less than $30,000 a year, and Hispanics are all less likely to purchase products online. Women are slightly more likely to purchase online than men, but not significantly so. With respect to online banking, the demographics are similar—those 65 and older are less likely than any age group to bank online, while those with at least some college are more likely than those with a high school diploma or less. Online banking is also more popular with men than women. No significant differences were found in terms of ethnicity (Pew Research Center, 2012). Other commentators have observed that children of poorer and less educated families spend considerably more time using their access devices for entertainment (movies, games, Facebook, and texting) than children from wealthier households. For all children and teenagers, the majority of time spent on the Internet is often labeled as "wasted time" because the majority of online use is for entertainment, and not education or learning (Richtel, 2012).

Type of Internet Connection: Broadband and Mobile Impacts

While a great deal of progress has been made in reducing glaring gaps in access to the Internet, there are still inequalities in access to broadband service. In 2015, around 91 million U.S. households had broadband service in their homes—75% of all households (eMarketer, Inc., 2015c). Research by the Pew Research Center indicates that broadband adoption levels are lower for older adults, those with low levels of education, and those with low household incomes. Rural residents, African Americans, and Latinos are also less likely to have a home broadband connection (Pew Research Center, 2013). For marketers, the broadband audience offers unique opportunities for the use of multimedia marketing campaigns, and for the positioning of products especially suited for this more educated and affluent audience. It is also important to note that just because a household does not have broadband access, it does not mean that household members do not use the Internet. About 50% of the non-broadband adopters do use the Internet, either from another location or via a smartphone. Certain groups are particularly reliant on smartphones for online access: younger adults in the 18–29 age group, those with low household incomes and levels of education, and non-whites (Pew Research Center, 2013a, 2013b, 2015c). The explosive growth of smartphones and tablet computers connected to broadband cellular and Wi-Fi networks is the foundation for a truly mobile e-commerce and marketing platform, which did not exist a few years ago.

Community Effects: Social Contagion in Social Networks

For a physical retail store, the most important factor in shaping sales is location, location, location. If you are located where thousands of people pass by every day, you will tend to do well. But for Internet retailers, physical location has almost no consequence as long as customers can be served by shipping services such as UPS or the post office or their services can be downloaded to anywhere. What does make a difference for consumer purchases on the Internet is whether or not the consumer is located in "neighborhoods" where others purchase on the Internet. These neighborhoods can be either face-to-face and truly personal, or digital. These so-called neighborhood effects, and the role of social emulation in consumption decisions, are well known for goods such as personal computers. In general, there is a relationship between being a member of a social network and purchasing decisions. Yet the relationship between "connectedness" (either offline or online) and purchase decisions is not straightforward or simple. People who score in the top 10%–15% of connectedness "do their own thing" to differentiate themselves and often do not share purchase decisions with friends. In fact, highly connected users often stop purchasing what their friends purchase. One can think of them as iconoclasts. The middle 50% of connected people very often share purchase patterns of their friends. One can think of these people as "keeping up with the Joneses" (Iyengar et al., 2009). A recent study of 6,000 social network users found that social networks have a powerful influence on shopping and purchasing behavior. An estimated 40% of social media users have purchased an item after sharing or favoriting it on Facebook, Pinterest, or Twitter. Facebook is the network most likely to drive customers to purchase, followed by Pinterest and Twitter. Unexpectedly, social networks increase research online, followed by purchase offline (sometimes referred to as ROPO), driving purchase traffic into physical stores where the product can be seen, tried, and then purchased. This is the opposite of the showrooming effect where consumers shop in stores, and then purchase online. The ROPO effect was found to be as large as the research offline and purchase online effect (Vision Critical, 2013; Schleifer, 2013; Sevitt and Samuel, 2013).

Membership in social networks has a large influence on discovering new independent music, but less influence on already well-known products (Garg, 2009). Membership in an online brand community like Ford's Facebook page and community has a direct effect on sales (Adjei et al., 2009). Amazon's recommender systems ("Consumers who bought this item also bought ...") create co-purchase networks where people do not know one another personally, but nevertheless triple the influence of complementary products (Oestreicher-Singer and Sundararajan, 2008). The value of social networks to marketers rests on the proposition that brand strength and purchase decisions are closely related to network membership, rank, prominence, and centrality (Guo et al., 2011).

CONSUMER BEHAVIOR MODELS

consumer behavior
a social science discipline that attempts to model and understand the behavior of humans in a marketplace

Once firms have an understanding of who is online, they need to focus on how consumers behave online. The study of **consumer behavior** is a social science discipline that attempts to model and understand the behavior of humans in a marketplace. Several social science disciplines play roles in this study, including sociology, psychology, and economics. Models of consumer behavior attempt to predict or "explain" what consumers purchase and where, when, how much, and why they buy. The expectation is that if the consumer decision-making process can be understood, firms will have a much better idea how to market and sell their products. **Figure 6.1** illustrates a general consumer behavior model that takes into account a wide range of factors that influence a consumer's marketplace decisions. Learning Track 6.2 contains further information about the cultural, social, and psychological background factors that influence consumer behavior.

PROFILES OF ONLINE CONSUMERS

Online consumer behavior parallels that of offline consumer behavior with some obvious differences. It is important to first understand why people choose the Internet channel to conduct transactions. **Table 6.2** lists the main reasons consumers choose the online channel.

While price is an important consideration, consumers also shop online because of convenience, which in turn is produced largely by saving them time. Overall transaction cost reduction appears to be a major motivator for choosing the online channel.

FIGURE 6.1	A GENERAL MODEL OF CONSUMER BEHAVIOR

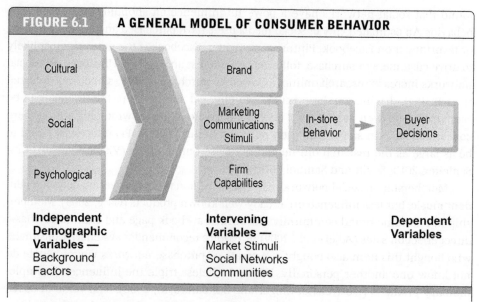

Consumer behavior models try to predict the decisions that consumers make in the marketplace.

SOURCE: Adapted from Kotler and Armstrong, 2009.

THE ONLINE PURCHASING DECISION

Once online, why do consumers actually purchase a product or service at a specific site? Among the most important reasons are price and the availability of free shipping. That the seller is someone whom the purchaser trusts is also a very important factor.

TABLE 6.2	WHY CONSUMERS CHOOSE THE ONLINE CHANNEL

REASON	PERCENTAGE OF RESPONDENTS
Lower prices	59%
Shop from home	53%
Shop 24/7	44%
Wider variety of products available	29%
Easier to compare and research products and offers	27%
Products only available online	22%
Online customer reviews	18%
Better product information available	7%
Promotion via e-mail or text	7%
Social media influence	1%

SOURCE: Based on data from eMarketer, Inc., 2014.

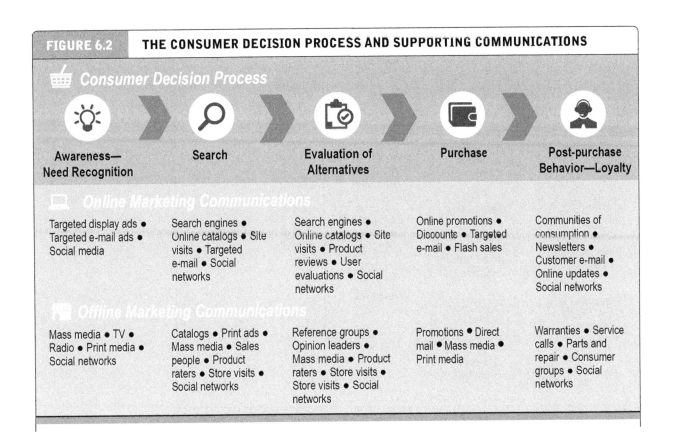

FIGURE 6.2   THE CONSUMER DECISION PROCESS AND SUPPORTING COMMUNICATIONS

The ability to make a purchase without paying tax and the availability of an online coupon are also significant factors.

You also need to consider the process that buyers follow when making a purchase decision, and how the Internet environment affects consumers' decisions. There are five stages in the consumer decision process: awareness of need, search for more information, evaluation of alternatives, the actual purchase decision, and post-purchase contact with the firm. **Figure 6.2** shows the consumer decision process and the types of offline and online marketing communications that support this process and seek to influence the consumer before, during, and after the purchase decision.

The stages of the consumer decision process are basically the same whether the consumer is offline or online. On the other hand, the general model of consumer behavior requires modification to take into account new factors, and the unique features of e-commerce that allow new opportunities to interact with the customer online also need to be accounted for. In **Figure 6.3**, we have modified the general model of consumer behavior to focus on user characteristics, product characteristics, and Web site and mobile platform features, along with traditional factors such as brand strength and specific market communications (advertising) and the influence of both online and offline social networks.

In the online model, Web site and mobile platform features, along with consumer skills, product characteristics, attitudes towards online purchasing, and perceptions

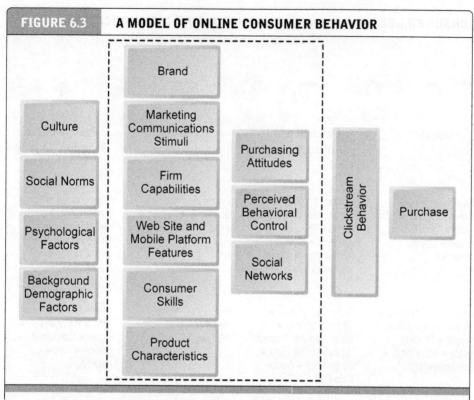

FIGURE 6.3   A MODEL OF ONLINE CONSUMER BEHAVIOR

In this general model of online consumer behavior, the decision to purchase is shaped by background demographic factors, several intervening factors, and, finally, influenced greatly by clickstream behavior very near to the precise moment of purchase.

about control over the online environment come to the fore. Web site and mobile platform features include latency (delay in downloads), navigability, and confidence in online security. There are parallels in the analog world. For instance, it is well known that consumer behavior can be influenced by store design, and that understanding the precise movements of consumers through a physical store can enhance sales if goods and promotions are arranged along the most likely consumer tracks. Consumer skills refers to the knowledge that consumers have about how to conduct online transactions (which increases with experience). Product characteristics refers to the fact that some products can be easily described, packaged, and shipped online, whereas others cannot. Combined with traditional factors, such as brand, advertising, and firm capabilities, these factors lead to specific attitudes about purchasing from an e-commerce firm (trust in the firm and favorable customer experience) and a sense that the consumer can control his or her environment online.

Clickstream behavior refers to the transaction log that consumers establish as they move about the Web, from search engine to a variety of sites, then to a single site, then to a single page, and then, finally, to a decision to purchase. These precious moments are similar to "point-of-purchase" moments in traditional retail. A study of over 10,000 visits to an online wine store found that detailed and general clickstream

clickstream behavior
the transaction log that consumers establish as they move about the Web

behavior were as important as customer demographics and prior purchase behavior in predicting a current purchase (Van den Poel and Buckinx, 2005). Clickstream marketing takes maximum advantage of the Internet environment. It presupposes no prior "deep" knowledge of the customer (and in that sense is "privacy-regarding"), and can be developed dynamically as customers use the Internet. For instance, the success of search engine marketing (the display of paid advertisements by search engines) is based in large part on what the consumer is looking for at the moment and how they go about looking (detailed clickstream data). After examining the detailed data, general clickstream data is used (days since last visit, past purchases). If available, demographic data is used (region, city, and gender).

SHOPPERS: BROWSERS AND BUYERS

The picture of Internet use sketched in the previous section emphasizes the complexity of behavior online. Although the Internet audience still tends to be concentrated among the well educated, affluent, and youthful, the audience is increasingly becoming more diverse. Clickstream analysis shows us that people go online for many different reasons. Online shopping is similarly complex. Beneath the surface of the €1.96 trillion B2C e-commerce market in 2015 are substantial differences in how users shop online.

Worldwide, about 1.4 billion people (about 45% of the Internet population) are "buyers" who actually purchase something online. In the United Kingdom, 88.2% of Internet users, age 14 and older, are buyers, while another 5.3% research products online ("browsers"), but purchase them offline (see **Figure 6.4**). With the teen and adult U.K. Internet audience (14 years or older) estimated at about 47 million in 2015, online shoppers (the combination of buyers and browsers, totalling almost 93.5%) add up to a market size of almost 44 million consumers.

The significance of online browsing for offline purchasing should not be underestimated. Although it is difficult to precisely measure the amount of offline sales

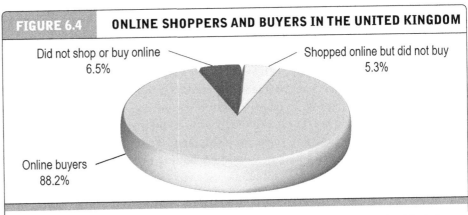

Over 85% of U.K. Internet users, age 14 and older, shop online on desktop computers and mobile devices, either by researching products or by purchasing products online. The percentage of those actually purchasing has increased to over 75%. Only about 5% do not buy or shop online.
SOURCE: Based on data from eMarketer, Inc., 2015d.

that occur because of online product research, Forrester Research estimates that U.S. Web-influenced retail sales will generate over $1.55 trillion in 2015, growing to around $1.8 trillion by 2018 (Forrester Research, 2014a).

E-commerce is a major conduit and generator of offline commerce. The reverse is also true: online traffic is driven by offline brands and shopping. While online research influences offline purchases, it is also the case that offline marketing media heavily influence online behavior including sales. Traditional print media (magazines and newspapers) and television are by far the most powerful media for reaching and engaging consumers with information about new products and directing them to the Web. Online communities and blogging are also very influential but not yet as powerful as traditional media. This may be surprising to many given the attention to social networks as marketing vehicles, but it reflects the diversity of influences on consumer behavior and the real-world marketing budgets of firms that are still heavily dominated by traditional media. Even more surprising in the era of Facebook, face-to-face interactions are a more powerful influence than participation in online social communities.

These considerations strongly suggest that e-commerce and traditional commerce are coupled and should be viewed by merchants (and researchers) as part of a continuum of consuming behavior and not as radical alternatives to one another. Commerce is commerce; the customers are often the same people. Customers use a wide variety of media, sometimes multiple media at once. The significance of these findings for marketers is very clear. Online merchants should build the information content of their sites to attract browsers looking for information, build content to rank high in search engines, put less attention on selling per se, and promote services and products (especially new products) in offline media settings in order to support their online stores.

WHAT CONSUMERS SHOP FOR AND BUY ONLINE

You can look at online sales as divided roughly into two groups: small-ticket and big-ticket items. Big-ticket items include computer equipment and consumer electronics, where orders can easily be more than €1,000. Small-ticket items include apparel, books, health and beauty supplies, office supplies, music, software, videos, and toys, where the average purchase is typically less than €100. In the early days of e-commerce, sales of small-ticket items vastly outnumbered those of large-ticket items. But the recent growth of big-ticket items such as computer hardware, consumer electronics, furniture, and jewelry has changed the overall sales mix. Consumers are now much more confident spending online for big-ticket items. Although furniture and large appliances were initially perceived as too bulky to sell online, these categories have rapidly expanded in the last few years. Free shipping offered by Amazon and other large retailers has also contributed to consumers buying many more expensive and large items online such as air conditioners. Refer to Figure 1.10 to see how much consumers spent online for various categories of goods in 2014.

INTENTIONAL ACTS: HOW SHOPPERS FIND VENDORS ONLINE

Given the prevalence of "click here" display ads, one might think customers are "driven" to online vendors by spur-of-the-moment decisions. In fact, only a tiny percentage of shoppers click on display ads to find vendors. E-commerce shoppers are highly intentional. Typically, they are focused browsers looking for specific products, companies, and services. Once they are online, a majority of consumers use a search engine as their preferred method of research for purchasing a product. Many will go directly to a online marketplace, such as Amazon or eBay, and some will go directly to a specific retail Web site. Merchants can convert these "goal-oriented," intentional shoppers into buyers if the merchants can target their communications to the shoppers and design their sites in such a way as to provide easy-to-access and useful product information, full selection, and customer service, and do this at the very moment the customer is searching for the product. This is no small task.

WHY SOME PEOPLE DON'T SHOP ONLINE

About 10% of Internet users do not shop or buy online. Why not? One of the most important factors cited by those who don't shop or buy online is the "trust factor," the fear that online merchants will cheat you, lose your credit card information, or use personal information you give them to invade your personal privacy, bombarding you with unwanted e-mail and pop-up ads. Secondary factors can be summarized as "hassle factors," like shipping costs, returns, and inability to touch and feel the product.

TRUST, UTILITY, AND OPPORTUNISM IN ONLINE MARKETS

A long tradition of research shows that the two most important factors shaping the decision to purchase online are utility and trust (Brookings Institute, 2011; Kim et al., 2009; Ba and Pavlou, 2002). Consumers want good deals, bargains, convenience, and speed of delivery. In short, consumers are looking for utility. On the other hand, in any seller-buyer relationship, there is an asymmetry of information. The seller usually knows a lot more than the consumer about the quality of goods and terms of sale. This can lead to opportunistic behavior by sellers (Akerlof, 1970; Williamson, 1985; Mishra, 1998). Consumers need to trust a merchant before they make a purchase. Sellers can develop trust among online consumers by building strong reputations of honesty, fairness, and delivery of quality products—the basic elements of a brand. Feedback forums such as Epinions.com (now part of Shopping.com), Amazon's book reviews from reviewers, and eBay's feedback forum are examples of trust-building online mechanisms (NielsenWire, 2012; Opinion Research Corporation, 2009). Online sellers who develop trust among consumers are able to charge a premium price for their online products and services (Kim and Benbasat, 2006, 2007; Pavlou, 2002). A review of the literature suggests that the most important factors leading to a trusting online relationship are perception of Web site credibility, ease of use, and perceived risk (Corritore et al., 2006). An important brake on the growth of e-commerce is lack of trust. Newspaper and television ads are far more trusted than online ads (Nielsen, 2011). Personal friends and family are far more powerful determinants of online purchases than membership in social networks (eMarketer, Inc., 2010). These attitudes have grown more positive over time, but concerns about the use of personal information by online marketers continue to raise trust issues among consumers.

6.2 DIGITAL COMMERCE MARKETING AND ADVERTISING STRATEGIES AND TOOLS

Online marketing has many similarities to, and differences from, ordinary marketing. (For more information on basic marketing concepts, see Learning Tracks 6.1 and 6.2.) The objective of online marketing—as in all marketing—is to build customer relationships so that the firm can achieve above-average returns (both by offering superior products or services and by communicating the brand's features to the consumer). These relationships are a foundation for the firm's brand. But online marketing is also very different from ordinary marketing because the nature of the medium and its capabilities are so different from anything that has come before.

There are four features of online marketing that distinguish it from traditional marketing channels. Compared to traditional print and television marketing, online marketing can be more personalized, participatory, peer-to-peer, and communal. Not all types of online marketing have these four features. For instance, there's not much difference between a marketing video splashed on your computer screen without your consent and watching a television commercial. However, the same marketing video can be targeted to your personal interests, community memberships, and allow you to share it with others using a Like or + tag. Marketers are learning that the most effective forms of online marketing have all four of these features.

STRATEGIC ISSUES AND QUESTIONS

In the past, the first step in building an online brand was to build a Web site, and then try to attract an audience. The most common "traditional" marketing techniques for establishing a brand and attracting customers were search engine marketing, display ads, e-mail campaigns, and affiliate programs. This is still the case: building a Web site is still a first step, and the "traditional" online marketing techniques are still the main powerhouses of brand creation and online sales revenue in 2015. But today, marketers need to take a much broader view of the online marketing challenge, and to consider other media channels for attracting an audience such as social media and mobile devices, in concert with traditional Web sites.

The five main elements of a comprehensive multi-channel marketing plan are: Web site, traditional online marketing, social marketing, mobile marketing, and offline marketing. **Table 6.3** illustrates these five main platforms, central elements within each type, some examples, and the primary function of marketing in each situation. Each of the main types of online marketing is discussed in this section and throughout the chapter in greater detail.

Immediately, by examining Table 6.3, you can understand the management complexity of building brands online. There are five major types of marketing, and a variety of different platforms that perform different functions. If you're a manager of a start-up, or the Web site manager of an existing commercial Web site, you face a number of strategic questions. Where should you focus first? Build a Web site, develop a blog, or jump into developing a Facebook presence? If you have a successful Web site that already uses search engine marketing and display ads, where should you go

TABLE 6.3	THE DIGITAL MARKETING ROADMAP		
TYPE OF MARKETING	**PLATFORMS**	**EXAMPLES**	**FUNCTION**
Web Site	Traditional Web site	Ford.com	Anchor site
Traditional Online Marketing	Search engine marketing	Google; Bing; Yahoo	Query-based intention marketing
	Display advertising	Yahoo; Google; MSN	Interest- and context-based marketing; targeted marketing
	E-mail	Major retailers	Permission marketing
	Affiliates	Amazon	Brand extension
Social Marketing	Social networks	Facebook	Conversations; sharing
	Micro blogging sites	Twitter	News, quick updates
	Blogs/forums	Tumblr	Communities of interest; sharing
	Visual marketing	Pinterest/Instagram	Branding; sharing
	Video marketing	YouTube	Engage; inform
	Game marketing	Chipotle Scarecrow Game	Identification
Mobile Marketing	Mobile site	m.ford.com	Quick access; news; updates
	Apps	2015 Ford Mustang Customizer	Visual engagement
		My Ford	Visual engagement
Offline Marketing	Television	2015 Ford F-150: This Changes Everything	Brand anchoring; inform
	Newspapers	Apple Shot on iPhone 6 campaign	Brand anchoring; inform
	Magazines	Apple Watch/Vogue Magazine	Brand anchoring; inform

next: develop a social network presence or use offline media? Does your firm have the resources to maintain a social media marketing campaign?

A second strategic management issue involves the integration of all these different marketing platforms into a single coherent branding message. Often, there are different groups with different skill sets involved in Web site design, search engine and display marketing, social media marketing, and offline marketing. Getting all these different specialties to work together and coordinate their campaigns can be very difficult. The danger is that a firm ends up with different teams managing each of the four platforms rather than a single team managing the digital online presence, or for that matter, marketing for the entire firm including retail outlets.

A third strategic management question involves resource allocation. There are actually two problems here. Each of the different major types of marketing, and each of the different platforms, has different metrics to measure its effectiveness. In some cases, for new social marketing platforms, there is no commonly accepted metric, and few that have withstood critical scrutiny or have a deep experience base providing empirical data. For instance, in Facebook marketing, an important metric is how many Likes your Facebook page produces. The connection between Likes and sales is still being explored. In search engine marketing, effectiveness is measured by how many clicks your ads are receiving; in display advertising, by how many impressions of your ads are served. Second, each of these platforms has different costs for Likes, impressions, and clicks. In order to choose where your marketing resources should be deployed, you will have to link each of these activities to sales revenue. You will need to determine how much clicks, Likes, and impressions are worth. We address these questions in greater detail in Chapter 7.

THE WEB SITE AS A MARKETING PLATFORM: ESTABLISHING THE CUSTOMER RELATIONSHIP

A firm's Web site is a major tool for establishing the initial relationship with the customer. The Web site performs four important functions: establishing the brand identity and consumer expectations, informing and educating the consumer, shaping the customer experience, and anchoring the brand in an ocean of marketing messages coming from different sources. The Web site is the one place the consumer can turn to find the complete story. This is not true of apps, e-mail, or search engine ads.

The first function of a Web site is to establish the brand's identity and to act as an anchor for the firm's other Web marketing activities, thereby driving sales revenue. This involves identifying for the consumer the differentiating features of the product or service in terms of quality, price, product support, and reliability. Identifying the differentiating features of the product on the Web site's home page is intended to create expectations in the user of what it will be like to consume the product. For instance, Snapple's Web site creates the expectation that the product is a delicious, refreshing drink made from high quality, natural ingredients. Ford's Web site focuses on automobile technology and high miles per gallon. The expectation created by Ford's Web site is that if you buy a Ford, you'll be experiencing the latest automotive technology and the highest mileage. At the location-based social network Web site for Foursquare, the focus is on meeting friends, discovering local places, and saving money with coupons and rewards.

Web sites also function to anchor the brand online, acting as a central point where all the branding messages that emanate from the firm's multiple digital presences, such as Facebook, Twitter, mobile apps, or e-mail, come together at a single online location. Aside from branding, Web sites also perform the typical functions of any commercial establishment by informing customers of the company's products and services. Web sites, with their online catalogs and associated shopping carts, are important elements of the online customer experience. **Customer experience** refers to the totality of experiences that a customer has with a firm, including the search, informing, purchase, consumption, and after-sales support for the product. The concept "customer experience" is broader than the traditional concept of "customer satisfaction" in that a much broader range of impacts is considered, including the customer's cognitive,

customer experience
the totality of experiences that a customer has with a firm, including the search, informing, purchase, consumption, and after-sales support for its products, services, and various retail channels

affective, emotional, social, and physical relationship to the firm and its products. The totality of customer experiences will generally involve multiple retail channels. This means that, in the customer's mind, the Web site, mobile site and apps, Facebook page, Twitter feed, physical store, and television advertisements are all connected as part of his or her experience with the company.

TRADITIONAL ONLINE MARKETING AND ADVERTISING TOOLS

Below we describe the basic marketing and advertising tools for attracting e-commerce consumers: search engine marketing, display ad marketing (including banner ads, rich media ads, video ads, and sponsorships), e-mail and permission marketing, affiliate marketing, viral marketing, and lead generation marketing.

online advertising
a paid message on a Web site, online service, or other interactive medium

Companies will spend an estimated €521 billion on advertising in 2015, and an estimated €156 billion of that amount on **online advertising**, which includes display (banners, video, and rich media), search, mobile messaging, sponsorships, classifieds, lead generation, and e-mail, on desktop, laptop, and tablet computers, as well as mobile phones (see **Figure 6.5**) (eMarketer, Inc., 2015e).

In the last five years, advertisers have aggressively increased online spending and cut outlays on traditional channels. By 2018, the amount spent on online advertising is expected to exceed the amount spent on television advertising.

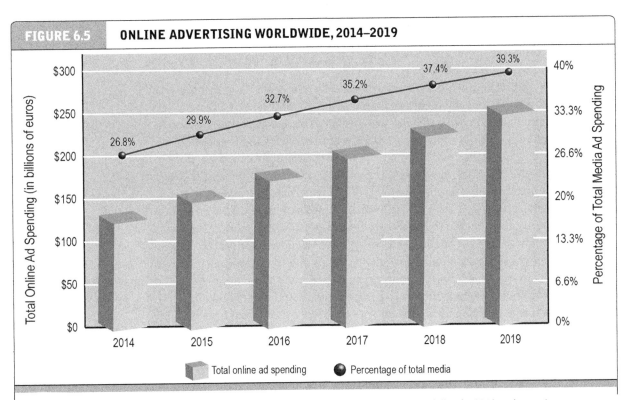

| FIGURE 6.5 | ONLINE ADVERTISING WORLDWIDE, 2014–2019 |

Worldwide spending on online advertising is expected to grow from €156 billion in 2015 to €257 billion by 2019, and comprise an increasing percentage of total media ad spending.

SOURCE: Based on data from eMarketer, Inc., 2015e.

TABLE 6.4	ONLINE ADVERTISING SPENDING IN THE UNITED STATES FOR SELECTED FORMATS (IN BILLIONS)		
FORMAT	2015	2019	AVERAGE GROWTH RATE
Search	$25.7	$36.8	9.9%
Banner ads	$12.1	$17.7	10.1%
Video	$7.8	$14.4	20.1%
Rich media	$5.2	$12.1	26.9%
Classifieds	$3.2	$3.9	5.3%
Sponsorships	$2.0	$3.2	12.5%
Lead generation	$2.2	$2.6	5.1%
E-mail	$0.27	$0.34	6.5%

SOURCE: Based on data from eMarketer, Inc., 2015m.

Table 6.4 provides some comparative data on the amount of spending for certain advertising formats in the United States. In 2015, the highest amount of spending is for paid search, followed by banner ads, but the fastest growing online ad formats are rich media and video ads.

Spending on U.S. online advertising among different industries is somewhat skewed. Retail accounts for the highest percentage (21%), followed by financial services (13%), automotive (12%), telecommunications (9%), leisure travel (9%), consumer electronics and computers (7%), consumer packaged goods (6%), pharmaceuticals and healthcare (5%), media (5%), and entertainment (4%) (Interactive Advertising Bureau/PricewaterhouseCoopers, 2015). Online advertising has both advantages and disadvantages when compared to advertising in traditional media, such as television, radio, and print (magazines and newspapers). One big advantage for online advertising is that the Internet is where the audience has moved, especially the very desirable 18–34 age group. A second big advantage for online advertising is the ability to target ads to individuals and small groups and to track performance of advertisements in almost real time. **Ad targeting**, the sending of market messages to specific subgroups in the population in an effort to increase the likelihood of a purchase, is as old as advertising itself, but prior to the Internet, it could only be done with much less precision, certainly not down to the level of individuals. Ad targeting is also the foundation of price discrimination: the ability to charge different types of consumers different prices for the same product or service. With online advertising, it's theoretically possible to charge every customer a different price.

Theoretically, online advertising can personalize every ad message to precisely fit the needs, interests, and values of each consumer. In practice, as we all know from spam and constant exposure to ads that are of little interest, the reality is very

ad targeting
the sending of market messages to specific subgroups in the population

different. Online advertisements also provide greater opportunities for interactivity—two-way communication between advertisers and potential customers. The primary disadvantages of online advertising are concerns about its cost versus its benefits, how to adequately measure its results, and the supply of good venues to display ads. For instance, the owners of Web sites who sell advertising space ("publishers") do not have agreed-upon standards or routine audits to verify their claimed numbers as do traditional media outlets. We examine the costs and benefits of online advertising as well as research on its effectiveness in Section 6.4.

Search Engine Marketing and Advertising

In 2015, companies will spend an estimated €75 billion on search engine marketing and advertising, about 48% of all spending for digital marketing. Briefly, this is where the eyeballs are (at least for a few moments) and this is where advertising can be very effective by responding with ads that match the interests and intentions of the user. The click-through rate for search engine advertising is generally 1%–4% (with an average of around 2%) and has been fairly steady over the years. The top search engine throughout Western Europe is Google, with over a 90% market share. **Search engine marketing (SEM)** refers to the use of search engines to build and sustain brands. **Search engine advertising** refers to the use of search engines to support direct sales to online consumers.

Search engines are often thought of as mostly direct sales channels focused on making sales in response to advertisements. While this is a major use of search engines, they are also used more subtly to strengthen brand awareness, drive traffic to other Web sites or blogs to support customer engagement, to gain deeper insight into customers' perceptions of the brand, to support other related advertising (for instance, sending consumers to local dealer sites), and to support the brand indirectly. Search engines can also provide marketers insight into customer search patterns, opinions customers hold about their products, top trending search keywords, and what their competitors are using as keywords and the customer response. For example, Pepsico, home of mega brands like Pepsi and Doritos, makes no sales on the Web, but has several branding Web sites aimed at consumers, investors, and shareholders. The focus is on building, sustaining, and updating the Pepsi collection of branded consumer goods. A search on Pepsi will generate numerous search results that link to Pepsi marketing materials.

Types of Search Engine Advertising Search engine sites originally performed unbiased searches of the Web's huge collection of Web pages and derived most of their revenue from banner advertisements. This form of search engine results is often called **organic search** because the inclusion and ranking of Web sites depends on a more or less "unbiased" application of a set of rules (an algorithm) imposed by the search engine. Since 1998, search engine sites slowly transformed themselves into digital yellow pages, where firms pay for inclusion in the search engine index, pay for keywords to show up in search results, or pay for keywords to show up in other vendors' ads.

---

search engine marketing (SEM)
involves the use of search engines to build and sustain brands

search engine advertising
involves the use of search engines to support direct sales to online

organic search
inclusion and ranking of sites depends on a more or less unbiased application of a set of rules imposed by the search engine

Most search engines offer **paid inclusion** programs, which, for a fee, guarantee a Web site's inclusion in its list of search results, more frequent visits by its Web crawler, and suggestions for improving the results of organic searching. Search engines claim that these payments—costing some merchants hundreds of thousands a year—do not influence the organic ranking of a Web site in search results, just inclusion in the results. However, it is the case that page inclusion ads get more hits, and the rank of the page appreciates, causing the organic search algorithm to rank it higher in the organic results.

Google claims that it does not permit firms to pay for their rank in the organic results, although it does allocate two to three sponsored links at the very top of their pages, albeit labeling them as "Sponsored Links." Merchants who refuse to pay for inclusion or for keywords typically fall far down on the list of results, and off the first page of results, which is akin to commercial death.

Pay-per-click (PPC) search ads are the primary type of search engine advertising. In **keyword advertising**, merchants purchase keywords through a bidding process at search sites, and whenever a consumer searches for that word, their advertisement shows up somewhere on the page, usually as a small text-based advertisement on the right, but also as a listing on the very top of the page. The more merchants pay, the higher the rank and greater the visibility of their ads on the page. Generally, the search engines do not exercise editorial judgment about quality or content of the ads although they do monitor the use of language. In addition, some search engines rank the ads in terms of their popularity rather than merely the money paid by the advertiser so that the rank of the ad depends on both the amount paid and the number of clicks per unit time. Google's keyword advertising program is called AdWords.

Network keyword advertising (context advertising), introduced by Google as its AdSense product in 2002, differs from the ordinary keyword advertising described previously. Publishers (Web sites that want to show ads) join these networks and allow the search engine to place "relevant" ads on their sites. The ads are paid for by advertisers who want their messages to appear across the Web. Google-like text messages are the most common. The revenue from the resulting clicks is split between the search engine and the site publisher, although the publisher gets much more than half in some cases.

Search engine advertising is nearly an ideal targeted marketing technique: at precisely the moment that a consumer is looking for a product, an advertisement for that product is presented. Consumers benefit from search engine advertising because ads for merchants appear only when consumers are looking for a specific product. Thus, search engine advertising saves consumers cognitive energy and reduces search costs (including the cost of transportation needed to do physical searches for products).

Because search engine marketing can be very effective, companies optimize their Web sites for search engine recognition. The better optimized the page is, the higher a ranking it will achieve in search engine result listings, and the more likely it will appear on the top of the page in search engine results. **Search engine optimization (SEO)** is the process of improving the ranking of Web pages with search engines by altering the content and design of the Web pages and site. By carefully selecting key words used on the Web pages, updating content frequently, and designing the site so

---

paid inclusion
for a fee, guarantees a Web site's inclusion in its list of sites, more frequent visits by its Web crawler, and suggestions for improving the results of organic searching

pay-per-click (PPC) search ad
primary type of search engine advertising

keyword advertising
merchants purchase keywords through a bidding process at search sites, and whenever a consumer searches for that word, their advertisement shows up somewhere on the page

network keyword advertising (context advertising)
publishers accept ads placed by Google on their Web sites, and receive a fee for any click-throughs from those ads

search engine optimization (SEO)
techniques to improve the ranking of Web pages generated by search engine algorithms

it can be easily read by search engine programs, marketers can improve the impact and return on investment in their Web marketing programs.

Google and other search engine firms make frequent changes to their search algorithms in order to improve the search results and user experience. Google, for instance, reportedly makes over 600 search engine changes in a year. Most are small unannounced tweaks. Recent major changes have included Panda, Penguin, Hummingbird, Knowledge Graph, and an unnamed algorithm that has been nicknamed Mobilegeddon. **Panda** was introduced in 2011 in an effort to weed out low quality sites from search results. Those sites with thin content, duplicate content, content copied from elsewhere on the Web, and content that did not attract high-quality hits from other sources were systematically pushed down in the search results. Google introduced **Penguin** in 2012 in an effort to punish Web sites and their SEO marketing firms who were manipulating links to their site in order to improve their rankings. The Google search engine rewards sites that have links from many other sites. What some marketers discovered is that Google could not tell the quality of these back links, and they began to manufacture links by putting their clients onto list sites, creating multiple blogs to link to their clients' sites, and paying others to link to their clients' sites. Penguin evaluates the quality of links to a site, and pushes down in the rankings those sites that have poor-quality back links.

Many search engines are attempting to capture more of what the user intended, or might like to know about a search subject. This is often referred to as semantic search. Google introduced **Hummingbird** in September 2013. Rather than evaluate each word separately in a search, Google's semantically informed Hummingbird will try to evaluate an entire sentence. Semantic search more closely follows conversational search, or search as you would ordinarily speak it to another human being.

Google introduced **Knowledge Graph** in 2012 as an effort to anticipate what you might want to know more about as you search on a topic or answer questions you might not thought of asking. Since 2013, results of Knowledge Graph appear on the right of the screen and contain more information about the topic or person you are searching on. Not all search terms have a Knowledge Graph result. Google displays information based on what other users have searched for in the past, as well as its database on over 1 billion objects (people, places, and things), and more than 18 billion facts.

In April 2015, Google released a new algorithm update (nicknamed Mobilegeddon) that made the "mobile-friendliness" of Web sites a much stronger ranking factor for mobile searches. Web sites that are not optimized for mobile now have a much lower ranking in mobile search results. And starting in November 2015, Google has announced that it will lower the search rank of mobile Web sites that display an ad that obscures the screen and asks users whether they would like to install the site's mobile app, on the grounds that such ads are less mobile-friendly. Companies that use such ads, such as Yelp, LinkedIn, Pinterest, and others, have charged that Google's new policy is in part an effort to protect its Web search revenue from mobile apps that lure users away from the Web.

Social Search **Social search** is an attempt to use your social contacts (and your entire social graph) to provide search results. In contrast to search engines that use a

---

Panda

change in the Google algorithm to eliminate low-quality sites from search results

Penguin

change in the Google algorithm to eliminate sites with low-quality back links

Hummingbird

semantic search component of Google's search algorithm

Knowledge Graph

function in Google's search engine that displays a selection of facts related to your search term that you may be interested in knowing more about

social search

effort to provide fewer, more relevant, and trustworthy results based on the social graph

mathematical algorithm to find pages that satisfy your query, social search reviews your friends' (and their friends') recommendations, past Web visits, and use of Like buttons. One problem with traditional search engines is that they are so thorough: enter a search for "smartphone" on Google and in .28 seconds you will receive 569 million results, some of which provide helpful information and others that are suspect. Social search is an effort to provide fewer, more relevant, and trustworthy results based on the social graph. Facebook's first effort to create a social search engine was Facebook Graph Search, which it launched in 2013. Graph Search produced information from within a user's network of friends supplemented with additional results provided by Bing. In December 2014, Facebook introduced a series of changes to Graph Search, dropping its relationship with Bing, rebranding the product as Facebook Search, and providing keyword search functionality that enables users to find people, photos, posts, videos, and links on Facebook by searching for words within a post. Results are ranked using a personalization algorithm based in part on the user's relationship to the poster.

Search Engine Issues While search engines have provided significant benefits to merchants and customers, they also present risks and costs. For instance, search engines have the power to crush a small business by placing its ads on the back pages of search results. Merchants are at the mercy of search engines for access to the online marketplace, and this access is dominated by a single firm, Google. How Google decides to rank one company over another in search results is not known. No one really knows how to improve in its rankings (although there are hundreds of firms who claim otherwise). Google editors intervene in unknown ways to punish certain Web sites and reward others. Using paid sponsored listings, as opposed to relying on organic search results, eliminates some, but not all, of this uncertainty.

Other practices that degrade the results and usefulness of search engines include:

- **Link farms** are groups of Web sites that link to one another, thereby boosting their ranking in search engines that use a PageRank algorithm to judge the "usefulness" of a site. For instance, in the 2010 holiday season, JCPenney was found to be the highest ranked merchant for a large number of clothing products. On examination, it was discovered that this resulted from Penney's hiring a search engine optimization company to create thousands of Web sites that linked to JCPenney's Web site. As a result, JCPenney's Web site became the most popular (most linked-to) Web site for products like dresses, shirts, and pants. No matter what popular clothing item people searched for, JCPenney came out on top. Experts believe this was the largest search engine fraud in history. Google's Panda series of updates to its search algorithms were aimed in part at eliminating link farms (Castell, 2014).

- **Content farms** are companies that generate large volumes of textual content for multiple Web sites designed to attract viewers and search engines. Content farms profit by attracting large numbers of readers to their sites and exposing them to ads. The content typically is not original but is artfully copied or summarized from legitimate content sites.

- **Click fraud** occurs when a competitor clicks on search engine results and ads, forcing the advertiser to pay for the click even though the click is not legitimate. Competitors

link farms
groups of Web sites that link to one another, thereby boosting their ranking in search engines

content farms
companies that generate large volumes of textual content for multiple Web sites designed to attract viewers and search engines

click fraud
occurs when a competitor clicks on search engine results and ads, forcing the advertiser to pay for the click even though the click is not legitimate

can hire offshore firms to perform fraudulent clicks or hire botnets to automate the process. Click fraud can quickly run up a large bill for merchants, and not result in any growth in sales. A study by the National Association of Advertisers estimated that advertisers would lose $6.3 billion in 2015 due to click fraud (Kirk, 2015).

Display Ad Marketing

In 2015, companies will spend around €68 billion on all forms of display ad marketing, about 44% of all spending for digital marketing. Around 6 trillion display ads will be served on desktop and mobile devices in 2015. The top five display ad companies in the United States are Facebook, Google, Twitter, Yahoo, and AOL, and together they account for 51% of U.S. display ad revenue. The Interactive Advertising Bureau (IAB), an industry organization, has established voluntary industry guidelines for display ads. Publishers are not required to use these guidelines, but many do. One objective of IAB is to give the consumer a consistent experience across all Web sites. The various types of ads are designed to help advertisers break through the "noise" and clutter created by the high number of display ad impressions that a typical user is exposed to within a given day. **Figure 6.6** shows examples of the seven core standard ad units, as specified by the IAB. According to Google, the top performing ad formats are the large rectangle, the medium rectangle, the leaderboard, and the half-page (Google Inc., 2015). Display ads consist of four different kinds of ads: banner ads, rich media ads (animated ads), sponsorships, and video ads.

banner ad
displays a promotional message in a rectangular box at the top or bottom of a computer screen

Banner Ads Banner ads are the oldest and most familiar form of display marketing. They are also the least effective and the lowest cost form of online marketing. A banner ad displays a promotional message in a rectangular box on the screen of a desktop computer or mobile device. A **banner ad** is similar to a traditional ad in a printed publication but has some added advantages. When clicked, it brings potential customers directly to the advertiser's Web site, and the site where the ad appears can observe the user's behavior on the site. The ability to identify and track the user is a key feature of online advertising. Banner ads often feature video and other animations. It's important to note that, although the terms banner ad and display ad are often used interchangeably, banner ads are just one form of display ad. Despite their limited effectiveness, advertisers will still spend about $12.1 billion on banner ads in 2015, about 44% of all spending on display ads, and 21% of total online ad spending.

rich media ad
ad employing animation, sound, and interactivity, using Flash, HTML5, Java, and JavaScript

Rich Media Ads Ads that employ animation, sound, and interactivity, using Flash, HTML5, Java, and JavaScript are referred to as **rich media ads**. They are far more effective than simple banner ads. For instance, one research report that analyzed 24,000 different rich media ads with more than 12 billion impressions served in North America over a six-month period found that exposure to rich media ads boosted advertiser site visits by nearly 300% compared to standard banner ads. Viewers of rich media ads that included video were six times more likely to visit the advertiser's Web site, by either directly clicking on the ad, typing the advertiser's URL, or searching

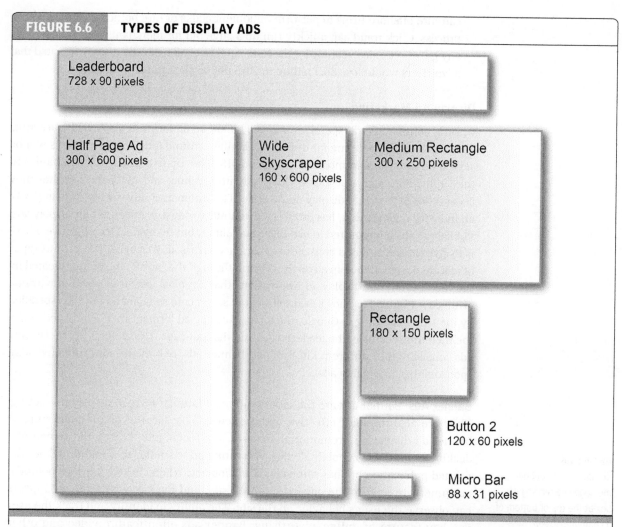

| FIGURE 6.6 | TYPES OF DISPLAY ADS |

Leaderboard
728 x 90 pixels

Half Page Ad
300 x 600 pixels

Wide Skyscraper
160 x 600 pixels

Medium Rectangle
300 x 250 pixels

Rectangle
180 x 150 pixels

Button 2
120 x 60 pixels

Micro Bar
88 x 31 pixels

In addition to the seven core forms of display ads shown above, IAB also provides standards for six new formats called Display Rising Star ad units.

SOURCE: Based on data from Interactive Advertising Bureau, 2011.

(MediaMind, 2012a). Recent research by the IAB indicates that its Rising Star ad units that can incorporate rich media elements deliver a 30% stronger brand lift than the traditional IAB core display ads with just one full exposure, increasing to over 40% when a consumer interacts with the ad. Rising Star ads also topped traditional display ads in terms of ad recall and were considered less annoying (IAB, 2015).

The IAB provides guidance for a number of different types of rich media ads, such as those that contain in-banner video, those that are expandable/retractable, pop-ups, floating versions, and interstitials. An **interstitial ad** (interstitial means "in between") is a way of placing a full-page message between the current and destination pages of a user. Interstitials are usually inserted within a single Web site, and displayed as the

interstitial ad
a way of placing a full-page message between the current and destination pages of a user

TABLE 6.5	TYPES OF VIDEO ADS	
FORMAT	DESCRIPTION	WHEN USED
Linear video ad	Pre-roll; takeover; ad takes over video for a certain period of time	Before, between, or after video
Nonlinear video ad	Overlay; ad runs at same time as video content and does not take over full screen	During, over, or within video
In-banner video ad	Rich media; ad is triggered within banner, may expand outside banner	Within Web page, generally surrounded by content
In-text video ad	Rich media; ad is delivered when user mouses over relevant text	Within Web page, identified as a highlighted word within relevant content

user moves from one page to the next. The interstitial is typically contained in its own browser window and moves automatically to the page the user requested after allowing enough time for the ad to be read. Interstitials can also be deployed over an advertising network and appear as users move among Web sites.

Because the Web is such a busy place, people have to find ways to cope with over-stimulation. One means of coping is known as *sensory input filtering*. This means that people learn to filter out the vast majority of the messages coming at them. Internet users quickly learn at some level to recognize banner ads or anything that looks like a banner ad and to filter out most of the ads that are not exceptionally relevant. Interstitial messages, like TV commercials, attempt to make viewers a captive of the message. Typical interstitials last 10 seconds or less and force the user to look at the ad for that time period. IAB standards for pre-roll ads also limit their length. To avoid boring users, ads typically use animated graphics and music to entertain and inform them. A good interstitial will also have a "skip through" or "stop" option for users who have no interest in the message.

The IAB also provides mobile rich media ad interface definitions (MRAID) in an effort to provide a set of standards designed to work with HTML5 and JavaScript that developers can use to create rich media ads to work with apps running on different mobile devices. The hope is make it easier to display ads across a wide variety of devices without having to rewrite code (Interactive Advertising Bureau, 2012).

video ad
TV-like advertisement that appears as an in-page video commercial or before, during, or after content

Video Ads Online **video ads** are TV-like advertisements that appear as in-page video commercials or before, during, or after a variety of content. **Table 6.5** describes some of the IAB standards for video ads. The most widely used format is the "pre-roll" (followed by the mid-roll and the post-roll) where users are forced to watch a video ad either before, in the middle of, or at the end of the video they originally clicked on. In 2014, the IAB released additional standards for five new in-stream and linear interactive video ad formats that enable advertisers to provide additional opportunities for consumer engagement.

Although from a total spending standpoint, online video ads are still very small when compared to the amount spent on search engine advertising, video ads are another fast growing form of online advertisement. The rapid growth in video ads is due in part to the fact that video ads are far more effective than other display ad formats. For instance, according to research analyzing a variety of ad formats, instream video ads had click-through rates 12 times that of rich media and 27 times that of standard banner ads (MediaMind, 2012). Research by the IAB indicates that interactive digital video has even greater impact than typical, non-interactive video formats, with interaction rates three to four times higher, and brand awareness heightened by more than 50% (Interactive Advertising Bureau, 2014).

There are many specialized video advertising networks that run video advertising campaigns for national advertisers and place these videos on their respective networks of Web sites. Firms can also establish their own video and television sites to promote their products. Retail sites are among the largest users of advertising videos. For instance, Zappos, the largest online shoe retailer, has a video for every one of its over 100,000 products.

Sponsorships A **sponsorship** is a paid effort to tie an advertiser's name to particular information, an event, or a venue in a way that reinforces its brand in a positive yet not overtly commercial manner. Sponsorships typically are more about branding than immediate sales. A common form of sponsorship is targeted content (or advertorials), in which editorial content is combined with an ad message to make the message more valuable and attractive to its intended audience. For instance, WebMD, the leading medical information Web site in the United States, displays sponsored pages on the WebMD Web site from companies such as Phillips to describe its home defibrillators, and Lilly to describe its pharmaceutical solutions for attention deficit disorders among children. Social media sponsorships, in which marketers pay for mentions in social media, such as blogs, tweets, or in online video, have also become a popular tactic. Sponsorships have also moved onto the mobile platform. For instance, Subaru sponsors an app called MapMyDogwalk, a GPS-enabled dog walking tool.

sponsorship
a paid effort to tie an advertiser's name to information, an event, or a venue in a way that reinforces its brand in a positive yet not overtly commercial manner

Native Advertising Advertising that looks similar to editorial content is known as **native advertising.** Native advertising is not new. Traditional native advertising includes television infomercials, newspaper advertorials, and entire sections of newspapers and magazines that are given over to advertisers, where the advertising looks similar to the rest of the publication. In the online world, native ads are most often found on social media, especially mobile social media, as part of a Facebook Newsfeed, Twitter Timeline, or Pinterest Promoted Pin. Mobile social networks do not have room for ads on the right side of the screen (the sidebar or right rail), and therefore native ads in the form of posts that look like other posts are the favored option.

native advertising
advertising that looks similar to editorial content

Typically, native ads mimic the editorial content around them. They appear outside the normal or expected area for ads and are labeled to indicate they are not editorial content, although in most cases the word "ad" is not used. On the Web or mobile screens, native ads are usually distinguished by a "sponsored" tag underneath the headline, often in a different color. Online native advertising is growing rapidly, especially on social networks. In 2015, native ad spending is expected to reach $4.3 billion (eMarketer, Inc., 2015f). Federal Trade Commission researchers found that 73% of online publishers offer native advertising, including the *New York Times*, which began the practice in 2014.

Researchers have found that 35% of online consumers cannot distinguish between editorial content and sponsored ads that look like editorial content, even if the ads are labelled as sponsored or promoted. Most consumers do not know what sponsored or promoted means. In a survey of 10,000 consumers, researchers found that consumers skip over labels like sponsored, and many do not understand the difference between paid and unpaid content (Franklin, 2013). Yet market researchers have found that native ads are far more influential with consumers. Consumers look at native ads 53% more frequently than display ads; native ads raise purchase intent by 18%; and consumers are twice as likely to share a native ad with a family member as a regular ad. Marketers and advertisers are opposed to labeling native advertising with the word "ad" and instead prefer other tags.

Native advertising is controversial. Critics contend that the purpose of native ads is to deceive or fool the consumer into thinking the ad has the same validity as the editorial content in media. The Federal Trade Commission held a conference in December 2013 to explore the native advertising phenomenon because of the potential to deceive consumers. Although the FTC has not as yet issued any specific guidelines with respect to native advertising, it has indicated that if publishers are involved in creating native advertising content, they can potentially be held liable for that content if it is misleading to consumers. Traditionally, the FTC has not held publishers responsible for misleading ads placed by advertisers (Lewis, 2015). Supporters argue that native ads add value by helping consumers, advertisers, and the media in which they are used (Federal Trade Commission, 2013).

Content Marketing Native advertising is usually focused on partnering with a specific publisher. **Content marketing** creates a content campaign for a brand and then tries to secure placement on a variety of Web site. Examples of content include articles, infographics, case studies, interactive graphics, white papers and even traditional press releases. The aim of content marketing is to increase visitors to a company's Web site, organic search rankings, and brand engagement via social media (Libert, 2015).

Advertising Networks In the early years of e-commerce, firms placed ads on the few popular Web sites in existence, but by early 2000, there were hundreds of thousands of sites where ads could be displayed, and it became very inefficient for a single firm to purchase ads on each individual Web site. Most firms, even very large firms, did not have the capability by themselves to place banner ads and marketing messages on thousands of Web sites and monitor the results. Specialized marketing firms called **advertising networks** appeared to help firms take advantage of the powerful marketing potential of the Internet, and to make the entire process of buying and selling

advertising networks
connect online marketers with publishers by displaying ads to consumers based on detailed customer information

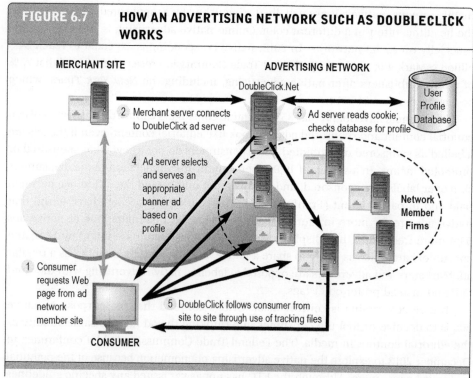

FIGURE 6.7 **HOW AN ADVERTISING NETWORK SUCH AS DOUBLECLICK WORKS**

MERCHANT SITE

ADVERTISING NETWORK
DoubleClick.Net

User Profile Database

2 Merchant server connects to DoubleClick ad server

3 Ad server reads cookie; checks database for profile

4 Ad server selects and serves an appropriate banner ad based on profile

Network Member Firms

1 Consumer requests Web page from ad network member site

5 DoubleClick follows consumer from site to site through use of tracking files

CONSUMER

Millions of publishers have audiences to sell, and pages to fill with ads. Thousands of advertisers are looking for audiences. Ad networks are intermediaries that connect publishers with marketers.

online ads more efficient and transparent. These ad networks have proliferated and have greatly increased the scale and liquidity of online marketing.

Advertising networks represent the most sophisticated application of Internet database capabilities to date, and illustrate just how different Internet marketing is from traditional marketing. Advertising networks sell advertising and marketing opportunities (slots) to companies who wish to buy exposure to an online audience (advertisers). Advertising networks obtain their inventory of ad opportunities from a network of participating sites that want to display ads on their sites in return for receiving a payment from advertisers everytime a visitor clicks on an ad. These sites are usually referred to as Web publishers. Marketers buy audiences and publishers sell audiences by attracting an audience and capturing audience information. Ad networks are the intermediaries who make this market work efficiently.

Figure 6.7 illustrates how these systems work. Advertising networks begin with a consumer requesting a page from a member of the advertising network (1). A connection is established with the third-party ad server (2). The ad server identifies the user by reading the cookie file on the user's hard drive and checks its user profile database for the user's profile (3). The ad server selects an appropriate banner ad based on the user's previous purchases, interests, demographics, or other data in the profile (4). Whenever the user later goes online and visits any of the network member sites, the ad server recognizes the user and serves up the same or different ads regardless of the site content. The advertising network follows users from site to site through the use of Web tracking files (5).

Advertising Exchanges, Programmatic Advertising, Real-Time Bidding Today, most online display advertising is being delivered by ad exchanges that use programmatic advertising and real-time bidding. An **ad exchange** is a digital marketplace that uses an automated auction-based method known as **programmatic advertising** to match supply and demand of online display advertising. Programmatic advertising uses a **real-time bidding (RTB) process** to match advertiser demand for display ads with publisher supply of Web page space. Publishers are able to sell their inventory of empty Web pages, often excess inventory that could not be sold directly. Want to contact males age 18 to 34, recent visitors to a car site, unmarried, high risk-taking profile, located in New York or California, urban home, and financial service industry employment? An ad exchange will allow you to bid in real time on this audience against other advertisers, and then manage the placement of ads, accounting, and measurement for your firm. Ad exchanges offer tremendous global scale and efficiency. One of the best known is Google's DoubleClick Ad Exchange, which is based on more than 100 ad networks (the supply side), and provides a computer-based market for buyers to purchase audiences (the demand side). This exchange sells audiences sliced into 1,600 interest categories. It displays more than 300 billion ad impressions a month across 2 million Web sites worldwide, and maintains or distributes more than 500 million user profiles of Internet users (Kantrowitz, 2013, 2015). These profiles are based on Web tracking files, offline purchase information, and social network data. Marketing firms, the buyers from publishers of Web sites, can target their audience and control the frequency and timing of ads during the day. The case study at the end of the chapter, *Programmatic Advertising: Real Time Marketing*, provides you with a further look at ad exchanges and real-time bidding.

Display Advertising Issues As with search engine advertising, online display advertising is not without its issues, which include both ad fraud (similar to click fraud) and concerns about viewability (whether display ads are actually being seen).

Ad Fraud. According to Interactive Advertising Bureau estimates, about 36% of all Web traffic is fake, and by extension, about the same percentage of clicks on ads are fake as well (Vranica, 2014). A study by the Association of National Advertisers and security company White Ops estimated that €5.7 billion will be lost worldwide as a result of ad fraud in 2015 (Kantrowitz, 2015). There are four primary sources of ad fraud. Botnets can be hired by publishers to click on their Web pages to create phony traffic. Second, a browser extension can insert ads into a premium publisher's Web site, and then list the ads as available on a programmatic ad exchange. Third, ad targeting firms can create bots that imitate the behavior of real shoppers, and then charge advertisers for successfully targeting consumers. Fourth, if you are a publisher looking to attract ads to your site, the simplest technique is simply to hire people in low-wage countries to click on your ads using a proxy server (Kantrowitz, 2014).

---

ad exchanges
auction-based digital marketplace where ad networks sell ad space to marketers

programmatic advertising
automated, auction-based method for matching demand and supply for online display ads

real-time bidding (RTB) process
used to match advertiser demand for display ads with publisher supply of Web page space

Large advertisers have begun to hire online fraud detection firms (a growth industry) to determine the extent of fraud in their campaigns. Verizon Wireless, L'Oreal, and Kellogg are among the firms that found millions of dollars of ad fraud in recent campaigns, and have demanded advertising networks to either reimburse them or generate real Web traffic in the amount of the fraud.

Viewability.   Recent research by Google revealed that 56% of the impressions served across its display advertising platforms, including DoubleClick, are not viewable. Previous research by comScore showed similar results: 54% of display ads, and 57% of video ads, were not in fact seen by people, even though advertisers were charged for generating ad impressions and serving ads (comScore, 2013). There are a number of reasons for this situation. First, there is no mechanism for measuring how many people actually see an online ad that has been served. The same is true of most offline print and TV advertising, although several methods and certifications have been developed over decades to accurately measure audience exposure. There are no such mechanisms for online advertising. Second, a large percentage of ads served appear lower down on the screen where users are less likely to go, or video ads on auto-play are playing in areas the user cannot see. Advertisers are still charged for ads that are served but not viewed. Unscrupulous publishers can place multiple ads on top of each other and charge multiple times for the same page space (Segal, 2014). Third, botnets can be programmed to click on ads on fraudulent Web sites, generating impressions and ad serves, but no one actually sees the ads. The Media Rating Council, an advertising industry group, released a very low standard for "viewability" in 2014: an ad is considered viewable if half of the ad can be viewed for at least one second. For video ads, half of the video needs to be viewable for two seconds (Hof, 2014). A revised version of the guidelines issued in August 2015 addressed some additional specific issues, but did not alter the baseline standard. The advertisers who pay for online ads are beginning to demand guarantees of viewability. Several companies, including comScore, are offering tagging technology that can partially measure viewability (Vranica, 2014). Unviewed ads are just as profitable as viewed ads for Web publishers and advertising agencies. For advertisers, they represent the half of marketing expenditures that is wasted.

Ad Blocking.   Over the past several years, use of ad-blocking software, which can eliminate display ads, pre-roll video ads, retargeted ads, and some types of native ads on desktops and laptops, has been growing. Ad blockers operate in a manner very similar to a firewall, recognizing and eliminating content based on IP address. Ad blockers have become very easy to install, with programs such as Adblock Plus offered as extensions for Firefox, Chrome, and other Web browsers. Currently, about 10% to 15% of Internet users in the United States are estimated to be employing ad blockers, with their most prevalent use among the younger, more technically advanced audience. Gaming, newsgroup/forums, and social network sites are the most frequently affected by ad-blocking. Although advertisers are not yet panicked about ad blocking, it is a trend that they are watching with increasing concern. Some Web sites, such as Wired, The Guardian, and OKCupid have made a direct appeal to their users to turn off their ad-blockers or to make a donation instead.

E-mail Marketing

direct e-mail marketing
e-mail marketing messages sent directly to interested users

When e-mail marketing began, unsolicited e-mail was not common. **Direct e-mail marketing** (e-mail marketing messages sent directly to interested users) was one of the first and most effective forms of online marketing communications. Direct e-mail marketing messages are sent to an opt-in audience of Internet users who, at one time or another, have expressed an interest in receiving messages from the advertiser. By sending e-mail to an opt-in audience, advertisers are targeting interested consumers. By far, in-house e-mail lists are more effective than purchased e-mail lists. Because of the comparatively high response rates and low cost, direct e-mail marketing remains a common form of online marketing communications. Other benefits of e-mail marketing include its mass reach, the ability to track and measure response, the ability to personalize content and tailor offers, the ability to drive traffic to Web sites for more interaction, the ability to test and optimize content and offers, and the ability to target by region, demographic, time of day, or other criteria. In 2015, although companies will spend a relatively small amount on e-mail marketing when compared to search and display ad marketing, e-mail marketing still packs a punch with solid customer response. Click-through rates for legitimate e-mail depend on the promotion (the offer), the product, and the amount of targeting, but average around 3%–4%. Despite the deluge of spam mail, e-mail remains a highly cost-effective way of communicating with existing customers, and to a lesser extent, finding new customers. Mobile devices have become the predominant method for accessing e-mail. A survey by Movable Ink showed that 67% of all email sent on its platform in the first quarter of 2015 were opened on a smartphone or tablet computer, while only 33% were opened on a desktop or laptop (Silverpop, 2015; eMarketer, Inc., 2015g).

E-mail marketing and advertising is inexpensive and somewhat invariant to the number of mails sent. The cost of sending 1,000 e-mails is about the same as the cost to send 1 million. The primary cost of e-mail marketing is for the purchase of the list of names to which the e-mail will be sent. This generally costs anywhere from 5 to 20 cents a name, depending on how targeted the list is. Sending the e-mail is virtually cost-free. In contrast, the cost to acquire the name, print, and mail a 5 x 7-inch direct mail post card is around 75 to 80 cents a name.

While e-mail marketing often is sales-oriented, it can also be used as an integral feature of a multi-channel marketing campaign designed to strengthen brand recognition. Personalization and targeting are major themes in e-mail marketing in 2015. For instance, Jeep created an e-mail campaign to a targeted audience who had searched on SUVs, and visited Chrysler and Jeep Facebook pages. The e-mail campaign announced a contest based on a game users could play online that involved tracking an arctic beast with a Jeep. Recipients could sign up on Facebook, Twitter, or the Jeep blog.

spam
unsolicited commercial e-mail

Although e-mail can still be an effective marketing and advertising tool, it faces three main challenges: spam, software tools used to control spam that eliminate much e-mail from user inboxes, and poorly targeted purchased e-mail lists. **Spam** is unsolicited commercial e-mail (sometimes referred to as "junk" e-mail) and *spammers* are people who send unsolicited e-mail to a mass audience that has not expressed any interest in the product. Spammers tend to market pornography, fraudulent deals and services, scams, and other products not widely approved in most civilized societies.

Legitimate direct opt-in e-mail marketing is not growing as fast as behaviorally targeted display ads and search engine advertising because of the explosion in spam. Consumer response to even legitimate e-mail campaigns has become more sophisticated. In general, e-mail works well for maintaining customer relationships but poorly for acquiring new customers.

While click fraud may be the Achilles' heel of search engine advertising, spam is the nemesis of effective e-mail marketing and advertising. The percentage of all e-mail that is spam averaged around 52.5% in the first 7 months of 2015, down about 10% from the comparable period in 2014 (Symantec, 2015). Most spam originates from bot networks, which consist of thousands of captured PCs that can initiate and relay spam messages (see Chapter 4). Spam volume has declined somewhat since authorities took down the Rustock botnet in 2011. Spam is seasonally cyclical, and varies monthly due to the impact of new technologies (both supportive and discouraging of spammers), new prosecutions, and seasonal demand for products and services.

Legislative attempts in the United States to control spam have been mostly unsuccessful. Thirty-seven states have laws regulating or prohibiting spam (National Conference of State Legislatures, 2015). State legislation typically requires that unsolicited mail (spam) contain a label in the subject line ("ADV") indicating the message is an advertisement, requires a clear opt-out choice for consumers, and prohibits e-mail that contains false routing and domain name information (nearly all spammers hide their own domain, ISP, and IP address).

The U.S. Congress passed the first national anti-spam law ("Controlling the Assault of Non-Solicited Pornography and Marketing" or CAN-SPAM Act) in 2003, and it went into effect in January 2004. The act does not prohibit unsolicited e-mail (spam) but instead requires unsolicited commercial e-mail messages to be labeled (though not by a standard method) and to include opt-out instructions and the sender's physical address. It prohibits the use of deceptive subject lines and false headers in such messages. The FTC is authorized (but not required) to establish a "Do Not E-mail" registry. State laws that require labels on unsolicited commercial e-mail or prohibit such messages entirely are pre-empted, although provisions merely addressing falsity and deception may remain in place. The act imposes fines of $10 for each unsolicited pornographic e-mail and authorizes state attorneys general to bring lawsuits against spammers. The act obviously makes lawful legitimate bulk mailing of unsolicited e-mail messages (what most people call spam), yet seeks to prohibit certain deceptive practices and provide a small measure of consumer control by requiring opt-out notices. In this sense, critics point out, CAN-SPAM ironically legalizes spam as long as spammers follow the rules. For this reason, large spammers have been among the bill's biggest supporters, and consumer groups have been the act's most vociferous critics.

In contrast, Canada's anti-spam law is one of the toughest in the world. Unlike the CAN-SPAM Act, Canada's law is based on an opt-in model and prohibits the sending of commercial e-mail, texts, and social media messaging unless the recipient has given his or her consent. Violations of the law can lead to penalties of up to $1 million for individuals and $10 million for organizations. The first phase of the law went into effect in July 2014. The law applies anytime a computer within Canada is used to send or access an electronic message, so companies located within the United States that send e-mail to Canada must comply with the law (French, 2014).

There have been a number of state and federal prosecutions of spammers, and private civil suits by large ISPs such as Microsoft. Volunteer efforts by industry are another potential control point. Notably, the Direct Marketing Association (DMA), an industry trade group that represents companies that use the postal mail system as well as e-mail for solicitations, is now strongly supporting legislative controls over spam, in addition to its voluntary guidelines. The DMA would like to preserve the legitimate use of e-mail as a marketing technique. The DMA has formed a 15-person anti-spam group and spends $500,000 a year trying to identify spammers. The DMA is also a supporter of the National Cyber-Forensics & Training Alliance (NCFTA), a nonprofit organization with close ties to the FBI. NCFTA operates a variety of initiatives aimed at combating cybercrime, including digital phishing via spam.

Affiliate Marketing

affiliate marketing
commissions paid by advertisers to affiliate Web sites for referring potential customers to their Web site

Affiliate marketing is a form of marketing where a firm pays a commission, typically anywhere between 4% to 20%, to other Web sites (including blogs) for sending customers to their Web site. Affiliate marketing generally involves pay-for-performance: the affiliate or affiliate network gets paid only if users click on a link or purchase a product (Robinson, 2014). Industry experts estimate that around 10% of all retail online sales are generated through affiliate programs (as compared to search engine ads, which account for more than 30% of online sales), and affiliate programs run by the Internet Retailer Top 500 have a median of 2,000 participating affiliates.

Visitors to an affiliate Web site typically click on ads and are taken to the advertiser's Web site. In return, the advertiser pays the affiliate a fee, either on a per-click basis or as a percentage of whatever the customer spends on the advertiser's site. Paying commissions for referrals or recommendations long predated the Web.

For instance, Amazon has a strong affiliate program consisting of more than 1 million participant sites, called Associates, which receive up to 10% in advertising fees on sales their referrals generate. Affiliates attract people to their blogs or Web sites where they can click on ads for products at Amazon. Members of eBay's Affiliates Program can earn between 50% and 75% of eBay's revenue on winning bids and Buy It Now transactions as well as between $20 and $35 for each active registered user sent to eBay. Amazon, eBay, and other large e-commerce companies with affiliate programs typically administer such programs themselves. Smaller e-commerce firms who wish to use affiliate marketing often decide to join an affiliate network (sometimes called an affiliate broker), such as CJ Affiliate and Rakuten Linkshare, which acts as an intermediary. Bloggers often sign up for Google's AdSense program to attract advertisers to their sites. They are paid for each click on an ad and sometimes for subsequent purchases made by visitors.

Viral Marketing

viral marketing
the process of getting customers to pass along a company's marketing message to friends, family, and colleagues

Just as affiliate marketing involves using a trusted Web site to encourage users to visit other sites, **viral marketing** is a form of social marketing that involves getting customers to pass along a company's marketing message to friends, family, and colleagues. It's the online version of word-of-mouth advertising, which spreads even faster and further than in the real world. In the offline world, next to television, word of mouth is the second most important means by which consumers find out about new products. And the most important factor in the decision to purchase is the face-to-face recommendations of parents, friends, and colleagues. Millions of online adults in the United States are "influencers" who share their opinions about products in a variety of online settings. In addition to increasing the size of a company's customer base, customer referrals also have other advantages: they are less expensive to acquire because existing customers do all the acquisition work, and they tend to use online support services less, preferring to turn back to the person who referred them for advice. Also, because they cost so little to acquire and keep, referred customers begin to generate profits for a company much earlier than customers acquired through other marketing methods. There are a number of online venues where viral marketing appears. E-mail used to be the primary online venue for viral marketing ("please forward this e-mail to your friends"), but venues such as Facebook, Pinterest, Instagram, Twitter, YouTube, and blogs now play a major role. For example, the most viral video ad of 2014 was a video featuring the singer Shakira that promoted the FIFA World Cup, with over 7.3 million shares and 560 million views as of August 2015 (Koerber, 2014).

Lead Generation Marketing

Lead generation marketing uses multiple e-commerce presences to generate leads for businesses who later can be contacted and converted into customers through sales calls, e-mail, or other means. In one sense, all Internet marketing campaigns attempt to develop leads. But lead generation marketing is a specialized subset of the Internet marketing industry that provides consulting services and software tools to collect and manage leads for firms, and to convert these leads to customers. Companies will spend an estimated $2.2 billion on lead generation marketing in 2015. Sometimes called "inbound marketing," lead generation marketing firms help other firms build Web sites, launch e-mail campaigns, use social network sites and blogs to optimize the generation of leads, and then manage those leads by initiating further contacts, tracking interactions, and interfacing with customer relationship management systems to keep track of customer-firm interactions. One of the foremost lead generation marketing firms is Hubspot, which has developed a software suite for generating and managing leads.

lead generation marketing
uses multiple e-commerce presences to generate leads for businesses who later can be contacted and converted into customers

SOCIAL, MOBILE, AND LOCAL MARKETING AND ADVERTISING

In this section we provide a very brief overview of the social, mobile, and local marketing and advertising landscape. Then, in Chapter 7, we provide a much more in-depth examination of social, mobile, and local marketing and advertising tools.

Social Marketing and Advertising

Social marketing/advertising involves the use of online social networks and communities to build brands and drive sales revenues. There are several kinds of social networks, from Facebook, Twitter, Pinterest, and Instagram, to social apps, social games, blogs, and forums (Web sites that attract people who share a community of interests or skills). In 2015, companies are expected to spend about €23 billion on social network marketing and advertising. Next to mobile marketing, it is the fastest growing type of online marketing. Nevertheless, in 2015, it represents only about 15% of all online marketing and is still dwarfed by the amount spent on search engine advertising and display advertising (eMarketer, Inc., 2015h).

Marketers cannot ignore the huge audiences that social networks such as Facebook, Twitter, Pinterest, and Instagram are gathering, which rival television and radio in size. In 2015, there were about 1.5 billion Facebook members, 320 million active Twitter users, around 400 million Instagram users, and around 100 million Pinterest members worldwide. It's little wonder that marketers and advertisers are joyous at the prospect of connecting with this large audience. Research has found that social network users are more likely to talk about and recommend a company or product they follow on Facebook or Twitter.

Social networks offer advertisers all the main advertising formats, including banner ads (the most common), short pre-roll and post-roll ads associated with videos, and sponsorship of content. Having a corporate Facebook page is in itself a marketing tool for brands just like a Web page. Many firms, such as Coca-Cola, have shut down product-specific Web pages and instead use Facebook pages.

Blogs and online games can also be used for social marketing. Blogs have been around for a decade and are a part of the mainstream online culture (see Chapter 2 for a description of blogs). Around 28 million people write blogs, and around 79 million read blogs in the United States. Blogs play a vital role in online marketing. Although more firms use Twitter and Facebook, these sites have not replaced blogs, and in fact often point to blogs for long-form content. Because blog readers and creators tend to be more educated, have higher incomes, and be opinion leaders, blogs are ideal platforms for ads for many products and services that cater to this kind of audience. Because blogs are based on the personal opinions of the writers, they are also an ideal platform to start a viral marketing campaign. Advertising networks that specialize in blogs provide some efficiency in placing ads, as do blog networks, which are collections of a small number of popular blogs, coordinated by a central management team, and which can deliver a larger audience to advertisers. For more information on social marketing using blogs, see Learning Track 6.3.

The online gaming marketplace continues to expand rapidly as users increasingly play games on smartphones and tablets, as well as PCs and consoles. The story of game advertising in 2015 is social, mobile, and local: social games are ascendant, mobile devices are the high-growth platform, and location-based advertising is starting to show real traction. The objective of game advertising is both branding and driving customers to purchase moments at restaurants and retail stores. In 2015, around 165 million Americans play games on their mobile phones, about 49 million play on consoles, while about 116 million play on tablets. Of the online gamers, about 86 million play social games, such as Jackbox Games' You Don't Know Jack. Advertisers are expected to spend about $310 million on in-game social game advertising in 2015 (eMarketer, Inc., 2015i).

Mobile Marketing and Advertising

Marketing on the mobile platform is growing rapidly and becoming a very significant part (42%) of the overall €156 billion online marketing spending. In 2015, spending on all forms of mobile marketing is estimated to be about €96 billion, and it is expected to almost double, to €182 billion, by 2019 (eMarketer, Inc., 2015e). A number of factors are driving advertisers to the mobile platform, including much more powerful devices, faster networks, wireless local networks, rich media and video ads, and growing demand for local advertising by small business and consumers. Most important, mobile is where the eyeballs are now and increasingly will be in the future: about 2.25 billion people access the Internet at least some of the time from mobile devices.

Mobile marketing includes the use of display banner ads, rich media, video, games, e-mail, text messaging, in-store messaging, Quick Response (QR) codes, and couponing. Mobile is now a required part of the standard marketing budget. In 2015, display ads are expected to be the most popular mobile advertising format in the U.S., accounting for about 51% of all mobile ad spending. Display ads can be served as a part of a mobile Web site or inside apps and games. Facebook is the leader in mobile display ad revenues, followed by Google and Twitter. Search advertising is also a popular format, and is expected to account for about 44% of U.S. mobile ad spending in 2015. Search ads can be further optimized for the mobile platform by showing ads based on the physical location of the user. Mobile messaging generally involves SMS text messaging to consumers offering coupons or flash marketing messages. Messaging is especially effective for local advertising because consumers can be sent messages and coupons as they pass by or visit locations. Video advertising currently accounts for a small percentage of mobile ad spending, but is one of the fastest growing formats. Ad networks such as Google's AdMob, Apple's iAd, Twitter's MoPub, inMobi (see the opening case), and Millennial Media are also important players in the mobile advertising market.

Apps on mobile devices constitute a marketing platform that did not exist a few years ago. Apps are a nonbrowser pathway for users to experience the Web and perform a number of tasks from reading the newspaper to shopping, searching, and buying. Apps provide users much faster access to content than do multi-purpose browsers. Apps are also starting to influence the design and function of traditional Web sites as consumers are attracted to the look and feel of apps, and their speed of operation. There are over 3 million apps available on Apple's App Store and Google Play and another million apps provided by Internet carriers and third-party storefronts like the Amazon Appstore, GetJar, and Appia. An estimated 2 billion people will use apps in 2015 worldwide (SocialMediaToday.com, 2013).

Local Marketing: The Social-Mobile-Local Nexus

Along with social marketing and mobile marketing, local marketing is the third major trend in e-commerce marketing in 2015–2016. The growth of mobile devices has accelerated the growth of local search and purchasing. New marketing tools like local advertisements on social networks and daily deal sites are also contributing to local marketing growth.

Spending on online local ads in the United States is estimated at around $36 billion in 2015. The mobile portion of local advertising spending is expected to reach $6.6 billion in 2015 (BIA/Kelsey, 2015a). In contrast, spending on traditional local advertising is expected to be flat during the same time period. The most common local marketing tools are geotargeting using Google Maps (local stores appearing on a Google map), display ads in hyperlocal publications like those created by Patch Properties, daily deals, and coupons.

The most commonly used venues include Facebook, Google, Amazon Local, LinkedIn, Yahoo, Bing, and Twitter, as well as more specific location-based offerings such as Google My Business, Yahoo Local, Citysearch, YP, SuperPages, and Yelp. The "daily deal" coupon sites, Groupon and LivingSocial, and location-based mobile firms such as Foursquare are also a significant part of this trend.

We examine social, mobile, and local marketing in much greater depth in Chapter 7.

MULTI-CHANNEL MARKETING: INTEGRATING ONLINE AND OFFLINE MARKETING

Without an audience, marketing is not possible. With the rapid growth of the Internet, media consumption patterns have changed greatly as consumers are more and more likely to engage with online media, from videos and news sites, to blogs, Twitter feeds, Facebook friends, and Pinterest posts. Increasingly, marketers are using multiple online channels to "touch" customers, from e-mail to Facebook, search ads, display ads on mobile devices, and affiliate programs. Forrester Research reports, for instance, that most customers purchased online following some Web marketing influence, and nearly half of online purchases followed multiple exposures to Web marketing efforts (Forrester Research, 2014a).

In 2013, for the first time ever, the average U.K. adult spent more time with digital media per day than the amount viewing TV. In 2015, the average U.K. adult will spend about 5 and a half hours a day online and using a mobile device for something other than telephone calls, compared to about three hours watching television (see **Figure 6.8**) (eMarketer, Inc., 2015a). An increasing percentage of media consumers multitask by using several media at once in order to increase the total media exposure. In this environment, marketers increasingly are developing multi-channel marketing programs that can take advantage of the strengths of various media, and reinforce branding messages across media. Online marketing is not the only way, or by itself the best way, to engage consumers. Internet campaigns can be significantly strengthened by also using e-mail, TV, print, and radio. The marketing communications campaigns most successful at driving traffic to a Web site have incorporated both online and offline tactics, rather than relying solely on one or the other. Several research studies have shown that the most effective online advertisements are those that use consistent imagery with campaigns running in other media at the same time.

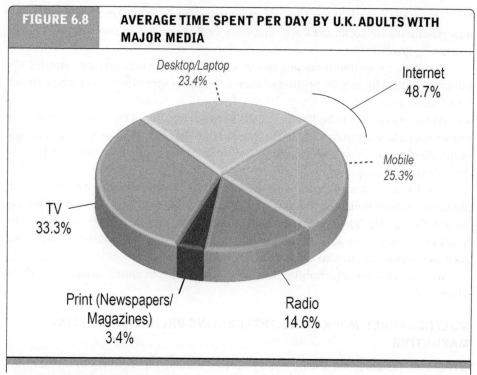

FIGURE 6.8	AVERAGE TIME SPENT PER DAY BY U.K. ADULTS WITH MAJOR MEDIA

Desktop/Laptop 23.4%

Internet 48.7%

Mobile 25.3%

TV 33.3%

Print (Newspapers/ Magazines) 3.4%

Radio 14.6%

Online marketing should be coupled with offline marketing to achieve optimal effectiveness.
SOURCE: Based on data from eMarketer, Inc., 2015a.

Insight on Business: Are the Very Rich Different from You and Me? examines how luxury goods providers use online marketing in conjunction with their offline marketing efforts.

OTHER ONLINE MARKETING STRATEGIES

In addition to the "traditional" online marketing and advertising tools we have previously discussed, such as search engine, display, and e-mail marketing, and the newer social, mobile, and local marketing and advertising tools, there are also a number of other, more focused online marketing strategies. Here we examine tools aimed at customer retention, pricing, and a strategy known as the "long tail."

Customer Retention Strategies

The Internet offers several extraordinary marketing techniques for building a strong relationship with customers and for differentiating products and services.

Personalization, One-to-One Marketing, and Interest-based Advertising (Behavioral Targeting)

No Internet-based marketing technique has received more popular and academic comment than "one-to-one" or "personalized marketing." **One-to-one marketing (personalization)** segments the market on the basis of individuals (not

one-to-one marketing (personalization) segmenting the market based on a precise and timely understanding of an individual's needs, targeting specific marketing messages to these individuals, and then positioning the product vis-à-vis competitors to be truly unique

INSIGHT ON BUSINESS

ARE THE VERY RICH DIFFERENT FROM YOU AND ME?

"Let me tell you about the very rich. They are different from you and me." So observed F. Scott Fitzgerald in the short story, "The Rich Boy." Palm Beach has its Worth Avenue, New York has its Fifth Avenue, Los Angeles has its Rodeo Drive, and Chicago has the Magnificent Mile. So where do the rich go to get that $5,000 cocktail dress or that $3,000 Italian suit online? It turns out they may not be so different from the rest of us: they look for online deals and situations where quality can be had at a bargain. At Net-a-Porter, an online luxury brand store and content site, for instance, you can find a Gucci two-tone silk wrap dress for $1,750 that looks smashing with a pair of Gucci patent-leather knee boots for $1,595. There's free shipping too!

Even experts find it hard to define what it means to be affluent. There are about 24 million households (20% of all U.S. households) with household income of $100,000 or above. These are often referred to as HENRYs (High Earnings, Not Yet Rich). But the really affluent (sometimes called the hyperaffluent) are those 2.4 million (the top 2% of U.S. households) that earn more than $250,000 a year. And then there are the 9 million households (0.7% of households) that earn more than $1 million a year. These are the ultra-rich.

Retail consumption in general is highly skewed: the wealthiest top 10% of households account for about 50% of all retail spending and over 35% of all e-commerce retail spending. Wealthy Americans are opening their wallets to spend on expensive clothing, accessories, jewelry, and beauty products. In fact, in 2014, the United States replaced China as the leader in luxury spending around the world. The trend is continuing in 2015, with 42% of the hyperaffluent intending to purchase more luxury items than in 2014, along with about 33% of the HENRYs, with over 80% indicating they plan to purchase luxury products online. A 2015 McKinsey report notes what consumers hear or see online influences almost 50% of luxury product buying decisions.

One of the largest fashion destinations is Net-a-Porter. Luxury goods designers would not even consider selling to the site when it initially launched in 2000. Affluent women in that period only bought clothes they had seen, touched and tried on. That all has changed in the last decade, and in 2014, Net-a-Porter had revenue of over $800 million. It currently sells over 400 of the world's most fashionable high-end brands from Gucci to Tory Burch and Burberry and was also recently selected by Chanel as the exclusive online vendor for Chanel's first fine jewelry collection. Net-a-Porter's Web site has 9 million visitors a month and it has 4 million followers on social media. The average customer is 39 years old, travels 11 times a year, has an average income of $282,000, and spends $21,000 a year on clothing. On balance, these customers are at the low end of the truly affluent or at the top end of the HENRYs. In 2015, Net-a-Porter launched an app called the Net Set in an effort to create a mobile social commerce network for luxury consumers. The app will provide a live feed of trending luxury items, and provide each designer with its own mobile brand portal.

Even the rich are not immune to the lure of a good deal. The problem is that luxury retailers are typically loath to offer sales because they believe sales detract from their reputations. To get around this problem, luxury retailers often offer "secret" discounts via flash e-mail campaigns and private online sales in which selected online customers are e-mailed alerts. Neiman Marcus calls them Midday Dash sales: two-hour online-only sales with 50% off on luxury goods that can be purchased only by clicking a link in the e-mail.

Luxury retailers have another dilemma: they need to attract not just the ultra-affluent, but also the aspirational HENRYs who are far more numerous and anxious to display their wealth. They need to be both exclusive and accessible. One solution is the so-called Mercedes Benz strategy: build luxurious but affordable cars for the HENRYs while maintaining a focus on high-end truly luxury models for the ultra-affluent. Mercedes Benz combines a dual level product strategy with effective use of social and mobile media. Mercedes' Facebook page is a main hub of interaction between the brand and its customers, with over 18 million fans entertained with sweepstakes, videos, images, news, and links to its blog for additional insight into why Mercedes is unique and worth all that money. Mercedes also uses Twitter, YouTube, Instagram, Pinterest, and a dozen mobile apps to engage a broader range of customers by providing personalized video tours of its cars.

The explosion of social media and the increasing investments in the online channel by luxury companies has reinforced and enlarged the community of those who explore, comment upon, and eventually purchase luxury goods. Luxury companies are more than doubling their fans on Facebook annually in recognition of the link between online and offline purchases. Burberry Group, the United Kingdom's largest luxury goods maker, reports that it obtains the most reach and most response from digital initiatives compared with other media. To promote the Burberry Body fragrance, the London-based company offered exclusive samples to its Facebook fans. It received more than 225,000 requests in little more than a week.

Developing an online marketing approach that increases a company's access to consumers while retaining an image of exclusivity was the challenge faced by Tiffany & Co. The company is in the enviable position of being perhaps the most famous jewelry company in the United States. Tiffany's offline marketing communications seek to engender feelings of beauty, quality, and timeless style—all hallmarks of the Tiffany brand. How does Tiffany maintain its approach on the Web, a medium that often emphasizes speed and flashy graphics over grace and elegance, and low-cost bargains over high-priced exclusive fashion? The Web, for the most part, is all about low prices and great deals—concepts that are anathema to the high-fashion merchants like Tiffany. The answer is apparent in a visit to the Tiffany Web site. The site features limited inventory, with a focus on high-resolution images of its exclusive and original designs in jewelry and apparel. There are no sales, coupons, discounts, or other offers although visitors can choose jewelry in lower price ranges (less than $250 for instance). The Web site and Facebook brand page reflect custom service and design, calm, and simplicity. The prices are equally exclusive: an exquisite Atlas Hinged Bangle in 18k rose gold and round brilliant diamonds for $9,000, and sunglasses for $500.

Today, Tiffany has shifted more of its direct marketing effort from the offline catalog to the online catalog and an increasing social media presence, including Facebook (over 7 million Likes), Instagram, Pinterest, Twitter, Tumblr, and YouTube. It has Web sites in 13 different countries, including Canada, the United Kingdom, Japan, and Australia. Tiffany sites carry over 2,100 products in six categories of goods: engagement, jewelry, watches, designers and collections, gifts, and accessories. In 2014, Tiffany's online sales were $256 million, 6% of its $4.25 billion worldwide sales, placing it in third place in the online jewelry industry.

SOURCES: "Affluents Give Digital the Luxury Treatment," eMarketer, Inc., July 9, 2015; "Net-A-Porter Unveils New Weapon in Luxury E-commerce Battle," by Phil Wahba, Fortune.com, May 12, 2015; "The Opportunity in Online Luxury Fashion," by Jennifer Schmidt et al., McKinsey & Company, February 2015; "Athena Magtail: Net-A-Porter's Porter," by Lucie Green, Lsnglobal.com, April 1, 2014; "Luxury Goods Worldwide Market Study Spring 2014," by Bain & Company, May 19, 2014; "Luxury Report 2014: Ultimate Six-Year Guide to the Luxury Consumer Market," by Unity Marketing Inc., January 2014; "The Luxury Consumer," by Patricia Orsini, eMarketer, Inc., November 2013; "Louis Vuitton Walks the Fine Luxury Line," by Renee Schultes, *Wall Street Journal*, April 14, 2013; "Luxury Marketing: Recreating the One-on-One Experience With Mobile," eMarketer, Inc. (Patricia Orsini), September 2012; "Affluents: Demographic Profile and Marketing Approach," eMarketer, Inc. (Mark Dolliver), January 2012; "Affluent Shoppers and Luxury Brand Retailers Online," eMarketer, Inc. (Jeffrey Grau), September 2011.

groups), based on a precise and timely understanding of their needs, targeting specific marketing messages to these individuals, and then positioning the product vis-à-vis competitors to be truly unique. One-to-one marketing is the ultimate form of market segmentation, targeting, and positioning—where the segments are individuals.

The movement toward market segmentation has been ongoing since the development of systematic market research and mass media in the 1930s. However, e-commerce and the Internet are different in that they enable personalized one-to-one marketing to occur on a mass scale. A recent survey found that over 90% of marketers either use or intend to use personalization for online customer interactions in 2015. Real-time personalization (data-driven personalization that is completed in under one second) is becoming an important tool, used by almost 60% of marketers surveyed (Evergage, 2015).

The Amazon and Barnes & Noble Web sites are good examples of personalization at work. Both sites greet registered visitors (based on cookie files), recommend recent books based on user preferences (stored in a user profile in their database) as well as what other consumers purchased, and expedite checkout procedures based on prior purchases.

behavioral targeting involves using the online and offline behavior of consumers to adjust the advertising messages delivered to them online, often in real time (milliseconds from the consumer's first URL entry). The intent is to increase the efficiency of marketing and advertising, and to increase the revenue streams of firms who are in a position to behaviorally target visitors. Because behavioral targeting as a label has somewhat unfavorable connotations, the online advertising industry, led by Google, has introduced a new name for behavioral targeting. They call it **interest-based advertising (IBA)**.

One of the original promises of the Web has been that it can deliver a marketing message tailored to each consumer based on this data, and then measure the results in terms of click-throughs and purchases. If you are visiting a jewelry site, you would be shown jewelry ads. If you entered a search query like "diamonds," you would be shown text ads for diamonds and other jewelry. This was taken one step further by advertising networks composed of several thousand sites. An advertising network could follow you across thousands of Web sites and come up with an idea of what you are interested in as you browse, and then display ads related to those interests. For instance, if you visit a few men's clothing sites in the course of a few hours, you will be shown ads for men's clothing on most other sites you visit subsequently, regardless of their subject content. If you search for a certain pair of shoes at Zappos, and Like them to your friends on Facebook, you will be shown ads for the exact same shoes at other sites (including Facebook). Behavioral targeting combines nearly all of your online behavioral data into a collection of interest areas, and then shows you ads based on those interests, as well as the interests of your friends. What's new about today's behavioral targeting is the breadth of data collected: your e-mail content, social network page content, friends, purchases online, books read or purchased, newspaper sites visited, and many other behaviors. And finally, ad exchanges take the marketing of all this information one step further. Most popular Web sites have more than 100 tracking programs on their home pages that are owned by third-party data collector firms who

behavioral targeting
involves using online and offline behavior of consumers to adjust the advertising messages delivered to them online

interest-based advertising (IBA) (behavioral targeting)
another name for behavioral targeting

then sell this information in real time to the highest bidding advertiser in real-time online auctions. Ad exchanges make it possible for advertisers to retarget ads at individuals as they roam across the Internet. **Retargeting** involves showing the same or similar ads to individuals across multiple Web sites. Retargeting has become a popular tactic, used by 88% of marketers surveyed in a recent poll, in large part due to its perceived effectiveness. Another recent survey found that over 90% of marketers believe retargeting ads performs equal or better than search advertising or e-mail. However, as more and more consumers use multiple devices, including mobile devices, for online access, the ability to retarget ads across devices is becoming a topic of great interest to marketers (Marin Software, 2014; AdRoll, 2015; eMarketer, Inc., 2015j).

There are four methods that online advertisers use to behaviorally target ads: search engine queries, the collection of data on individual browsing history online (monitoring the clickstream), the collection of data from social network sites, and increasingly, the integration of this online data with offline data like income, education, address, purchase patterns, credit records, driving records, and hundreds of other personal descriptors tied to specific, identifiable persons. This level of integration of both "anonymous" as well as identifiable information is routinely engaged in by Google, Microsoft, Yahoo, Facebook, and legions of small and medium-sized marketing firms that use their data, or collect data from thousands of Web sites using Web beacons and cookies. On average, online information bureaus maintain 2,000 data elements on each adult person in their database. The currency and accuracy of this data are never examined, and the retention periods are not known. Currently, there are no federal laws or regulations governing this data.

Earlier in the chapter we described search engine advertising in some detail. Search engine advertising has turned out to be the most effective online advertising format by several orders of magnitude, and provides more than 95% of the revenue of Google, the world's largest online advertising agency. Why is search engine advertising so effective? Most agree that when users enter a query into a search engine, it reveals a very specific intention to shop, compare, and possibly purchase. When ads are shown at these very moments of customer behavior, they are 4 to 10 times as effective as other formats. The author John Battelle coined the phrase and the notion that the Web is a database of intentions composed of the results from every search ever made and every path that searchers have followed, since the beginning of the Web. In total, this database contains the intentions of all mankind. This treasure trove of intentions, desires, likes, wants, and needs is owned by Google, Microsoft, and to a lesser extent, Yahoo (Battelle, 2003). Battelle later extended the concept of a database of intentions beyond search to include the social graph (Facebook), status updates (Twitter and Facebook), and the "check-in" (Foursquare and Yelp) (Battelle, 2010). The database of intentions can be exploited to track and target individuals and groups. Not only is this capability unprecedented, but it's growing exponentially into the foreseeable future. The potential for abuse is also growing exponentially.

The decline in the growth rate of search engine advertising caused the major search engine firms to seek out alternative forms of future growth, which include display, rich media, and video advertising on millions of Web publisher sites. Web publishers have responded by producing billions of pages of content. In this environment,

retargeting
showing the same ad to individuals across multiple Web sites

the effectiveness of display ads has been falling in terms of response rates and prices for ads. Behavioral targeting is an effective way to solve this problem and increase response rates. Behavioral targeting of both search and display advertising is currently driving the expansion in online advertising.

Behavioral targeting seeks to optimize consumer response by using information that Web visitors reveal about themselves online, and if possible, to combine this with offline identity and consumption information gathered by companies such as Acxiom. Behavioral targeting is based on real-time information about visitors' use of Web sites, including pages visited, content viewed, search queries, ads clicked, videos watched, content shared, and products they purchased. Once this information is collected and analyzed on the fly, behavioral targeting programs attempt to develop profiles of individual users, and then show advertisements most likely to be of interest to the user. More than 80% of North American advertisers use some form of targeting in their online display ads (Forrester Research, 2014b).

For a variety of technical and other reasons, this vision has, thus far, not been widely achieved. The percentage of ads that are actually targeted is unknown. Many advertisers use less expensive context ads displayed to a general audience without any targeting, or very minimal demographic targeting. The quality of the data, largely owned by the online advertising networks, is quite good but hardly perfect. The ability to understand and respond—the business intelligence and real-time analytics—is still weak, preventing companies from being able to respond quickly in meaningful ways when the consumer is online. The firms who sell targeted ads to their clients claim the targeted ads are two or three times more effective than general ads. There is not very good data to support these claims from independent sources. Generally these claims confound the impact of brands on targeted audiences, and the impact of the ads placed to this targeted audience. Advertisers target groups that are most likely to buy their product even in the absence of targeting ads at them. The additional impact of a targeted ad is much smaller than ad platforms claim. A research report based on real data from 18 ad campaigns on Yahoo, involving 18.4 million users, found that brand interest is the largest single factor in determining targeted ad effectiveness, and not the targeted ad itself (Farahat and Bailey, 2012). And marketing companies are not yet prepared to accept the idea that there needs to be several hundred or a thousand variations on the same display ad depending on the customer's profile. Such a move would raise costs. Last, consumer resistance to targeting continues. A recent survey found that nearly 70% of Americans are opposed to having companies track their online behavior even if they receive a free service or product. Over 60% of consumers do not believe that viewing more relevant ads is a fair trade-off for being tracked. Almost 90% say people should have the right to control what information is collected online and a significant majority would like to turn tracking off (Consumer-action.org, 2013). Some consumers find marketing messages that are too personalized to be "creepy." For example, suppose you visited the Hanes Web site to look at underclothing. How would you feel about receiving an unsolicited e-mail from Hanes thanking you for your visit and asking you to come back? How would you feel about getting a similar text message or telephone call, or being served a constant array of underclothing ads as you traverse the Web? What if a company mined your Pinterest pins, Facebook posts, or Twitter feed? Although some consumers might not be disturbed by this, many others find it to be "off-putting" at the very least. The public and congressional reaction to behavioral targeting is described more fully in Chapter 8.

Customization and Customer Co-Production Customization is an extension of personalization. **Customization** means changing the product—not just the marketing message—according to user preferences. **Customer co-production** means the users actually think up the innovation and help create the new product.

Many leading companies now offer "build-to-order" customized products on the Internet on a large scale, creating product differentiation and, hopefully, customer loyalty. Customers appear to be willing to pay a little more for a unique product. The key to making the process affordable is to build a standardized architecture that lets consumers combine a variety of options. For example, Nike offers customized sneakers through its Nike iD program on its Web site. Consumers can choose the type of shoe, colors, material, and even a logo of up to eight characters. Nike transmits the orders via computers to specially equipped plants in China and Korea. At the My M&M's Web site, customers can get their own message printed on custom-made M&Ms.

Information goods—goods whose value is based on information content—are also ideal for this level of differentiation. For instance, the *New York Times*—and many other content distributors—allows customers to select the news they want to see on a daily basis. Many Web sites, particularly portal sites such as Yahoo, MSN, and AOL, allow customers to create their own customized version of the Web site. Such pages frequently require security measures such as usernames and passwords to ensure privacy and confidentiality.

Customer Service A Web site's approach to customer service can significantly help or hurt its marketing efforts. Online customer service is more than simply following through on order fulfillment; it has to do with users' ability to communicate with a company and obtain desired information in a timely manner. Customer service can help reduce consumer frustration, cut the number of abandoned shopping carts, and increase sales.

Most consumers want to, and will, serve themselves as long as the information they need to do so is relatively easy to find. Online buyers largely do not expect or desire "high-touch" service unless they have questions or problems, in which case they want relatively speedy answers that are responsive to their individual issue. Researchers have found that online consumers strongly attach to brands when they have a problem with an order. Customer loyalty increases substantially when online buyers learn that customer service representatives are available online or at an 800-number and were willing and able to resolve the situation quickly. Conversely, online buyers who do not receive satisfaction at these critical moments often terminate their relationship with the business and switch to merchants that may charge more but deliver superior customer service (Ba et al., 2010; Wolfinbarger and Gilly, 2001).

There are a number of tools that companies can use to encourage interaction with prospects and customers and provide customer service—FAQs, customer service

customization
changing the product, not just the marketing message, according to user preferences

customer co-production
in the Web environment, takes customization one step further by allowing the customer to interactively create the product

chat systems, intelligent agents, and automated response systems—in addition to the customer relationship management systems described in the preceding section.

Frequently asked questions (FAQs), a text-based listing of common questions and answers, provide an inexpensive way to anticipate and address customer concerns. Adding an FAQ page on a Web site linked to a search engine helps users track down needed information more quickly, enabling them to help themselves resolve questions and concerns. By directing customers to the FAQs page first, Web sites can give customers answers to common questions. If a question and answer do not appear, it is important for sites to make contact with a live person simple and easy. Offering an e-mail link to customer service at the bottom of the FAQs page is one solution.

Real-time customer service chat systems (in which a company's customer service representatives interactively exchange text-based messages with one or more customers on a real-time basis) are an increasingly popular way for companies to assist online shoppers during a purchase. Chats with online customer service representatives can provide direction, answer questions, and troubleshoot technical glitches that can kill a sale. Leading vendors of customer service chat systems include LivePerson and ClickDesk. Vendors claim that chat is significantly less expensive than telephone-based customer service. However, critics point out this conclusion may be based on optimistic assumptions that chat representatives can assist three or four customers at once, and that chat sessions are shorter than phone sessions. Also, chat sessions are text sessions, and not as rich as talking with a human being over the phone. On the plus side, chat has been reported to raise per-order sales figures, providing sales assistance by allowing companies to "touch" customers during the decision-making process. Evidence suggests that chat can lower shopping cart abandonment rates, increase the number of items purchased per transaction, and increase the dollar value of transactions. "Click to call" or "live call" is another version of a real-time online customer service system, in which the customer clicks a link or accepts an invitation to have a customer service representative call them on the telephone.

Intelligent agent technology is another way customers are providing assistance to online shoppers. Intelligent agents are part of an effort to reduce costly contact with customer service representatives. **Automated response systems** send e-mail order confirmations and acknowledgments of e-mailed inquiries, in some cases letting the customer know that it may take a day or two to actually research an answer to their question. Automated shipping confirmations and order status reports are also common.

Pricing Strategies

As we noted in Chapter 1, during the early years of e-commerce, many academics and business consultants predicted that the Web would lead to a new world of information symmetry and "frictionless" commerce. In this world, newly empowered customers, using intelligent shopping agents and the nearly infinite product and price information available on the Internet, would shop around the world (and around the clock) with minimal effort, driving prices down to their marginal cost

frequently asked questions (FAQs)
a text-based listing of common questions and answers

real-time customer service chat systems
a company's customer service representatives interactively exchange text-based messages with one or more customers on a real-time basis

automated response system
sends e-mail order confirmations and acknowledgments of e-mailed inquiries

and driving intermediaries out of the market as customers began to deal directly with producers (Wigand and Benjamin, 1995; Rayport and Sviokla, 1995; Evans and Wurster, 1999; Sinha, 2000). The result was supposed to be an instance of the **Law of One Price**: with complete price transparency in a perfect information marketplace, one world price for every product would emerge. Frictionless commerce would, of course, mean the end of marketing based on brands.

But it didn't work out this way. Firms still compete for customers through price as well as product features, scope of operations, and focus. **Pricing** (putting a value on goods and services) is an integral part of marketing strategy. Together, price and quality determine customer value. Pricing of e-commerce goods has proved very difficult for both entrepreneurs and investors to understand.

In traditional firms, the prices of traditional goods—such as books, drugs, and automobiles—are usually based on their fixed and variable costs as well as the market's **demand curve** (the quantity of goods that can be sold at various prices). *Fixed costs* are the costs of building the production facility. *Variable costs* are costs involved in running the production facility—mostly labor. In a competitive market, with undifferentiated goods, prices tend toward their *marginal costs* (the incremental cost of producing the next unit) once manufacturers have paid the fixed costs to enter the business.

Firms usually "discover" their demand curves by testing various price and volume bundles, while closely watching their cost structure. Normally, prices are set to maximize profits. A profit-maximizing company sets its prices so that the *marginal revenue* (the revenue a company receives from the next unit sold) from a product just equals its marginal costs. If a firm's marginal revenue is higher than its marginal costs, it would want to lower prices a bit and sell more product (why leave money on the table when you can sell a few more units?). If its marginal revenue for selling a product is lower than its marginal costs, then the company would want to reduce volume a bit and charge a higher price (why lose money on each additional sale?).

In the early years of e-commerce, something unusual happened. Sellers were pricing their products far below their marginal costs. Some sites were losing money on every sale. How could this be? New economics? New technology? The Internet age? No. Internet merchants could sell below their marginal costs (even giving away products for free) simply because a large number of entrepreneurs and their venture capitalist backers thought this was a worthwhile activity, at least in the short term. The idea was to attract eyeballs with free goods and services, and then later, once the consumer was part of a large, committed audience, charge advertisers enough money to make a profit, and (maybe) charge customers subscription fees for value-added services (the so-called *"piggyback"* strategy in which a small number of users can be convinced to pay for premium services that are piggybacked upon a larger audience that receives standard or reduced value services). To a large extent, social network sites and user-generated content sites have resurrected this revenue model with a focus on the growth in audience size and not short-term profits. To understand the behavior of entrepreneurial firms, it is helpful to examine a traditional demand curve (see **Figure 6.9**).

Law of One Price
with complete price transparency in a perfect information marketplace, there will be one world price for every product

pricing
putting a value on goods and services

demand curve
the quantity of goods that can be sold at various prices

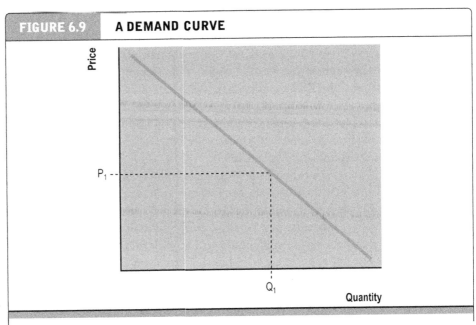

FIGURE 6.9 | **A DEMAND CURVE**

A demand curve shows the quantity of product (Q) that could be sold at various prices (P).

A small number of customers are willing to pay a great deal for the product—far above P_1. A larger number of customers would happily pay P_1, and an even larger number of customers would pay less than P_1. If the price were zero, the demand might approach infinity! Ideally, in order to maximize sales and profits, a firm would like to pick up all the money in the market by selling the product at the price each customer is willing to pay. This is called **price discrimination**—selling products to different people and groups based on their willingness to pay. If some people really want the product, sell it to them at a high price. But sell it to indifferent people at a much lower price; otherwise, they will not buy. This only works if the firm can (a) identify the price each individual would be willing to pay, and (b) segregate the customers from one another so they cannot find out what the others are paying. Therefore, most firms adopt a fixed price for their goods (P_1), or a small number of prices for different versions of their products.

What if the marginal cost of producing a good is zero? What should the price be for these goods? It would be impossible then to set prices based on equalizing marginal revenue and marginal cost—because marginal cost is zero. The Internet is primarily filled with information goods—from music to research reports, to stock quotes, stories, weather reports, articles, pictures, and opinions—whose marginal cost of production is zero when distributed over the Internet. Thus, another reason certain goods, such as some information goods, may be free on the Internet is that they are "selling" for what it costs to produce them—next to nothing. Content that is stolen has zero production costs. Content that is contributed by users also has zero production costs for the Web sites themselves.

price discrimination

selling products to different people and groups based on their willingness to pay

Free and Freemium Everyone likes a bargain, and the best bargain is something for free. Businesses give away free PCs, free data storage, free music, free Web sites, free photo storage, and free Internet connections. Free is not new: banks used to give away "free" toasters to depositors in the 1950s. Google offers free office apps, free e-mail, and free collaboration sites. There can be a sensible economic logic to giving things away. Free content can help build market awareness and can lead to sales of other follow-on products. Finally, free products and services knock out potential and actual competitors (the free browser Internet Explorer from Microsoft spoiled the market for Netscape's browser) (Shapiro and Varian, 1999).

Today, "free" is increasingly being implemented online as "freemium" to borrow a phrase from Chris Anderson's book *Free: The Future of a Radical Price.* The freemium pricing model is a cross-subsidy online marketing strategy where users are offered a basic service for free, but must pay for premium or add-on services. The people who pay for the premium services hopefully will pay for all the free riders on the service. Skype uses a freemium model: millions of users can call other Skype users on the Internet for free, but there's a charge for calling a land line or cell phone. Flickr, Google Sites, Yahoo, and a host of others offer premium services at a price in order to support free services. Pandora offers free Internet radio, but it includes advertisements. Premium service without ads costs about $55 a year. (See the Chapter 5 case study, *Freemium Takes Pandora Public,* for more information on Pandora and the freemium pricing strategy.)

"Free" and "freemium" as pricing strategies do have limits. In the past, many e-commerce businesses found it difficult to convert the eyeballs into paying customers. Free sites attract hundreds of millions of price-sensitive "free loaders" who have no intention of ever paying for anything, and who switch from one free service to another at the very mention of charges. The piggyback strategy has not been a universal success. "Free" eliminates a rich price discrimination strategy. Clearly some of the free loaders would indeed pay a small amount each month, and this revenue is lost to the firms who offer significant services for free. Some argue that everything digital will one day be free in part because Internet users expect it to be so. But the history of "free" includes broadcast television, which used to be "free" (it was advertising-supported), but the public eventually had no problem moving to cable television and DVDs as paid services. The exceptions to "free" are really valuable streams of information that are exclusive, expensive to produce, not widely distributed, unique, and have immediate consumption or investment value. Even in the age of the Internet, these digital streams will sell for a price greater than zero. There probably is no free lunch after all, at least not one that's worth eating.

Versioning One solution to the problem of free information goods is **versioning**—creating multiple versions of the goods and selling essentially the same product to different market segments at different prices. In this situation, the price depends on the value to the consumer. Consumers will segment themselves into groups that are willing to pay different amounts for various versions (Shapiro and Varian, 1998).

versioning
creating multiple versions of information goods and selling essentially the same product to different market segments at different prices

Versioning fits well with a modified "free" strategy. A reduced-value version can be offered for free, while premium versions can be offered at higher prices. What are characteristics of a "reduced-value version?" Low-priced—or in the case of information goods, even "free"—versions might be less convenient to use, less comprehensive, slower, less powerful, and offer less support than the high-priced versions. Just as there are different General Motors car brands appealing to different market segments (Cadillac, Buick, Chevrolet, and GMC), and within these divisions, hundreds of models from the most basic to the more powerful and functional, so can information goods be "versioned" in order to segment and target the market and position the products. In the realm of information goods, online magazines, music companies, and book publishers offer sample content for free, but charge for more powerful content. The *New York Times*, for instance, allows you to read 10 articles a month online for free, but if you want to read more, you must have a digital subscription. Some Web sites offer "free services" with annoying advertising, but turn off the ads for a monthly fee.

Bundling "Ziggy" Ziegfeld, a vaudeville entrepreneur at the turn of the twentieth century in New York, noticed that nearly one-third of his theater seats were empty on some Friday nights, and during the week, matinee shows were often half empty. He came up with an idea for bundling tickets into "twofers": pay for one full-price ticket and get the next ticket free. Twofers are still a Broadway theater tradition in New York. They are based on the idea that (a) the marginal cost of seating another patron is zero, and (b) a great many people who would not otherwise buy a single ticket would buy a "bundle" of tickets for the same or even a slightly higher price.

bundling

offers consumers two or more goods for a reduced price

Bundling of information goods online extends the concept of a twofer. **Bundling** offers consumers two or more goods for a price that is less than the goods would cost when purchased individually. The key idea behind the concept of bundling is that although consumers typically have very diverse ideas about the value of a single product, they tend to agree much more on the value of a bundle of products offered at a fixed price. In fact, the per-product price people are willing to pay for the bundle is often higher than when the products are sold separately. Bundling reduces the variance (dispersion) in market demand for goods.

Dynamic Pricing and Flash Marketing The pricing strategies we have discussed so far are all fixed-price strategies. Versions and bundles are sold for fixed prices based on the firm's best effort at maximizing its profits. But what if there is product still left on the shelf along with the knowledge that someone, somewhere, would be willing to pay something for it? It might be better to obtain at least some revenue from the product, rather than let it sit on the shelf, or even perish. Imagine also that there are some people in every market who would pay a hefty premium for a product if they could have it right away. In other situations, such as for an antique, the value of the product has to be discovered in the marketplace (usually because there is a belief that the marketplace would value the product at a much higher price than its owner paid as a cost). In other cases, the value of a good is equal to what the market is willing to pay (and has nothing to do with its cost). Or let's say you want to build frequent visits to your site and offer some really great bargains for a few minutes each day, or the whole day with a set time limit. Here is where dynamic pricing mechanisms come to the fore, and where the strengths of the Internet can be seen. With **dynamic pricing**, the price of the product varies, depending on the demand characteristics of the customer and the supply situation of the seller.

dynamic pricing
the price of the product varies, depending on the demand characteristics of the customer and the supply situation of the seller

There are a number of different kinds of dynamic pricing mechanisms. For instance, *auctions* have been used for centuries to establish the instant market price for goods. Auctions are flexible and efficient market mechanisms for pricing unique or unusual goods, as well as commonplace goods such as computers, flower bundles, and cameras.

Yield management is quite different from auctions. In auctions, thousands of consumers establish a price by bidding against one another. In *yield management*, managers set prices in different markets, appealing to different segments, in order to sell excess capacity. Airlines exemplify yield management techniques. Every few minutes during the day, they adjust prices of empty airline seats to ensure at least some of the 50,000 empty airline seats are sold at some reasonable price—even below marginal cost of production. Amazon and other large online retailers frequently use yield management techniques that involve changing prices hourly to stimulate demand and maximize revenues. Amazon can also track shopping behavior of individuals seeking a specific product, such as a laser printer. As the consumer searches for the best price, Amazon can observe the offering prices on other Web sites, and then adjust its prices dynamically so that when the user visits Amazon again, a lower price will be displayed than all other sites visited.

Yield management works under a limited set of conditions. Generally, the product is perishable (an empty airline seat perishes when the plane takes off without a full load); there are seasonal variations in demand; market segments are clearly defined; markets are competitive; and market conditions change rapidly (Cross, 1997). In general, only very large firms with extensive monitoring and database systems in place have been able to afford yield management techniques.

Surge pricing is a kind of dynamic pricing used by companies such as Uber. Uber uses a dynamic pricing algorithm to optimize its revenue, or as the company claims, to balance supply and demand. Prices have surged from two to ten times or higher during storms and popular holiday periods. Uber was sharply criticized for using this scheme in New York City during Hurricane Sandy in 2012. Critics claim the practice amounts to price gouging, which during an emergency is illegal in some states like New York. Uber counters that the higher prices bring more livery cars onto the streets, increasing supply just when needed. But surge pricing, like most dynamic pricing schemes, is not the same as an open auction, where price movements are transparent to all. Uber does not make its data on supply and demand available to the public. Therefore it is impossible to know if Uber prices go up during holidays and storms because demand exceeds supply or because Uber wants to increase profits. In July 2014, Uber reached an agreement with the New York State Attorney General to limit pricing surges during emergencies (Isaac, 2014).

A third dynamic pricing technique is *flash marketing*, which has proved extraordinarily effective for travel services, luxury clothing goods, and other goods. Using e-mail or dedicated Web site features to notify loyal customers (repeat purchasers), merchants offer goods and services for a limited time (usually hours) at very low prices. JetBlue has offered $14 flights between New York and Los Angeles. Deluxe hotel rooms are flash marketed at $1 a night. Companies like Rue La La, HauteLook, and Gilt Groupe are based on flash marketing techniques. Blink and you can easily miss these great prices. Gilt purchases overstocked items from major fashion brands and then offers them to their subscribers at discounted prices via daily e-mail and SMS flash messages. Typically, the sale of an item lasts for two hours or until the inventory is depleted. On many occasions, Gilt rises to the top of most frequently visited Web sites when it conducts a sale. Critics point out that these sites take advantage of compulsive shoppers and lead to overshopping for unneeded goods. In another example of mass retail dynamic pricing, in 2011, Amazon used its new cloud music service to offer a flash one-day sale of Lady Gaga's latest album for 99 cents. Response was so great that Amazon's cloud servers could not meet the demand, and the offer has not been repeated.

The Internet has truly revolutionized the possibilities to engage in dynamic, and even misleading, pricing strategies. With millions of consumers using a site every hour, and access to powerful databases, merchants can raise prices one minute and drop them another minute when a competitor threatens. Bait-and-switch tactics become more common: a really low price on one product is used to attract people to a site when in fact the product is not available.

Long Tail Marketing

Consider that Amazon sells a larger number of obscure books than it does of "hit" books (defined as the top 20% of books sold). Nevertheless, the hit books generate 80% of Amazon's revenues. Consumers distribute themselves in many markets according to a power curve where 80% of the demand is for the hit products, and demand for nonhits quickly recedes to a small number of units sold. In a traditional market, niche products are so obscure no one ever hears about them. One impact of the Internet and e-commerce on sales of obscure products with little demand is that obscure products become more visible to consumers through search engines, recommendation engines, and social networks. Hence, online retailers can earn substantial revenue selling products for which demand and price are low. In fact, with near zero inventory costs, and a good search engine, the sales of obscure products can become a much larger percentage of total revenue. Amazon, for instance, has millions of book titles for sale at $2.99 or less, many written by obscure authors. Because of its search and recommendation engines, Amazon is able to generate profits from the sale of this large number of obscure titles. This is called the **long tail effect**. See *Insight on Technology: The Long Tail: Big Hits and Big Misses.*

long tail effect

a colloquial name given to various statistical distributions characterized by a small number of events of high amplitude and a very large number of events with low amplitude

6.3   INTERNET MARKETING TECHNOLOGIES

Internet marketing has many similarities to and differences from ordinary marketing. The objective of Internet marketing—as in all marketing—is to build customer relationships so that the firm can achieve above-average returns (both by offering superior products or services and by communicating the product's features to the

INSIGHT ON TECHNOLOGY

THE LONG TAIL: BIG HITS AND BIG MISSES

The Long Tail is a name given to various statistical distributions characterized by a small group of events of high amplitude and a large group of events with low amplitude. Coined by *Wired Magazine* writer Chris Anderson in 2004, the Web's Long Tail has since gone on to fascinate academics and challenge online marketers. The concept is straightforward. Think Hollywood movies: there are a few big hits and also thousands of films that no one ever hears about. It's the legion of misses that make up the Long Tail. Anderson claimed to have discovered a new rule: no matter how much content you put online, someone, somewhere will show up to buy it. Rather than 20:80, Anderson suggested that Internet search, recommendation engines, and online social networks all enable niche products to be discovered and purchased. For example, eBay contains millions of items drawn from every Aunt Tilly's closet in the world and still seems to find a buyer somewhere for just about anything, generating revenue that would not be realized without an online marketplace.

On the Internet, where search costs are tiny, and storage and distribution costs are near zero, online retailers like Amazon and Alibaba are able to offer millions of products for sale compared to a typical bricks-and-mortar retailer like Walmart or Sears. Without physical stores to maintain, online merchants can save on overhead and labor costs and load up on inventory. Wherever you look on the Web, you can find a great many items that only a few people are interested in buying. But with over 3 billion people online, even a one-in-a-million product could find over 3,000 buyers. Researchers note that most shoppers have a taste for both popular as well as niche products.

One problem with the Long Tail is that people sometimes have difficulty finding niche products because they are—by definition—largely unknown.

The revenue value of low-demand products is locked up in collective ignorance. Here's where recommender systems come into play: although these systems can skew toward the most popular selections, they can sometimes guide consumers to obscure but wonderful works based on the recommendations of others. Netflix has spent millions in recent years on improving its recommender system, and Pandora's recommender system focuses on generating quality music without regard to popularity.

Search engine optimization is another area where marketers are trying to unlock the power of the Long Tail. Long-Tail keywords are phrases that a small but significant number of people might use to find products. For instance, instead of investing in keywords such as "shoes" or "men's shoes," a marketer focused on the Long Tail might choose a keyword like "purple all-weather running shoes." Google has rolled out various updates to its search algorithm that improve Long Tail searches. According to Google, Long Tail searches comprise as much as 50% of all Web queries, with approximately 20% of searches being extremely unique or never seen before. Google uses textual analysis to deliver better, more focused results for these searches. An increasing number of Internet users are using natural language searches (searches that are phrased in the way we would speak naturally, like "where is the nearest pizza place?") to find products and services. These searches are also a part of the Long Tail, and while big businesses tend to control the more frequently searched keywords, smaller businesses can focus on natural language and other Long Tail searches to dramatically improve their conversion rates.

Social networks also make the Long Tail phenomenon even stronger. A recent study found that popularity information of the sort produced in a social network spurs sales of niche products more than mainstream products because of the higher perceived quality of the niche product.

(continued)

Long Tail search is also pivotal for online sales of rare books. A 2014 study showed that used books sell for higher prices online than in physical stores. The study's authors surmised that book buyers are willing to pay a higher price because without the Web, they wouldn't have found the book they sought.

Anderson claimed that the Internet would revolutionize digital content by making even niche products highly profitable, and that the revenues produced by small niche products would ultimately outweigh the revenues of hit movies, songs, and books. But some newer research casts some doubt on the revenue potential in the Long Tail. Solid best sellers have expanded and produce the vast part of online media revenues. Netflix's most recent earnings report boasted record highs, which it credited to its growing group of original series and recently added blockbuster hits like the television series Friends, not the thousands of titles in its Long Tail. In fact, its DVD business, where most of its Long Tail titles are available, has only 5.5 million subscribers, compared to 62 million subscribers of its streaming service, which consists primarily of more popular movies and shows. Similarly, another study found that while the number of ISBNs of e-books in the Canadian market expanded rapidly in 2014, the number of ISBNs selling at least one copy remained unchanged. The situation is similar in the music industry. As music services compete to offer increasingly large catalogs of songs, the well-known artists do better, while each individual member of the growing Long Tail finds it harder to stand out amidst lesser-known peers. On mobile devices especially, "front end display" for music services and e-books is smaller than on desktop screens, and only the superstars get this valuable marketing real estate.

On the other hand, up-and-coming artists have fewer barriers to entry and more avenues than ever to promote themselves without the aid of major labels. Artists like violinist Lindsey Stirling started out in the Long Tail; she has put up her own videos on YouTube, and has since become a major commercial success. Indie music labels' percentage of the top 200 albums by sales grew from just 13% in 2001 to 35% in 2010. And would-be authors have more options to publish their works and market themselves, despite the low odds of penning a smash hit.

Both the Long Tail and the winner-take-all approaches have implications for marketers and product designers. In the Long Tail approach, online merchants, especially those selling digital goods such as content, should build up huge libraries of content because they can make significant revenues from niche products that have small audiences. In the winner-take-all approach, the niche products produce little revenue, and firms should concentrate on hugely popular titles and services. Surprisingly, contrary to what Anderson originally theorized, the evidence for online digital content increasingly supports a winner-take-all perspective.

SOURCES: "Netflix Wags Its Short Tail," by Justin Fox, Bloombergview.com, April 17, 2015; "Hidden in the Long Tail," *The Economist*, January 10, 2015; "Revisiting the Long Tail Theory as Applied to Ebooks," by Marcello Vena, Publishingperspectives.com, January 8, 2015; "The Long Tail And Why Your SEO Keyword Strategy Is Wrong," by Joshua Steimle, *Forbes*, December 23, 2014; "New Data on the Long Tail Impact Suggests Rethinking History and Ideas About the Future of Publishing," by Mike Shatzkin, Idealog.com, June 25, 2014; "Tales of Long Tail's Death Greatly Exaggerated," by Tracy Maddux, Billboard.com, June 17, 2014; "Why Alibaba's Long Tail Makes Amazon's Look Like a Bobcat's," by Matt Schifrin, *Forbes*, May 8, 2014; "The Death of the Long Tail," Musicindustryblog.com, March 4, 2014; "Winners Take All, But Can't We Still Dream," by Robert H. Frank, *New York Times*, February 22, 2014; "Blockbusters: Why the Long Tail Is Dead and Go-Big Strategies Pay Off," by Ginny Marvin, Marketingland.com, October 23, 2013; "How Google Is Changing Long-Tail Search with Efforts Like Hummingbird," by Rand Fishkin, Moz.com, October 18, 2013; "Microsoft, Apps and the Long Tail," by Ben Bajarin, Time.com, July 8, 2013; "Goodbye Pareto Principle, Hello Long Tail: The Effect of Search Costs on the Concentration of Product Sales," by Eric Brynjolfsson et al., *Management Science*, July 2012; "Recommendation Networks and the Long Tail of Electronic Commerce," by Gail Oestreicher-Singer, New York University, 2012; "Research Commentary—Long Tails vs. Superstars: The Effect of Information Technology on Product Variety and Sales Concentration Patterns," by Erik Brynjolfsson et al., *Information Systems Research*, December 2010; "How Does Popularity Affect Choices? A Field Experiment," by Catherine Tucker and Juanjuan Zhang, *Management Science*, May 2011; "From Niches to Riches: Anatomy of the Long Tail," by Eric Brynjolfsson et al., *MIT Sloan Management Review*, Summer 2006; "The Long Tail," by Chris Anderson, *Wired Magazine*, October 2004.

consumer). But Internet marketing is also very different from ordinary marketing because the nature of the medium and its capabilities are so different from anything that has come before. In order to understand just how different Internet marketing can be and in what ways, you first need to become familiar with some basic Internet marketing technologies.

THE REVOLUTION IN INTERNET MARKETING TECHNOLOGIES

In Chapter 1, we listed eight unique features of e-commerce technology. **Table 6.6** describes how marketing has changed as a result of these new technical capabilities.

TABLE 6.6	IMPACT OF UNIQUE FEATURES OF E-COMMERCE TECHNOLOGY ON MARKETING
E-COMMERCE TECHNOLOGY DIMENSION	SIGNIFICANCE FOR MARKETING
Ubiquity	Marketing communications have been extended to the home, work, and mobile platforms; geographic limits on marketing have been reduced. The marketplace has been replaced by "marketspace" and is removed from a temporal and geographic location. Customer convenience has been enhanced, and shopping costs have been reduced.
Global reach	Worldwide customer service and marketing communications have been enabled. Potentially hundreds of millions of consumers can be reached with marketing messages.
Universal standards	The cost of delivering marketing messages and receiving feedback from users is reduced because of shared, global standards of the Internet.
Richness	Video, audio, and text marketing messages can be integrated into a single marketing message and consuming experience.
Interactivity	Consumers can be engaged in a dialog, dynamically adjusting the experience to the consumer, and making the consumer a co-producer of the goods and services being sold.
Information density	Fine-grained, highly detailed information on consumers' real-time behavior can be gathered and analyzed for the first time. "Data mining" Internet technology permits the analysis of terabytes of consumer data every day for marketing purposes.
Personalization/ Customization	This feature potentially enables product and service differentiation down to the level of the individual, thus strengthening the ability of marketers to create brands.
Social technology	User-generated content and social network sites, along with blogs, have created new, large, online audiences where the content is provided by users. These audiences have greatly expanded the opportunity for marketers to reach new potential customers in a nontraditional media format. Entirely new kinds of marketing techniques are evolving. These same technologies expose marketers to the risk of falling afoul of popular opinion by providing more market power to users who now can "talk back."

On balance, the Internet has had four very powerful impacts on marketing. First, the Internet, as a communications medium, has broadened the scope of marketing communications—in the sense of the number of people who can be easily reached as well as the locations where they can be reached, from desktops to mobile smartphones (in short, everywhere). Second, the Internet has increased the richness of marketing communications by combining text, video, and audio content into rich messages. Arguably, the Web is richer as a medium than even television or video because of the complexity of messages available, the enormous content accessible on a wide range of subjects, and the ability of users to interactively control the experience. Third, the Internet has greatly expanded the information intensity of the marketplace by providing marketers (and customers) with unparalleled fine-grained, detailed, real-time information about consumers as they transact in the marketplace. Fourth, the always-on, always-attached, environment created by mobile devices results in consumers being much more available to receive marketing messages. One result is an extraordinary expansion in marketing opportunities for firms.

WEB TRANSACTION LOGS

transaction log
records user activity at a Web site

How can e-commerce sites know more than a department store or the local grocery store does about consumer behavior? A primary source of consumer information on the Web is the transaction log maintained by all Web servers. A **transaction log** records user activity at a Web site. The transaction log is built into Web server software. Transaction log data becomes even more useful when combined with two other visitor-generated data trails: registration forms and the shopping cart database. Users are enticed through various means (such as free gifts or special services) to fill out registration forms. **Registration forms** gather personal data on name, address, phone, zip code, e-mail address (usually required), and other optional self-confessed information on interests and tastes. When users make a purchase, they also enter additional information into the shopping cart database. The **shopping cart database** captures all the item selection, purchase, and payment data. Other potential additional sources of data are information users submit on product forms, contribute to chat groups, or send via e-mail messages using the "Contact Us" option on most sites.

registration forms
gather personal data on name, address, phone, zip code, e-mail address, and other optional self-confessed information on interests and tastes

shopping cart database
captures all the item selection, purchase, and payment data

For a Web site that has a million visitors per month, and where, on average, a visitor makes 15 page requests per visit, there will be 15 million entries in the log each month. These transaction logs, coupled with data from the registration forms and shopping cart database, represent a treasure trove of marketing information for both individual sites and the online industry as a whole. Nearly all Internet marketing capabilities are based on these data-gathering tools. For instance, here are just a few of the interesting marketing questions that can be answered by examining a site's Web transaction logs, registration forms, and shopping cart database:

- What are the major patterns of interest and purchase for groups and individuals?
- After the home page, where do most users go first, and then second and third?
- What are the interests of specific individuals (those we can identify)?
- How can we make it easier for people to use our site so they can find what they want?

- How can we change the design of the site to encourage visitors to purchase our high-margin products?
- Where are visitors coming from (and how can we optimize our presence on these referral sites)?
- How can we personalize our messages, offerings, and products to individual users?

Businesses can choke on the massive quantity of information found in a typical site's log file. We describe some technologies that help firms more effectively utilize this information below.

SUPPLEMENTING THE LOGS: COOKIES AND OTHER TRACKING FILES

While transaction logs create the foundation of online data collection at a single Web site, marketers use tracking files to follow users across the entire Web as they visit other sites. There are three primary kinds of tracking files: cookies, Flash cookies, and Web beacons. As described in Chapter 2, a cookie is a small text file that Web sites place on the hard disk of visitors' client computers every time they visit, and during the visit, as specific pages are visited. Cookies allow a Web site to store data on a user's computer and then later retrieve it. The cookie typically includes a name, a unique ID number for each visitor that is stored on the user's computer, the domain (which specifies the Web server/domain that can access the cookie), a path (if a cookie comes from a particular part of a Web site instead of the main page, a path will be given), a security setting that provides whether the cookie can only be transmitted by a secure server, and an expiration date (not required). First-party cookies come from the same domain name as the page the user is visiting, while third-party cookies come from another domain, such as ad serving or adware companies, affiliate marketers, or spyware servers. On some Web sites, there are literally hundreds of tracking files on the main pages.

A cookie provides Web marketers with a very quick means of identifying the customer and understanding his or her prior behavior at the site. Web sites use cookies to determine how many people are visiting the site, whether they are new or repeat visitors, and how often they have visited, although this data may be somewhat inaccurate because people share computers, they often use more than one computer, and cookies may have been inadvertently or intentionally erased. Cookies make shopping carts and "quick checkout" options possible by allowing a site to keep track of a user as he or she adds to the shopping cart. Each item added to the shopping cart is stored in the site's database along with the visitor's unique ID value.

Ordinary cookies are easy to spot using your browser, but Flash cookies, beacons, and tracking codes are not easily visible. All common browsers allow users to see the cookies placed in their cookies file. Users can delete cookies, or adjust their settings so that third-party cookies are blocked, while first-party cookies are allowed.

With growing privacy concerns, over time the percentage of people deleting cookies has risen. The more cookies are deleted, the less accurate are Web page and ad server metrics, and the less likely marketers will be able to understand who is visiting their sites or where they came from. As a result, advertisers have sought other methods. One way is using Adobe Flash software, which creates its own cookie files, known as Flash cookies. Flash cookies can be set to never expire, and can store about 5 MB of information compared to the 1,024 bytes stored by regular cookies.

Although cookies are site-specific (a Web site can only receive the data it has stored on a client computer and cannot look at any other cookie), when combined with Web beacons (also called "bugs"), they can be used to create cross-site profiles. Web beacons are tiny (1-pixel) graphic files embedded in e-mail messages and on Web sites. Web beacons are used to automatically transmit information about the user and the page being viewed to a monitoring server in order to collect personal browsing behavior and other personal information. For instance, when a recipient opens an e-mail in HTML format or opens a Web page, a message is sent to a server calling for graphic information. This tells the marketer that the e-mail was opened, indicating that the recipient was at least interested in the subject header. Web beacons are not visible to users. They are often clear or colored white so they are not visible to the recipient. You may be able to determine if a Web page is using Web beacons by using the View Source option of your browser and examining the IMG (image) tags on the page. As noted above, Web beacons are typically one pixel in size and contain the URL of a server that differs from the one that served the page itself.

Using cookies on mobile devices has been less effective. Regular cookies on the mobile Web are reset every time a user closes his or her mobile browser and in-app cookies can't be shared between apps, making both of limited utility. However, with the increasing numbers of people using mobile devices to access the Internet, it is not surprising that telecommunications companies have begun to use tracking files. In late 2014, it was revealed that Verizon Wireless and AT&T were inserting a tracking header called a Unique Identifier Header (UIDH) into HTTP requests issued to Web sites from mobile devices, enabling them to track the online activities of their subscribers. Commentators call these tracking headers zombie cookies, perma-cookies, or supercookies because they cannot be deleted the way that regular browser cookies can. Following an outcry by privacy advocates and an FCC investigation, AT&T reportedly stopped using supercookies, but Verizon continues, although allowing users to opt out of their use. However, a 2015 study found that 15% of mobile users around the world (including the United States) continue to be tracked by supercookies, and their use appears to be increasing.

deterministic cross-device tracking
relies on personally identifiable information such as e-mail address used to log into an app and Web site on different devices

probabilistic cross-device tracking
uses algorithms to analyze thousands of anonymous data points to create a possible match

In an effort to more effectively track consumers across devices, other cross-device tracking methods have begun to be developed. **Deterministic cross-device tracking** relies on personally identifiable information such as e-mail address used to log into an app and Web site on different devices. Facebook, Google, Apple, Twitter, and other companies that have very large user bases and have both desktop and mobile properties that require logins are the most likely to be able to effectively exploit deterministic matching. **Probabilistic cross-device tracking** uses algorithms developed by vendors such as Drawbridge, BlueCava, and Tapad to analyze thousands of anonymous data points, such as device type, operating system, and IP address, to create a possible match. This type of matching is, not surprisingly, less accurate than deterministic matching (Schiff, 2015; Whitener, 2015).

In November 2015, the Federal Trade Commission will host a workshop to examine the privacy issues involved with cross-device tracking, while the Network Advertising Initiative has indicated that it will issue guidance and standards on the use of such technologies. *Insight on Society: Every Move You Take, Every Click You Make, We'll Be Tracking You* further examines the use of tracking files.

DATABASES, DATA WAREHOUSES, DATA MINING, AND BIG DATA

Databases, data warehouses, data mining, and the variety of marketing decision-making techniques loosely called *profiling* are at the heart of the revolution in Internet marketing. **Profiling** uses a variety of tools to create a digital image for each consumer. This image can be quite inexact, even primitive, but it can also be as detailed as a character in a novel. The quality of a consumer profile depends on the amount of data used to create it, and the analytical power of the firm's software and hardware. Together, these techniques attempt to identify precisely who the online customer is and what they want, and then, to fulfill the customer's criteria exactly. These techniques are more powerful, far more precise, and more fine-grained than the gross levels of demographic and market segmentation techniques used in mass marketing media or by telemarketing.

In order to understand the data in transaction logs, registration forms, shopping carts, cookies, Web bugs, and other unstructured data sources like e-mails, tweets, and Facebook Likes, Internet marketers need massively powerful and capacious databases, database management systems, and analytic tools.

Databases

The first step in interpreting huge transaction streams is to store the information systematically. A **database** is a software application that stores records and attributes. A telephone book is a physical database that stores records of individuals and their attributes such as names, addresses, and phone numbers. A **database management system** (**DBMS**) is a software application used by organizations to create, maintain, and access databases. The most common DBMS are DB2 from IBM and a variety of SQL databases from Oracle, Sybase, and other providers. **Structured query language (SQL)** is an industry-standard database query and manipulation language used in relational databases. **Relational databases** such as DB2 and SQL represent data as two-dimensional tables with records organized in rows, and attributes in columns, much like a spreadsheet. The tables—and all the data in them—can be flexibly related to one another as long as the tables share a common data element.

Relational databases are extraordinarily flexible and allow marketers and other managers to view and analyze data from different perspectives very quickly.

Data Warehouses and Data Mining

A **data warehouse** is a database that collects a firm's transactional and customer data in a single location for offline analysis by marketers and site managers. The data originate in many core operational areas of the firm, such as Web site transaction logs, shopping carts, point-of-sale terminals (product scanners) in stores, warehouse inventory levels, field sales reports, external scanner data supplied by third parties, and financial payment data. The purpose of a data warehouse is to gather all the firm's transaction and customer data into one logical repository where it can be analyzed and modeled by managers without disrupting or taxing the firm's primary transactional systems and databases. Data warehouses grow quickly into storage repositories

profiling
profiling uses a variety of tools to create a digital image for each consumer

database
a software application that stores records and attributes

database management system (DBMS)
a software application used by organizations to create, maintain, and access databases

structured query language (SQL)
industry-standard database query language used in relational databases

relational databases
represent data as two-dimensional tables with records organized in rows and attributes in columns; data within different tables can be flexibly related as long as the tables share a common data element

data warehouse
a database that collects a firm's transactional and customer data in a single location for offline analysis

EVERY MOVE YOU TAKE, EVERY CLICK YOU MAKE, WE'LL BE TRACKING YOU

Advertising-supported Web sites depend on knowing as much personal information as possible about you. One of the main ways ad firms discover your personal information is by placing so-called "tracking files" on your computer's browser. There are several kinds of third-party tracking files on Web pages. Cookies are the best known. These simple text files are placed in your browser and assign a unique number to your computer, which is then used by advertisers to track you across the Web as you move from one site to another (without telling you). Web beacons (sometimes also referred to as Web bugs) are a little more pernicious. Beacons are small software files that track your clicks, choices, and purchases, and even location data from mobile devices, and then send that information, often in real time, to advertisers tracking you. Beacons can also assign your computer a unique number and track you across the Web. Tracking may also occur as you watch Adobe Flash-enabled videos, visit Web sites equipped with HTML5 local storage, and use apps on smartphones. Most Facebook apps, for instance, send personal information, including names, to dozens of advertising and Internet tracking companies.

So how common is Web tracking? In a recent study, researchers found a very widespread surveillance system. Only one site, Wikipedia, had no tracking files. Two-thirds of the tracking files came from companies whose primary business is identifying and tracking Internet users to create consumer profiles that can be sold to advertising firms looking for specific types of customers. The other third came from database firms that gather and bundle the information and then sell it to marketers. Many of the tracking tools gather personal information such as age, gender, race,

income, marital status, health concerns, TV shows and movies viewed, magazines and newspapers read, and books purchased. While tracking firms claim the information they gather is anonymous, this is true in name only. Scholars have shown that with just a few pieces of information, such as age, gender, zip code, and marital status, specific individuals can be easily identified. In 2012, a Web Privacy Census conducted by the University of California Berkeley Center for Law and Technology found that the total number of cookies on the top 100 Web sites had increased by 80%, from 3,600 when first measured in 2009 to over 6,400. The vast majority of these cookies (about 85%) were third-party tracking cookies, from over 450 different third-party hosts. Google's DoubleClick was the top tracker, and the most frequently appearing cookie keys were those associated with Google Analytics. Similar results were observed when looking at the top 1,000 and top 25,000 Web sites. One cause: growth of online ad auctions where advertisers buy data about users' Web browsing behavior. When you visit a site, your visit is auctioned and the winner gets to show you some ads. All this takes place in a few milliseconds so you don't know its happening. Welcome to the brave new world of Internet marketing!

The Privacy Foundation has issued guidelines for Web beacon usage. The guidelines suggest that Web beacons should be visible as an icon on the screen, the icon should be labeled to indicate its function, and it should identify the name of the company that placed the Web beacon on the page. In addition, if a user clicks on the Web beacon, it should display a disclosure statement indicating what data is being collected, how the data is used after it is collected, what companies receive the data, what other data the Web beacon is combined with, and whether or not a cookie is associated with the Web beacon. Users should be able to opt out of any data collection done by the Web beacon, and the Web beacon should not be used to collect information from Web pages of a sensitive nature, such as medical, financial, job-related, or sexual matters. Many sites have adopted the Network Advertising Initiative's (NAI) self-regulatory guidelines, but these are only voluntary, and these guidelines have done little to assuage fears from Web users that their privacy is at risk.

One roadblock involves the meaning of Do Not Track. Industry wants an opt-in, default Track Me feature on all Web sites, while the government and privacy groups are pushing for an opt-out Do Not Track feature in which the default is Do Not Track, and which users can switch off for all sites at ones In July 2013, a working group commissioned by the W3C proposed that Web users should be able to tell advertising networks not to show them targeted advertisements. In 2014, the W3C announced that it had made major progress, advancing its work to the "last call" phase of review from the outside world.

Nearly all browsers now offer users the option of using a Do Not Track feature. But users have to remember to turn it on. In addition, not all Web sites honor the Do Not Track request, because they are not legally obligated to do so. Major Web sites and the online advertising industry insist their industry can self-regulate and preserve individual privacy. However, this solution has not worked in the past. In 2014, major companies like Yahoo and AOL abandoned the Do Not Track standard, citing the lack of traction that Do Not Track has encountered across the rest of the Web. Although some bigger Web sites like Twitter and Pinterest do follow the Do Not Track guidelines, these defections are setbacks for the standard.

The situation in Europe is somewhat different. In 2009, Article 5.3 of Directive 2002/58/EC (Directive on Privacy and Electronic Communications) was amended by Directive 2009/136/EC, also known as the EU Cookie Law, which provides that Web sites must ask visitors for their consent before they can install most cookies (although not cookies considered necessary for the basic function of a Web site, such as session cookies that are used to track a shopping cart). The directive also applies to Flash and HTML5 local storage. The Directive was first passed in 2009, and by 2015, all of the countries in the EU with the exception of the Czech Republic and Estonia had enacted legislation enabling it. (Germany has not implemented the Directive on the grounds that German law already covers the topic, although some data protection authorities dispute this view.) However, compliance with the law remains very spotty, with consultants KPMG finding that more than half of the organizations it analyzed in the U.K were still not compliant. The U.K. legal firm Bristows made similar findings with respect to countries throughout the EU in its survey of the status of the implementation of, and compliance with, the EU Cookie Law in 2015.

SOURCES: "Status of Implementation of the Amendment to Article 5.3 of Directive 2002/58/EC (the "EU Cookie Law"), by Bristows LLC, June 5, 2015; "Do Not Track – The Privacy Standard That's Melting Away," by Mark Stockley, Nakedsecurity.sophos.com, August 26, 2014; "California Urges Websites to Disclose Online Tracking," by Vindu Goel, *New York Times*, May 21, 2014; "Yahoo Is the Latest Company Ignoring Web Users' Requests for Privacy," by Jon Brodkin, Arstechnica.com, May 1, 2014; "At Last, Some Progress on Do Not Track," Justin Brookman, Cdt.org, April 24, 2014; "'Do Not Track' Rules Come a Step Closer to an Agreement," by Somini Sengupta and Natasha Singer, *New York Times*, July 15, 2013; "Half of U.K. Organisations Not Compliant with EU Cookie Law," by Sooraj Shah, Computing.co.uk, May 29, 2013; "What You Need to Know About the EU Cookie Law," by Bobbie Johnson, Gigaom.com, May 25, 2013; "What Firefox's New Privacy Settings Mean for You," by Sarah A. Downey, Abine.com, March 29, 2013; "The Web Privacy Census," by Chris Jay Hoofnagle and Nathan Good, law.berkeley.edu/privacycensus.htm, October 2012; "Online Data Collection Explodes Year Over Year in US," eMarketer, Inc., July 19, 2012; "Online Tracking Ramps Up," by Julia Angwin, *Wall Street Journal*, June 17, 2012; "Microsoft's 'Do Not Track' Move Angers Advertising Industry," by Julia Angwin, *Wall Street Journal*, May 31, 2012; "Websites Using 14 Tracking Tools to Take Our Private Data, Says Truste Research," News.com.au, April 20, 2012; "Opt-Out Provision Would Halt Some, but Not All, Web Tracking," by Tanzina Vega, *New York Times*, February 28, 2012; "How Companies Learn Your Secrets," by Charles Duhigg, *New York Times Magazine*, February 16, 2012; "Latest in Web Tracking: Stealthy 'Supercookies,'" by Julia Angwin, *Wall Street Journal*, August 18, 2011; "WPP Ad Unit Has Your Profile," by Emily Steel, *Wall Street Journal*, June 27, 2011; "Not Me Dot Com," by Luke O'Neil, *Wall Street Journal*, June 18, 2011; "Show Us the Data. (It's Ours, After All)," by Richard Thaler, *New York Times*, April 23, 2011; "What They Know About You," by Jennfier Valentino-Devries, *Wall Street Journal*, July 31, 2010; "Sites Feed Personal Details to New Tracking Industry," Julia Angwin and Tom McGinty, *Wall Street Journal*, July 30, 2010; "Study Finds Behaviorally-Targeted Ads More Than Twice as Valuable, Twice as Effective as Non-targeted Online Ads," Network Advertising Initiative, March 24, 2010.

containing terabytes (trillions of bytes) of data on consumer behavior at a firm's stores and Web sites. With a data warehouse, firms can answer such questions as: What products are the most profitable by region and city? What regional marketing campaigns are working? How effective is store promotion of the firm's Web site? Data warehouses can provide business managers with a more complete awareness of customers through data that can be accessed quickly.

data mining
a set of analytical techniques that look for patterns in the data of a database or data warehouse, or seek to model the behavior of customers

Data mining is a set of analytical techniques that look for patterns in the data of a database or data warehouse, or seek to model the behavior of customers. Web site data can be "mined" to develop profiles of visitors and customers. A **customer profile** is simply a set of rules that describe the typical behavior of a customer or a group of customers at a Web site. Customer profiles help to identify the patterns in group and individual behavior that occur online as millions of visitors use a firm's Web site. For example, almost every financial transaction you engage in is processed by a data mining application to detect fraud. Phone companies closely monitor your cell phone use as well to detect stolen phones and unusual calling patterns. Financial institutions and cell phone firms use data mining to develop fraud profiles. When a user's behavior conforms to a fraud profile, the transaction is not allowed or is terminated (Mobasher, 2007).

customer profile
a description of the typical behavior of a customer or a group of customers at a Web site

There are many different types of data mining. The simplest type is **query-driven data mining**, which is based on specific queries. For instance, based on hunches of marketers who suspect a relationship in the database or who need to answer a specific question, such as "What is the relationship between time of day and purchases of various products at the Web site?", marketers can easily query the data warehouse and produce a database table that rank-orders the top 10 products sold at a Web site by each hour of the day. Marketers can then change the content of the Web site to stimulate more sales by highlighting different products over time or placing particular products on the home page at certain times of day or night.

query-driven data mining
data mining based on specific queries

Another form of data mining is model-driven. **Model-driven data mining** involves the use of a model that analyzes the key variables of interest to decision makers. For example, marketers may want to reduce the inventory carried on the Web site by removing unprofitable items that do not sell well. A financial model can be built showing the profitability of each product on the site so that an informed decision can be made.

model-driven data mining
involves the use of a model that analyzes the key variables of interest to decision makers

A more fine-grained behavioral approach that seeks to deal with individuals as opposed to market segments derives rules from individual consumer behavior (along with some demographic information) (Adomavicius and Tuzhilin, 2001a; Chan, 1999; Fawcett and Provost, 1996, 1997). Here, the pages actually visited by specific users are stored as a set of conjunctive rules. For example, if an individual visits a site and typically ("as a rule") moves from the home page to the financial news section to the Asian report section, and then often purchases articles from the "Recent Developments in Banking" section, this person—based on purely past behavioral patterns—might be shown an advertisement for a book on Asian money markets. These rules can be constructed to follow an individual across many different Web sites.

There are many drawbacks to all these techniques, not least of which is that there may be millions of rules, many of them nonsensical, and many others of short-term duration. Hence, the rules need extensive validation and culling (Adomavicius and Tuzhilin, 2001b). Also, there can be millions of affinity groups and other patterns in the data that are temporal or meaningless. The difficulty is isolating the valid, powerful (profitable) patterns in the data and then acting on the observed pattern fast enough to make a sale that otherwise would not have been made. As we see later, there are practical difficulties and trade-offs involved in achieving these levels of granularity, precision, and speed.

Hadoop and the Challenge of Big Data

Up until about five years ago, most data collected by organizations consisted of structured transaction data that could easily fit into rows and columns of relational database management systems. Since then, there has been an explosion of data from Web traffic, e-mail messages, and social media content (tweets, status messages), even music playlists, as well as machine-generated data from sensors. This data may be unstructured or semi-structured and thus not suitable for relational database products that organize data in the form of columns and rows. The popular term "Big Data" refers to this avalanche of digital data flowing into firms around the world largely from Web sites and Internet click stream data. The volumes of data are so large that traditional DBMS cannot capture, store, and analyze the data in a reasonable time. Some examples of Big Data challenges are analyzing 12 terabytes of tweets created each day to improve your understanding of consumer sentiment towards your products; 100 million e-mails in order to place appropriate ads alongside the e-mail messages; or 500 million call detail records to find patterns of fraud and churn. Big Data and the tools needed to deal with it really started with Google and other search engines. Google's problem: it has to deal with 3.5 billion searches a day, and within milliseconds, display search results and place ads. For fun, do a search on "Big Data" and you'll see Google respond with more than 47 million results in .39 seconds. That's much faster than you can read this sentence!

Big Data usually refers to data in the petabyte and exabyte range—in other words, billions to trillions of records, often from different sources. Big Data is produced in much larger quantities and much more rapidly than traditional data collection mechanisms. Even though tweets are limited to 140 characters each, Twitter generates more than 8 terabytes of data daily. According to the IDC technology research firm, data is more than doubling every two years, so the amount of data available to organizations is skyrocketing. The next frontier will be data derived from the Internet of Things (IoT). Making sense out of it quickly in order to gain a market advantage is critical.

Marketers are interested in Big Data because it can be mined for patterns of consumer behavior and contain more interesting anomalies than smaller data sets, with the potential to provide new insights into customer behavior, weather patterns, financial market activity, or other phenomena. For instance, Evrythng, an IoT platform company, is partnering with Trueffect, a digital ad firm, to develop ways that marketers can use data generated by connected appliances and other devices in order to directly communicate with and target advertising with consumers. However, to derive business value from this data, organizations need new technologies and analytic tools capable of managing and analyzing nontraditional data along with their traditional enterprise data. A recent survey found that while marketers say Big Data is their biggest opportunity, only 14% are confident in their use of Big Data (Tadena, 2015).

To handle unstructured and semi-structured data in vast quantities, as well as structured data, organizations are using Hadoop. **Hadoop** is an open source software frame-

Big Data
Big Data refers to very large data sets in the petabyte and exabyte range

Hadoop
a software framework for working with various big data sets

work managed by the Apache Software Foundation that enables distributed parallel processing of huge amounts of data across inexpensive computers. It breaks a Big Data problem down into subproblems, distributes them among up to thousands of inexpensive computer processing nodes, and then combines the result into a smaller data set that is easier to analyze. You've probably used Hadoop to find the best airfare on the Internet, get directions to a restaurant, search on Google, or connect with a friend on Facebook.

Hadoop can process large quantities of any kind of data, including structured transactional data, loosely structured data such as Facebook and Twitter feeds, complex data such as Web server log files, and unstructured audio and video data. Hadoop runs on a cluster of inexpensive servers, and processors can be added or removed as needed. Companies use Hadoop to analyze very large volumes of data as well as for a staging area for unstructured and semi-structured data before it is loaded into a data warehouse. Facebook stores much of its data on its massive Hadoop cluster, which holds an estimated 300 petabytes, about 30,000 times more information than the Library of Congress. Yahoo uses Hadoop to track user behavior so it can modify its home page to fit user interests. Life sciences research firm NextBio uses Hadoop and HBase to process data for pharmaceutical companies conducting genomic research. Top database vendors such as IBM, Hewlett-Packard, Oracle, and Microsoft have their own Hadoop software distributions. Other vendors offer tools for moving data into and out of Hadoop or for analyzing data within Hadoop. In addition, there are many new tools being developed for Big Data analysis in addition to Hadoop. One example is Spark, an open source product being supported by IBM that can deliver results faster than Hadoop.

MARKETING AUTOMATION AND CUSTOMER RELATIONSHIP MANAGEMENT (CRM) SYSTEMS

marketing automation systems

software tools that marketers use to track all the steps in the lead generation part of the marketing process

Marketing automation systems are software tools that marketers use to track all the steps in the lead generation part of the marketing process. The marketing process begins with making the potential customer aware of the firm and product, and recognizing the need for the product. This is the beginning of a lead—someone who might buy. From there, consumers need to find you as they search for products; they will compare your products with your competitors' offerings and at some point, choose to purchase. Software can help in each of these stages of the marketing process. A number of firms sell software packages that can visualize most of the online marketing activities of a firm and then track the progression from exposure to display ads, finding your firm on a search engine, directing follow-up e-mail and communications, and finally a purchase. Once leads become customers, customer relationship management systems take over the maintenance of the relationship.

customer relationship management (CRM) system

a repository of customer information that records all of the contacts that a customer has with a firm and generates a customer profile available to everyone in the firm with a need to "know the customer"

Customer relationship management systems are another important Internet marketing technology. A **customer relationship management (CRM) system** is a repository of customer information that records all of the contacts that a customer has with a firm (including Web sites) and generates a customer profile available to everyone in the firm with a need to "know the customer." CRM systems also supply the analytical software required to analyze and use customer information. Customers come to firms not just over the Web but also through telephone call centers, customer service representatives, sales representatives, automated voice response systems, ATMs and kiosks, in-store point-of-sale terminals, and mobile devices (m-commerce).

Collectively, these are referred to as "**customer touchpoints**." In the past, firms generally did not maintain a single repository of customer information, but instead were organized along product lines, with each product line maintaining a customer list (and often not sharing it with others in the same firm).

In general, firms did not know who their customers were, how profitable they were, or how they responded to marketing campaigns. For instance, a bank customer might see a television advertisement for a low-cost auto loan that included an 800-number to call. However, if the customer came to the bank's Web site instead, rather than calling the 800-number, marketers would have no idea how effective the television campaign was because this Web customer contact data was not related to the 800-number call center data. **Figure 6.10** illustrates how a CRM system integrates customer contact data into a single system.

CRMs are part of the evolution of firms toward a customer-centric and marketing-segment–based business, and away from a product-line–centered business. CRMs

customer touchpoints
the ways in which customers interact with the firm

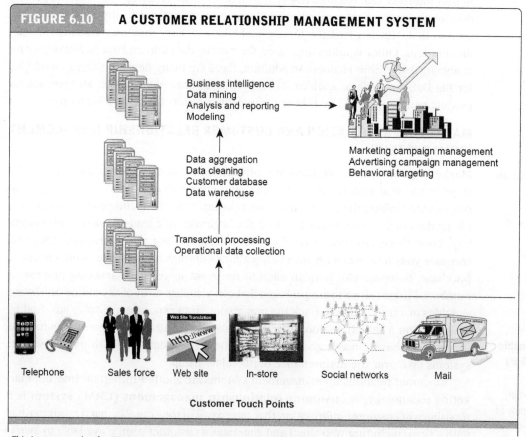

FIGURE 6.10   A CUSTOMER RELATIONSHIP MANAGEMENT SYSTEM

Business intelligence
Data mining
Analysis and reporting
Modeling

Marketing campaign management
Advertising campaign management
Behavioral targeting

Data aggregation
Data cleaning
Customer database
Data warehouse

Transaction processing
Operational data collection

Telephone   Sales force   Web site   In-store   Social networks   Mail

Customer Touch Points

This is an example of a CRM system. The system captures customer information from all customer touchpoints as well as other data sources, merges the data, and aggregates it into a single customer data repository or data warehouse where it can be used to provide better service, as well as to construct customer profiles for marketing purposes. Online analytical processing (OLAP) allows managers to dynamically analyze customer activities to spot trends or problems involving customers. Other analytical software programs analyze aggregate customer behavior to identify profitable and unprofitable customers as well as customer activities.

are essentially a database technology with extraordinary capabilities for addressing the needs of each customer and differentiating the product or service on the basis of treating each customer as a unique person. Customer profiles can contain the following information:

- A map of the customer's relationship with the institution
- Product and usage summary data
- Demographic and psychographic data
- Profitability measures
- Contact history summarizing the customer's contacts with the institution across most delivery channels
- Marketing and sales information containing programs received by the customer and the customer's responses
- E-mail campaign responses
- Web site visits
- Mobile app downloads

With these profiles, CRMs can be used to sell additional products and services, develop new products, increase product utilization, reduce marketing costs, identify and retain profitable customers, optimize service delivery costs, retain high lifetime value customers, enable personal communications, improve customer loyalty, and increase product profitability. The goal is what is known as a "360-degree" view that enables a company to know what its customers buy, how they browse, what kinds of communications and offers will engage them, and more. Leading CRM vendors include Oracle, SAP, Microsoft, Salesforce.com, and SugarCRM, many of which offer cloud-based versions of their CRM products. One issue facing cloud CRM providers and global companies that use those products is impending European Union data regulations that will require them to reassess how they use CRM data in order to avoid violating those regulations. All the major vendors offer cloud-based SaaS CRM applications.

6.4   UNDERSTANDING THE COSTS AND BENEFITS OF ONLINE MARKETING COMMUNICATIONS

As we noted earlier, online marketing communications still comprise only a small part of the total marketing communications universe. While there are several reasons why this is the case, two of the main ones are concerns about how well online advertising really works and about how to adequately measure the costs and benefits of online advertising. We will address both of these topics in this section. But first, we will define some important terms used when examining the effectiveness of online marketing.

ONLINE MARKETING METRICS: LEXICON

In order to understand the process of attracting prospects via marketing communications and converting them into customers, you will need to be familiar with online marketing terminology. **Table 6.7** lists some terms commonly used to describe the impacts and results of "traditional" online marketing such as display ads and e-mail campaigns. Metrics for social, mobile and local marketing are covered in Chapter 7.

The first nine metrics focus primarily on the success of a Web site in achieving audience or market share by "driving" shoppers to the site. These measures often substitute for solid information on sales revenue as e-commerce entrepreneurs seek to have investors and the public focus on the success of the Web site in "attracting eyeballs" (viewers).

Impressions are the number of times an ad is served. **Click-through rate (CTR)** measures the percentage of people exposed to an online advertisement who actually click on the advertisement. Because not all ads lead to an immediate click, the industry has invented a term for a long-term hit called **view-through rate (VTR)**, which measures the 30-day response rate to an ad. **Hits** are the number of HTTP requests received by a firm's server. Hits can be misleading as a measure of Web site activity because a "hit" does not equal a page. A single page may account for several hits if the page contains multiple images or graphics. A single Web site visitor can generate hundreds of hits. For this reason, hits are not an accurate representation of Web traffic or visits, even though they are generally easy to measure; the sheer volume of hits can be huge—and sound impressive—but not be a true measure of activity. **Page views** are the number of pages requested by visitors. However, with increased usage of Web frames that divide pages into separate sections, a single page that has three frames will generate three page views. Hence, page views per se are also not a very useful metric.

Viewability rate is the percentage of ads (either display or video) that are actually seen by people online. See page 403 for a further discussion of the issue of viewability.

The number of unique visitors is perhaps the most widely used measure of a Web site's popularity. The measurement of **unique visitors** counts the number of distinct, unique visitors to a Web site, regardless of how many pages they view. **Loyalty** measures the percentage of visitors who return in a year. This can be a good indicator of a site's Web following, and perhaps the trust shoppers place in a site. **Reach** is typically a percentage of the total number of consumers in a market who visit a Web site; for example, 10% of all book purchasers in a year will visit Amazon at least once to shop for a book. This provides an idea of the power of a Web site to attract market share. **Recency**—like loyalty—measures the power of a Web site to produce repeat visits and is generally measured as the average number of days elapsed between shopper or customer visits. For example, a recency value of 25 days means the average customer will return once every 25 days.

Stickiness (sometimes called *duration*) is the average length of time visitors remain at a Web site. Stickiness is important to marketers because the longer the amount of time a visitor spends at a Web site, the greater the probability of a purchase. However, equally important is what people do when they visit a Web site and not just how much time they spend there.

The metrics described so far do not say much about commercial activity nor help you understand the conversion from visitor to customer. Several other measures are more helpful in this regard. **Acquisition rate** measures the percentage of visitors who register or visit product pages (indicating interest in the product). **Conversion rate** measures the percentage of visitors who actually purchase something. Conversion

impressions
number of times an ad is served

click-through rate (CTR)
the percentage of people exposed to an online advertisement who actually click on the banner

view-through rate (VTR)
measures the 30-day response rate to an ad

hits
number of http requests received by a firm's server

page views
number of pages requested by visitors

viewability rate
percentage of ads that are actually seen by people online

unique visitors
the number of distinct, unique visitors to a site

loyalty
percentage of purchasers who return in a year

reach
percentage of the total number of consumers in a market who will visit a site

recency
average number of days elapsed between visits

stickiness (duration)
average length of time visitors remain at a site

acquisition rate
percentage of visitors who register or visit product pages

conversion rate
percentage of visitors who purchase something

TABLE 6.7	MARKETING METRICS LEXICON
DISPLAY AD METRICS	**DESCRIPTION**
Impressions	Number of times an ad is served
Click-through rate (CTR)	Percentage of times an ad is clicked
View-through rate (VTR)	Percentage of times an ad is not clicked immediately but the Web site is visited within 30 days
Hits	Number of HTTP requests
Page views	Number of pages viewed
Viewability rate	Percentage of ads that are actually seen online
Unique visitors	Number of unique visitors in a period
Loyalty	Measured variously as the number of page views, frequency of single-user visits to the Web site, or percentage of customers who return to the site in a year to make additional purchases
Reach	Percentage of Web site visitors who are potential buyers; or the percentage of total market buyers who buy at a site
Recency	Time elapsed since the last action taken by a buyer, such as a Web site visit or purchase
Stickiness (duration)	Average length of stay at a Web site
Acquisition rate	Percentage of visitors who indicate an interest in the Web site's products by registering or visiting product pages
Conversion rate	Percentage of visitors who become customers
Browse-to-buy ratio	Ratio of items purchased to product views
View-to-cart ratio	Ratio of "Add to cart" clicks to product views
Cart conversion rate	Ratio of actual orders to "Add to cart" clicks
Checkout conversion rate	Ratio of actual orders to checkouts started
Abandonment rate	Percentage of shoppers who begin a shopping cart purchase but then leave the Web site without completing a purchase (similar to above)
Retention rate	Percentage of existing customers who continue to buy on a regular basis (similar to loyalty)
Attrition rate	Percentage of customers who do not return during the next year after an initial purchase
VIDEO ADVERTISING METRICS	
View time	How long does the ad actually stay in view while it plays
Completion rate	How many viewers watched the complete video
Skip rate	How many viewers skipped the video
E-MAIL METRICS	
Open rate	Percentage of e-mail recipients who open the e-mail and are exposed to the message
Delivery rate	Percentage of e-mail recipients who received the e-mail
Click-through rate (e-mail)	Percentage of recipients who clicked through to offers
Bounce-back rate	Percentage of e-mails that could not be delivered
Unsubscribe rate	Percentage of recipients who click unsubscribe
Conversion rate (e-mail)	Percentage of recipients who actually buy

rates can vary widely, depending on the success of the site. The average conversion rate in the United States for e-commerce sites on traditional desktop computers was about 3.4% in 2014, compared to about 2.75% for tablet computers and 1.1% for smartphones. Clearly, Web sites viewed on desktops still remain the most effective vehicle for converting visitors into purchasers (Monetate, 2015). The **browse-to-buy ratio** measures the ratio of items purchased to product views. The **view-to-cart ratio** calculates the ratio of "Add to cart" clicks to product views. **Cart conversion rate** measures the ratio of actual orders to "Add to cart" clicks. **Checkout conversion rate** calculates the ratio of actual orders to checkouts started. **Abandonment rate** measures the percentage of shoppers who begin a shopping cart form but then fail to complete the form and leave the Web site. Abandonment rates can signal a number of potential problems—poor form design, lack of consumer trust, or consumer purchase uncertainty caused by other factors. Recent studies on shopping cart abandonment found abandonment rates ranging from 68% to 75% (Baymard, 2015). Among the reasons for abandonment were security concerns, customer just checking prices, couldn't find customer support, couldn't find preferred payment option, and the item being unavailable at checkout. Given that more than 80% of online shoppers generally have a purchase in mind when they visit a Web site, a high abandonment rate signals many lost sales. **Retention rate** indicates the percentage of existing customers who continue to buy on a regular basis. **Attrition rate** measures the percentage of customers who purchase once but never return within a year (the opposite of loyalty and retention rates).

Specific types of advertising have their own special metrics. For instance, for video ads, **view time** (how long the ad actually stays in view while it plays) and **completion rate** (how many viewers watch the entire video ad) are important factors. Research has shown that brand recall is significantly higher when the entire ad is watched, making the completion rate metric more meaningful to advertisers than the click-through rate (Adler, 2015).

E-mail campaigns also have their own set of metrics. **Open rate** measures the percentage of customers who open the e-mail and are exposed to the message. Generally, open rates are quite high, in the area of 50% or greater. However, some browsers open mail as soon as the mouse cursor moves over the subject line, and therefore this measure can be difficult to interpret. **Delivery rate** measures the percentage of e-mail recipients who received the e-mail. **Click-through rate (e-mail)** measures the percentage of e-mail recipients who clicked through to the offer. Finally, **bounce-back rate** measures the percentage of e-mails that could not be delivered.

There is a lengthy path from simple online ad impressions, Web site visits, and page views to the purchase of a product and the company making a profit (see **Figure 6.11**). You first need to make customers aware of their needs for your product and somehow drive them to your Web site. Once there, you need to convince them you have the best value—quality and price—when compared to alternative providers. You then must persuade them to trust your firm to handle the transaction (by providing a secure environment and fast fulfillment). Based on your success, a percentage of customers will remain loyal and purchase again or recommend your Web site to others.

browse-to-buy ratio
ratio of items purchased to product views

view-to-cart ratio
ratio of "Add to cart" clicks to product views

cart conversion rate
ratio of actual orders to "Add to cart" clicks

checkout conversion rate
ratio of actual orders to checkouts started

abandonment rate
% of shoppers who begin a shopping cart, but then fail to complete it

retention rate
% of existing customers who continue to buy

attrition rate
% of customers who purchase once, but do not return within a year

view time
how long the video ad actually stays in view while it plays

completion rate
how many viewers watch the complete video ad

open rate
% of customers who open e-mail

delivery rate
% of e-mail recipients who received e-mail

click-through rate (e-mail)
% of e-mail recipients who clicked through to the offer

bounce-back rate
percentage of e-mails that could not be delivered

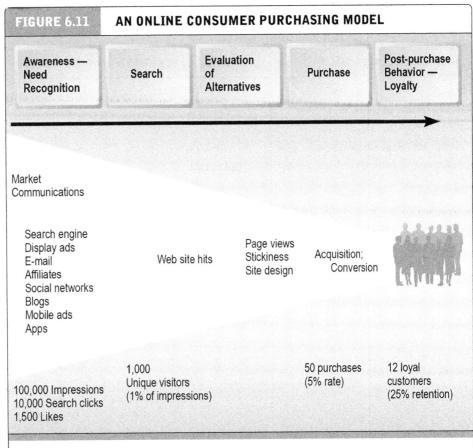

FIGURE 6.11	AN ONLINE CONSUMER PURCHASING MODEL

Awareness — Need Recognition	Search	Evaluation of Alternatives	Purchase	Post-purchase Behavior — Loyalty

Market Communications

Search engine
Display ads
E-mail
Affiliates
Social networks
Blogs
Mobile ads
Apps

Web site hits

Page views
Stickiness
Site design

Acquisition;
Conversion

100,000 Impressions
10,000 Search clicks
1,500 Likes

1,000
Unique visitors
(1% of impressions)

50 purchases
(5% rate)

12 loyal
customers
(25% retention)

The conversion of visitors into customers, and then loyal customers, is a complex and long-term process that may take several months.

HOW WELL DOES ONLINE ADVERTISING WORK?

What is the most effective kind of online advertising? How does online advertising compare to offline advertising? The answers depend on the goals of the campaign, the nature of the product, and the quality of the Web site you direct customers toward. The answers also depend on what you measure. Click-through rates are interesting, but ultimately it's the return on the investment (ROI) in the ad campaign that counts. More than 70% of marketing executives said they would spend even more on digital ads if ability to measure ROI improved (Tadena, 2015). Complicating matters is the difficulty of **cross-platform attribution**, which involves understanding how to assign appropriate credit to different marketing initiatives on a variety of platforms that may have influenced a consumer along the way to an ultimate purchase. There is increasing recognition that first-click and last-click models that focus, as their names indicate, on either the first or last marketing channel or advertising format that a consumer engages with prior to a purchase, are no longer sufficient.

cross-platform attribution

understanding how to assign appropriate credit to different marketing initiatives that may have influenced a consumer on the way to a purchase

TABLE 6.8	ONLINE MARKETING COMMUNICATIONS: TYPICAL CLICK-THROUGH RATES
MARKETING METHODS	**TYPICAL CLICK-THROUGH RATES**
Banner ads	.03%–.25%
Google enhanced search ads (Product Listing Ads)	2.8%–3.6%
Search engine keyword purchase	.70–5.0%
Video	.30%–1.65%
Rich media	.13%–.35%
Sponsorships	1.50%–3.00%
Affiliate relationships	.20%–.40%
E-mail marketing in-house list	3.0–5.0%
E-mail marketing purchased list	.01%–1.50%
Social site display ads	.15%–.25%
Mobile display ads	.09%–1.25%

SOURCES: Based on data from The Search Agency, 2014; eMarketer, Inc., 2015k; PointRoll, 2015; Vindico, 2015; industry sources; authors' estimates.

Table 6.8 lists the click-through rates for various types of online marketing communications tools. There is a great deal of variability within any of these types, so the figures should be viewed as general estimates. Click-through rates on all these formats are a function of personalization and other targeting techniques. For instance, several studies have found that e-mail response rates can be increased 20% or more by adding social sharing links. And while the average Google click-through rate is less than 1%, some merchants can hit 10% or more by making their ads more specific and attracting only the most interested people. Permission e-mail click-through rates have been fairly consistent over the last five years, in the 3%–5% range. Putting the recipient's name in the subject line can double the click-through rate. (For unsolicited e-mail and outright spam, response rates are much lower, even though about 20% of U.S. e-mail users report clicking occasionally on an unsolicited e-mail.) The click-through rate for video ads may seem low, but it is twice as high as the rate for banner ads. For instance, research by PointRoll found that adding video to a rich media campaign increased interaction rates by over 17% on average (PointRoll, 2015). "Interaction" means the user clicks on the video, plays it, stops it, or takes some other action.

How effective is online advertising compared to offline advertising? In general, the online channels (e-mail, search engine, display ads, video, and social, mobile, and local marketing) compare very favorably with traditional channels. This explains in large part why online advertising has grown so rapidly in the last five years. Search engine advertising has grown to be one of the most cost-effective forms of marketing communications and accounts for, in large part, the growth of Google. Direct opt-in e-mail is also very cost-effective. This is, in part, because e-mail lists are so inexpensive and because opt-in e-mail is a form of targeting people who are already interested in receiving more information.

A study of the comparative impacts of offline and online marketing concluded that the most powerful marketing campaigns used multiple forms of marketing, including online, catalog, television, radio, newspapers, and retail store. Traditional media like television and print media remain the primary means for consumers to find out about new products even though advertisers have reduced their budgets for print media ads. Consumers who shop multiple channels are spending more than consumers who shop only with a single channel, in part because they have more discretionary income but also because of the combined number of "touchpoints" that marketers are making with the consumers. The fastest growing channel in consumer marketing is the multi-channel shopper.

cost per thousand (CPM)
advertiser pays for impressions in 1,000-unit lots

cost per click (CPC)
advertiser pays prenegotiated fee for each click an ad receives

cost per action (CPA)
advertiser pays only for those users who perform a specific action

THE COSTS OF ONLINE ADVERTISING

Effectiveness cannot be considered without an analysis of costs. Initially, most online ads were sold on a barter or **cost per thousand (CPM)** impressions basis, with advertisers purchasing impressions in 1,000-unit lots. Today, other pricing models have developed, including **cost per click (CPC)**, where the advertiser pays a prenegotiated fee for each click an ad receives; **cost per action (CPA)**, where the advertiser pays a prenegotiated amount only when a user performs a specific action, such as a registration or a purchase; and hybrid arrangements, combining two or more of these models (see **Table 6.9**).

TABLE 6.9	DIFFERENT PRICING MODELS FOR ONLINE ADVERTISEMENTS
PRICING MODEL	DESCRIPTION
Barter	Exchange of ad space for something of equal value
Cost per thousand (CPM)	Advertiser pays for impressions in 1,000-unit lots
Cost per click (CPC)	Advertiser pays prenegotiated fee for each click ad received
Cost per lead (CPL)	Advertiser pays only for qualified leads or contacts
Cost per action (CPA)	Advertiser pays only for those users who perform a specific action, such as registering, purchasing, etc.
Hybrid	Two or more of the above models used together
Sponsorship	Term-based; advertiser pays fixed fee for a slot on a Web site

While in the early days of e-commerce, a few online sites spent as much as $400 on marketing and advertising to acquire one customer, the average cost was never that high. While the costs for offline customer acquisition are higher than online, the offline items are typically far more expensive. If you advertise in the *Wall Street Journal,* you are tapping into a wealthy demographic that may be interested in buying islands, jets, and expensive homes in France. A full-page black and white ad in the *Wall Street Journal* National Edition costs about $270,000, whereas other papers are in the $10,000 to $100,000 range.

One of the advantages of online marketing is that online sales can generally be directly correlated with online marketing efforts. If online merchants can obtain offline purchase data from a data broker, the merchants can measure precisely just how much revenue is generated by specific banners or e-mail messages sent to prospective customers. One way to measure the effectiveness of online marketing is by looking at the ratio of additional revenue received divided by the cost of the campaign (Revenue/Cost). Any positive whole number means the campaign was worthwhile.

A more complex situation arises when both online and offline sales revenues are affected by an online marketing effort. A large percentage of the online audience uses the Web to "shop" but not buy. These shoppers buy at physical stores. Merchants such as Sears and Walmart use e-mail to inform their registered customers of special offers available for purchase either online or at stores. Unfortunately, purchases at physical stores cannot be tied precisely with the online e-mail campaign. In these cases, merchants have to rely on less precise measures such as customer surveys at store locations to determine the effectiveness of online campaigns.

In either case, measuring the effectiveness of online marketing communications—and specifying precisely the objective (branding versus sales)—is critical to profitability. To measure marketing effectiveness, you need to understand the costs of various marketing media and the process of converting online prospects into online customers.

In general, online marketing communications are more costly on a CPM basis than traditional mass media marketing, but are more efficient in producing sales. **Table 6.10** shows costs for typical online and offline marketing communications. For instance, in 2015, the average cost for 30 seconds of commercial time during a prime-time network television broadcast is about $112,000, not including the cost to produce the advertisement. According to Nielsen, such an ad has an average CPM of $24.76. In contrast, a banner ad costs virtually nothing to produce and can be purchased for a cost of from $5–$10 per thousand impressions. Direct postal mail can cost 80 cents to $1 per household drop for a post card, while e-mail can be sent for virtually nothing and costs only $5–$15 per thousand targeted names. Hence, e-mail is far less expensive than postal mail on a CPM basis. **Effective cost-per-thousand (eCPM)** is a metric that measures return on investment from an ad by dividing the total earnings from the ad by the total number of impressions in thousands.

effective cost-per-thousand (eCPM) measures return on investment from an ad by dividing the total earnings from the ad by the total number of impressions in thousands

TABLE 6.10	TRADITIONAL AND ONLINE ADVERTISING COSTS COMPARED
TRADITIONAL ADVERTISING	
Local television	$1,500–$15,000 for a 30-second commercial; $45,000 for a highly rated show
Network television	$80,000–$600,000 for a 30-second spot during prime time; the average is $112,000
Cable television	$5,000–$8,000 for a 30-second ad during prime time
Radio	$100–$1,000 for a 60-second spot, depending on the time of day and program ratings
Newspaper	$120 per 1,000 circulation for a full-page ad
Magazine	$50 per 1,000 circulation for an ad in a regional edition of a national magazine, versus $120 per 1,000 for a local magazine
Direct mail	$15–$20 per 1,000 delivered for coupon mailings; $25–$40 per 1,000 for simple newspaper inserts
Billboard	$1,500–$30,000 for a large billboard for a 4-week period, with a minimum of 5–20 billboards
ONLINE ADVERTISING	
Banner ads	$5–$10 per 1,000 impressions, depending on how targeted the ad is (the more targeted, the higher the price)
Video and rich media	$20–$25 per 1,000 ads, depending on the Web site's demographics
E-mail	$5–$15 per 1,000 targeted e-mail addresses
Sponsorships	$30–$75 per 1,000 viewers, depending on the exclusivity of the sponsorship (the more exclusive, the higher the price)
Social network ads	$0.50–$3.00 per 1,000 impressions, with news feed ads at the high end of the range
Mobile display ads	$1.50–$3.25 per 1,000 impressions, including media costs, charges for first- or third-party data and service fees

MARKETING ANALYTICS: SOFTWARE FOR MEASURING ONLINE MARKETING RESULTS

A number of software programs are available to automatically calculate activities at a Web site or on a mobile device. Tracking the viewing and behavior of consumers across myriad devices and media channels is a much more difficult task. Other software programs and services assist marketing managers in identifying exactly which marketing initiatives are paying off and which are not.

The purpose of marketing is to convert shoppers into customers who purchase what you sell. The process of converting shoppers into customers is often called a

FIGURE 6.12 MARKETING ANALYTICS AND THE ONLINE PURCHASING PROCESS

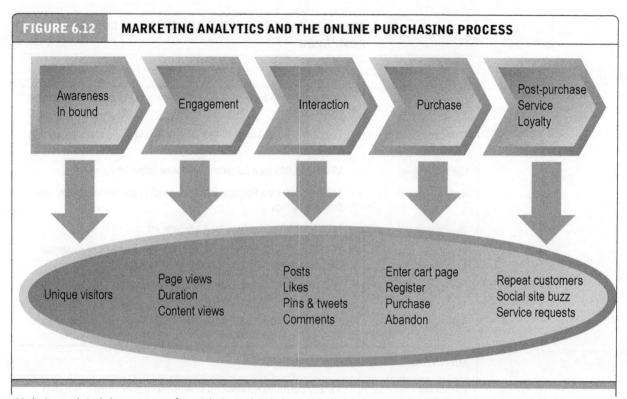

Marketing analytics help e-commerce firms to better understand consumer behavior at each stage of the online purchasing process.

"purchasing funnel." We have characterized this as a process rather than a funnel that is composed of several stages: awareness, engagement, interaction, purchase, and post-purchase service and loyalty. **Marketing analytics software** collects, stores, analyzes, and graphically presents data on each of the stages in the conversion of shoppers to customers (see **Figure 6.12**).

Marketing analytics packages can tell business managers how people become *aware* of their site, and where they come from (e.g., search, self-entered URL, e-mail, social campaigns, or off-line traditional print and TV ads), along with demographic, behavioral, and geographic information. Are shoppers coming from mobile devices, Facebook or Pinterest? This information can help managers decide the best ways to drive traffic, the so-called "in-bound" links to a site. Once on the Web site, analytics packages can record how *engaged* visitors are with the site's content, measured in terms of pages viewed and duration on site. This information can allow managers to change the design or their sites, or change the content viewers are seeing. For instance, video testimonials from product users may be much more engaging than expert reviews or user text comments. In a social marketing world, where consumers' opinions and behavior can be harvested and broadcast to their friends, an important intermediate step in the consumer conversion process is to encourage visitors to *interact* with your

marketing analytics software

collects, stores, analyzes, and graphically presents data on each of the stages in the conversion of shoppers to customers process on e-commerce sites

content and share their experiences, opinions, preferences, and behaviors with their friends, as well as other visitors to the site. Marketing analytics packages can track visitor interaction and help managers decide what content leads to higher levels of visitor interaction with friends and other visitors. The *purchase activity* on the shopping cart page is a major focus of analytics tools not just because this is where the revenue is generated, but also because this is where the customer frequently exits the entire site and the firm loses a potential sale. Current shopping cart abandonment is about 75% in the United States, with little change over the last few years, and higher in other countries (eMarketer, Inc., 2015l). This seems like an extraordinary rate but, like most of the indicators discussed in this chapter, abandonment is a complex phenomenon and often not what it seems. Consumers use carts like a shopping list, and don't complete the transaction immediately; they use it for price comparison and to know shipping costs, or taxes; they complete transactions later on a different device, such as a mobile phone. Another measure of near-purchase activity is the add-to-cart rate. Marketing analytics software can help managers tease out the meaning of behavior on a Web site's shopping cart page. Finally, marketing analytics can help managers discover customer *loyalty and post-purchase* behavior. In an increasingly social marketing environment, marketing managers need to know how their products and services are being talked about on other sites, Facebook pages, or Twitter tweets, often called "buzz" or sentiment analysis. Are the comments positive or negative? What is the source of negative comments? Possible candidates are poor quality, high costs, poor warranty service, and shipping issues.

The end objective of marketing analytics packages is to help business managers optimize the return on investment on their marketing efforts, and to do this by building a detailed understanding of how their consumers behave. Marketing analytics also allows managers to measure the impact of specific marketing campaigns involving, say, discounts, loyalty points, and special offers, as well as regional, or demographic-based campaigns. Aside from its role in enhancing management decision making, and optimizing the effectiveness of building an e-commerce presence, marketing analytics packages also enable a near real-time marketing capability where managers are able to change the content of a Web site, respond to customer complaints and comments, and align campaigns with trending topics or news developments, all in a near real-time manner (real-time may be a matter of minutes or at most 24 hours) (MarketingLand, 2015).

While there are a great many marketing analytics firms and software packages on the market, the leaders are Google Analytics, Adobe Analytics, IBM Digital Analytics, and Webtrends. Marketing analytics software is often part of a comprehensive package sold to corporations from hardware, to Web design tools, cloud services, and management expertise.

Programmatic Advertising:
Real-Time Marketing

The holy grail of advertising and marketing is to deliver the right message to the right person at the right time. If this were possible, no one would receive ads they did not want to see, and then no advertising dollars would be wasted, reducing the costs to end users and increasing the efficiency of each ad dollar. In the physical world, only a very rough approximation of this ideal is possible. Advertisers can buy television and radio spots, newspaper ads, and billboards based on broad demographics and interests of likely potential customers. The Internet promised to change this. On the Internet, ads supposedly could be targeted to individual consumers based on their personal characteristics, interests, and recent clickstream behavior. One early vision of e-commerce was a trade-off between privacy and efficiency: let us know more about you, and we will show you only the advertising and products you are interested in seeing, and even offer free content. E-commerce was supposed to end the mass advertising that exploded in the television era.

But contrary to popular impressions and the fears of privacy advocates, most of the display ads shown to site visitors are marvelously irrelevant to visitors' interests, both short-term and long-term. For this reason, the click-through rate for banner advertising is a stunningly low 0.03%, and the price of display ads has fallen to a few cents because of their poor performance. Check this out: visit Yahoo (the largest display advertiser on earth) on a desktop or laptop computer, look at the prominent ads shown on the right,

and ask yourself if you are really interested in the ad content at this moment in time. How about ever? Chances are slim you are interested at this moment, even if the ad is somewhat appropriate to your demographics. Often, it is an ad for something you are totally not interested in and never have been. Researchers have found that only 20% of Internet users find that display ads on Web sites are relevant to their interests. Programmatic advertising promises to improve the targeting of ads, decreasing costs for advertisers, and making the Web less annoying to consumers by showing them ads that really are of interest to them.

Programmatic advertising is an automated method that publishers use to sell their inventory (empty slots on their Web pages) to advertisers who want to buy ad space for their customers (brand and product owners looking to market their products and services). There are two kinds of programmatic advertising: auction-based real time bidding (RTB), and programmatic direct, where advertisers deal directly with publishers in a semi-automated environment.

Programmatic advertising platforms use Big Data repositories that contain personal information on hundreds of millions of online shoppers and consumers; analytic software to classify and search the database for shoppers with the desired characteristics; and machine learning techniques to test out combinations of consumer characteristics that optimize the chance of a purchase resulting from exposure to an ad. All of this technology is designed to lower the cost, increase the speed, and increase the efficiency of advertising in an environment where there are hundreds of millions of Web pages to fill with ads, and millions of online consumers looking to buy at any given moment. Programmatic advertising allows advertisers to potentially show the right ad, at the right time, to just the right person, in a matter of milliseconds. To the extent this is true, display advertising becomes more effective, and perhaps could become as effective as search-based advertising, where it is much more obvious what the searcher is looking for, or interested in, at the moment of search. In 2015, RTB digital display advertising will total an estimated $11 billion in the United States, about 42% of all online display advertising. Analysts believe programmatic advertising will grow to about $20 billion by 2016 and that by then, almost two-thirds of all U.S. ads will be placed programmatically.

Currently, 45% of online display advertising is still done in a non-automated, traditional environment that involves e-mail, fax, phone, and text messaging. This is the world of the traditional insertion order: if you want to advertise in a newspaper or magazine, call the ad department and fill out an insertion order. In this environment, firms who want to sell products and services online hire advertising agencies to develop a marketing plan. The ad agencies learn from the firms what kinds of people they would like to contact online. The ad agencies pay data brokers or advertising networks like DoubleClick to help them identify where the online ads should be placed given the nature of the product and the specific characteristics the producer firms are looking for. For instance, let's say a firm wants to market a new mountain bike to men and women, ages 24–35, who live in zip codes where mountain biking is a popular activity. Ad networks traditionally would direct the agency to direct purchases of ad space from Web sites that attract the mountain biking audience.

This traditional environment is expensive, imprecise, and slow, in part because of the number of people involved in the decision about where to place ads. Also, the technology used is slow, and the process of learning which of several ads is optimal could take weeks or months. The ads could be targeted to a more precise group of potential customers. While context advertising on sites dedicated to a niche product is very effective, there are many other Web sites visited by bikers that might be equally effective, and cost much less.

The process is very different in a programmatic environment. Ad agencies have access to any of several programmatic ad platforms offered by Google, Yahoo, AOL, Facebook, and many smaller firms. Working with their clients, the ad agency more precisely defines the target audience to include men and women, ages 24–35, who live in zip codes where mountain biking is a popular activity, have mentioned biking topics on social network sites, have e-mail where mountain biking is discussed, make more than $70,000 a year, and currently do not own a mountain bike. The ad agency enters a bid expressed in dollars per thousand impressions for 200,000 impressions to people who meet the characteristics being sought. The platform returns a quote for access to this population of 200,000 people who meet the characteristics required. The quote is based on what other advertisers are willing to pay for that demographic and characteristics. The quote is accepted or denied. If accepted, the ads are shown to people as they move about the Web, in real-time. As people come on to various Web sites they visit, the automated program assesses whether they meet the desired characteristics, and displays the mountain bike ad with milliseconds to that person. The programmatic platforms also track the responses to the ads in real time, and can change to different ads and test for effectiveness based on the platform's experience. Once the system learns from experience, it will focus on showing the most effective ads on the most productive Web sites. Programmatic direct (or premium) advertising uses the same platform, but publishers sell blocks of inventory to ad agencies rather than single impressions. This stabilizes their income, and puts them in closer contact with advertisers who can also exercise greater oversight over the publishers.

The auto industry is a large user of programmatic advertising. Car brands are highly focused on specific demographic groups, income levels, and aspirations. A programmatic campaign begins with the advertiser picking a demographic target, establishing a total budget for the campaign, and then choosing an RTB platform and competing for the delivery of an ad to that audience against other advertisers who may be other auto companies, retailers, or telecommunications providers. The ads are awarded and served automatically in millisecond-quick transactions handled by machines.

Despite its clear advantages, there are also several risks involved for all parties. Advertisers lose control over where their ads will appear on the Web. This is a threat to a brand if its products are shown on inappropriate sites. Advertisers lose some accountability for their expenditures because they cannot verify that their ads are actually being shown, and they must take the ad platform's word that indeed the ads are being shown to real people. This is a transparency issue. Ghost sites and ad fraud complicate the picture as well. There are thousands of ghost sites on the Web that do nothing but attract clicks using various ruses. Ad networks record this traffic

SOURCES: "Clorox Is Betting Big on Programmatic Advertising," by Jack Marshall, *Wall Street Journal*, September 4, 2015; "New Breed of Digital Publishers Just Say No to Ad Tech," by Mike Shields, *Wall Street Journal*, July 28, 2015; "US Auto Industry Sets Brisk Pace with Mobile Programmatic," by eMarketer, Inc., July 2, 2014; "Creating Ads on the Fly: Fostering Creativity in the Programmatic Era," by Debra Aho Williamson, eMarketer, Inc., April 2015; "Procter & Gamble CMO Pritchard: Programmatic Delivers Business Lift," by Sarah Sluis, Adexchanger. com, March 6, 2015; "Get With the Programmatic: A Primer on Programmatic Advertising," by Or Shani, Marketingland.com, August 22, 2014; "Programmatic Advertising Spreads Quickly Despite Nagging Problems, Says AOL Survey," by Robert Hof, Adage.com, August 13, 2014; "How Big Media Is Adapting to Automated Ad Buying," *Wall Street Journal*, June 27, 2014; "Proctor & Gamble Aims to Buy 70% of Digital Ads Programmatically," Adage.com, June 4, 2014; "Programmatic Buying Roundup," by Lauren Fisher, eMarketer, Inc., June 2014; "Programmatic Guaranteed," by Lauren Fisher, eMarketer Inc., May 2014; "Driving Programmatic Buying: Automotive Industry Will Invest Big in 2014," by Mike Hudson et al., eMarketer, Inc., January 2014; "Programmatic Everywhere? Data, Technology and the Future of Audience Engagement," IAB, November 4, 2013; "RTB Is the Most Overhyped Technology Ever: It's Useful for Extending the Reach of Mediocre Content, but Not for Subtle, Thoughtful Buys," by Joe Mohen, Adage.com, May 30, 2013.

and have little capability to determine if it is legitimate, and may show ads on these sites, which will generate fraudulent clicks that are paid for by the ad network and the advertising firm.

Given the risks, many of the largest advertisers initially did not use programmatic advertising, but that is rapidly changing. It was first used by publishers to sell inventory that was left over after the major ad campaigns had purchased the premium slots on Web pages. Programmatic platforms were inexpensive places to sell excess inventory. However, that is beginning to change as advertisers gain confidence and the platforms themselves improve their abilities to avoid inappropriate Web sites, purge ghost sites, and learn how to detect click fraud. In addition, a number of firms have stepped into the market with tools that address these concerns.

For instance, in 2014, Procter & Gamble announced that, going forward, it planned to buy 70%–75% of its U.S. digital media using programmatic methods. P&G is the largest advertiser in the country, spending $4.6 billion on advertising in the United States in 2014. In the past, P&G purchased premium online inventory at the top 100 comScore sites through several different ad agencies and tracked performance using its internal staff. According to P&G's Chief Marketing Officer Marc Pritchard, programmatic advertising has allowed P&G to more precisely target its advertising at a good price, providing a good return on investment. Other companies are following suit. Cleaning supply company Clorox is devoting about 50% of its entire digital budget to programmatic advertising in 2015.

However, some upstart Web publishers aimed at the millennial demographic are trying to buck the trend. Vox Media, Refinery29, and Mic have all rejected programmatic advertising and will only sell advertising space directly to advertisers. These publishers object on the ground that programmatic advertising can degrade Web site functionality by slowing down how fast Web pages load in browsers while also cluttering the site with ads. Whether other Web publishers will follow this lead remains to be seen.

Case Study Questions

1. Pay a visit to your favorite portal and count the total ads on the opening page. Count how many of these ads are (a) immediately of interest and relevant to you, (b) sort of interesting or relevant but not now, and (c) not interesting or relevant. Do this 10 times and calculate the percentage of the three kinds of situations. Describe what you find and explain the results using this case.

2. Advertisers use different kinds of "profiles" in the decision to display ads to customers. Identify the different kinds of profiles described in this case, and explain why they are relevant to online display advertising.

3. How can display ads achieve search-engine–like results?

4. Do you think instant display ads based on your immediately prior clickstream will be as effective as search engine marketing techniques? Why or why not?

6.6   REVIEW

KEY CONCEPTS

■ **Understand the key features of the Internet audience, the basic concepts of consumer behavior and purchasing, and how consumers behave online.**

- Key features of the Internet audience include the number of users online, the intensity and scope of use, demographics and aspects, the type of Internet connection, and community effects.
- Models of consumer behavior attempt to predict or explain what consumers purchase, and where, when, how much, and why they buy. Factors that impact buying behavior include cultural, social, and psychological factors.
- There are five stages in the consumer decision process: awareness of need, search for more information, evaluation of alternatives, the actual purchase decision, and post-purchase contact with the firm.
- The online consumer decision process is basically the same, with the addition of two new factors: Web site and mobile platform capabilities and consumer clickstream behavior.

■ **Identify and describe the basic digital commerce marketing and advertising strategies and tools.**

- A *Web site* is the major tool for establishing the initial relationship with the customer.
- *Search engine marketing and advertising* allows firms to pay search engines for inclusion in the search engine index (formerly free and based on "objective" criteria), receiving a guarantee that their firm will appear in the results of relevant searches.
- *Display ads* are promotional messages that users can respond to by clicking on the banner and following the link to a product description or offering. Display ads include banner ads, rich media, video ads, and sponsorships.
- *E-mail marketing* sends e-mail directly to interested users, and has proven to be one of the most effective forms of marketing communications.
- *Lead generation marketing* uses multiple e-commerce presences to generate leads for businesses who later can be contacted and converted into customers.
- *Affiliate marketing* involves a firm putting its logo or banner ad on another firm's Web site from which users of that site can click through to the affiliate's site.
- *Viral marketing* is a form of social marketing that involves getting customers to pass along a company's marketing message to friends, family, and colleagues.
- *Social marketing and advertising* involves using the social graph to communicate brand images and directly promote sales of products and services.
- *Mobile and local marketing and advertising* involves using display ads, search engine advertising, video ads, and mobile messaging on mobile devices such as smartphones and tablet computers, often using the geographic location of the user.
- *Multi-channel marketing* (combining offline and online marketing efforts) is typically the most effective. Although many e-commerce ventures want to rely heavily on online communications, marketing communications campaigns most successful at driving traffic have incorporated both online and offline tactics.
- *Customer retention techniques* for strengthening customer relationships include personalization, one-to-one marketing, and interest-based advertising, customization and customer co-production, and customer service (such as CRMs, FAQs, live chat, intelligent agents, and automated response systems).
- *Online pricing strategies* include offering products and services for free, versioning, bundling, and dynamic pricing.

■ Identify and describe the main technologies that support online marketing.

- *Web transaction logs*—records that document user activity at a Web site. Coupled with data from the registration forms and shopping cart database, these represent a treasure trove of marketing information for both individual sites and the online industry as a whole.
- *Tracking files*—Various files, like cookies, Web beacons, Flash cookies, and apps, that follow users and track their behavior as they visit sites across the entire Web.
- *Databases, data warehouses, data mining, and profiling*—technologies that allow marketers to identify exactly who the online customer is and what they want, and then to present the customer with exactly what they want, when they want it, for the right price.
- *CRM systems*—a repository of customer information that records all of the contacts a customer has with a firm and generates a customer profile available to everyone in the firm who has a need to "know the customer."

■ Understand the costs and benefits of online marketing communications.

- Key terms that one must know in order to understand evaluations of online marketing communications' effectiveness and its costs and benefits include:
  - *Impressions*—the number of times an ad is served.
  - *Click-through rate*—the number of times an ad is clicked.
  - *View-through rate*—the 30-day response rate to an ad.
  - *Hits*—the number of http requests received by a firm's server.
  - *Page views*—the number of pages viewed by visitors.
  - *Stickiness (duration)*—the average length of time visitors remain at a site.
  - *Unique visitors*—the number of distinct, unique visitors to a site.
  - *Loyalty*—the percentage of purchasers who return in a year.
  - *Reach*—the percentage of total consumers in a market who will visit a site.
  - *Recency*—the average number of days elapsed between visits.
  - *Acquisition rate*—the percentage of visitors who indicate an interest in the site's product by registering or visiting product pages.
  - *Conversion rate*—the percentage of visitors who purchase something.
  - *Browse-to-buy ratio*—the ratio of items purchased to product views.
  - *View-to-cart ratio*—the ratio of "Add to cart" clicks to product views.
  - *Cart conversion rate*—the ratio of actual orders to "Add to cart" clicks.
  - *Checkout conversion rate*—the ratio of actual orders to checkouts started.
  - *Abandonment rate*—the percentage of shoppers who begin a shopping cart form, but then fail to complete the form.
  - *Retention rate*—the percentage of existing customers who continue to buy on a regular basis.
  - *Attrition rate*—the percentage of customers who purchase once, but do not return within a year.
  - *Open rate*—the percentage of customers who open the mail and are exposed to the message.
  - *Delivery rate*—the percentage of e-mail recipients who received the e-mail.
  - *Click-through rate (e-mail)*—the percentage of e-mail recipients who clicked through to the offer.
  - *Bounce-back rate*—the percentage of e-mails that could not be delivered.
- Studies have shown that low click-through rates are not indicative of a lack of commercial impact of online advertising, and that advertising communication does occur even when users do not directly respond by clicking. Online advertising in its various forms has been shown to boost brand awareness and brand recall, create positive brand perceptions, and increase intent to purchase.
- Effectiveness cannot be considered without analysis of cost. Typical pricing models for online marketing communications include barter, cost per thousand (CPM), cost per click (CPC), cost per action (CPA), hybrid models, and sponsorships.

- Online marketing communications are typically less costly than traditional mass media marketing. Also, online sales can generally be directly correlated with online marketing efforts, unlike traditional marketing communications tactics.

QUESTIONS

1. What are some of the ways that gender, income, education, age, and ethnicity impact online purchasing behavior?
2. What are the primary differences between online and offline consumer behavior?
3. What is clickstream behavior and how is it used by marketers?
4. What is native advertising, and why is it controversial?
5. What are Web analytics and how do they help e-commerce firms better understand consumer behavior at the various stages of the online purchasing process?
6. What does the issue of ad viewability involve, and how is the ad industry responding to this problem?
7. What are the five main elements of a comprehensive marketing plan? What are some different platforms used for each?
8. List the differences among databases, data warehouses, and data mining.
9. What are three strategic questions that online marketing managers need to address?
10. What are the primary marketing functions of a Web site?
11. Name and describe three different types of search engine advertising.
12. What are some issues associated with the use of search engine advertising?
13. What is lead generation marketing?
14. What are the four features of social marketing and advertising that are driving its growth?
15. Explain why author John Battelle calls the Web a database of intentions.
16. What are two types of cross-device tracking?
17. What are four methods that online advertisers use to behaviorally target ads?
18. Shopping cart abandonment rates are typically 70% or higher. Why is this rate so high and what techniques can help improve this rate?
19. Define CTR, CPM, CPC, CPA, and VTR.
20. What advantages do rich media ads have over static display ads?

PROJECTS

1. Go to www.strategicbusinessinsights.com/vals/presurvey.shtml. Take the survey to determine which lifestyle category you fit into. Then write a two-page paper describing how your lifestyle and values impact your use of e-commerce. How is your online consumer behavior affected by your lifestyle?

2. Visit Net-a-porter.com and create an Internet marketing plan for it that includes each of the following:
   - One-to-one marketing
   - Affiliate marketing
   - Viral marketing
   - Blog marketing
   - Social network marketing

   Describe how each plays a role in growing the business, and create a slide presentation of your marketing plan.

3. Use the Online Consumer Purchasing Model (Figure 6 11) to assess the effectiveness of an e-mail campaign at a small Web site devoted to the sales of apparel to the ages 18–26 young adult market in the United States. Assume a marketing campaign of 100,000 e-mails (at 25 cents per e-mail address). The expected click-through rate is 5%, the customer conversion rate is 10%, and the loyal customer retention rate is 25%. The average sale is $60, and the profit margin is 50% (the cost of the goods is $30). Does the campaign produce a profit? What would you advise doing to increase the number of purchases and loyal customers? What Web design factors? What communications messages?

4. Surf the Web for at least 15 minutes. Visit at least two different e-commerce sites. Make a list describing in detail all the different marketing communication tools you see being used. Which do you believe is the most effective and why?

5. Do a search for a product of your choice on at least three search engines. Examine the results page carefully. Can you discern which results, if any, are a result of a paid placement? If so, how did you determine this? What other marketing communications related to your search appear on the page?

6. Examine the use of rich media and video in advertising. Find and describe at least two examples of advertising using streaming video, sound, or other rich media technologies. (Hint: Check the sites of Internet advertising agencies for case studies or examples of their work.) What are the advantages and/or disadvantages of this kind of advertising? Prepare a 3- to 5-page report on your findings.

7. Visit Facebook and examine the ads shown in the right margin. What is being advertised and how do you believe it is relevant to your interests or online behavior? You could also search on a retail product on Google several times, and related products, then visit Yahoo or another popular site to see if your past behavior is helping advertisers track you.

REFERENCES

Adjei, Mavis, and Stephanie Noble. "The Influence of C2C Communications in Online Brand Communities On Purchase Behavior." *Journal of the Academy of Marketing Science*, Vol. 38, No. 5 (2009).

Adomavicius, Gediminas, and Alexander Tuzhilin. "Using Data Mining Methods to Build Customer Profiles." *IEEE Computer* (February 2001a).

Adomavicius, Gediminas, and Alexander Tuzhilin. "Expert-Driven Validation of Rule-Based User Models in Personalization Applications." *Data Mining and Knowledge Discovery* (January 2001b).

AdRoll. "The Performance Marketer's Guide to Retargeting: Part 1." (2015).

Akerlof, G. "The Market for 'Lemons' Quality Under Uncertainty and the Market Mechanism." *Quarterly Journal of Economics* (August 1970).

Ba, Sulin, Jan Stallaert, and Zhang. "Balancing IT with the Human Touch: Optimal Investment in IT-Based Customer Service." *Information Systems Research* (September 2010).

Ba, Sulin, and Paul Pavlou. "Evidence on the Effect of Trust Building Technology in Electronic Markets: Price Premiums and Buyer Behavior." *MIS Quarterly* (September 2002).

Bakos, J. Y., and Erik Brynjolfsson. "Bundling and Competition on the Internet: Aggregation Strategies for Information Goods." *Marketing Science* (January 2000).

Battelle, John. "The Database of Intentions Is Far Larger Than I Thought." Battellemedia.com (March 5, 2010).

Battelle, John. "Search Blog." Battellemedia.com (November 13, 2003).

Baymard Research. "31 Cart Abandonment Rate Statistics." Baymard.com (May 8, 2015).

BIA/Kelsey. "U.S. Local Media Forecast 2015 Update." (April 22, 2015).

Brookings Institute. "Online Identity and Consumer Trust: Assessing Online Risk." (January 2011).

Castell, John. "Google Panda Explained for Website Owners." Linkedin.com (June 12, 2014).

Chan, P. K. "A Non-Invasive Learning Approach to Building Web User Profiles." In *Proceedings of ACM SIGKDD International Conference* (1999).

comScore (Andrea Vollman). "Viewability Benchmarks Show Many Ads Are Not In-View but Rates Vary by Publisher." (June 28, 2013).

Consumer-action.org. "Consumer Action 'Do Not Track' Survey Results." (May 5, 2013).

Corritore, C. L., B. Kracher, and S. Wiedenbeck, "On-line Trust: Concepts, Evolving Themes, a Model." *International Journal of Human-Computer Studies* (2006).

Cross, Robert. "Launching the Revenue Rocket: How Revenue Management Can Work For Your Business." *Cornell Hotel and Restaurant Administration Quarterly* (April 1997).

eMarketer, Inc. "Digital Set to Take Majority Share in UK Time Spent with Media in 2016." (September 29, 2015a).

eMarketer, Inc. (Alison McCarthy). "US Digital Users: Q1 2015 Forecast." (February 2015b).

eMarketer, Inc. "US Fixed Broadband Households, United States, 2013–2019." (February 2015c).

eMarketer, Inc. (Cindy Liu). "Worldwide Retail Ecommerce: The eMarketer Forecast for 2015." (July 2015d).

eMarketer, Inc. (Cindy Liu). "Worldwide Ad Spending: Q1 eMarketer's Estimates for 2015." (September 2015e).

eMarketer, Inc. (Paul Verna). "Native Video Advertising: Effective, But Still a Work in Progress." (January 20, 2015f).

eMarketer, Inc. (Lauren Fisher). "Email Benchmarks 2015: Are Performance Metrics Revealing Signs of Consumer Fatigue?" (August 12, 2015g).

eMarketer, Inc. "Social Network Ad Spending Worldwide, 2014–2015." (March 9, 2015h)

eMarketer, Inc. "US Social Network Ad Revenues, by Venue, 2013–2017." (September 2015i).

eMarketer, Inc. (Jeremy Kressman). "Cross-Device Search Marketing: As Search Goes Multidevice, Ad Targeting and Measurement Struggle to Keep Pace." (April 9, 2015j).

eMarketer, Inc. "Email CTRs: Nothing New, but Still a Problem." (May 18, 2015k).

eMarketer, Inc. "US Retail Ecommerce Metrics, by Device, Q2 2014 & Q2 2015." (July 30, 2015l).

eMarketer, Inc. "US Ad Spending: Q1 2015 Complete Forecast." (March 2015m).

eMarketer, Inc. "Reasons US Internet Users Buy Products Digitally Rather Than In-Store." (February 23, 2014a).

eMarketer, Inc. (Paul Verna). "Word of Mouth Marketing." (October 2010).

Evans, P., and T. S. Wurster. "Getting Real About Virtual Commerce." *Harvard Business Review* (November-December 1999).

Evergage. "Survey Report: Trends & Priorities in Real-Time Personalization." (June 2015).

Farahat, Ayman, and Michael Bailey. "How Effective is Targeted Advertising." International World Wide Web Conference Committee (April 26–20, 2012).

Fawcett, Tom, and Foster Provost. "Adaptive Fraud Detection." *Data Mining and Knowledge Discovery* (1997).

Fawcett, Tom, and Foster Provost. "Combining Data Mining and Machine Learning for Effective User Profiling." In *Proceedings of the Second International Conference on Knowledge Discovery and Data Mining* (1996).

Federal Trade Commission. "Blurred Lines: Advertising or Content?—An FTC Workshop on Native Advertising." (December 4, 2013).

Forrester Research. "US Cross-Channel Retail Sales Forecast, 2014 to 2018." (July 24, 2014a).

Forrester Research. "Refresh Your Approach to 1:1 Marketing: How Real-Time Automation Elevates Personalization." (August 18, 2014b)

Franklin, David J. "Consumer Recognition and Understanding of Native Advertisements." Federal Trade Commission (December 4, 2013).

French, Violet. "Canada's Tough New Anti-Spam Legislation: Beware Its Extra-Territorial Reach." Americanbar.org (January 2014).

Garg, Rajiv. "Peer Influence and Information Difusion in Online Networks: An Empricial Analysis." Carnegie Mellon University, School of Information Systems and Management, Working Paper, 2009.

Google Inc. "Guide to Ad Sizes." (accessed September 8, 2015).

Guo, Stephen, M. Wang, and J. Leskovec. "The Role of Social Networks in Online Shopping Choice: Information Passing, Price of Trust, and Consumer Choice." Stanford University (June 2011).

Hof, Robert. "The One Second Rule: New Viewability Metrics Exposes How Low Online Advertising Standards Still Are." *Forbes* (March 3, 2014).

Interactive Advertising Bureau. "Rising Stars Ads and Brand Equity." (February 9, 2015).

Interactive Advertising Bureau. "Digital Video Rising Starts Added to IAB Standard Ad Portfolio, Augmenting Sight, Sound & Motion with Interactivity at Scale." (February 10, 2014).

Interactive Advertising Bureau. "Mobile Rich Media Ad Definitions (MRAID)." (September 2012).

Interactive Advertising Bureau. "IAB Standards and Guidelines." Iab.net (September 2011).

Interactive Advertising Bureau (IAB)/PriceWaterhouse-Coopers. "IAB Internet Advertising Revenue Report: 2014 Full Year Results." (April 2015).

Isaac, Mike. "Uber Reaches Deal With New York on Surge Pricing in Emergencies." *New York Times* (July 8, 2014).

Iyengar, Raghuram, S. Han, and S. Gupta. "Do Friends Influence Purchases in a Social Network." Harvard Business School. Working Paper, 2009.

Kantrowitz, Alex. "Inside Google's Secret War Against Ad Fraud." Adage.com (May 18, 2015).

Kantrowitz, Alex. "Digital Ad Fraud is Rampant. Here's Why So Little Has Been Done about It." Adage.com (March 24, 2014).

Kantrowitz, Alex. "Just Look At How Google Dominates Ad Tech." Adage.com (October 18, 2013).

Kim, D., and I. Benbasat. "The Effects of Trust-Assuring Arguments on Consumer Trust in Internet Stores." *Information Systems Research* (2006).

Kim, D., and I. Benbasat. "Designs for Effective Implementation of Trust Assurances in Internet Stores." *Communications of the ACM* (July 2007).

Kim, Dan, Donald Ferrin, and Raghav Rao. "Trust and Satisfaction, Two Stepping Stones for Successful E-Commerce Relationships: A Longitudinal Exploration." *Journal of Information Systems Research* (June 2009).

Kirk, Jeremy. "Online Ad Industry Tries to Stamp Out Click Fraud." Pcworld.com (July 21, 2015).

Koerber, Brian. "The Top 20 Most-Shared Ads of 2014." Mashable.com (November 20, 2014).

Kotler, Philip, and Gary Armstrong. *Principles of Marketing, 13th Edition.* Upper Saddle River, NJ: Prentice Hall (2009).

Lewis, Truman. "FTC Warns Publishers to Be Careful with "Native Advertising." Consumeraffairs.com (June 5, 2015).

Libert, Kelsey. "Comparing the ROI of Content Marketing and Native Advertising." *Harvard Business Review* (July 6, 2015).

Marin Software. "The Performance Marketer's Retargeting Guide: Key Benchmarks, Challenges and Best Practices for Cross-Channel Success." (September 2014).

MediaMind Inc. "Consumers 27 Times More Likely to Click-Through Online Video Ads than Standard Banners." (September 12, 2012).

Mishra, D. P., J. B. Heide, and S. G. Cort. "Information Asymmetry and Levels of Agency Relationships." *Journal of Marketing Research.* (1998).

Mobasher, Bamshad. "Data Mining for Web Personalization." Center for Web Intelligence, School of Computer Science, Telecommunication, and Information Systems, DePaul University, Chicago, Illinois. (2007).

Monetate. "2015 Monetate Ecommerce Quarterly: Merchandise This." (2015)

National Conference of State Legislatures. "State Laws Relating to Unsolicited Commercial of Bulk E-mail (SPAM)." (January 9, 2015).

Nielsen Company. "Global Online Consumer Survey." (May 2011).

Oestreicher-Singer, Gail and Arun Sundararajan. "The Visible Hand of Social Networks." *Electronic Commerce Research* (2008).

Opinion Research Corporation. "Online Consumer Product Reviews Have Big Influence." Opinion Research Corporation (April 16, 2009).

Ostermiller, Jeremy. "After Addressing Initial Viewability, These Are the Metrics That Matter." Mediapost. com (June 26, 2015).

Pavlou, Paul. "Institution-Based Trust in Interorganizational Exchange Relationships: The Role of Online B2B Marketplaces on Trust Formation." *Journal of Strategic Information Systems* (2002).

Pew Research Center. (Amanda Lenhart). "Mobile Access Shifts Social Media Use and Other Online Activities." (April 9, 2015a).

Pew Research Center. (Andrew Perrin and Maeve Duggan). "Americans' Internet Access: 2000–2015." (June 26, 2015b).

Pew Research Center. (Aaron Smith). "U.S. Smartphone Use in 2015." (April 1, 2015c).

Pew Research Center. "Part 1: How the Internet Has Woven Itself into American Life." (February 27, 2014).

Pew Research Center. (Lee Rainie). "The State of the Digital Divides." (November 5, 2013).

Pew Research Center. (Kathryn Zickuhr and Aaron Smith). "Digital Differences." (April 13, 2012).

PointRoll. "2014 Benchmark Report." (March 5, 2015).

Rayport, J. F., and J. J. Sviokla. "Exploiting the Virtual Value Chain." *Harvard Business Review* (November–December 1995).

Richtel, Matt. "Wasting Time Is Divide in Digital Era." *New York Times* (May 29, 2012).

Robinson, Jim. "What You Need to Know About the Changing Affiliate Landscape." Marketingprofs.com (August 8, 2014).

Schiff, Allison. "A Marketer's Guide to Cross-Device Identity." Adexhanger.com (April 9, 2015).

Schleifer, Dan. "Which Social Network Makes Your Customers Buy?" *Harvard Business Review* (April 2, 2013).

Segal, David. "Web Display Ads Often Not Visible." *New York Times* (May 3, 2014).

Sevitt, David, and Alexandra Samuel. "Vision Statement: How Pinterest Puts People in Stores." *Harvard Business Review* (July–August, 2013).

Shapiro, Carl, and Hal Varian. *Information Rules: A Strategic Guide to the Network Economy.* Cambridge, MA: Harvard Business School Press (1999).

Shapiro, Carl, and Hal Varian. "Versioning: The Smart Way to Sell Information." *Harvard Business Review* (November–December 1998).

Silverpop. "2015 Email Marketing Metrics Benchmark Study." (2015).

Sinha, Indrajit. "Cost Transparency: The Net's Real Threat to Prices and Brands." *Harvard Business Review* (March-April 2000).

Socialmediatoday.com. "Mobile Apps: How Many People Use Apps?" (September 3, 2013).

Symantec. "Symantec Intelligence Report." (July 2015).

The Search Agency. "State of Paid Search Report—Q3 2014." (2014).

Tadena, Nathalie. "Marketers Say They Would Spend Even More on Digital Ads If Measurement Improved." *Wall Street Journal* (July 6, 2015).

Tobii/Mediative. "The Effectiveness of Display Advertising on a Desktop PC vs. a Tablet Device." (August 2012).

Van den Poel, Dirk, and Wouter Buckinx. "Predicting Online Purchasing Behavior." *European Journal of Operations Research*, Vol. 166, Issue 2 (2005).

Vindico. "2014 Annual Report." (April 13, 2015).

VisionCritical Corporation. "From Social to Sale: 8 Questions to Ask Your Customers." (June 2013).

Vranica, Suzanne. "A 'Crisis' in Online Ads: One-Third of Traffic is Bogus." *Wall Street Journal* (March 23, 2014).

Whitener, Michael. "Cookies Are So Yesterday; Cross-Device Tracking Is In—Some Tips." Iapp.org (January 27, 2015).

Wigand, R. T., and R. I. Benjamin. "Electronic Commerce: Effects on Electronic Markets." *Journal of Computer Mediated Communication* (December 1995).

Williamson, O. E. *The Economic Institutions of Capitalism*. New York: Free Press (1985).

Wolfinbarger, Mary, and Mary Gilly. "Shopping Online for Freedom, Control and Fun." *California Management Review* (Winter 2001).

Chapter 18
E Law

> " *The Congress shall have the power ... to promote the Progress of Science and useful Arts, by securing for limited Times to Authors and Inventors the exclusive Right to their respective Writings and Discoveries.* "
>
> —Article 1, Section 8, Clause 8 of the U.S. Constitution

Introduction to Intellectual Property and Cyber Piracy

The U.S. economy is based on the freedom of ownership of property. In addition to real estate and personal property, *intellectual property rights* have value to both businesses and individuals. This is particularly the case in the modern era of the Information Age, computers, and the Internet.

Federal law provides protections for intellectual property rights, such as patents, copyrights, and trademarks. Certain federal statutes provide for either civil damages or criminal penalties, or both, to be assessed against infringers of patents, copyrights, and trademarks. Trade secrets form the basis of many successful businesses, and they are protected from misappropriation. State law imposes civil damages and criminal penalties against persons who misappropriate trade secrets.

This chapter discusses trade secrets, patents, copyrights, and trademarks and protecting them from infringement, misappropriation, and cyber piracy.

And he that invents a machine augments the power of a man and the well-being of mankind.

Henry Ward Beecher
Proverbs from Plymouth Pulpit—Business

Intellectual Property

Intellectual property is a term that describes property that is developed through an intellectual and creative process. Intellectual property falls into a category of property known as *intangible rights*, which are not tangible physical objects.

Most persons are familiar with the fact that intellectual property includes patents, copyrights, and trademarks. It also includes trade secrets. For patents, think of Microsoft's patents on its Windows operating system. Microsoft has obtained more than ten thousand patents. For copyrights, think of music, movies, books, and video games. For trademarks, think of Nike's recognizable "*Just do it*" and Swoosh logo and McDonald's *Big Mac* and "*I'm lovin' it.*" For trade secrets, think of Coca-Cola Company's secret recipe for making Coca-Cola. Patents, trademarks, and copyrights give their owners or holders monopoly rights for specified periods of time. Trade secrets remain valuable as long as they are not easily discovered.

Intellectual property is of significant value to companies in the United States and globally as well. Over one-half of the value of large companies in the United States is related to their intangible property rights. Some industries are intellectual property intensive, such as the music and movie industries. Other industries that are not intellectual property intensive, such as the automobile and food industries, are still highly dependent on their intellectual property rights.

Because of their intangible nature, intellectual property rights are more subject to misappropriation than is tangible property. It is almost impossible to steal real estate, and it is often difficult to steal tangible property such as equipment, furniture, and other personal property. However, intellectual property rights are much easier to misappropriate. Think of counterfeit compact discs (CDs) and DVDs and fake designer purses. In addition, computers and cyber piracy make it easier to steal many forms of intellectual property. The misappropriation of intellectual property rights is one of the major threats to companies today.

intellectual property
Patents, copyrights, trademarks, and trade secrets. Federal and state laws protect intellectual property rights from misappropriation and infringement.

Where a new invention promises to be useful, it ought to be tried.

Thomas Jefferson

Trade Secret

Many businesses are successful because their **trade secrets** set them apart from their competitors. Trade secrets may be product formulas, patterns, designs, compilations of data, customer lists, or other business secrets. Many trade secrets do not qualify to be—or simply are not—patented, copyrighted, or trademarked. Many states have adopted the **Uniform Trade Secrets Act** to give statutory protection to trade secrets.

State unfair competition laws allow the owner of a trade secret to bring a lawsuit for *misappropriation* against anyone who steals a trade secret. For the lawsuit to be actionable, the defendant (often an employee of the owner or a competitor) must have obtained the trade secret through unlawful means, such as theft, bribery, or industrial espionage. No tort has occurred if there is no misappropriation.

The owner of a trade secret is obliged to take all reasonable precautions to prevent that secret from being discovered by others. If the owner fails to take such actions, the secret is no longer subject to protection under state unfair competition laws. Precautions to protect a trade secret may include fencing in buildings, placing locks on doors, hiring security guards, and the like.

Examples The most famous trade secret is the formula for Coca-Cola. This secret recipe, which is referred to by the code name "Merchandise 7X," is kept in a bank vault in Atlanta, Georgia. The formula is supposedly known by only two executives who have signed non-disclosure agreements. Another secret recipe that is protected as a trade secret is KFC's secret recipe of eleven herbs and spices for the batter used on the Colonel's Original Recipe Kentucky Fried Chicken.

Reverse Engineering

A competitor can lawfully discover a trade secret by performing **reverse engineering** (i.e., taking apart and examining a rival's product or re-creating a secret recipe). A competitor who has reverse engineered a trade secret can use the trade secret but not the trademarked name used by the original creator of the trade secret.

Example An inventor invents a new formula for a perfume. The inventor decides to not get a patent for her new formula (because patent protection is good only for twenty years). Instead, the inventor chooses to try to protect it as a trade secret, which gives her protection for as long a period of time as she can successfully keep it a secret. Another party purchases the perfume, chemically analyzes the perfume, and discovers the formula. The trade secret has been reverse engineered and the second party may begin producing a perfume using the inventor's formula.

Misappropriation of a Trade Secret

The owner of a trade secret can bring a **civil lawsuit** under state law against anyone who has **misappropriated a trade secret** through unlawful means, such as theft, bribery, or industrial espionage. Generally, a successful plaintiff in a trade secret action can (1) recover the *profits* made by the offender from the use of the trade secret, (2) recover for *damages*, and (3) obtain an *injunction* prohibiting the offender from divulging or using the trade secret.

Economic Espionage Act

Congress enacted the federal **Economic Espionage Act (EEA)**,[1] which makes it a federal *crime* to steal another's trade secrets. Under the EEA, it is a federal crime for any person to convert a trade secret to his or her benefit or for the benefit of others, knowing or intending that the act would cause injury to the owner of the trade secret. The definition of *trade secret* under the EEA is very broad and parallels the definition used under the civil laws of misappropriating a trade secret.

One of the major reasons for the passage of the EEA was to address the ease of stealing trade secrets through computer espionage and using the Internet. Confidential information can be downloaded onto a CD or Flash drive, placed in a pocket, and taken from the legal owner. Computer hackers can crack into a company's computers and steal customer lists, databases, formulas, and other trade secrets. The EEA is a very important weapon in addressing computer and Internet espionage and penalizing those who commit it.

The EEA provides for severe criminal penalties. The act imposes prison terms on individuals of up to fifteen years per criminal violation. An organization can be fined up to $10 million per criminal act. The criminal prison term for individuals and the criminal fine for organizations can be increased if the theft of a trade secret was made to benefit a foreign government.

The following case involves the misappropriation of a trade secret.

Ethics

Coca-Cola Employee Tries to Sell Trade Secrets to Pepsi-Cola

"What if you knew the markets they [Coca-Cola] were going to move into and out of ... and beat them to the punch."

—Letter to PepsiCo

In February 2007, former Coca-Cola secretary Joya Williams was convicted by a federal jury of conspiring to steal trade secrets and attempting to sell them to archrival PepsiCo for $1.5 million. Along with Williams, two other co-conspirators were arrested and pled guilty.

The conspiracy was initially foiled when rival PepsiCo produced a letter sent to the company by one of the co-conspirators that offered Coca-Cola trade secrets to the highest bidder. "What if you knew the markets they [Coca-Cola] were going to move into and out of ... and beat them to the punch," the letter stated. PepsiCo notified Coca-Cola officials and federal authorities, who initiated an investigation into the matter by the Federal Bureau of Investigation (FBI). Williams was fired as a secretary in Coca-Cola's global branding department when the initial allegations came to light.

The federal government brought criminal charges against Williams. During trial, prosecutors produced the letter as well as a videotape of Williams putting confidential documents and samples of Coke products that were still in development into her bag. According to court records, the stolen materials included details of an upcoming Coke product code-named Project Lancelot. Coke's 120-year-old "secret formula" recipe was not involved.

The jury returned a guilty verdict, and the trial court judge sentenced Williams to eight years in jail. The U.S. Court of Appeals upheld the decision. The Court stated that the sentence was justified based on the harm that Coca-Cola could have suffered if Williams and her co-conspirators had succeeded in selling its trade secrets to a rival and the danger to the U.S. economy these crimes pose. *United States v. Williams*, Web 2008 U.S. App. Lexis 6073 (United States Court of Appeals for the Eleventh Circuit, 2008)

Ethics Questions   Did Williams act loyally in this case? Did PepsiCo do what it was supposed to do in this case? How likely is it that PepsiCo would have paid Williams and her co-conspirators the money they demanded?

Patent

When drafting the Constitution of the United States of America, the founders of the United States provided for protection of the work of inventors and writers. Article I, Section 8 of the Constitution provides, "The Congress shall have Power ... To promote the Progress of Science and useful Arts, by securing for limited Times to Authors and Inventors the exclusive Right to their respective Writings and Discoveries." Pursuant to the express authority granted in the U.S.

Exhibit 1 PATENT APPLICATION FOR THE FACEBOOK SOCIAL NETWORKING SYSTEM

Constitution, Congress enacted the **Federal Patent Statute** of 1952[2] to provide for obtaining and protecting patents.

A **patent** is a grant by the federal government upon the inventor of an invention for the exclusive right to use, sell, or license the invention for a limited amount of time.

Patent law is intended to provide an incentive for inventors to invent and make their inventions public and to protect patented inventions from infringement. Federal patent law is exclusive; there are no state patent laws. Applications for patents must be filed with the **U.S. Patent and Trademark Office (PTO)** in Washington, DC.

U.S. Court of Appeals for the Federal Circuit

The **U.S. Court of Appeals for the Federal Circuit** in Washington, DC, was created in 1982. This is a special federal appeals court that hears appeals from the Board of Patent Appeals and Interferences of the U.S. Patent and Trademark Office and federal courts concerning patent issues. This Court was created to promote uniformity in patent law.

Patent Application

To obtain a patent, a **patent application** must be filed with the PTO in Washington, DC. The PTO provides for the online submission of patent applications and supporting documents through its EFS-Web system. A patent application must contain a written description of the invention. Patent applications are complicated. Therefore, an inventor should hire a patent attorney to assist in obtaining a patent for an invention.

If a patent is granted, the invention is assigned a **patent number**. Patent holders usually affix the word *patent* or *pat.* and the patent number on the patented article. If a patent application is filed but a patent has not yet been issued, the applicant usually places the words **patent pending** on the article. Any party can challenge either the issuance of a patent or the validity of an existing patent.

Exhibit 1 shows excerpts from the patent application for the Facebook social networking system (US Patent 20070192299).

Systems and Methods for Social Mapping

Abstract

A system, method, and computer program for social mapping is provided. Data about a plurality of social network members is received. A first member of the plurality of social network members is allowed to identify a second member of the plurality of social network members with whom the first member wishes to establish a relationship. The data is then sent to the second member about the first member based on the identification. Input from the second member is received in response to the data. The relationship between the first member and the second member is confirmed based on the input in order to map the first member to the second member.

Subject Matter That Can Be Patented

Most patents are **utility patents**, that is, they protect the functionality of the item. The term *patent* is commonly used in place of the words *utility patent*.

Only certain subject matter can be patented. Federal patent law recognizes categories of innovation that can be patented. These include:

- Machines
- Processes
- Compositions of matter
- Improvements to existing machines, processes, or compositions of matter
- Designs for an article of manufacture
- Asexually reproduced plants
- Living material invented by a person.

Abstractions and scientific principles cannot be patented unless they are part of the tangible environment.

Example Einstein's Theory of Relativity ($E = mc^2$) cannot be patented.

For centuries, most patents involved tangible inventions and machines, such as the telephone and the light bulb. Next, chemical and polymer inventions were patented. Then biotechnology patents were granted. More recently, subject matter involving the computer, Internet, and e-commerce has been added to what can be patented.

Requirements for Obtaining a Patent

To be patented, an invention must be (1) *novel, (2) useful*, and (3) *nonobvious*. An invention must meet all three of these requirements. If an invention is found to not meet any one of these requirements, it cannot be patented:

1. **Novel.** An invention is **novel** if it is new and has not been invented and used in the past. If an invention has been used in "prior art," it is not novel and cannot be patented.

    Example College and professional football games are often shown on television. It is often difficult, however, for a viewer to tell how far the offensive team must go to get a first down and keep possession of the football. Inventors invented a system whereby a yellow line is digitally drawn across the football field at the distance that a team has to go to obtain a first down. This "yellow line" invention qualified for a patent because it was novel.

2. **Useful.** An invention is **useful** if it has some practical purpose. If an invention has only theoretical benefit and no useful purpose, it cannot be patented.

    Example A cardboard or heavy paper sleeve that can be placed over the outside of a paper coffee cup so that the cup will not be too hot to hold serves a useful purpose. Many coffee shops use these sleeves. The sleeve serves a useful purpose and therefore qualifies to be patented.

3. **Nonobvious.** If an invention is **nonobvious**, it qualifies for a patent; if it is obvious, then it does not qualify for a patent.

    Example An invention called "Forkchops" was found to be nonobvious and was granted a patent. Forkchops consist of chopsticks with a spoon on one end of one of the chopsticks and a fork on one end of the other chopstick. Thus, when eating, a user can either use the chopstick ends or the spoon and fork ends.

    Example An inventor filed for a patent for a "waffle fry," which is a fried slice of potato with a waffle shape that is not as thick as a typical French fry but is thicker than a potato chip. Thus, the thickness of a waffle fry is somewhere in between the thickness of a French fry and a potato chip. The court rejected a patent for the waffle fry because it was obvious that a potato could be sliced into different sizes.

The following case involves a patent application.

CASE 1   *U.S. SUPREME COURT Patent*

Bilski v. Kappos, Director, Patent and Trademark Office

130 S. Ct. 3218, 177 L.Ed.2d 792, Web 2010 U.S. Lexis 5521 (2010)
Supreme Court of the United States

"The concept of hedging, described in claim 1 and reduced to a mathematical formula in claim 4, is an unpatentable abstract idea."

—Kennedy, Justice

Facts

Bernard Bilski and Rand Warsaw filed a patent application with the U.S. Patent and Trademark Office (PTO). The application sought patent protection for a claimed invention that explains how buyers and sellers of commodities in the energy market can hedge against the risk of price changes. The key claims are claims 1 and 4. Claim 1 describes a series of steps instructing how to hedge risk. Claim 4 puts the concept articulated in claim 1 into a simple mathematical formula. The remaining claims describe how claims 1 and 4 can be applied to allow energy suppliers and consumers to minimize the risks resulting from fluctuations in market demand for energy. The PTO rejected the patent application, holding that it merely manipulates an abstract idea and solves a purely mathematical problem. The U.S. Court of Appeals affirmed. Petitioners Bilski and Warsaw appealed to the U.S. Supreme Court.

Issue

Is the petitioners' claimed invention patentable?

Language of the U.S. Supreme Court

Section 101 specifies four independent categories of inventions or discoveries that are eligible for protection: processes, machines, manufactures, and compositions of matter. The Court's precedents provide three specific exceptions to Section 101's broad patent-eligibility principles: laws of nature, physical phenomena, and abstract ideas. The concepts covered by these exceptions are part of the storehouse of knowledge of all men free to all men and reserved exclusively to none.

Petitioners seek to patent both the concept of hedging risk and the application of that concept to energy markets. It is clear that petitioners' application is not a patentable process. Claims 1 and 4 in petitioners' application explain the basic concept of hedging, or protecting against risk. Hedging is a fundamental economic practice long prevalent in our system of commerce and taught in any introductory finance class. The concept of hedging, described in claim 1 and reduced to a mathematical formula in claim 4, is an unpatentable abstract idea. Allowing petitioners to patent risk hedging would preempt use of this approach in all fields, and would effectively grant a monopoly over an abstract idea. The patent application here can be rejected under our precedents on the unpatentability of abstract ideas.

Decision of the U.S. Supreme Court

The U.S. Supreme Court held that the concept of hedging is an abstract idea that cannot be patented.

Case Questions

Critical Legal Thinking
Is it often difficult for the U.S. Patent and Trademark Office to determine the patentability of claims in patent applications?

Ethics
Do you think that it was obvious that hedging is an abstract concept that cannot be patented?

Contemporary Business
Does the patent system promote or detract from business innovation?

Patent Period

In 1995, in order to bring the U.S. patent system into harmony with the patent systems of the majority of other developed nations, Congress made the following important changes in U.S. patent law:

- Utility patents for inventions are valid for *twenty years* (instead of the previous term of seventeen years).
- The patent term begins to run from the date the patent application is *filed* (instead of when the patent is issued, as was previously the case).

The United States still follows the **first-to-invent rule** rather than the *first-to-file rule* followed by some other countries. Thus, in the United States, the first person to invent an item or a process is given patent protection over a later inventor who was first to file a patent application.

Example On January 31, 2013, an inventor invents a chemical formula for a product that can be released into the air and eliminate air pollution. The inventor keeps her discovery secret, however. Two years later, another inventor invents exactly the same chemical formula. The next day, the second inventor files a patent application with the PTO and is issued a patent. The first inventor later discovers this fact and challenges the patent. The first inventor will win her patent challenge because she was the first to invent the invention. The second inventor, although the first to file for the patent, loses the patent.

After the patent period runs out, the invention or design enters the **public domain**, which means that anyone can produce and sell the invention without paying the prior patent holder.

Example On January 3, 2013, an inventor invents a formula for a new prescription drug. The inventor files for and is granted a twenty-year patent for this invention. Twenty years after the filing of the patent application, on February 1, 2033, the patent expires. At that time, the patent enters the public domain, and anyone can use the formula to produce exactly the same prescription drug.

One-Year "On Sale" Doctrine

Under the **one-year "on sale" doctrine**, also called the **public use doctrine**, a patent may not be granted if the invention was used by the public for more than one year prior to the filing of a patent application. This doctrine forces inventors to file their patent applications at the proper time.

one-year "on sale" doctrine (public use doctrine)
A doctrine that says a patent may not be granted if the invention was used by the public for more than one year prior to the filing of the patent application.

Example Suppose Cindy invents a new invention on January 10, 2013. She allows the public to use this invention and does not file a patent application until February 10, 2014. As a result, Cindy loses the right to patent her invention because she has waited over one year after her product has been used by the public before filing to patent her invention.

Provisional Patent Application

Congress enacted the **American Inventors Protection Act**, which permits an inventor to file a **provisional application** with the PTO so that the inventor has time to prepare and file a final and complete patent application with the PTO. This "provisional right" gives an inventor three months to prepare a final patent application.

provisional application
An application that an inventor may file with the PTO to obtain three months to prepare a final patent application.

In addition, the act requires the PTO to issue a patent within three years from the date of filing a patent application. The act provides that non–patent holders may challenge a patent as being overly broad by requesting a contested reexamination of the patent application by the PTO. This provides that the reexamination will be within the confines of the PTO; the decision of the PTO can be appealed to the U.S. Court of Appeals for the Federal Circuit in Washington, DC.

Patent Infringement

Patent holders own exclusive rights to use and exploit their patents. **Patent infringement** occurs when someone makes unauthorized use of another's patent.

patent infringement
Unauthorized use of another's patent. A patent holder may recover damages and other remedies against a patent infringer.

In a suit for patent infringement, a successful plaintiff can recover (1) money damages equal to a reasonable royalty rate on the sale of the infringed articles, (2) other damages caused by the infringement (e.g., loss of customers), (3) an order requiring the destruction of the infringing article, and (4) an injunction preventing the infringer from such action in the future. The court has the discretion to award up to treble damages if the infringement was intentional.

Design Patent

design patent
A patent that may be obtained for the ornamental nonfunctional design of an item.

In addition to utility patents, a party can obtain a design patent. A **design patent** is a patent that may be obtained for the ornamental nonfunctional design of an item. A design patents is valid for fourteen years.

Examples The design of a chair, a door knob, a perfume bottle, and the outside of a computer are examples of design patents.

Copyright

Article I, Section 8 of the Constitution of the United States of America authorizes Congress to enact statutes to protect the works of writers for limited times.

copyright
A legal right that gives the author of qualifying subject matter, and who meets other requirements established by copyright law, the exclusive right to publish, produce, sell, license, and distribute the work.

Pursuant to this authority, Congress has enacted copyright statutes that establish the requirement for obtaining a copyright. **Copyright** is a legal right that gives the author of qualifying subject matter, and who meets other requirements established by copyright law, the exclusive right to publish, produce, sell, license, and distribute the work.

Copyright Revision Act
A federal statute that (1) establishes the requirements for obtaining a copyright and (2) protects copyrighted works from infringement.

The **Copyright Revision Act** of 1976[3] currently governs copyright law. The act establishes the requirements for obtaining a copyright and protects copyrighted works from infringement. Federal copyright law is exclusive; there are no state copyright laws. Federal copyright law protects the work of authors and other creative persons from the unauthorized use of their copyrighted materials and provides a financial incentive for authors to write, thereby increasing the number of creative works available in society. Copyrights can be sold or licensed to others, whose rights are then protected by copyright law.

Tangible Writing

Only **tangible writings**—writings that can be physically seen—are subject to copyright registration and protection. The term *writing* has been broadly defined.

Examples Books, periodicals, and newspapers; lectures, sermons, addresses, and poems; musical compositions; plays, motion pictures, and radio and television productions; maps; works of art, including paintings, drawings, jewelry, glassware, tapestry, and lithographs; architectural drawings and models; photographs, including prints, slides, and filmstrips, greeting cards, and picture postcards; photoplays, including feature films, cartoons, newsreels, travelogues, and training films; and sound recordings published in the form of tapes, cassettes, CDs, and MP3 files qualify for copyright protection.

Registration of Copyrights

To be protected under federal copyright law, a work must be the original work of the author. A copyright is automatically granted when an author produces his or her work.

Example When a student writes a term paper for his class, he owns a copyright to his work.

In 1989, the United States signed the **Berne Convention**, an international copyright treaty. This law eliminated the need to place the symbol © or the word *copyright* or *copr.* on a copyrighted work. However, it is still advisable to place the copyright notice © and the year of publication and the author's name on many copyrighted works because it notifies the world that the work is protected by a copyright, identifies the owner of the copyright, and shows the year of its publication. This will help eliminate a defendant's claim of innocent copyright.

Example Copyright © 2012 Henry Richard Cheeseman.

Published and unpublished works may be registered with the **U.S. Copyright Office** in Washington, DC. **Registration of a copyright** is permissive and voluntary and can be effectuated at any time during the term of the copyright. Copyright registration creates a public record of the copyrighted work. A **copyright registration certificate** is issued to the copyright holder. Registration permits a holder to obtain statutory damages for copyright infringement, which may be greater than actual damages, and attorney's fees.

The **Copyright Term Extension Act**[4] of 1998 extended copyright protection to the following:

1. Individuals are granted copyright protection for their lifetime plus seventy years.
2. Copyrights owned by businesses are protected for the shorter of either:
   a. 120 years from the year of creation
   b. 95 years from the year of first publication

After the copyright period runs out, the work enters the **public domain**, which means that anyone can publish the work without paying the prior copyright holder.

Example If an author publishes a novel on April 1, 2003, and lives until August 1, 2037, his heirs will own the copyright until August 1, 2107.

The law in respect to literature ought to remain upon the same footing as that which regards the profits of mechanical inventions and chemical discoveries.

William Wordsworth
Letter (1838)

CONCEPT SUMMARY
COPYRIGHT PERIOD

Type of Holder	Copyright Period
Individual	Life of the author plus 70 years beyond the author's life
Business	The shorter of either 95 years from the year of first publication or 120 years from the year of creation

Copyright Infringement

Copyright infringement occurs when a party copies a substantial and material part of the plaintiff's copyrighted work without permission. The copying does not have to be either word for word or the entire work. A plaintiff can bring a civil action against the alleged infringer and, if successful, recover (1) the profit made by the defendant from the copyright infringement, (2) damages suffered by the plaintiff, (3) an order requiring the impoundment and destruction of the infringing works, and (4) an injunction preventing the defendant from infringing in the future. The court, in its discretion, can award statutory damages for willful infringement in lieu of actual damages.

The federal government can bring criminal charges against a person who commits copyright infringement. Criminal copyright infringement, including infringement committed without monetary gain, is punishable by up to five years in federal prison.

Fair Use Doctrine

A copyright holder's right in a work is not absolute. The law permits certain limited unauthorized use of copyrighted materials under the **fair use doctrine**. The following uses are protected under this doctrine: (1) quotation of the copyrighted work for review or criticism or in a scholarly or technical work, (2) use in a parody or satire, (3) brief quotation in a news report, (4) reproduction by a teacher or student of a small part of the work to illustrate a lesson, (5) incidental reproduction of a work in a newsreel or broadcast of an event being reported, and (6) reproduction of a work in a legislative or judicial proceeding. The copyright holder cannot recover for copyright infringement where fair use is found.

Examples A student is assigned to write a paper in class about a certain subject matter. The student conducts research and writes her paper. In her paper, the student uses two paragraphs from a copyrighted book and places these paragraphs in quotation marks and properly cites the source and author in a footnote. This is fair use for academic purposes. However, if the student copies and uses three pages from the book, this would not be fair use and would constitute copyright infringement whether she footnotes the author or not.

Example *Saturday Night Live* is a comedy television show that is on television on Saturday nights. *Saturday Night Live* often does parodies and satires on famous musicians. This is an example of parody fair use.

No Electronic Theft (NET) Act

In 1997, Congress enacted the **No Electronic Theft Act**[5], or **NET Act**, a federal statute that *criminalizes* certain copyright infringement. The NET Act prohibits any person from willfully infringing a copyright for the purpose of either commercial advantage or financial gain, or by reproduction or distribution even without commercial advantage or financial gain, including by electronic means. Thus, the NET Act makes it a federal crime to reproduce, share, or distribute copyrighted electronic works including movies, songs, software programs, video games, and the like.

Examples Violations include distributing copyrighted works without permission of the copyright holder over the Internet, uploading such works to a website, and posting information about the availability of such uploaded electronic works.

Criminal penalties for violating the act include imprisonment for up to five years and fines of up to $250,000. Subsequent violators may be fined and imprisoned for up to ten years. The creation of the NET Act adds a new law that the federal government can use to criminally attack copyright infringement and curb digital piracy.

The NET Act also permits copyright holders to sue violators in a civil lawsuit and recover monetary damages of up to $150,000 per work infringed.

The following feature discusses a federal law designed to protect digital copyright material.

Digital Millennium Copyright Act (DMCA)

A federal statute that prohibits unauthorized access to copyrighted digital works by circumventing encryption technology or the manufacture and distribution of technologies designed for the purpose of circumventing encryption protection of digital works.

Digital Law

Digital Millennium Copyright Act Makes It a Crime to Circumvent Encryption Technology

The Internet makes it easier than ever before for people to illegally copy and distribute copyrighted works. To combat this, software and entertainment companies have developed "wrappers" and **encryption technology** to protect their copyrighted works from unauthorized access. Not to be outdone, software pirates have devised ways to crack these wrappers and protection devices.

Software and entertainment companies lobbied Congress to enact federal legislation to make the cracking of their wrappers and selling of technology to do so illegal. In response, Congress enacted the **Digital Millennium Copyright Act (DMCA)**,[6] a federal statute that does the following:

- Prohibits unauthorized access to copyrighted *digital works* by circumventing the wrapper or encryption technology that protects the intellectual property
- Prohibits the manufacture and distribution of technologies, products, or services primarily designed for the purpose of circumventing wrappers or encryption technology protecting digital works

Examples Microsoft releases a new software program that it will license to users for a monetary fee. Microsoft has placed electronic encryption technology in the software to prevent illegal piracy of the program. A hacker develops software that cracks encryption technology. This is a violation

of the DMCA. The hacker then sells and distributes his software program to others. This is also a violation of the DMCA. One of these parties uses the software to break through Microsoft's antipiracy technology and obtains a copy of the Microsoft software program. This is a violation of the DMCA whether this party uses the Microsoft program or not. If this person uses the Microsoft program, he will be liable for copyright infringement.

Congress granted exceptions to DMCA liability to (1) software developers to achieve compatibility of their software with the protected work; (2) federal, state, and local law enforcement agencies conducting criminal investigations; (3) parents who are protecting children from pornography or other harmful materials available on the Internet; (4) Internet users who are identifying and disabling cookies and other identification devices that invade their personal privacy rights; and (5) nonprofit libraries, educational institutions and archives that access a protected work to determine whether to acquire the work.

The DMCA imposes civil and criminal penalties. A successful plaintiff in a civil action can recover actual damages from first-time offenders and treble damages from repeat offenders, costs and attorneys' fees, an order for the destruction of illegal products and devices, and an injunction against future violations by the offender.

Trademark

Businesses often develop company names, as well as advertising slogans, symbols, and commercial logos, to promote the sale of their goods and services. Companies such as Nike, Microsoft, Louis Vuitton, and McDonald's spend millions of dollars annually promoting their names, slogans, symbols, and logos to gain market recognition from consumers. The U.S. Congress has enacted trademark laws to provide legal protection for these names, slogans, and logos.

A **mark** is a is any trade name, symbol, word, logo, design, or device used to identify and distinguish goods of a manufacturer or seller or services of a provider from those of other manufacturers, sellers, or providers.

In 1946, Congress enacted the **Lanham (Trademark) Act**,[7] commonly referred to as the **Lanham Act**, to provide federal protection to trademarks, service marks, and other marks. This act, as amended, is intended to (1) protect the owner's

mark

Any trade name, symbol, word, logo, design, or device used to identify and distinguish goods of a manufacturer or seller or services of a provider from those of other manufacturers, sellers, or providers.

investment and goodwill in a mark and (2) prevent consumers from being confused as to the origin of goods and services.

Registration of a Mark

Marks can be registered with the U.S. Patent and Trademark Office (PTO) in Washington, DC. A registrant must file an application with the PTO wherein the registrant designates the name, symbol, slogan, or logo that he is requesting to be registered. A registrant must prove either that he has used the intended mark in commerce (e.g., actually used in the sale of goods or services) or states that he intends to use the mark in commerce within six months from the filing of the application. In the latter case, if the proposed mark is not used in commerce within this six-month period, the applicant loses the right to register the mark. However, the applicant may file for a six-month extension to use the mark in commerce, which is often granted by the PTO.

The PTO provides for the paper filing of the application or for the electronic filing of the application through its **Trademark Electronic Application System (TEAS)**. A party other than the registrant can submit an *opposition* to a proposed registration of a mark.

The PTO will register a mark if it determines that the mark does not infringe any existing marks, the applicant has paid the registration fee (approximately $375), and other requirements for registering the mark have been met.

Once the PTO has issued a registration of the mark, the owner is entitled to use the registered mark symbol ® in connection with a registered trademark or service mark. The symbol ® is used to designate marks that have been registered with the PTO. The use of the symbol ® is not mandatory, although it is wise to use the ® symbol to put others on notice that the trademark or service mark is registered with the PTO. Once a mark is registered, it is given nationwide effect, serves as constructive notice that the mark is the registrant's personal property, and provides that federal lawsuits may be brought to protect the mark. The original registration of a mark is valid for ten years, and it can be renewed for an unlimited number of ten-year periods.

While the application is pending with the PTO, the registrant cannot use the symbol ®. However, during the application period, a registrant can use the symbol **TM** for goods or **SM** for services to alert the public to his or her legal claim. TM and SM may also be used by parties who claim a mark for goods or services but have not filed an application with the PTO to register the mark. In summary, TM and SM are used to designate unregistered trademarks and service marks, respectively.

A party who sell goods and services using brand names and product or service names is not required to register these names with the PTO. The party who does not register a name with the PTO still has legal rights in the name and can sue to prevent others from using the name. The lawsuit will be in state court, however. A party can use the symbols TM and SM with his goods or services, respectively, even if there is no application pending at the PTO.

A party may file for the **cancelation** of a previously registered mark if the party believes that the registrant did not meet the requirements for being issued the mark or if a mark has been abandoned.

Sidebar glossary (left column)

Lanham (Trademark) Act (Lanham Act)
A federal statute that (1) establishes the requirements for obtaining a federal mark and (2) protects marks from infringement.

®
A symbol that is used to designate marks that have been registered with the U.S. Patent and Trademark Office.

WEB EXERCISE
Go to **www.coca-cola.com** to see trademarks of the Coca-Cola Corporation.

TM
A symbol that designates an owner's legal claim to an unregistered mark that is associated with a product.

SM
A symbol that designates an owner's legal claim to an unregistered mark that is associated with a service.

CONCEPT SUMMARY

MEANING OF SYMBOLS USED IN ASSOCIATION WITH MARKS

Symbol	Meaning
TM	Unregistered mark used with goods
SM	Unregistered mark used with services
®	Registered mark

Types of Marks

The word *mark* collectively refers to *trademarks, service marks, certification marks,* and *collective membership marks*:

- **Trademark.** A **trademark** is a distinctive mark, symbol, name, word, motto, or device that identifies the *goods* of a particular business.

  Examples *Coca-Cola* (The Coca-Cola Company), *Big Mac* (McDonald's Corporation), *Mac* (Apple Computer), *Intel Inside* (Intel Corporation), *Better Ingredients. Better Pizza.* (Papa John's Pizza), and *Harley* (Harley-Davidson Motor Company) are trademarks.

- **Service mark.** A **service mark** is used to distinguish the *services* of the holder from those of its competitors.

  Examples *FedEx* (FedEx Corporation), *The Friendly Skies* (United Airlines, Inc.), *Big Brown* (UPS Corporation), *Weight Watchers* (Weight Watchers International, Inc.), and *Citi* (Citigroup, Inc.) are service marks.

- **Certification mark.** A **certification mark** is a mark usually owned by a nonprofit cooperative or association. The owner of the mark establishes certain geographical location requirements, quality standards, material standards, or mode of manufacturing standards that must be met by a seller of products or services in order to use the certification mark. If a seller meets these requirements, the seller applies to the cooperative or association to use the mark on its products or in connection with the sale of services. The owner of the certification mark usually licenses sellers who meet the requirements to use the mark. A party does not have to be a member of the organization to use the mark.

  Examples A *UL* mark certifies that products meet safety standards set by Underwriters Laboratories, Inc. The *Good Housekeeping Seal of Approval* certifies that products meet certain quality specifications set by *Good Housekeeping* magazine (Good Housekeeping Research Institute). Other certification marks are *Certified Maine Lobster*, which indicates lobster or lobster products originating in the coastal waters of the state of Maine (Maine Lobster Promotion Council); *100% Napa Valley*, which is associated with grape wine from the Napa Valley, California (Napa Valley Vintners Association); and *Grown in Idaho*, which indicates potatoes grown in the state of Idaho (State of Idaho Potato Commission).

- **Collective membership mark.** A **collective membership mark** is owned by an organization (such as an association) whose members use it to identify themselves with a level of quality or accuracy or other characteristics set by the organization. Only members of the association or organization can use the mark. A collective membership mark identifies membership in an organization but does not identify goods or services.

  Examples *CPA* is used to indicate that someone is a member of the Society of Certified Public Accountants, *Teamster* is used to indicate that a person is a member of The International Brotherhood of Teamsters (IBT) labor union, and *Realtor* is used to indicate that a person is a member of the National Association of Realtors. Other collective marks are *Boy Scouts of America*, *League of Women Voters*, and *National Honor Society*.

Certain marks cannot be registered. They include (1) the flag or coat of arms of the United States, any state, municipality, or foreign nation; (2) marks that are immoral or scandalous; (3) geographical names standing alone (e.g., "South"); (4) surnames standing alone (note that a surname can be registered if it is accompanied by a picture or fanciful name, such as *Smith Brothers cough drops*); and (5) any mark that resembles a mark already registered with the federal PTO.

trademark
A distinctive mark, symbol, name, word, motto, or device that identifies the goods of a particular business.

service mark
A mark that distinguishes the services of the holder from those of its competitors.

certification mark
A mark that certifies that a seller of a product or service has met certain geographical location requirements, quality standards, material standards, or mode of manufacturing standards established by the owner of the mark.

collective membership mark
A mark that indicates that a person has met the standards set by an organization and is a member of that organization.

E-Commerce and Digital Law

Henry Cheeseman

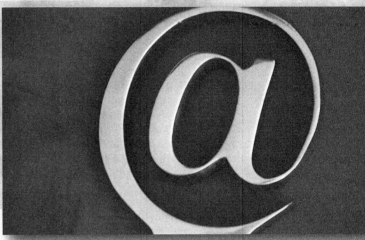

DIGITAL LAW AND E-COMMERCE
The development of the Internet and electronic commerce has required courts to apply existing law to online commerce transactions and e-contracts and spurred the federal Congress and state legislatures to enact new laws that govern the formation and enforcement of e-contracts.

Reyhan/Shutterstock

Learning Objectives

After studying this chapter, you should be able to:

1. Describe the laws that apply to e-mail contracts, e-commerce, and web contracts.
2. Describe e-licensing and the provisions of the Uniform Computer Information Transactions Act (UCITA).
3. Describe the provisions of the federal Electronic Signatures in Global and National Commerce Act (E-SIGN Act)
4. Describe laws that protect privacy in cyberspace.
5. Define *Internet domain names* and describe how domain names are registered and protected.

Chapter Outline

Introduction to E-Commerce and Digital Law

Internet

E-Mail Contracts
  DIGITAL LAW • *Regulation of E-Mail Spam*
  CASE 1 • *Facebook, Inc. v. Porembski*

E-Commerce and Web Contracts
  CASE 2 • *Hubbert v. Dell Corporation*
  DIGITAL LAW • *Electronic Signatures in Global and National Commerce Act (E-SIGN Act)*

E-Licensing
  DIGITAL LAW • *Uniform Computer Information Transactions Act (UCITA)*

Privacy in Cyberspace

Domain Names
  DIGITAL LAW • *New Top-Level Domain Names*
  DIGITAL LAW • *Federal Law Prohibits Cybersquatting on Domain Names*
  CASE 3 • *New York Yankees Partnership d/b/a The New York Yankees Baseball Club*

> *Through the use of chat rooms, any person with a phone line can become a town crier with a voice that resonates farther than it could from any soapbox. Through the use of Web pages, mail exploders, and newsgroups, the same individual can become a pamphleteer."*
>
> —Stevens, Justice
> *Reno v. American Civil Liberties Union, 521 U.S. 844 (1997)*

Introduction to E-Commerce and Digital Law

electronic commerce (e-commerce)
The sale of goods and services by computer over the Internet.

The use of the Internet and the World Wide Web to sell, lease, or license goods, services, and intellectual property through **electronic commerce**, or **e-commerce**, have exploded. Large and small businesses sell goods and services over the Internet through **websites** and registered *domain names*. Consumers and businesses can purchase almost any good or service they want over the Internet, using sites such as Amazon.com, eBay, and others. Businesses and individuals may register domain names to use on the Internet. Anyone who infringes on these rights may be stopped from doing so and is liable for damages.

In addition, software and information may be licensed either by physically purchasing the software or information and installing it on a computer or by merely downloading the software or information directly into a computer.

The 'Net is a waste of time, and that's exactly what's right about it.

William Gibson

Many legal scholars and lawyers argued that traditional rules of contract law do not adequately meet the needs of Internet transactions and software and information licensing. These concerns led to an effort to create new contract law for electronic transactions. After much debate, the National Conference of Commissioners on Uniform State Laws developed the *Uniform Computer Information Transactions Act (UCITA)*. This model act provides uniform and comprehensive rules for contracts involving computer information transactions and software and information licenses.

The federal government has also enacted many federal statutes that regulate the Internet and e-commerce. Federal law has been passed that regulates the Internet and protects personal rights while using the Internet.

This chapter covers Internet law, domain names, e-commerce, e-contracts, licensing of software, and other laws that regulate the Internet and e-commerce.

Internet

Internet (Net)
A collection of millions of computers that provide a network of electronic connections between the computers.

The **Internet**, or **Net**, is a collection of millions of computers that provide a network of electronic connections between the computers. Hundreds of millions of computers are connected to the Internet. The Internet's evolution helped usher in the Information Age. Individuals and businesses use the Internet for communication of information and data.

World Wide Web

World Wide Web
An electronic connection of millions of computers that support a standard set of rules for the exchange of information.

The **World Wide Web** consists of millions of computers that support a standard set of rules for the exchange of information called Hypertext Transfer Protocol (HTTP). Web-based documents are formatted using common coding languages. Businesses and individuals can access the web by registering with a service such as America Online (AOL).

Individuals and businesses can have their own websites. A website is composed of electronic documents known as webpages. Websites and webpages are stored on servers throughout the world, and these servers are operated by *Internet service providers (ISPs)*. Individuals view websites by using web-browsing software such as Microsoft Internet Explorer and Mozilla Firefox Each website has a unique online address.

The web has made it extremely attractive to conduct commercial activities online. Companies such as Amazon.com and eBay are e-commerce powerhouses that sell all sorts of goods and services. Existing brick-and-mortar companies, such as Walmart, Merrill Lynch, and Dell Computer, sell their goods and services online as well. E-commerce over the web will continue to grow dramatically each year.

E-Mail Contracts

Electronic mail, or e-mail, is one of the most widely used applications for communication over the Internet. Using e-mail, individuals around the world can instantaneously communicate in electronic writing with one another. Each person can have an e-mail address that identifies him or her by a unique address. E-mail is replacing telephone and paper communication between individuals and businesses.

Many contracts are now completed by using e-mail. These are referred to as **electronic mail contracts**, or **e-mail contracts**. E-mail contracts are enforceable as long as they meet the requirements necessary to form a traditional contract. This includes agreement, consideration, capacity, and lawful object. Traditional challenges to the enforcement of a contract, such as fraud, duress, intoxication, insanity, and other defenses may be asserted against the enforcement of an e-mail contract. E-mail contracts usually meet the requirements of the Statute of Frauds, which requires certain contracts to be in writing, such as contracts for the sale of real estate, contracts for the sale of goods that cost $500 or more, and other contracts listed in the relevant Statute of Frauds.

Often, the use of e-mail communication is somewhat informal. In addition, an e-mail contract may not have the formality of a paper contract that includes the final terms and conditions of the parties' agreement. The terms of the parties' agreement may have to be gleaned from several e-mails that have been communicated between the parties. In such case, the court can integrate several e-mails in order to determine the terms of the parties' agreement.

The following feature discusses a federal law that regulates spam e-mail.

electronic mail (e-mail)
Electronic written communication between individuals using computers connected to the Internet.

electronic mail contract (e-mail contract)
A contract that is entered into by the parties by use of e-mail.

Controlling the Assault of Non-Solicited Pornography and Marketing Act (CAN-SPAM Act)
A federal statute that places certain restrictions on persons and businesses that send unsolicited commercial advertising (spam) to e-mail accounts, prohibits falsified headers, prohibits deceptive subject lines, and requires spammers to label sexually oriented e-mail as such.

Digital Law

Regulation of E-Mail Spam

Americans are being bombarded in their e-mail accounts by **spam**—unsolicited commercial advertising. Spammers try to sell people literally anything. Spam accounts for approximately three-quarters of all business e-mail traffic. In addition, many spam messages are fraudulent and deceptive, including misleading subject lines. It takes time and money to sort through, review, and discard unwanted spam.

In 2003, Congress enacted the federal **Controlling the Assault of Non-Solicited Pornography and Marketing Act (CAN-SPAM Act)**.[1] The act (1) prohibits spammers from using falsified headers in e-mail messages, including the originating domain name and e-mail address; (2) prohibits deceptive subject lines that mislead a recipient of the contents or subject matter of the message; (3) requires that recipients of spam be given the opportunity to opt out and not have the spammer send e-mail to the recipient's address; and (4) requires spammers who send sexually oriented e-mail to properly label it as such. The Federal

Trade Commission (FTC), a federal administrative agency, is empowered to enforce the CAN-SPAM Act.

In effect, the CAN-SPAM Act does not can spam but instead approves businesses to use spam as long as they do not lie. The act provides a civil right of action to Internet access services that have suffered losses because of spam. The act does not, however, provide a civil right of action to individuals who have received unsolicited spam. The CAN-SPAM Act does not regulate spam sent internationally to Americans from other countries. In essence, the CAN-SPAM Act is very weak in helping consumers ward off the spam that deluges them daily.

In 2004, the FTC adopted a rule that requires that sexually explicit spam e-mail contain a warning on the subject line reading "SEXUALLY EXPLICIT." The FTC rule also prohibits the messages themselves from containing graphic material. The graphic material can appear only after the recipient has opened the e-mail message.

In the following case, the court was presented with an issue involving spam.

CASE 1   *E-Mail Spam*

Facebook, Inc. v. Porembski

Web 2011 U.S. Dist. Lexis 9668 (2011)
United States District Court for the Northern District of California

"The record demonstrates that defendants willfully and knowingly violated the statutes in question by engaging in the circumvention of Facebook's security measures."

—Fogel, District Judge

Facts

Facebook, Inc., owns and operates the social networking website located at **www.facebook.com**. Facebook users can admit friends to view the information they post on their Facebook site, and then others can ask to also be added as friends and so on. Facebook users must register with the website and agree to Facebook's Statement of Rights and Responsibilities (SRR). Facebook maintains strict policies against spam or any other form of unsolicited advertising by users. Facebook filed a lawsuit in U.S. District Court against Philip Porembski and PP Web Services, LLC, which was controlled by Porembski. Facebook alleged that Porembski registered as a Facebook user and was bound by the SSR. Porembski created PP Web Services LLC and was the sole person to act on its behalf. Through fraudulent misrepresentations, Porembski obtained over 116,000 Facebook users' account information. PP Web Services then sent more than 7.2 million spam messages to these Facebook users. Facebook alleged that the defendants' spamming activities violated the federal Controlling the Assault of Non-Solicited Pornography and Marketing Act (CAN-SPAM Act). Facebook sought damages and a permanent injunction against the defendants.

Issue

Have the defendants violated the CAN-SPAM Act?

Language of the Court

The record demonstrates that defendants willfully and knowingly violated the statutes
in question by engaging in the circumvention of Facebook's security measures. The court will award statutory damages of $50.00 per violation of the CAN-SPAM Act, for a total award of $360,000,000 under that Act. As a result of defendants' spam campaign, Facebook has received more than 8,000 user complaints, and more than 4,500 Facebook users have deactivated their accounts. Defendants have demonstrated a willingness to continue their activities without regard for Facebook's security measures or cease and desist requests. Thus, it is appropriate that defendants be permanently enjoined from accessing and abusing Facebook services. Facebook's request for permanent injunctive relief is granted.

Decision

The U.S. District Court held that the defendants had violated the CAN-SPAM Act, awarded Facebook $360,000,000 in damages, and issued a permanent injunction against the defendants.

Case Questions

Critical Legal Thinking
What is spam? Do you think that enactment of the CAN-SPAM Act was warranted?

Ethics
Did Porembski act ethically in this case? Will Facebook recover its awarded damages?

Contemporary Business
What would be the consequences if Facebook users were subjected to spam?

Internet Service Provider (ISP)

Internet service providers (ISPs) are companies that provide consumers and businesses with access to the Internet. ISPs provide e-mail accounts to users, Internet access, and storage on the Internet. ISPs offer a variety of access devices and services, including dial-up, cable, DSL, broadband wireless, Ethernet, satellite Internet access, and other services to connect users to the Internet. There are also web-hosting services that allow users to create their own websites and provide storage space for website users.

A provision in the federal **Communications Decency Act** of 1996 provides: "No provider or user of an interactive computer service shall be treated as the publisher or speaker of any information provided by another information content provider."[2] Thus, ISPs are not liable for the content transmitted over their networks by e-mail users and websites.

Communications Decency Act
A federal statute which provides that Internet service providers (ISPs) are not liable for the content transmitted over their networks by e-mail users and websites.

E-Commerce and Web Contracts

The Internet and **web contracts**, also called **e-contracts**, have increased as means of conducting personal and commercial business. Internet sellers, lessors, and licensors use web addresses to sell and lease goods and services and license software and other intellectual property over the Internet. Internet sellers, leasors, and licensors use web addresses to list the goods and services and intellectual property available and to provide the means for purchasing, leasing, or licensing these goods, services, and intellectual property. Internet sellers, lessors, and licensors, such as **www.amazon.com**, **www.dell.com**, **www.microsoft.com**, and others, use the Internet extensively to sell, lease, or license goods, services, and intellectual property. Assuming that all the elements to establish a traditional contract are present, a web contract is valid and enforceable.

In the following case, the court considered whether a web contract was enforceable.

Web contract (e-contract)
A contract that is entered into by purchasing, leasing, or licensing goods, services, software, or other intellectual property from websites operated by sellers, lessors, and licensors.

CASE 2   *Web Contract*

Hubbert v. Dell Corporation
835 N.E.2d 113 (2005)
Appellate Court of Illinois

"The blue hyperlinks on the defendant's Web pages, constituting the five-step process for ordering the computers, should be treated the same as a multipage written paper contract."

—Hopkins, Justice

Facts
Plaintiffs Dewayne Hubbert, Elden Craft, Chris Grout, and Rhonda Byington purchased computers from Dell Computer online through Dell's website. Before purchasing their computers, each of the plaintiffs configured the model and type of computer he or she wished to order from Dell's webpages. To make their purchase, each of the plaintiffs completed online order forms on five pages on Dell's website. On each of the five pages, Dell's "Terms and Conditions of Sale" were accessible by clicking on a blue hyperlink. In order to find the terms and conditions, the plaintiffs would have had to click on the blue hyperlink and read the terms and conditions of sale. On the last page of the five page

order form the following statement appeared: "All sales are subject to Dell's Terms and Conditions of Sale."

The plaintiffs filed a lawsuit against Dell, alleging that Dell misrepresented the speed of the microprocessors included in the computers they purchased. Dell made a demand for arbitration, asserting that the plaintiffs were bound by the arbitration agreement that was contained in the Terms and Conditions of Sale. The plaintiffs countered that the arbitration clause was not part of their web contract because the Terms and Conditions of Sale were not conspicuously displayed as part of their web contract. The trial court sided with the plaintiffs, finding that the arbitration clause was unenforceable because the terms and conditions of sale were not adequately communicated to the plaintiffs. Dell appealed.

Issue
Are Dell's Terms and Conditions of Sale adequately communicated to the plaintiffs?

(continued)

Language of the Court

We find that the online contract included the "Terms and Conditions of Sale." The blue hyperlink entitled "Terms and Conditions of Sale" appeared on numerous Web pages the plaintiffs completed in the ordering process. The blue hyperlinks on the defendant's Web pages, constituting the five-step process for ordering the computers, should be treated the same as a multipage written paper contract. The blue hyperlink simply takes a person to another page of the contract, similar to turning the page of a written paper contract. Although there is no conspicuousness requirement, the hyperlink's contrasting blue type makes it conspicuous.

The statement that the sales were subject to the defendant's "Terms and Conditions of Sale," combined with making the "Terms and Conditions of Sale" accessible online by blue hyperlinks, was sufficient notice to the plaintiffs that purchasing the computers online would make the "Terms and Conditions of Sale" binding on them. Because the "Terms and Conditions of Sale" were a part of the online contract, they were bound by the "Terms and Conditions of Sale," including the arbitration clause.

Decision

The appellate court held that the Terms and Conditions of Sale, which included the arbitration clause, was part of the web contract between the plaintiffs and Dell. The appellate court reversed the decision of the trial court.

Case Questions

Critical Legal Thinking
Should web contracts be treated any differently from traditional contracts?

Ethics
Did the plaintiffs act ethically in claiming that the Terms and Conditions of Sale were not included in their web contract with Dell? Do you read the terms and conditions of sale when you purchase goods over the Internet?

Contemporary Business
Do Internet sellers expect consumers to read the detailed terms and conditions of sale contained in web contracts?

The following feature discusses a federal statute that established rules for electronic contracts and electronic signatures.

Digital Law

Electronic Signatures in Global and National Commerce Act (E-SIGN Act)

In 2000, the federal government enacted the **Electronic Signatures in Global and National Commerce Act (E-SIGN Act)**.[3] This act is a federal statute enacted by Congress and therefore has national reach. The act is designed to place the world of electronic commerce on a par with the world of paper contracts in the United States.

Writing Requirement of the Statute of Frauds Met
One of the main features of the E-SIGN Act is that it recognizes electronic contracts as meeting the writing requirement of the Statute of Frauds for most contracts. Statutes of Frauds are state laws that require certain types of contracts to be in writing. The 2000 federal act provides that electronically signed contracts cannot be denied effect because they are in electronic form or delivered electronically. The act also provides that record retention requirements are satisfied if the records are stored electronically.

The federal law was passed with several provisions to protect consumers. First, consumers must consent to receiving electronic records and contracts. Second, to receive electronic records, consumers must be able to demonstrate that they have access to the electronic records. Third, businesses must tell consumers that they have the right to receive hard-copy documents of their transactions.

E-Signatures Recognized as Valid
In the past, signatures have been hand-applied by the person signing a document. However, in the electronic

commerce world, individuals provide verification in different ways: "What is your mother's maiden name?" "Slide your smart card in the sensor," or "Look into the iris scanner." But are electronic signatures sufficient to form an enforceable contract? The federal E-SIGN Act made the answer clear.

The E-SIGN Act recognizes **electronic signatures**, or **e-signatures**. The act gives an e-signature the same force and effect as a pen inscribed signature on paper. The act is technology neutral, however, in that the law does not define or decide which technologies should be used to create a legally binding signature in cyberspace. Loosely defined, a **digital signature** is some electronic method that identifies an individual. The challenge is to make sure that someone who uses a digital signature is the person he or she claims

to be. The act provides that a digital signature can basically be verified in one of three ways:

1. By something the signatory knows, such as a secret password, pet's name, and so forth
2. By something a person has, such as a smart card, which looks like a credit card and stores personal information
3. By biometrics, which uses a device that digitally recognizes part of the individual, such as fingerprints or the retina or iris of the eye

The verification of electronic signatures is creating a need for the use of scanners and methods for verifying personal information.

Counteroffers Ineffectual Against Electronic Agent

Many Internet sellers have websites that use electronic agents to sell goods and services. An **electronic agent** is any computer system that has been established by a seller to accept orders. Webpage order systems are examples of electronic agents.

Traditionally, when humans deal with each other face to face, by telephone, or in writing, their negotiations might consist of an exchange of several offers and counteroffers until agreed-upon terms are reached and a contract is formed. Each new counteroffer extinguishes the previous offer and becomes a new viable offer.

Most webpages use electronic ordering systems that do not have the ability to evaluate and accept counteroffers or to make counteroffers. Most state laws recognize this limitation and provide that an e-contract is formed if an individual takes action that causes the electronic agent to cause performance or promise benefits to the individual. Thus, counteroffers are not effective against electronic agents.

Example Green Company has a website that uses an electronic ordering system for placing orders for products sold by the company. Freddie accesses the Green Company's website and orders a product costing $1,000. Freddie enters the product code and description, his mailing address and credit card information, and other data needed to complete the transaction. The Green Company's web ordering system does not provide a method for a party to submit a counteroffer. After ordering the goods on the website, Freddie sends an e-mail to the Green Company, stating, "I will accept the product I ordered if, after two weeks of use, I am satisfied with the product." However, because Freddie has placed the order with an electronic agent, Freddie has ordered the product, and his counteroffer is ineffectual.

E-Licensing

Much of the new cyberspace economy is based on electronic contracts and the licensing of computer software and information. E-commerce created problems for forming contracts over the Internet, enforcing e-commerce contracts, and providing consumer protection. To address these problems, in 1999, the National Conference of Commissioners on Uniform State Laws (a group of lawyers, judges, and legal scholars) drafted the **Uniform Computer Information Transactions Act (UCITA)**. This act is discussed in the following feature.

Electronic Signatures in Global and National Commerce Act (E-SIGN Act)
A federal statute that (1) recognizes electronic contracts as meeting the writing requirement of the Statute of Frauds and (2) recognizes and gives electronic signatures (e-signatures) the same force and effect as pen-inscribed signatures on paper.

Uniform Computer Information Transactions Act (UCITA)
A model state law that creates contract law for the licensing of information technology rights.

Digital Law

Uniform Computer Information Transactions Act (UCITA)

The Uniform Computer Information Transactions Act (UCITA) is a model act that establishes a uniform and comprehensive set of rules that govern the creation, performance, and enforcement of computer information transactions. A computer information transaction is an agreement to create, transfer, or license computer information or information rights [UCITA 102(a)(11)].

The UCITA does not become law until a state's legislature enacts it as a state statute. Most states have adopted e-commerce and licensing statutes that are similar to many of the provisions of the UCITA as their law for computer transactions and the licensing of software and informational rights. The UCITA will be used here as the basis for discussing state laws that affect computer, software, and licensing contracts.

Unless displaced by the UCITA, state law and equity principles, including principal and agent law, fraud, duress, mistake, trade secret law, and other state laws, supplement the UCITA [UCITA § 114]. Any provisions of the UCITA that are preempted by federal law are unenforceable to the extent of the preemption [UCITA § 105(a)].

License

license
A contract that transfers limited rights in intellectual property and informational rights.

licensor
An owner of intellectual property or informational rights who transfers rights in the property or information to the licensee.

licensee
A party who is granted limited rights in or access to intellectual property or informational rights owned by a licensor.

exclusive license
A license that grants the licensee exclusive rights to use informational rights for a specified duration.

electronic license (e-license)
A contract whereby the owner of software or a digital application grants limited rights to the owner of a computer or digital device to use the software or digital application for a limited period and under specified conditions.

Intellectual property and information rights are extremely important assets of many individuals and companies. Patents, trademarks, copyrights, trade secrets, data, software programs, and such constitute valuable intellectual property and information rights.

The owners of intellectual property and information rights often wish to transfer limited rights in the property or information to parties for specified purposes and limited duration. The agreement that is used to transfer such limited rights is called a **license**, which is defined as follows [UCITA 102(a)(40)]:

License means a contract that authorizes access to, or use, distribution, performance, modification, or reproduction of, information or information rights, but expressly limits the access or uses authorized or expressly grants fewer than all rights in the information, whether or not the transferee has title to a licensed copy. The term includes an access contract, a lease of a computer program, and a consignment of a copy.

The parties to a license of intellectual property are the licensor and the licensee. The **licensor** is the party who owns the intellectual property or information rights and obligates him- or herself to transfer rights in the property or information to the licensee. The **licensee** is the party who is granted limited rights in or access to the intellectual property or information [UCITA 102(a)(41) and 102(a)(42)]. A **licensing** arrangement is illustrated in **Exhibit 1**.

A license grants the contractual rights expressly described in the license and the right to use information rights within the licensor's control that are necessary to exercise the expressly described rights [UCITA § 307(a)]. A license can grant the licensee the exclusive rights to use the information. With an **exclusive license**, for the specified duration of the license, the licensor will not grant to any other person rights in the same information [UCITA § 307(f)(2)].

E-License

Most software programs and digital applications are electronically licensed by the owner of the program or application to a user of a computer or digital device. An **electronic license**, or **e-license**, is contract whereby the owner of

Exhibit 1 LICENSING ARRANGEMENT

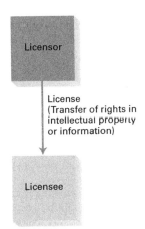

software or a digital application grants limited rights to the owner of a computer or digital device to use the software or a digital application for a limited period and under specified conditions. The owner of the program or application is the **electronic licensor**, or **e-licensor**, and the owner of the computer or digital device to whom the license is granted is the **electronic licensee**, or **e-licensee**.

Example Dorothy owns a computer and licenses a computer software program from SoftWare Company to use on her computer. Dorothy downloads the software onto her computer from SoftWare Company's website. There is an e-license between the two parties. SoftWare Company is the e-licensor, and Dorothy is the e-licensee.

Licensing Agreement

A licensor and a licensee usually enter into a written **licensing agreement** that expressly states the terms of their agreement. Licensing agreements tend to be very detailed and comprehensive contracts. This is primarily because of the nature of the subject matter and the limited uses granted in the intellectual property or informational rights.

The parties to a contract for the licensing of information owe a duty to perform the obligations stated in the contract. If a party fails to perform as required, there is a breach of the contract. Breach of contract by one party to a licensing agreement gives the nonbreaching party certain rights, including the right to recover damages or other remedies [UCITA 701].

licensing agreement
A detailed and comprehensive written agreement between a licensor and a licensee that sets forth the express terms of their agreement.

Privacy in Cyberspace

E-mail, computer data, and other electronic communications are sent daily by millions of people, using computers and the Internet. Recognizing that the use of computer and other electronic communications raises special issues of privacy, the federal government enacted the *Electronic Communications Privacy Act (ECPA)*.[4]

Electronic Communications Privacy Act

The **Electronic Communications Privacy Act (ECPA)** makes it a crime to intercept an electronic communication at the point of transmission, while in transit, when stored by a router or on a server, or after receipt by the intended recipient. An electronic communication includes any transfer of signals, writings, images, sounds, data, or intelligence of any nature. The ECPA makes it illegal to access stored e-mail as well as e-mail in transmission.

Electronic Communications Privacy Act (ECPA)
A federal statute that makes it a crime to intercept an electronic communication at the point of transmission, while in transit, when stored by a router or server, or after receipt by intended recipient. There are some exceptions to this law.

Example Henry owns a computer on which he sends and receives e-mail. Harriet learns Henry's access code to his e-mail account. Harriet opens Henry's e-mail and reads his e-mails. Harriet has violated the ECPA.

Exceptions to the ECPA

The ECPA provides that stored electronic communications may be accessed without violating the law by the following:

1. The party or entity providing the electronic communication service. A primary example is an employer who can access stored e-mail communications of employees using the employer's service.
2. Government and law enforcement entities that are investigating suspected illegal activity. Disclosure would be required only pursuant to a validly issued warrant.

Example John works for the National Paper Corporation. In his job, he has access to a computer on which to conduct work for his employer. John receives and sends e-mail that is work related. John also has access on his computer to the Internet. The National Paper Corporation investigates what John has been viewing on his computer and what is stored on his computer. During its investigation, the National Paper Corporation discovers that John has been viewing and storing child pornography images. The National Paper Corporation fires John for his conduct because it violates company policy, of which John is aware. Here, the National Paper Company did not violate the ECPA.

The ECPA provides for criminal penalties. In addition, the ECPA provides that an injured party may sue for civil damages for violations of the ECPA.

Domain Names

domain name
A unique name that identifies an individual's or company's website.

Most businesses conduct e-commerce by using websites on the Internet. Each website is identified by a unique Internet **domain name**.

Examples The domain name for the publisher of this book—Pearson Education—is **www.pearsonhighered.com**. The domain name for Microsoft Corporation is **www.microsoft.com**. The domain name for McDonald's Corporation is **www .mcdonalds.com**.

Registration of Domain Names

Domain names need to be registered. The first step in registering a domain name is to determine whether any other party already owns the name. For this purpose, InterNIC maintains a "Whois" database that contains the domain names that have been registered. The InterNIC website is located online at **www.internic.net**.

Domain names can also be registered at Network Solutions, Inc.'s, website, which is located at **www.networksolutions.com**, as well as at other sites. An applicant must complete a registration form, which can be done online. It usually costs less than $50 to register a domain name for one year, and the fee may be paid by credit card online. Some country-specific domain names are more expensive to register.

Domain Name Extensions

The most commonly used top-level extensions for domain names are set forth in **Exhibit 2**.

.com	This extension represents the word *commercial* and is the most widely used extension in the world. Most businesses prefer a .com domain name because it is a highly recognized business symbol.	
.net	This extension represents the word *network*, and it is most commonly used by ISPs, Web-hosting companies, and other businesses that are directly involved in the infrastructure of the Internet. Some businesses also choose domain names with a .net extension.	
.org	This extension represents the word *organization* and is primarily used by nonprofit groups and trade associations.	
.info	This extension signifies a resource website. It is an unrestricted global name that may be used by businesses, individuals, and organizations.	
.biz	This extension is used for small-business websites.	
.us	This extension is for U.S. websites. Many businesses choose this extension, which is a relatively new extension.	
.mobi	This extension is reserved for websites that are viewable on mobile devices.	
.bz	This extension was originally the country code for Belize, but it is now unrestricted and may be registered by anyone from anycountry. It is commonly used by small businesses.	
.name	This extension is for individuals, who can use it to register personalized domain names.	
.museum	This extension enables museums, museum associations, and museum professionals to register websites.	
.coop	This extension represents the word *cooperative* and may be used by cooperative associations around the world.	
.aero	This extension is exclusively reserved for the aviation community. It enables organizations and individuals in that community to reserve websites.	
.pro	This extension is available to professionals, such as doctors, lawyers, and consultants.	
.edu	This extension is for educational institutions.	

There are other domain name extensions available. Countries have country-specific extensions assigned to the country. Many countries make these domain name extensions available for private purchase for commercial use.

Exhibit 2 COMMONLY USED TOP-LEVEL EXTENSIONS FOR DOMAIN NAMES

WEB EXERCISE

Think up an Internet domain name you would like to use for a business. Go to the Network Solutions website, at **www.networksolutions.com**, and see if that name is available with the top-level domain extension .com.

WEB EXERCISE

Go to **www.networksolutions.com**. See if your name is available in the .name extension.

The following feature discusses the creation of new top-level domain names.

Digital Law

New Top-Level Domain Names

Prior to 2011, there were twenty-two **top-level domain names (TLDs)**, including .com, .net, .org, and .biz. However, it was often difficult to obtain a new domain name using these suffixes because many names had already been taken. In 2011, the **Internet Corporation for Assigned Names and Numbers (ICANN)**, the organization that oversees the registration and regulation of domain names, issued new rules that permit a party to register a domain name with new TLD suffixes that are personalized.

The new rules permit companies to have their own company name TLD, such as .canon, .google, .cocacola, and such. In addition, companies can obtain TLDs for specific products, such as .ipad or .prius. Such TLDs will help companies with the branding of their company names and products. New TLDs can also be registered for

(continued)

Pagadesign/iStockphoto

industries and professions, such as .bank, .food, .basketball, and .dentist.

Under the new rules, cities and other governmental agencies can register their names, such as .nyc (New York City), .paris (Paris, France), and .quebec (Quebec, Canada). Even persons sharing a cultural identity could have their own TLD, such as .kurd (for Kurds living in Iraq and elsewhere) or .ven (Venetian community, Italy). Another important change is that the new rules permit TLDs to be registered in languages other than English, including Arabic, Chinese, French, Russian, Spanish, and other languages.

Obtaining a new TLD does not come cheap. The cost to apply for a new TLD is about $200,000, and there is an annual maintenance fee of about $75,000. The cost should keep away many squatters, but it may also be

prohibitive for small businesses. To obtain a new TLD, a party must file a detailed 200-page application with ICANN, which will then process and investigate the application. The application process can take nine months or longer.

If there are multiple applicants for the same TLD, ICANN will determine the winner by applying specified criteria. Parties holding trademarks of the TLD are given preference over other applicants. A party who obtains a new TLD can license the use of the name to other parties and establish qualifications that must be met to obtain such a license.

The new rules are the biggest change in domain names in over four decades. The new rules substantially expand the number of TLDs available, permits companies and others to personalize their TLDs, and will change the way people find information on the Internet.

Cybersquatting on Domain Names

Sometimes a party will register a domain name of another party's trademarked name or famous person's name. This is called **cybersquatting**. Often the domain name owner will have registered the domain name in order to obtain payment for the name from the trademark holder or the famous person whose name has been registered as a domain name.

Anticybersquatting Consumer Protection Act (ACPA)

A federal statute that permits trademark owners and famous persons to recover domain names that use their names where the domain name has been registered by another person or business in bad faith.

Trademark law was of little help in this area, either because the famous person's name was not trademarked or because, even if the name was trademarked, trademark laws required distribution of goods or services to find infringement, and most cybersquatters did not distribute goods or services but merely sat on the Internet domain names.

The following feature discusses an important federal law that restricts cybersquatting.

Pagadesign/iStockphoto

Digital Law

Federal Law Prohibits Cybersquatting on Domain Names

In 1999, the U.S. Congress enacted the **Anticybersquatting Consumer Protection Act (ACPA)**.[5] The act was specifically aimed at cybersquatters who register Internet domain names of famous companies and people and hold them hostage by demanding ransom payments from the famous company or person.

The act has two fundamental requirements: (1) The name must be famous and (2) the domain name must have been registered in bad faith. Thus, the law prohibits the act of cybersquatting itself if it is done in **bad faith**.

The first issue in applying the statute is whether the domain name is someone else's famous name. Trademarked names qualify; nontrademarked names—such as those of famous actors, actresses, singers, sports stars, politicians, and such—are also protected. The second issue is whether the domain name was registered in bad faith. In determining bad faith, a court may consider the

extent to which the domain name resembles the trademark owner's name or the famous person's name, whether goods or services are sold under the name, the holder's offer to sell or transfer the name, whether the holder has acquired multiple Internet domain names of famous companies and persons, and other factors.

The act provides for the issuance of cease-and-desist orders and injunctions against the domain name registrant. The court may order the domain name registrant to turn over the domain name to the trademark owner or famous person. The law also provides for monetary penalties. The ACPA gives owners of trademarks and persons with famous names rights to prevent the kidnapping of Internet domain names by cyberpirates.

Examples The Academy Award–winning actress Julia Roberts was awarded the domain name **http://juliaroberts.com**

from a male registrant who had no legitimate claim to the domain name and was found to have registered the domain name in bad faith. The singer nicknamed Sting was not so fortunate because the word *sting* is generic, allowing someone else to originally register and keep the domain name **http://sting.com**.

The following case involves a domain name dispute.

CASE 3   *Domain Name*

New York Yankees Partnership d/b/a The New York Yankees Baseball Club
Claim Number FA0609000803277 (2006)
National Arbitration Forum

"Such use by Moniker is indicative of an intent to disrupt the business of the Yankees, and constitutes registration and use of the disputed domain name in bad faith."

—Kalina, Judge

Facts
The New York Yankees Partnership d/b/a/ The New York Yankees Baseball Club (Yankees) is among the world's most recognized and followed sports teams, having won more than twenty World Series Championships and more than thirty American League pennants. The Yankees own the trademark for the NEW YORK YANKEES (Reg. No. 1,073,346), which was issued to the Yankees by the U. S. Patent and Trademark Office (USPTO) on September 13, 1977. Moniker Online Services, Inc. (Moniker), registered the domain name **www.nyyankees.com**. Moniker operated a commercial website under this domain name, where it offered links to third-party commercial websites that sold tickets to Yankees baseball games and where it sold merchandise bearing the NEW YORK YANKEES trademark without the permission of the Yankees. The Yankees filed a complaint with the National Arbitration Forum, alleging that Moniker had registered the domain in bad faith, in violation of the Internet Corporation for Assigned Names and Numbers (ICANN) Uniform Domain Dispute Resolution Policy and seeking to obtain the domain name from Moniker.

Issue
Has Moniker violated the Uniform Domain Dispute Resolution Policy?

Language of the Arbitrator
The complaint has sufficiently demonstrated that Moniker's <nyyankees.com> domain name is confusingly similar to complainant's NEW YORK YANKEES mark. Moniker uses the <nyyankees.com> domain name to operate a website providing links to third-party commercial websites offering tickets to professional sporting events of the Yankees and merchandise bearing the Yankees NEW YORK YANKEES mark. There is no evidence in the record to suggest that Moniker is commonly known by the disputed domain name. Such use by Moniker is indicative of an intent to disrupt the business of the Yankees, and constitutes registration and use of the disputed domain name in bad faith.

Decision
The arbitrator held that Moniker had violated the Uniform Domain Dispute Resolution Policy and ordered that the **www.nyyankees.com** domain name be transferred from Moniker to the Yankees.

Case Questions

Critical Legal Thinking
Do you think that the element of bad faith was shown in this case? Why or why not?

Ethics
Did Moniker act ethically in obtaining and using the **www.nyyankees.com** domain name and website?

Contemporary Business
Do you think that many parties register domain names similar to existing famous trademarks? Why would they do this?

Web Exercise
Go to **http://www.nyyankees.com** to see the trademarks used by the New York Yankees professional baseball team.

Key Terms and Concepts

Anticybersquatting
   Consumer Protection
   Act (ACPA)
Bad faith
Communications
   Decency Act
Controlling the Assault
   of Non-Solicited
   Pornography and
   Marketing Act
   (CAN-SPAM Act)
Cybersquatting
Digital signature
Domain name
Electronic agent

Electronic Communi-
   cations Privacy Act
   (ECPA)
Electronic commerce
   (e-commerce)
Electronic license
   (e-license)
Electronic licensee
   (e-licensee)
Electronic licensor
   (e-licensor)
Electronic mail (e-mail)
Electronic mail contract
   (e-mail contract)

Electronic signature
   (e-signature)
Electronic Signatures in
   Global and National
   Commerce Act
   (E-SIGN Act)
Exclusive license
Internet (Net)
Internet Corporation for
   Assigned Names and
   Numbers (ICANN)
Internet service provider
   (ISP)
License

Licensee
Licensing
Licensing agreement
Licensor
Spam
Top-level domain name
   (TLD)
Uniform Computer
   Information
   Transactions Act
   (UCITA)
Web contract
   (e-contract)
Website
World Wide Web

Law Case with Answer

John Doe v. GTE Corporation

Facts Someone secretly took video cameras into the locker room and showers of the Illinois State University football team. Videotapes showing these undressed players were displayed at the website http://univ.youngstuds.com, operated by Franco Productions. The Internet name concealed the name of the person responsible. GTE Corporation, an ISP, provided a high-speed connection and storage space on its server so that the content of the website could be accessed. The nude images passed over GTE's network between Franco Productions and its customers. The football players sued Franco Productions and GTE for monetary damages. Franco Productions defaulted when it could not be located. Is GTE Corporation, the ISP, liable for damages to the plaintiff football players?

Answer No, GTE Corporation, the ISP, is not liable for damages to the plaintiff football players. A part of the federal Communications Decency Act of 1996 provides: "No provider or user of an interactive computer service shall be treated as the publisher or speaker of any information provided by another information content provider." Just as the telephone company is not liable as an aider and abettor for tapes or narcotics sold by phone, and the Postal Service is not liable for tapes sold and delivered by mail, so a web host cannot be classified as an aider and abettor of criminal activities conducted through access to the Internet. GTE is not a "publisher or speaker." Therefore, GTE cannot be liable under any state law theory to the persons harmed by Franco's material. Thus, GTE Corporation, the ISP, is not liable for the nude videos of the football players transmitted over its system by Franco Productions. *John Doe v. GTE Corporation*, 347 F.3d 655, **Web** 2003 U.S. App. Lexis 21345 (United States Court of Appeals for the Seventh Circuit)

Critical Legal Thinking Cases

1 Cybersquatting Ernest & Julio Gallo Winery (Gallo) is a famous maker of wines that is located in California. The company registered the trademark "Ernest & Julio Gallo" in 1964 with the U. S. Patent and Trademark Office. The company has spent over $500 million promoting its brand name and has sold more than four billion bottles of wine. Its name has taken on a secondary meaning as a famous trademark name. Steve, Pierce, and Fred Thumann created Spider Webs Ltd., a limited partnership, to register Internet domain names. Spider Webs registered more than two thousand Internet domain names, including http://ernestandjuliogallo.com. Spider Webs is in the business of selling domain names. Gallo filed suit against Spider Webs Ltd. and the Thumanns, alleging violation of the federal Anticybersquatting Consumer Protection Act (ACPA). The U.S. District Court held in favor of Gallo and ordered Spider Webs to transfer the domain name http://ernestandjuliogallo.com to Gallo. Spider Webs Ltd. appealed. Who wins? *E. & J. Gallo Winery v. Spider Webs Ltd.*, 286 F.3d 270, **Web** 2002 U.S. App. Lexis 5928 (United States Court of Appeals for the Fifth Circuit)

2 Domain Name Francis Net, a freshman in college and a computer expert, browses websites for hours each day. One day, she thinks to herself, "I can make money registering domain names and selling them for a fortune." She has recently seen an advertisement for Classic Coke, a cola drink produced and marketed by Coca-Cola Company. Coca-Cola Company has a famous trademark on the term *Classic Coke* and has spent millions of dollars advertising this brand and making the term famous throughout the United States and the rest of the world. Francis goes to the website www.networksolutions.com, an Internet domain name registration service, to see if the Internet domain name classiccoke.com has been taken. She discovers that it is available, so she immediately registers the Internet domain name classiccoke.com for herself and pays the $70 registration fee with her credit card. Coca-Cola Company decides to register the Internet domain name classiccoke.com, but when it checks at Network Solutions, Inc.'s, website, it discovers that Francis Net has already registered the Internet domain name. Coca-Cola Company contacts Francis, who demands $500,000 for the name. Coca-Cola Company sues Francis to prevent Francis from using the Internet domain name classiccoke.com and to recover it from her under the federal Anticybersquatting Consumer Protection Act (ACPA). Who wins?

3 E-Mail Contract The Little Steel Company is a small steel fabricator that makes steel parts for various metal machine shop clients. When Little Steel Company receives an order from a client, it must locate and purchase 10 tons of a certain grade of steel to complete the order. The Little Steel Company sends an e-mail message to West Coast Steel Company, a large steel company, inquiring about the availability of 10 tons of the described grade of steel. The West Coast Steel Company replies by e-mail that it has available the required 10 tons of steel and quotes $450 per ton. The Little Steel Company's purchasing agent replies by e-mail that the Little Steel Company will purchase the 10 tons of described steel at the quoted price of $450 per ton. The e-mails are signed electronically by the Little Steel Company's purchasing agent and the selling agent of the West Coast Steel Company. When the steel arrives at the Little Steel Company's plant, the Little Steel Company rejects the shipment, claiming the defense of the Statute of Frauds. The West Coast Steel Company sues the Little Steel Company for damages. Who wins?

4 Electronic Signature David Abacus uses the Internet to place an order to license software for his computer from Inet.License, Inc. (Inet), through Inet's electronic website ordering system. Inet's webpage order form asks David to type in his name, mailing address, telephone number, e-mail address, credit card information, computer location information, and personal identification number. Inet's electronic agent requests that David verify the information a second time before it accepts the order, which David does. The license duration is two years, at a license fee of $300 per month. Only after receiving the verification of information does Inet's electronic agent place the order and send an electronic copy of the software program to David's computer, where he installs the new software program. David later refuses to pay the license fee due Inet because he claims his electronic signature and information were not authentic. Inet sues David to recover the license fee. Is David's electronic signature enforceable against him?

5 License Tiffany Pan, a consumer, intends to order three copies of a financial software program from iSoftware, Inc. Tiffany, using her computer, enters iSoftware's website, http://isoftware.com, and places an order with the electronic agent taking orders for the website. The license is for three years at $300 per month for each copy of the software program. Tiffany enters the necessary product code and description; her name, mailing address, and credit card information; and other data necessary to place the order. When the electronic order form prompts Tiffany to enter the number of copies of the software program she is ordering, Tiffany mistakenly types in "30." iSoftware's electronic agent places the order and ships thirty copies of the software program to Tiffany. When Tiffany receives the thirty copies of the software program, she ships them back to iSoftware with a note stating, "Sorry, there has been a mistake. I only meant to order 3 copies of the software, not 30." When iSoftware bills Tiffany for the license fees for the thirty copies, Tiffany refuses to pay. iSoftware sues Tiffany to recover the license fees for thirty copies. Who wins?

6 License Metatag, Inc., is a developer and distributor of software and electronic information rights over the Internet. Metatag produces a software program called Virtual 4-D Link. A user of the Virtual 4-D Link program merely types in the name of a city and address anywhere in the world, and the computer transports the user there and creates a four-dimensional space and a sixth sense unknown to the world before. The software license is nonexclusive, and Metatag licenses its Virtual 4-D Link to millions of users worldwide. Nolan Bates, who has lived alone with his mother for too long, licenses the Virtual 4-D Link program for five years, for a license fee of $350 per month. Bates uses the program for two months before his mother discovers why he has had a smile on his face lately. Bates, upon his mother's urging, returns the Virtual 4-D Link software program to Metatag, stating that he is canceling the license. Metatag sues Bates to recover the unpaid license fees. Who wins?

7 E-Contract Einstein Financial Analysts, Inc. (EFA), has developed an electronic database that has recorded the number of plastic pails manufactured and sold in the United States since plastic was first invented. Using this data and a complicated patented software mathematical formula developed by EFA, a user can predict with 100 percent accuracy (historically) how the stock of each of the companies of the Dow Jones Industrial Average will perform on any given day of the year. William Buffet, an astute billionaire investor, wants to increase his wealth, so he enters into an agreement with EFA, whereby he is granted the sole right to use the EFA data (updated daily) and its financial model for the next five years. Buffet pays EFA $100 million for the right to the data and mathematical formula. After using the data and software formula for one week, Buffet discovers that EFA has also transferred the right to use the EFA plastic pail database and software formula to his competitor. Buffet sues EFA. What type of arrangement have EFA and Buffet entered into? Who wins?

8 E-License An Internet firm called Info.com, Inc., licenses computer software and electronic information over the Internet. Info.com has a website, http://info.com, where users can license Info.com software and electronic information. The website is operated by an electronic agent; a potential user enters Info.com's website and looks at available software and electronic information that is available from Info.com. Mildred Hayward pulls up the Info.com website on her computer and decides to order a certain type of Info.com software. Hayward enters the appropriate product code and description; her name, mailing address, and credit card information; and other data needed to complete the order for a three-year license at $300 per month; the electronic agent has Hayward verify all the information a second time. When Hayward has completed verifying the information, she types at the end of her order, "I accept this electronic software only if after I have used it for two months I still personally like it." Info.com's electronic agent delivers a copy of the software to Hayward, who downloads the copy of the software onto her computer. Two weeks later, Hayward sends the copy of the software back to Info.com, stating, "Read our contract: I personally don't like this software; cancel my license." Info.com sues Hayward to recover the license payments for three years. Who wins?

Ethics Cases

9 Ethics BluePeace.org is a new environmental group that has decided that expounding its environmental causes over the Internet is the best and most efficient way to spend its time and money to advance its environmental causes. To draw attention to its websites, BluePeace.org comes up with catchy Internet domain names. One is http://macyswearus.org, another is http://exxonvaldezesseals.org, and another is http://generalmotorscrashesdummies.org. The http://macyswearus.org website first shows beautiful women dressed in mink fur coats sold by Macy's Department Stores and then goes into graphic photos of minks being slaughtered and skinned and made into the coats. The http://exxonvaldezesseals.org website first shows a beautiful, pristine bay in Alaska, with the *Exxon Valdez* oil tanker quietly sailing through the waters, and then it shows photos of the ship breaking open and spewing forth oil and then seals who are gooed with oil, suffocating and dying on the shoreline. The website http://generalmotorscrashesdummies.org shows a General Motors automobile involved in normal crash tests with dummies followed by photographs of automobile accident scenes where people and children lay bleeding and dying after an accident involving General Motors automobiles. Macy's Department Stores,

the Exxon Oil Company, and the General Motors Corporation sue BluePeace.org for violating the federal Anticybersquatting Consumer Protection Act (ACPA).

1. What does the ACPA prohibit? What must be shown to find a violation of the ACPA?
2. Did BluePeace.org acted unethically in this case?
3. Who wins this case and why?

10 Ethics Apricot.com is a major software developer that licenses software to be used over the Internet. One of its programs, called Match, is a search engine that searches personal ads on the Internet and provides a match for users for potential dates and possible marriage partners. Nolan Bates subscribes to the Match software program from Apricot.com. The license duration is five years, with a license fee of $200 per month. For each subscriber, Apricot.com produces a separate webpage that shows photos of the subscriber and personal data. Bates places a photo of himself with his mother, with the caption, "Male, 30 years old, lives with mother, likes quiet nights at home." Bates licenses the Apricot.com Match software and uses it twelve hours each day, searching for his Internet match. Bates does not pay

Apricot.com the required monthly licensing fee for any of the three months he uses the software. After using the Match software but refusing to pay Apricot .com its licensing fee, Apricot.com activates the disabling bug in the software and disables the Match software on Bates's computer. Apricot.com does this with no warning to Bates. It then sends a letter to Bates stating, "Loser, the license is canceled!" Bates sues Apricot.com for disabling the Match software program.

1. What requirements must be met before Apricot. com can disable the Match software program?
2. Did Bates act ethically? Did Apricot.com act ethically?
3. Who wins this case and why?

Internet Exercises

1. Pick out a country. Use **www.google .com** or another Internet search engine and find the domain suffix is for this country.

2. Go to **www.rwgusa.net/bt.htm** to find out how to register a Bhutan .bt domain name. Go to **www.rwgusa .net/com_bt.htm** to find out how to register a Bhutan com.bt domain name.

3. The first step in registering a domain name is to determine whether any other party already owns the name. For this purpose, InterNIC maintains a "Whois" database that contains the domain names that have been registered. The InterNIC website is located at **www.internic.net**. Choose a domain name using the .com suffix and use **www.interic.net** to find out whether that name has been registered.

4. Domain names can be registered at Network Solutions, Inc.'s website, which is located at **www .networksolutions.com**. Choose a domain name using the .net suffix and use **www.networksolutions.com** to find out whether that name has been registered.

5. Use **www.google.com** or another Internet search engine and find an article that discusses the sale of a domain name. What was the domain name, and what price was it sold for?

6. Go to **http://msdnaa.oit.umass.edu/Neula.asp** and read the agreement. To what product does this license agreement apply?

Endnotes

1. 15 U.S.C. Sections 7701–7713.
2. 47 U.S.C. Section 230(c)(1).
3. 15 U.S.C. Chapter 96.
4. 18 U.S.C. Section 2510.
5. 15 U.S.C. Section 1125(d).

Index